"No other guide has as much to offer . . . these books are a pleasure to read."

Gene Shalit on the *Today Show*

★ ★ ★ ★ (5 star rating) "Crisply written and remarkably personable. Cleverly organized so you can pluck out the minutest fact in a moment. Satisfyingly thorough."

Réalités

"The information they offer is up-to-date, crisply presented but far from exhaustive, the judgments knowledgeable but not opinionated."

New York Times

"The individual volumes are compact, the prose succinct, and the coverage up-to-date and knowledgeable . . . The format is portable and the index admirably detailed."

John Barkham Syndicate

"They contain an amount of information that is truly staggering, besides being surprisingly current."

Detroit News

"These guides address themselves to the needs of the modern traveler demanding precise, qualitative information . . . Up-beat, slick, and well-put-together."

Dallas Morning News

". . . Attractive to look at, refreshingly easy to read, and generously packed with information."

Miami Herald

"These guides are as good as any published, and much better than most."

Louisville (Kentucky) *Times*

Stephen Birnbaum Travel Guides

Canada
The Caribbean, Bermuda, and the Bahamas
Disneyland
Europe
Europe for Business Travelers
Florida for Free
France
Great Britain and Ireland
Hawaii
Italy
Mexico
South America
United States
USA for Business Travelers
Walt Disney World

ADVISORY EDITOR
David Walker

CONTRIBUTING EDITORS
Janet Bennett, Helena Bentz, Tina Blackshare, Robert Bone, Al Borcover, James Bready,
David Breakstone, Patricia Brooks, Anita Buck, Jeff Burger, William Burk, Robert Butler,
Carol Campbell, Michael Carlton, Stacey Chanin, Don Chapman, Marie Chesny,
Shirley Christian, Jay Clarke, Thomas Coffey, James Cortese, Karen Cure, Sally Davy,
Teresa Morris Day, Katherine Dinsdale, John Doherty, Natilee Duning, Thomas Ellis,
Luise M. Erdmann, Walter Evans, Brenda Fine, John Firestone, Sam Fletcher,
James Frank, Janet Fullwood, Joel A. Glass, Mark Gottlieb, Paul Hagerman, Ben Harte,
Willard Hazelbush, Patricia Hetrick, Rosemary Peters Hinkle, Barbara Horngren,
Bill Jamison, Sam Jannerone, Lou Johnson, Michael Konon, Elliot S. Krane, Lori G. Kranz,
Linda Lampman, Pamela Marin, Antoinette Martin, Carole Martin, Alexandra Mayes,
Timothy McEnroe, Donald McMillin, Sandra Miller, Anne Millman, Bill Millman,
Laurie Nadel, Brooke Ramey Nelson, Marty Olmstead, Richard J. Pietschmann,
Daniel C. Pinger, Ann Pleshette, Mike Pulfer, Grace Renshaw, Steve Roberts,
Michael Robertson, Allan Rokach, William Ryan, Marie Rychman, William Schemmel,
Ellen Sherberg, Art Siemering, Douglas Smith, Jab Smith, Ronald Smith, Victoria Sprague,
Michael Steege, Jean Stewart, Jack Swanson, Rick Sylvain, Karen Tenney,
Charles Thurston, Diana Tittle, Robert Trumbull, Nikki Tureen, Ginny Turner,
Katherine Walker, Susan Walters, Hesh Weiner, Robert Wells, Mimi Whitefield,
Robert Wintner, Cathy Wood, Donald Woodward, Christine Zust

MAPS   COVER   SYMBOLS
B. Andrew Mudryk, Paul J. Pugliese   Robert Anthony   Gloria McKeown

A Stephen Birnbaum Travel Guide

Birnbaum's
UNITED
STATES
1987

Stephen Birnbaum
EDITOR

Brenda Goldberg
EXECUTIVE EDITOR

Kristin Moehlmann
Barbara Benton
Associate Editors

Kathleen McHugh
Assistant Editor

Eleanor O'Neill
Editorial Assistant

HOUGHTON MIFFLIN COMPANY/BOSTON 1986

For Alex, who merely makes all this possible

This book is published by special arrangement
with Eric Lasher and Maureen Lasher.

ISBN: 0-395-42334-1 (pbk.)
ISSN: 0749-2561 (Stephen Birnbaum Travel Guides)
ISSN: 0883-2501 (United States)

Printed in the United States of America

Q 10 9 8 7 6 5 4 3 2 1

Contents

GETTING READY TO GO

All the practical travel data you need to plan your vacation down to the final detail.

When and How to Go

Preparing

On the Road

Sources and Resources

THE AMERICAN CITIES

Thorough, qualitative guides to each of the 44 cities most often visited by vacationers and businesspeople. Each section offers a comprehensive report of the city's most compelling attractions and amenities, designed to be used on the spot. Directions and recommendations are immediately accessible because each guide is presented in consistent form.

DIVERSIONS

A selective guide to more than 25 active and/or cerebral vacation themes, including the best places to pursue them. Our intent is to point out where your quality of experience is likely to be highest.

For the Body

For the Mind

For the Spirit

DIRECTIONS

This country's most spectacular routes and roads, most arresting natural wonders, most magnificent parks and forests, all organized into 66 specific driving tours.

Midwest

West

A Word from the Editor

The broadening sophistication of travelers has made it essential that guidebooks also evolve, if only to keep pace with their readers. So we've tried to create a guide to the United States that's specifically organized, written, and edited for the knowledgeable traveler, for whom qualitative information is infinitely more desirable than mere quantities of unappraised data. We think that this guide — and the series of which it is a part — is the leader in a new generation of travel guides that are uniquely responsive to the needs and interests of today's travelers.

For years, dating back as far as Herr Baedeker, travel guides have tended to be encyclopedic, seemingly much more concerned with demonstrating expertise in geography and history than with any real analysis of the sorts of things that actually concern a typical tourist. But today, when it is hardly necessary to tell a traveler where New Orleans is, or that it was an important element in the development of the United States, it is hard to justify endless pages of historic perspective. In many cases, the traveler has been to New Orleans nearly as often as the guidebook editor, so the editor must provide new perceptions and suggest new directions to make the guide genuinely valuable.

That's exactly what we've tried to do in the Birnbaum travel guide series. I think you'll notice a fresh tone to the text as well as an organization and focus that are distinctive and different. And even a random examination of what follows will demonstrate a substantial departure from previous guidebook orientation, for we've not only attempted to provide information of a different sort, but we've also tried to present it in an environment that makes it particularly accessible.

Needless to say, it's difficult to decide what goes into a guidebook of this size — and what to omit. Early on, we realized that giving up the encyclopedic approach precluded the inclusion of every route and restaurant, and this fact helped define our overall editorial focus. Similarly, when we discussed the possibility of presenting certain information in other than strict geographic order, we found that the new format enabled us to arrange data in a way that we think best answers the questions travelers typically ask.

Large numbers of specific questions have provided the real editorial skeleton for this book. The volume of mail I regularly receive continually seems to emphasize that modern travelers want very precise information, and so we've tried to address this need and have organized the text in the most responsive way possible. If you want to know the best restaurant in Chicago or the best tennis camp for improving an erratic backhand, you will be able to extract that data easily.

Travel guides are, above all, reflections of personal taste, and putting one's name on a title page obviously puts one's preferences on the line. But I think

I ought to amplify just exactly what "personal" means. I am not at all a believer in the sort of personal guidebook that's a palpable misrepresentation on its face. It is, for example, hardly possible for any single travel writer to physically visit a thousand restaurants (and nearly that number of hotels) in any given year and provide accurate appraisals of each. And even if it were physically possible for one human to get through such an itinerary in a single year, it would of necessity have to be done at a dead sprint, and the perceptions derived therefrom would probably be even less valid than those of any leisurely layman visiting the same establishments. It is, therefore, impossible (especially in an annually revised guidebook *series* such as we have created) to have only one person provide all the data on the entire world.

I also happen to think that such individual orientation is of substantially less value to readers. Visiting a single hotel for one night, or eating one hasty meal in a restaurant, hardly equips anyone to provide meaningful appraisals that are of more than passing interest. No amount of doggedly alliterative or oppressively onomatopoeic text can camouflage a technique that is specious on its face. We have, therefore, chosen what I like to describe as the "thee and me" approach to restaurant and hotel appraisal, and in a somewhat more limited degree, to the sites and sights we have included in the other sections of the text. What this really reflects is personal sampling tempered by intelligent counsel from informed local sources, for these friends-of-the-editor are almost always residents of the city and/or area about which they are consulted.

We have also tried to be sure that our contributors have had a fair access to visitors so they may better solicit individual tourist reactions to the areas about which they contribute. It doesn't take long to discover whether a prospective contributor's tastes coincide with our own, and by the time we have assembled all the editors, researchers, writers, stringers, correspondents, and consultants that it takes to create an undertaking of this size, we have a fairly homogeneous group. We also find that these informed, insightful local correspondents are far more apt to hear about (or uncover) hard-to-locate gems that so often turn an ordinary visit into an exciting adventure. Furthermore, they are usually in the very best position to recognize and report on local consensus and consistency, and they represent a far better barometer of ongoing excellence than would any random encounter.

Despite this considerable number of contributors, very precise editing and tailoring keeps our text fiercely subjective. So what follows is designed to be the gospel according to Birnbaum, and represents as much of my own tastes and instincts as humanly possible. It is probable, therefore, that if you like your steak medium rare, routinely ask to have the MSG left out of Chinese food, and can't tolerate fresh fish that is overcooked, then we're likely to have a long and meaningful relationship. Readers with dissimilar tastes may be less enraptured.

I also think I ought to point out something about the person to whom this guidebook is directed. Above all, he or she is a "visitor." That means that such elements as restaurant choices have been specifically picked to provide that visitor with a representative, enlightening, hopefully exciting, and above all pleasant experience, rather than to provide an insider's guide for a constituency that already knows a city quite well. Since so many extraneous considerations can affect the reception and service accorded a regular restaurant patron, our choices can in no way be construed as a definitive guide to resident dining. We think we've got all the best in various price ranges, but they were chosen with a visitor's viewpoint in mind.

Just one example of how such choices were made is shown by the battle that waged over which French restaurant in New York City would be designated "best." Objective appraisals of the comparative cuisines of half a dozen perfectly marvelous Gallic establishments indicated that any one of them could reasonably qualify for the designation, and there was hardly a perceptible difference in the quality of the quenelles or the hauteur of the hollandaise. But there *was* a perceptible difference in how unknown diners were received and treated by the staffs of these various restaurants, and our final choice of *Lutèce* was as much due to its unusual hospitality to strangers as it was a nod to an extraordinary group of cuisineurs. We think this is especially precious information for a traveler to have at hand.

Other evidence of how we've tried to modify our text to reflect changing travel habits is most apparent in the section we call DIVERSIONS. Where once it was common for travelers to routinely take a two-week summer vacation — one likely to be spent at some ocean or lakeside where the vacationer's most energetic activity was scratching his or her stomach — travel has changed enormously in recent years. Such is the amount of perspiration regularly engendered by today's "leisurely" vacationer that the by-product of a modern holiday is often the need to take another vacation to recover from it. So we've selected every meaningful activity we could reasonably evaluate and have organized this material in a way that is especially accessible to activists of either an athletic or cerebral bent. So whether your preference is breaking your body in a downhill hurtle over America's most difficult ski terrain or whether you have a particular penchant for music festivals around the countryside, we've organized lots of hard information about just that particular activity. It is no longer necessary, therefore, to wade through fifty states' worth of extraneous text to find the best golf resort within a reasonable radius of where you'll be vacationing.

If there is one single thing that best characterizes the revolution and evolution of current holiday habits, it is that Americans now consider travel a right rather than a privilege. No longer is a trip to the far corners of this country or to Europe or the Orient necessarily a once-in-a-lifetime thing; nor is the idea of visiting exotic, faraway places in the least worrisome. Travel today translates as the enthusiastic desire to sample all of the world's opportunities, to find that elusive quality of experience that is not only enriching but comfortable. For that reason, we've tried to make what follows not only helpful and enlightening but also the sort of welcome companion of which every traveler dreams.

Finally, I should point out that every good travel guide is a living enterprise; that is, no part of this text is in any way cast in bronze. In our annual revisions, we refine, expand, and further hone all our material to better serve your travel needs. To this end, no contribution is of greater value to us than your personal reaction to what we have written, as well as information reflecting your personal experiences while trying our suggestions. We earnestly and enthusiastically solicit your comments on this book *and* your opinions and perceptions about places you have recently visited. In this way, we are able to provide the best sorts of information — including the actual experiences of the travel public — to make that experience more readily available to others. Please write to us at 60 E 42nd St., New York, NY 10165.

We sincerely hope to hear from you.

STEPHEN BIRNBAUM

How to Use This Guide

A great deal of care has gone into the special organization of this guidebook, and we believe it represents a real breakthrough in the presentation of travel material. Our aim has been to create a new, more modern generation of travel books, and to make this guide the most useful and practical travel tool available today.

Our text is divided into four basic sections in order best to present information on every possible aspect of an American vacation. This organization itself should alert you to the vast and varied opportunities available in this country — as well as indicating all the specific data necessary to plan a trip in the United States. You won't find much of the conventional "blue skies and beautiful beaches" text here; we've chosen instead to use the available space for more useful and purposeful information. Prospective American itineraries tend to speak for themselves, and with so many diverse travel opportunities, we feel our main job is to explain them and to provide the basic information — how, when, where, how much, and what's best — to let you make the most intelligent possible choices.

What follows is a brief summary of our four basic sections and what you can expect to find in each. We believe that you will find both your travel planning and en-route enjoyment enhanced by having this book at your side.

GETTING READY TO GO

This mini-encyclopedia of practical travel facts is meant to be a sort of know-it-all companion that has all the precise information you need to understand how to go about creating a journey through America. There are entries on nearly three dozen separate topics, including how to travel, what preparations to make before you leave, how to deal with possible emergencies while away from home, what to expect in the different regions of the US, what your trip is likely to cost, and how to avoid prospective problems. The individual entries are specific, realistic, and, where appropriate, cost-oriented.

We expect that you will use this section most in planning your trip, for its ideas and suggestions are intended to facilitate this often confusing time. Entries are intentionally concise, in an effort to get to the meat of the matter with little extraneous prose. This information is augmented by extensive lists of specific sources from which to obtain even more specialized information and some suggestions for obtaining travel information on your own.

THE AMERICAN CITIES

Individual reports on the 44 US cities most visited by tourists and businesspeople, researched and written by professional journalists on their own turf. Useful at the planning stage, THE AMERICAN CITIES is really designed to be taken with you and used on the spot. Each report offers a short-stay guide to its city within a consistent format: an essay, introducing the city as a contemporary place to live; *At-a-Glance,* a site-by-site survey of the most important (and sometimes most eclectic) sights to see and things to do; *Sources and Resources,* a concise listing of pertinent tourist information, meant to answer a myriad of potentially pressing questions as they arise — from something simple like the address of the local tourist office to something more difficult like where to find the best night spot, to see a show, to play tennis, or to get a taxi; and *Best in Town,* our cost-and-quality choices of the best places to eat and sleep on a variety of budgets.

DIVERSIONS

This section is designed to help travelers find the very best locations in which to satisfy their fondest vacation desires without having to wade through endless unrelated text. This very selective guide lists the broadest possible range of vacation activities, including all the best places to pursue them.

We start with a list of possibilities that will require some perspiration — sports preferences and other rigorous pursuits — and go on to report on a number of more cerebral and spiritual vacation possibilities. In every case, our suggestion of a particular location — and often our recommendation of a specific resort — is intended to guide you to that special place where the quality of experience is likely to be highest. So whether you opt for golf or tennis, scuba or whitewater rafting, tours of spectacular resorts or epic shopping areas, each entry is the equivalent of a comprehensive checklist to the absolute best in America.

DIRECTIONS

Here are a series of 66 American itineraries, from Maine's coastal islands to Hawaii's hidden beaches, to take you along this country's most beautiful routes and roads, most spectacular natural wonders, through our most magnificent national parks and forests. DIRECTIONS is the only section of the book organized geographically, and its itineraries cover the highlights of the entire country in short, independent segments that each describe journeys of one to three days' duration. Itineraries can be "connected" for longer trips or used individually for short, intensive explorations. Whether you are planning a major family vacation to cover thousands of miles or simply want to escape to the country, the format is adaptable to your end.

Each entry includes a guide to sightseeing highlights; a cost-and-quality guide to accommodations and food along the road (small inns, out-of-the-way restaurants, country hotels, and off-the-main-road discoveries); and suggestions for activities.

Although each of the sections has a distinct format and a unique function, they have all been designed to be used together to provide a complete package of travel information. Sections have been carefully cross-referenced, and you will find that as you finish an entry in one section, you are directed to another section and another entry, with complementary information. To use this book to full advantage, take a few minutes to read the table of contents and random entries in each section. This will give you an idea of how it all fits together.

Pick and choose information that you need from different sections. For example, if you are interested in a camping trip of some sort but have never been camping and don't really know where to go or how to organize yourself, you might well begin by reading the short, informative section on camping in GETTING READY TO GO. This would provide you with plenty of ideas on how to find a campsite, how to organize the trip, where to go for more information, what to take along. But where to go? Turn to DIVERSIONS for a listing of the best backpacking and camping sites in the country; a look through the selections will direct you to a route and a distance equal to your expertise. Perhaps you choose a walk along the Appalachian Trail in the Great Smoky

Mountains. Turn next to DIRECTIONS for suggestions on what to see along the way, including the Cumberland Gap. Once there, you might well decide to take a break to visit some of the nearby cities, Nashville or Louisville, Atlanta or even Memphis; all are fully covered in THE AMERICAN CITIES.

In other words, the sections of this book are building blocks to help you put together the best possible trip. Use them selectively as a tool, a source of ideas, a reference work for accurate facts, and a guidebook to the best buys, the most exciting sights, the most pleasant accommodations and delicious food, *the best travel experiences* you can have.

GETTING READY TO GO

When and How to Go

When to Go

The decision of when to travel may be forced upon you by the requirements of your schedule; more likely, you will have some choice, and will make the decision on the basis of what you want to see and do, what activities or events you'd like to attend, and what suits your mood.

CLIMATE: Below is a general description of the climate in various American regions to help you plan (all temperatures are given in the Fahrenheit scale). For a brief, city-by-city review of weather, see the *Climate and Clothes* entry in each city report in THE AMERICAN CITIES.

New England and Upstate New York: Connecticut, Maine, Massachusetts, New Hampshire, Upstate New York, Rhode Island, Vermont – The seasons are sharply defined: cold, snowy winters with temperatures in the 20s or lower (much lower in the northern regions of Maine, Vermont, and New Hampshire); short, temperate springs; warm summers in the 70s and 80s, often clear but sometimes humid, especially along the coasts; clear, crisp autumns with brilliant red, yellow, and orange foliage. Tourist season lasts almost around the year: in winter, for skiing and winter sports; summer, for the lakes, coastal resorts, and historic areas; autumn (especially the last two weeks of September and first two weeks of October), for foliage. Least crowded is spring. Best foliage routes: Vermont's Route 9; northwest Connecticut around Litchfield; the White Mountains and lakes of New Hampshire; Mohawk Trail in Massachusetts.

Mid-Atlantic: Delaware, District of Columbia, Maryland, New Jersey, New York City, Pennsylvania, Virginia, West Virginia – Temperatures ranging from below freezing in winter to upper 80s and into the 90s in summer, with cold, damp winters that can be brutal in windswept cities like New York. In the summer, humidity is high along the rivers, which is where many of the area's largest cities are located. Fall is pleasant with moderate temperatures. A long, temperate, flowering spring begins as early as March, continues into June, and is the region's finest season. Tourists visit the metropolitan areas in summer, when city dwellers spend their weekends in the country, and the cities are pleasantly uncrowded for visitors.

South: Alabama, Arkansas, Florida, Georgia, Kentucky, Louisiana, Mississippi, North Carolina, South Carolina, Tennessee – Anytime is a good time to visit the South, but fall and spring are the most temperate seasons. Winters range from the 40s inland to the 60s along the coast. Summer temperatures are in the 70s, 80s, and into the 90s. Events in the South are usually scheduled from January to May and from mid-September to October.

Midwest: Illinois, Indiana, Michigan, Missouri, Ohio, Wisconsin – Cold winters and hot summers mark the entire region. The northern states suffer the harshest winters, with heavy snowfalls and temperatures in the 0° to 20° range. In the more southerly parts of states — the Ohio River Valley section of Indiana, Illinois, Ohio, the southern tip of Illinois, and much of Missouri — winter temperatures average in the

30s. Summers across the region are hot, in the 80s and 90s, and can be blisteringly humid. Even so, summer is the most popular tourist season, when the colossal state fairs get into gear, and ethnic festivals are planned by towns large and small. Though the Midwest isn't as famous as New England for foliage, the leaves change just as dramatically, and are at their peak in mid-October in Manistee National Forest near Cadillac, Michigan, and in Mohican State Park in Ohio.

Plains: Iowa, Kansas, Minnesota, Nebraska, North Dakota, South Dakota – The Plains states offer short, pleasant springs and autumns. In the northern areas, the summer days are warm, nights cool, with snowy winters. Farther south the winters become milder, and the risk of hot, dry, 100° days in July and August increases. Tourist season is generally spring through the end of summer.

Rockies: Colorado, Idaho, Montana, Utah, Wyoming – A region of great diversity, the Rocky Mountain states include mountains, deserts, and flatlands. Except in the deserts of Colorado and Utah, evenings even in summer are cool. Low humidity and dependable sunshine distinguish the entire area. November to mid-April is skiing season; sightseeing and touring begin in spring and continue until the snows announce winter. In summer, desert temperatures can reach 110° and more, and it is best to visit early in the summer season. The Rockies are most famous as a winter — skiing — destination, but a marvelous and uncrowded western vacation can be a summer tour of those famous ski resorts: Aspen/Snowmass, Steamboat Springs, and Vail in Colorado; Big Sky, Montana; Jackson Hole, Wyoming; Park City and Sun Valley, Utah.

Southwest: Arizona, New Mexico, Oklahoma, Texas – This region boasts year-round sunshine and low humidity, as well as high temperatures. In Arizona and New Mexico, it can reach 110° and 115° in the summer, though temperatures in the northern sections are more likely to be in the 90s. The tourist season is December through April.

Far West: Alaska, California, Hawaii, Nevada, Oregon, Washington – For our purposes, the Far West is a rather artificially contrived category which comprises everything from southern California and the Hawaiian Islands to the great expanses of Alaska in the Arctic Circle. Not only is the vast range of temperature, climate, and geography within this huge area impossible to characterize neatly, but even along the Pacific Coast, from California to Washington, weather and temperatures are unpredictable, because of the various sea currents which affect weather conditions. In general, California north of Sacramento, Oregon, Washington, and Alaska are best seen in late spring through summer, when outdoor temperatures are warm. The winters can be quite cold, and in some coastal regions, rainy. Plan to visit Nevada, which is mostly desert, from October through April. Southern California and Hawaii are pleasant throughout the year, offering springlike weather almost anytime.

SPORTS: In the South and Southwest from Palm Springs to South Carolina, any season is warm-weather-sports season. The rest of the country plays according to the weather.

Tennis and golf are under way by March in most of the country and last well into October. In the North, in New England and Minnesota, for example, it is often as late as May before the mud clears, and cold sometimes stiffens knuckles by late September.

Since the most famous mountain climbing, hiking, and wilderness trips are in the Rockies, the Pacific Northwest, and northern New England, participants in these sports usually wait until summer, when the snow is clear, the mountain air is warmer, and less gear is required. Canoeing and rafting enthusiasts follow much the same schedule, though whitewater rafting enthusiasts take to the rivers following the first snowmelt in April or May.

Water sports, such as boating and sailing, get under way in the Northeast in late spring and continue through early fall, with most regattas and other events scheduled from July 4 through Labor Day. On the West Coast north of San Francisco, the season lasts longer, with regattas beginning in June and continuing into September.

The New England ski season starts in earnest around Christmas and lasts through March. A good year will bring skiers out much earlier, and if the snow lasts, the slopes will be busy into April. The season in the West is usually longer, beginning pretty dependably at Thanksgiving and lasting until early or mid-April. However, skiing conditions depend on the snow, and the determined skier should be prepared to make plans around the weather. Newspapers and radio stations in ski areas carry detailed daily ski-condition reports, often updated hourly. If you are planning to go a long distance and are uncertain of the conditions at your destination, call the management of the resort to get a complete report.

PARKS: Most national parks are open all year, closing only for Christmas and New Year's Day. However, many camping facilities in the parks close from October to April, and for a complete list of camping facilities and their opening and closing times, write the National Park Service, Department of Interior, Washington, DC 20240 (for a list of camping directories, guides, and other useful addresses, see *Camping, Hiking, Biking, RVs,* in this section). The most popular national parks, such as Grand Canyon, Zion, and Yosemite, keep some camping facilities open all year.

Parks will be crowded in the summer. Heaviest use is in July and August. To avoid crowds, consider a spring trip, when wild flowers are in bloom; or autumn, for changing leaves and clear weather. Two parks, the Everglades in Florida and Big Bend in Texas, are at their prime in winter.

CULTURAL EVENTS: The season for concerts, plays, art exhibits, dance, and other cultural events across the United States is October through April. New plays open on Broadway; regional theaters bring up their lights (see *Regional Theaters,* DIVERSIONS); major orchestras perform several nights a week; and art museums hold major exhibits, lectures, and film series (see *America's Great Museums,* DIVERSIONS). Schedules of events are available from the visitors and convention bureaus in most cities (addresses given in THE AMERICAN CITIES).

Summer programs are less formal, often outdoors, and usually less expensive (sometimes even free). Major cities offer full schedules of concerts and theater, as well as puppet shows and other entertainment for children. Many impromptu programs are set up in city parks. A helpful source for musical events is *Music Festivals in America* by Carol Rabin (Berkshire Traveller Press, Stockbridge, MA 01262; $8.95, plus $2 postage and handling). Exclusively summer events that cause national excitement are Saratoga Performing Arts Center, Saratoga Springs, New York; Tanglewood Music Festival in Lenox, Massachusetts; Wolf Trap Farm Park in Vienna, Virginia; and Aspen Music Festival in Aspen, Colorado. For a list of events, see *America's Music Festivals,* DIVERSIONS.

FAIRS AND CELEBRATIONS: Tobacco-chewing contests, flower festivals, state fairs, rodeos, horse shows, Indian ceremonies, ethnic festivals, and an endless number of similar events bring people together in all parts of the country. To find out about the events along your route, write to the state tourist boards, most of which publish a calendar of events (for the addresses, see *State Tourist Offices,* in this section). *A Guide to Fairs and Festivals in the United States* by Frances Shemanski (Greenwood Press, 88 Post Road W, Box 5007, Westport, CT 06881; $35) describes events alphabetically by state. The *Guide to Fairs, Festivals and Fun Events* by Janice and Stephen Gale (Sightseer Publications, Box 560182, Miami, FL 33156; $6.95) has a description and contact number or address for events in 18 eastern states from Maine to Florida. Though these guides are recommended, be sure to check dates and times as they are not always up to date. For a selection of the craziest and most interesting celebrations, contests, and festivities in the US, see *Oddities and Insanities,* DIVERSIONS.

Touring by Car

 DRIVING YOUR OWN CAR: Automobile travel is the most popular mode of transportation in the US, though not necessarily the least expensive. It costs about 28¢ a mile to drive an automobile in the US (cost varies with size and condition of car, price of gasoline, city or highway driving, etc.); only about 11¢ a mile to fly by commercial airline. Driving, however, becomes more economical with more passengers, and offers the great advantage of allowing you to explore inaccessible regions at your own pace and on your own schedule.

Automobile Clubs – To protect yourself in case of on-the-road breakdowns, you should consider joining a reputable national automobile club. The largest one is the American Automobile Association (AAA), with over 26 million members in chapters around the country, but numerous other clubs offer similar services. Any club should offer three basic services:

1. On-the-road insurance covering accidents, personal injury, arrest and bail bond, and lawyer's fees for defense of contested traffic cases.
2. Around-the-clock (24-hour) emergency breakdown service (including reduced rates on towing to nearest garage). AAA provides a country-wide list of AAA-approved garages; other clubs allow members to call any local mechanic and reimburse for cost of towing at a later date.
3. Travel and vacation planning service, including advice and maps.

These are the basic forms of service; specific policies and programs vary widely from club to club. Before joining any one, get information and brochures from several national clubs, and compare services and costs to find services which match your travel needs. Most clubs cost between $25 and $50 a year and include spouse and family in membership. Listed below are several of the largest US auto and travel clubs:

Allstate Motor Club: Run by Allstate Insurance; join through any Allstate agency; information from the Club, 30 Allstate Plaza, Northbrook, IL 60066 (312 291-5461).

American Automobile Association: Join through local chapters (listed under *Automobile Club of . . .* in the telephone book); information from national office, 8111 Gatehouse Rd., Falls Church, VA 22047 (703 222-6000).

Amoco Motor Club: Join through Amoco's office, PO Box 9049, Des Moines, IA 50369-0001 (515 225-4000 or 800 334-3300).

Gulf Auto Club: Join by writing PO Box 105287, Atlanta, GA 30348 (800 422-2582).

JTX Travel Club: Run by the Insurance Company of North America, Box 13901, Philadelphia, PA 19103 (215 241-4000; 800 262-5213 in Pennsylvania; 800 523-1965 elsewhere).

Montgomery Ward Auto Club: Join through credit manager at any Montgomery Ward store; national office, Box 803817, Chicago, IL 60680 (800 621-5151 in the continental US; 312 470-7487 elsewhere, call collect).

Motor Club of America: Open to residents of 30 states (protection extends to members traveling in all states); national office, 484 Central Ave., Newark, NJ 07107 (201 733-1234).

United States Auto Club Motoring Division: National office, PO Box 660460, Dallas, TX 75266-0460 (800 348-5058).

Oil Company Credit Cards – All major oil companies offer credit cards which can be used nationwide to buy gas, repairs, and most car parts at their respective service stations. A credit card will reduce the amount of money that you must carry on your trip. Applications for cards are available at service stations (Mobil stations have applications for Mobil cards only, etc.), and you will be granted a card if you have proven credit-worthiness — another credit card of any kind or an established credit rating. They are issued free, and usually take about a month for processing after application.

Charges are handled in two ways, and it is important to be aware under which system your card is working. A few companies — Amoco, for example — allow cardholders to carry charges from month to month. The cardholder pays a minimum each month, and the balance is carried over. For this privilege the cardholder is charged an interest rate (usually about 1½% a month) on the carried-over balance. If you spent $300 on gasoline during a two-week trip, you could spread the payment of this $300 over several months — virtually a "travel now–pay later" system, but you will end up paying more than $300.

Other companies — an example is Gulf — insist that the cardholder pay the full balance due at the end of each pay period (usually a month). While there is no extended credit (except for large repair bills, for which special arrangements can be made), neither is there an interest charge. There are advantages to both systems; when you consider a credit card, know which way it works and decide which is best for you.

Preparing Your Car – Always have your car thoroughly inspected before you leave on a trip, paying special attention to brakes and tires (including the spare). Always have liability insurance. Other suggestions:

1. Consult road maps. Many automobile clubs offer their members free maps and precise routings. Other travelers can get road maps free by writing to the state tourist boards (see *State Tourist Offices,* in this section). Maps are available at service stations, but due to budget cutbacks in the oil industry, most companies now charge for them. *Rand McNally's Road Atlas and Vacation Guide* (about $12.95) is excellent.
2. Make sure your car has the following equipment: spare tire, jack, wrench, and two wooden blocks; extra set of keys (well hidden); first aid kit; jumper cables/gloves; white towel for signaling and/or wiping windows.
3. Make the first days of your trip the shortest, and plan to drive 300-400 miles per day at the most (6-7 hours); this is a comfortable pace for most travelers. When traveling with children, plan on 200-250 miles a day (4-5 hours) at the most.
4. For current information on weather and road conditions, call the nearest AAA.

Breakdowns – If you break down on the road, immediate emergency procedure is to get the car off the highway, raise the hood as a signal that help is needed, and tie a white rag to the door handle or antenna, for the same reason. Don't leave the car unattended, and don't try any major repairs on the road.

Mechanics and Car Care – For any but the most simple malfunctions, you will probably need a mechanic. (Reliable mechanics are listed in THE AMERICAN CITIES .) An excellent series of booklets on car care, mileage, mechanical problems and their sources is published by Shell Oil in its *Shell Answer Man* series, available from Shell dealers or directly from the the company at PO Box 2463, Houston, TX 77001. Other suggestions for breakdowns and on-the-road car care:

1. Look for mechanics with certification. The National Institute for Automotive Service Excellence (NIASE) has certified 100,000 mechanics, many of whom work for local stations. The Automotive Service Council also certifies mechanics.
2. Have some idea what needs to be done. Oil needs to be changed approximately every 5,000 miles; a tune-up is needed every 12,000 miles (every 25,000 miles for

transistorized ignition cars); spark plugs need to be changed every 25,000 miles; fan and air conditioning belts, every 5,000 miles.

3. Get an estimate in writing on major repairs, and make sure there is a firm understanding that the mechanic will call you if any other problems arise. The average cost for service is between $18 and $35 per hour.

4. Be aware of dishonest practices. Some mechanics will cheat you. While checking oil they can "short-stick" the dipper so the full amount of oil in your engine doesn't register. Know your car's oil consumption, and watch while oil is being checked.

5. Recognize warning signals:
   - Fluid leaks: Spread paper and look for the following: brown or black fluid, *oil leak;* straw-colored fluid near wheel, *leaking brake fluid;* pink or reddish fluid, *automatic transmission leak;* colorless or greenish fluid near front, *radiator or hose leak.*
   - Car has trouble starting: May be a vapor lock caused by hot weather; a cold, wet rag on the fuel line and pump may help.
   - Rattle in rear: Loose muffler or tail pipe.
   - Rattling noise: Bent fan blade or loose pulley.
   - Loud squealing noise when wheel turns: Low power steering fluid.

6. If your car needs to be towed, agree in advance on the price and the station to which it will be towed. If you ask AAA clubs, they will often tell you which stations are not reliable.

SPEED TRAPS: Watch your speedometer in small towns. Not only do speed traps cost you a ticket, but they may also affect your future insurance rates.

SAFETY BELTS: Be aware that many states now require the use of safety belts. The driver and any front seat passengers must be belted in Connecticut, Hawaii, Idaho, Illinois, Indiana, Iowa, Louisiana, Michigan, Minnesota, Mississippi, Nebraska, New Jersey, New Mexico, New York, North Carolina, Ohio, Oklahoma, and Utah. In the District of Columbia, California, Massachusetts, and Washington, all passengers must use safety belts. In all 50 states and the District of Columbia, children up to age four must ride either in a child carrier or use safety belts.

SAVING ON GAS: Begin by planning your itinerary and making as many reservations as possible so that you don't waste gas figuring out where to go or stay. Drive early in the day when there is less traffic and heat. Leave your car at the hotel and take local transportation within cities. If it fits in with your plans, choose routes that are direct and avoid mountains or long hills.

Make sure that your tires are properly inflated and your engine is tuned correctly to cut your gas consumption. Avoid speeding — at 55 miles per hour, you can get 25% better mileage than at 70. You can also increase the number of miles you get per gallon by driving smoothly: Accelerate gently, anticipate stops, get into high gear quickly, and maintain a steady speed.

RENTING A CAR: No matter what the advertisements imply, renting a car is rarely as simple as signing on the dotted line and roaring off into the night. If you are renting for personal use, you will have to convince the renting agency that (1) you are personally credit-worthy; and (2) you will bring the car back at the stated time. This will be easy if you have a major credit card; all national agencies (see below) and most local rental companies accept credit cards in lieu of a cash deposit as well as for payment of your final bill. If you prefer to pay in cash, leave your credit card as a deposit and pay your bill in cash when you return the car.

If you don't have a national credit card, call the company several days in advance, give them your name, home address, information on your business or employer; the rental agency then runs its own credit check on you. In addition, you will have to leave a hefty deposit when you pick up the car — as much as $100 for each day you intend to keep the car.

Costs and Requirements – Renting is not cheap, but it is possible to economize by determining your own needs and then shopping around until you find the best deal. As you comparison-shop, keep in mind that rates vary considerably, not only from city to city, but also from location to location within the same city. It might be less expensive to rent a car in the center of a city rather than at the airport. Hertz might be cheaper in Tulsa, while Avis is more reasonable in New York. Usually, locally based companies are less expensive than the national giants. Ask about special rates or promotional deals such as weekend or weekly rates, bonus coupons for airline tickets, or 24-hour rates that include gas. Some companies have their version of the airlines' Super Saver fares — you can rent a car for as little as $140 a week with unlimited mileage if you pay for or reserve it 7 days in advance. There are two typical car rental deals:

1. Per-day charge, unlimited mileage: You pay a flat fee for each day you keep the car, but are not charged for mileage (an increasingly common alternative is to be given a certain number of miles free each day, and then charged on a per-mile basis over that number). If you plan to drive more than 100 miles, an unlimited mileage, flat fee is almost always the most economical arrangement.
2. Per-day, per-mile charge: You pay a flat fee for each day you keep the car (usually between $25 and $70) plus a per mile charge of 15¢ to 40¢.

Most rental firms require clients to be at least 21 years old and to have a valid driver's license.

Major national rental companies with toll-free telephone numbers are:

Ajax Rent-A-Car: continental USA except Boston, Las Vegas, and Newark, 800 367-2529; Boston, 800 225-2529; Las Vegas, 800 221-5391; Newark, 800 654-2529

American International Rent-A-Car: continental USA, 800 527-0202

Avis: continental USA except Oklahoma, 800 331-1212

Budget Rent-A-Car: continental USA except Nebraska, 800 527-0700

Dollar Rent-A-Car: continental USA except California, 800 421-6868

Hertz: continental USA, 800 654-3131

National Car Rental: continental USA, 800 328-4567; Alaska and Hawaii, 800 CAR-RENT

Sears Rent-A-Car: continental USA except Nebraska, 800 527-0770

Thrifty Rent-A-Car: continental USA and Canada, 800 367-2277

To economize on car rental, consider one of the firms that rent three- to five-year-old cars that are well worn but mechanically sound. One such company is Rent-a-Wreck (800 421-7253). While these cars often rent for half what major companies charge, they probably consume more gas than would a new, economy-size rental car.

Though the cost of gasoline has dropped considerably in the past year, it's something motorists often forget to budget into their car rental expenses. On the road, remember self-serve (where you do the pumping) is usually less expensive than full-serve. Also, remember to return the car with the tank *full,* since gasoline at the car rental pump is always much more expensive than gasoline you buy on the road.

Traveling by Plane

It *sounds* expensive to travel across the country via air, but it could be the most economical way to go if you must get to your destination quickly. Plane travel is actually cheaper per mile than travel by car (11¢ per mile to fly on a commercial airline; 28¢ to drive your own car).

If you do decide to fly, there are some basic facts you should know about the kinds of flights available, the rules governing air travel, and bargain fares now offered.

SCHEDULED AIRLINES: A number of airlines offer regularly scheduled flights in the US. Within their ranks are all the well-known major companies and many smaller, regional companies that are not so familiar.

Fares – Today's fares are changing so rapidly, even the experts have trouble keeping up with them. At one time the airlines were strictly controlled by the Civil Aeronautics Board (CAB), which dictated rates, routes, and consumer protection guidelines. Due to airline deregulation and the phasing out of the CAB, however, competition among airlines has been fierce in recent years, and many are suffering financially because of the resulting profusion of discounts on the market.

There are three basic fare categories for domestic flights — first class, coach (sometimes called economy), and excursion or other discount fares. A fourth category, called business class (an intermediate class between first and coach with many of the amenities of first class and more leg room than coach), has been added by many airlines in recent years.

A first-class ticket is your admission to a special section of the aircraft with larger seats, more leg room, better food, free drinks, and, above all, lavish attention.

Coach passengers sit more snugly, behind the first-class section, and receive standard meal service. Like first-class passengers, however, people paying the full coach fare are subject to none of the restrictions attached to cheaper discount fares. There are no advance booking requirements, no minimum stay requirements, and no cancellation penalties. Tickets are sold on an open reservation system: They can be bought for a flight up to the minute of takeoff if seats are available. If your ticket is round-trip, you can make your return reservation anytime you wish — months before you leave or the day before you return. Both first-class and coach tickets are generally good for a year, after which they can be renewed if not used, and if you ultimately decide not to fly at all, your money will be refunded.

Excursion and other discount fares are the airlines' version of a sale. Because it costs almost as much to run a half-empty plane as it does to run a full one, the airlines may, in an effort to fill all seats, offer lower prices to a limited number of people in the hope of attracting some who would not otherwise take the trip. They may cut down the number of reduced fares available per flight when they expect traffic paying full fare to be good and add more when they expect it to be poor. Needless to say, these reduced-rate seats are most limited at busy times such as holidays, when full-fare coach seats sell most quickly. Passengers fortunate enough to get a discount ticket sit with the full-fare coach passengers and receive the same basic services, even though they have paid anywhere between 20% and 50% less for the trip.

These discount or excursion fares may masquerade under a variety of names (Super Saver is the most common one), they may vary from city to city (what is available on the East Coast may not be available on the West Coast), but they invariably have strings attached. In general, the more restrictive they are, the cheaper they are. You usually must book the flight between 7 and 30 days in advance and often must pay for it shortly thereafter. You may well have to stay at your destination for a specified period of time; for example, no less than 7 days and no more than 30 days, or you may have to remain at your destination for at least one weekend day. Finally, you do *not* have the option of changing your plans after a certain point without losing money in the form of a cancellation penalty. If none of the above conditions apply, prospective passengers can be fairly sure that the number of seats per flight at this price is limited or that the fare came on the market with a set expiration date, either of which means they will have to move fast to be among the lucky ones.

Airlines have traditionally offered their most attractive special fares to encourage travel in slow seasons and to inaugurate and publicize new routes, but increasingly the stimulus for special fares is the appearance of upstart competitors offering bargain fares on the same route. These tend to be smaller carriers that can offer more for less because of lower overhead, uncomplicated route networks, and other limitations in their service. They include airlines such as People Express, which is no longer such a "small" airline. People Express is almost synonymous with "no frills," although it does have a first-class section (called Premium) on an increasing number of flights. It is important to note that tickets offered by the smaller airlines specializing in low-cost travel frequently are not subject to the same restrictions as the lowest-price ticket offered by the more established carriers. They may require no advance purchase or minimum and maximum stays, may involve no cancellation penalties, may be available one way or round trip, and may, for all intents and purposes, resemble the competition's high-priced full-fare coach. But never assume this until you know it's so.

Many major airlines now offer a bonus system to frequent travelers. After the first 10,000 miles, for example, you might receive a first-class ticket for the coach fare; after another 10,000 miles you might receive a discount on your next ticket purchase. The value of the bonuses continues to increase as you log more miles. Occasionally, airlines also have unlimited-mileage deals. For a flat fee (currently anywhere from $500 to $800, depending on whether you fly as part of a couple or travel alone, in low or high season), a traveler may fly anywhere in the US, logging an unlimited number of miles. Many restrictions apply, however, including the requirement that all stops be scheduled and the entire fare paid for a certain number of days in advance, and that all travel be completed in a minimum of 7 days and a maximum of 21 days.

To find out about the fares that are most useful to you, read the business and travel sections of your newspaper regularly or call the airlines directly. Ask about discount or promotional fares to the destination you desire, and ask about any conditions that might restrict booking or payment as well as penalties for canceling or changing your plans. Ask if there is a difference in price between midweek travel and weekend travel, or if there is a further discount for traveling early in the morning or at night. Ask also about packages, offered by most airlines. These may include car rental, accommodations, and dining or sightseeing features in addition to the air fare, and the combined cost of the packaged elements usually is considerably less than the cost of all of them purchased separately. Check the prices from cities nearby. Sometimes, for example, a promotional fare is offered in New York but not in Philadelphia, and it's enough of a bargain to warrant leaving from New York.

When you're satisfied that you've received the lowest possible price (you may have to call each airline desk several times, because different clerks will often quote different prices), make your booking. Then, to protect yourself against fare increases, purchase your ticket as soon as possible after you've received a confirmed reservation. Remember that tickets for excursion or discount fares often *must* be purchased by a specific date. Miss the deadline, and you lose the discount.

If you don't have the time and patience to investigate personally all possible air departures and connections for a proposed trip, remember that a travel agent can be of inestimable help. A good agent should have all the information on what flights go where and when and what categories of tickets are available on each. An increasing number also have computerized reservation links with a major carrier, in which case information on seat availability on all flights for the day you want to leave can result in reservation and confirmation in a matter of minutes.

Seats – Airline seats are usually assigned on a first come, first served basis when you check in, though some airlines permit you to reserve a seat when you purchase a ticket, and some go a step further by allowing you to visit a ticket office before departure to secure a boarding pass for the flight. Once this has been issued, airline computers show you as "checked in," and you effectively own the seat you have selected (this is also good insurance against being bumped from an overbooked flight and is, therefore, an especially valuable tactic for travel at peak holiday times).

There are a few basics to consider in choosing a spot. First, determine whether you want to sit in a smoking or nonsmoking section and if you prefer a window, aisle, or center seat. A window seat protects you from aisle traffic and has a view (unless you are over the wing); an aisle seat enables you to get up and stretch your legs without disturbing anyone. Center seats are less desirable, and seats in the last row are the least desirable, since they seldom recline all the way.

The amount of leg room you'll have (as well as chest room when the seat in front of you is in a reclining position) is determined by pitch, a measure of the front to rear spacing between seats. Since airplanes have tracks along which this spacing can be adjusted, the amount of pitch is a matter of airline policy, not the type of plane you fly. First-class and business-class seats have the greatest pitch, a fact that figures prominently in airline advertising. In economy class or coach, the standard pitch ranges from 33 to as little as 31 inches — downright cramped. Passengers with long legs are advised to choose a seat directly behind a door or emergency exit, since these seats often have greater than average pitch, or a bulkhead seat — that is, a seat in the first row of the cabin. (Avoid the first row if you want to watch the movie.) The number of seats abreast, another factor determining comfort, depends on a combination of airline policy and airplane dimensions. First and business classes have the fewest seats per row. Economy generally has 9 seats per row on a DC-10 or an L-1011, making either one slightly more comfortable than a 747, on which there are 10 seats per row. However, charter flights on DC-10s and L-1011s can have 10 seats per row and be noticeably more cramped than 747 charters, on which the seating remains at 10 per row.

Meals – Just as seating can be arranged in advance, special meals can be ordered before flight time. Most of the major airlines offer kosher, salt-free, low cholesterol, vegetarian, and other special meals at no extra charge. You should order what you want at the time you make your reservation or at least 24 hours before your flight.

Smoking – Regulations require that nonsmoking sections on airplanes be enlarged to accommodate all passengers who want to sit in them, provided they have a confirmed reservation and arrive at least ten minutes before boarding. Cigarette smoking is prohibited on planes of 30 or fewer seats and if the ventilation system is not functioning. Cigar and pipe smoking are prohibited on all flights.

Getting Bumped – A special air travel problem is the possibility that an airline will accept more reservations (and sell more tickets) than there are seats on a given flight. This is entirely legal and is done to make up for passengers who don't show up for a flight for which they have reservations. If the airline has oversold the flight and everyone does show up, the airline is subject to stringent rules laid down to protect travelers.

The airline first seeks ticketholders willing to give up their seats voluntarily in return for a negotiable sum of money or some other inducement, such as an offer of upgraded seating on the next flight or a voucher for a free trip at some other time. If there are not enough volunteers, the airline may bump passengers against their wishes. Anyone inconvenienced in this way, however, is entitled to an explanation of the criteria used to determine who does and does not get on the flight, as well as to compensation if the resulting delay exceeds certain limits. If the airline can put the bumped passengers on an alternate flight that gets them to their planned destination within 1 hour of the originally scheduled arrival time, no compensation is owed. If the delay is more than an hour, they must be paid denied-boarding compensation equivalent to the one-way fare to their destination (but not more than $200). If the delay is more than 2 hours beyond the original arrival time on a domestic flight, the compensation must be doubled. The airline may also offer bumped travelers a voucher for a free flight instead of the denied-boarding compensation. The passenger can choose either the money or the voucher (the dollar value of which may be no less than the monetary compensation to which the passenger would be entitled). The voucher is not a substitute for the bumped passenger's original ticket — the airline continues to honor that as well.

These rules do *not* apply to charters or to planes carrying less than 60 people. They also do not apply if the flight is canceled or delayed, or if a smaller aircraft is substituted due to mechanical problems. In such cases, some airlines provide amenities to stranded passengers, but these are strictly at the individual airline's discretion. Deregulation of the airlines has meant that the traveler must find out for himself what he is entitled to receive. A useful booklet, *Air Travelers' Fly Rights,* is available for $2.75 from the Superintendent of Documents, US Government Printing Office, Washington, DC 20402; stock number 003-006-00106-5.

To protect yourself against getting bumped, arrive at the airport early, allowing plenty of time to check in and get to the gate — an hour in advance if possible. If the flight is oversold, immediately ask for the written statement explaining the airline's policy on denied-boarding compensation and its boarding priorities. If the airline doesn't cooperate, file a complaint with both the airline and the appropriate federal consumer advocate (see below).

Delays and Cancellations – Each airline has its own policy for assisting passengers whose flights are delayed or canceled or who must wait for another flight because their original flight was overbooked. Most airline personnel will make new travel arrangements if this becomes necessary. If the delay is longer than 4 hours, the airline will sometimes pay for a phone call or telegram, a meal, and in some cases a hotel room and transportation to the hotel.

Caution: If you are bumped or miss a flight, be sure to ask the airline to notify other airlines on which you have reservations or connecting flights. When your name is taken off the passenger list of your initial flight, the computer automatically cancels all of your reservations unless you take steps to preserve them.

Baggage – Though domestic airline baggage allowances may vary slightly, in general all passengers may carry on board, without charge, one piece of luggage that will fit easily under a seat and whose combined dimensions (length, width, and depth) do not exceed 45 inches. Airlines like People Express (which actually charges $3 per bag to check luggage through to your destination) and those airlines now flying Boeing 757 and 767 aircraft (where the overhead luggage compartments are considerably enlarged) are far more liberal about carry-on luggage. A reasonable amount of reading material, camera equipment, and a handbag are also allowed. In addition, all passengers may check two bags in the cargo hold: one usually not to exceed 62 inches in combined dimensions, the other not to exceed 55 inches. No single bag may weigh more than 70 pounds. Charges for additional, oversize, or overweight bags are made at a flat rate on domestic flights, though the actual dollar amount varies from carrier to carrier. Sports equipment is also often subject to an excess-baggage charge regardless of how much other baggage you have checked.

If your luggage is not in the baggage claim area after your flight has arrived or if it is damaged, report the problem to the airline personnel immediately (some airlines disclaim liability for missing or damaged luggage that is not reported in writing within four hours of the arrival of the flight). Next, fill out a report form on your lost or damaged luggage. Finally, hold on to your claim check until you receive your baggage. Most airlines will give you some money at the airport for emergency purchases if your luggage cannot be readily located, but if it turns out your bags are truly lost and not simply delayed, do not then and there sign any paper indicating you'll accept an offered settlement. Since the airline is responsible for the value of your bags within certain statutory limits, you should take time to assess the extent of your loss (see *Insurance*).

The best way to reduce the chance of your luggage going astray is, when possible, to fly as many legs of a multistop journey on one airline, even if this means a longer wait between flights. Another wise measure to help ensure that your baggage arrives when and where you do is to remove all tags from previous trips and doublecheck the tag that the airline puts on your bag to make sure that it is coded for your destination. Airlines also require that you label your bags inside and outside with your name and address, and suggest you include (inside) a person to contact at your destination if possible. Always lock your luggage.

CHARTER FLIGHTS: By actually renting a plane or at least booking a block of seats on a specially arranged flight, charter operators have long been able to offer air transportation — often combined with a hotel room, meals, and other arrangements in a package — for less money than most regular fares on scheduled flights. Although charter fares were once the only bargains available, various discount fares on scheduled airlines are now often just as low, and they are usually more flexible. But charters to some popular vacation spots can still be the best buy.

You pay in convenience for what you save in money on a charter. If you are forced to cancel your flight, you could lose most or possibly all of your money unless you have cancellation insurance, which is a *must* (see *Insurance,* in this section). Charters have little of the flexibility of scheduled flights; you must leave and return on the scheduled dates; if you miss the plane, you lose your flight and your money — no refund.

Read all charter contracts carefully, noting what happens if you cancel and the circumstances under which the charterer may cancel (or change) a flight. Charter operators *may* cancel flights up to 10 days before departure; your money is returned in this event, but not necessarily in time to make new plans. (Also, be sure that any payments made to a charterer are deposited in an escrow account.)

CONSUMER INFORMATION: Consumers who feel they have not been dealt with fairly by an airline should make their complaints known. Begin with the customer service representative at the airport where the problem occurred, and if he or she cannot resolve the complaint, write to the airline's consumer office, attaching copies (never the originals) of any tickets, receipts, or other documents that back up your claims.

Until December 31, 1984, travelers with problems could also contact the Civil Aeronautics Board, which was responsible for overseeing the airline industry in a number of areas important to passengers. The Airline Deregulation Act of 1978, however, mandated the gradual phasing out of the CAB, though the law that abolished it did not abolish the consumer protection regulations it had established, nor its consumer assistance responsibilities. These responsibilities, along with many CAB employees, were transferred intact to the Department of Transportation. Passengers with problems that formerly fell under the CAB's jurisdiction — lost baggage, denied-boarding compensation, smoking rules, charter regulations, deceptive practices by an airline — should now write to the Office of Community and Consumer Affairs, US Department of Transportation, 400 Seventh St., SW, Room 10405, Washington, DC 20590, or call the office at 202 755-2220. Even so, consumer complaints should still be addressed initially to the airline that provoked them.

A charter flight or package should *always* be chosen with care. The Better Business Bureau in the home city of any charter company you are considering can tell you the complaints, if any, lodged against it. Also consult a reputable travel agent.

DISCOUNT TRAVEL SOURCES: An excellent source of information on economical travel opportunities is the *Consumer Reports Travel Letter,* published monthly by Consumers Union. It keeps abreast of the scene on a variety of fronts, including package tours, rental cars, insurance, and more, but it is especially helpful for its coverage of air fares, offering guidance on all the options from scheduled flights on major or low-fare airlines to charters and discount sources. For a year's subscription, send $37 to Consumer Reports Travel Letter, Subscription Dept., Box 5248, Boulder, CO 80322.

Still another way to take advantage of bargain air fares is open to those who have a flexible schedule. A number of organizations, usually set up as last-minute travel clubs and functioning on a membership basis, routinely keep in touch with travel suppliers to help them dispose of unsold inventory at discounts of between 15% and 60%. A great deal of the inventory consists of complete tour packages and cruises, but some clubs offer air-only charter seats and, occasionally, seats on scheduled flights. Members pay an annual fee and receive the toll-free number of a telephone hot line to call for information on imminent trips. In some cases, they also receive periodic mailings with information on upcoming trips for which there is more advance notice. Despite the suggestive names of the clubs providing these services, last-minute travel does not necessarily mean that you cannot make plans until literally the last minute. Trips can be announced with as little as a few days' or as much as two months' notice, but the average is from one to four weeks before departure. It does mean that your choice at any given time is limited to what is offered and, if your heart is set on a particular destination, you might not find what you want, no matter how attractive the bargains. Among these organizations are:

Discount Travel International, Suite 205, Ives Bldg., Narberth, PA 19072 (215 668-2182). Annual fee, $45.

Encore Short Notice, 4501 Forbes Blvd., Lanham, MD 20706 (301 459-8020). Annual fee, $36 per person, $46 per family.

Last-Minute Travel Club, 6A Glenville Ave., Allston, MA 02134 (617 254-5200). Annual fee, $25 per person, $30 per couple or family.

Moment's Notice, 40 E 49th St., New York, NY 10017 (212 486-0503). Annual fee, $45.

On Call to Travel, PO Box 11622, Portland, OR 97211 (503 287-7215). Annual fee, $45.

Stand Buys Ltd., 311 W Superior, Suite 414, Chicago, IL 60610 (312 943-5737 or 800 255-0200). Annual fee, $45.

Worldwide Discount Travel Club, 1674 Meridian Ave., Miami Beach, FL 33139 (305 534-2082). Annual fee, $45.

NET FARE SOURCES: The newest notion for supplying inexpensive travel services comes from travel agents who offer individual travelers "net" fares. Defined simply, a net fare is the bare minimum amount at which an airline or tour operator will carry a prospective traveler. It doesn't include the amount that would normally be paid to the travel agent as a commission. Traditionally, such travel agent commissions amount to about 8% on international tickets and 10% on domestic fares — not counting significant additions to these commission levels that are payable retroactively when agents sell more than a specific volume of tickets or trips for a single supplier. At press time, at least two travel agencies in the US were offering travelers the opportunity to purchase tickets and/or tours for the net price. Instead of making their income from conventional commissions, these agencies assess a fixed fee that may or may not provide a bargain for travelers; it requires a little arithmetic to determine whether you're better off with a net travel agent or one who accepts conventional commissions.

One net fare agency, *McTravel* (2335 Sanders Rd., Northbrook, IL 60062; 312 498-9390), will make a reservation for a domestic flight for a fixed fee of $8, will write a domestic ticket for $7, will reserve a place on an international flight for $20, and will write the international ticket for $10. Based on these fees, operative at press time, any international trip for which the ticket costs more then $400 looks like a good net buy; the breakeven on domestic tickets is somewhat lower. There's also the opportunity to economize further by making your own airline reservation, then asking *McTravel* only to write/issue your ticket. For travelers who reside outside the Chicago area, business may be transacted by phone and purchases paid for with a credit card.

Washington's World of Travel (1030 15th St., NW, Suite 942, Washington, DC 20005; 800 351-4495) doesn't sell individual airline tickets but does provide net price offerings if you're interested in a package tour or ocean cruise. It charges $50 for all travel transactions up to a total of $1,500; $100 for transactions between $1,500 and $5,000; and $150 for transactions over $5,000. The *WWT* fee applies to trips purchased for an entire family, so it's the cumulative cost of travel services purchased that determines the fee.

Touring by Train

 Almost all of the regularly scheduled passenger trains in the US are run by Amtrak, which serves most of the country's major cities and has made dramatic improvements in equipment and service. Routes, schedules, stations, and sample fares are given in the *National Timetable,* available at any Amtrak station or sales office (or through the national office at 400 N Capitol St., NW, Washington, DC 20001). You can reach Amtrak's computerized reservation service by calling 800 USA-RAIL. Agents can also provide information on tours, trains that connect with buses, and rail trips in Canada and even help with hotel reservations and car rental details.

ACCOMMODATIONS AND FARES: Amtrak fares are based on the quality of accommodation the passenger enjoys on the journey. Cheapest is basic transportation fare. Ordinarily this will buy a coach seat for the duration of the trip, but it guarantees only that the passenger has a right to transportation. Seats are allocated on a first come, first served basis. In addition to the seats, long-distance trains offer three classes of sleeping accommodations, for which the passenger pays significantly more: slumber-coaches, private rooms with lounge seats that convert to beds and a toilet and washstand; roomettes, larger rooms with chairs and fold-down beds; and full-sized bedrooms that can be combined into suites. The new Superliners have deluxe bedrooms; economy rooms, which are similar to a roomette with a toilet and washstand; and family bedrooms, which accommodate five people.

The cost of a coach seat — basic transportation fare — on a train will generally be something more than the cost of a bus ticket to the same destination, and something less than coach fare on a plane, except on such competitive routes as Boston to Washington, DC, where very inexpensive flights are available. For example, the Amtrak coach fare between Chicago and Seattle is about $130 more than bus fare, $170 less than coach fare on a plane. However, the plane makes the trip in a few hours; the train takes two days, and it is likely that anyone making the trip by train will want some kind of sleeping accommodations rather than just a coach seat. An economy room on that route costs about $50 less than the plane coach fare; and a deluxe bedroom about $160 more. So the cost of a train compared with that of a plane is very much relative to the level of comfort. From time to time, Amtrak also offers such promotional fares as a round-trip ticket for $7 more than the one-way fare.

BOOKING: Tickets may be obtained from Amtrak stations, travel agents, or on board the train (for an extra $3), and can be purchased with any major credit card or personal check. Reservations are mandatory for all club cars, sleeping cars, slumber-coaches, Metroliner coaches (high-speed electric trains that provide fast service between major cities), and on a number of other regular runs. Trains that require reservations are so marked in the *Timetable.* If you have difficulty reaching the reservation number, try early in the morning or late at night. Always allow extra time to make connections because trains are often late. If you have confirmed reservations and miss a connection because of a delayed train, Amtrak will provide overnight accommodations if necessary. Passengers can stop anywhere along their route for as long as they like, so long as they reach their final destination before their ticket expires (most tickets are good for a year). Sleeping car attendants should be tipped $1 a night.

BAGGAGE: In most stations, baggage can be checked through to destination up to one hour before departure (and should be claimed within 30 minutes after arrival). On long-distance runs, you will be allowed to carry on only enough baggage for essentials during the journey; you are allowed to check three pieces of luggage weighing a total of 150 pounds. Attendants on the train, or Red Caps in most stations, will give you free help with your luggage (tip about 50¢). Amtrak urges you to use only Red Caps.

TOURS: The USA Railpass is Amtrak's excursion rate, but it is not available to US citizens and can only be purchased in Europe. The pass entitles the holder to unlimited coach travel on Amtrak trains and routes for periods of 7, 14, 21, and 30 days. For US citizens, Amtrak sometimes offers Circle Fares, unlimited mileage and stopovers for a given time at a fixed fee. There is also an incredible variety of packages, or All Aboard American fares, in which the US is divided vertically into three zones and passengers can travel for a reduced round-trip fare based on the number of zones they cross. Recently, Amtrak has introduced a number of worthwhile tours, some connecting with boat, bus, or car packages. Brochures and details on Amtrak tours are available from Amtrak stations or from travel agents. Call USA-RAIL or write Amtrak Distribution Center, Western Folder Distributing Co., PO Box 7717, Itasca, IL 60143.

Touring by Bus

 Crisscrossing America's highways to serve nearly 10,000 cities and towns, bus companies are easily the country's most comprehensive public transport system. You can almost always get there by bus. Two major national bus companies, Continental Trailways and Greyhound, have depots in most cities across the country (listed in the yellow pages under Bus). Greyhound runs 3,000 buses over 70,000 miles of routes; Trailways' fleet is slightly smaller at 1,300 and covers 86,000 miles of highways. These two giants, with the many smaller independent firms in operation around the country, offer the most frequent, most economical transportation in America. Buses are undeniably slower than trains, planes, or private cars, and there is a trade-off of money saved for time spent en route.

ACCOMMODATIONS AND FARES: The cost of a bus trip is about 7¢ a mile, compared to 11¢ a mile by plane and 20¢ to 30¢ a mile by private car. The real savings in bus travel are most evident on long-distance, round-trip journeys. The difference between the train and bus fares on a one-way, New York–Philadelphia trip is about $7 (about $60 difference between bus and coach air fare). However, the difference between bus and train one-way rates from Denver to San Francisco is about $88. Lately the competition among bus companies is increasing, so that it is worth asking about promotional fares and checking with more than one company.

Bus passengers are allowed to stop anywhere along their route, as long as their entire journey is completed before the ticket expires. Most regular bus tickets are good for 30 days. If you don't use the ticket within that time, it may be returned for a full refund, or replaced by another ticket.

BOOKING: Reservations are not necessary on most bus routes; companies usually send as many buses as are needed to handle all passengers. Sightseeing tours and special programs (see below) require reservations and are subject to slightly different stopover rules. Both Greyhound and Trailways have unlimited travel tickets that allow the ticket holder to travel anywhere in the US on company routes (and often on the routes of smaller, connecting bus lines) for specified periods of time (7, 15, and 30 days). Special prices for these unlimited travel deals represent considerable savings. Greyhound's program is called Ameripass; Trailways offers Eaglepass.

SERVICES: Most buses are not equipped for food service. On long trips they make meal stops, and there is always food service of one kind or another in the terminals. It is not a bad idea to bring some food aboard. Almost all interstate, long-distance buses have air conditioning, heating, toilets, adjustable seats, and reading lamps.

FOR COMFORTABLE TRAVEL: Dress casually with loose fitting clothes. Be sure you have a sweater or jacket (even in the summer, air conditioning can make buses quite cool). Passengers are allowed transistor radios, but must use earphones. Choose a seat in the front near the driver for the best view, or in the middle between the front and rear wheels for the smoothest ride. Avoid the back near the toilet unless you smoke. Smokers are generally restricted to the last rows of any bus.

TOURS: Greyhound offers a wide variety of sightseeing bus tours. These include accommodations for overnight stays. For information on these tour programs, check with your Greyhound office. Dozens of tour operators offer a wide variety of bus or motorcoach tours in the US. One directory is the *Travel Agent Domestic Tour Manual* published by *Travel Agent* magazine, available in libraries. Travel agents also have this information.

Package Tours

A package tour is a travel arrangement that combines several travel services — transportation, accommodations, sightseeing, meals, etc. — into a one-price, one-booking package. The cost of the entire package is well below the combined price of the services if bought independently; and the passenger is freed from the bother of making any separate arrangements.

There are hundreds of package programs on the market today, offered by airlines, Amtrak, and the bus companies, as well as car rental companies, hotels, and travel companies. Many are built around sports activities like skiing. A typical package tour might include transportation to and from the destination, accommodations for the length of stay, a sightseeing tour of the area, and some meals. The price for this (especially if transportation were provided via charter flight) could be less than a round-trip coach airline ticket to the destination on a regularly scheduled flight.

One of the consumer's biggest problems is finding enough information to judge the reliability of a tour operator. First check to see if they are a member of the United States Tour Operators Association (USTOA), which has strict eligibility requirements. An operator must be in business for at least three years and carry a minimum of $1 million in professional liability insurance (similar to medical malpractice insurance). Write the USTOA, 211 E 51st St., New York, NY 10022, to receive a list of members. Also check the Better Business Bureau in your area to see if any complaints have been filed against the operator.

Since a retail travel agent usually intervenes between customer and tour operator, much depends on the candor and cooperation of the agent. Ask your travel agent a number of questions about the tour he or she is recommending. For example: Has the agent ever used the packages provided by this tour operator? How long has the tour operator been in business? Which and how many companies are involved in the package? If air travel is by charter flight, is there an escrow account in which deposits will be held, and, if so, what is the name of the bank?

This last question is very important. The law requires that tour operators deposit any charter passenger's deposit and subsequent payment in a proper escrow trust account. Money paid into such an account cannot legally be used except to pay for the costs of a particular package or as a refund if the trip is canceled. So to ensure safe handling of your money, make out your check to the escrow bank account. The law requires that the account number appear on any tour brochure, and it is usually found in that mass of minuscule type on the back. On the face of your check, write the details of the charter, including the destination and dates; on the back, print the words "for deposit only." Your travel agent may prefer that you make your check out to him, saying that he will then pay the tour operator the fee minus his commission. But it is perfectly legal to write your check this way, and if your agent objects too vociferously, consider taking your business elsewhere. If you don't make your check out to the escrow account, you lose all protection should the trip be canceled or the tour operator or travel agent fail. (Even the protection of escrow may not be enough to safeguard a traveler's investment, as recent bankruptcies and defaults by travel suppliers have served to illustrate. For information on insurance against such eventualities, see *Insurance.*)

Read package tour brochures carefully and with a grain of salt. Begin by assuming that the things that are not mentioned are not included in the price of the tour. Tour brochures often feature the lowest price at which a tour is offered, but this price may be available in off-season only, during midweek, at the cheapest hotel (which some travelers would not find satisfactory), or in such limited numbers that it is sold out at once. And remember: Prices quoted in brochures are based upon double occupancy (two people traveling together); if you travel alone, you will have to pay a single supplement (see *Hints for Single Travelers*). Tour brochures give prices of tours from the city of departure; if you don't live there, you must add transportation to and from that city.

Understand what is, and is not, included in a package. This may vary, but is generally spelled out in the fine print in the brochure. Read it and ask the following questions:

1. Does the tour include air fare (or other transportation), sightseeing, meals, transfers, taxes, baggage handling, tips, or any other services? Do you want all these services? If the brochure says "some meals" are included, exactly what does this mean — breakfast and dinner every day, or a farewell dinner the last night? Do you have a choice of food, or must you stick to a single menu?
2. What classes of hotels are offered?
3. Do you get a refund if you cancel? (If not — and stipulations vary widely between tour operators — get cancellation insurance.)
4. Can the operator cancel if not enough people join? (Usually the answer is yes.)
5. Is the price quoted in the literature guaranteed or can the tour operator increase it before departure?

Read the responsibility clause on the back page. Here the tour operator usually reserves the right to change services or schedules as long as you are offered equivalent service; this clause also absolves the operator of responsibility for circumstances beyond human control, like floods or famines, and of responsibility for injury to you.

Camping, Hiking, Biking, Recreational Vehicles

CAMPING: Fifty-eight million Americans go camping every year, and that can mean anything from backpacking with a pup tent to living in comfort in a plush recreational vehicle. There are almost 17,000 campgrounds serving these campers, some private, many in national or state parks and forests. Some excellent guides to campgrounds are, from Rand McNally: *Campgrounds & Trailer Parks* ($12.95), *Western Campgrounds & Trailer Parks* ($7.95), *Eastern Campgrounds and Trailer Parks* ($7.95); from Simon & Schuster: *North American Camp-*

ground Directory ($12.95), *Eastern Campground Directory* ($8.95), and *Western Campground Directory* ($8.95). *Free Campgrounds, U.S.A.,* by Mary Van Meer, describes over 6,500 free campgrounds and is available from the East Woods Press, 820 E Boulevard, Charlotte, NC 28203 ($9.95). In addition, the AAA has free camping guides for AAA members which give practical camping hints as well as lists of campgrounds and facilities. It is now possible to reserve campsites at several national parks through Ticketron as well as through many National Park Service offices.

Where to Camp – Campsites range from private facilities to state and national parks. For information on the national parks, request *Guide and Map: National Parks of the United States* from the National Park Service, Public Inquiries Office, 18th and C Sts., NW, Washington, DC 20240. Most national parks (even the famous ones like Yosemite, Grand Canyon, and Yellowstone) have adjacent extensive national forests with the same beautiful country. For a complete list of national forests, write for the free Forest Service brochure FS 13, *Field Offices of the Forest Service,* US Forest Service, Office of Information, PO Box 2417, Washington, DC 20013.

The National Park Service also encourages campers to use lesser-known national parks in its brochure *Lesser Known Areas of the National Park System,* usually available free from local offices of the Park Service or from the Superintendent of Documents, US Government Printing Office, Washington, DC 20402.

Organized Trips – If you want to go far afield with an experienced guide and other campers, contact these organizations:

American Forestry Association, 1319 18th St., NW, Washington, DC 20036 (202 467-5810 or 800 368-5748)

American Wilderness Alliance, 7600 E Arapahoe Rd., Suite 114, Englewood, CO 80112 (303 771-0380)

Appalachian Mountain Club, 5 Joy St., Boston, MA 02108 (617 523-0636)

Nature Expeditions International, PO Box 11496, Eugene, OR 97440 (503 484-6529)

Sierra Club, 730 Polk St., San Francisco, CA 94109 (415 981-8634)

Yosemite Institute, PO Box 487, Yosemite, CA 95389 (209 372-4441)

HIKING: If you would rather eliminate all the gear and planning and take to the outdoors unencumbered, park the car and go for a day's hike. There are fabulous trails in the United States (some of the very best are listed in *Wilderness Trips on Foot,* DIVERSIONS).

To make outings safe and pleasant, find out about the trails you plan to hike, and know your own limits. Choose an easy route if you are out of shape. Stick to the trails unless you are an experienced hiker or know the area well. If it is at all wild, let someone at the beginning of the trail know where you going, or leave a note on your car.

All you need to set out are a pair of sturdy shoes and socks, jeans or long pants to keep branches, poison ivy, and bugs off your legs, a canteen of water, a hat for the sun, and, if you like, a picnic lunch. It is a good idea to dress in layers, so that you can peel off a sweater or two to keep pace with the rising sun and replace them as the sun goes down. Make sure, too, to wear clothes with pockets or bring a pack to keep your hands free. Some useful and important pocket or pack stuffers include a jackknife, waterproof matches, a map, compass, and in snake areas, a snake bite kit.

BIKING: In choosing bike routes, long or short, look for ways to escape the omnipresent automobile and its fumes. Stick to back roads; use state highway maps which list secondary roads that the gasoline company maps ignore. Especially good riding is along old canal roads, abandoned railroad right-of-ways, and hard, packed beaches. Two sources of bike routes and roads are *The Bicycle Touring Book* by Glenda and Tim Wilhelm (Rodale Press; $14.95 cloth; $10.95 paperback) and *American Biking Atlas & Touring Guide* by Sue Browder (Workman; $5.95). For general biking information, try the *All New Complete Book of Bicycling* by Eugene A. Sloane (Simon & Schuster; $19.95) and *Anybody's Bike Book: The New Revised and Expanded Edition* by Tom Cuthbertson (Ten Speed Press; $8.95 cloth; $4.95 paperback).

Road Safety – While the car may be the bane of cyclists, cyclists who do not follow the rules of the road strike terror in the hearts of automobile drivers. Follow the same rules and regulations as motor vehicle drivers. Stay to the right side of the road. Ride no more than two abreast, or single file where traffic is heavy. Keep three bike lengths behind the bike in front of you. Stay alert to sand, gravel, potholes, and wet surfaces; make sure to wear bright clothes and use lights at dusk or night.

Choosing a Bike – A bicycle is the correct size for you if you can straddle its center bar with feet flat on the ground and an inch or so between your crotch and the bar. (Nowadays, because women's old-fashioned barless bikes are not as strong as men's, many women buy men's bicycles.) Seat height is right if your leg is just short of completely extended when you push the pedal to the bottom of its arc. Experienced cyclists keep tires fully inflated (pressure requirements vary widely, but are always imprinted on the side of the tire; stay within five pounds of the recommended pressure), and pedal at an even pace. For roadside repairs, and especially on longer rides, carry a tool kit of a bike wrench, screwdriver, pliers, tire repair kit, cycle oil, work gloves.

Tours – For a variety of bicycle tours, contact:

> *Backroads Bicycle Touring,* PO Box 1626-M50, San Leandro, CA 94577 (415 895-1783), for California, Yellowstone, and the Grand Tetons
>
> *Bicycling West,* PO Box 15128, San Diego, CA 92115-0128 (619 583-3001), for Oregon and California
>
> *Country Cycling Tours,* 140 W 83rd St., New York, NY 10024 (212 874-5151), for greater New York and the Northeast
>
> *Vermont Bicycle Touring,* Box 711, Bristol, VT 05443 (802 453-4811), for Vermont

General biking information is available through biking clubs in almost every city in the country (listed in the yellow pages under Clubs); a national biking organization is Bicycle USA, Suite 209, 6707 Whitestone Rd., Baltimore, MD 21207 (301 944-3399).

RECREATIONAL VEHICLES: The term recreational vehicles (or RVs) is applied to all manner of camping vehicles, whether towed or self-propelled. The level of comfort in an RV is limited only by the amount of money you choose to spend: It can be nothing more than an enclosed space for sleeping bags, or it can be a home on wheels, requiring electrical hookups at night to run the TV and kitchen appliances.

Towed RVs – Tow vehicles are hitched to cars or trucks and pulled. At their simplest, they are fold-down campers, tents on wheels that unfold into sleeping spaces. Fold-down campers weigh about 1,100 pounds and cost between $2,400 and $6,800. More elaborate are travel trailers, 10 to 30 feet long (average is about 22 feet), weighing up to 10,000 pounds, and costing as much as $30,000 (they start around $6,000).

Self-Propelled RVs – There are several styles of self-propelled vehicles:

1. Truck campers are converted pickup trucks with covered living units built on the truck body, often with sections extending over truck cabs. Cost and weight depend upon the size of the truck; but the living units alone cost between $6,500 and $8,500.
2. Van campers are just like store delivery vans, modified inside for living, sleeping, and dining. They cost anywhere from $21,000 to $30,000.
3. Mini/Class A motor homes are homes on wheels, with varying degrees of size and luxury. A mini costs between $25,000 and $45,000, a Class A starts around $30,000 and can cost as much as $70,000.

Gas Consumption – An RV undoubtedly saves the traveler a great deal of money on accommodations, and, if cooking appliances are part of the unit, on food. However, any RV increases gas consumption. It is most expensive to tow a large trailer camper, which decreases auto mileage by 50%. More economical, because smaller, is the fold-down tow camper, which will reduce normal car mileage by about 10% to 15%. Self-propelled RVs have no better mileage records. A truck camper gets about 20% less mileage than the same truck without camper, and an average Class A motor home gets only 7 to 12 miles per gallon of gas.

To reduce gas consumption, travel lightly (for every 100 pounds of weight, you use one percent more gas). Carry only the water you need on the road. Put everything inside your RV to reduce wind resistance and save on gas.

Renting – RVs are a poor choice for people who do not like to drive. They are not for people who want to leave housekeeping chores behind when they set off on vacation. They are sure to sour a person who cannot stand to do any maintenance or simple handyman chores, nor are they for people who need lots of privacy. The best way to introduce yourself to traveling by RV is to rent one. Some dealers will apply rental fees to the eventual price of purchase (check the yellow pages, and shop around for the best terms). For information on how to operate, maintain, choose, and use a recreational vehicle, see *Living in Style the RV Way,* a pamphlet available for $1.75 from the Recreational Vehicle Industry Association, PO Box 2999, Reston, VA 22090. You might also want to subscribe to *Trailer Life,* TL Enterprises, 29901 Agoura Rd., Agoura, CA 91301 ($16 a year).

Preparing

Calculating Costs

$ A realistic appraisal of your travel expenses is the most crucial bit of planning you'll undertake before your trip. It is also, unfortunately, one for which it is most difficult to give precise practical advice. Travel styles are intensely personal, and style to a great extent determines cost. Will you stay in a hotel every night? Will you eat every meal in a restaurant? Are you camping or picnicking? The "average" per diem costs we offer below are based on certain assumptions — every night in a hotel, every meal in a restaurant — that are hardly graven in stone. Never let published figures on the cost of travel frighten you out of taking a trip. You can always make economies and travel more cheaply. On the other hand, never get lulled into the feeling that you don't need to budget before you go. No matter how lush your travel budget, you will discover that without careful planning beforehand, and strict accounting along the way, you will spend more than you anticipated.

If you spend every night in a hotel or motel, and *if* you eat every meal in a modestly priced restaurant, you can expect to spend about $70 per person a day traveling. This figure does not include transportation costs. It does include accommodations (based on two people sharing a room), three meals, some sightseeing and other modest entertainment costs. It is based on recent figures of the average amount that Americans spent each day on trips of 200 miles or more, adjusted for inflation. It is, therefore, a national figure, and if it seems a bit arbitrary, bear in mind that as a raw figure it should represent no more than the broadest kind of guideline for daily costs.

However, adjusted for regional price differences it produces some figures that are much more useful. For example, overall prices in the Mountain West indicate that a day's travel costs about 5% less than this national figure. Travel in the Northeast or on the West Coast can cost from 15% to 30% more.

CALCULATING TRANSPORTATION COSTS: In earlier sections of GETTING READY TO GO we have discussed comparative costs of different modes of transportation, and the myriad special travel rates available through package tours, mid-week flights, train and bus budget deals. See each of the relevant sections for specific information. Transportation is likely to represent one of the largest items in your travel budget, but the encouraging aspect of this is that you can determine these costs before you leave. Fares will have to be paid in advance, especially if you take advantage of budget air travel or other special deals. Except for breakdown or repairs (for which you should budget something), car costs can be calculated by figuring mileage and average gas prices, based on your own experience.

A NOTE ON OUR HOTEL/RESTAURANT COST CATEGORIES: There are a great many moderate and inexpensive hotels and restaurants which we have not included in this book. Our *Best in Town* and *Best en Route* listings include only those places we think are best in their price range. We have rated our listings by general price categories: expensive, moderate, inexpensive. The introductory paragraph of each listing gives an indication of just what those categories mean within the context of local prices.

Planning a Trip

123 The merits of planning a trip carefully *before* you leave should be evident to even resolute nonplanners. But there are certain parameters within which each traveler must decide what to do, where to do it, how to get there, and how much to spend. You should consider these carefully even before you begin the time-consuming groundwork:

1. How much time do you have for the entire vacation, and how much of that do you want to spend in transit?
2. What interests and activities do you want to pursue (what makes the most pleasant break from your daily routine)?
3. What time of year are you going?
4. How much money is available for the entire vacation?

In addition, your general lifestyle will affect your decisions: What degree of comfort do you require; will you consider a tour, or do you want complete independence; how much responsibility for the trip do you want (will you consider a package trip)?

There is no lack of travel information in and on the United States. You can turn to travel agents, who specialize in planning and arranging trips (see *How to Use a Travel Agent,* in this section), to travel clubs such as AAA and other motoring organizations which have tour centers, and to general travel sources like books, guidebooks, brochures, and maps. State tourist boards and city convention centers provide vast amounts of literature of this sort for the asking (for details on getting travel information and a bibliography of travel books and sources, see this section, *For More Information* and *State Tourist Offices;* for city convention and tourist centers, see the *Sources and Resources* section of each city report in THE AMERICAN CITIES).

Make plans early. If you are flying and hope to take advantage of the considerable savings offered through discount fares or charter programs, you may need reservations as much as three months in advance. In high season, and in popular destinations, hotel and resort reservations are required months in advance (hotels inside Walt Disney World, for example, often demand a year's notice). Hotels require deposits before they will guarantee reservations. Be sure you have a receipt for any deposit.

Household details before you leave:

1. Arrange for your mail to be forwarded, held by the post office, or picked up daily at your house. Someone should check your door occasionally to pick up any unexpected deliveries. Piles of leaflets, circulars, packages, or brochures are an announcement to thieves that no one is home.
2. Cancel all deliveries (newspapers, milk, etc.).
3. Arrange for the lawn to be mowed at the regular times.
4. Arrange for care of pets.
5. Etch your social security number in a prominent place on all appliances (televisions, radios, cameras, kitchen appliances). This considerably reduces their appeal to thieves, and facilitates identification.
6. Leave a house key, your itinerary, and your automobile license number (if driving) with a relative or friend, and notify police that you are leaving and who has the key and itinerary.
7. Empty refrigerator, lower thermostat.
8. Immediately before leaving, check that all doors, windows, and garage doors are securely locked.

To further discourage thieves, it is wise to set up several variable timers around the house so that lights and even the television go on and off several times in different rooms of the house each night.

Make a list of any valuable items you are carrying with you, including credit card numbers and the serial numbers of your traveler's checks. Put copies in your luggage, purse, or pocket, and leave one copy at home. Put a label with your name and home address on the inside of your luggage, to facilitate identification in case of loss. Put your name and your business address on a label on the exterior of your luggage.

Review your travel documents. If you are traveling by air, check to see that your ticket has been filled in correctly. The left side of the ticket should have a list of each stop you will make (even if you are only stopping to change planes) beginning with your departure point. Be sure that the list is correct, and count the number of carbons to see that you have one for each plane you will take. If you have confirmed reservations, be sure that the column marked "status" says "OK" beside each flight. Have in hand vouchers or proofs of payment for any reservations paid in advance. This includes hotels, transfers to and from the airport, sightseeing, car rentals, special events, etc.

If you are traveling by car, bring your driver's license, auto registration, proof of insurance, gasoline credit cards, and auto service card if you have them, maps, books, flashlight, batteries, emergency flasher, first aid kit, extra car keys, and sunglasses. (For more information on preparing your car, see *Touring by Car,* in this section).

Finally, if you are traveling by plane, call to reconfirm your flight. While this is not required on domestic flights as it is on international flights, it is always advisable.

How to Pack

 Exactly what you pack on your trip will be a function of where you are going and when, and the kind of things you intend to do. As a first step, however, find out about the general weather conditions — temperature, rainfall, seasonal variations — at your destination. This information is included in the individual city reports of THE AMERICAN CITIES; other sources of information are airlines, travel agents, state tourist offices, and local convention and visitors bureaus.

Throughout the United States life is quite casual, and only at the most elegant resorts will you be required to have dressy clothes. If you are planning to be on the move — either in a car, bus, train, or plane — consider loose fitting clothes that do not wrinkle. Lightweight wools, knits, and drip-dry fabrics travel best, and prints look fresher longer than solids. Bring styles and colors of clothes that can be matched to give you as much variety with as few articles of clothing as possible.

The idea is to get everything into the suitcase and out again with as few wrinkles as possible. Put heavy items on the bottom toward the hinges of the suitcase, so that they do not wrinkle other clothes. Candidates for the bottom layer include shoes (stuff them with small items to save space), toiletry kit, handbags (stuff them to help keep their shape), and alarm clock. Fill out this layer with things that will not wrinkle or will not matter if they do, such as socks, bathing suit, gloves, and underwear.

If you get this first, heavy layer as smooth as possible with the fill-ins, you will have a shelf for the next layer of the more easily wrinkled items like slacks, jackets, shirts, dresses, and skirts. These should be buttoned and zipped, laid along the whole width of the suitcase, with as little folding as possible. When you do need to make a fold, do it on a crease (as with pants), along a seam in the fabric, or in a place where it will not show, such as shirttails. Alternate each piece of clothing, using one side of the suitcase, then the other to make the layers as flat as possible.

On the top layer, put the things you will want at once: nightclothes, an umbrella or raincoat, or a sweater. With men's two-suiter suitcases, follow the same procedure.

Then place jackets on hangers, straighten them out, and leave them unbuttoned. If they are too wide for the suitcase, fold lengthwise down the middle, straighten the shoulders, and fold the sleeves in along the seam.

SOME PACKING HINTS: Cosmetics and any other liquids should be packed in plastic bottles, or at least wrapped in plastic bags and tied. Prepare for changes in the weather or for atypical temperatures; on abnormally hot or cold days, be able to dress in layers so that as the weather changes, you can add or remove clothes as required.

Some travelers like to have at hand a small bag with the basics for an overnight stay, particularly if they are traveling by plane. Always keep necessary medicine, valuable jewelry, travel documents, or business documents in your handbag, briefcase, or hand luggage. Never check these things with your luggage.

For more information on packing clothes, send a stamped, self-addressed envelope to Samsonite Corporation, Samsonite Traveler Advisory Service, Dept. 20, PO Box 38300, Denver, CO 80238, for their free brochure *Getting a Handle on Luggage.*

How to Use a Travel Agent

To make the most intelligent use of a travel agent's time and expertise, it is necessary to know something of the economics of the industry. As client, you pay nothing for most services performed by the agent; in most cases, any money the travel agent makes on the time spent arranging your itinerary — booking reservations, advising about the best beach — comes from the principals who provide travel services — the airlines, hotels, cruise companies, etc. These commissions run anywhere from 7% to 15% of the total cost of the services — not a king's ransom for the total amount of time a good agent can spend on your whole trip.

This tradition may be changing, so that in some cases a travel agent may ask you to pay a fee for very personal service such as planning an intricate itinerary or making reservations at places that do not pay commissions. In most instances, however, you'll find that agents continue to provide their services at no charge.

The commission system implies two things about your relationship with an agent:

1. You will get better service if you arrive at the agent's desk with your basic itinerary already planned. Know roughly where you want to go, what you want to do. Use the agent to make bookings for you (which pay commissions) and to advise on facilities, activities, alternatives within the parameters of the basic itinerary you have chosen. You get the best service when you are buying commissionable items. There are few commissions in a camping or driving-camping tour; an agent is unlikely to be very enthusiastic about helping to plan one.
2. There is always the danger that an incompetent or unethical agent will send you to a place offering the best commission rather than the best facilities. The only way to be sure you are getting the best service is to have faith in your travel agent.

You should choose a travel agent with the same care with which you would choose a lawyer. You will be spending a good deal of money on the basis of the agent's judgment, and you have a right to expect that judgment to be mature, informed, and interested. At the moment, unfortunately, there are no real standards within the industry itself. The quality of individual agents varies enormously. While several states are in the process of drawing up legislation for licensing agents, which would at least ensure that anyone acting as a travel agent has met some minimum standards, only Ohio, Rhode Island, California, and Hawaii at present have any form of registration on their books. However, one industry organization, the American Society of Travel Agents (ASTA), requires its members to adhere to its strict Principles of Professional

Conduct and Ethics code. If you feel you have been improperly or unfairly dealt with, complaints can be made to ASTA's Consumer Affairs Dept., 4400 MacArthur Blvd., NW, Washington, DC 20007 (202 965-7520). The Association of Retail Travel Agents (ARTA) is a smaller but very highly respected trade organization similar to ASTA, and its member agencies and agents similarly agree to abide by its Code of Ethics. Complaints about an ARTA member's service can be made to ARTA's Grievance Committee, 25 S Riverside Ave., Croton-on-Hudson, NY 10520 (914 271-9000). More useful is the knowledge that any travel agent who has been in the business for at least 5 years and has completed the 18-month course of study conducted by the Institute of Certified Travel Agents, in Wellesley, Massachusetts, will carry the initials CTC (Certified Travel Counselor) after his or her name. This indicates a relatively high level of expertise.

Perhaps the best way to find a travel agent is by word of mouth. If the agent (or agency) has done a good job for friends over a period of time, it indicates a level of commitment and concern in your favor.

Hints for Handicapped Travelers

The travel industry has dramatically improved services to the handicapped in the past few years. Easy access facilities are far from universal, but the handicapped traveler can look to many new policies and a wide range of information sources to make traveling easier.

PLANNING: Your trip will be more comfortable psychologically as well as physically if you know that at the end of each day there are accommodations that suit your needs. For this you will need access guides to tourist facilities. Here are a few:

Access Amtrak: A Guide to Amtrak Services for Elderly and Handicapped Travelers published by the National Railroad Passenger Corporation (400 N Capitol St., NW, Washington, DC 20001; free).

Access Travel: Airports published by the Airport Operators Council International. Lists 472 airports worldwide, rating 70 features from location and size of parking spaces to width of corridors and accessibility of toilets. (Access America, Washington, DC 20202; free.)

Access to the World by Louise Weiss (Facts on File; $14.95). This is an excellent guide to handicapped travel, with airport access information.

Frommer's Guide for the Disabled Traveler: The United States, Canada, & Europe by Frances Barish (Simon & Schuster; $10.95). A sightseeing and access guide to seven of the most frequently visited US cities plus Hawaii.

International Directory of Access Guides, a free listing of over 450 domestic and international access guides (descriptions of the services in a particular locale that are barrier-free or have reduced barriers). RIUSA Travel Survey Dept., Rehabilitation World, 1123 Broadway, Suite 704, New York, NY 10010 (212 620-4040).

TravelAbility by Lois Reamy (Macmillan; $13.95) gives vast amounts of information on finding tours for handicapped travel; coping with public transport; finding accommodations, special equipment, travel agents.

The Wheelchair Traveler by Douglass R. Annand. Though now out of print, this city-by-city, state-by-state access guide to hotels and restaurants is still useful. Check your library.

For general information, write to the National Rehabilitation Information Center, Catholic University, 4407 Eighth St., NE, Washington, DC 20017 (202 635-5826).

An excellent aid to planning is offered by the Travel Information Center, Moss Rehabilitation Hospital (12th St. and Tabor Rd., Philadelphia, PA 19141, 215 329-5715). The center will provide detailed information on hotel accommodations, restaurants, touring sites, and other travel concerns. To keep abreast of developments in travel for the handicapped as they occur, you may want to join SATH (Society for the Advancement of Travel for the Handicapped; annual $40 membership fee), an organization whose members include travel agents, tour operators, and other travel suppliers as well as consumers. SATH publishes a quarterly newsletter, provides information on tours, and makes available a free 48-page guide, *The United States Welcomes Handicapped Visitors,* covering transportation, accommodations, insurance, and customs regulations. Send a stamped (39¢) self-addressed number 10 envelope to SATH, 26 Court St., Brooklyn, NY 11242 (718 858-5483). *The Itinerary,* a magazine for handicapped travelers published by Whole Person Tours (address below), is $7 for 6 issues a year.

TOURS: Various travel agencies and tour operators plan and sponsor group trips for handicapped travelers and also make arrangements for individual travelers. They include:

Access Tours for the Disabled, Directions Unlimited, 344 Main St., Mount Kisco, NY 10546 (718 263-3835)

Evergreen Travel Service/Wings on Wheels Tours, 19505M 44th Ave. W, Lynnwood, WA 98036-5699 (206 776-1184)

Flying Wheels Travel, PO Box 382, 143 W Bridge St., Owatonna, MN 55060 (507 451-5005 or 800 533-0363)

The Guided Tour, 555 Ashbourne Rd., Elkins Park, PA 19117 (215 782-1370)

Potomac Tours, 1314 Pennsylvania Ave., SE, Washington, DC 20003 (800 424-2969)

Sprout, 204 W 20th St., New York, NY 10011 (212 431-1265)

Whole Person Tours, PO Box 1084, Bayonne, NJ 07002 (201 858-3400)

BY CAR: Those traveling in their own cars will find that the problems are about the same as traveling locally. Hertz, Avis, and National have hand-control cars at some locations. There are only a limited number available; call well in advance.

BY PLANE: Airlines are required to take all disabled people if they give advance notice and can be evacuated in an emergency. This represents no real change in airline policy: Most airlines have always been accommodating in dealing with handicapped passengers' problems. And the situation has improved with the new Boeing 767s now used by United and American airlines, with new facilities for handicapped passengers.

If you are handicapped, try to fly at less crowded times for greater comfort, and book nonstop or direct flights to keep boarding to a minimum. Tell the airline when you call for a reservation about your handicap, and give advance notice if you need a wheelchair. Arrive at the airport at least 45 minutes in advance.

Passengers in wheelchairs should get a luggage tag for their wheelchairs when they check in. They should stay in their own chairs until they are transferred to a narrower airline chair at the door of the aircraft. Their wheelchairs will then be sent down to the luggage compartment. (Some airlines have restrictions on battery-operated chairs; inquire beforehand.) Usually people in wheelchairs are asked to wait until other passengers have disembarked. If you are making a tight connection, tell the attendant.

BY TRAIN: Amtrak has a 25% discount on round-trip travel. Whether you are riding a reserved or unreserved train, call in advance to make special arrangements or to reserve Amtrak's special seats for handicapped travelers. The newer Amtrak cars, such as the Amfleet trains and Metroliners (on the New York to Washington route), are boarded on the level at most stations. In other parts of the country, you will need to get Amtrak personnel to help with steps. Wheelchairs are available at most stations. Amtrak's new cars have special seats, properly equipped bathrooms, and special sleeping compartments for the handicapped. Older equipment presents many barriers, and a traveling companion can make the trip much easier. If necessary, Amtrak will recommend a professional traveling companion. Seeing-eye dogs may ride in the passenger cars at no extra charge.

BY BUS: Both Greyhound and Trailways offer special handicapped tickets whereby the handicapped passenger and a companion travel for the price of only one fare. The handicapped passenger must have a doctor's letter certifying the handicap and stating that one companion is enough to help with getting on and off the bus. (If you can manage the bus steps on your own, you are not required to have a companion.) Both bus companies will carry nonmotorized folding wheelchairs for free.

If you are traveling to national parks, make sure to get the Golden Access Passport for free admission for you and your traveling companions and a 50% discount on such facilities as camping and boat launching.

Hints for Traveling with Children

 Bring easily washed, stain-resistant clothes, and encourage each child to pack a small bag of toys and games. Have a toy or two close at hand for long waits and take simple snacks, like a small box of raisins or crackers, for those moments when hunger strikes and food is miles away.

FAMILY TRIPS: An alternative to long car trips arc holidays specifically planned for families, based on some adventure or activity exciting for all. A few examples:

A riverboat trip down the Mississippi on the *Delta Queen,* Delta Queen Steamboat Co., 30 Robin Street Wharf, New Orleans, LA 70130 (504 586-0631).

A train trip to Yosemite National Park organized by Yosemite Gray Line, PO Box 2472, Merced, CA 95344 (209 383-1563).

Rafting the Snake River in Idaho, with the Sierra Club, 730 Polk St., San Francisco, CA 94109 (415 981-8634).

Wagon train trip put together by L. D. Frome, Wagons West, Afton, WY 83110 (307 886-5240).

These are just a few of literally hundreds of vacations available throughout the country. One book of ideas, with the names and addresses of the companies that feature such adventures, is *Adventure Travel North America* by Pat Dickerman (Adventure Travel; $12.95). Also see *Traveling with Children in the USA* by Leila Hadley (Morrow; $4.95) and *What to Do with the Kids This Year: One Hundred Family Vacation Places with Time Off for You!* by Jane Wilford and Janet Tice (East Woods Press; $8.95).

Consider trading houses or apartments with people in the area where you would like to vacation. Join an organization that fosters such arrangements, such as Vacation Exchange Club, 12006 111th Ave., Youngtown, AZ 85363 (602 972-2186); or Holiday Exchanges, PO Box 5294, Ventura, CA 93003 (805 642-4879).

Colleges and universities are opening campuses to travelers during traditional academic vacations and in the summer. Some offer accommodations only (usually very cheap, in dormitory rooms); others open their recreational facilities and sports centers to visitors.

Try to find hotels that welcome children — that don't charge for children under a certain age, for example. In many of the larger chain hotels, the staffs are more used to noisy or slightly misbehaving children. These hotels are also likely to have swimming pools or game rooms — both popular with most young travelers. Write the hotel in advance to discuss how old your children are, how long you plan to stay, and to ask for suggestions on sleeping arrangements. Among the hotels known to welcome kids are *The Grand Hotel* on Mackinac Island in Michigan, the *Westin Crown Center* in

Kansas City, the *Houston Oaks Hotel* in Houston, the *Hyatt Regency* in Atlanta, the *Bonaventure* in Montréal, the *Polynesian Village* at Walt Disney World in Orlando, Florida, and, of course, the *Plaza,* with its Eloise myth intact, in New York.

For another family pleaser, consider staying as a guest on a farm or dude ranch, lists of which can be obtained from state departments of agriculture (see *Vacations on Farms and Ranches,* DIVERSIONS). Write to state tourist bureaus for the names of parks with overnight accommodations and marinas where families can rent houseboats. Theme parks make good family vacations. They offer entertainment, rides, and games for the whole family and accommodate the hamburger-and-ice-cream tastes of children (see *Amusement Parks and Theme Parks,* DIVERSIONS).

PLANNING: If you are spending your vacation traveling, rather than visiting one spot or engaging in one activity, pace the days with children in mind; break the trip into half-day segments, with running around or "doing" time built in; keep travel time on the road to a maximum of four or five hours each day. Involve children in the initial planning stage at home; if they are as excited about the trip as you are, everyone will enjoy it more.

BY CAR: Traveling by car, you can be flexible — making any number of stops at souvenir shops or snake farms, and meeting moods and emergencies as they arise. You can also take more with you, including items like ice chests and charcoal grills for picnics. Frequent stops for children to run around make car travel much easier. So do games and simple toys, such as magnetic checkerboards or drawing pencils and pads. *Games to Play in the Car* by Michael Harwood (Congdon & Weed; $6.95) lists 40 survival games.

BY TRAIN: Amtrak allows children under 2 (accompanied by an adult) to travel for free anytime. For older children it offers a series of programs that allow a family to travel by train at considerable savings by picking and choosing departure days. Children 2 through 11 travel for half price (that is, half the full adult fare) on Fridays and Sundays; on every other day, the cheapest rate for travel with children is by Family Plan — the head of household pays full fare, spouse and children 12 to 21 pay ½ fare, children ages 2 through 11 are charged ¼ fare. All long-distance trains with dining car service also offer special children's menus.

BY BUS: On Greyhound and Trailways, children 5 through 11 are charged half price (accompanied by an adult); one child under 5 may travel free on an adult's lap. At certain times, special promotions offer children under 12 a free trip during the week with a paying adult. Be sure any bus on which you travel with children — even on short runs — has a bathroom.

BY PLANE: Generally, children under 2 travel free. For children 2 to 17, prices vary from 25 to 50% off the adult fare. Watch for promotions when children with an adult fly free or at a deep discount (usually during the months of January and February), or when family fares extend discounts to spouses as well. Avoid night flights. Since you probably won't sleep nearly as well as your kids, you risk an impossible first day at your destination groggily taking care of your rested, energetic children. Nap time is, however, a good time to travel, especially for babies. Avoid commuter flights, and try to travel during off-peak hours when there are apt to be extra seats. When the plane lands and takes off, make sure your baby is nursing or has a bottle, pacifier, or thumb in mouth. This sucking will make the child swallow and clear stopped ears. For a small child a piece of hard candy will do the same thing. Newborns, whose lungs may not be able to adjust to the altitude, should not be taken aboard an airplane.

You are entitled to ask for a hot dog or hamburger in lieu of the airline's regular dinner when you make your reservation. Some, but not all airlines, have baby food aboard. While you should make sure to bring your own toys, ask about children's diversions. Some airlines, like Pan Am, have terrific packages of games, coloring books, and puzzles.

Some airlines may refuse to allow a pregnant woman to board if she is in her eighth or ninth month, because they fear that something could go wrong with an in-flight birth. Check with the airline ahead of time and carry a letter from your doctor stating that you are fit to travel and indicating the estimated date of birth.

THINGS TO DO: Special programs for children run the gamut from children's movies at museums and puppet shows in city parks to storytelling at a public library. Listings of these events, many of which are free, can usually be found in Friday or Sunday editions of city newspapers or at the city's visitors bureau or information center. Local or regional festivals, fairs, rodeos, parades, or other special events capture children's imaginations. For a list of these events, write to the tourist bureaus in the states you plan to visit. And ask about discounts; children often get discounts on everything from movies to monuments. Many hotels offer large reductions to families who all stay in the same room.

Hints for Single Travelers

Most travel bargains — all-inclusive tours, resort packages, cruises — are based on *double occupancy* rates, which means the per-person price is offered on the basis of two people traveling together, to fill a double room (and concomitantly to spend a good deal more on meals and extras). For exactly the same package, the single traveler will have to pay a surcharge, called a single supplement, which can add anywhere from 30% to 55% or more to the basic per-person rate.

The only real alternative to paying this penalty is to find a traveling companion. Even special "singles' tours" which promise no supplements are based on individuals sharing double rooms. There are several travel agents and tour operators around the US who help get single travelers together to share costs; some charge fees, others are free. All serve a national clientele.

Saga International Holidays: An organization for seniors over 60, including singles. There is no fee to be put on the mailing list. 120 Boylston St., Boston, MA 02116 (800 343-0273).

Singleworld· More of a "swinging singles" agency than Travel Mates (below). No age limits, but about two thirds of its clients are under 35 and more than half are women. Organizes singles' tours (on which shares can be arranged for approximately $20; if you don't share, you pay a single supplement). Also places sharers on existing package tours. Annual membership fee, $18. 444 Madison Ave., New York, NY 10022 (212 753-7595).

Travel Companion Exchange: Travelers of all ages and interests receive a membership brochure with brief descriptions of other club members and their travel interests. Annual membership fee, $60. Box 833, Amityville, NY 11701 (516 454-0673 or 516 454-0880).

Travel Mates International: For men and women of any age; arranges shares (on existing package tours) as well as organizing group tours for its own clients. Annual membership fee, $15. 49 W 44th St., New York, NY 10036 (212 221-6565).

Travel Partners Club: Run by and for travelers over 50, membership includes biographical listings and a bimonthly newletter. Annual membership fee, $30. PO Box 2368, Crystal River, FL 32629 (904 795-1117).

Certain cruise lines — Cunard, for example — have a sort of standby service for singles; you pay only the usual per-person charge for a double cabin if it has not been sold to a couple. Royal Cruise Line, 1 Maritime Plaza, Suite 660, San Francisco, CA 94111 (415 788-0610 or 800 227-5628) offers a guaranteed share rate for singles. One organization that caters exclusively to women, *Womantours,* features group and individual travel programs for women. 5314 N Figueroa St., Los Angeles, CA 90042 (213 255-1115). *The Women's Travel Guide: 25 American Cities* by Jane Lasky and Brenda Fine (G. K. Hall; $12.95) is a new publication aimed at the growing number of women travelers.

Hints for Older Travelers

No longer limited by three-week vacations or the business week, older travelers can take advantage of off-season, off-peak travel which is both cheaper and more pleasant than traveling in high season. Particularly attractive are cruises, wherein the crew takes care of all details, and special programs like the bus companies' Eaglepass and Ameripass, which offer unlimited travel for a fixed period of time (see this section, *Touring by Bus*).

DISCOUNTS: Senior citizens with identification are eligible for a huge variety of discounts in every city across the country. Although rules change from place to place and city to city, acceptable proof of eligibility (or age) is usually a driver's license, a membership card in a recognized senior citizens organization such as the American Association of Retired Persons (see below), or a Medicare card. Because senior citizen discounts are common but by no means standard, always ask about them before you pay — whether it's for a subway in Philadelphia or a campsite in Colorado. Discounts are available for local transportation in most American cities, for concerts, movies, museums, hotels, and dozens of other activities. Some states offer free hunting and fishing licenses to retired persons. Greyhound, Trailways, and Amtrak offer discounts. Several major airlines have initiated substantial flight discounts, along with hotel, car rental and tour reductions and bonus credits toward frequent flier programs. Of course, there are restrictions for the purchase and use of such fares. And depending upon local management, discounts are also available in some Marriott, Holiday Inn, Sheraton, Howard Johnson, Days Inn, Rodeway, and Treadway Inn hotels.

The National Park Service has a free Golden Age Passport, which entitles people over 62, and those in the car with them, to free entrance to all national parks and monuments as well as to discounts on campsites (available by showing Medicare card or driver's license as proof of age at any national park).

Travel Tips for Senior Citizens, a free booklet with general advice, is available from the State Department's Bureau of Consular Affairs, 220 21st St., NW, Washington, DC 20520. The booklet *101 Tips for the Mature Traveler* is available free from Grand Circle Travel, 347 Congress St., Boston, MA 02210 (617 350-7500; 800 221-2610). And *Travel Easy: The Practical Guide for People over 50* by Rosalind Massow (American Association of Retired Persons; $8.95) covers virtually every topic of interest to the mature traveler.

PACKAGE PROGRAMS: Many senior citizens' organizations take a great interest in promoting travel opportunities for their members. Among the most active of these organizations are:

American Association of Retired Persons (AARP), 1909 K St., NW, Washington, DC 20049 (202 872-4700). Membership costs $5 per year or $12.50 for three years.

National Association of Mature People, 2212 NW 50th St., Oklahoma City, OK 73112 (405 848-1832). Membership costs $9.95 per year for either an individual or a couple.

National Council of Senior Citizens, 925 15th St., NW, Washington, DC 20005 (202 347-8800). Membership costs $8 for an individual, $10 for a couple.

Numerous travel agencies and tour operators around the country specialize in organizing tours for older travelers. Three such are Gadabout Tours, 700 E Tahquitz Way, Palm Springs, CA 92262 (619 325-5556); and on the East Coast, Groups Unlimited, 3 E 54th St., 3rd Floor, New York, NY 10022 (212 751-9360) and Grand Circle Travel, 347 Congress St., Boston, MA 02210 (617 350-7500; 800 221-2610).

Educational travel is another option. Elderhostel runs programs (for those age 60 and up) from one to three weeks long at a vast number of schools and universities in the US and abroad. Contact Elderhostel, 80 Boylston St., Boston, MA 02116 (617 426-8056).

HEALTH: Medicare coverage is nationwide and will be honored by hospitals and doctors everywhere in the US, Puerto Rico, and the Virgin Islands. If you have specific medical problems, bring prescriptions and a "medical file":

1. Summary of medical history, current diagnosis.
2. List of drugs to which you are allergic.
3. Most recent electrocardiogram, if you have heart problems.
4. Your doctor's name, address, and phone number.

For a complete discussion of health for older travelers, Rosalind Massow's excellent *Now It's Your Turn to Travel* (Macmillan; $10.95) has a chapter on medical problems.

Insurance

The amount and kind of insurance you carry when you go on the road depends in large part on your own feelings about traveling, the insurance policies you have already, and your method of transport. There are five basic types of insurance any traveler should consider, though by no means are all — or any — a necessity:

1. Baggage and personal effects insurance
2. Personal accident and sickness insurance
3. Automobile insurance
4. Trip cancellation insurance
5. Flight insurance

These are options to be considered after you have established that your current medical and homeowner's (or tenant-homeowner's) policies are up to date and paid.

BAGGAGE AND PERSONAL EFFECTS INSURANCE: Ask your agent if baggage and personal effects are covered by your homeowner's policy regardless of where you lose them. If not, find out about the cost and coverage of a floater to protect you while you are away. A certain amount of coverage for loss or damage to baggage is part of the terms of the standard airline, train, or bus ticket, but it only applies while your bags are in the transportation company's care. (If you are driving, you must discuss protection with your insurance agent.) Furthermore, the limits of their liability may not be adequate: Most airlines insure luggage and contents for a maximum of $1,250 on domestic flights, and $9.07 a pound on international flights; Amtrak takes responsibility for a maximum of $500 per passenger; and the buses assume responsibility for considerably less, about $250 maximum per passenger. These maximum payments are not automatic; payments will be based on the value of the baggage and its contents.

If you are not otherwise protected and are carrying goods worth more than the maximum protection provided by these limits of liability, you should consider excess value insurance, available from the airlines for about $1 per $100 of protection provided (can be bought at the ticket counter at time of check-in) and from Amtrak for 50¢ for every $100 of protection. Excess value insurance is also included in certain of the combination travel insurance policies discussed below.

One note of warning: Be sure to read the fine print of any excess value or baggage insurance policy; there are often specific exclusions, such as money, tickets, furs, gold and silver objects, art and antiquities. And remember that ordinarily, insurance companies will pay the depreciated value of the goods rather than replacement value. To protect goods traveling in your luggage, have photos made of valuables, and keep a record of all serial numbers of such items as cameras, typewriters, radios, etc. (Original purchase receipts can also be useful in later litigation with the airlines.) This will establish that you do, indeed, own the objects. If your luggage disappears en route, or is damaged, deal with the situation immediately, at the airport, train station, or bus station. If an airline loses your luggage, you will be asked to fill out a Property Irregularity Report before you leave the airport. If your property disappears elsewhere, make a report to the police at once.

PERSONAL ACCIDENT AND SICKNESS INSURANCE: This insures you in case of illness on the road (hospital and doctor's expenses, etc.) or death in an accident. In most cases this is a standard part of life and health insurance policies, and anyone with average insurance coverage will be adequately protected while on vacation.

AUTOMOBILE INSURANCE: Every driver is required by law to have automobile insurance. Minimum coverage is determined by state law, but it is almost always too low to protect you adequately. A professional insurance agent should determine the amount of automobile insurance you should carry, but there are several major kinds of coverage you should have:

1. Liability insurance — Protection if you are sued for injuring another person or that person's property.
2. Uninsured motorist insurance — Protection if you or passengers in your car are injured by another motorist without insurance.
3. Accident insurance — Protection against liability for medical bills, loss of pay, other expenses of people injured in an accident for which you are at fault.
4. Comprehensive and collision insurance — Protection against damage to your car.

There are several ways to save money on car insurance. Many policies offer discounts for cars used in car pools, cars with low annual mileage (or compacts), and drivers with good driving records. Some states (New York and New Jersey are two) publish free booklets on car insurance coverage, how much and what kind to buy. Write the Department of Insurance in your state capital for any available information.

TRIP CANCELLATION AND INTERRUPTION INSURANCE: Most package tours, cruises, and charter flights require full payment a substantial period of time before departure. Although cancellation penalties vary, rarely will the passenger get more than 50% of this money back if forced to cancel within a few weeks of leaving. Therefore, if you are planning to take a package tour or a charter, you should have cancellation insurance to guarantee a full refund of your money should you, a traveling companion, or a member of your immediate family get sick, forcing you to cancel your trip or return home early. The key here is *not* to buy just enough insurance to guarantee full reimbursement in case of cancellation. The proper amount of coverage should be sufficient to reimburse you for the cost of having to catch up with a tour after its departure or having to travel home at full economy air fare if you have to forgo the return flight of your charter. There is usually quite a discrepancy between your charter air fare and the amount you would have to pay to travel the same distance on a regularly scheduled flight.

Cancellation insurance designed to cover a specific package is frequently offered by tour operators. Otherwise, it can be bought as part of a combination travel insurance policy sold through travel or insurance agents. Read any policy carefully before you buy it. Be sure it provides enough money to get you home from the farthest point on your itinerary should you have to forgo the return portion of a discounted flight and fly home at full fare. And check the fine print definition of "family members" and "pre-existing medical condition." Some policies will not pay if you become ill from a condition for which you have received treatment in the past.

DEFAULT AND/OR BANKRUPTCY INSURANCE: Although trip cancellation insurance usually protects you if you are unable to complete — or depart on — your trip, a fairly recent innovation is coverage in the event of default and/or bankruptcy on the part of the tour operator, airline, or other travel supplier. Some travel insurance policies now have this additional feature, and it is worth considering since it is no longer a remote possibility, given estimates that some 50 commercial passenger airlines have ceased operation since the advent of airline deregulation in 1978.

Should this type of coverage be unavailable to you (state insurance regulations vary, there is a wide difference in price, and so on), your best bet is to pay for airline tickets and tour packages with a credit card. The federal Fair Credit Billing Act permits purchasers to refuse payment for credit card charges where services have not been delivered, so the potential onus of dealing with a receiver for a bankrupt airline falls on the credit card company. Do not assume that another airline will automatically honor the ticket you're holding on a bankrupt airline, since the days when virtually all major carriers subscribed to a default protection program are long gone. Some airlines may voluntarily step forwrad to accommodate stranded passengers, but this is now an entirely altruistic act. Moreover, the value of escrow protection of a charter passenger's funds has lately come into question. While default/bankruptcy insurance will not ordinarily result in reimbursement in time for you to pay for new arrangements, it can assure that you will eventually get your money back; even independent travelers buying no more than an airplane ticket may want to consider it.

FLIGHT INSURANCE: Airlines have carefully established limits of liability for the death or injury of passengers. On tickets for international flights these are printed on the ticket: a maximum of $75,000 in case of death or injury; for domestic flights, the limitation is established by state law, with some few states (California, New York, Illinois) setting unlimited liability. But remember, these limits of liability are not the same thing as insurance policies; they merely state the maximum an airline will pay in the case of death or injury, and every penny of that is usually the subject of a legal battle.

This may make you feel that you are not adequately protected. But before you buy last-minute flight insurance from an airport vending machine, as many passengers do, consider the purchase in light of your total existing insurance coverage. A careful review of your current policies may reveal that you are already amply covered for injury and accidental death, sometimes up to three times the amount provided for by the insurance you'd buy at the airport.

If you buy your ticket with an American Express, Carte Blanche, or Diners Club credit card, you are issued automatic travel accident insurance at no extra cost. American Express automatically provides $100,000 in free insurance; Carte Blanche and Diners Club, $650,000. American Express offers additional coverage at extremely reasonable prices if you sign up in advance for it: $3 per ticket buys $250,000 worth of flight insurance, and $5.50 buys $500,000 worth; $11 provides $1 million worth of coverage.

COMBINATION POLICIES: A number of insurance companies offer all-purpose travel insurance packages that include baggage, personal accident and sickness, and trip cancellation insurance, and, sometimes, default and bankruptcy protection. They cover you for a single trip and are sold by travel agents, insurance agencies, and others. Sentry

Insurance's Travel Guard, the only policy endorsed by the American Society of Travel Agents (ASTA), is available through travel agents.

Mail and Telephone

 MAIL: Most main post offices are open 24 hours a day with at least a self-service section for weighing packages and buying stamps. In smaller cities and towns, hours are usually from 8 AM to 6 PM Monday through Friday and 8 AM to noon on Saturdays. Branch offices have shorter hours.

Stamps are also available at most hotel desks. There are vending machines for stamps in drugstores, transportation terminals, and other public places. Stamps cost more from these machines than they do at the post office, however.

Before you take a trip, fill in a change of address card (available at post office), which is the form you need to get the post office to hold your mail or send your first class mail to your vacation address. Generally, this free holding service lasts for a month, longer at the discretion of the post office. You can also have your third class mail sent on, but you will have to pay for this service.

If you want to receive mail in another city but do not know what your address will be, have it sent to you in care of General Delivery in the city or town you will visit. This is always the main post office in any large city. Have the sender put "Hold for 30 Days" on the envelope, and make sure that a return address is on the envelope so that the post office can return it if you are not able to pick it up. The post office will keep it only for 30 days. To claim this mail, go to the main post office in that city or town, ask for General Delivery, and present identification (driver's license, credit cards, birth certificate, passport). Mail must be collected in person.

If you belong to AAA or are an American Express customer, you can have mail sent to their offices in cities on your route. Envelopes should be marked "Hold for Arrival."

TELEPHONE: Public telephones are on hand just about everywhere if you are in a city or town. This includes transportation terminals, hotel lobbies, restaurants, drugstores, sidewalk booths, and along the highways. For a local call the cost is between 10¢ and 25¢.

Long-distance rates are charged according to when the call is placed: weekday daytime; weekday evenings; and nights, weekends, and holidays. Cheapest are calls you dial yourself from a private phone nights, weekends, holidays. It is always more expensive to call from a pay phone than it is to call from a private phone (you must pay for a minimum three-minute call). If the operator assists you, calls are more expensive. This includes credit card, bill-to-a-third-number, collect, and time-and-charge calls, as well as person-to-person calls, which are the most expensive. Rates are fully explained in the front of the White Pages of every telephone directory.

If you are planning to be away for more than a month, you may be able to save money by asking the telephone company to temporarily suspend your home telephone service. You can also arrange to have your calls transferred to another number.

Hotel Surcharges – When you are calling from your hotel room, inquire about any surcharges the hotel may have. These can be excessive, and are avoided by calling collect, using a telephone credit card (free from the phone company), or calling from a public pay phone.

Emergencies – 911 is the number to dial in an emergency in most cities. Operators at this number will get you the help you need from the police, fire department, or ambulance service. It is, however, a number that should be reserved for real emergencies only. If you are in one of the rare areas where 911 has not been adopted, dial "O" for the operator, who will connect you directly with the service you need.

On the Road

Credit Cards and Traveler's Checks

CREDIT CARDS: There are two essentially different kinds of credit cards available to consumers in the United States, and travelers must decide which kind best serves their interests. "Convenience" cards — American Express, Diners Club, Carte Blanche, are the most widely accepted — charge an annual membership fee but do not limit on the amount the cardholder may charge on the card in any month. However, the entire balance must be paid in full at the end of each billing period (usually a month), so the cardholder is not actually extended any credit — although deferred payment plans can usually be arranged for some types of purchases.

"Bank" cards, on the other hand, are often issued free, although some banks now charge a fee. They are real credit cards in the sense that the cardholder has the privilege of paying a minimum amount (1/36 is not atypical) of the total balance in each billing period. For this privilege, the cardholder is charged an interest rate — about 1½% a month or 18% a year — on the balance. In addition, there is a maximum set on the amount the cardholder can charge to the card, which represents the limit of credit the card company is willing to extend. Major bank cards are Visa (formerly BankAmericard) and MasterCard (formerly Master Charge).

Following is a list of widely used credit cards, with some of their key benefits to travelers and a telephone number to call for details..

American Express: Emergency personal check cashing at American Express or representative's office ($200 cash, $800 in traveler's checks); emergency personal check cashing for guests at participating hotels (up to $250 in US or Canada; $100 elsewhere) and, for holders of airline tickets, at participating airlines in the US (up to $50). Extended payment plan for cruises, tours, and plane tickets. $100,000 free travel accident insurance on plane, train, bus, and ship if ticket was charged to card; up to $1,000,000 additional low-cost flight insurance available. Contact: American Express Card, PO Box 39, Church St. Station, New York, NY 10008 (800 528-4800).

Carte Blanche: Emergency personal check cashing at participating Hilton hotels in the US (up to $1,000) and for guests at other participating hotels and motels (up to $250 per stay). Extended payment plan for airline tickets. $650,000 free travel accident insurance on plane, train, and ship if ticket was charged to card. Contact: Carte Blanche, PO Box 5824, Denver, CO 80217 (800 525-9135).

Diners Club: Emergency personal check cashing at participating Citibank branches worldwide (up to $1,000, with a minimum per check of $50 in the US and $250 overseas); emergency personal check cashing for guests at participating hotels and motels (up to $250 per stay). Qualified card members are eligible for extended payment plan. $650,000 free travel accident insurance on plane, train, and ship if ticket was charged to card. Contact: Diners Club, PO Box 5824, Denver, CO 80217 (800 525-9135).

Discover Card: Launched in early 1986 by Sears, Roebuck and Co., it provides cash advance at more than 500 locations nationwide and offers a revolving credit line for purchases at a wide range of service establishments. Other deposit, lending, and investment services are also available. For information, phone 800 858-5588.

MasterCard: Cash advance at participating banks worldwide. Interest charge on unpaid balance and other details are set by issuing bank. Check with your bank for information.

Visa: Cash advance at participating banks worldwide. Interest charge on unpaid balance and other details are set by issuing bank. Check with your bank for information.

TRAVELER'S CHECKS: With adequate proof of identification (credit cards, driver's license, passport), traveler's checks are as good as cash in most hotels, restaurants, stores, and banks. If you're traveling, they're even better because of their refundability; in the US, travelers can receive partial or full replacement funds the same day if their traveler's checks are lost or stolen and they have their receipt and proper identification. To avoid complications, keep your purchaser's receipt and an accurate listing by serial number of your checks in a separate place from the checks themselves. You can buy traveler's checks at any bank. Some companies offer more extensive services, making provisions for refunds on the weekends and after business hours. Here is a list of the major companies issuing traveler's checks and the number to call for refunds.

American Express: To report lost or stolen checks in the continental US, call 800 221-7282; in Alaska and Hawaii, call 800 221-4950.

Bank of America: To report lost or stolen checks in the US, except Alaska, 800 227-3460; from Alaska or outside the US, 415 624-5400, collect.

Barclays/Visa: To report lost or stolen checks in the US, call 800 227-6811.

Citicorp: To report lost or stolen checks in the US, call 800 645-6556.

Thomas Cook/MasterCard: To report lost or stolen checks in the US except New York State, Alaska, and Hawaii, 800 223-9920; from those states and from outside the US, 212 974-5696, collect.

Dining Out in America

American cities have undergone something of a restaurant revolution. In the last ten years, cities across the country, from Portland, Maine, to Portland, Oregon, have initiated renovation programs of the oldest sections of town. Often these are former port or warehouse districts, mercantile neighborhoods filled with fine 19th-century ironwork buildings which 100 years ago were in their prime and have since fallen into disrepair. Renovated, they become distinctive shopping areas, filled with gourmet food stores, art galleries, clothing or crafts boutiques, and . . . restaurants.

Built of simple wood and simpler bricks to accentuate the often stunning architecture of the original buildings, these restaurants — whether in Boston or St. Louis — sometimes seem strikingly similar in look and design, but they represent a new era for the traveler. America's largest cities have always had a diverse collection of restaurants, but eating out in smaller American cities, especially in the South, Midwest, and Plains states, used to offer little variety. The new generation of restaurants is beginning to change that. Generally moderately priced, run by owner-managers who care about food, they offer an eclectic selection of cuisines (Oriental and traditional American, vegetarian and meat dishes, haute cuisine and simple) with great care and real pride. We have listed our favorites in the *Eating Out* section in THE AMERICAN CITIES reports.

RESERVATIONS: Restaurants vary widely on reservation policies. At some, it is requisite (especially at more expensive and popular places in larger cities); other equally fine restaurants refuse to take reservations at all; the patron simply goes, and waits at the bar until a table is free. If you are planning a big night out, it certainly is advisable to call the restaurant early in the day to make a reservation or find out its policy. After-theater restaurants in New York almost always require booking. Every restaurant listing in *Best in Town* gives reservation policy and a telephone number.

Hotel restaurants often have specific serving times; plusher hotels usually have coffee shops as well as restaurants, and the coffee shops will offer more flexible hours (and are often open 24 hours a day).

Hotels and Motels in America

 Americans who travel frequently to Europe complain that the United States has few of the centuries-old, privately owned and personally run, tradition-conscious "little hotels" which can so grace a European visit. To a great degree this is a fair observation: There are fine old hotels in the US — New England inns, Southwestern haciendas, frontier stagecoach rest stops (you will find our pick of them listed in *Best in Town* in THE AMERICAN CITIES and *Best en Route* in DIRECTIONS) — which have been in continuous operation for a century or more and which can match the amenities of any European find; but by far the majority of travelers in the US will be staying at hotels and motels only a few years old, which are often part of national (or international) chains, and which are, to some degree, standardized in price and quality.

There is one great benefit in this standardization: The basic level of acceptable accommodations in the US is much higher than anywhere else in the world. The tourist in America, arriving in an unfamiliar town (or driving through a new region), can be safe in assuming that nearby there will be safe, clean, comfortable accommodations in an acceptable price range.

You can choose for yourself just what price range is acceptable. Some chains — like the Hyatt and Hilton hotels — offer luxury accommodations with all possible amenities. The hotels themselves are beautiful, the service excellent, the facilities complete; and the prices, as you would expect, are high — as much as $200 or more a night for a double. Other chains are more reasonably priced.

RESERVATIONS: It is best to make reservations for accommodations in the major US cities, even if you are traveling off-season. Most cities have convention centers, and hotel space can be limited if a large convention is being hosted at the same time you visit. All the hotel entries in the *Best in Town* sections of THE AMERICAN CITIES reports include phone numbers for reservations. Resorts, country inns, dude ranches, theme park hotels, and other special places should always be booked in advance, regardless of the season. Most major hotel and motel chains list their toll-free (800) reservation numbers in the white pages of the telephone directory, and any hotel within a chain can assure reservations for you at sister facilities. Many independent, nonchain hotels and motels are part of the American Reservation System (800 327-9157). Make sure to bring your reservation confirmation slip with you; it will increase your chances of getting a room if the hotel is overbooked. American Express, in conjunction with Hyatt and several other major hotel chains, offers an Assured Reservations Program. Any reservation made with an American Express credit card number will be held no matter how late you arrive. (Some hotels do this with any major credit card.) However, if you don't take the room, and fail to formally cancel, you will be charged.

BUDGET MOTELS: The budget motel is designed to offer basic accommodations (a comfortable bed, clean bathroom, central heating and air-conditioning) without services, bar or restaurant, or elaborate lobby. A double for a night can cost as little as $20–$25. The *Economy Motel Guide,* by Louise Delagran (Meadowbrook; $6.95) lists 2,800 such motels. Watch for:

> *Budget Host Inns* (over 125 throughout the US): 817 626-7064
> *Days Inn* (300 throughout the US): 800 325-2525
> *Econo-Travel Motor Hotels* (about 130, East Coast and South): 800 446-6900
> *Imperial 400* (400 throughout the US): 800 368-4400
> *Motel 6* (more than 315 throughout the US): 805 682-6666
> *Red Roof Inns* (65 throughout the Midwest): 800 848-7878
> *Regal 8* (about 50 throughout the Midwest): 800 851-8888

At hotels and motels in all price ranges, ask about minimum rates, weekend discounts, weekly rates, discounts for business travelers, special promotions, and special rates for children staying in their parent's room.

One way to save up to 25% on hotels is to send for the Council on International Educational Exchange's "Where to Stay: USA" discount card. It costs $12 and is good at more than 1,000 hotels and motels across the country. For information, contact CIEE, 205 E 42nd St., New York, NY 10017 (212 661-1450).

BED AND BREAKFAST: One of the most popular new forms of lodging is found via bed and breakfast networks, which provide a more personable, and sometimes less expensive, alternative to hotels and motels. Accommodations range from private homes and lovely mansions to small inns and guest houses with a Continental breakfast included (usually no private baths are offered). There can be a fine line, however, between "bed and breakfast" and "boarding house," so find out as much as you can before you book to avoid disappointment. The American Bed and Breakfast Association (PO Box 23294, Washington, DC 20026) can send you more information. Or consult any of several guidebooks on the subject; see the list in *For More Information,* in this section. The Bed & Breakfast League, 3639 Van Ness St., NW, Washington, DC 20008 (202 363-7767), and International Spareroom, PO Box 460, Helena, MT 59624 (406 449-7231), have nationwide listings. What follows are regional groups to contact for B&B information and reservations:

Northeast
> *Bed & Breakfast Associates of Bay Colony,* PO Box 166, Babson Park, Boston, MA 02157 (617 449-5302)
> *House Guests Cape Cod,* Box 8AR, Dennis, MA 02638 (617 398-0787)
> *New England Bed & Breakfast Centre,* 1045 Centre St., Newton Centre, MA 02159 (617 498-9819)
> *Nutmeg Bed & Breakfast,* 222 Girard Ave., Hartford, CT 06105 (203 236-6698)
> *Pineapple Hospitality,* 384 Rodney French Blvd., New Bedford, MA 02744 (617 990-1696)
> *Spirit of Massachusetts Bed & Breakfast Guide,* Massachusetts Division of Tourism, Dept. of Commerce and Development, 100 Cambridge St., 13th Floor, Boston, MA 02202 (617 727-3201)

Mid-Atlantic
> *The B&B Group (New Yorkers at Home),* 301 E 60th St., New York, NY 10022 (212 838-7015)
> *The Bed & Breakfast League,* 3639 Van Ness St., NW, Washington, DC 20008 (202 363-7767)
> *Bed & Breakfast of Philadelphia,* PO Box 680, Devon, PA. 19333 (215 688-1633)
> *New World Bed and Breakfast,* 150 Fifth Ave., Suite 711, New York, NY 10011 (212 675-5600)
> *Sweet Dreams & Toast,* PO Box 4835-0035, Washington, DC 20008 (202 483-9191)

Traveler in Maryland, 33 West St., Annapolis, MD 21401 (301 269-6232; 301 261-2233, DC area)

Urban Ventures, PO Box 426, New York, NY 10024 (212 594-5650)

South

A & A Bed & Breakfast of Florida, PO Box 1316, Winter Park, FL 32790 (305 628-3233)

Bed & Breakfast Atlanta, 1801 Piedmont Ave., NE, Suite 208, Atlanta GA 30324 (404 378-6026)

Bed & Breakfast Birmingham, Box 31328, Birmingham, AL 35222 (205 591-6406)

Bed & Breakfast Co., PO Box 262, South Miami, FL 33243 (305 661-3270)

Bed & Breakfast of the Florida Keys and Florida East Coast, PO Box 1373, Marathon, FL 33050 (305 743-4118)

Bed & Breakfast Mobile, PO Box 66261, Mobile, AL 36606 (205 473-2939)

Bed & Breakfast Montgomery, PO Box 886, Millbrook, AL 36054 (205 285-5421)

Guest Houses Reservation Service, Box 5737, Charlottesville, VA 22905 (804 979-7264)

Historic Charleston Bed & Breakfast, 43 Legare St., Charleston, SC 29401 (803 722-6606)

Kentucky Homes Bed & Breakfast, 1431 St. James Ct., Louisville, KY 40208 (502 452-6629; 502 635-7341)

Princely Bed & Breakfast, 819 Prince St., Alexandria, VA 22314 (703 683-2159)

The Travel Tree, PO Box 838, Williamsburg, VA 23187 (804 253-1571)

Midwest

Bed & Breakfast Chicago, PO Box 14088, Chicago, IL 60614 (312 951-0085)

Betsy Ross Bed & Breakfast, 3057 Betsy Ross Dr., Bloomfield Hills, MI 48013 (313 647-1158)

Buckeye Bed & Breakfast, PO Box 130, Powell, OH 43065 (614 548-4555)

West

American Family Inn/Bed & Breakfast San Francisco, PO Box 349, San Francisco, CA 94101 (415 931-3083)

B&B Ski America and Canada, PO Box 5346, Incline Village, NV 89450 (702 831-5350)

Bed & Breakfast International, 151 Ardmore, Kensington, CA 94707 (415 525-4569)

Bed & Breakfast in Arizona, 8433 N Black Canyon Hwy., Suite 160, Phoenix, AZ 85021 (602 995-2831)

California Houseguests International, 18533 Burbank Blvd., #190, Tarzana, CA 91356 (818 344-7878)

Digs West, 8191 Crowley Cir., Buena Park, CA 90621 (714 739-1669)

Eye Openers Bed & Breakfast, PO Box 694, Altadena, CA 91001 (213 684-4428; 818 797-2055)

Mi Casa–Su Casa Bed & Breakfast, PO Box 950, Tempe, AZ 85281 (602 990-0682)

Northwest Bed & Breakfast, 610 SW Broadway, Portland, OR 97223 (503 243-7676)

Pacific Bed & Breakfast, 701 NW 60th St., Seattle, WA 98107 (206 784-0539)

Travellers Bed & Breakfast, PO Box 492, Mercer Island, WA 98040 (206 232-2345, Seattle area)

Visitors Advisory Service, 1516 Oak St., #327, Alameda, CA 94501 (415 521-9366, San Francisco area)

Hawaii

Bed & Breakfast Hawaii, Box 449, Kapaa, HI 96746 (808 822-7771)

Religion on the Road

The surest source of information on religious services in an unfamiliar town is the desk clerk of the hotel or motel in which you are staying. In most cities, joint religious councils print circulars with the addresses and times of services of all the churches, synagogues, and temples in the city. These are often printed as part of general tourist guides provided by the local tourist and convention center, or as part of a "what's on" guide to the city. The local tourist council certainly can provide the information you need on services in the town. Many newspapers print a listing of religious services in their area in weekend editions. Often an entire page will be devoted to church and religious news.

You may want to use your vacation to broaden your religious experience by joining an unfamiliar faith in its service. This can be a moving experience, especially if the service is held in a church, synagogue, or temple that is historically significant or architecturally notable. You will almost always find yourself made welcome and comfortable.

Medical and Legal Help on the Road

MEDICAL HELP: You will discover, in the event of an emergency, that most tourist facilities — transportation companies, hotels, theme parks, and resorts — are equipped to handle the situation quickly and efficiently. Shout for help, and they will locate a doctor or ambulance. All hospitals are prepared for emergency cases, and even the tiniest of US towns has a medical clinic nearby. If you are on your own, you can get emergency help by dialing 911 or "0" (for Operator). You will be put into immediate contact with the service you require.

If you have a medical condition that may require attention on your trip, have your doctor at home recommend a physician in the areas you plan to visit. If you need a doctor unexpectedly, but it is not a severe emergency, you can call your own doctor for a recommendation in the area. If you are staying in a hotel or motel, ask for the house physician, who may visit you in your room or ask you to visit an office. (This service is apt to be expensive, especially if the doctor makes a "house" call to your room.) In larger cities, many hospitals have walk-in clinics designed to serve people who do not really need emergency service, but who have no place to go for immediate medical attention. You can also go directly to the emergency room. A phone call to a local hospital requesting the name of a doctor will usually turn up a name; some hospitals actually have referral services for this purpose. The medical society in most towns (or counties) will refer you to a member physician in the specialty you need (listed in the telephone book under the city or county medical society; for example, Des Moines Medical Society).

If you wear glasses, make sure you have an extra pair with you as well as your prescription. Also carry prescriptions for any medicines you might need on the trip.

Medic Alert sells identification tags that specify that the wearer has a medical condition — such as a heart condition, diabetes, epilepsy, or severe allergies — that may not be readily apparent to a casual observer. These are conditions that, if unrecognized at a time when emergency treatment is necessary (a time, incidentally, when you may be unable to speak for yourself), can result in tragic treatment errors. In addition to the identification emblems, a central file is maintained (with the telephone number clearly inscribed on the I.D. badge) where your complete medical history is available 24 hours a day via a telephone call. The cost of the I.D. bracelet or necklace depends on what sort of metal you select. For information contact: Medic Alert, PO Box 1009, Turlock, CA 95381-1009 (209 668-3333 or 800 468-1020 in California; 800 228-6222 elsewhere).

Intermedic, a division of Executive Health Examiners, provides access to a directory of English-speaking physicians in 200 cities in over 90 countries. The fee is $6 per year for an individual and $10 a year for a family. Each physician listed has provided Intermedic with data on his medical education, his professional experience, and his hospital affiliation; and each has indicated a willingness to respond promptly to calls from traveling Intermedic members. They have also agreed in writing to a ceiling on fees for any initial visit. For information contact: Intermedic, Inc., 777 Third Ave., New York, NY 10017 (212 486-8900).

Assist-Card International provides a number to call — 24 hours a day, 365 days a year — where complete emergency medical assistance can be arranged, including ambulance or air transportation to the proper treatment facilities, local lawyers for a case that is the byproduct of an accident, and up to $5,000 as a loan to post bail for a judicial proceeding that is similarly the result of an accident. They will also arrange for a flight home if the traveler is unable to complete his trip for medical reasons and will pay any fare differential that may be required. The organization also pays the first $3,000 in medical expenses and $500 in prescriptions. At press time, fees for the Assist-Card were $3 to $4 per day (sold in blocks of time). For information contact: Assist-Card Corporation of America, 347 Fifth Ave., New York, NY 10016 (212 752-2788 in New York or 212 686-1288, collect).

SOS Assistance also offers a program that covers medical emergencies while traveling. Again, members are provided with telephone access — 24 hours a day, 365 days a year — to a worldwide monitored multilingual network of medical centers. A phone call brings assistance ranging from telephone consultation to transportation home by ambulance or aircraft, and in some cases transportation of a family member to the place where you are hospitalized. The first $1,000 of sickness or accident bills are insured ($25 deductible). The service can be purchased for $15 a week, $45 a month, or $195 a year. For information contact: International SOS Assistance, 1 Neshaminy Interplex, Suite 310, Trevose, PA 19047 (215 244-1500 in Pennsylvania; 800 523-8930 elsewhere).

LEGAL AID: The best way to begin looking for legal aid in an unfamiliar area is with a call to your own lawyer. If you don't have, or cannot reach, your own lawyer, most cities offer lawyer referral services (sometimes called attorney referral services) maintained by county bar associations. There are over 335 such referral services in the US, and they see that anyone in need of legal representation gets it at a reasonable fee. (They are listed in the yellow pages under Attorney or Lawyer. In smaller towns, you will usually find a toll-free number that connects you to the service in the nearest larger city.) The referral service is almost always free. If your case goes to court, you are entitled to court-appointed representation if you can't get a lawyer or can't afford one.

Once you have found a lawyer, ask how many cases of this type the lawyer has worked on, and the arrangements to be made regarding fee and additional costs like medical or ballistics experts, transcripts, or court fees. For most violations, you will receive a citation at most. There are, however, the rare occasions when travelers find themselves in jail. Since obtaining a bond can be difficult away from home, the bail bonds offered by AAA and other automobile clubs are extremely useful (see *Touring by Car*). If you do not have this protection, ask to see a copy of the local bail procedures, which differ from state to state. A lawyer will be able to advise you on the alternatives you have in the state in which you are incarcerated.

Time Zones, Business Hours, Holidays

 TIME ZONES: East to west, the United States is divided into four time zones: Eastern, Central, Mountain, and Pacific. Each zone is an hour apart; when it is 8 PM in New York, it is 5 PM in Los Angeles. Alaska and Hawaii are both two hours behind Los Angeles time. To discover how these zones divide the country, check the map in the front of your telephone directory. Daylight Saving Time begins on the last Sunday in April and continues until the last Sunday in October. The only places that do not go on Daylight Saving Time are Arizona, Hawaii, Puerto Rico, the Virgin Islands, and parts of Indiana.

BUSINESS HOURS: Business hours throughout the country are fairly standard: 9 AM to 5 PM, Mondays through Fridays. While an hour lunch break is customary, employees often take it in shifts so that it rarely interrupts service, especially at banks and other public service operations. In Hawaii business hours run from 7:30 or 8 AM to 4 PM. Some California firms are also experimenting with these hours.

Banks are traditionally open from 9 AM to 3 PM Mondays through Fridays, although the trend is toward longer hours. In some areas they now open at 8 AM and stay open until 6 PM, especially at the end of the week. In addition they may remain open one evening a week until 8 or 9 PM, and some have hours on Saturdays.

Retail stores are usually open from 9:30 or 10 AM to 5:30 or 6 PM, Mondays through Saturdays. Most large stores, particularly department stores, are open *at least* one night a week until 9 PM. Blue laws, which close some stores, restaurants, and bars on Sundays, are controlled by cities in some areas, by states elsewhere. In major cities, grocery stores, delicatessens, and supermarkets are usually open Mondays through Saturdays from 9 AM to 9 PM, and some are open on Sundays as well. In fact 24-hour supermarkets are now operating in most regions. Drugstores are usually open from 8 AM to 9 PM, on weekdays. In major cities, at least one is usually open until midnight, or all night, and on Sundays; check the yellow pages.

HOLIDAYS: National holidays, when banks, post offices, libraries, most stores, and many museums are closed, include: January 1, New Year's Day; third Monday in January, Martin Luther King Jr. Day; third Monday in February, George Washington's Birthday; last Monday in May, Memorial Day (except in Alabama, Mississippi, and South Carolina, where it is not a legal holiday); July 4, Independence Day; first Monday in September, Labor Day; second Monday in October, Columbus Day (except in Alaska, Iowa, Mississippi, Nevada, North Dakota, Oregon, South Carolina, and South Dakota, where it is not a legal holiday); fourth Thursday in November, Thanksgiving; December 25, Christmas.

Drinking Laws

 Drinking is legal at 18 in Hawaii, Louisiana, and Vermont. In Idaho, Iowa, Minnesota, Montana, North Carolina, and Wyoming, legal age is 19. In Georgia drinking is legal at 20. The legal age is 21 in all other states with the following exceptions: In Colorado, Mississippi, and Wisconsin, it is legal to drink beer at 18, in Ohio and South Dakota at 19.

Laws on the availability of liquor run the gamut from Nevada's policy of "anytime, anywhere for anyone of age" to localities where drinking is strictly prohibited. Liquor laws are set by states, counties, and municipalities and towns, making generalizations terribly difficult. Regulations on the hours that bars and restaurants can serve liquor vary, though traditionally closing time in bars is between midnight and 3 AM.

Retail store sales are also restricted to certain hours in many states. Most states require liquor stores to close on holidays and Sundays. Some alcoholic beverages, however, may be purchased on Sundays (most often in restaurants) in almost all states. The following states, however, do not allow any Sunday sales: Louisiana, Mississippi, and Utah.

Some states maintain their own system of state liquor stores, which are usually the only place where you can buy hard liquor, and sometimes wine and beer as well. They include Alabama, Iowa, Maine, Montana, New Hampshire, North Carolina, Ohio, Oregon, Pennsylvania, Utah, Vermont, Virginia, Washington, and West Virginia.

It is possible to find dry counties or towns in all corners of the country. Usually, however, you will find a town just a few minutes away where the sale of liquor is legal. In Utah, beer is the only standard offering. Certain licensed restaurants are allowed to serve two-ounce bottles of mixed drinks, highballs, or wine, but only with meals.

Where the laws are tight, there are often private clubs. In states such as Kansas and Oklahoma, you can join private clubs through hotels and motels. Often you join the club with the price of your first drink. In localities that prohibit the serving of liquor, but not bottle sales, restaurants or clubs often furnish glasses, ice, and mix if the patron brings a bottle. This practice is also common in states where restaurants have difficulty getting liquor licenses.

Some states forbid the import of liquor: Arkansas, Georgia, Idaho, Michigan, and Pennsylvania. Some other states have quotas limiting imports to a quart or gallon. These are among the drinking laws least likely to be enforced. However, it is important to be aware of these laws, because if a state decides it is losing too much tax revenue to a neighboring state where liquor prices are lower, it will begin to crack down. It is wise, for example, not to buy a case of liquor in New Jersey in front of a policeman at the last liquor store before crossing into Pennsylvania.

Shopping and Tipping

SHOPPING: Large city or small town, wherever you travel there will be shopping centers, department stores, and small shops to provide the basic necessities (or that indispensable item you left at home). Many city department stores, like Filene's in Boston or Bloomingdale's in New York, are as much a part of the city scene as the very streets, and shouldn't be missed. Besides these two, other suggested stores are: Jordan Marsh in Boston; Lord & Taylor, Saks Fifth Avenue, Macy's in New York; Marshall Field in Chicago; Neiman-Marcus in Dallas; the May Company in Los Angeles.

Since supermarkets have become the most common source for food shopping, real farmers' markets have become tourist attractions. They are great places to take children, or to shop for picnics along the road. Several US cities have famous farmers' markets, including Haymarket in Boston, the Italian Market in Philadelphia, State Farmers' Market in Atlanta, and Soulard in St. Louis. (Some others are listed in individual city reports in THE AMERICAN CITIES.)

Other pleasant places to shop in the city are urban malls, such as Chicago's Water Tower Place, Salt Lake City's Trolley Square, San Francisco's Pier 39, Boston's Faneuil Hall Marketplace, and Manhattan's South Street Seaport.

Flea Markets – A growing phenomenon, especially on the East Coast, is that of flea markets, where all kinds of goods are offered in open stands. Located in country fields or empty parking lots, stadiums or skating rinks, some are occasional events advertised locally (watch the daily or weekly paper in the area in which you are traveling); others, usually in larger cities, are run on a permanent or semipermanent basis and advertised regularly. (See the entertainment section of the *New York Times.*) A few flea markets in the New York area:

Annex Fair and Antiques Flea Market, Ave. of the Americas at 25th St., New York, NY (212 243-5343, open Sundays April through October).

Barterama, Belmont Race Track, Elmont, NY (516 775-8774, open Saturdays, Sundays and Tuesdays).

Lambertville Antique and Flea Market, rt. 29, Lambertville, NJ (609 397-0456, open Saturdays and Sundays).

Redwood Country Flea Market, exit 64 off the Wilbur Cross Hwy., Wallingford, CT (203 269-3500, open Saturdays and Sundays).

Factory Outlets – Outlets are huge warehouse stores where companies unload their overruns and canceled orders at dramatically reduced prices — from 20% to 75% off the retail price. They also sell irregulars (slightly flawed pieces) and seconds (more severely flawed or damaged goods). These will be appropriately marked. Some companies, like Bass Shoes and Dansk housewares, have many stores, others just one or two. Factory outlets tend to be outside major urban areas, and several cities around the country have become known for having clusters of outlets nearby. Best known of these are Reading, Pennsylvania; Rochester, Minnesota; Sylvania, Ohio; and Louisville, Kentucky. Two urban areas known for outlets are Orchard Street in Lower Manhattan, New York City, and Fashion Row in Miami, Florida. The New England states are famous for blankets, leather, linen, and textiles; the Carolinas for furniture, linen, textiles, and towels; and Virginia and West Virginia for glassware and pottery.

At any factory outlet, be prepared for crowds, especially on Saturdays. Bear in mind that outlets are rarely centrally located and may take some time to find. (Usually you will need a car.) They can go out of business on short notice, so call in advance. Some of these factory outlets accept credit cards, but these are the ones that are likely to charge higher prices. To locate specific factory outlets, try these books:

Factory Outlet Shopping Guide Series by Jean Bird (available from PO Box 239AP, Oradell, NJ 07649; $3.95 each). Individual books cover Pennsylvania, New England, New Jersey, New York's Rockland County, New York City, Westchester County, and Long Island, North and South Carolina, Washington, DC, Maryland, Delaware, and Virginia.

The SOS Directory by Iris Ellis (9109 San Jose Blvd., Jacksonville, FL 32217; $10.95 including postage), listing 5,000 outlets throughout the United States.

Regional Specialties – In New England, New York, and Pennsylvania, look for good antiques. In addition to shops on Madison Avenue in New York or Pine Street in Philadelphia, you can find good buys in small antique stores along country roads if you are prepared to look through the junk and have a good sense of what items are worth. Vermont cheese and maple syrup, saltwater taffy along the New Jersey shore, and shoofly pie and pretzels in the Pennsylvania Dutch country are all specialties of their respective regions.

In the South there are interesting crafts, especially in the inland mountains. West Virginia is noted for handstitched quilts and quilted clothing and toys. Williamsburg, Virginia, reproductions of pewter, furniture, and other 18th-century items are justly famous. In Georgia you can buy local basketware, wood carving, handwoven wool, and ceramics. In the Blue Ridge Mountains, look for cornhusk dolls and a small wooden musical instrument called the Gee-Haw-Whimmy-Diddle. The Cherokees at Ocunaluf-tee Indian Village in North Carolina (see *A Short Tour of Indian America,* DIVERSIONS,

p. 785) sell handmade tomahawks, bows and arrows, pottery, basketwork, rugs, and feather headdresses.

In the Great Lakes region, consider homemade jams and relishes (especially in Iowa's country stores); American antiques in Illinois; hand-painted ceramics in Clay County, Indiana; wheel cheese and lace in Wisconsin; and pipes, moccasins, and handwoven Indian tribal rugs in Minnesota.

In the Southwest, Mexican, Indian, and "Old West" items are especially good buys. Serapes, tree-of-life candlesticks, and wool rebozos from across the border make nice gifts. The Indian specialties are pottery, Kaibab squaw boots, Navajo rugs, and silver and turquoise jewelry, as well as drums, dolls, and headdresses. And, of course, cowboy boots and ranch clothes from Arizona, New Mexico, and Texas. In the Rockies the same "Old West" focus prevails in many of the shops. Consider buckskin jackets or pants and tooled leather belts, boots, or hats. The region is not without its Indian specialties, but most special is Rocky Mountain jade jewelry.

The Far West, Alaska, and the northern states are the places to buy Eskimo crafts, which include ceremonial masks, dolls, carved whalebone sculpture, and jade items. American Indian crafts are available in Oregon and Idaho as well as in northern Nevada. Merchandise from the Orient is available in San Francisco's Chinatown, and Hawaii.

A Special Hint – For some particularly interesting souvenirs and gifts, look in the shops of museums, which often carry beautifully made reproductions from their collections — anything from prints and posters to jewelry, silver goods, sculpture. A special shopping bonanza is: the United Nations Gift Center in New York City (in the United Nations building), with gifts from around the world.

Ask any store about mailing your purchases home; it may save on sales taxes and will mean less to carry with you.

TIPPING: While tipping is at the discretion of the person receiving the service, 25¢ is the rock-bottom tip for anything, and 50¢ is the customary minimum for small services. In restaurants tip between 10% and 20% of the bill. Waiters in good restaurants expect 20%; for average service in an average restaurant, 15% is reasonable. If you serve yourself, as in a cafeteria, no tip is expected. Coat checks are worth about 50¢ a coat. For carrying luggage, tip bellboys $1 per person or couple, $2 if you have a lot of luggage. The doorman who unloads your car should receive $1. For any special service you receive in a hotel, a tip is expected — again 50¢ for a small service, ranging upward to $1 or more if someone really does something time consuming or out of the ordinary. Leave a hotel maid $1 a day.

Train personnel do not usually expect tips. The exceptions here are dining car waiters who expect 15% of the bill, sleeping car attendants who should get $1 a night, and porters, who expect 50¢ a bag, $1 if they do something extra. Taxi drivers should get about 15% of the total fare.

Sources and Resources

General Notes on Sports

 From Louisville, Kentucky, to Green Bay, Wisconsin, you can take in major seasonal sporting events during your travels. Here is some background on teams and events. See individual city reports in THE AMERICAN CITIES for specific ticket information.

AUTO RACING: There are five major automobile races in the United States each year:

The *Indianapolis 500* takes place on Memorial Day weekend each year at the Indianapolis Motor Speedway, 4790 W 16th St., Indianapolis, IN 46222 (317 241-2500).

The *Daytona 500* is held yearly in February at the Daytona International Speedway, Daytona Beach, FL 32015 (904 254-6767).

The *Long Beach Grand Prix* is held each April in Long Beach, California; information from 110 W Ocean Blvd., Suite A, Long Beach, CA 90802 (213 437-0341).

The *Detroit Grand Prix* is held in June: information, phone 313 259-5400.

The *Lowenbrau Grand Prix of Miami* is run every February on the streets of downtown Miami. For information call 305 662-5660.

For information on other important races: the Automobile Competition Committee for the United States, FIA, 1500 Skokie Blvd., Suite 101, Northbrook, IL 60062 (312 272-0090).

BASEBALL: Baseball is known as the national pastime, and with good reason. Its season opens in April and continues through the World Series in October. The professional teams are divided into two leagues, the National League and the American League. The National League (at 350 Park Ave., New York, NY 10022, 212 371-7300) includes Atlanta, Chicago Cubs, Cincinnati, Houston, Los Angeles, Montreal, New York Mets, Philadelphia, Pittsburgh, St. Louis, San Diego, and San Francisco. In the American League (at 350 Park Ave., New York, NY 10022, 212 371-7600) are Baltimore, Boston, California, Chicago White Sox, Cleveland, Detroit, Kansas City, Milwaukee, Minnesota, New York Yankees, Oakland, Seattle, Texas, and Toronto.

BASKETBALL: Professional basketball gets under way each year in October and keeps its fans watching the hoops through the playoffs in late May or early June. The National Basketball Association (NBA) oversees the sport and is divided into two conferences. The Eastern Conference includes Atlanta, Boston, Chicago, Cleveland, Detroit, Indiana, Milwaukee, New York Knicks, New Jersey Nets, Philadelphia, and Washington. In the Western Conference are Dallas, Denver, Golden State, Houston, Kansas City Clippers, Los Angeles Lakers, Phoenix, Portland, San Antonio, Seattle, and Utah Jazz. Information: the NBA, Olympic Tower, 645 Fifth Ave., New York, NY 10022 (212 826-7000).

FOOTBALL: Until the formation of the United States Football League (USFL) in 1982, this most popular of American spectator sports has been strictly under the aegis of the National Football League (NFL). The NFL season opens in September and culminates in the Super Bowl, which is held in mid-January in a warm-weather city like Los Angeles, Miami, Houston, or New Orleans, between the top teams of the two NFL conferences. The National Conference is made up of the Atlanta, Chicago, Dallas, Detroit, Green Bay Los Angeles Rams, Minnesota, New Orleans, New York Giants, Philadelphia, San Francisco, St. Louis, Tampa, and Washington. The American Conference consists of Buffalo, Cincinnati, Cleveland, Denver, Houston, Indianapolis, Kansas City, Los Angeles Raiders, Miami, New England, New York Jets, Pittsburgh, San Diego, and Seattle. Information: the NFL, 410 Park Ave., New York, NY 10022 (212 758-1500). The USFL consists of: the Arizona Outlaws, Baltimore Stars, Birmingham Stallions, Denver Gold, Jacksonville Bulls, LA Express, Memphis Showboats, New Jersey Generals, Oakland Invaders, Orlando Renegades, San Antonio Gunslingers, and Tampa Bay Bandits. The season runs from March through July. Information: the USFL, 52 Vanderbilt Ave., New York, NY 10017 (212 682-6363).

College football competition also takes place throughout the country from September through December. The Rose Bowl, which is the championship game between the winner of contests among the Midwest Big Ten universities and the top team in the Pacific Conference schools, is held January 1. For tickets contact the Rose Bowl, Pasadena, CA 91103 (818 449-4100). Another famous college contest is the Yale-Harvard game, which takes place either in New Haven (odd years) or Cambridge (even years) in November. It closes the Ivy League football season. For tickets, contact the Department of Athletics, Yale University, New Haven, CT 06520 (203 436-0100), or Athletic Department, Harvard University, Cambridge, MA 02138 (617 495-2211).

GOLF: Professional golf matches are held under the aegis of the Professional Golfers' Association of America (PGA). The three biggest matches on its tour include the Masters Golf Tournament, held in April in Augusta, Georgia; the United States Open, held in July at a different select course around the country each year; and the Professional Golfers' Association (PGA) Championship, held at a different premier layout every August. Contact the PGA of America for details, PO Box 12458, 100 Avenue of Champions, Palm Beach Gardens, FL 33418 (305 626-3600).

HOCKEY: From October through May the ice is hotly contested by the National Hockey League, whose membership is composed of Boston, Buffalo, Calgary, Chicago, Detroit, Edmonton, Hartford, Los Angeles, Minnesota, Montreal, New Jersey, New York Islanders, New York Rangers, Philadelphia, Pittsburgh, Quebec, St. Louis, Toronto, Vancouver, Washington, and Winnipeg. Its best teams compete for the Stanley Cup in May. For more information, contact: NHL, 500 Fifth Ave., 34th Floor, New York, NY 10110 (212 398-1100); or NHL, 1155 Metcalfe St., Suite 960, Montréal, Que., H3B 2W2 (514 871-9220).

HORSE RACING: Among the most prestigious national horse races are the Triple Crown races for three-year-olds. The Kentucky Derby is the first, held in early May at Churchill Downs (700 Central Ave., Louisville, KY 40208, 502 636-3541). Second is the Preakness Stakes, run in May at Pimlico Race Course (Baltimore, MD 21215, 301 542-9400). The final leg is the Belmont Stakes, held each year in June in Belmont Park (Elmont, NY 11003, 718 641-4700).

TENNIS: The major event in US tennis is the United States Open Tennis Championships at Flushing Meadow Park, held each year around Labor Day weekend. For specific information on this and other tournaments, contact the Tournament Players Club, 112 TPC Blvd., Ponte Vedra, FL 32082 (904 285-3301).

Weights and Measures

At some time in the future, the US may convert from the familiar units of measure (feet, yards, quarts, etc.) to the far easier and more logical metric system. Some highway signs, weight scales, and grocery labels already list both measurements. Metric conversions and equivalents are listed below.

APPROXIMATE EQUIVALENTS

Metric Unit	Abbreviation	US Equivalent
LENGTH		
millimeter	mm	.04 inch
meter	m	39.37 inches
kilometer	km	.62 mile
AREA		
square centimeter	sq cm	.155 square inch
square meter	sq m	10.7 square feet
hectare	ha	2.47 acres
square kilometer	sq km	.3861 square mile
CAPACITY		
liter	l	1.057 quarts
WEIGHT		
gram	g	.035 ounce
kilogram	kg	2.2 pounds
metric ton	MT	1.1 tons
ENERGY		
kilowatt	kw	1.34 horsepower

CONVERSION TABLES: METRIC TO US MEASUREMENTS

Multiply	by	to convert to
LENGTH		
millimeters	.04	inches
meters	3.3	feet
meters	1.1	yards
kilometers	.6	miles
CAPACITY		
liters	2.11	pints (liquid)
liters	1.06	quarts (liquid)
liters	.26	gallons (liquid)
WEIGHT		
gram	.04	ounces (avoir)
kilograms	2.2	pounds (avoir)

US TO METRIC MEASUREMENTS		
Multiply	**by**	**to convert to**
LENGTH		
inches	2.5	millimeters
feet	.3	meters
yards	.9	meters
miles	1.6	kilometers
CAPACITY		
pints	.47	liters
quarts	.95	liters
gallons	3.8	liters
WEIGHT		
ounces	28.	grams
pounds	.45	kilograms

TEMPERATURE

$$°F = (°C \times 9/5) + 32 \qquad °C = (°F - 32) \times 5/9$$

For More Information

Every city or region has at least one local guide — rarely available outside the area — which provides information on the nearby scene that is topical, detailed, and often amusing. While you are on the road, it will be well worth your time to browse the shelves of local bookstores. Before you leave on your journey, however, you can prepare by writing to city, regional, and state tourist authorities for information (see *State Tourist Offices*, p. 57, and *Sources and Resources* in THE AMERICAN CITIES); and by perusing books relevant to your special travel interests. The variety and scope of travel information in the United States today is astounding; below, a partial list of publications we have found particularly useful. Refer to individual chapters of GETTING READY TO GO for further lists of sources on specific topics.

NEWSLETTERS: A variety of newsletters provide up-to-date travel information in a simple format; most of the ones on the market today are monthly, eight-page reports that offer inside tips, detailed reports on destinations, and frank evaluations of travel bargains and opportunities in the US and abroad. Newsletters take no advertising, and can be good sources of disinterested — if subjective — judgments.

Consumer Reports Travel Letter (256 Washington St., Mt Vernon, NY 10553; 12 issues per year, $37)

Passport (20 N Wacker Dr., Suite 3417, Chicago, IL 60606; 12 issues per year, $45)

Travel Smart (40 Beechdale Rd., Dobbs Ferry, NY 10522; 12 issues, $29)

Travelore Report (225 S 15th St., Philadelphia, PA 19102; 12 issues per year, $25)

BOOKS: The list below comprises books we have seen and think worthwhile; it is by no means complete. Check the card catalogue of your library for other titles. Prices may have increased slightly in most recent editions.

Travel in the US

America by Train by Ira Fistell (Burt Franklin; $8.95)

Guide to the National Wildlife Refuges by Laura and William Riley (Doubleday; $19.95)

New America's Wonderlands: Our National Parks (National Geographic Society; $12.95, cloth)

Pictorial Travel Guide of Scenic America by E. L. Jordan (Hammond; $16.95, cloth)

Scenic Wonders of America (Random House; $21.45, cloth)

The U.S.A. Book by Hans Hannau (Doubleday; $9.95)

Wilderness U.S.A. (National Geographic Society; $9.95, cloth)

Facts and Information

Handbooks of the National Park Service, National Park Service, Public Inquiries Office, 1013 Interior Bldg., Washington, DC 20240 (202 343-4747)

Rand McNally Road Atlas and Vacation Guide (Rand McNally; $12.95)

Simons' List Book by Howard Simons (Simon & Schuster; $12.95, cloth; $5.95, paper)

Statistical Abstracts of the United States by the US Bureau of the Census (US Government Printing Office, no. 003-024-02680-5; $19)

Forests, Parks, and Camping

Free Campgrounds, U.S.A. by Mary Van Meer (East Woods Press, 820 E Blvd., Charlotte, NC 28203; $9.95)

Lakeside Recreation Areas by Bill and Phyllis Thomas (Stackpole; $8.95)

North American Campground Directory (Simon & Schuster; $12.95)

Pocket Book's Guide to the National Parks by Wallace Rhodes (Pocket Books; $3.95)

Rand McNally's Campgrounds & Trailer Parks (Rand McNally; $12.95)

Rand McNally's National Park Guide (Rand McNally; $8.95)

Wheelers RV Resort and Campground Directory (Print Media Services, 222 S Prospect Ave., Park Ridge, IL 60068; $8.95)

Walking and Backpacking

Adventure Travel North America by Pat Dickerman (Adventure Guides; $12.95)

Backpacking in North America: The Great Outdoors by Hilary J. Bradt and George N. Bradt (Bradt Enterprises; $7.95)

Guide to Backpacking in the United States by Eric Meves (Macmillan; $5.95, paper)

Walking: A Guide to Beautiful Walks and Trails in America by Jean Calder (Morrow; $3.95)

Bicycling

All New Complete Book of Bicycling by Eugene A. Sloane (Simon & Schuster; $19.95)

The American Biking Atlas and Touring Guide by Sue Browder (Workman; $5.95)

Anybody's Bike Book: The New Revised and Expanded Edition by Tom Cuthbertson (Ten Speed Press; $8.95, cloth; $4.95, paper)

The Bicycle Touring Book by Glenda and Tim Wilhelm (Rodale Press; $14.95, cloth; $10.95, paper)

Bicycle Tours in and around New York by Dan Carlinsky and David Heim (Hagstrom; $2.95)

Canoeing

Back to Nature in Canoes: A Guide to American Waters by Rainer Esslen (Columbia; $6.95)

Theme Vacations

The Adventure Vacation Catalogue (Simon & Schuster; $14.95)

American Travelers' Treasury: A Guide to the Nation's Heirlooms by Suzanne Lord (Morrow; $5.95)

Farm, Ranch & Country Vacations by Pat Dickerman (Adventure Guides; $11.95)

Fifty-one Capitols of America and Executive Mansions by Jean H. Daniel and Price Daniel (Country Beautiful Corp.; $15.95)

Vacation by Nancy Hayden Woodward (Penguin; $8.95)

Food

Where to Eat in America by William Rice and Burton Wolf (Random House; $7.95)

Historic Inns and Inexpensive Accommodations

Bed and Breakfast America: The Great American Guest House by John Thaxton (Burt Franklin, 235 E 44th St., New York, NY 10017; $8.95)

The Bed & Breakfast Guide (National Bed & Breakfast Association, 148 E Rocks Rd., Box 332, Norwalk, CT 06852; $9.95)

Bed & Breakfast North America (Betsy Ross Publications, 2057 Betsy Ross Dr., Bloomfield, MI 48013; $6.95)

Bed & Breakfast USA by Betty Rundback and Nancy Kramer (Dutton; $6.95)

The Bed 'n Breakfast Directory by Gail Parker (Posey Publications, PO Box 2612, Fairfield, CA 94533; $3.95)

Country Inns and Back Roads: North America (Berkshire Traveller Press; $9.95)

Country Inns of the Middle Atlantic States by Anthony Hitchcock and Jean Lindgren (Burt Franklin; $4.95)

Historic Country Inns of California by Jim Crain (Chronicle Books; $8.95)

Hotel and Motel Red Book (American Hotel Association, 888 Seventh Ave., New York, NY 10019; $45 plus $3.50 postage)

The Inn Book by Kathleen Neuer (Random House; $4.95)

The 1986-1987 National Directory of Budget Motels (Pilot Books, 103 Cooper St., Babylon, NY 11702; $4.95)

COMPUTER SERVICES: If you have a personal computer, there are many database services you can subscribe to that provide everything from airline schedules and fares to restaurant listings. Three such services are:

CompuServe (5000 Arlington Center Blvd., Columbus, OH 43200; 800 848-8199)

The Source (1616 Anderson Rd., McLean, VA 22102; 800 336-3330)

Travel Scan (5 Penn Plaza, New York, NY 10001; 800 435-7342)

State Tourist Offices

Below is a list of state tourist offices in all the US states (city tourist and convention centers are listed in THE AMERICAN CITIES section of this guide). These state offices offer a wide variety of useful travel information, most of it free for the asking. For best results, request general information on state facilities (several states have "travel kits" which include lists of hotels, tourist attractions, maps, etc.) as well as specific information relevant to your interests:

facilities for specific sports, tours and itineraries of special interest, accommodations in specific areas. Because most of the material you receive will be outsized brochures, there is little point in sending a self-addressed, stamped envelope with your request.

Alabama: Bureau of Tourism and Travel, 532 S Perry St., Montgomery, AL 36104 (205 261-4169 or 800 392-8096 in Alabama or 800 ALABAMA elsewhere except Alaska and Hawaii)

Alaska: Division of Tourism, Pouch E, Juneau, AK 99811 (907 465-2010)

Arizona: Office of Tourism, 1480 Bethany Home Rd., Suite 180, Phoenix, AZ 85014 (602 255-3618)

Arkansas: Department of Parks and Tourism, 1 Capitol Mall, Little Rock, AR 72201 (501 371-1511 or 800 482-8999 in Arkansas or 800 643-8383 elsewhere)

California: Department of Commerce, Office of Tourism, 1121 L St., Suite 103, Sacramento, CA 95814 (916 322-1396)

Colorado: Office of Tourism, 5500 S Syracuse Circle #267, Englewood, CO 80111 (303 779-1067)

Connecticut: Department of Economic Development, Tourism Division, 210 Washington St., Hartford, CT 06106 (203 566-3977)

Delaware: Tourism Office, Delaware Development Office, PO Box 1401, Dover, DE 19903 (302 736-4271 or 800 441-8846)

District of Columbia: Washington Convention and Visitor's Association, 1575 Eye St., NW, Suite 250, Washington, DC 20005 (202 789-7000)

Florida: Visitor Inquiry, Department of Commerce, 126 Van Buren St., Tallahassee, FL 32301 (904 487-1462)

Georgia: Tourist Division, Department of Industry and Trade, PO Box 1776, Atlanta, GA 30301 (404 656-3590)

Hawaii: Visitors Bureau, PO Box 8527, Honolulu, HI 96815 (808 923-1811)

Idaho: Travel Council, Room 108, Capitol Building, Boise, ID 83720 (208 334-2470 or 800 635-7820)

Illinois: Office of Tourism, Department of Commerce and Community Affairs, 620 E Adams, Springfield, IL 62701 (217 782-7139)

Indiana: Tourism Division, Department of Commerce, 1 N Capitol, Suite 700, Indianapolis, IN 46204-2243 (317 232-8860)

Iowa: Development Commission, Visitors and Tourism, 600 E Court Ave., Suite A, Des Moines, IA 50309 (515 281-3100)

Kansas: Department of Economic Development, Kansas Travel, Tourism, and Film Services Division, 503 Kansas Ave., 6th Floor, Topeka, KS 66603 (913 296-2009)

Kentucky: Department of Travel Development, Capital Plaza Tower, 22nd Floor, Frankfort, KY 40601 (502 564-4930)

Louisiana: Office of Tourism, PO Box 94291, Baton Rouge, LA 79291 (504 925-3860 or 800 231-4730)

Maine: Publicity Bureau, 97 Winthrop St., Hallowell, ME 04347 (207 289-2423)

Maryland: Department of Economic and Community Development, 45 Calvert St., Annapolis, MD 21401 (301 269-3517 or 800 331-1750)

Massachusetts: Division of Tourism, Department of Commerce and Development, 100 Cambridge St., Boston, MA 02202 (617 727-3201)

Michigan: Travel Bureau, Department of Commerce, PO Box 30226, Lansing, MI 48909 (517 373-0670 or 800 292-2520 in Michigan or 800 248-5700 elsewhere)

Minnesota: Office of Tourism, 240 Bremer Bldg., 419 N Robert St., St. Paul, MN 55101 (612 296-5029 or 800 328-1461)

Mississippi: Department of Economic Development, Division of Tourism, PO Box 849, Jackson, MS 39205-0849 (601 359-3414)

Missouri: Division of Tourism, Truman State Office Bldg., PO Box 1055, Jefferson City, MO 65102 (314 751-4133)

Montana: Travel Promotion Division, Department of Commerce, 1424 Ninth Ave. Helena, MT 59620 (406 444-2654 or 800 548-3390)

Nebraska: Division of Travel and Tourism, Department of Economic Development, PO Box 94666, 301 Centennial Mall S, Lincoln, NE 68509 (402 471-3796 or 800 742-7595 in Nebraska or 800 228-4307 elsewhere)

Nevada: Commission on Tourism, Capitol Complex, Carson City, NV 89710 (702 885-4322)

New Hampshire: Office of Vacation Travel, PO Box 856, Concord, NH 03301 (603 271-2343)

New Jersey: Department of Commerce and Economic Development, Division of Travel and Tourism, CN 826, Trenton, NJ 08625 (609 292-2470)

New Mexico: Economic Development and Tourism Dept., Bataan Memorial Building, Santa Fe, NM 87503 (505 827-6230 or 800 545-2040)

New York: Division of Tourism, State Department of Commerce, One Commerce Plaza, Albany, NY 12245 (518 474-4116 or 800 CALL NYS in the northeastern states)

North Carolina: Travel and Tourism Division, 430 N Salisbury St., Raleigh, NC 27611 (919 733-4171 or 800 VISIT NC)

North Dakota: Tourism Promotion Division, Capitol Grounds, Bismarck, ND 58505 (701 224-2525 or 800 437-2077)

Ohio: Office of Travel and Tourism, PO Box 1001, Columbus, OH 43216 (614 466-8844 or in Ohio, 800 282-5393)

Oklahoma: Division of Marketing Services, Tourism and Recreation Department, 500 Will Rogers Building, Oklahoma City, OK 73105 (405 521-2406 or 800 652-6552)

Oregon: Tourism Division, Economic Development Dept., 595 Cottage St., NE, Salem, OR 97310 (503 378-3451 or 800 233-3306 in Oregon or 800 547-7842 elsewhere)

Pennsylvania: Department of Commerce, Bureau of Travel Development, 416 Forum Building, Harrisburg, PA 17120 (717 787-5453)

Rhode Island: Department of Economic Development, Tourism and Promotion Division, 7 Jackson Walkway, Providence, RI 02903 (401 277-2601 or 800 556-2484, Maine-Virginia only)

South Carolina: Department of Parks, Recreation and Tourism, Division of Tourism, PO Box 71, Columbia, SC 29201 (803 758-2279)

South Dakota: Department of State Development, PO Box 6000, Pierre, SD 57501 (605 773-3301 or 800 843-1930)

Tennessee: Department of Tourist Development, PO Box 23170, Nashville, TN 37202 (615 741-2158)

Texas: Travel and Information Division, Department of Highways and Public Transportation, PO Box 5064, Austin, TX 78763 (512 465-7401)

Utah: Travel Council, Council Hall, Capitol Hill, Salt Lake City, UT 84114 (801 533-5681)

Vermont: Travel Division, 134 State St., Montpelier, VT 05602 (802 828-3236)

Virginia: Division of Tourism, Bell Tower, Capitol Sq., Richmond, VA 23219 (804 786-4484)

Washington: Tourism Development Division, Department of Commerce and Economic Development, 101 General Administration Building, Olympia, WA 98504 (206 753-5600 or 800 562-4570 in Washington or 800 541-WASH elsewhere)

West Virginia: Department of Commerce, Tourism Division, 1900 Washington St.

E, Building 6, Room B564, Charleston, WV 25305 (304 348-2286 or 800 624-9110 out of state)

Wisconsin: Division of Tourism, Box 7606, Madison, WI 53707 (608 266-2161 or, in or near Wisconsin, 800 ESCAPES)

Wyoming: Travel Commission, I-25 and College Dr., Cheyenne, WY 82002 (307 777-7777)

Camera and Equipment

 Vacations are everybody's favorite time for taking pictures. After all, most of us want to remember the places we visit — and show them off to others — through spectacular photographs. Here are a few suggestions to help you get the best results from your travel picture-taking.

BEFORE THE TRIP: If you're just taking your camera out after a long period in mothballs, or have just bought a new one, check it thoroughly before you leave to prevent unexpected breakdowns and disappointing pictures.

1. Shoot at least one test roll, using the kind of film you plan to take along with you. Use all the shutter speeds and f/stops on your camera, and vary the focus to make sure everything is in order. Do this well in advance of your departure so there will be time to have film developed and to make repairs, if they are necessary. If you're in a rush, most large cities have custom labs that can process film in as little as 3 hours.

2. Clean your camera thoroughly, inside and out. Dust and dirt can jam camera mechanisms, spoil pictures, and scratch film. Remove surface dust from lenses and camera body with a soft camel's hair brush. Next, use at least two layers of crumpled lens tissue and your breath to clean lenses and filters. Don't rub hard and don't use compressed air on lenses or filters because they are so easily damaged. Persistent stains can be removed by using a Q-tip moistened with liquid lens cleaner. Anything that doesn't come off easily needs professional attention. Once your lens is clean, protect it from dirt and damage with an inexpensive skylight or ultra-violet filter.

3. Check the batteries in the light meter, and take along extra ones just in case yours wear out during the trip.

EQUIPMENT TO TAKE ALONG: Keep your gear light and compact. Items that are too heavy or bulky to be carried with you will likely stay in your hotel room.

1. Most single lens reflex (SLR) cameras come with a conventional 50mm lens, a general purpose lens good for street scenes taken at a distance of 25 feet or more and full body portraits shot at normal distances. You can expand your photographic options with a wide-angle lens such as a 35mm, 28mm, or 24mm. These are especially handy for panoramas, cityscapes, and large buildings or statuary from which you can't step back. For close-ups, a macro lens is best, but screw-on magnifying lenses are an inexpensive alternative. Telephoto and zoom lenses are bulky and not really necessary unless you are shooting animals in the wild. If you want one such lens that gives a range of options, try a 35mm to 80mm zoom; it is relatively light, though expensive. Protect all lenses with a 1A or 1B skylight filter, which should be removed for cleaning only. And take along a polarizing filter to eliminate glare and reflection, and to saturate colors in very bright sunlight.

2. Travel photographs work best in color. The preferred and least expensive all-

around slide films are Kodachrome 64, Fujichrome, and Agfachrome. For very bright conditions, try slower film like Kodachrome 25. In places that tend to be cloudy, or indoors with natural light (as in museums), use a fast film such as Ektachrome 400, which can be "pushed" to ASA 800 or 1600, or 3M 1000 ASA film. Films tend to render color in slightly different ways. Kodachrome brings out reds and oranges. Agfachrome mutes bright tones and produces fine browns, yellows, and whites. Fuji is noted for its yellows, greens, and whites. Anticipate what you are likely to see, and take along whichever types of film will enhance your results.

If you choose film that develops into prints rather than slides, try Kodacolor 100 or 400 for bright, sunny days. For environments where there isn't much contrast — in the shade or on dark, overcast days — use Kodak Vericolor. Remember that multiple prints made from slide transparencies are generally better than those made from print negatives.

How much film should you take? If you are serious about your photography, pack one roll of film (36 exposures) for each day of your trip. If you are concerned about airport security X rays damaging your film, store it in lead-lined film bags sold in camera shops. (Film Shield, a company producing the lead-lined pouches, has just introduced a heavy-duty version that has twice the thickness of lead.) Photo industry sources say that incidents of damage to unprocessed film are minimal in the US, because low-dosage X-ray equipment is in use virtually everywhere. As a rule of thumb, film with speeds up to ASA 400 can go through security machinery in the US five times without any noticeable effect, but the new, very high speed film with an ASA rating of 1,000 should *never* be subjected to X rays, in the US or overseas. Use the lead pouches or ask to have your camera inspected by hand.

3. A small battery-powered electronic flash unit is handy for very dim light or at night, but only if the subject is at a distance of 15 feet or less. Flash units cannot illuminate an entire scene, and many museums do not permit flash photography, so take such a unit only if you know you will need it. If your camera does not have a hot-shoe, you will need a PC cord to synchronize the flash with your shutter.

4. Invest in a broad camera strap if you now have a thin one. It will make carrying the camera much more comfortable.

5. A sturdy canvas or leather camera bag — not an airline bag — will keep equipment organized and easy to find.

6. For cleaning, bring along a camel's hair brush that retracts into a rubber squeeze bulb. Also, take plenty of lens tissue as well, and plastic bags to protect cameras against dust.

7. Pack some extra lens caps — they're the first things to get lost.

SOME TIPS: For better pictures, remember the following pointers:

1. *Get close.* Move in to get your subject to fill the frame.
2. *Vary your angle.* Get down, shoot from above, look for unusual perspectives.
3. *Pay attention to backgrounds.* Keep it simple or blur it out.
4. *Look for details.* Not just a whole building, but a decorative element; not just an entire street scene, but a single remarkable face.
5. *Don't be lazy.* Always carry your camera gear with you, loaded and ready for those unexpected moments.

THE
AMERICAN
CITIES

ATLANTA

Until the 1960s, the world at large knew Atlanta mainly through the pages of Margaret Mitchell's *Gone With the Wind*. But then a pragmatic leadership steered it calmly through the stormy seas of social change, and an avalanche of favorable press turned the city — almost overnight — into America's urban sweetheart. Waves of ambitious entrepreneurs rushed in from across the country and around the world. Up went urban towers, ritzy hotels, glitzy restaurants, modern sports arenas, and shopping galleries where before there had been mostly red earth, pines, and kudzu.

In the early 19th century the city was nothing but a section of frontier forest coaxed away from the Creek Indians by the state of Georgia. A proposed rail route into the area from Tennessee was determined in 1837. A surveyor for the Western & Atlantic Railroad staked the southern terminus for the new right of way near where the Omni International complex now stands, calling the railroad workers' camp that grew on the site simply the Terminus.

Pretty soon they started calling it Marthasville, after the daughter of the governor who boosted the rail project. Then someone with the railroad feminized Atlantic into Atlanta and started using that name on train schedules. The city was chartered as Atlanta in 1847.

By the eve of the War Between the States, the city was a humming juggernaut whose 10,000 industrious citizens ran banks and stores and turned out munitions, railroad cars, food, and clothing for the Confederacy. Punished by devastation, Atlantans swiftly put their town back together and even invited the archfiend himself, General William Tecumseh Sherman, to witness the resurrection personally. Crusty old "War Is Hell" returned three times, was wined and dined, and was so impressed, he invested in the city's reconstruction effort.

Today's Atlanta, strung together by an overburdened network of freeways, is the financial, administrative, and distribution center and the cultural, retail, entertainment, transportation, and communications focus for a flourishing Sunbelt domain counting more than 34 million heads.

More than 30% of Georgia's manufacturing takes place in metropolitan Atlanta, and, at the latest reckoning, all but a handful of *Fortune* magazine's 500 largest corporations maintain national or regional offices and production facilities here. Attesting to the city's newest slogan, "The World's Next Great International City," about 35 nations operate consulates and trade offices.

And the city still thrives as a distribution point for travelers. After the Civil War, there was a familiar complaint about Atlanta: "Whether you're going to heaven or hell," people used to say, "you'll have to change trains in Atlanta." Today it's a change of planes, but the city's role is the same. Hartsfield International Airport, physically the world's largest jet terminal complex, annually runs neck and neck with Chicago's O'Hare in the number

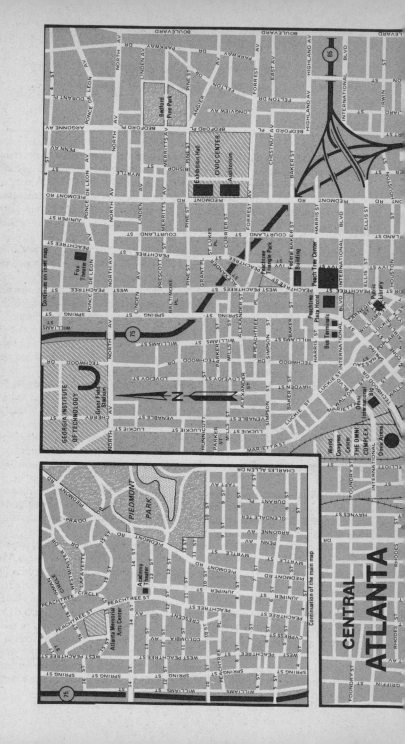

CENTRAL
ATLANTA

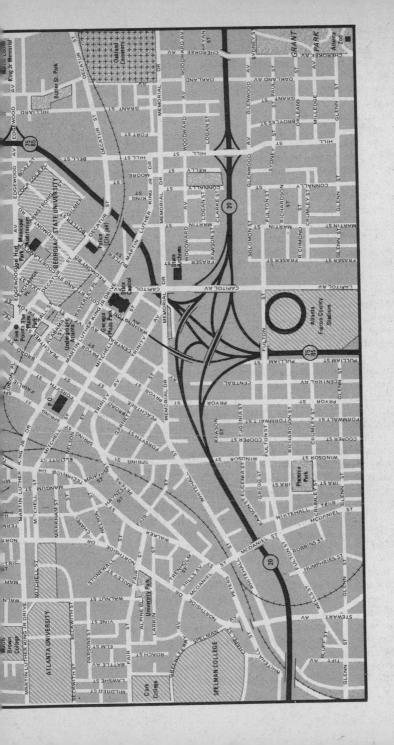

of passengers put on and taken off aircraft. Every year, more than 41 million passengers — half again as many as Europe's largest airports — pass through Hartsfield's color-coded concourses to and from Nashville, Seattle, Amsterdam, Mexico City, and a thousand and one other destinations.

Thanks to a transplanted Cincinnatian named Robert Edward (Ted) Turner III, Atlanta has also made a very big name for itself in the world of communications. Launched from a bankrupt UHF station in the early 1970s, Turner's Cable News Network and "Superstation WTBS" are now beamed across the country and to Europe and Japan as well. As a side effect, Turner's Atlanta Braves baseball team has fan clubs in some very unlikely out-of-state locales.

For shoppers from the far corners of Dixie, Peachtree Street is Fifth Avenue; here and in the suburban malls are found Atlanta's own retailers as well as trendy carpetbaggers from Beverly Hills, New York, and Paris. For Southerners in search of a good time, Atlanta is not known as "Hot-lanna" simply because a fellow named Sherman once burned it down.

Atlanta may be a hard-headed business giant, but it's also a town with a very large heart in which enlightened urban planning has integrated human needs and priorities into the civic structure. Clean-lined, functional skyscrapers are designed so that the inner space makes people comfortable rather than intimidated by overpowering monolithic anonymity. Sometimes, those designs even fulfill their aims. Older, inner-city neighborhoods like Midtown, Virginia/Highland, and Inman Park, once afflicted by urban blight, have been brought back to life largely by young Atlantans who thrive on urban diversity.

Culturally, the bleak days when Atlanta reigned unhappily over H. L. Mencken's "Sahara of the Bozarts" have passed into history. The new High Museum of Art, a feast of light and contemporary angles, has been highly acclaimed by art critics. The Atlanta Ballet and Atlanta Symphony are also well esteemed, and a score of lively companies have turned the town into a major center of regional theater.

A continuous influx of newcomers from across the US, Latin America, Europe, the Orient, Asia, Africa, and Canada has radically altered the city's personality through healthy infusions of diverse lifestyles and cultures. Philosophically, Atlantans span the spectrum from button-down conservative to ultra hip. A once-provincial town — where seldom was heard a non-Southern word — it no longer turns a surprised head at the sound of Korean or Thai or the sight of a sari on a MARTA bus or train.

Although natives have not, by a long shot, forsaken their passion for *Varsity Drive-In* chili dogs and fried peach pies, the glorious fried chicken at *Mary Mac's Tea Room,* or the barbecue and Brunswick stew at *Harold's,* it's far easier now to sample Oriental, Mexican, Italian, French, and even Ethiopian cuisine than it is to track down a traditional Southern table.

Atlantans can't figure for the life of them why anyone, for mere wealth and renown, would choose to live anywhere else. And in early spring, when dogwood and azalea cover the city's hillsides, residents insist that even Paris pales by comparison.

First-time visitors invariably feel at least a passing wave of disappointment. Were they subconsciously hoping to glimpse Miss Scarlett parading down

Peachtree in a flouncy frock, smuggled through the Yankee blockade by the outrageous Captain Butler? Southern belles may have gone the way of the steam locomotive, but Old Atlanta hasn't sashayed entirely out of existence. Way down in its heart it remains faithful to its Southern roots. Behind the modern skyscrapers, the nouvelle cuisine and sushi bars, expensive department stores and trendy European boutiques, there's an age-old code of soft speech and polite manners along with a sense of fierce regional pride that can turn politics and football games into replays of the Crusades.

Atlanta is the sort of city that requires more than just one look. An oft-repeated story about Atlanta Stadium says a great deal about the city's character. Ivan Allen, Jr., the mayor behind the stadium's construction in 1965, was fond of saying: "We built a stadium in 52 weeks, on land we didn't own, with money we didn't have, for a baseball team we weren't at all certain was coming."

As it turned out, the old Milwaukee Braves thoughtfully migrated south the next year to become the stadium's first major league tenant. Although the Braves have yet to fulfill their promise to win a World Series, Atlantans have never questioned their initial good judgment.

ATLANTA AT-A-GLANCE

SEEING THE CITY: The view from the 70th floor of *Peachtree Plaza Hotel*'s revolving *Sun Dial* restaurant is, in a word, spectacular. When the weather is clear, your eye sweeps from the planes arriving and taking off at Hartsfield International Airport (to the south) to the Blue Ridge Mountains (in the north). The *Sun Dial* can be reached only by an 80-second ride in one of the two glass elevators that skim up and down in the glass tubes affixed to the outside of the building. You will have to order something to eat or drink to spend any time there, and it's a good idea to make reservations first. Open daily till 1:45 AM for cocktails. Peachtree at International Blvd. (659-1400).

SPECIAL PLACES: You can walk around downtown Atlanta without much difficulty, but be warned, the streets aren't laid out in a neat, orderly grid. They roughly follow the paths of early — and now extinct — rail lines, because the early streets ran parallel to the old tracks. The result is a tangled web that often leaves visitors confused, as much by the erratic pattern as by the fact that at least half the streets seem to be named Peachtree, Circle, or Hills.

The good news is the public transportation system — MARTA — which is excellent, especially if you are downtown or near Peachtree Street. Not only do regular buses cruise downtown, but a special circular route (with buses every ten minutes) connects the major hotels and convention sites — Peachtree Center, the Civic Center, the Omni complex, and the World Congress Center.

DOWNTOWN

Peachtree Center – Half a block from that spectacular 80-second glass elevator ride that transports you from the heights of the *Sun Dial* restaurant is Peachtree Center, the shopping megastructure that surrounds Peachtree Plaza. Mazes of escalators whisk you to different levels of unusual shops, such as Hans Frabel's hand-blown glass atelier. Plants and vines hang everywhere. There are lakes and fountains here, too.

You can stop for a casual, relaxing meal in the center's courtyard restaurant. 230-233 Peachtree St. NE (659-0800).

Woodruff Park – A few blocks south of Peachtree Center, Woodruff Park is a gift from Atlanta's best-known anonymous donor, Coca-Cola millionaire Robert W. Woodruff, whose six-figure civic generosity has done more to change the face of the city than cosmetic surgery has done for Hollywood. (Emory University's Medical School is another large beneficiary of his anonymous largesse.) At lunch, hundreds of officeworkers, street people, wandering preachers, and Hare Krishna folk swarm into the park — a gentle crowd. Grab a hot dog or plate of shrimp fried rice at *Tokyo Shapiro's*, 62 Peachtree St., across from the park, and settle down on the grass. Peachtree, Edgewood, Pryor, and Auburn sts.

Martin Luther King Jr. Historic District – Within a five-block National Historic District near downtown are sites associated with the life and times of the late Nobel Peace Prize winner. These include his birthplace; Ebenezer Baptist Church, where he preached with his father; his tomb, guarded by an eternal flame and inscribed with the words "Free At Last"; the Interfaith Peace Chapel; a community center; and the Center for Social Change, which displays related papers, films, and memorabilia. Auburn Ave. at Boulevard NE (524-1956).

Georgia Capitol – Walk southwest to Martin Luther King Jr. Drive, then west again to the capitol. You can't miss it — it's the golden dome (regilded in 1981 with north Georgia gold leaf). If the legislature isn't in session, you can tour the Hall of Flags, the Hall of Fame in the rotunda, and the Museum of Science and Industry. Open weekdays. Free. Capitol Square SW (656-2844).

Federal Reserve Bank – Remember when dollar bills were silver certificates, not Federal Reserve notes? The dollar was worth a dollar in silver then. Not these days. But we're not complaining much — Federal Reserve notes seem to work just as well. If you want to see where they're made, walk over to Marietta Street, two blocks east of the Omni International, and look at the Corinthian-columned Federal Reserve Bank. Although the building is new, the Federal Reserve System's Sixth District headquarters has been here since 1914. Tours of the bank's operations and its Money Museum are available, but you must call in advance to schedule a visit. Open weekdays. Free. 104 Marietta NW (521-8747).

The Fox Theater – This grand movie palace has been around since 1929, and its past is as varied as its rococo facade. Built to be a Shriner Temple, the plans fell through and it opened — in all its Egyptian-Arabic-Moroccan splendor — as a movie house. For almost 30 years it was a popular family and date spot, but when Atlantans deserted downtown for the suburbs in the 60s, the Fox fell into disrepair. On the eve of its destruction a group called Atlanta Landmarks stepped in and saved it. Designated a national landmark in 1976, today it operates as a movie theater (a family film festival runs in the summer), a concert hall, and a stage for touring Broadway productions and big-name entertainment. A portion of every ticket goes toward ongoing restoration costs. The Fox seats 4,518 people, making it the country's second largest operating theater (after Radio City Music Hall in New York City). Tours of the hall are given from April through October on Mondays and Saturdays. Admission charge. 662 Peachtree St. NE (522-4345; for program and ticket information, 881-1977).

Omni International, Omni Coliseum, and Georgia World Congress Center – Grouped together at the edge of downtown, these three huge buildings are the heart of Atlanta's vital convention industry. The totally enclosed Omni International megastructure has shops, restaurants, office buildings, and the deluxe *Omni International Hotel.* Connected by a pedestrian bridge, the Georgia World Congress Center has now completed an expansion that makes it one of the country's largest and most modern exhibition halls. The Omni Coliseum, which looks rather like a rusty egg carton, seats

17,000 for sports events, rock concerts, circuses, and other large gatherings. 100 Techwood Dr. at Marietta St. NW (681-2163).

ENVIRONS

The Wren's Nest – The charming name was given to this Victorian cottage by its famous owner, Joel Chandler Harris, best known as the creator of Brer Fox, Brer Rabbit, and the other immortal Southern animal characters of the Uncle Remus stories. The house has original furnishings and lots of memorabilia from the life of the Atlanta storyteller. Open daily. Admission charge. 1050 Gordon SW (753-8535).

Chattahoochee Nature Center – The center is actually a 7-acre nature preserve on the peaceful banks of the Chattahoochee River, with animal exhibits and classes for both children and adults. Open daily. Voluntary admission charge. 9135 Willeo Rd., Roswell, 20 miles north of downtown (992-2055).

Piedmont Park – Three miles north of downtown, Piedmont is a spacious green place for swimming, tennis, jogging, picnics, and observing Atlantans at leisure. The Atlanta Arts Festival is held here annually in early May, and the Atlanta Symphony presents outdoor concerts in summer. The Atlanta Botanical Garden, on 60 acres in the park, has greenhouses, a Japanese garden, rose gardens, a Fragrance Garden for the blind, and a visitors center with classes and special programs. Open daily. Free. Piedmont Ave. between 10th and 14th sts. (876-5858).

The Cyclorama – The dramatic circular painting of the Civil War Battle for Atlanta (50 feet high and 400 feet in circumference) has been beautifully restored and enhanced by new sound and lighting effects. Skip the adjacent Atlanta Zoo, which is badly rundown and a depressing experience for anyone who cares about animals. Admission charge for both the Cyclorama and the zoo. Grant Park, 800 Cherokee Ave., 3 miles from downtown (624-1071).

Fernbank Science Center – Often overlooked by nonparents, the Fernbank has the Southeast's third largest planetarium, an observatory, and a nature trail leading through 70 acres of unspoiled forest. A see-and-touch museum, an electronic microscope laboratory, a meteorological laboratory, and an experimental garden also on the premises make this a fascinating place to spend an afternoon. Open daily. Admission charge. 156 Heaton Park Dr. NE (378-4311).

High Museum of Art – In late 1983, the High Museum moved out of the Woodruff Arts Center into a spectacular new home next door. The magnificent building is an architectural masterpiece in its own right, with an exterior of dazzling white enamel tiles and a central atrium flooded with natural light. The museum contains collections of American, European, and African art and a fine assemblage of decorative arts. Peachtree and 16th sts. (892-3600).

Robert W. Woodruff Arts Center – Originally dedicated to the 122 Atlanta art patrons who died in a 1962 air crash in Paris, the center has been renamed in honor of the Coca-Cola patriarch and arts benefactor, and in 1983 its art collection was moved to the new High Museum of Art. The center is now the home of the Atlanta Symphony Orchestra, the Alliance Theater, the Atlanta Children's Theater, and the Atlanta College of Art. It also sometimes features traveling art exhibitions. 1280 Peachtree St. NE (892-3600).

Atlanta Historical Society – Proceed north along Peachtree Road to W Paces Ferry Road. Turn left and look for Andrews Drive, site of the Atlanta Historical Society's 18-acre complex. The society's showpiece is Swan House, built in 1928 and designed by well-known Atlanta architect Philip Shutze in the Anglo-Palladian style. It is a magnificent exercise in a popular Italian Renaissance mode and is handsomely furnished in 18th-century antiques, many of which belonged to the former owners, prominent Atlantans Mr. and Mrs. Edward Inman. Adults can enjoy a fine building; kids can look for the swan hidden in the decoration of every room. Also on the grounds is the Tullie Smith house, an authentic 1840s "plantation plain" Georgia farmhouse reconstructed on the property with all its attached buildings. Nearby is the Inmans' coach house, now a pleasant restaurant, gift shop, and art gallery. Also on the property is the McElreath Memorial Hall, which houses the society's museum and its extensive Atlanta historical material, most of which is available to the public. A nature trail has been marked so you can learn about the region's ecology. Open daily. Admission charge for Swan and Tullie Smith houses. 3101 Andrews Dr. NW (261-1837).

Six Flags Over Georgia – Just outside the Perimeter Highway (I-285), this 276-acre amusement park has over 100 rides and live shows, including the Great American Scream Machine (fastest, tallest, and longest roller coaster in the world — until 1976) and the Great Gasp parachute jump (666 feet tall), which lets you free-fall for 30 feet. During the summer, there's a free fireworks display at closing time (11 PM). Open daily, late May through Labor Day; weekends, late March through November. Admission charge. 12 miles west of Atlanta on I-20 (948-9290).

Stone Mountain Park – There's a bit of something for everybody here: a cable car ride to the top, an old steam train, hiking trails, a lake where you can ride a riverboat or canoe, an 18-hole golf course, and an antebellum plantation. And that's not all. This is Mt. Rushmore South. The Confederate heroes Jefferson Davis, Robert E. Lee, and Stonewall Jackson have been drilled into the sheer face of a giant mass of exposed granite. The enormous bas-relief was begun — but not finished — by Gutzon Borglum, who went on to carve Mt. Rushmore. Resort facilities include campgrounds, restaurants, and motels. Open daily. Admission charge. 16 miles northeast of Atlanta on Rte. 78 (469-9831).

Kennesaw Mountain National Battlefield Park – The mountain and 2,800-acre park were the scene of one of the most important engagements in the Battle of Atlanta campaign. Attractions include a Civil War museum and defense lines. Open daily. Free. Off I-75; 25 miles from downtown, near Marietta (427-4686). Also in the vicinity is the Big Shanty Museum in Kennesaw. Its locomotive *General* was involved in a famous Civil War spy chase and was the subject of the Walt Disney movie *Great Locomotive Chase.* Open daily. Admission charge (427-2117).

Farmers' Market – Looking for that ole down-home feeling without trekking to Plains? Then drop down to the Georgia State Farmers' Market, the largest in the South. The colorful stalls and sheds spread across 146 acres, and for a buck and a quarter you can still get a juicy, black diamond watermelon or a mess of peaches. Just south of Perimeter Highway on I-75. Take the Thames Rd./Forest Park exit (366-6910).

Tara – Just about everybody comes to Atlanta looking for the legendary white-columned mansion. But, alas, Tara never existed, except in Margaret Mitchell's imagination and David O. Selznick's movie sets. If you're lucky, you'll be able to catch *Gone With the Wind* at a movie theater in town. It's shown frequently, and there's no better place to see it. Memorabilia and foreign editions of *GWTW* are on display at the Margaret Mitchell Room of the Atlanta Public Library, Peachtree and Forsyth sts. (688-4034).

■**EXTRA SPECIAL:** Just 35 miles northeast of Atlanta, *Lanier Islands* have been developed into a resort area. The 1,200 acres of hills and woods contain golf courses, tennis courts, and horseback riding and camping facilities. There are also sailboats and houseboats for rent. (Manmade Lake Lanier has 540 miles of shoreline.) *Stouffer's Pine Isle Resort Hotel* is on the grounds, too. Open daily. A parking permit is $3 daily. On I-85 (Lanier Islands information, 945-6701).

SOURCES AND RESOURCES

 TOURIST INFORMATION: For general information, brochures, and maps, contact the Atlanta Chamber of Commerce, Omni International (521-0845); or Atlanta Convention and Visitors Bureau, 235 Peachtree St. NE, Suite 1414 (521-6633). Exhibitions on Georgia tourism and industry are at the World Congress Center, Marietta and Magnolia sts. NW (656-7000). A covered pedestrian bridge links the center to the *Omni International Hotel.* Foreign visitors information and language help are available from the Atlanta Council for International Visitors, 235 Peachtree St. NE, Suite 202 (577-2248).

A Marmac Guide to Atlanta (Marmac Publishers; $8.95) is the most comprehensive guide to the city, with detailed chapters on sightseeing, dining, nightlife, museums, cultural activities, shopping, and other areas of interest.

Local Coverage – *Atlanta Constitution,* morning daily; *Atlanta Journal,* evening daily; *Atlanta* magazine, monthly.

Food – *Atlanta* magazine contains listings of most of the established restaurants and some newcomers. The Weekend section of the Saturday *Atlanta Journal-Constitution* offers complete dining, entertainment, and special events listings.

Area Code – All telephone numbers are in the 404 area code unless otherwise indicated.

 CLIMATE AND CLOTHES: Atlanta's temperatures vary from moderate winters to comfortable springs and falls to hot and humid summers. In the rainy winter months, December through March, it doesn't get much colder than 20°. May, September, October, and November tend to be the sunniest months. While Atlanta isn't exactly what you'd call dry, the average humidity hovers at 60%, which isn't intolerable either.

GETTING AROUND: Airport – Atlanta is served by Hartsfield International Airport, one of the world's largest and busiest. The airport's two terminals (North and South) are connected by a speedy and efficient subway system that runs every two minutes. Except during rush hours, a trip to the airport from downtown takes about 20 minutes; taxi fare should run about $13.50. Atlanta Airport Shuttle (525-2177) buses provide transportation to downtown hotels for $6 and to such suburban locations as Emory University, Lenox Square, and Colony Square for $9; buses depart from outside the airport terminals every 30 minutes. MARTA (Metropolitan Atlanta Rapid Transit Authority) bus #72 travels between the airport and downtown every 20 or 50 minutes (depending on the time of day) from 5:30 AM; the fare is 60¢ and exact change is required.

Bus – MARTA (Metropolitan Area Rapid Transit) is the backbone of Atlanta's public transportation system. Bus routes interlace the city, with frequent stops at downtown locations. Exact fare required. A new rapid rail system now runs 12 miles east-west and 12 miles north-south, connecting at the Five Points station downtown. When complete, the system will have 60 miles of tunnel and grade-level track. Each station has been designed by a different architect and decorated with murals, photos, and collages. MARTA maintains information booths at the intersection of Peachtree and West Peachtree, near the *Hyatt Regency Hotel,* and at Broad and Walton NE (522-4711).

Taxi – Atlanta isn't known for its efficient taxi services. Many are unclean, mechanically suspect, and often manned by drivers unfamiliar with local geography. Yellow Cab (522-0200) and London Taxi (681-2280) are among the more reliable.

Car Rental – All major national firms are represented.

MUSEUMS: The High Museum of Art, the Woodruff Arts Center, the Hall of Fame and Museum of Science and Industry in the capitol, and the Fernbank Science Center are described in *Special Places.*

Toy Museum of Atlanta – Thirteen rooms in this restored mansion are filled with antique dolls, trains, toy soldiers, and all sorts of games. Open daily. Admission charge. 2800 Peachtree Rd., 5 miles north of downtown (266-8697).

MAJOR COLLEGES AND UNIVERSITIES: There are nine important institutions of higher education in the metro area, each contributing to the cultural, as well as the academic, climate. They are Atlanta University, 223 Chestnut SW (681-0251); Atlanta College of Art, 1280 Peachtree NE (898-1164); Atlanta College of Business, 1280 W Peachtree NW (873-1981); Agnes Scott College, E College Dr., Decatur (373-2571); Emory University (famous for its medical program), 1380 S Oxford Rd. NE (329-6123); Georgia Institute of Technology, 225 North Ave. NW (894-2000); Georgia State University, University Plaza NE (658-2000); Interdenominational Theological Center, 671 Beckwith SW (525-5926); Oglethorpe University, 4484 Peachtree Rd. NE (261-1441).

SPECIAL EVENTS: The *Arts Festival of Atlanta* takes place in Piedmont Park in the spring. In September, the *Atlanta Greek Festival* is a potpourri of Greek costumes, movies, gifts, art, dances, and food. Greek Orthodox Cathedral of the Annunciation, 2500 Clairmont Rd. NE (633-5870). Best of all is the *Dogwood Festival,* the second week in April, when the city explodes in color (for information, call 892-0538). During the summer months, the *Atlanta Symphony Orchestra* plays outdoors in Piedmont Park on Sunday evenings.

SPORTS AND FITNESS: A major league city, Atlanta is home of the *Braves,* nest of the *Falcons* and *Hawks.*

Baseball – Atlanta *Braves* play at Atlanta–Fulton County Stadium, 521 Capitol Ave. SW. It can be difficult to get tickets, but try at 577-9100.

Basketball – The Atlanta *Hawks'* home games are played at the Omni, 100 Techwood Dr. NW (577-9600).

Bicycling – Bikes (and roller skates) may be rented at Skate Escape, 1086 Piedmont Ave. NE, across from Piedmont Park (892-1292).

Fishing – There's good fishing at Lake Allatoona, Lake Lanier, and Lake Jackson.

Fitness Centers – The Athletic Center of Atlanta has a track, exercise machines, and a sauna, and is one block from the North Avenue MARTA stop, 615 Peachtree St. at North Ave. (873-2633). Colony Square Athletic Club offers racquetball and aerobics classes, 1197 Peachtree at 14th St. (881-1632).

Football – The Atlanta *Falcons* (588-1111) play at the Atlanta–Fulton County Stadium.

Golf – The best public courses are at Stone Mountain and Lanier Islands.

Jogging – Run along Peachtree Street or Piedmont Road to Piedmont Park, about 1½ miles, and enter at 10th or 14th streets; roads in the park are closed to traffic. You can also run just past 14th Street to the Ansley Park and Sherwood Forest areas of Atlanta and along the wide residential streets. For more information, call Phidippides Sports Center (875-4268).

Tennis – The best clay courts are at the Bitsy Grant Tennis Center, 2125 Northside

Dr. NW (351-2774). Lanier Islands and Stone Mountain have good outdoor tennis courts, too. There are excellent public courts at the Blackburn Tennis Center, 3501 Ashford-Dunwoody Rd. (451-1061), and at the DeKalb Tennis Center, off Clairmont Rd., in suburban Decatur (482-8965).

Whitewater Rafting – Burt Reynolds (with some help from poet James Dickey) made North Georgia whitewater famous in the movie *Deliverance.* For an urban alternative, rent a raft at the Chattahoochee River Park at Hwy. 41 in NW Atlanta during the summer.

 THEATER: For complete performance schedules, check the local publications listed above. Among the best-known theatrical companies are the *Alliance Theater* and *Studio Theater* at the Woodruff Arts Center, Peachtree and 15th sts. (892-3600); *Academy Theater,* a trailblazer of new and experimental plays, 1337 Peachtree St. (892-0880); and *Theatrical Outfit,* Peachtree and 10th sts. (872-1009). The *Center for Puppetry Arts,* 1404 Spring St. (873-3089), has performances and exhibitions.

 MUSIC: The *Atlanta Symphony Orchestra* (892-3600) plays virtually year-round at the Woodruff Arts Center and gives a variety of indoor and outdoor concerts. Chamber music groups include the *Atlanta Virtuosi* (938-8611) and *Atlanta Chamber Players* (892-2414). The nationally honored *Atlanta Ballet* (873-5811) has a repertoire of classical and contemporary works. The *Ruth Mitchell Dance Company* (237-8829) performs originally choreographed ballet and jazz dancing at the Peachtree Playhouse, Peachtree and 13th sts. New York's *Metropolitan Opera* holds seven performances in Atlanta every May (262-2161, ticket information).

 NIGHTCLUBS AND NIGHTLIFE: Atlanta's nightlife covers the spectrum, with most places open nightly until 3 or 4 AM. There's excellent jazz at *Walter Mitty's Jazz Café,* 816 N Highland Ave. NE (876-7115). Disco thrives at *Limelight,* 3330 Piedmont Rd. NE (231-3520). Name comedians are featured at *The Punch Line,* 280 Hildebrand Dr. (252-LAFF). Tea dancing to the big band sound of the 1940s packs the mall of *Colony Square,* Peachtree and 14th sts. NE (892-6000), every Friday evening. Local and internationally known rock groups pack 'em in at *Moonshadow Saloon,* 1880 Johnson Rd. (881-6666). Cabaret-style shows are presented at *Upstairs at Gene and Gabe's,* 1578 Piedmont Rd. (874-6145). The best places to meet and mingle are *Peachtree Café,* 268 E Paces Ferry Rd. (233-4402); *Carlos McGee's,* 3035 Peachtree Rd. (231-7979); and *élan,* 4505 Ashford-Dunwoody Rd. (393-1333). The most convivial old-fashioned neighborhood bars are *Manuel's Tavern,* 602 N Highland Ave. (525-3447), and the *Stein Club,* 929 Peachtree St. (892-9466). *Reggie's British Pub* in the *Omni International* (525-1437) is a jolly good spot for a glass of ale, a steak and kidney pie, and a rousing game of darts. Magic acts and pranksters are the unique entertainment at *Tomfoolery,* 3166 Peachtree Rd. (231-8666).

SINS: Ladies and gentlemen of the night can be found in abundance in a string of striptease emporiums and gay bars on Peachtree Street between 6th and 14th sts.

For *idleness,* it's hard to beat rafting on the Chattahoochee River. You can rent rafts at Atlanta-Rent-A-Raft, near the river (952-2824).

Atlanta's *pride* is its Dogwood Festival, held each year in April. During this citywide observance, tours are suggested through the dogwood-laden drives to see and smell the flowers and covet the elegant homes.

LOCAL SERVICES: Business Services – Team Concept, 1925 Century Center NE (325-9754)

   Mechanics – Don Davis Gulf Service, 359 W Ponce de Leon Ave., Decatur (378-6751); Joe Winkler's Gulf Station, 2794 Clairmont Rd. NE (636-2940)

BEST IN TOWN

CHECKING IN: Today, Atlanta visitors can pick and choose from the most fabulous assortment of hotels in the country. You can also stay in a bed-and-breakfast inn very inexpensively. These are private homes, all of which rent rooms with adjacent baths, and they're scattered throughout the city. For information and reservations: Bed & Breakfast Atlanta, 1801 Piedmont Ave. NE, Suite 208, Atlanta 30324 (404 378-6026). Expect to pay $95 and up for a double in hotels we've classed as expensive; between $45 and $75 at places in the moderate category; under $45 in inexpensive places.

Ritz-Carlton, Atlanta – This authentic luxury hotel, with many elegant extras, attracts travelers with taste. Very close to the downtown financial district and right next door to the Georgia-Pacific Center, there are 472 rooms, along with the *Dining Room* for Continental dishes and *The Café* for lighter meals. 181 Peachtree St. NE (404 659-0400). Expensive.

Ritz-Carlton, Buckhead – Probably Atlanta's most fashionable hotel, the plush dining rooms and lounges are the places to be seen by local and visiting celebrities. The 573 rooms and suites are handsomely appointed with numerous luxuries. In the heart of the city's most upscale shopping, dining, and nightlife neighborhood. 3434 Peachtree Rd. NW (404 237-2700). Expensive.

Peachtree Plaza – The 70-story *Peachtree Plaza* is the world's tallest hotel. The 1,100-room *Plaza* has a ½-acre lake in its 7-story lobby. Regrettably, its rooms are far less spacious and barely adequate. Atop the cylindrical structure is the *Sun Dial* restaurant and lounge, our choice for a bird's-eye view of the city and the surrounding countryside. Peachtree at International Blvd. NW (404 659-1400). Expensive.

Omni International – Attached to the $70 million Omni complex, it resembles the set from a science fiction movie. Many of the 471 rooms have balconies overlooking all or part of the 14-story, 5½-acre Omni atrium. One Omni International NW (404 659-0000 or 800 241-5500). Expensive.

Hyatt Regency – Each of the 1,358 rooms in the main building has an outside balcony as well as a window overlooking the inner atrium. The adjoining tower has 200 additional rooms. The 327-foot-high revolving rooftop restaurant, *Polaris,* is reached via glass elevator. 265 Peachtree NE (404 577-1234). Expensive.

Atlanta Marriott Marquis – This predictably splashy property from local architect and developer John Portman opened in July 1985. One of the nation's largest hotels, with 1,647 rooms in a 50-story tower, it teems with restaurants, lounges, and shops and includes spacious convention facilities. Peachtree Center (404 521-0000). Expensive.

Atlanta Hilton & Towers – The 3-winged, 30-story, 1,250-room building has a group of small courtyards, each 7 stories tall. At the top are *Another World* and *Nikolai's Roof* (see *Eating Out*). The hotel provides 144 rooms for guests in wheelchairs or with other disabilities. Courtland and Harris NE (404 659-2000). Expensive.

The Waverly – A deluxe 533-room Stouffer hotel in the heart of a suburban shopping and office complex, it features a health club and several good restaurants among its amenities. 100 Galleria Pkwy. NW (404 953-4500). Expensive.

Hotel York of Atlanta – This tastefully rejuvenated older hotel, across from the Fox Theater, has 138 attractively decorated rooms, a restaurant serving Continental cuisine, and a cabaret with live entertainment. 683 Peachtree St. (404 874-9200). Moderate.

Atlanta Peachtree Travel Lodge – If you're looking for a smaller place, this 56-room facility could be what you want. It's not elegant, but it is comfortable. A swimming pool, too. 1641 Peachtree Rd. NE (404 873-5731). Moderate.

Radisson Inn Atlanta – Some 14 miles northeast of downtown, with 2 heated swimming pools, a café and lounge, lighted tennis courts, racquetball courts, and a barber. Only one room is equipped for handicapped guests; the other 399 are standard. Pets are welcome. I-285, Chamblee-Dunwood Rd. exit (404 394-5000). Moderate.

Days Inns – The Atlanta-based chain, now nationwide, offers nice, clean accommodations at very reasonable rates. Most inns (actually motels) have a swimming pool, playground, family restaurant, color TV; some have kitchenettes; none serves alcoholic beverages. Ten Atlanta locations, although the high-rise downtown, a block from Peachtree Plaza (300 Spring St.; 404 761-6500), may be the best value for the money in the city. For information on the others, call 404 320-2000.

 EATING OUT: The best place to get Southern cooking is still in a Southern home, but there are now some public places that run a pretty close second. Expect to pay $60 to $80 or more at restaurants in our expensive category; between $40 and $60 in the moderate range; $20 to $40 at places noted as inexpensive. Prices do not include drinks, wine, and tips.

Nikolai's Roof – With decor and atmosphere suggesting Czarist opulence, the *Atlanta Hilton*'s rooftop restaurant was originally intended to heighten the establishment's prestige, and not to serve as a big money-making operation — which is why it seats only 67 diners. Reservations are necessary weeks in advance, but if you want personal service by waiters in Cossack attire (who have memorized the evening's five-course menu), you'll find it worth the necessary advance planning. The food is French, but then the old Russian courts were also shamelessly Francophilic. Open daily. Reservations? Of course. Major credit cards. Atlanta Hilton, Courtland and Harris NE (659-2000). Expensive.

Savannah Fish Company – Fish and shellfish, flown in fresh from the Gulf of Mexico, the Pacific, and the North Atlantic, are the hallmark of this cozy restaurant in the *Peachtree Plaza Hotel.* Open daily. Major credit cards. Reservations recommended. Peachtree St. and International Blvd. (523-2500). Expensive.

Hedgerose Heights Inn – Pheasant, veal, beef, seafood, and fowl are served with either a French, Swiss, or German flair, and complemented by a fine wine list and very good service. Closed Sundays. Major credit cards. Reservations recommended. 490 E Paces Ferry Rd. (233-7673). Expensive.

La Grotta Ristorante Italiano – An elegant North Italian dining room. Delicious veal, pasta, and seafood dishes are matched by some of Atlanta's most professional service. Dinner only; closed Sundays. Reservations recommended. Major credit cards. 2637 Peachtree Rd. NE (231-1368); and 647 Atlanta St. (US 19), Roswell (988-0645). Expensive.

The Abbey – One of Atlanta's landmark churches has been converted into a "monastery" that serves French provincial dishes — escargots à la bourguignonne, tournedos à la béarnaise, etc. Dinner only. Reservations recommended. Major credit cards. 163 Ponce de Leon Ave. NE (876-8532). Expensive.

Coach and Six – You can get a good steak here and hearty black bean soup as well as seafood, veal, and very good drinks. Open daily. Reservations suggested. Major credit cards. 1776 Peachtree Rd. NW (872-6666). Expensive.

Hugo's – Well-prepared Continental dishes are served with flair, while harp music plays in the background. Open daily. Reservations recommended. Major credit cards. Hyatt Regency, 265 Peachtree NE (577-1234). Expensive.

Sidney's Just South – Unpretentious single-family cottage with additions tacked on over the years. First-rate Continental cuisine, good wine list, very friendly service. Open daily. Reservations necessary. Major credit cards. 4225 Roswell Rd. (256-5895). Expensive.

Pano's & Paul's – A classy restaurant hidden in a shopping center. Continental and American cuisine is served, but the kitchen promises it will prepare *anything* if requested far enough in advance. Dinner only. Reservations recommended. Major credit cards. West Paces Shopping Center (261-4739). Expensive.

Old Vinings Inn – This is a charming country cottage (about 20 minutes from downtown) full of delightful Gallic surprises. Hollandaises, béarnaises, and other delicious sauces complement the flavors of trout, Dover sole, beef, veal, and fowl. Closed Sundays and Mondays. Reservations recommended. No credit cards. 3020 Paces Mill Rd., Vinings (434-5270). Expensive.

Bone's – *The* place in town for prime beef and fresh seafood in clubby, convivial surroundings. It's very popular among executives and savvy out-of-towners. Closed for lunch on Saturdays. Reservations advised. Major credit cards. 3130 Piedmont Rd. (237-2663). Expensive.

The Brass Key – One of Atlanta's most distinguished restaurants, serving very good French/Continental cuisine in a setting reminiscent of Old Vienna. Closed Sundays. Reservations advised. Major credit cards. Peachtree Battle Shopping Center, 2355 Peachtree Rd. (233-3202). Expensive.

103 West – A creative array of richly sauced dishes and superior wines are complemented by Victorian floral prints, potted palms, and marble-topped tables. A memorable dining experience. Dinner only; closed Sundays. Reservations advised. Major credit cards. 103 W Paces Ferry Rd., Buckhead (233-5993). Expensive.

Carsley's – A very stylish place to enjoy the latest in food trends, new American cuisine. Crayfish pizza, Georgia quail with California chèvre, and mesquite-grilled chicken, beef, and seafood are just some of the selections. Open daily. Reservations advised. Major credit cards. On the Piedmont Rd. side of Tower Pl., Buckhead (261-6384). Expensive.

Lennox's – A piquant taste of Cajun country on busy Peachtree Road. Blackened redfish, soft-shell crabs, and trout are featured, along with many ingenious creations using shrimp and oysters. A chic and popular place. Open daily. Reservations advised. Major credit cards. 2225 Peachtree Rd. (351-0921). Expensive.

Gojinka – It's Atlanta's most authentic Japanese restaurant, claim local and visiting Asians, who rave about the sushi and sashimi. Very good tempura, sukiyaki, and yakitori, too. Closed Sundays. Reservations advised. Major credit cards. 5269 Buford Hwy., Pinetree Plaza Shopping Center, Doraville (458-0558). Moderate.

The Peasant Group – Some of Atlanta's favorite dining places are the locally owned Peasant restaurants, with innovative American/Continental meals served in a stylish and relaxed atmosphere. The group includes: *The Pleasant Peasant,* 555 Peachtree St. (874-3223); *The Country Place,* Colony Square, Peachtree and 14th sts. (881-0144); *Dailey's,* 17 International Blvd., downtown (681-3303); *Winfield's,* 100 Galleria Pkwy., Smyrna (955-5300); and *The Peasant Uptown,* Phipps Plaza, Peachtree and Lenox rds. (261-6341). Open daily. No reservations. Major credit cards. Moderate.

Dante's Down the Hatch – A late-night niche with a faithful coterie. Jazz lovers come to hear Paul Mitchell's Trio and assorted combos. The fondue/wine/cheese menu is an attraction on its own, and so is owner Dante Stephenson, who's usually there to recommend a vintage from his personally selected list. Open daily. Reservations suggested. Major credit cards. 3380 Peachtree Rd. (266-1600). Moderate.

Niko's – An always-lively Greek taverna, serving the best moussaka, dolmades, pan-fried squid, and baklava in town, along with Greek and American beers and wine. Open daily. Reservations for large groups. Some credit cards. 1803 Cheshire Bridge Rd. (872-1254). Moderate to inexpensive.

Pilgreen's – Tasty steaks, world-class onion rings, great drinks and service in a nostalgic roadhouse atmosphere have kept this a favorite with generations of Atlantans. Closed Sundays and Mondays. No reservations. Major credit cards. 1081 Lee St. (758-4669). Moderate to inexpensive.

Tito's – Good old Italian cooking draws crowds to this snug Virginia/Highland neighborhood eatery. Saltimbocca, veal Marsala, garlicky mussels, and pastas draped with rich sauces are among the specialties. Closed Sundays. No reservations. Major credit cards. 820 N Highland Ave. NE (874-8364). Moderate to inexpensive.

Pentimento – A smart little café that's popular with patrons of the High Museum and Woodruff Arts Center. The menu includes imaginative soups, salads, seafood, and chicken dishes, nicely complimented by a large selection of wines by the glass. Closed Sundays. Reservations advised. Major credit cards. In the Woodruff Arts Center, 1280 Peachtree St. (875-6665). Moderate to inexpensive.

Mary Mac's Tea Room – Atlanta's favorite place for honest, no-frills, Southern home cooking. Folks visit this maze of cheerful dining rooms for its delicious fried chicken, slow-simmered vegetables, breads, and desserts. Closed weekends. No reservations or credit cards. 224 Ponce de Leon Ave. NE (876-6604). Inexpensive.

El Toro – The zippiest enchiladas, tacos, burritos, and other Tex-Mex dishes served hereabouts. Closed Sundays. No reservations. Major credit cards. 4300 Buford Hwy. NE (321-9502); 5288 Buford Hwy. NE. (455-9677); 1775 Lawrenceville Hwy., Decatur (294-9906); and five other locations. Inexpensive.

Varsity – It's a scene right out of *American Graffiti* — a drive-in with singing car hops, an air of bedlam, and a menu of such All-American favorites as hot dogs, hamburgers, and sandwiches. Open daily. No reservations or credit cards. 61 North Ave. NW (881-1706). Inexpensive.

King & I – Spicy, exotic Thai dishes have made this friendly place a popular destination for adventurous Atlantans. Open daily. No reservations or credit cards. Ansley Sq. at Piedmont Ave. and Monroe Dr. (892-7743). Inexpensive.

Touch of India – This is where to go for the city's most expertly prepared tandoori dishes and curries. Open daily. Reservations accepted. Major credit cards. 970 Peachtree St., near 10th St. (876-7777). Inexpensive.

The Colonnade – A cheerful local landmark that's renowned for its friendly service and delicious steaks, seafood, fried chicken, vegetables, and other American and southern favorites. Closed Mondays. No reservations or credit cards. 1879 Cheshire Bridge Rd. (874-5642). Inexpensive.

The Blue Nile – Atlanta's most exotic little café, it treats the adventurous to spicy meat and vegetable dishes from Ethiopia. In the heart of a lively, diverse midtown neighborhood. Open daily. Reservations accepted. Major credit cards. 810 N Highland Ave. (872-6483). Inexpensive.

Harold's Barbecue – This quintessential Southern barbecue shack is a local legend for its grilled pork and beef sandwiches and hearty Brunswick stew. Closed Saturdays and Sundays. No reservations or credit cards. 171 McDonough Blvd. (627-9268). Inexpensive.

The Golden Buddha – This cheerful Emory University neighborhood place serves excellent Mandarin and Szechwan Chinese dishes, spiced to your liking. Open daily. Major credit cards. 1905 Clairmont Rd. (633-5252). Inexpensive.

Korea House – Zesty soups, grilled meats, stews, and seafood dishes, accompanied by kimchee, that fiery Korean staple. Open daily. Reservations accepted. Major credit cards. Peachtree and 6th sts. (876-5310). Inexpensive.

BALTIMORE

You might expect to find residents a shade defensive about Baltimore. Slipped quietly between the great cities of the Atlantic seaboard, like a note between the pages of a novel, the world just didn't think much about it. Commerce among Washington, Philadelphia, and New York went by on Baltimore's Beltway and Harbor Tunnel and was so favorably impressed by the smooth efficiency of the freeway system that it used to bypass the city every time.

But Baltimore has changed its image. Over the past decade, the city has undergone a miraculous transformation. The town has suddenly sparked to life with its dazzling new Inner Harbor, promenades, and marinas; a modern downtown business district; a rash of new restaurants, pubs, and hotels; an expanded airport; and a new tunnel.

The striking modern buildings and plazas of Charles Center, Baltimore's heart of business, Fort McHenry, the tiered iron stacks of the Peabody Library, the Sunpapers (among the nation's most distinguished newspapers), and the Johns Hopkins University and medical institutions provide the city with a contemporary cosmopolitan atmosphere, as well as a link to historic tradition. Perhaps best in Baltimore is the cuisine — the riches of the bay, so to speak, in hard or soft-shelled crabs, oysters (raw and stewed), clams, and shad roe — prepared in traditional Maryland style.

Baltimore's deepwater port on the Chesapeake Bay — the major Atlantic port for grain, coal, and spice — has always given residents a touch of smug satisfaction. Now its 45 miles of waterfront are further enhanced by a bright new centerpiece — Harborplace. This complex is the latest achievement in a long and concerted campaign to turn the city's decaying area of docks and piers into Baltimore's biggest asset. Once populated by derelict warehouses, debris, and pollution, the Inner Harbor is now the site of a pair of double-decker glass pavilions enclosing about 140 restaurants, cafés, and specialty shops. Also at Inner Harbor is the spectacular new National Aquarium, with its wonderful displays of marine life and even a tropical rain forest.

South of the harbor, the city's neighborhoods are being rejuvenated and restored into elegant residential areas. In the early 1970s, these blocks of row houses were the epitome of urban disaster. Through a city-sponsored program, countless row houses have been sold for $1 each to anyone who will restore the home and occupy it for 18 months. This successful homesteading program now extends across the city into Fell's Point, Stirling Street, Otterbein, Patterson Park, and Ridgely's Delight.

Baltimore residents are busy these days toasting the new charms of their town and, as ever, celebrating the old. The city is proud of its architecturally impressive City Hall, completed in 1875 in French Empire style. It represents something of the city's style. For the building's centennial, Baltimore spent some $11 million renovating the interior while preserving the best aspects of

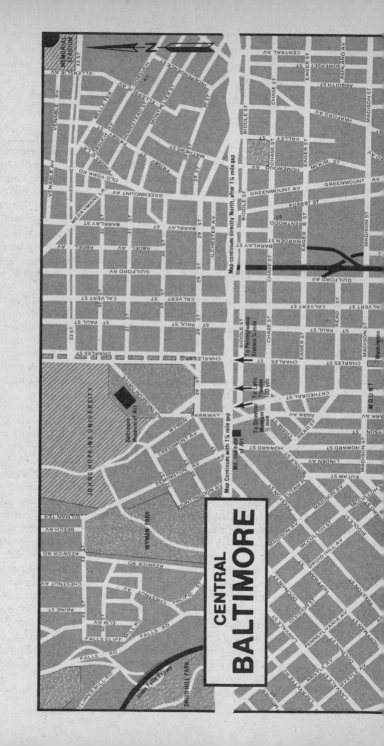

CENTRAL
BALTIMORE

the old decor. Outside, the only change is that the small round dome now gleams with gold leaf. Like the building itself, the city's assets can be perceived and appreciated most readily from the inside — which explains why so many people who happen upon Baltimore for one reason or another like what they find and stay. But you don't have to be a resident to like Baltimore. You simply have to visit.

BALTIMORE AT-A-GLANCE

SEEING THE CITY: Baltimore offers its finest panoramic view from the Top of the World Trade Center at the Inner Harbor. Downstream lies Fort McHenry, where the successful American repulsion of British forces in 1814 inspired Francis Scott Key to compose "The Star-Spangled Banner." To the northwest, the buildings and plazas of Charles Center stand out against the surrounding cityscape. At Pratt St. between South and Gay sts.

SPECIAL PLACES: Most of the notable sights in Baltimore are concentrated in a few nicely designed areas. Consequently, the best way to see the city is by walking. Buses and taxis, which serve the entire city, are convenient, but parking in the lots downtown isn't too difficult or expensive.

CHARLES CENTER AND DOWNTOWN

Charles Center – Built during the past two decades, Charles Center is a 33-acre plot of new office buildings, luxury apartment towers, overhead walkways, fountains, and plazas. Bounded by Lombard Street on the south, Saratoga Street on the north, Hopkins Place and Liberty Street on the west, and Charles Street on the east. (One of the city's oldest and grandest thoroughfares, Charles Street is also being revitalized, with shops and restaurants opening their doors to new business.)

Within the complex is One Charles Center, a 24-story tower of bronze-covered glass designed by Mies van der Rohe. Inside the Morris Mechanic Theater, such contemporary stars as Rudolph Nureyev and Lauren Bacall have performed. Charles and Baltimore sts.

Hopkins Plaza is the scene for many events, ranging from concerts by the Baltimore Symphony Orchestra to performances by lesser-known jazz ensembles and chamber groups (between Hopkins Pl., Charles, Baltimore, and Lombard sts.). Center Plaza, an oval plaza modeled after Siena's Palio, features a 33-foot bronze sculpture in the shape of a flame, designed by Francesco Somaini and presented to the city by the Gas and Electric Company (north of Fayette St. between Liberty and Charles sts.). Pedestrian ramps link Charles Center to the Convention Center and to the Civic Center, a sawtooth-roofed building that hosts circuses, ice hockey games, and rock concerts (201 W Baltimore St.).

Edgar Allan Poe Home and Grave – Poe lived here in the 1830s; he visited Baltimore again in 1849 long enough to die and be buried. (His grave is nearby, in the Westminster Presbyterian Church Cemetery at Fayette and Greene sts.) Home visiting hours are noon to 4 PM Wednesdays through Saturdays. 203 N Amity St. (396-7932, for information); graveyard tours are given on the first and third Friday evenings and Saturday mornings from April through October (528-2070).

City Hall – Still in use, the domed building is a monument to mid-Victorian design and craftsmanship. 100 N Holliday St. For tour information, call 396-1151.

Lexington Market – Since 1782 this colorful indoor marketplace has provided stalls for independent merchants, who sell a variety of goods. An addition, the Arcade, opened in October 1982, as the market celebrated its 200th anniversary. Today 100 kiosks and shops are in operation. You can lunch on Maryland seafood at its best — in the rough and at little expense — at *John W. Faidley Seafood,* one of the largest raw oyster bars in the world. Market is closed Sundays. 400 W Lexington and Eutaw sts.

MOUNT VERNON PLACE

This 19th-century bastion of Baltimore aristocracy now houses much of the 20th century's counterculture with its array of boutiques, plant stores, restaurants, and natural food shops. Reminders of bygone days remain in the lovely 19th-century merchant prince housefronts, the stately squares, and outstanding cultural institutions.

Walters Art Gallery – This extensive collection owned by the Walters family (who also owned railroads), and bequeathed to Baltimore, offers an impressive span of art from Ancient Near Eastern, Byzantine, and Classical archaeological artifacts to Medieval European illuminated manuscripts and painted panels, Italian Renaissance paintings, and 20th-century works. Admission charge. Charles and Centre sts. (547-9000).

Museum and Library of Maryland History – Examples of 18th- and 19th-century clothing, furniture, and silver, and general exhibitions. Closed Mondays. Library rich in genealogical material. Admission charge. 201 W Monument St. (685-3750).

Peabody Institute and Conservatory of Music – Worth a visit simply for a look at the magnificently designed library. Amid pillars and balconies, this 19th-century interior holds 300,000 volumes on its tiered, iron stacks that spiral upward six stories. Free student concerts. Mount Vernon Place at Monument and N Charles sts. For concert information, call 659-8124.

Washington Monument – The very first Washington Monument, designed by Robert Mills and completed in 1842. Washington's statue stands atop the monument's long shaft (a 228-step climb — there's no elevator) commanding an excellent view of the city, the harbor, and Mount Vernon Place. Small admission charge. Mount Vernon Place (752-9103).

NORTH

Baltimore Museum of Art – Noted for two especially fine collections: the Cone Collection of the French post-Impressionist period, with a wealth of Matisse's work; and the Wurtzburger collections of primitive art and modern sculpture. Also has restored rooms from 17th- and 18th-century Maryland mansions, and a new wing featuring American decorative arts and an outdoor sculpture garden. Closed Mondays. Admission charge for those 22 and over; free on Thursdays. Art Museum Dr. near N Charles and 31st sts. (396-7100).

INNER HARBOR

Harborplace – The dazzling kingpin in Baltimore's renaissance, Harborplace is carrying the heart of the city's business southward. In its two glass-enclosed pavilions you'll find a plethora of shops, restaurants, and market stalls — about 140 in all. On the first floor of the Light Street Pavilion is a marketplace where vendors hawk all manner of comestibles, while the upper level is chockablock with small eateries serving a diverse range of foodstuffs — everything from hot dogs to knishes. And whether you're looking for a crab mallet or a collector's comic book, chances are it's in the Sam Smith Market, where merchants sell a raft of unusual wares from their pushcarts and kiosks (also on the second floor). The Pratt Street Pavilion has its share of restaurants, boutiques, and specialty stores. At Pratt and Light sts.

The National Aquarium – The aquarium has an impressive series of audio-visual displays on marine life with a total of 5,000 specimens on 7 different levels. "People movers" carry you past the exhibits, which include sharks and dolphins, puffins living in their natural habitat, the largest coral reef in the US, and a reconstruction of Maine's coast with a hands-on display of shellfish and other shoreline creatures; finally, on the top floor, you can wander through a tropical rain forest. Open daily. Admission charge. Pier 3, Inner Harbor (576-3810).

Fort McHenry National Monument and Historic Shrine – Here in 1814, a young Maryland lawyer witnessed the successful resistance of American forces to heavy British mortar bombardment and was so inspired by the sight of the Stars and Stripes still fluttering against the morning sky that he wrote "The Star-Spangled Banner." Visitors can see the fort, the old powder magazine, the officers' quarters, the enlisted men's barracks, and then walk along Francis Scott Key's famed ramparts overlooking the harbor. Open daily. During the summer on weekend afternoons, drills and military ceremonies modeled after those of 1814 are performed by uniformed soldiers and sailors. Free. South of Inner Harbor, at the end of Fort Ave. (962-4290).

United States Frigate *Constellation* – The US Navy's oldest warship (1797), the *Constellation* (named by George Washington) defeated the French frigate *L'Insurgente* in America's first important victory at sea and was in service through World War II. Now the ship has daily tours. Small admission charge. Pier 1 of the Inner Harbor (539-1797).

Maryland Science Center and Planetarium – Covers the vastness of outer space in the planetarium and the complexity of inner space in the walk-through model of a single human cell. Open daily. Admission charge. At the southwest corner of the Inner Harbor (call 685-5225 for 24-hour information).

■**EXTRA SPECIAL:** Just 30 miles south of Baltimore on Route 2 (Ritchie Hwy.) lies *Annapolis.* The colonial charm of the first peacetime capital of the US is still preserved in Maryland's capital. Around town are lovely 18th-century buildings, including the old State House, still in use today, the Hammond-Harwood House, a Georgian home designed by William Buckland, and the campus of St. John's College, which appears much as it did to its most famous alumnus, Francis Scott Key. Also interesting is the US Naval Academy. The remains of John Paul Jones lie in the crypt of the chapel. The full brigade of midshipmen passes in formal parade review most Wednesdays at 3:30 PM on Worden Field. In town, the harbor is flanked by boutiques and restaurants.

SOURCES AND RESOURCES

TOURIST INFORMATION: The Baltimore Office of Promotion and Tourism offers useful tourist information, such as directions, maps, and brochures and daily events listings. Suite 310, 34 Market Pl. (752-8632 or 837-4636).
   Baltimore, Annapolis and Chesapeake Country Guidebook by James F. Waesche (Bodine and Associates; $4.95) is a good guide to Baltimore and the surrounding area.

Local Coverage – *The Sun,* morning daily; *The News American; The Evening Sun,* evening daily; *The Sunday Sun* and *Sunday News American* list the coming week's events. *Baltimore* is a monthly magazine with features on city life, restaurant listings, and calendars of events. All are available at newsstands.

Area Code – All telephone numbers are in the 301 area code unless otherwise indicated.

CLIMATE AND CLOTHES: Baltimore weather is fickle, neither the rigorous clime of the North nor the mild South. Unpredictable rain and frequent changes in wind direction make umbrellas advisable, particularly in the summer and early fall. In the summer, the weather can be hot and muggy, though the Chesapeake Bay exerts a modifying influence and brings relief with night-time breezes. The winter is cold with moderate snowfall. Spring is windy and pleasant.

 GETTING AROUND: Airport – Baltimore/Washington, DC International Airport (or BWI) is usually a 20-minute ride from downtown Baltimore via the Baltimore-Washington Expressway; taxi fare should run about $12. Train service is available from the airport to the city's downtown station for $5.50; a shuttle bus transfers passengers from the air terminal to the airport train station. Trains run eight times daily from the airport to downtown and seven times a day in the opposite direction. ABC Limo (859-3000), with a desk on the airport's lower level, charges $5 for transportation to most downtown hotels.

Bus – The Mass Transit Administration covers the entire metropolitan area. Route information and maps are available at MTA's main office, 300 W Lexington St. (539-5000).

Subway – The metro rail system offers limited access to much of the downtown area (659-2700).

Taxi – Cabs may be hailed on the street but are usually called by phone. Major companies are Yellow Cab (685-1212), Diamond (947-3333), Sun (235-0300), and BWI Airport Cab (859-1100).

Car Rental – Baltimore has offices of the major national firms. Reliable local service is provided by Baltimore Car and Truck Rental at 2303 N Howard St. (467-2900).

 MUSEUMS: The fine collections of the Baltimore Museum of Art, Walters Art Gallery, Maryland Historical Society, and Maryland Science Center are described in *Special Places.* Some other museums of note are:

B & O Railroad Museum – 901 W Pratt St. (237-2387); closed Mondays and Tuesdays

Babe Ruth Birthplace and Museum – 216 Emory St. (727-1539); open daily

Lacrosse Hall of Fame – on Hopkins' Homewood Campus in Newton H. White Athletic Center (235-6882); closed on weekends

Peale Museum – 225 Holliday St. (396-3523); closed Mondays

Streetcar Museum – 1901 Falls Rd. (547-0264); Sundays, noon to 5 PM

 MAJOR COLLEGES AND UNIVERSITIES: Johns Hopkins University, at 34th and Charles sts. (338-8000), and Johns Hopkins Hospital and Medical School, 600 N Wolfe (955-5000), are internationally renowned. Other notable schools are the Peabody Institute and Conservatory of Music, Mount Vernon Pl. (659-8100), Morgan State University, Hillen Rd. and Coldspring La. (444-3333), and Loyola, Charles St. and Cold Spring La. (323-1010). Goucher College is in suburban Towson on Dulaney Valley Rd. (337-6116).

 SPECIAL EVENTS: The *Maryland House and Garden Pilgrimage* lavishly demonstrates Baltimoreans' pride in their own backyards. This statewide event for garden lovers, held during the last week of April and the first week of May, is a series of self-guided tours through a group of outstanding homes and gardens. For details, contact the Pilgrimage offices at 1105A Providence Rd., Towson, MD 21204 (821-6933). Merriment abounds in May during the *Preakness Festival Week* of outdoor concerts, exhibitions, and performances preceding the famous horse race. Numerous ethnic fairs take place in warm weather and are held at a variety of city locations (see newspapers for listings). These festivities culminate in September in the *City Fair,* with everything from Old Country food to top-name entertainers. The *Harborlights Music Festival* is held every summer, usually July through September, at Baltimore's new 2,000-seat Pier 6 Pavilion. A variety of concerts — from symphony to pop — is given. For ticket information, call 727-5580. Pier 6 at Pratt St.

SPORTS AND FITNESS: Baseball – The *Orioles* play their home games at Memorial Stadium. Tickets for good seats may be hard to get (338-1300).
  Bicycling – A brochure describing several tours through the countryside is available at the Physical Fitness Commission, 201 W Preston St. (383-4040).

Fitness Centers – The Druid Hill YMCA opens its pool and equipment to visitors, 1609 Druid Hill Ave. (728-1600).

Football – The USFL *Stars* play at Memorial Stadium (576-STAR, for tickets).

Golf – Best public course is the 18-hole Pine Ridge, 3 miles north on Dulaney Valley Rd. (exit 27 on the Baltimore Beltway; 252-1408).

Horse Racing – The climax of the season is the *Preakness*, which ranks with the Kentucky Derby and the Belmont Stakes as one of the most important annual races. At the Pimlico Race Course, Belvedere and Park Heights aves. (542-9400).

Jogging – Run around the lake in Druid Hill Park. The Baltimore Office of Promotion and Tourism can provide a list of other routes.

Lacrosse – The Johns Hopkins *Blue Jays* (Homewood Field, Charles St. and University Pkwy.; 235-6882) are among the tops in the ranks of collegiate stickmen. Seats are usually available.

Steeplechase – As for another specialty, point-to-point races (with timber barrier jumps) are run in the valleys north of the city (Western Run, Worthington, Long Green) on Saturday afternoons during April and May.

Tennis – There are many courts in the city's parks. The best are at Clifton Park, Harford Rd. and 33rd St. (396-6101 for permit).

THEATER: For complete listings, see the publications cited above. Baltimore's theatrical offerings range from Broadway tryouts or road shows at the *Morris Mechanic Theater,* Charles Center (625-1400) to resident productions at *Center Stage,* Calvert St. at Monument (332-0033), to experimental works at the *Theatre Project,* 45 W Preston (539-3091).

MUSIC: The *Baltimore Symphony Orchestra,* which is highly regarded nationally, performs at the new Joseph Meyerhoff Symphony Hall, where the music can be appreciated in series concerts throughout the year, 1212 Cathedral St. (837-5691). For those more attuned to a syncopated beat, try to catch the *Left Bank Jazz Society* (call 945-2266 to learn where they're performing) or go to *Ethel's Place* (see below). Other musical programs are presented by well-known visiting artists; check the newspapers.

NIGHTCLUBS AND NIGHTLIFE: *Girard's* is the popular place for late-nighters: the disco music is loud, lighting is dim, and the clientele is voguish. Food served in early evening. Five minutes from downtown at 1001 Cathedral St. (837-3733). *Ethel's Place,* founded by jazz singer Ethel Ennis, features contemporary music and jazz by local and national talents. 1225 Cathedral St. (727-7077). *Shane's Restaurant-Cabaret* has a handsome turn-of-the-century decor and live entertainment. 1924 York Rd., Timonium (252-4100). The *Thirteenth Floor* in the *Belvedere Hotel* has a romantic piano bar and a great view of the city. 1 E Chase St. (547-8220). Entertainment at the many restaurants in Harbor Place ranges from piano music to stand-up comics.

SINS: The town that *prides* itself on its row houses, Johns Hopkins University, and the Basilica of the Assumption of the Blessed Virgin Mary also was the stomping ground of Blaze Starr — in her time, the highest paid exotic dancer in the US. Her former home-away-from-home, the *2 O'Clock*

Club, raunchy as ever, still thrives at 414 E Baltimore (752-5322), in the middle of Baltimore's version of Times Square — called the Block — just a hooker's stroll away from the city's police headquarters. An active redevelopment program will be changing this area, but currently the Block still swings with the boots-and-hot-pants set. To see how *lust* flourishes in an urban environment, visit the peepshow movies, pinball arcades, and pornographic bookstores along Baltimore Street that light up this murky strip of burlesque houses and strip joints.

Avarice claims its corner of Baltimore at the betting windows at Pimlico Race Course, Belvedere and Park Heights aves. (542-9400), especially in May during the Preakness Stakes, the second race in the famous Triple Crown for three-year-olds.

LOCAL SERVICES: Babysitting – Elizabeth Cooney Personnel Agency (323-1700)
    Business Services – Able Temporaries, 2 N Charles St. (685-8189)
    Mechanic – Plotkin's of Franklin Street, 600 W Franklin St. (728-5533)

BEST IN TOWN

CHECKING IN: Downtown Baltimore has its share of moderately priced ($45 to $70 a night for a double room) accommodations in its chain hotels. Many motorists check in here and take advantage of the free downtown parking. There are an increasing number of more expensive luxury hotels ($80 and way, way up) and several less costly hotels ($30 to $65) downtown. For B&B accommodations, contact Sharp-Adams, 33 West St., Annapolis, MD 21403 (301 269-6232; 202 261-2233 in the DC area).

Cross Keys Inn – Five miles from downtown (12 minutes via I-83, Jones Falls Expressway). A stop on the airport limousine run, the inn has a quiet atmosphere and is adjacent to the boutiques and specialty shops of Cross Keys Village Square. It has a good restaurant, coffee shop, lounge with entertainment, and a pool. 5100 Falls Rd. (301 532-6900). Expensive.

Hunt Valley Inn – In a suburban-industrial complex where office buildings and factories are attractively landscaped and discreetly set apart from one another, this 392-room spot is the place to stay if embarking on the Maryland House and Garden Pilgrimage or attending the spring's timber races in hunt country. In addition to the restaurant, bar, and breakfast-luncheon parlor, recreational facilities are available — a pool, tennis and golf courts. A Marriott Hotel. Shawan Rd. at I-83, in the Hunt Valley Cockeysville Business Park (301 666-7000). Expensive.

Hyatt Regency Baltimore – This glossy *Hyatt* on Baltimore's waterfront has 500 rooms, 27,000 square feet of meeting space, and a path connecting it to Harborplace and the Baltimore Convention Center. It's also only a short walk to the National Aquarium and the Maryland Science Center. Recreational facilities include tennis courts, jogging track, and swimming pool, and there's a coffee shop (with a waterfall) for snacks, a dining room in a parklike setting, and a formal restaurant on the rooftop level. 300 Light St., Inner Harbor (301 528-1234 or 800 228-9000). Expensive.

Tremont Hotel – Four blocks south of Mount Vernon Square, just off Charles Street, this hotel opened in 1984. The clientele tends toward executives looking for the privacy and amenities of an "all suites" hotel. Another attractive feature is guest privileges at the nearby Downtown Athletic Club. 8 E Pleasant St. (301 576-1200). Expensive.

Peabody Court – The same people responsible for the splendid restoration of Washington, DC's *Hay Adams Hotel* have brought similar distinctive qualities to this property in Baltimore's historic Mount Vernon Square, which has been transformed into a European-style hotel with polished service, antique decor, and a very good restaurant. Mount Vernon Place (301 727-7101 or 800 732-5301). Expensive.

Sheraton Johns Hopkins Inn – This is the most convenient, respectable hotel for visitors to Johns Hopkins Hospital or School of Medicine, near Baltimore's colorful Fell's Point. The 162-room *Sheraton* has a restaurant, a lounge, and a pool. 400 N Broadway (301 675-6800). Moderate.

Abbey Hotel – This hotel is close to Mount Vernon Place and downtown. Air conditioned, TV, and free coffee from 7 to 9 AM. No restaurant or parking lot, and some rooms lack private bath; but the best prices in the area. St. Paul and Madison sts. (301 332-0405). Inexpensive.

 EATING OUT: If you like eating, you'll be happy in Baltimore. From its regional specialty, seafood in the rough, to the authentic dishes of its Little Italy, there are restaurants to suit most palates and pockets. Our selections range in price from $50 or more for a dinner for two in the expensive range, $35 to $50 in the moderate range, and $30 or less in the inexpensive range. Prices do not include drinks, wine, or tips.

Tio Pepe Restaurant – A splendid choice for Spanish cuisine and an interesting atmosphere in the shadowy vaulted cellars of an old brick town house. The quality food, including paella à la Valenciana and a fresh fish-of-the-day preparation (not on the menu), and the professional service make this a favorite haunt of residents. Dinner daily and lunch on weekdays. Major credit cards. 10 E Franklin St. (539-4675). Expensive.

The Conservatory at the Peabody Court – Even if the cuisine were merely mediocre, a meal here would be enjoyable simply for the lovely view overlooking Mount Vernon's cultural institutions. Fortunately, the menu is quite commendable. One specialty is Virginia squab with poached quail eggs. Closed Mondays. Reservations necessary. Major credit cards. Mount Vernon Place (727-7101). Expensive.

Prime Rib – A hangout for figures in the city's political and entertainment worlds. Its prime rib *is* great, but no more so than the crab imperial. Major credit cards. 1101 N Calvert St., in Horizon House (539-1804). Expensive to moderate.

Sabatino's – What looks like Napoli is really the heart of Baltimore's Little Italy. Veal and shrimp Marsala are the specialties, appreciated by the locals who refer to the place familiarly as Sabby's. Spiro T. Agnew and Marvin Mandel both ate here right after their respective court convictions. You'll doubtless do better. Open daily for lunch and dinner. Major credit cards. 901 Fawn St. (727-9414). Moderate.

Olde Obrycki's Crab House – Roll back your sleeves, put on your bib, grab a mallet, and you're ready for a bout at Obrycki's. Here you spend all evening battling steamed crabs. There's plenty of support along the way in the warm family atmosphere. Open April through November only; closed Mondays; weekends, dinner only. Major credit cards. 1729 E Pratt St. (732-6399). Moderate.

Marconi's – The interior may not be pleasing to the eye, but the artistry is on the plate. The restaurant where, in a steady stream, Baltimoreans themselves go. The specialty of this Franco-Italian restaurant is fillet of sole prepared in a variety of delicious ways. Lunch and dinner; closed Sundays and Mondays. No reservations. 106 W Saratoga St. (752-9286). Moderate.

Haussner's – Everything abounds in this German restaurant from the fat Tyrolean dumplings to the draft Bavarian beer, to the Barbizon paintings and busts of

Roman emperors that cover the walls. The museum downstairs has a ball of string 300 miles long. Don't ask; we're just reporting the facts. Open Tuesdays through Saturdays for lunch and dinner. Reservations accepted for lunch only. Major credit cards. 3242 Eastern Ave. (327-8365). Moderate.

John W. Faidley Seafood – In the past hundred years, *Faidley's* has established itself as the place for oysters, crabs, and clams brought in fresh daily from the bay. The downtown lunch crowd regards a visit to *Faidley's* in Lexington Market — a vast assemblage of butchers and merchants — as the ultimate adventure. Open from 9 AM to 6 PM daily except Sundays. No credit cards. Paca at Lexington St. (727-4898). Inexpensive.

Harborplace – In addition to 33 food stalls, where you can find everything from Buffalo wings to chocolate-covered strawberries, the following restaurants have good food, harbor views, and moderate prices. In the Light Street Pavilion are: *The American Café,* with a light American menu and frequent live entertainment (962-8800); *City Lights,* featuring French cuisine and homemade desserts (244-8811); *Jean-Claude's Café,* also with French food (332-0950); *Phillips Harborplace,* with Chesapeake Bay seafood and a piano bar (685-6600); and *The Soup Kitchen,* with homemade soups, good salads, and desserts (539-3810). In the Pratt Street Pavilion are: *Mariner's Pier One,* with light fare, daily specials, weekend entertainment (962-5050); *Tandoor,* featuring Northern Indian cuisine cooked in special tandoori ovens (547-0575); *Taverna Athena,* with authentic Greek cuisine (547-8900); *Bamboo House,* with Chinese food (625-1191); and *Gianni's,* for North Italian (837-1130).

BOSTON

No matter how you approach Boston, you will be struck by the lovely siting of this city, which juts into the island-studded harbor and graces the banks of the Charles with its riverside parks and distinctive skyline — a poetic melding of the old and the new. Here are the narrow cobblestones where Boston's colonists walked, the Common where their cattle grazed, the churches they prayed in, and the tiny burying grounds that shelter their bones to this day. Here, too, are the bold buildings of government, the fortresses of finance, the colorful chaos of the open market, and the freewheeling spirit of the waterfront.

Anyone walking briskly could traverse this eventful terrain in an hour, but instead take the time to explore Boston at leisure, keeping an eye out for the little things — the odd quirks of architecture, the bright spots of whimsy and caprice. Spend a couple of hours in the North End, wandering along twisting streets barely wider than the ancient cowpaths they follow, or in the Back Bay, strolling down the broad avenues lined with stately town houses, and you will see much that is lovely or curious or amusing. Look for the famous brass nameplates and gas lamps of Beacon Hill, the intricate wrought-iron balconies along Commonwealth Avenue, the market refuse set into the pavement near Haymarket, and the grasshopper atop Faneuil Hall.

This grasshopper has had one of the best views of history in the making, for Faneuil Hall was the site of many Revolutionary protest meetings. Indeed, if it has been dubbed the Cradle of Liberty, Boston itself could be considered the hotbed of dissent in which the American Revolution was spawned. It is here that the impassioned protest "Taxation without representation is tyranny" was voiced; where Sam Adams roused the citizenry and organized the Boston Tea Party; and where Paul Revere began his midnight ride when the British approached.

The 19th century saw the rise of commerce in Boston; and the flowering of arts and letters — represented by such figures as Emerson, Hawthorne, Longfellow, and Thoreau — led to its reputation as the Athens of America. The boom of population and wealth combined with the increasing noxiousness of the Back Bay caused it to be filled in to provide land for the city's expansion. Though the affluent and influential clamored to build on its wide avenues and live in its grand homes, Henry James was less impressed: "It is all very rich and prosperous and monotonous . . . but oh, so inexpressibly vacant." Today, however, that barren landscape has been transformed by a century's growth of elms, magnolias, and fruit trees, and its houses have come to represent exceptional examples of Victorian architecture in America.

After half a century of neglect and deterioration, Boston has again been experiencing a renaissance, beginning with the creation of Government Center and the restoration of the city's historic neighborhoods. With the past revived for posterity, city planners turned their sights to the needs — or fancies — of a new generation of residents and visitors. In the 1970s, Faneuil Hall Marketplace became the prototype of a new concept of urban retail development when Benjamin Thompson and the Rouse Company successfully transformed the old, largely abandoned market buildings into a lively and congenial gathering place that thrives on a carnival atmosphere of jugglers, magicians, musicians, and street vendors outside, and eateries plain and fancy, trinket shops, and unusual boutiques inside. More recently, Copley Place, Lafayette Place, and Cambridge's Charles Square have added vitality to the city. By now, Boston's reputation as a bastion of conservatism and chilly Brahmins (remember "banned in Boston"?) has gone the way of history, replaced by an upbeat avant-garde image that is also reality.

Yet a civilized urbanity remains, a sense of ease combined with an abundance of opportunity. Step out of your hotel and Boston showers you with riches. Do you like art? Boston's museums are among the finest in the world and its galleries — both on Newbury Street and along Fort Point Channel — are worth a day in themselves. Music? The Boston Symphony is only the beginning. Baroque chamber music concerts are often sold out, jazz fans can sit through three sizzling sets in intimate underground cafés, and the biggest names in current folk and rock come back faithfully to sing in the clubs that gave them their start. There are drum and bugle corps, rock groups, early music ensembles, swing bands, and choral groups of all descriptions, not to mention the ever-popular Boston Pops.

The Opera Company of Boston and the Boston Ballet are world-renowned, and a variety of contemporary dance companies present frequent, innovative programs. Many Broadway shows come here, and theater groups stage everything from Shakespeare to experimental plays. Beside the many commercial movie houses showing first- and second-run films, the colleges and cultural centers are always sponsoring film festivals where you can catch your favorite Chaplin or Dietrich or Bogart epic.

These same colleges and cultural centers provide virtually unlimited opportunities for education and self-improvement, from the large academic communities like Harvard, MIT, and Boston University to the dozens of smaller institutions. The list of lectures open to the public on any given day is overwhelming.

For many people, Boston is, above all, a sports town. It's easy for Red Sox fans to indulge themselves at Fenway Park, which has ardent admirers nationwide. Fenway is one of the last of the great old urban ball parks, a cozy field where the stands are so close to the action that between pitches you can hear the tobacco juice hitting the grass — and that's real grass, mind you. Basketball and hockey fans flock to the Boston Garden, just a few blocks from Haymarket, where the Celtics and Bruins have been not infrequent world champions. Football followers have to drive to Foxboro to watch the New England Patriots, but the distance doesn't deter them. (Visitors should bear in mind that loyalties are intense in Boston. If you must cheer for the opposition, cheer softly.)

Politics often seems like another favorite sport in Boston. Mayor James Michael Curley will live forever in the novel *The Last Hurrah,* and the

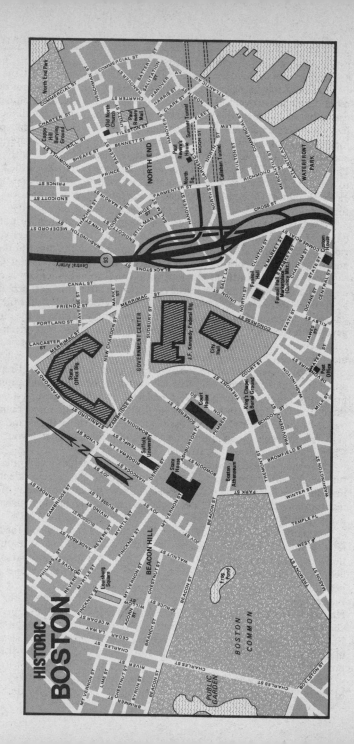

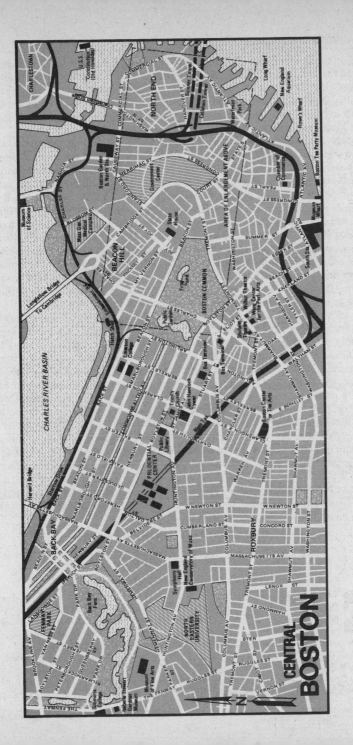

CENTRAL BOSTON

grandson of another mayor, "Honey Fitz" Fitzgerald, became the 35th president of the US, John F. Kennedy. Such names as Elliot Richardson and Henry Cabot Lodge loom large in our national consciousness, and Tip O'Neill, a North Cambridge boy, has stepped down after a lengthy tenure as Speaker of the House. But some run for more than election — Mayor Ray Flynn keeps in shape for the Boston Marathon as well.

Boston has long been known as "the home of the bean and the cod," but though scrod (as cooked cod fillets are called here) is found on many menus, it is harder and harder to find authentic baked beans. Local fishermen pride themselves in providing Boston's tables with the finest fresh fish and shellfish — especially lobster and clams. Two ethnic neighborhoods long known for their restaurants and groceries are Chinatown and the Italian North End. But today you can satisfy your desire for most any kind of cooking, be it Thai, Japanese, Portuguese, Indian, Mexican, or Greek, to name a few, and there has been an exciting proliferation of restaurants dedicated to creative nouvelle cuisine using the freshest seasonal produce. Bostonians bargain for their own at Haymarket, the traditional farmers' market adjacent to Faneuil Hall Marketplace. If you're in town on a Friday or Saturday, you shouldn't miss this chance to experience high-pitched excitement and local color.

For more peaceful and possibly healthful recreation, you are never more than a few blocks from a green oasis suitable for strolling, jogging, picnicking, or simply people-watching. Thanks to the genius and foresight of Frederick Law Olmsted, Boston enjoys several miles of continuous parkland known as the Emerald Necklace. Perhaps the prettiest jewel of them all is the Public Garden, with its ever-changing displays of luxuriant blooms arranged in intricate patterns and its graceful Swan Boats cruising the quiet pond. One of the best places for jogging — and Bostonians jog everywhere! — is the path along the Embankment (also called the Esplanade) of the Charles River, which provides plenty of aquatic as well as terrestrial scenery and in summer is the site of performances in the Hatch Shell, among them the famous July Fourth extravaganza of the Boston Pops Orchestra, led by John (*Star Wars*) Williams.

Boston has made the journey from its staid, Puritan beginning to its vibrant, cosmopolitan present, treasuring its past but eager to experience the new. You will enjoy the many stops along this route.

BOSTON AT-A-GLANCE

SEEING THE CITY: There are two unparalleled posts from which to view Boston: the John Hancock Tower's 50th-floor Observatory, and the 50th-floor Prudential Skywalk. The Hancock Tower gives you a spectacular panorama that even includes the mountains of southern New Hampshire (weather permitting), telescopes, recorded commentaries, a topographical model of Boston in 1775 (which is a must — we promise you'll be surprised), and a seven-minute film of a helicopter flight over the city. (Take the subway, the Green Line, to Copley Square.) Open daily. Admission charge. 200 Clarendon St., Copley Sq. (247-1977). Like the Hancock, the Prudential Skywalk offers an excellent 360° view, but the Pru also has a restaurant and bar on the 52nd floor. (Green Line, Auditorium or Prudential stop.) Skywalk and restaurant are open daily. Admission charge. Prudential Center, between Huntington Ave. and Boylston St. (236-3318). For another kind of overview, go to see the fascinating *Where's Boston?* exhibition and film (shown daily on the hour; afternoons on Sundays and holidays). Admission charge for film. Sack Cinema, Copley Pl. (267-4949).

SPECIAL PLACES: Boston is best seen on foot; the city is compact, and driving, even for residents, is hair-raising.

The Freedom Trail – The city has made it both easy and fun to track down the important sites from its colonial and Revolutionary past. Just follow the red brick (or red paint) line set into the sidewalk; it takes about two hours to walk its length without stops or side trips. To begin, take the Green or Red Line to Park Street and go to the Visitor Information Center on the Common, which has maps available. Or you can take a double-decker bus tour (see *Getting Around*).

Boston Common – A pastoral green, this is the nation's oldest park, set up in 1634. The earliest Bostonians brought their cows and horses here to graze. Today, you'll find their descendants engaging in free-form pastimes that range from music-making to baseball and skateboarding. We suggest starting your walking tour here. (It's advisable not to walk alone — and especially not at night — since the Common is often inadequately patrolled; you can park underneath the green in the Underground Parking Garage, open 24 hours daily.) For information on activities on the Common, call 267-6446.

State House – Facing the Beacon Street entrance to the Common, the gold-domed State House designed by Charles Bulfinch dates back to 1795. The gold leaf was added in 1874. You can enter through the side door of the right wing (the main door is hardly ever used). Inside, you can pick up pamphlets in Doric Hall and visit the Archives Museum in the basement. The Archives contain American historical documents, among them the original Massachusetts constitution, the oldest written constitution in the world (727-2816). There is also a library (727-2590). Closed weekends. Free. Beacon St. (727-2121).

Park Street Church and Granary Burying Ground – Built in 1809, the church witnessed William Lloyd Garrison's famous antislavery address in 1829 and heard the first singing of "My country, 'tis of thee" two years later. Open Tuesdays through Saturdays, July and August; otherwise by appointment. 1 Park St. (523-3383). In the 1660 cemetery next door are the graves of such Revolutionary notables as John Hancock, Samuel Adams, Thomas Paine, and Paul Revere and the parents of Benjamin Franklin. Look for the grave of Mary Goose, believed to be Mother Goose. Open daily.

City Hall – The focal point of Government Center, Boston's spacious new City Hall (1968), designed by Kallmann, McKinnell, & Knowles, sits in the middle of an 8-acre plaza that is often the scene of civic celebrations and politicking. Congress St. (725-4000).

Old State House – Sitting in the middle of State Street, surrounded by modern towers of law and finance, is this 18th-century seat of government, which served both the English colony and American state of Massachusetts until Bulfinch's State House was built. Now it is a museum of Boston history. Open daily. Admission charge. 206 Washington St. (242-5655). Across the street is a National Park Service visitors center, which provides useful information about Boston and sites in outlying areas. Open daily. 15 State St. (223-0058 or 242-5642).

Faneuil Hall Marketplace – These three large buildings have been a market since 1826 and still house eleven of the original tenants. Redesigned and opened between 1976 and 1978, the market has become a much-copied prototype of urban renewal. Over a million people per month — natives and tourists — partake of its multiplicity of stalls, restaurants, and shops. Plan to spend time wandering around and sampling its food, drink, and chic wares. The market takes its official name from adjacent Faneuil (pronounced Fan'l) Hall, a historic meeting house. Open daily (523-2980).

Beacon Hill – Walk along Mt. Vernon Street to see the stately old town houses that were (and are today) the pride of the first families of Boston. Look for the famous brass knockers, the charming carriage houses, and the intimate backyard gardens. A few blocks down is Louisburg Square, a rectangle of terribly proper houses facing a tiny park; this was once home to Louisa May Alcott and Jenny Lind, among others. Cobblestone Acorn Street, parallel to Mt. Vernon and Chestnut, is the most photographed in town.

North End – Paul Revere's House and Old North Church are both snugly tucked away among the narrow red brick streets of the North End, a colorful, Italian-American community with a lively street life and some excellent little restaurants (see *Eating Out*). To experience *la dolce vita*, stop at the *Caffé Paradiso* (255 Hanover St.) for cannoli, cappuccino, and people-watching.

Paul Revere's House – In addition to having housed the legendary Revolutionary hero, this place has the distinction of being the oldest wooden house in Boston. Before Revere lived here, one of the previous occupants was a sea captain who spent time in a Puritan pillory for "lewd and vicious behavior." Revere moved here in 1770 with his wife, mother, and five children. He had seven more children by his second wife, which is why his house was the only one on the block that didn't have to quarter British soldiers. Open daily. Admission charge. 19 North Sq. (523-1676).

Old North Church – Affectionately known as Old North, the official name of the church is Christ Church, built in 1723. On the night of April 18, 1775, sexton Robert Newman hung two lanterns outside to warn Bostonians that the British were coming by sea. His action and Paul Revere's famous ride were later immortalized by poet Henry Wadsworth Longfellow in a poem that you probably read in school. (The line you will want to remember is: "One if by land, two if by sea.") The church's original clock still ticks in the back and services are still held every Sunday. Open daily. Free. 193 Salem St. (523-6676).

Waterfront – Walk along Waterfront Park, with its invigorating views of the harbor and browse in the many new shops set in the renovated wharf buildings. On Long Wharf, the pier behind the Aquarium, you'll find the Custom House, built between 1845 and 1847, the ferry (summer only) across Cape Cod Bay to Provincetown (see *Cape Cod*, DIRECTIONS), and boats for harbor cruises and fishing excursions. For information, contact Baystate-Spray and Provincetown Steamship Company (723-7800) or Boston Harbor Cruises, Long Wharf (227-4320). The Massachusetts Bay Line leaves from Rowe's Wharf (542-8000).

New England Aquarium – One of the world's top collections of marine life, it served as the model for the National Aquarium in Baltimore. Taking center stage is the 180,000-gallon Giant Ocean Tank, the home of 1,000 aquatic specimens and a four-story coral reef. Divers regularly feed the multitudes of turtles, fish and sharks so they don't dine on each other. Exhibits re-creating environments such as tropical marine, northern waters and tidepool surround the saltwater tank. Penguins cavort in their own habitat called the Penguin Tray, and seals and dolphins perform aboard the floating pavilion *Discovery,* next door to the main building. A variety of films are shown in the auditorium, and there's an interesting gift shop. Blue Line, Aquarium stop. Open daily. Admission charge; children under 5 free. Central Wharf, Waterfront (742-8870).

BACK BAY

Arlington is the first of an alphabetically ordered series of streets created when the Back Bay was filled in during the mid-1800s. Broad streets and avenues were laid out in an orderly fashion, and along them wealthy Bostonians built palatial homes, churches, and public institutions. This area is a joy to walk and gives a better feeling of Victorian Boston than any other part of the city.

Public Garden – A treasure among city parks and a Boston tradition since 1861, the Garden has fountains, formal gardens, and trees labeled for identification. A special treat is a ride on the Swan Boats (remember Robert McCloskey's *Make Way for Ducklings?*), past the geese and ducks on the lake (open daily, mid-April through Labor Day, except on windy or rainy days; admission charge, group rates available; call 323-2700). Across Charles Street from the Common. Open daily. Free.

Commonwealth Avenue – Intended to replicate the broad boulevards of 19th-century Paris, with their mansard-roofed, stately homes, Commonwealth Avenue has fulfilled its early promise. Stroll down the shady mall, with its statues of famous Bostonians. In April, the magnolias are a special treat. On the corner of Clarendon Street stands the First Baptist Church, a splendid Romanesque structure designed by H. H. Richardson and completed in 1882. Open daily. Free. 110 Commonwealth Ave. (267-3148).

Newbury Street – This is where fashionable Bostonians shop. There are many art galleries and boutiques as well as a variety of restaurants and several outdoor cafés.

Copley Square – Seagoing vessels used to drop their anchors in Copley Square; now it harbors Richardson's magnificent Trinity Church. Open daily. Free (536-0944). The Boston Public Library (1885) is the oldest in the country. Step inside the Copley Square entrance for a quiet moment in the lovely central courtyard. Closed Sundays (536-5400). Across Dartmouth Street from the *Copley Plaza* is flashy Copley Place, a complex of hotels, fashionable shops (Neiman-Marcus, Tiffany, and the like), restaurants, movies, and an indoor waterfall.

OTHER SPECIAL PLACES

John F. Kennedy Library – This presidential library opened on October 20, 1979. Designed by I. M. Pei, it sits on the edge of a point of land projecting into Dorchester Bay, with a magnificent view of the Boston skyline and out to sea. The museum includes a half-hour film and an exhibit of documents, photographs, and memorabilia of JFK and his administration. There's also a section on his brother Robert F. Kennedy. By car, take the Southeast Expressway south to the JFK Library/UMass exit. The route to the library is well marked. Take the Ashmont train (Red Line) to Columbia; a shuttle bus takes you to the library. Open daily except certain holidays. Admission charge for adults; children under 16 free (929-4567).

Museum of Fine Arts – This is one of the world's great art museums, with comprehensive exhibits from every major period and in every conceivable medium. Special shows come and go frequently, many of them mounted in the West Wing, designed by I. M. Pei. The Monets are especially dazzling. Restaurant, snack bar, museum shop, and library. Arborway train (Green Line) Ruggles St. stop. Closed Mondays. Admission charge except Saturday mornings. 465 Huntington Ave., along the Fenway (267-9377 — A-N-S-W-E-R-S).

Isabella Stewart Gardner Museum – Mrs. Gardner, the widow of a Boston Brahmin, built this lovely Venetian *palazzo*, which she filled with her extraordinary collections of tapestries, stained glass, fine furniture, and paintings by masters like Rembrandt, Titian, and Corot. The courtyard is filled with blooms year-round. Free chamber music concerts are held frequently in the tapestry room, except in July and August (call 734-1359 for the schedule). A small café serves light lunches, in the garden in summer. Arborway train (Green Line), Ruggles St. stop. Closed Mondays. Suggested donation. 280 The Fenway (566-1401).

Institute of Contemporary Art – Exciting contemporary art in several media, including frequent series of interesting films. It's set in the halls of a 19th-century police station. Green Line, Auditorium stop. Hours vary seasonally; check before you go. Admission charge. 955 Boylston (266-5151).

Museum of Science and the Charles Hayden Planetarium – A wide variety of superb exhibitions illustrate the fields of medicine, technology, and space. Many of them involve viewer participation. You can watch a model of the ocean and a simulated lunar module in action. There's a special medical wing with anatomical and medical history and nutrition displays. Cafeteria and gift shop. Lechmere train (Green Line), Science Park stop. Open daily. Admission charge. Science Park, Charles River Dam (742-6088).

The Boston Tea Party Ship and Museum – Here you can board the *Brig Beaver II*, a full-size working replica of one of the three original ships in the Boston Tea Party. If you feel like it, you can even throw a little tea into Boston Harbor. The adjacent museum houses historical documents relevant to the period, as well as films and related exhibits. Red Line, South Station stop. Open daily. Admission charge. Congress St. Bridge at Fort Point Channel (338-1773).

USS *Constitution* – View the famous "Old Ironsides," the oldest commissioned ship in the US Navy and the proud winner of 40 victories at sea (242-5670). The adjacent shoreside museum displays related memorabilia and a slide show. City Square bus stop. Museum open daily. Admission charge. Boston Naval Shipyard, Charlestown (241-9078).

Bunker Hill Pavilion – Witness a vivid multimedia reenactment of the Battle of Bunker Hill on 14 screens, with 7 sound channels. Bet you thought the Americans won. Open daily, with shows every half-hour. Admission charge. Adjacent to USS *Constitution* (241-7575).

The Arnold Arboretum – Contained in these 265 acres of beautifully landscaped woodland and park are over 6,000 varieties of trees and shrubs, most of them labeled by their assiduous Harvard caretakers. Green Line, Arborway stop, or Orange Line, Forest Hills stop. Open daily. Free. The Arborway, Jamaica Plain (524-1717).

CAMBRIDGE

Harvard Square – Just across the Charles River from Boston, Cambridge has always had an ambience and identity all its own. Catering equally to the academic and professional communities, the Square is a lively combination of the trendy, traditional, and "upscale." It has the greatest concentration of bookstores in the country (many are open daily, late into the evening), movie options that range from vintage films like *Casablanca* to the latest from Hollywood and abroad, and the ever-present street musicians. When hunger pangs strike, everything from muffins to nouvelle cuisine awaits — with an authentic Italian ice to top it off. Red Line, Harvard Square stop.

Harvard Yard – This tree-filled enclave is the focal point of the oldest (1636) and most prestigious university in the country (the Law School is nearby, the Business School just across the river, the Medical School a bus ride away in Boston). Notice especially Massachusetts Hall (1720; Harvard's oldest building), Bulfinch's University Hall, and in the adjoining quadrangle Widener Library and Richardson's Sever Hall. Campus tours are given year-round; check at the information office in Holyoke Center (495-1573).

Fogg Museum – This neo-Georgian building houses Harvard's impressive collection of paintings, drawings, prints, sculpture, and silver as well as changing exhibitions. Open daily; closed weekends in summer. Admission charge. 32 Quincy St. (495-2387).

Harvard Museum of Natural History – On one short block parallel to Oxford Street is this complex housing the Natural History (comparative zoology), Peabody (anthropology), Geology, and Botanical museums. The Peabody houses extensive anthropological and archaeological collections, with an emphasis on South American Indians. There are also exhibitions on Africa and evolution as well as a fine gift shop. Reservations must be made for either group (495-2341) or individual (495-3045) tours. Open daily. Admission charge except on Saturdays from 9 to 11 AM. 24 Oxford St. (495-2463).

Longfellow House – George Washington and his troops billeted at this Tory Row house, built in 1759, at the beginning of the Revolutionary War. Longfellow bought it when he was a professor at Harvard and lived here until his death in 1882. (His children lived in neighboring Brattle Street homes.) Now it's a National Historic Site. Open daily. Admission charge. 105 Brattle St. (876-4491).

Radcliffe Yard – One of the Seven Sister colleges, Radcliffe has evolved from its historical role as Harvard's Annex to where its undergraduates are now fully integrated into the life of the university. Today Radcliffe focuses on special alternative programs for women at the graduate level and those involved in career changes. Its Schlesinger Library has one of the country's top collections on the history of women in America as well as an important culinary collection. Open weekdays. Free. 10 Garden St. (495-8647).

Old Burying Ground – Return to Garden Street and continue past Christ Church to the Old Burying Ground, also known as God's Acre. Graves here go back to 1635. Many Revolutionary War heroes and Harvard presidents are buried here. On the Garden Street fence, there's a mileage marker dating from 1754.

Massachusetts Institute of Technology – The foremost scientific school in the country, MIT opened its doors in Boston in 1861 and moved across the river to its Cambridge campus in 1916. In addition to its world-famous laboratories and graduate schools in engineering and science, its professional schools include the Sloan School of Management, the Center for Urban Affairs (with Harvard), and the School of Architecture. The architect I. M. Pei is an alumnus; next to his Green Building for the earth sciences is Calder's stabile *The Great Sail,* one of a superb collection of outdoor sculpture on the campus. Also worth noting are Saarinen's chapel and Kresge Auditorium, just off Mass. Ave. The Compton Gallery features changing technical exhibitions (77 Mass. Ave.; open weekdays; free) and the Hayden Gallery displays contemporary painting, photography, sculpture, and design (Memorial Dr.; closed Sundays; free). The new Wiesner Visual Arts Center, in the List Building, is another I. M. Pei, MIT landmark and also worth a visit for its interesting interior and its often provocative changing exhibitions (20 Ames St.; open daily; free). MIT campus tours are given year-round on weekdays at 10 AM and 2 PM. Red Line, Kendall Square stop. 77 Mass. Ave. (253-4795).

■ **EXTRA SPECIAL:** About 12 miles north of Boston on Route 107 is the town of *Salem.* The capital of the Massachusetts Bay Colony from 1626 to 1630, Salem earned a bitter name in American history as the scene of the witch trials, in which a group of women and children accused 19 villagers of witchcraft. The hysterical allegations resulted in the deaths of the accused. Several of the judges bitterly regretted their roles subsequently. Salem is also the site of Nathaniel Hawthorne's House of the Seven Gables (54 Turner St.). Hawthorne worked in the Salem Customs House and wrote the classic *The Scarlet Letter* at 14 Mall St. You can pick up a self-guiding cassette tour at the Chamber of Commerce, 18 Hawthorne Blvd. (744-0004). Like Boston, Salem has a history trail winding through its streets and port. The information booth provides maps and brochures. Open daily. Free. 18 Washington Sq. (744-0004).

While you're in the neighborhood, be sure to stop in at the Witch Museum, 19½ Washington Sq. N. Closed Thanksgiving, Christmas, New Year's. Admission charge (744-1692). The Witch House, site of some of the interrogations, radiates a claustrophobic, spooky feeling still, especially at night. (Some of the accused witches were confined here.) Open daily March to mid-December; other times by appointment. Admission charge. 9 North St. (744-0180). (You can get in the mood for this tour by picking up a copy of Arthur Miller's play *The Crucible.*)

For a cruise in the harbor, walk down to Salem Willows Pier; Pier Transit Cruises (744-6311). The Peabody Museum has fascinating scrimshaw carvings and nautical regalia from the early days of shipping and far-off ports. Closed Thanksgiving, Christmas, New Year's. Admission charge. 161 Essex St. (745-9500).

A couple of miles east of Salem, the shipbuilding town of *Marblehead* has interesting Colonial houses, places to sit and look at the harbor, and lots of boats. Toward evening, you can watch Marblehead fishermen unloading the day's catch.

SOURCES AND RESOURCES

TOURIST INFORMATION: For tourist information, maps, and brochures, visit one of the Visitor Information Centers — at City Hall, Boston Common, or the Hancock Tower — or call 267-6446. The Convention and Tourist Bureau and the Foreign Visitors Center have helpful information, too; open weekdays. Prudential Plaza W (536-4100).

A comprehensive guidebook is *In and Out of Boston (With or Without Children)* by Bernice Chesler (Globe Pequot Press; $9.95).

Local Coverage – *Boston Herald,* morning daily; *Christian Science Monitor,* Monday through Friday mornings; *Boston Globe,* morning daily; *The Boston Phoenix,* weekly; *Boston* magazine, monthly.

Food – *Robert Nadeau's Guide to Boston Restaurants* by Mark Zanger (World Food Press; $3.95) and *Boston* magazine's listings.

Area Code – All telephone numbers are in the 617 area code unless otherwise indicated.

CLIMATE AND CLOTHES: Autumn is the best time to see Boston. Days are generally clear and brisk, with temperatures in the 50s and 60s. At night it can drop into the 40s, with chilly winds. Winter can be formidable, with icy winds, snow, and sleet. If you intend to drive, make sure your car is properly equipped. Spring is brief and cool, and usually in the 60s. In summer, the mercury climbs into the 70s and 80s, although nights can be breezy and cooler.

GETTING AROUND: Airport – Just 3 miles from the center of the city, Logan International Airport handles both international and domestic traffic. The ride from the airport to downtown usually takes from 10 to 30 minutes, depending on traffic; taxi fare usually runs less than $10. Airways Transportation Company (267-2981) charges $4.25 for its bus service to major hotels in downtown Boston. Buses run on the hour and half-hour from 7 AM to 11 PM (Saturdays, hourly only). The most practical means of getting to Logan from virtually anywhere in the Boston area is by the MBTA (Massachusetts Bay Transit Authority) Blue Line trains, which cost 60¢ and run every 8 minutes (every 15 minutes on weekends) from 6 AM to midnight. From the train stop at downtown's Government Center station at City Hall Plaza, travel time to the airport is about 30 minutes. A water shuttle operated by Marina Bay Commuter (328-0600) also connects the city's downtown area with Logan (except in winter, when service is suspended). Boats sail across the harbor from Rowe's Wharf (400 Atlantic Ave.) to the airport every half-hour during rush periods; the trip takes about 10 minutes and costs $4.

Bus, Trolley, and Train – The Massachusetts Bay Transit Authority (MBTA) operates a network of subways (the Red, Blue, Green, and Orange lines) that are coordinated with a system of surface buses and trolleys. Exact change required. Service is fairly frequent during the day, less frequent at night, and nonexistent after about 12:30 AM. MBTA stations are marked with large, white circular signs bearing a giant T. For schedules, directions, timetables, and maps, call 722-3200. Red double-decker shoppers' buses start at the underground Common parking garage and circle the major retail areas: the Prudential Center, Newbury Street, Downtown Crossing, and Faneuil Hall Marketplace. They run every 15 to 20 minutes during store hours and cost 50¢. A double-decker bus tour of the Freedom Trail starts at the Visitor Information Center on the Common and costs $6; for details, call Hub Bus Lines, 739-0100.

Taxi – Boston has several taxi fleets, and you can hail them on the street, pick them up at taxi stands downtown, or call for them. Boston Cab (536-5010); Independent Taxi Operators Association (426-8700); Town Taxi (536-5000); Checker (536-7000); Yellow Cab, Cambridge (547-3000); Ambassador/Brattle Taxi, Cambridge (864-5000; 492-1100).

Car Rental – All major national firms are represented. Among the least expensive are American International Rent-A-Car, 209 Cambridge St. (Green or Blue Line, Government Center stop, 523-5441) or 341 Newbury St. (Green Line, Auditorium stop, 267-6661), and Ajax Rent A Car, Logan Airport (569-3550) or 424 Mass. Ave., Cambridge (497-4848).

 MUSEUMS: For a description of the New England Aquarium, Museum of Science, Fogg Museum, Museum of Fine Arts, Institute of Contemporary Art, Gardner Museum, Harvard Museum of Natural History, and Bunker Hill Pavilion, see *Special Places.* Other fine museums are:

Carpenter Center for the Visual Arts – Le Corbusier's only building in the US; 24 Quincy St., Harvard University, Cambridge (495-3216)

Children's Museum – Museum Wharf, 300 Congress St. (426-8855)

Boston Center for the Arts – 539 Tremont St.(426-5000)

Busch-Reisinger Museum – Harvard University, Cambridge (495-1694)

Ralph Waldo Emerson Memorial House – 28 Cambridge Turnpike, Concord (369-2236)

Gibson House – Victorian era; 137 Beacon St. (267-6338)

Museum of Afro-American History – Dudley Station, Roxbury (445-7400)

Society for the Preservation of New England Antiquities – 141 Cambridge St. (227-3956)

 MAJOR COLLEGES AND UNIVERSITIES: Boston is the country's ultimate college town, with tens of thousands of students, professors, and visitors from all over the world pouring onto the campuses every academic year. There are literally dozens of educational institutions, including the aristocratic New England prep schools. Harvard University (see *Special Places*) is the most prestigious in the country (Harvard Sq., Cambridge, 495-1000). MIT (see *Special Places*) produces scientists in all fields, many of whom continue in government research and consulting positions (77 Mass. Ave., Cambridge, 253-1000). In Boston itself, Boston University emphasizes the humanities. Check the bulletin boards and college newspapers for listings of campus events; Charles River Campus (353-2000). Other schools: Emerson College (130 Beacon St., 262-2010); University of Massachusetts/ Boston (Park Sq. and Columbia Point, 287-1900); Brandeis University (415 South St., Waltham, 647-2000); Endicott College (376 Hale St., Beverly, 927-0585); Tufts University (Medford-Somerville, 628-5000); Lesley College (29 Everett St., Cambridge, 868-9600); Wellesley College (Wellesley, 235-0320); Suffolk University (41 Temple St., 723-4700); Wheaton College (Norton, 285-7722); Simmons College (300 The Fenway, 738-2000).

SPECIAL EVENTS: The *Chinese New Year* is celebrated in Chinatown every February. *Patriots' Day* is observed the third Monday in April, which is also the day the famous *Boston Marathon* is run. The *Battle of Bunker Hill* is commemorated on June 17. *Saint's day celebrations* occur every weekend during July and August on Hanover St. in the North End. Male and female rowers compete in the *Head of the Charles Races,* the last Sunday in October. In even-numbered years, the *Harvard-Yale football game* is held in Cambridge.

SPORTS AND FITNESS: No doubt about it, Boston is one of the all-time great professional sports towns.

Baseball – The Boston *Red Sox* play at Fenway Park, 24 Yawkey Way. Green Line, Kenmore stop (267-8661).

Basketball – The Boston *Celtics* play at Boston Garden, 150 Causeway St. Green and Orange lines, North Station stop (523-3030; 523-6050).

Fishing – Deep-sea fishing boats leave from Long Wharf. Contact Boston Harbor Cruises (227-4320). You can rent boats, bait, and tackle from Hurley's Boat Rental, Houghs Neck, 136 Bay View, Quincy (479-1239); and Gamble's Landing, 15 Bayswater Rd., Quincy (471-8060).

Fitness Centers – Fitcorp has a track and workout equipment available, 133 Federal St. (542-1010).

Football – The New England *Patriots,* Sullivan Stadium, Rte. 1, Foxboro (262-1776).

Golf – There's a city course in Hyde Park, where the Parks and Recreation Department offers golf instruction. Contact George Wright Pro Shop, 420 West St., Hyde Park (364-9655). You can also take lessons at the Fresh Pond Golf Club, 691 Huron Ave., Cambridge (354-9130).

Hockey – The Boston *Bruins* play at Boston Garden, too (227-3200).

Jogging – Run along the banks of the Charles River on Memorial or Storrow Drive.

Racing – Thoroughbreds race at Suffolk Downs, Rte. C1, East Boston. Daily except Tuesdays and Thursdays (567-3900).

Sailing – You can rent boats from Marblehead Rental Boat Co., 83 Front St., Marblehead (631-2259); and in Boston at the Boston Sailing Center, 54 Lewis Wharf (227-4198).

Skiing – There's cross-country skiing at Weston Ski Track on Leo J. Martin Golf Course, Park Rd., Weston (894-4903), and at Lincoln Guide Service, Lincoln (259-9204). Lessons available.

Tennis – There are courts at Charles River Park Tennis Club, 4 Longfellow Pl. (742-8922).

THEATER: For information on performance schedules, check the local publications listed above.

Catch a Broadway show before it gets to Broadway. Trial runs often take place at the *Shubert Theatre,* 265 Tremont St. (426-4520); the *Colonial Theatre,* 106 Boylston St. (426-9366); the *Wilbur Theatre,* 246 Tremont St. (423-4008); and the *Wang Center for the Performing Arts,* 268 Tremont St. (800 223-0120). Or check out the *Charles Playhouse,* 74 Warrenton St. (426-6912). This is a much smaller and often livelier place, hosting consistently interesting contemporary plays. *The Next Move Theatre,* 1 Boylston Pl. (423-5572), performs new, experimental works — often satiric and political — with aplomb. The *American Repertory Theatre,* 64 Brattle St., Cambridge (547-8300), is based at Harvard's *Loeb Drama Center* and features an ever-changing bill of plays during the school year. In addition, there are dozens of smaller theater groups, including several affiliated with colleges, such as Boston University's *Huntington Theatre Company,* 264 Huntington Ave. in Back Bay (266-3913). *Boston Ballet Company* gives performances at the Wang Center (see above; 542-3945 for ballet information). Tickets for theatrical and musical events can be purchased through the Out of Town Ticket Agency, in the center of Harvard Square (492-1900); Ticketron (720-3400); Bostix, Faneuil Hall Marketplace (723-5181).

MUSIC: Almost every evening, Bostonians can choose among several classical and contemporary musical performances, ranging from the most delicate chamber music to the most ferocious acid rock. The *Boston Symphony Orchestra* performs at Symphony Hall, September through April, 251 Huntington Ave. (266-1492). In summer they perform at *Tanglewood Music Festival* in Lenox, Massachusetts. Selected members of the Boston Symphony Orchestra make up the *Boston Pops,* performing lighthearted orchestrations of popular music under the direction of John Williams. The Boston Pops Orchestra plays at Symphony Hall, April through July (266-1492), and gives free outdoor concerts in the Hatch Shell on the Charles River Esplanade in June and July. The *Opera Company of Boston,* with Sarah Caldwell, finally has an elegant home at 539 Washington St. (426-2786). For jazz, try *Montana's,* 160 Commonwealth Ave. (536-3556), *Ryles,* Inman Sq., Cambridge (876-9330), and the *Regattabar* in the Charles Hotel, Cambridge (864-1200). Top-name blues and pop musicians play here, too. For folk music, visit *Jonathan Swift's Pub,* 30B JFK St., Cambridge (661-9887), and *Passim's,* 47 Palmer St., Cambridge (492-7679).

NIGHTCLUBS AND NIGHTLIFE: A sophisticated and well-heeled crowd gathers nightly in the elegant *Plaza Bar* to listen to top-notch entertainers, *Copley Plaza Hotel* (267-5300). For vigorous popular music (mostly local), go to *Jack's,* 952 Mass. Ave., Cambridge (491-7800). TV celebrities, professional athletes, and those who want to meet them hang out at tiny, cozy *Daisy Buchanan's,* 240A Newbury St. at Fairfield St. (247-8516). *The Metro* features dancing to new wave music, has a video performance center, and is available for private parties; 15 Landsdowne St., Kenmore Sq. (262-2424). Devotees of hard rock should try the *Channel Club,* 25 Necco St., right beside the Fort Point Channel of the harbor (451-1050).

SINS: An awe-inspiring display of *avarice* can be witnessed in Filene's Basement every morning, about five minutes after the doors are opened. This is when bargain-mad shoppers storm the store, elbows out and aggression forward, searching for the special shipment of clothing that has just arrived from Neiman-Marcus or Brooks Brothers, marked way down.

Sloth is the word for lounging around the cafés of Boston and Cambridge on a Sunday afternoon, slowly drifting through a copy of the *New York Times.* If you're up too late to find a *Times,* the *Boston Globe* will do. Especially slow-moving hangouts, ideal for this pastime, are the *Harvard Book Store Café,* 190 Newbury St. (536-0095), and *Au Bon Pain,* at Holyoke Center Plaza in Harvard Square (497-9797).

Boston drivers are notorious throughout the eastern seaboard, and driving toward the Callahan Tunnel, the Tobin Bridge, or Cape Cod on any weekday afternoon after 3:30 PM will stimulate sufficient *anger* to make the reasons why all too clear.

Lust is the abiding spirit of the Combat Zone, in the downtown theater district on Washington St., a section of adult bookshops, X-rated films, bars, massage parlors, burlesque shows, and prostitutes.

LOCAL SERVICES: Babysitting – International Sitting Service, 1354 Hancock St., Quincy (472-7789); Child Care Resource Center, 552 Mass. Ave., Cambridge (547-9861)

Business Services – Bette James & Associates, 1430 Mass. Ave., Cambridge (661-2622)

Mechanic – Ray and Tom Magliozzi, at the Good News Garage, will repair anything for a fair price. 51 Landsdowne St., Cambridge, between Central Square and MIT (354-5383).

BEST IN TOWN

 CHECKING IN: Boston has some fine, old, gracious hotels with the history and charm you'd expect to find in this dignified New England capital. But Boston is in the midst of a hotel building boom, and there are now many modern places offering standard contemporary accoutrements. Expect to pay $120 or more for a double room at those places noted as expensive; between $75 and $95 in the moderate category; and inexpensive, under $75. Many of these hotels offer special weekend packages for relatively low rates. Reservations are always required, so write or call well in advance. For B&B accommodations, contact Bed & Breakfast Associates of Bay Colony, PO Box 166, Babson Park, Boston, MA 02157 (617 449-5302); Greater Boston Hospitality, Box 1142, Brookline, MA 02146 (617 277-5430); or write to the Massachusetts Division of Tourism (100 Cambridge St., 13th Floor, Boston, MA 02202) for its *Spirit of Massachusetts Bed & Breakfast Guide.*

Ritz-Carlton – The great lady of Boston hotels, quietly elegant, impeccably correct, and conveniently situated on the Public Garden, its 265 rooms a few steps from Newbury Street shops. The bar is the best place in town for a drink, and the upstairs dining room is superb. 15 Arlington St. (617 536-5700). Expensive.

Copley Plaza – This large (450 rooms), old hotel is on one of Boston's handsomest squares, convenient to Copley Place, Prudential Center, and Newbury Street shopping. Among its restaurants, *Copley's* offers very good food in a series of rich Victorian rooms, while the *Plaza Bar* features some of the great names in jazz. Copley Square (617 267-5300 or 800 225-7654). Expensive.

The Meridien – Distinctive red awnings mark this 1981 renovation of the landmark Federal Reserve Bank Building in the heart of the financial district. The 1922 Renaissance-revival structure was transformed with as little exterior alteration as possible; hence, there are 326 chic rooms and 22 suites, in 153 styles, all with a wet bar, 2 telephones, and 24-hour room service. Surrounded by greenery in a 6-story atrium is the French bistro *Café Fleuri;* its Sunday brunch is considered one of the best in Boston. *Julien,* the elegant dining room, honors the city's first French restaurant of 1794. Its nouvelle-inspired menu is the creation of Gerard Vie, owner of *Les Trois Marches* in Versailles. Health club with indoor pool, concierge, and lobby shops. 200 Franklin St., Post Office Sq. (617 451-1900 or 800 223-9918). Expensive.

Four Seasons – This $80 million, 15-story luxury hotel opened in 1985 across from the Public Garden. Fresh flowers fill the rich wood and marble lobby, and 19th-century artwork complements the decor. Its 288 rooms and suites each have a bar and 3 phones. There are also 2 restaurants, exercise rooms, and a pool. 200 Boylston St. (617 338-4400 or 800 268-6282). Expensive.

The Charles – This handsome red brick building is the centerpiece of the new Charles Square complex, set between the Charles River and Harvard Square. The 300 rooms are beautifully appointed and those on the 10th floor have teleconferencing and telecommunications facilities as well. Relaxation can be sedentary in the pleasant *Courtyard Café* and elegant *Rarities* restaurant or more active at the lavish Le Pli health spa, complete with an indoor pool. The *Regattabar* features live jazz by top names nightly. Full conference facilities. 840 Memorial Dr., Cambridge (617 864-1200). Expensive.

The Bostonian – Understated and small (155 rooms), this beautifully appointed hotel is across from the shopping and entertainment activities of Faneuil Hall Marketplace and just two blocks from the North End and the revitalized waterfront. The *Bostonian's* glass-enclosed rooftop *Seasons* restaurant discreetly overlooks the colorful bustle below. Faneuil Hall Marketplace (617 523-3600 or 800 343-0922). Expensive.

The Lafayette – Although centrally located in Downtown Crossing and part of the Lafayette Place complex of shops, restaurants, and an outdoor skating rink, this new luxury hotel reflects an Old World elegance. The 500 beautifully appointed guest rooms are grouped around four atriums. As befits a member of the Swissôtel group, the main dining room is the *Café Suisse;* for formal dining, the first-rate *Restaurant Le Marquis de Lafayette* offers creative Continental cuisine. Indoor pool, sun terrace, and saunas; 9 meeting rooms. 2 Ave. de Lafayette (617 451-2600). Expensive.

Dunfey's Parker House – This splendid, old 500-room hotel is right on the historic Freedom Trail, within easy walking distance of Beacon Hill, the Common, and Faneuil Hall Marketplace. The hotel's main restaurant (there are three) is *Parker's* (where Boston cream pie and Parker House rolls were invented); the *Last Hurrah,* a jolly Victorian room in the basement, is perhaps the liveliest, with good food and a terrific swing band. Tremont and School sts. (617 227-8600). Expensive.

Sheraton Boston – A huge, 1,400-room modern hotel in the Prudential Center, surrounded by fine places to shop. Its 4 restaurants, 3 cocktail lounges, and a year-round pool and health club provide plenty of diversion. Prudential Center (617 236-2000). Expensive.

The Colonnade – This distinguished 294-room hotel tries very hard to emulate the tradition of European luxury. There are large rooms, a (seasonal) rooftop pool, and *Zachary's* restaurant. Near the Prudential Center and Newbury Street. 120 Huntington Ave. (617 424-7000). Expensive.

Marriott on Long Wharf – A nautical motif envelops this new 400-room red brick luxury liner on the water at the foot of State Street. Its striking 5-story atrium is a highlight and provides the focus for the *Palm Garden Restaurant.* Two other restaurants, a ballroom, 5 conference rooms, an indoor-outdoor pool, and a health club offer multiple diversions. 296 State St. (617 227-0800 or 800 228-9290). Expensive.

The Westin – The opulent 36-story, 804-room property is one of three hotels in burgeoning Copley Place, a $500 million development adjacent to Copley Square. The hotel also has 2 ballrooms, 3 restaurants, and a meeting capacity of 2,000. 10 Huntington Ave. (617 262-9600 or 800 228-3000). Expensive.

Marriott in Copley Place – This 1,147-room giant is a focal point of the Copley Place development. Among its premium facilities are three restaurants, three bars, 36 meeting rooms, and the largest ballroom and most expansive exhibition area in any Boston hotel. For relaxation, there's an indoor pool, health club, and game room. 110 Huntington Ave. (617 236-5800 or 800 228-9290). Expensive.

Royal Sonesta – Tasteful renovations and sparkling additions to this flagship of the Sonesta chain have boosted its room count to 400. There are also 5 new eye-catching suites along with 3 restaurants, bars, pool, health club, the well-equipped Royal Sonesta Business Center, and conference rooms facing Boston across the Charles River. 5 Cambridge Pkwy. (near Kendall Sq.), Cambridge (617 491-3600 or 800 343-7171). Expensive.

Hyatt Regency Cambridge – The 500-room *Hyatt* in Cambridge features an enclosed central atrium with fountains, greenery, and glass-walled elevators. The revolving rooftop lounge offers a spectacular view of Boston, especially at sunset. On the Charles River, near MIT and Harvard (not easily accessible by public transportation). 575 Memorial Dr., Cambridge (617 492-1234). Expensive.

Embassy Suites – This distinctive hotel on the Charles River, opened in August

1985, has 10 conventional guest rooms and 310 luxurious suites. Amenities include complimentary breakfast, seven meeting rooms, restaurant, pool and sauna, and garage. Its location at the junction of two major traffic arteries makes it particularly attractive to businesspeople traveling by car. 400 Soldiers Field Rd., at the Allston exit of I-90, the Mass. Pike (617 783-0090). Expensive.

57 Park Plaza Hotel Howard Johnson's – They're pretty much the same everywhere. This one offers free parking, a year-round pool, and a location convenient to downtown. 351 rooms. 200 Stuart St. (617 482-1800 or 800 654-2000). Moderate.

Sheraton Commander – This mellow old 178-room hotel is directly on the Cambridge Common, within easy walking distance of Harvard University and Harvard Square. 16 Garden St., Cambridge (617 547-4800 or 800 325-3535). Moderate.

Chandler Inn – This modest, comfortable hotel conveniently sits between Copley and Park squares, near Copley Place. Recently renovated, it has 56 rooms and provides a Continental breakfast in its *Fritz Café,* where a light menu, cocktails, and weekend brunch are also available. 26 Chandler St. at Berkeley St. (617 482-3450). Inexpensive.

Howard Johnson's Motor Lodge – This modern, 205-room facility is on the Charles River, a few minutes' drive from both Harvard and MIT (not easily accessible by public transportation). Sauna and paddle tennis court. 777 Memorial Dr. (617 492-7777). Inexpensive.

 EATING OUT: Bostonians dine out less frequently than their New York friends; but when they do, they have their choice of several excellent restaurants. Our selection is based on outstanding quality, reliable service, and value. Expect to pay $75 or more for two at one of the places we've noted as expensive; between $40 and $75, moderate; and $40 or under, inexpensive. Prices do not include drinks, wine, or tips.

L'Espalier – Encompassing three floors of an Edwardian town house, this establishment exudes all the elegance, and then some, of its Back Bay neighborhood (but the service can be somewhat stuffy). Standouts on the Continental menu include poussin (a small chicken) in an artichoke sauce, and squab mousse in puff pastry. Closed Sundays. Reservations required. Major credit cards. 30 Gloucester St. (262-3023). Expensive.

Panache – A sparsely decorated place enlivened by bouquets of fresh and silk flowers, it serves some of the city's best Continental cuisine. Among the most successful dishes are grilled beef in red wine sauce, roast veal with a pesto sauce, and chocolate mousse. Closed Sundays and Mondays. Reservations necessary. Major credit cards. 798 Main St., Kendall Sq., Cambridge (492-9500). Expensive.

Restaurant Jasper – Chef Jasper White has an inventive touch, manifested skillfully in his unique treatment of such items as squab breasts and venison. He also makes his own pasta and serves it with equal flair — try the ricotta-filled tortellini in rabbit sauce. Closed Sundays. Reservations recommended. Major credit cards. 240 Commercial St. (523-1126). Expensive.

The Ritz-Carlton Dining Room – Large, lovely, serenely elegant, and one of only two places in town where you can enjoy a view of the Public Garden while dining with old-fashioned formality. The cuisine is Continental and very good and is served by an expert staff. Men must wear jackets and ties. Open daily. Reservations advisable. Major credit cards. 15 Arlington St. (536-5700). Expensive.

The Wild Goose Rotisserie and Grill – Guests may catch a glimpse of their goose being roasted to crisp, succulent perfection before enjoying it with game bird sausage, caramelized vinegar sauce, and braised red cabbage. Specials include whole roasted quail with chestnut stuffing and a thyme-scented duck ravioli made with fresh noodles. Open daily for lunch and dinner except Sundays, when only brunch is served. Reservations advised. Major credit cards. 300 N Market Bldg., Faneuil Hall Marketplace (227-9660). Expensive.

Le Bocage – This restaurant has some of the most consistently good French food available in New England. Both regional and classic entrées grace the menu, which changes to suit the season. A bright, efficient staff and a fine wine cellar add to the pleasurable dining. Closed Sundays. Reservations advised. Major credit cards. 72 Bigelow Ave., Watertown (923-1210). Expensive.

Maison Robert – Perhaps one of the finest French restaurants in the country, with food, drink, ambience, and service all worthy of top ranking. Owner-chef Lucien Robert has taught many of the French chefs in Boston and continues to prepare sauces for fish, fowl, and meat that defy imitation. Two dining areas, *Ben's Café* downstairs (on the patio in summer) and the elegant *Bonne Homme Richard* upstairs, are open for lunch and dinner. Brunch only on Sundays. Reservations necessary. Major credit cards. 45 School St. in the old City Hall (227-3370). *Bonne Homme Richard,* expensive; *Ben's Café,* moderate.

Hampshire House – Thoroughly evocative of 19-century Boston is this former mansion overlooking the Public Garden. The wood-paneled, clubby café-bar has piano music nightly, moose heads on the wall, and a fire blazing in the winter. It offers a simple Continental menu and a range of lighter fare. Upstairs, in the refined, eminently Victorian dining room, more elegant, traditional dishes are served. The basement houses the *Bull and Finch Pub,* a boisterous meeting, eating, and drinking place that was the inspiration for the television series *Cheers.* Open daily. Reservations desirable. Major credit cards. 84 Beacon St. (227-9600). Expensive to moderate.

Café Budapest – Gorgeously decorated in the lavish Eastern European tradition, and renowned for fine Continental and Hungarian cuisine. Avoid it on Saturday nights, when no reservations are accepted and hordes of hungry diners sometimes wait hours for tables. On weeknights this is a wonderful place to linger over superb strudel and some of the best coffee anywhere. Open daily. Reservations necessary. Major credit cards. 90 Exeter St. (266-1979). Expensive to moderate.

Harvest – This restaurant with a colorful dining room, lively bar, and (weather permitting) a secluded outdoor patio is tucked into a back corner of the former Design Research complex in Harvard Square. The menu features nicely executed international dishes in the nouvelle cuisine repertoire and fine salads and desserts. Open daily. Reservations advised. Major credit cards. 44 Brattle St. (492-1115). Expensive to moderate.

Locke-Ober Café – A splendid, albeit somewhat stuffy, tradition in probably the best-known of Boston's top restaurants. Though it was once a male bastion, today both sexes can eat at the handsome Men's Grill, with its glowing mahogany bar lined with massive silver tureens, its stained glass, snowy linens, and indefatigable gray-haired waiters. The food is identical in the less distinguished upstairs room — heavy on Continental dishes and seafood. Closed Sundays. Reservations essential. Major credit cards. 3 Winter Pl. (542-1340). Expensive to moderate.

Another Season – An intimate spot on Beacon Hill with murals evoking turn-of-the-century Paris. The menu changes every two weeks and features inventive Continental cuisine. Fresh seafood, a vegetarian entrée, and a marvelous array of desserts are always available. Closed Sundays; dinner only on Mondays and Saturdays. Reservations recommended. Major credit cards. 97 Mt. Vernon St. (367-0880). Expensive to moderate.

Lenora – This elegant restaurant features a mélange of nouvelle European food, prepared and served with skillful precision. The menu changes daily. Reservations advisable. Major credit cards. 1812 Mass. Ave., Cambridge (661-0191). Expensive to moderate.

St. Botolph – Actually a restored 19th-century brick town house, this two-floor restaurant sports a contemporary interior with exposed brick walls and a Continental menu with good, fresh seafood. Brunch is served on weekends. Reservations recommended. Major credit cards. 99 St. Botolph St. (266-3030). Moderate.

Anthony's Pier 4 – This massive place right on the harbor is predictably rigged out in a nautical motif. There's a commodious waterfront deck where you can have drinks and enjoy the view while you wait for your table. Good seafood, generous servings. Open daily. No dinner reservations. Major credit cards. 140 Northern Ave. (423-6363). Moderate.

Chart House – This restaurant occupies the oldest building on the waterfront, and the interior is a strikingly handsome arrangement of lofty spaces, natural wood, exposed red brick, and comfortable captain's chairs. The menu lists abundant portions of steak and seafood, with all the salad you can eat included in the reasonable prices. Open daily. No reservations, but the line moves pretty fast. Major credit cards. 60 Long Wharf (227-1576). Moderate.

Legal Sea Foods – If you don't mind waiting in line (no reservations), you'll find fresh and well-prepared seafood that we think is the best in Boston. Open daily. Major credit cards. *Park Plaza Hotel,* corner of Columbus and Arlington (426-4444); in the Chestnut Hill shopping mall, at 43 Boylston St. (277-7300); and 5 Cambridge Center, Kendall Sq., Cambridge (864-3400). Moderate.

Cornucopia – Off the beaten track between the Common and Lafayette Place is the historic home of the Peabody family. Here Nathaniel Hawthorne married Sophia, and Elizabeth opened the bookstore that became the meeting place for such literati as Emerson and Thoreau. Today, it has been renovated to accommodate a striking restaurant that features an eclectic blend of regional and ethnic dishes. The menu changes every two weeks. Lunch, weekdays only; dinner, Tuesdays through Saturdays. Reservations requested. Major credit cards. 15 West St. (338-4600). Moderate.

Kai Seki – This intimate Japanese restaurant in the Back Bay serves beautifully prepared traditional fare, including tantalizing tempura and sushi. A picturesque, private tearoom can be reserved for special occasions. The service is friendly and informative. Try the complete dinner, which is sumptuous and very reasonably priced. Closed Sundays. Reservations recommended. Major credit cards. 132 Newbury St. (247-1583). Moderate.

Tigerlilies – An enchanting spot in the heart of Beacon Hill, it offers al fresco dining in a peaceful courtyard in summer or the winter comfort of brick, tile, lilies, and a fire. The American nouvelle cuisine menu changes frequently but always includes seafood, pasta, and vegetarian dishes. Open daily. Reservations suggested. Major credit cards. 23 Joy St. (523-0609). Moderate.

Durgin-Park – Famed for generous servings of traditional Yankee roast beef, prime ribs, oyster stew, Boston baked beans, and Indian pudding. It's equally famous for its long, communal tables crowded with convivial diners and its brusque, no-nonsense waitresses. One of Boston's best values. (Another *Durgin-Park* has opened up in Copley Place, but we prefer the original.) Open daily. No reservations or credit cards. 340 Faneuil Hall Market Pl. (227-2038) and Copley Place (266-1964). Moderate to inexpensive.

North End Restaurants – Modestly priced Italian meals are available in dozens of little restaurants in Boston's oldest section, the North End. *Felicia's* has quite good North Italian cuisine, and Felicia herself, friend of countless Hub celebrities, oversees the preparation of such specialties as chicken verdicchio and cannelloni. Open daily. Reservations. Major credit cards. 145a Richmond St. (523-9885).

Lucia's is a warm neighborhood restaurant that unfailingly provides satisfying Italian food. Open daily. Reservations. Major credit cards. 415 Hanover St. (523-9148). Many locals swear the town's best pizza is tossed and baked at *Circle Pizza*, 361 Hanover St. (523-8787). Others claim the *European Restaurant* produces an even better pie. The *European* also has a large menu designed for the entire family. Open daily. Reservations. Major credit cards. 218 Hanover St. (523-5694). *Mother Anna's,* 211 Hanover St. (523-8496), and *Ida's,* 3 Mechanic St. (523-0015), are small-scale, home-style restaurants in the district noted for a fiercely loyal clientele and for authentic dishes cooked to order. Both are open daily, take reservations, and do not accept credit cards. All are moderate to inexpensive.

Rebecca's – White walls, blond wood furniture, and works by local artists dominate the comfortable, modern decor. The menu, described as new American, borrows from French, Greek, Indian, and Italian cuisines. Samplings include duck in green peppercorn sauce and shrimp sautéed with feta cheese, tomatoes, and olives. Open daily. No reservations. Major credit cards. 21 Charles St. (phone: 742-9747). Moderate to inexpensive.

Rubin's Kosher Delicatessen & Restaurant – One of only two true kosher restaurants in Boston, its chopped liver, potato latkes, and lean pastrami (hot or cold) are the genuine articles. Open Sundays through Thursdays; closes Fridays at 3 PM. Major credit cards. 500 Harvard St., Brookline (731-8787). Moderate to inexpensive.

Top of the Hub – This attractive restaurant on the 52nd floor of the Pru offers a spectacular view of the city and the harbor. It serves an interesting assortment of international dishes as well as all-American favorites like prime ribs, broiled scrod, lobster. Arrive early for the fixed-price Sunday brunch, or be prepared to wait in a long line. Open daily. Reservations accepted. Major credit cards. Prudential Tower, Back Bay (536-1775). Moderate to inexpensive.

Ye Olde Union Oyster House – This is the real thing, Boston's oldest restaurant. Daniel Webster himself used to guzzle oysters at the wonderful mahogany oyster bar, where skilled oyster-shuckers still pry them open before your eyes. Full seafood lunches and dinners are served upstairs, amidst well-worn colonial ambience. (One booth is dedicated to John F. Kennedy, once a frequent diner.) Don't miss the seafood chowder. Open daily. No reservations. Major credit cards. 41 Union St. (227-2750). Moderate to inexpensive.

Elsie's Lunch – This incomparable restaurant and sandwich shop has been serving food and drink to famished Harvard students for longer than anyone can remember. A great place to go when your feet are tired, or when you just want to fill up. Open daily. No reservations or credit cards. 71 Mt. Auburn St., Cambridge (354-8781 or 354-8362). Inexpensive.

The F&T Delicatessen and Diner – The relaxed, friendly, 1930s atmosphere in this pair of eateries draws regular customers from all over town. Fresh, flavorful deli meals are complemented by some of the most elegant cuisine available in any diner in eastern Massachusetts. Early bird breakfasts are a special treat in both. Diner closed weekends; deli closed Sundays. No credit cards. The deli and diner are both in the Cambridge Center section of Kendall Square in Cambridge at 304 and 310 Main St., respectively (547-3674, deli; 547-5820, diner). Inexpensive.

The Seventh Inn – Close to the Prudential Center on Newbury Street, this quiet, friendly restaurant has an eclectic menu: seafood, fresh vegetables and fruits, and desserts made with natural ingredients. The tempura is memorable. Nearly everything is prepared to order, and the variety of subtle seasonings and their aromas is delightful. Closed Sundays. Reservations accepted. Major credit cards. 272A Newbury St. (247-2475). Inexpensive.

Milk Street Café – Sandwiched into a sparkling niche of the financial district, this bustling vegetarian and fish cafeteria presents superb breakfasts and lunches. The muffins, smoked salmon platter, flavorful soups, and generous, artful quiches are perennial pleasers. Open weekdays. No credit cards. 50 Milk St. (542-2433). A second location is now open at 101 Main St., Kendall Sq., Cambridge (491-8286). Inexpensive.

CHARLESTON, SC

Charleston residents used to joke that their city was "the best-preserved secret on the Eastern seaboard." Standing on a peninsula where the Ashley and Cooper rivers flow into the Atlantic, Charleston's harbor is guarded by Fort Sumter, where the first shots of the Civil War were fired. (Charlestonians still refer to the War Between the States as "the Great War," and Robert E. Lee's birthday is observed as a holiday, as it is throughout much of the South.) With its architecturally gracious, historic buildings and magnificent gardens, Charleston had retained the flavor and charm of the Old South. But slow economic growth has been one of the consequences of this sleepy elegance. Charlestonians (like Bostonians or Virginians), however, tended to accept their city's lack of development as just another one of the continuing hardships of the post-Reconstruction era.

In their attempts to stimulate the local economy, city leaders tried to induce industry into the area, offering prime locations, tax incentives, and embroidered statistics about the available work force. But environmentalists opposed razing choice property for industrial parks. The conflict raged for years. The only common opinion was that tourism was not desirable. Charlestonians viewed tourists as long-necked, nosy people forever searching for bathrooms.

Then, early in 1975, Charleston was "discovered," like a rare, colorful, slightly chipped mollusk. Boosterism spread faster than the yellow fever in 1864. In the brief course of a year, "the best-preserved secret on the Eastern seaboard" metamorphosed into a national tourist attraction.

A new alliance of tourism-oriented entrepreneurs started a quarter-million-dollar promotion campaign. Old abandoned warehouses near Market Street were converted into boutiques, art galleries, studios, restaurants, and expensive town houses. Thirty new restaurants opened in 1976 (only half or a third are prospering), and the overall success of the Market Square renovation began to stimulate similar projects in other sections of the city.

In 1977, the Miss USA Beauty Pageant and the first Spoleto Festival USA were held in Charleston. Its more conservative citizens regarded the pageant's toothy grins and skimpy swimsuits as out of keeping with the city's traditional quaintness and suggested that events like the arts festival were preferable. As it worked out, the beauty pageant bombed — the city lost $70,000 — and any ideas about a repeat performance were abandoned. But the first American counterpart of Italian composer Gian Carlo Menotti's internationally acclaimed Spoleto Arts Festival was a great success, putting Charleston on the cultural map.

Even with its burgeoning renaissance, many of Charleston's residents feel the city has a long way to go before it acquires enough cosmopolitan flavor to accompany the scenery and architecture. But, they say, Charleston is beginning to reclaim its cultural heritage.

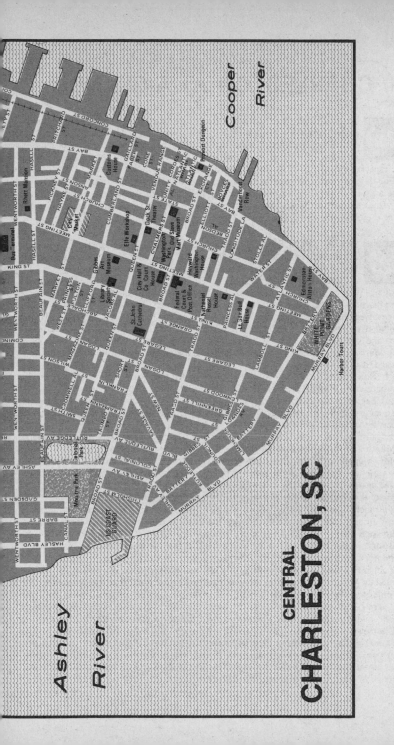

Ashley
River

Cooper
River

CENTRAL
CHARLESTON, SC

CHARLESTON AT-A-GLANCE

SEEING THE CITY: Charleston is set in that sea-level peninsula of south-eastern South Carolina known as the Lowcountry. There are no hills from which to get a good view of the city. Nicknamed the Holy City because of its many church spires, Charleston's best view is from the ground, looking up, especially at night, when floodlights illuminate the church spires.

For those determined to get a bird's-eye view, Hawthorne Aviation (744-2581) will take a group of three or more over the city for a moderate fee. You can also see the city from the harbor. Gray Line yachts depart at 2 PM daily (more often in summer) from the City Marina on Lockwood Dr. Admission charge (722-1112).

SPECIAL PLACES: The old city is approximately 7 square miles, and even a five-day visit could be spent walking without covering the same street twice. An evening stroll is most popular with residents.

Fort Sumter – A national monument, the fort where the first shots of the Civil War were fired sits on a small manmade island at the entrance to Charleston's harbor. Under federal attack from 1863 to 1865, Fort Sumter withstood the longest siege in warfare. The Confederates gave up the fort in February 1865. To the Union, it represented secession and treachery; to the Confederates, it meant resistance and courage. The fort can be reached only by boat. Fort Sumter Tours leave City Marina daily at 9:30 AM and 2:30 PM. Admission charge. Calhoun St. and Lockwood Dr. (722-1691).

Charles Towne Landing – Charleston was called Charles Towne in 1670 when the first permanent English settlers arrived. Now a state park, Charles Towne Landing has a number of restored houses, a full-scale replica of a 17th-century trading vessel, open-air pavilion with underground displays of artifacts found during archaeological excavations, and an Animal Forest with indigenous animals. Plenty of picnic tables, bike trails, and tram tours, too. Admission charge. 1500 Old Towne Rd. (556-4450).

Magnolia Plantation and Gardens – World famous for its abundance of colors and scents, Magnolia Gardens' 30 acres abound with 900 different varieties of camellias, 250 varieties of azaleas, and dozens of different exquisite plants, shrubs, and flowers. Listed in the National Register of Historic Places, Magnolia Gardens has been the home of the Drayton family since the 1670s. In addition to the boat tours, a small zoo, and a ranch exhibiting a breed of miniature horse, Magnolia Gardens offers canoeing, bird-watching, and bike trails through its 400-acre wildlife refuge. Open all year. Admission charge. 10 miles south on Rte. 61 (571-1266).

Boone Hall – If you ever imagined yourself as one of those romantic characters in *Gone With the Wind,* Boone Hall is the place where you can live your dream. The movie was actually filmed on the grounds of this 738-acre estate, formerly a cotton plantation. Settled by Major John Boone in 1681, Boone Hall has original slave houses intact. The ¾-mile Avenue of Oaks, planted in 1743, the famous restored mansion, and the 140-acre pecan groves attract visitors from all over the world. Open daily, except Thanksgiving and Christmas. Admission charge. 7 miles north on Rte. 17 (no phone).

Charleston Museum – The Charleston Museum, the oldest municipal museum in the country, has moved from its original facility, built in 1773, to a new complex and courtyard. It has impressive collections of arts, crafts, furniture, textiles, and implements from South Carolina's early days. Special film shows. Open daily except holidays. Admission charge. 360 Meeting St. (722-2996).

Provost Dungeon – Another grim reminder of what history was really like. The Provost Dungeon dates back to 1780. Here, the British imprisoned American patriots during the Revolutionary War, and reconstructed exhibits show how they were treated during their detention. Attached to the Provost are excavations from the Half Moon Battery (c. 1690), the original city wall built by the British. Open daily. Admission charge. East Bay St. at Broad, under the Exchange Building (792-5020).

Elfe Workshop – Thomas Elfe was an 18th-century cabinetmaker whose pieces now sell for as much as $80,000. Built between 1750 and 1760, the small scale of this mansion's furnishings and rooms may make you wonder if Thomas Elfe really was one. You can ask. The guides are friendly and well informed. (See *Sources and Resources.*) Closed Sundays. Admission charge. 54 Queen St. (722-2130).

■**EXTRA SPECIAL:** At *Middleton Place,* about 15 miles north of Charleston via Rte. 61, the self-sustaining world of a Carolina Lowcountry plantation is re-created daily by people in 18th-century costume. Built in 1755, Middleton Place features the oldest landscaped gardens in the country, laid out by Henry Middleton in 1741. The 1,000-year-old Middleton Oak and the oldest camellias in the New World flourish on the lush grounds. Arthur Middleton, a signer of the Declaration of Independence, is buried here. A national historic landmark, Middleton House is the site of the Spoleto Festival Finale in June, the Scottish Games in September, the Lancing Tournament in October, and Plantation Days (a dramatization of life on a plantation) in November. Open daily. Admission charge (556-6020).

SOURCES AND RESOURCES

TOURIST INFORMATION: The Arch Building used to be a public house for wagon drivers entering the city, a tradition of hospitality that has carried over to the present. It now houses the visitors center, where you can get advice or brochures on tours, hotels, and restaurants. The staff will assist you in making reservations. Open daily. Free. 85 Calhoun St. (722-8338) or write to PO Box 975, Charleston, SC 29402. Across the street, Your Charleston Connection provides a free shuttle to the historic district and makes reservations for tickets, lodging, and dining. 64 Calhoun St. (723-8145).

For information on events and performance schedules, call the Visitor Information Center (722-8338), the Charleston County Parks, Recreation and Tourism Commission (722-1681), or the Chamber of Commerce (577-2510).

Local Coverage – *Charleston News & Courier,* morning daily; *Evening Post,* evening daily.

Area Code – All telephone numbers are in the 803 area code unless otherwise indicated.

CLIMATE AND CLOTHES: Charleston's average temperature is 65°. Winters are mild, summers hot. March and April are the best spring months to visit, when the city is most accessible by foot and everything green and growing is abloom. In the fall, October and November are ideal.

GETTING AROUND: Airport – Charleston International Airport is a 20-minute drive from downtown; taxi fare should run about $15. Low Country Limousine provides van service from the airport to the downtown hotels for $7.

Bus – The South Carolina Electric and Gas Company operates the city bus system. 665 Meeting St. (722-2226). The Downtown Area Shuttle (DASH) operates on weekdays.

Taxi – Taxis are rather inexpensive and a better bet than buses; they must be ordered by phone. Call Yellow Cab (577-6565).

Car Rental – Major national agencies are represented at the airport.

Horse-Drawn Carriages – You can pick one up at 96 Market St., daily, from 9 AM till dusk. Night rates are available; reservations accepted. Charleston Carriage Co., 96 Market St. (577-0042).

MUSEUMS: The Charleston Museum is described under *Special Places.* Some other notable museums are:

Gibbes Art Gallery – 135 Meeting St. (722-2706)
Old Slave Mart Museum – 6 Chalmers St. (722-0079)

USS *Yorktown* – A World War II aircraft carrier, now a naval museum; on the east bank of the Cooper River (884-2727)

HISTORIC HOUSES: Edmonston-Alston House (1828) – 21 E Battery St. (722-7171)

Heyward-Washington House (1770) – 87 Church St. (722-0354)
Joseph Manigault House (1803) – 350 Meeting St. (722-0354)
Nathaniel Russell House (1808) – 51 Meeting St. (723-1623)

Candlelight tours of historic houses are conducted by the Preservation Society in October (722-4630). The Historic Charleston Foundation will guide you through 85 historic houses by day or candlelight. Mid-March through April. Modest admission charge. 51 Meeting St. (723-1623).

MAJOR COLLEGES AND UNIVERSITIES: The Citadel Military College of South Carolina, founded in 1842, is one of the few state-run military schools in the country. A full-dress parade takes place Fridays at 3:45 PM. West end of Hampton Park (792-6919).

SPECIAL EVENTS: *Spoleto Festival USA,* 17 days of chamber music, dance, jazz, opera and theater, begins every year in late May. For tickets, call 577-7863; for schedule information, call 722-2764. An array of local events, many free, make up *Piccolo Spoleto,* which coincides with the main festival; call 724-7305.

SPORTS AND FITNESS: Biking – Many of Charleston's parks have bike trails. Bikes may be rented from the Bicycle Shop, 283 Meeting St. (722-8168), or Charleston Carriage Co., 96 N Market St. (577-0042).

Fishing – The Isle of Palms fishing pier is open spring through fall; it's generally crowded, but in fact, the fishing is unexceptional. For really good surf fishing, try Capers Island and Dewees Island. Charter boats for deep-sea fishing are available through the Municipal Marina, but the best fishing is in the estuarine creeks that swim with bass, sheepshead, flounder, and trout (in fall and winter). In summer and fall the creeks are full of crabs. Crab, oyster, and creek fishing are especially good on Capers, Dewees, Bulls, Kiawah, and Seabrook Islands. There are some public oyster beds closer to Charleston. For fishing and hunting regulations, write: South Carolina Wildlife Resources Dept., PO Box 167, Columbia, SC 29202.

Fitness Centers – Living Well Fitness Center has exercise equipment, whirlpool, swimming pool, sauna, aerobic dancing, and exercise classes. 6750 Sam Rittenburg Blvd. (571-0130) and eight other locations.

Golf – Kiawah and Seabrook Islands have golf courses, but one of the most popular golfing areas in the country, Myrtle Beach, is only 98 miles north of Charleston on Rte. 17. This year-round resort, though increasingly tacky, has 28 golf courses, many of them first rate. Far better is Hilton Head Island, with more than a dozen golf courses of its own, including Harbour Town Golf Links, home of the annual Heritage Golf Classic. The resort accommodations offered at Hilton Head are far classier than those at Myrtle Beach.

Jogging – Run around Colonial Lake, on Ashley Avenue; for a nice 5-mile loop, run from Lockwood Drive to Battery, up East Bay Street, turn left onto Broad Street, right onto Meeting Street, and left onto Calhoun, which intersects with Lockwood.

Sailing – There's no place to charter sailboats in Charleston, but there are plenty of anchorages. Sailing regattas are held in the summer. If you're able to crew, go to the Municipal Marina. You'll usually be able to get on board for the day.

Swimming – Close to the city, Sullivan's Island and the Isle of Palms have fairly nice beaches, crowded in summer. Folly Beach, at the end of Folly Road (Rte. 171), usually gets a good crowd even though it's not well kept. North of Charleston, Capers Island and Dewees Island have more secluded beaches, probably because they're only accessible by boat. Both are state wildlife refuges.

Tennis – The courts at the resorts on Kiawah and Seabrook Islands are open to the public but can be expensive, and resort guests have priority. Try Shadowmoss Plantation Golf & Country Club, 20 Dunvegan Dr. (556-8251), for inexpensive public courts.

 THEATER: Built in 1736, the 463-seat *Dock Street Theater* — the oldest in the country — stages frequent performances of original drama, Shakespeare, Broadway, and 18th-century classics. Closed Sundays. Closed Saturdays during July and August. On the corner of Church and Queen sts. (723-5648). For up-to-date information and performance times, call the Chamber of Commerce (577-2510); the Visitor Information Center (722-8338); the Charleston County Parks, Recreation and Tourism Commission (722-1681). Schedules are erratic, so it's advisable to check in advance.

 MUSIC: For *Community Concert Association, Symphony Orchestra,* and *Civic Ballet* schedules, call the telephone numbers listed above. The *Robert Ivey Ballet* presents major concerts in the spring and fall (556-1343).

NIGHTCLUBS AND NIGHTLIFE: The best "happy hours" in town are at *Xanadu,* 35 Market St. (723-1084), and *Charleston Oyster Bar,* 70 State St. (723-1151). Both are within a two-block radius of Church and State streets. Also downtown is *Ashley's,* in the new *Sheraton Charleston Hotel,* 170 Lockwood Dr. (723-3000); and, for an intimate atmosphere, try *The Best Friend Bar* in the *Mills House Hotel,* 115 Meeting St. (577-2400). The best night spot north of town is the *Windjammer,* 1008 Ocean Blvd. (886-8596), a beer-and-billiards beach bar on the Isle of Palms. *Myskyn's Tavern,* 83 Market St. (577-5595), hosts jazz groups. *East Bay Trading Company* (corner East Bay and Queen sts.; 722-0722) is a converted warehouse filled with fun antiques and an unusual bar. Right next door at 159 East Bay St. is *Fanigan's* (722-6916), a favorite spot for businesspeople.

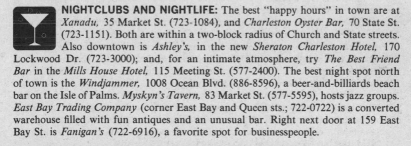 **SINS:** Look at the faces of the passengers in Charleston's romantic horse-drawn carriages, and you'll see the blissful glow of pie-eyed *sloth* that only the momentarily idle can experience.

Sometimes you can see *lust* on Folly Beach or the strands of Sullivan's Island, where the finest flowers of sweet-talking Southern womanhood spend weekends slathering each other with suntan oil. *Anger?* Watch the faces of the drivers of the cars forced down to the carriages' 2 mph clippity-clop. The city's *pride* is its collection of refurbished and immaculately maintained 18th-century homes.

LOCAL SERVICES: For information about local services, call the Chamber of Commerce (577-2510).

Business Services – For rapid-turnaround dictation service, Professional Word Processors, 315 Calhoun St. (577-0830)
Mechanic – Bowick Auto Service, 48 Pinckney St. (766-0804)

BEST IN TOWN

CHECKING IN: Expect to pay $80 and up for a double room in one of the places we've noted as expensive; and $50 to $75 at places listed as moderate; and under $50, inexpensive. For B&B accommodations, contact Historic Charleston Bed & Breakfast, 43 Legare St., Charleston, SC 29401 (803 722-6606).

Battery Carriage House – A few doors away from the Provost Dungeon, facing the harbor, this elegant hotel provides guests with canopied beds, a fully stocked bar in each room, and Continental breakfast in bed. Free bicycles, and complimentary wine to be sipped in the wisteria-draped, walled garden. There are only 10 rooms; make reservations well in advance. Price includes breakfast, all services. 20 S Battery (803 723-9881). Expensive.

Sword Gate Inn – In the heart of the old residential area, in a restored mansion. There are only 4 rooms, so reservations are required three to six months in advance for spring, one month in advance for the rest of the year. Breakfast and bicycles are included in the price of a room. 111 Trade St. (803 723-8518). Expensive.

Indigo Inn – Charleston's newest and most elegant hotel, the *Indigo* is furnished with 18th-century reproductions, and each of its 40 rooms has two four-poster, queen-size beds. Centrally located at 1 Maiden La. (803 577-5900). Expensive.

Lodge Alley Inn – This quiet, tasteful inn has 34 rooms, each with a fireplace, as well as 37 one- and two-bedroom suites and a penthouse. Adding to its allure, the inn is in Charleston's best shopping and sightseeing area. There's also a good restaurant and a lounge. 195 E Bay (803 722-1611). Expensive.

Sheraton Charleston Hotel – Near the historic district, this new *Sheraton* is set on the banks of the Ashley River, and some of its 350 rooms have balconies with river views. One of its dining rooms, the *Charleston Terrace,* emphasizes seafood and beef and offers a good selection of wines. Other facilities include pool, tennis courts, and jogging track. 170 Lockwood Dr. (800 325-3535). Expensive.

Planters Inn – Set in Charleston's historic district, this is the city's most elegant new inn. The building dates from the 1800s and was thoroughly renovated, under strict government rules, to maintain its original appearance. The public rooms are filled with antiques and the 43 spacious guest rooms (some with fireplaces) are furnished in period reproductions, including four-poster beds. *Silks,* the inn's very fine restaurant, features American cuisine. Concierge and 24-hour room service. 112 N Market St. (803 722-2345 or 800 845-7082). Expensive.

Heart of Charleston – Well run and conscientiously managed, the best thing about this 100-room contemporary motel is the people who own it. Within easy walking distance of the historic, shopping, and shipping districts, with a swimming pool, restaurant, and lounge. 200 Meeting St. (803 723-3451). Moderate.

Two Meeting Street Inn – A real "find" in Charleston, built in 1891 and similar to a European pension. The inn has been a guest home for more than 50 years.

Nine spacious rooms and a wide second-floor veranda overlook White Point Gardens and the harbor. It isn't ornate and will probably appeal to the more adventurous traveler. Rooms with private bath run about $65 or $70; rooms with a shared bath are about $20 less. 2 Meeting St. (803 723-7322). Moderate.

Days Inn Meeting St. – This 124-room hotel with a restaurant is in a very good location if seeing the city is top priority. 155 Meeting St. (803 722-8411). Moderate.

EATING OUT: Charleston used to be known as the kind of place where "you couldn't get a decent hot dog unless you knew somebody," but the times they are a-changing, and there are now more than enough interesting restaurants to whet your palate. Prices range from expensive ($40 or more for dinner for two without drinks, wine, or tips) to moderate ($25 to $35) to inexpensive (under $25) and do not include drinks, wine, or tips.

The Wine Cellar – Each night the chef prepares a different menu containing six French entrées. Meals are all six-course and prix fixe. Closed Sundays. Reservations required. Major credit cards. 35 Prioleau St. (723-3424). Expensive.

Robert's of Charleston – One of the city's top restaurants, the Châteaubriand prix fixe dinners are served by the owner-chef Robert Dickson. No extra charge for arias he sings as he serves. Open daily. Reservations required two weeks ahead. Major credit cards. 42 N Market St. (577-7565). Expensive.

82 Queen – There used to be just one restaurant at this address, but its popularity prompted the management to annex the building next door. Now, in addition to the seafood specialties served in *82 Queen*'s lovely 18th-century town house, the *82 Queen Café and Deli* offers lighter fare such as pasta salad and sandwiches. *The Wine Bar* serves no meals but is a nice spot for a pre- or post-dinner glass of wine. Open daily. Reservations advised. Major credit cards. 82 Queen St. (723-7591). Expensive.

East Bay Trading Company – Whimsical antiques decorate this converted warehouse. The menu features beef dishes, seafood, soups, and homemade desserts (including ice cream). Closed Sundays. Reservations advised. Major credit cards. Corner of East Bay and Queen sts. (722-0722). Expensive to moderate.

Marianne's – The regular dinner menu is French and excellent: beef, veal, seafood, and lamb. A late supper is also available from 11 PM to 1:30 AM, and features appetizers, soups, steaks, and omelettes. A good wine list is available. Dinner reservations advised. Major credit cards. 219 Meeting St. (722-7196). Expensive to moderate.

The Cotton Exchange – Although it features a Continental menu of beef, veal, and fresh seafood, most folks come here for duck, the house specialty, which the kitchen prepares in any of eight different ways. Closed Sundays. Reservations advised. Major credit cards. 36 Market St. (577-7137). Expensive to moderate.

Garibaldi – This small Italian café serves what may be best described as Italian home cooking. Spaghetti dishes are offered daily, as are regular specials, including seafood. Major credit cards. 49 Market St. (723-7153). Moderate.

Colony House Restaurant – In the same converted warehouse as the Wine Cellar, this is one moderately priced restaurant in Charleston that serves the best broiled or baked seafood in town. Open daily. Reservations advised. Major credit cards. 35 Prioleau St. (723-3424). Moderate.

The Last Catch – Some say that this place has the finest fresh seafood in town. Especially good is the *Coquilles St. Jacques*. Closed Sundays. Reservations advised. Major credit cards. Coleman Blvd. in Mt. Pleasant (884-2780). Moderate.

14 Market St. – A fascinating menu of Cajun, East Indian and Indonesian specialties. The lamb, seafood, and duck are favorites. A late-night breakfast is available

Thursdays through Saturdays. Closed Sundays. Reservations advised. Major credit cards. 14 Market St. (722-3180). Moderate.

Sprouts and Krauts – A food emporium with a restaurant serving healthful sandwiches, salads, and cheesy casseroles. Open daily for lunch and dinner. No reservations. Major credit cards. Marion Sq. (722-6726). Inexpensive.

The Marina Variety Store – Overlooking the Municipal Marina, this is a local favorite, especially at lunchtime. A simple, no-frills restaurant (lunch and dinner) serving seafood, fried chicken, homemade soups, and good burgers. Open daily. No reservations or credit cards. Municipal Marina (723-6325). Inexpensive.

CHICAGO

Ask a resident if Chicago has a soul, and you're likely to be greeted with a laugh. The third largest city in the country (the city proper has 2.9 million people; the metropolitan area, 7.6 million), ninth largest in the world, Chicago carries a long-standing reputation as a tough, cynical town. "Hog Butcher to the World," Carl Sandburg sang. Although Chicago lost that title to Omaha years ago, it is still one of the world's great cities. But despite its greatness, Chicago suffers from an inferiority complex, one that stems from the endless, inevitable comparisons to New York.

In fact, there is a unique allure to the place. It has inspired musicians to create a Broadway musical comedy (*Chicago*) and has been the scene of any number of Hollywood films. All of which may seem especially ironic if you consider that nobody really knows whether the Indian word *checagou* means "great and powerful," "wild onion," or "skunk." This long-standing linguistic controversy did not affect the songsters who created that legendary tribute to "Chicago, Chicago, that toddling town."

Chicago spreads along 29 miles of carefully groomed lakeshore. Respecting Lake Michigan, the people of Chicago have been careful not to destroy the property near the water with heavy manufacturing or industry. The lake is a source of water as well as a port of entry for steamships and freighters coming from Europe via the St. Lawrence Seaway. More than 82 million tons of freight are handled by Chicago's ports every year. The city is also the world's largest railroad center. The Chicago grain market is the nation's most important, and O'Hare Airport, its busiest. Nuclear research and the electronics industry came of age here. In 1942, the world's first self-sustaining nuclear chain reaction was achieved at the University of Chicago. Half the radar equipment used during World War II was made here, too. Today, Chicago's Association of Commerce and Industry proudly lists an amazing assortment of "number ones" in addition to those the city is most noted for: convention business, steel production, export trade, furniture marketing, mail order business, tool and die making, metal products, industrial machinery, household appliances, and radio and TV manufacturing.

People from all over the world have come here to live. In 1890, 80% of all Chicago residents were immigrants or children of immigrants. There are more Poles in Chicago than in any Polish city except Warsaw as well as sizable contingents from Germany, Italy, Sweden, and Ireland. People talk about "ethnic Chicago," which means you can find neighborhoods that will make you think you're in a foreign country. Chinatown stretches along Wentworth Avenue. Enclaves of Ukrainians and Sicilians live in West Chicago. The Greeks can be found on South Halsted and West Lawrence; Irish and Lithuanians around Bridgeport and Marquette Park; Latinos in Pilsen; Italians in an area bounded by the University of Illinois at Chicago, the Eisen-

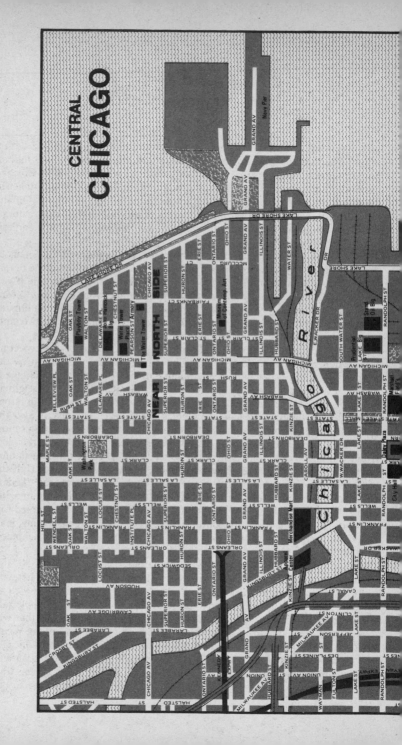

CENTRAL CHICAGO

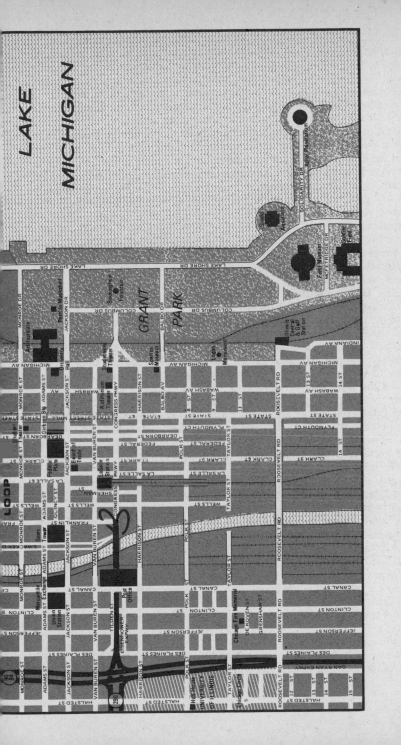

hower Expressway, the West Side Medical Center, and the black community. Polonia, which looks like a set for a 1930s Polish version of *West Side Story,* is mostly along Milwaukee. Nearly every nationality has a museum, and at least some of its customs have become public domain as well. There's a splendid array of inexpensive ethnic restaurants where you can get a whole meal for the price of an appetizer in a ritzier joint.

This cosmopolitan center had unprepossessing beginnings. Marquette and Joliet, the French explorers who provided the first record of the area, knew it as the Chicago Portage, one landmark on their route to the Chicago River from the Mississippi. A trading post was established in 1679. In the 1812 Fort Dearborn Massacre, 53 people were killed by Indians. Eighteen years later, the first parcels of land were sold — $40 to $60 per 15,000-square-foot plot. The city, incorporated in 1837, began to look as if it might amount to something when the Union Pacific Railroad connected it to San Francisco in 1869; two years later, on October 8, 1871, it was in ashes. Burning at the rate of 65 acres per hour ($125,000 damage per minute) and aided by a furious southwest wind, the Great Fire melted 15,000 water service pipes and 370 water meters, took 250 lives, left 90,000 homeless, and left 1,688 acres in rubble. The total damage was estimated at $196 million.

Like San Francisco after its earthquake, Chicago simply began to rebuild. And in the process, in the course of the following 50 years, a new urban architecture was born. Building quickly and furiously upon 4 square miles of charcoal, and abetted by simple clients whose aesthetics derived from their interests in the profits to be gained from efficient buildings rather than the glory to be garnered from neoclassical palaces, the Chicago architects *invented* the skyscraper; Frank Lloyd Wright pioneered the ground-hugging, prairie-style houses that became the prototypes for the suburban, single-family dwelling units we know today. In 1909, architect Daniel Burnham laid out a plan for the city's parks. Today, 576 of them stretch across 6,740 acres, not to mention 17 miles of clean public beaches and 35,350 acres of trail-crossed forest preserve on the outskirts.

The beaches are still clean and the forest acreage still pretty much unspoiled — a credit to the city planners who have, over the years, managed to keep Chicago alive and vibrant even as other downtown areas around the country have declined. While buildings elsewhere were being pulled down to make way for parking lots, Chicago was getting a handful of skyscrapers surrounded by pedestrian plazas studded with magnificent pieces of sculpture by Alexander Calder, Marc Chagall, Pablo Picasso, Claes Oldenburg, Joan Miró, and others. Lively lunchtime programs keep the plazas thronged with sightseers and Loop office workers alike in the summer.

In the same vein is the renovation of the venerable Marquette Building and the completion of the federally and city funded $17 million modernization of the State Street shopping area. So if you haven't seen Chicago for a while, you're likely to be astounded. Cars have been banned and buses only are permitted on State Street — what's left of it. Sidewalks have been widened to nearly 50 feet and covered with hexagonal, battleship-gray paving blocks; open-air cafés have sprouted; and modern bus stops, subway entrances, light poles, and newsstands have been constructed of Cor-Ten steel.

As part of the general facelifting, even Carson Pirie Scott, the turn-of-the-century department store designed by the celebrated Louis Sullivan, has restored its interior to match the Rococo splendor of its well-cared-for facade. Chicago has also been experiencing an architectural renaissance with the construction of major new office buildings, such as One Park Place, 333 Wacker Drive, One Magnificent Mile, and Helmut Jahn's State of Illinois Building.

If Chicago's modern face has improved with age, the same cannot be said of local politics. The successors to Mayor Richard Daley have not been able to maintain Chicago's old reputation as "the city that works," and municipal discord has become much more the order of the day. The 1983 mayoral election was a good example of the current roiling state of Chicago politics. The race was a close one, with the city sharply divided over the two candidates. After his election, Mayor Harold Washington called for unity and good will, though each has been in notably short supply as the mayor and City Council have continually battled over issues both small and significant. With another mayoral battle looming, it's hard to imagine Chicago's traditionally fractious political minorities and ethnic groups coming together behind a single banner.

Still, Chicago is quite a city, even if you consider just the ritzy Gold Coast and all those magnificent apartment buildings along the shore of Lake Michigan; the concert and lecture programs at the University of Chicago; the program of choral works at the neo-Gothic Rockefeller Chapel; the Rush Street bars; the Magnificent Mile — broad, shop- and gallery-lined Michigan Avenue. There are the Chicago Symphony Orchestra, the Lyric Opera, and the Art Institute, which has a world-famous collection of Impressionist and post-Impressionist paintings. You can enjoy jazz and blues till the wee hours of the morning. And if it's the kind of place that makes you want to sing — well, you won't be the first.

CHICAGO AT-A-GLANCE

SEEING THE CITY: The 110-story Sears Tower maintains a Skydeck on the 103rd floor. Open daily. Admission charge. Wacker and Adams sts. (875-9696). For a view from the north, visit the John Hancock Building (fifth largest in the world), fondly nicknamed "Big John." On the 95th floor are a bar and restaurant. Open daily. Admission charge. 875 Michigan Ave. (751-3681). For a river view, Wendella Sightseeing takes you by boat on the Chicago River and into Lake Michigan. Daily, mid-April through the first week in October. Admission charge. 400 N Michigan Ave. (337-1446). For an enjoyable, informative custom tour of Chicago (individuals or groups), contact Charlotte Kirshbaum, 399 Fullerton, Chicago 60614 (477-6509).

SPECIAL PLACES: A sophisticated public transport system makes it easy to negotiate Chicago's streets. You can explore the Loop, the lakefront, and suburbs by El train, subway, and bus. Culture buses take you to the art, science, and ethnic museums on Sundays and holidays during the summer.

THE LOOP

The Loop generally refers to Chicago's business district, which is encircled by the elevated train known as the El.

The ArchiCenter – The Exhibition Gallery, opened in 1982, has changing shows that feature points of interest in Chicago. Guided walking tours of the Loop (and other neighborhoods) daily, May-November; Tuesdays, Thursdays, and weekends the rest of the year. Chicago Highlights bus tours, Saturdays. Admission charge for tours. 330 S Dearborn, 1st floor (922-3431).

Art Institute of Chicago – Founded as an art school in 1879, the Art Institute houses an outstanding collection of Impressionist and post-Impressionist paintings, Japanese prints, Chinese sculpture and bronzes, and Old Masters. In the new Columbus Drive Addition, you can see some stained-glass windows by Chagall and the reconstructed trading room of the old Chicago Stock Exchange. Open daily. Admission charge; free Tuesdays. Michigan Ave. at Adams St. (443-3500 for recorded information or 443-3600).

Chicago Board of Trade – The largest grain exchange in the world. Stand in the visitors gallery and watch traders gesticulating on the floor, runners in colored jackets delivering orders, and an electronic record of all the trades displayed overhead. A new trading floor has been built to accommodate expanding markets. Open weekdays, 9 AM to 2 PM. Free. Jackson at La Salle St. (435-3590).

Chicago Mercantile Exchange and International Monetary Market – The show is much the same, only here you can sit down. Trading here does not stop suddenly. Each commodity has its own opening and closing time. Open weekdays, 8 AM to 3:15 PM. Free. 444 W Jackson (930-8249).

Marshall Field's – Chicago's most famous department store. When it was built in 1892 — before electric lighting was common — it was designed in sections, with shopping areas on balconies overlooking a skylit central courtyard. Later, the skylights were covered, one by a vivid blue and gold Louis Tiffany mosaic you can see by entering on the corner of Washington and State sts. *The Crystal Palace,* on the 3rd floor, serves unbelievable ice cream sundaes. Frango mint ice cream (a subtle mix of coffee, chocolate, malt, and mint) is a tradition. Open Mondays to Saturdays and the first Sunday of every month. Wabash, State, Randolph, and Washington sts. (781-1000).

NEAR SOUTH SIDE

Adler Planetarium – Exhibitions on everything from surveying and navigation instruments to modern space exploration devices, plus a real moon rock and an antique instrument collection that is one of the three best in the world — the best in the Western Hemisphere. You can see it all before or after the sky shows, which are what most people come for. There are five in all. Open daily. Free; admission charge to the sky shows. 1300 S Lake Shore Dr. on Museum Point (322-0304).

Field Museum of Natural History – Of the endless exhibitions on anthropology, ecology, botany, zoology, and geology, the most famous is the pair of fighting elephants in the Main Hall. Other standouts include the whole of Anniversary Hall, which explores the reasons for a natural history museum; the hands-on Place for Wonder, where youngsters can touch a dinosaur fish skeleton and try on ethnic masks; the Plants of the World hall with reproductions of about 500 plants from around the globe; the renovated Gem Hall; the full-scale model of a Pawnee earth lodge, where there are daily programs on Indian life; a display of prehistoric Egyptian tomb chapels; and an exhibition, Maritime Peoples of the Northwest Coast. The Hall of Chinese Jade and the display of Japanese lacquerware are also outstanding. Open daily. Admission charge; free on Thursdays. S Lake Shore Dr. at Roosevelt Rd. (922-9410).

Shedd Aquarium – The largest aquarium in the world, this one has 206 fish tanks and a collection of over 5,000 specimens: sturgeon from Russia, Bahamian angelfish, Australian lungfish, and a coral reef where divers feed the fish several times a day. Closed Christmas and New Year's. Admission charge; free on Thursdays. On Museum Point at 1200 Lake Shore Dr. (939-2426).

NEAR NORTH SIDE

Chicago Academy of Sciences – Particularly lively exhibitions on the natural history of the Great Lakes area, especially the reconstruction of a 350-million-year-old forest that stood on Chicago's present site, complete with humming insects and carnivorous dragonflies. There are also a "walk-through" cave and canyon. Open daily. Admission charge; free on Mondays. In Lincoln Park at 2001 N Clark St. (549-0606).

Chicago Historical Society – Pioneer crafts demonstrations, an outstanding collection of President Lincoln's belongings, and a Civil War slide show make this one of Chicago's most fascinating museums. New galleries focus on the city's beginnings and explore 19th-century American life through furniture and decorative objects. Open daily. Admission charge; free on Mondays. Clark St. and North Ave. (642-4600).

International College of Surgeons Hall of Fame – Full of medical curiosities: old examining tables, artificial limbs, an amputation set from the Revolution, a "bone crusher" used for correcting bow legs between 1918 and 1950(!). Finally, there's a fascinating display of prayers and oaths taken by doctors in different countries. Closed Mondays. Free. 1524 N Lake Shore Dr. (642-3555).

Lincoln Park Conservatory – Changing floral displays and a magnificent permanent collection that includes orchids, a 50-foot fiddle-leaf rubber tree from Africa with giant leaves, fig trees, and more ferns than you could ever imagine. Open daily. Free. In Lincoln Park, Stockton Dr. at Fullerton (294-4770).

Lincoln Park Zoo – The best thing about this zoo is that it has the largest group of great apes in captivity, now in a new Great Ape House (the rest of the zoo is undergoing extensive remodeling as well). There are, of course, the standard houses of monkey, tiger, lion, bear, and bison, plus the zoo's popular farm. Open daily. Free. In Lincoln Park at 100 W Webster (294-4660).

Museum of Contemporary Art – This small museum has always offered lively changing exhibitions, both retrospectives of the work of contemporary artists and surveys of 20th-century art movements and avant-garde phenomena; but only since a recent expansion has there been space enough to show off any appreciable portion of the fine permanent collection. The new area also features shows by Chicago artists, symposia, poetry readings, and other special events. Closed Mondays. Admission charge. 237 E Ontario (280-2660).

The Water Tower – This landmark, the sole survivor of the Great Fire of 1871, now serves as a visitors center. Open daily except holidays. N Michigan and Chicago aves.

Water Tower Place – This incredible, vertical shopping mall gets busier and better every year. Asymmetrical glass-enclosed elevators shoot up through an eight-story atrium, past shops selling dresses, books, gift items plus restaurants and a movie theater. Branches of *Marshall Field, FAO Schwarz,* and *Lord & Taylor* are here, along with the lovely *Ritz-Carlton Hotel,* stretching 22 stories above its 12th-floor lobby in the tower. Its skylit *Greenhouse Café* is great for tea or cocktails after a hard day of shopping. Michigan Ave. at Pearson St.

NORTH SIDE

Graceland Cemetery – Buried here are hotel barons, steel magnates, architects Louis Sullivan and Daniel Burnham — enshrined by tombs and miniature temples, and overlooking islands, lakes, hills, and views. A photographer killed while recording the controversial demolition of Sullivan's celebrated Chicago Stock Exchange is buried in a direct line with the grave of Sullivan himself. Guidebooks can be obtained from the gatekeepers. Open daily. Free. 4001 N Clark St. (525-1105).

SOUTH SIDE

Museum of Science and Industry – Some 2,000 displays explain the principles of science in such a lively way that the museum is Chicago's number one attraction. Longtime favorites: Colleen Moore's fairy-tale castle of a dollhouse with real diamond "crystal" chandeliers, the cunning Sears circus exhibition, a working coal mine, a walk-through human heart, and a captured German submarine. Open daily, but a madhouse on Saturdays and Sundays. Free. S Lake Shore Dr. at 57th St. (684-1414).

Pullman Community – Founded by George Pullman in 1880 as the nation's first company town, this early example of comprehensive urban planning is now a city, state, and national landmark. Walking tours conducted on the first Sunday of the month from May through October give you the story in detail; at other times you can find the Greenstone Church and other important sites on maps available at the *Florence Hotel,* a Pullman-era structure that serves as a visitors center of sorts (and provides lunch on weekdays, breakfast and lunch on Saturdays, and brunch on Sundays). A number of the many privately owned row houses are shown on special house tours held annually on the second weekend in October. West of the Calumet Expy. between 104th and 115th sts. (785-8181).

WEST

Garfield Park Conservatory – Here are 4½ acres under glass. The Palm House alone is 250 feet long, 85 feet wide, and 60 feet high; it looks like the tropics. There's a fernery luxuriant with greenery, mosses, and pools of water lilies. The cactus house has 85 genera, 400 species. At Christmas, poinsettias bloom; in spring, azaleas and camellias; at Easter, lilies and bulb plants; and in November, mums. Open daily. Free. 300 N Central Park Blvd. (533-1281).

OUTSKIRTS

Brookfield Zoo – Some 200 acres divided by moats and natural-looking barriers make this one of the most modern zoos in the country. There are special woods for wolves, a bison prairie, a replica of the Sahara, and a dolphin show. Olga the Walrus languishes in a pool. The new Tropic World features South American, Asian, and African birds, primates, and other animals. Open daily. Admission charge; free Tuesdays. 1st Ave. at 31st St. in Brookfield, 15 miles west of the Loop (242-2630).

Marriott's Great America – An extravagant roller coaster and a double-tiered carousel are the highlights of a theme park full of rides, some wild, some tame. Musical shows are performed throughout the season, and there's a special giant participatory play area for kids. It is also home to the world's largest motion picture experience. Open daily Memorial Day through Labor Day, weekends in May and from September to mid-October. Admission charge. I-94 at Rte. 132 in Gurnee (249-2020).

Lizzadro Museum of Lapidary Art – The collection of semiprecious stones and lapidary art is one of the most extensive in the US. About 150 exhibitions show off cameos, jade carvings, minerals, and fossils. Closed Mondays. Admission charge; free Fridays. 220 Cottage Hill, Elmhurst (833-1616).

Oak Park – Twenty-five buildings in this suburb, most of them remarkably contemporary looking, show the development of Frank Lloyd Wright's architectural style. The architect's residence/workshop and Unity Temple are open to the public, and there are daily tours (except on holidays). Admission charge. Edgar Rice Burroughs's and Ernest Hemingway's homes are here, too, along with numerous gingerbread and turreted Queen Anne palaces. The Oak Park Tour Center, based in the Frank Lloyd Wright Home and Studio, operates most area walking tours as well as a visitors center at 158

N Forest, where you can see photo exhibitions and take in an orientation program. At the Wright Plus Festival, the third Saturday in May, ten private homes are open to the public. For more information, phone 848-1978.

■**EXTRA SPECIAL:** You don't have to go very far from downtown to reach the *North Shore suburbs.* Follow US 41 or I-94 north. US 41 takes you through Lake Forest, an exquisite residential area, and Lake Bluff, site of the Great Lakes Naval Station. In Waukegan, *Mathon's Seafood Restaurant* has been delighting crusta-cean addicts since before World War II; two blocks east of Sheridan Rd. near the lake on Mathon Dr. (closed Mondays; 662-3610). Heading inland from Waukegan on Rte. 120 will take you directly to lake country, past Gages Lake and Brae Loch golf course, Grays Lake, and Round Lake where Rte. 120 becomes Rte. 134, continuing on to Long Lake, Duck Lake, and the three large lakes — Fox, Pis-takee, and Grass, near the Wisconsin border. All of these lakes offer water sports, fishing, golf, and tennis. On the northern border with Wisconsin, the 4,900-acre Chain O'Lakes State Park has campsites and boat rental facilities. Pick up Wilson Rd. north at Long Lake, then take Rte. 132 past Fox Lake. This will take you to US 12, which runs to Spring Grove and the state park (587-5512).

SOURCES AND RESOURCES

TOURIST INFORMATION: The Chicago Convention and Tourism Bureau, in the historic Water Tower at Michigan and Chicago aves. (225-5000), publishes a downtown map that pinpoints major attractions and hotels. The Chicago Visitor Eventline gives taped information on theater, sports, and special events (225-2323). Also get copies of the Chicago Transit Authority brochures: *The Chicago Street Directory,* which locates streets by their distance from State or Madison; the *CTA Route Map* of bus, subway, and El routes; and the *CTA Downtown Transit Map.* These are available at El stations, subway stations, libraries. For details, contact the Illinois Travel Information Center, 208 N Michigan Ave. (793-2094).

The best guidebook is *Chicago Magazine's Guide to Chicago* (Contemporary Books; $8.95), an insider's look at the city for residents and visitors alike. For self-guided walking tours, see Ira J. Bach's architecturally oriented *Chicago on Foot* (Rand McNally; $7.95).

Local Coverage – *Sun-Times,* morning daily; *Tribune,* morning daily; *Reader,* weekly; *Chicago* magazine, monthly.

Food – *The New Good (But Cheap) Chicago Restaurant Book* by Jill and Ron Rohde (Swallow; $2.95) and *Chicago* magazine's section of restaurant reviews.

Area Code – All telephone numbers are in the 312 area code unless otherwise indicated.

CLIMATE AND CLOTHES: They don't call it the Windy City for nothing. Fierce winter winds can knock you down, and wind-chill factors occasion-ally measure 47° below zero! The optimal visiting season is autumn, when temperatures are in the 60s and 50s; second best is spring. Summers are muggy, but the temperatures don't usually get higher than the 80s.

GETTING AROUND: Airport – O'Hare International Airport is about 25 miles west of the Loop and, depending on traffic, a 20- to 60-minute ride by cab; the fare should run about $25. Continental Air Transport (454-7800) charges $6.75 for its bus service to the airport from 24 city locations (includ-ing all the major hotels). The trip takes almost an hour, and buses run approximately every 30 minutes. Ask your hotel concierge for Continental's return schedule. Chicago Transit Authority (836-7000; 800 972-7000) O'Hare Line trains run from several downtown and North Side spots to O'Hare's main terminal in approximately 35 minutes; the fare is 90¢.

Midway Airport, which handles an increasing volume of domestic traffic, is 8 miles south of the Loop. A taxi ride to Midway from the Loop will take from 10 to 20 minutes and cost about $10. The No. 62 Archer Express bus (heading south) can be picked up from any stop along State St. in the Loop; transfer at Cicero Ave. to any southbound bus — they stop inside the airport. This ride takes about 30 minutes and costs $1. Continental Air Transport also provides bus service to the airport from the *Palmer House, Hyatt Regency,* and *Westin* hotels; schedules vary according to flights. The run to the airport takes about 40 minutes, and the cost is $6.

Bus, Subway, and El – Chicago Transit Authority operates bus, subway, and El services. For information, call 836-7000. You can take a do-it-yourself tour on public transport. One good round trip by public transportation starts in the Loop, goes through Lincoln Park, past the Historical Society, and into New Town on the No. 151 bus. When you've ridden enough, get off and catch the same bus going in the opposite direction. On Sundays and holidays, there is also a Culture Bus, which stops at the Art Institute, the Field Museum, the Shedd Aquarium, the Adler Planetarium, the Museum of Science and Industry, the Oriental Institute, and the DuSable Museum of African-American History. It operates every half-hour from 11 AM to 5 PM, June through August.

Taxi – Cabs can be hailed in the street or picked up from stands in front of the major hotels. You can also phone one of Chicago's taxi services: Yellow and Checker Cabs (829-4222); Flash Cab (561-1444); American United (248-7600).

Car Rental – All major national firms are represented.

 MUSEUMS: Chicago is paradise if you like going to museums. Those described in *Special Places* have plenty of company, including the following:
The Balzekas Museum of Lithuanian Culture – 4012 S Archer (847-2441)

Chicago Architecture Foundation, Glessner House – 1800 S Prairie (326-1393)
DuSable Museum of African-American History – in Washington Park, at 740 E 56th Pl. (947-0600)
Jane Addams's Hull House – A National Historic Landmark; Halsted St. at Polk (996-2793)
Oriental Institute at University of Chicago – 1155 E 58th at University (962-9521)
Polish Museum of America – 984 Milwaukee Ave. (384-3352)
Spertus Museum of Judaica – 618 S Michigan Ave. (922-9012)
The Telephony Museum – 225 W Randolph (727-2994)
Ukrainian Institute of Modern Art – 2320 W Chicago (227-5522)

Great sculpture and art can also be seen in the plazas of downtown skyscrapers. Bertoia's spellbinding *Sounding Sculpture,* at the Standard Oil Building, 200 E Randolph; *Flamingo,* a stabile by Alexander Calder, at Federal Center Plaza, Adams and Dearborn; Calder's gaily-colored mobile *Universe,* in the Sears Tower lobby, Wacker and Adams; sculptor Claes Oldenburg's 101-foot-high baseball bat, *Batcolumn,* at 600 W Madison; Chagall's *Four Seasons* mosaic, at First National Plaza, Monroe and Dearborn. (If you're there at noon, you might catch a free concert.) *Chicago's Picasso* (its formal title because no one could agree on a name), a giant sculpture, is at the Richard J. Daley Plaza, on Washington and Clark near the Chagall. (There are also free concerts at the plaza every weekday, weather permitting.) Joan Miró's *Chicago* sculpture mural is across the street from Daley Plaza. Buckingham Fountain, a Chicago landmark in Grant Park at Congress Parkway, is illuminated from May to September.

MAJOR COLLEGES AND UNIVERSITIES: Although far too big to be called a college town, Chicago has many fine universities. The University of Chicago, known for its economics and social science departments, has its main entrance at 5801 S Ellis Ave. (753-1234); University of Illinois at Chicago, at 601 S Morgan (996-3000); Illinois Institute of Technology, its Mies van der Rohe campus at 3300 S Federal (567-3000); Loyola University, at 820 N Michigan (670-3000) and 6525 Sheridan Rd. (274-3000); De Paul University, 25 E Jackson and in Lincoln Park at 2323 N Seminary (321-8000); Northwestern University at Chicago Ave. and Lake Shore Dr. (649-8649) and in Evanston (492-3741); Roosevelt University, 430 S Michigan Ave. (341-3500); Lake Forest College, Sheridan Rd., Lake Forest (234-3100).

SPECIAL EVENTS: Summertime is festival time. In June, the *Old Town Art Fair* is held in Lincoln Park; in July, sailboats race on Lake Michigan; and in August, the *Western Open Golf Tournament* is played at Butler National Golf Club in Oakbrook. The *Arlington Million,* the world's richest thoroughbred race, is held the last week of August at Arlington Park. The *Ravinia Festival,* a series of outdoor concerts by the Chicago Symphony Orchestra and other headliners, runs throughout the summer in Highland Park (728-4642). The first week in September brings a jazz festival to the Grant Park Bandshell (free).

SPORTS AND FITNESS: Plenty of major league action in town.
    Baseball – The *White Sox* play at Comiskey Park, 35th and Shields, off the Dan Ryan Expy. (924-1000). The *Cubs* play at Wrigley Field, Addison and Clark (281-5050).
Basketball – The NBA *Bulls,* 1800 W Madison (346-1122).
Bicycling – Chicago has a glorious bike path along the shore of Lake Michigan, running from the Loop to Evanston — about 11 miles. You can rent bikes in summer from the concession at Lincoln Park.
Fishing – After work, people flock to the rocks along the shore, casting nets for smelt. The rocks around Northwestern University at Evanston are especially popular. There's also an artificial island, attainable by footbridge, around Northwestern.
Fitness Centers – Body Elite, 445 W Erie (664-5710), and Combined Fitness Centre, 1235 N La Salle (787-8400), both allow nonmembers for a fee.
Football – The NFL *Bears* (663-5100) play at Soldier Field in Grant Park.
Golf – Chicago has 10 golf courses, some along the lakeshore. The most accessible municipal course is Waveland in Lincoln Park. The Chicago Park District offers golf instruction. For information, call 294-2274.
Hiking – Windy City Grotto, the Chicago Chapter of the National Speleological Society, organizes frequent field trips to cave country in southern Indiana and Missouri. For information, contact Windy City Speleonews, c/o Bill Mixon, 5035 N South Drexel, Chicago 60615. Chicago Mountaineering Club organizes weekend expeditions and teaches safe climbing techniques. They meet at the Field Museum every second Monday. For information, write to PO Box 1025, Chicago 60690. Sierra Club, 53 W Jackson (431-0158), also organizes outings.
Hockey – The NHL *Black Hawks* play in Chicago Stadium September through April (733-5300).
Horse Racing – Horses race at four tracks in the Chicago area:

Arlington Park, Euclid Ave. and Wilke Rd., Arlington Heights (255-4300)
Hawthorne, 3501 S Laramie, Cicero (652-9400)
Maywood Park, North and 5th aves., Maywood (343-4800)
Sportsman's Park, 3301 S Laramie, Cicero (242-1121)

Jogging – Run along Lake Shore Drive to Lincoln Park; there is a 5-mile track inside the park. Or simply do as many Chicagoans do and jog along the lakefront, accessible via numerous pedestrian walkways.

Polo – Summers at the Oak Brook Polo Club, 1000 Oak Brook Rd., Oak Brook (654-3060); during winter you can play indoors at the Chicago Armory, Chicago Ave. and Fairbanks.

Sailing – Lake Michigan offers superb sailing, but as experienced sailors can tell you, the lake is deceptive. Storms of up to 40 knots can blow in suddenly. Check with the Coast Guard before going out (219 949-7440). You can rent boats and take sailing lessons from City Sailors (975-0044). There are a few marinas between the Loop and Evanston; others, along suburban shores. Highland Park is one of the most popular city marinas.

Skiing – There are more than 50 ski clubs in the Chicago area. For information, contact the Chicago Metro Ski Council, PO Box 7926, Chicago 60680 (346-1268).

Swimming – Beaches line the shore of Lake Michigan. Those just to the north of the Loop off Lake Shore Drive are the most popular, and often the most crowded. Oak Street Beach along the "Gold Coast" is the most fashionable beach. If you go farther north, you'll find fewer people. The Chicago Park District offers swimming lessons at some of the 72 city pools. The best are at Wells Park and Gill Park. For information, call 294-2333.

Tennis – The city has 620 outdoor municipal courts. The best are at Randolph and Lake Shore Drive, just east of the Loop (294-4792). For other tennis information, call 294-2314.

THEATERS: For schedules and ticket information, consult the publications noted above or visit the HOT TIX booth at State St. and Madison (977-1755), where you can also purchase theater tickets at half price on the day of the performance. Many Broadway shows play Chicago before heading to the Big Apple. The main Chicago theaters are: *Shubert,* 22 W Monroe (977-1700); *Studebaker,* 418 S Michigan (435-0700); *Civic,* 20 N Wacker Dr. (346-0270); *Goodman,* 200 S Columbus Dr. (443-3800); *Blackstone Theater,* 60 E Balbo (977-1700); and the *Apollo Theater Center,* 2540 N Lincoln (935-6100).

Among Chicago's thriving Off-Loop theaters are *Organic Theater,* 3319 N Clark (327-5588); the *Goodman Studio Theater,* 200 S Columbus (443-3800), where award-winning playwright David Mamet is associate artistic director; *Victory Gardens Theater,* 2257 N Lincoln (549-5788), which is dedicated to the promotion of Chicago playwrights; *Steppenwolf Theater,* 2851 N Halsted (472-4141); *Wisdom Bridge Theater,* 1559 W Howard (743-6442); and *The Body Politic Theater,* 2261 N Lincoln (871-3000).

There are several good dinner theaters as well: *Martinique Drury Lane,* 2500 W 95th, Evergreen Park (779-4000); *Pheasant Run Theater,* Pheasant Run Lodge, Rte. 64, St. Charles (584-1454); and the *Candlelight Playhouse,* 5620 S Harlem Ave. in Summit, the first dinner theater in the country (496-3000).

MUSIC: Chicago isn't the musical desert that the Midwest is generally thought to be. Good music (and lots of it) can be heard all over the place. The world-renowned *Chicago Symphony Orchestra* plays Orchestra Hall, 220 S Michigan, in winter (435-8111), and Ravinia Park in Highland Park, March to October (433-8800). Outdoor concerts are also played in the new Petrillo Musicshell, behind the Art Institute between Jackson and Monroe on Columbus Dr. (294-2420). The *Lyric Opera of Chicago* performs at Civic Opera House, 20 N Wacker (332-2244). The Auditorium Theatre, a landmark designed by Louis Sullivan at 70 E Congress (922-2110), is another major hall.

NIGHTCLUBS AND NIGHTLIFE: You can take in Chicago's blues, folk, and jazz scene in informal pubs, cafés, and taverns. Among them are *Park West,* 322 W Armitage (929-5959); *B.L.U.E.S.,* 2519 N Halsted (528-1012); *Holsteins,* 2464 N Lincoln (327-3331); *Old Town School of Folk Music,* 909 W Armitage (525-7793); *The Vic,* 3145 N Sheffield (472-0366); and *Byfields,* in the *Ambassador East Hotel,* 1301 N State Pkwy. (787-6433). *The Second City* revue ensemble performs original, improvisational, and satirical skits, 1616 N Wells (337-3992).

SINS: Great metropolis that it is, Chicago nurtures sin in all its forms. *Pride?* Listen to Chicagoans compare their Art Institute, their museums, their Magnificent Mile, and their sports teams (especially the football *Bears* and the baseball *Cubs*) to those of any other city in the country. *Anger?* Suggest to the same people that Chicago might just still be the Second City (second, that is, to New York).

For a real pizza *glutton's* special — thickly crusted and slathered with toppings — check out *Gino's* or *Uno's.* Closet gluttons perch daintily on the wrought-iron ice cream chairs in Marshall Field's *Crystal Palace* on the third floor and order the giant special sundaes, which are so enormous that all but the very tallest ice cream freak has to bring the spoon down to his mouth instead of up.

LOCAL SERVICES: Babysitting – Check at your hotel for reliable services.

Business Services – Typing Unlimited, 400 N Michigan Ave. (321-0516)

Mechanics – ARCO station, 24-hour service, 665 N Dearborn (787-8164)

BEST IN TOWN

CHECKING IN: There are quite a number of interesting hotels in Chicago, varying in style from the intimate clubbiness of the *Tremont* and *Whitehall* to the supermodernity of the *Ritz-Carlton.* Unless otherwise noted, all listed here have at least one restaurant; your choice of eating places increases with the price of your room and the size of the hotel. Big hotels have shops, meeting places, nightly entertainment. Rates in Chicago are higher than in most other midwestern cities: You'll pay $125 to $175 for doubles in expensive hotels; $70 to $100 in those classified as moderate; and only as low as about $40 in those listed as inexpensive. If money is no object, ask for a room with a view. "Near North Side" hotels put you close to New Town, Lincoln Park, and Water Tower Place; Loop locations (about ten minutes away by taxi) are convenient to businesses and the fine, old downtown department stores. For B&B accommodations, contact Bed and Breakfast Chicago, PO Box 14088, Chicago, IL 60614 (312 951-0085).

Ritz-Carlton – Contemporary and chic, this beautifully appointed 430-room luxury establishment, a member of the fine Four Seasons chain, rises 20 stories above its 12th-floor lobby. In the spectacular Water Tower Place shopping complex, the *Ritz* has all the accouterments of elegance, including a fine health club and skylit indoor swimming pool. A recent renovation has left it looking spiffier than ever. Near North Side. 160 E Pearson (312 266-1000). Expensive.

Ambassador East – Now part of the Dunfey chain, this lovely old hotel was recently renovated but hasn't lost an ounce of charm (some say it looks better than ever). Notable for the many celebrities who visit, the *Ambassador East* also houses the famous *Pump Room* restaurant, a Chicago institution whose entryway is lined with photos of famous guests, who always dine in Booth One. Convenient location in the Gold Coast area; close to Lincoln Park, Rush Street, and the Magnificent Mile of Michigan Avenue. (Not affiliated with the *Ambassador West,* across the street). 1301 N State Pkwy. (312 787-7200). Expensive.

The Whitehall – Small, devoted to detail, and known for its elegance and its careful, courteous service. Its excellent restaurant is open only to members and registered guests. 226 rooms. 105 E Delaware Pl. (312 944-6300). Expensive.

The Tremont – The paneled lobby, with its elaborate moldings and chandeliers, is more like a private sitting room than a public foyer. Rooms are quite comfortable, with traditional elegance. The hotel is also the home of *Cricket's,* one of Chicago's best restaurants (see *Eating Out*). 100 E Chestnut (312 751-1900 or 800 621-8133). Expensive.

Chicago Hilton and Towers – Some $180 million — the most ever spent on a hotel renovation — has transformed this 30-story landmark building into an elegant, modern property. The former *Conrad Hilton* features 1,620 rooms, the most lavish of which is the 2-story Conrad Hilton Suite for $4,000 *a night.* Restored to their 1927 grandeur are the Great Hall and the Versailles-inspired Grand Ballroom. New facilities include a Fun and Fitness Center with an indoor running track, sundeck, exercise equipment, saunas, and whirlpools; a computerized business center; a 2-story atrium lounge, *Lakeside Green,* with views of Grant Park. *Buckingham's* is the fine dining room; the 24-hour café, *Pavilion,* features hot and cold buffets; *Kitty O'Shea's* is an Irish entertainment tavern, and *Fast Lane Deli* serves sandwiches and salads. There's also a 140,000-square-foot convention center, a parking garage, and 21 barrier-free rooms. 720 S Michigan Ave. (312 922-4400). Expensive.

Mayfair Regent – Quite a departure from the new high-rise hotels opening these days, the recently renovated *Mayfair* (formerly the *Lake Shore Drive Hotel*) is small enough to offer the ultimate in comfort and style — the ratio of employees to guests is 1 to 1. Dinner here is quite an elegant affair: The rooftop *Ciel Bleu* offers classic French cuisine and romantic views of Lake Michigan; *The Palm,* on the ground floor, has steaks as prime as those served by its New York counterpart. 181 E Lake Shore Dr. (312 787-8500 or 800 621-8135). Expensive.

The Westin Hotel, Chicago – Built in 1963, this growing deluxe near North Side hotel has a 754 rooms and a health club with sauna and steam room. The *Chelsea* restaurant serves Continental fare and the *Lion Bar* is a popular spot that's generally crowded with businesspeople. Near the Drake and the Hancock Center. N Michigan Ave. at Delaware (312 943-7200). Expensive.

Hyatt Regency Chicago – Over 2,000 rooms in two ultra-modern towers. Conveniently located between the Loop and N Michigan Ave. Fine dining at *Truffles.* 151 E Wacker Dr. (312 565-1000). Expensive.

Palmer House – A busy, 1,800-room giant, this is another Chicago tradition. The sumptuous, recently restored *Empire Room* is a visual delight; open for lunch only. You can also dine here at the *Palmer Steak House* and *Trader Vic's.* In the Loop on the new State Street mall. Monroe St. between State and Wabash (312 726-7500). Expensive.

Park Hyatt – Small, with 255 elegant rooms and suites, and as convivial as it is convenient to N Michigan Ave. and the historic Water Tower. Recently renovated (formerly the *Water Tower Hyatt*). 800 N Michigan Ave. (312 280-2222). Expensive.

Drake Hotel – A 700-room institution, with a graciousness not often found in hotels these days. The *Cape Cod Room* is Chicago's finest seafood eatery (see *Eating Out*). Near North Side. N Michigan Ave. at Lake Shore Dr. and Walton Pl. (312 787-2200). Expensive.

Sheraton-Plaza – This 346-room gem, with 96 suites, recently was redecorated. Just off Michigan Avenue. 160 E Huron St. (312 787-2900). Expensive

Hyatt Regency O'Hare – Ideal for a comfortable overnight stop between planes. Health club. 1,150 rooms. South River Rd. exit off Kennedy Expy. (312 696-1234). Expensive.

Allerton – Close to museums and shopping on Michigan Avenue, 10 minutes from the Loop. The 450-room *Allerton* is an economical but quite pleasant choice — and a steal in this location. 701 N Michigan Ave. (312 440-1500). Moderate.

The Bismarck – The *Walnut Room Restaurant* is a long-standing noontime tradition for Chicago politicos. There are 537 recently renovated rooms and some nice suites. 171 W Randolph at La Salle (312 236-0123). Moderate.

Richmont Hotel – Formerly the *Eastgate,* this property was completely overhauled and reopened in 1980 as a moderately priced alternative near the city's Magnificent Mile. There are 190 guest rooms, 2 meeting rooms, the *Café Richmont* lobby bar, and the *Rue Saint Clair,* which looks like a French bistro but serves American fare. 162 E Ontario St. (312 787-3580 or 800 621-8055). Moderate.

Holiday Inn City Centre – Architecturally more interesting than you might expect. Swimming pools and health club, indoor and outdoor tennis courts, racquetball, and free parking make this establishment's 500-odd rooms almost a bargain. 300 E Ohio (312 787-6100). Moderate.

Americana Congress – Not as large as the nearby *Palmer House* (1,000 rooms), this unit of the Best Western chain has a well-deserved reputation for personal attention. It also boasts a kosher kitchen and fine views of Lake Michigan and Grant Park. 520 S Michigan Ave. (312 427-3800). Moderate.

Holiday Inn Lake Shore – The best things about this 586-room *Holiday Inn* are its setting opposite the lake and Navy Pier and its relatively low rates, which are even more reasonable considering the outdoor pool. 644 N Lake Shore Dr. (312 943-9200). Moderate.

Holiday Inn of Elk Grove – Convenient to O'Hare. With 159 rooms and an outdoor pool, it's an economical choice for an overnight stop. Pets welcome. Transportation to the airport. 1000 Busse Rd. (312 437-6010). Moderate.

Avenue Motel – This budget establishment has only 78 rooms, and few amenities, but it's close to town. 1154 S Michigan Ave. (312 427-8200). Inexpensive.

Ohio House Motel – This 50-room property is centrally located, and the management provides a courtesy car to the Loop, daily from 8 AM to 4 PM. There's a coffee shop on the premises. Pets are welcome. 600 N La Salle St. at Ohio (312 943-6000). Inexpensive.

Grove Motel – An outdoor pool and low (for Chicago) prices make this 40-room motel a real find. Restaurant nearby. A half-hour drive from the Loop (longer in rush hour). 9110 Waukegan Rd., Morton Grove (312 966-0960). Inexpensive.

 EATING OUT: The city's restaurant business is booming, and some of the finest cooking in America can be found here. Expect to pay from $60 and up for two at those restaurants we've noted as expensive; between $40 and $60, for moderately priced meals; and under $40 at our inexpensive choices. Prices do not include drinks and wine, tips and taxes.

Le Perroquet – Subtle, sumptuous; undisputedly one of the best restaurants in the US. Expect a parade of wonders such as moules or a soufflé de crevettes Madras as hors d'oeuvres; salmon mousseline, venison filet, or quails as entrées; pastries to follow. Closed Sundays. Reservations necessary. American Express, Diners Club, and Carte Blanche. 70 E Walton (944-7990). Expensive.

Cricket's – In the style of the "21" Club in New York, with red-checkered table-cloths, bare floors, low ceilings, and walls festooned with corporate memorabilia, and a menu that includes chicken hash Mornay and various daily specials. A very good choice for Sunday brunch. Reservations essential. Major credit cards. *Tremont Hotel*, 100 E Chestnut (280-2100). Expensive.

Palm – Owned by the same people who run the well-known New York restaurants called *Palm* and *Palm, Too*, this eatery has a similar décor of sawdust-covered floors and walls hung with drawings of famous patrons. Also like its East Coast counterpart, the kitchen here specializes in producing great steaks and lobster. Closed Sundays. Reservations necessary. Major credit cards. *Mayfair Regent Hotel*, 181 E Lake Shore (944-0135). Expensive.

Le Français – One of the country's foremost French restaurants, it's well worth the 45-minute drive from Chicago. The surroundings are elegant, the service exceptional, and the cuisine, prepared by the French chef-owner Jean Banchet, remarkable. Among the specialties are *navarin de homard aux petites légumes* (lobster with sautéed fresh vegetables) and *aiguillette de canard à la rouennaise* (roast duckling in red wine sauce with duck and goose liver). Closed Mondays. Reservations essential. Major credit cards. 269 S Milwaukee, Wheeling, IL; take Kennedy Expy. to Rte. 294 north, Willow exit (541-7470). Expensive.

Doro's – Quite elegant North Italian cooking, much of it done at your table. Pasta made on the premises, superb veal, and four other categories of entrées, including grilled items, poultry, beef, and fish. Open daily for dinner. Reservations essential. Major credit cards. 871 N Rush St. (266-1414). Expensive.

La Cheminée – Rustic French, charming and small. Come here for great veal Florentine, steak au poivre, and duck à l'orange. The crabmeat-stuffed avocado and quiche Lorraine are perfect starters. Open daily for dinner. Reservations advised. Major credit cards. 1161 N Dearborn (642-6654). Expensive.

Biggs – In a restored Victorian mansion. The prix fixe menu changes every day, but the selection often includes beef Wellington, duck à l'orange, roast rack of lamb persillade, tenderloin tips sautéed with fresh mushrooms and served on wild rice. There's an extensive wine list. Open daily for dinner. Reservations necessary. Major credit cards. 1150 N Dearborn (787-0900). Expensive.

Jovan's – Prix fixe menus change daily depending on what's in the market; the cooking is taken very seriously. Pike mousse and quiche Lorraine are among the appetizers that appear frequently, along with interesting vegetables, dessert soufflés, and hand-dipped bonbons. Open weekdays for lunch; dinner daily except Sundays. Reservations required. American Express, Diners Club, and Carte Blanche. 1660 N La Salle (944-7766). Expensive.

95th – For food with a view, this is your best bet. Try the tournedos Rossini and lobster specialties. Open daily; lunch and dinner Saturdays; brunch and dinner Sundays. Reservations helpful. Major credit cards. 95th floor, John Hancock Center, 172 E Chestnut St. (787-9596). Expensive.

The Pump Room – A winning formula of fine cuisine, diligent service, and lovely decor have made the *Pump Room* a legend among Chicago restaurants. Continental dishes are the mainstays, but there are some nouvelle cuisine specialties; both are complemented by the restaurant's good wine list. Open daily. Reservations necessary. Major credit cards. 1301 N State Pkwy. (266-0360). Expensive.

Spiaggia – Expertly prepared North Italian cuisine — including unique pasta dishes, veal, and a grilled fish of the day — served in a beautiful setting. Open daily. Reservations advised. Major credit cards. 980 N Michigan (280-2750). Expensive.

The Bakery – Nearly every night you can get pork roast stuffed with Hungarian sausage, beef Wellington, roast duck with cherry sauce. Seasonal entrées include stuffed lamb, bouillabaisse, roast pheasant or goose. There's no menu; the waiters recite the night's choices. Closed Sundays and Mondays. Reservations required. Major credit cards. 2218 N Lincoln (472-6942). Expensive.

Ambria – Everything about this restaurant charms, from the comfortable setting to the menu's sophisticated variations on nouvelle cuisine. Calf's liver with cracked mustard seeds is a noteworthy entrée, and dinner might begin with a salad of sliced duck, pine nuts, and fresh pears with red currant dressing. Desserts are simply remarkable. There's also a *dégustation* dinner for four or more with samplings of many dishes. Closed Sundays. Reservations required. Major credit cards. 2300 N Lincoln Park W (472-5959). Expensive.

Nick's Fishmarket – The number of choices on the menu is bewildering, but the work of choosing is worth the effort. The cold appetizer assortment of shellfish is always a good bet, and try the pan-fried whole baby salmon or an abalone dish for an entrée. Closed Sundays. Reservations required. Major credit cards. First National Plaza, Monroe St. (621-0200). Expensive.

Printer's Row – Sophisticated American cuisine served in an elegant room. The hallmark vegetable and seafood pâtés are very good, and a roast breast of duck with corn crêpes is a standout entrée. Closed Sundays. Reservations advised. Major credit cards. 550 S Dearborn (461-0780). Expensive to moderate.

L'Escargot – Unpretentious and pleasant, with an emphasis on provincial French cooking, including a cassoulet — white beans, sausage, pork, and goose. There's always fresh fish and homemade pastries on the menu. Open daily. Reservations advised. Major credit cards. *Allerton Hotel,* 701 N Michigan (337-1717). Moderate.

Cape Cod Room – An institution. This seafood restaurant serves reliable fresh pompano, lobster, and other fish. Open daily. Reservations required. Major credit cards. *Drake Hotel,* 140 E Walton (787-2200). Moderate.

Chez Paul – Robert Hall McCormick's palatial mansion sets the scene for memorable meals of ris de veau Maréchal, salmon en croute beurre blanc, rognons de veau sautés Napoléon. Open weekdays for lunch; daily for dinner. Reservations essential. Major credit cards. 660 N Rush St. (944-6680). Moderate.

Lawry's The Prime Rib – The specialty here is prime ribs, served in three thicknesses with a big fresh salad with *Lawry's* special Famous French dressing. The salad is served with a chilled fork; the prime ribs, with Yorkshire pudding. And, of course, the seasoning salt that *Lawry's* made famous. Open daily; weekdays for lunch. Reservations suggested. Major credit cards. 100 E Ontario (787-5000). Moderate.

L'Épuisette – Small, with a good selection of seafood: turbot Véronique, crab in white wine and mushrooms, baked shrimp de Jonghe, red snapper Provençal. Dinner only; closed Mondays. Reservations advised. Major credit cards. 21 W Goethe St. (944-2288). Moderate.

Café Bohemia – Braised strips of African lion with Grand Marnier sauce, broiled antelope steak, and black bear stew are standard fare at this festive and comfortable place with paneled walls hung with stuffed moose and deer heads. Open weekdays; dinner only on Saturdays. Reservations accepted. Major credit cards. 138 S Clinton St. (782-1826). Moderate.

La Strada – An Italian restaurant with a reputation for its tableside preparation of such specialties as veal Forestiera, rich with mushrooms and artichokes in wine sauce. Other highlights include eggplant involtini and carpaccio. Closed Sundays. Major credit cards. 151 N Michigan (565-2200). Moderate.

Beau Thai – Lincoln Park's newest addition to the city's fine collection of Southeast Asian restaurants. Specialties include pad thai, a cold noodle dish; duck Beau Thai, cooked with cashews and vegetables; and sweet, creamy cold Thai coffee for dessert. Open daily. Reservations accepted on weekends only. Major credit cards. 2525 N Clark (348-6938). Moderate.

Hatsuhana – Delicious sushi and sashimi; tables as well as counter seating available. Open daily. Reservations advised. Major credit cards. 160 E Ontario (478-2486). Moderate.

Salvatore's – Diners at this handsome Italian restaurant may sit in a garden atrium or in the dining rooms — one of which is wood-paneled and the other decorated in classical Italian style. The menu features 14 kinds of homemade pasta and fresh fish specials that change daily, but the kitchen is most proud of its *castelle di Vitello* (roasted milk-fed veal) and *fettuccine alla Caroline* (green noodles with pine nuts, mushrooms, spinach, and cheese). Among the choices on the wine list are 114 varieties from Italy. Open daily. Reservations advised. Major credit cards. 525 W Arlington Pl. (528-1200). Moderate.

Szechwan House – The hot and sour soup and the crispy duck are just as appetizing as the chef's more unusual dishes, such as snails in spicy sauce and deep-fried ground shrimp wrapped in seaweed. Open daily. Reservations advised. Major credit cards. 600 N Michigan (642-3900). Moderate to inexpensive.

Carson's – Probably the best spareribs in the city. Salads with a creamy, anchovy-flavored dressing and tangy au gratin potatoes are the other lures. Don't dress up, for bibs (supplied) are essential. No reservations, so expect to wait for a table. Major credit cards. 612 N Wells St. (280-9200). Inexpensive.

Blackhawk – This Chicago institution is famous for its thick cuts of prime ribs, aged sirloins, and fresh Boston scrod — all served with a salad mixed right at your table. Good cheesecake. Usually crowded. Closed Sundays. Reservations advised. Major credit cards. 139 N Wabash (726-0100). Inexpensive.

Berghoff – Another Chicago tradition. Although the service is rushed, the meals are bountiful and the selection wide-ranging: ragout, schnitzel, steak, and seafood. Closed Sundays. Reservations accepted for groups of five or more. No credit cards. 17 W Adams (427-3170). Inexpensive.

Ed Debevic's – The latest creation of Rich Melman, king of Chicago restaurateurs — a 1950s diner that has crowds lining up outside. Burgers, chili, malts, fries, and a rollicking *American Graffiti* atmosphere. Open daily. No reservations or credit cards. 640 N Wells (664-1707). Inexpensive.

Greek Islands – A simple place where you can find thoughtfully prepared dishes such as gyros, squid, lamb, and fresh broiled red snapper. The decor isn't elegant, but the food is delicious. Open daily. Reservations are not necessary. Major credit cards. 200 S Halsted (782-9855). Inexpensive.

Febo's – A real "old neighborhood" restaurant where the North Italian cooking tastes like it came out of a family kitchen. Try the antipasto, followed by linguine Alfredo, cannelloni, tortellini, or chicken Alfredo in mushrooms and lemon-herb wine sauce. Closed Sundays. Reservations suggested. Major credit cards. 2501 S Western (523-0839). Inexpensive.

Jerome's – The room is warmly decorated and the service draws little complaint, but the food is the real attraction. In addition to a regular selection of meat, poultry, and fish, the kitchen turns out fresh bread and desserts and six to eight special dishes every day. Open daily. Reservations advised. Major credit cards. 2450 N Clark (327-2207). Inexpensive.

Chicago also has some interesting bistro-style restaurants. Try *Les Nomades,* 222 E Ontario St. (649-9010), or *Le Bastille,* 21 W Superior (787-2050).

CINCINNATI

Since most travelers seem to know little about Ohio's geography, it's worth stating that Cincinnati is not Cleveland. Cleveland is in the north, on Lake Erie. Cincinnati sits snugly in a basin of the north bank of the Ohio River, in the southwestern corner of the state, surrounded by tree-lined hills festooned with stately homes, on the border of Kentucky. Although resolutely businesslike and the headquarters of an unusually large number of well-known companies for a city its size (1.4 million people in the metropolitan area), Cincinnati does not consider itself as unredeemingly industrial as the cities of northern Ohio.

Originally called Losantiville, Cincinnati was founded in the 1780s and was renamed in honor of the Society of Cincinnati in 1790 by a member of that organization who happened to be passing through as the new governor of the Northwest Territory. "Losantiville!" he reportedly exclaimed. "What an awful name." The rest, as they say, is history.

Like river cities everywhere, Cincinnati has a lusty past. Soldiers were dispatched to protect its earliest settlers from the Indians, but the settlers soon came to fear the soldiers more than the Indians. William Henry Harrison visited not long before he became president and pronounced it "the most debauched place I ever saw." As late as 1901, Carrie Nation arrived on a temperance crusade, but failed to smash a single saloon window. "I would have dropped from exhaustion before I had gone a block," she told curious reporters. But, in succeeding years, seemliness somehow got the upper hand and lust was banished.

Longfellow called it the "Queen City of the West," and Winston Churchill said it was "the most beautiful of America's inland cities." In 1976, the *Saturday Review* called Cincinnati "one of the five most livable cities in the United States." Why the accolades? For one thing, Cincinnati's downtown is congenially vibrant, alive during the day and night. This is partly the result of substantial, continuing investment by the business community in an effort to stave off urban decay, the common enemy of cities. Leisure-conscious Cincinnati residents enjoy music, art, good food, and sports. Many are active volunteers on civic projects. In the center of town is 20th-century Fountain Square, which surrounds the majestic 19th-century Tyler-Davidson Fountain. Modern office buildings and ground-level shops line Fountain Square on the north and east. Across the street, Fountain Square South, one of the city's most ambitious private projects, is a new high-rise complex that has provided much-needed space for offices, hotels, and shops. The compact downtown area is easy to navigate. Because of its generally uncrowded streets and the 13-block-square Skywalk that connects many buildings, downtown Cincinnati can be easily explored on foot. Innumerable small restaurants, bars, and fast-food establishments exist to succor the footweary. Also within easy walk-

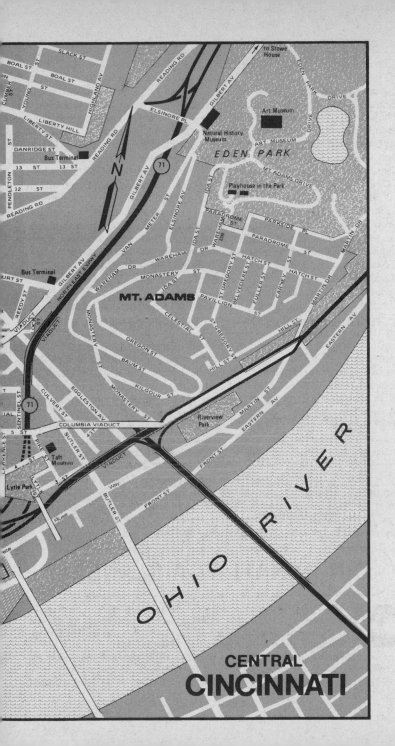

CENTRAL CINCINNATI

OHIO RIVER

EDEN PARK

MT. ADAMS

to Stowe House

Art Museum

Natural History Museum

ART MUSEUM

Playhouse in the Park

Bus Terminal

Taft Museum

Lytle Park

Riverview Park

SLACK ST
BOAL ST
BOAL ST
YOUNG ST
CUMBER ST
LIBERTY HILL
LIBERTY ST
HIGHLAND AV
DANRIDGE ST
13 ST
13 ST
12 ST
READING RD
PENDLETON
READING RD
READING RD
ELSINORE PL
GILBERT AV
EDEN PARK DRIVE
GILBERT AV
EDEN PARK DRIVE
MT ADAMS DRIVE
PARADROME ST
PARKSIDE PL
PARADROME ST
PARADROME ST
MARTIN DR
ELSINORE AV
IDA ST
IDA ST
METER ST
VAN DR
WAREHAM DR
WAREHAM DR
MONASTERY ST
WAREHAM DR
IDA ST
ST GREGORY'S ST
HATCH ST
HATCH ST
BELVEDERE ST
FULLER ST
FULLER ST
CARNEY
PAVILLION ST
CELESTIAL ST
ST GREGORY'S ST
HILL ST
MONASTERY ST
OREGON ST
BAUM ST
KILGOUR ST
EGGLESTON AV
MONASTERY ST
CULVERT ST
COLUMBIA VIADUCT
SENTINEL ST
REEDY ST
LOCUST ST
VIADUCT
VIADUCT
GILBERT AV
NORTHEAST EXPWY
Bus Terminal
Bus Terminal
URT ST
5 ST
4 ST
3 ST
PIKE ST
LYTLE ST
BUTLER ST
BUTLER ST
FRONT ST
FRONT ST
FRONT ST
MARTIN ST
EASTERN AV
EASTERN AV
EASTERN AV
LAWRENCE ST
Way
Pike
VIADUCT
71
71

ing distance from downtown are Riverfront Stadium (home of the Cincinnati *Reds* baseball team and the NFL *Bengals*) and Riverfront Coliseum (host to circuses, ice shows, rock concerts, and University of Cincinnati basketball).

Some 400,000 of the Cincinnati area's residents live in the city, many on the hillsides that ring the business district. Mt. Adams, to the northeast, and Clifton, directly north, are especially interesting. Mt. Adams is to Cincinnati what Greenwich Village once was to New York and Georgetown is to Washington: Bohemia at a price. Its slopes are covered by new and restored row houses, shops, and restaurants. Just north of Mt. Adams is Eden Park, where the Cincinnati Art Museum, Museum of Natural History, and Playhouse in the Park are found. Clifton is the site of the 35,000-student University of Cincinnati, a campus set in a residential district of baronial homes and interesting shops. Between Mt. Adams and Clifton, Mt. Auburn is undergoing extensive restoration in an effort to recapture some of the area's previous grandeur. Cincinnati residents are justifiably proud, too, of the superb Cincinnati Symphony and Opera Company, both housed in the Music Hall. The university's College Conservatory of Music also offers impressive musical programs. The Cincinnati Ballet also performs at the historic Music Hall.

Cincinnati people are friendly but reserved, sedately satisfied with their lives. Some residents will go so far as to admit the water tastes funny, but apart from that they tend to be laconic. Although there are many excellent restaurants and expensive shops, "fashionably dressed" in Cincinnati is conservative by big-city standards. People tend to play it safe rather than experiment, and this makes Cincinnati a city with class but no glamour. Most Cincinnati residents speak standard midwestern or Appalachian American English, with a couple of crucial exceptions. The expressions "three-way" and "four-way" do not refer to traffic signs; they refer to special toppings for native Cincinnati chili. "Please" is used to indicate that the listener did not understand a question and would like to have it repeated or clarified. "Square" is used interchangeably with "block" when describing directions or distances, as in "Lazarus's is three squares north of L. S. Ayre's." A "Pony Keg" is a convenience store, mostly for the dispensing of beer for off-premises consumption. Either "Cincinnat*i*" or "Cincinnat*a*" is correct. No Berlitz courses are available yet. But no matter what kind of English you speak, people in Cincinnati (or Cincinnata) will probably understand you. If you really get stuck, try a trusty international nonverbal: smile.

CINCINNATI AT-A-GLANCE

SEEING THE CITY: For the best view of Cincinnati, go to the top of the Carew Tower. You may see the original seven hills on which the town is said to have been built. Small admission charge. Children under six free. Groups of 15 or more get in for half price. 441 Vine (381-3448).

Another popular way to see the city is by riverboat. BB Riverboats' four vessels, the *Becky Thatcher, Mark Twain, Huck Finn* and *BB Funliner,* are available for one- to two-hour moonlight cruises or day-long adventures. They are moored at the foot of

Greenup St., Covington, KY (Cincinnati's sister city, across the river; phone 606 261-8500.) Or try Jubilee Riverboats, in Ludlow (606 581-0300).

SPECIAL PLACES: Cincinnati's relatively traffic-free streets make sightseeing on foot not only feasible but pleasant. There are many interesting shops and restaurants to stop at along the way.

Cincinnati Art Museum – This outstanding collection of paintings, sculpture, prints, and decorative arts fills more than 118 galleries and exhibition rooms (with an exceptionally fine section on ancient Persia). Ancient musical instruments, costumes, and textiles are also on view. Closed Mondays and holidays. Admission charge. Eden Park (721-5204).

Natural History Museum – The cavern and waterfall display here is the largest of its kind in the world. A wilderness trail features animals in their natural habitat. An Indian exhibition depicts early Ohio Indian life in life-size dioramas. Next door is the Planetarium. Closed Mondays. Admission charge. 1720 Gilbert Ave. (621-3889).

Harriet Beecher Stowe House – The author of *Uncle Tom's Cabin* often visited her parents' home here while doing research on her novel. In addition to a collection of Stowe memorabilia, the house has a number of exhibitions on black history. Closed Mondays. Admission charge. 2950 Gilbert Ave. (221-0004).

Taft Museum – William Howard Taft used this house for formal occasions during his presidency. It is now a museum of paintings, Chinese porcelain, and Duncan Phyfe furniture. Portraits and landscapes by Rembrandt, Turner, Goya, Gainsborough, and Corot line the walls. Open daily. Free. 316 Pike (241-0343).

Riverfront Stadium – Cincinnati is the self-proclaimed baseball capital of the world, and sports fans will enjoy touring the dugouts and back rooms of this 60,000-seat, artificial turf stadium. Tours by appointment during baseball season. Admission charge. 201 E 2nd St. (352-3779).

Contemporary Arts Center – "What is art?" is a puzzler as old as the Cincinnati hills, and the Contemporary Arts Center keeps many people in this good city wondering. Not only are there constantly changing modern paintings and sculpture, the center features multimedia exhibits aimed at dazzling the mind, the eye, and the mind's eye. Closed Sundays. Admission charge. 115 E 5th St. (721-0390).

Cincinnati Fire Museum – All kinds of old fire engines, paraphernalia, and some modern equipment, too. Closed Mondays. Children under 6 free. 315 W Court St. (621-5553).

Cincinnati Zoo – The second oldest zoo in the nation, known for its expertise in the propagation of rare and endangered species. There are more than 6,000 animals here. The most popular exhibits are the rare white Bengal tigers, the Bird of Prey Flight Cage, Outdoor Gorilla Exhibit, Children's Zoo, Insect House, and the new Cat House. Open daily. Admission charge. 3400 Vine St. (281-4700).

College Football Hall of Fame – A new collection of memorabilia of college football greats. The emphasis is on audio-visual displays and entertainment, including films and computerized information banks. Part of the Kings Island Theme Park complex, on I-71, 20 miles north of the city. Open weekends, off-season. (241-5410).

Sharon Woods Village – Life in 19th-century Ohio, with a representative group of pre-1880 buildings in a village setting. Closed Mondays and Fridays May to October. Admission charge. Sharon Woods, off Rte. 42 (563-9484).

Vent Haven Museum – This unique, entertaining museum across the state border in Kentucky has the largest known collection of ventriloquists' material in the world. In addition to about 500 puppets, there's a library of hundreds of books in eight languages, dating back to the 18th century. Summer tours by appointment. 33 W Maple Ave., Fort Mitchell, KY (606 341-0461).

■**EXTRA SPECIAL:** Just a couple of hours south of Cincinnati lies the best horse-breeding region in the US — *Kentucky Bluegrass* country. The drive on I-71/75 takes you through very green rolling hills and beautiful breeding farms. Stop for lunch at the relaxing *Beaumont Inn*, just west of Lexington, Kentucky, in Harrodsburg. Open March through mid-November (606 734-3381).

SOURCES AND RESOURCES

TOURIST INFORMATION: For maps and brochures, write or visit the Cincinnati Convention and Visitors Bureau, 200 W 5th St. (621-2142). It can also provide self-guided walking tour maps.

The best guide to events and places of interest is *Cincinnati* magazine, monthly, available at newsstands.

Local Coverage – *Cincinnati Enquirer,* morning daily and Sundays; *Cincinnati Post,* afternoon daily.

Food – *Cincinnati* magazine's annual restaurant guide, available from the Chamber of Commerce, gives the best information on where to dine. The *Cincinnati Enquirer, Post,* and the city magazine feature occasional restaurant columns and guides, too.

Area Code – All telephone numbers are in the 513 area code unless otherwise indicated.

CLIMATE AND CLOTHES: It's damp in Cincinnati. Winters tend to be wet and in the 30s, frequently much colder. Summers run into the sweaty 80s and 90s. Spring and fall, however, are more amenable, and a drive through the surrounding countryside in either season is a joy.

GETTING AROUND: Airport – Greater Cincinnati International Airport is about 13 miles southwest of the city in Kentucky. A trip to the airport by cab takes from 20 to 30 minutes and should cost around $15. Shortway Bus Co. (606 283-3702) provides both bus and limo transportation between the airport and Cincinnati's leading hotels. Buses run to and from the airport every half-hour (every 40 minutes on weekends) and the fare is $6.

Bus – Queen City Metro operates an excellent bus service. The bus stop signs carry numbers of the routes that stop there. Route maps are available from Queen City Metro, 6 E 4th St. (621-4455).

Taxi – Call Yellow Cab, 1110 Kenner St. (241-2100), or go to any of the major hotels, where cabs line up.

Car Rental – Major car rental agencies are represented at the Greater Cincinnati International Airport.

Horse-drawn Carriages – Three companies operate non-motorized transport in the Fountain Square area. Rates vary with the carriage and route.

MUSEUMS: Cincinnati's major museums — Cincinnati Art Museum, Natural History Museum, Taft Museum, Contemporary Arts Center, Cincinnati Fire Museum, and Vent Haven Museum — are described in detail under *Special Places.*

MAJOR COLLEGES AND UNIVERSITIES: The University of Cincinnati, Clifton (475-8000), has 35,000 students. Other notable schools are Xavier University, 3800 Victory Pkwy. (745-3000); the College of Mount St. Joseph, 5701 Delhi Rd. (244-4200); and the Art Academy of Cincinnati, Eden Park, (721-5205).

SPECIAL EVENTS: Ever since 1873, Cincinnati has been holding its annual *May Festival,* a series of choral and instrumental musical concerts at Music Hall, 1243 Elm (621-1919). In June, the *Ladies' PGA Championship* is held at Kings Island, Jack Nicklaus Sports Center, 3565 Kings Mills Rd. (241-5200). In mid-September, Cincinnati celebrates its German heritage with an *Oktoberfest,* along the lines of the famous Munich festival, in and around Fountain Square.

SPORTS AND FITNESS: Not only is Cincinnati one of the country's most enthusiastic baseball cities, it also has a National Football League team, the *Bengals.* Riverfront Stadium is easily accessible to downtown.

Baseball – Cincinnati *Reds* (421-4510) play at Riverfront Stadium (421-7337).

Basketball – University of Cincinnati (475-2287); and Xavier University (745-3411).

Bicycling – Bikes can be rented, in the summer, from Airport Playfield, Lunken Airport, Wilmer Ave. (321-6500).

Fishing – There's moderately good fishing at Lake Isabella and Winton Woods, the largest of the county lakes, and the "world series" of bass fishing contests is held on the Ohio River. Serious Cincinnati sportfishers drive four hours to Lake Cumberland and Kentucky Lake in southern Kentucky.

Fitness Centers – The YMCA provides a pool, sauna, equipment, and a track, as well as an outdoor jogging map, 1105 Elm St. (241-5348).

Football – Cincinnati *Bengals* (621-3550).

Golf – For spectators and golfers, Kings Island is far and away the best — the Jack Nicklaus Sports Center, 3565 Kings Mills Rd. (241-5200).

Horse Racing – Enthusiasts should check out the action at River Downs, 6301 Kellogg Ave. (232-8000); and Latonia racecourse, 7500 Turfway Rd., Florence, KY (371-0200).

Jogging – For a 6-mile jaunt, follow tree-lined Central Parkway to Ludlow Street and come back; or run back and forth across the Ohio River Suspension Bridge, designed by Brooklyn Bridge builder John A. Roebling.

Swimming – A good public pool is Sunlite Pool at Old Coney Island just before River Downs on Rte. 50 (231-7801). Call first to make sure it's open. There are lake beaches at nearby Hueston Woods in Butler County and Caesar's Creek in Warren County.

THEATER: Cincinnati has two major theaters. The *Taft* features touring companies, and has a spring, fall, and winter season, 5th and Sycamore (721-0411). *Playhouse in the Park* is a professional regional theater specializing in modern American and European plays and stages several musicals during the summer, Mt. Adams Circle, Eden Park (421-3888). The University of Cincinnati produces plays during the spring, summer, and fall on its *Showboat Majestic,* moored downtown (475-4163).

MUSIC: The internationally famous *Cincinnati Symphony Orchestra,* founded in 1895, has a September-May season at Music Hall, 1243 Elm (621-1919); its summer home is the Riverbend Music Center, 6295 Kellogg Ave. (232-5882). The *College Conservatory of Music* is one of the nation's oldest and most prominent professional music schools, on the University of Cincinnati campus, Clifton and Calhoun (475-6638). The *Cincinnati Ballet* performs at the downtown Music Hall and occasionally at the Taft. The *Cincinnati Opera* has been singing since 1921 at Music Hall.

NIGHTCLUBS AND NIGHTLIFE: Cincinnati is pretty much a couples' town. The most popular night spots are *Caddy's,* 230 W Pete Rose Way on the riverfront (721-3636); *Lucy's in the Sky,* Holiday Inn Queensgate, 8th and Linn (241-8660); *Rookwood Pottery,* 1077 Celestial, Mt. Adams (721-5456); and *Conservatory,* 640 W 3rd St., Covington, KY (491-6400).

SINS: Cincinnati *gluttons* are smug in the knowledge that the city boasts some of the best restaurants in the tristate area. Most notable are *Maisonette,* 114 E 6th St. (721-2260), and *Pigall's,* 127 W 4th St. (721-1345), excellent French restaurants that inspire you to ignore your pocketbook.
The *pride* of the city is the Cincinnati *Reds,* also known as the Big Red Machine. This hearty team managed to take the World Series in both 1975 and 1976, making the fans about as cocky and full of pride as any in the city's history.

LOCAL SERVICES: Business Services – Secretarial Office Services, Provident Bank Bldg. (651-1161) and Carew Tower (381-2277)
    Mechanic – Certified Car Care, 1507 Central Pkwy. (721-2886)
    Babysitting – Rock-a-Bye Sitters Registry, 7th and Vine (721-7440)

BEST IN TOWN

CHECKING IN: Although there are several hotels that qualify as comfortable, Cincinnati does not offer much in the way of really outstanding accommodations. You can expect to pay between $60 and $100 for a double at any of the hotels listed as expensive; $40 and $60 for those we consider moderate. For B&B accommodations, contact Buckeye Bed & Breakfast, PO Box 130, Powell, OH 43065 (614 548-4555).

Omni Netherland Plaza – Probably the finest hotel in the city after a recent $20 million total restoration. Connected by the Skywalk to the Convention Center, with lots of meeting space of its own (capacity for 1,200). In addition to its 620 rooms, suites are available (some are lovely duplexes). Dining can be either formal at *Orchids at the Palm Court* or a bit more casual at the *Café at the Palm Court.* 24-hour room service. 35 W 5th St. (513 421-9100). Expensive.

Clarion – Corporate executives stay at this very modern, 900-room downtown hotel with a heated outdoor swimming pool, health club, sauna, lounge, restaurant, barber, beauty shop, and free parking. 141 W 6th St. (513 352-2100). Expensive.

Westin – Opened in 1981, this is one of the newer downtown hotels. With 456 rather comfortable rooms, it is in the 17-story First National Bank Center. 500 Vine St. at Fountain Sq. (513 621-7700). Expensive.

Hyatt Regency – Opened in 1984, it has 487 rooms and 23 suites. Its *Champs Restaurant* features seafood and steaks; *Findlay's Restaurant* has more casual dining and a Sunday brunch. There's also a complete health club, including a swimming pool. Valet parking available. 151 W 5th St. (513 579-1234). Expensive.

Terrace Hilton Hotel – In addition to 350 rooms and suites, this attractive hotel has several restaurants: the *Gourmet Restaurant* on the top floor, the *Garden Terrace* on the 8th floor, and the very popular *Joe's Bar,* an intimate, rustic place on ground level that serves delicious deli sandwiches. 15 W 6th St. (513 381-4000). Expensive.

Kings Island Inn & Conference Center – A favorite of golfers, since it's near the Jack Nicklaus course, this Alpine chalet-style inn offers good accommodations in an attractive setting. In addition to its 194 rooms with queen-size beds, it has indoor and outdoor pools, playground, tennis courts, game room, cocktail lounge with entertainment, dining room, and bus service to Kings Island Theme Park. 5691 Kings Island Dr., Mason (513 241-5800). Expensive.

Vernon Manor – A tasteful restoration of a faded beauty. Handsome modern decor in the bar, restaurant, and other public space; 115 elegant sleeping rooms, each with its own steam bath. Barber shop and beauty salon. No pets. 400 Oak St. (513 281-3300). Expensive.

Holiday Inn — Downtown – Long-time residents remember this *Holiday Inn* as the one across the street from the former stadium and the old railroad station. It's not in the greatest neighborhood, but if you're looking for a 247-room, functional place to rest your head, this could be it. It has a swimming pool, two dining rooms, bar, and a nightclub. 8th and Linn (513 241-8660). Moderate.

 EATING OUT: Cincinnati's most notable gastronomic eccentricity is its chili, which is served over spaghetti, to which may be added cheese ("three-way"), cheese and raw onions ("four-way"), or cheese, raw onions, and beans ("five-way"). At our expensive listings, expect to pay at least $50 for two; between $20 and $40 at those places designated moderate; under $20 at places listed inexpensive. Prices do not include drinks, wine, or tips.

Maisonette – It may be in an unlikely spot, but it's one of the best French restaurants in the country. Its cuisine has consistently won every food award in the country. We recommend veal or lamb dishes. The service is extremely friendly. Jacket and tie required. Closed Sundays. Reservations required. Major credit cards. 114 E 6th St. (721-2260). Expensive.

Pigall's – A rival of *Maisonette;* some think it is already better. Established in 1956, it too has won top awards almost since its opening. Its lovely, formal blue-gray interior with teardrop chandeliers is reflected in smoked glass mirrors. For starters, try the *mousse de ris de veau et volaille* (sweetbreads), then treat yourself to the côte de veau with prosciutto and mushrooms. Jacket and tie required. Closed Sundays, Mondays, and holidays. Reservations required. Major credit cards. 127 W 4th St. (721-1345). Expensive.

The Precinct – A good choice for an evening of dining, dancing, and chatting with friends over what some say is the best steak in town. Other selections include veal, pasta, prime rib, and fresh seafood. *The Precinct* is also a lively night spot, with a disc jockey playing something for everyone. Five minutes from downtown. Open daily. Reservations necessary. Major credit cards. 311 Delta Ave. at Columbia Pkwy. (321-5454). Expensive.

China Gourmet – Highly praised for its variety of Chinese food and superior Szechwan dishes, this small, friendly restaurant is tucked away in a little shopping mall in Hyde Park, about 10 minutes from downtown. One of the city's restaurant critics called it the best Chinese restaurant west of New York. Open daily. Reservations recommended. Major credit cards. 3340 Erie Ave. (871-6612). Moderate.

Forest View Gardens – Waiters and waitresses sing your favorite operatic arias and serve tasty German food in a garden setting. Open Thursdays through Sundays. Reservations necessary. Major credit cards. 4508 N Bend Rd. (661-6434). Moderate.

Charley's Crab – Fresh fish is a rarity in landlocked Cincinnati, and this is one of the few places where it's available. The main selections are flown in fresh from the East Coast every day, and prepared simply and deliciously. Open daily. Reservations advised. Major credit cards. 9769 Montgomery Rd., 30 minutes from downtown on I-71 in Montgomery (891-7000). Moderate.

Lenhardt's – Hearty food for the famished, leaning heavily on schnitzels and sauerbraten. Closed Mondays. Reservations accepted. No credit cards. 151 W McMillan St. (281-3600). Moderate.

La Rosa's 580 – This is a convenient spot for Italian food, from simple pizza and spaghetti to elaborate veal and chicken dishes. The easy, relaxed pace is especially good for families. Closed Sundays. Reservations accepted. Major credit cards. 6th St. between Walnut and Main (421-2025). Inexpensive.

CLEVELAND

If you think there are no more chapters being written in the muscle and toil history of immigrant labor in America — that the story ended several decades ago with a final wave and the third generation — there is a book you should consult with some attention. It is called Cleveland, and you may find it a good deal more compelling than you'd expect.

Cleveland is a working city, and it always has been. Laid out in 1796 with strict attention to order and propriety by the surveyors of the Connecticut Company (led by Moses Cleaveland), its tidy New England pattern of straight streets around a public square was knocked into a cocked hat with the coming of industrialization. Cleveland's location at the confluence of Lake Erie and the Cuyahoga River provided a waterway that stimulated the growth of heavy industry — shipping, steel, iron, and construction. The city sprawled. Famous fortunes got their start. John D. Rockefeller parlayed an oil business into wealth beyond imagining; shipping magnates Sam Mather and Mark Hanna began their rise; the Van Sweringen brothers created a vast railroad and construction empire. But behind all this boom, and most of the money, was the muscle power of a largely immigrant work force that earned little more for its labor than the sweat of its own brow.

The workers have stayed, and so have the industries, and it is the continuing saga of their fortune together that makes Cleveland today something of a bellwether among middle-sized industrial US cities. For one thing, heavy industry is no longer the only game in town. Cleveland is now among the top ten US cities for major corporate headquarters. Rockefeller's Standard Oil has shown a continuing civic pride by spending $2 million on a new headquarters complex on Public Square, part of a nearly $1 billion building surge in Cleveland. Restoration work is booming as well. Tower City is a multimillion-dollar project that includes the Terminal Tower complex and its surrounding riverfront area. Playhouse Square, the largest restoration of its kind in the country, will resuscitate four 1920s theaters and some historic buildings in the Flats/Warehouse District. Today, Cleveland has a population of 600,000; Cuyahoga County, which includes the greater Cleveland area, a ring of wealthy suburbs, has 1.5 million people. Among the 59 suburbs in the county is Shaker Heights, considered one of the most affluent towns in the country. There, where the Shakers once threw off American industrial life to set up a rural commune, reside the most prosperous industrial and business leaders; it is a haven of sorts still.

But don't think Cleveland is getting effete or being abandoned by its industry. A drive along the Detroit-Superior Bridge over the flats shouldering the twists and turns of the Cuyahoga River — the steel mills belching flames into the sky, barges plunging up and down the river — shows Cleveland's muscles still flexing.

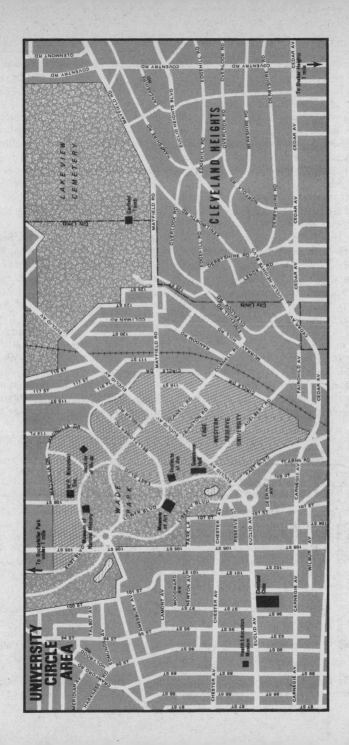

And that might be why, with all of its problems, there's something interesting about Cleveland. It's a city of the American Dream, bothered and bewildered, but with much to admire between the fret lines. Ethnocentricity is strong. Sons and daughters of immigrants who gladly took the toughest jobs at the poorest pay own their piece of the suburbs, but the old neighborhoods live on. Buckeye Road, where the Hungarians once crowded in such numbers that Cleveland was second only to Budapest in the number of Magyars calling it home, is still a substantial Carpathian community. Little Italy is an East Side enclave; Chinatown is on the fringes of downtown; and Tremont is a mixed ethnic neighborhood where God accepts the worship of a bewildering number of denominations and faiths. When you get right down to it, there's something genuinely American about the crazy-quilt ambience of Cleveland's neighborhoods.

You can buy anything you want in Cleveland, as a matter of fact, because somewhere, someone is selling it. The city has the attributes of a major cosmopolitan center. Besides the revitalized downtown shopping district, Coventry Road in Cleveland Heights is a smaller Greenwich Village, and Beachwood Place is a posh shopping mall in the suburb of that name. The Cleveland Orchestra is world renowned, and the Cleveland Museum of Art has one of the richest collections in the country.

You might hear along the way that Cleveland isn't the town it used to be, and in many ways it's not. It seems to be redefining and reshaping itself. After having survived industrialization, immigration, exploitation, and every other cultural shock wave to rattle urban America, Cleveland is a city not only still on its feet, but enthusiastic. It's a city where martinis for lunch are beginning to outnumber shot-and-beers at the bar; wing tips are becoming more evident than steel-toed boot. More people carry briefcases than lunch buckets to work.

What does it all add up to? Cleveland has diversity, history, energy, and a very friendly citizenry. It definitely deserves a close look.

CLEVELAND AT-A-GLANCE

SEEING THE CITY: Stouffer's *Top of the Town Restaurant* offers a panoramic view of Cleveland, the downtown, and Lake Erie with its recreation and shipping activity. 100 Erieview Plaza (771-1600). The Terminal Tower observation deck is open weekends from 11 AM to 3:30 PM and on holidays. Small admission charge. Public Sq. (621-7981). Trolley Tours (771-4484) conducts city tours daily at 10 AM, noon, and 2 PM.

SPECIAL PLACES: Many of Cleveland's most interesting sights are concentrated in the few areas served by public transportation. You'll want to stroll around, particularly in the University Circle area, which is the cultural heart of Cleveland, and in the lovely suburbs of Shaker Heights and Chagrin Falls.

DOWNTOWN

Public Square – In the heart of the business area, the Public Square is a good place to get one's bearings in Cleveland past and present. Statues pay tribute to the city's founder Moses Cleaveland, Tom Johnson, the populist reform mayor, and, with the Soldiers and Sailors Monument, to Cleveland's Civil War dead. Dominating the square are the 52-story Terminal Tower, built by the Van Sweringen brothers on the eve of the stock market crash that leveled their vast empire, and the recently completed world headquarters tower for the Standard Oil Company. Bounded by Euclid Ave., Superior Ave., and Ontario St.

The _Goodtime II_ Boat Tour – The tour on the river is the best introduction to "the Flats" or industrial valley along the river basin where Rockefeller and shipping magnates Sam Mather and Mark Hanna made their fortunes. The 500-passenger boat goes down the Cuyahoga as far as the steel mills. Departures daily from May through October except Mondays. Admission charge. E 9th St. Pier (531-1505).

The Arcade – This 19th-century marketplace is a multitiered structure topped by a stunning block-long skylight of steel and glass. Bookstores, boutiques, eateries, and galleries line the arcade. At lunchtime, local musicians offer free classical, pop, and jazz concerts. 401 Euclid Ave. (621-8500).

The Mall – This spacious rectangular mall is the location of all the government and municipal buildings and a well-designed plaza with a fountain. Buildings include City Hall, the Court House, the Public Library (which has over 3 million volumes and many WPA murals), and Public Auditorium overlooking Cleveland Stadium, home of the _Indians_ and _Browns_. Bounded by Lakeside Ave., St. Clair Ave., E 6th and E 4th sts.

UNIVERSITY CIRCLE AREA

Cleveland Museum of Art – Among the best museums in the country, this Greek-style marble building contains extensive collections of many periods and cultures; it's particularly strong on the medieval period, Oriental art, and paintings of Masters including Rembrandt, Rubens, and Picasso. Overlooks the Fine Arts Gardens of Wade Park with its seasonal flower displays. Auditorium features free films, lectures, and concerts. Closed Mondays. Free. 11150 East Blvd. at University Circle (421-7340).

Western Reserve Historical Society – The largest collection of Shaker memorabilia in the world is here, including inventions such as the clothes pin, the ladderback chair, and various farming implements and furnishings. There's also an extensive genealogical collection and exhibitions on Indians and pioneers. Closed Mondays. Small admission charge. 10825 East Blvd. (751-5722). Associated with the Crawford Auto-Aviation Museum with 200 antique autos and old airplanes. Displays trace the evolution of the automobile and describe Cleveland's prominence as an early car manufacturing center. Visitors can see how the old cars are given a new lease on life at the museum's restoration shop. Closed Mondays. Admission charge. 10825 East Blvd. at University Circle (721-5722).

Cleveland Museum of Natural History – Exhibitions of armored fish and sharks found preserved in Ohio shales, a 70-foot mounted dinosaur, skeletons of mastodon and mammoth, and Lucy, the most complete fossil evidence of early man. The museum also has a planetarium and observatory. Admission charge. Wade Oval Dr. at University Circle (231-4600).

Rockefeller Park – This 296-acre park features the Shakespeare and Cultural Gardens, a series of gardens, landscape architecture, and sculptures representing the 20 nationalities that settled the city. Between East Blvd. and Martin Luther King Jr. Dr. The Greenhouse displays include a Japanese Garden, tropical plants, and a Talking Garden with taped descriptions of plants for blind visitors. Open daily. Free. 750 E 88th St.

EAST SIDE

Cleveland Health Education Museum – A first of its kind, the museum has exhibitions on the workings of the human body and health maintenance. You can see everything here from the walk-through model of a human eye to Juno, the transparent woman, and the inspiring Wonder of New Life display. Admission charge. 8911 Euclid Ave. (231-5010).

Lakeview Cemetery – The plantings here are beautiful, the view fine, and the company illustrious. Among the natives buried here are President Garfield (you can't miss the monument), Mark Hanna (the US senator), John Hay (secretary of state under McKinley), and John D. Rockefeller (father of the fortune). The Garfield Monument offers a great view of downtown. Open daily. Free. 12316 Euclid Ave.

Coventry Road – This is Cleveland's answer to New York's Greenwich Village. Boutiques and shops offer unique fashions and arts. Sip unusual teas and coffees at *Arabica,* 2785 Euclid Heights Blvd., late at night, or try a sandwich and a milkshake at *Tommy's,* a local institution. 1820 Coventry Rd.

WEST SIDE

West Side Market – One of the largest Old World–style indoor markets in the country and a historic landmark. Fresh produce, meats, and baked goods are sold year-round on Mondays, Wednesdays, Fridays, and Saturdays. W 25th St. and Lorain Ave. (644-3386).

NASA Lewis Research Center – The NASA complex and its visitors center offer exhibitions, lectures, and films on aeronautics, energy, space travel, and communications. There are also tours of a propulsion systems laboratory and a supersonic wind tunnel. Open daily. Free. 21000 Brookpark Rd. (433-4000, ext. 731).

SHAKER HEIGHTS

One of the most affluent suburbs in America, Shaker Heights was developed in the early 1900s by brothers O. P. and M. J. Van Sweringen and now houses Cleveland's elite in lovely big old homes on wide, winding, tree-lined streets. The area was originally Shaker Lakes, the rural commune established by the 19th-century religious sect that left American industrial life for a religious regime featuring strict celibacy. Today, all that remains of the Shakers is the Shaker Historical Museum with its collection of artifacts (16740 South Park, 921-1201) and the Shaker Cemetery (Lee Rd. at Chagrin Blvd.).

■ **EXTRA SPECIAL:** *Canton,* home of the Pro Football Hall of Fame, is 53 miles south of Cleveland along I-77. Inside there are all kinds of mementos of the game and its players — uniforms, helmets, team pictures, a recording of Jim Thorpe's voice, a film on football, and a research library. Open daily. Admission charge. 2121 Harrison Ave. (456-8207). On the way, you may want to stop at Hale Farm Village, where you'll find homesteads, craft shops, and a working farm typical of those of the Western Reserve between 1825 and 1850. Closed Mondays. Admission charge. 2686 Oak Hill Rd., Bath (861-4573). You can also stop in Akron, rubber manufacturing capital of the world, for a tour of the Stan Hywet Hall and Gardens. Completed in 1915 by Frank A. Seiberling, founder of the Goodyear and Seiberling Rubber companies, the building is an excellent example of Tudor revival architecture, and the 65-room house contains original antique furnishings and artworks of the 14th through 18th centuries. The 70 acres of gardens are best in spring when thousands of tulips bloom. Closed Mondays. Admission charge for house tour. 714 N Portage Path, Akron.

SOURCES AND RESOURCES

TOURIST INFORMATION: The Cleveland Convention and Visitors Bureau is best for brochures, maps, and other information. 1301 E 6th St. (621-4110). For events, call 621-8860.

Local Coverage – *The Cleveland Plain Dealer,* morning daily; *Northern Ohio LIVE,* monthly; *Cleveland Magazine,* monthly. All are available at newsstands.

Food – Check the monthly restaurant listings in *Northern Ohio LIVE* and *Cleveland Magazine.*

Area Code – All telephone numbers are in the 216 area code unless otherwise indicated.

CLIMATE AND CLOTHES: Cleveland has cold and snowy winters that are followed by brief springs that give brief respite from damp winters and humid summers. Fall is generally the most pleasant season, with mild, sunny weather that often extends through November.

GETTING AROUND: Airport – Cleveland Hopkins International Airport is a 20- to 30-minute drive from downtown; taxi fare should run about $15. The Regional Transit Authority's Airport Rapid Transit train runs from the airport to downtown's Terminal Tower in the same amount of time but costs only $1.

Bus – Regional Transit Authority (RTA) serves both downtown and the outlying areas. Complete route and tourist information is available from the downtown office, 615 W Superior Ave. (621-9500).

Train – RTA Rapid Transit trains serve the city's east and west sides.

Taxi – Cabs can be hailed in the street in the downtown area around Public Square or ordered on the phone. Yellow-Zone Cab is the major company (623-1500).

Car Rental – Cleveland is served by the major national firms.

MUSEUMS: The Cleveland Museum of Art, the Western Reserve Historical Society, the Cleveland Museum of Natural History, the Cleveland Health Education Museum, and the Shaker Historical Museum are all described above in *Special Places.* In the future, visitors will be able to view the memorabilia of the likes of Elvis Presley, Chuck Berry, and Buddy Holly, for Cleveland has been chosen as the site of the *Rock 'n' Roll Hall of Fame.*

MAJOR COLLEGES AND UNIVERSITIES: Cleveland has close to 20 colleges and universities, including Case Western Reserve University (University Circle), one of the nation's leading research institutions; Cleveland State University (downtown); Baldwin-Wallace College (Berea); and John Carroll University (University Heights).

SPECIAL EVENTS: The *May Show Exhibit* at the Museum of Art kicks off spring and summer events, followed by *Riverfest* at the Port in June and the *Budweiser Cleveland Grand Prix* at Burke Lakefront Airport in July. In August, the *All Nations Festival* is held downtown and the *Feast of the Assumption* is celebrated in Little Italy. Fall festivities include the *Cleveland Air Show,* the *Annual Rib Burn-Off, Oktoberfest,* and the *Cleveland Art Focus.*

SPORTS AND FITNESS: Baseball – The American League's Cleveland *Indians* play at Cleveland Municipal Stadium from April to September. W 3rd St. and Lakeside Ave. (241-5555).

Basketball – The Cleveland *Cavaliers* play at the Coliseum from mid-October to early April. I-271 and Rte. 303 (659-9100).

Bicycling – From U-Rent-Um of America, 6683 W 130th St. (888-5100), or Easy Rider Bicycle Shop, 3974 E 131st St. (752-1748). The Cuyahoga Falls Reservation nearby has good biking trails.

Fitness Centers – The Thirteenth Street Racquetball Club has exercise equipment and a track. 1901 E 13th St. (696-1365).

Football – The Cleveland *Browns* play pro ball at the Stadium from August to January (575-1000).

Golf – Punderson State Park has the best public 18-hole golf course, at Rtes. 44 and 87 (564-5163).

Jogging – Run along Euclid Avenue to Public Square and on to the Flats; stop in at Herme's, 1607 Euclid, for a map and more information (or call 696-1542). Run at Cleveland State College at Euclid and Prospect.

Tennis – The best public courts are at Cain Park in Cleveland Heights, Superior Rd. at Lee Rd. (371-3000).

THEATER: For current offerings and performance times, check the publications listed above. Cleveland has a variety of theatrical offerings, some locally produced, others traveling shows. Best bets for shows: *Hanna Theatre*, 2067 E 14th St. (621-5000); *Cleveland Play House*, 8500 Euclid Ave. (795-7000); *Karamu House*, 2355 E 89th St. (795-7070); *Great Lakes Shakespeare Festival*, Ohio Theatre, 1511 Euclid Ave. (523-1755); *Eldred Theatre*, Case Western Reserve University Campus (368-2858).

MUSIC: The *Cleveland Orchestra* performs with noted soloists and guest conductors from October to mid-May in Severance Hall, 11001 Euclid Ave. at East Blvd. (231-7300). From June to September, it plays at Blossom Music Center, 1145 W Steels Corner Rd., Cuyahoga Falls (861-5674), as do pop and rock bands.

NIGHTCLUBS AND NIGHTLIFE: Current favorites: *Agora,* for rock or jazz, 1730 E 24th St. (696-8333); *Peabody's,* for folk or blues, 2140 S Taylor Rd. (321-4072); and *Club Isabella,* for jazz, 2025 Abington Rd. (229-1177).

For big-name entertainment, try *The Front Row Theatre,* 6199 Wilson Mills Rd. in Highland Heights (449-5000), or the *Play House Square Association,* 1621 Euclid Ave. (771-4444). The *Cleveland Comedy Club,* 2230 E 4th St. (696-9266), is open Wednesdays through Saturdays.

SINS: The city's area for adult entertainment is along Prospect Avenue between E 14th and 24th streets (adult cinemas, massage parlors, as well as Stagedoor Johnnies, Vegas Burlesque, and the New Era Burlesque, which has amateur nights).

The biggest party in town is on St. Patrick's Day, when Cleveland's proud Irish population comes out in full force.

LOCAL SERVICES: Babysitting – Ba-B-Sit Service Enterprises, 592 Cahoon Rd. (871-9595)

Business Services – Kelly Services, 33 Public Square (771-2800)

Mechanic – Park Auto Repair Co., 2163 Hamilton Ave. (241-7390)

BEST IN TOWN

CHECKING IN: Cleveland has many accommodations that are attractive, comfortable, and reasonably priced. In addition to the usual chains, there is an assortment of modern, locally owned hotels. Our selections range in price from $85 or more for a double room in the expensive category, $40 to $70 in the moderate range, and under $30 in the inexpensive list. A company called Private Lodgings, PO Box 18590, Cleveland, OH 44118 (216 321-3213), finds private residences in a variety of price ranges for those who'd rather not stay at a hotel.

Bond Court Hotel – A luxury hotel with a 22-story tower commanding a good view of Lake Erie, conveniently near the convention center. The service is fine and other features include indoor parking, coffee shop, lounge with entertainment, color TV, and an elegant dining room. 526 rooms. 777 St. Clair Ave. (216 771-7600). Expensive.

Stouffer's Inn on the Square – This hotel is always a surprise to guests, since its traditional elegance is so unlike most members of the chain. Special feature: a 10-story atrium complete with waterfall and swimming pool. 511 rooms and luxury suites. Four eating facilities; very good Sunday brunch. 24 Public Square (696-5600). Expensive.

Hollenden House – A favorite of business people because of its central location downtown. Features swimming pool and saunas, health club, free parking, color TV, coffee shop, lounge, and an excellent dining room specializing in aged beef and chops. 526 rooms. E 6th St. and Superior Ave. (216 621-0700). Moderate.

Marriott Inn – Near the airport, Cleveland's best motor inn. Its many recreational features include an indoor pool, therapy pool, sauna, miniature golf, putting green, volleyball, badminton. Also has free airport bus, lounge with entertainment, color TV, coffee shop, two dining rooms. 400 rooms. 4277 W 150th St. (216 252-5333). Moderate.

Clinic Inn Hotel – This modern high-rise is near the famous Cleveland Clinic. Features include indoor swimming pool, sauna, foreign language interpreters, color TV, coffee shop, and an Old English dining room. 410 rooms. E 96th St. and Carnegie Ave. (216 791-1900). Moderate.

Harley Hotel-West – Close to the airport, this 235-room hostelry also has in- and outdoor swimming pools, sauna, basketball, and free airport limousine service. 17000 Bagley Rd., near I-71 (216 243-5200). Moderate.

Beryl's Gold Coast Inn – This 40-room motor hotel offers good clean accommodations at the best prices around and throws in a free Continental breakfast too. Has TV, coin laundry, and is near cafés and restaurants. 11837 Edgewater Dr., 5 miles west of the city, one block north of US 6 (516 226-1616). Inexpensive.

EATING OUT: Cleveland has more than 100 different nationality groups who have brought with them distinctive old country recipes and appetites. Restaurants reflect this background with fine ethnic cuisine and a wide range of styles; haute cuisine in shimmering elegance to solid hamburgers in a casual atmosphere. Our selections range in price from $45 or more for a dinner for two in the expensive range, $25 to $35 in the moderate, and $20 or less in the inexpensive range. Prices do not include drinks, wine, or tips.

Giovanni's Ristorante – Pasta is prepared in delectable ways; the veal and sweetbreads are equally satisfying. The decor is quite elegant, so dress accordingly.

Closed Sundays. Reservations required. Major credit cards. 2550 Chagrin Blvd., Beachwood (831-8625). Expensive to moderate.

That Place on Bellflower – Set in a charming century-old carriage house, this is the fleur-de-lis of Cleveland's French restaurants. Specialties are veal Oscar and fresh salmon renaissance. In the summer, dining is al fresco. Closed Sundays. Reservations. Major credit cards. 11401 Bellflower Rd., at University Circle (231-4469). Moderate.

Pearl of the Orient – Chinese cuisine carefully presented, particularly the house specialty, Peking duck; also worth noting is the hot and sour soup. Open daily. Reservations required. Major credit cards. 20121 Van Aken Blvd., Shaker Heights (751-8181). Moderate.

Sutter's Restaurant – Known mostly for its veal dishes, the daily specials are also quite good and always include hearty potato pancakes. Make the finishing touch a rich chocolate torte that really does melt in your mouth. Closed Sundays and Mondays. Reservations for six or more. No credit cards. 726 E 140th St. (268-5257). Moderate.

Shujiro – Japanese simplicity is the keynote here, as demonstrated by such dishes as a delicate shrimp tempura and the house specialty, scampi. Sushi is also popular. Open daily. Major credit cards. Reservations recommended. 2206 Lee Rd., Cleveland Heights (321-0210). Moderate.

Noggins – The eclectic menu includes homemade pastas and fresh seafood; good wines. Open daily. Major credit cards. 20110 Van Aken Blvd., Shaker Heights (752-9280). Moderate to inexpensive.

Lopez y Gonzalez – Hearty portions of all-time Mexican favorites — *tacos al carbon,* for example — are washed down with a glass of Mexican beer or, better still, an oversized margarita. Mesquite-smoked game hen and duck and fresh fish dishes round out the menu. Closed Sundays. Major credit cards. 2066 Lee Rd., Cleveland Heights (371-7611). Moderate to inexpensive.

The Mad Greek – Moussaka, pastitsio, shish kabob, and Greek wine and liqueurs. Rustic inn atmosphere, with dining in the courtyard, weather permitting. Open daily. No reservations. Major credit cards. Cedar Rd. at Fairmont Blvd. (421-3333). Inexpensive.

The Balaton Restaurant – The atmosphere isn't much — bright lights and paper placemats — but the Hungarian food is the real thing. Specialties include homemade soups and strudel, dumplings, and Wiener schnitzel. No alcoholic beverages. Closed Sundays and Mondays. No reservations. No credit cards. 12523 Buckeye Rd. (921-9691). Inexpensive.

Corky & Lenny's – With a name like this, it could only be a deli, and it is. Cleveland residents claim that it's the best Jewish deli outside of New York City, and only New Yorkers may demur. Has the standard deli fare and plenty of the hustle-bustle as well. No reservations. No credit cards. 13937 Cedar Rd., University Heights (321-3310). Inexpensive.

DALLAS

Dallas is a paradox — both big city and small town. Gleaming glass monstrosities appear to rise daily in the downtown area, but Dallasites are just down-home good ol' boys at heart.

That is, if you can find a native Texan to talk to. Migration from the northern climes (with such major corporations as American Airlines relocating in the city) has doubled Dallas's population in 10 years. In less than 140 years, it has grown from a cabin on the banks of the Trinity River to a metropolitan area of almost 2 million (counting neighboring Fort Worth and surrounding suburbs). If Texas were a nation, Dallas would be its capital. More controversial is just how Texan it is; some residents claim it is quintessential Texas — the epitome of bigness and wealth. That claim has gained the city some enmity from other parts of Texas.

A few statistics: Dallas has more Cadillacs per capita than any major city outside the Arab world. Its gross annual sales exceed $2.5 billion, and its airport is larger than the island of Manhattan. These facts point to one thing: extraordinary wealth. Where does it come from? Oil, cotton, electronics, furniture, clothing, and insurance. It is this wealth, more than any other single factor, which determines what might be called the Dallas lifestyle. Historically, money was used to entice the railroads into the city. Today, it pays for glass skyscrapers that shine golden in the setting, rush-hour sun. It also stimulates leisure businesses, like discos and restaurants. At its best, the wealth has generated a number of progressive civic programs to improve the general quality of life. At its worst, it has led to a tasteless extravagance and a preoccupation with power and influence.

In 1940, an unpublished book written as part of the Texas Writers' Project (for the WPA) described the typical Dallas resident as someone who "wants the latest fashions from Fifth Avenue, Bond Street, and Rue de la Paix; the newest models in cars; and the best in functionally constructed, electrified, air conditioned homes, but prefers old-time religions with comfortable, modern trimmings and old-fashioned Jeffersonian democracy." If that picture is a touch too complacent to represent contemporary residents fairly, it nonetheless hits close to home. Dallas residents do have a fine sense of the good life, pursue it actively — and often achieve it.

There is a dark side to the dream, and though its impact diminishes year by year, it will not disappear. To millions of people throughout the world, Dallas is the city where President John F. Kennedy was killed on a November day in 1963. Memphis and Los Angeles bear no equivalent stigma for similar tragedies — the assassinations of Martin Luther King, Jr., and Robert Kennedy. But politically conservative, laissez-faire Dallas still suffers. Until recently, the mention of Dallas in any city outside Texas brought an automatic response of "Kennedy" or "assassination." Former Dallas Mayor Erik

CENTRAL
DALLAS

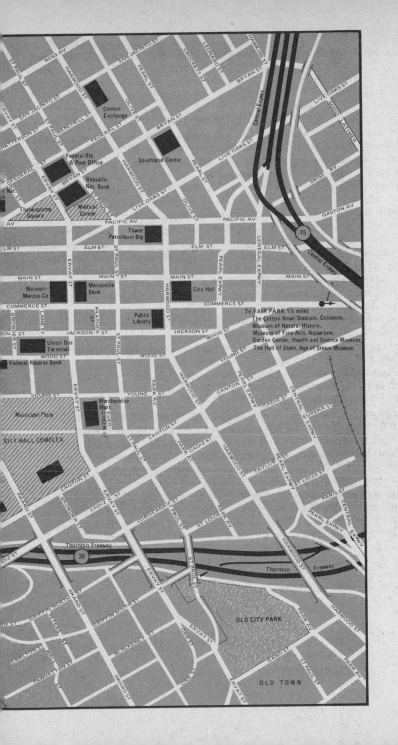

Johnson said, "In many places around the world, we became known as a city of hate — a city that killed a president." Years later, Dallas is still being silently blamed in the minds of millions, even though more than 25% of the city's residents weren't even alive in 1963. And tens of thousands have moved to Dallas since then, lured by the comfortable climate and jobs. But the place where President Kennedy was shot, and the Texas School Book Depository where Lee Harvey Oswald took aim, have become sites to which visitors are obsessively drawn; the Book Depository is the most-photographed site in Dallas — a bitter turn of events for a city that from the beginning has been an unabashed advertiser of its own virtues.

Dallas was founded in 1841 by a Tennessee lawyer named John Neely Bryan, who built a cabin at the junction of three forks of the La Santissima Trinidad River (the Most Holy Trinity) and then set about building it into a city with circulars and much enthusiastic word-of-mouth advertising. Within nine years 430 people had joined him. In later years he was committed to an insane asylum — not, it should be said, for his part in the Dallas venture, though putting a city in such a flat, arid, landlocked place might have been used as evidence. But it worked. With the help of a lot of oil, cattle, manufacturing, and several fortuitous technological revolutions, Dallas has become the eighth largest metropolitan area in the country.

That is not to say that all is perfect with the world beneath the Dallas sun. Unemployment is low, but those without work are just as unemployed as those in high unemployment areas. The rate of crime is high enough to worry anybody but the criminally intent, and city politics are still, for some, a gentleman's diversion. The Dallas County commissioners, by contrast, are viewed as ruffians because they comport themselves with the bellicosity and street savvy of Chicago aldermen.

Significantly, Dallas has never had the kind of racial turmoil other cities have suffered, and when the school desegregation plan was implemented here in 1976 there were few problems. But the racial tensions and separations that exist elsewhere exist here, too. They smolder and steam on street corners of this city's south side, and they are a cold undercurrent flowing beneath the manicured lawns of affluent white Dallas.

Perhaps, in all, it is not so surprising to discover that, at the heart of the bluff self-promotion that is so typically Texan and such standard Dallas-ese, there is a reflective reticence about the real nature of the city. Dallas is Texan, no doubt (the rest of the country can see that even if Texans can't agree); it is certainly American — in the problems it shares and the successes it enjoys and the future it mulls over. But the sum of these things does not quite equal the city itself. And it is this intangible "more" that fascinates residents — and keeps them thoughtfully silent.

DALLAS AT-A-GLANCE

SEEING THE CITY: For the best view of Dallas, go to the *Hyatt Regency Tower* with its revolving cocktail lounge, restaurant, and observation deck (admission charge). 400 S Houston St. (651-1234).

SPECIAL PLACES: Although attractions in Dallas are spread out, the museums are clustered together at Fair Park. Several amusement park complexes are in Arlington, 15 miles west of Dallas.

Fair Park – For three incredibly jammed weeks in October, Fair Park is the scene of the Texas State Fair, with all the superlatives you would associate with such an event: biggest, best, highest, widest, etc. For the rest of the year, Fair Park is the home of the Cotton Bowl, stadium for the New Year's Day college football game, and Fair Park Coliseum, Grand Ave. For information on State Fair activities, call 565-9931.

Museum of Natural History – In order to attract the Texas Centennial Exposition to Dallas in 1936, the city fathers built a group of museums at Fair Park. The Museum of Natural History, a Neoclassic, cream limestone building, contains a variety of fauna and flora from the Southwest. There are some interesting zoology and botany exhibitions, too. Open daily. Free. Ranger Circle, Fair Park (670-8457).

Dallas Museum of Art – The keystone of Dallas's new downtown Arts District houses the permanent collection of pre-Columbian art, African sculpture, and 19th-century modern and contemporary works that have been moved from the old museum at Fair Park plus some surprises. The Sculpture Garden, featuring works by Henry Moore and Ellsworth Kelly, is an urban oasis, replete with cascades and shade trees. The Dallas skyline is an impressive backdrop to the building designed by Edward Larrabee Barnes. Closed Mondays. Free. 1717 N Harwood (922-0220).

Aquarium – This one isn't the biggest or the best in the country, but it's the only one in Dallas. There are more than 325 species of native freshwater fish, cold- and tropical-water creatures — finned, scaled, and amphibious. If you like watching the fish and sea animals being fed, be sure to get here early — around 9 AM. Open daily. Free. 1st St. and Martin Luther King Ave. (670-8441).

Garden Center and Health and Science Museum – Next to the Aquarium, the Garden Center has delightful tropical flowers and plants with Braille markers. Open daily. Admission charge (428-7476). Just down the street, the Health and Science Museum features a fascinating series of anatomy, astronomy, and geology exhibitions. A free planetarium show enraptures planet-watchers and stargazers. Open daily. Free. Fair Park (670-8457).

The Midway and the Hall of State – As you walk along the Midway during the week, you will find it hard to imagine the frenetic carnival activity for which it is known. If you're here during the State Fair or on weekends May through September, you'll probably be swept into the frenzy, stopping only long enough to try winning a stuffed animal or doll at a shooting gallery or pitch 'n' toss. There is an assortment of spine-chilling, scream-inducing, turn-you-upside-down-and-inside-out rides for those who like thrills. There are also great food stands here — Greek, barbecue, and Mexican. At one end of the Midway, the Hall of State has paintings devoted to the heroes of Texas. It was built in 1936, for the Texas Centennial. Open daily. Free. The Midway.

The Age of Steam Museum – Will bring a lump to the throat of anyone who ever loved an old train, with steam engines and other railroad nostalgia. Open Sundays and during the State Fair. Admission charge. The Midway (691-7200).

Neiman-Marcus – The shrine of commercial elegance, the Neiman-Marcus department store has been known to induce orgies of money-spending. If you have an insatiable craving for wave-making machines, a computer chess game, or a biorhythm calculator, this is the place to satisfy it. These games, however, are among the more conservative items in stock. The really exotic stuff is not on display; it's listed in the Christmas catalogue. Three locations: Main and Ervay (downtown), North Park, and the Prestonwood Mall.

Farmers' Market – This is raunchy, down-home, earthy Texas. From 6 AM, farmers drive into town in their trusty ole pickups to sell the fruit and vegetables of their labor. The market consists of a tin-roof shelter and dozens of stalls, with any number of colorful characters standing around. The vegetables are fresher and a bit cheaper than anywhere else in town. Open daily. In May, there's a flower festival, in September a fall harvest, and in November an arts and crafts fair. 1010 S Pearl (742-5435).

Texas Stadium – Cowboys fans go crazy here. This open 65,100-seat stadium packs 'em in during home games and is also the scene of spirited SMU scrimmages. It's constructed to give you the feel of being in a theater or auditorium rather than a stadium, but critics point out that with the dome partially open, part of the field is always in shadow. Hwy. 183 at Loop 12 in Irving (438-7676).

Dallas Zoo – At one time an unkempt, run-down animal park, the Dallas Zoo has been rebuilt with newer facilities. It's now considerably more comfortable for the 2,000 mammals, reptiles, and birds that live within its 50 acres. Open daily. Admission charge. Marsalis Park, 621 E Clarendon Dr. (946-5154).

Texas School Book Depository – Known to millions of people around the world as the place where Lee Harvey Oswald hid, the Texas School Book Depository is the most-photographed site in Texas. It's now the home of the Dallas County Commissioners Court. 506 Elm.

John F. Kennedy Memorial – A 30-foot monument marks the spot where Kennedy fell. It has an indoor room for meditation, with the roof open to the sky. Main and Market sts.

Which Way to Southfork? – The question most asked by visitors is how to get to the mythical home of the Ewings. The building seen on TV's *Dallas* actually does exist. Formerly a private home, it was recently purchased by a real estate investor and soon will be transformed into a hotel of sorts — you can't rent a room, but you can rent the entire house. The ranch itself is being readied as a tourist attraction, replete with party barns and other amusements. It's not yet open to the public, but the exterior can be viewed by taking Highway 75 north to FM 544. Then drive 9 miles east to Murphy Rd. Turn left onto Murphy and continue for about 2 miles, and Southfork will soon appear on the right side of the road.

ARLINGTON

Six Flags Over Texas – A theme amusement park, Six Flags Over Texas motifs are based on different periods in Texas history: Spanish, Mexican, French, Republic of Texas, Confederacy, and the period since the Civil War. You can get a panoramic view of the Dallas and Fort Worth skylines from a 300-foot-high observation deck on top of an oil derrick. A narrow-gauge railway runs around the 145-acre grounds. Open weekends spring and fall, daily June through August. Admission charge. I-30 (formerly the Dallas–Fort Worth Turnpike) at Hwy. 360 (640-8900).

International Wildlife Park – A drive-through wildlife preserve, the only one of its kind in the Southwest. Thousands of animals roam freely around the 500-acre tract, and visitors can stop at many points along the six miles of safari trails. Open daily. Admission charge. 601 Lion Country Pkwy., Grand Prairie (263-2201).

Wax Museum of the Southwest – Definitely a cut above most of the genre. There are about 175 wax figures dispersed among 74 exhibits, including the car used by Bonnie and Clyde. This is a historical wax museum. Open daily. Admission charge, but children under three free. 601 E Safari Pkwy., Grand Prairie (263-2391).

White Water and Wet 'n Wild – These two Texas-size family recreation parks attract huge crowds on blistering summer weekends (weekdays are a bit less jammed). Waterslides, inner tube chutes, surfing pools, and children's play areas provide heat relief for all ages. White Water: Off I-30 at 701 E Safari Pkwy., Grand Prairie (263-1999); Wet 'n Wild: Across I-30 from Texas Stadium at 1600 Lamar Blvd. E (265-3013). Admission charge for both.

■ **EXTRA SPECIAL:** Dallas before its skyscrapers and highways was a simpler place whose lifestyle was reflected in unique architectural styles that combined Victorian grace with the less refined influence of the prairie. One of the few places still able to convey a sense of those earlier, unhurried days is *Old City Park,* an oasis of greenery and history close to downtown. Restored Victorian houses, a railroad depot, pioneer log cabins, and other historically significant structures have been moved in from various locales in North Texas and are now open for exploration. Open daily. Admission charge. Gano and St. Paul (421-5141).

SOURCES AND RESOURCES

TOURIST INFORMATION: For brochures, maps, and general information, contact the Dallas Convention and Visitors Bureau. 1507 Pacific (954-1111). The best guides are *Guide,* in the *Dallas Morning News,* and *Weekend,* in the *Dallas Times Herald;* both are published every Friday. Another good source of information is the *Dallas Observer* weekly tabloid.

Local Coverage – *Dallas Times Herald,* morning and evening daily; *Dallas Morning News,* morning daily; and *D* magazine, monthly.

Food – *D* magazine's restaurant section (monthly); the Dallas restaurant guide in *Texas Monthly* magazine; and the weekend guides published in Friday's newspapers.

Area Code – All telephone numbers are in the 214 area code unless otherwise indicated.

CLIMATE AND CLOTHES: Summers are blisteringly hot, with temperatures over 100. Sudden thunderstorms punctuate the dry, blazing heat. From October to January, the weather is mild, although it can be in the 70s one day and in the 30s the next. From January to March, there are occasional sharp cold snaps, and between March and June you can expect rain and dust storms.

GETTING AROUND: Airport – Dallas/Fort Worth Airport (or D/FW), the country's largest, is approximately 20 miles from downtown Dallas. In light traffic, the drive into the city takes about a half-hour; cab fare will run about $23. A service called the Link provides bus transportation from D/FW to downtown and Market Center hotels every 30 minutes; hourly to those in North Dallas. The Link runs daily from 6 AM to 10 PM and costs $8 or $10, depending on the destination.

Bus – Dallas Area Rapid Transit (DART) operates the bus service. For information, call 979-1111.

Taxi – There are taxi stands at most major hotels, but the best way to get one is to call Yellow Cab (426-6262).

Car Rental – All major national firms are represented.

MUSEUMS: The Dallas Museum of Art, the Museum of Natural History, the Health and Science Museum, the Age of Steam Museum, and Arlington's Southwestern Wax Museum are all discussed in detail in *Special Places.*

MAJOR COLLEGES AND UNIVERSITIES: Southern Methodist University (SMU) has a large campus with many activities (University Park; 692-2000). The University of Dallas campus is at 1845 E Northgate in Irving (721-5000).

SPECIAL EVENTS: The *Texas State Fair* runs for three weeks in October in Fair Park. For more information call 565-9931. College football teams face off annually at the *Cotton Bowl* on New Year's Day. In May, *St. Seraphin's Annual Festival* features Ukrainian dancing and food at European Crossroads. 2829 Northwest Highway (358-5574). The *Flower Festival* at Farmers' Market is another May event, 1010 S Pearl (742-5435). In September, Dallas's Greek Orthodox community sponsors a well-attended *Greek Food Festival* on the grounds of the Holy Trinity Church, 4005 Swiss Ave. (823-3509).

SPORTS AND FITNESS: Dallas has enough professional sports to satisfy just about everyone. A sampling:

   Baseball – Texas *Rangers* play at Arlington Stadium, 1600 Copeland Rd., Arlington (273-5100).

   Basketball – Dallas's NBA team, the *Dallas Mavericks,* plays at Reunion Arena, 777 Sports St. (748-1808).

   Bicycling – Dallas has some pretty trails in the White Rock Lake–East Dallas area and at Bachman Lake, off Northwest Highway near Love Field. You can rent bikes at Bachman.

   Fitness Centers – The Downtown YMCA has an indoor and an outdoor pool, tracks, squash and racquetball courts, exercise equipment, and a sauna, 601 N Akard at Ross, across from the Fairmont (954-0500).

   Football – Dallas *Cowboys* play at Texas Stadium, Texas 183 at Loop 12 (438-7676). The Cotton Bowl is held every New Year's Day at Fair Park (565-9931).

   Golf – There are several municipal courses in Dallas. Tenison Memorial is best known as the home of Lee Trevino. 3501 Samuell (823-5350).

   Jogging – For a 6-mile stint, head north on Akard, right onto Cedar Springs, then take Turtle Creek Boulevard, left onto Avondale, left onto Oak Lawn, left onto Irving, back to Turtle Creek, and retrace your steps home. Or take a bus (40 Bachman Bank or 43 Park Forest) to Bachman Lake for a 3-mile course, or to White Rock Lake (60 White Rock North on Commerce or East St.) for a 10-mile course.

   Tennis – Tennis is a year-round sport here, and it's terrifically popular. There are around 204 municipal courts. The best are at Sammuell Grand at 6200 Grand Ave. (821-3811) and at Fretz Park, Hillcrest and Beltline (233-8921).

THEATER: For a complete up-to-date listing on performance schedules, see the local publications listed above. The major Dallas theaters are: *Theatre Three,* 2800 Routh (871-3300); *Dallas Theater Center,* 3636 Turtle Creek (526-8857); *Stage #1,* 2914 Greenville Ave. (824-2552); and the *New Arts Theatre,* 702 Ross at Market (761-9064). The beautifully restored *Majestic Theatre,* 1925 Elm (880-0137), stages a variety of fine arts events.

MUSIC: For information on concerts, check local publications or call the following numbers. *Dallas Symphony Orchestra* (692-0203); *Dallas Opera* (871-0090); *Dallas Ballet* (744-4430); and *Rainbow-Ticketmaster* (787-2000) for pop-rock concerts.

NIGHTCLUBS AND NIGHTLIFE: Dallas crowds are so notoriously fickle that between the time of writing and the time of printing, everyone may have boogied on down the road to another hangout. Regardless of what's hot and what's not, there's never far to go. Nightlife in Dallas finds three major centers: Oak Lawn, just north of downtown; Greenville Avenue, a north-south artery chockablock with restaurants and nightclubs on the east side; and far North Dallas, the area north of LBJ Freeway. The West End Historical District of downtown Dallas also features several nightclubs; among the most popular is *The Stork Club* at 703 McKinney.

Among a concentration of popular clubs near the intersection of McKinney and Travis is one of the city's best jazz clubs, *Strictly Tabu*, 4111 Lomo Alto (528-5200). Variety is the spice of Greenville Avenue, where you'll find *Poor David's*, 1924 Greenville (821-9891), for every style of music from reggae to jazz to folk, and, just across the street, *Redux*, 1827 Greenville (827-1591), for popular local as well as nationally known entertainers. A few blocks north is the *Greenville Bar and Grill*, 2821 Greenville (823-6691), where rousing Dixieland acts are featured Thursdays and Sundays; the *Arcadia Theatre*, 2005 Greenville (823-3363), for live music events; *Fast and Cool Club*, 3606 Greenville (827-5544), a disco featuring 1960's R&B music; and *Popsicle Toes*, 5627 Dyer (368-9706), a jazz/funk club with dancing. In the upper Greenville area — the stretch above Mockingbird Lane — *Bowley & Wilson's*, 4714 Greenville (692-6470), features raunchy and rowdy comedy acts, while *Café Dallas*, in Old Town Shopping Center (987-0066), *Confetti*, two blocks east of Greenville at 5201 Matilda (369-6969), and *Studebakers* (with a fifties theme), in NorthPark East Shopping Center (696-2475), are three popular discos. *Club Mercedes*, 7035 Greenville (696-8686), is a new R&B club for the business set. There's country-western dancing at the *Longhorn Ballroom*, 215 Corinth (428-3128); *Belle Starr*, Southwestern and Central Expy. (750-4787); and at the *Dallas Palace*, 12215 Coit Rd. (385-0996). In far North Dallas, *Ravel's*, a dressy disco in the *Registry Hotel*, 15201 N Dallas Pkwy. (386-6000), packs 'em in on weekends. For something more avant garde, try the *500 Café*, 408 Exposition (821-4623), where poetry mixes with reggae and pop.

SINS: Humility has never been Texas' greatest virtue, especially regarding things Texan. In fact, Texans' *pride* is *pride;* and all the "biggests" and "bests" have become something of a laughing matter, even among Texans — and no less in Dallas than in other cities in the state. This metropolitan area's special claims to fame are the State Fair of Texas (three weeks in October); the Dallas *Cowboys'* Cheerleaders, who have been arousing *lust* in the hearts of men; and Neiman-Marcus, where you'll see the idle rich, among others, giving free rein to their acquisitive instincts, and hang the cost.

LOCAL SERVICES: Babysitting – Babysitters of Dallas, 5622 Dyer (692-1354)

Business Services – Kelly Services, Downtown, One Main Pl. (742-1721)

Mechanics – For American cars, Exxon Car Care, 5748 Live Oak (823-1351); for foreign cars, Fischer's Foreign Car Service, 4770 Memphis (630-2807)

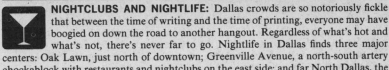

BEST IN TOWN

CHECKING IN: Dallas is the third most popular convention city in the country and has a considerable number of comfortable accommodations. Some hotels cater almost exclusively to conventions, so it may be difficult to book as an individual. It will save a lot of trouble if you inquire ahead of time. For something different and a little less expensive, try Bed & Breakfast Texas Style, a fast-growing service that offers lodging in private homes. Contact Ruth Wilson, 4224 W Redbird La., Dallas 75237 (214 298-5433 or 214 298-8586), for information. At the hotels below, expect to spend $105 and up a night for a double at those places we call expensive; between $60 and $90, moderate; $40 and under, inexpensive.

The Mandalay Four Seasons – This 27-story hotel dedicated to luxury is in Las Colinas, a new business center west of Dallas. It offers convenient access to both the Dallas–Fort Worth Airport and downtown, provides 24-hour room and valet service, and has a fine restaurant, *Enjolie*. 221 S Las Colinas Blvd., Irving (214 556-0800). Expensive.

The Mansion on Turtle Creek – Dallas's most elegant address exudes the kind of luxury and taste that make it worthy of its recent acceptance in the Leading Hotels of the World association. Custom-made furnishings, opulent bathrooms, and attentive service make this the best of the city's deluxe hotels. 2821 Turtle Creek Blvd. (214 559-2100). Expensive.

Fairmont – The morning paper is served with coffee, the restaurant is excellent, and you can generally indulge yourself at this luxurious 600-room hotel. Sunday brunch in the *Venetian Room* is the best and most elegant in Dallas. 1717 N Akard St. (214 720-2020). Expensive.

Plaza of the Americas – Part of the British Trusthouse Forte chain, its management was given carte blanche to hire the best help available — and that they did, from the staff at the coffee shop to the chef in the posh *Café Royal,* which features nouvelle cuisine and a well-stocked wine cellar. 650 N Pearl Blvd. at Bryan St. (214 747-7222). Expensive.

The Loew's Anatole – This addition to the luxurious hotel scene has two ultra-contemporary atriums with restaurants, bars, and the *Mistral* disco, popular for its state-of-the-art video and lighting systems, as well as tennis and racquetball courts. The red brick exterior looks more like a New York hospital than a Dallas hotel, but many residents find it a welcome change from monolithic rectangles of sparkling tinted glass. (214 748-1200). Expensive.

Hyatt Regency – The *Hyatt* has become one of Dallas's most popular hotels. It has an eye-catching silver-burnished exterior, a soaring atrium lobby, and a rooftop restaurant with a dynamite view. *Fausto's* restaurant has extravagant service, magnificent silver, with food that doesn't quite come up to the surroundings. 400 S Houston St. (214 651-1234). Expensive.

Amfac Hotel – This hotel is another popular convention spot. In addition to meeting rooms, it has a swimming pool, bar, and 24-hour café. Kids under 13, accompanied by an adult, free. At the Dallas/Fort Worth Airport (214 453-8400). Expensive.

The Adolphus – An elder giant among Dallas hotels, it has reopened after a $45 million renovation. The decor is turn-of-the-century elegant; rooms are large and individually appointed in the finest of taste. Its *Palm Bar* is a favorite lunch spot. 1321 Commerce (214 742-8200). Expensive.

The Registry – A new addition in far North Dallas that is a four-star attraction in itself. Tennis courts, indoor and outdoor pools, and fine restaurants lend it a resort ambience. Its disco, *Ravel's,* is one of the most popular in town. 15201 N Dallas Pkwy. (214 386-6000). Expensive.

The Westin Galleria – This luxury hotel with 440 balconied rooms opens onto that large and elegant shopping mall, the Galleria, which has some 200 stores and cinemas. Its amenities include a pool, jogging track, saunas, exercise facilities, parking garage, and three restaurants. Convenient to North Dallas business districts. 13340 N Dallas Pkwy. (214 934-9494). Expensive.

The Melrose – A small, premier hotel dating from the 1920s, its 185 rooms give it the hospitable feel of a country estate. A cozy, English-style lounge and an Art

Deco restaurant, the *Garden Court,* add to its appeal. 3015 Oak Lawn Ave. (214 521-5151). Expensive to moderate.

The Bradford Plaza – Small and handsomely refurbished, it's an intimate downtown hotel. *Sam's Bar and Grill,* the hotel eatery, is open 24 hours a day. 302 S Houston (214 761-9090). Expensive to moderate.

Harvey Hotel – An extremely good value in a pricey North Dallas neighborhood, this hotel has attractively appointed rooms and parking. 7815 LBJ Fwy. (214 960-7000). Moderate.

Ambassador Plaza Hotel – This recently renovated Dallas landmark has lots of period character. Near downtown. 1312 S Ervay (214 565-9003). Moderate.

The Summit – The *Summit* is one of the most attractive medium-priced hotels in the city. Its 379 rooms include many luxury suites. The hotel also has three restaurants. 2645 LBJ Fwy. (214 243-3363). Moderate.

Granada Royale Hometel – Suites with kitchens are standard in this Spanish-style hotel built around a soaring atrium. Convenient to downtown and Market Center. 2730 Stemmons Expy. (214 630-5332). Moderate.

La Quinta Motor Inns – If you're looking for a clean, inconspicuous place to sleep, try any of these motels. 4400 N Central Expy. (214 821-4220); Dallas/Fort Worth Airport, 4105 N Airport Fwy., Irving (214 252-6546); I-30 at NW 19th St., Grand Prairie (214 641-3021), near Six Flags amusement park; 13685 N Central Expy. (214 361-8200). Inexpensive.

Comfort Inn – If you're coming to Dallas/Fort Worth to see the Texas *Rangers* or ride the roller coaster at Six Flags Over Texas, this also offers decent, simple accommodations. A good budget choice. 150 rooms. 1000 N Watson Rd., Arlington (817 649-8811). Inexpensive.

EATING OUT: The restaurant business is booming in Dallas. Visitors can eat in a superlative place every night for a month and not repeat. Expect to spend $60 or more for two in those places we've listed as expensive; between $30 and $60, moderate; under $30, inexpensive. Prices do not include wine, drinks, or tips. (Parts of Dallas are "dry." Some restaurants serve drinks; at others, you must bring your own liquor. Call in advance to be sure.)

The French Room – Widely acclaimed as one of the city's best restaurants. Imaginative salads, rich lobster bisque, and entrées like the saddle of lamb in thyme and caviar sauce are standouts. In the *Adolphus Hotel.* Reservations a must. Major credit cards. 1321 Commerce (742-8200). Expensive.

Pyramid Room – A lavish French restaurant in the Fairmont Hotel. The pheasant roasted in a clay crock, sealed with pastry, and the fillet of sole with mushrooms, shrimp, and lobster baked in pastry are two of the exotic entrées regularly featured on the menu. The pompano flambéed in Pernod is superb, too, as are the famous soufflé desserts. The tab for two easily runs over $100. Open daily. Reservations a must. Major credit cards. 1717 N Akard St. (720-0220). Expensive.

The Mansion – As implied in the name, it's a handsomely refurbished private mansion. Quiet elegance, nouvelle cuisine, and polished service make dining here a memorable experience. 2821 Turtle Creek (526-2121). Expensive.

Mario's – This delightful restaurant offers a mixture of Italian and French dishes. Try the *scallopini alla Marsala* — tender escallops of veal sautéed in butter and drenched in a rich wine and mushroom sauce. Major credit cards. 135 Turtle Creek Village (521-1135). Expensive.

Old Warsaw – One of the oldest restaurants in Dallas, it features Continental cuisine with such selections as Dover sole, Châteaubriand, and rack of lamb. Various pâtés are also offered. Open daily. Reservations required. Major credit cards. 2610 Maple Ave. (528-0032). Expensive.

L'Entrecôte – A flashy newcomer that's earned a faithful following among residents. Its specialties include tempting veal dishes; steaks and soufflés are also favorites. Open daily. Major credit cards. 2201 Stemmons Fwy., in the Loew's Anatole Hotel (748-1200). Expensive.

Calluaud – This eatery is run by Guy and Martine Calluaud, who are descended from a long line of master French cooks. The menu changes daily. Closed Sundays. Reservations advised. Major credit cards. 2619 McKinney Ave. (823-5380). Expensive.

Routh Street Café – This innovative new restaurant uses regional produce in preparing southwestern cuisine. The five-course, fixed-price menu changes daily. Open for dinner Tuesdays through Saturdays. Reservations advised. Major credit cards. 3005 Routh St. (871-7161). Expensive.

Café Pacific – An interesting variety of American and European dishes are served in an attractive brass and glass setting. The clam chowder and seafood sauté are especially good. One of the most extensive and reasonably priced wine lists in town. Open daily. Reservations recommended. Major credit cards. 24 Highland Park Shopping Village (526-1170). Expensive to moderate.

Uncle Tai's – Some of the best Oriental food in Dallas is served at this elegant spot in the city's glitziest shopping mall. The crispy beef is a must; the two-color chicken Hunan style is extraordinary. Open daily. Reservations suggested. Major credit cards. The Galleria, near Dallas Pkwy. at LBJ (934-9998). Expensive to moderate.

Kirby's – A favorite choice of Dallas steak lovers, *Kirby's* is an old steakhouse with a warm atmosphere. The "extra-cut" sirloin is tops. Closed Sundays and Mondays. Reservations advised on weekends. Major credit cards. 3715 Greenville Ave. (823-7296). Moderate.

Newport's – At this pretty three-tiered dining room in downtown's historic West End, the grilled seafood dishes are especially recommended. Closed Sundays. Reservations accepted. Major credit cards. 703 McKinney Ave. (954-0220). Moderate.

La Trattoria Lombardi – Great food and good service have made this perhaps the most popular Italian restaurant in Dallas. The pasta and seafood dishes are standouts. Closed Sundays. Reservations advised. Major credit cards. 2916 N Hall St. (528-7506). Moderate.

Turtle Cove – This is a warm, intimate restaurant where the specialty is fresh seafood grilled Texas-style over a mesquite wood fire. Some vegetable dishes are mesquite-grilled, too. Open daily. Reservations accepted. Major credit cards. 2731 W Northwest Hwy. (350-9034). Moderate.

Jozef's – Some say that this is the best seafood restaurant in Dallas, with its Créole soup, smoked trout, and other fresh fish entrées. Open daily. Reservations advised. Major credit cards. 2719 McKinney (826-5560). Moderate.

Chiquita's – This isn't a Tex-Mex Americanized food joint — everything here is *really* Mexican. The carne asada Tampico-style is a filet sliced to triple its usual length and broiled over a hickory fire, then served with green peppers, onions, and soft tacos topped with ranchero sauce. Far and away one of the finest Mexican restaurants north of the border. Closed Sundays. No reservations. Some credit cards. 3810 Congress Ave. (521-0721). Moderate.

TGI Friday's – The bastion of the Greenville Avenue nightlife scene, and one of the first restaurants to settle there. It specializes in the simple things: good food and drink at reasonable price, in a spirited atmosphere. Open daily. Major credit cards. 5500 Greenville Ave. (363-5353). Moderate.

The Chimney – Swiss-Austrian establishment with one of the more esoteric menus found in the Southwest. Tournedos of Montana venison is a specialty, along with

Wiener schnitzel, veal Zürich, and Naturschnitzel. Closed Sundays. Reservations advised. Major credit cards. 9739 N Central Expy. at Walnut Hill, in Willow Creek Shopping Center (369-6466). Moderate.

Ranchman's Café – About an hour's drive north of Dallas, you'll come to the town of Ponder (pop. 208) and one of the most splendid little hometown cafés in Texas. The small restaurant's old wooden screen doors open into a room with longhorns and stirrups on the wall and an authentic country-and-western jukebox. Specialties are chicken-fried steak, T-bone steak, french fries, and possibly the best pecan pie in the country, along with other home-baked fruit pies. Open daily. No credit cards. Main St. (817 479-8221). Moderate.

St. Martin's – A well-chosen, reasonably priced wine list coupled with imaginatively prepared seafood specialties make this intimate restaurant a favorite with those who like to linger over a meal. Open daily. Major credit cards. 3022 Greenville (826-0940). Moderate.

Trail Dust Steak House – Exactly the kind of place visitors expect in Texas. The waitresses wear cowgirl garb, a country-western band entertains, and the food is straight off the ranch: steaks, red beans, potatoes, and salad. Don't wear a tie; if you do, the staff will cut it off and add it to the collection on the walls. Open daily. Reservations for large parties only. Major credit cards. 10841 Composite, at the Walnut Hill exit off Stemmons Expy. (357-3862). Moderate to inexpensive.

Andrew's – Its extensive menu has imaginatively concocted sandwiches as well as Créole and Tex-Mex meals. Popular with the happy-hour crowd. Open daily. No reservations. Major credit cards. Several locations: 7557 Greenville Ave. (363-1910); 10723 Composite (357-9994); 3301 McKinney (521-6535); 14930 Midway (385-1613). Inexpensive.

La Cave – This is a French wine bar where you can get wine or champagne by the glass. For a $1.50 cork fee, you can buy a bottle of anything in stock and drink it with your meal, to the music of Edith Piaf and other French artistes. La Cave serves cheese, pâté, tureen du chef, and other cold entrées. Reservations recommended for parties of six or more. Major credit cards. 2019 N Lamar (871-2072). Inexpensive.

Dickey's Barbecue – An unpretentious decor, but superior barbecued meats. The ribs, sausages, and beef are outstanding. Closed Sundays. No reservations. 14885 Inwood (233-3721). Inexpensive.

Dixie House – This chain of amiable eateries serves such down-home staples as chicken-fried steak, fried chicken, pot roast, and fresh vegetable dishes including black-eyed peas, okra, and greens. Homemade bread and pastries top off the satisfying menu. Several locations: 2822 McKinney (824-0891); 3647 W Northwest Hwy. (353-0769); 6400 Gaston Ave. (826-2412); 14925 Midway (239-5144); and 7778 Forest Lane (361-7221). Open daily. No reservations. Major credit cards. Inexpensive.

Grumbles – An informal eatery in the up and coming West End district of downtown Dallas, where many new restaurants are opening in renovated warehouses. Thick burgers and Créole specialties dominate the limited menu. Closed Sundays. No reservations. Major credit cards. Market and Ross (741-9212). Inexpensive.

Hoffbrau – At this popular, casual steakhouse, the beef is served drenched in butter sauce and accompanied by salad, bread, and potatoes. Open daily. No reservations. Major credit cards. 3205 Knox St. (559-2680). Inexpensive.

On the Border – Visit this place for a taste of Tex-Mex, particularly the *fajitas,* which are served sizzling on a hot platter and accompanied by a host of condiments. Outdoor tables placed on a good people-watching corner supplement those in the spacious dining rooms inside, where a sometimes boisterous atmosphere prevails. Special brunch menu on Sundays. Open daily. No reservations. Major credit cards. 3302 Knox St. (528-5900). Inexpensive.

S&D Oyster House – The restaurant's decor will remind you of almost every cozy little seafood joint you ever found along the Gulf Coast. It's almost always crowded; no reservations. Offerings include raw oysters, boiled and fried shrimp, and three kinds of broiled fresh fish. A house specialty is seafood gumbo. Only beer and wine. Major credit cards. 2701 McKinney Ave. (823-6350). Inexpensive.

Sonny Bryan's – Few would argue that *Sonny Bryan's* serves the best barbecue in Dallas, although some might take exception to the small, drab interior where school desks substitute for tables. Open daily. No reservations. No credit cards. 2202 Inwood Rd. (357-7120). Inexpensive.

DENVER

Denver sits a mile above sea level, sprawled across a sweeping plateau at the exact point where the high plains splash against the Rocky Mountains. Those 5,280 feet give residents a healthy lift that must be more than just psychological, because first-time visitors invariably comment on how healthy everyone looks — with a smiling, rugged, outdoorsy appeal that speaks of long acquaintanceship with Mother Nature and the code of the Old West. It can't be true that all Denver residents (1.6 million in the metropolitan area) are old mountaineers, but a goodly number of them are up here, way above the plains, for just one reason — the city's envied, spectacular toehold on the foot of the Rockies.

To be in Denver is to be aware, first and foremost, of the perennially snow-capped mountains that form the Continental Divide. The mountains look deceptively close, and many an unwary visitor has got the notion to stroll over to the foothills. In fact, it's 30 minutes by six-lane, interstate highway — not a morning's promenade. The RTD (Regional Transportation District) sends buses past the foothills (see *Getting Around*) to serve the communities where thousands of people reside. It's called "living up in the hills."

Denver, like the rest of Colorado, boasts 300-plus days of sunshine each year. Summer temperatures usually settle in the 80s and 90s, but in winter it's anybody's guess. One day might be sunny and 65°; the next may bring subfreezing temperatures. From time to time it does snow in Denver, but most of the white stuff stays in the mountains, to the delight of citizens and visiting schussers alike. More often winter brings Denver its notorious "brown cloud," which hovers over the area as a reminder that this old cowtown has grown up to become a big city with some big-city problems.

The energy crisis of the 1970s found several oil companies scurrying to Colorado to exploit its huge oil shale reserves. The accompanying influx of people and money spurred the construction of a number of modern skyscrapers both downtown and at the Denver Tech Center, at the south edge of the city. Though the oil shale — and the synthetic fuel — business dwindled, the city's skyline was permanently and dramatically changed.

Fortunately, the town's colorful past was not forgotten in the flurry of expansion. Larimer Square, on Cherry Creek (where the city's first settlers appeared in 1858), was restored and turned into an artistic corner of curio shops and cafés that irrationally manages to serve contemporary Denver while providing a sense of what the city used to be. A startling contrast nearby is the city's new 16th Street Mall, a mile-long pedestrian shopping area.

And though Denver's now a lot more like LA than the Old West, there are plenty of people trucking through the streets in flannel shirts, blue jeans, cowboy hats, and boots. If this gives the impression that Denver is a cowtown, don't be fooled. It is not. The Union Stockyards are no longer here, and the

CENTRAL
DENVER

only real cowboys and cowgirls on the streets come for a week in January to attend the National Western Stock Show and Rodeo. But people in Denver often dress that way, perhaps because of the history of the place, and it makes them feel more at home to look the part. A lot of people drift into Denver to check out the action, and you'll no doubt see an interesting assortment of *Easy Rider* biker types, young professionals, and nomads on their way to look for jobs at the ski resorts.

Denver has come a long way since it was a group of log cabins and tents hugging the junction of the Platte River and Cherry Creek. The commercial center of the West, Denver houses more gold bullion than anywhere outside Fort Knox (see *Special Places*). It has its own financial district, an art museum, Victorian mansions, and a zoo. But in spite of its green parks, small lakes, 16th Street Mall, and tree-lined residential streets, there is no question that the best scenery is out of town. The Queen City of the Plains is also the gateway to the Rockies, with its old mining towns, modern ski resorts, pristine lakes, and 14,000-foot mountain peaks. And that is one of the best things about Denver: You don't have to go very far to find the legendary clear air, blue sky, and wide open spaces.

DENVER AT-A-GLANCE

SEEING THE CITY: The best view of Denver is from the top of the capitol rotunda, where you can see the Rockies to the west, the Great Plains stretching, like an ocean, to the east, and Denver itself sprawled below. On the 13th step of the capitol is an inscription noting that you are exactly one mile above sea level. Between E 14th and E Colfax aves. (866-5000).

SPECIAL PLACES: It's a pleasure to walk around Denver. The downtown section has a number of Victorian mansions as well as the city's public institutions and commercial buildings.

United States Mint – Appropriately enough for a city that made its fortune in gold, Denver still has more of it than anyplace else in the country (except Fort Knox). On the outside, the Mint is a relatively unimpressive white sandstone Federal building with Doric arches over the windows. Inside, you can see money being stamped and printed and catch a glimpse of gold bullion, although the stuff on display is only a fraction of the total stored here. Most impressive is the room full of money just waiting to be counted. Closed on weekends. Free. Delaware St. between Colfax and 14th (844-3582).

Denver Art Museum – That imposing, rather odd building sparkling in the sun down the street from the Mint is the Denver Art Museum, a supermodern structure covered with a million glittering glass tiles. Designed by Gio Ponti, its interior is just as spectacular as its exterior. Be sure to visit the American Indian collection on the second floor — it has superlative costumes, basketry, rugs, and totem poles. Stop for lunch or a snack at the museum's terrace restaurant, weather permitting. Closed Mondays. Admission $1.50 to $2.50; children under six, free. W 14th Ave. and Bannock St. (575-2793).

Denver Public Library – This $3 million building houses a vast collection, including books, photographs, and historical documents related to the history of the West. The lower level, known as the basement, contains a splendid children's collection. Exhibitions on western life are on the main floor, and rare book lovers willing to hunt for the special collections will be delighted. Open daily. Free. 1357 Broadway (571-2345).

Colorado History Museum – The new Heritage Center has exhibitions on people who've contributed to Colorado history, period costumes from the early frontier days, and Indian relics. Many of the costumes were donated by members of old Denver families whose ancestors actually wore them. Life-size dioramas show how gold miners, pioneers, and Mesa Verde cliff dwellers used to live. Open daily. Free. 1400 Broadway (866-3682).

Capitol – The rotunda looks like the dome of the Capitol in Washington, DC, coated with $50,900 worth of Colorado gold leaf; the impressive marble staircases rate a look even if you don't want to climb to the top. There are 45-minute tours between 9:30AM and 3:30PM. Open daily. Free. Between E 14th Ave. and Colfax, at Sherman Ave. (866-5000).

Molly Brown House – When gold miner Johnny Brown and his wife Molly moved into their Capitol Hill mansion, Denver society snubbed them as nouveau riche. But Molly earned her place in city history, and, ironically, it's her former house that is now high on the "most visited" list. She is remembered for her earthy flair and keen intelligence and for taking charge of a lifeboat when the *Titanic* sank, commanding the men to row while she held her chinchilla cape over a group of children to keep them warm — which is how she came to be known as the "unsinkable Molly Brown." Closed Mondays in June, July, and August. Admission charge. 1340 Pennsylvania St. (832-4092).

Financial District – Seventeenth Street is the center of Denver's financial district, and there are quite a number of tall, modern bank buildings that will give you a proper sense of the economic stability and strength that characterizes such areas. During summer lunch hours, street musicians give concerts in the plazas outside the United Bank Center and the First Interstate Bank of Denver.

Larimer Street – Walk along the new 16th Street Mall to Larimer, Denver's most interesting shopping street. You'll pass the Daniels and Fisher Tower, a 1920s landmark said to be a copy of the campanile of Venice. It used to be the tallest building in town, but it has been overshadowed by more modern edifices. Larimer Street is lined with fascinating art galleries, curio shops, silversmiths, and cafés. Most interesting is Larimer Square, where various restaurants, crafts shops, and wine bars have been restored so that they retain the flavor of Denver's past (between 14th and 15th sts.).

City Park – A 640-acre park with two lakes, spreading lawns, Denver's Museum of Natural History (known for its exhibitions of animals in natural settings) and the Habitat Zoo. The museum was the first in the country to use curved backgrounds with reproductions of mountain flowers, shrubs, and smaller animals to give a feeling of the natural environment. Displays of fossils, minerals, gold coins, and birds. Open daily. Free (370-6363). The museum also houses the popular Gates Planetarium (370-6351) and the IMAX Theatre (370-6300), its newest addition. Both closed Mondays. Admission charge. The Habitat Zoo (575-2754) has designed a number of natural mountain environments for its animals. Open daily. Admission charge.

■**EXTRA SPECIAL:** There are so many gorgeous places to explore around Denver that it's almost unfair to single out any one in particular. *Rocky Mountain National Park* is, however, one of the most spectacular scenic areas of the US, and it's a perfect choice for a day trip. Within its 264,000 acres are dozens of mountains over the 12,000-foot mark, among them Bighorn Mountain and Longs Peak. The interior of the park offers the opportunity to cross the Continental Divide. You can rent horses and camping equipment in the town of Estes Park, at the northeast corner of the national park. To get there, take I-25 north for 50 miles, then Rte. 34 west. (See *Rocky Mountain National Park,* DIRECTIONS, for more information.)

SOURCES AND RESOURCES

TOURIST INFORMATION: For brochures, maps, and general information, contact the Colorado Hospitality Center, 225 W Colfax Ave. (892-1112). For information on skiing, contact Colorado Ski Country USA, 1410 Grant (837-0793) and at its airport booth.

Guestguide Magazine is the best guide to the Denver area; it's available at newsstands.

Local Coverage – *Denver Post* and *Rocky Mountain News,* morning dailies; *Denver* and *Colorado* magazines, monthly.

Food – *Denver* magazine; *Denver Post,* Friday edition.

Area Code – All telephone numbers are in the 303 area code unless otherwise indicated.

CLIMATE AND CLOTHES: Because of the altitude, Denver is pretty dry. Even when the temperature hits the 90s in summer (it hits 100 every five years!), it's not intolerable. Nights cool to the 70s. In fall and winter, the days are sunny and in the 60s, but nights can drop to the 20s. Denver is not usually hit by those mountain blizzards that the Weather Service reports as "sweeping the Rockies." And it only gets an average of 14 inches of precipitation a year, so you'll hardly need an umbrella.

GETTING AROUND: Airport – Denver's Stapleton International Airport is about a 20-minute drive from downtown; taxi fare to downtown runs $8 or $9. RTD (Regional Transportation District) buses leave for downtown Denver every half-hour from the airport terminal's east entry; fare is 70¢ during rush periods, 35¢ at other times.

Bus – RTD runs buses throughout the Denver area. For information, contact the Downtown Information Center, 626 16th St. (628-9000).

Taxi – Taxis cannot be hailed in the streets. Call Yellow Cab (292-1212) or Zone Cab (861-2323). There are cab stands at the airport, bus station, Union Station, and at most major hotels.

Car Rental – All major national firms are represented.

MUSEUMS: For a complete description of the Denver Art Museum, Colorado History Museum, Molly Brown House, and Museum of Natural History, see *Special Places.* Other notable museums are:

Buffalo Bill Museum – on Lookout Mountain is interesting, especially for children (526-0488). Buffalo Bill is buried on the grounds.

The Children's Museum – 2121 Crescent Dr., I-25 at 23rd Ave. (433-7433).

The Colorado Railroad Museum – 17155 W 44th Ave. (279-4591).

MAJOR COLLEGES AND UNIVERSITIES: The University of Denver makes its home within the city proper, at S University Blvd. and E Evans Ave. (871-2000). The University of Colorado is 20 miles northwest of the city, on Rte. 36, in Boulder (492-0111). The US Air Force Academy's bright, clean, spacious campus is 60 miles south of Denver on I-25, near Colorado Springs (472-1818).

SPECIAL EVENTS: The *National Western Stock Show and Rodeo* in January lasts a week and attracts cowfolk from all over. The Denver Art Museum's annual exhibition of western art runs from January through March. *Easter Sunrise Service* at Red Rocks Natural Amphitheater attracts thousands. In July and August, the University of Colorado at Boulder presents its annual *Shakespeare Festival.* And Larimer Square is the site of the *Oktoberfest* in guess what month?

 SPORTS AND FITNESS: Baseball – Denver *Zephyrs* play at Mile High Stadium, 1700 Federal Blvd. (433-8645).

Basketball – Denver *Nuggets* play at McNichols Sports Arena, 1635 Clay St. (893-3865).

Bicycling – Bikes can be rented from J & E Sports, 4365 S Santa Fe Dr. (781-4415).

Fishing – There's good fishing at Dillon Reservoir, west of Denver on I-70, and Cherry Creek Reservoir, just southeast of the city on I-225.

Fitness Centers – The Indian Springs Resort has relaxing, hot mineral baths, 302 Soda Creek Rd., one block south of Miner St., in Idaho Springs (623-2050). The International Athletic Club welcomes guests from the *Fairmont, Hilton, Holiday Inn,* and *Marriott;* it has exercise classes, tracks, racquetball and squash courts, sauna, massage; 1630 Welton (623-2100). The Yoga and Fitness Center offers exercise classes, 6th and St. Paul (320-6310).

Football – Denver *Broncos* of the NFL (433-7466) play at Mile High Stadium, 1700 Federal Blvd. (433-7466).

Golf – Among the 50 golf courses in the area, the best are Kennedy, 10500 E Hampden Ave. (751-0311); Park Hill, 3500 Colorado Blvd. (333-5411); and Wellshire, 3333 S Colorado Blvd. (756-6318).

Jogging – Follow the Highline Canal trail; or run in Washington Park, which is 4½ miles from downtown, or in City Park, 2 miles from downtown.

Racing – Greyhounds race at Mile High Kennel Club, 6200 Dahlia Rd. (288-1591). No one under 21 is admitted.

Skiing – Colorado ski country is famous all over the world. The slopes closest to the city are in Loveland Basin, 60 miles west on I-70; nearby Keystone and Arapaho Basin; and Winter Park, west on I-70, then north on Rte. 40. Former President Ford used to give news conferences on the slopes at Vail, a resort 100 miles west of Denver on I-70. Internationally acclaimed Aspen and Snowmass are about 190 miles southwest of Denver on I-70 and Hwy. 82 (see *Downhill Skiing,* DIVERSIONS).

Tennis – The best public courts are at Gates Tennis Center, 100 S Adams St. (355-4461).

 THEATER: For complete up-to-the-minute listings on theatrical and musical events, see local publications listed above. *Elitch Gardens* is one of the oldest summer theaters in the country, 4620 W 38th Ave. (458-8801). The University of Colorado at Boulder hosts a *Shakespeare Festival* every summer (see *Special Events*). The Denver Center for the Performing Arts presents Broadway productions as well as those of local companies, 14th and Curtis sts. (892-0987).

 MUSIC: *Red Rocks Amphitheater* is the site of big-name rock concerts. Park of the Red Rocks, US 285 (575-2637). The *Denver Symphony* plays from October through May at Boetcher Hall, 14th and Arapahoe sts. (592-7777). (Free concerts in City Park in June, July, and August.) *Heritage Square Opera House* south of the town of Golden, west on Rte. 6, stages opera (279-7881).

NIGHTCLUBS AND NIGHTLIFE: Big-name entertainment is available nightly at *Moulin Rouge* in the *Fairmont Hotel,* 1750 Welton St. (295-5821), but most of Denver's clubs are limited to singles spots on the new East Hampden Avenue strip. Popular places here are *Turn o' the Century* (779-1808), *Knick's* (740-9555), and *Bobby McGee's* (695-0700). The *Proof of the Pudding,* 7300 E Hampden Ave. (694-4884), offers live music and dancing in a basement restaurant. Larimer Square has *Josephina's* (623-0166) and *Basins Up* (623-2104). Off S Colorado Boulevard, in the town of Glendale, there's plenty of nightlife.

 SINS: To arrive in town only to discover that all the Texans got here first and that winter brings ground-hugging clouds of smog — that's an introduction to *anger* in Denver. Residents cool their outrage with *pride* thinking of Colorado's 52 mountain peaks at least 14,000 feet high. *Lust* flourishes even in the mountains: Denver's fading red-light district is on E Colfax. For dedicated topers, the suburb of Glendale, with its less stringent liquor laws, is the best place to go.

 LOCAL SERVICES: Babysitting – Family Care, 365 S Newcombe (980-9090); Domestic Perception, 2260 S Xanadu Way (745-4400)
    Business Services – Executive Services, 475 17 St., Suite 800 (293-3840); Record Executive Services, 11000 E Yale Ave. (771-8686)
  Mechanic – May D & F Goodyear Auto Center, 14th St. and Tremont Pl. (573-1502)

BEST IN TOWN

 CHECKING IN: Accommodations in Denver range from the ultra-deluxe, old-fashioned *Brown Palace* and *Oxford* to the modern, comfortable *Radisson, Fairmont,* and *Marriott.* Expect to pay between $90 and $150 at those places listed as expensive; between $50 and $80 at those in the moderate category; about $40 at places noted as inexpensive. Because the city is rather overbuilt with hotels, many offer very attractive weekend rates.

Brown Palace – Built in the 1890s, it was one of the first hotels to have a 9-story atrium lobby with balconies rimming it on every floor. The 231 rooms have been remodeled several times. 17th St. and Tremont Pl. (303 297-3111). Expensive.

Radisson Hotel – With an outdoor swimming pool and an ice skating rink that becomes a terrace in the summer, the standard, self-contained 752-room *Radisson* environment naturally includes a dining room, coffee shop, and cocktail lounge with entertainment. 16th and Court sts. (303 893-3333). Expensive.

Westin Tabor Center – Opened in 1985, this 430-room hotel is the centerpiece of the new Tabor Center, an office-hotel-retail complex on Denver's 16th Street Mall. A Continental dining room, pool, sauna, racquetball courts, and fitness center are among the facilities. 16th and Lawrence sts. (303 572-9100). Expensive.

Fairmont Hotel – This 26-floor beauty, with 540 rooms, has everything, including telephones in the bathrooms. Its *Moulin Rouge* dinner club and cocktail lounge offer top entertainment, and the *Marquis Room* challenges *Café Giovanni* as the swankiest (and finest) eating spot in town. 1750 Welton St. (303 295-1200). Expensive.

Marriott City Center Hotel – Opened in February 1982 on the lower 20 floors of the 42-story Arco Tower, in the heart of downtown Denver. Amenities include underground shopping and restaurants. 1701 California St. (303 297-1300). Expensive.

Oxford – A short stroll from the shopping attractions of the Tabor Center, Writer Square, and historic Larimer Square, the *Oxford* is a bit of history unto itself, having opened in 1891. A $12 million restoration (in 1979) turned this 82-room hotel into a Denver showplace. The *Sage, Oxford Club, Corner Room* jazz cabaret, and *Cruise Room Bar* (a registered historic landmark) are all local favorites. Features include complimentary Continental breakfast, sherry and biscuits served from alcoves on each floor, a health club, 24-hour room service, and complimentary limo within downtown. 17th St. and Wazee (303 628-5400). Expensive.

Denver Inn-Downtown – Originally part of the *Brown Palace*, this 230-room structure was converted into a separate establishment for the more budget-conscious traveler. Complimentary breakfast and access to health club provided. 17th St. and Tremont Pl. (303 296-0400). Moderate.

Holiday Inn Sport Center – Simple, comfortable rooms, some with excellent mountain views, less than a mile from the all attractions of downtown. Although the neighborhood is not one of the most desirable, the view of the Denver skyline from *Fans,* the 14th-floor restaurant and lounge, is spectacular. Shuttle service to and from downtown can be arranged, though we recommend that you provide your own transportation. Room service, outdoor swimming pool, and free airport shuttle. 1975 Bryant St. (303 433-8331). Inexpensive.

 EATING OUT: Gone are the days when dining in Denver inevitably meant broiling mule steak over an open fire, then spicing the meat with gunpowder. (Salt and pepper were scarce in the Old West.) Nowadays, there's quite a cosmopolitan selection of eating places, and two people can generally eat well for around $40. Expect to pay more than that at the restaurants listed below as expensive; between $30 and $35 at those places in the moderate category; inexpensive, under $25. Prices do not include drinks, wine, or tips.

Marquis Room – This restaurant in the *Fairmont Hotel* is the new and strong competition for *Café Giovanni.* It serves fine Continental and French cuisine in an elegant setting. Open daily for dinner; no lunch on Sunday. Reservations necessary. Major credit cards. 1750 Welton St. (295-5825). Expensive.

Café Giovanni – Its Continental cuisine, with French and Northern Italian flourishes, has earned high praise from Denver's restaurant reviewers. Try one of the daily seafood specials, with a soufflé for dessert. Closed Sundays. Reservations required. Major credit cards. 1515 Market St. (825-6555). Expensive.

Morton's of Chicago – Straightforward American cuisine, featuring huge portions of aged beef and arguably the best steak in town — certainly the most expensive. Closed Sundays. Major credit cards. Reservations accepted, and recommended, at most times. Tivoli Center, 901 Larimer St. (825-3353). Expensive.

The Sage – An ideal spot for a quick, elegant lunch or a romantic dinner in Denver's charming "LoDo" (lower downtown) district. Major credit cards. 17th St. and Wazee (628-5533). Moderate.

Downtown Broker – Tucked into an area that was once the basement vault and boardroom of a bank, tables are set in the cubicles customers once used to peer into their safe deposit boxes. This quaint touch of historical voyeurism heightens the palate, we think, and provides an added dimension to roast prime ribs and shrimp, the house specialties. (A bowl of shrimp is included with dinner.) Reservations required. Closed Sundays. Major credit cards. 17th and Champa sts. (292-5065). Moderate.

Wellshire Inn – For decades this has been southeast Denver's best-loved restaurant, serving creative American and Continental dishes. In a stately Tudor building on the Wellshire Golf Course (open to the public), just a 3-iron shot north of busy E Hampden. Popular with businesspeople for buffet breakfasts and leisurely lunches. Romantic evening atmosphere. Major credit cards. 3333 S Colorado Blvd. (759-3333). Moderate.

Buckhorn Exchange – It's not downtown, but you'll find the trip well worth the effort. Denver residents have been coming here for "umpteen million years" to feast on steaks in the shadows of big game trophy heads. Open daily. Reservations recommended. Major credit cards. 1000 Osage St. (534-9505). Moderate.

Chez Thoa – A French-Vietnamese eatery in the Cherry Creek shopping district, offering innovative French dishes as well as authentic Vietnamese specialties. Closed Sundays. Major credit cards. 158 Fillmore St. (355-2323). Moderate.

The Normandy – Consistent, well-prepared French cuisine and formal but friendly service in a Gallic setting. Closed Mondays. Major credit cards. 1515 Madison St. at E. Colfax Ave. (321-3311). Moderate.

Gasho of Japan – Specializing in teriyaki, sashimi, and sukiyaki, the chefs here prepare shrimp, vegetables, and other ingredients by your table. Open daily. Reservations advised. Major credit cards. 1627 Curtis St., at Prudential Plaza (892-5625). Moderate.

Brendles – This relative newcomer is rated "best in town" by many local reviewers. Recommended entrées include grilled veal loin chop and grilled duck breast; also try the smoked game for starters. The restaurant is in the basement of a warehouse on a rejuvenated lower downtown street near Larimer Square. Closed Sundays. Reservations advised. Major credit cards. 1624 Market St. (893-3588). Moderate.

La Loma – The best of Denver's many excellent Mexican restaurants, ideal for family dinners and quick, informal business luncheons. Comfortable, cheery ambience. Major credit cards. 2525 W 26th Ave. (433-8307). Inexpensive.

DETROIT

Poor mercurial Detroit. When its auto industry is percolating, there is dancing in the streets. When it isn't, the bread line forms to the right. Gluttonous prosperity or hard times — Detroit has tasted both, and usually in larger doses than other big cities with a more diversified industrial underpinning. Cars have been Detroit's lifeblood and its curse.

The inbound drive along I-94 from Metropolitan Airport provides more than subtle shadings of the Motor City, capital of the world's auto industry. Low-slung buildings of auto suppliers crowd the banks of the highway. At one bend is a giant tire the size of a ferris wheel. Farther along, the freeway skirts the leviathan Rouge manufacturing complex of Ford Motor Company, the largest industrial complex in the world, and the road's endless automobile billboards tick off auto production. More than just a digital readout, they are Detroit's electrocardiogram. But whether its vital signs are weak or strong, Detroit always manages to hang in there.

Like most of the Great Lakes country, Detroit's roots are French. When the king of France started wearing a beaver hat late in the 17th century, everyone in French society had to have one, too. This made trapping and exporting beaver fur a very lucrative venture for French trappers around Montreal and Quebec. Like any successful business, the beaver trade fell prey to unscrupulous operators, and entire canoeloads of pelts were hijacked along the Great Lakes. In 1701, Antoine de la Mothe Cadillac — who was to have an automobile named after him 200 years later   arrived in Detroit to protect legitimate voyageurs and their cargoes. Cadillac picked the strait between Lake St. Clair and Lake Erie for Fort Pontchartrain d'Étroit ("on the Straits"). After the French and Indian War, the fort became British, then was taken over by the Americans in 1796, 13 years after the Revolutionary War.

If its roots are French, subsequent Detroit history — its tree and branch — is indomitably American. Detroit's destiny was charted for it at the turn of this century when Henry Ford took the horseless carriage concept and applied mass production techniques. Detroit — and the world — hasn't been the same since. A historical plaque marks the site of the little two-story plant in uptown Highland Park where Model T's first sputtered to life.

Detroit's brontosaurus car-making plants went from wheels to weapons during World War II. Tides of war workers poured into the city and population zoomed. There was plenty of everything for everybody. That was, until Detroit fell into the same lockstep of other American cities. In the quietude of the 1950s, a middle-class exodus from the city began, and by the 1960s Detroit had become a case of classic American malaise: rings of wealthy suburbs around a neglected inner city — and its even more neglected residents. Degeneration of the core city has had severe consequences for Detroit. The mass exodus spurred city planners to allocate funds for endless concrete

CENTRAL
DETROIT

(Above) CULTURAL CENTER

(Below) DOWNTOWN AND CIVIC CENTER

Continuation of the main map
with 1½ mile gap between two parts

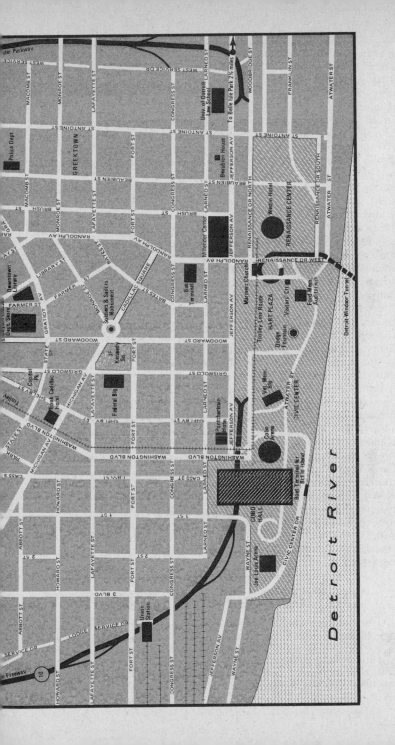

miles of freeways to connect the suburbs around the city, leaving the downtown area to shrivel.

At last something was done, and Detroit began coming back. Downtown districts left for dead seemed about to be reborn. There was a profusion of building, especially on the riverfront, along with new restaurants, and a recharged feeling among Detroiters. Then came the severe auto sales slump of the early 1980s, and the pace of rebuilding and revitalization slowed to a crawl — or stopped altogether. But, like an aging prizefighter who refuses to say uncle, Detroit is back; auto sales are up and optimism is boosting civic spirit.

Lording over modern Detroit is the Renaissance Center (known as RenCen), six circular towers of dark reflective glass surrounding an even taller tower, the 73-floor *Westin Hotel.* The dramatic office-shopping-hotel complex soars regally on the lip of the Detroit River, which separates the city from Canada. Trollies bounce down Washington Boulevard past colorful sidewalk cafés to the riverfront and the doorstep of RenCen.

Although RenCen has had its share of troubles both financially (it defaulted on its mortgage in 1983) and architecturally (its space age design isolates it both physically and emotionally from the surrounding downtown area), it was a necessary first step in the area's revitalization. Neighborhoods in its shadow are getting well again, and the Riverfront, a new twin-tower apartment complex, is leading a resurgence in downtown living. Across from RenCen is the $71 million Millender Center of shops, restaurants, apartments, and a spanking new *Omni International Hotel.* In Bricktown and Rivertown there is a host of new restaurants hopping inside old buildings; Greektown is a long downtown block of some of Detroit's best restaurants, as Greek as Zorba and as energized as Walt Disney World.

After cars, Detroit is a sports town. Baseball fans are justifiably proud of their Tigers. The Joe Louis Arena, named for one of Detroit's native sons, is the home of Detroit's pro hockey team, the Red Wings, and boxing. It's also on the revitalized riverfront alongside sprawling Cobo Hall, the city's cavernous convention center. There's the Pontiac Silverdome, with the world's largest inflated roof, for football and basketball. Detroit's Cultural Center and its Medical Center hug the city's main thoroughfare, Woodward Avenue, which separates Detroit's east and west sides.

Detroiters have a lot of good reasons to like themselves and where they live. After all, Detroit gave the world the Motown sound and the first ice cream soda, the first jazz club and cold duck, and the largest inventory of pistachios this side of the Middle East.

DETROIT AT-A-GLANCE

SEEING THE CITY: The best view of the city is from the top of the 73-story *Westin Hotel.* Part of the Renaissance Center, it is one of the city's most stylish and dramatic creations. Views are from the hotel's top three floors, called the Summit, with a revolving restaurant and cocktail lounge and an observation deck ($2 if you're not drinking or dining). Philip A. Hart Plaza on Jefferson at St. Antoine (568-8000). There are great skyline views of Detroit from rooms in the *Hilton International Windsor* and from Dieppe Gardens, a riverside park at the foot of Ouellette Avenue, Windsor's main street.

 SPECIAL PLACES: Down on the ground, Civic Center is a good place to begin sightseeing. We've divided the city into Civic Center, Cultural Center, and other Special Places.

CIVIC CENTER

Renaissance Center – Detroit's very own Oz, this city-within-the-city dominates Detroit's skyline. Dining, entertainment, designer boutiques, and more have made RenCen tick since it opened in 1977. Lately, however, it has been beset by hard times — it defaulted on its mortgage in 1983 and has lost a number of tenants. The fortress-like berms that surround the building add to its isolation from the rest of downtown. The huge complex is tied together by a maze of walkways, atriums, gardens — even an indoor lake. Prediction: With seven circular buildings to stroll around, first-timers will get lost. Everybody docs. Group tours are available (591-3611). Jefferson Ave. between Randolf and Beaubien sts.

Millender Center – Tethered to RenCen by an arcing skywalk over Jefferson Avenue, Millender is a smaller version of the office-shopping complex without the dizzying confusion. Both the Millender Center (222-1500) and the abutting *Omni Hotel* boast quality shops and restaurants.

Philip A. Hart Plaza – This once ragtag area of waterfront is now an upbeat people-place designed by the international sculptor Isamu Noguchi. What it lacks in grass, this paved esplanade makes up for in action. The $30 million Dodge Fountain spouts 30 computer-controlled water displays. It's also the home of Detroit's summer ethnic festivals of food and entertainment. In winter, there's an ice skating pavilion, à la Rockefeller Center. The Detroit River is alongside, with Windsor, Ontario, in the background.

Cobo Hall–Washington Boulevard Trolley – A charming, antique trolley car wends its way south from Grand Circus Park along Washington Boulevard and east to RenCen. (The conductor wears 1890 regalia.) The trolley runs through a new downtown section of sidewalk cafés, specialty shops, and covered parkways, past St. Aloysius Church, the *Book Cadillac Hotel,* and various airline and travel agency offices.

CULTURAL CENTER

Detroit Institute of Arts – An unusual collection of Great Masters and modern artists lines the walls, halls, and gardens here. Walking through the Institute of Arts will give you the chance to examine Peter Breughel's Flemish masterpiece *Wedding Dance* and Mexican artist Diego Rivera's gripping, provocative frescoes on the industrial life of Detroit. In the garden is a bust of Lincoln by Gutzon Borglum, Mt. Rushmore's sculptor. Closed Mondays. Donations accepted. 5200 Woodward Ave. (833-7900).

Detroit Public Library – This Italian Renaissance, white Vermont marble building houses books, paintings, stained glass windows, and mosaics. The Burton Historical Museum, an archive of material related to Detroit history, is one of the library's special collections. Closed Sundays and holidays. Free. Woodward and Kirby aves. (833-1000).

Detroit Historical Museum – The early days of Detroit are shown by models of early streets and railroads, period rooms, and exhibitions on horseless carriages and automobiles. In the basement stands a permanent display of actual storefronts from bygone eras. Closed Mondays, Tuesdays, and holidays. Donations accepted. Woodward and Kirby aves. (833-1805).

Wayne State University – Known for its innovative architecture rather than its football. A lot of buildings have gone up since 1960, among them a new medical center attached to the Wayne State medical school, reputed to be one of the best in the country. If you enjoy a college atmosphere, take a stroll on the campus. 650 W Kirby (577-2424).

Detroit Science Center – The hands-on displays here allow visitors to demonstrate scientific principles for themselves. This $5 million complex also features a domed space theater. Closed Mondays. Admission charge. 5020 John R St. (577-8400).

Children's Museum – A planetarium and collections of puppets and small animals. Kids love the life-size sculpture of the horse near the entrance — it's made out of automobile bumpers. Closed Sundays. Free. 67 E Kirby Ave. (494-1210).

OTHER SPECIAL PLACES

Belle Isle – This beautiful island park in the middle of the Detroit River was originally allocated for pasture by Monsieur Cadillac himself. About two miles long, Belle Isle has a children's zoo; the Dossin Great Lakes Museum, with displays of model ships (267-6440); an Aquarium (267-7159); and the Remick Music Shell, where the Detroit Concert Band plays for free in the summer. It's also a good place for picnics, biking, canoeing, and jogging. South of Jefferson, across the Gen. Douglas MacArthur Bridge (recreation office, 267-7115).

Boblo Boats – Every day between Memorial and Labor days, two 1,200-passenger steamers leave downtown Detroit for Boblo Island. The 26-mile boat ride takes about 1½ hours each way — the most pleasant way to see industrial Detroit and Canada. At Boblo Island, there's a large amusement park and local craftwork. Behind Cobo Hall, at 661 Civic Center Dr. (259-8055).

Greenfield Village and Henry Ford Museum – Legend has it that when Henry Ford couldn't find a copy of McGuffey's *Reader,* he feared such examples of Americana would disappear entirely unless he founded a museum. The result is here — and as you might expect, it has hundreds of splendid, antique automobiles and thousands of 19th- and 20th-century machines. Next-door Greenfield Village is a collection of transplanted houses of historical interest. Henry Ford couldn't be stopped — he bought McGuffey's school and had it reconstructed, along with Thomas Edison's Menlo Park laboratory and the first boarding house to have electricity. An English shepherd's cottage and Noah Webster's house are also here. Separate admissions for Greenfield Village and Henry Ford Museum. South of Michigan Ave. between Oakwood Blvd. and Southfield Fwy., Dearborn (271-1620).

Eastern Market – A carnival of sights, smells, and sounds, this has been a farmers' market since 1892. Saturdays are great fun, watching shoppers haggle over prices with merchants selling the freshest produce, meats, fish, poultry, and cheeses. Russell at Fisher Fwy. (833-1560).

Greektown – A downtown enclave of restaurants serving authentic Greek fare. Quaint shops, bakeries, and Old St. Mary's Church make an interesting stroll. Trappers Alley, a five-level mall full of restaurants, specialty shops, and Monroe's disco, is the new kid on the block. Monroe St. between Beaubien and St. Antoine.

Fort Wayne – French, British, American, and Canadian soldiers have all passed through this 15-acre fort in the line of duty. A museum focuses on Detroit's military history. Open Wednesdays through Sundays, May through November. Admission charge. W Jefferson at Livernois, at the Detroit River (297-9360).

Plant Tours – Long-abandoned auto plant tours have been revived with the opening of General Motors Hamtramck Assembly Center (972-6189). The Hiram Walker Distillery, 2072 Riverside Dr. E, in Windsor, Ont. (965-6611), offers tours in July and August.

■**EXTRA SPECIAL:** Detroit's biggest tourist attraction is just a mile away: *Canada.* In just a few minutes, you can enter a different country without having to go through the angst of getting a visa or changing money. You don't even need a passport if you're a US citizen — just a driver's license or birth certificate to prove citizenship. Don't expect any drastic change from Detroit, however. Windsor, Ontario, just across the river, is another automobile-producing city, with GM, Chrysler, and Ford Canadian plants. If you're looking for bargains, Ontario is a great place to buy English woolens, glassware, and china. The city is literally on Detroit's doorstep, and you can get there by bus or taxi to the tunnel, or by the Ambassador Bridge. The bridge is like Rome — all freeways lead to it.

SOURCES AND RESOURCES

TOURIST INFORMATION: The Metropolitan Detroit Convention and Visitors Bureau maintains a 24-hour "What's Line" directory of events (298-6262) and distributes free brochures and maps. 2 Jefferson Ave. (567-1170).

Visitor's Guide to Greater Detroit (Metropolitan Detroit Convention and Visitors Bureau; free) is the best guide to the area. Pick up a free *Detroit Monitor* or *Metro Times* for about-town happenings and attractions.

Local Coverage – *Detroit Free Press,* morning daily; *Detroit News,* morning and afternoon editions daily; *Royal Oak Tribune* and *Oakland Press* (Pontiac, both afternoon). *Key* (free), and *Where* and *Host* magazines are available at hotels. *Monthly Detroit* and *Metropolitan Detroit* are the popular city magazines.

Area Code – All telephone numbers are in the 313 area code unless otherwise indicated.

CLIMATE AND CLOTHES: Seasons usually procrastinate in Detroit. You might miss spring if you blink, and summer doesn't really peak until July. Autumn can be a day. The local joke is that if you don't like the weather, stick around because it'll change in five minutes. Temperatures range in the 70s and 80s in summer, and a light wrap might help for cool nights. Subfreezing temperatures are often the rule in January and February, so bundle up.

GETTING AROUND: Airport – Detroit Metropolitan Wayne County Airport handles most of the city's air traffic and is about a 30-minute drive from downtown; taxi fare to downtown runs approximately $25. Shortway Limousine (800 552-3700, from Detroit) provides bus transport to the downtown area from the airport's north and south terminals for $6.

Bus – For information on routes and schedules, call the Dept. of Transportation (933-1300).

Taxi – Cabs can be hailed in the street or picked up at the stands in front of hotels. Some of the cabs are licensed to cross over to Canada. If you prefer to call for a cab, we suggest Checker (963-7000) or Radio Cab (491-2600).

Car Rental – Car rental agencies are plentiful, with all major firms represented.

MUSEUMS: Detroit's major museums — the Detroit Historical Museum, Institute of the Arts, Children's Museum — cluster around the 5200 block of Woodward and are described under *Special Places.*

There are good tours of Henry Ford's *Fair Lane* mansion, on the Dearborn campus of the University of Michigan (593-5590), and the *Meadow Brook Hall* mansion, Adams Rd., in Rochester (377-3140).

MAJOR COLLEGES AND UNIVERSITIES: Wayne State University and medical complex, 650 W Kirby Ave. (577-2424); University of Detroit, 4001 W McNichols (927-1000); University of Michigan, 4901 Evergreen Rd. (593-5000); Oakland University, Walton Rd., Rochester (377-2100).

SPECIAL EVENTS: The *Detroit Grand Prix,* one of the stops on the international Grand Prix circuit, sends Formula One racers thundering through the downtown canyons every June. The friendship between Windsor and Detroit is celebrated in the *International Freedom Festival,* a series of events during Fourth of July week, highlighted by spectacular fireworks over the river. The *Montreaux Jazz Festival* has become quite an annual event the week surrounding Labor Day weekend. Concerts are held in Hart Plaza and at many other locations. Call Detroit Renaissance (259-5400) for details on the Grand Prix, Freedom Festival and Jazz Festival. *Michigan's Thanksgiving Day Parade,* a Detroit tradition since 1926, still marches on every Turkey Day (963-8300).

SPORTS AND FITNESS: Detroit wouldn't be Detroit without its top major league professional teams: the *Lions,* football; *Pistons,* basketball; *Red Wings,* hockey; and *Tigers,* baseball.

    Baseball – Home base for the American League *Tigers* is Tiger Stadium, Michigan at Trumbull (962-4000).

    Basketball – The *Pistons* play in the Pontiac Silverdome (338-4667).

    Bicycling – Rent at Belle Isle Park (267-7115).

    Fishing – Fishing is pretty good in the Detroit River, especially around Belle Isle. There are about 100 lakes in the area; we recommend Orchard Lake.

    Fitness Centers – The Renaissance Club in the *Westin Hotel* has a pool, outdoor track, exercise room, and sauna, Jefferson at St. Antoine (568-8000, ext. 8441).

    Football – The *Lions* (335-4151) play in the 80,000-seat, covered Silverdome. M-59 at Opdyke, Pontiac.

    Golf – Two of the better public courses are Rackham, 10100 W Ten Mile, Huntington Woods (398-8430), and William Rogell, 18601 Berg Rd. (935-5331).

    Hockey – *Red Wings* action is on the ice at Joe Louis Arena, Civic Center Dr. (567-7333).

    Horse Racing – Thoroughbred and harness horses race at Detroit Race Course/ Wolverine Harness Raceway, Schoolcraft at Middlebelt, Livonia (421-7170); Hazel Park Harness Races, 1650 E Ten Mile, Hazel Park (566-1595); Windsor Raceway, fall and winter harness racing, Hwy. 18, Windsor, Ont. (519 961-9545).

    Jogging – The ideal spot is Belle Isle Park. To get there, run 2½ miles east along Jefferson and ½ mile over the arched bridge; or take the Jefferson bus, then jog around the island's perimeter.

    Tennis – The City of Detroit operates several public courts. The best are at Palmer Park and Belle Isle. Call Parks and Recreation (224-1100) for schedule information.

THEATERS: Detroit's active theatrical life provides audiences with entertaining choices. There may be a Broadway-bound hit breaking in at the *Fisher Theater* year-round. 2nd at Grand Blvd. (872-1000). The *Birmingham Theater,* 211 S Woodward, Birmingham (644-3533), features straight drama and comedy, as does the *Meadow Brook Theatre* on the Oakland University campus. Their season runs from September to May at University Dr. east of I-75, Rochester (377-3300). Also very good are the *Hilberry Classic Theater,* 4743 Cass (577-2972), and the *Attic Theater,* 3031 W Grand Blvd. (875-8284).

MUSIC: You can find just about any kind of music in Detroit — symphonic, jazz, or soul. Detroit is the birthplace of Motown, the sound epitomized by the music of Stevie Wonder, the Supremes, and the Temptations. Today rockers like Bob Seeger call Detroit home. Rock and soul concerts are played at Cobo Arena, Jefferson at Washington Blvd. (224-1000); Pontiac Silverdome, M-59 at Opdyke, Pontiac (857-8000); Masonic Auditorium, 500 Temple (832-6648); Ford Auditorium, Jefferson at Woodward (224-1070); Royal Oak Music Theatre, 318 W 4th St. (546-7610); and Premier Center, 33970 Van Dyke (978-8700). The Ford Auditorium is the home of the *Detroit Symphony Orchestra,* whose concert season runs from September to May. Orchestra Hall offers dance and classical and jazz concerts, 3711 Woodward (833-3700). "Brunch with Bach" is presented on most Sundays at the *Detroit Institute of Arts,* 5200 Woodward Ave. (833-7900). *Meadow Brook Music Festival* offers summer symphonies and pop and jazz artists, Oakland University campus (377-2010). Top-name entertainers perform at the outdoor *Pine Knob Music Theater,* Sashabaw, north of I-75, Clarkston (647-7790). The summer jazz series, *P'Jazz,* begun in 1972, is held every Friday on the terrace of the *Hotel Pontchartrain* (965-0200). *Music Hall Center for the Performing Arts* hosts traveling dance and music concerts. The Fisher Theater is the new home of the *Michigan Opera Theater,* 6519 Second Ave. (874-7850).

NIGHTCLUBS AND NIGHTLIFE: *Gino's Surf Lounge* is a low-budget spot that has dancing and a floor show; 37400 E Jefferson, Mt. Clemens (468-2611). *Bennigan's,* 2555 Woodward, Bloomfield Hills (334-9810), and *Galligan's,* downtown (963-2098), are the places where singles mingle. *Baker's Keyboard Lounge* is the oldest jazz room in the country. Dizzy Gillespie, Les McCann, and Oscar Peterson play frequently; 20510 Livernois (864-2100). *Watt's Mosambique* features black jazz; 8406 Fenkell (864-0240). At the *Soup Kitchen Saloon,* there's jazz from Wednesdays through Sundays; 1585 Franklin (259-1374). *Windsor's Top Hat* has first-rate lounge acts; 73 University (963-3742).

SINS: In the *London Chop House* (see *Eating Out*), you can study *envy* as the diners on the east side of the salon watch the diners on the west side. At the *Lindell AC* (964-1122), patrons exude *pride* as they booze it up amid the bats, sticks, hoops, pucks, and pictures of local sports teams heroes.
   Detroit is also a very wealthy city, full of business, businesspeople, and, as you'd expect, hookers of all shapes, sizes, and proclivities. Adult movie houses, adult bookstores, and adult streetwalkers pander to *lust* along Woodward Avenue in Highland Park and the 8 Mile-Schaeffer area.

LOCAL SERVICES: Business Services – For photocopying, try Likity-Split, 140 W Lafayette (963-1999); Silver's, 151 W Fort (963-0000), has stationery and supplies.
   Mechanic – Downtown Auto Service, 1200 Cass Ave. (963-2744)

BEST IN TOWN

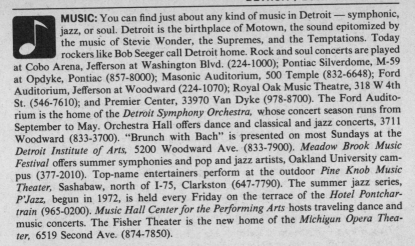

CHECKING IN: By expensive, we mean between $80 and $120 for a double room. Our moderate selections are in the $60 to $80 range; sadly, we found no hotels that met our requirements for an inexpensive recommendation. For inexpensive B&B accommodations, contact Betsy Ross Bed & Breakfast, 3057 Betsy Ross Dr., Bloomfield Hills, MI 48013 (313 647-1158).

The Westin – Previously known as the *Detroit Plaza,* this 1,400-room, 73-story round building has flair, no doubt about it. The lobby takes up the first eight stories, with fountains, trees, aerial walkways, specialty shops, and cocktail lounges (which are served by a traveling trolley) popping up everywhere. Three levels of bars and restaurants revolve. Unfortunately, the guest rooms are not nearly up to the standard of the public spaces. At the east end of Hart Plaza, on Jefferson at St. Antoine (313 568-8000). Expensive.

Hyatt Regency – Its 800 spacious, airy rooms overlook the landscaped park of the Ford World Headquarters. Round glass elevator pods, lit up like rockets, whisk guests to the upper floors, and a space age peoplemover takes shoppers to nearby Fairlane Shopping Center. Near Greenfield Village, Henry Ford Museum, and a University of Michigan campus, at Michigan and Southfield Freeway, Dearborn (313 593-1234). Expensive.

Omni International – Abutting the Millender Center of shops, restaurants, and apartments, this new 25-floor hostelry with 258 rooms fills Detroit's need for more downtown hotel space. There's also an exercise room and health club, meeting rooms, and restaurants. At the junction of RenCen and the Detroit-Windsor Tunnel (800 228-2121). Expensive.

Troy Hilton – On the lip of Detroit's big north-south interstate (I-75), convenient to K-Mart headquarters, chic shopping at Somerset Mall, and the Meadow Brook and Pine Knob theaters. Guests in any of the 401 rooms also have access to an indoor/outdoor pool, sauna, and jogging track. 1455 Stephenson Hwy. (800 482-3940). Expensive.

Hotel Pontchartrain – Detroiters call it "the Pontch." Built on the site of Fort Pontchartrain, this landmark property has just emerged from a $15 million facelift of its public areas and 430 guest rooms. Heavy reds, greens, and velvets have given way to soothing mauves, jades, and plums and a decidedly residential feel. And they've added a new health club. *Top of the Pontch* is open only for Sunday brunch and private gatherings. *Elaine's,* the fine dining room, serves Continental fare; lighter meals can be taken in *The Garden Court,* with its greenhouse atmosphere. P'jazz concerts happen here every Friday during the summer. 2 Washington Blvd. (313 965-0200 or 800 537-6624). Expensive.

Hotel St. Regis – The once-tacky *St. Regis* is now a small (117-room), elegant, European-style hotel. Its rooms and public areas are gracefully appointed, and the French Regency exterior is done in limestone and glazed brick with wrought-iron work and bay windows. The midtown location is ideal for guests with business with the corporate giants in the New Center area, 10 minutes from downtown. 3071 W Grand Blvd. (313 873-3000). Expensive.

Hilton International Windsor – Just across the Detroit River and commanding a sparkling view of Detroit's skyline from all of its 307 rooms, this new hotel features mini-bars in every room and two executive floors with concierge service. 277 Riverside Dr. W (519 973-5555). Moderate.

Dearborn Inn and Motor Hotel – The prototype for a string of combined airports and inns designed by Henry Ford in the 1920s. Ford envisioned an age of air travel, and he recognized that people on the move would require accommodations different from the standard hotels of the 1920s. Thus the 180-room *Dearborn Inn* was born. 20301 Oakwood, Dearborn (313 271-2700). Moderate.

Michigan Inn – Ideally suited if your business or pleasure is in suburban Southfield and environs. It's adjacent to shopping at sprawling Northfield Center, and there's a health club complete with indoor/outdoor pool, putting green, sauna, and tennis courts on the premises. The *Red Parrot Lounge* here is one of Detroit's popular after-work hangouts. 16400 J. L. Hudson Dr. (313 559-6500). Moderate.

EATING OUT: Detroit has a number of moderately priced restaurants serving everything from steaks, crêpes, and pheasant to natural foods and Coney Island hot dogs. And the nationalities represented include French, Middle Eastern, and Alsatian. Expect to pay $40 or more for two at expensive restaurants listed here; between $20 and $35, moderate; and under $20 in our inexpensive range. Prices are for two, and do not include drinks, wine, or tips.

London Chop House – Easily the most celebrated restaurant in town, boasting a 300-bottle wine list and a menu that changes daily. Specialties, naturally enough, are steaks and chops. By the way, status-conscious residents know who's important by checking out the west side of the bandstand; anyone who gets seated there really rates. Closed Sundays. Reservations required. Major credit cards. 155 W Congress (962-0278). Expensive.

The Summit – Perched on the 72nd floor of the *Westin Hotel* and revolving to give diners a 360° view of Detroit, the river, and Canada. The menu is limited to steaks, chops, and seafood. Open daily. Reservations recommended. Major credit cards. Renaissance Center (568-8000). Expensive.

1940 Chop House – Art Deco, supper-clubbish decor, and a menu to please any beef lover. Of 20 main courses, a dozen involve red meat — certified Angus beef from Kansas, succulent and seared over leaping flames by white-clad chefs in the exhibition kitchen. Closed Sundays. Reservations suggested. Major credit cards. 1940 E. Jefferson near RenCen (567-1940). Expensive.

Joe Muer's – Some people say this place serves the best seafood west of the Atlantic. Others say it's even better. Extravagant praise, no matter how sincere, can never substitute for firsthand experience, especially where seafood is concerned. Be prepared to wait in line, though. Joe Muer's doesn't take reservations. (A waiter will bring you a drink while you're standing.) Closed Sundays and holidays. Major credit cards. 2000 Gratiot (567-1088). Expensive.

Van Dyke Place – Detroit's most handsome restaurant is an old house decorated with walnut woods, marble fireplaces, and silk brocade draperies. Also an attraction is the delicious French cuisine. Closed Sundays and Mondays. Reservations required. Major credit cards. 649 Van Dyke Pl. (821-2620). Expensive.

Golden Mushroom – The menu changes with the mood of Milos Cihelka, one of the top chefs in town. Hope you're there when he's inclined to prepare his veal Oscar, calves' liver with green peppercorns, or roast rack of lamb persillade. Closed Sundays. Reservations advised. Major credit cards. Ten Mile at Southfield (559-4230). Expensive.

The Lark – A charming dining spot, this country inn features Continental cuisine. In fair weather, a mesquite barbecue is prepared outdoors. Closed Sundays and Mondays. Reservations required. Major credit cards. 6430 Farmington Rd., W Bloomfield (661-4466). Expensive.

333 East – Cuisine that can only be described as American trendy: grilled Pacific salmon, sautéed veal, breast of duck or chicken with herb and wine sauces for dinner; sandwiches, seafood pasta, and California-style pizza at lunch. Elegant yet unpretentious, with mirrors, American artwork, and Austrian shades to veil the glass wall overlooking Brush Street. Recommended for late dining downtown. Open daily. Major credit cards. 333 E Jefferson at the *Omni International Hotel* (222-7404). Expensive.

Money Tree – The kitchen here turns out interesting soups, fresh pasta, quiche, and crêpes. There's also an impressive pastry cart. Closed Sundays. Reservations advised. Major credit cards. 333 W Fort (961-2445). Expensive to moderate.

Charley's Crab – The seafood menu and the ragtime piano player are real crowd-pleasers. Open daily. Reservations accepted. Major credit cards. 5498 Crooks Rd. at I-75, Troy (879-2060). Moderate.

The Sheik – Hummus, pita bread, shish kebab, and other lamb delicacies, with a special reputation for salads. Closed Sundays. Reservations recommended. Major credit cards. 316 E Lafayette (964-8441). Moderate.

Pontchartrain Wine Cellars – Where cold duck was invented, with a unique French/New York style. Closed Sundays. Reservations recommended. Major credit cards. 234 W Larned (963-1785). Moderate.

The Louisiana Purchase – Cajun/Créole cooking in Windsor, Canada? Why not, especially when the food is authentic and the spices assertive. Chef-proprietor Cameron Lyon gets his seasonings direct from Cajun guru Paul Prudhomme, and several dishes — blackened fish and steak, oyster and brie soup and the sweet potato pecan pie — follow Prudhomme's recipes. Dixieland music, New Orleans graphics, and an old-house feel complete the picture. Closed Sundays and Mondays. Major credit cards. 3236 Sandwich, Windsor (519-255-7424). Moderate.

La Cuisine – The chef of this mite-sized French restaurant whistles up heavenly three-mustard kidneys, tasty fish soup, and more from his kitchen smack in the middle of the room. Closed Sundays and Mondays. Reservations necessary. Most major credit cards. 417 Pelissier, Windsor, Ont. (519 253-6432). Moderate.

New Hellas – The hub of Detroit's 1-block Greek community is as Greek as Greek can be, with moussaka, kalamari (squid), and baklava. Open daily until 3 AM. No reservations. Major credit cards. 583 Monroe (961-5544). Inexpensive.

FORT LAUDERDALE

For many Americans, the mention of Fort Lauderdale immediately calls to mind the 1960 movie *Where the Boys Are* (or its 1984 successor), which immortalized the seasonal migration of the nation's college students to Fort Lauderdale during spring break in search of sun and fun. After all these years, this ritual is still observed; annually, an estimated 30,000 young collegians flock to the Fort Lauderdale beaches between February and Easter. And with good reason: Fort Lauderdale claims to receive 3,000 hours of sunshine a year — more than anywhere else in the continental US — and the year-round average temperature is 75°.

In addition to its benign climate, Fort Lauderdale's proximity to the water has formed its character as a prime resort area. The city is virtually afloat: It and surrounding Broward County are bordered on the east by 27 miles of Atlantic Ocean coastline and beaches, on the west by that "river of grass," the Everglades. Between the two are 300 miles of navigable Intracoastal Waterway and an intricate network of canals that have led to Fort Lauderdale's being dubbed the "Venice of America."

While other resort areas count only their visitors, the Fort Lauderdale area also counts boats. There are nearly 30,000 permanently registered, and 10,000 or so more join their ranks during the winter months as the yachting crowd from as far away as Canada cruises to the area's warm waters. (Author John D. MacDonald's readers will recognize the Bahia Mar Yacht Basin as the place where the laid-back sleuth Travis McGee moors his houseboat, the *Busted Flush.*) Moreover, thousands of smaller craft — sailboats and powerboats — knife through these waters throughout the year. Even the Christmas holiday is celebrated in special Fort Lauderdale fashion, as hundreds of elaborately decorated and lighted boats and yachts take to the Intracoastal Waterway for the unusual Boat Parade from Port Everglades to Pompano Beach.

The city is named after Major William Lauderdale, who arrived in 1838 to quell the Seminole Indians and build a fort on the New River in an area of mosquito-infested, inhospitable mangrove swamps. The door for development first opened in the late 1890s, when the entrepreneur Henry Flagler began extending his Florida East Coast Railroad south from Palm Beach. A swamp drainage and reclamation project was undertaken in 1906, and canals were dug to create "finger islands," thus maximizing the city's waterside real estate. Fort Lauderdale was incorporated in 1911 and has welcomed millions of visitors ever since.

Today Fort Lauderdale is the largest — and by far the best known — of the 28 municipalities that constitute Broward County, the second most populous of Florida's 67 counties. The permanent population of just over 1 million swells each season as more than 3 million tourists pour in. To these guests, Fort Lauderdale and vicinity offer a wide choice of places to stay, from

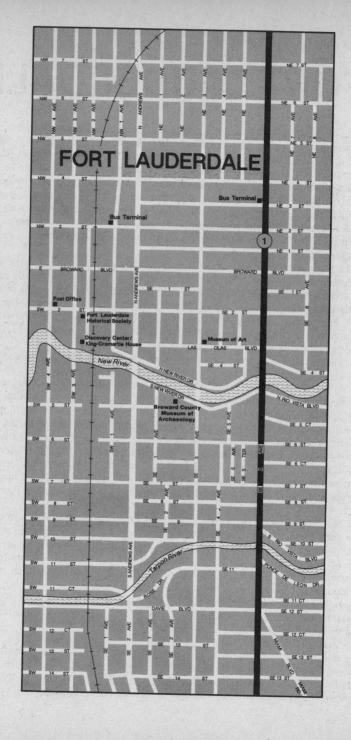

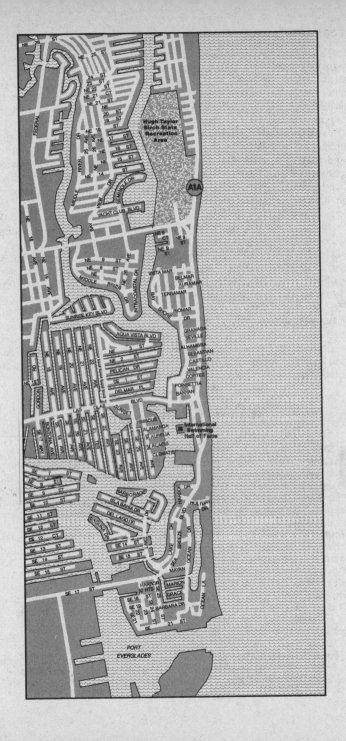

tiny motels to huge luxury hotels; more than 20,000 rooms can be found in the five major oceanfront communities. Even the most demanding diner will find satisfaction in the area's more than 2,500 restaurants, while its several nightclubs, discos, and theaters provide ample evening diversion. And in the sun-splashed daytime, those who tire of frolicking on the beach may work out on the approximately 50 golf courses and 550 tennis courts.

But Fort Lauderdale is not just sunshine and surf. It's also a bustling commercial city, and its pride, Port Everglades, is one of the nation's busiest cargo and passenger ports. City fathers recently undertook a refurbishment and expansion of Fort Lauderdale's downtown core, and a number of high-rise office buildings have sprung up, attracting new business. Furthermore, the cities that make up the greater Fort Lauderdale area are a diverse lot: Davie, whose residents prefer jeans and cowboy boots and hats, is one of the most "western" towns this side of the Pecos; it has dozens of farms, stables, saloons, country stores, and even a weekly rodeo. In Hollywood there's a Seminole Indian Reservation, and Hallandale is the home of the well-known Gulfstream Race Track. Dania, whose name reflects its early Danish settlers, is now called "the antiques center of the South" in recognition of its proliferation of antiques shops. Stretching away to the west of Fort Lauderdale are 65,000 fertile acres of fruit and vegetable farms, adding an agricultural side to the city's personality.

As more and more people discover its enviable lifestyle, the area continues to grow and evolve. Progress has its price, however, and Fort Lauderdale lovers will have to remain vigilant as developers draw closer and closer to the last available land — the eastern fringe of the Everglades.

AT-A-GLANCE

SEEING THE CITY: The most commanding view is from the *Pier Top Lounge* of the 17-story *Pier 66 Hotel* (2301 SE 17th St.). As the lounge makes one complete revolution each 66 minutes, a sweeping panorama unveils of the Atlantic Ocean and its beaches to the east, Port Everglades and Fort Lauderdale International Airport to the south, the city's many canals, sprawling suburbs, and the Everglades to the west, and more canals and the Intracoastal Waterway to the north.

Boat Tours – Fort Lauderdale is most easily and attractively seen by boat. The best cruise is offered by *Paddlewheel Queen,* which departs at 2 PM for a 2½-hour sightseeing cruise and at 7:30 PM for a 3-hour cruise, complete with live band and dinner; 2950 NE 32nd Ave. (564-7659). Other cruise boats include the *Jungle Queen,* at Bahia Mar Yachting Center on Rte. A1A (462-5596), and *The Spirit,* with lunch, dinner, and "moonlight party" cruises at 2:30, 7 and 10:30 PM respectively. Departs from dock across the street from the *Diplomat Hotel,* 3515 S Ocean Dr., Hollywood (458-4999). And what would the "Venice of America" be without gondolas? These can be rented, with or without guide, at Gondolas of America, 1007 Seabreeze Blvd., next to Bahia Mar (522-3333).

Tram Tours – A wonderful way to sightsee is aboard the open-air Voyager Sightseeing Train, which winds along an 18-mile route through old and new Fort Lauderdale, Port Everglades, "Millionaires Row," and some residential areas. 600 Seabreeze Blvd. (463-0401).

SPECIAL PLACES: The best way to get around Fort Lauderdale is by car.
Port Everglades – Because it has the deepest water of any port between Norfolk and New Orleans, Port Everglades attracts a lot of cargo and marine outfitting business, but it's also a popular port for luxury cruise ships that sail the world. Its seven passenger terminals each boast a different and bold design, the result of a $6 million remodeling of former warehouses. The port has two restaurants, one co-owned by Burt Reynolds, and a cocktail lounge. While there are no organized tours, visitors are free to roam at will from 6 AM to 6 PM. State Rd. 84, east of US 1 (523-3404).

Six Flags Atlantis – Spread over 65 acres, it's said to be the world's largest water theme park, with 80 rides and numerous shows and attractions, 5,000 square feet of video and other games; an Olympic pool; the world's longest waterslide (1 mile); an 82-foot-long tile mosaic of King Neptune; giant inner-tube rides; and bumper boats. Open daily. Admission charge. 2700 Stirling Rd., Hollywood (926-1000).

Malibu Castle Park – The brightly lit castle houses an amusement arcade with more than 125 games; the surrounding grounds contain a mini-raceway, two waterslides, bumper boats, water flume; miniature golf courses. Open daily. Charge for each activity. 1999 SW 33rd Pl. (462-8110).

Discovery Center – An integral part of downtown Fort Lauderdale's rejuvenated historic area, the facility is devoted to hands-on learning of things historic, artistic, and scientific. Closed Mondays. Admission charge. 231 SW 2nd Ave. (462-4115).

King-Cromartie House – A restored turn-of-the-century house now replete with fascinating antiques and furniture, found along the New River in the Himmarshee Village historic area. Tours depart from Discovery Center. Closed Mondays. Admission charge. 229 SW 2nd Ave. (764-1665).

Everglades Holiday Park – Savor what the famed ecological area is all about by birdwatching, taking airboat rides and special tours, or by renting boats or RVs. There's also a campground. Open daily. Free. 21940 Griffin Rd. (434-8111).

Flamingo Gardens – This unique jungle environment, with a botanical garden, museum, orange groves, alligators, flamingos, and a petting zoo, remains basically undisturbed by man. Open daily. Admission charge. 3750 Flamingo Rd., Davie (473-0010).

Hugh Taylor Birch State Recreation Area – Just across the street from the beach is this lush, tropical park with 180 acres ideal for picnicking, playing ball, canoeing, hiking. Open daily. Admission charge. 3109 E Sunrise Blvd. (564-4521).

John U. Lloyd Beach State Recreation Area – Many Fort Lauderdale residents consider this to be *the* place for picnicking, swimming, fishing, canoeing, and other recreation. There are 244 acres of beach, dunes, mangrove swamp, and hammock (a raised area of dense tropical vegetation). Park rangers lead nature walks during winter months. Open daily. Admission charge. 6503 N Ocean Dr., Dania (923-2833).

Ocean World – All the requisite aquatic creatures — sharks, alligators, sea lions, turtles, porpoises — are featured here in continuous 2-hour water shows. Visitors may also watch the porpoises show off in Davy Jones' Locker, a three-story circular tank, or the more than 40 sharks, sea turtles, and other fish in the Shark Moat. Boat tours, skyrides, and deep-sea fishing are also available. Open daily. Admission charge. 1701 SE 17th St. (525-6611).

Hollywood Broadwalk – A 2-mile, 24-foot-wide concrete ocean promenade bordered by a bicycle path. Lifeguard stations manned all year from 10 AM to 4 PM.

Spyke's Grove & Tropical Gardens – Florida is famous for its citrus; here's a chance to see a working grove up close. You can also hop aboard one of the hourly 15-minute tractor-pulled tram rides through the groves for a peek at various tropical birds and animals in their natural environment. Open daily. Free. 7250 Griffin Rd., Davie (583-0426).

International Swimming Hall of Fame – Many of the world's top swimming and diving competitions are held here, but its Olympic pool is open to the public when there's no meet. The adjoining museum houses unusual aquatic memorabilia from more than 100 countries. Open daily. Admission charge. 1 Hall of Fame Dr. (462-6536).

Topeekeegee Yugnee Park – With 150 acres, this is one of the area's larger parks. Visitors can enjoy all kinds of activities — swimming, boating, canoeing, picnicking, hiking, biking, roller skating, and miniature golf. One of its two waterslides is said to be the fastest in Florida. Open daily. Admission charge. 3300 N Park Rd., just off I-95, Hollywood (961-4430).

Seminole Indian Reservation – The Indian Village includes a museum, gift shop, demonstrations of alligator wrestling, and snake and turtle shows. Although commercial, for-profit bingo is not legal in Florida, it is here on the reservation. The bingo hall holds up to 1,400 people and is often full; winners have pocketed as much as $110,000 in a single game. There's an admission charge for the village and another for the bingo hall (this includes four bingo cards). Both open daily; the village is at 3551 N State Rd. 7, Hollywood (583-7112); the bingo hall is at 4150 N State Rd. 7, Hollywood (961-5140).

■**EXTRA SPECIAL:** To experience fully the tropical beauty and laid-back ambience that is Fort Lauderdale, drive east on Las Olas Boulevard past its chic boutiques and palm-lined streets. Continue through the Isles of Las Olas area, which is laced with canals and filled with fancy homes nestled among royal palm trees. Proceed on past the sailboat cove, where towering masts grope for the blue sky, and cruise over the small bridge to rt. A1A along the Atlantic Ocean. Turn north and drive along A1A and, at about 4 PM, stop at one of the hotel patio bars facing the ocean for a cocktail with the "end of the day" beach people. As it nears 5 o'clock, the beach will become nearly deserted, yet the ocean is filled with the multicolored sails of boats returning to safe harbor and cruise ships steaming out to distant corners of the world. Take off your shoes, walk along the sand at the water's edge — and let the images soak in.

SOURCES AND RESOURCES

TOURIST INFORMATION: The Broward County Tourist Development Council has just about everything visitors need in the way of maps, brochures, events schedules, and so on. 201 SE 8th Ave. (765-5508).

Local Coverage – *Fort Lauderdale Sentinel,* morning daily, and *Fort Lauderdale News,* afternoon daily, carry the week's upcoming events in their Showtime section on Fridays.

Area Code – All telephone numbers are in the 305 area code unless otherwise indicated.

CLIMATE AND CLOTHES: With the exception of occasional days in late December through February, when it can be chilly, the area generally enjoys warm weather, with daily temperatures averaging 75°. Swimming is possible almost every day. Fort Lauderdale is a very relaxed, informal city. Daytime clothing may be as casual as shorts and sandals; at night, more formal attire — a sport jacket and slacks for men and dresses for women — is usually worn at the fancier restaurants and night spots. Medium-weight clothing is best for winter, while lightweight tropical wear is necessary in the summer.

GETTING AROUND: Airport – Fort Lauderdale/Hollywood International Airport is a 10- to 15-minute drive from downtown; taxi fare should run about $5.50. Broward County Transit's #1 bus runs between the airport (opposite the main entrance on Federal Hwy.) and the downtown bus terminal at NW 1st St. and Andrews Ave.; fare is 50¢.

Bus – Broward County Transit services most of the area. A special 7-day, unlimited-use tourist pass can be purchased for a nominal sum at most hotels. For information, call 357-8400.

Taxi – While you can hail one on the street, it's best to pick one up at one of the major hotels and restaurants, or phone for one. The major cab companies are Yellow Cab (527-8600) and Broward Checker Cab (485-3000).

Car Rental – Fort Lauderdale is served by all the major national firms, two of which have their corporate headquarters in the city: Alamo, 1401 S Federal Hwy. (522-0000); and General Rent A Car, 3100 S Federal Hwy. (524-4635). There are also several regional agencies; look in the yellow pages.

MUSEUMS: The King-Cromartie House and Discovery Center are described in *Special Places.* Other museums include:
  Broward County Museum of Archaeology – 203 SW 1st Ave. (525-8778)
Fort Lauderdale Historical Society – 219 SW 2nd Ave. (463-4431)
Museum of Art – 1 E. Las Olas Blvd. (525-5500)

MAJOR COLLEGES AND UNIVERSITIES: Broward Community College has three campuses: central — 3501 SW Davie Rd., Davie; north — 1000 Coconut Creek Blvd., Coconut Creek; and south — 7200 Hollywood Blvd., Hollywood. Phone 475-6500 for information.

SPECIAL EVENTS: The *Venetian Festival* in January, on Las Olas Boulevard, marks Fort Lauderdale's special relationship with Venice; participants enjoy Italian food and dance as well as exhibitions of Venetian glass. Also on Las Olas Boulevard is the *Las Olas Art Festival,* a showing in March of the work of artists from all over the US. During April, the *Week of the Ocean* is observed by all of Broward County; it's a 9-day festival celebrating the interdependence between man and the sea with seafood samplings, a parade, a billfish tournament, and the like. In May, at the *Pompano Beach Fishing Rodeo,* fishermen compete for more than $250,000 in cash prizes, awarded for the largest catch. Also in May is the *International Swimming Hall of Fame Diving Meet,* attended by champion divers from many different countries. *The Oktoberfest* falls (naturally) in October and features lots of German food, drink, and music. The *Fort Lauderdale Boat Show,* the nation's largest, is held in November and attended by all the major boat builders displaying the latest boat models. Also in November is *Promenade-in-the-Park,* showcasing arts and crafts, food, and entertainment in Holiday Park. One of the world's most unusual Christmas celebrations has to be Fort Lauderdale's annual *Christmas Boat Parade,* a procession of about 100 boats, some with music and carolers, on the Intracoastal Waterway.

SPORTS: Baseball – Fans can watch spring training and preseason games from the first week in March through the first week in April. The New York *Yankees* play at Fort Lauderdale Stadium, 5301 NW 12th Ave. (776-1921); the Texas *Rangers* at Pompano Beach Municipal Stadium, 1700 NE 8th St., Pompano Beach (786-4113).

Fishing – There are lots of charter boat fishing operators at Bahia Mar Yachting

Center, 801 Seabreeze Blvd., across A1A from the beach (525-7174). Landlubbers fish 24 hours a day from the 1,080-foot Pompano Beach Fishing Pier, two blocks north of E Atlantic Blvd.

Fitness Centers – Nautilus Fitness Center, with certified instructors, offers all the standard Nautilus exercise equipment plus whirlpool, aerobic conditioning, and juice bar. 1624 N Federal Hwy. (566-2222).

Golf – There are more than 50 golf courses in the area. Among those open to the public are American Golfers Club, 3850 N Federal Hwy. (564-8760); Bonaventure, 200 Bonaventure Blvd. (389-8000); Rolling Hills, 3501 W Rolling Hills Circle, Davie (475-3010); and Jacaranda, 9200 W Broward Blvd., Plantation (472-5930).

Horse and Dog Racing – There's thoroughbred horse racing at Gulfstream Park on US 1, Hallandale (454-7000); and harness racing in winter, quarterhorse racing in summer, at Pompano Park Harness, 1800 SW 3rd St., Pompano Beach (972-2000). You can "go to the dogs" at Hollywood Greyhound Track, 831 N Federal Hwy., Hallandale (454-9400). Phone for racing dates.

Horseback Riding – There are many stables in the area. Among the larger ones are: Bar-B Ranch, 13607 Stirling Rd. (434-6175); Briarwood Farm, 4601 SW 118th Ave. (434-6640); Saddle Up Stables, 5125 SW 76th Ave. (434-1808); all in Davie. The county also operates stables at Tradewinds Park, 3600 W Sample Rd., Coconut Creek (973-3220).

Jai Alai – This Basque import is the area's most action-packed sport, with pari-mutuel betting adding spice. The season is November to mid-June, with a 3-day break in mid-November at Dania Jai-Alai, 301 E Dania Beach Blvd., Dania (428-7766).

Nature Hikes – The Broward Parks & Recreation Dept. sponsors a different nature walk each weekend during winter. Call for a schedule (765-5920).

Rodeo – The "Wild West" can be found at the Rodeo Grounds in Davie, where cowboys compete in bronco riding, calf roping, and other activities. Friday evenings. Admission charge. SW 65th Ave. (Rodeo Way) and 41st St. (434-7062).

Skating – It seems incongruous in a tropical city, but Fort Lauderdale residents love to ice skate. A favorite locale is Sunrise Ice Skating Center, 3363 Pine Island Rd. N, Sunrise (741-2366). Roller skating is at Topeekeegee Yugnee Park, 3300 N Park Rd., Hollywood (961-4430).

Swimming – The most crowded beach is along "the Strip," from Sunrise Boulevard to Bahia Mar. The Galt Ocean Mile is quieter, with an older crowd. Perhaps the quietest strand is the stretch between Galt Ocean Mile and NE 22nd St., and if you search you may find small pockets of peace in John U. Lloyd Beach State Recreation Area, 6503 N Ocean Dr., Dania.

Tennis – A number of the major hotels have tennis courts. Otherwise, only a few are open to the public. Among them are Crystal Lake Country Club, 3800 Crystal Lake Dr., Pompano Beach (943-3700); and Holiday Park Tennis Center, 701 NE 12th Ave. (761-2301).

THEATER: The area's major theaters are *Parker Playhouse,* 707 NE 8th St. (764-0700), which stars name actors in Broadway productions, and *Sunrise Musical Theater,* 5555 NW 95th Ave. (741-8600), which features Broadway musicals and individual stars in concert. Theatrical and cultural events are also staged at *War Memorial Auditorium,* 800 NE 8th St. (761-5381), and *Broward Community College,* 3501 SW Davie Rd. (475-6840). For current offerings, check the newspapers.

MUSIC: The *Fort Lauderdale Symphony Orchestra* usually plays at the War Memorial Auditorium (561-2997), which is also the site for performances of the *Opera Guild* (566-9913) during winter months; the latter often features visiting artists from New York's Metropolitan Opera. The *South*

Florida Symphony Orchestra stages several major productions at various sites; 1822 N University Dr., Plantation (474-7660). Student and guest chamber, jazz, opera, and symphonic performances are staged throughout the year at Broward Community College (475-6726).

NIGHTCLUBS AND NIGHTLIFE: Most hotels and larger motels offer music and/or comedy acts nightly. The *Diplomat,* 3515 S Ocean Dr., Hollywood (949-2442), features well-known stars during the winter. Growing in popularity are comedy clubs such as *The Comic Strip,* 1432 N Federal Hwy. (565-8887), which showcases New York and Los Angeles comics. *Musician's Exchange Cafe,* 729 W Sunrise Blvd. (764-1912), is the place to go for jazz; and *Cowboy's,* 4441 W Broward Blvd. (584-1774), for country music. For disco, try *Riverwatch* in the *Marriott,* 1881 SE 17th St. (463-4000); *Confetti's,* 2660 E Commercial Blvd. (776-4080); *Mr. Laff's,* 1135 N Federal Hwy. (561-3440); and *Banana Boat,* 2650 State Rd. 84 (791-5660). There's slow dancing and dinner at *Stan's,* 3300 E Commercial Blvd. (772-3777).

SINS: The city's *pride* is its weather and sandy beaches, upon which precious little construction has been permitted. *Avarice* gets a workout at the Seminole Indian Bingo Hall, 4150 N State Rd. 7 (961-5140). For *lust,* look to the "red-light" district up and down S Federal Highway.

LOCAL SERVICES: Babysitting – Children's Kingdom, 1016 NE 7th Ave. (522-4434)

   Business Services – Baker Secretarial Service, 3323 E Oakland Park Blvd. (566-7495)

Mechanics – Cork's, 1041 NE 30th Court, Oakland Park (565-0630), for foreign cars; Chuck's Oceanside Exxon, 3001 N Ocean Blvd. (561-3120), for American makes

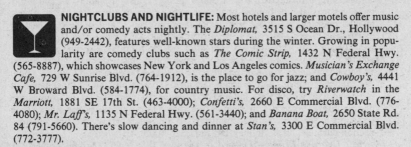

BEST IN TOWN

CHECKING IN: Fort Lauderdale's busiest period is winter, so if you plan to visit then, make reservations as far in advance as possible. During high season a double room listed in the expensive range could run $125 and up per night; $90 to $110 in moderate; and $65 to $80 in inexpensive. In the summer, occupancy (and room rates) drop. Note that a 2% tourist development tax and a 5% sales tax are added to all hotel bills.

Pier 66 – The 17-story octagonal hotel tower alongside the Intracoastal Waterway was the city's first luxury high-rise hotel. A recent multimillion-dollar refurbishing program has greatly enhanced its elegance and appeal. It has 252 spacious rooms, some of which have private balconies. Other amenities include 3 tennis courts, 2 swimming pools, a Jacuzzi, a large marina, a fitness center, 4 restaurants and 3 lounges. 2301 SE 17th St. (305 525-6666). Expensive.

Bahia Mar Quality Royale – This nautically themed hotel and marina at the Bahia Mar Yacht Basin at the southern end of "the Strip" has about 300 rooms, a restaurant, a coffee shop, and the *Spyglass Lounge,* with ocean views and nightly entertainment. 801 Seabreeze Blvd. (305 764-2233). Expensive.

Royce Resort – All of its 224 rooms have balconies that overlook either the Atlantic or the Galt Ocean Mile, and they've all just been refurbished and redecorated in soothing rose and mauve tones. The restaurant, *Cinnamon's,* offers a mostly Continental menu, and the patio-bar features live music and dancing on weekends.

The hotel is on the beach, has a pool, and offers sailboat rentals. 4060 Galt Ocean Dr. (305 565-6611). Expensive.

World of Palm-Aire – It's Fort Lauderdale's original (but still dazzling) spa — over 1,500 acres, 194 rooms, 37 tennis courts, 4 championship and 1 executive golf course, several racquetball courts, and 4 dining rooms. Special 3-, 4-, and 7-day packages may also be booked at the spa, whose program includes herbal wraps, facials, massage, whirlpool treatment, exercise classes, and other rejuvenating experiences. See also Resort Hotels, DIVERSIONS. 2501 Palm-Aire Dr. N, Pompano Beach (305 972-3300; 800 327-4960 outside Florida). Expensive.

Marriott's Harbour Beach – The city's newest and most expensive resort sits on 16 beachfront acres. Stunning public areas include 4 restaurants, 3 lounges, a pool bar, 5 tennis courts, and exercise facilities. There's also an 8,000-square-foot free-form pool with a waterfall and 50 cabanas. By contrast, the 645 rooms are disappointing, especially in view of the rates; however, suites are super. Free transport to the Bonaventure Country Club for golfers. Heavy meeting and convention clientele. 3030 Holiday Dr. (305 525-4000). Expensive.

Marriott Cypress Creek – Opened in October 1986, the 322-room property is adjacent to an 8-acre aquatic preserve in the burgeoning Cypress Creek area, north of the city. Facilities include an outdoor pool, a health club with saunas and lockers, a gift shop, plus parking for 350 cars. The 15-floor structure will also feature 2 restaurants, a 5,300-square-foot Grand Ballroom and 6 smaller meeting facilities. In the Cypress Park West complex (305 771-0440). Expensive.

Westin Cypress Creek – This 300-room luxury property, nearing completion at press time, will be the Westin chain's first foray into Florida. The 13-story property overlooks a 5-acre manmade lake and will feature a health club, large outdoor pool, and a lakeside jogging path. One restaurant will function as a private dining club, and there will be a casual restaurant and bar complex as well as an entertainment lounge. Two floors will offer concierge services. In the Radice Corporate Center (305 772-1331). Expensive.

Sheraton Yankee Clipper – "Moored" directly on the beach, its unusual architecture makes this landmark look like a ship, and the nautical theme — which provides a warm, clubby feeling — is also carried through indoors, too. Heated swimming pools, 505 rooms, and a restaurant; two lounges provide entertainment. 1140 Seabreeze Blvd. (305 524-5551). Moderate.

Marina Bay – An unusual place, with all 125 rooms in two-story houseboats on the New River, providing a tropical setting and maritime ambience. Two lounges with dancing, one of which is a private club, 13 tennis courts, a swimming pool, and boat slips complete the facilities open to guests. 2175 State Rd. 84 (305 791-7600). Moderate.

Riverside – Some 115 rooms in one of the city's oldest structures. The hotel has a sedate ambience and cozy lobby, with chandeliers, armchairs, touches of wicker, and a fireplace. There's also a restaurant and intimate lounge decorated with etched glass as well as a swimming pool and beautiful gardens. 620 E Las Olas Blvd. (305 467-0671). Moderate.

Ireland's Inn – This is a real find; although the decor is a bit old-fashioned, the hotel has 76 large rooms (some with kitchenettes), all immaculately kept. The pub lounge with sing-along bar is "homey." 2220 N Atlantic Blvd. (305 565-6661). Inexpensive.

Oakland Park Inn – It's a fine place to stay if being near the beach is not crucial. There are 32 hotel rooms, but the 105 poolside villas with living, dining, and bedroom available only with a year's lease. Other amenities are a heated whirlpool and putting green. 3870 N Andrews Ave. (305 563-1351). Inexpensive.

EATING OUT: There are nearly 2,500 restaurants in Fort Lauderdale. Many of these are well known and most are quite crowded during the winter season, so it's always a good idea to make reservations. Casual dress is accepted in most restaurants, though a few of the more expensive ones prefer gentlemen to wear jackets. Expect to pay $45 or more for dinner for two in a restaurant listed in the expensive range; $25 to $35 in the moderate; and $20 or less in the inexpensive. Prices do not include wine, drinks, or tips.

Casa Vecchia – Fine Northern Italian cuisine is served inside this lovely old house (built in the 1930s by the Ponds cold cream family), decorated with lots of plants, ceramics, and wrought iron. A courtyard adds to the charm, as does the view overlooking the Intracoastal Waterway. Open daily. Major credit cards. 209 N Birch Rd. (463-7575). Expensive.

Down Under – The kitchen at this spot alongside the Intracoastal Waterway prepares an eclectic menu of (at last look) 42 French, American, and seafood dishes. The atmosphere and decor seem similarly haphazard — plants abound, the brick walls are lined with old posters, and the large rooms are filled with tables placed rather closely together. Open daily. Major credit cards. 3000 E Oakland Park Blvd. (564-6984). Expensive.

Historic Bryan Homes – Two of the city's oldest homes have been refurbished and joined together to house this lovely, candlelit restaurant surrounded by landscaped grounds on the New River. The cuisine is new American and uses the freshest local and tropical ingredients. Closed Mondays. Major credit cards. 301 SW 3rd Ave. (523-0177). Expensive.

La Reserve – This French/Continental restaurant has a two-tiered, beam-ceilinged, candlelit dining room with sensational picture windows overlooking the Intracoastal Waterway. Boat dockage available. Open daily. Major credit cards. 3115 NE 32nd Ave. (563-6644). Expensive.

La Ferme – Marie-Paul Terrier welcomes customers with a smile and closely watches over their well-being while husband Henri tends to the kitchen, whipping up traditional and nouvelle delights. The restaurant is small and cozy, with a French Provincial decor and lace tablecloths. Closed Mondays. Major credit cards. 1601 E Sunrise Blvd. (764-0987). Expensive.

Christine Lee's – It's a branch of the popular Miami Beach restaurant serving Szechwan, Mandarin and Cantonese dishes. Surprisingly, it also has some of the best American-style steaks in South Florida. Open daily. Major credit cards. 6191 Rock Island Rd., Tamarac (726-0430). Expensive to moderate.

Mai-Kai – The large, rambling main dining room has a Polynesian decor, serves exotic drinks with its Polynesian, American and Cantonese food, and features Polynesian entertainment nightly (cover charge). The restaurant grounds boast lushly landscaped tropical vegetation. Open daily. Major credit cards. 3599 N Federal Hwy. (563-3272). Moderate.

Manero's – This family-run restaurant is large, noisy, and crowded; the walls are adorned with autographed photos of many of the celebrities who have eaten here. Steaks and seafood are featured. Open daily. Major credit cards. 2600 E Hallandale Beach Blvd., Hallandale (456-1000). Moderate.

Bobby Rubino's – The original rib joint has now expanded into a national chain, but it still serves the leanest barbecued ribs in town, usually accompanied by a delicious fried onion ring *loaf.* Barbecued chicken, steaks, and "combo platters" are also served. There are now five branches of this easygoing eatery; all are open daily and accept major credit cards: 4100 N Federal Hwy. (561-5305); 1430 SE 17th St. (522-3006); 6001 N Kimberly Blvd., N Lauderdale (971-4740); 3806 N University Dr., Sunrise (748-2000); 4520 W Hallandale Beach Blvd., Hallandale (987-5500). Moderate to inexpensive.

Old Florida Seafood House – It's a real find, where the seafood is consistently good and the prices reasonable. Try the raw bar — a selection of clams, oysters, shrimp, and other favorites. Open daily. Major credit cards. 1414 NE 26th St., Wilton Manors (566-1044). Moderate to inexpensive.

Carlos & Pepe's – The clientele at this popular hangout is eager and hungry; the setting is crowded but pleasant (light woods, green plants, and tile tables); and the menu is lighthearted Mexican (tacos, tortillas, and tostadas). Open daily. Major credit cards. 1302 SE 17th St. (467-7192). Inexpensive.

Papa Leone's – Papa Leone plays the organ every night at this small (only 18 candlelit booths and tables), old-fashioned, family-run, neighborhood Italian restaurant. Open daily. No credit cards. It's virtually invisible, next to Publix, at 2735 N Dixie Hwy., Wilton Manors (566-1911). Inexpensive.

Two Guys – Many natives will swear that these two guys serve the best pizza in Florida; both locations are casual, with cedar paneling, hanging plants, and ceiling fans. Open daily. Major credit cards. 701 S Federal Hwy. (462-7140); 391 N State Rd. 7 (792-8888). Inexpensive.

FORT WORTH

First, what Fort Worth is not: Fort Worth is not sleek, Fort Worth is not snooty, and Fort Worth is not the subject of any steamy television series. Fort Worth is not, to put it crudely, Dallas. And if ever on some feverish, less confident day long ago, its citizens wished it were, they've long since come to their senses. Fort Worth stands far apart from its flashy big sister 30 miles to the east, and its personality could not be more distinctly its own.

On the banks of the Trinity River, 50 miles south of the Oklahoma state line and 250 miles north of the Gulf of Mexico, Fort Worth acts as a geographic and cultural boundary between two very different parts of Texas. To the west of the city is raw and flat prairie, hardly more developed than it was a century ago, while to the east is Dallas, a flamboyant and wealthy town endowed with more pine trees and more pizzazz. A successful blend of both worlds, Fort Worth has a natural and rugged charm. Dallas writer Jerry Flemmons describes the difference between the two cities thus: "Dallas grew into a huckster city of contrived haute culture. Fort Worth became a comfortable, ambitious town with a high society always one generation removed from flour sack underwear."

Comparisons aside, the history of Fort Worth is an interesting one. Founded as a frontier army post in 1849 by Major Ripley Arnold to provide protection against frequent and ferocious Indian attacks, Fort Worth was named for the Mexican War hero William Jenkins Worth. The settlers who took refuge in this stronghold considered it the very edge of civilization, since all that existed west of Fort Worth were hundreds and hundreds of wild, dry miles of Indian territory. After the Civil War, Fort Worth emerged as a key stop on the Chisholm Trail, a route cut through Texas and Oklahoma along which millions of longhorns were driven north to market in Kansas. Enormous stockyards were built in what is now North Fort Worth, and entrepreneurs wasted no time in building an assortment of saloons and dance halls to accommodate the wants and needs of the weary cowhands and smooth-talking cattle barons who came to trade. These moneyed cattlemen became the first incarnation of Fort Worth gentry; they built mansions along Pennsylvania Avenue in which entire floors were devoted to ballrooms and ladies' dressing rooms were filled with gowns bought in the East.

When the first of nine railroads came to Fort Worth in 1876, the city acquired a new role as a meat-packing and shipping center. Then in 1917 oil was discovered and Fort Worth experienced a new boom — in population and wealth. And while cattle and oil have remained the bedrock of Fort Worth's economy, since World War II many technological and defense industries have prospered here; three such corporate giants are the Tandy Corporation, Bell Helicopter, and General Dynamics. Today, Fort Worth has a growth rate that is more than double the national pace, and the per capita income remains

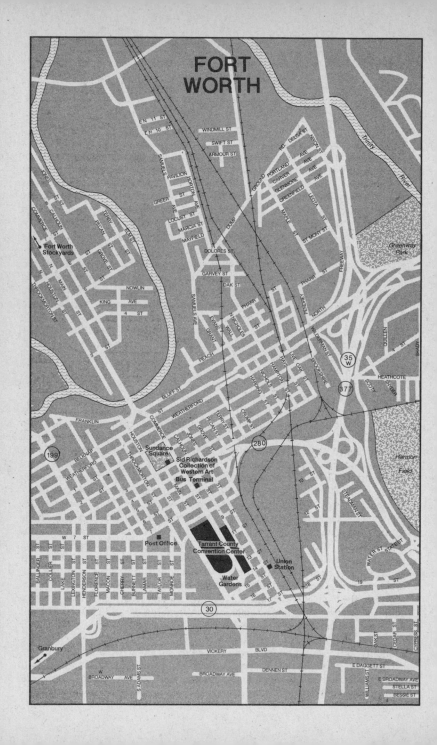

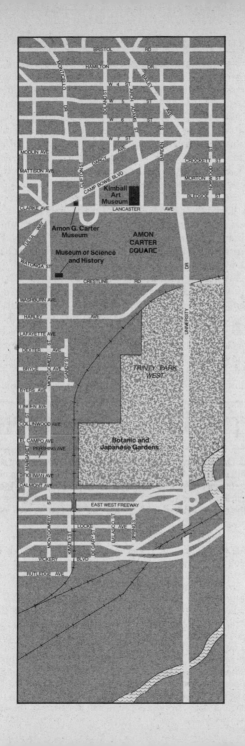

14% above the national average while the cost of living is 10% below.

Fort Worth's broad-based economy is just one example of the city's real drawing card, its diversity. Another example is the several different faces of the city. Downtown Fort Worth is in the midst of an unprecedented construction spurt that's more than doubling the city's existing office space. The area has the look of a city being built simultaneously in two different centuries: refurbished turn-of-the-century structures stand just a few feet from modern high-rises. And in North Fort Worth the stockyards have been declared a National Historic District. Although the stockyard area has certainly been duded up for the tourist trade, it hasn't lost its original Old West charm, its for-real cowboy clientele, or its earthy smell and soft background music of braying livestock. Due west of downtown is Fort Worth's artistic and cultural center, Amon G. Carter Square, a cluster of museums that's among the best west of the Mississippi. Sustained completely by family money, Fort Worth's museums grew up with the city, supported by a citizenry not because it had to but because it wanted to.

Despite its many facets, "Cowtown" (as Fort Worth was nicknamed) suffered for many years from a whopping identity crisis. Always overshadowed by supposedly more sophisticated Dallas, it simply settled for playing second fiddle. Then, slowly, visitors started coming to Fort Worth to see the historic stockyards; the Amon G. Carter and Kimbell museums began to gain acceptance and acclaim in the international art market; and the city's business leaders were acknowledged "big dogs" by anybody's standards. Suddenly, the people of Fort Worth realized that their city's idiosyncratic mix of cattle, culture, and commerce is just what makes it a very special place.

FORT WORTH AT-A-GLANCE

SEEING THE CITY: Panoramic views of Fort Worth turn up serendipitously over a hill or around a corner, but the best one is from the esplanade from the east entrance of the Amon G. Carter Museum. Get a king-sized scoop of homemade ice cream from the *Front Porch* (across Camp Bowie Boulevard), then enjoy the rolling lawn of the Kimbell Art Museum as well as a spectacular view of downtown.

SPECIAL PLACES: One of the nicest things about Fort Worth is that sightseeing is easy. All the museums are within walking distance of one another; the stockyard area is best seen on foot; and the botanical gardens and zoo are across the street from each other.

Fort Worth Stockyards – Wear your jeans to prowl around the north side of Cowtown. The stockyard area includes livestock exchange buildings; Cowtown Coliseum, the home of the world's first indoor rodeo; and brick-paved Exchange Avenue, where you can pick up a Stetson and a pair of lizardskin boots or down some Texas Longneck beer in a watering hole, such as the *White Elephant Saloon,* 106 E Exchange (624-1887), that's been serving cowboys for more than 100 years. Any Monday through Thursday you can do some shopping at a cattle auction. N Main St. and Exchange Ave.

Kimbell Art Museum – Architect Louis Kahn's last work opened in 1973 and is considered one of the most important and beautiful small art museums in the country. Its permanent collection dates from pre-Columbian America to the early twentieth century, with an emphasis on European art. Closed Mondays. Free. 3333 Camp Bowie Blvd. (332-8451).

Amon G. Carter Museum of Western Art – Best known for its paintings by Frederic Remington and Charles M. Russell, the museum also features an extensive collection of sculpture, painting, and photography by many other twentieth-century artists. 3502 Camp Bowie Blvd. (738-1933).

Museum of Science and History – Formerly called the Children's Museum, it includes the Hall of Medical Science, Man and His Possessions, and Computer Technology. Also part of the museum is the Omni Theater, a remarkable computerized 70mm multi-image projection and sound system — the largest of its kind in the world. Closed Mondays. Admission charge. 1501 Montgomery (732-1631).

Sundance Square – This charming square is formed by Commerce, Houston, Second, and Third streets downtown and is bordered by an interesting collection of boutiques, craft shops, restaurants, and art galleries. Main Street, which bisects the square, is notable for its red brick sidewalks, period streetlamps, and turn-of-the-century buildings. At 309 Main Street is the well-known Sid Richardson Collection of Western Art (332-6554), which features more than 100 paintings by the western artists Frederic Remington and Charles M. Russell. Special concerts and events are often held here (390-8700).

Water Gardens – The opening scenes of the science fiction movie *Logan's Run* were shot at this water wonderland, where some 19,000 gallons of water pour over pebbled concrete sculptures every minute. Open daily. Free. South of the convention center between Commerce and Houston streets.

Log Cabin Village – Six cabins from the 1850s have been restored and furnished with period antiques. Costumed "villagers" demonstrate typical pioneer crafts — weaving, quilting, etc. Open daily. Admission charge. 2100 Log Cabin Village near the zoo and botanical gardens (926-5881).

Botanic and Japanese Gardens – The Botanic Gardens encompass several acres for exploring and studying hundreds of different plant species and varieties of roses. Within are the Japanese Gardens, tranquil arrangements of trees and shrubs, bridges, pools, waterfalls, and teahouses. Open daily. Admission charge for Japanese Gardens only. 3220 Botanic Garden Dr., off University Dr. (870-7686).

Fort Worth Zoological Park – Part of Forest Park, with picnic tables and a small amusement park, the Fort Worth zoo contains America's largest herpetarium, a lovely rain forest with rare and exotic birds, and an outstanding collection of mammals. Adjacent to the zoo is the longest miniature train ride in the country. It's a leisurely and scenic 5-mile trip covering the length of several parks. Open daily. 2727 Zoological Park Dr., off University Dr. (870-7050).

Thistle Hill – Built in 1903, this elegant old house is the last one remaining from the days when the rich cattle barons built their flashy mansions along Pennsylvania Avenue. Closed Saturdays. Free. 1509 Pennsylvania Ave. (336-1212).

Six Flags Over Texas – About 30 minutes east of Fort Worth, in Arlington, this famous amusement park features more than 95 rides, shows, and other attractions. Open weekends only in spring and fall; daily, June through August. Admission charge. I-30 at Hwy. 360 (640-8900).

White Water – A great place to spend a blistering Texas day. Attractions include a surfing pool, waterslides, inner tube rapids, and a children's play area. 6 miles from Six Flags at I-30 and Beltline Rd. (214 263-1999).

■ **EXTRA SPECIAL:** Fort Worth may be typically Texan, but you really haven't seen the state until you've visited at least one of its small towns. *Granbury,* an easy 30 minutes southwest of Fort Worth on Hwy. 377, has admittedly taken advantage of its charming eccentricities and attracted some tourist trade. But the appeal of the agricultural community has only been heightened. A limestone courthouse dominates a town square ringed with craft shops, ice cream parlors, and restaurants, all in 19th-century buildings. In fact, Granbury is so full of Old West buildings that it's entered in the National Register of Historic Places in Washington, DC. The Granbury Opera House (on the Square on Pearl St.) features drama, comedy, and music. (Reservations are advised: PO Box 297, Granbury, TX 76048; 573-9191.) Surrounding Granbury is a manmade lake of the same name with beautiful camping and picnicking facilities; the Chamber of Commerce (573-1622) may provide further information. For a country-style buffet, try the local favorite, the *Nutt House* restaurant. "Country-style buffet" means you go through a line, cafeteria style, pick yerself up some grits (pronounced *gree-*uts), red beans, and maybe some ham, and set down at a long table. The *Nutt House,* like many establishments in Granbury, is closed Mondays (121 E Bridge St.; 573-9362).

SOURCES AND RESOURCES

 TOURIST INFORMATION: For brochures, maps, and general information, contact the Fort Worth Convention and Visitors Bureau, 700 Throckmorton (336-8791).

Local Coverage – The *Fort Worth Star-Telegram* is published mornings, evenings, and Sundays.

Food – *Texas Monthly,* the state magazine, publishes reviews of Fort Worth's best restaurants. *D* magazine also lists Fort Worth restaurants.

Area Code – All telephone numbers are in the 817 area code unless otherwise indicated.

 CLIMATE AND CLOTHES: The official word is that Fort Worth's average daily temperature during the spring is 65°; summer, 84°; fall, 66°; and winter, 47°. But don't let rumor or averages fool you: you can plan on summer scorchers or some pretty nippy winter days.

 GETTING AROUND: Airport – Dallas/Fort Worth Airport (or D/FW), the country's largest, is usually about a 40-minute drive from downtown Fort Worth; cab fare should run about $32. Bus transportation between D/FW and the downtown hotels is provided by the city-operated Citran Airport service (870-6200), which costs $6.

Bus – Citran provides bus service throughout Fort Worth; to check on routes and schedules, call 870-6200.

Taxi – The best way to get a cab is to phone for one. Try Yellow Cab (335-3333).

Car Rental – All the major national car rental agencies are represented.

Trolley – Six rubber-tired trolleys provide service to and from downtown to the historic stockyard district and to the museum complex. Call 870-6200 for schedule and stop information.

 MUSEUMS: The Kimbell Art Museum, the Amon G. Carter Museum, and the Museum of Science and History are described under *Special Places.* Also of interest is the *Fort Worth Art Museum,* 1309 Montgomery (738-9215), a collection of 20th-century sculpture and paintings.

 MAJOR COLLEGES AND UNIVERSITIES: Texas Christian University has especially distinguished drama and music departments and offers performances year-round in Ed Landreth Auditorium. 2800 S University Dr. (921-7000). Texas Wesleyan College is also in Fort Worth, 3101 E Rosedale

(534-0251), as is the Southwestern Baptist Theological Seminary, the largest Baptist seminary in the world, 2001 W Seminary Dr. (923-1921).

 SPECIAL EVENTS: Any child who spent any time at all in the Fort Worth Independent School District can tell you the highlight of the year comes during the 12 days in late January or early February when the *Southwestern Exposition and Fat Stock Show* comes to town. Schoolchildren have one day designated as Stock Show Day and receive free tickets, but the world's oldest indoor rodeo, midway, and stock show is fun for anyone. Contact the Fort Worth Convention and Visitors Bureau, 700 Throckmorton (336-8791) for more information.

Other special events are *Mayfest,* an annual celebration with food, music, and games on the banks of the Trinity River the first weekend in May; the *Chisholm Trail Roundup,* a 3-day festival of street dances, chili cook-offs, and gunfights staged in the Stockyards area in June; the *Shakespeare in the Park* series at the Trinity Park Playhouse in late June, when spectators bring picnic suppers and enjoy the free performances; *Pioneer Days,* a 3-day western wingding held in September in the Stockyards; *Oktoberfest,* the first weekend in October; and the *National Cutting Horse Futurity,* held the second week in December at Will Rogers Coliseum, one of the premier western events in the country, with some of the highest monetary awards anywhere outside the racetrack.

 SPORTS AND FITNESS: Baseball – The *Texas Rangers* play at Arlington Stadium, 1700 Copeland Rd. (273-5100).

Bicycling – The Dept. of Parks, 2222 W Rosedale (870-7000), provides maps of scenic biking trails that circle Forest and Trinity parks.

Fitness Centers – The coed YMCA downtown provides a pool, track, and racquetball courts, 512 Lamar (332-3281). Another fitness center is President's, 6833 Green Oaks Rd. (738-8910).

Golf – There are 11 country clubs and 9 municipal courses in Fort Worth. The Colonial National Invitation is held at Colonial Country Club, 3735 Country Club Circle, in May (927-4200).

Jogging – Maps of the jogging trails around Forest and Trinity parks are available from the Dept. of Parks, 2222 W Rosedale (870-7000).

Tennis – The Mary Potishman Lard Tennis Center near Texas Christian University offers 22 outdoor and 5 indoor courts to the public. Open daily. Admission charge. 3609 Bellaire (921-7960).

 THEATER: *Casa Mañana* ("the house of tomorrow") is probably Fort Worth's best-known playhouse, 3101 W Lancaster at University Dr. (332-6221). A theater-in-the-round, it mounts a variety of dramatic productions. Others include the *Fort Worth Theater,* 3505 Lancaster (738-6509); the *Circle Theater,* 3460 Bluebonnet Circle (921-3040); and the *Hip Pocket Theater,* which performs outdoors, 1620 Las Vegas Trail N (246-1269).

MUSIC: The *Fort Worth Opera,* the *Fort Worth Symphony Orchestra,* and the *Fort Worth Ballet* all give performances at the Tarrant County Convention Center, 1111 Houston. For ticket information, contact Central Tickets (429-1181). Fort Worth's Grammy-winning *Texas Boys Choir* was called the best in the world by composer Igor Stravinsky; concerts are given in a variety of places (738-5420). The *Schola Cantorum of Texas* is a 50-member chorus that also performs in different venues (737-5788). For a very different kind of music that will appeal to the whole family, check out *Johnnie High's Country Music Revue* in Will Rogers Auditorium, 3001 W Lancaster (481-4518).

NIGHTCLUBS AND NIGHTLIFE: Without a doubt, the place you'll want to be able to say you've been in Fort Worth is *Billy Bob's Texas,* the world's largest honky-tonk, with a real bullring *and* a mechanical bull as well as 42 (count 'em) bar stations, 2520 N Commerce (429-5979). The *White Elephant Saloon,* 106 E Exchange (624-1887), is another popular watering hole that features barbecue and country music; it's in the historic Stockyards area. The *Caravan of Dreams,* 312 Houston (877-3000), an avant-garde performing arts center, has a jazz and blues nightclub. At *MacArthur's,* on Anderson Rd. off Camp Bowie (735-8851), the music is more eclectic; and *The Hop,* 2905 W Berry (923-9949), has a mixed bag of jazz, rock, and good food.

 SINS: Back when the West was yet to be won, Fort Worth's downtown was a hotbed of licentiousness known as Hell's Half Acre. These days the sinning is all but supervised in legitimate dens of iniquity like *Billy Bob's.* Exchange Avenue's bawdy saloons are the best bets for old-time hell-raising.

 LOCAL SERVICES: Babysitting Services – Children's World, 6301 McCart Ave. (292-2041)
   Business Services – Kelly Services (332-7807)
   Mechanics – American cars: Hostetter Services, 4800 E Lancaster (536-5685); foreign cars: Overseas Motors, 2824 White Settlement Rd. (332-4181)

BEST IN TOWN

 CHECKING IN: At the hotels listed below, expect to pay $80 or more for a double room for a night in the expensive category, $45 to $80 for moderate, and $30 for inexpensive. While Fort Worth has no shortage of traditional hotels, another alternative, Bed and Breakfast Texas-Style, offers lodging and either Continental or Texas-style breakfasts in private homes in the city's most desirable neighborhoods. Rates vary from budget to comfortable and deluxe, $20 to $60. Write to Ruth Wilson, 4224 W Red Bird La., Dallas 75237 (214 298-5433).

Worthington Hotel – This lovely European-style hostelry is downtown, across the street from Sundance Square. There are 509 rooms, including 69 luxury suites, 2 outdoor tennis courts, indoor pools, fully equipped athletic club, 24-hour private dining service, and a fine restaurant called *Reflections.* 200 Main St. (817 870-1000). Expensive.

Hyatt Regency – A renovated old Texas hotel, it has retained more of the city's original western flavor than any of the others. One block north of the convention center, at 815 Main St. (817 870-1234). Expensive.

AMFAC Hotel and Resort – This elegant hotel within the airport complex is a good place to stay if you're planning to divide your time between Dallas and Fort Worth or visit the amusement parks between the two cities. Big, convenient, and busy, it has 1,450 rooms, 7 restaurants, 36 holes of golf, 10 racquetball courts, and 3 indoor and 4 outdoor pools. Ask about family rates. PO 619025, D/FW Airport (214 453-8400). Expensive.

The Stockyards Hotel – This historic three-story hotel, dating to cowboy boom-town days, reopened in 1984 after extensive renovations. Much is made of the time Bonnie and Clyde put up here. Smack in the middle of the Stockyards district, it's a popular choice among tourists since *Billy Bob's, The White Elephant,* numerous restaurants, and other attractions are all within walking distance. Check out the saddles that serve as bar stools in the hotel barroom. 109 E Exchange (817 625-6427). Expensive.

Fort Worth Hilton – It's right in the heart of downtown, near the convention center and overlooking the Water Gardens. There are 435 rooms in twin high-rise towers, an indoor pool, and *The Fountain Square* restaurant. 1701 Commerce St. (817 335-7000). Moderate.

Green Oaks Inn – This older hotel is a bit out of the way but conveniently across the street from an 18-hole golf course, and its 300 rooms overlook a lush garden area, 2 swimming pools, and a winding brook that falls to a fish-stocked pond. 6901 W Freeway at State Hwy. 183 (817 738-7311). Moderate.

EATING OUT: In a city called Cowtown you'd naturally expect good beef, but natives pride themselves more on ferreting out superior Tex-Mex and chicken-fried steak. Both are available in Fort Worth, along with some better-than-average Continental fare and a surprising assortment of ethnic eats. Expect to spend more than $50 for a meal for two in a restaurant listed as expensive; $30 to $50 for moderate; and less than $30 for inexpensive. Prices do not include drinks, wine, or tips.

Michel – Such a class act is still a novelty in Fort Worth, but the quality here is hardly beginner's luck. The fixed-price ($38.50), four-course dinners are masterful presentations of Continental favorites. Closed Sundays. Reservations. All credit cards. 3851 Camp Bowie Blvd. (732-1231). Expensive.

The Carriage House – This longtime favorite of the Fort Worth establishment combines a Continental menu with a comfortably elegant decor. Open daily; brunch only on Sundays. Reservations advised. Major credit cards. 5136 Camp Bowie (732-2873). Expensive.

Tours – Despite it's unimpressive shopping center location, this is a good choice for its admirable and original interpretations of Continental cuisine. Closed Sundays. Reservations advised. Major credit cards. 3429B W 7th St. (870-1672). Expensive to moderate.

Ristorante Lombardi – This Fort Worth outlet of the popular Dallas restaurant serves Northern Italian cuisine in a pretty setting downtown. Closed Sundays. Reservations advised. Major credit cards. 300 Main St. in Sundance Sq. (877-1729). Moderate.

Szechuan – If you hanker for Chinese food in Cowtown, this is the place to go — heaping portions, helpful service, and an extensive menu. The house specialties are heartily recommended. Open daily. Reservations accepted. Major credit cards. 5712 Locke (738-7300). Moderate.

The Balcony – This dressy, romantic restaurant overlooks Camp Bowie Boulevard and serves Continental cuisine. Broiled lamb chops and lobster are the specialties. Closed Sundays. Reservations advised. Major credit cards. 6100 Camp Bowie (731-3719). Moderate.

Le Cafe Bowie – An intimate eatery, where the beef, veal, and poultry dishes are served with a crisp salad, the soup of the day, and warm, buttery bread. Open daily. Reservations. Major credit cards. 4930 Camp Bowie Blvd. (735-1521). Moderate.

Cattleman's Steak House – The portraits of blue-ribbon beef that grace the walls in this Stockyard stronghold are a little-needed reminder of each T-bone's heritage. Many of the cowboy customers are urban, but look carefully, since old-timers still like to splurge here. Open daily. No reservations. All credit cards. 2458 N Main (624-3945). Moderate.

Joe T. Garcia's – This famous North Fort Worth dive serves Tex-Mex food family-style to crowds that arrive fully expecting to line up out front for more than an hour on weekends. The wait is eased (and the food improved) by a couple of stout, delicious frozen Margaritas. Open daily. No reservations. No credit cards. 2201 N Commerce (626-4356). Moderate.

Hedary's – Everything is fresh and flavorful at this Lebanese restaurant, where customers may watch their dinners being prepared. Try the chicken with lemon, veal sausages, grilled lamb chops, and fresh pita bread. Closed Mondays. No reservations. All credit cards. 3308 Fairfield in Ridglea Center (731-6961). Moderate.

Angelo's – Hearty barbecue with the finest of trimmings is all this Fort Worth institution offers. But what more could one ask for than an icy beer and a paper plate heaped with tangy ribs (served after 5 PM only) or barbecued beef plus a scoop of potato salad, coleslaw, a pickle, some onion sauce, and bread. Closed Sundays. No reservations. No credit cards. 2533 White Settlement (332-0357). Inexpensive.

Benito's – This is the best place in Fort Worth to sample a variety of Mexican dishes. The standard Tex-Mex combos are available, but the more authentic Mexican fare — menudo (tripe), homemade tamales, and chile relleños — hasn't been tamed for American tastebuds. They're delicious. Open daily. No reservations. No checks or credit cards. 1450 W Magnolia (332-8633). Inexpensive.

Carshon's – Split-pea soup and corned beef on rye aren't exactly the stuff of Fort Worth's fame, but this spruced-up deli is touted statewide. Closed Mondays. No reservations. No credit cards. 3133 Cleburne Rd. (923-1907). Inexpensive.

Massey's – No theory of evolution has been more often debated than how Massey's chicken-fried steak came to be. To date, it's an unsurpassed delight — tender beef and a crunchy crust topped with thick and creamy gravy. Open daily. No reservations. Major credit cards. 1805 Eighth Ave. (924-8242). Inexpensive.

The Wine Seller – A cozy bistro featuring well-prepared Continental fare along with cheese and pâté boards and, of course, an ample wine selection. Closed Sundays. Reservations accepted. Major credit cards. 6120 Camp Bowie (737-2323). Inexpensive.

Edelweiss – German food and an oompah band are the draws at this popular family place. The sauerbraten comes highly recommended. Closed Sundays. No reservations. Major credit cards. 3801A Southwest Blvd. (738-5934). Inexpensive.

HARTFORD

East Coast residents used to joke that Hartford was an oasis on the highway between New York and Boston, for Hartford's unexpected beauty surprises many visitors. At first glance, the city's crystal skyscrapers, rising suddenly on the flat Connecticut River valley horizon, sparkle like Disney fantasy castles. However, the glitter is disarming. The majestic exterior of Connecticut's most dramatic cityscape masks one of the most pragmatic urban identities in the country. Hartford is the insurance capital of the United States. It is here, amid the graceful towers, that nearly every major domestic insurance company decides its policy regarding premiums and payments, decisions that, in some way or another, probably affect you. This bit of news is hardly likely to be first in your mind when you enter Hartford, however. Initial impressions are likely to be more aesthetic. But Hartford is more than just a pretty city or the state capital or a thriving business center; it is beginning to generate a lot of excitement as a place in which to enjoy oneself.

Although the Dutch visited and established a trading post in the area in the 1620s, Hartford was permanently settled by malcontents from Cambridge, Massachusetts, in 1636. For many years a lively port, here molasses, coffee, spices, and tobacco were stored in large warehouses, then shipped to other destinations on the Connecticut River. An important tobacco-growing region, the Connecticut River valley was the site of the first cigar factory in the United States. Even today, the broad, green banks of the river stretch away, checkered by an intriguing patchwork of white cloth squares that shield the sensitive tobacco leaves from too much light. Hartford is still the marketing center for Connecticut Valley tobacco.

In the middle of this productive agricultural area, Hartford retains the essence of a historic New England township, a source of joy for anyone curious about American architecture during our nation's formative years. Colonial, post-Revolutionary, and 19th-century houses sit in spacious gardens. The renovated Old State House, where statesmen gathered to debate issues of the day as far back as 1796, is open to visitors. Mark Twain, creator of Tom Sawyer and Huck Finn, spent many years in Hartford, and his home, as well as the nearby house of *Uncle Tom's Cabin* author Harriet Beecher Stowe, are favorite stopping points along Hartford's literary trail.

And juxtaposed in the same city is a dramatic, revitalized downtown area. Some 134,000 people live in Hartford. With Springfield, Massachusetts, 25 miles to the north, the urban area population climbs to more than 1 million.

Hartford's insurance business alone employs around 50,000 people. The Connecticut state government employs even more. Bradley International Airport, between Hartford and Springfield, gives western New Englanders an alternative to the frenzy of Boston and New York airports. Visitors arriving

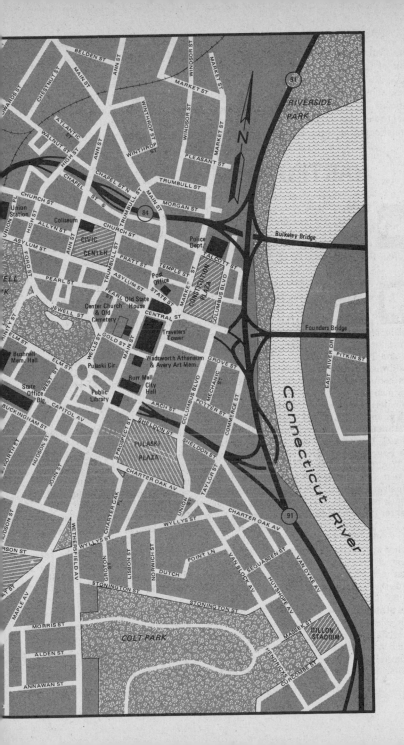

from Canada or the Caribbean can also be spared the more chaotic environment of the larger cities.

Hartford's Civic Center has sparked a proliferation of new restaurants and cafés, some in creatively restored buildings. Streets that used to fold up at nightfall are now alive with bar-hoppers, diners, tourists, and residents of downtown apartments. With its new image, Hartford is fast becoming a sophisticated, enthusiastic visitors' center with a magnetism all its own.

HARTFORD AT-A-GLANCE

SEEING THE CITY: The top of the Travelers' Tower offers the best view of the city, 527 feet above the madding crowd in the Travelers' Insurance Company building. There are 72 steps to climb before reaching the very top. Open weekdays from May until the last Friday in October. Reservations are required. Free. 700 Main St. (277-0111).

SPECIAL PLACES: Walking through Hartford can be highly enjoyable, especially since the city combines classical and contemporary architectural styles. Capitol Hill is a good place to begin.

Capitol Hill – The seat of the state government, the capitol atop the hill is distinguishable by its gold dome. Statues and bas-reliefs decorating the building commemorate events in Connecticut history. Guided tours on weekdays. Near Capitol Ave. and Trinity (566-3662).

Baldwin Museum of Connecticut History – Three and a half centuries of Connecticut's heritage are packed into this museum with exhibitions tracing the growth of major manufacturers in the state. Most notable are the collection of Colt firearms and a Columbia automobile, built when Hartford's auto industry rivaled Detroit's. Closed Sundays and holidays. 231 Capitol Ave. (566-3056).

Bushnell Park – Bushnell is to Hartford what Central Park is to New York. In fact, Frederick Law Olmsted, who designed Central Park, also worked on Bushnell. The Knox Foundation, a private charitable organization, has donated an antique carousel with Wurlitzer band organ to the Bushnell Park Carousel Society, a nonprofit corporation that sells annual $10 individual and $25 family memberships to support the carousel; members can then ride free. Nonmembers need only spend a quarter for a ride. Bounded by Trinity, Elm, Ford, Wells, and Jewell sts. (246-7739).

Center Church – In 1636, the Reverend Thomas Hooker of Cambridge, Massachusetts, led a group of 100 men, women, and children and 160 head of cattle to Hartford, at the time a Dutch trading post. On the site of the Old State House, in 1638, he preached a revolutionary doctrine: "The foundation of authority is laid, first, in the free consent of the people." Hooker's ideas were incorporated into Connecticut's royal charter in 1662, and the minister became known as the founding father of the state. Outside the church is a cemetery, in use from 1640 to 1803. First Church of Christ on Main St. (249-5631).

Old State House – At one time an active meeting house for statesmen, this Federal building designed by Charles Bulfinch is now a museum. Colonial furniture and other artifacts date to 1796, when the Old State House was built. Now privately owned, the museum was refurbished in 1979, and a new souvenir and craft shop added. Closed Mondays. Free. Main and State sts. (522-6766).

Wadsworth Atheneum – The oldest art museum in the country, with eclectic collections of prehistoric relics, paintings, and sculptures, and some new galleries displaying American art from 1630 to the present. Open all year. Admission charge; free on Thursdays. Main St. and Atheneum Sq. N (278-2670).

Avery Art Memorial – Attached to the Wadsworth Atheneum, Avery has an independent collection of Great Masters (Rembrandt, Wyeth, Daumier, Picasso, Goya, Cézanne, Whistler, and Sargent). Open all year. 25 Atheneum Sq. N (278-2670).

Morgan Memorial – Also part of the Wadsworth Atheneum, this museum was started by J. P. Morgan, a Hartford citizen who left home to make his fortune. Fine collections of Middle Eastern and Oriental archaeological relics, Meissen china, and firearms, especially those made by Colt, a local enterprise. Open all year. 590 Main St. (278-2670).

Nook Farm – A 19th-century writers' community, the former Nook Farm estate contains several authors' houses. Mark Twain lived in a riverboat-shaped brick, stone, and wood three-story house with brown and orange brick patternwork. Harriet Beecher Stowe, author of *Uncle Tom's Cabin,* lived only slightly less elaborately in a brick house next door. A 45-minute tour takes you through the premises. Closed holidays. Admission charge. Mark Twain Memorial, 351 Farmington Ave. (525-9317). Harriet Beecher Stowe House, 77 Forest St. (525-9317).

■ **EXTRA SPECIAL:** For a beautiful drive on winding, narrow roads through romantic pine forests and cozy New England towns, take a drive west on Rte. 44 to Rte. 202. About 30 miles from the city is Litchfield, a dazzling village of huge white mansions set around a classic American village green. Continue on Rte. 202 for about 12 miles until you reach New Preston, on the shore of Lake Waramaug. *The Inn on Lake Waramaug,* a 25-room country inn, serves healthy, home-cooked meals (off Rte. 45, New Preston; 868-0563). Continue south on Rte. 47, one of the best antiques centers in New England, for about 12 miles. In Woodbury, *Curtis House* claims to be Connecticut's oldest inn. Opened in 1754, it has 18 bedrooms, most of which have large, canopied beds. Large lunches and dinners include freshly baked hot muffins and lovely desserts (263-2101). Take Rte. 6, going northeast, to return to Hartford.

SOURCES AND RESOURCES

TOURIST INFORMATION: The Greater Hartford Convention and Visitors Bureau distributes brochures, maps, and general tourist information. 1 Civic Center Plaza (728-6789). It operates a visitors center at the Old State House. Closed Mondays. Main and State sts. (522-6766).

Local Coverage – *Hartford Courant* (the oldest daily newspaper in continuous circulation), morning daily; *Connecticut Magazine,* monthly; *The Hartford Advocate,* a free alternative news and entertainment publication, weekly.

Food – *The Complete Menu Guide to Hartford Restaurants,* by John A. Russo, Jr. ($4.95), lists menus for over 100 restaurants.

Area Code – All telephone numbers are in the 203 area code unless otherwise indicated.

CLIMATE AND CLOTHES: Hartford's humidity is a problem in the summer when temperatures reach the 80s and 90s; winters are snowy, generally in the 20s and 30s; spring and fall are delightful.

GETTING AROUND: Airport – Bradley International Airport is about 12 miles from downtown Hartford. The drive usually takes 20 to 30 minutes, and taxi fare should run about $16. Airport Taxi (627-0213) provides hourly bus service to the downtown area from 6:35 AM to 11:20 PM (less often on weekends) for $4.25.

Bus – The state-owned Connecticut Company operates the municipal bus service. 53 Vernon St. (525-9181).

Taxi – It's very difficult to get a cab in the street. Pick up a cab during the day in front of the *Sheraton Hartford, Parkview Hilton,* and *Summit* hotels, or call Yellow Cab, 666-6666.

Car Rental – All major national firms are represented at the airport as well as downtown. Budget Rent-a-Car is the cheapest local service. Asylum and High sts., next to the *Parkview Hilton,* lobby (278-4440).

 MUSEUMS: Museum aficionados will love the abundance of art and historical collections in Hartford. Wadsworth Atheneum, the Avery Art Memorial, Morgan Memorial, and the Old State House are described above in *Special Places.* Other notable museums are:

Butler-McCook Homestead – 396 Main St. (522-1806)
Connecticut Historical Society – Elizabeth St. (236-5621)
Science Museum of Connecticut – 950 Trout Brook Dr., West Hartford (236-2961)

 MAJOR COLLEGES AND UNIVERSITIES: Trinity College, at Summit, Vernon, and Broad sts. (527-3151); St. Joseph College, Asylum Ave. W Hartford (232-4571); University of Hartford, 200 Bloomfield Ave. W Hartford (243-4100).

 SPECIAL EVENTS: The *Festival of Lights* is held every year on Constitution Plaza the day after Thanksgiving, when thousands of tiny white lights are turned on by a child picked through a lottery. Santa Claus always makes a dramatic appearance, arriving on top of the the United Technologies building in a helicopter and descending in a window washer's gondola made up to look like a sleigh. *Wintertainment,* a new two-day festival in January, features events ranging from fireworks to snow sculpture contests and dogsled races. *A Taste of Hartford,* also held at Constitution Plaza the weekend before Memorial Day, is a giant block party with music, dancing, and booths set up by over 60 restaurants to offer samples of their specialties. The *Connecticut Family Folk Festival* fills Elizabeth Park on the city's west side with the sounds of guitars, fiddles, and dulcimers during the second weekend of August.

 SPORTS AND FITNESS: Fishing – For the best fishing, try Wethersfield Cove.

Fitness Centers – The YMCA has a pool, squash and racquetball courts, and a track, 160 Jewell at Ann St.. (522-4183).

Golf – There are 24 golf courses in the Hartford area. The best public course is in Goodwin Park. PGA pros compete in the Greater Hartford Open every July at Tournament Players Club, Cromwell.

Hockey – The *Hartford Whalers* NHL team plays at the Hartford Civic Center (727-8080).

Jogging – The perimeter of Bushnell Park, across from the YMCA, is ⅞ mile; other running courses include Goodwin Park, 1½ miles from downtown, with a 2-mile perimeter; and Elizabeth Park, 2 miles from downtown, with a 2½-mile perimeter.

Skiing – There's excellent cross-country skiing at the Metropolitan District Commission reservoir in West Hartford. Downhill enthusiasts like Mt. Southington, 20 minutes south on I-84; Powder Ridge Ski Area, 20 minutes south on I-91; and Mt. Tom, 45 minutes north on I-91.

Swimming – The Connecticut River is acceptable for boating but not clean enough for swimming, even though it may look tempting on a hot day, Hartford residents recommend swimming at the YWCA. Admission charge. 135 Broad St. (525-1163). YMCA, 160 Jewell at Ann St. (522-4183).

Tennis – The best public courts are at Elizabeth Park, Prospect and Asylum aves.; at the State Armory on Capitol Hill; there are indoor courts at In-town Tennis (246-2448).

THEATER: For complete up-to-the-minute performance schedules, check the newpapers listed above. Hartford's main theaters are the *Hartford Stage Company,* 50 Church St. (527-5151); and touring companies frequently bring Broadway productions to *Bushnell Memorial Hall,* 166 Capitol Ave. (246-6807).

MUSIC: Concerts, operas, symphonies, and ballets are performed at Bushnell Memorial Hall, 166 Capitol Ave. (246-6807); and Goodspeed Opera House, in East Haddam, 30 minutes south on Rte. 9 (873-8668). The Civic Center, 1 Civic Center Plaza (727-8080), features rock concerts.

NIGHTCLUBS AND NIGHTLIFE: Hartford's cafés are great places for listening to music. The selection varies from place to place, from night to night, so call ahead. At *Boppers,* 22 Union Pl. (549-5801), a DJ plays oldies but goodies from the back of a real 1957 convertible, parked in the center of the dance floor. The bar at *Shenanigan's,* 1 Gold St. (522-4117), is an authentic Art Deco diner that's been taken apart and rebuilt inside the restaurant. For disco dancing, try *Lorien,* 187 Allyn St., (525-1919), or *Le Jardin,* 121 Allyn St. (547-1190). Most lively gay bar is the *Lost and Found Café,* 81 Pope Park Hwy., #4 (241-5000).

SINS: *Hartford's Civic Center* and surrounding *Constitution Plaza* are points of *pride* in the city; this complex of office buildings bordering the Connecticut River is especially beautiful at Christmas, when it sparkles with thousands of tiny white lights. A good place to practice *sloth.*

Ditto for the magnificent carousel — a stained glass pavilion full of wooden horses assembled from merry-go-rounds of generations past — in Bushnell Park.

LOCAL SERVICES: Babysitting – Care-At-Home, 243 Farmington Ave. (728-1165)

Business Services – Headquarters Companies, One Corporate Center (247-8300) and City Place (275-6500)

Mechanic – Hartford Auto Repairs, 12 S Whitney St. (232-2236)

BEST IN TOWN

CHECKING IN: Hartford has an unexceptional collection of comfortable hotels. The *Parkview Hilton* does offer free local calls, and serves free coffee in guest rooms (some of which have waterbeds). The *Sheraton-Hartford, Summit* and *Holiday Inn* offer in-room movies. Expect to pay $80 and up at places noted as expensive, $60 to $80 in the moderate category, and $55 or less in the inexpensive range. For B&B accommodations, contact Nutmeg Bed & Breakfast, 222 Girard Ave., Hartford, CT 06105 (203 236-6698).

Sheraton-Hartford – Connected to the Civic Center, this 407-room hotel gives the indoor sports enthusiast a wider range of facilities than any other Hartford hotel. The indoor heated pool has a lifeguard on duty. There's also a whirlpool, sauna, exercise room, and recreation room. The café-bar features nightly entertainment and dancing. In-room movies are also available. Cribs for infants are free. Trumbull St. at Civic Center (203 728-5151). Expensive.

Parkview Hilton – Overlooking Bushnell Park and the capitol, it was completely refurbished in 1981 and offers 410 rooms, 3 restaurants, and an entertainment center. Ford and Pearl sts. (203 249-5611). Expensive.

The Summit – In the middle of Hartford's ultra-modern, exceptionally well landscaped raised mall, Constitution Plaza. In addition to having a café-bar and dining room, the 296-room *Summit* offers free in-room movies. 5 Constitution Plaza (203 278-2000). Expensive.

Holiday Inn – On the fringe of downtown, with easy access to I-84 and I-91, this high-rise property features free parking for guests and an outdoor pool. It's a popular choice among corporate travelers. 50 Morgan St. (549-2400). Moderate.

Ramada Inn – If you're looking for a central hotel with basic conveniences at a good price, this is your best bet in Hartford. Its 96 rooms have recently been refurbished. It has a restaurant and café. Parking is free. 440 Asylum St. (203 246-6591). Inexpensive.

 EATING OUT: The number and varieties of foreign cuisines available in the city are gradually increasing, but most of the best restaurants still feature traditional Hartford fare: American-Italian cooking, or the steaks-chops-seafood routine. Expect to pay between $30 and $50 at restaurants designated as expensive; between $20 and $30 at those we've listed as moderate; $20 or less at inexpensive places. Prices do not include drinks, wine, or tips.

Hubbard's Park – This restaurant has one of the city's most sophisticated settings for dining out, with lots of chrome and glass and waiters in black tie. The cuisine is nouvelle and rarely fails to please. Eating here in the daytime is particularly enjoyable since there's a good view of Bushnell Park, across the street. Open daily. Reservations advised. Major credit cards. 26 Trumbull St. (728-0315). Expensive.

Spencer's – In the restored Linden apartment building (one of the city's most exclusive), this is actually two restaurants in one. The formal, Edwardian-style dining room features a Continental bill of fare, while the *Tavern* serves lighter meals in a more casual atmosphere. Open daily. Reservations advised. Major credit cards. 10 Capitol Ave. (247-0400). Expensive.

L'Américain – On the fringe of downtown, this eclectic restaurant inside a renovated factory is a favorite of the business community. Open daily. Reservations advised. Major credit cards. 2 Hartford Sq. (522-6500). Expensive.

Frank's Restaurant – A favorite of state politicians; traditional Italian-American dishes. The manicotti is considered excellent, and the veal superb. Frank's is especially busy before and after hockey games and Civic Center events, so call ahead for reservations. Open daily except Sundays in July and August. Major credit cards. In the Cityplace Complex at 185 Asylum St., across from Hartford Civic Center (527-9291). Moderate.

Honiss' Oyster House – After a hiatus of several years (following the demolition of its original location), this Hartford institution — which once counted Mark Twain and P. T. Barnum among its regular patrons — has reopened at the downtown *Ramada Inn.* The fare is traditional New England seafood, nothing fancy, but all fresh and tasty. The decor is historic Hartford with a sampling of the hundreds of vintage photos that lined the walls of the original restaurant. Open daily. Reservations suggested. Major credit cards. 440 Asylum St. (246-6591). Moderate.

Brown Thomson & Co. – In the Richardson Building complex, which also includes a shopping mall, this antiques-encrusted restaurant offers the most extensive menu in town — 125 separate items. Sandwiches, Mexican food, and delicacies such as fried ice cream are included. This is where the young people of Hartford meet these days. Major credit cards. 942 Main St. (525-1600). Inexpensive.

HONOLULU

Honolulu stretches along a 20-mile strip of land between the Pacific Ocean and the 3,000-foot mountains of Oahu, the major island of the state of Hawaii. In the past 20 years the city has outgrown this narrow strip and risen up the mountains along ridges and deeply cleft valleys; it reaches into the sea with a multitude of docks and marinas that run, off and on, from Pearl Harbor to the first grand sweep of magnificent Waikiki Beach — and magnificent it is, even poised against a backdrop of high-rise hotels several blocks deep. At night the homes up in the heights glitter above the city, and beyond them — 10 minutes from downtown — are the tropical mountain rain forests, as prolific and luxuriant as ever.

Private sailors and yachtsmen know Honolulu as one of America's trimmest, cleanest port cities. To landbound Americans it is something more — the country's most foreign metropolis, an American city that stubbornly refuses to feel quite like America. Small wonder, when you consider that less than 100 years ago — until 1893, to be exact — it was the capital of a foreign country, a monarchy ruled by a queen: a Pacific Ocean island nation with its culture, arts, and world view rooted in the South Seas. In 1893 reigning Queen Liliuokalani was overthrown by Americans living in the islands, and five years later the islands were annexed as a US territory. They became American, but they were — are — still the islands, and that ain't Baltimore. About 2,500 miles southwest of Los Angeles, Honolulu is just short of halfway between the continental US and Tokyo, a relationship that more than once has given rise to awe and some misgivings.

The sense of disorientation is not all one-sided. The "mainland" is what residents call the rest of the United States (and if you want to keep their respect you will never refer to it as "stateside" since Hawaii, too, is a state, and proud of it), and to many residents the other 49 states represent the strange and sometimes rather frightening culture of the *haoles.* Pronounced "*how*lees," this old Hawaiian word for outsiders has, in the 20th century, come to mean Caucasians — a segment of the population well outnumbered by Orientals and Polynesians in Hawaii. To native Hawaiians, *haoles* in the past have represented Yankees who don't understand pidgin and who seem eager to bull their way into business and social success. The fact that they no longer automatically succeed in these objectives represents a change not uniformly felt, and sometimes overlooked, in the islands today.

Islanders in general, and Honolulu residents in particular, are unabashedly fond of dubbing their island home "paradise." But it is sometimes an uneasy Eden, with a history that has often been violent and tragic. Early-19th-century American missionaries experienced severe hardships here; but in the pitched battles between missionaries and western shippers and merchants for the hearts and minds of the native population, it was the Hawaiians who lost almost everything. They were converted to Christianity and lost their culture; they were taught to read, write, and count, and were decimated by foreign diseases to which they had no immunity. Only today is the long-dormant pride of culture emerging among descendants of the original Polynesian Hawaiians.

Other groups came to live in the islands, too, gradually making Honolulu a cosmopolitan city. When the economy required hard labor for the sugar plantations in the late 19th century, unskilled workers were recruited from all over, especially from Japan and China. When their contracts expired, many stayed on, marrying and spawning the lovely racial mix that characterizes contemporary Honolulu society. More than half the marriages in Hawaii today are interracial.

With the attack on Pearl Harbor — December 7, 1941 — Honolulu entered the consciousness of most mainland Americans. Martial law was declared throughout the islands, and for millions of American servicemen Hawaii became the jumping-off point for the Pacific theater. They called Oahu "the Rock," and they hated it.

They don't hate it anymore. Almost 5 million visitors a year pour into the Honolulu airport and drop more than $4 billion into the Hawaiian coffers as they come. Honolulu's green outback may be carpeted with sugar and pineapple plantations, but plantations no longer support the economy. Tourism is the vital juice of Hawaii, and most of it gets squeezed out in Honolulu. (And among the visitors are a goodly number of ex-GIs who hated the Rock. The most popular tourist destination is the beautiful memorial that floats over the sunken USS *Arizona*. One million people a year see it.)

Honolulu — the eleventh largest city in the country — is a modern metropolis struggling with modern problems. A few decades ago Waikiki was a sparsely settled peninsula along a swamp, 3 miles southeast of town. There was an unobstructed view of Diamond Head, and the tallest structure in town was the 10-story Aloha Tower, from which ship traffic was controlled. No more, no more. Forests of high-rises dwarf the Tower and Waikiki has its share of dope dealers, pickpockets, and prostitutes. But Chinatown is still in the center of town, with its noodle factories and small restaurants reminiscent of a port town 100 years ago. And within Honolulu is a taste of everything Hawaiian, and a flavor of far seas beyond.

HONOLULU AT-A-GLANCE

SEEING THE CITY: For an eye-popping view of the shoreline, take the outdoor glass elevator to the top of the *Ilikai Hotel* (1777 Ala Moana Blvd.; 949-3811). There are equally spectacular views from atop the *Sheraton Waikiki* (2255 Kalakaua Ave.; 922-4422) and from *Nicholas Nickolas,* atop the *Ala Moana Americana* (410 Atkinson St.; 955-4811). For another good perspective, visit the 10th-floor observatory in the Aloha Tower, with a panorama that stretches from the airport to Diamond Head. At the bottom of Fort Street Mall (537-9260).

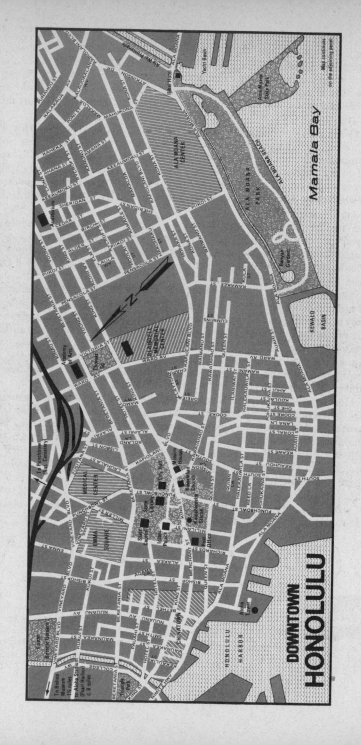

DOWNTOWN HONOLULU

Mamala Bay

Map continues on the adjoining page

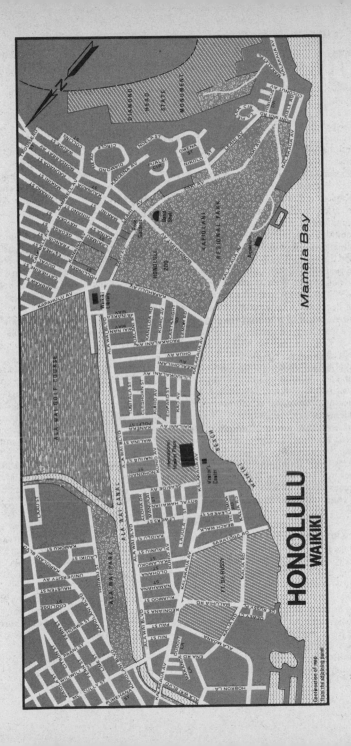

HONOLULU
WAIKIKI

Mamala Bay

Continuation of map
from the adjoining panel

SPECIAL PLACES: Although it is now considerably overbuilt, Waikiki is nonetheless an attractive center for wandering. We suggest getting to know your neighborhood first with a 3-mile walking tour.

Diamond Head – Guarding the southeasternmost boundary of Waikiki, this 760-foot volcanic crater is a world-famous landmark. You can climb around the slopes of Diamond Head along the tricky trail that begins at a gate off Makalei Place or you can drive into the crater through a tunnel to a state park inside. For park information, call the State Parks Dept., 548-7455.

Kapiolani Park – This 220-acre park, named for the wife of Kalakaua, the last king of Hawaii, has enough special places to keep you busy for more than a few hours. Just off Monsarrat Ave., the Kodak Hula Show (833-1661) is performed at 10 AM Tuesdays through Fridays. Get there early if you want a seat. Drift along toward the scent of the Kapiolani Rose Garden on the corner of Paki and Monsarrat. Kalakaua Ave., named after the good king, begins here. Pronounced "ka-la-cow-wah," it is the principal thoroughfare of Waikiki.

Waikiki Beach – Just outside the park, alongside Kalakaua Ave., begins the famous, 2½-mile-long curve of Waikiki Beach, one of the most famous beaches and surfing spots in the world. The 2- to 5-foot waves that are standard along the shoreline for much of the year are perfect for novices and amateurs. (On the few days in the summer when they reach 15 feet, Waikiki's waves should be avoided by all but experts.) Several hotels along Waikiki — for example, the *Outrigger,* 2335 Kalakaua Ave. (923-0711; ask for Beach Services) — provide instruction and surfboards.

International Marketplace – A great place to poke around outdoor stalls underneath a giant banyan tree festooned with lanterns. (A souk, Hawaiian style, is what we call it.) You can pick up all kinds of exotic junk and treasures you just can't live without. 2330 Kalakaua Ave.

Royal Hawaiian Shopping Center – Stretching three blocks along the ocean side of Kalakaua Avenue, this three-level outdoor mall is Waikiki's largest shopping complex, with everything from Hawaiian crafts to designer clothes, plus daily performances of music and Hawaiiana as well as several restaurants serving a variety of cuisines. 2201 Kalakaua Ave. (922-0588).

Fort DeRussy Army Museum – Weapons used by ancient Hawaiians, weapons captured from the Japanese, and weapons used by US soldiers in campaigns from the Spanish-American to the Korean War are on display here. In addition, there are uniforms worn at various times by US forces as well as those of the enemy. The most fascinating items are the Hawaiian weapons made long ago from shark's teeth and the newspaper accounts of the US involvement in World War II following the invasion of Pearl Harbor. Closed Mondays. Kalia Rd. (543-2687).

DOWNTOWN

Mission Houses Museum – This museum complex contains the earliest American buildings in Hawaii. The white frame house was shipped around Cape Horn in pieces, then reassembled in 1821 by the first missionaries. The buildings have been intelligently restored, and excellent guides are available (and give a good thumbnail sketch of basic Hawaiian history). Open daily. Admission charge. 55 S King St. (531-0481).

Kawaiahao Church – Across from the Mission Houses, Kawaiahao Church is also known as the Westminster Abbey of Hawaii. It was designed by Hawaii's first minister and constructed out of 14,000 coral blocks cut from a local reef. King Lunalilo is buried in the front yard. Services are conducted in English and Hawaiian at 10:30 AM on Sundays. Open daily. Free. King and Punchbowl sts. (538-6267).

Chinatown – Chinatown is on the easternmost fringe of downtown and spills across the Nuuanu Stream into Aala Triangle Park. There are open-air meat, fish, and vegetable markets; herb shops selling age-old medications; and elderly people who still dress in traditional costume. This is also the "sin" quarter of Honolulu, where sleazy sex shows compete for customers with family-style chop suey houses. A walking tour of Chinatown with an optional lunch (a real bargain) takes place on Tuesdays at 9:30 AM, starting from the Chinese Chamber of Commerce, 42 N King St. (533-3181).

Iolani Palace – With elaborate surroundings, Iolani Palace sits in state, receiving tribute from admirers. Highly revered by historians and sentimentalists alike, the palace was the final residence of monarch and songwriter Queen Liliuokalani. In fact, she was imprisoned there following the 1893 revolution and wrote some of her famous songs, including "Aloha Oe," while in detention. Iolani was built by King David Kalakaua in 1882. In 1883, he placed a crown on his own head in what is now Coronation Bandstand, where, every Friday at noon, the Royal Hawaiian Band gives free, informal concerts. Palace tours are given Wednesdays through Saturdays; tickets should be reserved a few days in advance. King and Richards sts. (538-1471; for reservations, 523-0141).

State Capitol – Built in 1969, for $25 million, the capitol takes its inspiration from the natural history of the islands. All of its features — columns, reflecting pools, courtyard — reflect aspects of Hawaii's environment. Outside the capitol stands a beautiful bronze statue of Queen Liliuokalani and the controversial modern statue of Father Damien, the hero of the leprosy settlement at Kalaupapa on the island of Molokai. 400 S Beretania St. (548-2211).

OTHER SPECIAL PLACES

Ala Moana Center – This is one of the world's largest shopping centers. Built in 1959, when Hawaii achieved statehood, the Ala Moana Center has more than 200 stores selling quality clothing, antiques, carpets, furniture, fabrics, and art made at home and imported from other countries. Ala Moana Blvd. across from Ala Moana Park.

Arizona Memorial – More than a million people a year come to honor the American sailors who perished on the USS *Arizona,* sunk when the Japanese bombed Pearl Harbor on December 7, 1941. The only boat tour of the Memorial departs from the vistors center daily except Mondays. The National Park Service operates a large museum, with exhibitions and films. At Kewalo Basin near Waikiki you can buy a ticket for a half-day Pearl Harbor cruise that passes the memorial but does not allow for a visit (422-0561).

Bishop Museum – Near the beginning of Likelike (pronounced "leekay-leekay") Highway, in the working-class neighborhood called Kalihi, this prestigious museum houses the greatest collection of Hawaiiana in the world. Founded in 1899, it is the center for most of the anthropological research done throughout Polynesia and the Pacific. In addition to excellent displays, the museum features daily performances of Hawaiian music and dance. Open daily. Admission charge. 1525 Bernice St. (847-1443).

Foster Botanic Gardens – Often overlooked by tourists, this cool, tranquil retreat in the middle of the city is a living museum of growing things. The #4 bus from Waikiki will bring you close to the garden at Nuuanu and Vineyard. Open daily. Admission charge. 180 N Vineyard Blvd. (531-1939).

Honolulu Academy of Arts – Across Thomas Square from Blaisdell Center, the Academy of Arts has Oriental art and some European and American works. Interesting items include a Japanese ink and color handscroll dating from 1250, John Singleton Copley's *Portrait of Nathaniel Allen,* and Segna di Bonaventura's *Madonna and Child.* Closed Mondays. Free. 900 S Beretania St. (538-3693).

National Memorial Cemetery of the Pacific – Also known as Punchbowl crater, this cemetery is the Arlington of the Pacific. In prehistoric times it was the site of human sacrifices. Now, more than 20,000 servicemen lie buried among its 112 peaceful acres overlooking downtown Honolulu. Commercial bus and van tours visit Punchbowl, but if you're on your own, you'll need a car or taxi. Take Puowaina Drive to its end.

■**EXTRA SPECIAL:** Honolulu is the great jumping-off point for *island-hopping* expeditions. Hawaiian Air (537-5100) flies to the islands of Kauai, Maui, Hawaii, and Molokai daily, and less frequently to Lanai; Aloha Airlines (836-1111) and Mid Pacific Air (836-3313) serve all but Lanai; Royal Hawaiian Air Service (836-2200) has flights to each of the islands except Kauai. There are also several commuter carriers, often offering even lower fares. Kauai, the oldest of the islands, is known for golf at the *Princeville Resort* courses, sunny Poipu Beach, and the spectacular Na Pali coast. Maui offers valleys, waterfalls, beaches, and the crater of the dormant Haleakala Volcano. Hawaii is the home of Mauna Loa and Kilauea, two of the most active volcanoes in the world. On Lanai, only 17 miles long, the main draw is plenty of pineapples. The Dole Company owns most of the island, and its land is devoted to cultivating the spiny, delicious fruit. Molokai, 37 miles long, a relatively untouched ranchers' island, allows you to see a rural side of Hawaii. There are, however, resorts at Kaluakoi and along the east coast should you wish to stay awhile.

SOURCES AND RESOURCES

TOURIST INFORMATION: For information, maps, and brochures, contact the Hawaii Visitors Bureau, 2270 Kalakaua Ave., Room 804 (923-1811). *Oahu Destinations, Guide to Oahu, This Week,* and *Spotlight Hawaii* are free booklets available in most hotel lobbies. Also see our own *Hawaii 1987.*

Local Coverage – *Honolulu Advertiser,* morning daily; *Honolulu Star-Bulletin,* evening daily; *Honolulu* magazine, monthly.

Area Code – All telephone numbers are in the 808 area code unless otherwise indicated.

CLIMATE AND CLOTHES: In ancient times, the Hawaiians had no word for weather. They did, however, have words for two seasons — winter and summer. Winter, which runs from about October through April, means daytime highs reaching the mid-70s and low 80s, dropping into the low 60s at night. There can be several short rains in a day. You can count on 11 hours of daylight — short by Hawaiian standards. Summer temperatures hover around the mid- to upper 80s; rains are less frequent, and you get about 13 hours of daylight, more vacation for your money.

GETTING AROUND: Airport – Honolulu International Airport is about a 20- to 25-minute drive from Waikiki (in moderate traffic), slightly less from the downtown area. Cab fare to Waikiki should run $14 to $16, $8 to $10 downtown. The Gray Line (834-1033) provides bus service from the airport to Waikiki hotels for $5; buses leave from outside the baggage claim area every 20 minutes during most of the day (hourly in the morning and at night). The Gray Line trip to Waikiki can take anywhere from 45 minutes to 1½ hours, depending on the location of your hotel.

Bus – TheBus, as the municipal transit line is called, is the least expensive, most convenient way to get around Honolulu. You can get a map of bus routes at your hotel, at Ala Moana Center, or from the Honolulu Dept. of Transport, Mass Transit Lines (MTL), 725 Kapiolani Blvd. (531-1611).

Taxi – Technically, it's illegal for taxis to cruise or pick up passengers on the street, although it's often done. To be sure of finding a cab, call for one. Some reliable companies are: SIDA (836-0011), Charley's (955-2211), and Aloha State Taxi (847-3566).

Car Rental – One of the best local car rental firms is Tropical (836-1041), but check some of the smaller companies; they sometimes offer a better deal. Dollar (926-4200), Budget (922-3600), and other major agencies are represented at the airport and have offices in Waikiki as well.

Pedicab – These chromium versions of rickshaws, operated by healthy-looking college students, are available to the daring for short rides in the open air of Waikiki. Be sure to check rates with the driver before riding.

MUSEUMS: The Army Museum, Bishop Museum, and Honolulu Academy of Arts are described under *Special Places.* Another notable museum is the *Polynesian Cultural Center,* 1½ hours from Waikiki in Laie (923-1861). Each of the seven model villages on the 42-acre grounds represents a Polynesian culture: Maori, Tahitian, Samoan, Fijian, Tongan, Marquesan, and Hawaiian. People live and work as they would on their native islands. Throughout the day there is Polynesian entertainment featuring the villagers (the most authentic South Seas Show on Oahu). Closed Sundays. Admission charge (923-1861 or 293-3333).

MAJOR COLLEGES AND UNIVERSITIES: The University of Hawaii, in Manoa Valley (948-8855); Brigham Young University, at Laie (293-3211); Chaminade University of Honolulu (735-4811); Hawaii Pacific College, downtown (544-0239); Hawaii Loa College (235-3647).

SPECIAL EVENTS: Special events are held year-round. Here are a few highlights:

January: The annual *Hula Bowl College All-Star Football Classic* is played in Aloha Stadium and the *Chinese New Year* is celebrated in Chinatown (sometimes in February).

February: Early in the month, the nationally televised 4-day *Hawaiian Open International Golf Tournament,* at the Waialae Country Club in the Kahala District (sometimes late in January).

June: On June 11, *Kamehameha Day* honors the conqueror of the islands with a long parade.

July: In even-numbered years, the *Trans-Pacific Yacht Race* finishes off Diamond Head.

September: The *Waikiki Rough Water Swim* is held over a 2-mile course, ending at Duke Kahanamoku Beach in front of the *Hilton Hawaiian Village Hotel. Aloha Week* is Honolulu's biggest celebration. It features canoe races, luaus, balls, athletic events, parades and more.

October: The *Honolulu Orchid Society Show* is held at the Neal S. Blaisdell Center, with lei-making and flower-arranging demonstrations as well as floral displays.

December: Contestants in the *Honolulu Marathon* run from the Aloha Tower to the bandshell in Kapiolani Park. December 7 is *Pearl Harbor Day,* commemorated by a service at the Arizona Memorial.

SPORTS AND FITNESS: Hawaii is one of the world's great centers for water sports. Surfing and swimming contests are held often. Aloha Stadium is the site of the Hula Bowl college football game each January, football and baseball games at other times; Halawa Heights (488-7731). Basketball and boxing events are held at the Neal S. Blaisdell Center, 777 Ward Ave. (521-2911).

Bicycling – Bikes can be rented from Aloha Funway Rentals, 1984 Kalakaua Ave. (942-9696).

Fishing – Fishing enthusiasts from all over the world flock to Hawaiian waters. Fishing boats can be chartered from Coreene C's Sport Fishing Charters (536-7472), or Island Charters (536-1555). Most boats leave from Kewalo Basin, at the end of Ward Ave., just across Ala Moana Blvd.

Fitness Centers – King Street Courts has tennis and racquetball courts, S King St. between Isenberg and McCully (944-9960). The YMCA has a pool, racquetball court, sauna, exercise machines, and weights, 401 Atkinson Dr., across from Ala Moana Center (941-3344). For a treat, set up an appointment with the massage (acupressure) specialist at the *Moana Hotel,* 2365 Kalakaua Ave. (922-3111).

Golf – There are 15 public golf courses on Oahu. These include Ala Wai Golf Course, (732-7741); Pali Golf Course, Kaneohe (261-9784); *Makaha Resort Golf Course* (695-9544) and Makaha Valley Country Club (695-9578), both in Makaha; and the *Turtle Bay Hilton* (293-8811), Kuilima.

Jogging – Run along Kalakaua Avenue to Kapiolani Park, where a group meets at the bandstand at 7:30 AM every Sunday from March through December for a short lecture and a run. The distance around the park is 1.8 miles; to tack on more mileage, continue along Kalakaua to Diamond Head Road and circle the base of Diamond Head. The road turns into Monsarrat Avenue, which leads back to Kalakaua (4½ miles altogether). Or take Diamond Head Road as far as Kahala Avenue, one of the island's most beautiful runs. Another: the 2-mile perimeter of Ala Moana Park.

Skindiving – Dan's Dive Shop, 660 Ala Moana Blvd. (536-6181), rents diving gear, offers instructions for beginners, and has brush-up courses for those with some experience. Out near Makaha, call Leeward Dive Center (696-3414).

Surfing – The quest for the perfect wave attracts surfers from all over the world. Most hotels along the Waikiki Beach have surfing instructors and concessions that rent surfboards, canoes, and catamarans. The most famous surfing beach is Sunset Beach on the other side of the island.

Swimming – With Waikiki Beach generally very crowded, an alternative is to head for beaches on the other side of the island. Equally spectacular settings include Sandy Beach and Makapuu, where just about everyone bodysurfs; Waimanalo and Kailua, where swimming and windsurfing are popular; and on up the coast to Kahana and the legendary surfing beaches of the North Shore. Many beaches are dangerous for swimming; stick to those with lifeguards.

Tennis – There are public courts at 40 places around Oahu. Try the ones at Ala Moana Park, Diamond Head Tennis Center, Kapiolani Tennis Courts, or King Street Courts.

THEATERS: You can get tickets at the door for most plays and musicals in Honolulu. The main theaters are *Blaisdell Memorial Center Concert Hall,* Ward and King sts. (537-6191); *Honolulu Community Theater,* Makapuu and Aloha aves. (734-0274). Also check for performances at the *Waikiki Shell* (521-2911).

MUSIC: The *Honolulu Symphony* plays at the Blaisdell Center Concert Hall (537-6191). Rock musicians appear at the Blaisdell Center Arena (521-2911) or sometimes at Aloha Stadium (487-3877) or the Waikiki Shell (521-2911).

NIGHTCLUBS AND NIGHTLIFE: With a large tourist industry to support it and a Hawaiian musical tradition to provide the raw material, it does indeed seem that Kalakaua Avenue — and plenty of side streets — swing from about 8 PM until dawn, most nights of the week. Hawaii's most famous singer and entertainer, Don Ho, plays the *Hilton Dome,* 2005 Kalia Rd., in the Hilton Hawaiian Village (949-4321). The Brothers Cazimero frequently perform at the *Royal Hawaiian*'s Monarch Room and are the most popular and enduring of Hawaii's musical entertainers. There's also a piano bar at the *Sheraton-Waikiki,* 2255 Kalakaua Ave. (922-4422), and, for jazz, try *Trapper's* at the *Hyatt Regency,* 2424 Kalakaua Ave. (922-9292). Popular discos include *Annabelle's,* atop the *Ilikai Hotel* (949-3811); *Bobby McGees,* at the *Colony Surf,* 2885 Kalakaua Ave. (922-1282); and *Hula's,* 2103 Kuhio Ave. (923-0669), with a mixed crowd ranging from punk to gay. *Lavender Follies* presents a very polished and popular transvestite revue, with optional cocktails or dinner, daily except Sundays, 286 Beach Walk (923-8411).

SINS: Being a Polynesian Hawaiian is a point of *pride* nowadays in Honolulu. You'll see a fine display of Hawaiian *anger* simply by saying, "I'm from the States." Islanders are too.

The city has go-go dancers, strippers, massage girls, and booksellers adept at pandering to every kink — everything needed to satisfy any category of *lust.* It outdoes itself at the *Club Hubba-Hubba,* 25 N Hotel St. (536-7698), in the center of the red-light district. Sidewalk stewardesses regularly turn up along Kalakaua Avenue, with prices seeming to decline in direct ratio to the distance from the prime Waikiki hotel strip.

LOCAL SERVICES: Babysitting – Wesley Child Care Center, 1350 Hunakai St. (735-1688)

Business Services – Una May Young, Suite 3206, Manor Wing, Sheraton-Waikiki Hotel, 2255 Kalakaua Ave. (922-4422)

Mechanic – Toguchi Chevron Service Station, 825 N Vineyard Blvd. (845-6422)

BEST IN TOWN

CHECKING IN: Some say that Waikiki is a solid wall of hotels today, but that's not entirely true. Nevertheless, there are a confusing number of choices. Hotels vary in personality, so do a bit of careful checking before picking one. Remember, it's not just a place to sleep; it will also serve as your tropical headquarters during your Honolulu visit. Expect to pay $175 or more for a double at those places we've listed as very expensive; around $85 and up at hotels classed as expensive; between $50 and $80 at those designated moderate; under $45 at hotels listed as inexpensive. For B&B accommodations, contact Bed & Breakfast Hawaii, Box 449, Kapaa, HI 96746 (808 822-7771).

Kahala Hilton – A deluxe, modern, 372-room resort in the prestigious Kahala district, between Waialae Golf Course and Waialae Beach. The *Kahala* consists of a main 12-story building, beachside bungalows, and a 2-story wing. Its 6½ acres include an 800-foot beachfront and a tropical lagoon stocked with dolphins and other aquatic playmates. The *Kahala*'s reputation is based on excellent service. 5000 Kahala Ave. (808 734-2211 or 800 367-2525). Very expensive.

The Halekulani – Since $125 million was spent to rebuild this old cottage hotel in the heart of Waikiki Beach, it has become the most elegant place to stay in the area. Expansive ocean views, tropical decor, fine dining in the *Orchid* and *La Mer,* two of Honolulu's best restaurants, and sunset cocktails served at its oceanfront bar are only the highlights. 2199 Kalia Rd. (808 923-2311 or 800 367-2343). Very expensive.

Hilton Hawaiian Village – Not to be confused with the *Kahala* (which is run by Hilton International), the *Hawaiian Village* is owned by the Hilton Hotels Corporation chain, which is currently spending $80 million to upgrade this gigantic, 2,600-room resort campus, with five main structures spread over 22 acres. The best rooms are, generally, in the Rainbow Tower, with the widest, prettiest section of beach right outside the door. The exotic trees and plants that fill the grounds are all identified. The Rainbow Bazaar shopping area has lots of unusual items on display. 2005 Kalia Rd. (808 949-4321). Expensive.

Hyatt Regency – The two octagonal towers atop the ritzy Hemmeter Center are a visual landmark among the concrete blocks along Kalakaua Avenue. The Great Hall, with its outdoor tropical garden, 3-story waterfall, and massive hanging sculpture, is a sightseeing spot in its own right. Each of its 1,234 rooms is handsomely furnished, and the art on the walls is invariably worth looking at. The suites feature some authentic antiques and original oil paintings. Guests on the Regency Club floors have their own complimentary bar and a concierge. The pool deck is one of the most attractive in Honolulu, and the bars, cafés, and restaurants in the complex are among the very best on the beach. The service is first rate. One cavils only with the placement of the reception area, which is easily confused with the rest of the shopping area. Major credit cards. Hemmeter Center, 2424 Kalakaua Ave. (808 922-9292 or 800 228-9000). Expensive.

Royal Hawaiian – Fondly known as "the Pink Palace" or "Pink Lady," this 525-room hotel was *the* place to stay in the 1930s, when luxury cruise liners steamed into Honolulu with elegant passengers who stayed on for months. The pink stucco Mediterranean-style building retains its glittering chandeliers and long corridors, although it has changed hands since its 1927 opening and is now under the wing of Sheraton. The beach is wide and particularly nice, but the rooms vary. Avoid the new tower — it's awfully dull. The gracious, older rooms are really what give this place its charm. 2259 Kalakaua Ave. (808 923-7311 or 800 325-3535). Expensive.

Ilikai Hotel – Frequently used as a location for the once-popular TV series *Hawaii Five-O,* this 800-room tower isn't exactly in the center of the action, which some consider a major asset. It is pretty close to the Duke Kahanomoku section of Waikiki beach and has a great view of the Ala Wai Yacht Harbor, a dynamite outdoor glass elevator, and a good restaurant, *Champeaux's.* There are also 2 swimming pools and 6 tennis courts. 1777 Ala Moana Blvd. (808 949-3811 or 800 228-3000). Expensive.

Sheraton Waikiki – Once the largest hotel in Waikiki — 1,852 rooms — until it was surpassed by the *Hilton Hawaiian Village,* it still boasts the greatest number of units in one building. Lanais on the Pacific side loom over the ocean as precipitously as from a cliff. It's a splendid sensation if you don't suffer from vertigo, and the sunsets are often memorable. Here's all that's expected from a big hotel: There is never a paucity of taxis, it's a pick-up point for every major local tour operator, TheBus stops right outside, and there is just about every kind of restaurant you could crave — except a truly first-class one. 2255 Kalakaua Ave. (808 922-4422 or 800 325-3535). Expensive.

Holiday Inn Waikiki Beach – Although the rooms provide no more than the standard *Holiday Inn* level of style and comfort, they can boast some of the best views of the Pacific and Diamond Head found in Waikiki. The hotel occupies a terrific site: just outside the hustle-bustle of the strip, next door to Kapiolani Park and the Honolulu Zoo, and across the street from the loveliest stretch of Waikiki Beach. The *Captain's Table,* an easygoing eatery that looks out at the sea, is a good place to sample your first mahimahi. 2570 Kalakaua Ave. (808 922-2511 or 800 465-4329). Expensive to moderate.

Moana Hotel – A Victorian grande dame, perhaps a wee bit past her prime, that hasn't changed much since opening in 1901 and clings to another age. In addition to its great location on the beach, the *Moana* is known for its Robert Louis Stevenson tree, more than 100 years old. When making reservations, specify a room in the old building if that's what you want; there is also a modern wing. If you'd like air conditioning, mention that, too. 2365 Kalakaua Ave. (808 922-3111 or 800 325-3535). Expensive to moderate.

Waikiki Surf – This is one of the "finds" of Honolulu. In a semi-residential part of Waikiki, it's friendly, clean, decorated in blue and green, quiet, and delightfully inexpensive. Some rooms have kitchenettes. Perhaps best of all, the 288-room *Waikiki Surf* has two companions — the 102-room *Waikiki Surf East* (422 Royal Hawaiian Ave.) and the 110-room *Waikiki Surf West* (412 Lewers St.) — owned and managed by the same people. The original *Waikiki Surf* is at 2200 Kuhio Ave. (for all three: 808 923-7671 or 800 367-5170). Inexpensive.

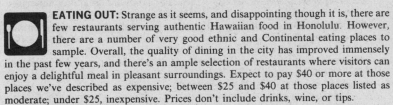

EATING OUT: Strange as it seems, and disappointing though it is, there are few restaurants serving authentic Hawaiian food in Honolulu. However, there are a number of very good ethnic and Continental eating places to sample. Overall, the quality of dining in the city has improved immensely in the past few years, and there's an ample selection of restaurants where visitors can enjoy a delightful meal in pleasant surroundings. Expect to pay $40 or more at those places we've described as expensive; between $25 and $40 at those places listed as moderate; under $25, inexpensive. Prices don't include drinks, wine, or tips.

The Third Floor – One of the best restaurants in Honolulu (so named because it's on the third floor of the *Hawaiian Regent Hotel*) has elegant parquet tables, high-backed rattan chairs, a small fountain, and a fish pond. Between courses, look up at the ceiling to examine a fine display of heraldic banners. Among the house specialties are medallion of veal Forêt Noire and rack of spring lamb. For dessert there are Polynesian fruits with kirsch and, wonder of wonders, real Irish coffee. Open daily. There is a $15 minimum. Reservations necessary. Major credit cards. 2552 Kalakaua Ave. (922-6611). Expensive.

Maile Restaurant – A staff of kimono-clad waitresses, who give expert, unobtrusive service, serve roast duckling Waialae (with bananas, peaches, litchi, and oranges) and fresh island chicken (poached in white wine with tarragon) among the other house specialties. Open daily. Reservations advised. Major credit cards. *Kahala Hilton Hotel,* 5000 Kahala Ave. (734-2211). Expensive.

Nick's Fishmarket – This is one of the best fish restaurants in Honolulu. Don't let the earthy name confuse you; *Nick's* is a plush establishment with individually controlled lighting systems for customers seated at banquettes. Expensive live Maine lobsters are available, but this is a better place to sample fresh island fish, such as opakapaka, mahimahi, and ulua. The combination Seafood Louis Salad is enormous and beautifully prepared. Open daily. Reservations advised. Major credit cards. *Waikiki Gateway Hotel,* 2070 Kalakaua Ave. (955-6333). Expensive.

John Dominis – An extraordinary restaurant much favored by well-to-do Honolulu residents, it stands at the end of a most unpromising street of warehouses and light industries, on a promontory overlooking the Kewalo Basin and the Pacific. The smell of fresh fish is everywhere. At a central island lavishly laden with fruits of the sea, a chef shucks oysters, steams clams, and makes broth. In saltwater pools surrounded by substantial dining tables, spiny lobsters and carp clamber and swim around. Mainland specialties, such as Maine lobster and Alaskan king crab, all arrive fresh, but this is the ideal place to sample the local seafood. Ono (wahoo), hapuu (grouper), and opelu (mackerel) are all available in season. The cioppino, a stew of soft- and hard-shell seafood and fresh fish cooked in tomatoes, herbs, and spices, is unbeatable. This is also one of the few restaurants in the city with a first-class bar serving decent drinks. Open daily for dinner. Major credit cards. Reservations necessary. 43 Ahui St. (523-0955). Expensive.

The Willows – One of the most famous restaurants in the city and *the* place to sample traditional Hawaiian dishes. *The Willows'* celebrated Poi Dinner offers many of these, including poi itself, steamed laulau, sweet potato, chicken luau, lomi salmon, limu kohu, green onion, fresh pineapple, and haupia. If these seem too exotic, the curry dishes, leavened with coconut milk, are superb. This is also the perfect place for wearing an aloha shirt or muumuu for the first time — the rural, tropical atmosphere of palm trees and thatched roofs seems to call for it. Open daily. Reservations necessary. Major credit cards. 901 Hausten St. (946-4808). Expensive.

Michel's – At most beachfront restaurants in Honolulu, the cooking takes a back seat to the view. *Michel's* is not one of them. For a start, the decor does not suggest a mere extension of sand and ocean. The dining room is elegant and subdued. Although there are occasionally deft local touches, such as prosciutto served with papaya, most of the dishes tend to be classic. Even the opakapaka is served véronique style with a champagne sauce added. The roast veal with cream sauce and the lobster bisque with cognac are memorable. Jacket required for dinner. Reservations necessary. Major credit cards. In the *Colony Surf Hotel* at 2895 Kalakaua Ave., Diamond Head (923-6552). Expensive.

Canlis – Sometimes called *Canlis Broiler,* it is one of the most attractive restaurants in the city. An old-timer on the Waikiki dining scene, it is famous for its salads and desserts and for topping all meat dishes with a touch of vermouth. Other specialties are steaks, chops, and seafood broiled over kiawe wood. 2100 Kalakaua Ave. (923-2324). Expensive.

Bagwells – The fine Continental menu and gracious service at this elegant dining room on the third floor of the *Hyatt Regency Waikiki Hotel* makes a meal here worth the stiff price. Save room for a soufflé for dessert. Open daily. Reservations advised. Major credit cards. 2424 Kalakaua Ave. (922-9292). Expensive.

Nicholas Nickolas – Magnificent views from atop the 40-floor *Ala Moana Americana Hotel* are a counterpoint to the soft lights and elegant decor of Honolulu's newest "in" restaurant, opened by the same Nick who made *Nick's Fishmarket* a Waikiki classic. The extensive menu focuses on both American and Continental specialties, ranging from prime ribs to lamb, with pastas, soups, salads, and catch-of-the-day entrées in between. Open daily for dinner, with live entertainment until 3:30 AM. Reservations required. Major credit cards. 410 Atkinson Dr. (955-4811). Expensive.

Keo's Thai Cuisine – A fine place to sample Thai cuisine, which can be flavorful and fiery, although the kitchen here will prepare milder versions of its hottest specialties if requested. Mint-flavored spring rolls make a delicious appetizer, and cold sweet tea is a good accompaniment for the spicier dishes. Reservations required. 625 Kapahulu Ave. (737-8240). Expensive.

Andrews – The steamed clams in herbs and spices, the tender fried calamari, and the veal dishes are carefully prepared and presented with considerable flare at one of Honolulu's less touted Italian rstaurants. Linens, crystal, and silver set the tone for a relaxed evening in pleasant surroundings. Open daily for lunch and dinner. Major credit cards accepted. Ward Centre, 1200 Ala Moana Blvd. (523-8677). Expensive to moderate.

Banyan Gardens – Taking its cue from the legendary *Willows, Banyan Gar-*

dens (same owners) features a similar menu in a most relaxed and beautiful garden setting right in the heart of Waikiki. Hawaiian shrimp curry, prepared with the finest herbs and freshly ground spices, is worthy of a recommendation, along with spinach timbale (custard served with a velvety cheese sauce) as an appetizer and a calorie-busting sky-high pie for dessert. Open daily for lunch and dinner. Live entertainment from 8:30 PM. Major credit cards. 2380 Kuhio Ave. (923-2366). Moderate.

Bon Appetit – The look is that of an elegant bistro in the French provinces, with cane-back chairs and light pink linen. The menu is imaginative and includes an unusual scallop mousse, seafood soup with saffron, snails in puff pastry, and sliced breast of duck with peppercorn sauce. Closed Sundays. Reservations advised. Major credit cards. In the Discovery Bay complex at 1778 Ala Moana Blvd. (942-3837). Moderate.

Trattoria – A number of connoisseurs insist that this charmingly decorated restaurant is the top entry in the Italian food category in Honolulu. For one thing, the chef doesn't overload the menu with tomato paste, and many dishes are cooked al burro — delicately, in butter, instead of doused in olive oil. The lasagna is well worth tasting. Open daily. Reservations advised on weekends. Major credit cards. *Cinerama Edgewater Hotel,* Kalia Rd. and Beach Walk (923-8415). Moderate.

Ray's Seafood – A quiet, relaxing place to enjoy savory steamed clams, an appetizing catch of the day, and more. Open daily; lunch weekdays only. Major credit cards. Waikiki Shopping Plaza, 2250 Kalakaua Ave., 4th floor (923-5717). Moderate.

Il Fresco – The restaurant's high tech design and tables laden with linen and crystal are right in tune with its location in the chic Ward Center, an upscale shopping mall between Waikiki and downtown Honolulu. The menu is varied, with specialties ranging from Kona crab to pasta. Open daily. Major credit cards. Ward Center (enter on Auahi St.), 1200 Ala Moana Blvd. (523-5191). Moderate.

TGI Friday's – The Honolulu version of this genre features antique furnishings, a friendly bar, an extensive 16-page menu, and surprisingly good food at modest prices. Best known for its potato skins — stuffed with anything from cheddar cheese and bacon to crab Stroganoff — this eatery also serves an array of quiches, omelettes, salads, and desserts. No reservations. Open daily. 950 Ward Ave. (523-5841). Moderate.

The Stuffed Potato – Despite its name, this inconspicuous eatery with indoor and patio seating is most notable for the delicious meat, fish, and pasta dishes prepared by the owner-chef. Bring your own beer and wine, easily bought at a nearby convenience store. 2109 Kuhio Ave. (922-0102). Moderate to inexpensive.

It's Greek To Me – The setting amid the shops of the Royal Hawaiian Center is more convenient than charming, but the food is recommended for quality, price, and the speed with which it is served. Open daily for all meals. Major credit cards accepted. 2201 Kalakaua Ave. (922-2733). Inexpensive.

Bueno Nalo – The coconut wireless (as the local grapevine is called) gives this eatery high marks for its Mexican cooking — chile rellños, chimichangas, and such. It's a casual place, where guests bring their own wine or beer and wait for tables. No reservations. Open daily for lunch and dinner. 41-865 Kalanianaole Hwy., Waimanalo (259-7186). Inexpensive.

Cafe Guccini – The warm welcome at this low-key café is followed by fine pasta, rich cappuccino, and tempting desserts. 2139 Kuhio Ave. (922-5287). Inexpensive.

Laulima – Innovative, tastily prepared vegetable dishes are created by chef Alan Young at this vegetarian restaurant. 2239 S King St. (947-3844). Inexpensive.

Mandarin – Here you are given huge portions of Shanghai steamed dumplings and

Mongolian beef, sautéed with green onions and red peppers. It's best to go with a group of four or more and order family style — passing around several different dishes. Open daily. Reservations advised. Major credit cards. 942 McCully St. (946-3242). Inexpensive.

King Tsin – This spicy favorite serves up very tasty hot and sour soup. The crackling chicken is chopstick-lickin' good, as is the Hunan pork sautéed with broccoli. Open daily. Reservations advised. Major credit cards. 1486 S King St. (946-3273). Inexpensive.

HOUSTON

Houston is dazzling to the newcomer. Its downtown mushrooms unexpectedly from the flat Texas prairie in a striking display of modern architecture. The city stretches for miles in all directions, apparently without limits. Massive expressway systems, always busy, pump traffic in and out of the metropolis that's been called the "golden buckle of the Sunbelt." Although a century and a half old, the past has been all but wiped out, overrun by a sense of newness and bravado of the prosperity in the here and now and a promise of more to come. For Houston is the 20th century's incarnation of the 19th-century dream of industrial progress.

Houston is the fourth largest city in the country (with a metropolitan population of 1.7 million) and has been one of the fastest growing. About 250 companies have relocated major operations in the city since 1970, and, until recently, there were enough jobs to accommodate the 1,538 newcomers arriving each week. Fueling most of this boom was oil. For a while, Houston was thriving and seemed immune to the economic ills that worried the rest of the country. However, the sparkle started to fade in 1982, when oilfield equipment manufacturers made their first massive layoffs and Houston's unemployment rate rose. The worldwide oil glut has compounded local problems, and at the moment Houston is fighting hard to emerge from an energy-based depression.

These problems have been added to the chaos that was one price of Houston's boom in the 1970s. The city grew lots faster than its civic services, and every sort of urban trauma was magnified as a result. There are still no zoning laws, little evidence of city planning beyond the downtown, insufficient mass transit, congested traffic, and consequently often oppressive air pollution.

When a 19th-century traveler described Houston as a place "where one can no longer rationalize or explain what he sees," he spoke honestly not only of Houston past but of Houston present and, undeniably, of Houston future. It's the place where there are no state or city income taxes, but you still have to register cowbrands at the courthouse.

In Houston, the original bit of good luck came in the form of oil, and that was as true in the founding of the city as residents wish it would be today. In 1836, even before the first street existed, founders J. K. and A. C. Allen, brothers from New York, were advertising their new town nationwide as the state's garden spot. In reality it was humid, marshy, and mosquito-infested. People came anyway, enticed by the Allens' grandiose descriptions, cheap land, and the promises of great money-making opportunities.

Little did the newcomers realize how closely luck was following them. At the turn of the century, oil was discovered 90 miles away, and Houston found itself in the middle of the great Texas oil boom. In 1914, civic leaders built a ship channel 32 miles inland to the city, creating a fairweather port. By the

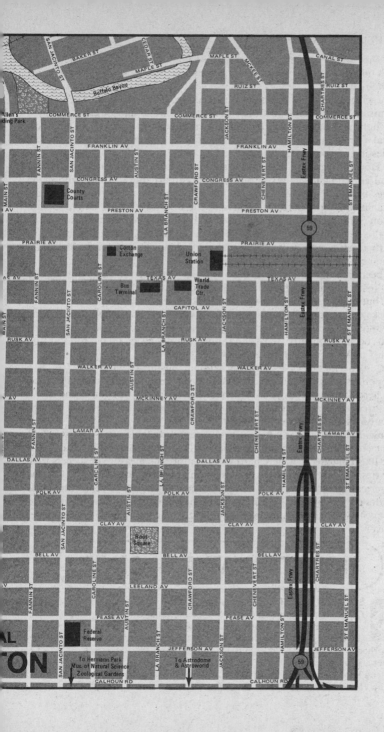

1960s the two — oil and port — combined to make Houston one of the world's major petrochemical centers, creating the backbone of the city's economic strength.

Pure science as well as technology has reinforced this strength. The Lyndon B. Johnson Space Center has been the focal point of almost every manned space flight and has earned Houston the moniker "Space City." The Texas Medical Center, noted for cancer research, is one of the largest medical facilities in the country.

But Houston's growth extended to more than science and business. Similar cultural enrichment has taken place, in large part due to those who made fortunes here. Their bullish attitude has provided the city with some of the best facilities for the performing arts in the Southwest. The Grand Opera, Houston Symphony, and Alley Theater, the established resident company, are highly acclaimed nationally. The arts are thriving, patronized by a citizenry that seems to be dedicated to making its home as renowned for cultural achievement as for boldness in business.

It's been said that Houston has two seasons — eternal summer outside and winter inside, borne on gusts from ubiquitous air conditioners. The climate *is* hot, but being outdoors is a way of life, not a seasonal occupation. Municipal parks equipped with fine facilities for swimming, golf, tennis, and hiking are abundant. Open-air concerts, Shakespeare in the park, and sidewalk art festivals occur frequently year-round. Just 50 miles away, Galveston Bay and the Gulf of Mexico are a haven for water enthusiasts.

The city's emergence as an international business center has lent it a cosmopolitan image unique to the South. Over forty foreign consulates have offices here. In the streets, you'll still hear Texas drawls, but you'll also detect many foreign accents. Restaurants, especially those in the Montrose district, offer cuisines from all over the globe.

Things are still happening at a furious, unpredictable pace. Houston is a city once more in the process of finding itself, a feisty frontier that draws new people like a magnet — where hard work is more the measure of success than family ties. Despite recent setbacks, Houstonians still think of their city as one of America's greatest, and it's hard for a newcomer not to sense this pride even after only a day here. Given the energetic human forces at work, it's hard to believe that Houston cannot weather the current slump to emerge stronger than ever.

HOUSTON AT-A-GLANCE

SEEING THE CITY: The revolving *Spindletop* cocktail lounge atop the *Hyatt Regency* turns on the Houston panorama. One revolution takes in all of Space City. To the south stands downtown, to the north an industrial area and the ship channel, industrial sprawl to the east, and Houston's residential neighborhoods to the west. 1200 Louisiana (654-1234).

Stationary, but splendid for a view of the downtown skyline, is Sam Houston Park. 515 Allen Pkwy. Dominating the cityscape are the futuristic Pennzoil Towers, designed by Philip Johnson, and the city's other big oil headquarters, Shell and Tenneco.

SPECIAL PLACES: A car is a necessity for mobility in the Houston sprawl. Mass transit is unreliable and not always accessible. Several of the attractions are concentrated in a few areas, so you can park and walk, but otherwise, you'll be driving from place to place.

Museum of Natural Science – Each of the 13 halls in the largest such institution of the Southwest pertains to a different natural science including two subjects near and dear to the wallets of Houstonians — oil and space. You can learn how oil is formed, see a model of an offshore oil rig, or manipulate a working model of a fault — by turning a wheel you can create an earthquake. The space exhibit includes reproductions of the lunar Rover (the real one is still up there) and a model of the space capsule used by John Glenn. Not as endearing, but also on display, are Ecuadorian shrunken heads and a Diplodocus dinosaur skeleton. The Museum of Medical Science displays the human body — yours. You can listen to the rhythm of your heartbeat or test your lung capacity, or, if you're too modest to put yourself on display, skip it and visit the Burke Baker Planetarium. Open daily. Free. 5800 Caroline St. in Hermann Park (526-4273).

Houston Zoological Gardens – One of the best zoos around, this abounds with some rarely seen animals in unusual settings. Vampire bats, flying squirrels, and bush babies inhabit a red light district where time is reversed and you can see the bats feeding on blood at 2:30 in the afternoon. The Tropical Bird House has over 200 exotic birds in a rain forest. But our favorite is the Gorilla House, where the royal couple of the jungle swing in primordial splendor complete with waterfalls, vines, moats, and skylighting. There's also a children's zoo where kids can make contact with creatures from four regions of the world. Open daily. Free. S Main at Bissonnet in Hermann Park (523-5888).

Museum of Fine Arts – With Neoclassical beginnings and finishing touches by Mies van der Rohe, this structure could house most anything — and it does, including the Ima Hogg collection of Southwestern Indian art with pottery and kachina dolls, an extensive collection of Frederic Remington's works, a pre-Columbian gallery, and a modern sculpture garden with Alexander Calder's "Crab." Closed Mondays. Free. 1001 Bissonnet (526-1361).

The International Strip – On the main drag of Montrose, one of the city's oldest residential neighborhoods, natives and visitors come to browse through antique shops, foreign bazaars, art galleries, boutiques, flea markets, and off-beat book shops. The art festivals held in October and April are the largest in the South. Sidewalk cafés and restaurants allow patrons to try dishes from around the world, linger in a wine-tasting shop, or just hang out in a tree house bar. A *Moveable Feast* is great for health food sandwiches (3827 Dunlavy; 528-3585). The Strip is also the showplace for exotic nightlife, everything from bellydancing to body painting. More sedate, but also in the neighborhood is the Rothko Chapel, a meditation chapel with works by Russian-born painter Mark Rothko (3900 Yupon; 524-9839). The Strip extends from the 100 to 1800 block of Westheimer.

River Oaks – If you're wondering where all that old oil money went, you'll find that no one's tried to hide it. Here are the palatial mansions and huge estates of Houston's super-rich, who still have it and flaunt it. River Oaks Blvd. between Westheimer and the Country Club.

Galleria Center – This stunning, glass-domed, three-level edifice shows how the wealth is spread, Houston style. Among the stores here are *Neiman-Marcus, Lord & Taylor, Sakowitz, Tiffany's,* and *Way Out West* (western wear), and across the street is *Saks Fifth Avenue.* There's also a skating rink on the ground floor. Open daily. 5015 Westheimer (621-0656).

Sam Houston Park – One of the few signs that there was an old Houston, this project of the Harris County Heritage Society encompasses a restored country church, homes, and shops, depicting the lifestyle of 19th-century Houstonians. The Kellum-Noble House is the oldest brick house in Houston, and contains pioneer equipment and furnishings, and the Cherry House is a Greek Revival home furnished with American Empire antiques. Tours begin at the office (515 Allen Pkwy.; 759-1292). Open daily. Admission charge. Allen Pkwy. and Bagby St.

Astrodome – Besides serving as home for the Astros, Oilers, and the University of Houston Cougars, this $36 million domed stadium, big enough to accommodate an 18-story building (standing) or 66,000 spectators, with the world's largest and most dazzling scoreboard (474 feet long and 4 stories high, complete with pyrotechnical display when the home team scores), is Texas' most visited attraction. There are guided tours of the Dome at 11 AM, 1, and 3 PM, featuring a multimedia blowout on the scoreboard. Open daily. Admission charge. 4¾ miles southwest at I-610 and Kirby Dr. (799-9544).

Astroworld – Also part of Astrodomain, Houston's version of a theme park offers 70 acres of entertainment, including 11 theme amusement parks, water-skiing spectaculars, trained dolphin shows, and high-diving feats. The Texas Cyclone Roller Coaster induces its share of rave reviews, screams, and nausea. Open daily June through August and weekends during spring and fall. (Check locally for shortened or extended hours.) Admission charge. 9001 Kirby Dr., across from the Astrodome (799-1234).

San Jacinto Battleground – The 570-foot-tall San Jacinto Monument marks the spot where Sam Houston defeated Mexican General Santa Anna to win Texas' independence. The 460-acre state park also includes a Museum of Texas History tracing the region's development from the Indian civilization through Texas' annexation by the United States; the museum also houses the battleship *Texas,* veteran of both world wars. Closed Mondays (open daily in the summer). Free. Farm Road 134, off Hwy. 225, 21 miles east of downtown Houston (479-2431).

Port of Houston – From an observation platform atop Wharf 9, visitors can see the turning basin area of this country's third largest port. To inspect some of the elaborate industrial-shipping developments, take an excursion along the ship channel aboard the MV *Sam Houston* (make reservations well in advance). No trips on Mondays or in September. Free. Gate 8, off Clinton Dr. (225-4044).

Lyndon B. Johnson Space Center – Until you actually fly Trans-Universe to the moon, this is the closest you can get to the experience. This 1,620-acre campus-like facility is the training ground for the Gemini, Apollo, and Skylab astronauts, and the monitoring center for the NASA manned space flights. The visitors center displays craft that have flown in space, moon rocks, and a lunar module, and the Mission Control Center houses some of the most sophisticated communications computer data equipment in the world. Visitors are welcome at the Control Center and the Skylab Training Room on guided tours, available by reservation. NASA films are shown throughout the day in the auditorium. Open daily. Free. 25 miles SE of downtown Houston via I-45 (483-4321).

■**EXTRA SPECIAL:** Just 51 miles south of Houston along I-45 is *Galveston Island,* a leading Gulf Coast resort area. Stewart Beach is the principal public beach and there's good swimming, surfing, sailing, water skiing, and deep-sea fishing (reservations taken at boats on Piers 18 and 19 of the Galveston Yacht Basin). Seafood restaurants, art galleries, and restored turn-of-the-century homes are in the former vacation destination of the oil magnates clustered around Strand Blvd.

SOURCES AND RESOURCES

TOURIST INFORMATION: The Houston Convention and Visitors Council is best for brochures, maps, and general information. 3300 Main St. (523-5050). Many banks also provide free visitor information kits, as does the Chamber of Commerce. 1100 Milam (651-1313).

The revised edition of *Texas Monthly's Guide to Houston* by Felicia Coates and Harriet Howle (Mediatex Communications Corp.; $3.95) is a comprehensive guide. *The Intrepid Walker's Guide to Houston* by Eli Zal and Doug Milburn ($2.95) is the best guide to the network of underground tunnels connecting major downtown buildings and other off-the-beaten-track walking tours.

Local Coverage – The *Post,* morning daily; the *Chronicle,* evening daily; the *Tribune,* weekly, published Thursdays. All are available at newsstands.

Food – Check *Best Restaurants Texas* by Ann Valentine, Derro Evans, and James Medlin (101 Productions; $2.95) and the *Texas Monthly Guide.*

Area Code – All telephone numbers are in the 713 area code unless otherwise indicated.

CLIMATE AND CLOTHES: In the summer, Houston is hot and humid. Winds from the Gulf of Mexico create warm summer nights, and keep the winters and the rest of the year relatively warm. During the winter, light jackets are advisable. Dress is informal and lightweight clothes are most comfortable, but indoors air-conditioning is in full force during the hot months so you'd be wise to carry a sweater.

GETTING AROUND: Airport – The city's main airports are Houston Intercontinental and William P. Hobby Airport. Those familiar with Houston traffic allow about 45 minutes to reach either one from the downtown area (note that it is not unusual for rain, fog, or the nightly rush hour to practically double this time). Yellow Cab charges a flat rate of $20 for the trip between Intercontinental and downtown. Taxi fare into the city from Hobby should run about $12. Trailways (759-6500) operates shuttle service from Intercontinental to its four downtown terminals. Buses leave every half-hour, and tickets ($5) can be purchased at stands outside each of the airport's three terminals.

Bus – Metropolitan Transit Authority of Harris County serves downtown and the suburbs, but the system can be confusing and unreliable. Mini-buses run in the downtown shopping area. For route information contact the main office, 401 Louisiana (635-4000).

Taxi – Cabs can be ordered on the phone, picked up in front of hotels and terminals, or, with some difficulty, hailed in the street. Major companies are Sky-Jack's (523-6080) and Yellow Cab (236-1111). Be warned, however, that taxi rates are rather high.

Car Rental – Because Houston is a huge, sprawling city whose backbone is its extensive freeway system, a car is the most practical mode of travel. Try to avoid being caught in Houston's rush hour, when traffic is impossibly snarled. All the major national firms serve Houston. Local service is provided by Greater Houston Leasing, 3231 Audley (528-0873), and Thrifty Rent-A-Car at Hobby Airport (644-3351) and Intercontinental Airport (449-0126).

MUSEUMS: The Museum of Natural Science and the Museum of Fine Arts are described under *Special Places.* Other notable Houston museums are:
Bayou Bend – Early American furnishings, 1 Westcott St. (529-8773)
Contemporary Arts Museum – 5216 Montrose at Bissonnet (526-3129)

MAJOR COLLEGES AND UNIVERSITIES: Among Houston's educational institutions are Rice University (6100 S Main St.; 527-8101), which has a good reputation for its engineering and science schools; University of Houston (4800 Calhoun Rd.; 749-1011); and the Texas Medical Center (between Fannin St. and Holcombe Blvd.; 792-2121).

SPECIAL EVENTS: Check the publications noted above for exact dates. For two weeks in late February and early March, Houston cowboys come out in full force and descend on the Astrodome complex for the *Houston Rodeo and Livestock Show.* There's plenty of action — rodeo events and country and western concerts. During April and October, local and regional artists show their stuff in the *Westheimer Art Show,* an outdoor arts and crafts festival on Westheimer Rd. Most Houston area hotels are filled for the 4-day *Offshore Technology Conference,* the world's biggest oil industry show, in late April and early May.

SPORTS AND FITNESS: Tickets to professional games can be picked up at Ticket Connection, 2031 Southwest Fwy. (524-3687).

Ballooning – The *Rainbow's End Balloon Port* sends 'em up weekend mornings at dawn when the winds are calm. You can watch the balloonists rise to the occasion, and if they don't, join them for breakfast. 18710 Montgomery Rd. (466-1927).

Baseball – The National League's Houston *Astros* play at the Astrodome from April to September, I-610 and Kirby Dr. (799-9555).

Basketball – The National Basketball Association's *Rockets* play from December to April at the Summit, 10 Greenway Plaza (627-0600).

Bicycling – Rent from Recycled Cycles, 7921 Westheimer (977-1393). A good bike trail runs from the Sabine Street Bridge (just east of Allen's Landing) along Buffalo Bayou to Shepherd, and back along the Memorial side of the Bayou. The City of Houston Parks and Recreation Dept. offers a list of other bike routes. 2999 S Wayside (641-4111).

Fishing – Best for fishing is Galveston, where you can wet a line in the Gulf of Mexico off piers or from deep-sea charters that leave from Piers 18 and 19 of the Galveston Yacht Basin.

Fitness Centers – The YMCA has a pool, indoor and outdoor tracks, exercise classes, and handball and racquetball courts, 1600 Louisiana (659-8501).

Football – The *Oilers* play at the Astrodome (797-1000).

Golf – Best public course for the duffer is in Hermann Park, 6110 Golf Course Dr. (529-9788). The most challenging of the municipal courts is in Brock Park, 8201 John Ralston Rd., off Old Beaumont Hwy. (458-1350).

Jogging – Most running is done along a 3-mile loop in Memorial Park, 4 miles from downtown and reached on foot from Buffalo Bayou or by taking the No. 16 Memorial or the No. 17 Tanglewood bus. Other possibilities are Hermann Park, via South Main, and the well-used trails along Ellen Parkway.

Rodeo – On Saturday nights year-round, the *Simonton Rodeo* rounds 'em up with real live rodeo followed by country and western dancing, on Westheimer Rd., 45 minutes west of the city (346-1534).

Swimming – There are 42 municipal pools in Houston, open from June through Labor Day. The Hermann Park pool is convenient. 2020 Hermann Dr. (641-4111).

Tennis – The municipally run Memorial Tennis Center has 18 Laykold courts, showers, lockers, tennis shop, and practice court. 600 Memorial Loop Dr. (641-4111). There are free courts in most of the city parks.

THEATER: For current offerings check the daily and weekly publications listed above. *The Alley Theater,* Houston's established and acclaimed resident company, performs everything from classical drama to experimental plays, October to May, at 615 Texas Ave. (box office, 228-8421). During the summer, the *Miller Outdoor Theater* offers a variety of entertainments, all free, ranging from pop concerts, *Frank Young's Theater Under the Stars* musical extravaganzas, to a Shakespeare Festival, at 100 Concert Dr. in Hermann Park (622-8887). Colleges and universities in the area produce plays and musicals.

 MUSIC: Jones Hall for the Performing Arts provides a home for Houston's own companies as well as offering concerts and performances throughout the year by internationally renowned artists and companies. The nationally acclaimed *Houston Symphony Orchestra* performs there from September to May; the *Houston Ballet,* the only resident professional ballet company in the Southwest, from September to March; and the *Houston Grand Opera* from September to March at 615 Louisiana in Civic Center (222-3415). All give free performances at the Miller Theater in the summer. Big rock concerts are held at the Summit throughout the year. 10 Greenway Plaza (961-9003).

 NIGHTCLUBS AND NIGHTLIFE: Depending on what you want, you can unwind or recharge at one or more of Houston's night spots. Current favorites for progressive country music, Texas style, and local color: *San Antone Rose,* 1641 S Voss Rd. (977-7116), or *Gilley's Club,* 4500 Spencer Hwy. in Pasadena, on Houston's southeast perimeter (946-9842); for jazz, *Rockefeller's,* 3620 Washington (864-9365); *Al Mark's Melody Lane Ballroom,* for ballroom dancing, 3027 Crossview (785-5301); *Jet Set Club International,* for disco, 3315 Mangum (680-3232).

 SINS: While conservative Dallas plods along congratulating itself on the Dallas Cowboys' Cheerleaders, Houstonians are hustling bucks, far earthier in their tastes and tone. The Chamber of Commerce won't talk about it, but massage parlors, adult bookstores, and pornographic movie houses are flourishing all over town. *Lust* is an urge easily satisfied hereabouts, especialy in these days of economic downturn, though the play-for-pay breed is strongly challenged by the party-prone masses that pack Houston's bars and roadhouses — especially on Friday nights.

Everyone in town aspires to the good life in posh suburban River Oaks, where rich folk get their hair frosted, play tennis, and try to do each other in. People might call it *sloth,* though it requires a lot of effort to do nothing elegantly. Among those who haven't yet made it, the stupendous mansions along River Oaks Boulevard inspire *envy.*

 LOCAL SERVICES: Business Services – Business Services of Houston, 2537 S Gessner (780-7335)

   Mechanics – Altenberg's Garage for American cars, 2306 Brazos (523-2837); for foreign cars, Freeman's Auto Service, 3540 Oak Forest Dr. (681-9484)

BEST IN TOWN

 CHECKING IN: Houston's hotel industry rode the crest of the city's boom during the 1970s, with new — and usually luxurious — hotels springing up almost daily. As a result, hotels are now the most overbuilt segment of the city's real estate industry. Hence it is no longer impossible to get a room during the annual Offshore Technology Conference. And although many hotels are having problems filling their available inventory of rooms, rates are still increasing. Expect to pay $100 and up a night at a hotel we list as expensive; $75 in the moderate range, and about $50 in the inexpensive category.

The Remington on Post Oak Park – Considered the top of the line in Houston. Built by Rosewood Hotels, it offers all the amenities of a top European hotel plus 3 restaurants, a bar, lounges, a swimming pool, recreational deck, boutique, and more. 1919 Briar Oaks Dr. (713 840-7600). Expensive.

Westin Oaks and Westin Galleria – Smack in the middle of the luxurious Galleria Mall, the ideal spot for a shopping spree. The *Oaks* at 5011 Westheimer Rd. (713 623-4300), with 400 rooms, is the older but no less grand facility. At the other end of the mall is the 400-room *Galleria,* 5060 W Alabama (713 960-8100), which is every bit as fine. Really big spenders can splurge on the Crown Suite at the *Oaks,* a penthouse with two fireplaces, 2½ baths, a banquet table for 14, and a grand piano — all for about $800 a night. Other features include a pool, cafés, entertainment and dancing, and access to ice-skating, a running track, and indoor tennis. Pay garage. Expensive.

Inn on the Park – In the new Riverway complex and part of the superb Four Seasons chain, the hotel overlooks a scenic bayou area populated by live swans and features an interesting sculpture garden. Amenities include 2 restaurants, a cabaret, health club, outdoor jogging track, 4 tennis courts, and garage. In Riverway at Post Oak La. and Woodway Dr. (713 871-8181). Expensive.

Lancaster – A small, elegant hotel in a restored 1926 brick building with the air of private British club. Oriental carpets and original oils fill the lobby; each of the 85 rooms and 8 suites is done up with antiques and a four-poster bed. Guests and the theater crowd (Jones Hall for the Performing Arts and the Alley Theater are across the street) enjoy the nouvelle accents on Gulf Coast seafood in the *Lancaster Grille.* Other features include a multilingual staff, concierge, 24-hour room service, access to health club. 701 Texas Ave. (713 228-9500 or 800 231-0336) Expensive.

Meridien Houston – Part of the chain owned by Air France. As expected, the 363-room hotel has a certain Gallic style — from its concierge to the nouvelle cuisine in its restaurant (which some say is the best in town). Designed for the well-heeled tourist and upper-echelon executive. Downtown, in Allen Center (713 759-0202). Expensive.

Embassy Suite – All two-room suites, with a complimentary full breakfast and two-hour open bar daily. Free shuttle bus to downtown terminal. Health club and game room. 9090 Southwest Fwy. (713 995-0123). Moderate.

Holiday Inn at Greenway Plaza – Strategically located between downtown and the Galleria on one of the city's main arteries. King-size beds available. There's an outdoor pool, cafeteria, live entertainment, and a gift shop. 2712 Southwest Fwy. (713 523-8448). Moderate; inexpensive on weekends.

Rodeway Inn at Greenway Plaza – Another well-sited property with modest accommodations. Features include a restaurant, meeting, and banquet facilities. 3135 Southwest Fwy. (713 526-1071). Inexpensive.

There are several moderate to inexpensive motel chain facilities scattered about Houston, including *Ramada, Best Western, La Quinta, Days Inn, Trave-Lodge,* and *Texian Inn.* Features and rates are standard for what one has come to expect from such chains. The deciding factor then is location: along the Katy Freeway or Southwest Freeway if one is visiting the outlying suburbs; along Buffalo Speedway or South Main to be near the Astrodome; inside Loop 610 of the Southwest Freeway to shop at the Galleria; North and Eastex freeways for the Intercontinental Airport area; and Galveston Freeway for Hobby Airport and — much farther out — the Johnson Space Center.

 EATING OUT: Besides offerings of fine regional foods — chili parlors and Mexican restaurants abound — Houston has a great variety of cuisines including seafood fresh from the Gulf of Mexico, Continental, Chinese, Greek, and down-home Southern meals. Expect to spend about $60 for a dinner for two at restaurants in the expensive range, $20 to $40 in the moderate range, and $20 or less in the inexpensive range. Prices do not include drinks, wine, or tips.

Brennan's – A bit of New Orleans' Vieux Carré in Houston. Patio tables and a lovely pillared dining room are the setting for fine food. Louisiana-style and Créole specialties make this branch as pleasurable as its counterparts in New Orleans, Dallas, and Atlanta. Open daily. Reservations advised. Major credit cards. 3300 Smith (522-9711). Expensive.

Cadillac Bar – The current Houston favorite for fine Mexican cuisine. Try the queso flameado con chorizo (melted white cheese with sausage) with tender tortillas for starters. Ask about house specialties, which include such exotic dishes as mesquite-smoked kid. Open daily. Reservations advised. Major credit cards. 1802 Shepherd at I-10 (862-2020). Expensive.

Foulard's – Fine French cuisine served in a formal setting. Oysters Foulard are a good beginning, and the chocolate soufflé with Grand Marnier is a perfect ending. You won't be disappointed by the courses in between, either, especially if you try the six-course prix fixe dinner (for the truly hungry only). Open daily. Reservations advised. Major credit cards. 10001 Westheimer, in the Carillon West Mall (789-1661). Expensive.

Harry's Kenya – This lushly formal restaurant (with a safari motif) is named for the legendary African hunter Harry Selby, the model for the Peter McKenzie character in Robert Ruark's novel *Something of Value.* Its excellent Continental cuisine is enlivened with dishes such as venison and wild boar. Only a few steps from downtown hotels, complimentary shuttle service takes diners to performances at Jones Hall, the Alley Theater, and the Music Hall. Closed Sundays. Reservations suggested. Major credit cards. 1160 Smith (650-1980). Expensive.

Ruth's Chris Steak House – A true Texas establishment, redolent with the aroma of fine beef cooking; decorated with oil company paraphernalia, and much appreciated for its prime cuts: fillet, porterhouse, and strip steak. Closed Sundays. Reservations suggested. Major credit cards. 6213 Richmond (789-2333). Expensive.

Maxim's – Consistently fine food of the haute cuisine category and what is probably the most extensive wine cellar in the Southwest. The decor is somewhat overwhelming, but once you start eating, you'll forget all about the pink and green overtones. The menu is weighted toward Gulf seafood, which is prepared well, but the beef is also prime. Chocolate mousse or brandy freeze for dessert are excellent. Closed Sundays. Reservations advised. Major credit cards. 3755 Richmond (877-8899). Expensive.

Tony's – Owner Tony Vallone is on hand most of the time to oversee this stronghold of elegance in this otherwise purposely informal city. Punctilious service by waiters in black tie, understated wood-paneled decor, and fresh flowers provide the back-drop for excellent Continental food. The pâtés and salads are impeccable. Of the entrées, veal piccata with truffles and mushrooms and red snapper noisette, with hazelnuts, are the best. Try the Grand Marnier soufflé for dessert, but remember to order it at the beginning of the meal. Closed Sundays. Reservations advised. Major credit cards. 1801 Post Oak S (622-6778). Expensive.

Uncle Tai's Hunan Yuan – Uncle Tai made his name and reputation in New York City, then headed south to start his own place, and people in Houston couldn't be happier. This family-run restaurant offers impeccable service, and from the Tricolored Lobster to Uncle Tai's Texas-Hunanese-style chicken, the food is uniformly wonderful. Open daily. Reservations advised. American Express and Diners Club accepted. 1980 S Post Oak Rd. (960-8000). Expensive.

Bombay Palace – Indian cuisine is enjoying growing popularity in Houston, and this place is a great favorite. The best dishes prepared in the tandoor — the special Indian clay oven — are chicken, lamb, and prawns. Open daily. Reservations advised. Major credit cards. 3901 Westheimer (960-8472). Moderate.

Las Cazuelas – Deep in the heart of Houston's barrio, this gathering place serves simple, hearty Mexican fare. Try the caldo de res, a beef broth with potato, beef, and corn on the cob, and the delicious huevos con chorizo (eggs and sausage) rolled up in a tortilla and served with guacamole and a special sauce. Open 24 hours daily. Major credit cards. 2219 Fulton (223-0095). Moderate.

Romero's – Tasty and interesting Italian and Continental dishes are complemented by a good list of wines. Some favorites on the menu are veal piccata, blackened redfish, and angel-hair pasta with shrimp and crabmeat. Closed Sundays. Major credit cards. 2400 Midlane (961-1161). Moderate.

Ouisie's Table and Traveling Brown Bag Lunch Company – Fresh, excellent ingredients coupled with an imaginative, constantly changing menu make *Ouisie's* more than a fad. The homemade soups and the chilled crisp salads, a peppery onion pâté, and the perfectly cooked fresh fish are among the best in town. Closed Sundays. Major credit cards. 1708 Sunset (528-2264). Moderate.

Ninfa's – A local must for Mexican fare that seems to be on everyone's list, so you may have to wait in line. But it's worth it, particularly for the tacos al carbon (tortillas wrapped around barbecued pork or beef) and chilpanzingas (ham and cheese wrapped in pastry, fried, and topped with sour cream). There are seven locations now, but the downtown site is still the best. Open daily. No reservations on weekends. Major credit cards. 2704 Navigation (228-1175). Moderate.

San Jacinto Inn – This weathered old inn is next to the San Jacinto Battleground. The freshly cooked seafood dinner comes in great waves of shrimp cocktail, stuffed crabs, tenderloin of trout or red fish, fried chicken, french fries, and hot biscuits with fruit preserves. Closed Mondays. Reservations. Major credit cards. Battle-ground Rd., off Hwy. 225 (479-2828). Moderate.

Zorba the Greek Café – Fried shrimp and seafood platters, and Greek dishes like tiropitakia (phylo filled with feta cheese), leg of lamb, and a great Greek salad. The place looks like a beer parlor, and is, but they also have retsina. Closed Sundays. No reservations. No credit cards. 202 Tuam (528-1382). Moderate.

Captain Benny's Half Shell – Boiled shrimp, freshly shucked oysters, juicy crayfish in season, and lightly fried shrimp are all dished out to the crew of regulars who jam the place. You may have to stand, but you'll find the people-watching and the food worth it. Closed Sundays. No reservations. No credit cards. 7409 S Main (795-9051). Inexpensive.

Chili's – It's easy to guess the house specialty — the real hot stuff, served steaming, spicy, and thick, concocted from a secret Texas recipe. Otherwise, the jumbo hamburgers and homemade french fries make a solid meal at an easy price. Open daily. No reservations. Major credit cards. 5930 Richmond (780-1654). Inexpensive.

The Health Seekers – Refreshing salads, vegetable sandwiches and dishes, some meat platters, fresh juice drinks, and, coolest of all, frozen yogurt. It's all good for you. Open daily. No reservations. Major credit cards. 5080 Richmond Ave. (963-0795). Inexpensive.

Otto's – Aficionados argue over the merits of various styles of barbecue sauce. If you crave the East Texas sweet variety, ride over to *Otto's* and sample good beef, ribs, links, or ham awash in the delightful stuff. Closed Sundays. No credit cards. 5502 Memorial (864-8526). Inexpensive.

Szechuan East – Some of the spiciest Chinese food around. The fowl dishes are especially good, and best of all is the spicy duck. Open daily. No reservations. Major credit cards. 5300 N Braeswood (729-9443). Inexpensive.

INDIANAPOLIS

Like quite a few other midwestern cities, Indianapolis is not likely to excite you at first. There are those endless handsome neighborhoods — big trees, big yards, big houses — in an endless procession above 38th Street. Posh suburbs. Elegant shopping malls. The kind of city that might make you assume that it'd be a nice place to live — for a while.

But as in other cities, first impressions are deceptive. This is partly because of the lack of widespread information about the out-of-the-ordinary places that keep the citizens happy, partly because a lot of vociferous visitors left before they got to the heart of the place under the placid surface, partly because residents took their Indianapolis pleasures for granted. But in the last few years, all that taking for granted has come to a halt. At just about the same time the residents of cities all over the Midwest were realizing that this part of the country was a pretty fine place to live after all, and talking up their cities, and patting themselves on the back for living there, and feeling smug, Richard Lugar took over as Indianapolis's mayor.

He consolidated the city and county governments in an effort to smooth city finances. The downtown area — which had begun to decline only insofar as the movie houses had nearly all gone to the suburbs, and the better part of the more affluent shops and shoppers had followed them — began to blossom. The old city market — vaulted in cast iron and chockablock with fresh produce stands, fish stands, stands for meats, sausages, cheeses, spices, coffees, and tea — was among the first of the institutions to get fixed up instead of torn down. A Convention Center and elegant *Hyatt Regency* soon appeared, along with an arena nearby; the latter provides a home for the Indiana Pacers basketball team and such special events as concerts and ice shows. Monument Circle has been transformed into a clean park that's neatly surrounded by red bricks. The new Hoosier Dome Complex, a 63,000-seat stadium, features sports events as well as conventions and trade shows. Its facilities have already lured the NFL Colts from Baltimore in a very controversial, acrimonious transfer.

Meanwhile, the excitement spread to the suburbs. Boutiques that had been quietly gaining fame and financial security during the preceding ten years were joined by scores of others, particularly on the North Side. Broad Ripple — a village in its own right before the city grew around it and took it in — boomed as bath shops and kitchen shops took over quaint little frame houses along its side streets. The same thing is happening to Zionsville, another small village not quite part of Indianapolis's hustle and bustle. A new shopping center, Keystone at the Crossing, has added something like a bazaar to the city scene. Restaurants sprout, then flourish. The cornfield that some people had called Indianapolis is getting to look pretty lush.

INDIANAPOLIS AT-A-GLANCE

 SEEING THE CITY: Indianapolis has some breathtaking vantage points. The highest point is in Crown Hill Cemetery, at the grave of author James Whitcomb Riley. (John Dillinger and Benjamin Harrison are also buried at Crown Hill, which is a National Historic Site.) Entrance at 3402 Boulevard Pl. (925-8231). Soldiers and Sailors Monument gives you the best overview of the layout of the city. Small admission. Monument Circle, downtown (631-6735). The view from *La Tour,* the 35th-floor restaurant at the top of the Indiana National Bank Tower, is also exceptional. 1 Indiana Sq. (635-3535).

 SPECIAL PLACES: You'll find Indianapolis an easy place to get around. Numbered streets always run east and west, and the number of the streets represents the number of blocks north of Washington St. Most of the great places in Indianapolis are spread out north of Washington St.

Union Station – The biggest news in town is the revitalization of the once-decrepit railroad terminal into an eating-entertainment-shopping area à la Faneuil Hall Marketplace in Boston and South Street Seaport in New York. Centrally located across from the Convention Center and Hoosier Dome, the three-block structure opened in April 1986 and features nearly 40 restaurants, 5 nightclubs, and a variety of shops. The highlight is the 275-room *Holiday Inn* — the first ever placed in an existing structure — with even a few Pullman cars available for lodging (637-1888).

Indiana State Museum – This entertaining museum relates the natural and cultural history of the state. Free. 202 N Alabama, at Ohio (232-1637).

Scottish Rite Cathedral – A vast Tudor Gothic structure with a 54-bell carillon, two organs, and an interior that looks like 3-D lace turned into wood. Free tours on weekdays only. 650 N Meridian (635-2301).

James Whitcomb Riley Home – Indiana's underrated poet laureate lived in this comfortable house between 1892 and 1916; the whole area has been recently restored, as it might have been then. Admission charge. 528 Lockerbie (631-5885).

Benjamin Harrison Memorial Home – This 16-room Victorian mansion, built in 1875 for the 23rd US president, has been fitted out with the Harrisons' own furnishings. Admission charge. 1230 N Delaware (631-1898).

Indianapolis Motor Speedway – Minibuses will take visitors around the 2½-mile oval on which the 500-mile race is held every year on the last Sunday in May. You can also visit the IMS Museum, where race cars from the early days are on display. Admission charge. 4790 W 16th (241-2500).

Indianapolis Museum of Art – By any standards, a truly remarkable museum. Its Krannert Pavilion contains a wide-ranging collection of American, Oriental, primitive, and 18th- and 19th-century European art. The Clowes Pavilion, adjacent, has rooms full of medieval and Renaissance art, plus some watercolors by Turner, ranged around a skylit, plant-filled courtyard. In the gardens are modern sculptures, including Robert Indiana's *LOVE,* and a wonderful, geometrical fountain. The grounds were originally the riverview estate of the Lilly family. Their mansion now shows off a collection of English, French, and Italian 18th-century decorative art. Admission charge for the third-floor and mansion exhibitions; the pavilions are free. 1200 W 38th St. (923-1331).

The Children's Museum – This is the largest children's museum in the world. Kids can ride a turn-of-the-century carousel, spelunk in a simulated limestone cave, and see a real mummy and the largest collection of toy trains on public display. Also featured are antique fire engines, a furnished Hoosier log cabin, and two major galleries full of

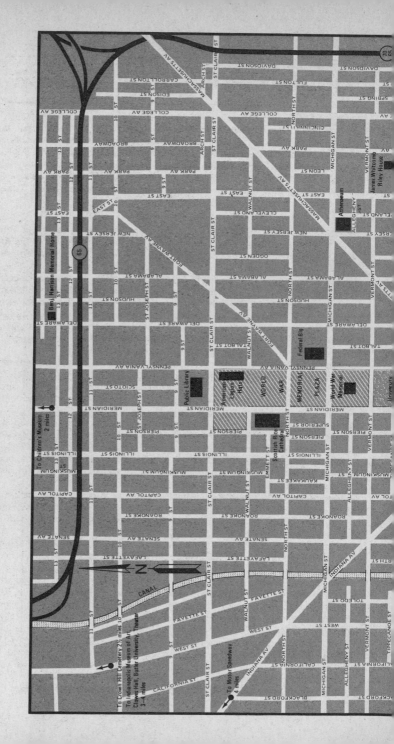

CENTRAL
INDIANAPOLIS

hands-on displays exploring the natural and physical sciences. Special programs are held regularly. Closed Mondays from Labor Day through Memorial Day. Free. 3000 N Meridian (924-5437).

Zionsville – A mid-19th-century restored village. The streets are now full of ritzy shops. Good for a long afternoon. 86th St. north to Zionsville Rd.

Conner Prairie Pioneer Settlement and Museum – A 25-building museum village portraying the life of central Indiana pioneers about 1836. Annual events include Indiana Spring (late April), an old-fashioned Fourth of July bash, and quaint Christmastime festivities. Closed Mondays. Admission charge. 13400 Allisonville Rd., about 20 miles northeast of Monument Circle via Rte. 37 and I-465 (776-6000).

SOURCES AND RESOURCES

TOURIST INFORMATION: The Indianapolis Convention and Visitors Association, 100 S Capitol (639-4282), and the Indiana Tourism Development Division, 1 N Capitol, Suite 700 (232-8860 or 800-2WANDER), supply brochures and general tourist information.

Local Coverage – *Indianapolis Star,* morning daily and Sundays; *Indianapolis News,* afternoon daily.

Area Code – All telephone numbers are in the 317 area code unless otherwise indicated.

CLIMATE AND CLOTHES: Indianapolis has typical midwestern weather — beautiful springs, steamy summers, mild autumns, and moderately cold winters with varying amounts of snow.

GETTING AROUND: Airport – Indianapolis International Airport is a 15-minute drive from downtown; taxi fare should run about $8. AAA Limousine Service offers frequent van service from the airport to most downtown hotels for $6.80 or less, depending on the number of passengers. Metro Transit's #8 Washington St. bus provides public tranportation between the airport and downtown; for the return trip, catch the bus on Washington between Illinois and Meridian streets. The fare is $1; exact change is required.

You *can* get around by public transportation, but a car is more convenient since Indianapolis is a sprawling city.

Bus – Service has improved in recent years, and some lines operate 24 hours — but check before you go. Metro Transit (635-3344).

Taxi – Phoning Yellow Cab (637-5421) is the surest way to get one.

Car Rental – All the big national companies are represented here.

MUSEUMS: The Indianapolis Museum of Art, the Indiana State Museum, the Children's Museum, and the Conner Prairie Pioneer Settlement and Museum are described in *Special Places.* Also interesting:

The Museum of Indian Heritage – 6040 DeLong Rd., in Eagle Creek Park (293-4488)

MAJOR COLLEGES AND UNIVERSITIES: The combined campus of Indiana and Purdue universities is modern and beautifully designed. 1100-1300 W Michigan (635-8661). The campus of Butler University is farther north, at Sunset Ave. and W 46th St. (283-8000). The J. I. Holcomb Observatory and Planetarium sits at the campus's north end (283-9333).

SPECIAL EVENTS: *The Indianapolis 500 Race* — the world's biggest single-day sporting event — is held at the Speedway every Memorial Day weekend. One Saturday night in June, thousands crowd Monument Circle downtown for the *Mid-Summer Fest,* a music fair. Almost as exciting is the *Indiana State Fair,* in August. Indianapolis is also offers the *US Open Clay Court Championships* in a modern tennis stadium in August; and the *National Championship Drag Races* are held at Raceway Park every Labor Day weekend. In September, the *To Market to Market Ball* is held to benefit the City Market; you shop for your dinner at the food stalls and dance to the music of an orchestra outside.

SPORTS AND FITNESS: Baseball – The Indianapolis *Indians,* affiliated with the Cincinnati Reds, play in Bush Stadium at 1501 W 16th (632-5371).
   Basketball – The NBA Indiana *Pacers* play in the Market Square Arena, 300 E Market (639-2112).
   Fishing – Panfish at Eagle Creek Reservoir, 7602 Walnut Point Rd. (293-5555). Farther out of town: Geist and Morse Reservoirs, and, about 2 hours south and much larger, Monroe Reservoir, near Bloomington.
   Fitness Centers – Silhouette National Health Spa, 6407 E Washington (356-7223) and three other locations. The pool at the YMCA is also available, 860 W 10th, by Wishard Hospital (634-2478).
   Football – The Indianapolis *Colts* of the NFL play in the Hoosier Dome, 100 S Capitol (632-4321).
   Golf – There are three good public courses near Riverside Park, 3501 Cold Spring Rd., and eight others around the city. For information on all of them, call the Parks and Recreation Dept. (924-9151).
   Hockey – The Indianapolis *Checkers* play at Market Square Arena, 300 E Market (639-2112).
   Ice Skating – November to March at Ellenberger City Park, 5301 E St. Clair (353-1600), and Perry City Park, 415 E Stop 11 Rd. (888-0070). Also, October through March, at the Coliseum, State Fairgrounds (927-7536), and year-round at the Carmel Skadium, 1040 Third SW (844-8888).
   Jogging – Take advantage of the walkways around the capitol, at Capitol and Washington Street, in the early morning and evening. Joggers also use Military and University parks and the World War Memorial area downtown. Another possibility is the campus of Indiana and Purdue universities, 1100 W Michigan.
   Tennis – Most high school courts are open to the public. Municipal courts can be found throughout the city. For specific locations, call 924-9151.

THEATER: The professional *Indiana Repertory Theater* has grown by leaps and bounds in the last few years, 140 W Washington St. (635-5252). Indianapolis also has the *Civic Theater,* 1200 W 38th (923-4597), the oldest continuously active civic theater in the US. Community theater can be found at the *Christian Theological Seminary,* 1000 W 42nd (924-1331). For dinner theater, *Beef 'N Boards,* 9301 Michigan Rd., NW (872-9664), features stars of TV, Broadway, and Hollywood. In July and August there are musicals under the stars at *Hilton U. Brown Theatron,* 304 W 49th (926-1581).

MUSIC: The Circle Theater is where the *Indianapolis Symphony Orchestra* plays most of its concerts (639-4300). The Murat Theatre is the home of the *Indianapolis Opera Company* (638-4600). The *Butler Ballet* performs in winter and spring at Clowes Hall (283-9231).

NIGHTCLUBS AND NIGHTLIFE: For dancing: *Quincy's,* 2544 Executive Dr. (248-2481). Young singles patronize *Friday's,* 3502 E 86th (844-3355). *Crackers Comedy Club,* 8702 Keystone Crossing (846-2500), features nationally known comedians Wednesdays through Saturdays; reservations recommended. There are also some promising nightclubs in the rejuvenated Union Station, across from the Convention Center.

SINS: Ever since the mayor's office found that the greatest obstacle to the growth of the Hoosier capital was its poor self-image, the city has been spitting and polishing, demolishing and building. with such enthusiasm that *pride* has routed humility.

LOCAL SERVICES: Babysitting – Most hotels can help you arrange for sitters. Failing that, contact Kinder Care, with several locations in the city (849-1944, headquarters).

    Business Services – Manpower Inc. of Indianapolis, 251 N Delaware (635-1001)

    Mechanic – Approved Auto Repair Service (923-1500), affiliated with AAA Motor Club, gives locations and phone numbers of reputable shops.

BEST IN TOWN

CHECKING IN: All the expected chains are here — most of them immediately off I-465, which rings the city, or I-65, which run diagonally through it. Inexpensive doubles run under $40, moderately priced rooms range from $45 to $65, expensive rooms from $90 to $130. Rates are usually higher during Indianapolis 500 weekend and the National Drags. Call the Indiana Tourism Development Division (800-2WANDER) for a list of local bed and breakfast facilities.

The Hyatt Regency Indianapolis – An imposing red brick edifice built around a 20-story central atrium lobby. With 500 rooms, 5 restaurants, lounges, and shops. 1 S Capitol Ave., opposite the Convention Center (317 632-1234). Expensive.

The Hilton at the Circle – The glass elevator that rises and falls through the 370-room hotel allows riders to look out at Monument Circle; the *Top of the Hilton* restaurant offers the same lovely view. 34 W Ohio (317 635-2000). Expensive.

Embassy Suites at Claypool – All accommodations here are fully equipped suites — 348 of them, each with bedroom, living room, and a kitchen. The hotel also has a pool, steam room, and two whirlpools. The first three floors of the building make up the Claypool complex of shops and restaurants. Illinois and Washington sts. (317 635-1000). Expensive.

Radisson Plaza – Within walking distance of some of the city's best shops and restaurants, it's convenient as well as comfortable. Amenities include a pool, Jacuzzi, exercise room, and men's and women's saunas. 8787 Keystone Crossing (317 846-2700). Expensive.

The Atkinson – An older, 233-room hostelry with taste and style — and beautiful Empire antiques in the lobby. Illinois and Georgia sts. (317 639-5611). Moderate.

Sheraton Meridian – In a neighborhood of older, well-maintained apartment buildings, this 280-room property is close to the Children's Museum. Pleasant and modern, it has an indoor-outdoor swimming pool, a sundeck, and a health club. 2820 N Meridian (317 924-1241). Moderate.

Holiday Inn North – Features a beautiful Holidome, a small sports complex with a pool, Jacuzzi, saunas, and other facilities for rest and relaxation. 3850 DePauw Blvd. (317 872-9790). Moderate.

Indianapolis Motor Speedway Motel – Next to the racetrack, with many amenities, including a golf course next to the Speedway Museum. 4400 W 16th St. (317 241-2500). Inexpensive.

Days Inn South – The pleasant swimming pool makes the typical low rates especially noteworthy. On US-31 south and I-465 (317 788-0811). Inexpensive.

 EATING OUT: Indianapolis has always had more than its share of steak-and-baked-potato places and very few notable ethnic eateries. But this situation is slowly changing. Excluding drinks, taxes, and tips, you'll pay $40 and up for a meal for two in restaurants listed below as expensive, $25 to $30 at those marked moderate, and less than $20 at inexpensive places. Prices do not include drinks, wine, or tips.

Chanteclair sur le Toit – Entrées and desserts are flambéed at the table while strolling violinists entertain. Veal Oscar is among the Continental specialties. Open for dinner only; closed Sundays. Reservations recommended. Major credit cards. At the *Holiday Inn–Airport*, 2501 S High School Rd. (243-1040). Expensive.

La Tour – At the top of the Indiana National Bank Tower, with a menu as ambitious as the view is gorgeous. When the kitchen is at the top of its form, it is very, very good. Closed Sundays. Reservations advised. Major credit cards. 1 Indiana Sq. (635-3535). Expensive.

New Orleans House – Visit this relatively plain establishment with a very empty stomach. Unless you're ravenous, it's impossible to do justice to the extravagant all-you-can-eat seafood buffet. Allow 2½ to 3 hours to consume your fill of oysters and clams on the half shell, chowders and Créole dishes, crab legs and lobster. Open daily for dinner only. Reservations required. Major credit cards. 8845 Township Line Rd. (872-9670). Expensive.

The Glass Chimney – Some of the city's best Continental fare appears on the carefully set tables of this consistently fine establishment in a charming old house. Open for dinner daily except Sundays. Reservations required. Major credit cards. 12901 N Meridian (844-0921). Expensive.

Waterson's – Entrées prepared by this kitchen vary, based on what's freshest and best at the market. *Always* on the menu, however, is the house's special sinful dessert, the Chocolate Concord. Closed Sundays. Reservations advised. Major credit cards. At the *Radisson Plaza*, 8787 Keystone Crossing (846-2700). Expensive.

Jonathon's Restaurant & Pub – English country accents fill the four dining rooms of this tasteful place specializing in American cuisine. They also do a fine New York strip, veal Oscar, and prime ribs. Darts, backgammon, and chess are played in the Old English style pub. Open for lunch and dinner daily; brunch served from 10:30 AM to 2 PM on Sundays. Reservations suggested. Major credit cards. 96th and Keystone Ave. (844-1155). Expensive.

St. Elmo's – A local tradition for steaks and potatoes since 1902, and as wonderful as ever. Open for dinner daily except Sundays. Reservations recommended. Major credit cards. 127 S Illinois (635-0636). Expensive to moderate.

Adam's Rib – Prime ribs are the specialty, but fresh fish is flown in daily, and the menu always lists one exotic viand like venison, rattlesnake, or antelope. The salad bar is one of the best in town. Open for lunch on weekdays, for dinner except Sundays. Reservations recommended. Major credit cards accepted. 40 S Main, in Zionsville (see *Special Places;* 873-3301). Expensive to moderate.

The Greenhouse – As the name suggests, plants richly adorn the premises, creating a cool, lush atmosphere in which to enjoy the Continental cuisine. A full bar and jazz entertainment thrives upstairs. A buffet is served on Sundays. Open daily. Reservations recommended. Major credit cards. 8702 Keystone Crossing (844-4556). Expensive to moderate.

Milano Inn – The best place for Italian fare. Open daily for lunch and dinner. Reservations recommended. Major credit cards. 231 S College Ave. (632-8834). Moderate.

Hollyhock Hill – One of Indianapolis's several family-style restaurants. Steaks, fried chicken, and vegetables in generous portions. Open Tuesdays through Sundays for dinner, for lunch on Sundays. Reservations suggested. Major credit cards. 8110 N College Ave. (251-2294). Moderate.

James Tavern – Warmly decorated in wood and gingham, with guests seated before one of many fireplaces to dine on steak, seafood, or fowl. The pleasant waiters are kept busy serving up house specialties like peanut soup and apple walnut pie. Open daily; brunch only on Sundays. Reservations recommended. Major credit cards. 8601 Keystone Crossing (844-7848). Moderate.

Rosa Corona – Mexican fare from south of the border in an elegant and festive setting. There are also two bars, a greenhouse, and a lounge. Open daily. Reservations recommended. Major credit cards. 8650 Keystone Crossing (848-5202). Moderate.

Shapiro's – Indianapolis's best deli, with food served cafeteria style. Open daily for lunch and dinner. No reservations or credit cards. 808 S Meridian (631-4041). Moderate to inexpensive.

Paramount Music Palace – A lively family pizza place and ice cream parlor that features "the mighty Wurlitzer theater pipe organ," which plays all kinds of music. Closed Mondays. No reservations or credit cards. I-465 at E Washington St. (352-0144). Inexpensive.

KANSAS CITY, MO

Surrounded by rich farmlands and grazing fields, Kansas City owes a lot to its agricultural heritage, and agribusiness is the backbone of its economy. Kansas City is first in the nation as a farm distribution center and hard wheat market; second in grain elevator capacity; third as a feeder cattle market. However, don't expect to hear any of these sterling statistics from the average — and always helpful — Kansas City person-in-the-street. Residents are skittish as wild horses about anything that seems to reinforce Kansas City's ingrained "cowtown" image.

For most of its 130-year history, travelers have regarded Kansas City as a one-night stand between the Rockies and Chicago. Residents, naturally, don't see it that way. With more than a million people tucked away in the urban area of rolling woodland, limestone bluffs, and the Kansas and Missouri rivers, Kansas City is the heart of the "breadbasket of the world." It is called the City of Fountains, because of its hundreds of beautiful fountains, many of them European; some, centuries old. It is also a city of art. J. C. Nichols, developer of the Country Club Plaza and residential district, imported more than a million dollars' worth of statuary and other art in the 1920s, not for museums, but for the boulevards and parkways. In fact, Kansas City has more boulevards than Paris — 140 miles of wide, graceful, tree-lined streets and parkways.

But the resemblance to Paris does not extend to the cold, haughty condescension that Parisians show to outsiders. A visitor to Kansas City will inevitably be asked — and asked — what he or she thinks of the place. It may even get a little annoying, but Kansas City folk are self-conscious about their hick-town image and go out of their way to ask a lot of well-meaning questions to reassure you and make sure you're having a good time.

The Nelson-Atkins Museum of Art is one of the top museums in the United States. Classical music events, repertory drama, and a wide range of pop concerts provide enough entertainment to keep anybody busy. Kansas City's breezy, contented lifestyle has a lot to do with its increasing popularity. Dynamic, without succumbing to a frantic pace, Kansas City has been experiencing a rapid but orderly growth cycle — one, however, that has not disturbed its fluid rhythm of life. It is a center of gracious living, magnificent mansions, and old wealth.

The city has certainly come a long way from the days of Rodgers and Hammerstein's musical *Oklahoma!* In those days, went the song, Kansas City "went and built a skyscraper seven stories high — about as high as a building ought to go." A number of private building ventures are still changing the skyline with complexes like the Crown Center, the overwhelming "city within a city," and Westport Square, which is filled with young shopkeepers and artisans who have re-created the charm of old Kansas City by restoring

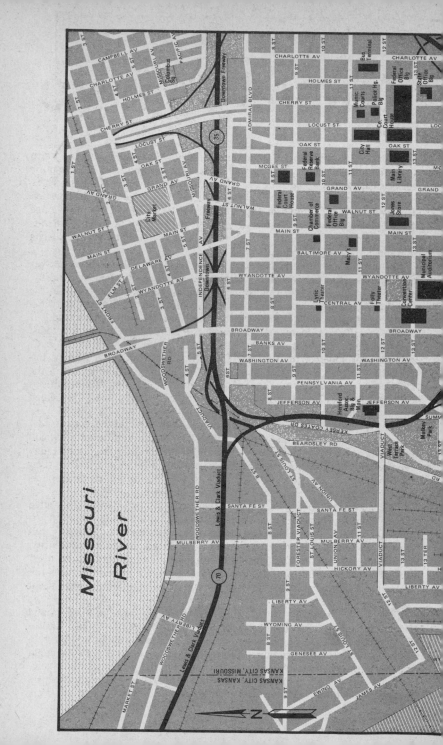

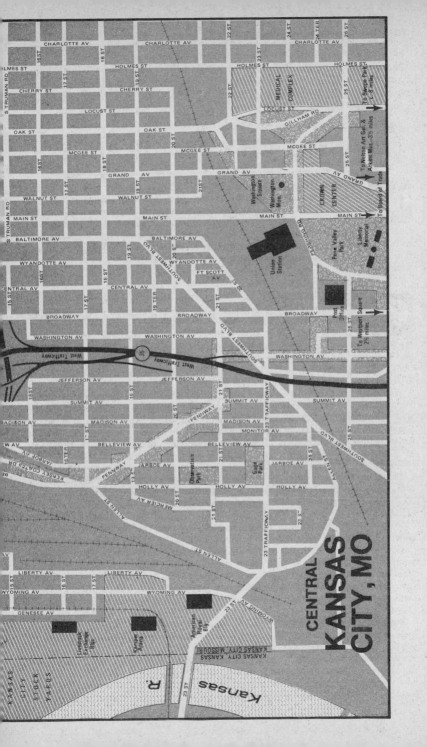

CENTRAL
KANSAS
CITY, MO

the old Victorian buildings. The nation's first shopping center, Country Club Plaza, resembles a tile-roofed Moorish city rather than an impersonal suburban behemoth of glass and brick. But some things Rodgers and Hammerstein wrote still apply. Everything is "up to date in Kansas City," and visitors are more often than not delightfully surprised to find it beautiful as well.

KANSAS CITY AT-A-GLANCE

SEEING THE CITY: One of the best views of Kansas City is from the Observation Tower on the 30th floor of City Hall. Open weekdays. Free. Oak between 12th and 13th sts. (274-2000). Even more dramatic is the view from atop the Liberty Memorial, the great limestone column at the south edge of the downtown area, from which you'll see massive Union Station (second in size only to New York's Grand Central), the downtown skyline, and Crown Center. Closed Sundays and Mondays. Small admission charge. Memorial Dr. just west of 27th and Main sts.

SPECIAL PLACES: Kansas City's three major shopping complexes are self-contained units in which a visitor can be immersed for an entire day.
  Crown Center – This $300 million development is the brainchild of the late Joyce Hall, founder of Hallmark Cards. We suggest starting out from the lobby of the super-elegant *Crown Center Hotel,* dominated by a tropical rain forest and waterfall that winds its way down the limestone hillside on which the hotel was built. Then move on to the shops, where more than 50 stores offer everything from fine art to ski equipment. 2450 Grand (274-8444).
  Westport Square – "Westward, ho!" used to echo across the field that is now Westport Square. It was here that pioneers outfitted themselves for the great journey west. Although times have changed, the tradition of seeking out supplies at Westport Square is solidly implanted in the consciousness of Kansas City residents. A lot of work has gone into restoring the old buildings, many of which date to the 1850s. Broadway at Westport Rd. (931-2855).
  Country Club Plaza – A few blocks south of Westport Square, Country Club Plaza is Disneyland for grownups. More than $1 million worth of statues, fountains, and murals line the shaded walks of this spectacular Spanish- and Morrish-style residential shopping center with over 150 shops, restaurants, and nightclubs. 4629 Wornall Rd. (753-0100).
  Nelson-Atkins Museum of Art – The Nelson is renowned for its comprehensive collection of art, from the ancient Sumerian civilization (3000 BC) to works by contemporaries. Egyptian, Greek, Roman, and medieval sculpture and a reconstructed medieval cloister make this more than just a museum of Old Masters, although there are plenty of classics on the walls — Titian, Rembrandt, El Greco, Goya, the Impressionists, Van Gogh — and contemporary Andy Warhol. It also houses a fine Oriental collection. Closed Mondays, major holidays. Admission charge except Sundays. 4525 Oak St. (561-4000).
  Swope Park – This 1,772-acre park has two golf courses, a swimming pool, picnic areas, a zoo, and the Starlight Theater (333-9481), where popular musicals and concerts are performed in the summer under the stars. 5600 E Gregory.
  Kansas City Stockyards – At the nation's largest stocker and feeder market, you can see what a Kansas City steak looks like before it gets to your table. Depending on how you react to the cattlemen in action, you may or may not look forward to a hefty meal of the beef that helped make Kansas City famous. There are frequent cattle

auctions at the stockyards. Visitors are welcome at the Sales Pavilion of the Livestock Building Tuesdays, Wednesdays, and Thursdays. 16th and Genesee (842-6800).

Benjamin Stables on the Santa Fe Trail – Benjamin Stables is a complex of barns, fields, and blacksmith's shop that re-creates an early western town. Horse-drawn carts, wagons, and carriages are visible everywhere. There are sleigh rides and hayrides, and horseback riding for those who want to ride the old Santa Fe Trail. Call one day in advance for a tour. Open weekdays. 6401 E 87th at I-435 (761-5055).

Worlds of Fun – This 140-acre family theme park has more than 60 rides. The adjacent Oceans of Fun (459-9283) is a huge aquatic park that's open in the summer. Worlds of Fun is open daily from June until early September; weekends only from mid-April to late May and in September and October. Admission charge. On I-435, just north of the Missouri River, at Parvin Rd. (454-4545).

Missouri River Excursions – A relaxing way to spend a few hours. Cruises leave from Westport landing at the foot of Grand Ave. (842-0027).

■**EXTRA SPECIAL:** Just 8 miles east of downtown Kansas City in Independence, Missouri, is the *Harry S. Truman Library and Museum.* Remember "The buck stops here"? So should you, if you're a Truman fan. Even if you're not, you might become one after a visit. Open daily except Thanksgiving and New Year's Day. Admission charge for adults; children and educational groups free. On US 24 at Delaware (833-1225). While you're there, stop for a meal at *Stephenson's Apple Farm.* Just up the road a piece from the Truman Library and Museum is *Fort Osage,* a reconstruction of the trading post established by explorer William Clark of the famous Lewis and Clark team. Open daily during daylight hours. About 22 miles northeast of Independence on US 24, in Sibley, Missouri (249-5737).

SOURCES AND RESOURCES

TOURIST INFORMATION: The Kansas City Convention and Visitors Bureau has a 24-hour hotline (474-9600) for the latest information on city activities. It also provides brochures, maps, and a restaurant and hotel guide. City Center Square Bldg., Suite 2550, 1100 Main St. (221-5242).

Local Coverage – *Kansas City Times,* morning daily; *Kansas City Star,* afternoon daily.

Food – *The Kansas City Restaurant Guide* (from the Convention and Visitors Bureau; free).

Area Code – All telephone numbers are in the 816 area code unless otherwise indicated.

CLIMATE AND CLOTHES: Kansas City's midwestern climate is notorious. It's fine in the spring and fall, but the winters are rough (frequently the thermometer never rises above freezing in January). and the summers are hot and humid. Rain is particularly likely in spring.

GETTING AROUND: Airport – Kansas City International Airport is usually a 30- to 40-minute drive into the city; cab fare should run about $20 to $25. If cabs are not readily available at the airport, call the dispatcher at 471-5000. The green KCI Airport Express buses run from the airport to the major downtown and plaza area hotels every 30 minutes, on the hour and half-hour. Tickets are $8.50 and can be purchased at Gate 63 in Terminal C (take the inter-airport red buses to this terminal). Return schedules vary; ask for a timetable at your hotel or call 243-5950.

Bus – The Kansas City Metro Bus covers the downtown area (221-0660).

Taxi – Call Yellow Cab (741-5000).

Car Rental – The best way to see Kansas City is by car. Major car firms are represented.

MUSEUMS: The Nelson-Atkins Museum of Art and the Harry S. Truman Library and Museum are described in *Special Places.* Other fine Kansas City museums are:

Agriculture Hall of Fame – I-70 to Bonner Springs (721-1075)

1859 Jail and Museum – 217 N Main St., Independence, MO (252-1892)

Kansas City Museum of History and Science – 3218 Gladstone (483-8300)

Liberty Memorial Museum – The country's only museum devoted to World War I, Memorial Dr. just west of 27th and Main sts; free

Shawnee Methodist Mission and Indian Manual Labor School – Indian Mission, 53rd and Mission Rd., Fairway, KS (913 262-0867)

Wornall House – Civil War restoration, 61 Terrace and Wornall (444-1858)

MAJOR COLLEGES AND UNIVERSITIES: The University of Missouri–Kansas City, 51st and Rockhill Rd. (276-1000).

SPECIAL EVENTS: *American Royal Horse and Livestock Show,* November, at Kemper Arena, 1700 Wyoming (421-6460).

SPORTS AND FITNESS: Kansas City has professional baseball and football teams.

Baseball – The Kansas City *Royals,* Harry S. Truman Sports Complex, I-70 and Blue Ridge Cutoff (921-8000).

Bicycling – Bikes can be rented in summer at Shelter House One in Swope Park, at the main entrance, Swope Pkwy. and Meyer Blvd.

Fitness Centers – K. C. Fitness Center offers pools, exercise equipment, aerobics classes, and a track, 5030 Main St., on the plaza (753-6767); Town & Country Health Club, on the 5th floor of the *Crown Center Hotel,* has a pool, steam room, sauna, and coed whirlpool, 1 Pershing Rd., in Crown Center (474-4400).

Football – The NFL Kansas City *Chiefs,* Harry S. Truman Sports Complex, I-70 and Blue Ridge Cutoff (924-9400).

Golf – The best is at River Oaks, 140 and US 71, in Grandview (966-8111).

Horseback Riding – Benjamin Stables Trail Town on the old Santa Fe Trail, 6401 E 87th at I-435 (761-5055).

Jogging – Penn Valley Park, near the *Crown Center Hotel* (25th to 33rd St. and Pershing Rd.); Jacob L. Loose Park inner and outer loops, 1½ blocks from the *Alameda Plaza;* Ward Parkway, a large, lovely boulevard (pick it up at the Alameda and run south).

Tennis – There are more than 200 public tennis courts in the Kansas City metro area. Most are free. Swope Park has good courts at the picnic area north of the Starlight Theater. At 4747 Nichols Parkway, there are year-round courts. For reservations call 531-0761.

THEATER: For the latest information on theater and musical events, call 474-9600. The city's *Theater League* (421-7500) presents touring companies of Broadway hits in the Midland Center for the Performing Arts, 1228 Main. Dramatic and musical productions are also booked into the Music Hall in the Municipal Auditorium, 200 W 13th (421-8000); at the Lyric Theater, 10th and

Central (471-7344); and the Folly Theatre, 12th and Central (842-5500). From July to September and January to March, the *Missouri Repertory Company* performs in the Spencer Theater on the University of Missouri campus (276-2704). The Starlight Theater in Swope Park, an under-the-stars amphitheater, features musical comedy and concerts with top-name stars from May to mid-September (333-9481). Kansas City has two dinner playhouses, *Tiffany's Attic,* 5028 Main (561-7921); and the *Waldo (not* Waldorf) *Astoria,* 7428 Washington (561-9876).

MUSIC: For up-to-date data on concert happenings, call 474-9600 or check the newspapers. The *Kansas City Symphony* season, from November through May, features internationally known conductors and soloists. Performances are held on Fridays and Saturdays in the Lyric Theater, 11th and Central (471-7344). There are two opera seasons, in April and October at the Lyric. The operas are in English. Jazz still thrives in Kansas City; call the Municipal Jazz Commission hotline (931-2888) for information on jazz events. Another good source of information on current musical offerings is the Concert Connection (276-1171), sponsored by the UMKC Conservatory of Music. To find out who's playing at the clubs, check the arts section of the Sunday *Kansas City Star.*

NIGHTCLUBS AND NIGHTLIFE: In the last decade, Kansas City's after-dark scene has picked up so that now it's one of the most lively in the Midwest. The liquor laws are still a bit antiquated: Missouri bars close at 1 AM. Bars are closed on Sunday, although restaurants and hotels may serve drinks. Kansas taverns serve 3.2% beer and private clubs only may serve liquor by the drink. Singles action is liveliest at *Houlihan's Old Place,* 4743 Pennsylvania (561-3141), which also has good food. Best bet for out-of-towners is to park on the plaza or near Westport Square and bar hop. There are dozens of clubs and bars — some with live entertainment — within easy walking distance of each other. Westport Square is very casual; the plaza is a bit more formal, and some restaurant-bars require a coat and tie. The best gay bars are on Main St. between 50th and 51st sts.

SINS: Kansas City may think of itself as the Paris of the Plains, and the citizens get apoplectic with *anger* when any outsider suggests that their city is not quite as cosmopolitan as it pretends. But the fact of the matter is that in Paris prostitutes are as easy to find as a good meal, and in Kansas City they aren't. Which has less to do with food in Kansas City (*gluttony* thrives at places like *Arthur Bryant's*) than with an attitude toward prostitution that is as American as apple pie. But a few working women can usually be spotted along Main or on Troost between 31st and 39th streets. As for overweening *pride,* it depends on who you ask. Some folk will rave about the revolving restaurants and the fancy shopping malls, and some people go bonkers over the boulevards and the fountains.

LOCAL SERVICES: Business Services – AAA Secretarial Service (531-4615)
  Mechanic – Glenn Freely Auto Repair (421-2436)

BEST IN TOWN

CHECKING IN: Expect to pay $90 and up for a double in hotels categorized as expensive; and $70 to $80 in those places designated as moderate.
Crown Center Hotel – Built on a huge chunk of limestone known as Signboard Hill because of the commercial embellishments that used to deco-

rate it, this 730-room ultramodern hotel is part of the Crown Center complex. It integrates the limestone face of the hill into the lobby, where there is a winding stream, 5-story waterfall, and tropical rain forest. It has 7 restaurants, including *Trader Vic's*, and numerous shops and boutiques. 1 Pershing Rd. in Crown Center (816 474-4400 or 800 228-3000). Expensive.

Alameda Plaza – A sumptuous building with 359 elegantly appointed rooms in beautifully landscaped grounds on Country Club Plaza. Wornall Rd. at Ward Pkwy. (816 756-1500). Expensive.

The Hyatt Regency – Kansas City's fanciest hotel is also its most notorious since the collapse, in July 1981, of two of the three skywalks that spanned its huge, glass-topped lobby. The rubble of the disaster is gone, the three suspended walks have been replaced by a single elevated ramp resting solidly on pillars, and probably no other public building in America has undergone more inspections and safety tests. South of the downtown loop; McGee at Pershing Rd. (816 421-1234 or 800 228-9000). Expensive.

Vista International – Built on what used to be known as "the strip," where jazz and bootleg gin flowed all night in the many clubs along its length, this hotel has recaptured the spirit of this bygone era in its own ambience. Part of the major facelift of the downtown Convention Center area, it has 572 rooms and suites, the formal *Harvest* restaurant, *Lilly's Restaurant and Wine Bar,* and the *12th Street Rag* nightclub. Features include a nonsmoking floor, 2 outdoor tennis courts, and a health club with indoor pool, sauna, Nautilus and David equipment, and aerobics. Operated by Hilton International. 200 West 12th St. (816 421-6800). Expensive.

Hilton Airport Plaza Inn – Ideal if you're more interested in traveling than downtown sightseeing. In addition to 360 comfortable rooms, there are 2 heated swimming pools — indoor and outdoor; a sauna, whirlpool, a health club, putting green, and tennis courts, as well as 2 dining rooms, a coffee shop, and bar with entertainment. I-29 and NW 112th St. (816 891-8900). Moderate.

Radisson-Muehlebach – The king of downtown hotels, acquired by the Radisson chain and given a major facelift. Most of its 700 rooms have been redecorated, the lobby and restaurant have undergone a major overhaul, but the the 1920s aura has been preserved. No pool or sauna here, but its style makes it popular with business-people and conventioneers. 12th and Baltimore (816 471-1400). Moderate.

Doubletree Hotel – The once-sleepy bedroom community of Johnson County, Kansas, are now buzzing with business thanks to the industrial growth along I-435 and I-35 southwest of downtown Kansas City. The sumptuous *Doubletree* is geared to the needs of visitors with business in that part of town. 10100 College Blvd. (913 451-6100). Moderate.

 EATING OUT: Kansas City has great steaks and good French food. Its very best eatery, however, is a barbecue restaurant, and that's a fact. Visitors can select a high-priced haute cuisine restaurant or one that will provide superb food at more moderate prices — although you'll find Kansas City prices reasonable everywhere. We recommend calling ahead for reservations at all the places listed below. Expect to pay $45 or more for dinner for two at those places listed as expensive; $25 to $35 at those places listed as moderate; under $20 at restaurants listed as inexpensive. Prices do not include drinks, wines, or tips.

American – Many Kansas City people say this is the best in town. Certainly, it's the fanciest. The *American* has French moderne decor and a menu featuring bluepoint oysters on the half shell, Nova Scotia salmon, Gulf shrimp creole with rice pilaf, fresh sea bass sautéed with mushrooms in white wine, rock salt hobo steak, Montana elk with lingonberries and mushroom caps, and braised South

Dakota pheasant in juniper sauce. Open daily. All credit cards. In the *Crown Center Hotel,* 25th and Grand (471-8050). Expensive.

Alameda Rooftop Restaurant – The menu is oppressively pretentious, but this is a great place from which to see the glittering city spread below as you dine on excellent roast rack of lamb, seafood, and beef. The cold gazpacho is palate-tingling. Reservations are especially necessary if you want to sit near a window. Open daily. All credit cards. Ward and Wornall on the plaza (756-1500). Expensive.

The Peppercorn Duck Club – A knockout eatery in the *Hyatt Regency.* The decor is Olde English and the food is sumptuous, especially the roast duckling. The chocolate dessert bar is appropriately sinful and the service is attentive almost to a fault — you can hardly sniffle without someone handing you a hankie. Reservations advised. Major credit cards. McGee at Pershing Rd. (421-1234). Expensive to moderate.

Bristol Bar and Grill – One of the best seafood restaurants in the Midwest is found at the Country Club Plaza. A New York actress who eats here when she's in town says the fish is better than back home on Long Island. The decor is a pleasant blend of Victorian architecture and modern art; ask to be seated in the back room beneath the huge Tiffany leaded glass dome. The bar is a popular after-work watering hole for KC's upwardly mobile bunch. Reservations advised. Major credit cards. 4740 Jefferson (756-0606). Expensive to moderate.

Plaza III – While *Houlihan's* next door excels at trendiness, the venerable *Plaza III* sticks to the basics. Seafood lovers will delight in the Sausalito seafood sauté, with its garlic butter and heavy cream sauce; the Steak Imperial is stuffed with crabmeat; the desserts are heavenly. Open daily. Reservations accepted. Major credit cards. 4749 Pennsylvania Ave., on the plaza (753-0000). Expensive to moderate.

Golden Ox – In the heart of the stockyards, near Kemper Arena, where the wranglers who work the steers take their food breaks. Good, solid American cooking here, and arguably the best steaks in town, served with potato, garlic bread, and salad. Open daily. Call to see if reservations are necessary. All credit cards. 1600 Genesee (842-2866). Moderate.

Savoy Grill – A turn-of-the-century restaurant cherished by Kansas City residents that serves very fine seafood and steaks. The most outstanding feature of the *Savoy* is its 1903 Victorian mirrored bar and stained-glass windows, giving you the feel of early Kansas City. Closed Sundays. Reservations accepted. Major credit cards. 9th and Central (842-3890). Moderate.

Stephenson's Apple Farm Restaurant – Down-home cooking has made this fine restaurant's reputation. Hickory-smoked pork ribs, chicken gizzards, beef brisket, steak, and homemade pie in a rustic American setting make this well worth a trip out to Independence, even if you have no interest in Harry S. Truman. Open daily. Reservations recommended. Major credit cards. US 40 at Lea's Summit Rd., South Independence (373-5400). Moderate.

Houlihan's Old Place – A casual dining spot serving soups, mushroom burgers, crab Newburg, eggs Benedict, quiches, omelets, roast duck, banana splits, and, of course, Kansas City steaks. Lavishly decorated in Gay 90s style, some people say it looks like a Wild West bordello. Decide for yourself. Open till the wee hours, daily. Reservations accepted. Major credit cards. 4743 Pennsylvania, Country Club Plaza (561-3141). Moderate to inexpensive.

Arthur Bryant's Barbecue – This eatery has acquired a reputation of legendary proportions, thanks in part to Calvin Trillin's book *American Fried* (in which he claims this is the best restaurant in America!). In fact, 95 pounds of Bryant's barbecued ribs and beef were flown to New York for Trillin's publication day party. To check it out, you'll have to wait in line — but the huge sandwiches, French fries, and free "brownies" (ends of brisket) make it all worthwhile. Closed Sundays and the month of January. No reservations. No credit cards. No atmosphere. But who cares? 1727 Brooklyn (231-1123). Inexpensive.

Happy Family – If you're in the area, try this delightful family-run teahouse for its satisfying Chinese fare. Modest decor, modest prices, but very, very pleasant. Open daily. No credit cards. 8623 W 95th St., Overland Park, Kansas (913 383-3110). Inexpensive.

LAS VEGAS

There may be no other place on earth so forbidding and yet so alluring as Las Vegas, that glittering oasis in the midst of mountainous Nevada desert. To some it's a 24-hour city of fantasy, to others an unending nightmare. How you feel about it may just depend on your tolerance for the phantasmagorical. But whether it's loved as a vacation paradise or damned as "Sin City," the maze of contradictions that are bred here make the place fascinating.

With the legalization of gambling in Atlantic City and the probability of legalization elsewhere, a new age is dawning. Since the 1940s Las Vegas reigned as the unchallenged gambling resort of the world, and it is not about to surrender its throne without a fight. A sense of competition has swept the city, and several of the older hotels have received dramatic facelifts while the new structures that continue to spring up place special emphasis on "extras" and "freebies."

Visitors are shown one face of Las Vegas: the facade of "Entertainment Capital of the World." But this doesn't begin to describe it. The cavernous air conditioned vastness of countless Strip casinos aims at total sensory bombardment with a maelstrom of sights and sounds: the ringing bells and flashing lights of the slot machines, the rolling wheels of fortune, the dice dancing on the green tables, the smoke-filled air mixed with a heavy undercurrent of free-flowing alcohol. Throngs of people crowd the casinos at every hour of the day and night. In Las Vegas, time doesn't matter. There are no clocks in the casinos, and most places offer breakfast and dinner 24 hours a day at such bargain prices that it might make sense to eat both at one sitting. Cocktail waitresses keep the thirst quenched by bringing drinks on the house for those gambling steadily. The casinos offer these extras so that Vegas visitors can spend their time indulging in the town's one overwhelming obsession — the desire to gamble. If gratification is not found instantly, there is a choice of a few hundred other places whose neon signs blare bigger and better attractions.

Just venture outside on the Strip (in Las Vegas, going outside is a big step) and you will see one after another huge hotel-casino: *Caesars Palace,* the *Sahara,* the *Sands, Aladdin, MGM Grand.* The names promise magic, but it's mostly an optical illusion. Underneath those opulent exteriors and plush decors is a foundation of sand. Certainly, some of the biggest names in entertainment perform here and everyone flocks to see them, but the real business is gambling; anything else is done simply to draw people to the casinos. That's the real trick and that's what keeps Las Vegas going. Money is god here and it created poker chips in its own image. It also created some vast resort complexes — castles built on the desert that promise paradise at the next throw of the dice.

But if you do manage to break the spell of the casinos and get outside

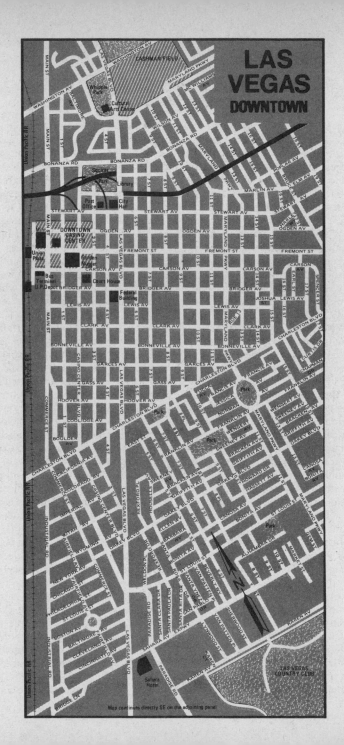

Map continues directly SE on the adjoining panel

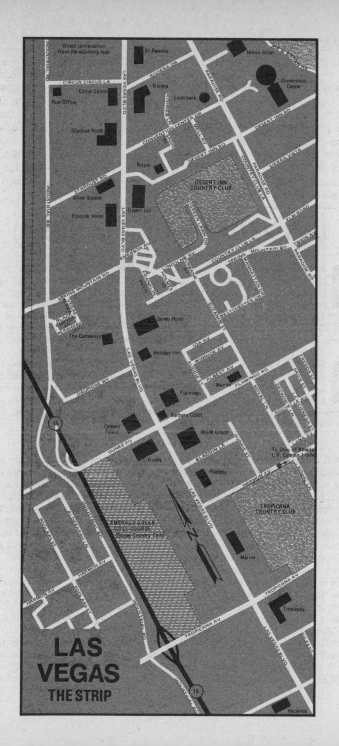

LAS VEGAS
VEGAS
THE STRIP

— outside the Strip and outside town — you will discover that the world outside is worth a good deal more than the few rounds of golf or tennis between poker games. Contrary to preconceived notions of the desert as a lifeless, joyless, uniformly bland stretch of rock and sand, you will value the treeless expanse for its incredible beauty — a magnificent variety of colors, and the utter freedom of its open spaces. Within miles of Las Vegas, but on the other side of the barrier of unreality, lie the dramatic red and white sandstone formations of Red Rock Recreation Area and the subtle desert colors of the Valley of Fire. These, with the nearby cool green mountains of Mt. Charleston and the manmade Lake Mead, make the desert as attractive a proposition as the Strip.

LAS VEGAS AT-A-GLANCE

 SEEING THE CITY: The *Top O' Mint Restaurant* offers a panoramic view of Las Vegas. As you ascend in the glass elevator, all of downtown Las Vegas glitters around you. As you reach the top, the expanse of surrounding desert appears, and your eye is drawn to the neon of the Strip, a long stream of hotels and casinos, and beyond to the south, the green heights of Mt. Charleston. In the *Mint Hotel,* 100 E Fremont St. (385-7440). You can also try the *Top of the Landmark,* 364 Convention Center Dr. (733-1110), for a spectacular 360° view.

 SPECIAL PLACES: Gambling is the name of the game in Las Vegas. The cultural aspects of the city are limited, and its history has been all but obliterated by its rapid growth. But the surrounding area is rich in outdoor diversions that can fill your days with a wide variety of noncasino pleasures, leaving the nights for the air conditioned paradise of green felt, dazzling neon, and showgirl entertainment.

THE STRIP

If gambling is the game, the Strip is the place. Shining brightly in the desert sun, this 5-mile boulevard just south of town glows more intensely at night, ablaze with the glittering opulence of a seemingly never-ending stream of hotels. The sky's the limit here, and one after another of the big hotels offer it — the *Sahara, Circus Circus,* the *Riviera,* the *Silver Slipper,* the *Sands, Caesars Palace,* the *Tropicana,* and the *Dunes.* From slot machines, poker, and blackjack to the esoteric keno and baccarat of the casinos, to the production spectaculars with a cavalcade of stars in the main showrooms, to 24-hour breakfasts or dinners, it's all here and rolling around the clock. Las Vegas Blvd., just south of the city along US 91. A few highlights are:

Caesars Palace – Las Vegas's stab at ancient Rome, *Caesars Palace* outdoes its namesake in gaming. The only other similarities are the Romanesque names of casino areas and showrooms, and the fact that cocktail waitresses and keno runners dress in distinctive mini-togas. Otherwise, it's the plushest of the plush, with more red velvet carpets than the total number of Caesar's battles. Superstars perform nightly; be sure to make reservations. 3570 Las Vegas Blvd. (731-7110).

Circus Circus – There's gambling on the ground and gamboling up above in this tent-shaped casino where trapeze and high-wire artists, clowns, acrobats, and dancers perform to the music of a brass band. The observation gallery at circus level is lined with food and carnival stands. Children are permitted in the gallery but not on the casino floor, so bring them along and everyone can have their own circus. Circus open 11 AM to midnight. Free. 2880 Las Vegas Blvd. (734-0410).

Wet 'n Wild – A 26-acre family-oriented water playground with a surf lagoon, water chutes, rapids, flumes, and even pearl diving. Family rates and discount tickets are available at the Strip hotels. Open daily, May through October. On the Strip between the *Sahara* and *El Rancho* hotels.

Convention Center – One of the world's major convention destinations, this is Las Vegas's center. This modern steel structure is a million-square-foot complex that can seat 7,200 in the rotunda. On Paradise Rd., next to the *Las Vegas Hilton*, off the Strip (733-2323).

DOWNTOWN

Golden Nugget Hotel and Casino – The most spectacular hotel downtown, and one of the most glamorous in Las Vegas, it has recently undergone a $75 million expansion and renovation. Additions include the $50 million Town House Tower with just 27 duplex suites, a jewel-box *Cabaret Lounge*, *Elaine's* and *Stefano's* restaurants for fine dining, and a 500-seat theater-ballroom. The exterior of the building has been encased in Italian marble and all the old neon is but a memory. A must-see during your visit. 129 E Fremont St. (385-7111).

THE OUTDOORS

Hoover Dam and Lake Mead – Completed in 1936, Hoover Dam is an awesome monument to man's engineering capabilities, a 726-foot-high concrete wall that tamed the mighty Colorado River and supplies electricity to Las Vegas and California. Daily tours. Admission charge. Lake Mead, produced when the Colorado backed up behind the dam, is, at 115 miles long, one of the largest manmade lakes in the world. Fishing (bass, crappie, and catfish), swimming, and boating are available year-round. The visitors center for Hoover Dam (293-8367) and headquarters of Lake Mead National Recreation Area (293-4041) are 30 minutes south of the city on Boulder Hwy. (US 93).

Mt. Charleston – Just 35 minutes north of the city, Mt. Charleston dramatically exhibits the effect of increased elevation with a wide variety of trees and wildlife. Plenty of cool fresh mountain air. During the winter months, snow covers the ground and temperatures often hover below freezing at the Lee Canyon ski slopes while vacationers swim in Las Vegas hotel pools just half an hour away. Tonapah Hwy. north to Rte. 39.

Red Rock Recreation Area – A beautiful desert locale featuring red and white hues of sandstone formations, and spectacular views of steep canyons. Just a few miles farther west, the Spring Mountain State Park has Old West buildings on a ranch that has belonged to such well-known capitalists as Howard Hughes and the German Krupp family (of armament notoriety). State rangers lead tours through the old buildings. W Charleston Blvd., 15 and 20 miles west of the city.

■ **EXTRA SPECIAL:** Just 2 hours northwest of Las Vegas lies *Death Valley*, the hottest, driest, and lowest area in the US. It is also starkly beautiful. The high mountains surrounding the 120-mile-long valley have isolated it, and of the 600 species of plants that have been identified there, 21 grow nowhere else on earth. The variety of the colors and textures of nature in the raw is remarkable, from the jagged bluish rock salt formations of Devil's Golf Course, to the smoothly sculpted golden dunes of Mesquite Flat, to the rich reds and purples of Telescope Peak at sunrise. *Scotty's Castle*, an eccentric and intricate mansion built in the middle of this expanse by a Chicago millionaire, is the area's most incongruous wonder. Because of extremely high temperatures in the summer, the best time to visit the valley is from November through April. Information on self-guided auto tours and planned walking tours and programs is available November through April at the visitors center at Furnace Creek (714 786-2331). Tonapah Hwy. north (I-95) to Beatty, then take the Death Valley Junction cutoff straight into the park. (See also *Death Valley,* DIRECTIONS.)

SOURCES AND RESOURCES

TOURIST INFORMATION: The Las Vegas Chamber of Commerce is best for brochures, maps, suggestions, and general tourist information. 2301 E Sahara Ave. (457-4664).

Local Coverage – *Review Journal,* morning and evening daily; *Las Vegas Sun,* morning daily. Several weekly entertainment guides are available at newsstands.

Area Code – All telephone numbers are in the 702 area code unless otherwise indicated.

CLIMATE AND CLOTHES: In the middle of the desert, Las Vegas summers are hot and dry. Winters are pleasant and mild, and outdoor activity takes place year-round. Bring along a sweater for the indoors; high-powered air conditioners are in use everywhere. Dress is casual during the day; at night the showtime dress can be formal and elegant, but it's optional.

GETTING AROUND: Although Las Vegas is not really a large city, the heat, dust, and wind make walking difficult. If you are going any farther than a hundred yards or so, you'll probably do better on wheels.

Airport – McCarran International Airport is a 20-minute drive and $8 cab ride from the Strip; allow 10 minutes and $5 more to reach downtown. Whittlesea-Bell Co. (384-6111) provides transportation to Strip hotels for $2.75; to downtown hotels for $4.25. For return service, call 2 hours before flight time. Plan to arrive at the airport at least an hour before flight time, since the distances between the main entrance and the check-in gates are great, and the newness of the facility — which has recently undergone a $300 million expansion — can cause a bit of confusion in matching passengers with their flights.

Bus – The Las Vegas Transit System covers the downtown area and the Strip. The discount commuter ticket offers a real savings if you expect to use the buses frequently. Route information is available at 1550 Industrial Rd. (384-3540).

Taxi – Cabs can be hailed in the street, ordered on the phone, or picked up at taxi stands in front of hotels. Major companies are Western Cab (382-7100); Whittlesea Cab (384-6111); Yellow Cab (382-4444).

Car Rental – The large national firms serve Las Vegas, though the cheapest local service is provided by *Dollar Rent-A-Car,* at McCarran Airport (739-8408); *Abbey Rent-A-Car,* 3745 Las Vegas Blvd. S (736-4988); and *Allstate,* 5175 Rent Car Rd. (736-6147).

MUSEUMS: Las Vegas hotels have commercial art exhibitions with works of well-known artists. *Herigstad's Gallery* has art shows as well as works for sale. Closed Sundays. 2290 E Flamingo Rd. (733-7366). Also worth a visit is *Minotaur Fine Arts Ltd.* (737-1400) in the Fashion Show Mall. Open daily.

The University of Nevada at Las Vegas has a *Museum of Natural History* with collections of Indian artifacts and live desert reptiles. Open daily. Free. 4505 S Maryland Pkwy. (739-3381).

The *Mineral Collection,* which is also on the campus, displays 1,000 specimens from the area and around the world. Closed weekends. Free. Science Hall, Room 103.

MAJOR COLLEGES AND UNIVERSITIES: The University of Nevada at Las Vegas is the largest school in the area, with an enrollment of 12,000. 4505 S Maryland Pkwy. (739-3011).

SPECIAL EVENTS: During the *Helldorado Festival* held for four days in May, the city celebrates its Western heritage with rodeos, parades, beauty contests, and, for those who want some slower-paced action, a beardgrowing contest. The *Jaycees State Fair* takes place in August at the Convention Center and has carnival acts, magic shows, rides, livestock and craft exhibits.

SPORTS AND FITNESS: Las Vegas offers a wide variety of sporting events and fine facilities.

    Basketball – The University of Nevada at Las Vegas has fielded one of the finest collegiate basketball teams in the nation for several years. They play from November to February in the Thomas & Mack Center, an 18,000-seat arena. Tickets are usually available, but for good seats, your hotel bell captain or casino pit boss would be helpful (739-3267).

    Betting – If you want to bet on almost any athletic event taking place outside of Nevada, numerous race and sports books dot the city. The facilities in *Caesars Palace,* 3570 Las Vegas Blvd. S (731-7110), and the *Stardust Hotel,* 3000 Las Vegas Blvd. (732-6111), are the most lavish on the Strip. Union Plaza's Book tops the downtown locales. 1 Main St. (386-2110).

    Boxing – If punching is your bag, the major hotels promote many boxing matches. Major bouts between professional heavyweight contenders are held from time to time at *Caesars Palace,* the *Riviera,* and the *Showboat.*

    Fitness Centers – The health club at *Caesars Palace* has a whirlpool, steam room, and exercise equipment, but no pool, 3570 Las Vegas Blvd. S, 15th floor (731-7110). The Aristocrat Health Spa, in the *Hilton,* has a sauna, whirlpool, and massage, 3000 Paradise Rd., 3rd floor on the pool deck (732-5111). A new, multimillion-dollar facility has been added to the *Desert Inn,* 3145 Las Vegas Blvd. (733-4571).

    Golf – Dozens of courses dot the desert landscape. Most of the Strip hotels have championship-quality courses, but the Sahara Country Club, 1911 Desert Inn Rd. (796-0013), and the Desert Inn Country Club, 3145 Las Vegas Blvd. S (733-4444), are the best. For lower prices, try the public courses. Best bet is the Municipal Golf Course. which offers a reasonable challenge and good greens. Washington Ave. and Decatur Blvd. (878-4665).

    Jogging – It's possible to run right along the Strip between Flamingo Road and Spring Mountain, where there are no cross streets to slow the pace (about ½ mile each way); stay on the *Caesars Palace* side. Another possibility is Squires Park, ½ mile from downtown; or drive to Sunset Park, 7 miles from downtown, or Bob Baskin Park, W Oakey Blvd. at Rancho Dr. The *Las Vegas Hilton* has an enclosed jogging track next to the hotel.

    Tennis – Almost all the Strip hotels have good tennis facilities open to the public. Indoor courts are available at the Cambridge Tennis Club, 3890 Swenson Ave. (735-8153).

THEATER: For current performances, check the publications listed above. Outside of the entertainment at the Strip hotels, there is not that much in the way of theater. But a few new additions and old standbys keep the curtains raised. The best bet for shows is the *Repertory Theater at Judy*

Bayley Hall, University of Nevada at Las Vegas campus (739-3641). The Clark County Community College and other local companies are featured in *Theatre Under the Stars,* outdoors at the Spring Mountain Ranch in late June and early July. The creative sets make fine use of the environment, and the acting is first-rate. Tickets at the Ranch, on Spring Mountain Rd., 18 miles west on Charleston Blvd. (875-4141).

 MUSIC: Symphony concerts, opera, jazz, and the *Nevada Dance Theatre* are featured throughout the year at Artemus W. Ham Concert Hall and the Judy Bayley Theatre on the UNLV campus. For tickets, call 739-3011.

 NIGHTCLUBS AND NIGHTLIFE: When it comes to nightlife, Las Vegas is king. The city never sleeps, and can keep visitors who want to keep the same hours entertained all night. The Strip hotels offer a wide variety of entertainment. There are nightly production spectaculars, with dancing girls, lavish costumes and sets, and all kinds of specialty acts. Most extravagant are *Jubilee* at the *MGM,* 3645 Las Vegas Blvd. S (739-4111), and *Beyond Belief* at the *Frontier,* 3120 Las Vegas Blvd. S (731-0110). Other notables of this genre are *Lido de Paris* at the *Stardust,* 3000 Las Vegas Blvd. S (732-6111); *Splash* at the *Riviera,* 2901 Las Vegas Blvd. S (734-5110); *Folies Bergère* at the *Tropicana,* 3801 Las Vegas Blvd. S (739-2222); and *City Lites* at the *Flamingo Hilton,* 3555 Las Vegas Blvd. S (733-311).

In the main showrooms of all the other hotels on the Strip, a constant parade of stars perform twice nightly to audiences of 800 to 1,200 people in each hotel, either at the early show, when dinner is available, or later, when drinks are the rule. There's no cover charge but the minimum runs about $10 to $35 per person for dinner shows and $6 to $35 for late shows. You should keep a few things in mind when you are trying to get reservations to these big productions: Houseguests get first priority for many shows, so consider staying at the hotel which has the show you want to see. Always call early in the morning, or better still, go in person. Most hotels do not take show reservations more than two days in advance. The reservation booths open in the morning and stay open till show time, and the earlier you get there the better. If you've been gambling a good deal, ask the pit boss for assistance, and if you haven't you might try tipping the bell captain and hoping for the best.

Often overlooked are the casino lounges, where lesser-known performers (many of whom become better known) perform for just the cost of your drinks.

Favorite nonhotel clubs are: *Victoria's Disco,* 740 S Decatur Blvd. (878-8595); *Botany's,* 1700 E Flamingo Rd. (737-6662); *Tramps,* 4405 W Flamingo Rd. (871-1424). *Top of the Landmark* has dancing, *Landmark Hotel* (733-1110); and the *Silver Dollar Saloon,* 2501 E Charleston Blvd. (382-6921), live country-western music.

Las Vegas presents the best-known burlesque/striptease artists in the world. Tops (or topless, more likely) are: *The Crazy Horse Saloon,* 4034 Paradise Rd. (732-1116); *Palomino Club,* 1848 Las Vegas Blvd. N (642-2984); the *Cabaret,* 4416 Paradise Rd. (733-8666); and *Bogie's,* 4375 Las Vegas Blvd. S (736-0668).

 SINS: Sad to say, Las Vegas is not the US sin capital it once was, but in Nye County — about 40 miles from the Strip — prostitution is legal. Flashily togged women who linger long on any one spot, particularly barstools, are usually likely candidates to satisfy *lustful* urges — for a price. And there are still a number of bartenders and bellboys who live by the motto, "Anything can be arranged." If all you really want to do is look, the floor shows in all the big hotels are well stocked with long legs and full bosoms.

It is considered the height of *avarice* and gauche insensitivity to forget to tip a dealer working for you on your big win. Local protocol dictates that you toss a few largish chips his or her way. Never openly hand over money. This could be considered even worse than ignoring him altogether, and he will not be able to accept the gratuity.

 LOCAL SERVICES: Babysitting – Sandy's Sitter Service, 24-hour service, 953 E Sahara (731-2086)

Business Services – Abacus and Quill, 3355 Spring Mountain Rd. (873-1552); Manpower Temporary Services, 314 Las Vegas Blvd. N (386-2626)

Mechanic – Stiver's Exxon, 1550 W Oakey Blvd. (385-2407)

Wedding Bells Are Always Ringing in Las Vegas – If you are at least 18 (16 with parental consent), and you feel a sudden urge to legally merge, it's easy to tie the knot on the spot. Just apply at the Las Vegas Marriage License Bureau; there's not even a blood test or waiting period. Pay a modest fee, say "I do," and the deed is done. They don't call this place the "Wedding Capital of the World" for nothing. Open round the clock on Fridays and Saturdays; till midnight Sundays through Thursdays. Clark County Courthouse, 3rd and Carson sts. (385-3156).

BEST IN TOWN

CHECKING IN: In Vegas, the hotel's the thing. The Strip (Las Vegas Blvd. South) is a 3-mile stream of hotel-casinos and motels, nearly matched in number — though usually not in quality — by the downtown "Glitter Gulch" area. Competition is fierce among the major hotels and keeps room costs modest and on a par with one another. Expect to pay $95 and up for a double room per night in the expensive range; $40 to $60, moderate; around $20 to $35, inexpensive.

Caesars Palace – The current quality leader, this is the ultimate Las Vegas hotel. Even the most basic of its 1,600 rooms are ornate, while the suites are sumptuous, with large classical statues to make you feel right at home if you've just flown in from ancient Rome. The service is excellent, and the location — midway on the Strip — puts guests right in the middle of the action. It has big-name entertainment, cafés, bars, restaurants, pool, tennis, golf privileges, meeting rooms, shops, and free parking. Reservations are a must during the summer, especially on holiday weekends. 3570 Las Vegas Blvd. S (702 731-7110). Expensive.

MGM Grand Hotel – Rebuilt after a fire in 1980, it is now more spectacular than ever, with an overall Golden Era movie theme. There are 6 fine restaurants, a shopping mall, the Hall of Fame gallery of stars statues, the Ziegfeld Room for production numbers, the Celebrity Room for top-name entertainment, and even a movie theater that presents MGM screen classics. 3,000 rooms. 3645 Las Vegas Blvd. (702 739-4111). Expensive.

Las Vegas Hilton – With 3,100 rooms, it surpasses even the *MGM Grand* for the title of "Biggest in Vegas." The *Hilton* is a small city, with even a "children's hotel" to occupy younger guests while their parents attend to casino business. Off the Strip near the Convention Center, it's not in the middle of the glitter, but neither is it in the center of traffic. With entertainment, café, bars, restaurants, large recreation center with pool, tennis, health club, putting greens and golf privileges, shops, free parking. 3000 Paradise Rd. (702 732-5111). Expensive to moderate.

Golden Nugget – Probably the most glamorous downtown hotel, it combines an overall turn-of-the-century look with a dazzling decor of marble, brass, and crystal in its casino, entertainment rooms, and restaurants. 129 E Fremont St. (702 385-7111). Expensive to moderate.

Sahara Hotel – First stop on the Strip, and notable for its quietly elegant decor and traditional sense of taste. This friendly sophistication characterized Las Vegas a long time ago but exists in fewer hotels each year. Here the service is personalized and excellent. Has star entertainment, café, bar, pools, health club, meeting rooms, shops. 1,000 rooms. 2535 Las Vegas Blvd. S (702 737-2111). Moderate.

Aladdin Hotel – The decorating scheme at this 1,000-room hotel features a *Thousand and One Arabian Nights* atmosphere. A while ago Aladdin rubbed his lamp, and out came upgraded facilities and a 7,500-seat theater. Also has cafés, bars, restaurants, pools, meeting rooms, shops, tennis, free in-room movies. 3667 Las Vegas Blvd. S (702 736-0111). Moderate.

Union Plaza – A large (1,020-room) hotel, with the most complete facilities downtown, at the entranceway to the downtown "Glitter Gulch" action. Facilities include a pool, tennis courts, café, bar, restaurant, shops, meeting rooms, and casino. 1 Main St. (702 386-2110). Moderate.

Mint Hotel – A Del Webb property, this modern 300-room high-rise combines a touch of class with good service amidst a dark and relaxing decor. The casino and dining areas have been expanded, and it also has a pool and an amusement arcade for children, parking, and casino. 100 E Fremont St. (702 385-7440). Moderate to inexpensive.

Circus Circus Hotel – Of all the hotels on the Strip, the only one really dedicated to family entertainment (at family prices). With a full-scale circus operating complete with sideshows, there's something for everyone. Lots for the children — carousel, clown-shaped swimming pool; for the adults, cafés, bars, meeting rooms, health club, sauna. 1,500 rooms. 2880 Las Vegas Blvd. S (702 734-0410). Inexpensive.

Motel 6 – Good clean accommodations at the best prices in town. The bargain is worthwhile since hotel-motel rooms get little use in Las Vegas, and most of the time you're in them, you're asleep. Also, you get a pool for your money. 758 rooms. 196 E Tropicana (702 736-4904). Inexpensive.

Mini Price Motor Inn – Just as it says, mini prices, and just off the Strip. 2550 S Rancho (702 876-2410). Inexpensive.

EATING OUT: Probably the only sure bet in Vegas is the food. Between hotels, restaurants, and casinos there's plenty to eat, and the food is much better than standard hotel or nightclub fare. From the Continental cuisine of the hotels' main restaurants to "all-you-can-eat" buffets, Las Vegas features quantity and quality. Though the offerings are basically American — steaks and seafood — there are a number of good ethnic restaurants. So eat up, and take advantage of the bargains in the casinos that are subsidized by gambling revenues; you're probably paying for them anyway. Our restaurant selections range in price from $55 or more for a dinner for two in the expensive range; $30 to $45 in the moderate range; and $20 or less, inexpensive. Prices do not include drinks, wine, or tips.

Palace Court – Considered the ultimate in dining grace in Las Vegas. Candelabra, vermeil flatware, and handblown crystal are the accouterments of an unforgettable experience. Sommeliers pour wine from the hotel's distinguished wine cellar. Dinner nightly. Reservations advised. Major credit cards. 3570 Las Vegas Blvd. S (731-7110). Expensive.

Monte Carlo Room – Decorated in red velvet and crystal, this small hideaway in the *Desert Inn Hotel* has an almost homey atmosphere (though the home would have to belong to the Vanderbilts). Specialties include steak marchand de vin and veal dornandig, and the service is first rate. Open nightly. Reservations recommended. Major credit cards. 3145 Las Vegas Blvd. S (733-4444). Expensive.

Claudine's – This posh room is a welcome relief from the gaudy atmosphere of the *Holiday Casino's Riverboat.* Specialties such as escargots Bourguignonne with Pernod and hazelnut butter, and oysters Florentine precede the excellent charcoal-broiled steaks. Open nightly. Reservations suggested. Major credit cards. 3740 Las Vegas Blvd., S. (369-5000). Expensive.

Aristocrat – A charming 80-seat restaurant featuring Continental cuisine in the Rancho Circle area. Open daily. Reservations advised. Major credit cards. 850 S Rancho Dr. (870-1977). Expensive.

André's – A French restaurant in an old home, this is a favorite of the crowd in the downtown area. Open daily. Reservations advised. Major credit cards. 401 S 6th St. (385-5016). Expensive.

Liberace's Tivoli Gardens – Formerly the antique shop owned by the performer, the restaurant was built to his exacting specifications. Dinners are served on exquisite china and on tables valued at $30,000. Music nightly, naturally, and lots of celebrities in attendance. Open daily. Reservations advised. Major credit cards. 1775 E Tropicana (739-8762). Expensive.

House of Lords – The *Sahara Hotel's* try at a ritzy British pub serves fine steaks and seafoods. Best are sole, trout, and salmon, flown in from the Coast, and tournedos of beef if you really want to be swept away — thick chunks of filet mignon in a delicate hollandaise sauce. Open nightly. Reservations advised. Major credit cards. 2535 Las Vegas Blvd. S (735-2111). Expensive.

Hugo's Cellar – Should you arrive in Las Vegas on a Friday, head here for a bountiful New England clambake. Boiled lobster, steamed clams, oysters Rockefeller, and corn on the cob are served on a giant platter along with your choice of salad, hot bread, steamed vegetables, and dessert. Dinner nightly. Reservations advised. Major credit cards. In the *Four Queens* hotel. 202 E Fremont St. (385-4011). Expensive to moderate.

Don the Beachcomber – Another *Sahara Hotel* restaurant; Polynesian cuisine amid tropical surroundings — real giant palms, flowing brook, and mellow background music. For a variety of flavors, try the High Chief Special — assorted appetizers including fried shrimp, egg roll and crab puff, main dishes of Cantonese pork, chicken with almonds, beef soya, with fried rice. Open nightly. Reservations advised. Major credit cards. 2535 Las Vegas Blvd. S (735-2111). Moderate.

Alpine Village Inn – Best are the portions of good Swiss and German food — the wurst plates of all varieties, and the huge kettles of thick, dark German chicken soup that are meant for two but could actually feed the entire Swiss Family Robinson. Restaurant also features a Ratskeller with a piano player and lots of German beers. Open nightly. Reservations suggested. Major credit cards. 3003 Paradise Rd. (734-6888). Moderate.

Rafters – A San Francisco–style restaurant with some of the best seafood in town. Joe Thompson, a native of the Golden Gate city, has shipments flown in daily from Fisherman's Wharf. Try the splendid bouillabaisse, which comes topped with a whole soft-shell crab. Dinner nightly. Reservations recommended. Major credit cards. 1350 E Tropicana (739-9463). Moderate.

Battista's Hole in the Wall – Plentiful Italian pastas for dinner, helped along by all the wine you can drink, and an occasional Italian aria by Battista himself, to create the proper mood. Closed Sundays. Reservations advised. Major credit cards. 4041 Audrie, across from the *MGM Grand* (732-1424). Moderate.

LimeLight – A lively family-run Italian establishment, serving such specialties as chicken Florentine, veal scalloppine marsala with demi-glaze, and sea bass poached with chablis, leeks, and cream. Lunch, weekdays only; dinner, nightly. Major credit cards. 2340 E Tropicana (739-1410). Moderate.

The Bootlegger – Cozy, nestled in a quiet area about 3 miles from the Strip and specializing in Italian dishes. The sunken pit lounge area is a good place to relax after a day at the casinos. Closed Mondays. Reservations accepted. Major credit cards. 5025 S Eastern Ave. (736-4939). Moderate.

Chateau Vegas – Continental cuisine in elegant surroundings, backed up by soft music and a harpist. Best are the Italian veal and any of the steaks. Open daily. Reservations suggested. Major credit cards. 565 Desert Inn Rd. (733-8282). Moderate.

Golden Steer – In a town that has to revise the phone books twice a year just to keep up with the comings and goings of things, 17 years in the same place attest to a strong tradition. The decor is luxurious western and the offerings top-notch, from the steaks (try the Diamond Lil prime ribs) to the toasted ravioli, and the extensive wine list. If you give a day's notice, you can have a special delicacy: pheasant, goose, quail, chukar (partridge), or roast suckling pig. Open daily. Reservations advised. Major credit cards. 308 W Sahara Ave. (384-4470). Moderate.

Waldemar's – In a setting reminiscent of a German grotto, chef Waldemar prepares dishes from an open-spit roaster. Also highly recommended are the goulash, beef shashlik, and, for dessert, wife Janina's homemade plum cake, heaped with freshly whipped cream. Open daily for lunch and dinner. Reservations suggested. Major credit cards. 2202 W Charleston (386-1995). Moderate.

Starboard Tack – For years, a local favorite. Now a sister restaurant, the *Port Tack,* also offers romance and good food in a larger setting with an attractive sunken fireplace. Open 24 hours. Reservations recommended. Major credit cards. *Starboard,* 2601 Atlantic St. (457-8794); *Port,* 3190 W Sahara Ave. (873-3345). Moderate.

State Street – This late-night restaurant, with an atmosphere reminiscent of Chicago in the 1930s, is run by Gianni Russo, who performed in the film *The Godfather.* Delicious Italian food is served until dawn. Open daily. Reservations advised. Major credit cards. 2570 State St. (733-0225). Moderate.

Viva Zapata – A cut above most Mexican places in price, but worth the difference. The atmosphere is modern and informal, decorated with baskets, fresh flowers, and posters. The food is excellent, and the flautas (tortillas stuffed with beef, vegetables, and cheese, and sautéed with avocado sauce) are really something special. Open daily. Reservations advised. Major credit cards. 4972 S Maryland Pkwy. (736-6630) and 3540 W Sahara (873-7228). Moderate.

Library Buttery and Pub – The atmosphere is a combination of an expansive library and a traditional English pub. Extensive menu has a wide range of entrées, but best are chicken Angelo (in tomato sauce with baby onions) and veal piccante. Open 24 hours. Reservations suggested. Major credit cards. 200 W Sahara Ave. (384-5200). Moderate.

Carlos Murphy's Irish Mexican Café – Sounds strange, but with a touch of American nostalgia and multitudes of memorabilia, this warmly decorated café offers specialties such as quiche, crêpes, Irish stew, and Mexican dishes. Open daily. No reservations. Major credit cards. 4770 S Maryland Pkwy. (798-5541). Moderate.

El Burrito Café – This small authentic Mexican restaurant seats only 30, but the quality of the food would keep it full if it were twice as big. Offers several fine combination plates. The chicharrones, burritos stuffed with fried pork bits, are extra special. Open daily. Reservations advised. No credit cards. 1919 E Fremont St. (387-9246). Inexpensive.

Golden Wok – This Chinese restaurant has been so successful that it now has a second location. Open daily. 4760 S Eastern (456-1868); 504 S Decatur (878-1596). Inexpensive.

Vineyard – On the exterior of the Boulevard, one of Las Vegas's three enclosed shopping malls, this quaint Italian eatery offers a fine antipasto salad bar and specialties such as chicken cacciatore and veal cutlet Parmigiana. Open daily. Reservations for six or more. Major credit cards. 3630 S Maryland Pkwy. (731-1606). Inexpensive.

Buffets – If all-you-can-eat sounds good to you, you can spend all your time in Las Vegas doing just that. Virtually every Strip hotel and most of the downtown hotels have buffet lunches and dinners, where, for a couple of dollars, you can have as much as you can handle from an array of salads, fish, chicken, pasta, occasionally roast beef, and dessert. Best bets are the *Golden Nugget,* 129 E Fremont St. (385-7111); *Caesars Palace*'s *Palatium,* 3570 Las Vegas Blvd. S. (731-7110); the *Riviera,* 2901 Las Vegas Blvd. S (734-5110); the *Sahara,* 2535 Las Vegas Blvd. S (737-2111); *Holiday Casino,* 3475 Las Vegas Blvd. S (732-2411); the *Fremont,* 2nd and Fremont sts. (385-3232).

For something really special, try the weekend Champagne Brunch at *Caesars Palace* — a feast for the eyes as well as the tastebuds with its beautifully arranged selections of freshly baked pastries, fresh melons, eggs, bacon, ham, sausage, and all the champagne you can drink. 3570 Las Vegas Blvd. S (731-7110). Inexpensive.

LOS ANGELES

Whatever you have heard — or think you know — about Los Angeles is probably wrong. Or misleading. Or hyperbole. This is a city that leads the league in misconceptions. To set the record straight on a few points:

- Despite the palm trees, Los Angeles is not a tropical city.

- Although Los Angeles does have a harbor, the city is not on the Pacific; it is 20 miles inland.

- One cannot swim comfortably in the Pacific during the winter, when cold Alaskan currents often drop the water temperature into the 50s.

- Debilitating smog is rare, usually occurs in summer, and is often confined to a small area.

- It is possible to visit Los Angeles happily without spending all one's time driving a car.

- The arts — music, theater, dance — can be readily enjoyed and are actually flourishing.

- The city has more people than swimming pools.

- Sunglasses are not issued to residents at birth.

Los Angeles, like it or not, is a city of dreams, myths, and misunderstandings. It is our nation's Olympus, where certain of our gods live and cavort and where both good and bad are inflated to larger-than-life proportions. Rarely have a city's virtues, excesses, shortcomings, and sins been exaggerated with such glee and small regard for current fact. Yes, certainly there is glitter and foolishness and often much about which to chuckle. Yes, admittedly there are the curses of occasionally snarled traffic, torrential rains, and eye-tearing smog.

But much of the rest can be sublime.

To begin with, the 3 million or so people who live in LA (8 million in the metropolitan area; it's become the second largest city in the country) care little about their city's skewed — and skewered — reputation. They are there, most of them, not for the glitz and the hijinks but for the quality of life.

There is no doubt that Los Angeles is one of the most beautifully situated and climate-blessed of the world's major cities. Because of the mile-high San Gabriel Mountains that skirt Los Angeles on the north and the Santa Monica Mountains that bisect it, the city enjoys magnificent vistas and offers the unusual opportunity for secluded hillside living in the midst of a vast metropolis. Such lofty ranges also give rise to the accurate statement that this is one of the few places on the globe where it is possible in the same day to both ski and surf (though you'd better wear a wetsuit while surfing to avoid freezing).

On the other hand, many visitors are stunned to learn that Los Angeles isn't always favored with blue skies and perpetual sunshine. Southern California is actually an area of weather extremes. Late summer and early fall are usually the hottest times of year, when the dust-dry Santa Ana winds blow out of the nearby eastern desert to elevate temperatures into the 90s — and sometimes 100s — and escalate temperaments into the danger zone. This is when, wrote LA crime novelist Raymond Chandler, wives finger the sharp edges of knives and study the contour of their husbands' necks. Oddly enough, spring and early summer can bring the most miserable weather of the year — chill fog and dull, overcast skies. Winter is the rainy season and can be glorious or awful — and normally is both, in spurts — depending on the weather patterns churning out of the Pacific. Rainfalls can be quick and violent and give way to clear warm days and cool nights.

Despite these vicissitudes, it is virtually inevitable that New Year's Day will dawn bright and sunny, with 80° temperatures, and that the achingly beautiful panoramas seen by the tens of millions watching the Rose Bowl game on television will only reinforce the LA legend.

Los Angeles traces its origins to a dusty little settlement founded in 1781 by the Spanish colonial governor, who gave it the monumental name of El Pueblo de Nuestra Senora la Reina de los Angeles de Porciuncula. By 1850, after California was ceded to the United States as a result of the Mexican-American War, it had a population of a mere 1,610, and at the turn of the century, it was the home of only a few more than 100,000 residents. Still largely citrus groves and bean fields, it retained much of the character of its Spanish and Mexican roots — and remained that way until the massive American migration to the West Coast began in the 1920s. California was the country's last frontier, a chance to start a new life and make one's fortune, and the city, along with the state, boomed. In the 1930s, the area attracted those rendered homeless and near hopeless by the Great Depression; in the 1940s, servicemen on their way home from World War II stopped here to put the past behind them. The 1950s and 1960s saw LA develop into a center for new industries — the technological and aerospace industries of the future.

In spite of such dynamic growth (or perhaps because of it), Los Angeles continued to derive its perceived civic persona from the sunny weather, from a beach culture that embraced only a tiny fraction of the population, and from its association with the sometimes bizarre world of the motion picture industry. Almost coincidentally, it had also begun to develop in the 1920s, with the arrival of the early movie moguls and their studios from New York, and later came to include the television and music businesses as well. The city found it difficult to be taken seriously. To much of the rest of the nation, Los Angeles was "the Coast," a place dismissed laughingly and almost by rote as provincial and self-absorbed.

Meanwhile, however, things were rapidly changing in the City of the Angels. Spearheaded by local leaders frustrated by the lopsided, frivolous image of their city, Los Angeles began an effort to shed its second-class mantle. The archaic ordinance that limited downtown buildings to the height of City Hall (presumably for earthquake protection) was scrapped, and a

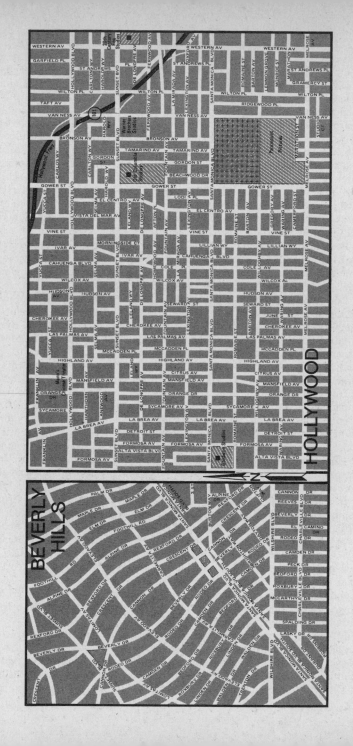

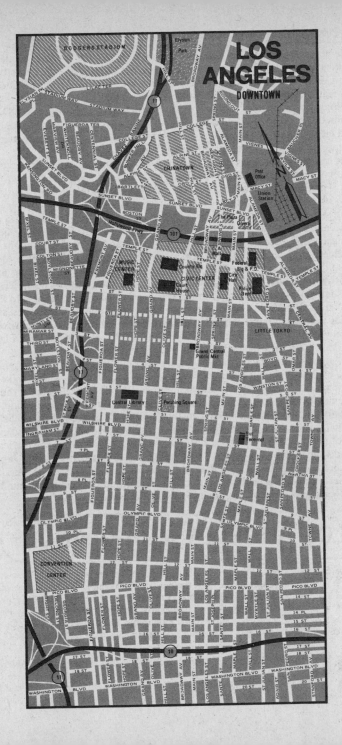

skyline began to rise. Major league sports arrived in 1958 with the Dodgers from Brooklyn, followed by professional teams in the top rank of basketball, football, and hockey. Finally, in 1964, the city proudly opened the ambitious, multitheater complex called the Music Center.

No longer was Los Angeles referred to by such amusing epithets as "Double Dubuque." In the last two decades LA has grown up to become a sophisticated city that boasts some of the finest hotels, restaurants, shopping, nightlife, museums, and cultural events in the nation.

Over the years, Los Angeles has also become a favorite vacation destination and now welcomes more than 41 million visitors annually from all over the world. They are lured to LA, not only by its salubrious weather and the chance of glimpsing a movie or TV personality, but also by its theaters offering stage productions, symphony orchestras, opera and light opera companies, dance companies, museums, and scores of top professional and college sporting events. Specific areas of Los Angeles have become attractions in themselves: Hollywood and its Mann's Chinese Theater, with cement footprints and handprints of the stars; Beverly Hills and its expensive shops and Rolls-Royce lifestyle; Westwood, with its footloose university town ambience; the casual but wealthy beach communities stretching from Malibu to the Palos Verdes Peninsula. In addition, the more traditional tourist sites and activities continue to draw many visitors to Los Angeles and its environs — Disneyland, Universal Studios, Movieland, Knott's Berry Farm, Six Flags Magic Mountain, Marineland, the *Queen Mary,* and so on.

Los Angeles still has its critics, to be sure. The city's vast size — 465 square miles, a bit less than half of the *entire state* of Rhode Island — may make it seem uncomfortably spread out and sometimes difficult to negotiate for those accustomed to more compact and centralized places. But most people find LA a pleasant and easy city in which to live and to visit. Beneath the official municipal veneer, away from the sunshine and removed from the artificial glitter of show biz, Los Angeles has an essentially solid and All-American soul. Add the fascination of the city's ethnic mix — Mexican, Chinese, Japanese, Korean, and Thai — as well as its environmental meld of sea, mountain, and desert, and Los Angeles emerges from its shroud of fable to assume its logical position as one of the great cities of the world.

LOS ANGELES AT-A-GLANCE

SEEING THE CITY: There are at least three great places to go for a fantastic view of Los Angeles. The most famous is Mulholland Drive, a twisting road that winds through the Hollywood Hills. Another is the top of Mt. Olympus, in Laurel Canyon, near Sunset Boulevard. The 34-story, 464-foot City Hall Tower has a sweeping view of downtown, the mountains, and the Pacific Ocean. Open daily. Free. City Hall East, near south end of Los Angeles Mall (485-2891).

SPECIAL PLACES: A walk along Hollywood Boulevard from Vine Street to Highland Avenue will delight the heart of anyone who loves the era of those great movies that made Hollywood famous. However, Hollywood is no longer the physical center of film production, and its glamour is, sadly, long gone. X-rated movies now seem to outnumber the kind of films that made the area world-renowned. Keep in mind that most residents would never contemplate walking down Hollywood Boulevard after dark. During the daytime, however, most Hollywood streets are crowded, bustling, and safe. There is a lot to enjoy here, much of it for little or no cost.

OLD HOLLYWOOD: MEMORIES AND EMPTY BUILDINGS

Mann's Chinese Theater – Known to movie fans around the world as Grauman's Chinese Theater, this is probably the most visited site in Hollywood. If you wander down Hollywood Boulevard toward Highland Avenue looking for the Grauman's sign, you'll never find it, though. Several years ago, Ted Mann took the theater over and added it to his movie chain. As the new proprietor, he felt within his rights to take down the sign that had made Syd Grauman famous and replace it with his own. But he caused considerable controversy. The Chinese Theater forecourt is world-famous for its celebrity footprints and handprints immortalized in cement. If you join the crowd of visitors outside the box office, you'll probably find your favorite star of the 1920s and 30s. If you buy a ticket to get in, you'll be treated to one of the world's most impressive and elaborate movie palaces. The ornate carvings, the very high, decorative ceiling, the traditionally plush seats, the heavy curtains that *whoosh* closed when the film ends, and the enormous screen itself are all part of a Hollywood that no longer exists. The Chinese Theater is one of those movie theaters that gives children some idea of what parents mean when they talk about how moviegoing has changed since their own childhood. 6925 Hollywood Blvd. (464-8111).

Hollywood Wax Museum – If the Chinese Theater makes you nostalgic for the faces belonging to the disembodied prints, stop in at the Hollywood Wax Museum. If you've been leery of wax museums ever since you watched Vincent Price coat his victims in wax in the famous movie *House of Wax,* we hasten to reassure you that there is no such hanky-panky going on in the back rooms here. Marilyn Monroe, Clark Gable and Jean Harlow, Paul Newman, Gary Cooper, Barbra Streisand, Raquel Welch, Sylvester Stallone as Rambo, and many more fill the star-studded display cases. There's also a horror chamber, a re-creation of *The Last Supper,* and a documentary about the history of the Academy Awards with film clips from winners like *Gone With the Wind* and *Mary Poppins.* Open daily. Admission charge; children under 6 free. 6767 Hollywood Blvd. (462-8860).

Hollywood Studio Museum   If nostalgia is what you seek, you can also find it at the largest single historical movie artifact in existence. Called the DeMille Barn, it was designated a California Cultural Landmark in 1956 and presently houses the Hollywood Studio Museum. Cecil B. DeMille used this structure, a rented horse barn, as a studio when he made the first feature — *The Squawman* — ever shot in the town of Hollywood. Inside today are a replica of DeMille's office and stills from silent motion pictures. The outside of the building is interesting, too: When it was on the back lot of Paramount Studios, it often was used in Westerns and for many years was seen as the railroad station in the *Bonanza* TV series. Closed Sundays and Mondays. Admission charge. 2100 N Highland (213 856-6000).

Paramount Pictures – At one time, RKO studios adjoined the Paramount lot. After RKO folded in 1956, its studio became the home of television's Desilu Productions, which in turn sold its property to next-door Paramount. Close to the Bronson Avenue intersection with Melrose is the famous Paramount Gate, the highly decorative studio entrance that many people will remember from the film *Sunset Boulevard.* The Gower Street side of today's Paramount was the old front entrance to RKO. At what used to be 780 Gower Street, you will now find simply an unimpressive back door to Paramount, painted in that dull, flat beige many studios use to protect their exterior walls. The door no longer bears its old marquee with distinctive Art Deco neon letters spelling out RKO, the numbers have been torn from the front steps, and the Art Deco front doors are gone. RKO is just a memory now. Paramount extends from Melrose Ave. on the south to Gower St. on the west, Van Ness Ave. on the east, and Willoughby Ave. on the north (468-5000).

Gower Street – This was once the center for so many small film studios that it became known in the film business as Gower Gulch. It was also nicknamed Poverty Row because so many of its independent producers were perpetually strapped for production money. Poverty Row's most famous studio was Columbia Pictures, which ultimately grew healthy enough to acquire most of the smaller parcels of studio real estate in the neighborhood. Columbia's old studios still stand at Gower Street and Sunset Boulevard, although Columbia moved out several years ago. It found a new home in Burbank at the Warner Brothers Studio, which was then renamed The Burbank Studios (TBS). The two film companies operate TBS as a rental facility for film and TV production today. When Columbia vacated its Hollywood property, some of its sound stages were used for a time as indoor tennis courts. Today they have become film studios once more, available for rent to independent production companies.

Warner Brothers – In the late 1920s, when Warner's was introducing "talkies" to America, its pictures were filmed here. It was also the home of Warner's radio station at the time, KFWB. Today the old studio is the headquarters for KTLA-TV and KMPC radio. The stately southern mansion that served as Warner's administration building still stands on Sunset Boulevard. Sunset Blvd. and Van Ness Ave.

Samuel Goldwyn Studios – Originally built by Mary Pickford and Douglas Fairbanks, the old Samuel Goldwyn studios became United Artists in 1919, when Pickford and Fairbanks were joined by Charlie Chaplin and D. W. Griffith. In 1980 Warner Brothers purchased the lot as a site for its television production activities. Santa Monica Blvd. and Formosa Ave., West Hollywood.

Selznick Studios – Nothing can compare with the old Selznick studios, where David O. Selznick produced *Gone With the Wind, Rebecca,* and *Intermezzo.* It was built by silent film director Thomas Ince, a Southerner who wanted his administration building to look like a typical Georgia mansion. Millions of filmgoers have seen Ince's mansion as the opening logo of the Selznick film classics. The once-beautiful Selznick studio is now a rundown rental facility, but it still retains some of its old majesty. If you imagine the gardens restored to their original condition and the buildings freshly painted, it's possible to get a feel for how it used to be. It was here that Selznick filmed the burning of Atlanta in *Gone With the Wind.* He had to film it before the other scenes so that the back lot could be cleared of sets and props to make room for other production activities. Jefferson and Ince blvds., Culver City.

Hollywood Museum – Among the exhibitions here that preserve and glorify the Golden Age of the movies are costumes, old cameras and projectors, wardrobe sketches, miniatures used as props in horror films, and a chariot used by Cecil B. DeMille in four pictures. Open daily. Admission charge. 7051 Hollywood Blvd. (213 465-3773).

Max Factor Beauty Museum – The only museum in the world devoted to makeup is housed in the famous Max Factor Building, just off Hollywood Boulevard, where (since the 1940s) the stars came to have their faces painted, to have their hair styled, and to be fitted for wigs or toupees. The displays document the history of the company, which is synonymous with the history of makeup in film. One of the most unusual is a collection of special head blocks of famous stars, used to create wigs and toupees without the actors and actresses having to spend hours being fitted and styled. Open weekdays. Free. 1666 N Highland Ave. (213 856-6000).

Hollywood Bowl Museum – Celebrating some 60 years of the bowl through pictures and artifacts, this collection includes costumes from early ballet productions and mementos of some of the 150 world-famous conductors who have led the Los Angeles

Philharmonic Orchestra in performances here. Open Wednesdays through Saturdays. Free. 2301 N Highland Ave. (213 850-2059).

"HOLLYWOOD": ALIVE AND WELL

"Hollywood," as we refer to the film business, is no longer geographically located in the district bearing that name. If your nostalgic walking tour of Old Hollywood has made you curious about modern production methods, we suggest a tour of one of the following Los Angeles studios:

Universal Studios – The combination movie studio tour and theme park has been attracting more than 3 million people a year. In 1915, Universal Pictures established a mammoth studio on 420 acres of what was then a chicken farm. Land in the eastern part of the San Fernando Valley was pretty cheap, and Universal's founder, Carl Laemmle, was smart enough to buy a lot of it. As a result, the modern Universal, a division of MCA, found itself with more than enough room to make movies and television shows, as well as build a theme park. The Universal Studio tours, launched in 1964, are conducted on trams, complete with guides, and take about 175 people per tour. Some of the highlights include a special stunt show, a working quicksand pit, the *Battle of Galactica,* where you're captured by Cylons, a look at some of the 34 sound stages and other production facilities, a special-effects demonstration, a burning house, and a collapsing bridge. You'll also see the house used in Alfred Hitchcock's *Psycho,* a street from *The Sting,* the colonial street from *Airport 77,* a flash flood, a runaway train, the parting of the Red Sea, an attack on the tour tram by the 24-foot "shark" from *Jaws,* a waterfall, and the Doomed Glacier Expedition, where you get to plunge down an Alpine avalanche. If you're ready for all that, you can visit Universal Studios any day of the week. Admission charge; children under three free. Hollywood Fwy. to Lankershim exit, Universal City (818 508-9600).

The Burbank Studios – If you want something a little lower key than the Universal extravaganza, try The Burbank Studios. It's now the home of Warner Brothers and Columbia Pictures as well as many independent production companies. Nothing on the tour is staged, so visitors watch whatever is happening on that particular day. Not only do you get to see some actual shooting whenever possible, you also see a lot of behind-the-scenes action — scenery construction, sound recording, and prop departments. Since TBS tours are limited to 12 people (with children under 10 not permitted), reservations are required a week in advance.. Open weekdays. Admission charge. 4000 Warner Blvd. (818 954-1744).

NBC Television Studios – Another traditional behind-the-scenes tour, NBC offers you the chance to see television studios, set construction, makeup and wardrobe departments, and to participate in some of the magic of TV in the new Sound and Special Effects Center. Tours are escorted by NBC pages, who take you, when possible, to such sets as Johnny Carson's *Tonight* show. There are 15 people on each tour, which takes about 1¼ hours. Open daily except Easter, Thanksgiving, Christmas, and New Year's Day. Admission charge. 3000 W Alameda Ave., Burbank (818 840-3537).

20th Century–Fox – If you're interested in taking a peek at a working film studio other than on an official tour, you will be happy to know you can enter the 20th Century–Fox lot from Motor Avenue in Hollywood and drive the entire length of the cobblestone street from *Hello, Dolly!* before reaching the security gate. (Carol Channing will not be there to sing for you, though.) The street, built for the 1969 musical, is now being used for filming TV programs and commercials. The facades of the various buildings resemble New York in the 1890s, including the New York Public Library. It's one of the most interesting film studio sets in town, and it's free. Open daily. Pico Blvd. and Motor Ave., just west of Beverly Hills.

HollywoodOn Location** – You don't have to visit the studios to see the stars. Hollywood**On Location**publishes a daily list of where and when current TV series, movies, and videos are filming in and near LA. It's available weekdays at 9:30 AM. A fee covers the list (which includes times and street address), maps pinpointing locations, and everyone in the car. 8644 Wilshire Blvd., Beverly Hills (659-9165).

Beverly Hills – After a hard day on the lot, movie stars return to their Beverly Hills mansions for a good night's sleep. Even during the sunshiny daylight hours, Beverly Hills is remarkably tranquil, with nary a person walking on the residential streets. Without a doubt the most affluent and elegant suburb in Southern California, Beverly Hills is a must-see. If you want to window-shop or purchase high fashion clothing or leather, stroll along Rodeo Drive between Santa Monica and Wilshire boulevards. If you want to make sure you don't succumb to an impulse to buy anything, go on Sunday, when the stores are closed. Gray Line offers van and limousine tours (481-2121).

DOWNTOWN LOS ANGELES

To see a Los Angeles that most people don't know about, take a walking tour downtown.

The Plaza – If you ever wondered what the place looked like before shopping centers were created, step across the Plaza and marvel. The Plaza is a wide square, the scene of monthly fiestas. The Old Plaza Church, built by a captured pirate in 1818, has a curious financial history: It was partially paid for by the sale of seven barrels of brandy. The city's first firehouse is here, too. For a complete repertory of colorful local anecdotes, take a narrated walking tour of the Plaza. For information, contact El Pueblo de los Angeles State Historical Park on the Plaza. 845 N Alameda St. (628-1274).

Olvera Street – Music from the Plaza fiesta spills into Olvera Street, a block-long pedestrian alley filled with colorful Mexican shops, restaurants, and spicy food stalls. The oldest house in Los Angeles is here — the 1818 Avila house, made of adobe. The first brick house is also here, but now it's a restaurant.

Los Angeles Civic Center and Mall – An unusually quiet, well-landscaped city mall, with tropical plants, gentle splashing fountains, and sculpture half hidden among the lush greenery. It's the first mall of shops and restaurants to be built on City Hall property (at Main and Los Angeles sts.). The Triforium tower of glass cylinders occasionally flashes brightly colored lights in time to music — a symphony of light and sound composed and conducted by a computer. For one of the best views of the city, make sure you get to the top of City Hall Tower at the south end of the mall. Open daily. Free (485-2891).

Third and Broadway – Several places in this area are worth noting. First is the skylit, 5-story indoor court of the Bradbury Building, now a registered historic landmark. You can ride an old hydraulic elevator to the top balcony and walk down a magnificent staircase guaranteed to evoke visions of bygone splendors. Across the corner from the Bradbury Building is the Million Dollar Theater — Syd Grauman's first; it's currently a Spanish-language picture palace inside but it has a fascinating exterior. Just south of the theater is the entrance to the Grand Central Public Market, a conglomerate of stalls selling food from all over the world.

Little Tokyo – This is the social, economic, cultural, and religious center of the largest Japanese-American community in the US. There's a specialty shopping center here as well as many restaurants. First and San Pedro sts. (620-8861).

Central Library – To catch your breath, get out of the heat, or read for a while, walk to the Central Library, considered to be one of the first modern buildings in LA (built in 1926). Inside, in addition to the books, magazines, and periodicals, you'll find splendid murals of California history by Dean Cornwall. Closed Sundays and holidays. Free. 630 W 5th St. (612-3200).

Music Center – The best time to visit the Music Center is during a concert or performance, but it's worth seeing anytime. The Ahmanson Theater stages classical dramas, comedies, and international premieres and is also the base for a branch of the

Center Theatre Group, a well-respected professional repertory company. The Mark Taper Forum, a theater in the round, houses the branch of the Center Theatre Group that specializes in experimental material. The Dorothy Chandler Pavilion, a 3,200-seat auditorium trimmed in gold and red velvet, is home to the Los Angeles Philharmonic. The orchestra season runs from October to May; other musical and dance groups, including the Joffrey Ballet, perform the rest of the year. You can take a guided tour of the theaters. First and Grand sts. (972-7211).

Chinatown – Chinatown has the usual assortment of restaurants, vegetable stores, and weird little shops selling ivory chess sets and acupuncture charts. The 900 block of N Broadway.

Farmers Market – "Eat your liver." No, we're not quoting your mother, we're quoting Yossarian, the hero of *Catch-22* (book by Joseph Heller, movie by Mike Nichols). Yossarian used to say "eat your liver" all the time, and at the Farmers Market you can do just that. You can also eat anything else within the realm of gastronomic imagination. You'll find 150 stalls of American, Mexican, Italian, Chinese, and vegetarian food, and any number of exquisite bakeries and fruit and candy shops. If you don't like to eat standing up, there are tables set among the aisles of this indoor, covered market. It's a great place to be hungry. Open daily. 6333 W 3rd St. and Fairfax (933-9211).

Griffith Park – If you thought Texas had the biggest of everything, you're mistaken. This is the largest municipal park in the country. Griffith has three golf courses, a wilderness area and bird sanctuary, tennis courts, three miniature railroads, a carousel, pony rides, and picnic areas within its 4,043 acres. Not only that — this is where you'll find the famous Los Angeles Zoo, home to 2,500 mammals, birds, and reptiles. Open daily except Christmas. Admission charge; children under 5 free. 5333 Zoo Dr. (666-4090). If you like railroads, you'll love Travel Town, a unique outdoor museum of old railroad engines, cars, railroad equipment, and fire trucks. The Griffith Observatory (2800 E Observatory Rd.; 664-1191) near Mt. Hollywood houses a 500-seat planetarium theater, a twin-refracting telescope, and the Hall of Science. Park facilities are open daily (665-5188).

Six Flags Magic Mountain – A 260-acre family theme park, featuring more than 100 rides, shows, and other attractions, this is the new home of Bugs Bunny and his Looney Tunes friends in Bugs Bunny World. In addition to the mighty Colossus (a huge, wooden roller coaster) and the spine-tingling Revolution (a 360° vertical loop coaster), there's also the challenge of a whitewater rafting experience, a ride that simulates Olympic bobsledding, and a magic show run by the Wily Rabbit. The dolphin show and a children's village and petting zoo are also worthwhile. 25 minutes north of Hollywood on the Golden State Fwy., Magic Mountain exit in Valencia (818 367-2271).

Ports o' Call Village – Some 59 specialty shops here feature merchandise from around the world. You can relax by taking a boat or helicopter tour of Los Angeles Harbor and dining in your choice of 25 restaurants and snack shops. Open daily. Free. Berths 76-79 at the foot of the Harbor Fwy. in San Pedro (831-0287).

Redondo Beach Marina – A delightful waterfront recreation showplace, the marina offers a pier restaurant extending over the ocean, boat cruises, and sportfishing. Open daily. Free. 181 N Harbor Dr., Redondo Beach. Take the Harbor Fwy. to the Torrance Blvd. exit and proceed west to the ocean (374-3481).

Los Angeles County Museum of Art – There are special exhibits in the Frances and Armand Hammer wing, and a dazzling permanent collection in the Ahmanson Gallery, which includes pre-Columbian art, tapestries, and paintings from the 18th century to today. The Leo S. Bing Theater offers special films and concerts. Closed Mondays. Admission charge. 5905 Wilshire Blvd. (937-2590).

Forest Lawn Memorial Park – A major tourist attraction, Forest Lawn is a huge cemetery calling itself a memorial park, which advertises on huge billboards overlooking the freeways. On the grounds you'll find a stained glass window depicting *The Last Supper* and spectacular artwork of the crucifixion and the resurrection. Forest Lawn is the home of the largest religious painting in the world, Jan Styka's 195-by-45-foot *The Crucifixion.* Open daily. Free. 1712 S Glendale Ave., Glendale (818 241-4151).

Marineland – Dolphins, killer whales, and acrobatic sea lions perform at this world-famous oceanarium. Snorkels, masks, swimsuits, wetsuits — even towels and hair dryers — are available for those who wish to swim in the world's only swim-through aquarium. Large windows allow other visitors to watch the swimmers. Exhibitions include walruses, waterfowl, and an amazing assortment of fish. Open daily, April through September; October through March, open Mondays and Tuesdays for guided tours only. Admission charge. San Diego Freeway south to Hawthorne Blvd., then south to Palos Verdes Dr. 6610 Palos Verdes Dr. S, Palos Verdes Peninsula (377-1571).

Queen Mary – Now permanently docked in Long Beach. When she was launched in 1936, a transatlantic voyage on the *Queen* was the ultimate travel experience of the time. She was "relaunched" in 1971, after retiring from a long, exciting career on the high seas. You can tour the 81,000-ton ship stem to stern and can even spend the night — the original 390 staterooms are operated by the Wrather Port Properties as a hotel. Also at the site is Howard Hughes's *Spruce Goose,* the world's largest all-wood airplane. Open daily. Admission charge. Long Beach Fwy. to *Queen Mary* exit (435-3511).

Catalina Island – It's two hours by boat from San Pedro or Long Beach to Catalina Island, where you can spend the day wandering around the flower-filled hills, looking at the ocean, swimming, sightseeing, playing golf, or riding horses. There are places to stay overnight, but be sure to reserve in advance during the summer. Boats to Catalina leave daily from Catalina Landing, 330 Golden Shore Blvd., Long Beach, and from the Catalina Terminal Building, foot of Harbor Fwy., Berths 95 and 96, San Pedro. Boats are operated by Catalina Cruises (775-6111).

ORANGE COUNTY

Disneyland – For many people, this is the most compelling magnet in all of Southern California — and the inspired creation that forever changed the image of theme and amusement parks. If you've ever wished upon a star and longed to make your way toward the glittering spires of Fantasyland, a trip to this incredibly clean, colorful, and diversified amusement park is essential. You will undoubtedly encounter one of your favorite Disney characters promenading down Main Street, a re-creation of a typical 1890s American street. 40 minutes from downtown LA, Disneyland is open daily. Admission charge. 1313 Harbor Blvd., Anaheim (714 999-4000).

Movieland Wax Museum – About a 10-minute drive from Disneyland, with more than 200 movie and television stars in wax, molded into stances from their most famous roles. The original props and sets from many films are here, too. Recently opened is the Chamber of Horrors, 15 sets with wax figures re-creating the special effects that made movies such as *Psycho* and *The Exorcist* famous. Open daily. Admission charge. 7711 Beach Blvd., Buena Park (714 522-1154 or 213 583-8025).

Knott's Berry Farm – The theme is the Old West. An old-fashioned stagecoach and authentic steam coach will take you around the grounds, past rides called the Corkscrew, Whirlwind, Log Ride, Sky Jump, Loop Trainer, and bumper cars. There are also a mine train, Montezooma's Revenge, a forward/backward loop roller coaster, and Camp Snoopy, an entertainment area for kids. Knott's Berry Farm has top country and western artists performing frequently, and a great ice show at Christmastime. Open daily. Admission charge. 10 minutes from Disneyland at 8039 Beach Blvd., Buena Park (714 827-1776).

■**EXTRA SPECIAL:** For one of the most spectacular drives in California, follow the Pacific Coast Highway (Rte. 1) north to *Santa Barbara,* about 95 miles from LA.

Santa Barbara is a picturesque California mission town facing the Pacific, where bright bougainvillea flowers purple and magenta against classic white adobe houses, and small clapboard buildings recall the 19th-century settlers. A walking tour of the historic district might well begin at Ortega Street, named for an explorer who guided one of the first expeditions into California in 1769. From Ortega, it's six blocks along Spanish, vine-hung, hacienda-lined streets to State Street, where the architecture turns Victorian. Santa Barbara has a couple of interesting country inns. You can stay overnight at the *Upham Hotel,* an 1871 wooden structure furnished comfortably with antiques. 1404 De La Vina (805 962-0058). The *Cold Spring Tavern,* about 10 miles northwest from Santa Barbara on Rte. 154, goes back to the old stagecoach days. Chili is popular at lunch. At dinner, the menu tends more toward chicken, steak, and game. Open daily for lunch and dinner. 5995 Stagecoach Rd. (805 967-0066).

SOURCES AND RESOURCES

TOURIST INFORMATION: For free information, brochures, and maps, contact the Greater Los Angeles Visitors and Convention Bureau, 501 Figueroa St. (624-7300).

The best guides to Los Angeles are *Where Can We Go This Weekend? — 1-, 2-, and 3-Day Travel Adventures in Southern California* (J. P. Tarcher; $5.95); *L.A.'s The Place: The Vacation Planner's Guidebook* by Ronni Schwartz ($14.95).; and Richard Alleman's *The Movie Lover's Guide to Hollywood* (Harper Colophon; $12.95), which delivers all the lowdown on places associated with movies and movie stars in Hollywood and the greater Los Angeles area.

Local Coverage – *Los Angeles Times,* morning daily; *Los Angeles Herald-Examiner,* morning daily; *Los Angeles* magazine, monthly; *California* magazine, bi-weekly.

Food – To keep absolutely up to date, check the restaurant listings in *Los Angeles* or *California* magazine.

Area Code – Telephone numbers are in the 213 area code unless otherwise indicated.

CLIMATE AND CLOTHES: Summers are hot and dry, with temperatures in the 90s; winters are rainy and cooler, registering in the 70s during the day and the 50s at night.

GETTING AROUND: It's always more convenient to have a car for exploring Los Angeles; however, there *are* buses, taxis, and tour operators.

Airports – Los Angeles International Airport (known as LAX) is the city's major airport and handles all international and most domestic traffic. The drive downtown from LAX takes about an hour, depending on traffic, and taxi fare should run about $25. Although city buses do stop at the airport, a more efficient alternative is one of the private transport companies. Airport Service (723-4636) buses leave from the lower level of each terminal every half-hour for downtown hotels; every hour or hour and a half for Hollywood hotels. The fare for either trip is $6. Supershuttle (777-8000) offers transportation by van from LAX to the Wilshire district and down-town hotels for $15 (less if traveling with others). At the airport, Supershuttle can be summoned through the courtesy phones in the baggage claim area or by calling 1-800-554-0279. For the return trip, call at least 4 hours ahead for a pickup at your hotel.

Bus – The best way to get from Los Angeles International Airport to the major Los Angeles and Orange County hotels is via Airport Service buses; information is available at kiosks near the lower roadway, outside the airport's baggage claim facilities. For route information on scheduled city buses, call the Southern California Rapid Transit District (273-0910 in the Beverly Hills/West LA area; 626-4455 in Hollywood/central LA; and 818 781-5890 in the San Fernando Valley).

Car Rental – All major firms are represented throughout Greater Los Angeles.

Taxi – Check at your hotel desk; different firms serve different areas.

Tours – Gray Line offers tours of downtown LA (Music Center, Chinatown, Little Tokyo, Olvera St., etc.) and the Hollywood–Beverly Hills area as well as Disneyland, Universal Studios, and Knott's Berry Farm. 1207 W 3rd St. (481-2121).

MUSEUMS: The Los Angeles County Museum of Art is described in *Special Places.* Other fine museums in LA are:

J. Paul Getty Museum – 17985 Pacific Coast Hwy. Malibu (459-8402)
Los Angeles Children's Museum – 310 N Main St. (687-8800)
Museum of Science and Industry – 700 State Dr. (744-7400)
Natural History Museum – 900 Exposition Blvd. (744-3411)
George C. Page Museum – 5801 Wilshire Blvd. (857-6311)
Norton Simon Museum of Art – 411 W Colorado Blvd., Pasadena (818 449-6840)

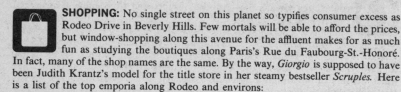

SHOPPING: No single street on this planet so typifies consumer excess as Rodeo Drive in Beverly Hills. Few mortals will be able to afford the prices, but window-shopping along this avenue for the affluent makes for as much fun as studying the boutiques along Paris's Rue du Faubourg-St.-Honoré. In fact, many of the shop names are the same. By the way, *Giorgio* is supposed to have been Judith Krantz's model for the title store in her steamy bestseller *Scruples.* Here is a list of the top emporia along Rodeo and environs:

Abercrombie & Fitch – A trendy new version of the aristocratic old sporting goods store. 9424 Wilshire Blvd.

Bally of Switzerland – High-style shoes. 340 Rodeo Dr.

Brentano's – Books, adult games, posters, lithos. 9528 Wilshire Blvd.

Carroll & Co. – Ivy league clothing for men and women. 466 N Rodeo Dr.

Alfred Dunhill of London – Tobacco and smoking accessories. 136 S Rodeo Dr.

Wally Findlay Galleries – Fine art. 339 N Rodeo Dr.

Cecil Gee – British clothing for men. 346 N Rodeo Dr.

Giorgio – Chic clothing for men and women; has stand-up bar and complimentary drinks for shoppers. 273 N Rodeo Dr.

Gucci – Italian leather goods, jewelry, clothing, accessories. 347 N Rodeo Dr.

Hermès – Fine leather goods from France. 343 N Rodeo Dr.

Fred Joaillier – Expensive jewelry. 401 N Rodeo Dr.

Jurgensen's – Gourmet foods. 409 N Beverly Dr.

Frances Klein – Antique jewelry. 310 N Rodeo Dr.

David Orgell – Silver and china. 320 N Rodeo Dr.

Superior Stamp & Coin – Gold coins and rare stamps. 9301 Wilshire Blvd.

Tiffany & Co. – Fine jewelry. 9502 Wilshire Blvd.

MAJOR COLLEGES AND UNIVERSITIES: There are three major university campuses spread through the LA area, in addition to dozens of colleges and junior colleges. The University of California (UCLA) is known to college football fans as the Bruins. UCLA's main campus is at 405 Hilgard Ave. (825-9111). The University of Southern California (USC) has the Trojans. USC's campus is at Exposition Blvd. and Hoover St. (743-2311). California Institute of Technology's main campus is at 1201 E California Blvd., Pasadena (818 356-6326).

SPECIAL EVENTS: There are more special events than we could possibly list here. For complete listings, check the local publications listed above or call the Greater Los Angeles Visitors and Convention Bureau (239-0200). Annual attractions include: *Pasadena Rose Bowl,* the traditional New Year's Day gridiron spectacle; *Glen Campbell Open Golf Tournament,* Pacific Palisades, in February; *Camelia Festival,* Temple City, in February; *UCLA Mardi Gras,* in April; *Renaissance Pleasure Faire,* in Agoura, in April; *Disneyland's Easter Parade; Sidewalk Arts Festival,* Westwood, in May; *Manhattan Beach Art Festival,* Manhattan Beach, in June; *Fourth of July* fireworks at Anaheim Stadium and Pasadena Rose Bowl; *All-Star Shrine Football Game,* Pasadena Rose Bowl, in July; *Festival of Arts and Pageant of the Masters,* Laguna Beach, in July; *SeaFest,* Long Beach, in August; *International Surf Festival,* Redondo Beach, in August; *Los Angeles County Fair,* Pomona, in September; *Hollywood Christmas Parade,* Hollywood, in November.

SPORTS AND FITNESS: There is no question that Southern California is a paradise for sports lovers.

Baseball – The Los Angeles *Dodgers,* Dodger Stadium, 1000 Elysian Park Ave. (224-1500); California *Angels,* Anaheim Stadium, 2000 State College Blvd., Anaheim (714 937-6700).

Basketball – The *Lakers* play at the Forum, Manchester Blvd. and Prairie Ave., Inglewood (673-1300, 674-6000).

Bicycling – Biking is great around the Westwood UCLA campus, Griffith Park, and the 28-mile bike path running from Marina del Rey to the Palos Verdes Peninsula.

Fishing – Fishing and sailing boats can be rented from Rent-A-Sail, 13560 Mindanao Way, Marina del Rey (822-1868). Fishermen catch halibut, bonito, and bass off the LA shores. Sportfishing boats leave daily from San Pedro, 22 minutes from downtown Los Angeles, site of the LA port and from the Redondo Beach Marina in Redondo Beach.

Fitness Centers – Nautilus Plus, on the ground floor of the International Tower building, offers aerobics classes and has a Jacuzzi and sauna. 888 9th St. at Figueroa (488-0095).

Football – Champions of the Big 10 and Pacific 8 college conferences meet in the Pasadena Rose Bowl every New Year's Day. UCLA plays its home games at the Rose Bowl, and USC plays at the Coliseum, 3911 S Figueroa (747-7111). The NFL *Rams* play at Anaheim Stadium (714 937-6767) and the *Raiders* at the Coliseum. The USFL *LA Express* also play at the Coliseum.

Hockey – The *Kings* make their home at the Forum (673-1300, 674-6000).

Horse Racing – If you like to spend your nights at the track, make tracks for Los Alamitos. There's harness, quarterhorse, and some thoroughbred racing, and the season runs from mid-October to mid-August. Take Freeway 605 south to Katella Ave. exit in Orange County (431-1361 or 714 995-1234). If you prefer daytime action, try Hollywood Park between mid-April and late July and from early November to Christmas Eve. Near Los Angeles International Airport between Manchester and Century blvds. (677-7151). There's also racing at Santa Anita Park, Huntington Dr. and Baldwin Ave. (818 574-7223), in Arcadia, from late December to mid-April and October through November.

Jogging – Downtown, run around Echo Park Lake (a little less than a mile); get there by going up Sunset and taking a right onto Glendale. In Griffith Park, run in the woodsy Ferndale area near the Vermont Avenue entrance; get to the park via the Golden State Freeway and watch for the sign to turn off. In Westwood, UCLA has a hilly 4-mile perimeter course and a ¼-mile track. Four blocks from Century City, Cheviot Hills Park, at 2551 Motor Ave., has a runners' course. And in Beverly Hills, jog in Roxbury Park, entrance at 471 S Roxbury Dr. and Olympic, or along the 1½-mile stretch of Santa Monica Boulevard between Doheny and Wilshire. Jogging is also popular along the oceanside bike path between Marina del Rey and the Palos Verdes Peninsula.

THEATER: There is no shortage of stages in LA, despite the overshadowing presence of the film industry. The *Center Theater Group*, a professional repertory company, performs at the Music Center's *Ahmanson Theater* and *Mark Taper Forum*. For information about either, call 972-7211. Other Los Angeles theaters include: the *Doolittle Theater*, 1615 Vine St., Hollywood (462-6666). The *Shubert Theater* is in the ABC Entertainment Center, 2020 Ave. of the Stars, Century City (553-9000; for credit card reservations, call 800 762-7666). The *Westwood Playhouse* is near the UCLA campus at 10886 Le Conte Ave., Westwood (208-5454). The *Pantages Theater* is at 6233 Hollywood Blvd. (216-6666). Tickets for all major events can be ordered over a telephone charge line called Teletron (410-1062) or from Ticketron outlets at most Sears and Tower Records stores; call 641-8321 for the nearest location.

MUSIC: All kinds of music can be heard in LA's concert halls and clubs. The *Los Angeles Philharmonic* plays at the Dorothy Chandler Pavilion, Music Center (972-7211). The *Hollywood Bowl*, 2301 N Highland Ave., Hollywood (850-2000), is a 17,630-seat hillside amphitheater that features famous guest entertainers as well as being the summer home of the Philharmonic. Leading popular performers in a wide range of musical styles play year-round at the *Universal Amphitheater*, Hollywood Fwy. at Lankershim Blvd. (818 980-9421). The *Greek Theater*, 2700 N Vermont Ave. (216-6666), is an outdoor bowl with concerts by top names from April through October. The *Roxy Theater*, 9009 Sunset Blvd. (276-2222), is also good for concerts. For country and western music, check out the *Palomino Club*, 6907 Lankershim Blvd., North Hollywood (818 983-1321).

NIGHTCLUBS AND NIGHTLIFE: Anything goes in LA, especially after dark. Swinging nightspots open and close very quickly, since the restless search for what's "in" keeps people on the move for newer night scenes. *Doug Weston's Troubador Club* pioneered a number of top rock music acts, at 9081 Santa Monica Blvd., West Hollywood (276-6168). Another place which seems to be able to hold its own is *Whisky A Go Go*, 8901 Sunset Blvd. (652-4202).

SINS: Overindulging in the City of the Angels seems to be a native way of life. A good bout with *gluttony* is easy to arrange at any of LA's many Mexican restaurants around Olvera Street. Either sit down to one enormous feast of tacos, chile relleños, enchiladas, and tamales, or eat your way slowly from one end of the market to the other, stopping at each of the outdoor stands, and dripping hot sauce over the counters of embroidered blouses, huaraches, perfumed candles, and Mexican ceramics.

The beaches of LA offer plenty of space for a *sloth*ful dropping out. You can find a few feet of sand, anywhere from Malibu to the Palos Verdes Peninsula, and spread your blanket or towel out for a day in the sun. Cover your body with oil, turn on the radio or cassette recorder, lie back, close your eyes, and watch the yellow spots behind your lids. You needn't move until the sun has your head swimming or the passers-by have managed to slowly cover you in a gritty coating of sand. At that point it is straight into the water for a quick surrender to the force of the tides and waves, sometimes known as body surfing.

For *lust*, Los Angeles is prepared to accommodate any taste. Some of the more accessible scenes are at the empire of massage parlors (advertised in the *LA Free Press*, the well-known underground newspaper) serving tastes that range from simple good health to the exotic to the ultimate kink; *Tony Roma's* or the *Rangoon Racquet Club* for a heavy dose of singles mixing; or simply the top of Mulholland Drive, looking out over the city below, where you have to arrange for companionship beforehand, but need only park and negotiate steering wheels and gearshifts for a lusty good time of your own.

LOCAL SERVICES: Babysitting – Babysitters Guild Agency, 6362 Hollywood Blvd., Hollywood (469-8246); Weston's Services Agency, 8230 Beverly Blvd., LA (274-9228); Community Service Agency, 19562 Ventura Blvd., Suite 200, Tarzana (818 345-2950)

Business Services – HQ, 1901 Ave. of the Stars, Suite 1774, Century City (277-6660); Century Secretarial Service, 2040 Ave. of the Stars, Suite 400, Century City (277-3329); Just-a-Sec, 500 S Sepulveda, Suite 400 (472-9521)

Mechanics – The best bet is membership in one of the major automobile clubs.

BEST IN TOWN

CHECKING IN: Los Angeles is the city where you stand the best chance of checking in alongside a movie star, although, obviously, you'll be paying more for the possible privilege of rubbing shoulders with cinematic royalty. If you're looking for someplace simply to shower and sleep, you'll be happier at one of the smaller hotels or motor hotels sprinkled throughout the area. Generally speaking, accommodations are less expensive in the San Fernando and San Gabriel valleys than in Hollywood or downtown. Expect to pay $130 and up for a double room at those places we've bracketed as very expensive; between $95 and $130 at those places listed as expensive; under $75 at moderate places. For B&B accommodations, contact Eye Openers Bed & Breakfast, PO Box 694, Altadena, CA 91001 (213 684-4428 or 818 797-2055), or California Houseguests International, 18533 Burbank Blvd. #190, Tarzana, CA 91356 (818 344 7878).

Bel-Air – This beautiful California mission–style hotel, splashed with purple and magenta bougainvillea and surrounded by splendid gardens, has recently been completely renovated by its new owner, Rosewood Hotels, controlled by Caroline Schoellkopf, of the mega-rich Hunt family of Texas. It now offers 92 elegant rooms and lovely public areas. Set in 11½ acres in a canyon, it's as private as you're likely to want and you'll need a car. 701 Stone Canyon Rd., West LA (213 472-1211). Very expensive.

The Beverly Hills – The *Polo Lounge* is a famous watering spot for movie moguls and producers — a place to be seen, if you're someone who people will know they've seen once they see you. We think the 268 rooms are a little on the musty side, but that's part of the charm. Show-biz action is pretty heavy at poolside. Stargazers can watch enraptured from a cabana, while eating lunch ordered from room service. 9641 Sunset Blvd., Beverly Hills (213 276-2251). Very expensive.

The Beverly Wilshire – Just walk out the front door into the middle of the elegant Beverly Hills shopping district. The mood here is more businesslike and subdued, less Hollywood flash, than at the *Beverly Hills.* In the new tower wing, all the rooms are done in different color schemes, furniture styles, and themes — but it's more expensive than the older wing. There are 450 rooms and suites and an award-winning restaurant, *La Bella Fontana.* If you like to read, you'll be very happy with the Brentano's bookstore downstairs — it's open late. 9500 Wilshire Blvd., Beverly Hills (213 275-4282). Very expensive.

The Century Plaza and Tower – A 1,072-room property with a lot of convention business. Its new wing, The Tower, has luxurious lodgings and a full-service business center. There are several fine restaurants on the premises, the best being Japanese (*Yamato*), and plenty of shops to browse in. Because of its location in Century City, near the ABC Entertainment Center, a car is recommended, but there are usually cabs lined up outside and the hotel has a complimentary town car service for trips within a 5-mile radius. 2025 Ave. of the Stars, Century City (213 277-2000). Very expensive.

Westwood Marquis – The current favorite among businessfolk who really know quality. Originally built to house UCLA students, it has now been converted to first-class digs. The attractive high-rise holds 256 suites, and the bustling college town of Westwood is all around. The *Garden Terrace Room* offers a terrific brunch, and the UCLA running track is not a half-mile away. 930 Hilgard Ave., Westwood (213 208-8765). Very expensive.

The Westin Bonaventure – This 1,500-room giant is a premier convention hotel. The hotel's mirrored towers are an LA skyline landmark, and it is especially convenient for downtown activities. Rooms are pretty pedestrian for the high prices. 404 S Figueroa St. (213 624-1000). Very expensive.

L'Ermitage – No relation to the restaurant of the same name, this hotel has a European ambience, 114 suites, a rooftop Jacuzzi and pool, a piano lounge, and its own fine *Café Russe.* It is very well run and blissfully low key. Should buy better pillows, however. Parking available. 9291 Burton Way, Beverly Hills (213 278-3344). Very expensive.

The Biltmore Hotel – Generally considered the grand dame of downtown hotels, its dramatic interiors combine the classical architecture typical of European palaces with contemporary luxury. The fine French restaurant *Bernard's* is another plus, as are an indoor pool and Jacuzzi. 515 S Olive St. (213 624-1011). Very expensive.

Bel Air Sands – This spot has reopened in the process of renovation. It's completely refurnished, with added amenities and a light, breezy atmosphere. All 162 rooms have balconies, and there are two swimming pools, tennis court, cocktail lounge, and dining room. Free parking and limo transportation to the Beverly Hills shopping district and elsewhere in the immediate area. 11461 Sunset Blvd. (213 476-6571). Very expensive.

The Beverly Hilton – Many fans say this is the best of the whole Hilton lot. It's not as convenient to downtown Beverly Hills as the *Wilshire,* and if you plan to spend a lot of time in the hotel you'll be happy here, since this is another one of those self-contained hotels which caters to every need. *Trader Vic's* is a consistently good restaurant in the hotel. 9876 Wilshire Blvd., Beverly Hills (213 274-7777). Very expensive to expensive.

Barnabey's – This just may be the best hotel value in Southern California. Here's the charm of an English country inn, less than 3 miles from Los Angeles International Airport and within walking distance of Manhattan Beach. All public and guestrooms are furnished with antiques. Dine in the *Drawing Room* and drink in *Rosie's Pub.* Sepulveda Blvd. at Rosecrans Ave., Manhattan Beach (213 545-8466). Very expensive to expensive.

Le Bel Age – The new sister property to the fine *L'Ermitage,* this hotel is also European in tone. Its 198 suites are gracefully decorated with hand-carved rosewood and pecan wood furnishings complemented by pastel color schemes. *La Brasserie* is the hotel's casual French café, and *Le Bel Age,* its more formal dining room, serving nouvelle Russe cuisine. Other amenities include a heated rooftop pool and limousine service to the Beverly Hills and Century City areas. 1020 N San Vicente Blvd., W Hollywood (213 854-1111). Expensive.

Shangri-la – This classic steamship-style Art Moderne building facing the ocean is as interesting for what it doesn't offer as for what it does. For example, it doesn't have a pool or a restaurant, room service (except for complimentary Continental breakfasts), or even much parking. It does have trendy Art Deco decor and, since it got some free publicity a couple of years ago in singer Randy Newman's *I Love LA* video, an even trendier show-biz clientele. Diane Keaton, Bill Murray, Cybill Shepherd, Newman, and his videomaker cousin Tim all stay here — sometimes for months at a time. It's a stylish place, but since the *Shangri-la* is in Santa Monica, not Beverly Hills, it's fairly low key. There are only 55 units, consisting of studios, one- and two-bedroom suites, and penthouses, all recently refurbished and upgraded. All have ocean views, although in some you have to crane your neck to get a good look. Most have kitchens. 1301 Ocean Ave., Santa Monica (213 394-2791). Expensive.

Sheraton Grande – This may well be the first Sheraton hotel to earn a five-star rating. If it isn't, it won't be for lack of trying. For starters, there's butler service and a fully stocked butler's pantry on every floor, complimentary morning beverage and newspaper, and shoes placed outside guestrooms at night return polished in the morning. Each of the 470 rooms is tastefully decorated, with a sitting area that includes a desk or writing table. Conference and entertainment space is all first class and includes a ballroom, meeting rooms, teleconferencing, and, during the daytime, use of a four-movie-theater complex in the building. For recreation, try the pool or cross the pedestrian bridge over the street to the Los Angeles Racquet Club, with its gym, running track, and courts. 333 S Figueroa (213 617-1133). Expensive.

Sheraton Premiere – This gray glass Art Deco tower provides every guest room with expansive views of either downtown LA, the Hollywood Hills, or the San Fernando Valley. The tower's top five floors are strictly butler-serviced suites; there are 450 rooms in all. This hotel also has a good setup for conventions: Besides having its own ballroom, hospitality suites, tiered seminar facility, and teleconferencing equipment, if necessary it can join forces with its neighbor, the *Sheraton Universal Hotel*. Other features include two restaurants, two lounges, an outdoor heated pool, spa, concierge, staff, and a garage for 700 cars. 555 Universal Terrace Pkwy., Universal City (818 506-2500). Expensive.

The New Otani Hotel & Garden – Conveniently within walking distance of the Music Center, the *Otani* has 448 rooms featuring Japanese luxury and service in a lovely gardenlike setting. Amenities include a shopping arcade and a Japanese health club. 120 S Los Angeles St. (213 629-1200). Expensive.

Hyatt Regency – Like the Hyatt Regencys in San Francisco and Atlanta, this one boasts a spectacular open-lobby design. This 500-room, super-modern luxury hotel is another convention favorite. *Pavan* is an expensive, Continental restaurant which is among downtown's best. 711 S Hope St. (213 683-1234). Expensive.

Sheraton Plaza–La Reina – This conference center is Sheraton's largest California hotel. It features 810 rooms and comprehensive convention facilities, and *Landry's*, a fine restaurant. 6101 Century Blvd. (213 642-1111). Expensive.

Safari Inn – If you're planning to visit The Burbank Studios, you'll find this more convenient than the Beverly Hills or downtown hotels. The spacious valley environment gives you more of a sense of being in the open. 105 rooms. 1911 W Olive Ave., Burbank (818 845-8586). Moderate.

Farmer's Daughter Motel – Across the street from the Farmers Market and CBS television studios, this 66-room Best Western hotel offers you the chance to be in the middle of an active part of town. There's also a heated pool, and all of the rooms have refrigerators. 115 S Fairfax (213 937-3930). Moderate.

Mikado Best Western Hotel – The twisting canyon roads separating Hollywood from the San Fernando Valley are among the most scenic parts of LA. The

Mikado is set between Coldwater and Laurel canyons, where cottages and modern glass and wood homes hang dramatically from cliffs, propped up only by stilts. The 58-room *Mikado* has a pool, Jacuzzi, restaurant, and cocktail lounge. Guests receive complimentary American breakfast. Pets are welcome, too. 12600 Riverside Dr. (818 763-9141). Moderate.

EATING OUT: In spite of the plethora of good restaurants in LA, finding one can be as hard as locating that proverbial needle in the haystack. A lot of places reward the unsuspecting first-timer with outstretched palms, unhonored reservations, and tables next to the kitchen door. Some of the places you've probably read about in the movie columns or heard about on television are among the worst offenders. With few exceptions, a restaurant's popularity with the show-biz crowd is inversely proportional to the excellence of its kitchen. If you have to spread cash around to crack the front door in hopes of sitting alongside someone famous, you can be pretty sure that neither the food nor the expected guests will be worthwhile. Our choices are below. Expect to pay $60 or more for two at those places we've listed as expensive; between $35 and $50, moderate; under $25, inexpensive. Prices do not include drinks, wine, or tips.

L'Ermitage – A typical meal in this handsome old mansion could start with the velvety-smooth mousse of duck livers with juniper, followed by sautéed veal filet with apple brandy, concluding with an individual chocolate soufflé. Too special a place to waste on just an ordinary night, so celebrate something — anything — while you're here. (Maybe you could celebrate that you're willing to spend $150 for a dinner for two.) Closed Sundays. Reservations necessary. Major credit cards. 730 N La Cienega Blvd. (652-5840). Expensive.

Rangoon Racquet Club – This place gets two very different types of crowds. The singles set congregates in the *Rangoon* bar but rarely stays to dine. An older and more elegant group turns up for lunch and dinner. Be sure to leave room for the huge stemmed strawberries and orange slices dipped in dark chocolate. Closed Sundays. Reservations advised. Major credit cards. 9474 Little Santa Monica Blvd., Beverly Hills (274-8926). Expensive.

Le St. Germain – Another favorite where special selections vary from day to day. The roasted Norwegian salmon with caviar butter sauce, veal chop with red wine sauce and truffles, and breast of duck with sherry vinegar sauce are delicious. Fresh fruit for dessert, as well as fancier sweets. Closed Sundays. Reservations required. Major credit cards. 5955 Melrose Ave. (467-1108). Expensive.

Le Restaurant – A quaint and unassuming decor provides the backdrop for yet another of LA's fine French establishments. All entrées, as well as appetizers, are carefully prepared. Service is just as meticulous. Closed Sundays. Reservations required. Major credit cards. 8475 Melrose Pl. (651-5553). Expensive.

The Bistro Garden – The very same Beverly Hills celebrities who have parked their Rolls-Royces up the street at *The Bistro* for years are now making its sister restaurant the "in" spot. Lunch is especially chic with popular fare like bratwurst with hot potato salad. Reservations required. Major credit cards. 176 N Canon Dr., Beverly Hills (550-3900). Expensive.

Valentino – Devotees generally describe the cuisine as Italian, and the homemade pasta certainly bears them out. But there's also a world of other choices on the eclectic menu — starters such as timballo (rolled baby eggplant) or crespelle (corn crêpes stuffed with seafood) and entrées like grilled fresh shrimp wrapped with swordfish and dressed with lime juice. The casually elegant spot boasts an impressive wine cellar: some 50,000 bottles, including Italian, French, German, and California labels. Open Mondays through Saturdays for dinner; Fridays for lunch as well. Reservations required. Major credit cards. 3115 Pico Blvd., Santa Monica (829-4313). Expensive.

Chasen's – A Beverly Hills institution for about 50 years, people come to enjoy a host of chef's specialties; the spinach salad and chili are also worth sampling. Closed Mondays. Reservations advised. No credit cards. 9039 Beverly Blvd. (271-2168). Expensive.

Palm – A local branch of New York's famous steakhouse. The thick prime steaks and Maine lobsters are as succulent as their New York counterparts. Food is consistently good, and the service tends to be very friendly and attentive. Open daily. Reservations recommended. Major credit cards. 9001 Santa Monica Blvd., West Hollywood (550-8811). Expensive.

Tracton's – Fresh Florida stone crabs aren't easy to find in LA, but they're a specialty here, served — when in season — as an appetizer or as a super-giant-sized main course. Also try the green goddess dressing on the tomato and anchovy salad. Open daily. Reservations advised. Major credit cards. 16705 Ventura Blvd., Encino (818 783-1320). Expensive.

L'Orangerie – Under high ceilings and among the potted palms you'll find one of the city's most attractive dining rooms, and some of the most exciting dishes as well. The mostly French menu offers soft scrambled eggs, topped with caviar, a spicy fish soup, sea bass (with a touch of Pernod), and first-class desserts like the apple tart or a puff pastry, filled with raspberries and sweet cream. Open daily for dinner. Reservations required. Major credit cards. 903 N La Cienega Blvd. (652-9770). Expensive.

Rex Ristorante – In an Art Deco building in the heart of downtown and filled with Lalique, oak paneling, and brass, it duplicates the dining room of *The Rex*, an Italian passenger liner of the 1920s. Each evening there's a six-course special dinner or à la carte dining on specialties that include tagliolini with tomato and fresh basil, ravioli stuffed with sea bass in lobster sauce, shrimp with broccoli in tarragon sauce, lamb cutlet in thyme with baby artichokes, or kidneys with sweet-breads in black olive sauce. On the mezzanine level there's a full bar featuring soft dance music. Open weekdays for lunch and dinner. Reservations required. Major credit cards. 617 S Olive (627-2300). Expensive.

Mr. Chow – The highly stylized Chinese cuisine here is even better than at Michael Chow's original London restaurant. Start with fried dumplings, Chinese noodles, or gambei (fried seaweed). Twice-fried beef is an excellent, if spicy, main course. Peking duck is best of all, and is often available even if not ordered in advance. There are numerous desserts, but the lychee nuts are particularly good. Open daily. Reservations necessary. Major credit cards. 344 N Camden Dr., Beverly Hills (278-9911). Expensive.

The Windsor – This award-winning restaurant is noted for its wide variety of beef dishes. Though the atmosphere is somewhat formal, it's particularly popular with the Dodger Stadium crowds. Open daily. Reservations recommended. Major credit cards. 3198 W 7th St. (382-1261). Expensive.

Le Dome – One of the most interesting of LA's French restaurants. It opened as a brasserie with various grilled dishes (the thick veal chop is a wonderful introduction) but added more traditional haute cuisine in response to patron pressure. The atmosphere is chic, understated, comfortable. Open daily. Reservations required. Major credit cards. 8720 Sunset Blvd. (659-6919). Expensive.

Monty's – An all-around, mouth-watering favorite, *Monty's* serves great steamed clams, barbecued spareribs, the thickest, juiciest prime ribs in LA, tempting scampi, and shrimp Monty (bacon-wrapped and stuffed). The charcoal-broiled swordfish is habit-forming. Open daily. Reservations recommended. Major credit cards. 17016 Ventura Blvd., Encino (818 783-1660). Expensive.

Dynasty Room – Continental French food is served in a restaurant that showcases original artwork and artifacts from China's T'ang Dynasty. The chicken breast with black angel hair pasta is one of several winning combinations. Other recommended offerings include veal and lamb chops and fresh swordfish. But much of the restaurant's popularity is probably owed to its "menu minceur," which offers health-conscious dinners — appetizer, main course, and dessert — that total less than 500 calories. Open daily for dinner. Reservations preferred. Major credit cards. *Westwood Marquis Hotel,* 930 Hilgard Ave., Westwood (208-8765). Expensive to moderate.

Spago – Owner Wolfgang Puck describes his unusual menu as California cuisine. Although entrées include roasted baby lamb, grilled salmon and tuna, and pasta that's made daily, this restaurant is best known for its "gourmet" pizzas — with toppings like duck sausage, goat cheese, oregano, and tomato or smoked lamb, eggplant, and roasted peppers. Baked in a wood-burning brick oven, they arrive at the table sizzling hot and crispy. Open daily. Tops among the trendy set, so reserve about three weeks ahead. Major credit cards. 1114 Horn Ave. at Sunset Blvd. (652-4025). Expensive to moderate.

Pane Caldo Bistrot – An unpretentious Italian ristorante with a great view of the city's famed hills. What it lacks in fancy appointments it more than makes up for with careful food preparation, generous portions, and reasonable prices. A complimentary appetizer and basket of focaccia arrive with the menu to ease the difficult task of choosing among Tuscan specialties such as warm bell pepper salad, risotto with asparagus, tagliatelle with porcini, spinach tortelloni with butter and sage, osso bucu (veal shank with vegetable sauce), and a selection of 14 individual pizzas. Try the ultra-rich tira mi su or a wedge of sinfully good crème caramel for dessert. Lunch and dinner; closed Sundays. Reservations recommended. Major credit cards. 8840 Beverly Blvd. (274-0916). Moderate.

Scandia – One of the city's best, but we feel obliged to warn you that *Scandia* overbooks and often sends guests to the bar to wait for an eternity. The bar isn't large enough to handle crowds, so it's generally impossible to sit down or get close enough for a drink. Go at lunchtime, or after 10:30 PM, but by all means avoid the 7–10 PM crunch. A typical meal might begin with Scandia's Viking Platter (tiny blinis flavored with aquavit and topped with Danish caviar and sour cream), followed by virgin lobster (tiny fried Norwegian lobster tails), or tournedos Theodora (filet mignon split and garnished with goose liver). Closed Mondays. Reservations are necessary, but avoid rush hour. Major credit cards. 9040 Sunset Blvd., W Hollywood (278-3555). Moderate.

Peppone – Possibly the best Italian restaurant in LA, tucked away in a tiny West Los Angeles shopping center. Splendid pastas and veal dishes are the cornerstones of the evening. Reservations absolutely required. Major credit cards. 11628 Barrington Ct. (476-7379). Moderate.

The Mandarin – Northern Chinese cooking in elegant surroundings instead of the usual plastic, pseudo-Oriental decor. Not on the menu, but well worth remembering as an appetizer is the minced squab wrabbed in lettuce leaves; also, be sure to try the spicy prawns. Reservations recommended. Major credit cards. 430 N Camden Dr., Beverly Hills (272-0267). Moderate.

Madame Wu's Garden – Imaginative Oriental decor. Mostly Cantonese food, with some Szechwan selections. Tossed shredded chicken salad makes a good appetizer, and Wu's beef and cashew shrimp are fine entrées. One of our favorites is sizzling go ba, a bubbling combination of chicken, ham, shrimp, mushrooms, water chestnuts, shredded bamboo shoots, and other vegetables. Stay away from the sweet-and-sour pork. Open daily. Reservations recommended. Major credit cards. 2201 Wilshire Blvd., Santa Monica (828-5656). Moderate.

Musso & Frank Grill – It really is a grill, in Hollywood since 1919, and apparently not redecorated once (not that its regulars — film people, journalists, the moiling LA middle class — want it to change one iota). Orthodox American food and the kind of place the cachet of which is having no cachet; an LA classic. Reservations recommended. Major credit cards. 6667 Hollywood Blvd. (467-7788). Moderate.

Pacific Dining Car – Steak — cut on the premises from aged, corn-fed beef — is the house specialty, although the menu also offers four types of fresh fish every day. The restaurant *is* a real dining car (plus an additional building) that's been in its downtown location since 1921. Open daily. Reservations required. VISA and Mastercard. 1310 W Sixth St. (483-6000). Moderate.

Garden Terrace – This gazebo-like room with green and white decor suggests summertime dining all year. What really draws crowds are the elaborate Sunday buffet brunches, with omelettes prepared to order and freshly carved roast beef, ham, and turkey as well as platters laden with fresh fruit, pâtés, smoked salmon, and salads. Excellent dry champagne flows nonstop throughout the meal. Open daily for lunch. Brunch on Sundays only; reservations should be made days ahead. Major credit cards. *Westwood Marquis Hotel,* 930 Hilgard Ave., Westwood (208-8765). Moderate.

Lawry's California Center – From May to October this restaurant is open in an outdoor garden surrounding the Lawry's (the sauce people's) headquarters. Mexican and/or barbecued specialties are the lunchtime fare, while in the evening there's a choice of steak, fresh fish, or hickory-smoked chicken. Each entrée comes with fresh corn-on-the-cob, a green vegetable, and hot herb bread. Preceding the main course is a salad of crisp, crunchy vegetables accompanied by your choice of Lawry's dressings. Open daily for lunch; Wednesdays through Sundays for dinner. Reservations preferred. Major credit cards. 570 West Ave. 26 (224-6850). Moderate.

Cock 'n Bull – A legendary establishment, the *Cock 'n Bull* has held forth on Sunset Strip since the 1930s. Lunch and dinner are served buffet-style. English brunch served Sundays. A great place for well-behaved kids who are always hungry. Open daily. Reservations required. Major credit cards. 9170 Sunset Blvd. (273-0081). Moderate.

A Thousand Cranes – Besides having such a beautiful name, this Japanese restaurant is well versed in the traditional art of serving beautiful food. It has several tatami rooms and a Western dining room. Reservations recommended. Major credit cards. In the *New Otani Hotel,* 120 S Los Angeles St. (629-1200). Moderate.

The Gingerman – Hollywood celebrities have really taken to Patrick O'Neal and Carroll O'Connor's local branch of New York's Gingerman pub. At dinner the pepper steak is first-rate, and the country paté makes a fine starter. *The Gingerman* serves supper most days until 12:30 AM and usually musters a good crowd for those wee hours. Open daily. Reservations recommended for dinner; not necessary for supper. Major credit cards. 369 N Bedford Dr., Beverly Hills (273-7585). Moderate.

Le Cellier – Another restaurant notorious for overbooking, but the prices are good and the quality makes it superior to many more expensive restaurants. On Wednesdays only, there's a fresh salmon baked in brioche and topped with a light caviar sauce. Reserve a portion or two when you call to book your table. Closed Mondays. Be prepared to wait a half-hour or more, even with reservations. Major credit cards. 2628 Wilshire Blvd. (828-1585). Moderate.

El Cholo – LA is glutted with places promising authentic south-of-the-border cooking, but this is the best, without question. Around for more than 50 years, and its burritos and combination plates are real knockouts. Open daily. There's usually a wait even with reservations; they're advised anyway. Major credit cards. 1121 S Western Ave. (734-2773). Inexpensive.

Anna's – This is a good late-night place for Italian food. A highlight of the diverse menu is linguine Sorrento al cartoccio (linguine topped with shellfish, prepared in a bag, and served from it at your table). Open daily. Reservations advised. Major credit cards. 10929 W Pico Blvd., West LA (474-0102). Inexpensive.

Sida – Rather difficult to find in Canoga Park, and woefully short on charm, but it makes up for it with excellent Thai food, such as noodles made on the spot to complement chicken, cold meat, and vegetable dishes. A wonderful introduction to Thai cuisine. Reservations not required. Visa and MasterCard only. 21109 Sherman Way, Canoga Park (818 703-9480). Inexpensive.

Nate 'n Al – Where unrepatriated Easterners go for a hot pastrami or corned beef fix. A block or so from the *Beverly Wilshire Hotel*. No reservations. Diners Club and Carte Blanche only. 414 N Beverly Dr., Beverly Hills (274-0101). Inexpensive.

The Twin Dragon – Less formal than *Madame Wu's,* with a solid repertoire of top-notch northern Chinese food. A lot of families bring their children here, and it's pretty noisy. Open daily. Reservations are unnecessary. Major credit cards. 8597 W Pico Blvd. (657-7355). Inexpensive.

The Bicycle Shop – An informal café perfect for a leisurely lunch or a casual dinner. Paté, quiche, onion soup, and a wide variety of crêpes and sandwiches make up the menu. Older children may be intrigued by the many different types of bicycles hanging from the ceiling. Open daily. Reservations are not essential. Visa and MasterCard only. 12217 Wilshire Blvd., West LA (826-7831). Inexpensive.

Chicago Pizza Works – The pizzas are deep-dish style and served with your choice of a wide range of toppings. Other offerings include lasagna, spaghetti, salads, and desserts. There are also over 100 beers to choose from. Open daily. Reservations not needed. Visa and Mastercard only. 11641 Pico Blvd. (477-7740). Inexpensive.

Hamayoshi – This restaurant, one of the reasons Japanese diplomats request an appointment in Los Angeles, is a sushi bar for connoisseurs, favoring flatfish of all kinds — a list not to be equaled at almost any other sushi house. The place is small and simple, and customers sometimes have to wait outside for a spot. Open daily; no lunch on weekends. Reservations advised. Major credit cards. 3350 W 1st St. (384-2914). Inexpensive.

The Rib Joint – Known as R.J.'s, this is the place for sumptuous spare ribs, seafood, and salads. Portions are very generous and best accompanied by the Anchor Steam beer on draft. The salad bar is splendid, and the chocolate cake is colossal. Open daily. Reservations advised. Major credit cards. 252 N Beverly Dr. (274-7427). Inexpensive.

And finally, for dessert, try the luscious ice cream at *Häagen-Dazs Ice Cream Shoppe,* 904 S Barrington Ave., West LA (820-1666) or 15615 Ventura Blvd., Encino (818 788-3118); or at *Swensen's Ice Cream Factory,* 1051 Broxton Ave., Westwood (208-6785).

LOUISVILLE

Everyone knows one thing about Louisville: Once a year the town is host to that amazing horse race and attendant carousal called the Kentucky Derby. There are two seasons in Louisville: Derby Week (the first week in May) and the rest of the year. But there is a good deal to that "other" season, and Kentucky's largest city is too often dismissed as a one-horse-race town.

Louisville (pronounced *loo-ee-ville* by visitors, and *looavul* — sounding a little like *interval* — by residents) combines aspects of the big city and the small town in its character. It is a blend of urbanity and provincialism, tradition and progressivism — the product of the city's traditional role as fence-sitter between North and South.

The fence the city sits on is the Ohio River, which also serves as the boundary between Kentucky and Indiana. The city has a population of 298,000, but the metropolitan area extends into four Kentucky counties and three in southern Indiana, so Louisville is the economic, social, and cultural center of 965,000 people.

Louisville's development as an industrial town is impressive. The city was actually settled in 1778 as an informal military base; it was the point from which George Rogers Clark drove the British and the Indians from the Midwest. The appearance of steamboats on the Ohio in the early 19th century turned a lazy river town into a booming port, and today more tonnage passes through Louisville than through the Panama Canal. The city itself produces more than half the world's bourbon as well as substantial amounts of such varied products as cigarettes, chemicals, and appliances.

It's a city of "has and has not." Actors Theatre of Louisville has been called the "Broadway of the Midwest" by national critics. The Louisville Orchestra is the only city orchestra in the world with its own recording label. And don't forget the lovely parks, the good old country cookin', or the leisurely cruises up the Ohio on the steamboat *Belle of Louisville*.

What it hasn't got is a variety of places to go after — or for that matter, before — the cruise. It's hard to find a good meal after midnight. In the city named for Louis XVI of France, good French restaurants are few.

Louisville keeps trying, though. Visitors will find its will to improve itself as inspiring as they find its reverence for tradition charming. In recent years, there's been a veritable renaissance downtown. The Riverfront Plaza/Main Street area is now the home of the new Kentucky Center for the Arts, which features all manner of cultural programs; a natural history museum housed in an 18th-century warehouse; and an array of fine shops and restaurants. A few blocks south, on 4th Avenue, is a modern shopping complex.

You get the feeling that Louisville wants to be a big city. In the southern tradition, though, it's just been taking its time.

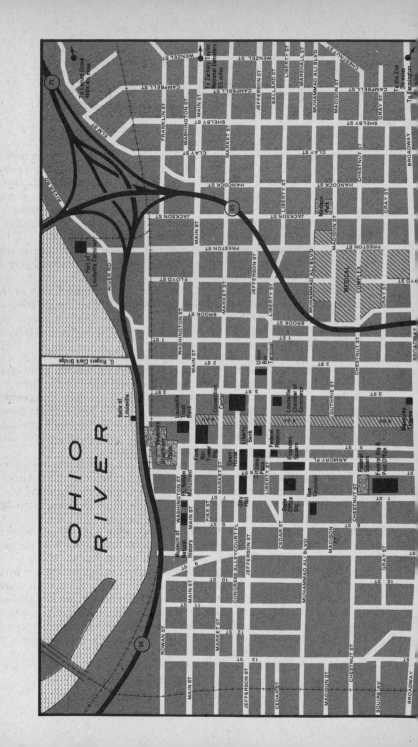

CENTRAL LOUISVILLE

LOUISVILLE AT-A-GLANCE

 SEEING THE CITY: The *Spire* restaurant and cocktail lounge on the 19th floor of the *Hyatt Regency Louisville* revolves to show views of downtown Louisville, the Ohio River, and, when it's not too hazy, southern Indiana across the river. 320 W Jefferson (587-3434).

 SPECIAL PLACES: The best way to get around Louisville is by car. You can walk around downtown, but attractions like Churchill Downs, historic old homes, and the lovely surrounding countryside a few miles from the center of town require transportation.

Museum of History and Science – Locally oriented exhibitions trace the development of the Ohio River valley from its geological origins to its modern status as the major waterway for four states. Open daily. Admission charge. 727 W Main St. (587-3137, recorded information; 589-4584).

Belvedere-Riverfront Plaza – This open plaza overlooks an impressive expanse of the Ohio — two bridges spanning the river with barges and tugboats streaming down in between. North of Main St. between 4th Ave. and 6th St.

Kentucky Center for the Arts – Music, dance, and theater are on the bill at the city's new performing arts center. There's also a restaurant and gift shop, and visitors are welcome. 5 Riverfront Plaza (584-7777).

KentuckyShow! – An entertaining multimedia presentation shown in a restored 1920s movie house that aims to convince viewers that Kentucky is a lot more than tobacco, horses, and bourbon. Open daily. Admission charge. 651 4th Ave. (585-4008).

Louisville Zoological Gardens – The zoo offers a pleasant afternoon outing for the whole family, but be prepared to do some walking. Instead of cramped cages, the animals' terrain is spacious and attractive. There's also a children's zoo. Closed Mondays. Admission charge. 1100 Trevilian Way (459-2184).

Louisville Galleria – The 40 stores and 10 restaurants in the city's most elegant shopping complex offer everything from high fashion to fast food. It's all under glass — 12,392 panes, to be exact. Closed Sundays. 4th Ave. between Liberty St. and Muhammad Ali Blvd. (584-7170).

Belle of Louisville – You can board one of the last of the 19th-century-style steamboats for a cruise up the Ohio River as it winds its way east through rural fields of Kentucky and Indiana into the river's navigatory past. Cruises leave once a day, daily except Mondays, and there is also a dance cruise Saturday nights. Memorial Day through Labor Day. Tickets at Steamer office at 4th Ave. and River Rd. or in the boarding line at the foot of 4th St. (582-2547).

Farmington – Built according to Thomas Jefferson's plans, the 19th-century home of Judge John Speed is an outstanding example of Federal architecture. Open daily. Admission charge. 3033 Bardstown Rd. (452-9920).

Old Louisville – The homes in Old Louisville (2nd to 6th streets and Ormsby to Eastern Parkway) are fine examples of 19th-century Victorian architecture. You can visit the Information Center year-round for a free walking tour. 1340 S 4th St. in Central Park (635-5244).

Locust Grove – Another fascination for architecture fans, this Georgian plantation was the last home of George Rogers Clark. Open daily. Admission charge. 561 Blankenbaker La. (897-9845).

Churchill Downs – By far Louisville's largest attraction, the Kentucky Derby draws some 100,000 people to Churchill Downs on the first Saturday in May. The twin-spired track is packed with fans sipping mint juleps, shedding a few tears at the sound of "My Old Kentucky Home," and, if they're lucky, catching a glimpse of some of the world's most expensive horseflesh. If you can stand the unabashed sentimentality, the crowds, and the expense (accommodations are sold at a substantial premium on Derby weekend), the Derby is worth the trip — at least once. Reserved seats for the race are hard to come by (they're held by box owners), but all you need to join the general admission party in the infield is $20 — and a lot of nerve. For information, write to Churchill Downs, PO Box 8427, Louisville, KY 40208 (502 636-3541).

The spring meet begins in May; closing dates vary. The fall meet is daily in November. At other times the grounds are open, and so is the new Kentucky Derby Museum, where visitors can view racing memorabilia, watch a 360° panorama on the race, and through "hands-on" exhibitions test your Derby trivia skills and explore the mysteries of pari-mutuel betting. Daily except Derby Day. Admission charge. 700 Central Ave. (634-0676).

■ **EXTRA SPECIAL:** About a 1½-hour drive from Louisville is the restored *Shaker Village* at Pleasant Hill, Kentucky. The Shakers were a 19th-century communal religious group who believed in hard work and celibacy. Although only a few members of the sect survive (in New Hampshire and Maine), they developed a distinct architecture, based on simple lines and sturdy functionalism. A nonprofit corporation has taken over this village, set in scenic rolling fields and farmlands, and has restored 27 buildings, including a meeting hall, homes, and shops. You can spend an afternoon taking a self-guided tour and viewing Shaker crafts demonstrations, stay overnight in rooms furnished with Shaker reproductions, and dine in a restaurant featuring some of the best country cooking in the state. No liquor or tipping. Room and restaurant reservations a must. Off US 68, 7 miles east of Harrodsburg (606 734-5411).

SOURCES AND RESOURCES

TOURIST INFORMATION: The visitors center provides lists of current events, maps, and other tourist information. Ask for the excellent Louisville Information Kit, Founder's Square at 5th St. and Muhammad Ali Blvd. (582-3732).

Local Coverage – *Louisville Courier-Journal,* morning daily; *Louisville Times,* afternoon daily, publishes *Scene Magazine* on Saturdays with complete listings of the coming week's events. Available at newsstands.

Area Code – All telephone numbers are in the 502 area code unless otherwise indicated.

CLIMATE AND CLOTHES: The general tendency is toward mild winters, brief but exquisite springs and falls, and overbearingly humid, long, and polluted summers. But save the bets for the thoroughbreds; a snow in April or a 65° day in December isn't too long a shot.

GETTING AROUND: Airport – Louisville's Standiford Field airport, 5 miles south of downtown, handles only domestic flights. Depending on the traffic, the drive to the airport can take anywhere from 10 to 30 minutes and taxi fare will run about $10. The airport limosine service costs $3.75 and makes stops at a few hotels, but most hotels in town offer courtesy vans to pick up registered guests. The city's TARC buses stop near the airport's main entrance and travel downtown for 35¢; for the return trip, buses can be picked up along the southbound side of 1st Street.

Bus – TARC bus system serves the downtown area adequately during the day but is limited in the suburbs and after dark downtown. Route information is available at the Transit Authority Office, 1000 W Broadway (585-1234).

Taxi – Cabs must be ordered by phone and are often slow to respond. The major company is Yellow Cab (636-5511).

Car Rental – Most national firms have offices at the airport, and Hertz has an office downtown in the *Hyatt Regency* hotel, 320 W Jefferson (589-0951).

 MUSEUMS: Museums not mentioned in *Special Places:*
Kentucky Railway Museum – La Grange Rd.and Dorsey La.(245-6035)
Rauch Planetarium – also on the U of L campus, behind the museum (588-6664)
J. B. Speed Art Museum – 2035 S 3rd St., adjacent to the University of Louisville (636-2893)
Zachary Taylor National Cemetery – 4701 Brownsboro Rd. (893-3852)

 MAJOR COLLEGES AND UNIVERSITIES: The University of Louisville, a four-year state school, is the area's oldest educational institution (between Eastern Pkwy. and Floyd St. south of 3rd St.; 588-5555).

 SPECIAL EVENTS: The week preceding the race, the *Kentucky Derby Festival* unwinds with a parade, music, hot-air balloons, and a race between the *Belle of Louisville* and *Delta Queen* steamboats. Many events free; write the festival, 224 W Muhammad Ali Blvd., Louisville 40202 (584-6383). The free *Bluegrass Music Festival* is held the first weekend after Labor Day on the Belvedere.

 SPORTS AND FITNESS: Baseball – The Louisville *Redbirds,* members of the American Association, play at the Kentucky Fair and Exposition Center. Off I-264 (367-9121).
Basketball – The Continental Basketball Association Louisville *Catbirds* play at Louisville Gardens, 6th St. and Muhammad Ali Blvd. (589-2300).

Bicycling – Rent from Highland Cycle, 1737 Bardstown Rd. (458-7832). Cherokee Park has good bike trails in hilly terrain.

College Sports – University of Louisville's basketball and football teams play at the Kentucky Fair and Exhibition Center, off Watterson Expressway (I-264). (588-4192).

Fitness Centers – The Louisville Athletic Club has a lot to offer: a rooftop pool, exercise classes, steam room, sauna, whirlpool, and racquetball and squash courts; towels are provided, and there's a lounge and restaurant as well; 5th and Muhammad Ali, at the red awning (583-3871; call ahead). The YMCA has a pool, gym, racquetball court, and indoor track, 2nd and Chestnut (587-6700).

Golf – Two good 18-hole courses are Iroquois Park (Newcut Rd. and Southern Pkwy.; 363-9520) and Seneca Park (Taylorsville Rd. and Cannons La.; 458-9298).

Horse Racing – In addition to racing at Churchill Downs (April-July, November), the Louisville Downs has trotting races in the summer and after Churchill Downs' season is over. 4520 Poplar Level Rd. (964-6415).

Jogging – For a 3-mile run, start at the *Hyatt Regency Hotel* on 4th Ave. Run north to Main St., turn right onto Main St., turn left at 2nd St., and head across Clark Memorial Bridge; then retrace your tracks.

Tennis – The Louisville Tennis Center has the best outdoor courts in the area. Open during spring and summer, Trevilian Way, across from the Louisville zoo (452-6411). Indoor courts are available right across the river at the Kentuckiana Convention and Sport Center, 520 Marriott Dr., Clarksville, Indiana (812 283-0785).

 THEATER: For current offerings, check the papers noted above. *Actor's Theatre,* a regional company, performs traditional productions and avant-garde plays from September through May, 316 W Main St. (584-1205). Touring repertory groups, including Broadway road shows, play at the Kentucky Center for the Arts, 5 Riverfront Plaza (584-7777).

 MUSIC: The *Louisville Orchestra,* the *Kentucky Opera Association,* and the *Louisville Ballet Company* perform at the Kentucky Center for the Arts, 5 Riverfront Plaza (584-7777).

 NIGHTCLUBS AND NIGHTLIFE: Current favorites include the *Phoenix Hill Tavern,* which features popular music and a large rooftop beer garden, 644 Baxter Ave. (589-4630); *City Lights,* for dancing to live music, 117 W Main St. (582-3943); *Louisville Palace,* for big-name performers, 625 4th Ave. (589-0100); *Downtowner,* gay disco with female impersonators, straights welcome, 105 W Main St. (583-1166).

 SINS: Clearly it is the Kentucky Derby and all the trappings that accompany it — big hats, mint juleps, and shmaltzy renditions of "My Old Kentucky Home" — that bring out the deepest *pride* in Louisville residents. Churchill Downs is the setting, the best three-year-old horses in the racing game are the performers, and the citizens of the world are the spectators at this traditional and classic event.

Even *gluttony* has a racetrack flavor in Louisville. The concoction of chocolate, bourbon, and nuts called Derby Pie is a sure winner. The exact recipe is a secret and is protected by a patent. Only the original can be called Derby Pie on menus (so avoid "Famous Horserace Pie" or other imitators). Served at numerous restaurants.

 LOCAL SERVICES: Babysitting – We Sit Better, Inc., of Louisville, Starks Bldg., 455 4th Ave. (583-9618)
    Business Services – Hospitality C Services, Legal Arts Bldg., 7th and Market sts. (587-0933)
  Mechanics – Lee's Gulf Service, 301 E Breckinridge (583-6912); Smith Imported Car Service, 1250 E Broadway (583-4724)

BEST IN TOWN

 CHECKING IN: Louisville's broad selection of accommodations ranges from standard large hotels to a resort-style motel with a lake and wave-making swimming pool. The more expensive hotels cost $95 to $135 per night for a double room, though they may have some less expensive accommodations in the moderate category ($65 to $80). Inexpensive hotels are in the $40 to $65 range. For B&B accommodations, contact Kentucky Homes Bed & Breakfast, 1431 St. James Ct., Louisville, KY 40208 (502 452-6629; 502 635-7341).

Hyatt Regency – One of Louisville's best stopping places, it features an 18-story atrium, spacious rooms, and several restaurants, including the revolving *Spire.*

It also has a pool, Jacuzzi, and tennis courts. 320 W Jefferson (502 587-3434).
Expensive.

Seelbach Hotel – The charm of a bygone era is combined with modern amenities
here. A showplace in the early 1900s, the hotel has undergone extensive renovation
aimed at re-creating its turn-of-the-century appearance. There are 324 guest rooms
in all, a restaurant, 3 bars, a Georgian-style ballroom, 24-hour room service, and
valet parking. The hotel adjoins the new Galleria shopping complex. 500 4th Ave.
(502 585-3200). Expensive.

The Brown – Built in the 1920s, this architectural landmark has found new life as
a Hilton. From the marble-floored lobby and archway-filled mezzanine to the
wood interior of the *English Grille,* it's a real piece of Louisville history. Two
restaurants (try a Hot Brown turkey sandwich, invented at the hotel), cocktail
lounge. 4th and Broadway. (502 583-1234). Expensive to moderate.

The Galt House – Though the decor is imitation extravagant — felt wallpaper, red
plush carpets, and new "antiques" — the hotel is adjacent to Riverfront Plaza, has
a fine view of the Ohio, and is convenient for downtown shopping. Facilities
include two cocktail lounges, an outdoor swimming pool, and 3 restaurants, one
with a revolving section (the view is better than the food). 140 N 4th St. (502
589-5200). Moderate.

Marriott Inn – This resort-style hotel features some unusual extras: a "Wave-Tek"
ocean, which is really a huge swimming pool with mechanically created waves; a
real 11-acre lake with boating and fishing; 10 lakefront villas; and a floating bridal
suite on the lake. It also has a health club, babysitting service, and a restaurant
and cocktail lounge. 2 miles north of downtown off I-65 at 505 Marriott Dr.,
Clarksville, Indiana (812 283-4411). Moderate.

Holiday Inn Downtown – This comfortable hotel offers good service and excellent
facilities for a modest price — indoor/outdoor swimming pools, sauna, 2 restaurants, and a cocktail lounge with entertainment. 120 W Broadway (502 582-2241).
Inexpensive.

Howard Johnson's Motor Lodge – Good value, with all the standard features:
pool, color TV, restaurant, and cocktail lounge. 100 E Jefferson St. (502 582-2481).
Inexpensive.

 EATING OUT: Our restaurant selections range in price from $40 to $60 for
dinner for two in the expensive range, $25 to $40 in the moderate range, and
$25 and below in the inexpensive range. Prices do not include drinks, wine,
or tips.

Casa Grisanti – Louisville's best restaurant offers carefully prepared Italian cuisine
(try especially the veal), a good wine list, and attentive service. Closed Sundays.
Reservations advised. Major credit cards. 1000 E Liberty St. (584-4377). Expensive.

New Orleans House – Eat all you want from an elaborate seafood smorgasbord of
15 different sea items, including crab legs, steamed shrimp, shrimp Créole, smoked
fish, and a wide variety of salads. Closed Sundays. Reservations advised. Major
credit cards. 412 W Chestnut St. (583-7231). Expensive.

The Oak Room – Antique furnishings combine with a Continental menu and formal
service to make dining here an elegant affair. Try the medallions of venison with
quail or grilled swordfish. Open daily, including a sumptuous Sunday brunch.
Reservations a must. Major credit cards. 500 S 4th Ave., in the *Seelbach Hotel*
(585-3200). Expensive.

Kienle's German Delicatessen and Restaurant – The food is wonderful —
and heavy. Wiener schnitzel, sauerbraten, and the homemade mushroom and
cauliflower soups are highlights. Beer only. Closed Sundays and Mondays. No

jeans or children under 12. Reservations required. No credit cards. Shelbyville Rd. Plaza (897-3920). Moderate.

Bristol Bar & Grill – A popular spot featuring Continental cuisines along with lighter meals and salads. Open daily. Reservations only for parties of eight or more. Major credit cards. 1321 Bardstown Rd. (456-1702). Moderate to inexpensive.

Hasenour's – Steaks are the specialty, but the seafood and daily specials are also reliable in this popular neighborhood restaurant. There's a wide variety in both food and price, and the drinks are among the most masterfully mixed in town. Major credit cards. 1028 Barret Ave. (451-5210). Moderate to inexpensive.

Old Stone Inn – Take a half-hour's ride in the country to this 18th-century landmark, which serves good, old-fashioned southern food like fried chicken, country ham, and fresh vegetables. Closed Mondays and Tuesdays and December through March. No liquor. Reservations advised. Major credit cards. Take I-64 East to US 60 North in Simpsonville (722-8882). Moderate to inexpensive.

Mamma Grisanti – Owned by the same family that operates *Casa Grisanti.* The pasta is just about perfect at *Mamma's,* ranging from fettuccine Alfredo to lasagna and chicken tetrazzini. Special prices for children; very good service. Open daily. Reservations advised. Major credit cards. 3938 Dupont Circle (893-0141). Inexpensive.

MEMPHIS

A modern southern city in the southwestern corner of Tennessee, Memphis is much more economically and psychologically in tune with the Mississippi and Arkansas cotton and soybean belt than with Tennessee mountain country. In the early seventies the press gave the city a bum rap by calling it "a backwater river town." Residents took offense at what seemed to them a willful misrepresentation of a quite genuine Memphis trait — that slow, unflustered approach to life entirely fitting in a town with the southern credentials Memphis carries. But there was an element of truth in the snipe which residents recognized and set out to correct.

Everyone has heard the cliché that New York City is a great place to visit but you wouldn't want to live there. For a good while, Memphis — named in 1819 for the Egyptian city of Memphis — was known as just the reverse: a great place to live, but you wouldn't necessarily want to visit. Today, Memphis is a good place to live and is fast becoming a good place to visit, too. In fact, the city is so sure of its charms that Marshall Murdaugh of "Virginia is for lovers" fame has been hired to change its reputation.

The 846,000 people in the Memphis area *do* live at a somewhat slower pace than people in other parts of the country. Sitting high on the bluffs overlooking the Mississippi at the mouth of the Wolf River, the 19th-century city was one of the busiest ports in the United States and the site of the largest slave market in the central South. Memphis lost its city charter for a year in 1878 when the yellow fever epidemic forced more than half its population to move to St. Louis (the half that could afford to move), but it survived as a shipping center. Today, more than one-third of the US cotton crop is still marketed through Memphis.

Memphis is basically a conservative town, both in politics and economics. One theory for this, advanced by residents, is that because the wealth in Memphis was accumulated over the decades through cotton, and because the process of accumulation was so slow, the community leaders are reluctant to spend. Memphis is *not* like Houston, with its fast-flowing oil money, or Atlanta, which leaped ahead of all southern cities to become a tourist haven, in Memphis terms, almost overnight.

Memphis is a beautiful city with thousands of trees, magnificently landscaped lawns, and spacious parks, sitting atop the Mississippi bluff and surrounded by scores of fishing lakes. Outdoor activities (hunting, fishing, golf, water skiing, speedboat racing, auto racing, tennis, etc.) abound.

A few uniquely American phenomena are headquartered in Memphis. The late King of Rock, Elvis Presley, lived in and is buried on the grounds of his Memphis mansion, Graceland. It draws more visitors to the city than any other single attraction. And Holiday Inns and Federal Express were born and are based in Memphis, organizations built on a bedrock of shrewd business judgment and old-fashioned southern faith. Not an unusual combination in this very southern city.

MEMPHIS AT-A-GLANCE

SEEING THE CITY: The best way to see Memphis is by drifting along the legendary Mississippi. Captain Jake Meanley's *Memphis Queen* paddleboat takes you along the river. The cruise takes about an hour and a half. It leaves daily, from March through December, from Memphis Downtown Harbor, Monroe Ave. and Riverside Dr. (527-5694).

SPECIAL PLACES: A natural place to start a tour of Memphis is alongside the riverbanks. From there, you can wander through downtown, wending your way out to the suburbs.

Mud Island – Legend has it that Mud Island, measuring 1 by 5 miles, was formed by mud deposits clinging to a gunboat sunk during the Civil War. Residents are sure it was a Union gunboat, because, they say, Confederate gunboats were unsinkable. Mud Island is the site of a $63 million tribute to the history and heritage of the Mississippi, with exhibits on its legends, music, and people; a 5,000-seat outdoor amphitheater; a five-block scale model of the river; and restaurants, shops, a river museum, marina, and picnic area. Enter on Front St. between Poplar and Adams (528-3595).

Beale Street – Renovated buildings along this historic street, which saw the birth of the blues in the early 1900s, contain specialty shops, restaurants, bars, and offices. At the corner of Beale and Third is W. C. Handy Park, and at Beale and Main, Elvis Presley Plaza; both feature statues honoring these two international artists from Memphis. At 329 Beale is the Old Daisy Theater, run by the Center for Southern Folklore, which serves as the interpretive center for the new Beale Street and presents the show *If Beale Street Could Talk.* Closed Mondays, except on holiday weekends. Live concerts on Friday and Saturday nights. Admission charge (527-8200 or 726-4205).

Victorian Village – Homes and churches in this downtown area date back to the 1830s and feature a variety of architectural styles, among them late Victorian, Neoclassic, Greek Revival, French, and Italianate. The Fontaine House and the Mallory-Neely House are open to the public daily. 100 to 700 block of Adams St.

Overton Square – A 15-minute drive from downtown, the square has restaurants and bistros, jazz trios and rhythm and blues bands, specialty shops, an art gallery, and a professional theater. Madison at Cooper.

Libertyland – At the Fairgrounds, a mile from the square on East Parkway, this theme park reflects nostalgia and patriotism (its roller coaster is aptly named the Revolution). Open weekends beginning in the spring, daily from mid-June through August. Admission charge; children under 3 free. Fairgrounds (274-1776).

Memphis Pink Palace Museum and Planetarium – The museum is built of pink Georgia marble, and features exhibitions on the natural and cultural history of the mid-South. Closed Mondays. Admission charge. 3050 Central Ave. (454-5600).

Chucalissa Indian Village – A reconstructed village where Choctaw Indians live and work. Grass huts and a ceremonial house and museum are on the site, and Indian tools, weapons, and pottery are displayed. Closed Mondays. Admission charge. 6 miles south of downtown, adjoining Fuller State Park on Indian Village Dr. (785-3160).

Memphis Zoo and Aquarium – The complete range of lions, tigers, monkeys, and birds can be found in this well-designed city zoo. An aquarium adjoins the animal sections. Closed Thanksgiving, Christmas Eve, Christmas, and icy days. Admission

charge; free from 3:30 to 5 PM on Saturdays. Overton Park, off Poplar Ave. (726-4775, recording; for further information, 726-4787).

Graceland – Elvis Presley's home is the most popular site in Memphis. The white-columned southern mansion is now open to the public, and Elvis fans can also stroll through the 14-acre estate, well shaded by oak trees, and pay respects at the grave of Elvis, his mother, father, and grandmother. Don't forget to look closely at the Musical Gate at the foot of the winding circular driveway. It has a caricature of Elvis with guitar and a bevy of musical notes in ornamental iron. Elvis's plane, the *Lisa Marie,* is also on display. Closed Tuesdays. Admission charge; make tour reservations in advance. 3764 Elvis Presley Blvd. in Whitehaven, South Memphis (332-3322 in Tennessee; 800 238-2000 elsewhere).

Sun Recording Studio – Elvis, Johnny Cash, Jerry Lee Lewis, Carl Perkins and other recordings artist cut their first records here. Restored and operated by Graceland Division of Elvis Presley Enterprises. Open by appointment. Admission charge. 706 Union (332-3322).

■**EXTRA SPECIAL:** About 2½ hours away by car, *Shiloh National Military Park* lets visitors follow the sequence of a famous Civil War battle, the 1862 Battle of Shiloh. Points of interest are clearly marked, and visitors can walk or drive along a 10-mile route. Pre-Columbian Indian mounds are also visible along the way. A 25-minute movie about the Battle of Shiloh is shown in the visitors center. Closed Christmas. Off US-64 in Shiloh (689-5275).

SOURCES AND RESOURCES

TOURIST INFORMATION: The Convention and Visitors Bureau of the Memphis Area Chamber of Commerce is the best place for general information. 203 Beale St. (526-1919).

Key magazine and the *Convention and Visitors Guide* are the best sources for Memphis activities.

Local Coverage – *Memphis Commercial Appeal,* morning daily; *Memphis* magazine, monthly.

Area Code – All telephone numbers are in the 901 area code unless otherwise indicated.

CLIMATE AND CLOTHES: Memphis humidity is formidable. Even though temperatures seldom drop below the 30s in winter, it's wet. The worst month is February, when it occasionally snows. July and August get dripping hot as the temperature climbs into the 90s and 100s; dress coolly.

GETTING AROUND: Airport – Memphis International Airport is usually about a 30-minute drive from downtown and midtown; taxi fare should run about $14. The Airport Limousine Service (346-1200) meets incoming flights and takes passengers to the city for $5. When returning to the airport, call in advance for a pickup. Although public bus #20 stops at the terminal building, a transfer to bus #13 is required to get downtown. The fare is 95¢.

Bus – Memphis buses generally run between 5 AM and 8 PM during the week, with limited service on the weekend. Information, routes, from Memphis Area Transit Authority, 1370 Levee Rd. (274-6282).

Taxi – There are taxi stands near the bus station and at the airport. It's best to call Yellow Cab (526-2121).

Car Rental – The major national firms have agencies in Memphis. A reliable local firm is Thrifty Rent-A-Car, 2230 E Brooks (345-0170).

MUSEUMS: The Memphis Pink Palace Museum is famous for natural history exhibitions (see *Special Places*). Other museums are the *Memphis Brooks Museum of Art* (American and European art), Overton Park (722-3500); and *Dixon Gallery and Gardens* (French and American Impressionist art) 4339 Park Ave. (761-5250). Both are closed Mondays.

MAJOR COLLEGES AND UNIVERSITIES: Memphis State University (454-2040); Rhodes College (274-1800); University of Tennessee, Memphis (528-5500).

SPECIAL EVENTS: The *National Indoor Tennis Tournament* is held in February. The *Memphis in May International Festival* stretches from late April into early June. Highlights of the Festival are the *International Children's Festival, International Cooking Contest* (barbecue), *Beale Street Musical Festival* and a *Sunset Symphony* on the banks of the Mississippi. *Great River Carnival* (formerly the *Cotton Carnival*) in early June, has parades, a midway, music and a riverside pageant. In September one of the ten largest fairs in the country, the *Mid-South Fair*, takes place. In December is college football's *Liberty Bowl.*

SPORTS AND FITNESS: Baseball – The Memphis *Chicks* (short for Chickasaw Indians, who once lived in the area) play at Tim McCarver Stadium, renamed for the Memphis-born former catcher for the Philadelphia *Phillies.* The Chicks are a Southern League farm club for the Kansas City Royals. Tim McCarver Stadium, Fairgrounds (272-1687).

Fishing – There are fish in the lakes, mostly bass, bream, crappies, and catfish. Sardis Lake is a good bet; Meeman-Shelby Forest, a 14,000-acre park with two large lakes.

Fitness Centers – The Peabody Health Club, in the *Peabody Hotel,* offers aerobics classes and a sauna, 149 Union (525-1600).

Football – The Memphis *Showboats,* of the USFL, play from February through June at Liberty Bowl Stadium (795-9334).

Golf – The $300,000 PGA Danny Thomas Memphis Classic is played every June at the Colonial Country Club, a private course 10 miles east of the city on I-40. The best public golf course is Galloway, 3815 Walnut Grove Rd. (685-7805).

Jogging – Run in Audubon Park on Park Avenue, and Overton Park on Poplar Avenue.

Swimming – Some of the lakes are polluted. The nearest good swimming pool is Maywood, just across the state line in Olive Branch, Mississippi. Admission charge. 422 S Maywood Dr. (601 895-2777 or 767-7241).

Tennis – The best year-round public courts are at Audubon Tennis Center, 4145 Southern (685-7907), and John Rodgers Tennis Complex, Midtown (523-0094).

THEATER: *Playhouse on the Square,* Overton Square (726-4656); *Theater Memphis,* 630 Perkins Ext. (682-8323); *Orpheum Theater,* 89 Beale St. (525-3000); *Circuit Playhouse,* 1705 Poplar Ave. (726-5521); *Gaslight Dinner Theater,* 1110 E Brooks Rd. (396-7474).

MUSIC: Big-name country and rock concerts are played at *Mid-South Coliseum,* Fairgrounds (274-7400), and *Dixon-Meyers Hall* at the Cook Convention Center, 255 N Main (523-7645). Headliners appear at the *Mud Island Amphitheater* from May through September (take the monorail on

Front St. between Poplar and Adams; 528-3595) and at the *Orpheum Theater,* 89 Beale St. (525-3000), year round.

NIGHTCLUBS AND NIGHTLIFE: Memphis blues originated on Beale Street, with W. C. Handy, and is performed nightly at *Blues Alley,* 60 S Front St. (523-7144) and *Club Handy,* 340 Beale St. (521-0213). Other popular downtown nightspots include *Number One Beale* (525-1116) and the *Anchor Bar* at Captain Bilbo's (526-1966). Both are in the Beale Street Landing Emporium, a shopping and restaurant complex at the corner of Beale and Wagner. In midtown, the Overton Square area at Madison and Cooper, try *TGI Friday's* (725-7737), *Bombay Bicycle Club* (726-6055), or *Folk's Sea Folly* (722-8461). Best bets elsewhere are *Trivia,* 4730 Poplar Ave. (761-2880), and *Confetti,* 5100 Poplar Ave. (761-0990).

SINS: In its early days Memphis was a rough, tough, hard-drinking river town where "whiskey was two-bits a gallon." It began to go conservative in the 1940s, when political boss Ed Crump "got religion" and closed the red-light district. Since then Memphis has had its sinful ups and downs, but in recent years it has struck a happy medium with the redevelopment of downtown and the renewal of Beale Street — several blocks of shops, restaurants, and nightclubs — that opened in 1983.

And *lust?* Well, Memphis women are endowed with southern charm. But a word of caution: Don't be fooled by their gracious veneer; it masks a formidable and independent will.

LOCAL SERVICES: Babysitting – Crosstown Christian Daycare and Elementary School provides 24-hour, 7-day service for children 15 months and older. 1258 Harbert (725-4666).

    Business Services – Business Office Services, Memphis International Airport (345-5965)

    Mechanics – Lamb's Auto Service, 3343 Millbranch (345-5875); A. S. Martin & Sons, 411 Monroe (527-8606)

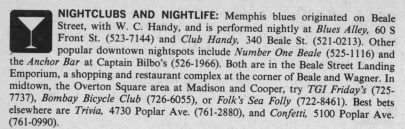

BEST IN TOWN

CHECKING IN: Restoration of the 400-room *Hotel Peabody* is complete, and the construction of a new *Holiday Inn Crowne Plaza* convention center has recently been completed. There's an abundance of *Holiday Inns* (six, to be exact) — hardly surprising since the chain makes its headquarters in Memphis. Other chains, such as *Ramada, TraveLodge,* and *Sheraton,* are also represented. Expect to pay between $60 and $90 for a double at the hotels mentioned here.

The Peabody – Mississippi author David Cohn wrote in 1935 that "the Delta begins in the lobby of the Peabody and ends on Catfish Row in Vicksburg." Built in 1925, the 13-story, 400-room hotel reopened in 1981 after a $20 million renovation. A focal point of the elegant Renaissance lobby is a travertine marble fountain in which the *Peabody* ducks — trained mallards — swim each day. Sixteen square marble columns support a mezzanine balcony; the ceiling is graced by ornate woodwork and stained glass skylights. *Chez Philippe* is the hotel's fancy restaurant; *Dux,* its theme restaurant. (Incidentally, neither restaurant serves duck.) For music and dancing, there's the *Skyway,* a rooftop nightclub. The *Plantation Roof* affords splendid views of the river and city. The hotel's lower level has a pool,

snack bar, health club, beauty shop, barber shop, and shoeshine parlor. 149 Union
Ave. (901 529-4000). Expensive to moderate.

Hyatt Regency – This circular, 27-story, all-glass structure is known affectionately
as "the glass silo." The 400-room hotel, on the eastern outskirts of town, has a
swimming pool, café, and bar with nightly entertainment and dancing, free parking, free cots, and cribs. Pets welcome. Children under 18 free. 939 Ridge Lake
Blvd. (901 761-1234). Moderate.

Holiday Inn Crowne Plaza – Part of the new executive-oriented Crowne Plaza
division of Holiday Inn, focusing on the affluent business traveler, this hotel,
adjacent to the Memphis Convention Center, offers 415 rooms, pool, health club,
and sauna. *Chervil's* is the ambitious restaurant, and there's a coffee shop and
24-hour room service, as well. 250 N Main (901 527-7300). Moderate.

EATING OUT: The city's natives are quick to say "There ain't no good eatin'
places in Memphis," but this is a bum rap. While it's true there are hundreds
of fast-food franchise outlets in every section of the city, a visitor still can
dine well, feast on some of the best barbecue anywhere, or enjoy home-
cooked meals. Our restaurant selections range in price from $38 for two in the expensive
range; around $20 for two, moderate; under $20, inexpensive. Prices do not include
drinks, wine, or tips.

Justine's – Often acclaimed as one of the nation's notable restaurants, and de-
servedly so. The French cooking here is first rate. Baking is done on the premises.
A rather formal ambience prevails in this antebellum mansion, however. Jacket
and tie are required. So are reservations. Closed Sundays. Major credit cards. 919
Coward Pl. (527-3815). Expensive.

Folk's Folly – This is a steak house supreme, serving the largest bits of beef in
Memphis. Vegetables are prepared Cajun-style — that's New Orleans French. Try
the sautéed mushrooms or fried dill pickles. Humphrey Folk, a John Wayne type,
owns the restaurant. According to local legend, he opened it to help his girlfriend,
who always wanted to run a restaurant. Open daily. Reservations advised. Major
credit cards. 551 S Mendenhall (767-2877). Expensive.

Grisanti's – This North Italian restaurant features spicy food and a chance to swap
insults with owner Big John Grisanti, a legend on the city's nightlife circuit. The
cannelloni, manicotti, and veal are highly recommended. The blind can order from
a Braille menu. Closed Sundays. Reservations accepted for ten or more. Major
credit cards. 1489 Airways Blvd. (458-2648). Moderate.

Captain Bilbo's – Have a drink at the bar and listen to nightly entertainment while
viewing beautiful sunsets on the Mississippi River. And don't be surprised if an
Illinois Central Gulf Railroad train rumbles past — the railroad track is only 22
feet from the restaurant's windows. Next, enjoy the excellent salad bar, seafood
gumbo, steaks, and fish. Open daily. Reservations accepted for groups of 12 or
more. Major credit cards. 263 Wagner (526-1966). Moderate.

Rendezvous – In a basement in a back alley, this classic little place is chock full
of Memphis memorabilia. It's as much a museum as a restaurant, and it serves
the best barbecue ribs, beef, and pork in town. Closed Sundays, Mondays, and
holidays. No reservations. Major credit cards. General Washburn Alley, off S 2nd
and behind the *Ramada Inn* (523-2746). Inexpensive.

Pete and Sam's – Pound for pound, the best all-around restaurant in town; serves
dynamite Italian-American food. Order anything, the steak is as good as the pizza.
There are two Memphis locations, but try the original on Park Avenue. Open
daily. Reservations are a good idea. Major credit cards. 3886 Park (458-0694).
Inexpensive.

MIAMI-
MIAMI BEACH

Difficult as it is to find adults actually born in Miami, practically all residents regard themselves — somehow — as natives. The year-round population of Miami is 1¾ million. This figure swells immensely during the winter months, when millions of "snowbirds" arrive. ("Snowbird" is a tricky term as used in Miami; it refers primarily to tourists escaping the northeastern freeze but can just as easily describe South Americans in town for a midsummer shopping spree.) Sprawling across 2,054 square miles of land (the metropolitan area also encompasses 354 square miles of water), Miami is a huge and cosmopolitan metropolis; yet it has managed to maintain a provincial quality in spite of commercialized efforts to identify it as a tropical New York City.

This is in part due to the way in which the metropolitan area is organized. Greater Miami (actually Metropolitan Dade County) is composed of 27 municipalities and a scattering of totally unincorporated areas. This breeds something of a small-town attitude in residents who have a chauvinistic interest in their own small enclaves. They identify with the whole city — it is, after all, all Miami — but they live where they live.

In even larger part, it is due to a deeply rooted tradition of hospitality and neighborliness that can only be described as somehow "southern" — even while admitting that a large number of those residents who display it most openly are either recent arrivals or part-time snowbirds.

From an early small settlement consisting primarily of Indians, Miami only began to grow after one Julia Tuttle tickled the fancy of a railroad tycoon with some orange blossoms. According to the story told here, Tuttle was an early settler who was eager to see Miami become part of a railroad hookup with the rest of the state. She petitioned railroad magnate Henry Flagler to extend his Florida East Coast Railroad from Palm Beach to Miami. He seemed in no great hurry to do so until the Big Freeze of 1894 devastated most of Florida's fruit and vegetable crops. Most, but not all. When he received a box of frost-free orange blossoms from Tuttle, he suddenly got her point. Soon enough Miami had rail access to the rest of the world.

It wasn't long until the rest of the world was glad of access. Attracted by year-round warmth and sunshine, thousands of new residents began pouring into the area, only one step behind hundreds of shrewd and even occasionally honest entrepreneurs. Miami and Miami Beach became glittering wintertime destinations, and later began drawing vacationers in summer as well. While Miami Beach still remains tourist-oriented, Miami has developed into a flourishing international business hub. They are together an attractive combination that lures a wide variety of visitors.

Jolted a few years ago into the realization that their fun and sun city had begun to lose its good reputation, the local government began implementing a series of major programs dedicated to restoration and redevelopment. Renewing the beaches, sprucing up oceanfront hotels, cleaning up the Miami River, expanding the park system, and enforcing strict environmental laws to protect the delicate marine ecology reflected a determination to keep the good life good.

That Miami still has the good life is attested to by the waves of new residents who settle in one or another of Miami's municipalities each year (a fact that sits uneasily with long-time residents, torn as they are between the need for steady economic growth and the desire to maintain the quality of life). Today, the majority of these new residents are Spanish-speaking, many of them from the steady flow of refugees from Cuba, others fleeing violence in Central America, while still others are affluent Venezuelans and Colombians who occupy their Miami homes only part of the year. This has turned metropolitan Miami into a city where you can buy anything from fried bananas to Chilean wine and where Spanish is the first language of more than 50% of the year-round inhabitants. However, there is also an only slightly smaller tide of new resident and regular visitors from the Caribbean islands, Britain, and Europe, bringing Miami such things as Jamaican-Chinese restaurants, Haitian grocery stores, and elegant French restaurants.

Coral Gables is Miami's prestigious planned community, conceived and built by entrepreneur George Merrick. Elegant gates to the city are still standing in various spots around the Gables, relics of Merrick's grand scheme to build "a place where castles in Spain are made real." Strict building codes prevail here, and woe to the newcomer who tries to put a flat roof on his home. In a county where almost all the streets are laid out in a simple north-south-east-west numbered grid, Coral Gables sticks to its Spanish and Italian street names and layout. Just 10 minutes from the airport, it has also become the favored locale for multinational corporations doing business in Latin America.

South Miami, adjacent to the Gables, is reminiscent of an Anywhere, USA, crossroads town. Farther south, in an unincorporated part of Dade County called Kendall, lie expensive estates with pools and tennis courts, where not so long ago there were only extensive mango and avocado groves.

Closer to downtown Miami is the area known as Coconut Grove, a base for wealthy year-round and winter residents and not so wealthy colonies of artists and writers. Here, crafts shops stand next to expensive boutiques, health food stores sit alongside posh restaurants, and old Florida houses of coral rock nestle close to modern high-rises. Luxurious yachts and sailboats lie in Biscayne Bay, and the Grove's younger generation lies all over Peacock Park. Little Havana is part of the center city but is really a small world unto itself, with its Latin culture intact.

Also in a class by themselves are the communities of Miami Beach and Key Biscayne. Besides its glittering hotel row, the Beach (and the small manmade islands between it and the mainland) houses some of the most luxurious waterfront homes in Greater Miami. Cuban refugees who arrived during the boatlifts a while ago have begun to share South Beach with retired and

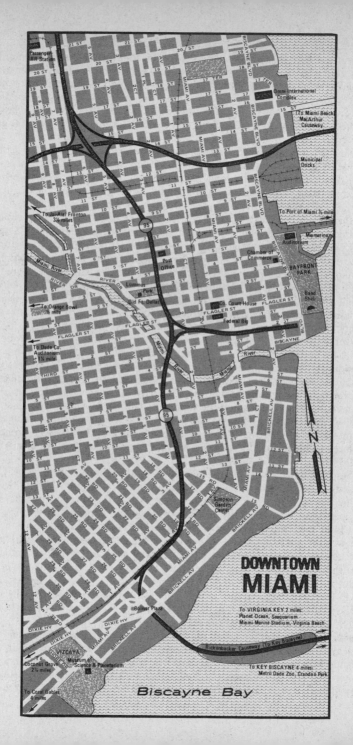

DOWNTOWN
MIAMI

To VIRGINIA KEY 2 miles:
Planet Ocean, Seaquarium
Miami Marine Stadium, Virginia Beach

Biscayne Bay

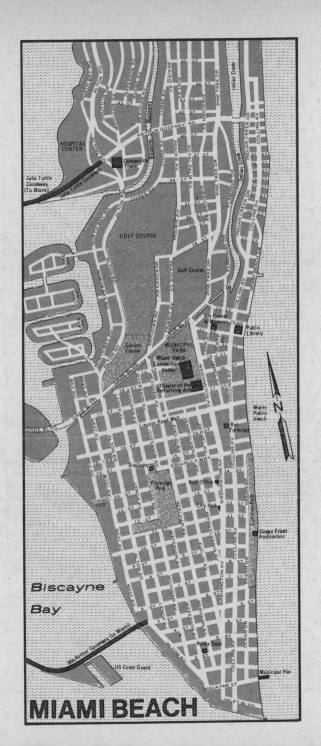

MIAMI BEACH

semi-retired Northeasterners. Key Biscayne has rows of luxury high-rises, simple bungalows, and excellent beaches.

With a mean annual temperature of 75.3°, with 40,000 registered boats, miles of improved beaches, 57 marinas, 11,829 acres of parks, 354 square miles of protected waters, and 3,200 more of sheltered waters, Miami's vital statistics support its reputation as a sunny, water-oriented resort. Yet in recent years, the city has become a major urban area, with an economic diversity associated with cities of comparable size. To a large extent, this is a result of the Latin American–Caribbean connection. Population has grown by 40% since the early 1970s, and employment has doubled in local business and industry. Indeed, the export trade is expected soon to overtake tourism as the number one industry. Traditional tourist migration from the Northeast has slowed, a good part of it stopped midstate by the growing attractions of the Tampa–Walt Disney World–Orlando–Daytona axis. Reports of Miami's drug- and race-related flare-ups have made headlines across the country and have doubtless discouraged certain potential visitors. Still, this area was once a small village stuck on the side of a swamp, and it became America's single greatest tourist magnet. It's probably not true, as an old Florida legend claims, that a race of giants once lived here, but it surely is true that Miami today possesses a gigantic will that wants most to grow. It's hard to believe it will not have its way.

MIAMI–MIAMI BEACH AT-A-GLANCE

SEEING THE CITY: The *Omni Gallery Lounge* at the *Omni International* (1601 Biscayne Blvd.) looks out over downtown; the *700 Club* atop the *David William Hotel* (700 Biltmore Way) in Coral Gables offers a panoramic view of the area; *Horatio's,* on the roof of the *Coconut Grove Hotel* (2649 S Bayshore Dr.) commands a fine view of Biscayne Bay.

Miami is largely a waterfront city, and one of the best ways to get to know it is by boat. Besides the *Island Queen,* which leaves from Miamarina (see *Special Places,* below), Nikko's Gold Coast cruises set sail out of Haulover Marina, 10800 Collins Ave. (945-5461), twice each day.

A bus tour of Miami highlights is given by American Sightseeing Tours, 4300 NW 14th St. (871-4992).

For a different view of the city, you can take a helicopter flight over Miami Beach from Watson Island on MacArthur Causeway. Open year-round (377-0934).

SPECIAL PLACES: The best way to see Greater Miami is by car.

Port of Miami – Every week thousands of people depart on Caribbean cruises from here, making Miami the world's largest cruise port. Cruises aren't free, but watching the tourist-laden ocean liners turn around in the narrow channel that leads to the open sea is. Open daily. Ships leave Fridays, Saturdays, Sundays, and Mondays from 4 to 7 PM.

Miamarina – Sightseeing and charter boats berth in this downtown marina. You can board the *Island Queen* for a 2-hour circle cruise of Biscayne Bay, viewing waterfront estates and residential islands daily (379-5119). Admission charge. 5th St. and Biscayne Bay.

Bayfront Park – This splash of green along Biscayne Bay lined with royal and coconut palms is a nice place to sit and watch the world of Miami sail or stroll by. The Kennedy Memorial Torch of Friendship symbolizes the relationship of the United States and Latin American countries. Open daily. Free. NE 5th to SE 2nd St.

Little Havana, Calle Ocho (8th Street) – The real Latin Flame, however, burns in this community, founded by Cubans who left after Castro's takeover. Shops feature handmade jewelry, dolls, and works of art. Fruit stands, bakeries, restaurants, and coffee stalls offer authentic Latin food. Try *Malaga* for lunch or dinner — roast pork with rice and black bean sauce, then flan (a custard covered with caramel syrup) for dessert (740 SW 8th St.; 858-4224), followed by a cup of espresso at a sidewalk stall. You can watch cigars being hand-rolled by Cuban experts in exile at Padron Cigars (1566 W Flagler St.; 643-2117).

Metro-Dade Cultural Center – This huge $25 million downtown complex, designed by Philip Johnson, houses the Center for the Fine Arts (375-1700; admission charge), which features traveling exhibitions, the Historical Museum of South Florida (375-1492; admission charge), with exhibitions on Spanish exploration, Indian civilization, and maritime history, and the Miami-Dade Public Library (375-BOOK). The Metro-Dade Cultural Center is at 101 W Flagler St.

Metrozoo – Here, in Miami's cageless zoo, Bengal tigers lounge before a replica of a Cambodian temple; and the mountains, streams, and bridges inside the new free-flight aviary evoke the natural habitat of the Asian birds inside. The air conditioned monorail whisks through the aviary. Open daily. Admission charge. 12400 SW 152nd St. (251-0401).

Planet Ocean – The International Oceanographic Foundation maintains this multimillion-dollar permanent exhibition that tells the story of the world's oceans in films and exhibitions (including a real submarine and a real iceberg). Open daily. Admission charge. 3979 Rickenbacker Causeway, Virginia Key (361-9455 or 361-5786).

Miami Seaquarium – Once you've learned all about the oceans, you can see who lives there at the world's largest tropical marine aquarium. Among the 10,000 creatures swimming around the tidepools, jungle islands, and tanks under a geodesic dome are killer whales, sharks, sea lions, and performing seals and dolphins. The real stars, though, are Flipper, of TV fame, and Lolita, a killer whale. Open daily. Admission charge. On Rickenbacker Causeway across from Planet Ocean (361-5703).

Miami Marine Stadium – This 6,500-seat roofed grandstand on Biscayne Bay hosts Miami's big shows as well as powerboat races, water shows, outdoor concerts, and fireworks displays. Check newspapers. 3601 Rickenbacker Causeway (361-6732).

Villa Vizcaya – This palatial estate is where International Harvester magnate James Deering reaped his personal harvest. The 70-room Venetian palazzo, furnished with European antiques, precious china, and artworks spanning 18 centuries, is surrounded by 30 acres of formal gardens. Open daily. Admission charge. 3251 S Miami Ave., just off US 1 (579-2708; 579-4626).

Museum of Science and Space Transit Planetarium – Exhibitions on a coral reef and the Everglades are enlightening, and there's a participatory science arcade. The planetarium has several shows daily, and if you are really inspired you can search for the stars yourself with the Southern Cross Observatory telescope atop the building in the evenings. Open daily. Admission charge. 3280 S Miami Ave. (854-4242).

Fairchild Tropical Gardens – Founded by a tax attorney with a touch of the poet in him, this might just be one of the most lyrical tax shelters imaginable — 83 acres of paradise with tropical and subtropical plants and trees, lakes, and a rare plant house with an extensive collection of unusual tropical flora. Tram rides are available through the grounds complete with intelligent commentary. Open daily. Admission charge. 10901 Old Cutler Rd. (667-1651).

Parrot Jungle – More of the tropics, but this time, screaming, colorful, and talented. Not only do these parrots, macaws, and cockatoos fly, but they also ride bicycles, roller skate, and solve math problems. If you don't believe it, just wait till you see the flamingos on parade — all amid a jungle of huge cypress and live oaks. Open daily. Admission charge. 11 miles south off US 1 at 11000 SW 57th Ave. (Red Rd.) and Killian Dr. (666-7834).

Monkey Jungle – The monkeys wander, run free, and swing from trees while visitors watch from inside a wire cage. Naturally, some chimp stars perform, and there are also orangutans, gibbons, and an Amazonian rain forest with South American monkeys in natural habitats. Open daily. Admission charge. 22 miles south off US 1, at 14805 SW 216th St. (235-1611).

Orchid Jungle – Jungle trails wind through this huge orchid display, more species and colors than you thought existed. Open daily. Admission charge. South of Miami off US 1 in Homestead, 26715 SW 157th Ave. (247-4824).

Preston B. Bird & Mary Heinlein Fruit and Spice Park – Some 20 tropical acres feature over 250 species of fruit, nut, and spice trees and plants. Guided tours by Parks Dept. naturalists include samplings of seasonal fruits. Open daily. Free. 35 miles southwest of Miami off US 1 at Coconut Palm Dr. and Redland Rd. (247-5727).

Miami Beach – At one time, this 8-mile-long island east of the mainland was renowned for its glittering seaside resorts, but over the years its image has been tarnished by crime and racial unrest. Recent efforts at renewal and redevelopment have improved the situation, bringing tourists back to the flashy *Fontainebleau Hilton* and the other big-name hotels that line Collins Avenue, the main drag. A $64 million beach renourishment program created a 300-foot strand extending from Government Cut to Haulover Inlet, and a beach boardwalk runs 1.8 miles from 21st to 46th sts. Miami Beach attractions (besides the sun, sand, and star-studded nightlife) include the Miami Beach Garden and Conservatory, with a beautiful display of Florida's native flora (2000 Convention Center Dr.) and the Bass Museum of Art, with a permanent collection ranging from the Old Masters to the Impressionists (2121 Park Ave.; 673-7530). The southern end of the island, between 5th or 6th street and 20th or so, is designated as a National Historic District for its many Art Deco buildings.

■ **EXTRA SPECIAL:** For a refreshing change, drive south along US 27 through miles of Miami's little-known farmland. You can stock up on fresh fruits and vegetables at numerous stands or go right out into the U-Pic fields and choose your own. Forty miles south of Miami (turnoff on US 1) is *Everglades National Park,* a unique and extremely diverse subtropical wilderness with some of the best natural-ist-oriented activities anywhere in the world. This 1½-million-acre preserve features alligators, raccoons, manatees, mangroves, and thousands of rare birds, all in their natural habitats. For complete details see DIRECTIONS. Farther south along US 1 stretch the *Florida Keys,* a chain of islands connected by an Overseas Highway. Here you'll find everything from the only living coral reef in the continental United States (which you can see in all its glory only by skin diving, snorkeling, or in a glass-bottom boat) at John Pennekamp State Park in Key Largo to great fishing possibilities and better food: conch chowder, and Key lime pie. For complete details see DIRECTIONS.

SOURCES AND RESOURCES

TOURIST INFORMATION: The Greater Miami & the Beaches Tourism Council is best for brochures, maps, and general tourist information; open weekdays. 555 17th St., Miami Beach (673-7070). The Miami Office of Information and Visitors Dept. of Tourism Office can also provide information. 174 Flagler St., 10th floor (579-6327). For information on fairs, art shows, and events in the area's parks, call the Dade County Leisure Line (547-PARK).

Local Coverage – *Miami Herald,* morning daily, publishes the Weekend section on Fridays with a schedule of upcoming events; *Miami News,* afternoon daily has a similar Upbeat section; *Miami* magazine, monthly, includes a What's Going On section, with a calendar of events for the month.

Area Code – All telephone numbers are in the 305 area code unless otherwise indicated.

 CLIMATE AND CLOTHES: Miami is warm all year with average daily temperatures of 75.3° and lots of sunshine. Summer clothes and beach attire are most comfortable, except during infrequent winter cold spells when medium-weight clothing and sweaters should be worn. Temperatures can also get cool indoors where air-conditioning prevails. In the big hotels, men dress in jackets and ties, and women usually wear cocktail dresses.

 GETTING AROUND: Airport – Miami International Airport is usually a 15-minute drive from downtown and about a half-hour from Miami Beach, longer during rush periods. Taxi fares average $10 to downtown, $12 to mid–Miami Beach. Red Top (526-5764) has van service every 30 to 45 minutes from the airport to hotels in downtown Miami for $6, to those in Miami Beach for $7. Call Red Top 24 hours in advance when returning to the airport; pickups are made 2 hours before flight time.

Metrorail – Metrorail, an elevated rail system, went into operation in 1984 from the Dadeland shopping mall in the Kendall area to downtown Miami, beyond to the Civic Center. The second phase extended it out to Hialeah; fare, $1. The Metromover rail system on a 1.9-mile downtown loop began service in June 1986; fare, $1. For information, call 638-6700.

Bus – Metrobus serves downtown Miami, Collins Avenue on Miami Beach, Coral Gables, and Coconut Grove fairly well, but service to other areas tends to be slow and complicated. A special shuttle bus covers the central downtown area, and links the downtown Metrorail station at Government Center to the Brickell financial district and the Omni complex. For information on routes, schedules, and fares, call 638-6700.

Taxi – You can sometimes hail a cab in the street, but it's better to order one on the phone or pick one up in front of any of the big hotels. Major cab companies are Yellow Cab (444-4444), Super Yellow Cab (888-7777), Metro Taxi (888-8888), and Central Cab (532-5555).

Car Rental – Miami is served by the large national firms; rates here are the cheapest in the country.

 MUSEUMS: Villa Vizcaya, the Museum of Science and Space Transit Planetarium, and the museums in the Metro-Dade Cultural Center are described in some detail in *Special Places.* Other museums are:

Cuban Museum of Arts and Culture – The cultural heritage of Miami's Cuban community, 1300 SW 12th Ave. (858-8006)

Lowe Art Museum – 1301 Stanford Dr., on the University of Miami campus in Coral Gables (284-3535)

Metropolitan Museum and Art Center – 1212 Anastasia Ave., Coral Gables (442-1448)

 MAJOR COLLEGES AND UNIVERSITIES: The University of Miami in Coral Gables (1200 San Amaro Dr.) has an enrollment of 17,000. Florida International University is a four-year degree college with two separate campuses (SW 8th St. and 107th Ave., NE 151st St. and Biscayne Blvd.).

Miami Dade Community College, with three campuses, is the largest junior college in the country (11380 NW 27th Ave., 11011 SW 104th St., and 300 NE 2nd Ave.).

SPECIAL EVENTS: Miami is the site of the annual *Orange Bowl Parade,* nationally televised from Biscayne Blvd. each New Year's Eve as a prelude to the *Orange Bowl* football classic played on New Year's night. Two of the country's largest boat shows are held each year, the *Dinner Key Boat Show* in Coconut Grove in October, and the *International Boat Show* at the Miami Beach Convention Center in February. Miami Beach hosts the *Festival of the Arts* each February, and the *Coconut Grove Art Festival* in the same month draws many away from the beach to stroll the shady lanes of this artists' haven. Also in February, the *Lowenbrau Grand Prix of Miami* attracts top racing drivers to the downtown run on Biscayne Blvd. between Flagler and NE 8th sts. (662-5660). In March, in Little Havana, natives and visitors alike head for Calle Ocho (8th St.) for *Carnaval Miami,* a 9-day festival.

SPORTS AND FITNESS: Baseball – Fans can watch preseason games of the Baltimore *Orioles,* whose spring training camp is in Miami; they often play the New York *Yankees,* who train in nearby Fort Lauderdale (635-5395). The University of Miami Hurricanes play at Mark Light Stadium on campus at 1 Hurricane Dr., corner of Ponce de Leon and San Amaro (284-2655).

Bicycling – Rent from Dade Cycle Shop, 3216 Grand Ave. in Coconut Grove (443-6075). There are over 100 miles of bicycle paths in the Miami area, including tree-shaded lanes through Coconut Grove and Coral Gables. A self-guided bicycle tour of Key Biscayne originates in Crandon Park. Dade County Parks & Recreation Dept. will provide more information (call 579-2676).

Boating – Greater Miami is laced with navigable canals and has many private and public marinas with all kinds of boats for rent. Sailboats are available from Dinner Key Marina, Bayshore Dr., Coconut Grove.

Fishing – Surf and offshore saltwater fishing is available year-round. The boardwalks on the Rickenbacker and MacArthur causeways and the Haulover Beach Fishing Pier (10880 Collins Ave., Miami Beach; admission charge) are popular fishing spots. There's also plenty of freshwater action in canals and backwaters, including the Everglades and Florida Bay. Charter boats offer a half day and full day of deep-sea fish, snapper, grouper, yellowtail, pompano, and mackerel trips from Miamarina, Bayfront Park at 5th St. (374-6260); Crandon Park Marina (361-1281); and Haulover Marina, 10800 Collins Ave. (947-3525).

Fitness Centers – Sportrooms, with four locations around Miami, has racquetball courts, exercise rooms, and aerobics classes. For information, call 944-8500 (N Miami), 443-4228 (Coral Gables); 556-4222 (Hialeah); 596-2677 (S Dade).

Football – Miami is the home of the NFL *Dolphins,* and Dolphin-mania infects the entire city during the football season, so for good seats go to the Orange Bowl, 1501 NW 3rd St., Gate 14, in advance (643-4700). The University of Miami Hurricanes also play football at the Orange Bowl; for tickets and information, contact the University of Miami ticket office, 1 Hurricane Dr., Coral Gables (284-2655), or go to the Orange Bowl.

Golf – More than 35 golf courses are open to the public. Some of the best are Kendale Lakes, 6401 Kendale Lakes Dr. (382-3930); Biltmore, 1210 Anastasia Ave., Coral Gables (442-6485); Miami Springs, 650 Curtiss Pkwy., Miami Springs (888-2377); Bayshore, 2301 Alton Rd., Miami Beach (532-3350); Palmetto, 9330 SW 152nd St., Miami (238-2922); and Key Biscayne, 6700 Crandon Blvd., Key Biscayne (361-9139).

Horse and Dog Racing – Betting is big in Miami. Hialeah racetrack, 2200 E 4th Ave., Hialeah (887-4347), is worth a visit not just for the action, but to see the beautiful grounds and clubhouse and the famous flock of pink flamingos (they're in the opening of TVs *Miami Vice*). There is also thoroughbred horse racing at Gulfstream Park, US 1 at Hallandale Beach Blvd. (944-1242), and at Calder, 21001 NW 27th Ave. (625-1311). Greyhound racing is held at Flagler, NW 37th Ave. and 7th St. (649-3000), and Biscayne, 320 NW 115th St. (754-3484). Check the racing dates before heading to the track.

Jai Alai – From December through April there's jai alai (a Basque game resembling a combination of lacrosse, handball, and tennis) and betting action nightly at the Miami Jai-Alai Fronton, the country's largest. You can pick up tickets at the gate or reserve them in advance, 3500 NW 37th Ave. (633-6400).

Jogging – Run along South Bayshore Drive to David Kennedy Park, at 22nd Avenue, and jog the Vita Path; or jog in Bayfront Park, at Biscayne and NE 4th St.

Nature Walks – There are nature walks at Fairchild Tropical Gardens and Preston B. Bird & Mary Heinlein Fruit and Spice Park, but the Parks & Recreation Dept. offers frequent guided tours through natural hammocks, tree forests, bird rookeries, and even through water (a monthly marine walk and nature lesson and dousing at Bear Cut, Key Biscayne). For information contact the Parks Dept. office (662-4124).

Skating – For outdoor roller skating, Coconut Grove is the place. You can rent skates at Sandy's Skates, 3001 Grand Ave., Coconut Grove (447-8888). For hard-hit snowbirds, head north to Broward County for year-round ice skating at Sunrise Skating Center, 3363 Pine Island Rd. (741-2366).

Swimming – With an average daily temperature of 75°, and miles of ocean beach on the Atlantic, Miami Beach and Key Biscayne offer some great places for swimming, all water sports, and another prime activity, sun worshiping. Some of the best beaches are:

Bill Baggs State Park. This long beach with sand dunes, picnic areas, fishing, boat basin, restored old lighthouse, and museum is a favorite of residents. At Cape Florida, the far south end of Key Biscayne.

Crandon Park Beach, a 2-mile stretch lined with shade trees, picnic tables, barbecue pits, ample parking. Drive to the far end for private cabanas rented by the day or week. Rickenbacker Causeway to Key Biscayne.

Haulover Beach is a long stretch of beautiful beach, good for surfing and popular with families. Marina, sightseeing boats, charter fishing fleets, restaurants, and fishing pier. A1A north of Bal Harbour.

Miami Beach. Several long stretches of public beach at various places, including South Beach for surfers (5th St. and Collins Ave.), Lummus Park with lots of shaded beaches (north of South Beach on Collins Ave.), and North Shore Beach with landscaped dunes and oceanfront walkway (71st St. and Collins Ave.). There are also small public beaches at the ends of streets in the midst of Hotel Row.

Tennis – Many hotels have courts for the use of their guests and there are also public facilities throughout the county. Some of the best are Flamingo Park with four hard courts, 1245 Michigan Ave. (673-7761); Biltmore, 1150 Anastasia, Coral Gables (442-6565); Tamiami, 10901 Coral Way, (223-7076); North Shore Center, 350 73rd St., Miami Beach (673-7754); and Tropical Park, 7900 SW 40th St., Miami (223-8710).

 THEATER: For current offerings, check the publications listed above. Miami's resident repertory company, *The Players,* performs everything from classical plays to experimental theater from October to May at the Coconut Grove Playhouse, 3500 Main Hwy. (442-4000). *The Miami Beach Theater of the Performing Arts* offers touring plays and musicals, including some pre- and post-Broadway shows, 1700 Washington Ave. (673-8300). The Gusman Cultural Center, 174 E Flagler St. (374-2444), and the Dade County Auditorium, 2901 W Flagler St. (545-3395), book theatrical and cultural events year-round. The *Miami Ballet Company,* 5818 SW 73rd St. (667-5985), holds several productions during the winter season.

MUSIC: Visiting orchestras and artists perform in Miami at the Gusman Cultural Center, 174 E Flagler St. (374-2444), and at Dade County Auditorium, 2901 W Flagler St. (545-3395), or in Miami Beach at the Theater of the Performing Arts, 1700 Washington Ave. (673-8300). The *Greater Miami Opera Association,* 1200 Coral Way (854-1643), stages several major productions in the winter season, as does the *South Florida Symphony Orchestra,* 1822 N University Dr., Plantation (1-474-7660).

NIGHTCLUBS AND NIGHTLIFE: The Diplomat Hotel's *Cafe Cristal,* 3515 S Ocean Ave., Hollywood (949-2442), features top-name entertainers. For a "flesh and feathers" revue, head for the *Sheraton Bal Harbour,* 9701 Collins Ave. (865-7511). Other good night spots are: *Greenstreet's,* 2051 Le Jeune Rd., Coral Gables (445-2131); *Casanova's,* 740 E 9th St., Hialeah (883-8706), for disco; *Les Violins,* 1751 Biscayne Blvd. (371-8668), and *Flamenco,* 991 NE 79th St. (751-8631), for, what else, flamenco shows; and *The Forge,* 432 Arthur Godfrey Rd., Miami Beach (538-8533), for contemporary music.

SINS: *Avarice* thrives most openly at Hialeah Race Track, 2200 E 4th Ave. (887-4347), where the thoroughbreds race and the hopeful place their bets. *Lust* lives in the red-light district in northeast Miami, along Biscayne Boulevard and NE 2nd Ave., between NE 50th St. and the 79th St. Causeway, and in virtually every resort hotel bar and lobby.

LOCAL SERVICES: Business Services – Stephan Secretarial Services, 2731 Ponce de Leon Blvd., Coral Gables (446-9500)
   Mechanics – Martino, for foreign and American cars, 7145 SW 8th St. (261-6071); Lejeune-Trail Exxon, for American makes, 801 SW 42nd Ave. (446-2942)

BEST IN TOWN

CHECKING IN: Winter is the busy season, and reservations should be made well in advance. In winter, a double room in the very expensive range will run $140 and up per night; $130 to $140 in expensive, and $85 to $110 in moderate. In summer, most hotels cut their rates, so shop around. For information about B&B accommodations, contact: Bed & Breakfast Co., PO Box 262, South Miami, FL 33243 (305 661-3270).

The Alexander – Miami Beach's first "new" oceanfront hotel since 1970, this elegant yet surprisingly homey place metamorphosed from former luxury apartments at a cost of $35 million. A chandeliered portico, a grand lobby with a curving stairway and antiques from the Cornelius Vanderbilt mansion in New York, and 211 spacious, antique-filled suites are all impressive, as is *Dominique's* French restaurant, with a main dining room overlooking the ocean. Roasted rack of lamb and exotic appetizers such as rattlesnake salad, alligator tails, and buffalo sausage are specialties. The grounds include an acre of tropical gardens, 2 lagoon swimming pools — 1 with its own waterfall — and 4 soothing whirlpools; a private marina and golf and tennis facilities are nearby. In a price range of its own, with rooms starting at $200. 5225 Collins Ave., Miami Beach (305 865-6500 or 800 327-6121). Very expensive.

Mayfair House – This all-suite hotel, part of the Mayfair Mall complex, opened in 1985. Each of the 186 suites has a terrace with Jacuzzi and small dining area, where a complimentary Continental breakfast with lots of tropical fruit is served each morning. There are two restaurants and a rooftop pool with bar. 3000 Florida Ave. (305 441-0000 or 800 433-4555). Very expensive.

Sonesta Beach Hotel and Tennis Club – This top-class resort is on the beach at Key Biscayne, complete with a tennis club offering 10 Laykold courts (3 lighted) and instruction by two pros, an Olympic-size swimming pool, and a fitness center. In addition to the 300 guest rooms, there are also villas with from two to five bedrooms. 350 Ocean Dr. (305 361-2021). Very expensive.

Fontainebleau Hilton – Recently given a facelift to the tune of $60 million, it is still far more glitzy than glittering. The hotel's lagoon-like pool has a grotto bar inside a cave. Award-winning *Dining Galleries* are especially popular for Sunday brunch. Fully equipped spa; 1,208 rooms. 4441 Collins Ave., Miami Beach (305 538-2000). Very expensive.

Grand Bay Hotel – Run by Italy's CIGA chain and done in high style, the 181-room hotel overlooks Biscayne Bay and sits right next to the equally tony Mayfair Mall. Guests have been unanimous in applauding the high quality of the facilities and service. It houses the fashionable *Regine's* nightclub. 2669 S Bayshore Dr., Coconut Grove (305 858-9600). Expensive.

Omni International – This 10½-acre complex includes 165 shops, 6 movie theaters, 10 restaurants, an amusement area, tennis courts, a sundeck, and rooftop pool. There are 500 rooms and suites. 1601 Biscayne Blvd. (305 374-0000). Expensive.

Key Biscayne – The Key's first and still most delightful hotel, with a quiet and peaceful atmosphere amid soft tropical decor. Features a private beach, 8 tennis courts, pitch-and-putt golf course, and 3 dining rooms. 100 rooms and 75 villas. 701 Ocean Dr., Key Biscayne (305 361-5431). Expensive.

Doral-on-the-Ocean – At the top of this 420-room high-rise is the *Starlight Roof Supper Club,* but the beach gets top billing here. Other highlights include shops, pool, and free bus to the Doral Country Club west of Miami, built around four championship 18-hole golf courses with tennis, sauna, and health club. 4833 Collins Ave., Miami Beach (305 532-3600). Expensive.

Hotel Inter-Continental Miami – This city-center hotel, formerly the *Pavillon,* is built in the grand old hotel tradition. The 646 rooms have marble baths and Oriental furniture along with other luxurious appointments. Facilities include 4 restaurants, 3 lounges, a swimming pool, tennis and racquetball courts, a jogging trail, and a 150-seat auditorium. 100 Chopin Plaza (305 577-1000). Expensive.

Riverparc – Quiet and modern, offering only suites, 129 in all. Of the 28 different styles, perhaps most lavish is the Presidential Suite, with two bedrooms, living room, and its own dining room. All units have refrigerators and mini-bars, about half have Jacuzzis. 100 SE 4th St. (305 374-5100). Expensive to moderate.

Biscayne Bay Marriott – On the marina, it offers 605 coral or mint green rooms, a majority with bay views. The brass and marble lobby is comfortably welcoming, and the 2 restaurants serve fresh seafood, as does the hotel's oyster bar. A 3rd-floor skybridge connects the *Marriott* to the Omni International shopping and hotel complex. 1633 N Bayshore Dr. (305 374-3900). Moderate.

Hyatt Regency – This riverside hostelry is part of Miami's convention and conference complex in the heart of downtown. The top two floors feature Hyatt's Regency Club, with complimentary Continental breakfast, private lounge, and other extras. Two restaurants, one of which features Continental cuisine. 400 SE 2nd Ave. (305 358-1234). Moderate.·

Holiday Inn – Across from the University of Miami, this motel is a good spot for visitors to the southwest area. The rooms are comfortable and there's a popular restaurant. 1350 S Dixie Hwy. (305 667-5611). Moderate.

EATING OUT: Much of Miami socializing centers around restaurant dining, so beware the long waiting lines during the winter season (December through April) when snowbirds swell the ranks of regular diners. Residents always make advance reservations. Expect to pay $50 or more for a dinner for two in the expensive range; $30 to $40 in the moderate; and $25 or less in the inexpensive range. Prices do not include drinks, wine, or tips.

Café Chauveron – Transplanted from New York City to Bay Harbor without the slightest disturbance of its famous soufflés, it's a French restaurant in the grand manner. Everything is beautifully prepared, from coquille de fruits de mer au champagne to soufflé Grand Marnier. Docking space if you arrive by boat. Open daily but closed from June through early October. Reservations necessary. Major credit cards. 9561 E Bay Harbor Dr., Bay Harbor Island, Miami Beach (866-8779). Expensive.

The Forge – Prime ribs and Java steak are the specialties on the otherwise Continental menu here, with an extensive wine list. . This attractive restaurant is decorated with Tiffany lamps, carved ceilings, and chandeliers. There's also a lounge with entertainment. Open daily. Reservations required. Major credit cards. 432 Arthur Godfrey Rd., Miami Beach (538-8533). Expensive.

Raimondo's – In a plain brick building in Coral Gables, *Raimondo's* doesn't offer much atmosphere, but the food is as good as ever. Daily specials are posted, but spaghetti carbonara and red snapper meunière are also excellent. Open daily. Reservations advised. Major credit cards. 4612 S LeJeune Rd. (666-9919). Expensive.

The Bistro – Intimate atmosphere, with a classic French menu including fresh fish specials. There's also a good, reasonably priced wine list. Open daily. Reservations suggested. Major credit cards. 2611 Ponce de Leon Blvd., Coral Gables (442-9671). Expensive.

Gatti – In Miami Beach since 1924, this family-owned restaurant remains in its original stucco house. The North Italian cuisine is excellent. Closed Mondays and May through October. Reservations suggested. Major credit cards. 1427 West Ave., Miami Beach (673-1717). Expensive.

Vinton's – Spread across the ground floor of the old *La Palma Hotel,* an elegant choice, with foot pillows and fresh flowers for the ladies and sherbet served midway through dinner to refresh the palate. Superb duck with raspberry sauce, salmon in sorrel sauce, and lots of fresh seafood. Some dishes flambéed tableside. Closed Sundays. Reservations advised. Major credit cards. 116 Alhambra Circle, Coral Gables (445-2511). Expensive.

Joe's Stone Crab – By now, this famous old (since 1913) South Beach restaurant is a Miami tradition, big, crowded, noisy, and friendly (get there by 6:30 or you'll have to wait). The stone crabs are brought in by Joe's own fishing fleet. People come here for serious eating, ordering tons of the coleslaw, hash brown potatoes, and Key lime pie that can keep dedicated diners waiting in line for up to two hours. Open daily; closed from May 15 to October 15. No reservations.

Major credit cards. 227 Biscayne St., Miami Beach (673-0365). Expensive to moderate.

Le Manoir – In a former bakery, very good traditional French food is served at reasonable prices. Big hit is the Friday night bouillabaisse. Closed Sundays. Reservations necessary. Major credit cards. 2534 Ponce de Leon Blvd., Coral Gables (442-1990). Expensive to moderate.

Cafe Martinique/English Pub – These two restaurants share a building, but the resemblance ends there. The two-level *Cafe Martinique* is set in a tropical garden and specializes in French/Continental cuisine and seafood amid very Gallic Art Deco surroundings. The *Pub,* dismantled in England and shipped here, is dark, atmospheric, and . . . pubbish. Prime ribs are the specialty. Both open daily. Reservations advised. Major credit cards. 320 Crandon Blvd., Key Biscayne (361-5481). Expensive to moderate.

Monty Trainer's – A casual atmosphere pervades this bayside eatery in Coconut Grove. Guests can arrive either by car or boat (100 dock spaces are available for diners), then enjoy a meal on a palm-fringed terrace. Open daily. Reservations not necessary. Major credit cards. 2560 S Bayshore Dr. (858-1431). Expensive to moderate.

Embers – As you might have guessed, the food here is hickory-grilled — steak, ribs, chicken, duck, lobster, shrimp, stone crabs, and so on. Everything comes with homemade bread, salad, potato, and relishes, and all the grilling is done over the barbecue pit out in front. Considering the casual food, the surroundings are surprising: chandelier, candlelight, pink tablecloths, and flowers. Open daily. Reservations suggested. Major credit cards. 245 22nd St., Miami Beach (538-4345). Moderate.

Kaleidoscope – Indoor-outdoor dining amidst palms and hanging plants on the 2nd floor of a Coconut Grove building. Good veal Oscar and duckling for dinner; tasty salads for lunch. Reservations recommended. Major credit cards. 3112 Commodore Plaza (446-5010). Moderate.

Centro Vasco – Next to jai alai, this is Miami's favorite Basque import. Specializes in filet Madrilene de Centro Vasco, seafood paella, arroz con mariscos. A great sangria is made right at your table. Open daily. Reservations advised. Major credit cards. 2235 SW 8th St. (643-9606). Moderate.

Marshall Major's – Some people call Miami the Bronx with palm trees. Whether or not that's true, Major's ranks with New York delis – pastrami, corned beef, home-style flanken, boiled chicken and vegetables, all served in huge portions. There's an Early Bird Special for dinner. Open daily. No reservations. Visa and MasterCard only. 6901 SW 57th Ave. (665-3661). Moderate to inexpensive.

Versailles – Authentic Cuban food and a lively ambience characterize this Little Havana landmark. A favorite of Latins and knowledgeable gringos. Wonderful Cuban sandwiches, black beans, and rice. Open daily till the wee hours. No reservations. Major credit cards. 3555 SW 8th St. (445-7614). Inexpensive.

The Spiral – The best bets at Miami's first vegetarian restaurant are tempura, salads, and vegetable sandwiches. Open daily. No reservations. Major credit cards. 1630 Ponce de Leon Blvd., Coral Gables (446-1591). Inexpensive.

My π – At this low-key eatery with Tiffany lamps and lots of natural wood, pizza is the specialty, but it looks more like quiche with a thick crust and slices of tomatoes on top. Also featured are burgers, salads, and soup. No reservations. MasterCard and Visa only. 9541 S Dixie Hwy., South Miami (666-3325); 235 Sunny Isles Blvd., Miami Beach (947-9052). Inexpensive.

Malaga – This traditional Cuban restaurant in Little Havana is a good place to get acquainted with the cuisine. Best are standards like fried whole snapper, spiced pork, arroz con pollo. Open daily. Major credit cards. 740 SW 8th St. (858-4224). Inexpensive.

Wolfie Cohen's Rascal House – A Miami Beach institution that might be described as a deli, whose eclectic, 500-item menu carries everything from knishes to chicken parmigiana. Open daily. No reservations or credit cards. 17190 Collins Ave. (947-4581). Inexpensive.

MILWAUKEE

Milwaukee is the kind of place that grows on you gradually, like contentment with a cold glass of beer. And beer is the word you immediately associate with Milwaukee. Only in 1889 was brewing the city's principal industry, but Milwaukee residents loyally claim they consume more beer than anyone else in America. Two of the nation's six largest breweries are making beer in the city that grew up around a French-Canadian trading post, and their presence is so pervasive that you smell malt in the air.

The city's role as a lake port was primarily responsible for its early growth. Here, Lake Michigan receives the waters of the Milwaukee, Menominee, and Kinnickinnic rivers. With so much water around, it's easy to see why Milwaukee used to be a swamp. But the resourceful pioneers who arrived in 1833 discovered plenty of gravel left by a departing glacier ten thousand years earlier. They were fast with a shovel, and before long, New Englanders were parceling off Milwaukee real estate and selling it to each other.

The sailing ships brought loads of immigrants in the 19th century — first the Irish, fleeing the potato famine; then the Germans, including those who left home after the abortive revolutions of 1848; and in years following a variety of ethnic groups, among them the Poles, now Milwaukee's second largest ethnic group. (The Poles gave the city kielbasa sausage, a dietary staple on the South Side.)

During the latter half of the 19th century, Milwaukee called itself the German Athens. As late as the 1880s, two out of every three Milwaukee residents who bought a daily paper chose to read the news in the language of Goethe. The city's Germanic era ended in a flurry of divided loyalties and ill will during World War I. The Deutscher Club changed its name to the Wisconsin Club, sauerkraut became liberty cabbage, and the Germania Building was called the Brumder Building until recently, when it took back its original name.

Although Milwaukee's European heritage has been considerably diluted over the years, stubborn local conviction insists that food ought to be piled high on the plate, that no one ought to thirst for long, and that a householder who doesn't keep his lawn cut is a menace to civilization. With a downtown district that seems too small for a metropolitan population of 1.4 million and an Old World respect for homey virtues and tidy streets, Milwaukee impresses a lot of people as an overgrown small town. Where else but in Milwaukee would everyone quit work for a sausage break, as employees of Usinger's wiener works do each morning, to sample the product? Where but at County Stadium would a bratwurst be nearly as popular with hungry fans as a hot dog? A bratwurst on a poppy seed roll in one hand, a beer in the other, and the home team hitting homers — now that's Milwaukee living!

But there is lots more to the place than sauerbraten and suds. Milwaukee's

lakefront has been compared to the Bay of Naples — not, it must be admitted, by the Neopolitans, but by the people who live here. Much of the shore belongs to the local taxpayers, including those who fish there for everything from smelt to coho salmon. (Milwaukee residents claim that no one lives more than half an hour from where the fish are biting.) When the weather is warm, the beaches within five minutes of downtown are crowded, even though Lake Michigan is generally too chilly for leisurely swimming.

Everyone celebrates the annual opening of Wisconsin's deer season, with thousands of hunters scurrying toward the woods and North Country taverns. Milwaukee County is proud of its park system, its zoo, its golf courses, and horticultural exhibits in glass domes that rise south of the Menominee Valley. The Milwaukee Symphony plays at the Performing Arts Center, and there are first-rate repertory and ballet companies. A downtown natural history museum and an art museum on the lakefront round out the city's cultural life. Urban problems are less severe in Milwaukee than in other cities of comparable size. The odds are pretty good you won't get mugged walking downtown after dark, and any political scandals you hear about are likely to be mild in comparison to those of other major cities. Milwaukee works hard to uphold its tradition of honest politicans and upright public servants.

Still, as nearly anyone you ask will admit, the city is no San Francisco, New Orleans, or New York. And ever since the early days, when a certain rival lakeport pulled ahead in the competition to attract settlers, it's been clear it's no Chicago. But the people who live in the community that made beer famous take comfort in that.

MILWAUKEE AT-A-GLANCE

 SEEING THE CITY: The 41-story First Wisconsin Center, Milwaukee's tallest building, anchors the eastern end of Wisconsin Avenue at Lake Michigan. Arrange a free visit to the top-floor observatory deck by calling 765-5733. 777 E Wisconsin Ave.

 SPECIAL PLACES: Milwaukee River divides the downtown area into east and west segments of unequal size (walking east you soon run into the beautiful Lake Michigan shoreline).

DOWNTOWN WEST

Wisconsin Avenue West – Walking west from the bridge along Wisconsin Avenue, Milwaukee's principal shopping street, you pass Gimbel's, on the same site that John Plankinton, a pioneer butcher, started his career with one cow and boundless ambition. He became a millionaire, and gave a start to packing tycoons Philip Armour and Patrick Cudahy. The blocks between Gimbel's and the Boston Store have been converted into a the Grand Avenue shopping mall.

Joan of Arc Chapel – On the campus of Marquette University. This is the medieval chapel where Joan of Arc prayed before being put to torch — not here in Milwaukee, but in the French village of Chasse, from whence the chapel was transported stone by stone. One of those stones reputedly was kissed by Joan before she went to her death, and is said to be discernibly colder than the others. Open daily. Free. 601 N 14th St. (224-7700).

The Alex Mitchell Home – Now quarters of the Wisconsin (formerly Deutscher) Club, this was originally the house of General Billy Mitchell's grandparents. A Scot, Alex Mitchell arrived in Milwaukee with a carpetbag full of money and established the first bank. Banks were illegal at the time, but that didn't stop him. He called it an insurance company. Later he became a railroad president. 900 W Wisconsin Ave.

Milwaukee Public Museum – Has the fourth largest collection of natural history displays in the country, including a "Streets of Old Milwaukee" section, showing the city in the 19th century. Discreetly hidden away in an upstairs bedroom is the sink that once belonged to Kitty Williams, a famous Milwaukee madam. Open daily except major holidays. Admission charge. 800 W Wells St. (278-2700).

Milwaukee County Historical Museum – Built in a former brewer's bank before World War I, this is the most interesting part of the Convention Hall/MECCA Complex, which includes an arena for sports activities and facilities for meetings. The museum has an archive and numerous exhibitions on the city's history, several of which are especially entertaining for children. Open daily. Free. 910 N 3rd St. (273-8288).

Père Marquette Park – Between the museum and the river, this park is named after the explorer-priest who stopped briefly in Milwaukee during a canoe trip through the Great Lakes area. Local legend insists that he landed here, although the site was then part of an extensive tamarack swamp along the Milwaukee River.

DOWNTOWN EAST

Wisconsin Avenue East – Wisconsin Avenue, east of the river, is a shopper's haven, with numerous fine stores. Shops on several nearby cross streets have been lovingly restored to their 19th-century origins. Across from the *Pfister Hotel* is the Milwaukee Club, whose members are the city's ruling elite.

Milwaukee War Memorial, Milwaukee Art Museum – On the lakefront, where Lincoln Memorial Drive crosses Wisconsin Avenue, the original building was designed by Eero Saarinen. The Art Museum has recently doubled its size; its permanent collection includes Old Masters, contemporary art, and primitive painting and sculpture. It also runs the Villa Terrace Decorative Arts Museum at 2220 N Terrace Ave. Outside, Lake Michigan provides a powerful backdrop for sculpture. The museum is closed Mondays. Admission charge. 750 N Lincoln Memorial Dr. (271-9508).

Cathedral Square – Between Jackson and Jefferson streets, this square dates back to Milwaukee's territorial days. Except for the tower, St. John's Cathedral was nearly destroyed by fire in 1935. On the west side of the square, Skylight Theater offers musical plays and vest pocket operas. If you feel like a snack, turn left on Jefferson to #761, where *George Watts & Son's* interesting silver shop has a restaurant tucked away on the second floor.

City Hall – Milwaukee's best-known landmark, this building with the tall tower (393 feet) was designed in 1895 so taxpayers could drive their buggies up in the rain to pay real estate taxes without getting wet. In the tower above the arched entry, Old Sol, a 20-ton bell, gathers dust. In 1922 citizens complained about the noise of Old Sol tolling, and city fathers ordered it stilled. N Water St. at Wells St.

OTHER SPECIAL PLACES

Annunciation Greek Orthodox Church – The last major building designed by Wisconsin-born architect Frank Lloyd Wright. You can tour the saucer-shaped structure daily except Sundays. Admission charge. 9400 W Congress St. (461-9400).

Whitnall Park – One of the larger municipal parks in the country, Whitnall includes the 689-acre Boerner Botanical Gardens, with sunken gardens, nature trails, and exhibitions. Open daily. Free (425-1130). Also on the park grounds is the Todd Wehr Nature Center, a wildlife preserve for hikers and strollers. Open daily; closed Sundays in winter. Free (425-8550).

Milwaukee County Zoo – Among the most famous zoos in the country, this one allows the animals to roam free in natural habitats. Kids adore the miniature railroad and children's zoo. Open daily. Admission charge. 10001 W Blue Mound Rd. (771-5500).

Schlitz Audubon Center – The 180 acres of undisturbed grazing area once provided pasture to brewery horses weary from pulling beer wagons. It's a good place to wander and wonder at days gone by. Closed Mondays. Admission charge; free to members of Audubon Center. 1111 E Brown Deer Rd. (352-2880).

Harbor Cruises – Iroquois Boat Line offers 2-hour trips along the Milwaukee River. Daily from Memorial Day through Labor Day. Admission charge. Clybourn St. Bridge dock (354-5050).

■**EXTRA SPECIAL:** For an interesting day trip, take I-94 west for 78 miles to *Madison,* capital of the state and home of the *University of Wisconsin*'s 1,000-acre, Big Ten campus. Drop in at the information center at Memorial Union on Park and Langdon streets to pick up a map and find out what's happening on campus. You'll find more than enough to keep you busy here, with an art center, geology museum, planetarium, observatory, and arboretum to see. The four lakes around Madison — Mendota, Monona, Waubesa, and Kegonsa — are great for fishing and swimming. If you continue driving west (toward the Iowa border), you'll find yourself in Wisconsin cheese country.

SOURCES AND RESOURCES

TOURIST INFORMATION: For information, maps, and brochures contact the Visitor Information Centers at 828 N Broadway and 161 W Wisconsin (273-3950, 276-6080). The public service bureau in the lobby of the Journal Building, 4th and State, is also helpful.

Local Coverage – *Milwaukee Sentinel,* morning daily; Milwaukee *Journal,* after-noon daily; *Milwaukee* magazine, monthly.

Area Code – All telephone numbers are in the 414 area code unless otherwise indicated.

CLIMATE AND CLOTHES: Summer and fall are generally pleasant, but expect sudden change when the wind shifts to the east. Even in July or August, pack a sweater. In winter, be prepared for bitter winds. The sub-zero cold is formidable.

GETTING AROUND: Airport – General Mitchell Field handles the city's domestic and international air traffic and is a 15-minute drive from down-town; taxi fare should run about $12. An economical share-a-ride program is available to those heading to the same destination; make arrangements through the Ground Transportation Coordinator, directly outside the baggage claim area. Milwaukee County Transit buses also provide service downtown for 80¢ (exact change required). Airport Limousine (282-8200) leaves every half-hour for downtown hotels ($4.70) as well as hotels in the western and northern metro areas ($9.50).

Bus – During the summer, a shuttle bus runs from the lakefront to the courthouse, mostly along Wisconsin Avenue. For information on bus schedules, contact Milwaukee County Transit System, 4212 W Highland Blvd. (344-6711).

Taxi – There are taxi stands at most major hotels, but we recommend phoning City Veterans Taxi (933-2266) or Yellow Cab (271-1800).

Car Rental – Most major car rental firms are represented. For a reliable local car rental agency, contact Selig Chevrolet, 10200 W Arthur Ave., West Allis (327-2300), or Econo-Lease, 3504 W Wisconsin Ave. (933-1040).

 MUSEUMS: The Milwaukee Public Museum, Milwaukee County Historical Society Museum, and Milwaukee War Memorial and Art Center are described in *Special Places*. Milwaukee has other museums a-plenty, among them:

Charles Allis Art Museum – 1630 E Royall Pl. (278-8295)
Old World Wisconsin – 25 miles SW in Eagle, Wisconsin (425-4860)
Captain Frederick Pabst Mansion – 2000 W Wisconsin Ave. (931-0808)
Brooks Stevens Auto Museum – 10325 N Port Washington Rd. (241-4185)

 MAJOR COLLEGES AND UNIVERSITIES: Marquette University (13,000 students) 11th and 18th sts. on Wisconsin Ave. (224-7700); University of Wisconsin–Milwaukee (25,000 students) Kenwood Blvd. and Downer Ave. (963-1122).

 SPECIAL EVENTS: *Summerfest* is held every June and July on the lakefront. Amusement park rides, rock and jazz concerts are part of the celebrations. *Lakefront Festival of the Arts* is held outdoors near the Milwaukee Art Center in the middle of June with music, food, arts and crafts exhibits. The *Circus Parade,* revived in 1985, promises to become an annual July event. The *Wisconsin State Fair* takes place for two weeks in mid-August on the fairgrounds adjoining I-94 west of downtown. The weekend before Thanksgiving, *Holiday Folk Fair* features ethnic food, music and entertainment. MECCA complex, Kilbourn Ave.

 SPORTS AND FITNESS: Baseball – The Milwaukee *Brewers* play at County Stadium, 201 S 46th St. (933-9000).
    Basketball – The Milwaukee *Bucks* and Marquette *Warriors* play at the Arena, 500 W Kilbourn Ave. (271-2750).

Bicycling – Bikes can be rented from East Side Cycle and Hobby Shop, 2031 N Farwell Ave. (276-9848); Wilson Park Schwinn Cyclery, 2033 W Howard Ave. (281-4720).

Fishing – Salmon and trout as big as 30 pounds are caught in Lake Michigan, from shore and breakwater. You can use launching ramps at McKinley Marina and near South Shore Yacht Club for $3 to $5. Half-day boat charters cost about $125 for a party of six, including bait and tackle, and are offered by numerous firms (see the yellow pages under Fishing Parties — Charter).

Fitness Centers – The YMCA has a pool, track, sauna, weights, and massage, 9250 N Green Bay Rd. (354-9622).

Football – Green Bay *Packers* play at County Stadium, 201 S 46th St. (342-2717).

Golf – The best public golf course is at Mee-Kwon Park, 6333 W Bonniwell Rd., Mequon (242-1310).

Hockey – The Milwaukee *Admirals* play at the Arena.

Ice Skating – In winter, many parks open rinks. For year-round ice skating (indoors), try Wilson Park Center, 4001 S 20th St. (281-4610); Northridge Ice Palace, 9225 N 76th St. (354-1751).

Jogging – Run in Lake Front Park, near War Memorial Center, on the beach, sidewalk, or oval track.

Polo – Sundays in summer Milwaukee's polo teams compete at Uihlein Field, Good Hope Rd. and N 70th St. (no phone).

Skiing – Currie, Dretzka, and Whitnall parks have ski tows, and mostly beginners' trails. Cross-country skiers may use all county parks. The Whitnall Park trails are particularly good.

Swimming – Seven public beaches along the lakefront have lifeguards and dressing facilities. The water is usually chilly, even in August. For information on the 17 public pools, call 278-4343.

Tennis – Try North Shore Racquet Club, 5750 N Glen Park Rd. (351-2900), or Le Club, 2001 W Good Hope Rd. (352-4900). In warm weather, numerous county parks have courts available for nominal fee.

 THEATERS: For complete listings on theatrical and musical events, see local publications listed above. *Milwaukee Repertory Theater* is based at Performing Arts Center, 929 N Water St. (273-7121). *Pabst Theater* stages a variety of shows, 144 E Wells St. (271-3773), and the *Riverside Theater,* 116 W Wisconsin Ave. (271-2000), features stage shows by top performers. Other theaters include: *Skylight Theater,* 813 N Jefferson St. (271-8815); *Theatre X,* 820 E Knapp St., for experimental drama (278-0555); *Melody Top,* featuring musicals in summer (271-8815).

 MUSIC: *Milwaukee Symphony, Milwaukee Ballet Company,* and *Florentine Opera Company* play at Performing Arts Center, 929 N Water St. (273-7121). "Music Under the Stars" concerts are held in Washington and Humboldt parks on Friday and Saturday nights in July and August.

 NIGHTCLUBS AND NIGHTLIFE: For jazz, visit the *Red Mill,* 1005 S Elm Grove Rd. (782-8780). *Park Avenue,* 500 N Water St. (765-0891), is a lively disco for the under-30 crowd; *Rumors,* in the *Marriott* at 375 S Moorland Rd. in Brookfield (786-1100), has dancing to top-40 hits and caters to well-dressed young professionals; *La Playa,* atop the *Pfister Hotel and Tower,* (276-4448) has touch dancing to a 10-piece combo with a spectacular view; and *Papagaio,* 515 N Broadway (277-0777), features top-40 music for an older clientele. For dinner with piano music, try *Chip & Py's,* 815 S 5th (645-3435).

 SINS: *Gluttony* takes rather a strange form in this Midwestern city, with Milwaukee boasting the largest per capita consumption of popcorn anywhere in the world. If this sounds sissy to you, you might consider it is also the largest consumer of brandy in the entire US, though residents make a habit of cutting their drinks with 7-Up or sugared club soda.

If you want a *sloth*ful afternoon, grab your binoculars and head off to the *Schlitz Audubon Center,* 1111 E Brown Deer Rd. There are plenty of nature walks to stroll along and an amazing variety of birds to spy on. It's also easy enough to find an old reliable tree to curl up under for a lazy afternoon nap.

LOCAL SERVICES: Babysitting – Nannys Ltd. (961-0515); Deerwood Center (355-3655)

Business Services – National Business Offices, 2300 N Mayfair Rd. (259-9110), also at 2040 W Wisconsin Ave. (933-0636); National Bookkeeping Service, 759 N Milwaukee St. (276-6655)

Mechanics – Midtowne Mobil Servicenter, 2630 W Wisconsin Ave. (342-7726); Suburban Motors, Thiensville (242-3737); for foreign cars, Tosa Imports, 6102 W North Ave. (771-2340)

■ **THE BEERS THAT MADE MILWAUKEE FAMOUS:** If you're wondering where the smell of malt is coming from, follow your nose to one of the big breweries, where you'll be escorted through the facilities and given samples of the frothy wares (unless you're a child, in which case you only get to look): Miller's, 3939 W Highland Blvd. (931-2000); Pabst, 917 Juneau Ave. (347-7300). All welcome visitors except on holidays, when everyone stays home testing the product.

BEST IN TOWN

CHECKING IN: Milwaukee's hotels range from the elegant, older *Pfister* and the modern *Hyatt Regency* to the functional *Red Carpet Inn* near the airport. You can expect to pay between $80 and $105 for a double at those places designated expensive; between $55 and $75 in the moderate category; about $45 or $50 at inexpensive places.

Pfister – Catering to visiting and local elite since the 1890s. For a while, it looked as if the 330-room establishment was sliding gently downhill, but the present owners have brought it back to the level of elegance that enchanted Enrico Caruso and several presidents. The bronze lions in the lobby are named Dick and Harry, by the way, and the best views of the lake are in rooms 8, 9, 10, or high up in the new tower in the romantic lounge, *La Playa.* 424 E Wisconsin Ave. (414 273-8222). Expensive.

Hyatt Regency – This new $28 million, 18-story hotel is the first large hotel to be built in Milwaukee in many years and has helped to end a chronic shortage of rooms for conventions. And, by no coincidence, it is next to the downtown convention center. Topping the 485-room structure, with its atrium lobby, is a revolving restaurant. 4th and Kilbourn (414 276-1234 or 800 228-9000). Expensive.

The Marc Plaza – The largest hotel in Milwaukee since 1927, its 540 rooms have gone through extensive renovation during their long career. Updated facilities include a heated indoor swimming pool and sauna. 509 W Wisconsin Ave. (414 271-7250). Expensive to moderate.

Marriott Inn – Stands out among the many motels on the outskirts of town. It has 254 rooms (one especially equipped for paraplegics), an indoor heated pool, and a popular disco, *Rumors.* 375 S Moorland Rd., Brookfield (414 786-1100). Moderate.

Hilton Inn – Overlooking the Milwaukee River, this 164-room hostelry includes such amenities as king-size beds and an indoor pool. The adjoining *Anchorage* restaurant is noted for its seafood. On the Milwaukee River, near the Hampton Ave. exit of I-43 (414 962-6040). Moderate.

Red Carpet Inn – Near the airport, next to a convention hall, this property has 400 rooms, 2 heated swimming pools, and handball, tennis, and racquetball courts. If you're intrigued by Milwaukee's favorite sport, you'll be delighted to find out it's close to a bowling alley. 4747 S Howell Ave. (414 481-8000). Moderate to inexpensive.

EATING OUT: Visiting Milwaukee without sampling the wiener schnitzel would be like going to New Orleans's French Quarter and living on Big Macs. They used to say you could get any kind of food in Milwaukee as long as it was German, but these days it's easier to feast at Polish, Chinese, Italian, Greek, Japanese, Serbian, and American restaurants as well. Expect to pay between $35 and $50 for two at those places listed as expensive; between $25 and $35, in the moderate category; under $20 in the inexpensive bracket. Prices don't include drinks, wine, or tips.

Karl Ratzsch's – Ranked as one of Milwaukee's top dining spots for many years, specializing in Teutonic cuisine since the days when the city called itself the German Athens. Open daily. Reservations advisable on weekends. Major credit cards. 320 E Mason St. (276-2720). Expensive.

John Ernst's Café – Even older and still a favorite of members of the brewing aristocracy, serving since 1878. Decorated with steins, German clocks, and posters. You can get steak, but to do as the local populace does it's better to order "sauerbraten mit dumplings, ja?" Closed Mondays. Reservations advisable on weekends. 600 E Ogden Ave. (273-5918). Expensive.

Pfister Hotel's English Room – Fairly exotic for Milwaukee, this is the place if you suddenly develop an overwhelming craving for crêpes flambées or pheasant with truffles. Flaming dishes are prepared at your table with appropriate theatrical flourish. Open daily. Reservations necessary on weekends. Major credit cards. 424 E Wisconsin Ave. (273-8222). Expensive.

La Rôtisserie and Polaris – These two restaurants are in the new *Hyatt Regency* hotel. The former overlooks the 18-story lobby/atrium and specializes in duck roasted on a spit. The latter, revolving slowly atop the *Hyatt*'s roof, offers a more limited menu but a better view. Open daily. Reservations recommended. Major credit cards. 4th and Kilbourn (276-1234). Expensive.

Le Restaurant – In the nearby suburbs, offering what some insist is the most interesting food in the area. The menu, which changes daily, emphasizes seafood, fowl, and beef. Piano music on Friday and Saturday nights. 149 N Green Bay Rd., Thiensville (242-2280). Expensive.

Mader's – Another family-run place going back to shortly after the century's turn, decorated in Bavarian style. For years, the late Gus Mader offered a reward to anyone who could finish his 3½-pound pork shank. The prize? Another 3½-pound pork shank, to be eaten in the same sitting. Open daily. Reservations recommended on weekends. Major credit cards. 1037 N 3rd St. (271-3377). Expensive to moderate.

The Beer Baron's – In the elegant former headquarters of the brewery once run by Valentin Blatz, this popular downtown eatery suits diners in the mood for anything from a fancy meal to a sandwich or an elaborate salad. An adjoining saloon matches the high standards of the pioneer brewers. In July and August, lunch is served on the sidewalk café. Reservations advised. Major credit cards. 1120 N Broadway (272-5200). Expensive to moderate.

Toy's Chinatown – The family that owns this elaborate downtown Chinese restaurant has been serving Milwaukee residents for three generations, so when you eat here, you're not just getting egg rolls, you're getting tradition. Unless you order hundred-year-old duck eggs, you can be sure of fresh Cantonese dishes, like sweet and sour shrimp, spare ribs, and chow mein. Open daily. Reservations recommended on weekends. Major credit cards. 830 N 3rd St. (271-5166). Moderate.

Old Town – At this Serbian restaurant you can dine to the tune of tinkling tamburitzas. Fine, you say, but what is Serbian food? Well you might ask. We did, and were delighted to find it means sizzling lamb dishes cooked somewhat spicier than similar Greek and Turkish dishes. Closed Mondays. Reservations advised on weekends. Major credit cards. 522 W Lincoln Ave. (672-0206). Moderate.

Jake's Delicatessen – If corned beef on rye appeals to you more than goose à la Tivoli or souvlaki, head for *Jake's*. All kinds of people eat here, from local millionaires to penniless kreplach lovers. You can sit at a booth, at a counter, or take your pastrami sandwich with you in a paper bag. Try the specials — they're giant knockwurst-like sausages. Open daily. Reservations advised. No credit cards. 1634 W North Ave. (562-1272). Inexpensive.

Bavarian Inn – This inn sits in a park owned by Germanic clubs, but its dining room is open to the public daily except Mondays. The food is good, the atmosphere informal, and Sunday buffet is one of the best bargains in town. You can help yourself to as much as you like. Be sure to bring a big appetite to do it justice. Closed Mondays. Reservations advised on weekends. Major credit cards. Take the Silver Spring exit from I-43 north, turn south on N Port Washington Rd., then west on Lexington to 700 W Lexington Ave. (964-0300). Inexpensive.

MINNEAPOLIS-
ST. PAUL

Describing the Twin Cities is like describing your children: They can be very different and yet you love them for their unique qualities; and you can never forget that they are products of much the same history. Vibrant and culturally eclectic, Minneapolis and St. Paul complement one another, each lending something extra to the other's character.

Just how these characters differ may not be as apparent to the visitor as it is heartfelt by the resident. But even long-time Minneapolis residents get lost in St. Paul (or say they do), and they are quick to reassure the outsider that people from St. Paul get just as confused in Minneapolis.

Minneapolis is the larger of the two cities, and has been for almost a century, but St. Paul is the state's capital. St. Paul is the older, settled in the 1850s by Irish and German Catholics, the city with a tradition of "old wealth" that, by reputation at least, looks down its nose at nouveau riche Minneapolis; but as an old industrial and railroad center, St. Paul suffers more pollution than its twin, which has cleaner industries and more room to grow.

In the past decade, however, St. Paul has enjoyed an enthusiastic revival. A large-scale redevelopment brought $903 million in new buildings to the downtown area. Town Square Park is a four-level, glass-enclosed park, filled with flowing streams, waterfalls, and trees. Fine shops and enticing eateries are just a skywalk away from 100 retail stores, professional services, and government offices. Grand Avenue and the Ramsey Hill redevelopment combine 2 miles of epicurean delights and innovative shops with restorations of Victorian architecture in F. Scott Fitzgerald's old stomping ground. Future plans for St. Paul include a World Trade Center, which is scheduled for completion in 1987. The 40-story building will be the tallest in the city and the hub of international business in the region.

As for the flamboyant twin, Minneapolis, Nicollet Mall is the heart of downtown shopping and business. The city retains its natural beauty through an outstanding park system, while creating residential neighborhoods of distinct character and ethnic variety. And the riverfront area has a new vitality since the resuscitation of the old warehouse district with attractive shopping areas and restaurants.

A steady increase in filming activity has contributed to the status of the Twin Cities as the fourth largest film production center nationally; it's seventh in terms of advertising and public relations business.

At the junction of the Mississippi and Minnesota rivers, the Twin Cities region was discovered by French explorers in the late 17th century. It remained relatively undeveloped until the 1850s, when the Indian territory west of the Mississippi was opened for settlement. Situated at the first navigable point on the Mississippi, Minneapolis and St. Paul became major shipping points for timber, flour, furs, and other natural resources.

South of Franklin Street, St. Paul and Minneapolis are divided by the Mississippi, but Twin Cities residents don't perceive the river as the boundary. The University of Minnesota campus spans both sides of the river, but retains a Minneapolis address. About 50 miles in diameter, the metro area absorbs diversified industries and businesses that have spread throughout the two cities; St. Paul has attracted more of the steel and chemical plants over the years, while Minneapolis is home of cleaner industries like electronics. Traditional rivals, in recent years the two cities have opted for a joint approach toward solving mutual urban problems. Water, pollution, sewage, and transportation are dealt with efficiently on a "metro area" basis.

Although St. Paul initially led in population, Minneapolis surpassed its twin around 1880 and has been Minnesota's largest city ever since. With a population of 2 million, the unified Twin Cities metro area is the third fastest growing urban region in the United States — and the fifteenth largest. Its 936 lakes and 513 parks contribute to Minneapolis–St. Paul's unusual pastoral beauty.

Part of the charm of the metro area can be directly attributed to an almost religious sense of tithing on the part of the more responsible corporations and their principals. They feel, perhaps, that the quality of life in the Twin Cities is unique and worth supporting. The first car pools in the United States were started by the 3M Corporation to help employees conserve energy. Corporate and individual response to the arts is exemplary; perhaps business leaders realize that the relative isolation of the Twin Cities (at least 400 miles from another major city) requires a full measure of cultural and sports activities to provide the nonbusiness pleasures demanded by talented employees.

The cultural scene in Minneapolis–St. Paul is outstanding. The world-famous Guthrie Theater makes its home here, as does the Minnesota Orchestra — a full-time symphony. The only full-time chamber orchestra in the United States, the St. Paul Chamber Orchestra, performs to packed houses. The Minneapolis Institute of Arts, the Walker Art Center, the Ordway Music Theater, the Twin Cities' two science centers, the Minnesota Opera, and the cities' many historical collections and art galleries are responsible for Minneapolis–St. Paul's reputation as the cultural center of the Midwest. And the St. Paul radio program "Prairie Home Companion" with host Garrison Keillor, a delightful takeoff on the Grand Ole Opry that is broadcast on National Public Radio, is attracting a national audience.

Minneapolis–St. Paul residents don't even mind the severe winter weather. They enjoy it with a vigor by snowmobiling, ice fishing, and skiing. Twin Citians like where they live no matter what the season.

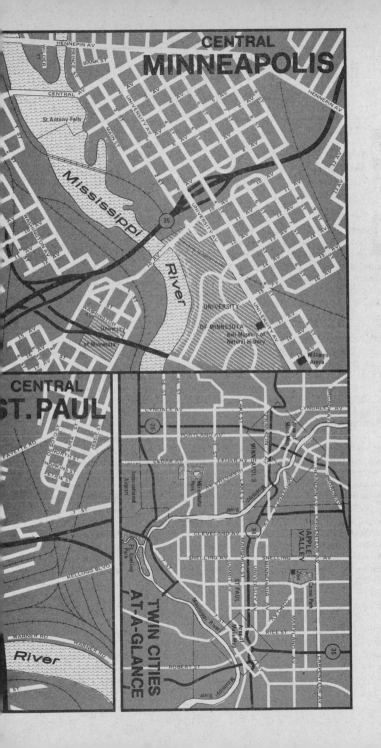

MINNEAPOLIS–ST. PAUL AT-A-GLANCE

 SEEING THE CITY: Although the IDS and Multi-Foods buildings are taller, the best view of the area is from the observation deck of the 32-story Foshay Tower (9th St. at 2nd Ave). Closed in winter. St. Paul is built on seven hills, like Rome, and while there's no place as romantic as Hollywood's Mulholland Drive, there are a few drives with good views. One of the best is the Pennsylvania Avenue hill.

 SPECIAL PLACES: The most extraordinary feature of downtown Minneapolis and St. Paul is their interior skyways, an interconnected belt of pedestrian malls and escalators lacing in and out of shops, banks, and restaurants at the second-story level. When it's below zero, you may still walk around comfortably without a coat. At street level, courtyards, gardens, fountains, and sculpture form attractive plazas. In Minneapolis, travelers may check in at one of two hotels connected to the skyway, the *Marquette,* and the *Amfac.* St. Paul's skyway connects to the *Holiday Inn* (see *Checking In).*

MINNEAPOLIS

The Minneapolis Institute of Arts – Architecturally classical, the Institute houses Old Masters, Chinese and Egyptian art, Revere silver, and historical exhibitions. In addition to the museum collections, the Institute's Society for Fine Arts presents classical films, recitals, and lectures. A model for other arts institutions around the country, the Institute is also the home of the Minneapolis College of Art and Design and the Children's Theater Company and School. Open every day. Admission charge. 2400 3rd Ave. S (870-3200).

The Guthrie Theater – Internationally acclaimed for its superb productions, the Guthrie Theater features a resident professional repertory company which presents ensemble productions of classical and modern drama. The contemporary theater building can seat more than 1,400 people in a 200-degree arc around an open stage. After a nationwide search for a hospitable metropolitan environment in which to locate a repertory theater, Sir Tyrone Guthrie selected Minneapolis. His choice has been borne out by the enthusiastic, loving support of audiences and patrons. The theatrical season generally runs from May to February. Concerts are performed throughout the year. 725 Vineland Pl. (377-2224).

Walker Art Center – Named after T. B. Walker, a local patron of the arts, the center, in the Guthrie building, complements the classical Institute of Arts by focusing on post-Impressionist and contemporary art. The Walker also features alternating exhibits, innovative film programs, and concerts. Pretheater dinners are served in the Walker restaurant. Closed Mondays. Free except for special exhibitions. 725 Vineland Pl. (375-7600).

Minnehaha Park – In his poem "Hiawatha," Longfellow immortalized the "laughing waters" of Minnehaha Falls along the Mississippi. In addition to the splendor of the Falls, you can picnic near a statue of Minnehaha herself and brave Hiawatha. Free. Minnehaha Pkwy. and Hiawatha Ave. S.

Minneapolis Grain Exchange – An ornate hall the size of a large school gym, the exchange is a loud, hectic place where futures and samples of actual grains are bought and sold. You can take a guided tour through the world's largest grain exchange, but you must make reservations in advance. Visitors balcony open daily. Tours, Mondays-Fridays. 400 4th St. S (338-6212).

Orchestra Hall – Music has had an appreciative audience in the Twin Cities since the turn of the century. The hall houses the Minnesota Orchestra, formerly the Minneapolis Symphony, an orchestra which played its first concert in 1903 and has been playing classical and symphonic pop music to responsive audiences ever since. Though spartan in appearance, the new Orchestra Hall is renowned for its superior acoustics. 1111 Nicollet Ave. (371-5656).

Minnesota Zoo – Set in the rolling hills of Apple Valley, this 500-acre, state-funded zoological park provides a natural environment for Siberian tigers, musk oxen, moose, and other northern animals. A pair of beluga whales joins other aquatic species in the Aquarium, and a five-story indoor tropical environment houses jungle fauna and flora. Zoo lovers will find this one among the nation's best. Open daily. Admission charge. 12101 Johnny Cake Ridge Rd., Apple Valley, 25 minutes south of the city on Hwy. 35 (432-9000).

ST. PAUL

Como Park – Minneapolis–St. Paul has a multitude of parks. The largest is St. Paul's Como Park, which dates from Victoria's reign. A 70-acre lake, a small zoo, a golf course, and children's rides contribute to its popularity. In addition, there are special floral gardens and a conservatory where summer concerts are held. Open daily. Free. Lexington Pkwy. and W Como Blvd. (zoo: 488-5572; gardens: 489-1740).

State Capitol – St. Paul is Minnesota's political center, and its capitol is one of the most important buildings in the state. Set on a hill, its giant dome — a replica of one designed by Michelangelo in Rome — is one of the state's outstanding landmarks. More than 25 varieties of marble, limestone, sandstone, and granite were used to construct the building. Free guided tours given daily. The Minnesota Historical Society building is on the edge of the capitol grounds. Founded in 1849, ten years before Minnesota became a state, the society houses records of pioneer days. Open daily. Free. University Ave. between Wabasha and Cedar sts. (296-2881).

St. Paul's Cathedral – The center of the Roman Catholic archdiocese, this cathedral is a replica of St. Peter's in Rome. Architecturally notable for its 175-foot-high dome and a central rose window, the cathedral has a special Shrine of the Nations where visitors from all around the world can meditate and pray. Open daily. Free. 239 Selby Ave. (228-1766).

Science Museum of Minnesota – This $3.5 million complex combines a 635-seat theater for the performing arts, a 300-seat auditorium, an art gallery, a rooftop lounge, and the pièce de résistance, the science museum. Featuring natural history, environmental, geological exhibitions and films, the science center is immensely popular with residents. Open daily. Free. 30 E 10th St. (221-9488).

William L. McKnight Science Center – The Science Center — named after the founding father of the 3M Company — is among the most advanced science centers in the US. Part of the Science Museum of Minnesota, the high point of this new science complex is its "omnitheatre" — a floor-to-ceiling hemispheric screen surrounding the audience and tilted at 30° so that viewers will see the screen in front of them rather than above, as in conventional planetarium-type theaters. Closed Mondays. Admission charge. 505 Wabasha (221-9400).

Fort Snelling State Park – The oldest landmark in the Twin Cities, one of the first military posts west of the Mississippi. Not very far west, however: Fort Snelling sits high on a bluff overlooking the junction of the Mississippi and Minnesota rivers. You can see what life was like here during the 1820s. People in costume demonstrate early crafts, and parade in military formation. Fife and drum bands perform in summer. The history center is open weekdays year-round. Fort Snelling is open daily, May through

October. Admission charge. Highways 5 and 55, 6 miles southwest of the city (726-9430).

■**EXTRA SPECIAL:** *St. Croix Valley,* 25 miles northeast of Minneapolis–St. Paul, offers several stops for a day's outing. Stillwater, birthplace of Minnesota, is within easy striking distance of the Afton Alps, Trollhaugen, and Snowcrest mountains for skiers. In Stillwater, visit the *Grand Garage and Gallery* on Main Street, with shops and galleries. It has food, but a better eating stop is *Brine's Meat Market and Lunchroom,* which has *The Employees Lunchroom* upstairs, open to *anybody* employed *anywhere,* with great bratwurst, pastrami, and chili. On the Wisconsin side of the tour is Somerset, which has one of the greatest summer activities in the entire world: tubing down the Apple River. You get carted upriver about 4 miles, plunked into an inner tube, and sent drifting back to Somerset. The river flows quickly at the outset but widens and slows down, and the ride is tranquil into town.

SOURCES AND RESOURCES

TOURIST INFORMATION: The Greater Minneapolis Chamber of Commerce and the Minneapolis Convention and Tourist Commission have an information booth in the IDS building, 15 S 5th St. (348-4330).

    Minnesota Explorer, a 24-page guide to events throughout the state published three times a year, is free from the Minnesota Office of Tourism, 240 Bremer Bldg., 419 N Robert St., St. Paul 55101 (296-5029 or 800 328-1461).

Local Coverage – *Minneapolis Star-Tribune,* daily; *St. Paul Pioneer Press/Dispatch,* daily. *The Reader* (distributed free in the Mall and downtown hotels) lists activities in the Twin Cities. *Mpls.–St. Paul* and *Twin Cities* magazines, available monthly at newsstands, give full details on what's what.

Food – *Twin Cities: Guide,* by Lori Morse (Dorne; $8.95), includes a restaurant guide. *Minneapolis–St. Paul Epicure* ($5.95) shows menus from restaurants in all price ranges.

Area Code – All telephone numbers are in the 612 area code unless otherwise indicated.

CLIMATE AND CLOTHES: In winter, be prepared for the worst. The average winter temperature is 19°, but it can drop to 35° below zero, and snow has been known to fall as early as October. Summer temperatures are generally in the 70s and 80s.

GETTING AROUND: Airport – Minneapolis/St. Paul International Airport is a 20- to 30-minute drive from the downtown area of either Twin City; cab fare should run about $15. Minneapolis-Suburban Airport Service (726-6400 or 827-7777) provides transportation from the airport to Minneapolis hotels for $5.50; Capitol City Airline Service (726-9598) handles the St. Paul hotel transfers for $4. Metropolitan Transit Commission buses 7C and 7E run between the airport and downtown Minneapolis, stopping along Washington Avenue every 40 minutes; to get to the airport from downtown St. Paul, take bus 9B on 6th St. and transfer to the 7C or 7E at Fort Snelling. The fare is 75¢.

Bus – Minneapolis–St. Paul bus systems are a model of efficiency studied by other cities. They run from 6 to 1 AM. Express buses make the trip between Minneapolis and

St. Paul in 15 minutes. Passengers' queries are handled by an extensive switchboard. Metropolitan Transit Commission, 560 6th Ave. N, Minneapolis (827-7733).

Taxi – As in many other cities, taxis are impossible to get when you really need them and plentiful when you don't. Most are radio-dispatched. There are some taxi stands. The largest cab company is Yellow Cab, 2812 University Ave. SE (331-8294); in St. Paul, 167 Grand Ave. (222-4433).

Car Rental – All major firms are represented. A good local agency is Dollar Rent-A-Car, at the airport (726-9494).

 MUSEUMS: The pride of Minneapolis–St. Paul is the Twin Cities' cultural wealth, and a visit to the many fine museums is well worth it. The Minneapolis Institute of Arts, the Walker Art Center, the Science Museum of Minnesota, and the McKnight Science Center are described in *Special Places.* Some others are:

American Swedish Institute – 2600 Park Ave., Mpls. (871-4907)
Bell Museum of Natural History – 17th and University SE, Mpls. (373-2423)
James J. Hill House – 240 Summit Ave., St. Paul (297-2555)
Minneapolis Planetarium – 300 Nicollet Mall, Mpls. (372-6543)
Minnesota Museum of Art – 75 W 5th St., St. Paul (292-4355)
Minnesota Transportation Museum – W 42nd St. and Queen Ave., S Mpls. (890-9455). Streetcar rides, Memorial Day through Labor Day.
Ramsey House – 265 S Exchange St., St. Paul (296-0100)

 MAJOR COLLEGES AND UNIVERSITIES: About 55,000 students attend the University of Minnesota, one of the Big Ten universities; the campus sprawls across the east and west banks of the Mississippi. Escorted tours are available. University Ave. SE (373-2126).

 SPECIAL EVENTS: The *Aquatennial Festival* in late July features sailboat races, a torchlight parade, and "Queen of the Lakes" beauty contest. *Minnesota State Fair,* 11 days, ending Labor Day at Como and Snelling aves., St. Paul. *St. Paul Winter Carnival,* late January or early February, is a citywide celebration.

 SPORTS AND FITNESS: Professional Sports – The new 60,000-seat Hubert H. Humphrey Stadium (500 11th Ave. S) houses major league baseball and football teams. For information on games call: *Twins* (baseball; 375-1116), *Vikings* (football; 333-8828). The Metropolitan Sports Center, 7901 Cedar Ave. S, is home of the *North Stars* and the *Strikers* hockey teams. For *North Star* tickets, call 853-9300; for *Strikers* tickets, phone 854-5450.

Biking – There are bike trails around Lake Harriet, Lake Calhoun, and Lake of the Isles in Minneapolis; Lakes Como and Phalen in St. Paul. Bicycles may be rented from Rent-N-Roll, 1615 W Lake St. (825-4080), and at Lake Como, St. Paul (488-1477).

Fishing – Twelve fishing lakes are in the Twin Cities metro area; the best is Lake Minnetonka, which has 177 miles of shoreline. 15 miles west on Hwy. 12. Within the city limits, Lake Calhoun has a fishing dock.

Fitness Centers – The La Salle Sports & Health Club has exercise equipment, a sauna, and a whirlpool, La Salle and 8th St. (332-6761).

Golf – There are 18 courses in Minneapolis–St. Paul. Best is Meadowbrook Golf Course, 201 Meadowbrook Rd. at Goodrich Ave., Mpls. (929-2077).

Horse Racing – Canterbury Downs, 25 miles west of downtown Minneapolis, has thoroughbred and harness racing from mid-April through mid-November (445-3644).

Ice Skating – The cities clear, test, and maintain outdoor rinks on many of the lakes. Indoor ice arenas offer some free time for public skating. Consult telephone directory for locations and numbers.

Jogging – Run to Loring Park via Marquette Avenue and West Grant Street (about 1½ miles) and then around the park (.8 mile). A more ambitious run leads to Lake of the Isles, 2½ miles from downtown, and from there to several other lakes: Cedar Lake to the west or Lakes Calhoun and Harriet to the south; the perimeter of each lake is about 3 miles. Another route is along the Mississippi on East or West River Road, by the University of Minnesota.

Skiing – Best are Afton Alps Ski Area, Inver Hills, and Buck Hill.

Swimming – There are public swimming beaches at 23 lakes in and around the Twin Cities area. Open June to August.

Tennis – There are many lighted, outdoor courts as well as indoor courts (ranging from $6.50 to $9 per hour) available throughout the cities.

 THEATER: In addition to the *Guthrie,* Minneapolis–St. Paul has more than a dozen theaters. The universities and colleges also produce plays and musicals. Best bets: *Guthrie* (377-2224); *Children's Theater Company* (874-0400); *Chimera Theater,* 30 E 10th St., St. Paul (293-1043).

 MUSIC: For a complete schedule of musical happenings, check the newspapers, especially *St. Paul Pioneer Press/Dispatch* "Entertainment" on Thursday; *Minneapolis Star-Tribune* "Preview" on Friday. The copper-capped, glass-walled Ordway Music Theater, 345 Washington St. (224-4222), presents performances by the *St. Paul Chamber Orchestra,* the *Minnesota Opera,* the *Schubert Club,* and the *Minnesota Orchestra.* There are outdoor summer concerts at Lake Harriet in Minneapolis and at Lake Como in St. Paul.

 NIGHTCLUBS AND NIGHTLIFE: *Gallivan's Downtown* in St. Paul, 354 Wabasha (227-6688), features professional entertainment and a piano bar. The *Manor,* 2550 W 7th St. (690-1771), provides ballroom dancing Wednesdays through Saturdays. *Scotty's* is a café and disco named for F. Scott Fitzgerald, 36 S 7th St., Mpls. (338-8311). *Duff's* caters to a sports crowd, 21 S 8th St., Mpls. (332-3554); The *Carleton Celebrity Room,* 8350 24th Ave. S, Mpls. (854-9300) has Las Vegas–style dinner theater with top-name performers. The *Continental Room* at McGuire's Inn of Arden Hills, 1201 W County Rd. E, St. Paul (636-4123), also presents well-known entertainers. Bob Dylan began his singing career in the West Bank area near the University of Minnesota, where there are a number of small clubs and cafés.

Rupert's, 5410 Wayzata Blvd., Mpls. (544-5035), boasts a 10-piece band cranking out jazz, swing, and pop tunes Tuesdays through Saturdays. Singles flock to *Sommer-fields* in the *Ramada Inn,* 4200 W 78th St. (831-4200), or *Shiek's,* 115 S 4th St. (341-2332). The former Greyhound Bus Depot in Minneapolis is now *First Avenue & 7th Street Entry,* a nightclub featured in local rock star Prince's film *Purple Rain* (338-8388).

 SINS: The twin cities are blessed with one of America's finest regional theaters, the Tyrone Guthrie. *Pride* in this 1,487-seat repertory showplace reaches six to eight peaks a year, once for each production staged. It would be criminal for people who consider themselves cultured to visit Minneapolis and not see at least one of these highly professional masterpieces. Or to be in St. Paul without attending a performance of the world-famous St. Paul Chamber Orchestra.

The sin of *anger* grips Twin Citians on two main issues. The new Minnesota Zoo, created by an act of the state legislature, was to be self-supporting, but instead has required continued appropriation of funds to keep it going.

The $55 million domed Hubert H. Humphrey Stadium, raises some voices as well. Twin Citians paid a liquor tax for several years for a stadium with 60,000 seats but no parking facilities.

LOCAL SERVICES: Business Services – Airport Business Services, 1408 Northland Dr., (452-8215); A-1 Secretarial Services, Pioneer Building, Suite 219, St. Paul (228-1907).

Mechanics – Fisher Liberty and Towing Service provides excellent 24-hour road service at extremely reasonable prices. 1022 Hennepin Ave. (338-6953). Pat's Mobile Service, 1010 W 7th St., St. Paul (292-8482).

Babysitting – Dayton's department store, 700 Nicollet Mall, has a three-hour sitting service during store hours (375-2288). The YWCA cares for children from three months to five years old; make reservations 24 hours in advance. Minimum sitting assignment is four hours. 1130 Nicollet Ave. (332-0501). We Sit Better is part of a nationwide service organization, with 200 sitters on its Minneapolis staff. Minimum assignment is four hours (three at motels), and you must pay the sitter's transportation (375-0932). Ramsey County Day Care Referral (298-4260).

BEST IN TOWN

CHECKING IN: There are a number of places near the Minneapolis–St. Paul International Airport, in the suburb of Bloomington, as well as some new and newly renovated hotels downtown. Expect to pay $90 or more for a double room in one of the hotels we've listed as expensive; $70 to $90 in the moderate range; and around $50 in inexpensive places.

L'Hôtel Sofitel – The first North American link in the French hotel chain offers a concierge, the latest issues of Parisian magazines, and real croissants for breakfast. Many of the 300 rooms have bidets. Continental elegance includes an indoor heated pool, sauna, babysitting service, bars, and dancing. Children under 12 admitted free, but for the rest of us it's pricey. I-494 and Hwy. 100, Bloomington (612 835-1900). Expensive.

Marquette Hotel – Connected to the interior skyway in the IDS center, offering gracious, spacious accommodations in the middle of downtown. Princess Margaret has stayed here. Steam baths in rooms. Bar, beauty shop, drugstores, café, babysitting service, heated parking; 285 rooms. 710 Marquette Ave., Mpls. (612 332-2351). Expensive.

Hotel St. Paul – A beautifully restored Victorian hotel that's shining again after a $20 million facelift. Crystal chandeliers sparkle in the lobby and elegant Biedermeier-style furniture decorates the guest rooms, some of which have lovely views over Rice Park. The hotel also has a notable and pricey restaurant, *L'Étoile.* 350 Market St., St. Paul (612 292-9292). Expensive.

Nicollet Island Inn – It's hard to believe that this lovely hotel was once a manufacturing plant. In the early 1980s, a massive renovation of the long-neglected building produced a rather plain exterior but an interior awash in turn-of-the-century style and charm. None of the 24 guest rooms is the same, though all have a homey and comfortable decor: beds with puffy comforters, wing chairs and walls covered in pretty print fabrics, and gleaming wood armoires and writing desks usually topped with a vase of fresh flowers. Room rates include Continental breakfast and the morning newspaper. The *River Room* serves American cuisine and the *Captain*

John Tapper Pub has complimentary snacks at cocktail time. 95 Merriam, Nicollet Island, Mpls. (612 623-7741). Expensive.

Hyatt Regency Minneapolis – Another glitzy Hyatt, this one is in Nicollet Mall, just a short hop from the airport. There are 540 tasteful rooms and suites and a Regency Club floor for extra-special service. *The Terrace* is the hotel's more casual eating spot; *The Willows Restaurant* has fancier, Continental fare; *The Willows Lounge* features entertainment every night but Sunday. 1300 Nicollet Mall (612 370-1234). Expensive.

Amfac Hotel at City Center – This new 32-floor glass tower (which is linked to the city's enclosed skyway system) is as modern and up to date as the many services it offers guests. It's particularly suited for those in town on business since one whole floor is like a small convention center, with rooms appropriate for both small and large functions. The hotel also has two notable restaurants: *Gustino's* for North Italian cuisine and *The Fifth Season* for American dishes from all around the country. 30 S 7th St., Mpls. (612 349-4000). Expensive.

Minneapolis Plaza – An elegant, modern, 304-room hotel in Nicollet Mall with a top-floor cabaret and a fine view of the Mississippi. When the Metropolitan Opera plays Minneapolis–St. Paul, the cast stays here. With the *Stradavarious* lounge, a heated pool, barber and beauty shops, babysitter service, free parking. Children under 17 free. 315 Nicollet Mall (612 332-4000). Expensive to moderate.

Radisson Hotels – The *Radisson South* is the tallest and largest hotel in Bloomington, with 578 rooms, an indoor heated pool, sauna, restaurants, bar, dancing, entertainment, free parking. I-494 and 100 Bloomington (612 835-7800). *Radisson St. Paul* has 480 rooms (3 for paraplegics), a revolving rooftop restaurant, lounge, indoor heated pool and garden court, entertainment, dancing, barber and beauty shops, sundeck, in-room movies. 11 E Kellogg Blvd. (612 292-1900). The *Radisson Plaza* (scheduled to open December 1986) will have 363 rooms, restaurants, a lounge, and access to Plaza VII exercise equipment, sauna, and whirlpool. 35 S 7th St., Mpls. (no phone at press time). Two other *Radisson* properties are the *Radisson Metrodome,* 210 Cedar Ave., Mpls., with 266 rooms (612 333-4646), and *Radisson University,* 615 Washington Ave. SE, Mpls., with 308 rooms (612 379-8888). All are expensive to moderate.

Normandy Inn – In the heart of downtown Minneapolis, this cozy hostelry offers 230 cozy rooms. It occupies a full block and has a pool, conference and banquet rooms, whirlpool, sauna, and adequate parking. Two dining rooms; one serves full dinners, the other light lunches. 405 S 8th St. (612 370-1400). Inexpensive.

 EATING OUT: You can find almost any kind of food in the Twin Cities area, from high-priced, exquisitely prepared Continental cuisine to Japanese food or kosher delicatessen. In fact, Minneapolis–St. Paul is considered a great eating-out town. Prices range from $50 or more for a dinner for two in the expensive range, $30 to $50 in the moderate, and $30 or less, inexpensive. Prices do not include drinks, wine, or tips.

Lowell Inn – The closest thing to a New England inn that you'll find in the Midwest. Gracious, family-style Minnesota meals. The menu includes beef fondue, and gigantic drinks are another special feature. Open daily. Reservations essential. Major credit cards. 102 N 2nd St., Stillwater (a northeast suburb of St Paul; 439-1100). Expensive.

The Orion Room – High atop the IDS Center, 50 stories up, the view from three seating levels, is magnificent. Specialties, including rack of lamb, Châteaubriand, wild rice soup, pheasant, and Dover sole — and impressive tableside presentation — enhance the spectacular setting. Open daily. Reservations suggested. Major credit cards. IDS Center, 80 S 8th St., Mpls. (372-3772). Expensive.

Blue Horse – Winner of innumerable awards over the years, this gracious, intimate restaurant is consistently cited as the Twin Cities' finest. The chef devotes full, loving attention to every dish. The pasta is specially prepared and comes highly recommended. Closed Sundays. Reservations necessary. Major credit cards. 1355 University Ave., St. Paul (645-8101). Expensive to moderate.

Fuji Ya – If you're in the mood to sample the gentle, tranquil mood and food of Japan, then this is the place. Reiko Weston, who came to the Twin Cities as a war bride, charmed discriminating diners first with conventional Japanese fare, then with showbizzy teppan yaki cuisine, and most recently with a sushi bar. The view of Lock #1 on the Mississippi complements the settling effects of the food and service. Closed Sundays. Reservations advised. Major credit cards. 420 1st St., Mpls. (339-2226). Moderate.

Lexington Restaurant – An unpretentious neighborhood restaurant in St. Paul, with steaks, prime ribs, lamb shanks, and seafood. Well-prepared cocktails. Closed Sundays. Reservations recommended. No credit cards. 1096 Grand Ave. (222-5878). Moderate.

Murray's – Well known for its hickory-smoked shrimp appetizers, award-winning silver butterknife steak, and homemade rolls and dressing. The decor is in the 1940s tradition, and there is music and dancing later in the evening. Closed Sundays. Reservations advised. Major credit cards. 26 S 6th St., Mpls. (339-0909). Moderate.

Forepaughs – The charm and elegance of the Victorian age is preserved in this restaurant, where French cuisine is served in a gracious 19th-century former home. Free parking and shuttle service to the Ordway Theater provided. Reservations advised. 276 Exchange St., St. Paul (224-5606). Moderate.

Le Café Nicollet – The simple and authentic French menu includes such interesting items as fish terrine with horseradish and vegetable pâté with fresh tomato-basil sauce. There is a wide selection of appetizers (try the escargots with artichoke hearts) and desserts such as chocolate mousse cake and orange Bavarian torte. Nice wine list, too. Closed Sundays. Reservations advised. Major credit cards. 1350 Nicollet Mall, Mpls. (874-8636). Moderate.

Leeann Chin's Chinese Cuisine – This cavernous space used to be the Union Depot. Now lofty columns, smoked mirrors, and a rosy beige decor provide a warm backdrop for stunning Oriental vases, jade, ivory carvings, and whimsical modern Chinese paintings. A buffet with everything from fun kin soup and cream cheese wontons to lemon chicken and almond cookie ice cream is served for both lunch and dinner. Open daily. Reservations advised. Major credit cards. Union Depot Pl. at 4th and Sibley, St. Paul (224-8814). Moderate to inexpensive.

St. Anthony Main – An entire development of eating establishments and specialty shops on rustic Main Street, on the Mississippi. *Anthony's Wharf:* East Coast cuisine comes to Minneapolis, offering fresh lobster, fresh scallops, rainbow trout, and swordfish. No reservations. Major credit cards. 201 SE Main St., Mpls. (378-7058). Moderate. *GuadalaHARRY's:* This popular restaurant captures the true south-of-the-border atmosphere and offers Mexican pizza and chimichangas. No reservations. Major credit cards. 201 SE Main St., Mpls. (378-2233). Inexpensive. For dessert, stop by *Häagen-Dazs* for all-natural, out-of-this-world ice cream.

Black Forest Inn – Near the Institute of Arts, the inn serves bratwurst and sauerkraut dinners, wiener schnitzel, and other honest, substantial German fare. The restaurant evolved from a tavern that used to serve only beer. It still offers German beers, and you can enjoy drinking in the outdoor beer garden. The jukebox plays opera. Open daily. Reservations advised. Major credit cards. 1 E 26th St., Mpls. (872-0812). Inexpensive.

Chi Chi's – No matter where one springs up, you're certain to find them lining up to partake of the Mexican cuisine done with American know-how. *Chi Chi's* popularity is due in no small part to the pleasant atmosphere (rotating fans, sprawling plants, and stucco walls), hefty margaritas and the chain's knack for using the freshest ingredients available. Specialties include chimichangas and Mexican fried ice cream. Expect a wait because the portions are large and reasonably priced. Open for lunch and dinner. No reservations. Major credit cards. Two locations: 7717 Nicollet Ave., Richfield (866-3433); 389 N Hamline, St. Paul (644-1122). Inexpensive.

Ciatti's Italian Restaurant – There's a good selection of Italian dishes, including a variety of pastas served with different sauces, and a menu listing over 30 entrées; some non-Italian dishes are also available. Desserts, like the Amaretto torte, are delicious. Open daily. No reservations. Major credit cards. 1346 La Salle S, Mpls. (339-7747). Inexpensive.

What's the best local place for barbecue? That question has always been followed by lively debate in Minneapolis. Current favorites include *Market BBQ* (28 Glenwood Ave.; 333-1028) preferred by long-time residents for ribs cooked to dry, smoky perfection over a wood fire. And then there's *Rudolph's Bar-B-Que* (1933 Lyndale Ave. S; 871-8969, or 815 E Hennepin Ave.; 623-3671), which took top honors in the National Rib Cook-Off in August 1985 for its sloppy, piquant-sauced ribs served up with a great side of coleslaw.

NASHVILLE

Hundreds of thousands of hero-worshiping country music fans from around the country come to Nashville every year, by the busload, for the afternoon or the weekend, to take a tour of the homes of the stars and cruise past the houses where Minnie Pearl, Pat Boone's parents, and dozens of others live. Afterward, when the final "ooh" is "aahed," they take in a performance of the Opry.

The Grand Ole Opry, a 2½-hour country music extravaganza that takes the title as the longest-running radio program in the US, is justifiably Nashville's biggest drawing card. Something that inspires so many people can't be all bad, and even if you hate country music, you can't fail to be amused by the spectacle. Onstage in the very fancy Grand Ole Opry House — completed in March 1974 to the tune of some $13 million — there are guitarists in glittery, rhinestoned leisure suits; busty female vocalists with curly manes and slinky dresses (or little-girl outfits that seem strangely incongruous with the bodies underneath), or cloggers who stomp up a storm in a blizzard of ruffly white petticoats. Every time a new performer comes onstage, the fans whistle, clap, jump up and down in their seats, then scramble up the aisles to be the first to get an autograph or snap a picture. Sometimes so many flashbulbs pop off at once that it seems as if a giant strobe is flickering over the audience. Onstage, friends and families of the performers look on from church pews moved from the old Ryman Auditorium, where the Opry spent the better part of 30 years, or mill around in the wings, never bothering to make themselves inconspicuous. It's hard to tell the hangers-on from the stars, who, meanwhile, are twanging away onstage or signing autographs backstage, in the manner of true professionals.

Which they all are. If you've seen Robert Altman's film *Nashville,* you've got a pretty fair idea that this city is far from being the simple hillbilly heaven portrayed in the songs that pour out of the one-square-mile area of South Nashville known as Music Row. The country music business, which is concentrated here, is a multimillion-dollar industry, getting bigger all the time. There are scores of large recording studios, a number of major music publishers, more than a hundred talent agencies, and countless record pressing plants, marketing firms, and production houses. The Opry House is the largest broadcast studio in the world. TV shows by the score are taped in Nashville. The odds are even that when you come for a visit you can sit in on a taping, and when you do, you'll find out why audiences you hear at the beginning of some live TV shows are clapping so madly: Studio people close to the stage urge them on like cheerleaders.

But for all that, Nashville is also a southern city, with all the traditions of gentility that characterize the breed, and you don't have to stay here for very long before you understand from whence came the nickname, "the Athens

of the South." The town that annually goes berserk for the Country Music
Fan Fair is also home to many colleges and universities, countless plantation
mansions, and the world's only full-scale replica of the Greek Parthenon.
There are symphony orchestra concerts and lovely old suburban neighborhoods which by no stretch of the imagination could you call nouveau riche.
The Cheekwood Botanical Gardens boasts one of the finest growths of boxwood in the US.

Like other American cities of half a million, Nashville has its slums. And
its eyesores: highways lined with what seems like an endless procession of
fast-food joints, chain coffee shops with plastic signs, streams of neon lights,
and garishly illuminated used-car lots. But beyond that, and beyond the
occasional silliness of the country music mania, there is something about the
place that can't fail to catch your imagination. There's unabashed, unpretentious good humor almost everywhere you go. There are dozens and dozens
of nifty little Southern-cooking restaurants (called "meat'n'threes" because
their entrées generally consist of meat with a choice of three home-cooked
vegetables) and hole-in-the-wall nightclubs with stages so small that fiddlers
can barely keep from bowing the banjo players.

NASHVILLE AT-A-GLANCE

SEEING THE CITY: On a clear day, from the observation deck on the 31st
floor of the Life & Casualty Building, you can see 26 miles in all directions.
Even rainy days can be interesting: A peculiarity of the building's L-shaped
design makes raindrops fall up instead of down. Closed Sundays and holidays. Small admission charge. 4th and Church sts. (244-2130).

SPECIAL PLACES: The outstanding attractions are clustered within a couple of miles of the downtown area, and ranged along the southern and
eastern outskirts of the metropolitan area.

DOWNTOWN

Fort Nashborough – A partial reconstruction of the pioneer fort where Nashville
began back in 1779, when a small band of settlers under the leadership of James
Robertson arrived on the west bank of the Cumberland River. In five cabins, costumed
guides show how the settlers chopped wood, tended gardens, carded and spun wool,
made candles and lye soap, cooked meals (in pots hanging from iron hooks in immense
stone fireplaces), and entertained themselves with singing. Closed Sundays and Mondays. Admission charge. 170 1st Ave. N at Church St. (255-8192).

The Ryman Auditorium – Home of the Grand Ole Opry between 1943 and March
16, 1974. You can climb up onto its creaky wood stage, and see mementos of the stars
of days gone by. The Ryman, Mecca to country music lovers, was built in 1891 by a
riverboat captain, Tom Ryman, who had found religion and wanted to help others do
the same. Open daily. Admission charge. 116 5th Ave. N (254-1445).

MUSIC ROW

The Country Music Hall of Fame and Museum – Memorabilia of country music
stars — Elvis Presley's solid gold Cadillac, comedienne Minnie Pearl's straw hat complete with dangling price tag, Chet Atkins's first guitar, rare film footage of Patsy Cline

and earlier country singers, etc. — interesting more for the reverence with which your fellow visitors view it all than the objects themselves. Open daily. Admission charge. On Music Row at 4 Music Sq. E (256-1639).

Studio B – Elvis Presley, Chet Atkins, Charley Pride, Eddy Arnold, and a score of other greats recorded for RCA at this famous studio in the 1950s and 1960s. Guides will tell you its history, talk about the Nashville recording industry, and let you act as a recording engineer at a "mix-down" session, in which the sixteen tracks recorded by the artists are put onto two tracks before delivery to the record presser. Admission charge to Studio B is included in the Hall of Fame entry fee. Open daily. 806 17th Ave. S (242-9414).

Riverfront Park – Recently renovated by the Metro Parks Department, this park on the Cumberland is a little heavy on the concrete, but Metro hires local bands to play on Saturday nights during the summer, and sheltered tables make for nice noon picnicking on cooler days (259-6399 for entertainment information).

EAST

The Grand Ole Opry – This long country-music-star-studded spectacular is well worth the planning it takes to get tickets. More than a third of the 60-odd acts under contract to the Opry will perform in a given night, and you're bound to like some if not all of them. There are shows Fridays at 7:30 PM and Saturdays at 6:30 and 9:30 PM, and matinees and a second Friday show during the peak-season months when Opryland USA is open. Reserved-seat tickets sell out months in advance for summer shows. General admission tickets go on sale Tuesdays at 9 AM the week of the show, at the Opryland box office only. The nearer to summer, the earlier you must arrive to get a ticket. Information Center, 2802 Opryland Dr. (889-3060).

Opryland USA – Music from Broadway and the hit parade and just about any other kind of melody that has ever been called music, along with foot-tapping bluegrass, carry out the American-music-is-great motif at this new-style family theme park. The *General Jackson* — a re-creation of an old showboat — carries passengers from Opryland to downtown Nashville and back. Open daily in summer, and weekends in spring and fall. Admission charge. Information Center, 2802 Opryland Dr. (889-6611).

The Hermitage – Once the home of President Andrew Jackson, the old plantation home is now a museum devoted to the Jackson family. Tulip Grove, a Greek Revival house completed in 1836, is also on the grounds, 12 miles east of downtown in Hermitage. Open daily; last tour at 4:30 PM. Admission charge (889-2941).

SOUTH

Belle Meade Mansion – Inside the century-old rock walls that edge the 24-acre estate, Belle Meade Mansion is just a shadow of its former self, but even its shadow is impressive: There are immense pillars and ornate plaster cornices outside, and, inside, Adamesque moldings and a splendid double parlor. Open daily. Admission charge. Harding Rd., at Leak Ave. US 70 S (352-7350).

The Parthenon – A full-scale replica of the ancient Greek building; the building material is not marble but a steel-reinforced conglomerate. Its four bronze doors are the largest in the world. Inside, displays include reproductions of the Elgin marbles, plus pre-Columbian art and various changing exhibitions. Closed Mondays. Donation suggested. In Centennial Park at 25th Ave. N and West End Ave. (259-6358).

Travellers' Rest – The remarkably finely detailed home of John Overton, one of Nashville's first settlers, restored, expanded, and filled with furniture, letters, and memorabilia that tell the story of Tennessee's settlement and civilization. Open daily. Admission charge. 636 Farrell Pkwy. 6 miles south of downtown Nashville via Franklin Rd., which is US 31 (832-2962).

Tennessee Botanical Gardens and Fine Arts Center – Cheekwood, a Georgian mansion built in the 1930s, is now a museum with art shows and traveling exhibitions. You may be more impressed, though, by the elegant Palladian window, or the chandelier (once the property of a countess), or the swooping spiral staircase (which used to be a fixture of Queen Charlotte's palace at Kew). Outdoors: formal gardens, a wisteria arbor, wildflower gardens, a Japanese sand garden, greenhouses, horticultural exhibits, and an outstanding boxwood garden. Closed Mondays. Admission charge. Forrest Park Dr., 7 miles west of town via West End Ave., then Belle Meade Blvd. (352-5310).

■ **EXTRA SPECIAL:** You'll see the announcements for tours of the homes of the stars on big billboards on the way into town, and even if you ordinarily hate group excursions, you may like these. While you're getting a glimpse into what makes Nashville tick, you can also enjoy some delightful southern-accented speech and the colorful language that seems to be the mark of Nashville citizenry. Each of the following offers several all-day, half-day, or evening tours: *Gray Line,* 501 Broadway (244-7330); *Grand Ole Opry Tours,* 2808 Opryland Dr. (889-9490); *Nashville Tours,* 2626 Music Valley Dr. (889-4646); *Country and Western Tours,* 2416 Music Valley Dr. (883-5555); and *Stardust Tours,* 1504 Demonbreun St. (244-2335).

SOURCES AND RESOURCES

TOURIST INFORMATION: For brochures, maps, general tourist information, and all kinds of other help, your best bet is to write the Nashville Area Chamber of Commerce, 161 4th Ave. N, Nashville 37219; to phone 259-3900; or to stop in at the official Tourist Information Center at exit 85 on I-65 N just east of downtown.

The *Nashville Visitor's Guide,* published annually by the Chamber in conjunction with *Nashville!* magazine, is as comprehensive a city guide as you'll see anywhere.

Local Coverage – The *Tennessean,* morning daily; the *Nashville Banner,* afternoon daily. The former publishes a complete events listing on Fridays and Sundays; the latter on Thursdays. *Nashville!* magazine publishes a monthly events calendar. All are available at newsstands.

Food – Check the *Nashville City Guide* or the *Nashville Visitor's Guide* for a comprehensive restaurant guide.

Area Code – All telephone numbers are in the 615 area code unless otherwise indicated.

CLIMATE AND CLOTHES: Nashville's temperatures hover around the 80s in summer, dropping into the 40s and 30s (occasionally into the 20s or lower) between November and February. It gets humid in the summer, and you can expect thunderstorms from March through late summer. Expect rain in the spring and in October and November.

GETTING AROUND: Airport – Metropolitan Nashville Airport is a 15- to 20-minute drive from downtown (30 minutes or more during rush hours), and cab fare will run about $10. Airport Limo (367-2305) provides frequent van service to downtown Nashville hotels from the airport; $8 for single passengers, less if traveling with others.

Bus – You need a car to manage conveniently. However, buses are available (route information, 242-4433).

Taxi – Nashville's principal cab companies are Yellow (256-0101) and Checker (254-5031).

Car Rental – Major national car rental agencies can be found in Nashville.

 MUSEUMS: In addition to those described above in *Special Places,* you'll want to investigate the following:

The Cumberland Museum and Science Center – Closed Mondays. Admission charge except Tuesdays. 800 Ridley Ave. (259-6099).

The Tennessee State Museum – in the Tennessee Performing Arts Center (741-2692), with a branch devoted to military history in the War Memorial Bldg. Frequent exhibitions of local arts and crafts. Free. 7th and Union sts. (741-5383).

 MAJOR COLLEGES AND UNIVERSITIES: Of the dozen-plus colleges and universities in Nashville, Vanderbilt, West End at 21st Ave. (322-7311), is perhaps the most famous, as its nickname, "the Harvard of the South," would suggest. The city is also the home of Fisk University, 17th Ave. N (329-8500), one of the US's most noted predominantly black colleges.

 SPECIAL EVENTS: The *Opryland Gospel Jubilee* brings gospel bands, choruses, and lots of extra music to the theme park every year over Memorial Day weekend (see *Special Places*). Also in May is the *Tennessee Crafts Fair,* one of the largest shows in the South. For information, write PO Box 150704, Nashville, TN 37215 (383-2502). The second Saturday of May is the *Iroquois Steeplechase,* the daylong series of eight races that's the oldest amateur steeplechase meet in the US. Old Hickory Blvd. in Percy Warner Park, 11 miles south of Nashville. For information: PO Box 22711, Nashville 37202 (373-2130). The *International Country Music Fan Fair,* a June event, brings thousands for five days of spectacular shows, autograph sessions, concerts and a Grand Masters Fiddling Contest. For more information write: Fan Fair Information, Grand Ole Opry, 2804 Opryland Dr., Nashville 37214 (889-3060). In October, there's the *National Quartet Convention,* five days of top-name gospel singing at the Nashville Municipal Auditorium. For information: National Quartet Convention, 54 Music Sq. W, Nashville, TN 37203 (320-7000). In February, Charlie Daniels holds his annual *Volunteer Jam,* with surprise guest artists (past performers include Billy Joel, Willie Nelson, and Crystal Gayle) at Municipal Auditorium. For tickets, contact Municipal Auditorium (259-6217 or 327-1711) *early* in January.

SPORTS AND FITNESS: Baseball – The Nashville *Sounds,* a Triple-A farm team for the Detroit *Tigers,* play in Greer Stadium on Chestnut, between 4th and 8th aves. S (242-4371).

Fishing and Boating – Two manmade lakes — Old Hickory (822-4846) and Percy Priest (889-1975) — are a 20-minute drive from downtown, and several others are within an hour or so. Black bass, rock bass, striped bass, walleye, sauger, northern pike, crappie, bluegill, and sunfish are the standard catch. Call the Resource Management office at each lake for boat and equipment rental details. The Tennessee Wildlife Resources Agency, PO Box 40747, Ellington Agricultural Center, Nashville 37204 (741-1512), can provide details about other lakes in the area.

Fitness Centers – The YMCA offers an indoor and a roof track, racquetball, exercise equipment, and a sauna, 1000 Church (254-0631). Work-It-Out, 1602 21st Ave. S (321-4003), has exercise classes at about $4 per session.

Golf – There are ten public courses in Nashville. Best 18-holers are at Harpeth Hills, Old Hickory Blvd., off Rte. 431 S (373-8202); McCabe Park, 46th Ave. N at Murphy Rd. (297-9138); Nashville Golf and Athletic Club, Moore's Lane in Franklin (794-

6616); Shelby Park Golf Course, 20th Ave. and Fatherland St. (227-9973); and Two
Rivers Course, Two Rivers Pkwy. near Opryland (889-9748).

Jogging – Follow Church Street (which turns into Elliston Place) to Centennial
Park, about 1½ miles from downtown and near Vanderbilt University; or drive or take
the West End Belle Meade bus (from 6th and Church, or Deaderick at 4th or 6th) to
Percy Warner Park. Jogging in either area after dark is not recommended.

Stock Car Racing – All-Pro and American Speed Association racing on a ⅝-mile
track at the Tennessee State Fairgrounds every Saturday night from April through
mid-October, Wedgewood Ave. between 4th and 8th aves. S (726-1818).

Swimming – Wave Country, on Two Rivers Pkwy., near Opryland, is the Southeast's largest surf-producing swimming pool. Open May-September. Admission charge
(885-1052).

Tennis – The major public facility is in Centennial Park, West End and 25th aves.
N, where there are 13 courts open from March through October. Admission charge.
For more information, call 259-6399. Indoor tennis at Nashboro Village Racquet Club,
2250 Murfreesboro Rd. (361-3242).

 THEATER: For touring Broadway shows and regional companies: the
Tennessee Performing Arts Center, 505 Deaderick St. (741-2787). Lively
children's theater and classics for adults: the *Nashville Academy Theatre*
(the city's resident professional company), 724 2nd Ave. S (254-6020). The
Tennessee Repertory Theatre performs four plays yearly in the Polk Theater of the
Tennessee Performing Arts Center (see above). Two small companies that perform
recent works are the *John Galt Theater,* 2318 West End (327-0049), with performances
from September through May; and *The Circle Players* (327-4048), who present several
plays each year, either at the Johnson Theatre of the Tennessee Performing Arts Center
or at the Alternate Circle Theater, 1703 Church St. For dinner theater, try the *Barn
Dinner Theater,* 8204 Hwy. 100 (646-3111).

 MUSIC: The *Nashville Symphony Orchestra* holds concerts from September
through May in the Tennessee Performing Arts Center. The symphony box
office is at 208 23rd Ave. N (329-3033). On Friday and Sunday nights during
June, July, and August, there are musical programs at *Centennial Park.* For
information, call the Parks and Recreation Department's activities number (259-6399).
Chamber music is offered at Cheekwood on weekends, at Fisk, and at Blair School of
Music on the Vanderbilt campus. Often it's free.

 TV SHOW TAPINGS: National network specials, syndicated shows, and
programs for cable TV's Nashville Network are taped frequently in the Opry
House and in the TV studio behind it. Schedules are handed out as you enter
Opryland or you can call ahead (889-6611). Tickets are always free.

 NIGHTCLUBS AND NIGHTLIFE: For music, this is a hard town to beat.
Even motels can sometimes turn up good entertainers. Check newspapers
and the *Nashville Visitor's Guide* for a thorough rundown of places to hear
country music.

For the best in a concentrated area, however, visit Printer's Alley downtown, where,
along with some strip-tease joints and seedy-looking bars, there are standouts like the
Captain's Table, a silver-and-white-linen-tablecloth sort of place (251-9535), and *Boots
Randolph's,* which features Boots (when he's in town), comedy acts, and a house band
(256-5500). For bluegrass, try the *Bluegrass Inn,* at the rear of 1914 Broadway at the
edge of the Vanderbilt campus (320-0624), or the *Station Inn,* 402 12th Ave. S (255-
3307). Four places to hear local talent play jazz, rock, country, and folk music are:

Bluebird Café (which also has fine lunches and dinners daily except Sundays), 4104 Hillsboro Rd. (383-1461); *J.C.'s*, 2227 Bandywood Dr. (383-8160); *The Boardwalk Café*, 4214 Nolensville Rd. (832-5104); and the *Bullpen Lounge* at the *Stock Yard Restaurant*, 901 2nd Ave. N (255-6464). *Zanies Comedy Showplace*, 2025 8th Ave. (269-0221), features stand-up comedians nightly.

 SINS: The *pride* of Nashville is heard throughout the world on every jukebox, dance floor, and radio station. It is country music supreme, with headquarters at the Grand Ole Opry. But music abounds throughout the city in honky-tonks, bars, music clubs, and an enormous number of recording studios that produce the largest number of top-selling albums in the world.

Lower Broadway is the place for *lust* with massage parlors, peep shows, and topless joints.

 LOCAL SERVICES: Babysitters – If you think you might need one, ask your hotel or motel to make the arrangements when you book your room. **Business Services –** Executive Park Office Services, 4741 Trousdale Dr. (331-2300); Nashville Secretarial Services, 1612 Church St. (329-2436)

Mechanics – People come from all the way across town to have their domestic cars fixed at Garrett Amoco Service, 2600 Lebanon Rd., Donelson, near Opryland (883-1386); for foreign cars, try Stubblefield Brothers, 317 6th Ave. S (255-5453). Also good are Robinson's Chevron, 2801 McGavock Pike, at Exit 96 of I-65, about 5 miles north of downtown (883-2261), and J&L Auto Service (American cars only) at the Texaco at 2508 Nolensville Rd. (331-4249).

(BEST IN TOWN)

 CHECKING IN: There are dozens of new motels in Nashville — some parts of large chains, some parts of small chains, and a few independents. Prices generally range from $80 and up per night for a double room in an expensive hotel; $45 to $75 for accommodations in hostelries we've classified as moderate; and as low as $30 in an inexpensive place.

The Hermitage – Built in 1910, this showpiece structure of Beaux-Arts classic design is now a luxury hotel featuring 112 suites — with three phones and two color TVs in each. It also has an oak-paneled bar, a fine dining room, and a Rolls-Royce as the hotel limousine. 231 6th Ave. N, downtown (615 244-3121 or 800 342-1816). Expensive.

The Hyatt Regency – Like its fellows in the chain, this 478-room hotel has glass elevators to whisk you up through a vast skylit lobby, the elegant *Café Troubadour* (great for desserts and specialty sandwiches), and a good restaurant, *Hugo's*. 623 Union St., downtown (615 259-1234 or 800 228-9000). Expensive.

The Opryland Hotel – This 1,068-room hotel is near the Opry and Opryland (but 20 minutes from downtown). Good entertainment at its *Stagedoor, Saloon,* and *Staircase* lounges. The *Old Hickory Room* is one of the city's better (and more expensive) restaurants. The hotel also has a beautiful indoor park with suspended walkways. 2800 Opryland Dr. (615 889-1000). Expensive.

Vanderbilt Plaza – Most guests either love or hate this 342-room hotel's architecture and its severely modern stone lobby, all part of an office complex. But everyone usually agrees that it's an elegant place to stay. There's a pleasant English pub-style bar, casual dining at *Impressions,* and a more formal atmosphere and fancier menu at *Chancellor's.* Across the street from the Vanderbilt campus. 2100 West End Ave. (615 320-1700). Expensive.

Hermitage Landing Beach Cabins – On Percy Priest Lake, with lake activities — fishing, boating, swimming — at your doorstep. 20 units with kitchenettes (5 have fireplaces). Rte. 2 on Bell Rd. (615 889-7050). Expensive to moderate.

Holiday Inn, Vanderbilt – Standard *Inn* high-rise, but close to Vanderbilt University and a horde of good restaurants and across the road from the Parthenon and Centennial Park. This 300-room *Holiday Inn* is near some good night spots and has a lively bar of its own. 2613 West End Ave. (615 327-4707). Moderate.

Knights Inn South – This new, no-frills motel has 114 rooms; some units have kitchenettes. I-24 at Harding Pl. (615 834-0570). Inexpensive.

 EATING OUT: Nashville is, as they say, a good eating town, with lots of small, unpretentious restaurants where you'll find fried chicken and shrimp, steaks, home-style vegetables, and the like. An inexpensive meal will cost two of you 20 or less, a moderate one about $20 to $30, and an expensive one anywhere from $30 up. Prices do not include drinks, wine, or tips.

Julian's – Sophisticated French cuisine, featuring roast quail in peach sauce, fresh salmon, and veal aux champignons. A specialty is hot dessert soufflés. The restaurant is in an old house, complete with white columns and plants. Closed Sundays. Reservations recommended. Major credit cards. 2412 West End Ave. (327-2412). Expensive.

Mario's – Owner Mario Ferrari serves up North Italian dishes, lasagna, and a variety of Italian veal specialties — alongside photos of himself taken with celebrities who stop by when they're in town. Closed Sundays. Reservations recommended. Major credit cards. 1915 West End Ave. (327-3232). Expensive.

Arthur's – Seven-course Continental dining and plush decor characterize this chic eating place. The menu changes daily, but specialties include Dover sole, beef Wellington, and veal Normandy. Open daily. Reservations recommended. Major credit cards. The Mall at Green Hills, off Abbott-Martin Rd. (383-8841). Expensive.

Christopher's – Tucked underneath a shopping plaza, this quiet haven has an intimate, elegant atmosphere, with chamber music in the background. The menu is Continental, and service is attentive but unobtrusive. Open daily. Reservations advised. Major credit cards. Belle Meade Shopping Center on West End Ave. (385-5900). Expensive.

Samaina – Don't be put off by its boring, whitewashed brick setting; this is one of the city's best and most authentic ethnic restaurants. Traditional Greek dishes are served in the small but agreeable dining room. Closed Mondays. Major credit cards. 19th Ave. S at West End (329-0004). Moderate.

Tavern on the Row – The new "in" spot for celebrities and lots of others. Good tavern atmosphere, outside seating in summer, plenty of noise and confusion, and surprisingly good food. Closed Sundays. Major credit cards. 26 Music Square E (255-3900). Moderate.

The Bluebird Café – With an atmosphere similar to that of European cafés, it serves tasty meat and vegetarian specials as well as a large selection of salads, sandwiches, and tempting desserts. Open daily, but on Sundays only in the evening, for desserts and music. Reservations not necessary. Major credit cards. 4104 Hillsboro Rd. (383-1461). Moderate to inexpensive.

Metropole – Excellent, inexpensive Lebanese specialties in a small Mom-and-Pop restaurant that makes every effort to be elegant and romantic. Try the Mazza, a feast of Mediterranean appetizers for two. Open daily, lunch only on Sundays. Major credit cards. 200 Broad (329-2897). Inexpensive.

Chinatown – An escape from the red plastic tablecloths found at almost every other Chinese restaurant in Nashville, it's a good spot for quiet conversation and tasty Hunan, Szechwan, and Mandarin food. Open daily. Major credit cards. 3813 Hillsboro Rd. (269-3275). Inexpensive.

Miss Daisy's – For refined Southern entrées and desserts. Open daily for lunch; dinner daily except Sundays. 4029 Hillsboro Rd. (269-5354). Inexpensive.

The Elliston Place Soda Shop – Good lunches and dinners served by waitresses who look as if they're about to tell you to eat all your vegetables. The tile and chrome decor is beautifully intact from the 1940s. Closed weekends. Reservations not necessary. No credit cards. 211 Elliston Pl. (327-1090). Inexpensive.

The Gaslight Beef Room – At Opryland USA, this steak and baked potato place is convenient if you're going to the Opry. Best are the homemade rolls. Open any time Opryland is open (see *Special Places*). Reservations not necessary. Major credit cards. 2802 Opryland Dr. (889-6611). Inexpensive.

Loveless Motel Restaurant – Fried chicken, homemade biscuits, and peach and blackberry preserves, plus country ham (salty, the way it's supposed to be) with gravy. Breakfast anytime; reservations recommended. Closed Mondays. No credit cards. Rte. 5, Hwy. 100 (646-9700). Inexpensive.

West End Cooker – This chain offers some of the best Southern cooking in town — nothing fancy, but plenty of big salads and stick-to-your-ribs main courses in a pleasant atmosphere. Open daily for lunch and dinner. Major credit cards. 2609 West End Ave. (327-2925). Inexpensive.

NEW HAVEN

To most visitors, New Haven is Yale, and Yale is New Haven. Certainly, the university dominates the city center, with 200 buildings spreading across much of New Haven's downtown section. And as the city's largest single employer, Yale could qualify as New Haven's major industry, if the production of literate graduates can be properly called an industry.

But there was a New Haven long before there was a Yale. The city was established in 1638; Yale moved to New Haven from Old Saybrook, Connecticut, in 1716 and wasn't even called Yale until two years later. And the city has always had the kind of diverse population that Yale discovered as a goal to work toward in the late 1960s.

An early trading center with a good harbor on Long Island Sound, New Haven really established its character in the 19th century, when the construction of the New Haven Railroad and the arrival of Irish, Italian, Polish, and Eastern European Jewish immigrants provided all the ingredients for heavy industry (the first repeating rifle was a New Haven product, which, like a number of young, ambitious Yale students, helped settle the frontier).

Today New Haven is a city of strong contrasts. There is the "Hill Section," a miserable slum of ugly old wooden buildings, once occupied by Irish railroad workers; but there is also Hillhouse Avenue, described by Dickens as the loveliest street in America. The avenue is flanked by beautiful Victorian mansions of red brick, set back from the street by spacious landscaped gardens. One of the homes, the Aaron Skinner house, is an outstanding example of Greek Revival architecture.

Many of New Haven's neighborhoods have retained their particular ethnic characteristics, although the city has undergone a population loss in recent decades, down about 25,000 from a high of 163,000 in the late 1930s. Neat wooden houses line the streets of Fair Haven, where many Irish live, and the Wooster Square area, with its large Italian population. Lace-curtain Irish and aristocratic Yankees live in the exclusive homes in Westville and on Wooster Square itself. The efforts of city officials were the principal factor in keeping these neighborhoods intact and desirable during the 1950s and 60s, when New Haven was confronted with deterioration and the threat of wholesale suburban exodus. New Haven was not allowed to degenerate into a massive slum surrounding an Ivy League enclave.

New and modern buildings standing side by side with the genteel 19th-century homes create a sharp contrast of architectural styles. But the presence of Yale creates an even more distinct mixture of cultures. The university and city have coexisted for two and a half centuries, sometimes on good terms, sometimes not. Currently the two administrations are battling over finances; as a nonprofit educational institution, Yale is exempt from taxes, but the city wants money in lieu of taxes, which the university is reluctant to give. Nevertheless, town and gown are on good terms, mostly due to the efforts of A. Bartlett Giamatti, Yale's president from 1978 to 1986, who originally went to Yale on a scholarship.

Yale gives the town a number of its valuable libraries and galleries — the Peabody Museum of Natural History, the Yale Collection of Musical Instruments, the University Art Gallery, and the Center for British Art. The town, in turn, supplies the university with workers, and complements its collections with three beautiful churches on the Green, the New Haven Historical Society, and a score of good restaurants. Like an old married couple that has suffered bitter disappointments in the past and still harbors ancient grievances, the bond between town and university is hardly perfect; but if this particular marriage wasn't made in heaven, it was most certainly contracted on the New Haven Green, around which town and gown are intertwined, presumably forever. Despite what others may think, both "Yalies" and "townies" know that New Haven wouldn't be New Haven without Yale and Yale really wouldn't be Yale outside New Haven.

NEW HAVEN AT-A-GLANCE

 SEEING THE CITY: Once used by the Quinnipiac Indians for smoke signals, the 359-foot summit of New Haven's eastern cliff in East Rock Park still commands a panoramic view of the area — the city centered around the Green, the Yale campus, the harbor, and, on a clear day, 18 miles down Long Island Sound to Bridgeport.

 SPECIAL PLACES: New Haven, the first architecturally planned city in the US, was designed for walking. Laid out in nine squares, the Green is still the main square. Almost everything of interest is nearby, in a 30-block area whose cultural and historic scope transcends its geographic limits.

The Green – The 16-acre square of grass, trees, and shrubbery in the city center remains today the focal point of New Haven activity as it was for early-17th-century settlers. Originally all public buildings were on the Green, as well as cows and pigs to keep the grass down. All the animals are now gone. The only buildings left are three churches, two of Georgian and Federal style and one Episcopal church of Gothic Revival, all built between 1812 and 1815.

New Haven Colony Historical Society and Museum – A large model offers a look at New Haven of 1640, and other collections span the city's historical development over the past three centuries. Closed Mondays. Free. 114 Whitney Ave. (562-4183).

Yale Campus and Facilities – Named for East India trader and donor Elihu Yale, the university, founded in 1701, is one of the most distinguished educational institutions in the world. The campus is lovely with its ivy-covered Gothic buildings, charming green courtyards, and examples of contemporary architecture. The best way to see the campus is to take a free university tour led by student guides well versed in college lore and anecdotes. The tour begins at the Old Campus with its Gothic and Romanesque structures, including the oldest of the ivy-covered buildings, Connecticut Hall, and proceeds to Memorial Quadrangle, Harkness Tower, *Mory's,* and the newer Yale structures such as the Ezra Stiles and Morse colleges and the Beinecke Rare Book Library. Tours are given twice daily throughout the year starting at the University Information Office, Phelps Archway, 344 College St. (436-1907).

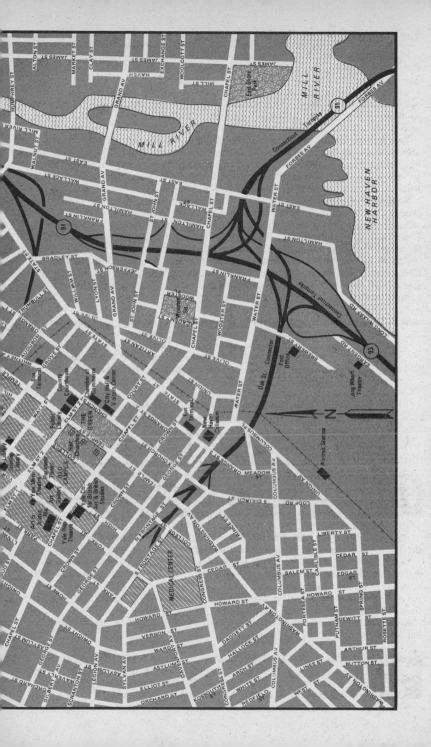

Peabody Museum of Natural History – Exhibits on evolutionary history: a huge skeleton of a brontosaurus, the Pulitzer Prize–winning *Age of Reptiles* mural by Ralph Zallinger, the Hall of Mammals. Open daily. Small admission charge; free on Tuesdays. 170 Whitney Ave. (436-0850).

University Art Gallery – This fine collection includes John Trumbull's original paintings of the American Revolution. Samples of ancient Greek and Roman art and architecture. Closed Mondays. Free. 1111 Chapel St. (436-0574).

Yale Center for British Art and British Studies – Designed by Louis I. Kahn, it features works of Hogarth, Constable, Turner, Stubbs, and Blake. The paintings are hung in bright, open galleries which create the atmosphere of an English country house and provide optimal viewing. There are more British works here than anyplace outside Britain. Closed Mondays. Free. 1080 Chapel St. (436-3909).

Shubert Performing Arts Center – This historic theater, once the preeminent staging ground for Broadway plays and musicals, has been restored to its original 1914 elegance, thus spurring a performing arts and retail renaissance in the College and Chapel streets area. Productions include both national touring groups and local performers. 247 College St. (624-1825).

Palace Performing Arts Center – Directly across the street from the Shubert Center, this newly renovated concert hall complements New Haven's performing arts scene with a number of modern dance productions each year and an impressive musical performance schedule including everything from rock 'n' roll to classical.

■**EXTRA SPECIAL:** Some 60 miles east of New Haven on I-95 is the town of *Mystic,* where the fastest clipper ships and the first ironclad vessels were built in the 19th century. The town has been restored as a 19th-century seaport. You can stroll along the waterfront of the Mystic River or down the cobblestone streets lined with reproductions of quaint seaport homes. The Mystic Seaport Museum has an outstanding collection featuring the *Charles W. Morgan,* a large wooden whaling ship in service more than 80 years, and the *Joseph Conrad,* one of the last squareriggers ever built. For more information, see DIRECTIONS.

SOURCES AND RESOURCES

TOURIST INFORMATION: The New Haven Convention and Visitors Bureau is best for maps, brochures, and general information; downtown at 155 Church St. (787-8367). Also at Exit 47 of I-95 (787-8318), from May through October. Yale has its own information center at Phelps Archway, 344 College St. (436-1907).

Enjoying New Haven, A Guide to the Area by Jane Byers and Ruth McClure ('Round-the-Town Publications; $4.95) is a good guide to the city.

Local Coverage – The *New Haven Journal-Courier,* morning daily; the *New Haven Register,* evening daily and Sundays; the Friday *Register* lists the coming week's attractions. Available at newsstands.

Food – *Best Restaurants in Southern New England* by Patricia Brooks (101 Productions; $4.95) has many New Haven listings.

Area Code – All telephone numbers are in the 203 area code unless otherwise indicated.

CLIMATE AND CLOTHES: Umbrellas are an important item in New Haven. On Long Island Sound, the city gets a lot of rain. The sea breeze, which gives some pleasant relief during the humid summers, the spring, and the fall, becomes raw during the cold and snowy winters.

GETTING AROUND: Airport – Tweed–New Haven Airport is a 15-minute drive from downtown, and taxi fare will run about $6. The Connecticut Transit bus that heads this way is not recommended for those with luggage, since it stops two blocks away. Tweed–New Haven handles only domestic flights. Those with international connections can get to JFK and La Guardia in New York City and Newark International in northern New Jersey by contacting Connecticut Limousine (878-2222); the ride to any of the three from its terminal on Brewery St. at Long Wharf (behind the New Haven post office) will take approximately 2 hours and cost from $21 to $24.

Bus – Connecticut Transit serves the downtown area and the suburbs. Route information and guides are available at 470 James St. (624-0151).

Taxi – Cabs can be ordered on the phone. They can be hailed in the street, but free taxis are rare. The largest company is Yellow Cab (562-4123).

Car Rental – New Haven has offices of all the national firms.

MUSEUMS: With Yale's fine collections and New Haven's Historical Society, all cultural bases are loaded in the city. Two special collections reach interests further afield:

Beinecke Rare Book and Manuscript Library – 121 Wall St. (436-8438)

Yale Collection of Musical Instruments – Open Tuesdays through Thursdays, 1 to 4 PM, and Sundays, 2 to 5 PM. 15 Hillhouse Ave. (436-4935)

MAJOR COLLEGES AND UNIVERSITIES: Yale University (see *Special Places*). Other educational institutions in the area are the University of New Haven, 300 Orange Ave. in West Haven (932-7000), and Southern Connecticut State College, 501 Crescent St. (397-4000).

SPECIAL EVENTS: The *New Haven Jazz Festival,* a series of concerts featuring well-known artists, runs from early July through mid-August. The 20-kilometer *Road Race* takes place annually on Labor Day, and the *New Haven Bed Race* is held in early September. The weekend before Thanksgiving of odd-numbered years, the Harvard-Yale football game takes place, with all the fanfare of a traditional rivalry, at the Yale Bowl.

SPORTS AND FITNESS: Fitness Centers – The Downtown Racquet Club has racquetball, squash, and basketball courts, sauna, and Nautilus equipment, 230 George St. (787-6501).

Football – Yale has teams in all major sports, but the biggest are the *Bulldogs,* who play football at the Yale Bowl. Between Derby Ave. and Chapel St. Call the Athletic Association for tickets (436-0100).

Hockey – The New Haven *Nighthawks* of the American Hockey League play from October to April at the New Haven Coliseum, 275 S Orange St. (787-0101).

Horse Racing – Although there is no racetrack nearby, OTB has taken on a new meaning here with an $8 million racing theater, complete with a 24-by-32-foot screen and 40 betting windows. The "grandstand" seats 1,800. Open six afternoons (not Tuesdays) and six evenings (not Sundays) a week, it's called *Teletrack* (789-1943) in the Long Wharf area.

Jogging – Run along Whalley Avenue, which is hilly, to Edgewood Park, about 2 miles north; Amity Road provides a more rural setting; Fountain Street and Litchfield Road are other options. Every Monday at 6:15 PM a Fun Run leaves from Running Start, 93 Whitney Ave. and Trumbull St. (865-6244).

Skiing – Best facilities nearby are at Powder Ridge in Middlefield, Connecticut, 21 miles on I-91 (exit 16) to E Main St. in Meriden; from there follow the signs to Powder Ridge.

Tennis – There are many good outdoor courts for the public in the city. Municipal courts at Bowen Field (Munson St. between Crescent St. and Sherman Ave.) are free while the College Wood Courts (Orange and Cold Spring sts.) have a small fee. Yalies get preference at university courts but the public is welcome. Derby and Central aves.

THEATER: For up-to-date offerings and performance times, check the publications listed above. New Haven is the home of a well-known professional repertory company, the *Long Wharf Theatre Company,* with productions of classics, musicals, contemporary works, and experimental theater, in a former warehouse in the meat and produce terminal. Closed in the summer. 222 Sargent Dr. (787-4282; see *Regional American Theater,* DIVERSIONS). *Yale Repertory Theatre,* 1120 Chapel St. (436-1600), also has experimental theater and classic plays.

MUSIC: The *New Haven Symphony Orchestra* gives concerts from October through April at Woolsey Hall on the Yale campus (ticket information, 776-1444). For information about the Yale chorus, student groups, and visiting artists, call University Information at 436-1907.

NIGHTCLUBS AND NIGHTLIFE: Nightspots come and go in New Haven. The *Top of the Park,* at the *Sheraton Park Plaza Hotel,* has the best view of the city at night and no cover charge. 155 Temple St. (772-1700). *Toad's Place,* 300 York St. (777-7431), features top-name entertainment. *Partners,* mostly for gays, has drag entertainment. 365 Crown St. (624-5510).

SINS: In New Haven, Yale is the city's *pride* — the kind of pride that can easily precede a fall. University people think they're better than townspeople; townspeople seek to limit the university's influence by withholding permission for such expansion items as new dorms. It's not that such strained town-and-gown situations are unusual among college cities, but New Haven manages to be a little worse than most because the pride (some call it arrogance) of Yalies is so fierce. Here, when the going is roughest, the only place you'll spot the twain meeting is in Wooster Square, in the heart of the city's huge Italian neighborhood, over pizza at diners like *Sally's, Pepe's,* and *The Spot.* (Each has its loyal following; *gluttony* flourishes at each.)

LOCAL SERVICES: Business Services – Audubon Copy Shoppe, 50 Whitney Ave. (865-3115)
 Mechanic – Libby's Sales and Service, 60 Printer's La. (772-1112)

BEST IN TOWN

CHECKING IN: Everything is easy to find in New Haven, but visitors will certainly be frustrated in their search for a grand old traditional hotel — it's simply not there. What does exist is as easy to find in New Haven as anywhere else — branches of the familiar chains, which offer moderately priced accommodations ($70 to $80 per night for a double room). There are also inexpensive rooms downtown ($35 to $45 per night), which can be a real find if you've seen one too many chains. For B&B accommodations, contact: Bed & Breakfast Ltd., PO Box 216, New Haven, CT 06513 (203 469-3260).

Park Plaza Hotel – Downtown, with a rooftop restaurant that features a view of New Haven at night, plus music and dancing. 155 Temple St. (203 772-1700). Moderate.

Holiday Inn – Also downtown, with a pool and a restaurant. 30 Whalley Ave. (203 777-6221). Moderate.

The Colony Inn – The old *Midtown Motor Lodge,* closed for several years, has been completely refurbished and renamed. As close to Yale as you can get without being in a classroom. 1157 Chapel St. (203 776-1234). Moderate.

Hotel Duncan – A small, old hotel near Yale (so near, in fact, that students sometimes live here). But there are rooms available for visitors, travelers, and the student-at-heart. 1151 Chapel St. (203 787-1273). Inexpensive.

 EATING OUT: For folks who consider eating far more important than sleeping, New Haven is the place for you. What the city lacks in fancy overnight accommodations, it makes up for in an abundance and variety of restaurants. A two-minute walk through the center of town will turn up several worthwhile eateries tucked away in basements and other unlikely corners. Because there are many potential diners in the city, restaurants are highly competitive, and prices are generally reasonable. Most of the restaurants are in the moderate ($20 to $30 for a dinner for two) to inexpensive range ($15 and under) though there are a few that are more expensive ($40 and up). Prices do not include tax, drinks, or tip.

Leon's – This family-run restaurant is rich in Italian food. The specialty is chicken Eduardo, prepared in a light butter and garlic sauce, but mussel and clam dishes are also good. Closed Mondays. Reservations for large parties in private rooms only. Major credit cards. 321 Washington Ave. (777-LEON). Expensive.

Delmonaco's – The decor is strictly Valentino — Valentino posters on the wall and sometimes an old Valentino silent film to dine by. And the food is southern Italian. Inspired by the atmosphere, the chef has created two dishes designed to raise passions in the blood: fresh fish on linguine topped with a·whole lobster, and a variety of meats mixed with peppers and onions, cooked in a secret sauce. Both terrific, both called the Chef's Specials. Closed Tuesdays. Reservations advised. Major credit cards. 232 Wooster St. (865-1109). Expensive.

Basel's – Everyone and everything here is Greek, from the large portions of moussaka to the waitresses in flowery peasant dresses, who dance to the live Greek bouzouki music (Friday and Saturday nights) and get everyone into the act, Greek or not. Closed Sundays and Mondays. Reservations suggested. Major credit cards. 993 State St. (624-9361). Moderate.

Old Heidelberg – One of the city's basement restaurants, this one has a real Yale flavor, complete with students, beers, steaks, and pictures of generations of varsity heroes lining the walls. Open daily. Reservations suggested. Major credit cards. 1151 Chapel St. (777-3639). Moderate.

Hatsune – A fine Japanese restaurant serving original country style fare with over 100 kinds of sushi. Decorated in the style of a Japanese farmhouse, it offers one of the more exotic dining experiences in New Haven. Open daily. Reservations advised. Major credit cards. 93 Whitney Ave., corner of Trumbull St. (776-3216). Moderate.

Hunan Wok – New Haven's best Chinese restaurant, serving Hunan, Szechwan, and Mandarin cuisine in a warm and friendly atmosphere. Open daily. Reservations and take-out available. Visa and MasterCard. 142 York St. (776-9475). Moderate.

Elm City Diner – An atypical Art Deco diner, favored by theatergoers for its late night menu. Nouvelle cuisine. Piano bar Friday and Saturday nights. Open daily. No reservations. Major credit cards. 1226 Chapel St. (776-5050). Moderate.

Fitzwilly's – This place is always jumping with students, residents, and visitors.

Good quiche, homemade soups, and complete dinners are offered. Open daily. No reservations. Major credit cards. 338 Elm St. (624-9438). Inexpensive.

Claire's Corner Copia – Even after expanding and redecorating, *Claire's* is still packed at mealtimes, with good reason. Here you'll find the best homemade food away from home. Soups are nothing short of wonderful, as are the breads and cakes (the carrot cake is widely acknowledged to be the finest in the city). Open daily. No reservations or credit cards. 1000 Chapel St. (562-3888). Inexpensive.

Pepe's – Pepe claims to have invented the pizza. You might not believe him but you'll have to agree that in an area where pizza-making is fine art, Pepe's takes the pie. Closed Tuesdays. No reservations. No credit cards. 157 Wooster St. (865-5762). Inexpensive.

Louis' Lunch – This tiny place, which looks like an English pub, claims to be the birthplace of the hamburger. Whether this is true or not, the burgers are great — big, juicy, and charcoal grilled. And don't ask for ketchup — they don't have it and to ask is considered an affront to the quality of the product. Open weekdays till 4:30 PM. No reservations. No credit cards. 263 Crown St. (562-5507). Inexpensive.

Picnic on the Green – Part of the redesigned Chapel Square Mall and composed of over a dozen eateries. Seating is along a window wall overlooking the New Haven Green. The *Atticus Bookstore Café* is a special treat. Open daily. Chapel Square Mall mezzanine. 900 Chapel St. Inexpensive.

NEW ORLEANS

Jazz musicians call it the Big Easy, and down in New Orleans jazzmen are called professors. If anyone can transmit a feeling for New Orleans, it is probably the professors. Not because they are formally educated — they're not, and some can't even read music — but they can *improvise;* and in New Orleans, that's what it's all about.

The past has been a double-edged sword for New Orleans. Not even its port on the Mississippi — second in trade only to New York City harbor — has shaken it out of a certain Old South torpor. The city (with a metropolitan population of about 1,190,000) lacks manufacturing and heavy industry, and throughout its long history as a center of trade and source of great wealth for some, it has maintained a European, 18th-century air. For the rich it has ever been a sophisticated, cultured haven; for the poor — many of whom are black — it has offered little hope of betterment over the years. The poverty just seems to roll along like the river; and little has appeared to change it. But at the same time, this torpor has managed to protect the city's charms, where in a different place they might have fallen long ago before the trumpet of civic progress.

Initially, New Orleans was something of a hot property, traded back and forth between governments. The French were first attracted in the early 1700s by the area's deep, swift harbor; named for the regent of France, Philippe, Duc d'Orléans, it served as the capital of the French territories in America from 1723 to 1763, when a Bourbon family pact transferred it to Spanish rule, until it was ceded back to France in 1800. Two important things developed from all this swapping and ceding: the Créole culture, unique to the New World and descended from French and Spanish parents; and one of the greatest bargains of the century. Napoleon sold New Orleans and the entire Louisiana Purchase to the United States for $15 million in 1803, doubling the size of the country's territory. In 1815, to protect this wily investment, General Andrew Jackson and his Kentucky militiamen teamed with anyone and everyone — including the pirate Jean Lafitte, the Choctaw Indians, numerous Créoles, and some black slaves — to defeat the British in the Battle of New Orleans. The War of 1812, unfortunately, had ended, some time earlier, somewhat dampening the victors' spirits. (News of the peace had not yet reached the combatants.) Jackson secured the Mississippi River for America, and New Orleans began to grow as a major port for the cotton, sugar cane, and indigo crops grown on surrounding plantations and as a kind of Old World cosmopolitan center in the midst of the deep South. The terrain is basically flat plains of the river delta — the Mississippi flows to the south, and the sea-sized Lake Pontchartrain borders the city on the north.

Today, the Vieux Carré or French Quarter, the main area of interest in New Orleans, reflects and preserves the New Orleans style. Protected by a powerful

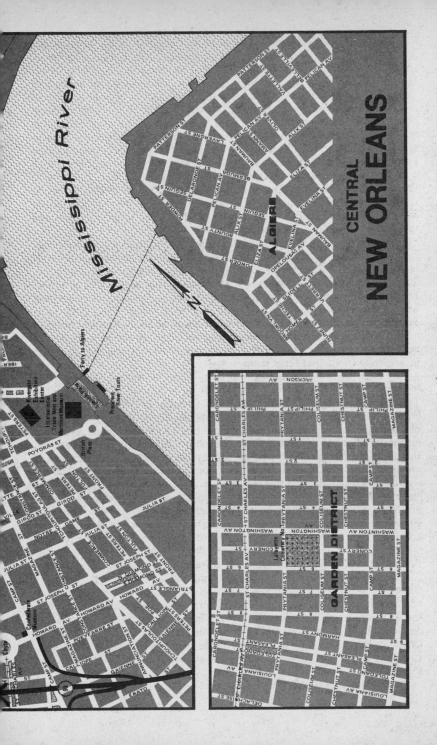

CENTRAL
NEW ORLEANS

Mississippi River

ALGIERS

GARDEN DISTRICT

Vieux Carré Commission, which regulates construction and modification of the area, the architecture is a blend of French and Spanish colonial (and their hybrid, Créole) standing side by side. A fine example of the mixture of cultures and styles is the Cabildo, once the headquarters of Spanish colonial rule. The impressive structure features wide Spanish arches and a French mansard roof. Flanking the European-style Jackson Square are the imposing St. Louis Cathedral and the Pontalba apartments, which contain a French-style arcade and beautiful cast ironwork on the balconies, seen throughout the French Quarter. And there is a lot more; the renovated French Market, with a history dating back 200 years, still has a colorful atmosphere and some of the best café au lait on either side of the Atlantic. The way to see the French Quarter is also old-fashioned — by strolling down the cobblestone streets and allowing your eyes to direct you. It's the kind of place where you relax and take it easy — the charms surround you.

In New Orleans, though, you don't just see and feel the city, but you must taste what it has to offer — Créole food, a highly developed regional style blending classical French cuisine with Spanish and American Southern, enhanced by spices and seasonings from American Indian, African, and West Indian recipes. The results are so good that they say down in New Orleans when a Créole goes to heaven, the first thing he asks Saint Peter is where he can find the jambalaya (a fragrant stew of shrimp, oysters, tomatoes, and rice) or gumbo filé (a spicy soup of shrimp, crabmeat, okra, oyster, herbs, and rice). Seafood is a Créole staple, as are fresh vegetables and veal, and the city is rich in fine restaurants that serve it up in style.

And then there is the Carnival Season — an extravagant blow-out that begins shortly after Christmas and builds up steam till Mardi Gras (Fat Tuesday) preceding Ash Wednesday. The tradition of Mardi Gras in New Orleans was begun over 100 years ago by a social club, the Mystick Krewe of Comus. Other private clubs picked up the idea, and thus began a series of elaborate balls and parades whose tradition continues today. The balls are still the principal event of New Orleans society. A well-known businessman is crowned King; the Queen is a debutante from a prominent family. But all the world loves a parade, and the Mardi Gras has gone public (though private balls still are held). In addition to the traditional parades with elaborate floats, marching jazz bands, doubloons and trinkets tossed to the crowds, the entire French Quarter, St. Charles Avenue, and Canal Street are jammed. And celebrate they do in all manner of the word. Also parading on Mardi Gras is a black krewe, led by King Zulu, who shares some of the spotlight with the Big Shot of Africa. Zulu meanders throughout downtown New Orleans throwing painted coconuts, doubloons, and beads. The annual He Sheba costume competition for transvestites colorfully jams already jammed Bourbon Street. Each year, two parades of magnificently decorated trucks follow the Rex parade, with the occupants throwing trinkets just like the maskers on the floats. Costumed marching clubs dance and weave their way toward Canal St. behind small Dixieland jazz bands before Rex takes to the streets. In recent years, new krewes parade in the suburbs on Mardi Gras after the Rex parade.

Mardi Gras is both the best and the worst of times to visit New Orleans.

The revelry and spectacle reach great heights, but so, too, do the hotel prices and the frenetic pace. There are other festivals which offer New Orleans in a different mood, without the crowds of the Mardi Gras (see *Special Events*).

The Jazz and Heritage Festival is a special event, but there's no dearth of music anytime. The place that started off such great jazzmen as Louis Armstrong, Buddy Bolden, Joe "King" Oliver, Kid Ory, and Jelly Roll Morton still swings. The Old Mint, which has been renovated, is the permanent home for excellent exhibitions on how it all began with a merging of Afro-American and European rhythms. At Preservation Hall, Dixieland jazz is played every night; and in countless honky-tonks on Bourbon Street the beat goes on. New Orleans still has brass band funerals where a marching band accompanies the procession from the church to the cemetery, playing solemn marches and hymns. As soon as the services are over, the rhythm picks up and the theme changes to something like "I'll Be Glad When You're Dead You Rascal You." The mourners begin prancing and cavorting behind the band, picking up others who join in the "Second Line" though they probably don't even know who died. But it doesn't really matter because when you leave the Big Easy, New Orleans folk act like you're on your way to the Bigger Easy, and send you off easily. Regardless of where you go afterward though, while you're there, it's hard not to join in. And why not? As they say in New Orleans, if you ain't gonna shake it, what did you bring it for?

NEW ORLEANS AT-A-GLANCE

SEEING THE CITY: The revolving bar in the *Top of the Mart* restaurant, on the 33rd floor of the International Trade Mart, offers the best view of the city, the Mississippi River as it cuts the crescent shape of New Orleans, and the barges, ocean liners, and ferries as they move up and down the river. 2 Canal St. at the river (522-9795).

River Tours – On the free ferry you can ride back and forth to Algiers. The *Bayou Jean Lafitte* steamboat gives a tour from the Toulouse Street Wharf through the bayou country to Bayou Barataria, home of the famous pirate. Open daily. Admission charge. The paddlewheel steamboat *Natchez* has daily runs up and down the river. Admission charge. The big side-wheeler steamboat the *President* sails from the dock at the foot of Canal St. for dance cruises on weekend nights. Admission charge (586-8777).

SPECIAL PLACES: Nestled between the Mississippi River and Lake Pontchartrain, New Orleans' natural crescent shape can be confusing. North, south, east, and west mean very little here; New Orleans residents keep life simple and use "lakeside" or "riverside" as directions.

VIEUX CARRÉ

Jackson Square – This stately square was once the town square of the French colonial settlement, and the scene of most of New Orleans' history, from hangings to the transfer ceremony of the Louisiana Purchase. Rebuilt in the 1850s with the equestrian statue of Andrew Jackson, the hero of the Battle of New Orleans, the square is a pleasant place to sit and watch New Orleans go by, against a setting of charming brick facades of the surrounding buildings. Heads no longer roll here, but an occasional open-air jazz concert does, and the only hangings are on the iron fence bounding the area, where local artists display their work, and some draw portraits. Traffic is usually rerouted from the area, leaving a pedestrian mall. 700 Chartres St. bordered by Chartres, St. Ann, St. Peter, and Decatur sts.

St. Louis Cathedral – Built in 1794, this beautiful Spanish building features towers, painted ceilings, an altar imported from Belgium, and markers for those buried in the sanctuary in French, Spanish, Latin, and English. Tours given daily. Donations requested. 700 Chartres St., across from Jackson Square (525-9585).

The Cabildo – Once the headquarters of Spanish rule and the site of the Louisiana Purchase and now part of the Louisiana State Museum. The architecture reflects the Spanish influence in its wide arches; the French influence with its mansard roof; and American with the emblems near the roof. Exhibits focus on New Orleans' interesting heritage with historical displays on French and Spanish colonial Louisiana (including portraits and documents, and even a death mask of Napoleon Bonaparte). Between the Cathedral and the Cabildo is Pirate's Alley, a narrow passageway that is the scene of frequent outdoor art shows. Closed Mondays. Small admission charge. At the corner of Chartres and St. Peter sts. (568-6968).

The Presbytère – Used as a courthouse during the Spanish colonial period, it is also part of the Louisiana State Museum and features mostly touring exhibitions. Closed Mondays. Small admission charge. At the corner of Chartres and St. Ann sts. (568-6968).

Pontalba Apartments – Built in the 1850s, this row of town houses features distinctive cast ironwork on the balconies, and a French-style arcade. Rich in New Orleans history, the Pontalba apartments and shops have seen the comings and goings of the French aristocracy, Jenny Lind, Sherwood Anderson, and William Faulkner. Today, ice cream parlors and small shops line the ground floors and some very fortunate New Orleans residents live above. Jackson Square at St. Ann and St. Peter sts.

The Moon Walk – Named for former mayor Moon Landrieu, the title's a bit misleading. But this promenade alongside the Mississippi River shows "Ol' Man River" at its best as it winds its way along the crescent shape of the city (the only resemblance Moon Walk has with the moon). The Mississippi is deep and swift at New Orleans and the port, which can accommodate oceangoing vessels, is second in tonnage only to New York. Across the levee from Decatur St. at Jackson Square.

French Market – A farmers' market for two centuries, the French Market still has a colorful atmosphere with stands under large old arches offering everything in the way of fresh vegetables and fruits (try the Louisiana oranges, sugar cane, and the sweet midget bananas), meats, and fish including live crab, turtle, shrimp, catfish, and trout. The covered section has cafés, candy shops, and gift shops. *Café du Monde* is a New Orleans institution featuring marvelous café au lait (half coffee and chicory, half hot milk) and beignets (square French donuts). The café never closes, and the market is open daily. Extending down Decatur St. from St. Ann.

Beauregard-Keyes House – Although George Washington never slept here, almost everyone else lived in this Federal house, including the novelist Frances Parkinson Keyes, chess player Paul Morphy, and Confederate General P. G. T. Beauregard; quite a few of another sort died here in a Mafia battle in 1909. The house has period furniture, a collection of dolls, and Keyes memorabilia. Closed Sundays. Admission charge. 1113 Chartres St. (523-7257).

Madame John's Legacy – Built in 1727 and survivor of the great fire of 1794, this house is one of the oldest remaining in the Mississippi Valley. The house is an excellent example of the Créole "raised cottage," with its brick-paved first floor used for storage below the dwelling area and for protection against floods and dampness, a service wing with a double stairway, and a courtyard. The Louisiana State Museum has renovated the house and furnished it as an authentic example of 18th-century New Orleans lifestyle. Closed Mondays. Small admission charge. 632 Dumaine St. (568-6968).

Royal Street – There really was a streetcar named Desire, and in the 19th century it used to run along Royal St. Though the streetcar is gone, desire for the old days remains and some of it can be fulfilled by a stroll down this street, famous for its antique shops and highly distinctive architecture.

Historic New Orleans Collection – Scholarly archives, a preserved French Quarter restaurant, gift shops, and historic exhibitions. Closed Sundays and Mondays. 533 Royal St. (523-4662).

Old Mint – Opened in 1982 and part of the Louisiana State Museum, the Mint contains a Mardi Gras exhibition and a collection of jazz memorabilia. Jazz lovers will find souvenirs of the patron saints of jazz — Louis Armstrong's first horn, Bix Beiderbecke's cuff links, and instruments played by members of the Original Dixieland Jazz Band. Fine displays trace the development of jazz from its Afro-American rhythms and the European brass band tradition to current progressive strains. Closed Mondays. Admission charge. 400 Esplanade Ave. (568-6968).

Preservation Hall – What's recorded in the jazz collection at the Mint still happens every night at Preservation Hall. Features traditional New Orleans Dixieland played by a different band from a group of six. No booze, sparse surroundings, but the real jazz thing. Open nightly. Small admission charge. 726 St. Peter St. (523-8939).

Bourbon Street – Though the street was named for the French royal family, it actually has a lot more in common with the drink, which, along with anything else potable, can be found here in abundance (and New Orleans establishments have added many drinks to the bartender's list, including the absinthe frappe and the Hurricane. Round the clock the honky-tonks offer live jazz, which gets wild in the wee hours, and live booze, which gets wicked the morning after. A hot strip since the postwar years, Bourbon Street also has lots of strip joints and peep shows, where, even if you stay outside, you'll get more of an eyeful than a peep as the hawkers swing the doors open to lure customers. Among the hottest spots is *Lafitte's Blacksmith Shop,* 941 Bourbon St., where pirate Jean Lafitte is purported to have had a blacksmith shop, now a bar where the forge is still flaming; others are the *Old Absinthe House,* 240 Bourbon St., a barroom since 1826, for rhythm and blues, and *Lulu White's Mahogany Hall,* for Dixieland jazz. 309 Bourbon St.

St. Louis Cemetery Number One – The last stop in the Vieux Carré, this old New Orleans cemetery with its tombs designed by earlier architects is literally a diminutive necropolis. The marshy ground dictated aboveground burial, and the monuments are interesting for their structure, inscriptions, and number of remains inside (to solve overcrowding, tombs are opened, and the remaining bones are moved deeper into the vault to accommodate new arrivals). If you're interested, the caretaker will give you a tour. Among the prominent buried here are Étienne de Boré, the first mayor of New Orleans; Paul Morphy, the chess player; and Marie Laveau, a 19th-century Voodoo Queen. Open daily. Free admission, but small charge for tours. (It's best not to wander around alone.) 400 Basin St.

DOWNTOWN AND THE GARDEN DISTRICT

Canal Street – Where the French Quarter ends, the business district begins, and the transition is sharp, from narrow cobblestone streets to a wide, main boulevard. The International Trade Mart, a glass skyscraper, is the center of companies dealing in foreign trade and home of the Louisiana Maritime Museum (with good displays on the Mississippi's navigatory past, and a fine collection of models of battleships, steamers, sailboats, naval weapons and equipment). Closed weekends. Small admission charge. River Wing of 2 Canal St. at the river (581-1874).

Garden District – Above Canal Street and the business district is the lovely Garden

District, once the center of 19th-century American aristocracy, still preserving its old style. The houses, mainly Victorian and Greek Revival in design, are set back from the street with wide, shady gardens of oak, magnolia, camellia, and palm trees. The district is a great place to stroll anytime (or take the St. Charles Ave. streetcar), but during the two-week Spring Fiesta in April there are tours of the private homes. For information, contact Spring Fiesta Headquarters, 826 St. Ann St. (581-1367). Bounded by Magazine St., St. Charles Ave., Jackson Ave., and Louisiana Ave.

CITY PARK AND LAKE PONTCHARTRAIN

New Orleans Museum of Art – This attractive Greek Revival building has fine permanent collections including the Samuel H. Kress Collection (Italian renaissance and baroque masterpieces), 19th-century French salon paintings, works by Degas, pre-Columbian art, African art, and Spanish colonial paintings. Closed Mondays. Admission charge. In City Park (488-2631).

Lake Pontchartrain – New Orleans' other body of water, this large saltwater lake has swimming and fishing at the beach, on Lake Shore Drive. Best is the drive over the Lake Pontchartrain Causeway, the longest overwater highway bridge in the world — 24 miles across open water, and for eight miles in the center, you are completely out of sight of land; there's only Lake Pontchartrain for as far as the eye can see. I-10 leads to the Causeway. Toll.

■**EXTRA SPECIAL:** Somewhere out there in Louisiana country was once the heart of the *Old South,* and it still beats faintly along the banks of the Mississippi. Little over 100 years ago sugar cane was king in Louisiana, and large plantations established commercial empires, as well as an entire social system, around it. A few of these plantations have been restored and are open to visitors who want to see what that period was like, at least for the people on top. And the life that the southern gentry created for themselves really is something to see. The most interesting plantations are within an hour's drive of New Orleans. Houmas House (72 miles west on River Rd.), which was used for the filming of Hush, Hush, Sweet Charlotte, looks just like a plantation should — a big, white mansion with stately columns and lovely grounds with huge, old oak trees and formal gardens. There is an excellent tour through the house, which has a circular staircase, rare antiques, a widow's walk for river gazing, and outside, garçonnière, little windmill-shaped structures where young men were sent to live independently when they came of age. San Francisco (42 miles west along River Rd.) is an attractive structure — Flamboyant Steamboat Gothic with lots of Victorian trim, elaborate ceiling paintings, and, over the front door, a mirror that reflects the Mississippi River.

SOURCES AND RESOURCES

TOURIST INFORMATION: The New Orleans Tourist Information Center provides a wealth of information on the city's attractions, including maps, brochures, and personal help. 334 Royal St. (566-5011).

New Orleans by Carolyn Kolb (Doubleday; $3.95) is the most comprehensive guide to New Orleans and the surrounding area. Another good source is *The Pelican Guide to New Orleans* by Tommy Griffin (Pelican; $2.95).

Local Coverage – *The New Orleans Times-Picayune/The States-Item,* daily.

Food – Check *The Revised New Orleans Underground Gourmet* by Rima and Richard Collin (Simon & Schuster; $3.95), and *New Orleans Restaurant Guide* by Rima and Richard Collin (Strether and Swann; $3.95).

Area Code – All telephone numbers are in the 504 area code unless otherwise indicated.

CLIMATE AND CLOTHES: New Orleans weather is subtropical with high humidity, temperatures, and substantial rainfall. Moderated by the Gulf of Mexico winds, summer temperatures hover around 90°, while winter temperatures rarely drop to freezing. Summers can get unbearably sticky.

GETTING AROUND: Airport – New Orleans International Airport is a 45-minute drive from the downtown area, and taxi fare should run about $18. The Louisiana Transit Co. (737-9611) runs an Airport-Downtown Express bus on a 10- to 25-minute schedule from downtown at the corner of Loyola and Tulane aves.; fare, 90¢. Gray Line Tours (464-0611) also provides transportation from the airport to downtown hotels for $7.

Bus – New Orleans Regional Transit Authority provides efficient bus and streetcar service throughout the city. The St. Charles Ave. streetcar offers a scenic ride through the Garden District (board at Canal and Baronne sts.). Complete information is available at the Regional Transit Authority office, 1001 Howard Ave., 15th floor, (569-2600).

Taxi – Cabs can be ordered on the phone, hailed in the streets, or picked up at stands in front of hotels, restaurants, and transportation terminals. Major cab companies are Yellow-Checker Cab (525-3311); United Cab (522-9771).

Car Rental – All major car rental companies have offices in New Orleans.

MUSEUMS: The New Orleans Museum of Art, the Old Mint, the Louisiana State Museum, the Historic New Orleans Collection, and the Louisiana Maritime Museum are described above in *Special Places.* Other notable New Orleans museums are:

Confederate Museum – 929 Camp St. (523-4522)
Pharmacy Museum – 514 Chartres St. (524-9077)

MAJOR COLLEGES AND UNIVERSITIES: Tulane University, 6400 St. Charles Ave. (865-5000), is New Orleans' most prominent educational institution, known primarily for its medical and law schools. Loyola University, 6300 St. Charles Ave. (865-2011), which has an enrollment of over 4,000 students, is also in the city. The University of New Orleans, the Lakefront (286-6000), is the area's largest school.

SPECIAL EVENTS: When it comes to special events, none tops New Orleans' *Mardi Gras,* an extravagant succession of parades, carnivals, and balls that begin January 6 and continue through Ash Wednesday. (For a fuller description, see the New Orleans essay).

As if the Mardi Gras is not enough, two weeks later the *Spring Fiesta* begins with "A Night in Old New Orleans." After the coronation of the queen, there is a carriage parade through the French Quarter. For the next two weeks the town is literally laid open. For information, contact the Fiesta Association, 826 St. Ann St. (581-1367).

Since 1969 New Orleans has been driving home the point that there just ain't no better place for jazz than the *New Orleans Jazz and Heritage Festival,* held every May. The top names in jazz perform at a number of places throughout the city, while all kinds of bands — ragtime, traditional New Orleans Dixieland, Cajun — and folk and blues musicians entertain outside on the Fair Grounds. All come together as jazz stars join in late night jam sessions in the French Quarter. More than just music for the soul, the Heritage includes something for the stomach and plenty of it. All kinds of Créole and Cajun food, the New Orleans specialties, are available on the Fair Grounds.

The *New Orleans Food Festival, Bastille Day,* and *La Fête,* all held every July, celebrate the city's heritage with musical, sports, cultural, and culinary events.

SPORTS AND FITNESS: The biggest thing in New Orleans sports is the Superdome, the world's largest domed stadium. You can take 15-minute tours daily of the 27-story arena with a capacity of 97,000. The Superdome hosts the New Year's Day *Sugar Bowl* football classic.

Bicycling – Both City Park and Audubon Park are good for riding.

College Football – The Tulane University *Green Wave* team plays at the Superdome from late September through November (861-9283).

Fishing – On Lake Pontchartrain, and within easy distance of the Gulf of Mexico, New Orleans is a fishing paradise (for fishermen, not fish). The best spot is Empire, 52 miles south on Rte. 23 where you can rent boats or take a charter to go after king mackerel, white trout, and red snapper, at Battistella's Marina (523-6068). You can fish in Lake Pontchartrain for bass, speckled trout, and red fish off the seawall along Lake Shore Drive or rent a boat from Ed Lombard's bait center at Chef Menteur.

Fitness Centers – In the *Hilton,* the Rivercenter Tennis Club has a sauna, whirlpool, outdoor track, aerobic classes, and tennis and racquetball courts, 2 Poydras St., at the river (587-7242).

Football – The NFL's New Orleans *Saints* play at the Superdome from August to December. Tickets are available at the Superdome box office (522-2600). 1500 Poydras St. at La Salle St.

Golf – Golf is popular year-round, and the best courses for the public are the four 18-hole courses at City Park, Esplanade Ave. southwest of French Quarter (283-3458), and the course at Audubon Park, 473 Walnut (861-9511).

Horse Racing – There are two seasons for racing and pari-mutuel betting: winter season at Fair Grounds Race Track, 1751 Gentilly Blvd. (944-5515) from Thanksgiving Day to mid-April; summer season at Jefferson Downs, Kenner La. (466-8521) from mid-April to early November.

Jogging – Audubon Park, 3 miles from downtown, has a popular 3-mile course; run or take the streetcar on St. Charles Avenue to get there.

Swimming – You can swim during the summer at the Olympic-sized pool in Audubon Park, St. Charles Ave. (587-1920).

Tennis – City Park has 45 good public courts of various composition, open year-round; there's a small fee (482-2230).

THEATER: For up-to-date offerings and performance times, check *The New Orleans Times-Picayune/The States-Item.* New Orleans has several theaters that offer performances, some locally produced, others traveling shows. Colleges and universities in the area also produce plays and musicals. Best bets for shows: *Theatre of the Performing Arts,* 801 N Rampart St. (522-0592); *Saenger Performing Arts Center,* 143 N Rampart St. (888-8181).

MUSIC: Classical concerts and opera are heard at *Theatre of the Performing Arts,* 801 N Rampart St. (522-0592); *New Orleans Opera Guild* has eight productions from September to May (525-7672); the *New Orleans Philharmonic Symphony* performs from September to May at the *Orpheum Theater,* 129 University Pl. (525-0500). Jazz is the big story in New Orleans music, and when it comes to jazz, it's time for:

NIGHTCLUBS AND NIGHTLIFE: New Orleans is a night town, and the jazz gets better and the drinks stronger (at least it seems that way) as the night wears on. At any one time there is an astonishing array of jazz being played in the city: top names and talented local musicians playing traditional New Orleans jazz, progressive, blues, rock, or folk music.

Current favorites are: *Pete Fountain's Night Club,* in the *Hilton* on Poydras St. (523-4374), featuring the renowned jazz clarinetist; *Tyler's Beer Garden,* 5234 Magazine St. (891-4989), for jazz; *Lulu White's Mahogany Hall,* 309 Bourbon St. (525-5595), for Dixieland music by the Dukes of Dixieland; and the *Maple Leaf Bar,* 8316 Oak St. (866-9359), for ragtime and rhythm and blues. *Preservation Hall* is the place for pure jazz (no drinks) by traditional New Orleans bands, 726 St. Peter St. (523-8939). Favorite bars: *Napoleon House and Bar,* 500 Chartres St. (524-9752); *Lafitte's Blacksmith Shop,* 941 Bourbon St. (523-0066); *Old Absinthe Bar,* 400 Bourbon St. (525-8108); *Pat O'Brien's* (home of the Hurricane), 718 St. Peter St. (525-4823).

 SINS: The Big Easy, as the "professors" or jazzmen of New Orleans call their city, is one of the hottest and funkiest places in the US. And it is not difficult for its uniquely complicated citizenry to find a lot in which to have *pride.* From the French, Spanish, African, and native American roots that form New Orleans' culture, a variety of music has been born and nurtured that is richer, more imaginative, and more influential than that from any other single source in the Western Hemisphere, and possibly the world. And Mardi Gras is a time when all the other musical forms, such as combined Indian-African chanting hymns, suddenly emerge in public places, letting outsiders in on a kind of music they can hear nowhere else in the world. And as if this isn't enough to engender a deep sense of pride, the New Orleans cooking, language, architecture, and pace of life are just as wonderful.

The cooking will particularly interest visitors who are up for a chance to indulge in a little *gluttony.* If you start the day with poached eggs and crab meat, turtle soup, and a slice of peanut butter ice cream pie, how far do you have to go to achieve the goal of overindulgence? There is still gumbo, jambalaya, stewed okra, oyster loaf, and shrimp rémoulade to get to at lunch and dinner.

Lust is the main business of Bourbon Street in the French Quarter, though it may be the music that made its name. On both sides of the street, and in every other doorway, there is a lady of the night ready to offer her services to any taker. There is nothing undercover or oblique about the action here, that is not New Orleans' way.

 LOCAL SERVICES: Business Services – Dictation Incorporated, open 24 hours daily, 1552 Washington Ave. (895-8637)
   Mechanic – Doody and Hank's Service, 719 O'Keefe (522-5391)

BEST IN TOWN

 CHECKING IN: Hotels in New Orleans are usually more than just places to stay after spending a day (and half the night) seeing the city. Many of the hotels reflect the influence of French, Spanish, and/or Louisiana colonial architecture and often a measure of charm. The service in these hotels is generally excellent. No matter where you stay or what you pay, make reservations well in advance, particularly during Mardi Gras and the Carnival season, from Christmas to Ash Wednesday (this includes Sugar Bowl Week, which precedes the football classic on New Year's Day). Slightly higher rates prevail during these periods. In general, however, the spate of hotel building that coincided with New Orleans' ill-fated World's Fair of 1985 has tended to keep the local hotel business very competitive and rather reasonable — especially on weekends. Expect to pay $100 to $160 a night for a double room (and way up — particularly for suites) in the expensive range, $75 to $95 in the moderate scale, and $45 to $70 in the inexpensive category. Many of the more expensive hotels have excellent weekend promotional packages.

Pontchartrain Hotel – With 100 individually decorated rooms and suites with many French provincial antique furnishings, this hotel is a favorite of celebrities and traveling dignitaries. Its service is truly worth the name. It has an excellent restaurant, the *Caribbean Room* (see *Eating Out*), serving Créole specialties and a bar with a jazz pianist nightly. 2031 St. Charles Ave. (504 524-0581). Expensive.

Royal Orleans Hotel – On the site of the famous St. Louis Hotel, amid the hustle and bustle of the Vieux Carré. The lobby is luxurious Italian marble, most of the 356 rooms rooms are elegantly furnished, and there is conscientious service. Features the *Esplanade Lounge,* popular with the late-night crowd, *Café Royale, Touche-Bar,* a three-level night spot, the fine *Rib Room* for dining, a rooftop pool, shops, garage. 621 St. Louis St. (504 529-5333). Expensive.

Maison de Ville – Probably the finest small hotel in the French Quarter, it's actually a variety of accommodations: the main house, with wonderfully restored former slave quarters; a town house with four apartments; and, most notable, the Audubon Cottages (named for the naturalist, who lived and painted here a century ago), each of which has a patio with access to a small swimming pool. It is in these cottages that the best of French Quarter ambience is felt. 727 Toulouse St. (504 561-5858). Expensive.

Grenoble House – A stately, mostly brick guest house retreat in the French Quarter, named — appropriately — after France's historic walled city. The 17 suites with kitchens are handsomely decorated with antiques, and some have an exposed brick fireplace. The garden patio features a heated pool, whirlpool spa, and a built-in barbecue pit, which guests are encouraged to use. 329 Dauphine St. (504 522-1331). Expensive.

Soniat House – Formerly the *Felton House,* this remarkable pair of town houses has been beautifully restored, and everything possible has been done to reinforce the feeling that guests are living in the New Orleans of 150 years ago. Guest rooms are filled with antique furniture, often including canopied beds and Victorian loveseats. 1133 Chartres St. (504 522-0570). Expensive.

The St. Louis Hotel – This elegant 68-room hotel is one of the city's newest. In the tradition of Parisian hotels, it offers personal service, rooms with French period furnishings, and tastefully landscaped courtyards with fountains. *Louis XVI* features nouveau French cuisine, and *Savoir Faire* is a French bistro. 730 Bienville St. (504 581-7300). Expensive.

New Orleans Hilton – A downtown 1,200-room resort by the river, with a fine view and the International Rivercenter, an entertainment development that includes a cruise ship terminal, a tennis club, and a luxury shopping mall. Also has a pool, health club, sauna, and garage. Special features are *Le Café Bromeliad's* Sunday champagne brunch; *Rainforest Club* with a diet buffet (a calorie count on each item); *Pete Fountain's* nightclub, featuring the famous jazz clarinetist; *Winston's,* offering five-course nouvelle cuisine dinners; and *Kabby's Seafood Restaurant,* with a Sunday seafood brunch and Dixieland jazz. 2 Poydras St. at the Mississippi River (504 561-0500). Expensive.

Windsor Court – A new, luxuriously British-style hotel with 40 deluxe rooms and 290 suites. Its afternoon teas are so popular that you may need a reservation. Every room, public and private, is richly decorated and comfortable. 300 Gravier St. (504 523-6000). Expensive.

Westin Canal Place – There are remarkable panoramic city views from the 11th-floor lobby of this new hotel atop Canal Place — the shopping mall — with 380 top-quality rooms of varying sizes and views. 100 Rue Iberville (504 566-7006). Expensive.

Méridien – This new 505-room hotel on Canal Street in the shopping district is directly on the Mardi Gras parade routes. The French atmosphere is thick, especially in the casual *Le Bistro* restaurant as well as in the more elegant and expensive *Henri* restaurant. Health club, pool. 614 Canal St. (504 525-6500). Expensive.

Fairmont – They say New Orleanians wept when its predecessor, *The Roosevelt,* was sold to the Fairmont interests. But they weep no more. The *Fairmont*'s owners have successfully wedded the charms of San Francisco and New Orleans and produced an efficient, 758-room enterprise. At the fine *Sazerac Restaurant,* topers can sample the Sazerac cocktail or the famed Ramos gin fizz. The *Blue Room* has dinner dancing and top acts. *Bailey's* is a 24-hour restaurant-bar. Also a heated pool and 2 tennis courts. University Pl. (504 529-7111). Expensive.

Monteleone – At the gateway of the Vieux Carré, this old 600-room hotel maintains a friendly atmosphere while offering the amenities of a larger operation. Features rooftop pool and bar, revolving lounge, *Steaks Unlimited Dining Room, Le Café,* garage. 214 Royal St. (504 523-3341). Expensive to moderate.

Prince Conti – Converted from an old mansion, this 50-room inn retains all of its charm, from the carriageway entrance through the lovely French château lobby to the rooms with authentic antique furnishings. In the morning, Continental breakfast is brought up to the room; in the afternoon, *Le Petit Bar* serves cocktails. 830 Conti St. (504 529-4172). Expensive to moderate.

Inter-Continental New Orleans – A new presence in the business district, with New Orleans jazz musicians entertaining in the public rooms, afternoon tea, and 3 restaurants: *Pete's Pub, The Terrace,* and excellent *Les Continents.* 500 comfortable rooms. 444 St. Charles Ave. (504 525-5566). Expensive to moderate.

The Columns – An unusual hotel in the Garden District, perfect for travelers who care less about creature comforts (not every room boasts a private bath) and more about immersing themselves in the ambience of early New Orleans. A recent refurbishment has modernized rooms. If the bar looks familiar, you know it from films like *Pretty Baby* and *Tightrope.* The St. Charles Ave. streetcar runs by the front door. 3811 St. Charles Ave. (504 899-9308). Expensive to moderate.

Cornstalk Hotel – This old Victorian home is surrounded by a New Orleans landmark — a wrought-iron fence showing ripe ears of corn shucked on their stalks, ready for harvest, and pumpkin vines. The interior is something of a landmark, too — a grand entrance hall and lobby with antique mirrors and crystal chandeliers. The 14 rooms feature four-poster beds, and you can take Continental breakfast there, in the front gallery, or on the patio. 915 Royal St. (504 523-1515). Moderate.

French Quarter Maisonnettes – A converted Vieux Carré mansion with carriageway drive of flagstones and a spacious patio, the inn is a quaint and friendly place to stay. Each of the 7 rooms is luxuriously private, right on the patio. The owner presents each guest with a printed, personal folder listing places to go, what to see and do in the city, and offering advice and suggestions for activities. 1130 Chartres St. (504 524-9918). Inexpensive.

Quality Inn Midtown – Convenient and modestly priced, with an excellent restaurant featuring Maine lobster, boiled Créole beef brisket, and shrimp cocktail. Pool, café, bar, meeting rooms. 102 rooms. 3900 Tulane Ave. (504 486-5541). Inexpensive.

EATING OUT: The city abounds with restaurants. Most are good. Many are excellent. And all reflect the distinctive cuisine of New Orleans, Créole cooking — shaped through the years by the cultures of France, Spain, America, the West Indies, South America, African blacks, and the American Indian. Seafood is king in Créole recipes, and the nearby waters are a rich kingdom, providing crab, shrimp, red snapper, flounder, Gulf pompano, and trout. Vegetables in season, fowl, veal, and fresh herbs and seasonings are culinary staples that fill out the court and have made this strongly regional style a royal art. There are many fine expensive and moderately priced restaurants. Inexpensive restaurants and even department stores serve up New Orleans specialties, gumbo, po' boy sandwiches, and red beans and rice on Mondays, a New Orleans tradition. Our selections range in price from expensive at $65 or more for a dinner for two, $35 to $45 in the moderate range, and $20 or less in the inexpensive range. Prices do not include drinks, wine, or tips.

Le Ruth's – The best restaurant in New Orleans. Owner and chef Warren Le Ruth has spent his career in New Orleans preparing French and Créole food, and serves consistently fine dishes — oysters and artichoke soup, soft-shell crab with lump crabmeat and meunière sauce, veal Marie with crabmeat, frogs legs meunière, homemade desserts, mandarin ice, or the exquisite almond torte. He also bakes his own bread. Closed Sundays and Mondays. Reservations a must. Major credit cards. 636 Franklin St. in Gretna, 4½ miles across the Mississippi River Bridge from Canal St. (362-4914). Expensive.

Antoine's – Established in 1840, and one of the oldest restaurants in the country, it still offers a grand gastronomic experience, although some say the service is slipping. The waiters know the daily fare well and it pays to listen to their suggestions. Specialties include tournedos with Créole red wine sauce, pompano en papillote, oysters Rockefeller, filet de boeuf Robespierre, soufflé potatoes, and baked Alaska. Though the decor is somewhat sparse — white tiled floors and mirrored walls — *Antoine's* has a great wine cellar and picturesque private dining rooms. Closed Sundays. Reservations advised. Major credit cards. 713 St. Louis St. (581-4422). Expensive.

Caribbean Room – The *Pontchartrain Hotel's* exceptional dining room serves French and Créole cuisine. The menu is imaginative, and specialties are beautifully served — trout Véronique (poached and topped with green grapes and hollandaise sauce), crabmeat Biarritz (lump crabmeat with whipped cream dressing and topped with caviar), pompano Pontchartrain (with soft-shell and buster crabs), and, if you can go the distance, mile-high ice cream pie. An elegant buffet is served Sunday mornings. Everything (including the pie) is prepared under the watchful eye of the owner and founder, who lives in the hotel and dines in the Caribbean Room. Open weekdays for lunch; daily for dinner. Reservations and jackets required. Major credit cards. 2031 St. Charles Ave. (524-0581). Expensive.

Christian's Restaurant – A quaint place known for its French and Créole menu. The redfish au poivre vert (a broiled filet served with green peppercorn cream sauce) is highly recommended. Closed Sundays and Mondays. Reservations necessary. Major credit cards. 3835 Iberville (482-4924). Expensive.

Corinne Dunbar's – In this exquisitely furnished antebellum home, the kitchen prepares old family Créole recipes. The service and the ambience are both delightful. Closed Sundays and Mondays. Reservations required. No credit cards. 1617 St. Charles Ave. (525-2957). Expensive.

Galatoire's – No matter who you are or who you think you are, you stand in line on the sidewalk like everyone else when the house is full. But both the wait and the possible humiliation (depending on who you think you are) are worth it. This favorite of New Orleans residents has great French and Créole dishes, a distinctive atmosphere with ceiling fans and mirrored walls, and knowledgeable waiters.

Specialties include trout Marguery with shrimp, shrimp rémoulade, oysters en brochette, eggs Sardou (artichokes and spinach over poached eggs), and crêpes maison filled with currant jelly. Open for lunch and dinner; closed Mondays. No reservations or credit cards. 209 Bourbon St. (525-2021). Moderate.

Brennan's – Although the food is as good as ever, it's become so popular that the atmosphere is very hectic and the service declining. However, the saying goes that you haven't really had a full day in New Orleans unless you've started it with breakfast at *Brennan's* — poached eggs with hollandaise and marchand de vin sauce, creamed spinach, or New Orleans style with crabmeat, turtle soup, and maybe bananas Foster (bananas with ice cream and liqueur) for a flaming dessert, and certainly café Brulot (coffee with Curaçao and orange rind). Open daily. Reservations necessary. Major credit cards. 417 Royal St. (525-9711). Moderate.

Versailles – This relative newcomer to the New Orleans scene improves each year. Its menu is a good mix of French, German, and Créole. One fine appetizer is the Versailles escargots en croute — classic snails bourguignon served in a hollowed-out bun made of New Orleans French bread. Main course specialties include duck à la Flamande, rack of lamb persillade, veal financière with sweetbreads, bouillabaisse Marseillaise, and veal farci with crabmeat. On the ground floor of the Carol Apartments at the edge of the Garden District. Closed Sundays. Reservations advised. Major credit cards. 2100 St. Charles Ave. (524-2535). Moderate.

Commander's Palace – This longtime favorite in an old mansion in the Garden District has been operated for the past several years by a branch of the *Brennan's* restaurant family. The unusual "jazz brunch" offered on Saturdays and Sundays features traditional and exotic poached egg dishes accompanied by New Orleans jazz. Dinner specialties include trout pecan, crabmeat imperial, turtle soup, lemon crêpes, and filet mignon. Open daily. Reservations advised. Major credit cards. 1403 Washington Ave. (899-8221). Moderate.

Arnaud's – This once-noble Vieux Carré restaurant, founded in 1918 by Count Arnaud Cazenave, has rejoined the ranks of New Orleans' best. Its traditional menu has been shortened and strengthened: Many dishes were eliminated; some that originated here and became famous were retained; a few were added. You can't miss with shrimp Arnaud (a spicy rémoulade), trout meunière, and caramel custard. The dining areas also have been refurbished, but not at the sacrifice of the old France–old New Orleans decor — crystal chandeliers and flickering gas lanterns. Open daily. Reservations advised. Major credit cards. 813 Bienville St. (523-5433). Moderate.

Masson's Restaurant Français – This elegant French restaurant near the lakefront has a strong local following. Chef-owner Ernest Masson visits France frequently to bring back recipes for the latest in haute cuisine. He tries them out for a while and if they are assez haute, he adds them to the offerings on the already fine menu — oysters Albert, seafood crêpes, and marinated rack of lamb. Open daily. Reservations advised. Major credit cards. 7200 Pontchartrain Blvd. (283-2525). Moderate.

Alonso's – This typical New Orleans neighborhood restaurant and bar specializes in seafood. The main attraction is the very large, very good, and very cheap seafood platter. It contains the traditional hot seafood, plus a few seasonal items like crayfish or soft-shell crab, and some boiled shrimp or crab tossed in for good measure. Don't expect your party to be served together — you get it while it's hot. Extremely crowded on Friday nights. Closed Sundays. No reservations. No credit cards. 587 Central Ave. (about 6 miles from Canal St.) (733-2796). Inexpensive.

Central Grocery Company – This grocery store has been here since 1906 and still stocks flour, beans, and other staples in barrels to sell by the pound. More popular, however, are the great take-out Italian sandwiches, cheeses, and salads. Open daily. No credit cards. 923 Decatur (523-1620). Inexpensive.

K-Paul's Louisiana Kitchen – When we have time to eat only one meal in New Orleans, we eat it here. One of the city's most celebrated chefs, owner Paul Prudhomme (and family) dishes up dozens of tempting Cajun specialties, including 17 varieties of gumbo. The pièce de résistance is a hot Cajun martini served in a Mason jar. Closed weekends. No reservations. American Express only. 416 Chartres St. (524-7394). Inexpensive.

Ye Olde College Inn – In the university section, daily dinner plates, shrimp rémoulade, red beans and rice, oyster loaf, french-fried onion rings, and a good bar. The Créole vegetables, especially the eggplant and stewed okra, are at the top of their class. Open daily. No reservations. No credit cards. 3016 S Carrollton Ave. (866-3683). Inexpensive.

Mandina's – Of the vast number of places that offer po' boy sandwiches, this small family-style restaurant does it best with Italian sausage and roast beef. The large servings of meatballs and spaghetti, gumbo, and jambalaya will not take too big a bite out of your pocket. Open daily. No reservations. No credit cards. 3800 Canal St. (482-9179). Inexpensive.

Gumbo Shop – This pleasant little shop in the Vieux Carré serves up some of the best gumbo around — and in Gumbo City that's saying something. Open daily. No reservations. Major credit cards. 630 St. Peter St. (525-1486). Inexpensive.

D. H. Holmes – You can get a good and filling lunch or snack at this department store for just a few dollars. The daily specials are usually good, and the turtle and vegetable soups are great. Closed Sundays. No reservations. Major credit cards. 819 Canal St. (561-6321). Inexpensive.

NEW YORK CITY

A first-time visitor trying to capture New York City in a single phrase may find a situation similar to the legendary blind man who tried to describe an elephant. Your first impression of this enormously diverse city can easily be distorted by the specific neighborhood in which you happen to land. An uninitiated tourist in the Tottenville section of Staten Island would likely surprise neighbors back home with descriptions of rolling farmland, rural ambience, and settings seemingly more appropriate to Iowa than to this country's most cosmopolitan center. That same stranger standing in the ruins of the South Bronx would horrify friends with tales of a "war zone" reminiscent of Dresden after the bombings. And seeing the corner of 59th Street and 5th Avenue for the first time, our fledgling traveler couldn't help but be impressed with the incredible elegance of surroundings whose gaudy opulence has few equals in the world. The question, then, is which is the real New York?

The answer is that New York is all these things. In a way, a visitor has his choice of the New York City he wishes to visit, and it's a simple matter to be insulated from all potential unpleasantness. A tourist's terrain in New York is traditionally limited to Manhattan and, indeed, generally bordered by the Hudson and East rivers and 34th and 96th streets. Within this relatively narrow geographic area stand New York's most famous hotels, its elegant restaurants, and its most famous theaters, cinemas, museums, and fine shops.

It is, therefore, sometimes difficult for a visitor to reconcile the entertaining New York of his own experience with the troubled and troublesome New York described in the newspapers. It is hard to understand matters of want and welfare while window-shopping in the chic, dramatic boutiques of Madison Avenue or craning one's neck up the canyons of Park Avenue. But in fact the tourist's New York and the most crowded residential areas of the city seldom intersect, and it is unlikely that the reality of New York's municipal malaise will ever intrude on the tourist's consciousness — unless he or she specifically sets out to see the city's other face.

New York offers an array of distractions unequaled anywhere on earth. Nowhere are there more museums of such a consistently high quality. Nowhere are there restaurants of such striking ethnic diversity. Nowhere is there more varied shopping for more esoteric paraphernalia, and nowhere in the world does the pace of city life and the activities of the populace more dramatically accent a city's vitality and appeal.

Just as Americans hardly ever refer to themselves simply as Americans — they are Southerners, Texans, Californians, and the like — New York's 7 million residents are similarly chauvinistic about the specific enclaves of their city. Though in theory New York is composed of five boroughs — Manhat-

NEW YORK
AT-A-GLANCE

Van Cortlandt
Museum
Van Cortlandt
Park
Ft. Tryon Park
The Cloisters
George Washington
Bridge
Poe Cottage
N.Y.
Hall of
Fame
Botanical
Gardens
Bronx Zoo

Grant's Tomb
Riverside Church
Yankee
Stadium
Columbia
University
Cathedral
Bronx Museum
of Art
BRONX
HARLEM

NEW JERSEY
Hudson River
Riverside Park
CENTRAL PARK
Guggenheim
Museum
Triboro
Bridge
East River

Circle Line
Pier
Gracie
Mansion
Lincoln
Tunnel
MANHATTAN
Roosevelt
Island
LaGuardia
Airport

AREA OF
MAIN MAP
Queensboro Bridge
Midtown
Tunnel
Shea Stadium

Holland
Tunnel
East River
QUEENS BLVD
Corona Park

Newark Bay
Area of
Inset Map
QUEENS

Ellis Island
Brooklyn
Heights

Statue
of Liberty
Governors
Island
Brooklyn
Academy of Music
Aqueduct
Race Track

Staten Island Ferry
New York
Harbor
Navy
Yard
Brooklyn
Botanical Gardens
ATLANTIC

Staten
Island Zoo
Prospect
Park
Brooklyn
Museum
JFK Airport

STATEN
BROOKLYN
Bay
Ridge
EXPRESSWAY

ISLAND
Verrazano
Narrows Bridge
JAMAICA
BAY

Sheepshead Bay

Coney
Island
Brighton
Beach
Manhattan
Beach

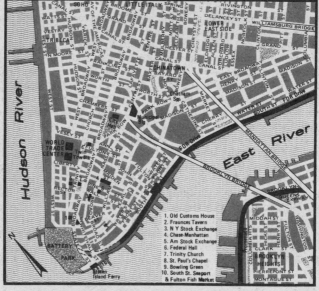

Hudson River

SOHO
CANAL ST
LITTLE ITALY
SPRING ST
RIVINGTON ST
WATTS ST
BROOME ST
DELANCEY ST
WILLIAMSBURG BRIDGE
VESTRY
TRIBECA
GRAND ST
LOWER
EAST SIDE
N MOORE
CANAL ST
GRAND ST
FRANKLIN ST
CHINATOWN
CANAL ST
CHAMBERS ST
BAYARD ST
MADISON ST
HENRY ST
MADISON ST
WATER ST
EAST BROADWAY
FDR DRIVE
VESEY ST
Municipal
MADISON ST
CHERRY
East River
WORLD
TRADE
CENTER
TWIN
Towers
FDR DRIVE
MANHATTAN BRIDGE
LIBERTY
BROOKLYN BRIDGE
QUEENS EXPWY
RECTOR
MIDDAGH ST
BEAVER
CLARK ST
BATTERY
PARK
COLUMBIA
BROOKLYN
HEIGHTS
PIERREPONT ST
MONTAGUE ST

1. Old Customs House
2. Fraunces Tavern
3. N Y Stock Exchange
4. Chase-Manhattan
5. Am Stock Exchange
6. Federal Hall
7. Trinity Church
8. St. Paul's Chapel
9. Bowling Green
10. South St. Seaport
& Fulton Fish Market

Staten
Island Ferry

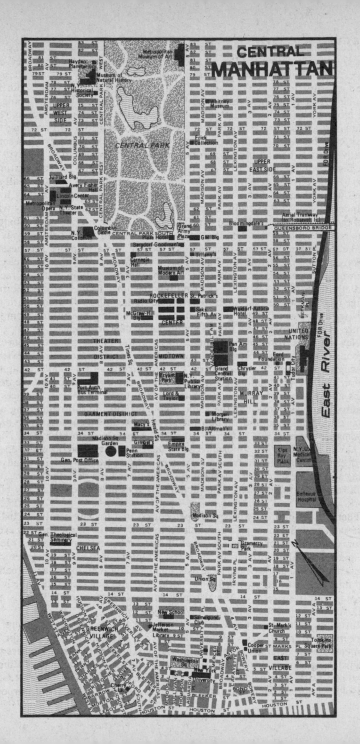

tan, Queens, Brooklyn, the Bronx, and Richmond (Staten Island) — everyone understands that Manhattan is "The City."

So a visitor to New York should not feel at all self-conscious about his insular orientation, since residents of Flushing (in Queens) talk of going to the city with the same undertone of long-distance travel adventure as residents of Kansas City. Brooklynites have been known to avoid crossing the East River for years at a time, and many think of themselves as living in some relatively rural hamlet quite separate and entirely distinct from the evils of the Big Town. And there are farmers on Staten Island who haven't ventured into Manhattan in a generation. Yet all are lifetime New Yorkers, and all are filled with especially fierce pride in the area of the city in which they live.

Indeed, New York is truly the capital of this country in almost every way, and the presence of the United Nations enclave in the middle of Manhattan makes it possible to describe the city as the capital of the world as well. It is likely that you will find more French people in Paris, more Japanese in Tokyo, and more Africans in Dakar, but it is *unlikely* that any other city in the world boasts so large a population of these cosmopolitan cultures, races, and ethnic entities as New York. And one has only to pick any of a broad range of midtown restaurants to experience dining elbow-to-elbow with the very same figures who, just hours before, were deciding everything from the future of world commerce to the maintenance of world peace.

New York is also the communications capital of the planet. From the Avenue of the Americas come most of the decisions that determine television viewing — not only in this country, but around the world — and while the majority of TV production facilities are firmly based in California, the decisions about what will be produced are usually made in executive offices in Manhattan. New York has the same dominance in radio broadcasting and magazine publishing, and though the city is now down to only three daily newspapers, at least two of them — the *New York Times* and the *Daily News* — have national impact. Books, records, and even motion pictures all depend on decisions originated in New York for everything from creativity to advertising and financing, and they reflect what has often been described as the bias of the eastern establishment. The capital of that establishment is clearly New York.

There is, in addition, widespread perception that for any creative artist to succeed, she or he must gain recognition in New York. In the theater, every actor, writer, director, designer, singer, dancer, musician, and composer feels the magnetic pull of Broadway. Painters, sculptors, writers of every description, cartoonists, jingle rhymers, artists, and charlatans all focus their creative and financial yearnings toward New York. Whether one wants to make it on the stage, on the screen, on the airwaves, in bookstores, or on billboards, the path to success must eventually traverse New York.

Just as hard to characterize as the geography of this city is the attempt to stereotype a typical New Yorker. The city is notable, first of all, for its immense ethnic diversity, and there are large segments of the city where the English language is hardly ever heard. From the obvious examples of Chinatown and Little Italy to the less apparent Slavic and Hasidic enclaves, centuries-old tradition is maintained through rigid authoritarianism and purposeful segregation. Though New York's ethnic ghettos are initially invisible and completely unofficial, they are often most stringently maintained by their residents.

Other New Yorkers use these enclaves to their own benefit and regularly visit ethnic neighborhoods to attend "foreign" festivals during the year. The Chinese New Year is nowhere more intensely celebrated than on Mott Street, and one would be hard pressed to develop a more authentic case of Italian indigestion than can be suffered during the San Gennaro Festival on Mulberry Street each fall. New Yorkers, whose culinary horizons probably reach farther afield than those of any other civic population on earth, regularly plumb the depths of such exotica as Greek specialties wrapped in grape leaves, Lebanese shish kebabs, Slavic pirozhkies, and German wursts. A visitor who does not sample as many ethnic cuisines as possible is indeed wasting a special opportunity.

New York's cultural and gastronomic leadership is only slightly less important to the nation and the world than its financial ascendancy. Just walking through the Wall Street area provides a dramatic impact and reaffirms that the city has a firm hold on world commerce. Visitors' galleries at the New York Stock Exchange and some of the commodity exchanges provide the unique opportunity to watch capitalism in action in its wild state, and nowhere is the sense of the enormity of American industry and the scope of commercial trading more keenly felt.

Trading has a long history in New York City, for it was here that the original $24 worth of trinkets and baubles bought the island of Manhattan from the Indians who may (or may not) have been its owners. Depending on one's point of view, the Indians were either boldly deceived on the price or they made one of the best real estate deals in the city's history.

That original island of Manhattan, a near wilderness traversed by several streams and rivers, bears little resemblance to the island as it presently exists. Various landfill and reclamation projects have enlarged it over the years, and just a brief glance today at the west side of the Battery Park area (at the southernmost tip) indicates that expanding the island's real estate is still very much an active enterprise.

Through the years, New York has resisted any exclusive European identification, and its current cast indicates very little influence of the passage from Dutch hands to English and the subsequent domination of first one group of immigrants and then another. In this sense, it is a singularly liberated city, feeling little allegiance to any single ancestor or antecedent. From this polyglot past springs the New York feeling that it is really a nation unto itself.

In all the world, New York has no equal. Its ability to prosper in spite of its monumental problems testifies to its strength and resilience more dramatically than can any analytic essay. That its residents choose to continue to live amid its many municipal shortcomings highlights the fact that its excitement and challenges far outweigh its discouragements, and the inclination of tourists from all over the world to visit its buildings and byways continues to make it the single most popular city for tourists. This ongoing appeal amply justifies New York's avowed preeminence and ensures its continued attraction as the greatest magnet in America. It is, above all, a city that revels in its ability to tantalize the curious and strongly attract the interest of those who live elsewhere.

NEW YORK AT-A-GLANCE

SEEING THE CITY: New York is, to put it simply, the most complex city in the world. People who have lived here all their lives don't even know all of it — its size and diversity challenge even the most ambitious. The best bet for the visitor who wants to feel the magic of New York and to understand how the city is laid out is to take it all in from one of several vantage points:

Brooklyn Promenade – Standing on this walkway at dusk, with the lights of Manhattan shimmering across the East River, you'll get an idea of the magnitude and beauty of the city. In lower Manhattan the towers of the World Trade Center rise before you, and the Brooklyn Bridge spans the river to your right. Farther north stand the Empire State Building and the United Nations Secretariat Building, landmarks of midtown. The easiest way to get here is via the IRT 7th Avenue subway line, Clark St. stop.

World Trade Center – The elevator to the observation deck of Two World Trade Center whisks you more than a quarter of a mile above the street. There is an enclosed deck on the 107th floor and a promenade on the roof above the 110th floor. Manhattan spreads out to the north, Brooklyn is on the east, on the west is New Jersey, and to the south lies New York Harbor, leading to the Atlantic Ocean. Open daily from 9:30 AM to 9:30 PM. Tickets are sold on the mezzanine level of Tower Two. Liberty and West sts. (466-7397).

Empire State Building – Although many tourists prefer the newer and higher World Trade Center observation deck, the old queen of New York attracts more than 1.5 million people a year — the Art Deco design is more romantic than anything in the World Trade Center (even if Deborah Kerr never kept her appointment with Gary Grant here in *An Affair to Remember*). You can feel the breeze from the 86th floor or ascend to the glass-enclosed 102nd floor. Don't be surprised if in the evening the top of the building is bathed in colored lights — it's the city's newest way to commemorate holidays and special occasions. Open daily from 9:30 AM to 11 PM. Admission charge. 34th St. and 5th Ave. (736-3100).

Views from Above and Below – You get some of the most dramatic views of New York when entering the city by car. The three western access routes have special features: the Holland Tunnel access road from the N. J. Turnpike, leading into lower Manhattan, offers a panorama of the southern tip of the island; the Lincoln Tunnel access road offers a view of Manhattan's West Side; and the George Washington Bridge, linking New Jersey and the Upper West Side, has spectacular views of the Hudson, the city's long shore along the river, and the New Jersey Palisades, as well as being a work of art itself, best seen from a distance, from the river, or while driving north on the West Side Highway.

Tours – Many of the tour companies in the city will help you get your bearings before setting out on your own. *Gray Line,* 900 8th Ave., between 53rd and 54th sts. (397-2600), provides good bus tours. *Circle Line Sightseeing Yachts* offers an interesting 3-hour guided boat trip around Manhattan from the middle of April until mid-November. Boats leave from Pier 83 at the foot of W 43rd St. and the Hudson River (563-3200). Most spectacular is *Island Helicopter*'s ride around Manhattan. Though the price is considerable ($30-$50 for flights ranging from 5 to 17 minutes), you won't forget this trip soon. At E 34th St. and the East River (718 895-1626).

SPECIAL PLACES: Manhattan is a 12½-mile-long island stretching 2½ miles at its widest point. Avenues run north and south, streets run east and west. Fifth Avenue is the dividing line between addresses designated east and those designated west. For example, 20 E 57th Street is in the first block of 57th east of 5th Avenue; 20 W 57th Street is in the first block west of 5th Avenue. New York grew from south to north, street by street and neighborhood by neighborhood. The oldest parts of the city are around the docks in lower Manhattan and in the financial district.

The best way to discover the city and enjoy its incredible variety and ethnic diversity is by direct contact — walking through the neighborhoods. You will want to take taxis or public transport between areas — distances can be great — but have no hesitation about walking once you've arrived. The much-touted reputation of New Yorkers for aloofness and unfriendliness simply isn't true. Just watch what happens when you ask directions on a bus or subway (except during rush hours, when things are, admittedly, a bit primitive). We suggest a copy of the *Flashmaps! Instant Guide to New York* (Flashmaps; $4.95), which has the most accessible and best-organized series of maps of New York neighborhoods we've seen.

LOWER MANHATTAN

Statue of Liberty – Given by France as a symbol of friendship with the United States, this great lady has been guarding the entrance of New York Harbor since its dedication in 1886. To celebrate its centennial in 1986, "Liberty Enlightening the World" was given a major facelift, and a new museum was added to its base. New lighting makes the statue even more dazzling than ever after dark. The Circle Line (269-5755) runs from Battery Park to Liberty Island; the cost of the trip includes admission to the statue and to the Museum of Immigration (732-1236) at the base. You can see the statue from a distance and the southern tip of the city by riding the Staten Island Ferry, still one of the world's great transportation bargains at 25¢. The Ferry Terminal is next to Battery Park (the South Ferry Stop on the IRT 7th Ave. line).

Ellis Island – Visible from the Statue of Liberty or Battery Park, Ellis Island served as a processing center for immigrants from 1892 to 1954. More than 121 million people passed through this island on their way to a new life in the land of opportunity. These aging shells of buildings were the sites of joy and heartbreak; many immigrant families were separated here when some members were refused entry to the US because of bad health or lack of money. Ellis Island, now run by the National Park Service, has been closed for renovation since 1984. The Great Hall — the centerpiece of the immigration process — is expected to open as part of a restored complex, scheduled for completion sometime in 1987. Check with Circle Line to see if it is running trips to the island from Battery Park (269-5755).

Governors Island – Groups can visit this island in New York Harbor from April through October. Now a Coast Guard base, the island's two pre-1800 structures are the Governor's House and Fort Jay. Free tours for groups of ten to fifty (no individual tours) can be arranged by writing to the Special Services Division, Building 110, Governors Island, NY 10004 (668-7255).

Battery Park – Twenty-one acres of green, overlooking New York Harbor, this is the spot for picnics on hot summer days. There's a statue of Giovanni da Verrazano, the pilot of the *Dauphine,* the ship that reached Manhattan in 1524 (Verrazano was later killed by cannibals in the Caribbean). Castle Clinton, built as a fort in 1807, has functioned as an opera house, an immigrant landing depot, and as an aquarium at various times. Its latest incarnation is as a ticketing center for the Statute of Liberty ferry. Bordered by State St., Battery Pl., and the river.

Battery Park to Wall Street – This area is a lovely place to wander on weekends, when the empty streets emphasize the incongruity of the Chase Manhattan building and the World Trade Center surrounded by the 17th- and 18th-century buildings on Pearl Street, Bowling Green, and Hanover Square. Two buildings of particular note are the India House on the south side of Hanover Square (1837) and the old US Custom House (the new Custom House is in the World Trade Center), which was built in 1907 in Neoclassic style. Another turn-of-the-century building at 56 Beaver St. until recently housed *Delmonico's Restaurant,* the meeting place of lower Manhattan's elite.

Fraunces Tavern Museum – This building, the site of Washington's farewell to his officers in 1783, contains memorabilia of the American Revolution (including Washington's hat). The *Fraunces Tavern* restaurant occupies the ground floor. Most of the area around it is slated for renovation as a historic area. Open weekdays except when a new exhibition is being prepared. Free (special shows are sometimes staged on Sundays, and a fee is charged). 54 Pearl St. (425-1778).

New York Stock Exchange – A tree stands in front of the stock exchange to commemorate the tree under which the first transaction took place in 1792. Today, close to 1,600 corporations are listed on the big board. You can observe the action from a glass-enclosed gallery reached via the visitors' entrance at 20 Broad St. Open weekdays. Free (623-5167). The American Stock Exchange (86 Trinity Pl.) no longer has a visitors gallery. If you want to see real emotion, head for the Coffee, Sugar, and Cocoa Exchange, 4 World Trade Center (938-2018), which makes the Stock Exchange seem like a London tea party.

Federal Hall – This national historic site served as the British headquarters during the Revolution and was later the seat of American government. George Washington was sworn in as president here in 1789. Open weekdays. Free. At the corner of Wall and Broad sts. (264-8711).

Trinity Church – The church faces Wall Street, which is appropriate, because it has been a wealthy parish since it was first granted a charter by William III in 1697. One of the local citizens who aided in building the church was Captain Kidd, the notorious pirate who was hanged in London in 1701. The present building was completed in 1846, but the graveyard beside the church is even older. William Bradford, Jr., Robert Fulton, and Alexander Hamilton are buried here. For years, the Trinity Church steeple was the highest point on the New York skyline. During the summer, the church sponsors lunch-hour entertainment, called the Noonday Café, for downtown workers in the south courtyard. Classical concerts are held year-round on Tuesdays at 12:45 PM in the church. At Broadway and Wall sts. (285-0800).

St. Paul's Chapel – The oldest church building in Manhattan, this fine example of Colonial architecture was erected in 1766 on what was then a field outside the city. George Washington worshiped here. On the corner of Broadway and Fulton St. (732-5564).

World Trade Center – A world in itself. At 1,350 feet each, its two towers are not the tallest buildings in the world (the CNR Tower in Toronto is at 1,815 feet), but close to it. In order to build the center, 1.2 million yards of earth and rock were excavated (they're now in the Hudson River). The concourse has shops and some excellent restaurants (see *Best in Town*), including *Windows on the World, The Big Kitchen,* and the *Market Dining Room.* Not all World Trade Center businesses involve trade, but the Custom House is here, as are the Commodity Exchange and the Cotton and Mercantile Exchanges. Open daily. Free. Bounded by West, Church, Liberty, and Vesey sts. (466-4170).

City Hall – This is the third City Hall of New York; it was built in 1803 and contains the office of the mayor and the City Council chamber. The original construction cost half a million dollars, and in 1956 the restoration cost some $2 million (times change). The building was a site of great importance to New York's and America's history: Lafayette visited in 1824; Lincoln's body lay in state in 1865; and, in the 1860s, City Hall and Tammany Hall (Park Row and Frankfort St.) were controlled by Boss Tweed, the powerful corrupt political figure who dominated New York politics until the 1870s.

Other city government buildings nearby include the Municipal Building on the northeast corner of City Hall Park, the United States Court House, across from Foley Square, the New York County Courthouse next door, the Federal Office Building on the other side of Lafayette St., and the Hall of Records. City Hall Park has a statue of Nathan Hale, the patriot of the Revolution, who was executed here in 1776. Today, protestors of every persuasion gather in the park to "fight City Hall." Open weekdays. Free. In a triangular park between Park Row, Broadway and Chambers St.

South Street Seaport and the Fulton Fish Market – In July 1983, stage one of the South Street Seaport renovation was completed, enlivening the area with new shops and restaurants and additional space for the South Street Seaport Maritime Museum. The Museum Block is an entire row of rejuvenated buildings (some dating to the 1700s) with room for exhibitions, shops, and offices. The Schermerhorn Row of renovated 19th-century warehouses is also alive with retail outlets and the South Street Seaport Museum Visitors Center. All of these changes have not substantially altered the area's famous old Fulton Fish Market, where, from about 2 to 8 AM, trucks still deliver fresh fish to the wholesale outdoor market. But the old market is now joined by another building called the Fulton Market, with restaurants, cafés, and food stalls. Among the many eateries are two of New York's oldest seafood restaurants, *Sweets* (Fulton at South St.; 344-9189 or 825-9665; closed weekends), and *Sloppy Louie's* (92 South St.; 509-9694). For years, these veterans of the Fulton Fish Market served the freshest seafood at rock-bottom prices in simple quarters. When the seaport was renovated, the restaurants moved into more sanitized surroundings, with proper dining rooms and higher prices — and, unfortunately, lost their boisterous atmosphere and earthy appeal. At least the portions remain hearty and the fish is as fresh as ever. Also of interest are the historic boats docked at Piers 15 and 16, where summertime pop and jazz concerts are staged. The new three-story Pier 17 Pavilion adds even more shops and restaurants to the riverside complex. Fulton St. between South and Water sts.

Brooklyn Bridge – You can stroll from Manhattan to Brooklyn by crossing the Brooklyn Bridge on a pedestrian walk. You'll get a good view of the city, and a close look at this engineering feat. The 6,775-foot bridge, which spans the East river at a height of 133 feet and is considered by many to be one of the most beautiful bridges in the world, was completed in 1883 and cost $25 million. Many workers were seriously injured during its construction, and a number of people have since committed suicide by jumping from it. Always open. Free (unless someone succeeds in selling you title to the bridge). Take the IRT Lexington Ave. line to Worth St.–Brooklyn Bridge station.

Chinatown – The best way to get the feel of New York's Chinese neighborhood is to hit the streets, especially Mott, Bayard, and Pell. More than 10,000 people live in this area of crowded, narrow streets, and the Chinese population spills into neighboring Little Italy. Although the Chinese community here is not as large as the one in San Francisco, it is authentic. You'll know when you reach Chinatown by the pagoda-shaped telephone booths and stores that sell shark fins, duck eggs, fried fungi, and squid. Herbs are lined up next to aspirin in the pharmacies. This is where Chinese shop, and uptowners and out-of-towners follow their lead. Don't miss the good, inexpensive restaurants, the tea parlors, or the bakeries. Try the dim sum at lunchtime (steamed or fried dumplings filled with seafood, pork, or beef). Sundays are a good time to visit the area, but if you can, come during the Chinese New Year (held on the first full moon after January 21). The celebration is wild and woolly, with fireworks, dancing dragons, and throngs of people. While you'll get the best sense of Chinatown from the streets, if you want historical perspective, stop by the Chinese Museum, which houses exhibitions from the first dynasty to the present. Open weekdays. Admission charge. 8 Mott St. (964-1542).

Little Italy – Italian music from tenement windows, old men playing bocce, old women dressed in black checking the vegetables in the markets, store windows with religious articles, pasta factories, and the ubiquitous odor of Italian cooking fill this neighborhood, which has the reputation of being one of the safest areas in the city. Mulberry Street is the center of Little Italy, but the area stretches for blocks around and blends into parts of SoHo and Greenwich Village. Even Bleecker Street, toward 7th Avenue, has a decidedly Italian flavor, with bakeries selling cannoli and cappuccino sandwiched between Middle Eastern restaurants and stores selling Chinese window shades. Little Italy is thronged during the festivals of San Gennaro and St. Anthony. In late September, San Gennaro covers Mulberry Street from Spring to Park. St. Anthony fills Sullivan Street, from Houston to Spring, in mid-June. The festivals attract people from in and out of the city with game booths, rides, and most of all, enough food and drink (both Italian and "foreign") for several armies. Bordered by Canal and Houston sts. and the Bowery and Ave. of the Americas.

The Bowery – There is nothing romantic about New York's Skid Row. On this strip are people who have failed — alcoholics and dope addicts, both old and young. If you drive west on Houston Street, you'll get a look at some of the inhabitants — they'll wipe your windshields whether you like it or not and expect some change for their trouble. Recently, however, the Bowery has had some new settlers; a few theaters and music places have moved in. The area also has some good places to shop; specialties include lamps and restaurant supplies. The stores have relocated here because of the proximity to one of the most interesting shopping markets in the world: the Lower East Side. Between 4th St. and Chatham Sq.

The Lower East Side – This area is probably the largest melting pot in the city. Its Sunday market is an experience that shouldn't be missed. Eastern European Jews, many of whom are Hasidim (an ultra-religious sect, recognizable by the men's earlocks, called pais, and their fur hats and long black coats), sell their wares for rock bottom prices; you'll have to bargain if you want the best prices, and these merchants are formidable opponents. The area is also home to Puerto Ricans, blacks, and various other groups; you will hear Yiddish, Spanish, and even some Yiddish-accented Spanish.

The Lower East Side was where Eastern European Jews, fleeing Czarist persecution and pogroms, first settled during their massive migration from 1880 to 1918. Many of the streets, including Rivington, Hester, Essex, and Grand, still look the way they did then. To really get a taste of the area, try the food at the *Grand Dairy Restaurant* (341 Grand St.), knishes at *Yonah Schimmel's* (137 E Houston St.), hot dogs at *Katz's Delicatessen* (205 E Houston St.), or a Romanian "broilings" at *Sammy's* (157 Chrystie St.).

SoHo – The name means "South of Houston Street" (pronounced *How*-stun). SoHo leads a double life. On weekends, uptown New Yorkers and out-of-towners fill the streets to explore its trendy stores, restaurants, and art galleries. During the week, SoHo is a very livable combination of 19th-century cast-iron buildings, spillovers from Little Italy, off-off-Broadway theater groups, and practicing artists. At night, the streets are empty and you can see into the residential lofts of the old buildings; some are simple, open spaces, others are jungles of plants and Corinthian columns. *Fanelli's*, on the corner of Mercer and Prince streets, is one of the oldest bars around and a hangout for residents. Many artists are now moving to Tribeca (the triangle below Canal — get it?), which is south and west of SoHo and has better loft pickings. SoHo is between Canal and Houston sts., Broadway and Hudson St.

The East Village – Famous during the 1960s as the center of the New York counterculture, this section has become gentrified, with a growing number of art galleries, restaurants, and night spots competing for space with poor artists and various ethnic groups (the largest of which is Ukrainian, but there are also Armenians, Czechs, Germans, Russians, Poles, Jews, blacks, and Hispanics, many of whom live in low-income housing projects). St. Mark's Place, between Second and Third avenues, was once the city's psychedelic capital. It is still a lively block, chockablock with inexpensive restaurants, shops featuring styles from hippie to punk, and generally hops at all hours of the day and night. Two streets south is what could be considered India Row: numerous Indian restaurants line East 6th Street between First and Second avenues. (Some parts of the East Village, especially east of Avenue A, remain seedy; don't wander here after dark unless you know where you're going.) Astor Place, on the border of the East and West villages, is the site of Cooper Union (good for free concerts and lectures) and the Public Theater, 425 Lafayette St. (598-7150), Joe Papp's creation, where you'll find some of the best serious drama (both contemporary and classical) and experimental theater as well as progressive jazz. You might want to have a drink at *McSorley's Old Ale House,* 15 E 7th St. (473-8800), a fixture in the East Village for years. A few blocks north is the spiritual home of the village, St. Mark's-in-the-Bouwerie, on the corner of 2nd Ave. and 10th St. The church still sponsors community activities, especially poetry readings by some of the best poets in New York. The East Village has housed many writers, from James Fenimore Cooper (6 St. Mark's Pl.) to W. H. Auden (77 St. Mark's Pl.) to LeRoi Jones — now Imamu Baraka (27 Cooper Sq.). Bounded by Lafayette St. and the East River, Houston and 14th sts.

GREENWICH VILLAGE

You can and definitely should stroll around the West Village (as residents know it) at night. The area is filled with surprises. You've probably heard of Bleecker Street, the slightly tawdry gathering place of tourists and the high school crowd from the suburbs, or of Washington Square Park, with its musicians, mimes, and street people. But you might not have pictured Grove Court, the lovely and secluded row of 19th-century houses near the corner of Grove and Bedford Streets (where O. Henry lived), or the Morton Street pier on the Hudson River, from which you can see the Statue of Liberty on a clear day. But the Village is more than this. It is an activist neighborhood, struggling to keep control of this famous, much-loved neighborhood. There are meat-packing factories from the 1920s, old speakeasies turned into restaurants, a miniature Times Square on W 8th Street, and immaculate (and expensive) brownstones on quiet, tree-lined streets. Get a map (you'll need it — there's nowhere else in Manhattan where W 4th Street could bisect W 12th Street) and wander. Or you can ask directions — villagers love to help and it's a nice way to meet them. You can eat, go to the theater, sip cappuccino in an outdoor café, hear great jazz, and find your own special places. Bounded by 5th Ave. on the east, the Hudson River on the west, Houston St. on the south, and W 14th St. on the north.

Washington Square – A gathering place for students from New York University, frisbee aficionados, volleyball players, modern-day Bohemians, and people who like to watch them all. The Arch is New York's answer to the Arc de Triomphe. Buildings surrounding the square include the New York University library, administration buildings, and law school. The north side of Washington Square has some lovely homes, including #7, where Edith Wharton lived. Bounded by extensions of W 4th St., MacDougal St., Waverly Pl., and University Pl.

Bleecker Street – Strolling down Bleecker Street from La Guardia Place to 8th Avenue you'll pass outdoor cafés, head shops, falafel parlors, jazz clubs including the *Village Gate* (Bleecker and Thompson sts.), Italian grocery stores, and a myriad of restaurants. You should also wander down some of the side streets, like Thompson, MacDougal (Bob Dylan's old stomping ground), and Sullivan. Have a cappuccino at *Caffè Reggio* (119 MacDougal). Beyond 7th Avenue, the side streets become more residential; try Charles Street, W 10th Street, and Bank Street for examples of how the upper middle class lives in the Village. You'll also pass Christopher Street, the center of gay life in Manhattan (although the toughest part of it comes alive on West Street, by the West Side Highway, on weekend nights).

Fifth Avenue – Where the wealthy Villagers live. The Salmagundi Club, built in 1853 at 47 5th Avenue (near 12th Street), is the last of the imposing private mansions that once lined the avenue. On the streets between 5th and the Avenue of the Americas (which the natives call 6th Avenue) you can see expensive brownstones. The New School for Social Research, 66 W 12th St., has courses on everything from fixing a leak to ethnomusicology. From Washington Sq. north to 14th St.

Avenue of the Americas – One of the most unusual buildings in the village is the Jefferson Market Library, on 6th Avenue and 10th Street, with a small garden alongside. Built in 1878 in Italian Gothic style, it served as a courthouse for many years. Across the street is *Balducci's,* 424 6th Ave., an Italian market with a wide variety of exotic foods, plus fresh fruit and vegetables. *Famous Ray's Pizza,* 465 6th Ave. at 11th St. (243-2253) — the place on the corner with the long lines — is considered the source of some of the best pizza in the city. (Note that many pizza places in the city have "Ray's" in their names, but this is the one everyone raves about.)

Farther west (between 6th Ave. and Hudson St. and W Houston and Christopher sts.) is a series of small winding streets with some especially interesting places to visit. At 75½ Bedford Street is the house in which Edna St. Vincent Millay and John Barrymore once lived (not at the same time) — it's only nine feet wide. *Chumley's,* 86 Bedford St., used to be a speakeasy during Prohibition and still has no sign on the door — but it does have good food and poetry readings inside. Commerce Street is a small side street lined with lovely old buildings, including the Cherry Lane Theater, one of the city's oldest. Morton Street, one block south, is often mistaken for Hester Street, because it was the site of the filming of *Hester Street,* the 1975 film about the Lower East Side Jewish immigrants. Another block south is Leroy Street with St. Luke's Place, a row of 19th-century houses. Number 6 Leroy was built in 1880 and was the home of New York Mayor Jimmy Walker. If you walk to the end of the block and north on Hudson Street, you'll come to the *White Horse Tavern,* 567 Hudson St., Dylan Thomas's hangout on his trips to New York City. Go in and have a drink.

14TH STREET TO 34TH STREET

Gramercy Park – A few blocks north of Greenwich Village, Gramercy Park is one of the few places where you can get a feel for what Manhattan used to be like. The park itself is open only to local residents, but on a sunny day you can see nannies with their privileged young charges sitting on the benches in the shadows of the 19th-century mansions that surround the park. A few blocks north of Gramercy Park on Lexington Avenue are dozens of little Eastern Indian shops selling splendid assortments of spices, saris, cotton blouses, jewelry, and food. E 21st St. and Lexington Ave.

Chelsea – An eclectic residential neighborhood in the West 20s, between 7th and 10th Avenues, where you can find elegant brownstones next door to run-down, four-story, walk-up tenements. The *Chelsea Hotel,* W 23rd St. and 9th Ave., has earned an important place in literary history. Thomas Wolfe, Brendan Behan, Dylan Thomas, and Arthur Miller slept and wrote in its rooms. Andy Warhol made a four-hour movie about its raunchier inhabitants. For a sojourn into tranquillity, step into the inner courtyard of General Theological Seminary, a gift to the city in 1817 by Clement C. Moore, author of *A Visit from Saint Nicholas.* Open daily (except when special use is being made of it), 2 to 5:30 PM weekdays, 9 AM to 5 PM weekends. Free. 175 9th Ave. (243-5150).

MIDTOWN (34TH STREET TO 59TH STREET)

West 34th Street – A major shopping street, this is the home of the traditional mercantile giant *Macy's* as well as *B. Altman's* (technically on East 34th Street) and scores of boutiques selling blue jeans, blouses, underwear, shoes, records, and electronic gear. The main shopping district runs along 34th Street from 8th Avenue east to

Madison Avenue, with a number of smaller, expensive shops lining the street as far east as Third Avenue. The hub of 34th Street is Herald Square, where Broadway intersects the Avenue of the Americas (6th Avenue).

Madison Square Garden, Felt Forum, and Penn Station – A huge coliseum-arena, office building, and transportation complex. The Garden's 19,500 seats are usually fully packed when the New York Knicks (NBA basketball) and the New York Rangers (NHL hockey) play home games, when the Ringling Brothers and Barnum & Bailey Circus comes to town, or whenever there is a major exhibition, concert, or convention. The Felt Forum, a 5,000-seat subsidiary hall that's part of the Garden complex, is the site of boxing matches, concerts, and smaller exhibitions. Penn Station is Amtrak's major New York terminal (for Amtrak information, 736-4545). No guided tours. 4 Pennsylvania Plaza, W 33rd St. between 7th and 8th aves. (564-4400 for Garden and Forum information).

Garment District – The center of the clothing and fashion industries. On any weekday during office hours, you can see racks of the latest apparel being pushed through the terrifically hectic streets. Along 7th and 8th Aves. from 30th to 39th sts.

The Empire State Building – The first skyscraper in New York to be attacked by King Kong. The 102-story Art Deco edifice was erected in 1931 and became the symbol of the city for decades. There is an open-air observation deck on the 86th floor to which millions of tourists have been whisked over the years to gaze in awe at the surrounding New York skyline and another glass-enclosed viewing area on the 102nd floor. Open daily, 9:30 AM to 11 PM. Admission charge. W 34th St. and 5th Ave. (736-3100).

Jacob K. Javits Convention Center – Much delayed and over budget, this glass and steel monolith designed by I. M. Pei, covering 22 acres along the Hudson River, will host the bigger synods and conventions that outgrew the now closed New York Coliseum. The complex runs for 5 blocks between 11th and 12th avenues and encompasses 1.8 million square feet of space, making it one of the world's largest buildings. It has more than 900,000 square feet of indoor exhibition space, another 50,000 square feet outside, and a 15-story atrium. The kitchens produce banquet meals for up to 10,000, while the cafeteria serves 1,500 people an hour. State-of-the-art meeting facilities include a sophisticated audio-visual system and soundproofing throughout its 131 separate meetings rooms, with simultaneous translation in up to 8 languages. There's also a VIP lounge, a press room, a video information center, and a cocktail lounge. The only thing missing is a garage. 655 W 34th St. (216-2000).

Times Square – Every New Year's Eve, Times Square is where thousands of New Yorkers and visitors welcome in the New Year. Although the height of mad celebration reaches its pinnacle at that time, Times Square is always crowded. The quality of the crowds, however, leaves much to be desired. In spite of its reputation as one of the major crossroads of the world, Times Square is mainly the hangout of drug pushers, pimps, hookers, junkies, and assorted street peddlers attempting to fence stolen goods. It is also the center of the city's tackiest sex industry. To the naked eye, it is nearly wall-to-wall porn shops and hard-core movies. Proposals for rehabilitation have been almost as numerous as the prostitutes on parade. A sign of a possibly brighter future comes in the form of the new 50-story *Marriott Marquis* convention hotel (see *Checking In*), built on the site of the Helen Hayes and Morosco theaters, W 42nd St., where Broadway crosses 7th Ave. Plans for the rebuilding of most of 42nd Street, from the Avenue of the Americas to 9th Avenue, also appear finally to be coming to fruition.

Broadway and the Theater District – Just north of Times Square, you'll find the colorful marquees and billboards for which New York is famous. The lights are still pretty dazzling, twinkling on and off in a glittering electric collage. On most nights, the side streets are jammed with people from 7:30 to 11 PM. The legitimate theaters are mostly clustered between W 42nd and W 50th sts. to the east and west of Broadway.

New York Public Library – A couple of blocks east of Times Square, this dignified old building is a good place to sit and catch your breath. Sit on the front steps, between the famous lion statues, or in Bryant Park behind the library, where there are lunchtime concerts during the summer. The park is not, however, very safe after dark. New Yorkers generally prefer to sit on the steps near the stone lions. Inside the library is New York's largest reference collection of books, periodicals, and exhibits of graphic art, as well as a gift store, and a Gutenberg Bible worth $3 million. Tours are given Mondays through Saturdays at 11 AM and 2 PM. Closed Sundays. Free. E 42nd St. and 5th Ave. (340-0849).

The Chrysler Building – The princess of the skyline. Its distinctive, graceful spire, decorated with stainless steel, now sparkles with more than its usual brilliance since the installation of hand-blown fluorescent lights around its peak. Although it has long ceded the title of tallest on the skyline, this twinkling, Art Deco building of the 1930s remains, to many New Yorkers, the most beautiful of all. There are no tours or observatories, but the small lobby with its exquisite elevator doors is worth a trip. 405 Lexington Ave. at 42nd St.

The Ford Foundation Building – If you happen to be wandering through New York at sunrise and climb the stairs between 1st and 2nd avenues on 42nd Street, you'll see the bronzed windows of the Ford Foundation building catch the first rays of the sun, reflecting copper-colored light into the sky. At other times, the building is just as dramatic. Built around a central courtyard containing tropical trees and plants, it is the only place in Manhattan where you can feel as if you're in a jungle. It's one of the great New York experiences — especially on snowy afternoons. Open weekdays. Free. 320 E 43rd St. (573-5000).

Tudor City – A nearly forgotten pocket of the city, this 1920s neo-Tudor apartment complex is one of the most romantic parts of the city. An esplanade overlooks the East River and the United Nations. Home to many diplomats and UN employees, Tudor City serves as an international campus. (According to local legend, Tudor City used to be where executives and industrialists housed their mistresses in the 1930s and 1940s.) The long, curved staircase leading to the sidewalk opposite the United Nations is known as the Isaiah Steps because of the biblical quote carved into the wall. Between E 42nd and E 43rd sts. at 1st Ave.

The United Nations – Although the UN is open all year, the best time to visit is between September and December, when the General Assembly is in session. Delegates from nearly 150 nations gather to discuss the world's problems, and sessions are open to the public. The delegates' dining room is also open to the public for lunch weekdays throughout the year. Overlooking the East River, it room offers a lovely international menu and the chance to overhear intriguing conversations. Reservations are essential; pick up a pass in the lobby. There are guided tours of the UN. Open daily. Admission charge for tour. 1 Dag Hammerskjold Plaza, E 42nd St. and 1st Ave. (754-7713).

Rockefeller Center – A group of skyscrapers originally built in the 1930s, Rockefeller Center is best known for the giant Christmas tree in December, for its ice skating rink, and for Radio City Music Hall, a theatrical landmark and home of the Rockettes (757-3100). There are tours of the center and the observation tower as well as tours of NBC television studios from 30 Rockefeller Plaza (the RCA Building) daily except Sundays. 5th Ave. between 48th and 51st sts. (489-2947).

St. Patrick's Cathedral – A refuge from the crowds of 5th Avenue, it's the most famous church in the city. Dedicated to Ireland's patron saint, it stands in Gothic splendor across the street from Rockefeller Center in the shadow of the skyscrapers. Resplendent with gargoyles on the outside, stained glass windows and magnificent appointments on the inside, St. Patrick's is a good place for rest, contemplation, and prayer. Catholic services are held daily. 5th Ave. between E 50th and E 51st sts. (753-2261).

Sixth Avenue – Officially known as Avenue of the Americas, but no true New

Yorker calls it that. Sixth Avenue between 42nd and 57th streets is particularly breathtaking at dusk, when the giant glass and steel buildings light up. In the basement of the McGraw-Hill Building (6th Ave. and W 48th St.) is *The New York Experience* (869-0345), a dazzling multimedia show about the Big Apple. You travel through a replica of an old-fashioned El train to get to the show. Open daily. Admission charge.

Museum of Modern Art – A must. The masterpieces of modern art hanging on the walls include Wyeth's *Christina's World*, Monet's *Water Lilies*, and Van Gogh's *Starry Night*. A renovation project completed in 1984 gave MOMA twice as much gallery space and expanded study and library facilities. The most dramatic alteration is a four-story glass Garden Hall overlooking the sculpture garden. The museum's collection is now installed in chronological order, and, by following a suggested route, visitors can see the history of modern painting and sculpture unfold. Closed Wednesdays. Admission charge; on Thursdays evenings, admission is on a pay-as-you-wish basis. 11 W 53rd St. (708-9480).

Fifth Avenue – Although the street runs from Washington Square straight up to Spanish Harlem, when New Yorkers refer to 5th Avenue they usually mean the stretch of the world's most sophisticated shops between Rockefeller Center at 50th Street and the *Westin Plaza Hotel* at the southeastern corner of Central Park at Central Park South (59th St.). *Saks, Gucci, Tiffany's, Cartier, Bergdorf Goodman,* and, for children, *FAO Schwarz* make walking along the street an incredible test in temptation. Stop in at *Steuben Glass* on the corner of 55th Street and marvel at its permanent collection of sculpted glass depicting mythological and contemporary themes. Fifth Avenue is the dividing line between east and west in New York street addresses. It is the only New York avenue that runs perfectly straight along a north-south axis.

Grand Army Plaza – This baroque square, with its central fountain just across the street from the southeast corner of Central Park, faces the regal *Westin Plaza Hotel,* the General Motors Building, and the hansom cabstand where horse-drawn carriages (some guided by drivers in top hats and tails) wait to carry clients through Central Park. If you have a lover, be sure to arrange to meet here at least once. Be sure, too, to take at least one ride through the park in a hansom cab, preferably at dusk or very, very late. Central Park South and 5th Ave.

Central Park – More than 50 blocks long but only 3 blocks wide, this beloved stretch of greenery designed by Frederick Law Olmsted and Calvert Vaux in the 1860s is now a National Historic Landmark. New Yorkers use it for everything — jogging, biking, walking, ice skating, riding in horse-drawn hansom cabs, listening to concerts and opera, watching Shakespearean plays, demonstrating, flying kites, boating, gazing at art, and playing all kinds of ball games. The Central Park Zoo, between E 61st and E 65th sts. on 5th Ave., is being taken over by the New York Zoological Society, which runs the Bronx Zoo and which is planning major changes for this mid-Manhattan menagerie. During its renovation you can still visit the Children's Zoo (10¢ admission) and the sea lions' pool. These two areas will be spruced up when the main zoo reopens sometime in 1988. Open daily. Free. Central Park is bounded by Central Park South (W 59th St.) on the south, W 110th St. on the north, 5th Ave. on the east, and Central Park West on the west. For information on park events call 755-4100.

UPPER EAST SIDE

The Metropolitan Museum of Art – Perhaps the finest museum this side of the Louvre; more than 2 million people visit every year. You could easily spend days walking through the impressive sections displaying the costumes, ceramics, metalwork, armor, mummies, paintings, drawings, sculpture, photographs, and mosaics of dozens of different periods and countries. The special exhibitions are really special. There is a cafeteria and two gift shops. Films and lectures are presented throughout the year, and a distinguished concert series (570-3949) is held from September through May. Closed Mondays. Suggested admission: $4. 5th Ave. at 82nd St. (535-7710).

The Guggenheim Museum – Designed in 1959 by Frank Lloyd Wright, this white circular building has spiraling ramps along its inner walls so you can travel through the collections by following the curves of the building. While it is given over primarily to exhibitions of contemporary art, some patrons feel that its architecture is more impressive than the collection it houses. Closed Mondays. Admission charge. 1071 5th Ave., between E 88th and E 89th sts. (360-3500).

Yorkville and Gracie Mansion – An interesting ethnic neighborhood of mostly German and Eastern European families. There are plenty of restaurants, beer halls, and delicatessens selling wiener schnitzel, sauerbraten, wurst, and kielbasa. Gracie Mansion, the official residence of the Mayor of New York, sits in a garden that is part of Carl Schurz Park alongside the East River. The park is popular with joggers and dog-walkers. The best time to visit is at dawn, when the eastern sky comes to life. Yorkville stretches from E 80th to E 89th sts. between Lexington and York aves. Gracie Mansion and Carl Schurz Park are at E 88th St. and East End Ave.

Roosevelt Island – A self-contained housing development in the middle of the East River. Roosevelt Island, accessible from Manhattan by tramway or bus from Queens, offers a unique view of midtown Manhattan. A loop bus encircles the island, which has restricted automobile traffic. The aerial tramway leaves each side every 15 minutes daily except during rush hours, when it leaves every 7½ minutes. The tram costs $1 (subway tokens are also accepted). Manhattan terminal at E 60th St. and 2nd Ave. (753-6626).

UPPER WEST SIDE

Columbus Circle and New York Coliseum – The southwestern corner of Central Park is dominated by a statue of Christopher Columbus and a traffic circle. On the western side of the circle stands the New York Coliseum, once the site of major events such as the annual auto, boat, and antiques shows. A multi-use project, incorporating a hotel, residential area, and commercial and retail space, will replace it. W 59th St. and Central Park West.

Lincoln Center – If you have ever seen Mel Brooks's film *The Producers,* you have probably retained an image of the glowing lights of a fountain shooting into the air with an exuberance to match the enthusiasm of actors Zero Mostel and Gene Wilder. That's the Lincoln Center fountain, and it's just as magnificent in real life. The pulsing water and light are dramatically framed by the Metropolitan Opera House, a contemporary hall with giant murals by Marc Chagall. The performing arts complex also contains Avery Fisher Hall (home of the New York Philharmonic), the New York State Theater, (home of the New York City Ballet), the Vivian Beaumont Theater, the Juilliard Building, and the Library and Museum of the Performing Arts (see *Theater* and *Music* sections, below). Guided tours through the major buildings are conducted daily and last about an hour. Admission charge for tour. Broadway and W 66th St. (877-1800).

The American Museum of Natural History – A cornucopia of curiosities. The anthropological and natural history exhibitions in the form of life-size dioramas showing people and animals in realistic settings have made this one of the most famous museums in the world. The dinosaurs on the 4th floor are the stars of the show. Free guided tours leave from the main-floor information desk. Open daily. Donations accepted. Central Park West and W 79th St. (873-4225).

Hayden Planetarium – An amazing collection of astronomical displays on meteorites, comets, space vehicles, and other galactic phenomena. The sky show, in which constellations are projected onto an observatory ceiling, is one of the great New York sights. Subjects of the sky shows include lunar expeditions, the formation of the solar system, and UFOs. Open daily. Admission charge. Central Park West and W 81st St. (873-8828).

The Cathedral of St. John the Divine – The largest Gothic cathedral in the world, with a seating capacity of 10,000. It is irreverently nicknamed St. John the Unfinished, for a chronic shortage of funds has allowed only two thirds of the impressive church to be completed since work began in 1892. Stonemasons, who most recently put down their trowels in the late 30s, picked them up again in 1979, with plans to finish the interior of the Crossing and the two towers' spires by the year 2000. There is a stunning collection of Renaissance and Byzantine art inside, and an exquisite time to see it all at its best is on Christmas Eve at midnight mass. Guided tours of the cathedral and the stoneyard are conducted daily. Open daily. Free. Amsterdam Ave. and W 112th St. (678-6922).

Columbia University – The Big Apple's contribution to the Ivy League. Although more than 27,000 students attend classes here, the campus is spacious enough to avoid a sense of crowding. Around the campus are a number of interesting bookstores, restaurants, and bars. The *West End Café,* Broadway and W 113th St. (666-8750), is a long-standing student favorite, and it was from here that Jack Kerouac went forth to lead the Beat Generation of the 1950s. On weekdays at 3 PM, from September through May, free guided tours of campus leave from 201 Dodge Hall. Open daily. Free. Broadway and W 116th St. (280-1754).

Riverside Church – Perched on a cliff overlooking the Hudson River, Riverside is an interdominational Christian church with a functioning carillon tower and an amazing statue of the Angel Gabriel blowing the trumpet. The white building next to the church is known as "the God Box" because many religious organizations (among them, the National Council of Churches and the Interfaith Council on Corporate Responsibility) are headquartered here. The carillon tower is open daily; free guided tours of the Church Sundays at 12:30 PM. W 120th St. between Riverside Dr. and Claremont Ave. (222-5900).

Grant's Tomb – Who is buried in Grant's tomb? Suffice it to say, You-Know-Who and his wife, Mrs. You-Know-Who, are entombed here in a gray building topped with a rotunda and set in Riverside Park. A word about the park: Don't wander in after dark. Grant's tomb is officially known as General Grant National Memorial. Closed Mondays and Tuesdays. Free. Riverside Dr. and W 122nd St. (666-1640).

The Cloisters and Fort Tryon Park – Without a doubt one of the most unusual museums in the country, if not the world. The Cloisters, a branch of the Metropolitan Museum, consists of sections of cloisters that originally belonged to monasteries in southern France. It houses an inspiring collection of medieval art from different parts of Europe, of which the Unicorn Tapestries are the most famous. Recorded Medieval music echoes through the stone corridors and courtyards daily; Medieval and Renaissance concerts are held on Sundays in November, December, March, and April. Set in Fort Tryon Park along the Hudson River, the Cloisters offers a splendid view of the New Jersey Palisades, the George Washington Bridge, and the Hudson River. Closed Mondays. Admission charge. Closest intersection is Washington Ave. and W 193rd St. (923-3700).

Harlem – Most visitors to New York — black or white — are uncomfortable at the thought of entering Harlem, and it is intimidating. But there is much to see there, and a visit has the undeniable effect of shattering the monolithic association with threat and violence that attends most people's image of the community. Harlem, starting in earnest at 110th Street and stretching to about 160th Street, is a community filled with neighborhoods of families as concerned about community problems as families in other neighborhoods throughout the city.

In the words of a New York police officer: "The best way to see Harlem is by driving or in a cab. Take a bus rather than a subway if you are using public transportation."

The nicest part of Harlem is the landmark block called "Strivers Row" — 138th Street between Seventh and Eighth avenues — a string of turn-of-the-century brownstones designed by Stanford White. Penny Sightseeing Company conducts three-hour guided tours of Harlem on Tuesdays, Thursdays, and Saturdays, from March through December. For reservations, contact its office at 303 W 42nd St., Suite 504, at 8th Ave. (246-4220).

BROOKLYN

Mention Brooklyn to most Manhattanites and you'll probably hear, "Oh, I never go to Brooklyn" or some similar wise-aleck remark. People who do not know the borough think purely in terms of the book *A Tree Grows in Brooklyn* or 1930s gangster movies in which Brooklyn-born thugs make snide remarks out of the sides of their mouths while chewing on cigars. Actually, Brooklyn has a lot of trees (more than Manhattan) and some charming neighborhoods that are more European in character than American. Not only is it greener, it is also considerably more peaceful than Manhattan, even though it has 3 million people and bills itself as "the Fourth Largest City in America."

Brooklyn Heights – The most picturesque streets of classic brownstones and gardens can be found in this historic district. Not only does the Promenade facing the skyline offer the traditional picture-postcard view of Manhattan, but the area behind it retains an aura of dignity that characterized a more gracious past. Montague Street, a narrow thoroughfare lined with restaurants and shops selling ice cream, candles, old prints, flowers, and clothing, runs from the East River to the Civic Center, a complex of federal, state, and municipal government buildings. To get to Brooklyn Heights from Manhattan, take the IRT 7th Avenue line to Clark Street; or, better yet, walk across the Brooklyn Bridge and bear right. The district extends from the Brooklyn Bridge to Atlantic Avenue and from Court Street to the Promenade. For information on events in the Heights, contact the Brooklyn Heights Association, 55 Pierrepont St. (718 858-9193).

Atlantic Avenue – Lebanese, Yemeni, Syrian, and Palestinian shops, bakeries, and restaurants line the street, purveyors of tahini, Syrian bread, baklava, halvah, assorted delicious foodstuffs, Arabic records, and books. There is even an office of the Palestinian Red Crescent, an official branch of the International Red Cross that has been helping victims of the wars in Lebanon. Occasionally, women in veils make their way to and from the shops, some incongruously carrying transistor radios. The most active street scene takes place between the waterfront and Court Street along Atlantic Ave.

Park Slope – An up-and-coming restoration district, the Slope resembles the Chelsea section of London, with many beautiful, shady trees and gardens. It feels more like a town than part of the city, especially at night, when the only sounds are the birds and the wind rushing through the trees. A large part of Park Slope has been designated a historic district and there are some truly impressive town houses here. Grand Army Plaza, a colossal arch commemorating those who died in the Civil War, stands at the end of the Slope that extends along the western edge of Prospect Park. Seventh Avenue, two blocks from the park, is an intriguing shopping street where you can get old furniture, stained glass, ceramics, houseware, flowers, health food, vegetables, and toys. Saturday afternoons get pretty lively. To get to Park Slope from Manhattan, take the IRT 7th Avenue line to Grand Army Plaza or the IND D train to the 7th Avenue exit.

Prospect Park and the Brooklyn Botanic Gardens – Prospect Park, another Olmsted and Vaux creation, has more than 500 acres of gracefully landscaped greenery with fields, fountains, lakes, a concert bandshell, an ice skating rink in winter, a bridal path, and a zoo. The Botanic Gardens, 1000 Washington Ave. (718 622-4433), contain serene rose gardens, hothouses with orchids and other tropical plants, cherry trees, a Zen meditation garden, and hundreds of flowers and shrubs. Closed Mondays. Free. From Manhattan, take the IRT 7th Avenue line to Grand Army Plaza and walk up the hill along Flatbush Avenue or take the IND D train to Prospect Park.

The Brooklyn Museum – In addition to its outstanding permanent anthropological collections on American Indians of both the northern and southern hemispheres, this museum hosts terrific traveling exhibits. In the permanent collection are fine exhibits of Oriental arts, American painting and decorative arts, and European painting. The roster of artists whose work is permanently displayed includes Van Gogh, Rodin, Toulouse-Lautrec, Gauguin, Monet, and Chagall. Closed Tuesdays. Suggested donation: $2. From Manhattan, take the IRT 7th Avenue line to Eastern Parkway. 200 Eastern Pkwy. and Washington Ave. (718 636-5000).

Bay Ridge – Although Brooklynites have been fond of this Scandinavian waterfront community for years, it took the film *Saturday Night Fever* to bring it to national attention. Bay Ridge is dominated by the world's longest suspension bridge, the Verrazano-Narrows Bridge, which connects Brooklyn with Staten Island. (Some people say this bridge goes from nowhere to nowhere else, but they fail to appreciate its finer aesthetics.) Although chances are you won't see John Travolta tripping down 4th Avenue, you will see a lot of people who look like the character he played in the film, and you'll also get to see the bridge rising over the tops of houses, shops, restaurants, and discos. A bike path runs along the edge of the Narrows from Owls Head Pier, the pier of the now-defunct Brooklyn–Staten Island ferry, all the way to the Verrazano-Narrows Bridge. The pier has recently been renovated and is a great place for fishing, watching the ships come in, and looking at a wide-angle view of lower Manhattan. To get to Bay Ridge from Manhattan, take the BMT RR train to 95th St.

Coney Island – If you've seen the classic film *The Beast from 20,000 Fathoms,* you no doubt remember the climactic final scene in which the beast is shot down from the top of a roller coaster called the Cyclone. As the monster falls, he destroys half of Coney Island. But fear not, gentle reader, Hollywood's illusion is a far cry from reality — although some disenchanted residents wish it were a lot closer to the truth. Now a long strip of garish amusement park rides, penny arcades, hot dog stands, and low-income housing complexes, Coney Island is jam-packed in summer, eerily deserted in winter. Weekends in the summer are the worst time to visit. Weekday evenings are considerably less frenetic. You can ride the Cyclone (if they ever solve their liability insurance problems), one of the most terrifying roller coasters on the East Coast, and the Wonder Wheel, a giant Ferris wheel alongside the ocean, but the parachute jump, which is Coney Island's landmark and can be seen for miles, is no longer operational. There are honky-tonk bars along the boardwalk, where country and western singers compete with the sound of the sea. If you get a sudden craving for Italian food, head for *Gargiulo's,* 2911 W 15th St. (718 266-0906) for some good Neapolitan dishes. The ultimate offbeat New York treat is to have hot dogs at *Nathan's* at 2 in the morning. Surf and Stillwell aves. Take IND F, D, or B trains to Coney Island from Manhattan.

Sheepshead Bay – More like a New England fishing village than part of New York, fishermen sell their catch on the dock in the early afternoon. Charter boats that take people out for the day leave very early in the morning. For the best view of the scene, cross the wooden footbridge at Ocean Avenue and walk along the mile-long esplanade. A few blocks south of the bay is Manhattan Beach, one of the smaller city beaches. Brighton Beach, a few blocks to the east, joins Manhattan Beach with Coney Island. To get to Sheepshead Bay from Manhattan, take the IND D train to Sheepshead Bay.

THE BRONX

If you intend to visit the Bronx, don't ask for directions from someone from Brooklyn. Because of a local prejudice, residents of these boroughs look down on each other. With 1.5 million inhabitants, the Bronx is smaller than Brooklyn; it's the only borough in the City of New York that is joined to the mainland. Although all the points of interest listed here are safe for visitors, some sections of the Bronx are the most dangerous parts of New York City. The South Bronx has been nicknamed Fort Apache by the police, and one officer advises staying clear of any place south of Fordham Road.

Bronx Zoo – One of the most famous zoos in the world, it houses more than 3,000 animals who live amid 250 acres. Elephants, tigers, chimps, seals, rhinos, hippos, birds, and buffalos are the favorites. To get there from Manhattan, take the IRT 7th Ave. #2 Express to Pelham Pkwy.; walk west to the Bronxdale entrance (for other routes, call the zoo). Open daily. Admission charge Fridays through Mondays; other days free; parking, $2.50. At Fordham Rd. and Bronx River Pkwy. (367-1010).

The New York Botanical Gardens – Adjoining the zoo to the north, the 230-acre gardens have an unspoiled, natural forest area. This is what New York looked like BP (before people). The Enid A. Haupt Conservatory (closed Mondays) with its 11 pavilions — each with a totally different environment — is a special treat. Other highlights include a rose garden, azalea glen, daffodil hill, conservatory, botanical museum, and restaurant. Well worth the trip, especially in the spring. From Manhattan take the IND D train to Bedford Park Station. Open daily. Admission charge for the Conservatory except Wednesdays; parking, $2.50. Southern Blvd. south of Mosholu Pkwy. (220-8700).

The Van Cortlandt Museum – One of the few remaining 18th-century Dutch estates, this one is lovingly preserved with carefully restored furnishings. Women in colonial garb escort you through the premises. Take the IRT 1 train from Manhattan to W 242nd St. Closed Mondays. Admission charge for adults only. In Van Cortlandt Park north of W 242nd St. and Broadway (543-3344).

Bronx Museum of the Arts – This museum moved into its new, permanent home in 1983. Its changing exhibitions have two themes: contemporary art and the artistic expression of the many ethnic groups who live in the borough. Classical music concerts, film programs, poetry readings, and dance performances are held throughout the year. From Manhattan, take the IRT 4 to 161st St. or the IND D to 167th St. Closed Fridays. Free. 1040 Grand Concourse at 165th St. (681-6000).

The Edgar Allan Poe Cottage – A tiny cottage, adequately cramped to inspire claustrophobia in anyone larger than a gnome, sits incongruously in the middle of the Grand Concourse. Poe lived here during his final years and it now contains his personal belongings. Open daily. Admission charge. 3266 Bainsbridge Ave., at Grand Concourse and Kingsbridge Rd. (881-8900).

Yankee Stadium – A landmark. Here, in this 70,000-seat stadium, batted the late, great Babe Ruth, Joe DiMaggio, and dozens of other baseball stars. Take the IND D train from Manhattan to 161st St. Open during baseball season. 161st and River sts. (293-6000).

The Hall of Fame of Great Americans – Bronze-cast busts of great American presidents, poets, and people noted for achievement in the sciences, arts, and humanities. About 100 busts stand on podiums set atop columns. The Hall is on the Bronx Community College campus; from Manhattan take the IND D train to 183rd St. or the IRT 4 train to Burnside Ave. Open daily. Free. W 181st St. and University Ave. (220-6312).

STATEN ISLAND

Much closer to New Jersey than New York, Staten Island is the Big Apple's most remote borough and, with 250,000 people, its least populous. Since the Verrazano-Narrows Bridge opened in 1964, Staten Island has been filling up with suburban housing developments and shopping centers. However, a few farms remain in southern Staten Island. To find them, take the bus marked Richmond Ave. at the ferry terminal. Getting around Staten Island by public transportation takes a long time. Driving is recommended if at all possible.

Staten Island Zoo – Considerably smaller than the Bronx Zoo, this zoo is near a lake in Barret Park. Its specialty is reptiles, and snakes of all descriptions coil and uncoil in glass cases. Open daily. Admission charge; free Wednesdays. Broadway and Clove Rd. (718 442-3101).

Jacques Marchais Center for Tibetan Art – One of the esoteric treasures of the city, this is also one of the best-kept secrets in the metropolitan area. A reconstructed Tibetan prayer hall with adjoining library and gardens with Oriental sculpture, the Center sits on a hill overlooking a pastoral, un–New York setting of trees. The Tibetan *Book of the Dead,* other occult tomes, prayer wheels, statuary, and weavings are on display. Open April through November; weekends only. Admission charge. 338 Lighthouse Ave. (718 987-3478).

SOURCES AND RESOURCES

TOURIST INFORMATION: The New York Convention and Visitors Bureau, 2 Columbus Circle (397-8242), is an excellent source for tourist information and assistance. Its office carries hotel and restaurant information, subway and bus maps, descriptive brochures, and current listings of the city's entertainment and activities, and it is staffed with multilingual aides. The New York Chamber of Commerce and Industry can mail informative brochures and pamphlets to people planning to move to the New York area. Some of the details may be out of date, but the literature can be helpful. Contact the Chamber at 200 Madison Ave., New York, NY 10016 (561-2020).

Visitors who require assistance in an emergency — anything from a lost wallet to a lost child — should stop at the Traveler's Aid Services office on 42nd St. between Broadway and 7th Ave. (944-0013); open weekdays 8:30 AM to 6 PM. There is also a branch at Kennedy Airport (718 656-4870); open weekdays 10 AM to 10 PM, weekends 3 to 10 PM.

A fascinating book about the city is *New York: A Guide to the Metropolis, Walking Tours of Architecture and History* by Gerald Wolfe (New York University Press; $12.95). There are countless other guides cramming the shelves at any good-size bookstore.

Local Coverage – The *New York Times,* morning daily; the *Daily News,* morning daily; and the *New York Post* morning and afternoon daily; and the weekly *Village Voice.* Also, the weekly magazines *The New Yorker* and *New York.*

Food – *Restaurants of New York,* by Seymour Britchky (Random House; $10.95); *The All New Underground Gourmet,* by Milton Glaser and Jerome Snyder (Simon and Schuster; $4.95); *Best Restaurants New York,* by Stendahl (101 Productions; $4.95).

Area Code – All telephone numbers in Manhattan and the Bronx are in the 212 area code; numbers in Brooklyn, Queens, and Staten Island have the 718 area code, as noted.

CLIMATE AND CLOTHES: The best times to visit New York are in the spring — mid-April to mid-May — and in the fall — mid-September through October — when temperatures are comfortable, in the high 60s to low 70s. Winter and summer are extreme, averaging in the 80s and up in July and August, in the 20s or below during the months of hard winter. However, the weather should not determine your visit since most of what makes New York great takes place indoors, and air conditioning and central heating are standard. New Yorkers dress informally for most events; anything in good taste goes. Remember, there is no rainy season as such — it can happen any day of the year. Be prepared. And during the warm months, a sweater or a wrap is usually welcome after an hour or so of sitting in an air-conditioned place. Wintertime can be quite cold; boots, hats, gloves, and a heavy coat are necessities.

GETTING AROUND: Airports – New York City is served by three major airports: John F. Kennedy International (JFK), La Guardia (for domestic flights), and Newark International, across the Hudson in New Jersey. It takes 50 to 60 minutes to reach JFK from midtown Manhattan by cab and costs about $23. La Guardia from midtown is a 30- to 45-minute ride, with a fare of around $15. Newark International from midtown is the meter amount (usually $40), plus $10 and tolls; one fare covers up to four or five passengers and their luggage (except trunks, which are 50¢ extra).

Quick and relatively inexpensive transportation is available via several bus lines. Carey Transportation (718 632-0500) provides service from 125 Park Ave. at 42nd St., the Air Trans Center at the Port Authority Bus Terminal, and the Eastern Airlines office at 10 Rockefeller Plaza to both New York City airports. Buses leave every 20 or 30 minutes. One-way fare to JFK is $8, $6 for La Guardia; Carey also runs a shuttle between these two airports. New Jersey Transit handles service to Newark International out of the Port Authority Bus Terminal (564-8484), on 8th Ave. between 40th and 42nd sts. Purchase tickets ($5) at the Air Trans Center desk on the ground floor of the terminal's North Wing. Buses depart every 10 to 30 minutes and the trip takes about a half-hour. Olympia Trails (964-6233 in New York, 589-1188 in New Jersey) provides coach service every 20 minutes from Newark International's North, A, B and C terminals to the World Trade Center and Grand Central Terminal; the fare is $5. Newark International Airport–New York City Mini Bus Service is yet another alternative. It takes passengers from the airport to midtown Manhattan hotels for $10 to $14.

New York Helicopter (800 645-3494) offers daily flights from midtown's 34th St. Heliport to JFK in 18 minutes, to La Guardia in 6 minutes, and to Newark in 10 minutes; all fares are $58 one way. On weekdays there is also service between all three airports and the World Trade Center in downtown's financial district.

If luggage is light, travelers headed for JFK from Manhattan or Brooklyn can take the JFK Express, a combination bus and subway airport connection. The service operates every 20 minutes and is $7. For a subway map and more information see *Subways,* below.

The fare on New York City buses and subways (and the Roosevelt Island tramway) is $1, no matter how far you travel.

Bus – New York City buses run frequently. There are more than 200 routes and over 4,500 buses in operation. Although slower than subways, buses bring you closer to your destination, stopping about every two blocks. The main routes in Manhattan are north-south on the avenues, and east-west (crosstown) on the streets, as well as some crisscross and circular routes. Check both the sign on the front of the bus and the one at the bus stop to make sure the bus you want stops where you are waiting. Be sure to have exact change for the basic fare (subway tokens are acceptable), and ask for a transfer, should you need one, when you board the bus. Bus drivers do not make change nor do they accept bills. Transfers should be obtained from the bus driver at the time of paying your fare; they are free. Most bus routes operate 24 hours a day, seven days a week, but a few do not run late at night or on Sundays. Free bus maps are available at Grand Central and Penn Stations, or by sending a stamped, self-addressed No. 10 envelope to the New York Transit Authority, 370 Jay St., Brooklyn, NY 11201, Attn.: Maps.

Subways – No doubt about it, the New York subway system is confusing. But that is no reason to avoid it. Its convenience and speed can't be duplicated by any other form of transportation, and the intelligence of its overall design is awesome. Basically, there are three different subway lines, with express and local routes serving all city boroughs except for Staten Island (reached via the Staten Island Ferry). The most extensive line is the IRT, which originates in Brooklyn and transverses Manhattan en route to the Bronx. The IRT has two main divisions: the 7th Avenue line, which serves the West

Side of Manhattan, and the Lexington Avenue line, which covers the East Side. You can go from east to west (crosstown) on the shuttle (SS) between Grand Central Station and Times Square. The IND serves Brooklyn, Queens, Manhattan, and the Bronx. The BMT serves Brooklyn, Queens, and Manhattan. The subway is the most heavily used means of city transportation (over 3 million people ride it daily on 230 miles of track) and is mobbed during rush hours, weekdays from 7:30 to 9:00 AM and from 4:30 to 7:00 PM. You buy tokens at booths in the subway stations and insert them in turnstiles to enter the subway. Pick up a free subway map at the Convention and Visitors Bureau, or check the complete map in the yellow pages of the Manhattan phone book or the maps posted in every station and in each subway car. The subway system operates 24 hours a day. For further information, call the NY Transit Authority (330-1234).

Taxi – The handiest and most expensive way to get around the city is by cab. Cabs can be hailed almost anywhere and are required to pick you up and deliver you to your specified destination. Cabs can be identified by their yellow color and are available if their roof light is on. Cabbies expect a 20% tip. There is a 50¢ surcharge on fleet cab fares between 8 PM and 6 AM; red and white stickers are on both front doors of cabs that impose the extra charge.

Car Rental – New York is served by all the major car rental companies as well as a host of small local firms.

 MUSEUMS: The Guggenheim, Museum of Modern Art, Metropolitan Museum, Hayden Planetarium, American Museum of Natural History, the Cloisters, the Brooklyn Museum, the Jacques Marchais Center for Tibetan Art, and the Fraunces Tavern Museum are described in *Special Places*. Other notable New York museums are:

American Craft Museum – 45 W 45th St. (869-9422)
Asia Society – 725 Park Ave. (288-6400)
Center for African Art – 54 E 68th St. (861-1200)
Cooper-Hewitt Museum – A branch of the Smithsonian Institution, featuring textiles and material arts, 2 E 91st St. (860-6868)
The Frick Collection – 1 E 70th St. at 5th Ave. (288-0700)
International Center of Photography – 5th Ave. at 94th St. (860-1777)
The Jewish Museum – 1109 5th Ave. (860-1889)
The Morgan Library – 29 E 36th St. (685-0610)
El Museo del Barrio – Hispanic art, 1230 5th Ave. (831-7272)
Museum of American Folk Art – 125 W 55th St. (581-2474)
Museum of the American Indian – 3750 Broadway at 155th St. (283-2420)
Museum of Broadcasting – 1 E 53rd St. (752-7684)
The Museum of the City of New York – 5th Ave. at 103rd St. (534-1672)
Museum of Holography – 11 Mercer St. (925-0526)
New-York Historical Society – 170 Central Park West (873-3400)
The Studio Museum in Harlem – 144 W 125th St. (864-4500)
The Whitney Museum of American Art – Madison Ave. at E 75th St. (570-3676); new branch in the Philip Morris building, Park Ave. at 42nd St. (878-2550)

 SHOPPING: This city is like no other for acquiring material possessions. It is the commercial center and the fashion capital of the country, and styles that originate here set the trends for fashionable folk from Portland, Maine, to Portland, Oregon. The scope of merchandise available approaches the infinite, and there's a price range for every budget. To help you find products and services, the yellow pages offers a free where-to-buy-it hot line called *Cityphone* (675-0900).

Bloomingdale's, **A World unto Itself** – This is the place for fashionable Upper East

Siders and anyone else who aspires to those heights. Whether you want to pick up satin running shorts or a sheer evening gown, you'll probably find it here. Saturdays on the main floor is something of a social event — anyone who cares to be anyone is here shopping and being seen. Lexington Ave. at 59th St., (355-5900 or 705-2000).

Bookstores – The publishing capital of the world, New York has a wealth of literary worth. Leaders among its outlets include *Barnes and Noble,* 105 5th Ave. at 18th St. (807-0099), 600 5th Ave. at 48th St. (765-0590), and three other locations, which carries a wide selection at bargain prices. *Scribner's,* 597 5th Ave. (486-2700), *B. Dalton,* 666 5th Ave. (247-1740), and at three other Manhattan locations, and *Doubleday,* 673 5th Ave. (953-4805), all carry a broad variety of new titles and trade books. *The Strand,* 828 Broadway at 12th St. (473-1452), has a huge collection of old and used books and even some rare manuscripts. *Rizzoli,* 31 W 57th St. (759-2424), is best known for its collection of art books. *Gotham Book Mart,* 41 W 47th St. (719-4448), specializes in contemporary literature, poetry, theater, and film. *Kitchen Arts & Letters,* 1435 Lexington Ave. (876-5550), is a bookstore and gallery exclusively devoted to food and wine.

Boutiques and Specialty Shops – Fifth Avenue in the East Fifties and Madison Avenue in the East Sixties and Seventies are lined with boutiques that carry haute couture at haute prix, but looking is free. The names are an encyclopedia of style: *Versace, Kenzo, Sonia Rykiel, Daniel Hechter, Emanuel Ungaro, Saint Laurent, Armani, Valentino, Gucci,* and the like. Other interesting, superb merchandise can be found in shops such as *Ménage à Trois,* 760 Madison at 65th St. (249-0600), with fine shirts for men and women in linen and silk; *Alcott & Andrews,* Madison Ave. at 44th St. (818-0606), for fine, color-coordinated classics for women; and *Diane B.,* 729 Madison Ave. at 64th St. (759-0988), and in SoHo at 426 W Broadway (226-6400), for casual-chic clothes by the trendiest of designers. Also on the cutting edge of fashion are the styles at *Charivari Workshop,* 441 Columbus Ave. at 81st St. (496-8700), and at four other locations around town. For casual, Italian sweaters in the latest styles, visit one of the city's many *Benetton* stores (there are a few on Fifth Avenue in the East Forties). For the finest in raincoats, there's *Burberrys,* 9 E 57th St. (371-5010), and *Aquascutum,* 680 Fifth Ave. (975-0250). *Ashanti,* 872 Lexington Ave. (535-0740), specializes in stylish clothes for larger women. *Loehmann's,* 19 Duryea Pl., off Flatbush Ave. in Brooklyn (718 469-9800), and 9 W Fordham Rd. (near Jerome Ave.) in the Bronx (295-4100), carries some of the best bargains in women's clothing found anywhere. You can get designer goods, with the labels removed, at 25% to 50% off the retail price.

Indoor urban malls are a new phenomenon in New York City; they first arrived in 1984 with the glitzy *Trump Tower,* 725 5th Ave. between 56th and 57th sts. The tenants in the tower's six-story marble and mirrored atrium are among the world's most opulent (and most expensive) vendors: *Harry Winston's Petit Salon, Asprey's, Boehm Porcelain, Buccellati* (silversmiths), *Charles Jourdan* (men's and women's shoes), *Martha* and *Lina Lee* (both for women's fashions), *Loewe* (leather goods), *Pineider* (stationery and fine writing implements), and *Norman Crider Antiques.*

On the other side of town, *Herald Center,* opened in 1985, spans the block between W 33rd and 34th sts. on 7th Ave.; about 70 retail and restaurant outlets are in operation. The directory is a bit less exclusive than Trump Tower's, but many prestigious names are in residence, such as *Ann Taylor, Alfred Dunhill,* and *Charles Jourdan.*

Department Stores – *Macy's,* Broadway at 34th St. (695-4400), is the quintessential New York department store. You can buy what you need and choose from a large assortment of high-quality, stylish goods, but most people come here for the total experience of shopping — browsing, watching, and buying. Macy's basement emporium, The Cellar, is designed as a street lined with shops, which carry everything from fruits and vegetables to housewares, and restaurants, including the *Cellar Grill*, which serves a variety of pizza, pasta, and grilled meats. *B. Altman*, at 5th Ave. and 34th St. (679-7800), has a good selection of women's and men's clothing and housewares. *Lord & Taylor*, 5th Ave. and 39th St. (391-3344), has stylish, rather conservative clothing and a bright, airy atmosphere that makes browsing enjoyable. *Saks Fifth Avenue*, 5th Ave. and 49th St. (753-4000), is where you can be sure to get whatever is chic this season. *Bonwit Teller*, 10 E 57th St. (593-3333), seems to be a cross between *Lord & Taylor* and *Saks*. *Bergdorf Goodman*, 5th Ave. and 57th St. (753-7300), is the epitome of elegant shopping. In some haute couture salons, you sit in a parlor overlooking Central Park while salespeople bring merchandise for you to examine, then escort you to the fitting room. *Henri Bendel*, 10 W 57th St. (247-1100), carries an impressive selection of trendy clothes. *Alexander's*, 731 Lexington Ave. at 58th St. (593-0880), carries medium-quality goods, though you can find some excellent buys there during its numerous sales and markdowns. *Abraham and Strauss*, 420 Fulton St. in downtown Brooklyn (718 875-7200), carries a complete stock of moderately priced goods.

Jewelry and Gems – Diamonds are a girl's best friend, they say, and so as not to limit ourselves, we'll include emeralds, rubies, sapphires, gold, silver, and other precious metals. And so as not to discriminate, we'll include men, too. Without a doubt, the most famous of all luxury emporiums is *Tiffany & Co.*, 727 5th Ave. at 57th St. (755-8000). If you must have something from Tiffany's but can't afford a necklace or ring, you can purchase a novelty like a silver bookmark or toothpaste roller. Across the street, *Harry Winston*, 718 5th Ave. at 56th St. (245-2000), has display cases, but most of the jewels are kept in an inner sanctum. After conferring with a salesperson, the items you wish to see are brought for your inspection. *Cartier*, at 5th Ave. and 52nd St. (753-0111), is renowned for highly polished silver and some of the world's finest jewelry and accessories. For bold Brazilian jewelry, stop in at *H. Stern*, 645 5th Ave. at 51st St. (688-0300). For splendid glass sculpture, bowls, trays, and goblets, go to *Steuben Glass*, 5th Ave. and 56th St. (752-1441). And for the ultimate in European style and craftsmanship, there's no jeweler who exceeds the talent of *Bulgari*, 795 5th Ave. at 61st St. (486-0086). Known for quality and quantity in pearls is *Mikimoto*, 608 5th Ave. (586-7153).

If your budget is limited, you may want to do your gem shopping along 47th Street between 5th and 6th avenues. That's the heart of New York's wholesale jewelry district and the best place to find sparkling stuff at mortal prices. *Colon's* (27 W 47th St.) is an especially worthwhile stop for quality and fair prices; and if you're planning to get married (or even reaffirm your vows), *Bill Schifrin* (Booth 86 at the National Jewelers Exchange, 4 W 47th St.) is a good place to stop; it has the largest collection of wedding rings in the world.

Kitchen Equipment – The Bowery is New York's kitchenware and lamp district, where large wholesale houses such as the *Federal Restaurant and Supply Company*, 202 Bowery St. (226-0441), offer some commercial products at very reasonable prices. At *Professional Kitchens*, 932 Broadway, 2nd floor, between 21st and 22nd sts. (254-9000), a retail outlet for commercial cooking supply companies, you will find a good, complete selection of kitchen equipment. *The Bridge Company*, 214 E 52nd St. (688-4220), has four floors of kitchenware. You can find every possible domestic and imported item here, from cherry pitters to egg slicers. Selecting a single pot or pan could occupy several hours or a full day, given the number and variety on display.

Knickknacks – *Jenny B. Goode*, 1194 Lexington Ave. at 81st St. (794-2492), sells amusing nostalgia and contemporary adaptations (soft-sculpture, penny candy, mugs with gorgeous gam handles, radios disguised as giant Oreo cookies) that are a serendipitous delight. *Mythology*, 370 Columbus Ave. (874-0774), has a wonderful selection of antique toys, modern robots, rubber stamps with hundreds of designs, and plastic food that looks good enough to eat. *The Belle Epoch*, 211 E 60th St. (319-7870), has very interesting tabletop antiques as well as a lovely collection of antique jewelry. *Mixing Times,* 2403 Broadway (595-1505), offers contemporary reproductions of Tiffany lamps, Art Deco jewelry, and collectibles of various periods.

Round the world in a unique way with a trip to *The United Nations Souvenir Shop,* UN Bldg., 1st Ave. at 47th St. (754-7702), featuring handicrafts, ethnic clothing, native jewelry, indigenous toys — lots of beautiful things from every UN nation.

Luggage and Leather Goods – You'll have no trouble finding a wide selection of high- and low-priced luggage and leather goods in New York. *Hermès,* 11 E 57th St. (751-3181), is known the world over for spectacular silk scarves and ties, saddles and other fine leather goods in a variety of exotic skins, all at heart-stopping prices. *Louis Vuitton,* 51 E 57th St. (371-6111), has a large selection of leather goods (made in France) sporting the famous "LV" logo. However, if you prefer interlocking "G"s, visit *Gucci,* 685 and 689 Fifth Ave. (826-2600). For elegant, high-quality merchandise that's only slightly less pricey, try *Crouch & Fitzgerald,* 400 Madison Ave. (755-5888), *Mark Cross,* 645 5th Ave. (421-3000), or *T. Anthony,* 480 Park Ave. (750-9797). Along less expensive lines, you will run into several reasonable leather goods and luggage stores during your strolls around the East and West Sides and the Lower East Side.

Men's Clothes – Manhattan has fashions to fit every man's taste, from the ultra-expensive chic at *Bijan* (by appointment only), 5th Ave. between 54th and 55th sts. (758-7500), to *Billy Martin's Western Wear,* Madison Ave. at 75th St. (861-3100), to the discounted conservative styles at *Merns Mart,* 75 Church St. (227-5471). *Brooks Brothers,* 346 Madison Ave. (682-8800) and 1 Liberty Plaza downtown (682-8595), *J. Press,* 16 E 44th St. (687-0850), and *F. R. Tripler,* Madison Ave. at 46th St. (922-1090), all offer expensive, high-quality conservative business suits and other classic menswear; *Burton Clothing,* 14 E 41st St. (685-3760), and *St. Laurie,* 897 Broadway (473-0100), carry similar merchandise with slightly lower price tags. *Paul Stuart,* Madison Ave. at 45th St. (682-0320), offers an expensive but less strictly traditional collection of top-quality clothing, while *Barney's,* 111 7th Ave. at 17th St. (929-9000), has an eclectic array of goods that ranges from Hickey Freeman to Bill Blass to the top European designers. For Italian *alta moda* in SoHo, try *Di Mitri,* 110 Greene St. (431-1090).

Poster and Print Shops – *The Old Print Shop,* 150 Lexington Ave. at 29th St. (683-3950), has a huge collection of early American prints, watercolors, and paintings ranging in price from $10 to $20,000. For contemporary theater posters and some collector's items, try the *Triton Gallery,* 323 W 45th St., between 8th and 9th aves. (765-2472). Rare movie posters are available at *Yesterday,* 174A Ninth Ave. (206-0499).

Records – There are a number of places where you can get good prices on records. *Sam Goody's,* at 235 W 49th St. (246-1708) and branches throughout the city, stocks new labels, classical, jazz, and foreign music as well as audio equipment. Two chain stores, *King Karol* and *Disco-Mat,* carry a lot of labels at prices lower than standard retail stores. Disco-Mat's main store is at 716 Lexington Ave. at 58th St. (759-3777). King Karol's main store is at 126 W 42nd St. (354-6880). *Tower Records,* at Broadway and 4th St., is the world's largest record store and is open until midnight every day of the year; there's also a branch uptown at Broadway and 66th St. *J & R Music World* at 33 Park Row (349-0062) has the best selection of new and hard-to-find jazz records at good prices. *House of Oldies* at 35 Carmine St. (243-0500) specializes in discs from the past. *Gryphon Record Shop,* 606 Amsterdam Ave. (874-1588), has 40,000 out-of-print records.

Sheets and Pillowcases – For good buys on top-brand and designer sheets and pillowcases, New York is definitely the place. At *Ezra Cohen,* 307 Grand (925-7800), *H & G Cohen Bedding Co.,* 306 Grand St. (226-0818), and *J. Shachter,* 115 Allen St. (533-1150), you can find all the major brands at a 25% to 30% discount. J. Shachter also specializes in custom comforters that can be made from any fabric you wish. (All are closed Saturdays and open Sundays; typical of the stores on the Lower East Side).

Shoes – All of the expensive, top shoe designers are represented: *Ferragamo*, 730 5th Ave. at 57th St. (246-6211), for men, and 717 5th Ave. at 56th St. (759-3822), for women; *Bally of Switzerland*, 711 5th Ave. between 55th and 56th sts. (751-9082) and at three other Manhattan locations, for men and 689 Madison Ave. at 62nd St. (751-2163), for women; *Bruno Magli*, 681 5th Ave. (355-3280), for men only; *Charles Jourdan*, 725 5th Ave. in Trump Tower (644-3830) and 769 Madison Ave. at 66th St. (628-0133); *Carrano*, 677 5th Ave. (752-6111), and at two other Manhattan locations; and *Maud Frizon*, 49 E 57th St. (980-1460). For a few brands of imported women's shoes under one roof, visit *I. Miller*, which also has its own label, on 5th Ave. at 57th St. (581-0062). For well-made men's boots and shoes, stock up at *McCreedy and Schreiber* at 37 W 46th St. (719-1552) or 213 E 59th St. (759-9241). *Designer Shoes*, 150 W 26th St. (675-1550), has a wide selection of women's shoes at discount prices.

Special Shopping Districts – The ultimate shopping experience is on the *Lower East Side* of Manhattan, if you're up to it. Along Orchard Street, Delancey Street, and all the side streets, you'll find incredible bargains in all manner of clothing, housewares, foam padding; but finding them is only half the battle. Then you have to fight for them, and the haggling begins. The merchant says something along the lines of, "I couldn't give you this for a penny less than $12," to which you respond that it's not worth more than 50¢, and usually you come to terms, apparently unsatisfactory to both of you. A lot of the selling is done in a mixture of Yiddish, English, and Spanish — particularly the counting — and if you know any or all three, you'll do better than wholesale. See *Special Places* for more on the Lower East Side.

Sporting Goods – The most elegant sporting goods store is *Abercrombie & Fitch* at South Street Seaport (809-9000); another branch was scheduled to open in Trump Tower late in 1986. *Herman's*, New York's best-known sporting goods chain, has everything, but *Paragon* says it has more. At either one, you can find just about every piece of sporting gear and wear under the sun. *Herman's* stores are at 110 Nassau (233-0733), 135 W 42nd St. (730-7400), 39 W 34th St. (279-8900), and 845 3rd Ave. (688-4603). *Paragon* is at 867 Broadway at 18th St. (255-8036).

Thrift Stores – Most thrift stores carry a variety of merchandise, from men's and women's clothing to household items and appliances to furniture. The best area for thrifting in New York is the Upper East Eighties along 1st, 2nd, and 3rd aves. Unfortunately, many of the secondhand clothes stores in New York carry the price tags of fine antique stores. Some interesting places to try are *Stuyvesant Square Thrift Shop*, 1704 2nd Ave. (831-1830); *Irvington House Thrift Shop*, 1534 2nd Ave. (879-4555); *Thrift Shop East*, 1430 3rd Ave., (744-5429); and *Spence-Chapin Corner Shop*, 1424 3rd Ave. (737-8448).

Toys – Once immersed in the enchanting world of children's toys at *FAO Schwarz*, GM Bldg., 5th Ave. and 58th St. (644-9400), adults have as difficult a time as children leaving empty-handed. They have every kind of toy — from precious antiques and mechanical space ships to simple construction sets and building blocks. The prices are very high. *Penny Whistle Toys*, at 1283 Madison Ave. (369-3868) and 448 Columbus Ave. (873-9090), and *Dolls and Dreams*, 1421 Lexington Ave. (876-2434), also have quality merchandise. Teachers as well as parents favor *Childcraft's* two stores — 155 E 23rd St. (674-4754) and 150 E 58th St. (753-3196) — for educational toys, games, and crafts, many of which, including the anatomically correct dolls, are made in Europe and are unique in the US.

Trendy Gear – There are several large outlets in New York for the stylish military attire that has put practical army surplus clothes and gear on the fashion pages. The best stores for work shirts, pea jackets, navy pants, jeans, combat boots, and other surplus attire, which have the unique combination of being both "in" and inexpensive, are *I. Buss,* 738 Broadway (242-3338); *Parachute,* 121 Wooster St. (925-8630); *Unique Clothing Warehouse,* 718 and 726 Broadway (674-1767), and *Hudson's,* 97 3rd Ave. at 13th St. (473-7320).

Uniquely New York – Probably nowhere else on earth could you find everything from earplugs to fine silver under one roof. *Hammacher Schlemmer,* 147 E 57th St., between 3rd Ave. and Lexington (421-9000), has it all. And what they don't have, whether it's a chotchka or a real white elephant, they'll try to order.

47th St. Photo, 67 W 47th St. (260-4410), is a bare-bones bargain center for cameras, computers, and other electronic gear with excellent discounts and a huge selection (some 5,000 items in stock). The tiny 2nd-floor headquarters as well as its branches, at 115 W 45th St. and 116 Nassau St., tend to be chaotic with customers. Closed Friday afternoons and Saturdays; open Sundays.

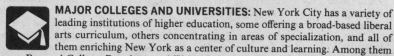 **MAJOR COLLEGES AND UNIVERSITIES:** New York City has a variety of leading institutions of higher education, some offering a broad-based liberal arts curriculum, others concentrating in areas of specialization, and all of them enriching New York as a center of culture and learning. Among them are: Barnard College, Broadway and W 116th St. (280-5262); the City College of City University, Convent Ave. and W 138th St. (690-6741); Columbia University, Broadway and W 116th St. (280-1754); Cooper Union, 3rd Ave. and 7th St. (254-6300); Fordham University, Columbus Ave. and 60th St. (841-5100), and at E Fordham Rd. and 3rd Ave., Bronx (579-2000); Hunter College, 695 Park Ave. (772-4000); Jewish Theological Seminary of America, Broadway and W 122nd St. (678-8000); Juilliard School of Music, Lincoln Center Plaza (799-5000); Mannes College of Music, 150 W 85th St. (580-0210); New School for Social Research, 66 W 12th St. (741-5600); New York University, Washington Sq. (598-1212); Parsons School of Design, 5th Ave. and 12th St. (741-8900); Pratt Institute, 200 Willoughby Ave., Brooklyn (718 636-3600); Queens College, 65–30 Kissena Blvd., Queens (718 520-7000); Union Theological Seminary, 3041 Broadway at Reinhold Niebuhr Pl. (W 123rd St.; 662-7100); Yeshiva University, Amsterdam Ave. and W 186th St. (960-5400).

 SPECIAL EVENTS: January-February, *Chinese New Year Celebration and Dragon Parade,* Chinatown; January, *National Boat Show,* Javits Convention Center; March 17, *St. Patrick's Day Parade,* 5th Ave.; May, *Ninth Avenue International Festival;* May and September, *Greenwich Village Outdoor Art Show,* Washington Square; first Sunday in June, *Puerto Rican Day Parade,* 5th Ave.; June, *JVC Jazz Festival,* throughout city; June-August, *Miller Music on the Pier,* Pier 84; July-August, free *Shakespeare Festival,* Delacorte Theater, Central Park; free performances, *NY Philharmonic, Metropolitan Opera,* all boroughs; late August-September, *US Open Tennis Championships,* USTA National Tennis Center, Queens; September, the ten-day *Festival of San Gennaro,* patron saint of the Neapolitans, Mulberry St. Little Italy; September-October, New York Film Festival, Lincoln Center; October, *Columbus Day Parade,* 5th Ave.; late October, *NYC Marathon;* early November, *Horse Show,* Madison Square Garden; *Macy's Thanksgiving Day Parade,* Broadway, Herald Square; December, *Christmas Tree Lighting,* Rockefeller Plaza; November-January, *The Great Christmas Show,* Radio City Music Hall.

 SPORTS AND FITNESS: New York is a sports-minded city, offering a great variety of spectator and participatory activities. It is the home of the *Yankees* and *Mets, Jets* and *Giants* (though the latter two now play in New Jersey), *Rangers* and racetracks, and countless tennis players, swimmers, bikers, runners, joggers, and walkers, to name but a few of the major activities.

Baseball – The season, April through early October, features the *Mets* (National League) at Shea Stadium, Flushing, Queens (718 507-8499), and the *Yankees* (American League) at Yankee Stadium, Bronx (293-6000). Tickets are usually available at the many Ticketron outlets throughout the city (central ticket information, 977-9020).

Basketball – The area features the *Knicks*, playing at Madison Square Garden (564-4400), and the *Nets*, whose home is the Brendan Byrne Arena at the Meadowlands Sports Complex in East Rutherford, New Jersey, during the regular season from late October to early April (201 935-8888, for ticket and schedule information).

Bicycling – There are over 50 miles of bike paths in the city, with Central Park in Manhattan and Prospect Park in Brooklyn the two most popular areas. Most roadways within the parks are closed to traffic from May through October, except in rush hour on weekdays. They are closed on weekends year-round. Bikes can be rented in the parks or on nearby side streets.

Billiards and Bowling – Extremely popular with many New Yorkers. Pool halls and bowling alleys are plentiful throughout the city. Consult the yellow pages for the location most convenient to you.

Boxing – Major bouts are still fought at Madison Square Garden (564-4400), and the *Daily News* continues to sponsor the Golden Gloves competition every winter.

Fitness Centers – The Rivereast Health Club offers classes, a pool, whirlpool, saunas, and exercise equipment, 614 2nd Ave. at 34th St. (689-4043). On the West Side, the Hudson Health Club, in the *Henry Hudson Hotel*, has a pool, track, steam room, gym, and yoga and other classes, 353 W 57th St. near 9th Ave. (265-6100).

Football – During the September–December season, the *Jets* and the *Giants* play at Giant's Stadium at the Meadowlands Sports Complex in East Rutherford, New Jersey (about 6 miles from midtown). Tickets to any of the NFL games are hard to get due to the great number of season subscribers. For Giants ticket information, call 201 935-8222; for Jets tickets, call 201 421-6600. The USFL New Jersey *Generals* also play at Giants Stadium at the Meadowlands. Columbia University leads the collegiate football scene, with its games played at Baker Field (280-2541).

Golf – For up-to-date information on current golf tournaments, call the Metropolitan Golf Assn. (914 698-0390). The Dept. of Parks press office (360-8141) can provide a complete list of public courses and how to get on them.

Handball – Try Central Park's courts, north of the 97th St. transverse.

Hockey – Tickets are expensive and scarce during the early October to early April season, featuring the *Islanders*, at the Nassau Coliseum (516 794-9100), and the *Rangers*, Madison Square Garden (564-4400). The New Jersey *Devils* play across the Hudson at the Brendan Byrne Arena (201 935-3900).

Horseback Riding – Horses can be rented and boarded at the Claremont Riding Academy, 175 W 89th St. (724-5100). There are almost 50 miles of bridal paths in the city, most in Central Park.

Horse Racing – Harness racing is at Yonkers Raceway, in lower Westchester County, nightly except Sundays (562-9500), and at Roosevelt Raceway in Westbury, Long Island (718 357-3838). The Meadowlands, East Rutherford, New Jersey (201 935-8500), has both harness and flat racing nightly, except Sundays. Thoroughbreds also run during the day at Aqueduct Race Track in Queens (641-4700), or Belmont Park Race Track in Elmont, Long Island (641-4700). Aqueduct and Belmont are closed Tuesdays. Both racetracks have separate seasons; they are never open at the same time.

Jogging – Undoubtedly the most popular sport in New York, with enthusiastic runners in all the city parks; paths at Riverside Park, near W 97th St., around the Central Park Reservoir, 85th St., and the promenade along the East River, between E 84th and 90th sts.

Ice Skating – From October to April, you can show off your figure eights at the famous Rockefeller Center rink (757-5731); the new Rivergate Ice Rink, 401 E 34 St.

(689-0035); and from mid-November to mid-February at Lasker Rink, Central Park (397-3142). (The Parks Dept. operates a shuttle bus to Lasker from the 59th Street entrance of the park; call 360-8141.) For indoor skating year-round, try Skyrink, 450 W 33rd (695-6555).

Swimming – Several dozen indoor and outdoor pools are operated by the Parks Dept. Indoor pools are open most of the year, except Sundays and holidays, and usually until 10 PM weekdays. Call the Parks Dept. press office (360-8141) for particulars. Check the yellow pages for pools at the YMCA and YMHA.

Ocean swimming is a subway or bus ride away. Jones Beach State Park, Wantagh, Long Island, 30 miles outside the city, is the most popular. It is a beautifully maintained, enormous stretch of sandy beach, and includes surf bathing, swimming and wading pools, lockers, fishing, outdoor skating rinks, paddleball, swimming instruction, restaurants, and day- and nighttime entertainment. Beaches maintained by the city are Orchard Beach in the Bronx; Coney Island Beach and Manhattan Beach, Brooklyn; and Riis Park and Rockaway Beaches in Queens.

Tennis – Courts maintained by the Parks Dept. require a season permit. One of the larger privately owned clubs that will rent by the hour is the Midtown Tennis Club, 341 8th Ave. (989-8572). Check the yellow pages for other locations.

THEATER: There are devoted New York theatergoers who wouldn't dream of stepping inside a Broadway theater. They prefer instead the city's prolific off-Broadway and off-off-Broadway circuit, productions less high-powered but no less professional than the splashiest shows on Broadway. On the other hand, there are theater mavens who've never seen a performance more than three blocks from Times Square and who can remember every detail of the opening night of *My Fair Lady.* If their reminiscences don't have you running to the nearest box office for front-row seats to the season's biggest hit, you are made of stone.

Broadway signifies an area — New York's premier theater district, the blocks between Broadway and 9th Avenue running north of Times Square from 42nd Street — and a kind of production — the "big show" that strives to be the smash hit of the season and run forever. The glitter of the area has turned a bit tacky since the halcyon days of the Great White Way, but a renovation of the area is in the planning stage and may eventually turn things around. In any case, the productions remain as stellar as ever.

Off-Broadway and off-off-Broadway signify types of theater (playhouses producing shows that qualify as off-Broadway are strewn from the Lower Village to the Upper West Side) that have developed in response to the phenomenon of Broadway. Off-Broadway productions are smaller in scale, with newer, lesser-known talent, and are likely to feature revivals of classics or more daring works than those on Broadway. Off-off-Broadway is more experimental still, featuring truly avant-garde productions with performances in coffee houses, lofts, or any appropriate makeshift arena. Off-Broadway often costs half of the price of a Broadway ticket, and the price of a seat in an off-off-Broadway is usually even less.

You should take advantage of all three during a visit. The excitement of a Broadway show is incomparable, but the thrill of finding a tiny theater in Soho or the West Village in which you are almost nose to nose with the actors is undeniable. Planning your theater schedule is as easy as consulting any of the daily papers (they all list theaters and current offerings daily, with comprehensive listings on Fridays or Saturdays) or looking in the "Goings On About Town" column in *The New Yorker* or "Cue" Theater Guide in *New York* magazine, which lists current theater fare under headings of "Broadway," "Off-Broadway," and "Off-Off-Broadway."

Broadway tickets can be quite expensive (they average $15 to $47, depending on where you sit and when you go), but that needn't be a deterrent to seeing as many shows as you would like. The TKTS stands, 47th St. at Broadway in Times Square and 2

World Trade Center in lower Manhattan (354-5800), sell tickets at half price, plus a service charge of a dollar or two, for a wide range of Broadway and off-Broadway productions; tickets are sold on the day of performance after 3 PM for evening shows, after noon for matinees. You must line up for the tickets; there are no reservations.

Theater Companies – *Circle Rep,* 99 7th Ave. South (924-7100); *Manhattan Theatre Club,* at the Space at City Center, 131 W 55th St. (246-8989); *The Public,* 425 Lafayette St. (598-7150); *La Mama ETC,* 74A E 4th St. (475-7710); *Jean Cocteau Repertory,* 330 Bowery (677-0060); *Ridiculous Theatrical Company,* 1 Sheridan Sq. (691-2271); and *Roundabout,* 100 E 17th St. (420-1360 or 420-1883). All can provide a schedule of offerings and performance dates.

 MUSIC: New York is a world center for performing artists. It presents the best of classical and nonclassical traditions from all over the world, in a variety of halls and auditoriums, filled with appreciative, knowledgeable audiences.

Lincoln Center for the Performing Arts, completed in 1969, represents the city's devotion to concerts, opera, and ballet, and is on Broadway and 65th St. (general information, 877-1800). It consists of: *Avery Fisher Hall,* home of the *NY Philharmonic* (874-2424); *NY State Theater,* featuring the *NY City Ballet* and *NY City Opera* (870-5570); *Metropolitan Opera House,* for the opera and the *American Ballet Theatre* (362-6000); *Damrosch Bandshell,* an open-air theater used for free concerts; the *Juilliard School* for musicians, actors, and dancers (799-5000); and *Alice Tully Hall,* home of the Chamber Music Society (362-1911). In addition, all the auditoriums in Lincoln Center present other musical events and recitals. While in the area, visit the *NY Public Library at Lincoln Center,* a unique library and museum of the performing arts (870-1630). Guided tours of Lincoln Center are available daily (877-1800).

Other major halls are: *Carnegie Hall,* 57th St. and 7th Ave. (247-7800); *City Center,* 131 W 55th St. (246-8989); *Symphony Space,* Broadway at 95th St. (864-5400); *Kaufmann Auditorium,* 92nd St. and Lexington Ave. (427-4410); *Grace Rainey Rogers Auditorium,* 5th Ave. and 82nd St. (570-3949), in the Metropolitan Museum; and *Brooklyn Academy of Music,* 30 Lafayette Ave. (718 636-4100). Also check music and dance listings in the newspapers and *New York* and *The New Yorker* magazines. The TKTS booth in Times Square, which sells discount theater tickets, now has a counterpart on W 42nd Street for those interested in buying half-price tickets to music and dance events on the day of the performance. The booth, open daily from noon to 7 PM, is on the 42nd Street side of Bryant Park, just behind the New York Public Library, between 5th Ave. and Ave. of the Americas (382-2323).

 NIGHTCLUBS AND NIGHTLIFE: The scope of nightlife in New York is as vast as the scope of daily life. Cultural trends strongly affect the kinds of clubs that are "in" at any given time and their popularity has a tendency to peak, then plunge rather quickly. Old jazz and neighborhood clubs, on the other hand, remain intact, catering to a regular local clientele. They offer various kinds of entertainment, and many stay open until the wee hours of the morning serving drinks and food. It is a good idea to call all the clubs in advance to find out when they are open and what shows or acts they are offering; or consult the "Cue" listings in *New York* magazine. Many of the city's nightclubs with live entertainment and/or dancing have cover charges of about $15.

The current focus of the trendy crowd is on clubs that offer rock and contemporary or new wave music with some disco mixed in as well. In addition to their lavish stereo systems, many of these clubs also feature videos, live bands, a few bars, and lots of room for dancing. Most popular are: *The Ritz,* 119 E 11th St. (228-8888); *Heartbreak,* 179 Varick St. (691-2388); *The Cat Club,* 76 E 13th St. (505-0090); *Limelight,* 660 6th Ave. (807-7850); *Area,* 157 Hudson St. (226-8423), which is completely redecorated according to its new theme every six weeks; and dance palace extraordinaire, *The Palladium,* 126 E 14th St. (473-7171).

For everything from swing to disco, try the *Red Parrot,* 617 W 57th St. at 12th Ave. (247-1530), with its own 20-piece orchestra.

Among the nightclubs with food and drink that feature live music — including rock, soul, rhythm and blues, reggae, jazz and top 40 music — *Sweetwaters,* 170 Amsterdam Ave. (873-4100); and *Mikell's,* 760 Columbus Ave. (864-8832). You can eat, dance to, and hear country-style music and bluegrass at *O'Lunney's Steak House,* 915 2nd Ave. (751-5470). *The Bitter End,* 147 Bleecker St. (673-7030), and *The Bottom Line,* 15 W 4th St. (228-7880), often offer traditional blues and jazz. Country music notables entertain, and are entertained, at the *Lone Star Cafe,* 61 5th Ave. (242-1664), when they come to New York. The *Eagle Tavern,* 355 W 14th St. (924-0275), is good for country, bluegrass, and Irish music.

Even though discos are no longer the city's hottest spots, there are still a fair number of chic places where it's offered, such as *Regine's,* 502 Park Ave. (826-0990). The famous Brooklyn hangout where the movie *Saturday Night Fever* was filmed, *2001 Odyssey,* 802 64th St. (718 238-8213), still draws a crowd. For dancing to a Latin beat, try the *Sounds of Brazil (S.O.B.)* supper club, 204 Varick St. (243-4940). If you prefer disco on wheels, try *The Roxy,* 515 W 18th St., between 10th and 11th aves. (675-8300), Sundays through Wednesdays (Thursdays through Saturdays are reserved for dancers), or *Empire Roller Disco,* 200 Empire Blvd., Brooklyn (718 462-1570). As for good, clean traditional ballroom fun with American and Latin live dance music, the famous *Roseland Dance City,* 239 W 52nd St. (247-0200), definitely deserves a whirl — it holds up to 4,000 dancers.

For a low-key, elegant evening of dancing to live music, a good show and dinner, try *Jimmy Weston's,* 131 E 54th St. (838-8384) or *Freddy's Supper Club,* 308 E 49th St. (888-1633). The *Rainbow Room,* 30 Rockefeller Plaza (757-9090), also has good cheek-to-cheek dancing music and dazzling views of the city from the 65th floor of the RCA Building. The adjacent *Rainbow Grill* (757-8970) also has a dance floor and an entertaining musical revue.

Among the small, intimate supper clubs with good food, a nice, informal atmosphere, and low-key, quality entertainment, we recommend the *Café Carlyle,* in the *Carlyle Hotel,* 35 E 76th St. (744-1600). Lively, casual "showcase" clubs, where singers, comedians, and performers of all kinds test their new material on reliably loud but not always appreciative audiences, include *Caroline's,* 332 8th Ave. (924-3499), *The Improvisation,* 358 W 44th St. (765-8268), and *Catch a Rising Star,* 1487 1st Ave. (794-1906). *The Magic Towne House,* 1026 3rd Ave. (308-2733), is a unique weekend spot where you can catch some good magic acts.

The largest concentration of singles bars in New York can be found on 1st and 2nd (some on 3rd) avenues, between 61st and 80th streets. If you walk along either one of these you will probably find a likely looking place. Be sure to check out the *Adam's Apple,* 1117 1st Ave. (371-8650); *Maxwell's Plum,* 1181 1st Ave. (628-2102); *T.G.I. Friday's,* 1152 1st Ave. (832-8512); and *Septembers,* 1442 1st Ave. (861-4670). If you like sitting around a piano, listening to, requesting, and even singing your favorite tunes, *The Village Green,* 531 Hudson St. (255-1650), *Knickerbocker Saloon,* 33 University Pl. (228-8490), and *Oliver's Restaurant,* 141 E 57th St. (753-9180), can fill the bill as well as satisfy your appetite.

The Village Vanguard, 178 7th Ave. S (255-4037), *The Village Gate,* Bleecker and Thompson sts. (475-5120), *Sweet Basil,* 88 7th Ave. S (242-1785), *Lush Life,* 184 Thompson St. (228-3788), *The Blue Note,* 131 W 3rd St. (475-8592), and *Seventh Ave. South,* 21 7th Ave. S (242-4694), feature top jazz artists. Some of the more casual, neighborhood-type jazz clubs with reasonable prices and a relaxed atmosphere are *Arthur's Tavern,* 57 Grove St. (242-9468); *The Angry Squire,* 216 7th Ave. (242-9066); *Bradley's,* 70 University Pl. (228-6440); *The West End Jazz Room,* 2911 Broadway

(666-8750). For nostalgia and more traditional jazz sounds, try *Fat Tuesday's*, 190 3rd Ave. (533-7902), or *Michael's Pub*, 211 E 55th St. (758-2272).

Cabarets and floor shows have been making something of a comeback. *Cafe Versailles*, 151 E 50th St. (753-3884), is the place for gorgeous showgirls and flashy production numbers, while popular comedy revues are featured at *Palsson's*, 158 W 72nd St. (595-7400). *Chippendales*, 1110 1st Ave. at 61st St. (935-6060), offers all-male strip shows "for women only" Wednesdays through Saturday nights.

Gay bars are scattered throughout New York, but the Upper West Side, in the Seventies, and Christopher Street in the West Village distinguish themselves as gay areas. Christopher Street, especially, is noted for its cruising bars.

 SINS: New York is a city of vast extremes, with an opulence equal to any metropolis in the world and poverty harsh enough to force people to live in steam tunnels, bombed-out shells of old cars, doorways, and on park benches. One might expect *anger* to seethe throughout this urban madland, but while it's not uncommon to see people walking down the street talking fiercely to themselves, a much more violent response can be raised by visitors who blithely announce, "It's a great place to visit, but I wouldn't want to live here."

For all their normally frenetic pace, New Yorkers can be seen at their *slothful* best at lunchtime in Central Park or in such vest-pocket enclaves as Paley Park (between Madison and 5th avenues on 53rd Street).

New York fairly boils over with *lust*, mostly of a very unattractive variety. The 42nd Street–Times Square area, extending up 8th Avenue as far as 50th Street, is slowly being cleaned up but still includes both homosexual and straight pornographic establishments, including peep shows, strip shows, massage parlors, and street women. Pornographic cinemas dot the city, with conglomerations around the Times Square area and Penn Station. Be forewarned: Street prostitutes in New York are among the most dangerous in the world, and muggings and robbery are a frequent by-product of an encounter with one of them.

New York could well be called the *gluttony* capital of the world. Ice cream freaks craving banana splits, sundaes, floats, or frosteds should head for *Agora's* (corner of E 87th and 3rd Ave.), *Serendipity 3* (225 E 60th St.), or *Swensen's Ice Cream Factory* (1246 2nd Ave. and 14 W 4th St.). Pessimists can satisfy their gloomy perspectives as well as their appetites by dropping into *Mary Elizabeth's* (E 37th between 5th and Madison) and asking for the most delicious doughnut holes ever baked. And for cheesecake fanciers, New York's creamiest is in Brooklyn at *Junior's* (386 Flatbush Ave. at DeKalb).

You'll have all you can do to keep your *envy, avarice,* and consummate *greed* in check as you romp through such palaces of the privileged as *Gucci, Cartier,* and *Tiffany's*. It is scant comfort to know these are but three of the nonpareil shops that will stir your basest instincts.

And when it comes to *pride,* New York chauvinism is rivaled only by the amount of criticism the city takes. From Yankee Stadium to the World Trade Center, you will hear again and again that New York has the best of everything — restaurants, museums, shopping, art, theater, music and dance, career opportunities — and the most interesting cross section of American culture in the country.

LOCAL SERVICES: Babysitting – Ask at the hotel desk for recommended babysitting services.

Business Services – A Steno Service (682-4990) and Ann H. Tanners Co. (687-2870) for secretarial services; Rainbow Enterprises (764-6070), for taping and immediate transcription of meetings and seminars; and Video Monitoring Service (736-2010), for taping television appearances

Limousine Service – London Town Cars (988-9700)

Mechanics – 24-hour road service and minor repairs: Executive Towing, 510 W 36th St. (947-5610)

BEST IN TOWN

 CHECKING IN: New York City is still one of the hardest places in the world to find an empty hotel room between Sunday and Thursday nights, and a rash of new properties have opened up to alleviate the problem. However, don't expect this increased supply to offset inflation's upward push on room rates in the foreseeable future. Do expect to pay $175 or more — often lots more — for a very expensive room for two in Manhattan; $120 to $160 for an expensive one; $85 to $120 for a moderately priced room; and $85 or less for an inexpensive one. These prices include no meals. *Note:* Many of these hotels offer special weekend packages for relatively low rates. The packages include a variety of amenities — from just a room to a room plus breakfast/dinner, champagne, theater tickets, and parking. Reservations are always required, so write or call for information well in advance.

An alternative to taking a standard hotel room is a new Bed & Breakfast plan run by Urban Ventures. Accommodations are in private homes, include a Continental breakfast, and cost from $28 to $60 per night. For a brochure, contact Urban Ventures, PO Box 426, New York, NY 10024 (212 594-5650). Another organization providing a somewhat similar service is The B&B Group (New Yorkers at Home), 301 E 60th St., New York, NY 10022 (212 838-7015).

Pierre – The most luxurious stopping place in midtown, with the most august clientele. The elegance is low key but consistent, and the rooms with a park view command the highest of already heady prices. Operated by the superb Four Seasons group on the most attractive corner of the city, it is *the* place to stay. 5th Ave. and 61st St. (212 838-8000 or 800 462-1150). Very expensive.

Regency – Where the movers and shakers of America now stay when they're in New York. More business is probably conducted in the dining room here at breakfast than in all of the rest of the country during a normal business day. Its modern architecture does not detract at all from its appeal, and a recent basement-to-roof restoration and refurbishing has only added to its luster. Park Ave. and 61st St. (212 759-4100). Very expensive.

Ritz-Carlton – Brought to you by the same people responsible for the *Tremont* and *Whitehall* hotels in Chicago and the *Fairfax* in Washington, D.C. The luxury touches here (in the shell of the old *Navarro*) are chintz and Chippendale in the rooms, Courvoisier and chocolates on the nightstand at bedtime, leather banquettes and firelight in the *Jockey Club* restaurant, and a park view for guests in front rooms. 112 Central Park South (212 757-1900 or 800 223-7990). Very expensive.

Carlyle – The leader among luxurious uptown hotels, where the Kennedy family traditionally stays. Noted for its quiet and serenity, with prices to match the high level of service. 35 E 76th St. (212 744-1600). Very expensive.

Plaza Athénée New York – Small and sumptuous, this is the new US edition of the celebrated *Plaza Athénée* in Paris. The management strives to look as unlike a hotel as possible and prides itself on personal attention to its guests. There are 160 rooms and 34 suites, all furnished with French antiques. 37 E 64th St. (212 734-9100 or 800 223-5672). Very expensive.

Westin Plaza – Eloise isn't romping in the halls anymore, but it's hardly an effort to "skipperdee" up to one of the rooms facing Central Park. Recent refurbishing has restored most of the old sparkle, and this is the first hotel NYC visitors think of when they imagine a luxurious urban hostelry. Erratic, but mostly elegant. 5th Ave. and 59th St. (212 759-3000 or 800 228-3000). Very expensive.

St. Regis – Right in the heart of the best New York shopping, it remains a favorite with international visitors. The *King Cole Bar* is a popular late-afternoon rendezvous, But the hotel operation still relies on a reputation that hasn't been accurate since the Sheraton folks took over. 5th Ave. and 55th St. (212 753-4500). Very expensive.

United Nations Plaza – Beautifully integrated modern design, from the sleek, green-tinted glass exterior through the dark green marble reception area to the top 10 floors. Subtly hued rooms provide magnificent city views. Both a truly international staff and exceptional facilities — including a tennis court, heated pool, and exercise room — are provided to pamper all guests. E 44th St. and 1st Ave. (212 355-3400). Very expensive.

Mayfair Regent – For those New York visitors who stay at the *Gritti* in Venice and the *Hotel du' Cap* in the south of France. There are just 150 suites, plus the nonpareil *Le Cirque* restaurant. Uncompromising elegance and superb service. Park Ave. at E 65th St. (212 288-0800). Very expensive.

Essex House – Since Nikko Hotels of Japan took over in mid-1985, this 40-story landmark overlooking Central Park has undergone a multimillion-dollar enhancement program and a distinct transformation in style. In addition, a new two-level lounge with conference center and special amenities for business travelers was opened on the 19th floor. 160 Central Park South (212 247-0300). Very expensive.

Lowell – Little expense has been spared in turning this once undistinguished property into an authentic gem, an Art Deco delight. The smallish rooms are perfect for a modestly proportioned king, and most have a working fireplace (a log costs $3.50). The overall feeling is one of being a guest in a very well bred New York town house — on what's arguably the most stylish block in Manhattan. 28 E 63rd St. (212 838-1400). Very expensive.

New York Marriott Marquis – A predictably pedestrian convention hotel designed by John C. Portman, this 50-story, 1,876-room addition to Times Square tries to make up for a lack of distinction in room design with a 37-floor open atrium that is long on glitz, short on class. *The View,* a three-tier rotating rooftop restaurant, overlooks the city, and the 8th-floor revolving lounge overlooks Broadway. 1535 Broadway (212 398-1900). Very expensive.

Helmsley Palace – The *Palace* combines the landmark Henry Villard houses with a 51-story high-rise and has beautifully restored, elegant public rooms decorated in marble, crystal, and gold as well as modern guest rooms. Guests must use the 50th Street side entrance for checking in, but thereafter enter through the wrought-iron gates on Madison Avenue. 455 Madison Ave. at 50th St. (212 888-7000 or 800 221-4982). Very expensive.

Grand Hyatt – You won't find more dazzle east of Broadway than at the *Hyatt.* Formerly the *Commodore,* it has been reincarnated with sleek modern lines, mirrored glass, and shiny chrome. The centerpiece of the multilevel lobby is the tiered, marble fountain crowned by a 77-foot bronze sculpture. On the lobby's upper level is the *Sungarden,* a glass-enclosed bar and cocktail lounge that overhangs the hotel's entrance and the busy 42nd Street traffic. The 1,400 smallish guest rooms are dressed in rich, earthy tones that are brightened daily with fresh flowers. 109 E 42nd St. (212 883-1234 or 800 228-9000). Very expensive.

Berkshire Place – Built in 1926, the old *Berkshire* hotel has been resuscitated with dash and considerable understated flair. Most impressive is the Atrium Lobby, a mirrored lounge accented with soft shades, creating a quite comfortable and intimate atmosphere. Gaining momentum on the culinary scene is the pretty

Rendez-vous Restaurant serving both classic French and nouvelle cuisine. 21 E 52nd St. (212 753-5800 or 800 228-2121). Very expensive.

Parker Meridien – Billing itself as New York's "first French hotel," this establishment provides guests with the elegance of a European hostelry. There are 600 luxurious rooms plus apartments, bars, and *Le Restaurant Maurice,* serving nouvelle cuisine. The sports-minded will enjoy Club Raquette for racquetball, handball, and squash, and the rooftop running track that encircles the enclosed pool where the views of Central Park are lovely. The hotel also has banquet and meeting facilities. 118 W 57th St. (212 245-5000). Very expensive.

Westbury – The tapestries at the entrance are Belgian; the soft pink carpeting in the marble lobby, Irish — as befits this tranquil, European-style hotel with its large international clientele. Completely redecorated over the past few years, the *Westbury* has retained its crystal chandeliers in the lobby and its brass doorknobs engraved with the hotel's address. Its *Polo Restaurant* serves nouvelle cuisine. 15 E 69th St. (212 535-2000 or 800 223-5672). Very expensive.

No. 1022 – There are only three suites and a studio in this elegant town house on the Upper East Side, but each is decorated as if it were part of a handsome residence. Two of the suites have large skylights and fireplaces, the other has its own terrace. Amenities include antiques, original artwork; room service is provided by the excellent *Jack's* restaurant on the ground floor. 1022 Lexington Ave. (212 697-1536). Very expensive.

Waldorf-Astoria – A legend on Park Avenue, divided between the basic hotel and the more opulent (and more expensive) Towers. The degree of comfort delivered here is consistent with the hotel's reputation. *Peacock Alley* is a favorite cocktail rendezvous, and the clock in the middle of the lobby may be New York's favorite meeting place. 301 Park Ave. (212 355-3000). Very expensive to expensive.

New York Hilton – An enormous modern structure near Rockefeller Center and one of New York's largest hotels, it's a bit antiseptic in ambience, but about as efficiently run as any hotel with more than 2,000 rooms can be. A favorite meeting and convention site. Pets allowed. 1335 Ave. of the Americas between 53rd and 54th sts. (212 586-7000). Very expensive to expensive.

Morgan's – The ultimate contemporary hotel, without so much as a sign out front. Stereo cassette players and component TVs with stereo sound are a standard amenity in every room (VCRs and movies are also available), bathrooms are pure high tech, and artwork is by avant-garde photographer Robert Maplethorpe. The only traditional touch here is the Brooks Brothers–style linens. All things considered, it's not surprising that the hotel's 154 rooms are usually occupied by a trendy, young, international clientele. 237 Madison Ave. (212 686-0300 or 800 334-3408). Very expensive to expensive.

New York Helmsley – A shining glass skyscraper on 42nd Street, this executive-oriented facility has special services available for the business traveler — secretaries, telex, photocopying, meeting rooms, and other extras. For dining, there's *Mindy's,* a Continental restaurant, and for drinks and piano music try *Harry's New York Bar.* 212 E 42nd St. (212 490-8900 or 800 221-4982). Very expensive to expensive.

Doral Tuscany – In the middle of attractive Murray Hill, it is a name not often known outside the city's immediate environs. Guests who know it well treasure the service and atmosphere. 120 E 39th St. (212 686-1600). Expensive.

Vista International – The first hotel to be built in Manhattan's Wall Street vicinity in over 100 years, it sits between the World Trade Center towers facing New York Harbor. A full range of special services is available for business travelers. Other highlights include the indoor Executive Fitness Center, with first-rate sports equipment; the *Greenhouse* and *American Harvest* restaurants, offering very good

American regional specialties; and the *Tall Ships Bar,* a popular after-work meeting place. 3 World Trade Center (212 938-9100). Expensive.

Sherry-Netherland – It's a little less renowned than the *Westin Plaza* and the *Pierre* (its immediate neighbors), but the accommodations here are hardly less elegant. The location is superb, and this is a luxurious stopping place truly worthy of the description. It now boasts the *Harry Cipriani* restaurant, run by the Arrigo family that made *Harry's Bar* in Venice a legend. 5th Ave. and 59th St. (212 355-2800). Expensive.

Mayflower – A favorite with ballet and concert buffs. Guests enjoy large, comfortable rooms with pantries that once served the permanent residents. All rooms either have been or will be refurbished in a major renovation begun in 1982. Quite close to Lincoln Center. 15 Central Park West, between 61st and 62nd sts. (212 265-0060 or 800 223-4164). Expensive.

New York Penta – Formerly the *Statler Hilton,* the *Penta* has changed management and has been undergoing a top-to-bottom renovation. Its guest rooms were first to be redone; at press time, the final phase — the lobby and restaurants — was scheduled for completion by the grand reopening in 1986. 401 7th Ave. (212 736-5000). Expensive.

Golden Tulip Barbizon – Not to be confused with the *Barbizon Plaza,* this East Side establishment was formerly a residential hotel for women only, but a thorough refurbishing has turned it into one of New York's newer tourist hotels. A comprehensive health spa on the premises will be a unique feature in a facility in this price range. 140 E 61st St. (212 838-5700 or 800 223-1020). Expensive to moderate.

Roosevelt – The hotel has recently changed ownership and undergone redecoration and restoration. The accommodations are clean and comfortable and its *Crawdaddy* restaurant has one of the area's most popular after-work bars. A good value (and location) for business travelers. Madison Ave. at 45th St. (212 661-9600). Expensive to moderate.

Sheraton Centre – This 50-story modern monolith, once the *Americana,* has been taken over by the Sheraton chain. It's always busy; the rooms are quite comfortable, and it's only a short walk to the theater. The top five floors, called the *Sheraton Towers,* are for more exclusive "business class" clients. 7th Ave. and 52nd St. (212 581-1000). Expensive to moderate.

Wyndham – Though admittedly overshadowed by better-known neighbors like the *Pierre, Westin Plaza,* and *Sherry-Netherland,* this extremely convenient hotel has been fondly described as a posh country inn; a fine, small London hotel; and a private club. It's a particular favorite among actors, and chintz plays a rather large part in its breezy decor. It takes a certain self-sufficiency to enjoy the *Wyndham*'s special appeal; there's no room service, the hotel restaurant is closed on weekends, and the front door is locked at night. 58th St. between 5th Ave. and Ave. of the Americas (212 753-3500). Moderate.

Algonquin – Long known as a favorite among literary types, the hotel's reputation is most closely connected to the days of the "round table" in its fine restaurant. The personal attention accorded by the management is visible everywhere, and, if anything, the hotel has improved with age. 59 W 44th St. (212 840-6800). Moderate.

Salisbury Hotel – Owned by the Calvary Baptist Church, this hotel has a small, welcoming lobby and newly painted, nicely sized pastel rooms (all with refrigerators and pantries, but no stoves). It's a favorite with buyers and musicians, who like the hotel's location near 5th Avenue and Carnegie Hall. 123 W 57th St. (212 246-1300). Moderate.

Milford Plaza – Out-of-towners usually come to Manhattan for Broadway's bright nightlife and the *Milford* is smack in the center of New York's theater district.

All kinds of money-saving tour packages are available, and while rooms are small, they're pleasant. The neighborhood, however, is the pits! 270 W 45th St. at 8th Ave. (212 869-3600). Moderate.

Royalton – Midtown hotels can be budget-benders, but this one — in the theater district, and spic and span with color TV and telephone — is quite reasonable. 44 W 44th St. (212 730-1344). Moderate to inexpensive.

Wales – This comfortable, reasonably priced hotel is in a very appealing neighborhood, close to Central Park and the Metropolitan and Guggenheim art museums. It offers more than 50 individually decorated rooms and suites, some with kitchenette, four-poster bed, or tile fireplace, all with cable television. 1295 Madison Ave. (212 876-6000). Moderate to inexpensive.

Shoreham – On a fashionable block off Fifth Avenue, this small hotel has 75 good-size rooms that are pleasantly decorated and have modern bathrooms. Although the hotel has no dining room, each guest room has an electric coffeemaker and small refrigerator. 33 W 55th St. (212 247-6700). Inexpensive.

Empire – Across the street from Lincoln Center, accommodations here are sufficiently comfortable and clean, and the food service is pretty good. 44 W 63rd St. (212 265-7400). Inexpensive.

Olcott – By no means plush, but certainly comfortable and adequate, this is a typical New York residential hotel that offers some transient accommodations. Spacious facilities and a homey atmosphere are its advantages. Most rooms are suites, with a living room, bedroom, kitchen, and bathroom. All rooms have air conditioning. Reservations should be made several weeks in advance. 27 W 72nd St., only one block from Central Park (212 877-4200). Inexpensive.

Gorham – The variety of room-and-bed combinations possible, together with the fact that all units contain a kitchenette, dining table, and color TV, make the *Gorham* a great boon to families traveling with children. 136 W 55th off 6th Ave. (212 245-1800). Inexpensive.

Century Paramont – The enormous lobby is always alive with flight crews and tour groups — about 70% from abroad. Most of the 700 air-conditioned rooms are smallish but cheerful. 235 W 46th near Broadway (212 764-5500). Inexpensive.

Chelsea – A New York architectural and historic landmark where Dylan Thomas, Arthur Miller, Lennie Bruce, Diego Rivera, Martha Graham, and others have made their New York home. The atmosphere in this 19th-century structure is distinctly unmodern, unhomogenized, and unsterilized. There is a large permanent occupancy, with about 200 rooms available for transients. Rooms vary in structure, price, and facilities — some have a kitchen, a fireplace, and a bathroom, and others have none of the above. For the adventurous only; make reservations well in advance. 222 W 23rd St. (212 243-3700). Inexpensive.

EATING OUT: New York City is, plain and simply, the culinary capital of the world. It is possible that there are more good French restaurants in Paris or more fine Chinese eating places in Taiwan, but no city in the world can offer the gastronomic diversity that is available in New York. If there is one compelling reason to come to New York, it is to indulge exotic appetites that cannot be satisfied elsewhere, and it is not unusual for dedicated eaters to make several pilgrimages to New York each year simply to satisfy their sophisticated palates.

Regrettably, New York's tastiest cuisine does not come cheap, though there are places to dine around the city where you need not pay in 30-, 60-, and 90-day notes. But as in most places, you get what you pay for, and you should expect to pay $80 or more for two in the restaurants that we've noted as expensive. Moderate restaurants will run between $50 and $80 per couple, and in inexpensive establishments you can expect to spend from $25 to $40 and less for a meal for two. These price ranges do not include drinks, wine or tips. Unless otherwise noted, reservations are essential.

The Four Seasons – The *Pool Room* is perhaps the most beautiful dining room in the city, with a proprietorship that is not only creative but extremely able. Although the menu is interesting from top to bottom, desserts deserve special mention, and there's one called Chocolate Velvet that is merely ecstasy. Special "spa cuisine" provides careful calorie and sodium monitoring for the health-conscious. The *Grill Room* is currently the luncheon favorite of New York's power elite. Closed Sundays. Major credit cards. 99 E 52nd St. (754-9494). Expensive.

Lutèce – New York's (and perhaps this country's) finest French restaurant, with service and atmosphere to match the extraordinary cuisine. Of all the premier restaurants in New York, this is the one most hospitable to strangers willing to pay the price for deluxe French food. If you have the option, dine in the comfortable upstairs room, though the enclosed garden is a treat in New York City. André Soltner runs this incredible bastion of gastronomic delight with a firm hand, but you'd still best be prepared for a check that will total well into three figures. An excellent way to sample the combination of classic dishes, innovative nouvelle creations, and Alsatian specialties is to order the menu de dégustation, a tasting of six or seven courses. Make reservations a month in advance. Closed Sundays. Accepts only American Express, Carte Blanche, and Diners Club credit cards. 249 E 50th St. (752-2225). Expensive.

Le Cirque – The tables are too close together, the noise level can be deafening, and reservations are as hard to come by as an invitation to Buckingham Palace. Still, the remarkable French food that comes out of the kitchen is enough to make legions of dedicated diners put up with the less than perfect atmosphere. Everything on the menu is special and prepared perfectly. Remember, however, that the main reason for dining here is to taste the sublime crème brulée for dessert. Nowhere in the world is it prepared better. Major credit cards. 58 E 65th St. (794-9292). Expensive.

La Caravelle – A traditional bastion of classic French cuisine with all of the attendant hauteur, this is often the choice of New York's smartest set. Menus are unalteringly interesting, and the kitchen is not merely competent but innovative. Closed Sundays. Major credit cards. 33 W 55th St. (586-4252). Expensive.

Palm – The best sirloin steak in New York in an atmosphere so unattractive that it's the restaurant's prime appeal. Sawdust covers the floor, tables and chairs are refugees from a thrift shop, but the steaks are just great. The largest (and most expensive) lobsters in New York are served here. *Palm, Too,* across the street, is a branch serving identical food and takes care of the overflow. Closed Sundays. Reservations accepted for lunch but not dinner. Major credit cards. 837 2nd Ave. (687-2953). Expensive.

Christ Cella's – A creditable eatery that specializes in sirloin steak. The decor is attractive, the service is efficient, and it's a favorite of advertising and publishing types. Not quite up to its own old standards but still worth a visit. Closed Sundays. Major credit cards. 160 E 46th St. (697-2479). Expensive.

Spark's – Nothing (except the food) is admirable: the entry to the dining room is the most cramped and uncomfortable in town, the decor is early bordello, and the service is oppressive at best. Still, the steaks are superb, the wine list is genuinely extraordinary, and it's a chance to experience at first hand the level of abuse that is an integral part of New York City life. Closed Sundays. Major credit cards. 210 E 46th St. (687-4855). Expensive.

La Grenouille – Soft green walls and glorious floral arrangements provide a romantic setting in which to sample such house masterpieces as les grenouilles Provençales (frogs' legs); thin, sautéed calves' liver Bercy; and roast duck. Be prepared, however, for a very hauty, condescending attitude if you're not known to the staff. Closed Sundays. American Express and Diners Club credit cards. 3 E 52nd St. (752-1495). Expensive.

The Quilted Giraffe – Among the prime temptations at this highly regarded restaurant are entrées such as grilled Norwegian salmon and moist, crisp-skinned confit of duck with garlic potatoes. An alternative to the prix fixe dinner is a tasting menu offering five small courses; similarly, the Grand Dessert provides a sampling of such pleasures as a hazelnut waffle with vanilla ice cream and maple sauce. The two intimate dining rooms have only 17 tables; be sure to reserve about a month in advance. Closed weekends. Major credit cards. 955 2nd Ave. (753-5355). Expensive.

Windows on the World – Somewhat overpriced (though interesting) menu that is extremely ambitious, but the food is less a lure than *the* best view of Manhattan. Try to sit along the north wall, where you'll have all of glittering Manhattan spread out at your feet. If you don't care to spend the price of dinner, stop for a drink in the bar and enjoy the superb hors d'oeuvres. The *Cellar in the Sky* room here serves an interesting prix fixe menu with a wide choice of wines — but no view. Open daily. Major credit cards. 1 World Trade Center (938-1111). Expensive.

Coach House – Not as highly regarded as it once was but still generally considered one of New York's best "American" restaurants. The black bean soup is a tradition here, as is the rack of lamb and the superb chocolate cake. Another attraction is its Greenwich Village location, across from some interesting Federal row houses. Closed Mondays. Major credit cards. 110 Waverly Pl. (777-0303). Expensive.

The "21" Club – The legendary atmosphere and unquestionable cachet are what lure most visitors, but since the original owners sold most of their equity, there's been a discernible decline in camaraderie. Still, the preparation of fresh game here is excellent. Ties are always required, and if you're not a regular or a celebrity, sometimes the welcome isn't very warm. The upstairs dining room is more elegant and quiet, but those who wish to see and be seen usually adorn the wall on the left as you enter the downstairs bar and dining room. Closed Sundays and summer weekends. Major credit cards. 21 W 52nd St. (582-7200). Expensive.

The Russian Tea Room – With enough blinis to float diners down the Volga, this attractive restaurant is an almost obligatory stop for any visitor who plans to attend a concert at adjacent Carnegie Hall. Try the borscht or chicken Kiev or abide by the waiter's suggestions and let your Slavic instincts have free rein. Open daily. Major credit cards. 150 W 57th St. (265-0947). Expensive.

Tavern-on-the-Green – One of New York's most beautiful dining establishments. In winter, the snow-covered trees trimmed with tiny white lights outside the Crystal Room make a dazzling display. Best of all at Christmastime but only slightly less spectacular in summer. Open daily. Major credit cards. Central Park West and 67th St. (873-3200). Expensive.

Cafe Luxembourg – The interior here runs to Art Deco, bright lights, and noise, with everyone appearing to be looking around for someone famous. The location, near Lincoln Center, is especially welcome to concertgoers. The cuisine is nouvelle, and while the boudin blanc — chunks of seafood wrapped in a crinkly spinach covering — is an imaginative and light first course, specials tend to be uneven. For the best look at the chic crowd, come late (between 11 PM and 3 AM). Open daily. Major credit cards. 200 W 70th St. (873-7411). Expensive.

Parioli Romanissimo – Ensconced in an attractive East Side town house and frequented by the "beautiful people," the tables at this classy spot are among the most difficult to book in the city. Those who succeed dine on pricey (at least $75 per person) but delicious Italian specialties. Opt for a meaty main course like veal chop giardiniera and then splurge on the chocolate torte for dessert. Service is notoriously chilly, and even when reservations are in hand, expect a wait. Closed Sundays and Mondays. American Express, Diners Club, and Carte Blanche only. 24 E 81st St. (288-2391). Expensive.

Chanterelle – Here on a dingy corner in SoHo is a tiny, simply elegant dining room, with dark wood wainscoting, eggnog-colored walls, tables draped in starched white linen, and a pretty pressed tin ceiling hung with brass chandeliers. The prix fixe menu leans toward nouvelle. Begin with seafood sausage, then choose such entrées as salmon en papillote, rack of lamb, duck in sherry vinegar, or sautéed soft-shell crabs, all accompanied by crisply stir-fried squash mixed with zucchini blossoms and other vegetables. A cheese board is offered, and dessert might be chocolate pavé, a dense, rich, mousselike cake. Make reservations about 3 weeks in advance. Closed Sundays and Mondays. Major credit cards. 89 Grand St., corner of Greene St. (966-6960). Expensive.

Gloucester House – The most elegant seafood center in the city. Fresh biscuits are a particular delight and help salve the impact of some frankly staggering prices. A fine place to dine, but a real budget-bender. Closed only Thanksgiving and Christmas. Major credit cards. 37 E 50th St. (755-7394). Expensive.

Peter Luger – The best porterhouse (T-bone) steak in town, lurking in the shadows under the Brooklyn side of the Williamsburgh Bridge. The neighborhood is hardly fashionable, but the food is first class. No menu, but try the thick-sliced onions and tomatoes under the special barbecue sauce, and be sure to taste the best home-fried potatoes the city has to offer. Open daily. No credit cards. 178 Broadway, Brooklyn (718 387-7400). Expensive.

Manhattan Ocean Club – Both the lower-level and upstairs dining rooms of this fine seafood house near Lincoln Center are reminiscent of a museum, with white walls, Grecian columns, and Picasso plates and prints displayed behind glass. The real attraction is the fresh, delicious fish and shellfish — the spicy blackened redfish and the buttery red snapper are particularly good. The dessert cart winner is something called "bag of chocolate," the dark, rich shell filled with white chocolate mousse and topped with fresh raspberries, all of it in a light raspberry purée. Open daily. Major credit cards. 57 W 58th St. (371-7777). Expensive.

Il Nido – A superb menu of Northern Italian specialties and the highest standards of service are the hallmarks of Adi Giovannetti's attractive East Side establishment. Crostini of polenta with a sauce of mushroom and chicken liver is the perfect starter, to be followed by fritto misto (mixed fried fish), crostacei marinara (shellfish in marinara sauce), or any of a host of other house specialties. Closed Sundays. Major credit cards. 251 E 53rd St. (753-8450). Expensive.

Il Cantinori – A welcome addition to New York's stable of Northern Italian restaurants that's on one of the city's loveliest blocks. A beamed ceiling, terra cotta floor, and chairs of wood and straw create the charming ambience inside. Begin with risotto nero (a rice delicacy in squid ink) or ravioli alla fiorentina (dumplings of spinach and ricotta cheese) before an entrée of excellent fish or game. For dessert, try the restaurant's version of the popular Italian confection tirami su, espresso-soaked ladyfingers and sweet mascarpone cheese. Open daily. Major credit cards. 32 E 10th St. (674-6044). Expensive.

Riveranda *and* Empress *of New York* – The food may not be the best in town, but the experience of dining on the city's only restaurant-yacht is worth the tab. It's delightful to have dinner and dance while cruising the Hudson River and New York Harbor past the glittering Manhattan skyline. There are luncheon and Sunday brunch cruises as well. Advance reservations and tickets required. Major credit cards. Sailings from Pier 62 on the Hudson River at W 23rd St. (929-7090). Expensive.

Maxwell's Plum – Actually three establishments in one: a popular singles bar, a streetside café, and an elegant dining room. Decor consists of cut glass of every color and variety, and there's not a more visually spectacular dining room in the city. This is the New York City scene about which you've read. Open daily. Major credit cards, but limits on the amounts that can be charged. 1181 1st Ave. at 64th St. (628-2100). Expensive to moderate.

The Water Club – The decor at this restaurant/barge in the East River is naturally nautical, but with restraint, since the view is decorative enough: river traffic and the twinkling lights of the Manhattan and Queens skylines. The menu, too, is nautical, with similar restraint. Appetizers range from oysters and smoked salmon to Beluga caviar, entrées from Maryland crab cakes to Dover sole (with a delicately flavored beurre blanc) and lobster — but you can also order pâté plus filet mignon or the lovely roast duck with chestnuts and poached pear. Open daily. Major credit cards. It's tricky to get there, so take a cab. East River at 30th St., on the northbound service road of the FDR Drive (683-3333). Expensive to moderate.

Trattoria da Alfredo – One of those superb small restaurants found only in a city like New York, offering the finest Northern Italian fare. Special, inventive pasta dishes are featured in an alternating group of specialties not found on the menu, and these should be your focus when you dine here. Make reservations a week in advance, and bring your own wine. Closed Tuesdays. No credit cards. 90 Bank St. (929-4400). Moderate.

Cafe 43 – A welcome addition to the theater district, this French brasserie-style restaurant offers an array of interesting dishes, beautifully presented — chicken with pine nuts, duck confit, swordfish in tarragon sauce — and a wide selection of good wines by the glass. There's a prix fixe menu for those who are particularly budget conscious. Major credit cards. 147 W 43rd St. (869-4200). Moderate.

Santa Fe – Less trendy than many of the new Mexican eateries that have sprung up around the city; there are no hanging plants, no neon signs, no ear-splitting conversational roar. Instead, crisp linens and salmon-colored walls hung with Mexican weavings provide a serene setting for nicely tart margaritas and well-prepared southwestern dishes. Just a few blocks from Lincoln Center. Open daily. Major credit cards. 72 W 69th St. (724-0822). Moderate.

Grotta Azzurra Inn – Neapolitan specialties are served in a basement in the heart of Little Italy. Lobster fra diavolo exacts an awesome price, but it's worth the tariff. The garlic bread is like no other in this world, and it guarantees that you won't be bothered by vampires for years. Closed Mondays. No reservations. No credit cards. 387 Broome St. (925-8775). Moderate.

Azzurro – A tiny storefront on the Upper East Side demonstrates the unexpected delicacy of Sicilian cooking. Grilled fish, fine pasta specials, and delectable vino santo. The waiters are all cousins; Mama is in the kitchen. Open daily. No credit cards. 1625 Second Ave. (517-7068). Moderate.

Shun Lee Palace – Chef T. T. Wang is one of New York City's two most talented Chinese cooks, and his menu here includes the most exciting Oriental temptations ever inscribed. If you can somehow round up a group of ten to dine together, you might be interested in ordering Wang's special Chinese feast. It's beyond belief. Open daily. Accepts only American Express, Diners Club, and Carte Blanche credit cards. 155 E 55th St. (371-8844). Moderate.

Shun Lee West – Same as above, this time very near Lincoln Center. Actually, this recently refurbished dining room is the better of the two *Shun Lee* emporiums run by Michael Wong. Open daily. Major credit cards. 43 W 65th St. (595-8895). Moderate.

Kitcho – Soups are notably delicate, and teriyaki grills of meat or fish are tastefully seasoned with ginger and sweet sake (rice wine) at this authentic Japanese restaurant. Try such delicacies as kushi-katsu — crisp, deep-fried chunks of pork — or to-banyaki — marinated and grilled meat or fish with broiled vegetables. Closed Saturdays. American Express and Diners Club only. 22 W 46th St. (575-8880). Moderate.

Café des Artistes – One of New York's most romantic restaurants, in a West Side apartment house. Appetizers and main dishes are all first rate, but the real lure are the desserts. Save room, for they've an unusual special offering that includes a sample of every dessert on the menu. For those with a sweet tooth, it's like visiting paradise. The most beautiful Sunday brunch in town. Open daily. Major credit cards. 1 W 67th St. (877-3500). Moderate.

Raga – A carved wooden gateway, tall carved columns, heavy silk fabrics, and antique musical instruments mounted on the walls provide the opulent setting for one of New York's finest Indian restaurants. Lobster Malabar, gosht vindaloo, and meat, poultry, and seafood specialties broiled in the stone tandoor are particularly good here. Most evenings musicians play the sitar, tabla, and flute for an unobtrusive background. Open daily. Major credit cards. 57 W 48th St. (757-3450). Moderate.

Bon Temps Rouler – The name means "Let the good times roll," and there's no better place to do just that than this converted bar in deepest Tribeca. The food is Créole-Cajun, the decor rises slightly above minimal, and the mood and the jukebox are funky. Start with the sweet, spicy alligator sausage, the tasso and ham quesadilla, or Louisiana gumbo. Move on to voodoo stew or grilled redfish with love sauce. The food can be very hot, so ask for the spice level you prefer. To soothe your palate, don't resist the bread pudding in whiskey sauce for dessert. Closed Sundays. American Express only. 59 Reade St. (near Broadway) (513-1333). Moderate.

Quatorze – Despite its slightly seedy location on the periphery of Greenwich Village, this is an attractive, convivial bistro. Diners may eat either at the marble-topped bar or in the pale yellow dining room with oak floor, white linen-draped tables, and a wall of red velvet banquettes. Try the chicory and bacon salad in a dressing of hot vinaigrette then the grilled salmon in choron sauce or the grilled chicken. Choose the crispy, warm apple tart for dessert. The short wine list includes some interesting, reasonably priced offerings. Open daily. American Express only. 240 W 14th St. (206-7006). Moderate.

America – The menu is as big (and varied) as its namesake — a staggering 175-plus dishes, representing every corner of the country and the ethnic groups that inhabit it — including dishes like the American-as-apple-pie Blue Plate Special and a peanut butter and jelly sandwich. The food ranges from good to fair, and the service is best described as leisurely. With its high, exposed ceiling and mural-covered walls, *America* looks like a warehouse-cum-loft, with an elevated bar that, despite its football field dimensions, is jammed most nights. Open daily. Major credit cards. 9-13 E 18th St. (505-2110). Moderate.

The Ballroom – When it opened a few years ago, this very pretty bistro in the Garment District introduced a new twist to Manhattan dining — the tapas bar. A changing, varied menu of tapas (*tapa* is Spanish for "appetizer") is spread along a lengthy bar, and patrons either nibble their way through dinner at the bar or head for the dining room, where waiters circulate with trays of tapas. There's also a very tempting menu of main courses and a dessert table that's as much a feast for the eyes as the tastebuds. Closed Sundays and Mondays. Major credit cards. 253 W 28th St. (244-3005). Moderate.

Sabor – A tiny, unprepossessing eatery in the heart of Greenwich Village, this restaurant serves up simple, Cuban-based cuisine, such as white bean soup, red snapper in green sauce, baked chicken scented with cumin, and shrimp in lime sauce. The baked coconut dessert, with cinnamon, sherry, and a dollop of whipped cream, is a must. Major credit cards. 20 Cornelia St. (243-9579). Moderate.

Cockeyed Clams – The best seafood-per-dollar value in New York. Tables are close and the dining room can get quite noisy, but you won't find a better lobster or piece of snapper in the city for these prices. Open daily. No credit cards. 1678 3rd Ave at 94th St. (831-4121). Moderate.

Odéon – Opened in 1980 in a gray cast-iron building, this refurbished cafeteria is in the midst of Tribeca. Pass up the menu's standard fare and sample the more innovative works of Patrick Clark, the young chef. Look for entrées such as squab with shiitake mushrooms and wild rice, and roast loin of lamb with white peppercorns. A dessert worth trying is crêpes with praline butter and apricot liqueur. Major credit cards. 145 W Broadway (233-0507). Moderate.

Village Green – Don't be dismayed by this restaurant's rather shabby-looking location. Inside, you'll find the two-story dining room elegant yet cozy: linen-draped tables shining with crystal and silver and a fire snapping away in the hearth. The menu is Continental, the food always well prepared, and the service friendly. Closed Sundays and Mondays. Major credit cards. 531 Hudson St. (255-1650). Moderate.

Hatsuhana – A Japanese restaurant that's still winning kudos from some of New York's toughest restaurant critics. The sushi, sashimi, and tempura are about the tastiest in town. Closed Sundays. Reservations for dinner only. Major credit cards. 14 E 48th St. (355-3345). Moderate.

Carolina – Southern and southwestern dishes grilled over hickory and mesquite are specialties. Although the red pepper shrimp can be disappointingly mild, the crab cakes are light and succulent, the corn bread flavorful, and the slaw creamy and delicious. The green chile soufflé is a tasty starter and the chocolate mud pie and tangy lime pie tempting finales. Note that the rear "garden room" can be noisy and traffic through the front room disconcerting; ask for a table to the right of the entrance. 355 W 46th St. (245-0058). Moderate.

Sammy's Roumanian Steak House – The last survivor of a long, Lower East Side tradition of ethnic meat restaurants. Traditional Eastern European favorites are featured, as is old country music of a sort you're not likely to hear in any other establishment. The makings for egg creams are set right on the table — an experience you don't usually find this side of Anatefka. Open daily. Major credit cards. 157 Chrystie St. (475-9131). Moderate.

Gage & Tollner – Holding forth at this stand since 1889, it's worth a visit, if only to watch the gaslight glowing in the evening. Specialties include lobster Newburg and crabmeat Virginia. Among the specialties are 15 separate styles of potatoes. Closed Sundays. American Express and Diners Club only. 374 Fulton St., Brooklyn (718 875-5181). Moderate.

Malaga – Delicious, reasonably priced Spanish specialties such as paella, shrimp in garlic sauce, and fish in salsa verde make this a neighborhood favorite. Try to sit in the front room, because the tin ceiling in the back room reverberates with noise when it's crowded. Open daily. Major credit cards. 406 E 73rd St. (737-7659 or 650-0605). Moderate to inexpensive.

Au Tunnel – Onion soup, mussels, frogs' legs, and minute steak typify the French provincial dishes featured by this theater district bistro since 1950. Try the noisette de Veau or tripes à la mode de Caen. The original high standards have not changed a whit. Closed Sundays. American Express only. 250 W 47th St. (582-2166). Moderate to inexpensive.

Pamir – A small, family-run restaurant specializing in Afghan (much like Indian) cooking. The delicately seasoned lamb dishes are very good. Open daily. MasterCard and Visa only. 1437 2nd Ave. (734-3791). Inexpensive.

Manhattan Brewing Company – Pub grub in the ever-crowded *Tap Room* here runs to oysters, shepherd's pie, hot open-faced sandwiches of roast beef or turkey, and the like, but the real reasons to visit are the brewed-on-the-premises beers and ales. Closed Mondays. 40-42 Thompson St. (219-9250). Inexpensive.

Carnegie Delicatessen – The quintessential New York deli. The sandwiches are enormous, far too big to put in a normal human mouth. Corned beef and pastrami are king; waiters provide entertaining banter (to help pass the time). Communal tables; no atmosphere save the frantic 7th Avenue scene. Open daily. No reservations. No credit cards. 854 7th Ave. (757-2245). Moderate to expensive.

Tennessee Mountain – Some of the meatiest baby back ribs in town come from this casual SoHo outpost. The gentle tomato-based sauce is also used to flavor the barbecued chicken, and don't miss the fried onion rings. Open daily. Major credit cards. 143 Spring St. (431-3993). Inexpensive.

The Hard Rock Cafe – More a monument to rock 'n' roll than a restaurant, this funky spot — akin to the original in London — sports all manner of memorabilia: the guitars of Eric Clapton, Pete Townsend, and Bo Diddley, gold records of the Rolling Stones, and Prince's purple coat. Check out the 45-foot guitar-shaped bar and the 1959 Cadillac Biarritz jutting out from the 2nd floor. The menu is your basic hamburgers and shakes; the music can be very loud. Popular with the younger set, the cafe draws between 1,500 and 2,400 patrons a day. Major credit cards. 221 W 57th St. (489-6565). Inexpensive.

Il Bocconcino – The celebrity photographs in the window date back to *la dolce vita* days, when Gilberto was a *papparazzo* in Rome. Now he and co-owner Giorgio run this modest but congenial Greenwich Village spot, with lace curtains, white tablecloths, and some murals of Italianate architecture to remind them of home. Sample the bruschetta (Roman garlic bread), then follow with pasta, chicken, veal, seafood, or a meal of Gilberto's pizza. Sidewalk tables in summer. Open daily. Major credit cards. 168 Sullivan St. (982-0329). Inexpensive.

Green Tree – For a taste of the old country, head to this family-run Upper West Side establishment. Hungarian waiters load down your table with specialties of their homeland — chicken or cold cherry soup, stuffed cabbage, and Hungarian goulash. For dessert try the palacsintas, crêpes filled with cheese or apricot jam. Closed Sundays. No credit cards. 1034 Amsterdam Ave. at 111th St. (864-9106). Inexpensive.

Hunan House – Among Chinatown's best, this pleasant restaurant specializes in the subtly spiced food of the province of Hunan. Start off with fried dumplings or hot and sour soup, then have Hunan lamb, prepared with scallions; Changsha beef, done in a hot sauce with broccoli; or Confucius prawns with cashews. Open daily. No reservations. American Express only. 45 Mott St. (962-0010). Inexpensive.

Harvey's Chelsea Restaurant – Etched-glass windows, polished brass rails, and baroque wood paneling make this turn-of-the-century bar a delightful oasis in an otherwise dreary neighborhood. The best choice on the menu is the tasty fish and chips, accompanied by a frosty draft. Reservations advised. No credit cards. 108 W 18th St. (243-5644). Inexpensive.

OKLAHOMA CITY

On April 22, 1889, the United States opened the theretofore protected federal lands of central Oklahoma to settlement by white men. Between dawn and dusk more than 10,000 people poured across these unrelieved prairie midlands staking claims and laying out homesteads as if pursued by The Furies. By nightfall a city of flickering campfires and roughly marked claims outlined the farthest extents of the city born so abruptly, and in such a fever, on the open prairie.

If it was a moment of dreams fulfilled for the settlers, it was the bitter end of a promise to the Indians who had been "given" Oklahoma years before. The area had become American in 1803 as part of that most fabulous of real estate deals, the Louisiana Purchase. Almost immediately, it was declared Indian Territory, and what remained of Native American tribes throughout the US, from the forests of New England to the bayous of the South, were arbitrarily and compulsorily moved there (see *A Short Tour of Indian America*, DIVERSIONS). The land was owned and administered by the federal government, but dedicated to use for, and by, the Indians. This commitment lasted all of about 60 years. By the end of the Civil War, the area was halved, the western half becoming Oklahoma Territory, the eastern half remaining Indian Territory. From then until 1907, when both territories became the State of Oklahoma, the Indians lost land as the open and to-be-settled areas were extended.

But for the settlers, the area that was to be Oklahoma City represented one precious commodity — space, inexpensive land on which to establish homes. Just how ambitious they were, and how many of them there were, is still evident: By area Oklahoma City is one of the largest American cities, with 621 square miles within its municipal borders. And more than ambitious, they were lucky: Beneath the surface of their jealously guarded homesteads percolated a sea of oil, and Oklahoma became the city with oil derricks downtown (even in front of the capitol). Oil meant money, and with the money came a level of sophistication that a prairie town otherwise could scarcely have expected. In the last couple of years, the bounty of black gold has been less apparent as the worldwide oil glut has cut revenues and severely increased unemployment. Oklahomans avidly seek other sources of income as they wait for the energy industry to stabilize and oil prices to rise.

Today Oklahoma City has a population of over 800,000 people. Oil is still a mainstay of the economy, but the giant Oklahoma City Air Materiel Area (Tinker Air Force Base) employs more than 19,000 civilians and 3,600 military personnel. The FAA Aeronautical Center, including the Civil Aeromedical Institute, is at the city's bustling Will Rogers World Airport. More than 2 million passengers fly to and from Oklahoma City annually. The city is also a shipping point for wheat and cotton grown in surrounding areas. The OKC feeder market is the third largest cattle market in the country. The University of Oklahoma School of Medicine with its affiliate hospitals, Research Building, Medical Research Foundations, and Veterans Hospital is considered one of the best in the nation.

Sports and religion play a big part in the lives of residents. OKC (or The City, as residents refer to it) is practically the center of what is commonly known as the Bible Belt. More than 45 denominations are represented in the city's 500 churches, from Zen Buddhist to Baptist (admittedly more Baptists than Buddhists). The fervor of spirit is not all religious, however. Every autumn, "Big Red" fever sweeps the city as the University of Oklahoma starts the football season.

Because of its wide-open spaces, Oklahoma City is mainly residential, with plenty of yard to mow between homes. Local real estate is a relative bargain, especially during the current economic malaise. A house and land that would cost more than $200,000 in the eastern part of the country currently costs less than half that amount here. What's more, the residential area is surrounded by lovely lakes, which are great for fishing and sailing (even ice sailing).

OKLAHOMA CITY AT-A-GLANCE

SEEING THE CITY: *Eagles Nest* restaurant, on top of the 20-story United Founders Life Tower, offers a view of the city as well as fine seafood specialties. 5900 Mosteller Dr. (840-5655).

SPECIAL PLACES: Most of the major attractions are not within walking distance. The city's Masstrans system provides bus service to all points of interest. For bus information, call 235-RIDE. You can also rent a car.

State Capitol – This is one of the few capitols in the nation that does not have a dome. It's probably the only one with an active oil well on the grounds. (The capitol was built before prospectors struck oil. When it was, derricks went up everywhere.) The capitol complex consists of four buildings. Most interesting is the main building, of granite and limestone, with pillars and a wide staircase in front, a statue of a cowboy in the lobby, and murals of Oklahoma history in the halls. Open daily. Free. Lincoln Blvd., between 22nd and 23rd sts. (521-2011).

Oklahoma Historical Society – An astounding collection of Indian artifacts, presenting aspects of Indian history from diggings that go back from AD 400 and 500 to the days of Custer and Buffalo Bill. The library has one of the most complete archives of historical documents on American Indians in the US. Open daily. Free. On the southeastern section of the capitol grounds, 2100 Lincoln Blvd. (521-2491).

Omniplex – The only Egyptian mummy in Oklahoma makes its home here. Part of the Foundation complex, the Gerrer Museum and Art Gallery has a number of curios from ancient times, as well as some Renaissance paintings, carved ivory figurines, and contemporary Americana. The Kirkpatrick Planetarium presents sky shows and hosts traveling Air Force exhibitions. Open daily. Admission charge. 2100 NE 52nd St. (424-5564, recording; 424-5545, tour information).

Oklahoma City Zoo – Captivity seems to agree with the more than 2,000 animals, birds, and reptiles here, perhaps because they're left to wander freely in natural settings. The zoo has been so successful in raising animals in captivity that many are sent here

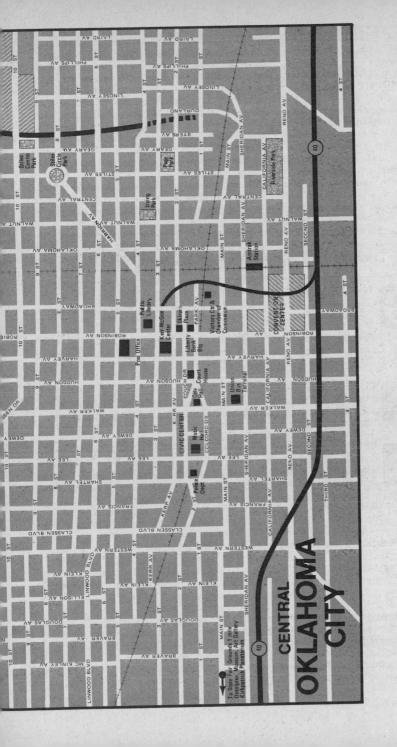

CENTRAL
OKLAHOMA
CITY

from other parts of the country to breed. (You might catch a couple of baboons on a wild weekend.) A Safari train covers the exhibitions. There's also an Iron Horse train. Open daily. Admission charge. Eastern Ave. and NE 50th St. (424-3343).

National Cowboy Hall of Fame – Hi-ho, Silver! Cowboys, real and fictional, line the halls of this good-natured museum. In addition to art and scupture, there are dioramas, relief maps showing migration paths, and a model village of early days. Also, plenty of saddles and exhibitions on movie cowboys. Western heroes visit at least once a year. Open daily. Admission charge. 1700 NE 63rd St. (478-2250).

Enterprise Square – A learning center that uses contemporary educational techniques, entertainment, and audience participation to communicate the fundamentals of the US economic system. 2501 E Memorial (478-5190).

White Water – At this amusement park, visitors can body-surf in the Wave Pool, take a slow ride over the rapids in an inner tube, or slide down White Lightning (the tallest water slide in the world). Open May through September. Admission charge. W Reno and Portland (943-9687).

SOURCES AND RESOURCES

 TOURIST INFORMATION: Oklahoma City Convention and Tourism Bureau has brochures and maps; Main and Gaylord (278-8910).
 Local Coverage – *Daily Oklahoman,* morning daily; *Journal Record,* daily for business and law news.
 Food – *Downtowner* magazine, weekly.
 Area Code – All telephone numbers are in the 405 area code unless otherwise indicated.

 CLIMATE AND CLOTHES: The weather is very changeable. Changeable means that in winter it can be 12° in the morning and 45° or 50° in the afternoon. In the summer it's often 100° or higher, but the wind keeps it from being totally unbearable. The winds often gust from 35 to 40 miles an hour.

 GETTING AROUND: Airport – Will Rogers World Airport is a 20-minute drive from the downtown area; taxi fare should cost about $12. Metro Airport Limo Service (681-3311) provides transportation from the airport to downtown at rates that vary according to the number of passengers on a particular trip: $11.50 for one, $5.75 and less for two or more.
 Bus – Masstrans operates frequent buses; 300 E California (235-RIDE).
 Taxi – There are taxi stands in front of the big hotels and at major intersections. For dependable service, call Yellow Cab (232-6161).
 Car Rental – Every major national firm is represented.

 MUSEUMS: National Cowboy Hall of Fame and Oklahoma Historical Society are described in *Special Places.* Other Oklahoma City museums are:
 The Air Space Museum – 2100 NE 52nd St. (424-1443)
 Kirkpatrick Center – 2100 NE 52nd St. (427-5461)
 National Softball Hall of Fame – 2801 NE 50th St. (424-5266)
 Oklahoma Art Center – 3113 Pershing Blvd., Fair Park and Plaza Circle (946-4477)
 Oklahoma Heritage Association – 201 NW 14th St. (235-4458)
 Oklahoma Museum of Art – 7316 Nichols Rd. (840-2759)
 Oklahoma State Firefighters Museum – 2716 NE 50th St. (424-3440)
 Photography Hall of Fame and Museum – 2100 NE 52nd St. (424-4055)

MAJOR COLLEGES AND UNIVERSITIES: University of Oklahoma (Norman; 325-0311); Oklahoma State University (Stillwater; 624-5000); Oklahoma City University (2423 NW Blackwelder; 521-5000); Bethany Nazarene College (6729 NW 39th Expressway; 789-6400).

SPECIAL EVENTS: College football season, September-December; *Greater Oklahoma Thunderboat Classic* on Lake Overholser in August; *World Championship Quarter Horse Show & Sale,* November; *Spring Arts Festival,* April; *Festifall,* September; *Fall Arts Festival,* October; *Masquerade on Paseo,* October.

SPORTS AND FITNESS: Baseball – The *'89ers* play at All Sports Stadium, Fairgrounds Park, 10th and May (946-8989).

    Fishing – The best fishing is at Lake Hefner and Lake Overholser, twin lakes 20 miles northwest of the center of town, between McArthur and Council rds.

    Fitness Centers – The International Fitness Center has a pool, exercise equipment, and aerobics classes, 5900 Mosteller Dr., in the United Founders Life Tower (843-9408). The YMCA has a pool, track, weights, and squash, handball, and racquetball courts, 125 NW 5th St. (232-6101).

    Football – College games are held at Owen Stadium at the University of Oklahoma in Norman (325-0311), and Lewis Field at Oklahoma State University, Stillwater (624-5746).

    Golf – The best city course is at Lincoln Park, Eastern Ave. and NE 50th St.

    Jogging – It's possible to run to Memorial Park, at NW 32nd and Classen; in the park is a posted map showing 2- to 8-mile routes. Run around Lake Hefner, in Stars and Stripes Park, off Hefner Road, or the less-traveled Lake Overholser, west of downtown and reachable only by car; or take the No. 11 or 12 bus to Westwood and run around Woodson Park (1½ miles).

    Sailing – There's good sailing (and ice sailing) on Lake Hefner and Lake Overholser.

    Tennis – There are good public courts at Memorial Park, 32nd and Classen, and at Will Rogers Park, 36th and Portland.

THEATER: *Stage Center* at Myriad Gardens, 400 W Sheridan (239-7333), is a modern complex with two stages. The *Lyric Theater* hosts a professional summer stock company that performs musicals from June through August, NW 25th and Blackwelder (528-3636). *The Jewel Box Theatre,* 3700 N Walker (521-1786), presents innovative, contemporary productions.

MUSIC: *Oklahoma Symphony Orchestra* and traveling entertainers play at the Music Hall, Civic Center, 201 Channing Sq. (232-4292 or 23-MUSIC). Oklahoma City University music school sends opera singers to the Met. Check out their performance schedules by calling 521-5000.

NIGHTCLUBS AND NIGHTLIFE: *Doc Severinson's* has top-of-the-chart entertainers, 201 N Meridian (946-1144); and *The Bowery,* 31st and Classen (524-3316), features new wave music including live appearances by top performers.

SINS: Oklahoma City residents take great *pride* in the fact that in less than 100 years the city has grown from a modest boomtown of 10,000 to a thriving metropolis of more than 800,000 spread out across 900 square miles, with plenty of elbow room and space to grow.

LOCAL SERVICES: Business Services – Kelly Services, 3030 NW Expressway (946-4309)

Mechanic – Ray's Tire and Auto Service, 5201 N Pennsylvania (842-1427)

BEST IN TOWN

 CHECKING IN: Expect to pay $80 and up for a double room at hotels listed as expensive and about $60 in the moderate category.

The Richmond Hotel – A new 50-suite property with tastefully decorated rooms and a good restaurant, *The Fairfax.* It's also close to some of the city's best shopping. NW Highway at Blackwelder (405 840-1440). Expensive.

Vista International at Waterford – The city's newest — and certainly its most ambitious — hotel, the *Vista* has 196 rooms and suites that are graciously appointed with lovely cherry wood armoires and other traditional pieces. For dining, its more formal restaurant is *The Waterford,* with a Continental menu; the *Veranda Room* serves lighter fare. And for relaxing, there's a well-equipped health spa with outdoor pool, tennis courts, and jogging track, Nautilus, sauna, whirlpool, and squash courts. 63rd at Pennsylvania (405 848-4782). Expensive to moderate.

Sheraton Century Center Hotel & Towers – This modern building in the heart of downtown has 400 rooms, brightly splashed in orange, rich brown, and beige tones. Outdoor pool, disco, and restaurants. 1 N Broadway (405 235-2780). Expensive to moderate.

Park Suite – A lovely new hotel offering 237 one- and two-bedroom suites exclusively, opening onto balconies overlooking a central atrium. Dining room. Meridian and SW 18th (405 682-6000). Moderate.

Holiday Inn City Center – If you're looking for convenience, this is probably your best bet. Sitting right in central downtown, it's closest to the Civic Center Music Hall and theaters. Outdoor pool. 204 rooms. 520 W Main (405 232-4444). Moderate.

 EATING OUT: Oklahoma City is known for its choice steaks. Restaurants are spread out across the city, rather than concentrated into one area. Expect to pay $40 at an expensive restaurant; between $15 and $20 at those we've classed as moderate; under $15 at the inexpensive one. Prices are for a meal for two, without drinks, wine, or tip.

The Fairfax – Decorated with dark wood paneling, oversized armchairs, and brass fixtures sparkling by candlelight, *The Fairfax* is recommended as much for its Continental cuisine as its appealing decor. Open daily. Reservations required. Major credit cards. In the *Richmond Hotel* on NW Hwy. at Blackwelder (842-3519). Expensive.

Christopher's – An intimate bistro serving French or Continental meals (lamb, duck, steaks, and seafood). Closed Sundays. Reservations necessary. Major credit cards. 2920 NW Grand Blvd. (943-8395). Expensive.

The Haunted House – For quiet, relaxed dining in a house that's reportedly haunted. House specialties focus on steak and seafood. When you make your reservations ask for directions; it's hard to find. Closed Sundays and holidays. Major credit cards. 1 mile east of Cowboy Hall of Fame, just off I-44 (478-1417). Expensive to moderate.

Alberta's Tea Room – A restaurant with a quiet atmosphere and fine food and service. *Alberta's* menu is the culmination of years of creative cooking, with homemade rolls, steak, fresh shrimp in a luscious rémoulade sauce, and other specialties. Open for lunch only; closed Sundays. Reservations required for parties of five or more. Major credit cards. French Market Mall at 63rd and N May (842-3458). Moderate.

Molly Murphy's House of Fine Repute – Waiters and waitresses here are actually performers who dress up like comic and storybook characters. The menu features steak and chicken, and the Bacchus feast, a platter of steak, chicken, vegetables, and fruit. Open daily. No reservations. Major credit cards. 1100 S Meridian (942-8588). Moderate.

Santa Fe Crossing – A good choice for lovers of Mexican food, it also has a charming southwestern-desert decor. Open daily. Reservations not necessary. Major credit cards. 36 W Memorial Pkwy. (755-9030). Moderate.

Oklahoma Line – Barbecue is king here, a hearty variety stirred up from beef ribs, brisket, and smoked sausages. Prime ribs, pork loin, and duck and chicken are also well prepared. There's even homemade ice cream for dessert. 1226 NE 63rd St. (478-4955). Inexpensive.

The Brick's – "Old style country cooking" is how they describe the menu; chicken fried steak (with the mandatory cream gravy), meat loaf, ham, and turkey are the staples. Homemade bread is featured, and there are homemade cookies for dessert. Basic food, for basic tastes. 3110 N Portland St. (942-0618). Inexpensive.

OMAHA

Whenever a stand-up comic wants to take a shot at a cowtown, he invariably aims at Omaha. Omaha has a lot of cows, and cows are a sure laugh. The blizzards and thundershowers are funny, too, but they obscure the target. What the comic fails to mention is that the Wizard of Oz also came from Omaha (as he admits when he's been debunked), and though it's no Emerald City, it has considerable appeal.

Nebraska's largest city (metropolitan population of 377,000) strikes a nice compromise between the friendly ways of a small town and the cultural sophistication of a far larger city. Omaha is the industrial center of the Great Plains and maintains one of America's largest shopping centers, but also has relatively clean air, a low crime rate, and free-flowing traffic. A good art museum, an ambitious opera, a symphony, and a zoo, provide evidence that Omaha is no longer just an overgrown cowtown, though the cows continue to be pretty important citizens.

Omaha is on the west bank of the Missouri River, and, with its suburbs, spreads out across 89 square miles of rolling midwestern terrain. The river, which runs 2,723 miles from southwest Montana to join the Mississippi north of St. Louis, has played an important role in the city's historic and economic development. Founded in 1854 by a ferryman from Council Bluffs, the raw young river town bristled with gunfighters and gamblers. In 1868, saloon keepers outnumbered teachers, and undertakers outnumbered clergymen. But its location on the river and the naming of the city by President Lincoln as the eastern terminus of the transcontinental railroad in 1862, assured Omaha's future prosperity. During the following decades, the prairie gave way to stockyards, plants, and warehouses. Today barges transport grain, farm products, and machinery on the Missouri, and the transcontinental railway lines converge in the home of Union Pacific. Omaha is a major center of grain and livestock markets, meatpacking, insurance, and is the headquarters of the Air Force's Strategic Air Command.

Despite its advantageous position, Omaha's collective ego is sensitive about being so far removed from America's cultural capitals. But this situation, too, has its assets. Residents are proud that many silly notions ballyhooed elsewhere never really catch on in Omaha. And some of them never even arrive. Swinging night spots are not that common, but the sunsets are beautiful. The Gerald Ford Birthsite is now a pleasant park. And there are many places to rustle up an Omaha steak, which is a carnivore's justly celebrated slab of pleasure.

Though the downtown area has been in a slow state of decline for twenty years, and many of the businesses have moved out to West Omaha, which sprawls with shopping centers, fast-food chains, and apartment complexes, a relatively recent "Return to the River" movement has generated renewed

interest in the downtown area. New government and university buildings and
a library have already been built. In place of deteriorated buildings near the
river, a key section of the new Central Park Mall has been completed, lined
with stores, fountains, and even an artificial stream that will someday stretch
to the river.

OMAHA AT-A-GLANCE

SEEING THE CITY: *Maxine's,* a restaurant and lounge atop the *Red Lion
Inn,* offers the best view of Omaha — the metropolitan area, the Missouri
River, and farther east to the small industrial town of Council Bluffs and
the bluffs themselves, which are wind-blown deposits of soil that have
formed steep hills, unusual for midwestern terrain.

SPECIAL PLACES: Omaha is spread out. You can walk around downtown
or take the bus, but it's best to have a car to visit the places of interest on
the outskirts of town, and in West Omaha, which is the thriving business
center.

Central Park Mall – Reclaimed from a decayed commercial and warehouse district,
this new urban park will stretch a mile east to the Missouri River when completed.
Lined with an artificial stream, pond, and waterfall, the Mall is already the site of
festivals and free concerts in nice weather. 14th and Douglas sts.

Union Pacific Historical Museum – In Union Pacific National Headquarters, the
museum recalls this line's colorful history as a transcontinental trailblazer, displaying
everything from thumbcuffs, used by railroad detectives to disable miscreants, to President Lincoln memorabilia (including a replica of his funeral car). Closed Sundays. Free.
1415 Dodge St. (271-3530).

The Old Market – Once Omaha's wholesale produce center, the market is now an
ever-changing collection of small shops, restaurants, pubs, art and craft galleries,
pinball arcades, and plant stores. Among the most interesting of the galleries is Artists'
Cooperative, which features contemporary and abstract prints, sculptures, and paintings by 30 of the area's best artists. At *Spaghetti Works,* you can have lunch or dinner
— all the spaghetti and as much of the works (bread, salad, sauces) as you can eat for
a song. 11th and Howard sts.

Antiquarium – Near but not part of the Old Market, the Antiquarium has the real
old stuff, from rare 19th-century manuscripts to over a half-million used books at
bargain prices. Closed Sundays. 1215 Harney St. (341-8077).

Joslyn Art Museum – This monolithic chunk of pink marble holds some of the finest
midwestern and western collections around as well as exhibitions of international art
through the ages. Features the Maximilian-Bodmer Collection of paintings done while
on the Belgian Prince's Upper Missouri River Expedition of 1833-34. Also has 19th-
century western landscapes of Albert Bierstadt, paintings by Remington, Russell,
Catlin, and the Stewart-Miller Collection, focusing on the Great Plains of the 1830s.
Closed Mondays. Admission charge. 2200 Dodge St. (342-3300).

Boys Town – An internationally famous institution for homeless boys, it was
founded in 1917 by Father Flanagan in the belief that there is no such thing as a bad
boy, given a good Christian upbringing and education. Self-conducted tours of the
campus, which has 65 buildings including grade and high schools, a trade school, gyms,
a fine philatelic and numismatic center, and 350 good boys. Open daily. Free. 138th
and W Dodge Rd. (498-1350).

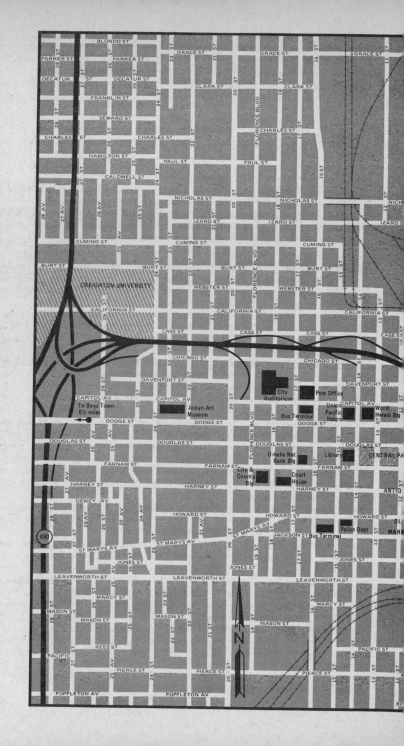

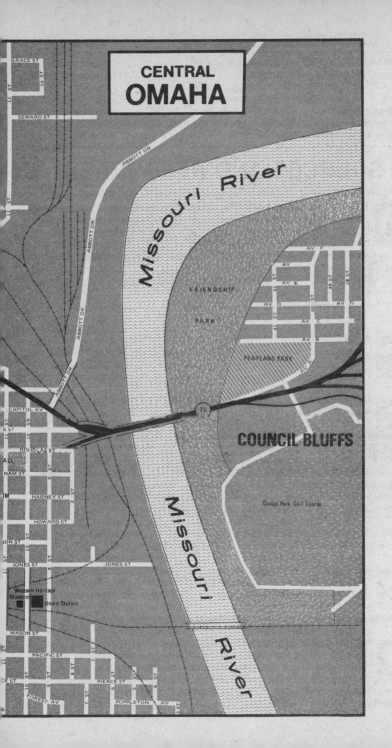

CENTRAL
OMAHA

■**EXTRA SPECIAL:** Fifty miles southwest of Omaha along I-80 is *Lincoln,* the state's capital and second largest city. The University of Nebraska State Museum (14th and U sts., in Morrill Hall) has excellent displays of the geology and animal life of the Great Plains from prehistoric to modern times, as well as the world's largest mammoth. The 400-foot capitol is an impressive sight, visible for miles around, and features a glazed dome with the Indian Thunderbird design, topped by a 32-foot statue of *The Sower.*

SOURCES AND RESOURCES

TOURIST INFORMATION: The Omaha Convention and Visitors Bureau (444-4660) publishes brochures and maps of attractions that are available in all the hotels. For timely information on scheduled cultural events, call the bureau's Events Hotline (444-6800).

Local Coverage – *Omaha World-Herald,* morning and evening daily, publishes Sunday *Entertainment* magazine which lists the coming week's events.

Food – Weekend editions of the *Omaha World-Herald* are your best bet for current information.

Area Code – All telephone numbers are in the 402 area code unless otherwise indicated.

CLIMATE AND CLOTHES: Seasons are distinct and there is daily variety, perhaps a bit too much for some when the mercury drops to 15° below or rises to 105° above. Omaha is mostly sunny, with evening showers and thunderstorms occurring frequently between April and September.

GETTING AROUND: Airport – Omaha's Eppley Airfield is a 10-minute drive from downtown; cab fare should run about $6. Airport Limousine (342-1131) vans are available at the airport to take passengers to some West Omaha hotels. (This service is free to registered guests at the *Omaha Marriott, New Tower,* and *Embassy Suites.*)

Bus – Metropolitan Area Transit provides efficient service for the city and Council Bluffs. For route information contact Metro Area Transit, 2615 Cuming St. (341-0800).

Taxi – Cabs can be picked up at taxi stands in front of major hotels or at the airport, or can be ordered on the phone. Major companies are Happy Cab (339-0110 or 331-8294); Checker Cab (342-8000); Safeway Cab (342-7474); and Yellow Cab (341-9000).

Car Rental – Omaha has offices of the major national firms and inexpensive service is provided by Thrifty, 2323 Abbott Dr. (345-1040).

MUSEUMS: In addition to the Joslyn Art Museum and the Union Pacific Historical Museum (see *Special Places*), there are:

Strategic Aerospace Museum – Open daily. 12 miles south on US 75 (292-2001)

Western Heritage Museum – Closed Mondays. 801 S 10th St. (444-5071)

MAJOR COLLEGES AND UNIVERSITIES: The University of Nebraska at Omaha at 60th and Dodge sts. (554-2800), with an enrollment of 15,000, and the Medical Center, 42nd St. and Dewey Ave. (559-4000) are both part of the University of Nebraska system. Creighton University (enrollment 5,000) is a private institution founded in 1878 by the Creightons, early settlers of the territory, 2500 California St. (280-2700).

SPECIAL EVENTS: The Ak-Sar-Ben *World's Championship Rodeo* in late September features bull riding, calf roping, wild broncos, livestock collections, and country-and-western entertainers.

 SPORTS AND FITNESS: Baseball – The American Baseball Association's Omaha *Royals* play their home games at Rosenblatt Stadium from May to September; 13th St. and Murphy Ave. (734-2550). In June, the stadium is the site of the NCAA Baseball World Series; tickets available at City Auditorium, 1804 Capitol Ave. (346-1323).

Fitness Centers – The Omaha Athletic Center has a sauna, weights, and exercise equipment, 2010 N 66th St., on Blondo (551-2228); the YMCA provides a pool, track, and racquetball courts, 20th St. and Howard (341-1600).

Golf – There are two excellent public golf courses: Benson at 5333 N 72nd St. (571-5940) and Applewood at 6111 S 99th St. (339-2020).

Horse Racing – For racing and pari-mutuel betting, Ak-Sar-Ben is ranked among the country's finest tracks. The season is from April through July, 63rd and Center sts. (554-8800).

Jogging – Run in Memorial Park; on the University of Nebraska at Omaha or Creighton University campuses; or in the Dundee area, off Dodge, especially along Underwood Street, which is lined with lovely, old homes.

Tennis – Dewey Park has fine outdoor public tennis courts, at 500 Turner Blvd. (444-4980), and Hanscom Park offers indoor public courts, 3200 Creighton Blvd. (444-5584 or 444-5585).

 THEATER: For current offerings, check the publications listed above. The *Omaha Community Playhouse,* where Henry Fonda got his start, puts on a large variety of productions year-round, using amateur performers and a professional staff, 6915 Cass St. (553-0800). The *Firehouse Dinner Theater,* 514 S 11th St. (346-8833), has professional local and outside actors who perform in comedies and dramas throughout the year.

 MUSIC: The *Omaha Symphony* performs with featured guest artists from September to May, and *Opera/Omaha* presents three operas from November to April, both at the Orpheum Theater, a restored vaudeville palace at 409 S 16th St. The City Auditorium has entertainment all year from rock and pop concerts to Triumph of Agriculture shows. Tickets for all Orpheum and Auditorium events are available at the Auditorium Box Office, 1804 Capitol Ave. (346-1323), or at Brandeis Stores ticket centers.

 NIGHTCLUBS AND NIGHTLIFE: *The Howard Street Tavern* is a two-fisted bar with the best in blues, jazz, rock, and bluegrass music, at 11th and Howard sts. (342-9225). Other hot spots are: *Arthur's Le Grille,* 8025 W Dodge Rd. (393-6369); *Chicago,* 3529 Farnam St. (346-7300), for chatting up; and *Club 89,* 89th and H sts. (339-8989), for cabaret.

 SINS: *Lust* is alive, if not exactly kicking, in Omaha. Ladies of the night once again ply the streets of downtown after dark, thanks to a recent change in state law that reduced their crime to a misdemeanor. For a pornographic book or movie, though, you'll still have to cross the state line to Council Bluffs, Iowa. As for other vices, any old-timer can probably recommend a spot where people fish illegally. *Gluttony* has never had a problem being indulged in Omaha, and it flourishes daily at the city's several bountiful buffets. *V. Mertz Restaurant,* 1022 Howard (345-8980), offers an elegant, inexpensive Sunday brunch.

LOCAL SERVICES: Business Services – Professional Typing Services, 900 S 74th St. (397-0309)

   Mechanics – Anderson's Amoco Service, 7911 W Dodge Rd. (393-2722)

BEST IN TOWN

CHECKING IN: Several of the national chains have good representatives in Omaha. Our selections range in price from around $75 and up for a double room per night in the expensive category, $50 and up in the moderate range, and $45 and under, inexpensive.

Embassy Suites – A Spanish-style building with a gleaming tiled fountain courtyard and indoor garden. The 188 suites have kitchens, living rooms, hide-a-bed couches, free full breakfasts. Facilities also include wet bars, indoor heated pool, whirlpools, and sauna to dry it all out. 7270 Cedar St., 1½ miles north of I-80, exit 72nd St. (402 397-5141). Expensive.

Red Lion Inn – Its location across the street from City Auditorium makes it Omaha's busiest convention hotel, with 456 rooms. The revolving bar of the rooftop restaurant, *Maxine's*, offers a panoramic view of the city. Free parking in adjacent garage. 1616 Dodge St. (402 346-7600). Expensive.

Omaha Marriott – This 303-room hotel is within walking distance of the city's largest shopping center, the Westroads. 10220 Regency Circle, just southeast of the I-680 Dodge St. exit (402 399-9000). Expensive.

New Tower – Centrally located, this 340-room hotel has good standard accommodations with modern furnishings and design. Features a domed indoor pool, saunas, whirlpool baths, and a cocktail lounge. 7764 Dodge St. (402 393-5500). Moderate.

Holiday Inn – Nebraska's largest hostelry (503 rooms) features 2 restaurants, 2 lounges with live entertainment, "Holidome" (enclosed swimming pool), putting green, electronic games, shuffleboard, and bar. 3321 S 72nd St., just north of I-80, exit 72nd St. (402 393-3950). Moderate.

Thrifty Scot Motel – In one of the city's busiest hotel areas, *Thrifty Scot*'s brand of basic hospitality includes color television, free Continental breakfast, plus *Perkins' Cake and Steak* restaurant next door. 7101 Grover, just north of I-80, exit 72nd St. (402 391-5757). Inexpensive.

EATING OUT: There really are a lot of cows out here, and when visitors eat out they quickly learn why. Omaha restaurant offerings run the gamut from prime ribs to hamburgers. Steaks are big here, and folks are proud of the local product — the beef is terrific. This is not fertile ground for vegetarians. Besides steakhouses, there are several ethnic eateries plus a handful of Continental restaurants. Our selections range in price from $50 up for a dinner for two in the expensive range, $30 to $45 in the moderate, and $25 and under in the inexpensive range. Prices do not include drinks, wine, or tips.

The French Café – Of Omaha's restaurants that specialize solely in French cuisine, this one carries an aura of glamour and buzzes with excited conversation. Specialties include veal, rack of lamb, a daily fresh-fish dish, French onion soup, rich desserts, and an extensive wine list, all served in an elegant yet comfortable atmosphere. It's decorated with antiques, brassworks, and fresh flowers. Closed Sundays. Reservations advised. Major credit cards. 1017 Howard St. (341-3547). Expensive.

Blue Fox – The Continental menu with a sprightly Greek accent is the creation of owner/chef George Kokkalas. Everything — from appetizers to desserts —

is made from scratch, and the fish and other seafoods are flown in fresh. The veal dishes and rack of lamb are very good. Closed Sundays. Reservations advised. 11911 Pierce Court; just off 119th and Pacific sts. in the Boardwalk Shopping Center (330-3700). Expensive.

Salvatore's – A restaurant that serves a wide range of Italian dishes as well as other fine Continental cuisine. There's a notable wine list and the owner sometimes sings opera. Closed Sundays. Reservations advised. Major credit cards. 4688 Leavenworth St. (553-1976). Expensive to moderate.

Gallagher's – The long menu runs the gamut from light to hearty fare — burgers to quiche. Opulent decor is set off by a stained-glass skylight. Open daily. Reservations suggested. Major credit cards. 10730 Pacific St. (393-1421). Moderate.

Imperial Palace – An artfully decorated alternative to the usual Chinese storefront restaurant. The menu embraces several of the cuisines of Northern China and the sinus-clearing specialties of Szechwan. Although a newcomer, *Imperial Palace* has gained a reputation as Omaha's best Oriental restaurant. Open daily. Reservations accepted. Major credit cards. 627 N 109th Plz. (496-1888). Moderate.

Firmature's Sidewalk Café – At this green oasis within the city's most elegant shopping center, the all-encompassing menu ranges from lighter fare — omelettes, crêpes, and such — to steaks and seafood. Specialty of the house is Omaha's most coveted prime ribs. The New Orleans Brunch served on Sundays is worth missing a sermon for. Open daily. Reservations advised. Major credit cards. 153 Regency Fashion Court (397-9600). Moderate.

Mister C's – Although the decor here might be a little tacky — twinkling lights reminiscent of Italian street carnivals, an iridescent mural of Venice on one wall, a backlighted diorama of a Sicilian village on another — the food is quite good. Specialties are Omaha steaks and Italian pasta; homemade soup appears on every table nightly except Saturdays, and strolling musicians play requests nightly. *Mister C's* may be the busiest steakhouse in Omaha, and despite its formidable capacity, there's often a wait to get in. Mister C himself greets one and all. Open daily. Reservations advised. American Express only. 5319 N 30th St. (451-1998). Moderate to inexpensive.

Neon Goose – This glitzy café/bar covers an entire block facing the city's old Union Station, just a short walk south of the Old Market area. Its menu runs from burgers to fresh seafood and it is known for a very good Sunday brunch. Closed Mondays. No reservations. Major credit cards. 1012 S 10th St. (341-2063). Moderate to inexpensive.

Bohemian Café – Besides an impressive collection of Jim Beam bottles, which speaks for itself, the café features a full line of Eastern European specialties, like boiled beef in dill gravy, sweet and sour cabbage, roast duck, liver-dumpling soup, and kraut. Open daily. Reservations. Major credit cards. 1406 S 13th St. (342-9838). Inexpensive.

Michaels' II – When *mamacitas* do the cooking, they do it right. Consistently excellent Mexican food — spiced to sting, but not to start a fire — served in an unpretentious bar atmosphere. Open daily. No reservations. No credit cards. 1919 Missouri Ave. (733-9666). Inexpensive.

To corral a prime Omaha steak, try either of Omaha's classic steakhouses, *Johnny's* or *Ross'*. In both places all is the way it should be, big and heavy, from the cowtown decor, where huge tables and chairs leave plenty of room to rassle with the beef to that pure slab of well-marbled pleasure itself, which can weigh in at as much as 20 ounces (not including the potato, spaghetti, bread, and salads that normally come along with the main ingredient). *Johnny's* (4702 S 27th St., 731-4774). *Ross'* (909 S 72nd St., 393-2030). Both closed Sundays. Both take reservations and credit cards. Expensive to moderate.

ORLANDO

Orlando was just another good-sized American city until 1971, when Walt Disney's dream park opened nearby. The number of hotel and motel rooms shot from 6,300 to more than 44,000 in the next few years. The $300 million Orlando International Airport, whose glass, concrete, and steel structure is considered the state of the art in airport design, was constructed within a decade to handle the dramatically increased traffic, and it soon became the fastest-growing airport in the US.

In short, Orlando had come a long way since it started out as a campground for soldiers fighting the bloody Seminole Indian War in the early nineteenth century, and it was formally established in 1857. But despite several growth spurts — in 1880, when a railroad line was run from the city of Sanford; in the 1920s, just before the Great Depression; in 1956, with the opening of an important defense plant; and in 1961, when President Kennedy declared that the US would place a man on the moon within the next ten years and thereby launched the space industry in Central Florida — Orlando drifted into and through the twentieth century on the commerce of oranges and cows. And since the area was always more or less farmland, much of Orlando today is short on antique charm and long on look-alike apartment developments, fast-food restaurants, used car lots, and other none-too-lovely marks of the modern age.

What many people don't realize until they spend a little more time here is that the city has its beauty spots as well. Though parts of its downtown may seem sad and decaying, other sections have recently been renovated and spruced up. The city also boasts the elegant *Harley Hotel* and the lively Church Street Station entertainment complex, which attracts residents from the little towns around Orlando for a night out. The entire area is neat and clean as a pin, and as Church Street Station caught on, a number of other buildings in the neighborhood were turned into atmospheric restaurants and clubs.

Then there's Winter Park, one of Orlando's small towns-cum-suburbs. There are lovely neighborhoods where the lawns are broad and velvety and dotted with palms or huge old live oaks thickly veiled with Spanish moss. The houses are sprawling and of gleaming white stucco, with roofs of red-orange ceramic tile in the Spanish style. The shops and restaurants in the small "downtown" commercial area can hold their own among sophisticates anywhere in the country.

Moreover, Orlando is something of an outdoors paradise. The more than 2,000 spring-fed lakes in the area take care of the water sport scene, and the 85 publicly owned and operated parks and recreation facilities offer golf, tennis, jogging, and lots more. Residents as well as visitors take advantage of the abundant recreational facilities at Walt Disney World, some 20 miles southwest of downtown, especially after-dark entertainment and the three championship golf courses.

ORLANDO AT-A-GLANCE

 SEEING THE CITY: For most visitors, the Orlando area's premiere panorama is the one from *Top of the World* in Walt Disney World's *Contemporary Resort.* Whether you see it at sunset, when rosy light gilds the spires of Cinderella Castle, or at night, when tiny white lights glitter along the rooflines, it's absolutely stunning.

 SPECIAL PLACES: Walt Disney World alone requires 3 days — and even 6 days would not do justice to all its shows, sporting facilities, restaurants, and attractions. When the rest of Orlando is also considered, it's easy to see how time can really fly during a visit.

ORLANDO AND ENVIRONS

Florida Cypress Gardens – It's said that you'd have to visit 70 countries at different times of the year to see all the plants that can be viewed in a single day at this 223-acre attraction developed back in the mid-1930s. The famous water ski shows, in which athletes ski barefoot and backward, are also well worthwhile. Open daily. Admission charge. Rt. 540, Winter Haven (351-6606).

Gatorland Zoo – In a couple of hours here you see *thousands* of alligators. Open daily. Admission charge. US 17-92-441N near Kissimmee (855-5496).

Sea World – The world's largest marine park ranks among Orlando's must-sees thanks to the high quality of the animal displays. Don't miss the Shamu Experience, in which three 4,000-pound killer whales perform balletic leaps and rolls, and the Shark Encounter exhibition, which includes a film showing an incredible shark-feeding frenzy sequence and a glass tunnel that lets you walk "through" a huge pool full of sharks. Open daily. Admission charge. 7007 Sea World Dr., Orlando (351-3600).

Wet 'n Wild – Among connoisseurs of water slides, this aquatic play park full of water-based thrill rides gets top marks. Bring a bathing suit, and prepare for long lines on summer afternoons. Varying hours, depending on the season. Admission charge. 6200 International Dr., Orlando (351-3200).

WALT DISNEY WORLD

The fact that Walt Disney World attracts some 23 million visitors annually says just about everything that anyone needs to know about the basic appeal of Walt Disney's greatest dream-come-true. Less obvious is the sheer extent of the place. For instance, the Magic Kingdom, the well-known rides and attractions area with the Cinderella Castle and other landmarks of American pop culture, occupies just 98 of the 27,400 acres of WDW's property. EPCOT Center, which opened in the fall of 1982 to great fanfare, is more than twice as large — and that still leaves 27,000 acres for the villas and hotels, shopping, a nonpareil swimming hole, golf courses, tennis courts, and a huge nature preserve. The main telephone number at WDW is 824-4321.

Magic Kingdom – The glittering Cinderella Castle, the magical heart of the Magic Kingdom, sets the mood for this marvel of a park full of nooks and crannies, lush landscaping, restaurants, shops, shows, and "adventures" — boat rides, roller coasters, and other amusements that transcend themselves because they're incorporated into elaborate sets full of artificial plants, robotic people, and sound effects.

Top attractions include Pirates of the Caribbean and Jungle Cruise in the park's

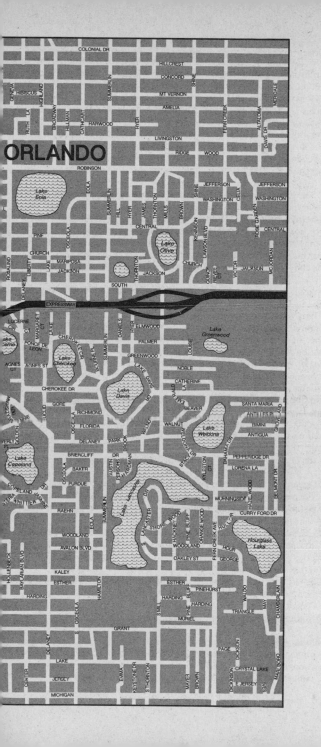

Adventureland section; the implacably cute Country Bear Jamboree and Big Thunder Mountain Railroad in Frontierland; the beautiful Haunted Mansion in Liberty Square; the wild Space Mountain in-the-dark coaster in Tomorrowland; Fantasyland's It's A Small World, with mechanical dolls and folk costumes; and the Hall of Presidents in Liberty Square, where a Disney-manufactured Abraham Lincoln stands up and talks as though he were Abe in the flesh.

During summer evenings and school holiday periods, be sure to see the Main Street Electrical Parade. The floats, made of metal frameworks studded with a million twinkling lights, are stupendous; the music, very tuneful. The 5 minutes of fireworks presented shortly after the end of the first of the two runnings of this parade are equally impressive.

EPCOT Center – Something like a world's fair but executed with the considerable technical skills, creativity, and financial resources of the Disney organization, EPCOT Center has two "entertainment worlds": Future World and World Showcase. Future World examines often controversial concepts such as energy and agriculture, while World Showcase brings nations of the world to life with the same extraordinary devotion to detail that makes the Magic Kingdom so enchanting. Appropriate entertainment, ethnic food, and lively shops stocked with wares made in the featured nations round things out.

At EPCOT Center, as in the Magic Kingdom, there are a few attractions that visitors simply must not miss. In Future World, these include the ride inside the round ball known as Spaceship Earth, the Listen to the Land boat ride in The Land pavilion, the Journey into Imagination ride, the stunning new 3-D movie *Captain EO* (starring Michael Jackson), and the electronic funhouse known as the Image Works (all in the Journey into Imagination pavilion); and the shows in the World of Motion, Horizons, and Energy pavilions. In World Showcase, you should see the movies in the Canada, China, and France pavilions, which take the travelogue to new heights, and the technologically marvelous show at the American Adventure.

Walt Disney World Shopping Village – The shops here stock everything from baby bonnets to silk dresses, from thousand-dollar bottles of wine and toy soldiers to stuffed animals — and then some. You can sit on a bench and watch the boats on the lagoon — or rent one yourself on the spot. Best of all, for R&R, there's the wonderful *Baton Rouge Lounge,* aboard the gleaming white riverboat known as *Empress Lilly,* and *Cap'n Jack's,* across the lagoon, where you can get huge, tart, unique-to-WDW strawberry margaritas.

River Country – It's next to impossible to go through childhood without developing a few fantasies about the perfect swimming hole. River Country is just such an animal, and it's full of curvy water chutes where even blasé grownups can't help but grin, even roar, with delight. A Disney must.

Discovery Island – Crisscrossed by footpaths, this tranquil 11½-acre landfall in Bay Lake is the home of dozens of birds — some in cages or huge aviaries, others running free; their chirps, tweets, crows, and caws nearly drown out the sounds of the little motorboats zipping across surrounding Bay Lake.

Behind the Scenes – There isn't a Magic Kingdom visitor around who wouldn't like to see Disney character costumes being made or talk to a Disney artist in person. The Wonders of Walt Disney World program makes precisely this kind of experience available to youngsters, and Disney Learning Adventures does the same for adults.

Hoop-Dee-Doo-Revue – Perhaps the most memorable of all WDW's lively live entertainment is this dinner show, wherein a round of singing, dancing, and wisecracking keeps audiences whooping it up until their sides are as sore from laughing as their stomachs are full of country-style vittles. Reservations are required well in advance (824-8000).

SOURCES AND RESOURCES

 TOURIST INFORMATION: For details, contact the Orlando Area Chamber of Commerce, Tourism Development Dept., Box 1234, Orlando, FL 32802 (425-1234); Orlando Convention and Visitors Bureau, 7680 Republic Dr., Orlando, FL 32819 (345-8882); and Walt Disney World Co., Box 40, Lake Buena Vista, FL 32830 (824-4321).

Local Coverage – There are what's-doing sections in Friday's *Orlando Sentinel,* a daily, and in *Orlando* magazine. We immodestly believe that the best guide to the area is our own companion volume, *Steve Birnbaum Brings You the Best of Walt Disney World* (Houghton Mifflin; $8.95).

Area Code – All telephone numbers are in the 305 area code unless otherwise indicated.

 CLIMATE AND CLOTHES: Spring and fall enjoy temperatures averaging in the mid-70s. From November through March, warmer clothing is a must for evening. Always pack something for unseasonably warm or cool weather.

 GETTING AROUND: Airport – Orlando International Airport is 12 to 15 miles from the city's downtown area and 28 miles from the gates of Walt Disney World. Cab fare from the airport to Orlando averages around $12, $30 to WDW. Airport Limousine (859-4667) provides transportation from the airport to the major downtown hotels for $11 and to WDW for $10. Reserve a seat upon landing at the airport; a van should depart about 20 minutes later. American Sightseeing Tours (859-2250) has bus service from the airport to many hotels. City buses run hourly between the airport and Orlando's downtown terminal at Pine and Central; the fare is 60¢. Call 841-8240 for more information.

Bus – Gray Line (422-0744) and Rabbit (291-2424) are among the operators providing transportation from hotels all over the city to the major attractions. American Sightseeing Tours (859-2250) has service from the airport to many hotels. Hotel desks can provide details.

Taxi – Several firms provide service, among them City Cab (422-5151), Yellow Cab (699-9999), and Ace Taxi (859-7514).

Car Rental – Most major car rental firms are represented. Orlando has one of the largest number of fleet vehicles of any US city, and the rates (most with unlimited mileage) are relatively modest.

 MUSEUMS: Orlando has a handful of noteworthy small institutions:

Loch Haven Art Center – permanent displays of paintings and sculpture and frequent special exhibits, 2416 N Mills Ave. (896-4231).

Morse Gallery of Art – noted for its collection of Tiffany stained glass, 151 E Welbourne Ave. in Winter Park (645-5311).

Orlando Science Center – 810 E Rollins St. (896-7151).

 MAJOR COLLEGES AND UNIVERSITIES: University of Central Florida, Alafaya Trail (275-2000); Rollins College, Winter Park (646-2000).

SPECIAL EVENTS: The *Scottish Highland Games* in January draw huge crowds for Highland dancing and bagpipe competitions. The *Winter Park Sidewalk Art Festival,* the third weekend of March, is one of the Southeast's most prestigious such events. Zellwood's *Sweet Corn Festival,* in late May, features corn on the cob by the crate and plenty of toe-tapping music. The *Florida State Air Fair,* held in Kissimmee in October, has performances by the US Navy's Blue Angels. At Walt Disney World, beautiful decorations are put up at Christmastime, and there are parties and extra-large fireworks displays on New Year's Eve. The Fourth of July also occasions additional pyrotechnics.

SPORTS AND FITNESS: Baseball – The Minnesota *Twins* hold their spring training at Orlando's Tinker Field in late February and early March. The Orlando *Twins,* a farm team, play here in summer (849-2105). The Houston *Astros* prepare for the season at Osceola Stadium in Kissimmee (933-5500).

Fishing – Bass anglers flock to Florida's third largest lake, Tohopekaliga. To find out about nearby fishing camps, contact the Kissimmee–St. Cloud Convention and Visitors Bureau (847-5000).

Fitness Centers – The YMCA, 433 N Mills Ave., Orlando (896-6901), has an indoor pool, weight room, gymnasium with Nautilus equipment, outdoor track, and racquetball facilities.

Football – The USFL Orlando *Renegades* (843-USFL) play at Orlando Stadium from August through January, as do the University of Central Florida *Knights* (849-2105) in the fall.

Golf – Walt Disney World has three public courses: Magnolia and Palm at the *Disney Inn* and Lake Buena Vista Golf Course (824-3625).

Jogging – Around Lake Eola in downtown Orlando, and on a trail at Fort Wilderness and on the roads of WDW.

Swimming – Wet 'n Wild and WDW's River Country (see *Special Places*) are good bets for a dip, and most hotels have pools. Within the boundaries of WDW, there are especially good-size pools at *Contemporary Resort* (824-1000), *Royal Plaza* (828-2828), and *Buena Vista Palace* (827-2727).

Tennis – It's possible to play on the many lighted Walt Disney World courts (where court reservations, lessons, rental rackets, and even a partner-finding service are available; 824-1000, ext. 3578). Or you can play for a small fee on Orlando parks courts (849-2161). *Americana Dutch Resort Hotel, Hotel Royal Plaza, Buena Vista Palace, Hilton at Walt Disney World Village, Holiday Inn Main Gate-East, Hyatt Orlando, Ramada Resort Hotel, Sheraton-Lakeside Inn, Grand Cypress Hyatt Regency, Court of Flags, Orlando Vacation Resort, Orlando Marriott, Wyndham Hotel Sea World,* and *Sheraton World* are among the establishments with courts for guests.

THEATERS: *Mark Two* features a buffet meal followed by a Broadway-style musical with a professional cast, 3376 Edgewater Dr. (422-3191). At *King Henry's Feast,* a five-course repast is served in true Elizabethan style (no forks), while some of the Bard's characters perform, 8984 International Dr. (351-5151). The *Civic Center of Central Florida* features musicals, dramas, and mysteries, 1010 E Princeton St. (896-7365).

MUSIC: Programs of dance, music, and theater are often presented at the Mayor Bob Carr Performing Arts Centre, 401 Livingston St. (843-8111).

NIGHTCLUBS AND NIGHTLIFE: Once a pair of decaying hotels in a depressed section of none-too-lively downtown Orlando, the *Church Street Station* complex of bars and restaurants is now a very big deal, and nobody grumbles too much — on the way home — about the cover/entrance charge. There's Dixieland to keep things lively at vast, wood-floored *Rosie O'Grady's Good Time Emporium,* bluegrass at the brick-floored, plant-and-wicker-decked *Apple Annie's Courtyard,* disco in *Phineas Phogg's Balloon Works,* traditional American and Continental food at *Lili Marlene's,* and barbecue and all the fixings at the *Cheyenne Saloon & Opera House.* Be aware that the charge for many specialty drinks includes the price of the glass (you turn it in at the gift shop for a refund). Children are welcome. 129 W Church St. (422-2434).

In Winter Park, there's *Cheek to Cheek,* 839 N Orlando Ave. (644-2060), a good place for dancing to top-40 music. *Park Avenue,* 4315 N Orange Blossom Trail (295-3750), has a huge dance floor and great sound system.

And WDW itself has a variety of night spots, from the elegant, intimate *Empress Lilly Lounge* and the comfortable *Village Lounge,* which attracts top jazz entertainers, to the mad, merry *Baton Rouge Lounge,* which features Disney's own more than competent musician-comedians.

 SINS: *Lust* thrives in the topless bars along Orlando's South Orange Blossom Trail.

 LOCAL SERVICES: Babysitting – Both *Polynesian Village Resort* and *Contemporary Resort* have child care facilities. Kindercare, the children's center at WDW, is suitable for youngsters ages 2 through 12 (827-KIDS).

Business Services – Business Innovations, 1093 S Semoran Blvd., Bldg. 1, Winter Park (671-8611), and Custom Communications, 7040 Lake Ellenor Dr., Orlando (855-2242)

Mechanics – Allied Auto Repair, 5829 Old Winter Garden Rd., Orlovista (293-3773); Don's Chevron, 2610 Edgewater Dr., Orlando (425-7372); the Car Care Center, Floridian Way, Walt Disney World (824-4813)

(BEST IN TOWN)

 CHECKING IN: Most Orlando-area accommodations are clustered along International Drive and nearby Sand Lake Road at the Orlando city limits, 10 to 15 minutes' drive from WDW; along US 192, which runs east and west and intersects I-4 near WDW (actually in Kissimmee, and closer to WDW); and inside WDW itself. Expect to pay $125 to $190 for a double at those places designated as expensive; $80 to $120 for those identified as moderate; and $50 to $75 at inexpensive spots — occasionally less in quiet periods in winter.

Walt Disney World–owned Properties – For both facilities and convenience, the hotels and villas owned by the Disney organization can't be beat, and unless your budget prohibits it, you should make every effort to set yourself up in one of them. *Contemporary Resort,* a bustling high-rise with a pair of 3-story wings, has magical views, a lake's-edge location, 2 terrific swimming pools, and one of the biggest game rooms anywhere. *Polynesian Village Resort,* on lushly landscaped grounds in several buildings by a lake, is only slightly more tranquil. Both are on the monorail line — and exceptionally convenient to both the Magic Kingdom and

EPCOT Center. The understated *Disney Inn* (the old *Golf Resort*) is nearby, not on the monorail, but has a pleasantly relaxed atmosphere. Close to the array of shops at WDW Shopping Village are a fair number of spacious contemporary villages: *Club Lake Villas, Fairway Villas,* and *Vacation Villas.* All of them are especially good values for families. The octagonal *Treehouse Villas* — built on stilts, surrounded by pines and peacocks, and equipped with kitchens — are utterly delightful. Also lovely are the luxurious trailers at *Fort Wilderness Campground,* which come complete with bathrooms, color televisions, and fully equipped kitchens. All properties are expensive. For details, phone WDW Central Reservations (305 824-8000).

Walt Disney World Village Hotel Plaza – The six hotels here, within walking distance of Walt Disney World Shopping Village, are nearly as convenient as the WDW-owned properties, and a couple of them are a bit less pricey. Also, small discounts on WDW admission tickets are available to guests at *Hotel Plaza* properties. Our favorites in the complex are *Buena Vista Palace,* which boasts 870 handsomely decorated rooms embellished with Mickey Mouse telephones and old-fashioned ceiling fans (as well as air conditioning), plus outstanding sporting facilities (305 827-2727 or 800 327-2990); the 814-room *Hilton at Walt Disney World Village* has a Youth Hotel that recommends it to guests with children (305 827-4000); also attractive is *Hotel Royal Plaza,* a 17-story high-rise with a pair of 2-story wings, plus tennis courts and a good swimming pool (305 828-2828 or 800 327-2990). *Howard Johnson's Resort Hotel,* another sleek high-rise with a 6-story annex, is also handsome (305 828-8888 or 800 654-2000). Note that reservations for all of these properties can be made through WDW Central Reservations (305 824-8000). All are expensive.

Marriott's Orlando World Center – Opened in the spring of 1986, this 1,503-room, 27-story resort hotel commands nearly 200 beautifully landscaped acres, just minutes away from Walt Disney World's EPCOT Center. Features include a 6-story lobby atrium, 4 swimming pools, 12 lighted tennis courts, an 18-hole Joe Lee golf course, fully equipped health spa, game room, 10 restaurants and lounges, and specialty shops. World Center Dr., Orlando (305 239-4200). Expensive.

Hyatt Regency Grand Cypress – This glittering, $110 million, 750-room luxury hotel, with a 170-foot atrium lobby modeled after the *Hyatt Regency Maui,* is the star of an 800-acre complex that has more facilities than most visitors can ever use, including one of the largest free-form swimming pools anywhere. The golf course, restricted to guest use, is a Jack Nicklaus gem. 1 Grand Cypress Blvd., Lake Buena Vista (800 228-9000). Expensive.

Wyndham Hotel Sea World – This new $86 million, 782-room property rises 10 stories above an enormous atrium complete with free-flying birds and exotic fish. A fitness center, 6 tennis courts, pool, 4 restaurants, and convention facilities round out the offerings. 6677 Sea Harbor Dr. (305 351-5555). Expensive to moderate.

Orlando Marriott Inn – The 1,079 smart rooms here — arranged in 2-story stucco-walled villas scattered around landscaped grounds — are popular with business travelers, but ideal for any visitor in search of serenity. 8001 International Dr. (305 351-2420). Moderate.

Park Plaza – Orlando's answer to New England's country inns has plenty of charm, even if the rooms don't always measure up to the palm-and-antique-decked lobby. 307 Park Ave. S, Winter Park (305 647-1072). Moderate.

Days Inn–Lake Buena Vista – An especially good value very close to Walt Disney World Village and EPCOT Center. There are 203 rooms, a pool, restaurant, and game room. 12799 Apopka-Vineland Rd., Lake Buena Vista (305 239-4441). Inexpensive.

EATING OUT: The last decade's growth has attracted chefs from all over the world, so first-class dining experiences are easy to find. Expect to pay between $40 and $70 for two at those places listed as expensive; between $30 and $40 in the moderate category; and under $30 in the inexpensive bracket — excluding drinks, wine, and tips.

Empress Room – Elegant (but cordial) service and Louis XV surroundings, replete with crystal and gold leaf make this WDW room in the *Empress Lilly* riverboat a favorite among Orlando residents out for a big celebration. Jackets required for men. Open daily. Reservations necessary well in advance. Major credit cards. Walt Disney World Village, Walt Disney World (828-3900). Expensive.

Le Cordon Bleu – The unpretentious decor here gives no hint of the quality of the artichoke bottoms filled with crabmeat and glazed with Mornay sauce, snails in garlic butter, rack of lamb, and other specialties at this favorite eating spot. Closed Sundays. Reservations necessary on weekends. Major credit cards. 537 W Fairbanks, Winter Park (647-7575). Expensive.

Chefs de France – Three of France's finest chefs — Paul Bocuse, Roger Vergé, and Gaston LeNôtre — firmly based the menu here on nouvelle cuisine, with very good results. Gleaming napery, sparkling brass, etched glass, and all manner of turn-of-the-century touches make the decor as appealing as the food. There's also a separate menu "for the little gourmet" (for kids under 12) at reduced prices. A first-rate bistro thrives upstairs. Open daily. Reservations necessary (but available only in person at EPCOT Center). Major credit cards. World Showcase, EPCOT Center, Walt Disney World. Expensive.

Maison & Jardin – An elegant spot with high ceilings, widely spaced tables, and vast windows that take in the surrounding formal gardens, this restaurant that local wags have nicknamed "Mason Jar" serves ambitious fish, meat, and fowl preparations. Major credit cards. 430 S Wymore Rd., Altamonte Springs (862-4410). Expensive.

Park Plaza Gardens – Garden-like awnings, skylights, and greenery make a lovely backdrop for tasty, well-sauced meals. Open daily. Reservations accepted for dinner only. Major credit cards. 319 Park Ave. S, Winter Park (645-2475). Expensive.

Barney's Steakhouse – Voted the citizens' favorite steakhouse in an *Orlando Sentinel* reader survey, *Barney's* also has a huge salad bar. Open daily. Reservations accepted only for parties of eight or more. Major credit cards. 1615 E Colonial Dr., Orlando (896-6864). Moderate.

La Cantina – Orlando residents line up for as much as an hour for the huge steaks and Italian specialties here. Closed Sundays and Mondays. No reservations. Major credit cards. 4721 E Colonial Dr., Orlando (894-4491). Moderate.

East India Ice Cream Company – Imaginative breakfasts, big sandwiches at lunch and dinner, unusual flavors of ice cream made on the premises, and an antique-like, brick-floored setting are the drawing cards. Open daily. No reservations or credit cards. 327 Park Ave. S, Winter Park (628-2305). Inexpensive.

Orient IV – Orlando's best for Szechwan and Hunan-style Chinese cooking. Open daily. Reservations accepted. Major credit cards. 104 Altamonte Ave., Altamonte Springs (830-4444). Inexpensive.

Other Walt Disney World Restaurants – Most first-time visitors are surprised at just how far the WDW food offerings stray from the well-trod hamburgers-and-hot-dogs path — and then dive right into steak and kidney pie, fettuccine all' Alfredo, amaretto-flavored soufflés, or any number of other exotic foodstuffs served at EPCOT Center's *World Showcase*. Another pleasure is that even cafeterias and fast-food eateries have a bit of atmosphere that makes them just a little special. Where you eat at WDW will be determined by where you are at mealtimes. Below are a few of the more noteworthy spots.

In the Magic Kingdom, *Crystal Palace,* an old-fashioned glass-and-plant-filled cafeteria on Main Street, is very pretty. *Town Square Café* nearby serves delicious Monte Cristo sandwiches. *King Stefan's Banquet Hall* in Cinderella Castle has service by waitresses (but you must reserve in person, first thing in the morning). EPCOT Center offers even greater variety. In Future World, try *The Farmers Market* in The Land, where each of a half-dozen stands serves soups or salads, barbecue, cheese items, baked potatoes, and other savory specialties. Upstairs, at *The Land Grille Room,* are unusual American foods and scrumptious cheese bread. At the Living Seas Pavilion, try the fresh seafood at *Coral Reef Restaurant,* complete with a panoramic view of a living underwater coral reef. *Stargate* serves unique breakfast pizzas. In World Showcase, don't miss Canada's low-ceilinged, stone-walled *Le Cellier,* a cafeteria that offers a tasty Canadian pork and potato pie called tourtière; Italy's *Alfredo's,* for tasty Italian food; Germany's *Biergarten,* for its hearty food and oom-pah entertainment; Mexico's *San Angel Inn Restaurante,* which takes Mexican food far beyond tacos; and China's *Nine Dragons Restaurant,* where meals are prepared in a variety of provincial Chinese cooking styles. Dinner reservations, a must at many restaurants, must be made in person in Earth Station; to get them, arrive at the front gate a half-hour before the published park opening, decide where to eat, and send the speediest member of your group to book your table when the park opens. (Be aware that by an hour later most restaurants are usually booked for prime dinner hours.) Lunch reservations can be made at the restaurant in person on the day of the seating or at Earth Station. Booking procedures sometimes change, so confirm the preceding information on arrival at WDW (824-4321).

At *Contemporary Resort,* consider the elegant *Gulf Coast Room* for a big occasion or the viewful *Top of the World* for its bountiful breakfast and Sunday brunch buffets. The superb banana-stuffed French toast served in *Polynesian Village Resort's Tangaroa Terrace* is worth a detour. At *Disney Inn's Garden Gallery,* there's delicious french-fried ice cream at lunch and dinner.

In Walt Disney World Village, the comfortable, unassuming *Village Restaurant* has fine lake views. Aboard the *Empress Lilly* riverboat, there's the charming *Fisherman's Deck* and the hearty Victorian *Steerman's Quarters,* with a picture-window view of a churning paddlewheel.

Travelers with children should make note of the special breakfasts and dinners with Disney characters in attendance (824-4321; 824-8000 for reservations).

PHILADELPHIA

An American visiting Philadelphia for the first time is bound to leave with a new appreciation of what the United States stood for when it was founded. It's not merely a question of the neatly preserved pockets of historic buildings. It has to do with the Philadelphians themselves. They have a way of talking about "our history" that naturally seems to include a visitor, even if your first reaction is to think "Our history? I don't live here." A few hours spent walking through streets that look like illustrations in history books you read as a child will bring home the notion that this is, truly, the America you learned about in school.

But it's not a textbook experience. The tradition in which the city was born, the inextricable marriage of politics and conscience, is everywhere evident. Even on bitterly cold days, you are likely to see human rights vigils at Independence Mall, across the street from the buildings in which the Bill of Rights and the Constitution were drafted, and where the Declaration of Independence was signed. Residents don't pass even small demonstrations without at least slowing down to read the signs; and a protest too small to warrant media attention in New York is often reported in detail here. A longtime resident, who opposed the Vietnam War, says he often comes to gaze at the Tomb of the Unknown Revolutionary Soldier in Washington Square. "I just come to read the inscription ('Freedom is a light for which many men have died in darkness'). I ask myself what I would have done then. Of course, I can't say. But I do know that those people acted on their conscience. They had to fight. They weren't heroes, so much as real people making ethical decisions. Like we did during the Vietnam War."

When William Penn founded Philadelphia in 1682, on a flat, fertile site between the Delaware and Schuylkill rivers, he advertised his colony as a place of religious freedom, christening it "The City of Brotherly Love." Thousands of persecuted Europeans left their homes and came to this New World city to create lives for themselves that would enable them to live in accord with their beliefs. By 1750, Philadelphia was the leading city in the colonies. In 1752, the Liberty Bell emerged from a foundry in England. It had been designed to mark the 50th anniversary of William Penn's Charter of Privileges. A precursor of later documents, such as the Universal Declaration of Human Rights, the Charter declared, "Proclaim liberty throughout all the land, unto all the inhabitants thereof." When the colonies broke away from Great Britain in 1776, the Bell cracked upon being put to use. (It was recast by a Philadelphia foundry.) From 1790 to 1800, the first Congress of the United States met in Congress Hall. Philadelphia only relinquished its role as the nation's capital when the District of Columbia became the permanent headquarters of the federal government.

The city now has a population of 1.6 million (4.7 million in the metropoli-

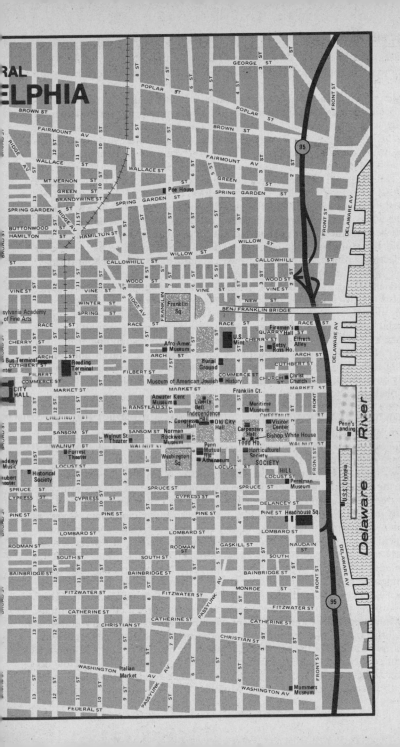

tan area). To this day it follows Penn's original plans, laid out around four spacious parks (one in each quadrant of the city). Today's Philadelphians still live in the city's 18th-century town houses, trimmed with cream-colored wooden shutters, and they pray in the same churches as did George Washington, Benjamin Franklin, and John Adams. You begin to discover Philadelphia as you walk along the narrow red brick, dovetail-patterned sidewalks that lead through narrow alleys to reveal hidden gardens and courtyards. These parts of the city look remarkably like the 18th-century sections of London.

And it's not all solemn. Walking along Market Street between the river and City Hall, you will discover a quickening pace amid a typical hodgepodge of chain stores selling clothing, drugs, novelties, pastries, ice cream, nuts, records, stereos, and radios. Market Street can suddenly start to pulse with disco music, while the street vendors peddling balloons and pretzels dance in place to the beat; at the same time, an old blind man with a tin cup in front of a 5¢ and 10¢ store wails the blues in a voice strong enough to be heard over the electronic music, the rushing crowds, and the buses. Throughout the day, people wander through Wanamaker's, one of the city's oldest and most prominent department stores. A delightful place for shopping and browsing, it boasts the city's most famous meeting place — the bronze bald eagle statue on the main floor of the store's seven-story atrium. The holiday season brings a special tradition to Wanamaker's, when people congregate around the eagle to gaze at a brilliant show of lights and to listen to resounding triumphal strains of the organ that sound like a cross between a church and an ice skating rink. The best view is from the main floor, where you can see the lovely gold pipes and behold the architectural splendor of the six layers of white balconies trimmed in gold.

Almost directly behind Wanamaker's is the city's most famous landmark, William Penn's statue on City Hall. The city's founder crowns a dome that, in turn, caps what can only be described as an architectural extravaganza of portholes, turrets, wedding cake statuettes, Ionic, Doric, and Corinthian columns and pillars. Until 1984, Billy Penn's statue (as residents call it) was, by law, the tallest fixture on the skyline. After a lengthy debate, the rule declaring that nothing in the city exceed the 548-foot height of the statue was overturned, and a contractor was allowed to erect two taller buildings. Diagonally behind Penn's left shoulder stands the giant clothespin — yes, a sculpted clothespin — which dominates the plaza in front of the Atlantic Richfield building. The old-fashioned wooden clip clothespin towers several stories above street level, in funny juxtaposition to the solid, ornate City Hall.

Philadelphia's sense of humor cuts loose every New Year's Day, when the Mummers Parade struts down Broad Street, playing tunes like "Oh, Dem Golden Slippers." A tradition since 1901, it is Philadelphia's Mardi Gras, incorporating the ebullient New Year's customs of several ethnic communities. Mummers' suits (don't call them costumes) are extraordinary fantasies of brightly colored silk, sequins, gold braid, feathers, pointed hats, and veils. Prizes are awarded for the best, some of which are on display at the Mummers Museum, where you can also listen to recordings of parade music. How do you get to be a Mummer? According to a former resident, you have to be invited to participate by one of the Mummers Clubs — usually a storefront social club in the ethnic neighborhoods of South Philly (where the *Rocky* movie series has been filmed). Because of the competitiveness among rival clubs and neighborhoods, coming from West Philly makes you ineligible. Once you're in the club, you can spend the rest of the year practicing an instrument like the ukulele or banjo, learning the songs and steps to the Mummers Strut. Mothers in the neighborhood often spend the year designing and sewing the suits, although there are some commercial establishments like Pierre's on Walnut Street which supply outfits.

In recent years Philadelphia, like so many cities, has been in the course of restoration. Slums have been swept away, and crumbling chunks of the business district have fallen to the wrecking ball, giving way to better housing and commercial facilities. This, in turn, has stimulated residents to return to the city from the suburbs. The Society Hill riverfront restoration project is a case in point. Named for the Free Society of Traders, an early British company, Society Hill had deteriorated over the years. But with ingenuity, determination, and creative use of space, it was transformed into what has since been called "the textbook example of how to improve urban environment in America." Concern for keeping the city livable has resulted in rezoning some of the downtown streets into traffic-free pedestrian malls. Now you can browse along Chestnut Street, Philadelphia's popular shopping street, without breathing exhaust fumes or dodging in and out of traffic to cross to the other side. You can also wander along the Delaware River, taking in the sights and sounds of the riverfront shops on Front Street, and the boats berthed in the docks. And, if you're feeling extravagant or just want to delight your shopping eye, be sure to visit the Bourse. Standing not 500 feet from the Liberty Bell, this restored, turn-of-the-century building offers elegant shops and restaurants.

Every July, Philadelphia celebrates the signing of the Declaration of Independence. The bicentennial celebrations of 1976 focused national attention on the place where it all began. But when the firecrackers stopped and the 200-year anniversary became just another page in the calendar, the bicentennial displays were not torn down; they were, instead, integrated into the network of historic sites that people come from all over the world to see.

Philadelphia residents used to joke that the next-door state of New Jersey had been created only so that Philly residents would have somewhere to go on the weekend. But nowadays people joke, "I went to Philadelphia on Sunday — and it wasn't closed."

PHILADELPHIA AT-A-GLANCE

 SEEING THE CITY: You don't have to run up the steps of the Philadelphia Museum of Art the way Sylvester Stallone did in his *Rocky* movies. You can walk up to get the same far-reaching view of the skyline. Inside, you'll find an impressive collection of paintings, drawings, sculpture, and graphic art from all periods and countries. Closed Mondays and holidays. Admission charge (for the museum, not the view). 26th and Parkway (763-8100).

For a different but equally appealing view of Philadelphia, go to City Hall Tower.

Visitors are welcomed in the Tower waiting room and then taken up to the observation deck, which offers views of the city, its surrounding rivers, and the New Jersey shoreline. Open weekdays. Free. At Broad and Market sts. (686-4546).

You can also see Old Philadelphia by horse-drawn carriage. Tours depart from the carriage stand on Chestnut between 5th and 6th streets daily, weather permitting, from March through December; by appointment only in January and February. Charge for carriage tours (922-6840).

 SPECIAL PLACES: Philadelphia's tight city blocks and narrow streets make it great for walking, not driving. Streets, laid out in checkerboard fashion, are easy to understand, but they are always choked with traffic. It's best to park your car at your hotel. Philadelphia's main places of interest are clustered in Independence Hall National Historical Park and around Fairmount Park in West Philadelphia.

INDEPENDENCE HALL HISTORICAL AREA

Visitor Center – This is a good place to launch a tour of the historical area and pick up maps and brochures. Open daily. Free. 3rd and Chestnut sts. (597-8974).

Independence National Historical Park – "The most historic square mile in America." This is what everyone comes to see. Within the park, you'll find the major Colonial and Revolutionary era buildings, which we've listed separately, below. Open daily. Free. The general park area runs from 3rd to 7th St. between Chestnut and Walnut sts. (597-7018; 627-1776 for a 24-hour recording).

Independence Hall – When you think of Philadelphia, this is probably the first image that comes to mind. The solid tower, massive clock, and graceful spire are unmistakable. Early colonists called it the State House. Here, the Declaration of Independence was signed, and 11 years later, the Constitution was written. Open daily, with guided tours. Free. 5th and Chestnut sts. (597-8974).

Congress Hall – The first US Congress met here, between 1790 and 1800. George Washington delivered his final congressional address in these halls; here, too, the Bill of Rights was adopted. In 1800, the seat of federal government moved to the District of Columbia. Open daily. Free. 6th and Chestnut sts. (597-8974).

Old City Hall – The first US Supreme Court issued judgments from the bench inside this building. The Court moved to new headquarters in Washington, DC, in 1800. Inside, an audio-visual show gives you an idea of what life was like in post-Revolutionary Philadelphia, with an emphasis on the formative years of the federal judiciary. Open daily. Free. 5th and Chestnut sts. (597-8974).

Independence Mall – Across the street from the Halls, this leafy stretch of grass, fountains, and tree-lined walks contains the glass pavilion housing the Liberty Bell. It was moved from Independence Hall so more people could see it and touch it. Open daily. Free. Market and 5th sts. (597-8974).

Carpenters' Hall – So named because it housed the Carpenters' Company Guild during the colonial era (before unions). The oldest building organization in the US still owns the hall, and early carpentry tools are on display. In 1774, the First Continental Congress met here. Closed Mondays; also closed Tuesdays in January and February. Free. 320 Chestnut (925-0167).

Todd House – Before she became Dolley Madison — wife of fourth president James, famed as First Lady and society hostess — she was Dolley Payne Todd, whose husband, the young Quaker lawyer John Todd, died in the yellow fever epidemic of 1793. Their home, built in 1775, is typical of middle-class residences of the period. Free guided tours, by reservation only, must be arranged in person at the Visitor Center (see above). Open daily. 4th and Walnut sts. (597-8974).

Bishop White House – While the Todd House reflects a middle-class lifestyle, this home typifies the affluence of people such as Bishop William White, a politically active Episcopalian minister (from the 1770s to the 1790s) who served as rector of both Christ Church and St. Peter's. Open daily. Free. 3rd and Walnut sts. Can be combined with a tour of the Todd House. Sign up at the Visitor Center (597-8974).

Christ Church – Benjamin Franklin sat in pew 70. George Washington prayed here, too. The original church was built in 1695; this, a larger one, was erected in 1745. It's still in use. Open daily. Donation suggested. 2nd St. above Market St. (922-1695).

Christ Church Burial Ground – Throw a penny on the grave of Benjamin and his wife, Deborah Franklin. It's a Philadelphia custom. Tours by appointment. Open daily May through October. 5th and Arch sts. (923-1100).

Betsy Ross House – Where, tradition says, George Washington directed Elizabeth Ross, an upholsterer's widow, in the stitching of the first American flag. According to the Philadelphia Historical Commission, however, Betsy Ross never lived here and had nothing to do with the first US flag. Make up your own mind, after you've seen this tiny cottage filled with household items and memorabilia allegedly pertinent to that famous seamstress. Open daily. Free. 239 Arch (627-5343).

Elfreth's Alley – The oldest continuously occupied residential street in America, dating back to 1690. Only one block long, six feet wide, it is lined with 200-year-old houses. Usually the first weekend in June, Elfreth's Alley holds its annual pageant. North of Arch St., running between Front and 2nd sts. For more information, call the museum at #126 (574-0560).

Headhouse Square – Only survivor of the many middle-of-the-street markets that once flourished in the city. Built in 1775, it has good restaurants and revitalized shops. In summer, there are crafts demonstrations and concerts. 2nd and Pine.

Mummer's Museum – The city's pop history is lovingly preserved in this memorial in South Philadelphia, in the heart of where Mummery began. The outside is tile as dazzling as a Mummer's suit. Inside are memorabilia, history, sound recordings. Closed Mondays. Admission charge. 2nd St. at Washington Ave. (336-3050).

Franklin Court – Benjamin Franklin came to Philadelphia in 1723. In his later years Franklin resided in a brick house on this site. He died here in 1790. Although the house itself is no longer standing (it was demolished in 1812), three of the surrounding houses designed by Franklin are here, along with an 18th-century garden with a mulberry tree (planted by the National Park Service in 1976 — because Franklin had one), a print shop, and a post office. An underground museum has Franklin stoves and a phone where you can "dial-an-opinion" from Benjamin Franklin. Open daily. Free. Running from Chestnut to Market between 3rd and 4th sts. (597-8974).

USS *Olympia* – The oldest steel-hulled American warship afloat, the *Olympia* was Commodore George Dewey's flagship at Manila Bay in the Spanish-American War. Open daily. Admission charge. Penn's Landing (922-1898).

Boathouse Row – A collection of Victorian boathouses used by collegiate and club oarsmen. The hub of many national competitions. East River Dr., running along the east bank of the Schuylkill River, north of the Museum of Art.

WEST PHILADELPHIA

Fairmount Park – Approximately 8,000 acres of meadows, gardens, creeks, trails, and 100 miles of bridle paths for joggers, bicyclists, softball players, fishermen, and picnickers. The Fairmount Park Trolley Bus (879-4044, for information), a replica of a Victorian conveyance, is a pleasant way of getting around the park and also seeing some of Philadelphia. On Mondays and Tuesdays (daily December through March) there is a 2½-hour narrated tour of the Society Hill section of the city, Center City, and parts of the park, stopping at one of the seven restored historic mansions: Cedar Grove, Sweetbriar, Lemon Hill, Mount Pleasant, Strawberry, Woodford, and Laurel Hill. Wednesdays through Sundays, April through early December, the bus makes

90-minute rounds of the park with on-off privileges at all of the mansions. Don't miss the Christmas tour the first weekend in December, which takes in the mansions and Horticultural Society, decorated in colonial holiday styles. (Closed Mondays and Tuesdays. Admission charge. For guided tours, call 787-5449.) Park open daily. Free. The park begins at Philadelphia Museum of Art and extends northwest on both sides of the Wissahickon Creek and Schuylkill River.

Philadelphia Zoo – Established in 1874, this is the nation's oldest. More than 1,600 animals, reptiles, and birds make their home within its 42 acres. There are several natural habitat displays, a children's zoo, and a safari monorail aerial tram. Open daily, except holidays. Admission charge except on Mondays from November through February. 34th St. and Girard Ave. (387-6400).

Philadelphia Museum of Art – Outstanding collections of all periods and schools, housed in a sweeping Greco-Roman building. Limited access on Tuesdays; closed Mondays and holidays. Admission charge except on Sundays until 1 PM. 26th and Parkway (763-8100).

Franklin Institute Science Museum – Ben Franklin would have traded his kite for one day in this remarkable science museum, with Fels Planetarium and four huge floors jammed with exhibitions on anatomy, aviation, and space exploration. Open daily. Admission charge. 20th St. and Parkway (564-3375; planetarium, 563-1363).

Rodin Museum – Sculpture, sketches, and drawings make up the largest collection of Auguste Rodin's work outside France. An afternoon can easily be spent wandering through the halls and gardens. Foreign language tours are available by appointment. Closed Mondays and holidays. Free; donations accepted. 22nd and Parkway (763-8100).

OTHER SPECIAL PLACES

City Hall – The most distinctive landmark in Philadelphia. Critics have called it "an architectural nightmare." Others praise its elaborate decor: sculpture, marble pillars, alabaster chandeliers, ceilings with gold leaf, carved mahogany, and walnut paneling. The Tower, at William Penn's feet, looks out to the Delaware and Schuylkill rivers (smog permitting). The business district fans out from City Hall. Guided tours of the tower and offices are offered weekdays. Free. At Broad and Market sts. (686-2250).

Rittenhouse Square – Named after David and Benjamin Rittenhouse, who designed the first astronomical instruments in the United States toward the end of the 18th century. Today, Rittenhouse Square is one of the loveliest, most elegant residential areas of the city. Handsome brownstones and high-rise apartment houses surround a green park, where people from all over town congregate. Art shows, flower shows, and concerts take place here in spring and summer. At 18th and Walnut.

United States Mint – Watch coins being minted. This facility can produce 10,000 coins per minute. At each marked observation post, a pushbutton activates a taped commentary on the different stages of the minting process. Historic coins are exhibited in the Relic Room, and a special counter sells proof sets and medals. Accessible to people in wheelchairs. Closed Sundays and national holidays. Free. 5th and Arch sts. (597-7350).

Edgar Allan Poe House – The poet composed his epic to the raven, and his chilling story *The Murders in the Rue Morgue* in these quarters. He lived here for three years, with his mother-in-law and young bride. A must for Poe addicts. Closed only on major holidays. Free. 532 N 7th (597-8780).

Pennsylvania Horticultural Society – The formal gardens of the 18th century are recreated here, with flowers, shrubs, and pruned trees typical of the era. This is the oldest horticultural association in the US, with a library devoted to botanical subjects. Open weekdays. Free. 325 Walnut (625-8250).

Reading Terminal Market – Shoppers of all persuasions come to foray for fresh ground horseradish, study French brie, and snack at oyster bars. Check out the home-made soups and hot-from-the-oven shoofly pie. Ice cream at *Bassett's* is a must. Closed Sundays. 12th St. just north of Market (922-2317).

Italian Market – Also known as Rocky's market. This is part of Sylvester Stallone's famous jogging trail, in South Philly. 9th St. and Washington Ave.

■ **EXTRA SPECIAL:** Even if you've never played the song "Washington at Valley Forge" on a kazoo, you've undoubtedly heard of the place. General George Washington and 11,000 Revolutionary troops retreated to *Valley Forge* during the winter of 1777-78. The site of their camp and training grounds is now a state park. The visitors center has a film and museum (open daily, but weekends are best — when the park's historical buildings and brigade huts are open). Closed Christmas. Free. Take Schuylkill Expressway to Valley Forge exit (about 20 miles). Take Route 363 north to the park (783-7700).

SOURCES AND RESOURCES

 TOURIST INFORMATION: Right in the heart of the city, only steps from City Hall, is the Philadelphia Visitors Center, with maps, brochures, and other information. Ask specifically for CAP's (a commercial/civic organization) free brochures: *Center City Philadelphia Map of Shopping, Dining & Cultural Attractions* and *Philadelphia in the Spring* (or one of the other three seasons, depending on your interest). 16th St. at John F. Kennedy Blvd. (568-6599). For a recording on what to see and where to go, call the Philly Fun Phone (568-7255), which operates 24 hours a day.

Foreign visitors can stop in at the Council for International Visitors (withs 24-hour emergency language translation), Civic Center Blvd. at 34th St. (879-5248).

Local Coverage – *The Inquirer,* morning daily; *The Daily News,* afternoon daily; *Philadelphia* magazine, monthly.

Food – *Philadelphia* magazine's restaurant listings or the CAP brochure.

Area Code – All telephone numbers are in the 215 area code unless otherwise indicated.

 CLIMATE AND CLOTHES: Winter temperatures in Philadelphia generally hover in the 20s and 30s. Spring and autumn are the best times to visit — temperatures then are usually in the 50s to 70s. Summer tends to be hot and sticky, with temperatures in the 80s and 90s.

 GETTING AROUND: Airport – Philadelphia International Airport is a 30-minute drive to Center City (up to an hour during rush periods); taxi fare should run about $17. Knights Limousine (632-4685) has van service every 15 minutes from the airport to Center City hotels at $5 per person, to City Line Ave. hotels for $7.50, and to other points in the city for $6. Knights also serves Northeast Philadelphia with rates starting at $17.75 for a single passenger and $10 more for each additional person. The SEPTA (Southeastern Pennsylvania Transportation Authority) Airport Express train (574-7800) makes the 20-minute trip to the city's main terminal, 30th St. Station, for $3.50 during peak periods, $2 at other times. Trains stop at most of the airport terminals every half-hour.

Bus – SEPTA (Southeastern Pennsylvania Transportation Authority) will take you everywhere, by bus, trolley, or subway. A good SEPTA map showing routes for all public transportation is available at newsstands (call 574-7800 for information). The

#76 bus runs daily except Sundays and takes you up and down the city's main shopping thoroughfare on Chestnut Street between 19th and 5th sts.; 50¢.

Car Rental – Philadelphia is served by all the national firms.

Taxi – Costly, but for short hops to transport three or four people, it's worth it. Hail them in the street or do as Philadelphians do and pick them up in front of the 30th Street train station, the Greyhound bus terminal, or the nearest hotel, which is where most of them wait for customers. Call Yellow Cab (922-8400), Quaker City Cab (728-8000), or United Cab Association (625-2881).

MUSEUMS: Independence National Historic Park, Philadelphia Museum of Art, Rodin Museum, and the Franklin Institute Science Museum, described in *Special Places,* are only a few of Philadelphia's museums. Some of the other notable museums are:

Academy of Natural Sciences – 19th St. and the Parkway (299-1000)

Afro-American Historical and Cultural Museum – 7th and Arch (574-0380)

Athenaeum – Library and historic documents, 219 S 6th St., Society Hill (925-2688)

Attwater Kent Museum – Local history, 15 S 7th St. (922-3031)

Barnes Foundation – Art; Fridays through Sundays only; reservations helpful, 300 N Latch's La., Merion Station (667-0290)

Civic Center – Variety of exhibitions, 34th and Civic Center Blvd. (823-7400)

Fireman's Hall Museum – 2nd and Quarry sts. (923-1438)

Historical Society of Pennsylvania – 1300 Locust St.(732-6200)

Institute of Contemporary Art – U. of Pennsylvania, Meyerson Hall, 34th and Walnut sts. (898-7108)

Library Company of Pennsylvania – Rare books, 1314 Locust (546-2465)

Museum of American Jewish History – 55 N 5th St. (923-3811)

Mutter Museum – Medical history, 19 S 22nd St. (561-6050)

Pennsylvania Academy of Fine Arts – The oldest art school and museum in the country, Broad and Cherry sts. (972-7600)

Perelman Antique Toy Museum – 270 S 2nd St. (922-1070)

Philadelphia Maritime Museum – 321 Chestnut St. (925-5439)

Please Touch Museum – Terrific hands-on exhibitions for children 7 years and under, 210 N 21st St. (963-0667)

Print Club – Prints and photography, 1614 Latimer (735-6090)

Norman Rockwell Museum – 6th and Walnut (922-4345)

Rosenbach Museum – Former private house containing porcelains, antiques, graphic art, 2010 Delancey Pl., between Spruce and Pine (732-1600)

University of Pennsylvania Museum – 33rd and Spruce (898-4000)

Wagner Free Institute of Science – 17th St. and Montgomery Ave. (763-6529)

MAJOR COLLEGES AND UNIVERSITIES: Philadelphia's colleges and universities are among the best in the country. Foremost is the University of Pennsylvania, founded by Benjamin Franklin in 1740. 34th and Walnut (898-5000). Others include: Temple University, Broad St. and Montgomery Ave. (787-7000); Drexel University, 32nd and Chestnut (895-2000); La Salle College, 20th and Olney (951-1000); St. Joseph's College, 5600 City Line Ave. (879-7300); Haverford College, Haverford (896-1000); Swarthmore College, Swarthmore (447-7000); Bryn Mawr College, Bryn Mawr (645-5000); Villanova University, Villanova (645-4500).

SPECIAL EVENTS: *The Mummers Parade,* a Philadelphia tradition on January 1, is eight hours of string bands strutting up Broad Street in elaborate costumes. Spring comes to the city during the second week in March when the *Philadelphia Flower and Garden Show* is held at the Civic Center,

34th and Civic Center Blvd. Come fall, *Super Sunday,* usually the second Sunday in October, is a day of free culture at institutions along the Benjamin Franklin Parkway with folk dancing, flea markets, music, food, and mobs of people. The *Philadelphia Craft Show,* held the first or second weekend in November at the 103rd Engineers Armory at Drexel University, displays and sells a wide variety of crafts by area artisans.

 SPORTS AND FITNESS: Whether you like to watch or do it yourself, there's enough sports activity to satisfy even the fanatics.

Baseball – From April to September, the *Phillies* chase the pennant at Veterans Stadium, Broad St. and Pattison Ave. (463-1000).

Basketball – Pro basketball's *76ers* pack them in at the Spectrum, Broad St. and Pattison Ave., from October to April (339-7676).

Bicycling – Rent from the Fairmount Bicycle Rental (closed Sundays) behind the Art Museum, Boathouse Row and E River Dr. (765-9118). Some 10.6 miles of Fairmount Park are devoted to bike paths.

Boating – Within the city you can rent rowboats and canoes for the Schuylkill River at the East Park Canoe House on E River Dr. (225-3560).

Fitness Centers – Your hotel facilities may prove your best bet. The Queen Village Racquetball & Fitness Club provides a pool, whirlpool, sauna, racquetball courts, and exercise equipment at one-day guest rates, 325 Bainbridge St. (922-7900).

Football – The NFL *Eagles* (463-5500) play at Veterans Stadium.

Golf – Try to get invited to a country club. If you can't, your next best bet is to try the public city course at Cobbs Creek, 7800 Lansdowne Ave. (877-2724).

Hockey – Hardest to get are tickets to the *Flyers,* who play ice hockey at the Spectrum from October to May. Best bet is to try a center city ticket agency (or call 755-9700).

Horse Racing – Philadelphia Park has thoroughbred racing at Street and Richlieu rds. (632-5770).

Jogging – In Fairmont Park, run along the banks of the Schuylkill River; enter the park at Eakins Oval.

Skiing – Everybody goes to the Pocono Mountains, two hours away in northeastern Pennsylvania. Best bets: Camelback Mountain, Tannersville (717 629-1661), Big Boulder, Lake Harmony (717 722-0101), and Jack Frost, Whitehaven (717 443-8425).

Tennis – The nation's number one indoor event, the US Pro Indoor, is held annually at the Spectrum in late January. The city owns more than 200 all-weather courts and Fairmount Park also has that many. Call the City Recreation Dept. at 686-3600.

 THEATER: Broadway- and off-Broadway-bound shows, or post-Broadway reruns, are all performed at three major houses and a dozen other theaters. *Forrest Theater* at 1114 Walnut (923-1515) has year-round offerings, as do *Walnut Street Theater,* 9th and Walnut (574-3550), and *Walnut Theater,* 2030 Sansom St. (963-0345). The *Annenberg Center* at 3680 Walnut St. (898-6791) has three theaters that present a wide variety of plays and musicals and house the Philadelphia Drama Guild, the Annenberg Subscription Series, and the Philadelphia Festival Theater for New Plays.

 MUSIC: The *Philadelphia Orchestra* under conductor Riccardo Muti performs at the Academy of Music, a classic 1847 building at Broad and Locust sts. (893-1930). In summer, they play at the Mann Music Center, Fairmount Park (567-0707), where rock concerts are also held.

 NIGHTCLUBS AND NIGHTLIFE: Philadelphians prefer cabarets to Las Vegas–type shows. Best bets: *Café Borgia,* 406 S 2nd St. (574-0414), a café with Left Bank ambience and sophisticated jazz; *Rick's Cabaret,* 757 S Front (389-3855), featuring an assortment of live entertainment and dancing;

Chestnut Cabaret, 3801 Chestnut (382-1201), ranging from rock 'n' roll to rhythm and blues; and *Middle East,* 126 Chestnut (922-1003), with bellydancers. Comics perform upstairs from *Middle East* at *Comedy Works* (922-5997), at *The Comedy Factory Outlet,* 31 Bank St. (386-6911), and at *Going Bananas* on 2nd St. between South and Bainbridge (925-3470). *Palumbo's,* 824 Catherine (627-7272), has long been a citadel of family-style entertainment.

SINS: If you want to see *sloth* at its well-dressed best, take a stroll around City Hall, at Broad and Market streets. Not only is the building replete with 19th-century statuary goddesses, but the offices exude the vapors of languishing bureaucrats, the product of a still thriving patronage system.

Across from City Hall, at 15th and Market streets, is Claes Oldenburg's *Clothespin,* a piece of sculpture that produces real *anger* among the city fathers, who think it is fashionable to hate contemporary art. If you hate contemporary art, the 45-foot chrome and steel monument to laundry and the Eiffel Tower will probably make you mad, too.

Gluttony can be indulged in many forms in Philadelphia. You can start with an orgy of ice cream at *Hillary's* at 437 South St., 1207 Walnut St., or 1929 Chestnut St., and then get down to the gritty Philly reality of the Italian Market, 9th St. at Washington Ave. Staggering quantities of the good things in life are just waiting to be taken home. Mussels come by the bushel in large brine-filled barrels; rice and exotic golden grains pour from their sacks; skinned rabbits, hot Italian sausage, and provolone cheeses swing from the ceilings; and there is plenty to nibble on while picking and choosing.

LOCAL SERVICES: Business Services – CPS Services, Philadelphia Center Hotel, 1725 John F. Kennedy Blvd. (563-1542)
  Mechanic – Center City Service (24-hour garage), 427 N Broad (922-7021)

■ **TAKE SOME PHILADELPHIA HOME WITH YOU:** "Tastykakes" are what exiled Philadelphia residents dream about. The little packages of cakes and pies are available at most grocery stores. But the biggest food thrill is Bassett's ice cream, available around the city.

BEST IN TOWN

CHECKING IN: Hotels range from durable, famous places to sleek, new spots with loud, lively lobbies. But there are very few really good inexpensive hotels. Expect to pay $100 to $150 or more for a double in any of those places we've listed as very expensive; between $75 and $100, expensive; between $50 and $75, moderate. Most hotels offer weekend packages at significantly reduced rates. For B&B accommodations, contact Bed & Breakfast of Philadelphia, PO Box 680, Devon, PA 19333-0680 (215 688-1633).

Barclay – A quiet, stylish stalwart, only steps from Rittenhouse Square and the Walnut Street shops. Its restaurant is a favorite with the monied Main Line crowd. Though the 240 rooms are not regal, they are comfortable and tastefully furnished. 237 S 18th St. (215 545-0300). Very expensive.

Four Seasons Hotel – The height of elegance, the 377-room *Four Seasons* opened in 1983 and filled up quickly with convention bookings. Featuring such touches as a mini-bar in each room, twice-daily maid service, and a complimentary shoeshine, there are also two restaurants: *The Fountain* has been winning very high praise for its menu, which changes frequently and emphasizes local favorites — and a courtyard café during the summer. Other amenities include meeting rooms and a health spa with a pool, exercise room, sauna, and whirlpool. Typical first-rate *Four Seasons* service. One Logan Sq. (215 963-1500). Very expensive.

The Palace Hotel of Philadelphia – Another relative newcomer to the city's hotel scene, this 280-room British-owned property is furnished in 18th-century English reproduction pieces and carved French-style beds. Features include restaurant and lounge, outdoor pool, and reciprocal arrangements with city health clubs. 18th and Parkway (215 963-2222 or 800 223-5672). Very expensive.

Hershey Philadelphia – A first-class 450-room contemporary hotel in the center of the city, it features extensive meeting facilities, 2 restaurants, 3 cocktail lounges, and nightly entertainment. The athletically inclined can use the pool, indoor jogging track, racquetball courts, exercise room, and game room or relax in the sauna and whirlpool. Broad and Locust sts. (215 893-1600). Very expensive.

The Latham – The 145 rooms are inviting, with bright floral bedspreads, marble topped bureaus and nightstands, and graceful French writing desks. Chocolates on the pillow at night are one of the ways the hotel pampers its guests. A favorite of businesspeople who seek a central location and good service. Its café, *Bogart's* (see *Eating Out*), and bar are places to see and be seen. 17th and Walnut (215 563-7474). Very expensive.

Franklin Plaza – This large, lavish gem is one of the city's best, and only four blocks from City Hall, a few steps from the parkway. Facilities include 800 modern rooms, racquetball courts, health club, underground parking, meeting rooms, and 4 restaurants. 17th and Vine sts. (448-2000). Very expensive.

Adams Mark – Across from the *Marriott,* this 515-room property was completely refurbished in 1983. The decor, featuring furnishings from around the world, is tasteful and elegant. Amenities include 2 restaurants, 2 lounges, nightly entertainment, meeting rooms, indoor and outdoor pools, sauna and whirlpool, racquetball courts, and exercise rooms. Free parking. City Line Ave. and Monument Rd. (215 581-5000). Very expensive.

Hilton – Slightly away from the mainstream with its Civic Center location, but close enough to most sites to remain convenient. Rooftop restaurant, discotheque, coffee shop, and indoor pool. 400 rooms. Civic Center Blvd. at 34th St. (215 387-8333). Very expensive to expensive.

Marriott – Comfortable modern decor with 4 restaurants, 3 swimming pools (1 indoors), and ice skating (weather permitting). Stores, restaurants, and night spots line the highway near the hotel. Check into "great escape" weekend packages. 750 rooms. City Line Ave. and Monument Rd. (215 667-0200 or 800 228-9290). Expensive.

Holiday Inn–Center City – Good location, near the Penn Center complex. Indoor pool, standard amenities. Within walking distance of major museums, a mile from Independence Mall. Free indoor parking. 304 rooms. 18th and Market (215 561-7500). Expensive.

Sheraton Inn–University City – Convenient to the University of Pennsylvania campus, with free parking and a restaurant called *Smart Alex,* whose disc jockeys provide evening entertainment. Outdoor pool. 377 rooms. 36th and Chestnut sts. (215 387-8000). Expensive.

Howard Johnson's – Near Valley Forge, with an outdoor pool, restaurant, cocktail lounge, entertainment, and free in-room movies. 168 rooms. Rte. 202, N and S Gulph Rd., King of Prussia (215 265-4500). Expensive to moderate.

Quality Inn–Center City – With 284 rooms in the heart of the museum district and within walking distance of most major city attractions, the style is casual comfort.

Amenities include restaurant, lounge, outdoor pool, and free parking. 22nd and Parkway (215 568-8300). Moderate.

Holiday Inn–Midtown – Small, scrupulously maintained 160-room motor inn with a good location and an outdoor pool. Near theaters, and just a stroll away from all the best shops. Free indoor parking. 1305 Walnut (215 735-9300). Moderate.

Penn Center Inn – This pioneer high-rise motor inn built in 1962 and continues to keep house competently in its 304 rooms. Has a small gym and sauna. Free indoor parking. 20th and Market (215 569-3000 or 800 523-0909). Moderate.

Philadelphia Best Western – Recently taken over by the chain, this 350-room hotel offers guests an indoor pool, restaurant, and free parking. It's also convenient to City Line shops and restaurants. City Line and Presidential Blvd. (215 477-0200). Moderate.

George Washington Motor Lodge – We're certain George Washington would have preferred staying here during his cold Valley Forge encampment. Its facilities include 330 rooms, a restaurant, cocktail lounge, and indoor/outdoor pool. Rte. 202 and Warner Rd., King of Prussia (215 265-6100). Moderate.

EATING OUT: The city boasts quite a few outstanding restaurants. In fact, in recent years Philadelphia has been enjoying something of a restaurant renaissance with both spacious and intimate places opening their doors, many offering very fine dining experiences. Expect to pay $75 or more for two in those places we've listed as very expensive; $50 to $70 in the expensive category; $20 to $40, moderate; $15 or less, inexpensive. Prices do not include drinks, wine, or tips.

Le Bec Fin – Usually the best in town and, at its best, one of the finest restaurants in the country. Imaginative French food by Georges Perrier, a master chef from Lyon who has lately grown a touch erratic. Still, quenelles with lobster sauce are exceptionally good, as are the lavish desserts. Closed Sundays. Make weekend reservations well in advance as the restaurant seats only 60. Lunch served weekdays. Prix fixe dinner, around $70 per person. American Express and Diners Club. 1523 Walnut (567-1000). Very expensive.

DiLullo Centro – Opened in 1985 in a renovated theater, this large establishment has world-class atmosphere and small restaurant quality. Opulence is everywhere, from a bronze food-presentation table and glass elevator to Impressionist murals. The menu features a wide variety of pasta and seafood dishes. Closed Sundays. Reservations suggested. Major credit cards. 1407 Locust St. (546-2000). Expensive.

Bogart's – Like the movie set of *Casablanca,* with wooden ceiling fans and tinkling piano. You won't find Bogie belting one down at the bar, but you will find Continental dishes and a well-dressed crowd. Open daily. Reservations suggested. Major credit cards. *Latham Hotel,* 17th and Walnut (563-9444). Expensive.

The Garden – Seafood and French country cooking in a stylish old town house. You can eat outdoors in the courtyard when the weather's good, or station yourself at the cozy Oyster Bar in the front room. Closed Sundays. Reservations advised. Major credit cards. 1617 Spruce (546-4455). Expensive.

La Terrasse – A glass-enclosed terrace where a tree grows amid the dining tables is the focal point of this small, lively French restaurant near the University of Pennsylvania campus. Favorite of artistic and academic types as well as other professionals. Good for Sunday brunch or late snacks. Open daily. Reservations advised. Major credit cards. 3432 Sansom St. (387-3778). Expensive.

Top of Center Square – Expansive windows in each of the four dining rooms on the 41st floor of the First Pennsylvania Bank building provide a panorama of the city. Request the east dining room to see the beautifully lighted City Hall and Billy Penn statue towering above. There is a varied and delicious menu of meats and seafoods. Open daily. Reservations advised. Major credit cards. 1500 Market St. (563-9494). Expensive to moderate.

The Frög – The blackboard menu changes constantly, but is generally adventurous. Expect dishes like sautéed vegetarian eggplant steak, grilled tandoori chicken breast, and an extraordinary chocolate mousse. A favorite hangout for newspaper, TV, and modeling crowds. Open daily. Reservations necessary. Major credit cards. 1524 Locust St. (735-8882). Expensive to moderate.

October – An autumnal decor pervades this cozily romantic restaurant where the chefs are dedicated to regional American cuisine. Treat yourself to a New Orleans blackened redfish or savor cioppino, a Portuguese fisherman's stew of lobster, mussels, and other seafood delicacies. Open daily. Reservations recommended. Major credit cards. 26 S Front St. (925-4447). Expensive to moderate.

The Fishmarket – Always crowded at lunch, so get there early. The featured seafood entrées vary according to the day's catch, but the high quality of preparation never wavers. The crab quiche is fabulous, as is the yellowtail snapper and bouillabaisse. Open daily. Reservations recommended. Major credit cards. 124 S 18th St. (567-3559). Moderate.

Old Original Bookbinder's – Philadelphia's best known restaurant, with mahogany and gleaming leather. Many love it, many hate it. The seafood is as much of a legend as many of the celebrities who dine here. Open daily. Reservations recommended. Major credit cards. 125 Walnut (925-7027). Moderate.

Bookbinder's Seafood House – The better (and less expensive) of the two restaurants bearing this famous name. Happy, bustling, serving the same well-prepared, simple food, fresh from the ocean. Open daily. Reservations advised. Major credit cards. 215 S 15th (545-1137). Moderate.

Head House Inn – Complete a tour of historic Philadelphia with a meal at this quaint corner inn. The atmosphere is colonial, but the menu is strictly contemporary, with a good selection of lamb, veal, and seafood. Lighter fare includes French onion soup, quiches, and salads. Open daily. Reservations advised. Major credit cards. 2nd & Pine sts. (925-6718). Moderate.

Miss Headly's Wine Bar – This eatery in the old section of the city is loved by its customers for the peaceful, quiet atmosphere and wines, cheeses, desserts, and Pakistani dishes. Closed Sundays. Major credit cards. 56 S 2nd St. (922-0763). Moderate.

The Imperial Inn – In Chinatown, an ambitious, well-prepared menu of Mandarin and Szechwan dishes. Open daily. No reservations. Major credit cards. 941 Race (925-2485). Moderate to inexpensive.

Hunan – Elegant and subdued, though the Oriental music plays a tad too loudly to be considered background. Service is brisk and cordial and the traditionally prepared regional Chinese food is quite good: Peppers stuffed with ground pork and spices and topped with black bean sauce — the owners' favorite — will excite the taste buds as it scorches the palate. Häagen-Dazs ice cream is served along with more traditional desserts. Open daily. Reservations advised. Major credit cards. 1721 Chestnut St. (567-5757). Moderate to inexpensive.

USA Café at The Commissary – Specializing in "the cuisine of the American Southwest with some Louisiana overtones," the café has a look as modern as its menu: streamlined tubes of orange neon run along the deep blue ceiling. The food is tasty and imaginatively prepared, from the batter-fried peppers stuffed with crabmeat and Monterrey Jack cheese to the barbecued ribs. *The Commissary*, downstairs, is a handsome cafeteria with a simpler menu — mostly salads, omelettes, and pasta. *Café:* closed Sundays; reservations advised; moderate to inexpensive. *Commissary:* open daily; inexpensive. Both accept major credit cards. 1710 Sansom St. (569-2240).

H. A. Winston & Co. – Dozens of burger permutations in an atmosphere that's warm, cozy, and comfortable. Open daily. Reservations are not necessary. Major credit cards. Front and Chestnut sts. (928-0660) and 1500 Locust St. (546-7232). Inexpensive.

Famous Delicatessen – Famous among Philadelphia residents, and for its celebrity customers, to which the picture-lined walls will attest. Monstrous hot pastrami, roast beef, and corned beef sandwiches. No-frill eating, the food comes on paper plates. Open daily until 6 PM. No reservations. No credit cards. 700 S 4th St. (627-9198). Inexpensive.

Harvest – Enjoy a wide variety of American dishes, some prepared with a North African or European touch, at this cafeteria-style restaurant (waiters will serve dinner). Seafood and game are emphasized. Closed Sundays. Major credit cards. Stock Exchange Bldg., 19th and Market sts. (568-6767). Inexpensive.

Melrose Diner – With its 50-year history, fanatically devoted staff, and round-the-clock crowds, this is as much a Philly institution as the scrapple it serves. Food preparation is fastidious, right down to the refiltered water and the coffee specially brewed in a custom-made urn. Waitresses wearing coffee-cup-shaped pins with clock faces (the diner's logo; a tiny knife and fork form the hands) serve up scrapple and eggs, cutlets, burgers, creamed chipped beef on toast, and other no-frills fare. The homemade desserts are popular takeout items. Open daily. No reservations. No credit cards. Broad St. and Snyder Ave. (467-6644). Inexpensive.

Pete's Pizza – Convenient to the Franklin Institute, Please Touch, and other museums, the menu here includes Philadelphia hoagies, grinders, and burgers in addition to pizza. It also claims to have the city's best stromboli. Open daily until 1 AM. 116 N 21st St. (567-4116). Inexpensive.

PHOENIX

Phoenix: the Los Angeles of the future? If it sounds unthinkable, consider these facts: In 1960, Phoenix had a population of 439,000; now its citizenry numbers over 900,000. It's among the fastest growing metropolises in the US. Its major industries are electronics and aerospace, both businesses coming of age with the next millennium — not just future-oriented, but damn near futuristic. People are flocking to the Southwest, and in many cases landing in Phoenix and its environs. If residents view this turn of events with some satisfaction, they are not oblivious to the dangers ahead. Most people come here for just one thing — the environment: relatively smog-free, clear, boiling in summer but beautiful for the lungs. Nothing threatens the environment like numbers, and the numbers of Phoenicians keep growing. And not one is willing to sacrifice oxygen or scenery to the future.

The scenery is frankly spectacular. The city takes a back seat to the awesome beauty of the Valley of the Sun (as the area around Phoenix is called). From the top of nearby South Mountain one sees the Valley stretch away in all directions, with the checkerboard of Phoenix's main avenues crisscrossing far into the northern horizon. East and west, suburbs extend for 50 miles (Glendale, Avondale, Sun City, and Youngtown to the west; Scottsdale, Tempe, and Mesa eastward toward the fabled Superstition Mountains). In the northeast, there's no mistaking the Valley's most distinctive landmark, Camelback Mountain. If you were to draw an imaginary line down its rugged, red haunches, you'd have the boundary between Phoenix and Scottsdale, the city's fashionable, artistic suburb.

As the eye follows the palisades of the Superstitions along the eastern horizon, it picks out the far mountain chain which cradles the crashing Salt River, lifeblood of the city and the Valley. The Salt has been irrigating the Valley for more than 1,000 years, and some of its canals follow water paths created by ancient Hohokam Indians.

What ancient history Phoenix has is associated with its first residents, the Indians. The city itself is little more than 100 years old, and Arizona has only been a state since 1912. But it cherishes its Indian past. Ringed by reservations, the Valley has a number of museums devoted to indigenous cultures, as well as art galleries featuring the work of local Indian artists.

If you think the desert is all sand dunes, you'll be delightfully surprised by the abundance of plant life. There are at least a dozen different species of cactus, one of which, the saguaro, with its thick, tall torso and upraised arms, is the state symbol. You'll also be surprised by residents' attitude toward distance. They consider it nothing to drive 200 miles for a picnic or a swim. (By the way, you'll need a car to get around here. Everything is spread out.)

Everything is also dependent on the weather, generally fantastic in winter and *incredibly* hot in summer. In winter, the Valley bustles with thousands

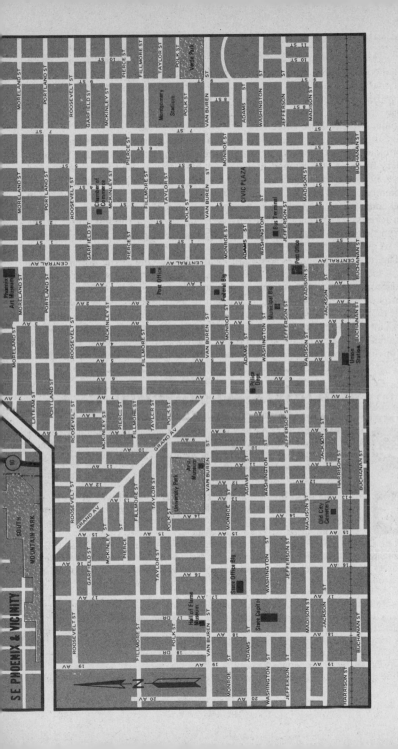

SE PHOENIX & VICINITY

of "snowbirds" escaping the northern and eastern cold. Except for the occasional cold snap or cloudburst, it's possible to play tennis and golf all winter. But make no mistake. It gets cold after dark. Sometimes, the temperature drops below freezing. Even during the daytime, coats or sweaters are almost always necessary. Oddly enough, though, Phoenix gets most of its rain in the summer — what little there is.

By June, Phoenix metamorphoses into an oven. The snowbirds forsake the mountain-rimmed bowl to return to their spring gardening, and residents scurry from air conditioned house to air conditioned car to air conditioned office. Daytime temperatures climb over the century mark most days through September. On a really cool night the mercury might plunge to 70°! On weekends, Phoenix becomes a ghost town as people flee to the cooler mountain forests. You'll understand why Arizona is one of the few states in the nation that doesn't have Daylight Saving Time. Arizonans can't wait for the sun to go down.

The heat also generates some tall local legends. One of the hottest-selling items in souvenir shops is an ordinary-looking twig called a "lizard stick." An accompanying tag informs the buyer that this stick is used by Arizona lizards during the summer. The crafty critters, it alleges, carry the stick in their mouths as they run from burrow to burrow. When their feet get too hot, they jam the stick into the sand, and climb it to give their feet a rest. It won't be taken amiss if you raise a skeptical eyebrow at these gadgets. They sell a lot of them here, but save your wonder for the fabulous Phoenix desert.

PHOENIX AT-A-GLANCE

 SEEING THE CITY: As you look out on Phoenix from South Mountain ponder on the words of an Indian prayer to Corn Mother and Sun Father: "Oh, it is good, you provide. It is the ability to think. It is the wisdom that comes. It is the understanding."

 SPECIAL PLACES: Street numbers start at zero in the center of downtown. Central Avenue, the business and financial district, runs north and south, bisecting the city into east and west. Numbered avenues lie to the west of Central, numbered streets to the east.

State Capitol – The building will give an idea of what granite from the Salt River Mountains looks like when put to constructive use. The murals inside depict Arizona's discovery and exploration in the 16th century. The Department of Library and Archives on the 3rd floor contains historical material. Closed weekends and holidays. Free. W Washington and 17th Ave. (255-4675).

Heard Museum – A fascinating anthropological collection of artifacts from ancient Indian civilizations in Arizona. The kachina doll collection, donated by Senator Barry Goldwater, is consistently interesting for neophytes as well as experts. Changing exhibitions feature contemporary American Indian sculpture, paintings, and drawings. Gift shop carries fine Indian jewelry, crafts, and artwork. Open daily except holidays. Admission charge. 22 E Monte Vista (252-8848).

Phoenix Art Museum – Specializes in contemporary art from the Southwest; other collections lean toward North American art in general (including Mexican), with a small exhibition of Renaissance, 17th-, and 18th-century material. Closed Mondays and major holidays. Admission charge except Wednesdays. 1625 N Central (257-1222).

Pueblo Grande Museum and Indian Ruins – Pueblo Grande is on the site of a former Hohokam Indian settlement. By climbing to the top of a mound marked into seven stations, you can see the ruins which are believed to have been occupied from 200 BC to AD 1400, when the Hohokam vanished without a trace. Phoenix municipal archaeologists are continuing their excavations. Open daily except holidays. Admission charge. 4619 E Washington (275-3452).

Desert Botanical Gardens – Half of all the varieties of cactus in the world are planted on the grounds, and self-guiding tours and booklets help identify the prickly flora. Open daily. Admission charge. Papago Park (941-1217).

Phoenix Zoo – When you're done walking around the Botanical Gardens, take a leisurely drive through desert rock formations to Phoenix Zoo, which covers more than 125 acres in another section of Papago Park. (You can stop to picnic in the park.) Two of the most popular attractions are the oryx herd, and Hazel, the gorilla, and her offspring Fabayo. There are more than 1,000 animals altogether. Open daily. Admission charge. 5810 E Van Buren (273-7771).

Scottsdale – This re-created western community with hitching posts is a haven for artists and art lovers. Scottsdale's Fifth Avenue is lined with galleries (see *Museums* and *Galleries*) featuring Indian art, handicrafts, and jewelry. Every Thursday evening from 7 to 9, October through May, the community sponsors an "art walk" through town. In Scottsdale, taking a walk is an aesthetic adventure. Take McDowell Rd. east to Scottsdale Rd. north.

Cosanti Foundation – The architect Paolo Soleri maintains a workshop here, with a model of Arcosanti, his megalopolis of the future. His sculpture and windbells are on display, too. Open daily except major holidays; call for tour information. Donation. 6433 E Doubletree Rd., Scottsdale (948-6145).

Taliesin West – The future owes much of its shape to the innovative imagination and technical expertise of the master architect Frank Lloyd Wright. His former office and school, Taliesin West (pronounced tal-ly-*ess*-en), offers the chance to see what goes into planning and designing those marvelous, ultramodern structures. Closed on rainy days and holidays. Admission charge. Scottsdale Rd. north, to Shea Blvd. east, to 108th St. north, to Taliesin West in Scottsdale (948-6670).

The Borgata – Not the place for bargain-priced jeans or a pound of sugar, it's one of the most opulent retail operations this side of Beverly Hills — and one of the most unusual anywhere. The Borgata houses about 50 boutiques and restaurants in a setting redolent of an old Italian village. It's well worth a visit, even if you can only afford to cast amazed glances at the price tags. Open daily. 6166 N Scottsdale Rd., Scottsdale.

■ **EXTRA SPECIAL:** For a picturesque day trip through open desert, take the Black Canyon Highway north, to Cordes Junction, then travel west through the old territorial capital of Prescott to *Sedona*, famous for its dramatic red cliffs. At Sedona, take a breathtaking drive up Oak Creek Canyon to *Flagstaff*, or complete the circle by driving back to Verde Valley, returning via the Black Canyon Highway. Be sure to stop in *Jerome*, the ghost town too ornery to die. A community of artists now lives in the old wooden buildings that cling precariously to the steep mountainside of this former copper mining town. Jerome has great curio and antiques shops specializing in mining paraphernalia and one of the best restaurants in Arizona, the *House of Joy*. The food is Continental, the prices are reasonable, and it's open only on weekends (so reservations are a must; 634-5339).

496

SOURCES AND RESOURCES

 TOURIST INFORMATION: For maps, brochures, and information, contact Phoenix and Valley of the Sun Convention and Visitors Bureau, 505 N 2nd St. (254-6500), or Arizona Office of Tourism, 1480 E Bethany Home Rd., Suite 180 (255-3618).

The best guide is *Phoenix* magazine's *City Guide* (Phoenix Publishing; $4.95).

Local Coverage – *Arizona Republic,* morning daily; *Phoenix Gazette,* evening daily; *Scottsdale Daily Progress,* afternoon daily; *New Times,* weekly; *Phoenix* magazine, monthly.

Food – *100 Best Restaurants in the Valley of the Sun,* by John and Joan Bogert (ADM; $2.95).

Area Code – All telephone numbers are in the 602 area code unless otherwise indicated.

 CLIMATE AND CLOTHES: Try not to visit in summer, when it's more than 100°. Fall, winter, and spring are dry, warm, and sunny. Temperatures range from daytime highs of between 60° and 80°, to nighttime lows of about 35° to 50°.

 GETTING AROUND: Getting around Phoenix is next to impossible without a car.

Airport – Sky Harbor International Airport is usually just a 10-minute drive from downtown, and, depending on the cab company, taxi fare will run from $7 to $14. (Fares have been deregulated and now vary widely, so be sure to agree on a price before getting into a cab.) Sky Harbor Limousine (275-8501) offers transportation from the airport to downtown for $8; for the return trip, reserve 24 hours in advance. Phoenix Transit (257-8426) buses stop at each of Sky Harbor's three terminals every half-hour and make the trip downtown for 75¢.

Bus – There are buses, but service is sketchy, with interminable waiting periods, erratic schedules, and no buses at all at night and on Sundays. However, you can call Phoenix Transit System (257-8426) for schedule information. Greyhound runs buses to Tempe and Mesa (248-4040).

Taxi – Call Yellow Cab (252-5071).

Car Rental – All major national firms are represented. Rent A Wreck (252-4897) is among the cheapest.

 MUSEUMS: Heard Museum, Phoenix Art Museum, and Pueblo Grande Museum, are described in *Special Places.* Other museums in Phoenix are:

Arizona Mineral Museum – 1826 W McDowell (255-3791).

Hall of Flame Museum – No kidding. A collection of firefighting paraphernalia from 1725; 6101 E Van Buren. (275-3473).

 ART GALLERIES: Although Phoenix does have some interesting art galleries, most of the finest are in Scottsdale, within walking distance of one another. They exhibit a rich and vast array of art forms — paintings, sculpture, graphics — and many are devoted to American Indian art and contemporary western art. Some of the best are:

Artistic Gallery – Artists include the nationally acclaimed R. C. Gorman; 7077 E Main St., Scottsdale (945-6766).

Suzanne Brown Gallery – Contemporary western art, from abstract to representational; 7156 E Main St., Scottsdale (945-8475).

Marilyn Butler Fine Art – Fritz Scholder is among the gallery's artists; 4160 N Craftsman Court, Scottsdale (994-9550).

Hand and the Spirit – Tapestries, ceramics, jewelry, and other American crafts; 4222 N Marshall Way, Scottsdale (946-4529).

Elaine Horwitch Galleries – Contemporary sculpture and paintings by a wide variety of artists; 4211 N Marshall Way, Scottsdale (945-0791).

Gallery McGoffin – The country's only batik gallery; 902 W Roosevelt, Phoenix (255-0785).

Lovena Ohl Gallery – Indian arts and crafts, from primitive to contemporary; Mercado Verde, 7373 Scottsdale Mall, Scottsdale (945-8212).

 MAJOR COLLEGES AND UNIVERSITIES: A lot of concerts and plays take place on campuses. Check publications listed above for details. The largest and most active campus is Arizona State University, Apache Blvd., Tempe (965-9011). Phoenix College, 1202 W Thomas Rd. (264-2492), and American Graduate School of International Management, 59th Ave. and Greenway Rd., Glendale (978-7011), sponsor concerts and activities, too.

 SPECIAL EVENTS: The *Phoenix Open Golf Tournament* takes place in January; other golf tournaments are played throughout the year. In mid-March, the *World Championship Rodeo* is held at Veterans Memorial Coliseum, 1826 W McDowell. In October, the *Arizona State Fair* fills up the State Fairgrounds. In November, the annual *Thunderbird Balloon Race* takes place at the American Graduate School of International Management in Glendale.

 SPORTS AND FITNESS: The year-round sun makes Phoenix ideal for watching or participating in outdoor athletics. (In summer, get up early and play before it gets too hot.) In winter and spring, there's dog racing at Greyhound Park, 40th and E Washington sts. (273-7181), and horse racing at Turf Paradise, 19th Ave. and Bell Rd. (942-1101).

Basketball – NBA Phoenix *Suns* play at Veterans Memorial Coliseum, 1826 W McDowell (258-6711). The Arizona State University *Sun Devils* have come to national attention during the past few seasons. They play at Sun Devil Stadium on the campus in Tempe (965-2381).

Bicycling – Rent bikes from Airplane and Bicycle Works, 4400 N Scottsdale Rd., Scottsdale (949-1978).

Fishing – Trout, bass, and crappie can be caught at Apache Lake and Salt River.

Fitness Centers – The YMCA offers exercise classes and massage and has a pool and outdoor track, 350 N First Ave. (253-6181).

Football – The USFL *Arizona Outlaws* (275-2233, for tickets) play at Sun Devil Stadium on the Arizona State University campus in Tempe.

Golf – There are 68 courses in Phoenix. The best public course is Encanto Municipal (253-3963).

Horseback Riding – Hourly rentals at Ponderosa Stable, 10215 S Central (268-1261), and South Mountain Stable, 10001 S Central (276-8131). All Western Stables, 10220 S Central (276-5862), also rents horses by the hour.

Inland Surfing – If you've always wanted to surf but can't quite brave the force of the ocean, Big Surf (947-2477) at 1500 N Hayden Rd. in Tempe is a good place to break in. There are artificial beaches and waves, and you can rent equipment. Closed Mondays and October through February; open weekends only in September. Admission charge.

Jogging – An enclosed haven for runners on scorchingly hot days is the air conditioned Paradise Valley Mall (6 to 10 AM, before it is officially open to shoppers, in northeast Phoenix at the intersection of Tatum and Cactus; 996-8840). Under the sun, run along the banks of the Arizona Canal (pick it up beside the *Biltmore Hotel*) or the Grand Canal, reachable by jogging about a mile north along Central Avenue; Encanto Park, about ¾ mile from downtown, also attracts runners.

Swimming – The Salt River is good for swimming, too. There are 40 municipal pools in Phoenix. Every large park has one. Try the pool at Coronado Park, N 12th St. and Coronado Rd.

Tennis – Phoenix Tennis Center has 22 lighted courts for night games, 6330 N 21st Ave. (249-3712).

Tubing – Arizona's most popular summer sport. On any given weekend, as many as 20,000 residents strap beer-filled ice chests and their behinds to old inner tubes and float down five or ten miles of free-flowing Salt River, below Saguaro Lake, just north of Mesa. The trip is free and you can buy tubes — the bigger the better — at gas stations and stands along the route. This utterly relaxing pastime is called "tubing down the Salt."

 THEATER: There's quite a lot of drama in Phoenix and Scottsdale. World-renowned performers like the late Sir Michael Redgrave have come to play Shakespeare in the past. Check the local publications listed above for schedules. The major theaters include: *Phoenix Little Theater,* 25 E Coronado Rd. (254-2151); *Gammage Auditorium,* a Frank Lloyd Wright building on the campus of Arizona State University in Tempe (965-3434). Scottsdale has a *Shakespearean Festival* in late winter. Scottsdale Center for the Arts, Civic Center Plaza, Scottsdale (994-2787).

 MUSIC: *Phoenix Symphony* (264-4754) and *Arizona Opera Company* (262-7272) play at Symphony Hall, 225 E Adams; *Scottsdale Symphony* and *Arizona Ballet Theater* play at Scottsdale Center for the Arts, 7383 Scottsdale Mall (994-2787). Traveling dance troupes play Gammage Auditorium and Scottsdale Center for the Arts. Nationally known rock performers and classical musicians appear at Gammage Auditorium. Rock groups also give concerts at Veterans Memorial Coliseum, 1826 W McDowell (258-6711).

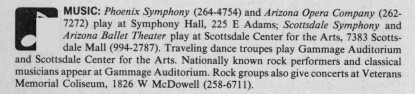 **NIGHTCLUBS AND NIGHTLIFE:** One of the most popular nightspots in Phoenix is *Oscar Taylor* at Biltmore Fashion Sq. (956-5705), which offers a great happy hour and a decor that's reminiscent of Chicago during Prohibition. Another good meeting place is *TGI Friday's,* 1851 E Camelback (266-8443), behind the Colonnade Shopping Center.

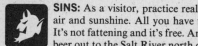 **SINS:** As a visitor, practice real Phoenix *gluttony.* Gorge yourself on fresh air and sunshine. All you have to do is go outside and take a deep breath. It's not fattening and it's free. And to enjoy *sloth,* take a chest full of ice-cold beer out to the Salt River north of Mesa and plunk it onto an old inner tube. Plunk yourself right down next to it and let the tube and the river do all the work. Tubing down the Salt allows you to remain utterly inert while you travel, guzzling beer all the way.

 LOCAL SERVICES: Business Services – Alison's Secretarial Service, 3270 E Camelback Rd. (955-3542).

   Mechanic – Sheets Union 76 Service, 4042 N 7th St. (277-7025).

   Babysitting – Arizona Babysitters Service, 4214 N 48th Dr. (247-0260).

BEST IN TOWN

CHECKING IN: If you're going to Phoenix on business, you'll probably want to stay downtown. If it's a vacation visit, you can't beat the resorts, which offer full recreational activities and valley tours. Meals are usually included in the room rate at a resort. Expect to pay between $140 and $200 for a double room at an expensive resort; between $75 and $100 at an expensive hotel; and around $25 at our inexpensive listing. For B&B accommodations, contact Bed & Breakfast in Arizona, 8433 N Black Canyon Hwy., Suite 160, Phoenix, AZ 85021 (602 995-2831).

Arizona Biltmore – The first, and still among the most luxurious in the valley, this 506-room resort is first class in every way. Golf and tennis facilities are outstanding, and so are the swimming pools. Individual guests may be put off by the hordes of convention and meeting goers who always seem to dominate the premises. The dining room serves fine Continental cuisine. 24th St. and Missouri (602 955-6600). Expensive.

The Boulders – Opened in 1985 by the Rockresort group (though now owned by the CSX Corp.), this is a "rock resort" in another sense, too: It's set on 1,300 acres of desert foothills at the base of a towering pile of boulders. The 120 adobe-colored casitas blend beautifully with the surroundings, and each contains a room with a wet bar and working fireplace. There are also tennis courts, golf courses, and horseback riding. Carefree, about 30 miles north of Phoenix (602 488-9009). Expensive.

Camelback Inn – This is among the largest resorts in the state — 423 rooms, mostly in two-story cottages. It's set among the beautiful Camelback Mountain foothills and has swimming pools, golf, and tennis facilities. The cowboy cookouts are great fun. 5402 E Lincoln Dr., Paradise Valley (602 948-1700). Expensive.

Phoenician Golf and Tennis Resort – Scheduled to open for the 1987-88 winter season, this $150 million property at the base of legendary Camelback Mountain will have over 500 rooms, individual casitas, several restaurants, an 18-hole championship golf course and clubhouse, tennis, and health spa. 6000 E Camelback Rd., Scottsdale (602 956-0200). Expensive.

Phoenix Hilton – A Phoenix fixture, previously known as the *Adams Hotel*. The 538 large rooms all have magnificent views and there's an old-time feeling at the quaint bar, with swimming pool, good coffee shop, and a good dining room. Central and Adams (257-1525). Expensive.

Stouffer-Cottonwoods Resort – It's easy to relax at this resort while admiring the Camelback Mountains in the distance, sniffing the piñon-perfumed air, and basking in the bright Arizona sun. The 170 fresh and comfortable rooms have a southwestern decor. A jitney connects the hotel with nearby shopping, and there's a pool, putting greens, and jogging trails. Golf and horseback riding are nearby. 6160 N Scottsdale Rd., Scottsdale (602 991-1414). Expensive.

Registry Resort – A good choice for those who want to go first class, this busy place has 3 pools, 2 18-hole golf courses, a complete fitness center, and nightly entertainment. Its *La Champagne* (see *Eating Out*) restaurant is considered one of the valley's best, and Sunday brunch in the *Phoenician Room* combines danceable jazz with a remarkable array of food. 7171 N Scottsdale Rd., Scottsdale (602 991-3800). Expensive.

Doubletree Inn – A nice hotel that's convenient to Scottsdale Center for the Arts, the Scottsdale Mall, and the town's numerous boutiques. An added bonus is the

Rotisserie Bar & Grill, which features southwestern cuisine and a stylish piano bar that's open late every night but Sunday. 7353 E Indian School Rd., Scottsdale (602 994-9203). Expensive.

Marriott's Mountain Shadows Resort – With a 1,500-seat grand ballroom and 10 meeting rooms, it's no wonder this place is popular with convention groups and business travelers. And after all those meetings, guests can relax by taking advantage of the 3 pools, 2 Jacuzzis, 8 tennis courts, and 3 18-hole golf courses. The *Sunset Terrace* restaurant has a lovely view overlooking Camelback Mountain, and the *Crystal Terrace* has both dining and dancing. 5641 E Lincoln Dr., Scottsdale (800 228-9290). Expensive.

Hermosa Inn – Long one of the valley's most exclusive guest ranches and tennis resorts, it advertises that it is "not just a resort, it's an attitude." That sounds like hype until you check in and find Jacuzzi baths, rooms with gas fireplaces, wet bars, and a staff that gives VIP treatment to every guest. The setting seems far removed from the rat race, but civilization is only minutes away — if you want it. 5532 N Palo Cristi Rd., Paradise Valley (602 955-8614). Expensive.

SunBurst Resort Hotel and Conference Center – A Santa Fe decor enhances the refurbished *SunBurst,* which has as much to offer outdoors as in. Amenities include a freeform pool, a spa, a lively lounge, and a restaurant (the *Desert Rose*) with very good American and Continental cuisine. 4925 N Scottsdale Rd., Scottsdale (602 945-7666). Expensive.

Granada Royale Hometel – Run by a hotel chain whose goal is to provide guests with a homey atmosphere, and since 95% of the guests return, it appears that the management is successful. Accommodations are in two-room suites with kitchens; breakfasts and late afternoon cocktails are free; and tipping is not permitted. 5001 N Scottsdale Rd., Scottsdale; 1515 N 44th St., and 3101 N 32nd St. in Phoenix (800 528-1100). Expensive.

Westcourt – Ultramodern, boasting more original artworks than many galleries; specially commissioned lithographs decorate its 300 luxury rooms and suites. In the city next to the gargantuan Metrocenter — packed with shops and restaurants — it also has a dining room called *Trumps.* 10220 N Metro Pkwy. E (602 997-5900). Expensive.

Pointe at Tapatio Cliffs – Patterned after the successful *Pointe at Squaw Peak,* this mountainside resort has attractive Spanish-southwestern architecture and luxurious amenities. The dazzling *Etienne's Different Pointe of View* restaurant is a high-tech mountaintop facility that serves fine French cuisine. 11111 N 7th St. (602 866-7500). Expensive.

Hyatt Regency Scottsdale – Built on the Gainey Ranch development, this brand-new, $75 million, 489-room luxury resort offers all the basic recreational facilities (swimming pool with swim-up bar, 8 tennis courts, 27 holes of championship golf, health club, and Jacuzzi) as well as a few extras (lawn tennis and croquet). After all that exercise, guests can sate their hunger and quench their thirst at the 2 restaurants, entertainment lounge, or lobby bar. 8777 E Via de Ventura, No. 115, Scottsdale (800 228-9000). Expensive.

Radisson Scottsdale Resort – The desert landscaping here provides a placid retreat from the hustle-bustle of nearby downtown Scottsdale. There are 220 rooms, including suites and casitas, plus 2 pools, 8 lighted tennis courts, an exercise parcourse, and numerous other amenities. The main restaurant, *Ride 'n Rock,* has a western theme and serves steaks, seafood, and live entertainment. 7601 E Indian Bend Rd., Scottsdale (602 991-2400 or 800 228-9822). Expensive.

Loews Paradise Valley Resort – This 20-acre, $40 million facility offers 380 rooms including 27 suites, 2 pools, a health club and spa, 2 racquetball courts, and 6 tennis courts. There are several restaurants, including the romantic *Bouchon,* where the American cuisine embraces everything from peanut soup to buffalo T-bone steaks. 5401 N Scottsdale Rd., Scottsdale (602 947-5400). Expensive.

Hyatt Regency – Play tennis after dark, swim, or relax those aching muscles in the whirlpool. This elegant, 711-room newcomer has a fine restaurant and an over-priced coffee shop. 2nd and Adams (602 257-1110 or 800 228-9000). Expensive.

Pointe at Squaw Peak – A lovely southwestern decor characterizes this mountain-side resort, which manages to remain almost fully booked even during the summer. The American and Continental *Pointe of View* is one of several good restaurants here. 7677 N 16th St. (602 997-2626). Expensive.

Phoenix Crescent – Part of a self-contained corporate center, this brand-new 362-room hotel caters to the business traveler. Features include a pool, tennis courts, health club, and restaurant, as well as a location that is convenient to the airport and the rapidly expanding North Phoenix commercial center. 2620 W Dunlap Ave. (943-0200). Expensive to moderate.

Holiday Inn – This modern 139-room hotel near the financial district has a swim-ming pool, whirlpool, and a good restaurant. Pets are welcome. 2nd Ave. at Osborn (602 248-0222 or 800 465-4329). Moderate.

Friendship Inn 6 – Smaller and quieter than the others, this 68-unit inn is also kinder to your budget. There's also a heated swimming pool. 201 N 7th Ave. (602 254-6521). Inexpensive.

 EATING OUT: Best bets in Phoenix are Mexican food and steaks. Expect to pay $60 or more for a meal for two at an expensive restaurant; between $35 and $50 at a moderate restaurant; under $25 at a selection noted as inexpensive. Prices do not include drinks, wine, or tips.

The Golden Eagle – Although this restaurant is expensive, the view over the valley and the quick and attentive service make you feel it's worth it. The Continental menu features some southwestern specialties, including roast buffalo and pheasant; also try the stuffed trout. Since only men are routinely handed the menu with the price listings, women should specify whether they wish one also. Closed Sundays, Christmas, and New Year's. Reservations recommended. Major credit cards. 201 N Central, atop the Valley Bank Center, Phoenix (257-7700). Expensive.

Steven – As fashionable a place as fashionable Scottsdale has to offer, the decor is a stylish blend of Art Deco and southwestern contemporary; and the kitchen — best with grilled dishes — blends domestic standouts with a healthy dose of Continental fare. Closed on Christmas. Reservations advised. Major credit cards. 4333 N Brown Ave., Scottsdale (941-4936). Expensive.

Vincent's French Cuisine – Surrounded by a $3 million collection of 16th- to early-20th-century artwork, all catalogued and up for sale, diners savor French specialties, such as veal with forest mushrooms and fresh fish flown in from France daily, from a menu that changes nightly. Closed Mondays and all of late July and August. Reservations recommended. Major credit cards. 8711 E Pinnacle Peak Rd., Scottsdale (998-0921). Expensive.

Mancuso's – The decor here will transport you to an Italian Renaissance castle and the Continental cuisine will make you want to applaud. So will the service and the prices of entrées, which include soup, salad, and more. Open daily. Reservations recommended. Major credit cards. 6166 N Scottsdale Rd., Scottsdale (948-9988). Expensive.

Avanti – This place has a six-page menu of Northern Italian and Continental dishes. Open daily. Reservations advised. Major credit cards. Two locations: 3102 N Scottsdale Rd., Scottsdale (949-8333); 2728 E Thomas Rd., Phoenix (956-0900). Expensive.

Palm Court – Tuxedoed waiters prepare much of the food at your table at this dining room in the *Scottsdale Conference Resort.* While gazing out on Camelback Mountain and Lake McCormick, you can select from the brief but tempting à la carte Continental menu. Recommended are the bibb lettuce salad, the lobster bisque, and the rack of lamb. Open daily. Reservations advised. Major credit cards. 7700 E McCormick Pkwy., Scottsdale (991-3400). Expensive.

Voltaire – The most popular entrée is sand dab — a white fish from the sole family that the chef blankets with egg batter and sautés with lemon butter — but the rack of lamb, medallions of veal, and boned chicken in champagne sauce are just as good. Closed Sundays, Mondays, and summer. Reservations advised. Major credit cards. 8340 E McDonald, Scottsdale (948-1005). Expensive.

La Champagne – Part of the prestigious *Registry Resort,* this ambitious restaurant has Continental cuisine, black-tie service, and a long, wide-ranging wine list. A pianist provides soothing background music. Open daily. Reservations advised. Major credit cards. 7171 N Scottsdale Rd., Scottsdale (991-3800). Expensive.

Tomaso's – The latest effort of a successful valley restaurateur, this eatery is known for its Northern Italian cuisine. Open daily. Reservations advised. Major credit cards. 7243 E Camelback Rd., Scottsdale (947-5804). Expensive.

Rick's Café Americana – The kitchen at this loving re-creation of the nightclub in *Casablanca* turns out dependable, diverse Continental fare. A pianist plays and takes requests in the lounge. Closed on Christmas. Reservations advised. Major credit cards. 8320 N Hayden, Scottsdale (991-2233). Expensive to moderate.

Pointe of View – As its name implies, this restaurant gives its diners an impressive panorama of the valley. Specialties include tableside flambées and Cajun cooking. Reservations recommended. Major credit cards. 7677 N 16th St., Phoenix (997-5859). Moderate.

Famous Pacific Fish Co. – Good service and bargain prices are simply extras. This place is really special for its combination of Mexican mesquite charcoal broiling and fresh seafood. The nautical ambience is delightful, too. Don't miss the New England clam chowder, which may not be the "world's finest" (as the menu claims) but certainly comes close. Closed on major holidays. Lunch reservations only. Major credit cards. 4321 N Scottsdale Rd., Scottsdale (941-0602). Moderate.

Don & Charlie's – If your appetite is bigger than your budget, try this restaurant. The menu's American dishes may seem standard, but just wait till they arrive at your table. Steaks are huge and perfectly cooked, and the meaty pork ribs are good, too. Closed on Thanksgiving. Reservations advised. Major credit cards. 7501 E Camelback Rd., Scottsdale (990-0900). Moderate.

Armenia – In the mood for something different? Try the Middle Eastern cuisine — lamb, beef, chicken, and shrimp kabobs are the specialties. There is also a good number of vegetarian dishes. Closed on Christmas and New Year's. Reservations advised. Major credit cards. 7055 E Indian School Rd., Scottsdale (994-4717). Moderate.

Monti's La Casa Vieja – A valley landmark. Serves some of the best steaks anywhere. It's always crowded but the service is good. Side dishes are plentiful. Open daily. Reservations for lunch only. Major credit cards. 3 W First, Tempe (967-7594). Moderate.

Asia House – A unique concept offering meals at one price, with different rooms devoted to Chinese, Japanese, and Mongolian cuisines. Select the type of meal you want when you call to make reservations. The Japanese room has low tables; the Mongolian, a circular table set under a *yurt* (a Mongolian tent). All the food is excellent, but the Mongolian meal is an experience. Closed Mondays. Reservations essential. Major credit cards. 2310 E McDowell, Phoenix (267-7461). Moderate.

Kamnitzer's Terrace – The regularly updated international menu is imaginative, and the chef clearly knows his stuff. Other enticements include prices that spell value and unforgettable desserts. Closed weekends and major holidays. Reservations recommended. Major credit cards. 2020 N Central Ave., Phoenix (256-0283). Moderate.

Lunt Avenue Marble Club – If the name isn't enough to draw you in, it has great deep-dish pizza, too, and one of the best sandwich selections in the state. Closed on Christmas. Reservations accepted. Major credit cards. Five locations: 1212 E Apache Blvd., Tempe (968-9859); 6202 N Scottsdale Rd., Scottsdale (998-3505); 2770 W Peoria (863-9791); 2 E Camelback Rd. (265-8997), Phoenix; 1371 N Alma School Rd., Chandler (899-6735). Moderate.

Ninth & Ash – In a quiet neighborhood in a rebuilt turn-of-the-century home, diners are served in two intimate first-floor rooms plus upstairs during winter and on a lovely covered patio in summer. Service is friendly and professional, and the price is right. The list of entrées is small but imaginative and varied; highlights range from baby back pork ribs to scallops Florentine to veal cordon bleu. Closed Sundays and major holidays. Reservations advised. Major credit cards. 850 S Ash, Tempe (968-6193). Moderate.

Pinnacle Peak Patio – No trip to Arizona would be complete without a visit to a real, by-God western cowboy steakhouse. This one's the oldest and most famous, with two-pound Porterhouses broiled over mesquite coals and served with sourdough bread and pinto beans. Don't wear a tie! Closed only on Thanksgiving and Christmas. No reservations. Major credit cards. 10426 Pinnacle Peak Rd., Scottsdale (949-7311). Moderate.

The T-Bone – An out-of-the-way real find that's never crowded. It has basically the same menu as *Pinnacle Peak* but with a fantastic night view of the valley. Food is brought by entertaining, gun-totin' waitresses, and you get to help yourself to a filling salad. Closed on Thanksgiving, Christmas, and the first two weeks in July. Reservations unnecessary. Major credit cards. End of 19th Ave. south of Dobbins, Phoenix (276-0945). Moderate.

Pink Pepper – A few years ago, the valley had only one Thai restaurant; now there's more than a dozen. The ultramodern *Pink Pepper* is the prettiest of the lot, and since it uses moderation when sprinkling on the spices, it's a good place for the uninitiated to try this often hot-as-fire cuisine. The soups with lemon grass and coconut milk are tops, as are the meat dishes with Phonaeng curry. Open daily. Reservations accepted. Major credit cards. 2003 N Scottsdale Rd., Scottsdale (945-9300). Inexpensive.

Los Olivos – A family operation for more than three decades, this is the valley's oldest Mexican restaurant. A thoroughly modern decor belies its age, but the food explains its longevity. Try such house specialties as sour cream enchiladas and carne asada, then walk off the meal by strolling over to the adjacent Scottsdale Center for the Arts. Closed on Easter. Reservations accepted. Major credit cards. 7328 E Second St., Scottsdale (946-2256). Inexpensive.

Aunt Chilada's – Authentic Mexican cuisine is the specialty of this family restaurant. Try the Whole Aunt Chilada: chimichangas, bean burritos, tamales, guacamole, sour cream, and homemade flour tortillas served with fideo (Mexican pasta) instead of rice. Don't worry; it serves two. Open daily. Reservations for parties of six or more. Major credit cards. 7330 N Dreamy Draw Dr., Phoenix (944-1286). Inexpensive.

The Original Hamburger Works – If all you want is a good burger, wander over to the vicinity of Phoenix College and partake of giant hamburgers with all the fixin's. The decor is rustic 1880s, with advertising posters from the turn of the century on the walls. Open daily except major holidays. No reservations. No credit cards. 2801 N 15th Ave., Phoenix (263-8693). Inexpensive.

PITTSBURGH

Like the mythical phenix, Pittsburgh has risen from its ashes — almost literally. For more than a hundred years, it was one of the most important industrial cities in the world, producing one fifth of all the steel made in the United States. But with prosperity came pollution and the image of a one-industry town; it had become something of an urban slag heap dubbed Steel Capital, USA.

Then, having lost ground to fierce competition from abroad, the domestic steel industry declined, forcing Pittsburghers to adapt. Over the past three decades civic leaders and residents have made a concerted effort to clean up the air, put some green underfoot, and promote the city as a vital and vibrant place to live. To some degree, they have succeeded. Once-smoggy skies are now clear, revealing stunning skylines, healthy rivers, and more trees per capita than any other city in the US. Indeed, the Renaissance has garnered some hefty praise: Pittsburgh was rated the country's most livable city in Rand McNally's 1985 *Places Rated Almanac*.

Pittsburgh is still an important commercial city. Within the one-half square mile that comprises the downtown area known as the Golden Triangle, 16 of the world's 500 leading corporations maintain their offices. The top six bring in more than $1 billion in revenue annually. Pittsburgh is also an international leader in the fields of chemical, plastic, nuclear, and general scientific research.

A metropolis of 2.3 million people, the city is spread out around the confluence of the Allegheny and Monongahela rivers. The Point, where the rivers join to form the Ohio River, has been strategically important as far back as the years before the French and Indian War. This confluence was a point of contention and, later, the site of vicious conflict between France and Great Britain, at that time colonial rivals. It was not far from the Point, in 1754, that the young George Washington, then an ardent British officer, ordered an attack on a French encampment, thereby inadvertently triggering the Pennsylvania phase of the French and Indian War. In 1758, British troops managed to secure control of the river forks, which enabled them to ensure their domination of North America. They built the formidable Fort Pitt at the Point, naming the battlement in honor of England's prime minister, William Pitt.

Even as Fort Pitt's military importance declined, Pittsburgh developed as a commercial town and river port. As the center for transporting westward-bound pioneers and supplies, the "Key to the West" did a thriving business, selling flatboats loaded with glass, home furnishings, hardware, drygoods, and farm products. In 1760, the largest coal seam ever struck in the United States was discovered on Mt. Washington. With this coal and the iron ore that was shipped from nearby, Fort Pitt became industrial as well as commercial.

Iron foundries multiplied, and during the Civil War Pittsburgh was the "arsenal of the North." It was also a magnet for magnates. The roster of tycoons who made their fortunes in Pittsburgh includes Thomas Mellon, Andrew Carnegie, and Henry Clay Frick.

As the industries flourished, the immigrants flocked to this burgeoning center of employment. Besides future tycoons like Frick and Carnegie, stonemasons and other Old World artisans also came, craftsmen who created much of the ornate stone and metal work found in Pittsburgh's older buildings and bridges. And there are many bridges in Pittsburgh — 1,700 at last count.

The cleaner current environment heightens the enjoyment of Pittsburgh's cultural activities, many of which are the legacy of the giants of industry. Thomas Mellon and Andrew Carnegie endowed several art institutions; Henry Clay Frick gave the city a museum, and the Henry Heinz family of the famous "57 varieties" contributed a performing arts center. The wealth also helped underwrite education, recreation, and health care. Today Pittsburgh has 28 colleges, 4 universities, 170 research and development facilities, a internationally acclaimed symphony, and more golf courses per capita than any other city in the country. For a city its size, Pittsburgh is an amazingly friendly place. It is not uncommon for strangers to wish each other a good day on their way to work or for visitors asking directions to be personally escorted to their destination — or given an ad lib tour. Pittsburghers are very proud of their city, a pride that is well justified.

(PITTSBURGH AT-A-GLANCE)

SEEING THE CITY: Go to the top of Mt. Washington via the Duquesne or Monongahela inclines for a sweeping 17-mile view of the confluence of the Allegheny, Monongahela, and Ohio rivers. Duquesne is at W Carson St. (381-1665); Monongahela, in operation since 1870, is at E Carson St., behind the Freight House Shops of Station Square (231-5707). Exact change (60¢) is required. Pittsburgh's original blast furnace can be seen on the south side of the Monongahela River, between the two inclines.

For a more down-to-earth view, take one of several different cruises on the Gateway Clipper fleet, from the dock at Station Square. The captain aboard the 2-hour sightseeing cruise ($6 for adults, $4 for children), will highlight points of interest along all three rivers. The *Goodship Lollipop* has clowns to keep children occupied while parents enjoy the sights on its 1-hour cruise (adults $4; children $3). Reservations are required for the dinner cruise ($17 to $20 per person), which leaves the dock daily at 7 PM. Specialty cruises include a tour of the river lock system and an excursion to Waterford Race Track, Wheeling, West Virginia. Some cruises are seasonal; call 355-7980 for information.

SPECIAL PLACES: There are three main sections of the city in which you'll find most of Pittsburgh's places of interest. The Golden Triangle encompasses the downtown area; North Side, old homes, the restored "Mexican War Streets," and parks; Oakland, museums and cultural institutions.

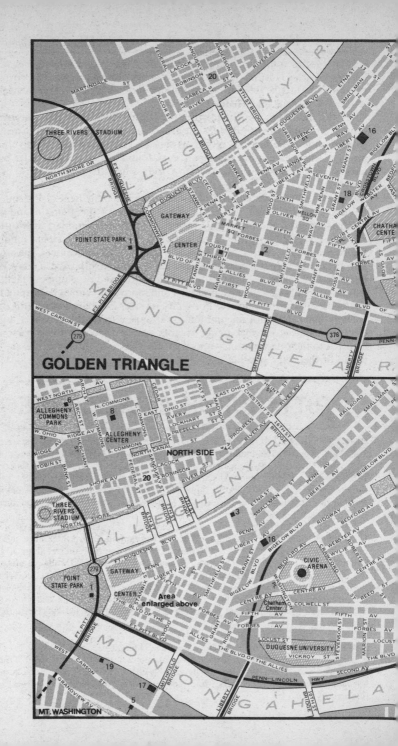

CENTRAL
PITTSBURGH

LANDMARKS

1. Fort Pitt Museum
2. Bank Center
3. David L. Lawrence Convention Center
4. Heinz Hall
5. Monongahela Incline
6. West Park Conservatory—Aviary
7. PPG Place
8. Buhl Planetarium
9. Cathedral of Learning
10. Carnegie Museum and Library
11. Mellon Institute
12. Phipps Conservatory
13. Historical Society of Western Pennsylvania
14. Frick Fine Arts Building
15. Pittsburgh Playhouse Theater Center
16. Penn. Central Station
17. Pittsburgh & Lake Erie Station
18. U.S. Steel Building
19. First Blast Furnace
20. "Mexican War" District

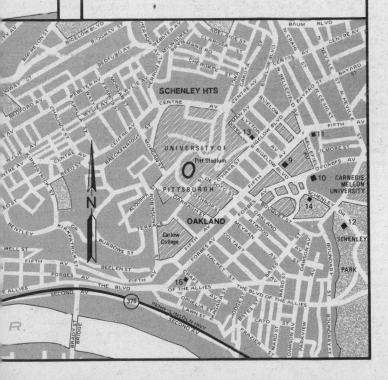

GOLDEN TRIANGLE

Though most of the major attractions are within walking distance, use the just finished subway for quick crosstown transportation.

Point State Park – At the tip of the Golden Triangle, it covers 36 acres of broad walks and spacious gardens on the banks of the river junction, Point State Park contains Fort Pitt Blockhouse, a 1764 fortification, and Fort Pitt Museum, with exhibitions on the French and Indian War and early Pennsylvania history. The park is free and open daily (281-9284); the museum is open Wednesdays through Sundays. Admission charge.

Bank Center – Once a financial hub, these four turn-of-the-century buildings are now an indoor bazaar. Under a stained-glass skylight and amid marble columns and gleaming brass are shops, cinemas, and restaurants. After browsing in the boutiques, have espresso, antipasto, or quiche in the atrium's café as you watch the parade pass by. 307 Fourth Ave.

PPG Place – The "crown jewel" in Pittsburgh's skyline is a plaza surrounded by six modern Gothic buildings, all with a mirrored-glass facade, designed by Philip Johnson and John Burgee. On the ground floor of PPG 1 is the Wintergarden, open to the public for civic functions. An array of international food establishments and retail boutiques runs throughout buildings 2 through 6. Summer concerts are given in the plaza. Off Stanwix St.

One Oxford Center – This office tower at Grant and Fourth streets has three lower floors dedicated to designer shops like Charles Jourdan, Gucci, and Bill Blass. Elegant restaurants, some featuring live jazz, are there when you've had your fill of shopping.

Civic Arena – Recognizable by its stainless steel roof — the largest retractable dome in the world — this is the home of the Pittsburgh *Penguins* hockey team and the Pittsburgh *Spirit* soccer team. The circus, dog show, and top-name concerts are also held here. Bordered by Washington and Crawford sts., Bedford and Centre aves.

David L. Lawrence Convention Center – The city's newest exposition hall (opened in 1980), it has 131,000 square feet of space and hosts the home show and the Pittsburgh Folk Festival every May. Call 565-6000 for a schedule of upcoming events. Penn Ave.

The Liberty Center – Next to the convention center and connected to it by a bridge, this multi-use facility was scheduled to open late in 1986 and feature 4 floors of retail shops, 2 international restaurants, an entertainment lounge, a fitness center, and 20,000 square feet of garden space.

Heinz Hall – A very classy movie theater in 1926, Heinz Hall is now an acoustically balanced, stately auditorium, home of the Pittsburgh Symphony, Pittsburgh Opera, and Civic Light Opera, and host to performing arts troupes. Worth a look for its ornate decorations. Guided tours by appointment. Admission charge. 600 Penn Ave. (392-4800 for tour; 281-5000 for tickets).

NORTH SIDE

To get to the North Side from the Golden Triangle, cross Sixth Street Bridge, then proceed north to the Allegheny Center Mall. Crosstown buses leave from Horne's, at Penn Avenue and Stanwix Street.

Allegheny Observatory – With a 30-inch-diameter refractory lens — a very powerful telescope — this observatory is acclaimed as one of the world's best. Amateur astronomers can scan the heavens or partake in the illustrated lectures. Open Wednesday, Thursday and Friday evenings by appointment, April through October. Free. Riverview Park off Perrysville Ave. (321-2400).

Pittsburgh Aviary – Close to 260 species of birds chatter away in walk-through and enclosed exhibitions. A good place to escape from 20th-century urban America with the advantage that you can slip back into it once you've recharged your battery.

Open daily. Admission charge. Ridge Ave. and Arch St., Allegheny Commons (322-7855).

Children's Museum – Tots and preteens can play with video equipment, operate puppets they know from television, and participate in a kid clinic where they are the doctor to an injured dummy. Admission charge. Open daily. Seasonal hours. Call 322-5058 for recording of hours and special events. Old Post Office Bldg., Allegheny Square.

Buhl Science Center – One of the first and best sky shows in the country. Entertaining exhibitions on astronomy and other branches of science allow you to pedal a bicycle to generate electricity, push a button to activate the rotation of planets in our solar system, and monitor voice patterns on an oscilloscope. A weird-looking Zeiss projector is used for "Sky Dramas" in the Theater of the Stars. Open daily. Admission charge. Allegheny Square (321-4300).

OAKLAND

Cathedral of Learning – Part of the University of Pittsburgh, this imposing 42-story Gothic tower is the only skyscraper of classrooms in the country. A special attraction is the 19 Nationality Rooms on the first floor, devoted to each of the city's major ethnic groups. Open daily. Free. Bigelow Blvd. and 5th Ave., (624-6000).

Carnegie Institute – In one building are housed the main branch of the Carnegie Libraries, an art collection with masterpieces from the French Impressionists, 10,000 dinosaurs, an extensive mineral and gem collection, and much more. Closed on Sunday mornings and Mondays. Donation. 4400 Forbes Ave., (622-3289).

Phipps Conservatory – Rare tropical and domestic fragrant blossoms flourish in the greenhouses and gardens of this 2½-acre publicly owned conservatory. Annual flower shows are in spring, fall and during Christmas. The 13 greenhouses are only a fraction of the greenery of surrounding Schenley Park, which covers 422 acres. Schenley has a lake, tennis courts, baseball fields, a golf course, an ice skating rink, picnic areas, and nature trails. Conservatory (admission charge) and park open daily. Schenley Park (255-2375).

Historical Society of Western Pennsylvania – Curious bottles of antique glass, hand-carved furniture, and other memorabilia line the halls, walls, and shelves. You can peruse old documents on Pennsylvania history in the library. Closed Sundays and Mondays. Free. 4338 Bigelow Blvd. (681-5533).

Pittsburgh Zoo – Not only does this zoo have more than 2,000 animals spread over 75 acres but an indoor Aquazoo as well, with tanks full of domestic trout and pike, and esoteric species like penguins and piranhas. Nocturnal animals are on display in the Twilight Zoo (a children's zoo that operates from May to October). Open daily. Admission charge. Highland Park (441-6262).

Frick Art Museum – A magnificent Renaissance mansion houses Great Masters from the Renaissance through the 18th century. Marie Antoinette's furniture is on display in an ornate living room. The eclectic collection comprises Russian silver, Flemish tapestries, and Chinese porcelains. Closed Mondays and Tuesdays. Free. 7227 Reynolds St. and S Homewood Ave., Point Breeze (371-7766).

■**EXTRA SPECIAL:** For a total change of environment and mood, drive across the state border to *West Virginia,* still a relatively isolated part of the country — three fourths of the state is forest. Take I-70 to exit 6 (Washington, Pennsylvania), then follow Rte. 18 to Rte. 844. In West Virginia, the road becomes Rte. 27, and it will take you to *Drovers Inn* in Wellsburg, where you can feast on hearty, home-cooked American food (304 737-0188). *Wellsburg* is near Meadowcroft Village, in Avella, Pennsylvania, a restored early-19th-century farming community spaciously rebuilt on a wide tract of land. Open daily June-October, Saturdays and Sundays in November; closed December-May. Admission charge (2½ miles off Rte. 231; 412 587-3412). In Wheeling, West Virginia, there are outdoor summer concerts in Oglebay Park (304 242-3000); and country music concerts at Brush Run Park near the airport (304 232-1170).

SOURCES AND RESOURCES

 TOURIST INFORMATION: For information on places of interest and events contact the Visitor Information Center in Gateway Center, the Golden Triangle. The VIC is run by the Greater Pittsburgh Convention and Visitors Bureau, 4 Gateway Center (281-7711), which offers a variety of city guides. For recorded information on daily events, call 391-6840.

Local Coverage – *Post-Gazette,* morning daily; *Press,* evening daily; *Market Square of Pittsburgh,* weekly.

Food – The restaurant sections of *Pittsburgh* magazine and *Key — This Week in Pittsburgh* magazine.

Area Code – All telephone numbers are in the 412 area code unless otherwise indicated.

 CLIMATE AND CLOTHES: Pittsburgh has a moderate climate with frequent precipitation year-round. Summer temperatures climb into the 80s; winters drop into the 20s. About 200 days of the year are cloudy.

 GETTING AROUND: Airport – Greater Pittsburgh International Airport is a 40-minute ride from downtown; taxi fare should cost about $25. Airport Limousine (262-2525) provides service every 20 or 30 minutes from the airport to the *Westin William Penn, Pittsburgh Hilton & Towers,* and *Hyatt Pittsburgh* hotels for $7.

Bus – Port Authority Transit provides efficient bus service (231-5707).

Taxis – To get a taxi, call Yellow Cab (665-8100).

Car Rental – All major national firms are represented.

Van Service – Peoples Cab (441-5334).

 MUSEUMS: The Fort Pitt Museum, Children's Museum, Buhl Science Center, Carnegie Institute, Historical Society of Western Pennsylvania, and Frick Art Museum are described in *Special Places.* Other museums worth noting are:

Art Institute of Pittsburgh – 536 Penn Ave. (263-6600)

Old Economy Museum and Village – 14th and Church sts., Ambridge (266-4500)

Pittsburgh Center for the Arts – 5th and Shady aves. (361-0873)

 MAJOR COLLEGES AND UNIVERSITIES: University of Pittsburgh, Forbes Ave., Oakland (624-4141); Chatham College, 5th Ave. and Woodland Rd. (365-1100); Duquesne University, Blvd. of the Allies (434-6000); Carnegie-Mellon University, Schenley Park (578-2000).

 SPECIAL EVENTS: The *Three Rivers Arts Festival,* displaying the work of over 600 artists, spans 17 days in June. Performing arts and a film festival are a small part of the Carnegie Institute–sponsored festivities. The *Pittsburgh Folk Festival,* an ethnic fair and entertainment spectacular, takes place the weekend before Memorial Day weekend at the David L. Lawrence Convention Center. The *Shadyside Art Festival* takes place in Shadyside in early August. The festive *Three Rivers Regatta,* the first weekend in August, features the Grand Prix of Formula I boat racing, Steamboat Races for the Mayors Cup, the race of the River Belles, and the not-to-be-missed "Anything That Floats" race. A hot-air balloon race, live music, and aerobatic and water ski shows enliven the event. Schenley Park becomes a racetrack of yesteryear during the *Pittsburgh Vintage Grand Prix* the third weekend in August. And from the end of May through mid-August, the *Three Rivers Shakespeare Festival* stages three productions at the Stephen Foster Memorial. Point State Park is the site of celebrations over July 4th and Labor Day weekends.

SPORTS AND FITNESS: Baseball – The *Pirates* play at Three Rivers Stadium, Stadium Circle, North Side (323-1150).

    Bicycling – There are no bike rental shops in town, but the county parks (like North and South parks) have rental facilities.

Canoeing, Kayaking – You can canoe and kayak through exciting whitewater rapids in the Laurel Highlands. Canoe, Kayak and Sailing Craft offers lessons and guided tours, 712 Rebecca Ave., Wilkinsburg (371-4802).

Fishing – The City Parks and Recreation Dept. runs a group fishing program at Panther Hollow in summer. You can rent rods and reels (255-2355).

Fitness Centers – The YMCA has a pool, racquetball courts, track, and exercise classes, 304 Wood St. (227-3800).

Football – The *Steelers'* home grid is also at Three Rivers Stadium (323-1200).

Hiking – There are quite a few hiking programs. For information on Parks Dept. nature tours and programs for the handicapped, contact Schenley Nature Center, Schenley Park (681-2272). For information on hiking, backpacking, canoeing, and camping in the area, contact the Sierra Club (561-0203).

Hockey – The *Penguins* play at Civic Arena, Washington Pl., Center and Bedford Ave. (642-1800).

Horse Racing – Fans have a choice of the Meadows, Washington, Pennsylvania (563-1224), or Waterford Park, Chester, West Virginia (304 387-2400).

Horseback Riding – Hit the trail in South Park. You can rent a horse or sign on for a hayride at Valleybrook Stables (835-9687). If you bring your own horse, you can board it at Morning Star Stables (655-9793).

Ice Skating – Gliding's good from October to March at an outdoor rink in Schenley Park (521-8579) or indoors year-round at Mt. Lebanon Ice Rink (561-3040).

Jogging – Point State Park, where the Allegheny and Monongahela meet; Schenley Park; and North Park (get there by car).

Scuba Diving – In Pittsburgh? Check it out. Sub-Aquatics gives a 36-hour course in essentials with tips on local lakes and water-filled quarries, 1593 Banksville Rd. (531-5577).

Soccer – The *Pittsburgh Spirit Soccer Club* also plays at the Civic Arena (642-1800).

Swimming – There are swimming pools throughout the city. Ream Playground has a good one, Merrimac and Virginia (431-9285).

Tennis – The best municipal courts are at Mellon Park. There are excellent suburban courts at North and South parks.

THEATERS: Pittsburgh's theatrical scene is pretty lively, especially in summer when *Park Players* and *Pittsburgh Puppet Theater* take to the parks. For information, call 255-2354. *The Pittsburgh Public Theater,* Allegheny Square (321-9800), and *Heinz Hall,* 600 Penn Ave. (281-5000), are the city's most prestigious theaters. *Pittsburgh Playhouse Theater Center* produces plays for both children and adults, 222 Craft Ave. (621-4445).

Carnegie-Mellon Theater Co. performs at Kresge Theater, Carnegie-Mellon University, Schenley Park (578-2407). *Chatham College Theater* presents modern classics

(365-1100). There are dinner theaters at *Apple Hill Playhouse,* Lamplighter Restaurant, Delmont (468-4545), and *Little Lake Dinner Theater,* Rte. 19 south, Donaldson's Crossroads (745-6300, 745-9883).

 MUSIC: The world-famous *Pittsburgh Symphony Orchestra* performs from September through May at Heinz Hall, 600 Penn Ave. (281-5000). Summertime the air fills with music. The *American Wind Symphony* performs at Point State Park (681-8866). Jazz can be heard at the Aviary, string ensembles at the Conservatory, and folk music on Flagstaff Hill. The Parks Dept. coordinates schedules (255-2390). For jazz events, dial MUS-LINE.

 NIGHTCLUBS AND NIGHTLIFE: *Cliff Side* offers a glittering nightscape, 1208 Grandview Ave., Mt. Washington (431-6996). For nightscape glitter, take the Duquesne Incline to Grandview Ave. atop Mt. Washington. Have drinks and enjoy the view at the adjacent *Tin Angel* (381-1919) and dine a few steps away at *Cliff Side* (431-6997). For disco, there's *Mirage,* 105 6th St. (281-0349).

SINS: It's a long way from Shady Side and Fox Chapel, the affluent areas to which the *avaricious* in Pittsburgh aspire, to Liberty Avenue; but from the look of that street's massage parlors, peep show palaces, and other strongholds of *lust* in the city, some of that money must be filtering down. Pittsburgh's point of *pride?* A $6 billion construction program, Renaissance II, will brighten the inner face of the city within the next 5 years.

 LOCAL SERVICES: Babysitting – All hotels have babysitting services. There are no independent child care services, however.
   Business Services – Allegheny Personnel Services, Arrott Bldg. (391-2044)
Mechanic – Drugmand's Arco, 304 Virginia Ave. (431-1130)

BEST IN TOWN

 CHECKING IN: For a city of this size, the hotel choices are surprisingly small, and the quality of the accommodations run only from fair to mediocre. All the hotels listed below are in the expensive category; expect to pay $80 or more for a double.

Hyatt Pittsburgh – Conveniently near Civic Arena and Exhibit Hall, the 400 rooms here have all been redecorated. The improvement is very apparent, and the top two Regency floors offer the best accommodations in town. *Hugo's Rotisserie* serves a moderately priced lunch and buffet dinner, with roast duckling the specialty of the house. You can get an inexpensive meal at *QQ's Café.* Both open daily. Chatham Center (412 471-1234). Expensive.

Pittsburgh Greentree Marriott – The *Marriott* livens up its 500-room facility with a swimming pool, a putting green, a whirlpool, sauna, and exercise room. You can enjoy entertainment or disco nightly in the *Trolley Bar* or dinner at the *Grand Pier.* 101 Marriott Dr., Crafton (412 922-8400). Expensive.

Pittsburgh Hilton & Towers – Standing at the edge of Point State Park with an incomparable view of the three rivers, this is currently the leader in a town where great hotels are notable by their absence. Some of its 800 rooms overlook the park, others face the Gateway Center smaller parks. Gateway Center (412 391-4600). Expensive.

Sheraton Inn — Station Square – A 300-room riverside hotel with cocktail lounges, and two restaurants: *Reflections,* with a good seafood buffet on Thursdays and Fridays; and *Mr. C's,* has a sumptuous Sunday brunch. Near Station Square's shops and restaurants. Smithfield and Carson sts. (412 261-2000). Expensive.

The Westin William Penn – A $30 million renovation undertaken by the new Westin management has reinstated this property's status. Since the building was declared a National Historic Landmark, the exterior remains unchanged; the most striking alterations are found in the 595 enlarged and modernized guest rooms. The *Terrace Room* is the formal dining room, offering Continental fare; the more casual *La Plume* is open at lunchtime only. Mellon Sq. (412 281-7100). Expensive.

 EATING OUT: The city's restaurant choices are far better than its selection of hotels, and there is a broad spectrum of ethnic eateries all over the landscape. These are most enthusiastically recommended, for they offer a quality of food preparation and diversity of menus far greater than those found at the anonymous "Continental" restaurants. Expect to pay $35 or more for two at a restaurant we've noted as expensive; between $25 and $35, moderate; under $20 at a place listed as inexpensive. Prices don't include drinks, wine, or tips.

Hyeholde – Just a few minutes from the Pittsburgh airport, there is a medieval castle. Or at least what looks like one, with wooden beams, slate floors, European tapestries, and spacious grounds. The dinner menu changes daily but usually consists of classic dishes — filet mignon, trout, breast of fowl — prepared with the freshest ingredients. Bread and desserts are homemade, and don't pass up the Hyeholde trifle. The wine list is the most extensive in the area. Closed Sundays. Reservations advised. Major credit cards. 190 Hyeholde Dr., Coraopolis (264-3116). Expensive.

Lawrence's – Across from Heinz Hall, this new favorite of performing arts patrons specializes in veal and seafood prepared with a light touch. Try veal Lawrence in a gentle sauce of artichokes, onions, mushrooms, and hearts of palm. Dinner is preceded by complimentary crudités and concludes with luscious pastries or a plate of seasonal fruits that's on the house. Closed Sundays. Reservations advised. Major credit cards. 610 Penn Ave. (391-1414). Expensive.

Tambellini's – The outstanding selection here includes lemon sole, lobster tail, scallops, shrimp, oysters, crabmeat and frogs legs. The spinach salad is crunchy, and the homemade gnocchi irresistible. Closed Sundays. No reservations or credit cards. 860 Saw Mill Run Blvd. (481-1118). Expensive.

Top of the Triangle – Atop the 64-story, triangular US Steel Building, this restaurant provides diners with a gorgeous 3-mile panoramic view. The oak walls add a certain warmth that modern decor often lacks. There's nightly entertainment in the glass-enclosed cocktail lounge. Stouffer's provides the food. Open daily. Reservations advised. Major credit cards. 600 Grant St. (471-4100). Expensive.

Le Pommier – Everything is made on site at this elegant (yet homey) new restaurant in the heavily Slavic South Side — from starter stocks and sourdough country bread to ice cream and bountiful apple desserts (*Le Pommier* means "apple tree"). Proprietors Jim (he's a doctor) and Christine Dauber (she's chief cook, he handles everything else) serve a cross between classic French fare and nouvelle cuisine: chicken breast stuffed with chèvre is a favorite as is the chocolate cake filled with Grand Marnier–laced chocolate mousse. Closed Sundays. Reservations necessary. Major credit cards. 2104 E Carson St. (431-1901). Expensive to moderate.

Arthur's – Though one of Pittsburgh's newest, this small restaurant in the city's oldest office building provides an attractive early American decor with four working fireplaces. The menu includes Continental and American dishes; the smoked meats and fish are excellent (all smoking is done on the premises). Some specialties are German onion beer soup and veal stuffed with smoked scallops and mozzarella cheese, served with spinach noodles in a Marsala wine and mushroom sauce. Closed Sundays. Reservations advised. Major credit cards. 209 4th Ave. (566-1735). Expensive to moderate.

Grand Concourse – This elegant remake of the old Pittsburgh and Lake Erie Railroad Terminal is the best thing to happen to Pittsburgh's restaurant scene in years. Beautiful wood, stained glass, and gleaming brass surround diners who devour excellent seafood — oysters, shrimp, clams, crab — and especially a tangy seafood chowder that is served in a pewter tureen. One Station Sq. (261-1717). Expensive to moderate.

Sgro's – In a sylvan setting 20 minutes from the city, this is a relaxing place to dine at one of the area's best country clubs. Prime ribs and seafood are the specialties, and service is gracious. Closed Sundays. Reservations accepted. Major credit cards. Campbell's Run Rd., off the Parkway West (787-1234). Expensive to moderate.

The Balcony – A charming restaurant in Shadyside's shopping quarter serving soups, fresh fish, vegetarian dishes, and imaginative sandwiches with a homey touch. Live jazz entertainment. Closed Sundays. Reservations advised. Major credit cards. 5520 Walnut St. (687-0110). Moderate.

Tequila Junction – A short walk from the city, across the Smithfield Street Bridge, will take you to the Freight House Shops at Station Square, where you can lunch or dine south of the border. In a romantic brick and adobe inn, sip a strawberry margarita followed by one of the many tasty Mexican entrées, such as crabmeat enchilada or chili Colorado. Open daily. No reservations. Major credit cards. Freight House Shops, Station Square (261-3265). Moderate.

Sir Loin Inns – Cheerful pub featuring an extensive full-course dinner menu of steaks, beef, and seafood, complemented by homemade soup, giant bowls of salad, and very good bread. If you can manage, try one of their desserts, too. Open daily. Reservations only for five or more. Major credit cards. 5841 Forbes Ave. (521-8710). Moderate.

Samreny's – Actually the full name is Samreny's Cedars of Lebanon Restaurant. And there's a full menu of Middle Eastern dishes, like shish kebab, stuffed cabbage and grape leaves, kibbi nayaa (rice with pine nuts), heaping green salads, baklava, and other rich, rare pastries. The decor includes a delightful collection of antique water pipes. Open daily. Reservations accepted. No credit cards. 4808 Baum Blvd. (682-1212). Inexpensive.

PORTLAND, OR

One of the most important things to bear in mind when you visit Portland is that it's likely that you will be made to feel welcome. Under no circumstances, however, must you let on that you'd actually like to live here. You *will* want to live here, if you've got any sense, even after just one visit; but better to lie about it. Portland residents are that sensitive.

They're not unfriendly, mind you. It's simply that the city is beautiful — always ranking high on metropolitan "quality of life" surveys — and with an enlightened government and determined citizenry, it's getting better all the time. Even the eruptions of Mt. St. Helens haven't left any scars.

Portland stretches along the Willamette River (one of the few rivers in the country that flows north) just below the point where it joins the Columbia. The confluence provides Portland with a deep, freshwater port that serves oceangoing vessels, and because the city straddles the Willamette, ships dock beneath downtown bridges. By river some 110 miles from the ocean, Portland is a seaport. Around the whole metropolitan area, like the brackets of parentheses, are the Northwest's two most imposing mountain ranges — the Cascades in the east, the Coast Range to the west.

The city is divided neatly into its east and west sides by the Willamette; each side has its own atmosphere (east side, homey; west side, posh. The elegant, downtown shopping district is very west side). The two segments of the city are connected by 11 bridges. The whole city is then divided into five large sections: North, Northeast, Northwest, Southeast, Southwest. Sounds confusing, but it actually makes finding places very easy with a local map, since every address includes an area designation (SW, NE, N, etc.).

For the most part, the city is flat, hugging its major waterways, lakes and ponds, with hundreds of parks spread across its metropolitan area. Now and then, a group of forested hills raises an imperious eyebrow — some residential, others intentionally undeveloped. In the east, the city holds up three fingers of small, residential mountains, as if pointing to the great mountains to the east, and 11,235-foot Mt. Hood in the Cascades, an hour away.

The Greater Portland Area stretches from the foothills of Mt. Hood to the western plains of the Coast Range; more than one million people live in this four-county area.

The city was incorporated in 1845 by New England settlers — it's named for Portland, Maine. When the great crash of 1893 closed banks across the country, one pioneer Portland merchant, Aaron Meier, took his bags of gold to banker Henry Corbett. The next morning, as the rest of the nation's banks failed, Corbett stood tall and firm in the middle of his bank's lobby — properly attired in frockcoat and top hat — with Meier's gold piled conspicuously around him. There was no closure in Portland that day.

When Scottish shipper Donald Macleay bequeathed 107 acres to the city

CENTRAL
PORTLAND, OR

The city is divided into 5 sectors, by Burnside Rd., The river, and by Williams Av.
All streets within each sector have prefixes: NW, NE, SW, SE and N., respectively.

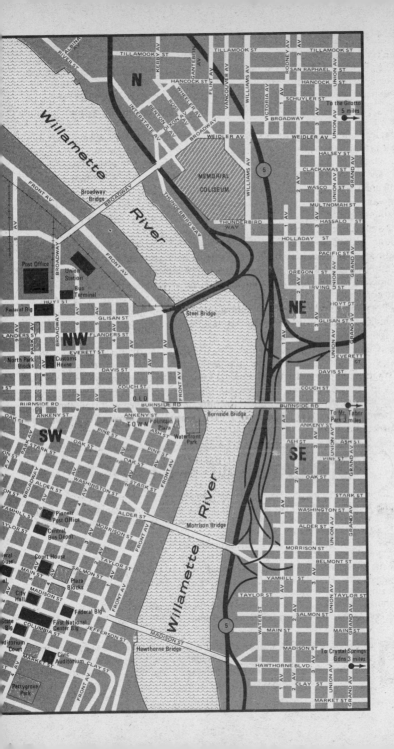

at the turn of the century, it was with the stipulation that no wheeled vehicle *ever* be allowed to enter the premises. The city agreed, and has even expanded Macleay's trust. Today, Macleay Park stands in the middle of the city, untouched by exhaust fumes or bicycle tread, part of nearly 5,000 acres of dense forest — a green velvet buffer for hikers, bird-watchers, and nature lovers.

Macleay anticipated the attitude of modern Portlanders with admirable skill. In recent years, the city has torn up some 24 blocks right out of the heart of the west side business district to build a brick-covered, tree-lined pedestrian mall, spotted with fountains and sculpture. Along the Willamette River, which creates the city's natural seaport, the old factories have been razed, and greenways are spreading out with smug brilliance. By order of the people, the Willamette River has been cleaned up, and riverboating, salmon fishing and water skiing are now commonplace.

Along with the rest of the state, Portland has banned the use of fluorocarbons in aerosol sprays, abolished the sale of beer and soda in nonreturnable cans and bottles, and is seriously discussing mandatory use of seat belts in all automobiles. Portland is a potent force in civic activism.

After taking a long look at the first 40-story building to go up in its business area, Portland moved swiftly to assure that no other such building would be built higher. It has thus saved its panorama of mountains and wooded hillsides for succeeding generations.

The City of Roses, Portland has also proven a thorn in the side of some industry. All new buildings must pass inspection as early as the initial planning stages, and the powerful Historical Landmarks Commission works constantly to protect Portland's historic buildings. On its list of protected properties are several iron-fronted buildings, plus one sycamore and one elm tree, each planted by founding parents and each continually bursting the seams of downtown sidewalks.

PORTLAND AT-A-GLANCE

SEEING THE CITY: Portland offers several exceptional vantage points from which to see the city, the valley in which it lies, and the mountains beyond. Two of the best are:

Pittock Acres Park – The grounds of the former Pittock Mansion (see below), 1,000 feet above the city. At your feet are the port, business section, the Willamette River, and the southeast residential areas. In the distance are the Cascade Mountains — Mt. Hood in Oregon, Mt. Rainier, Mt. Adams, and Mt. St. Helens in Washington. 3229 NW Pittock.

Washington Park – The best view is from the International Rose Test Gardens, looking east toward mountains in the background. 400 SW Kingston.

SPECIAL PLACES: Portland was made for walking. Her founders frequently built homes in the west hills and walked to work along the waterfront. Especially on the west side, major points of interest are within walking distance of one another.

WEST SIDE

Portland Center for the Performing Arts – The newest dazzler on the city's roster of flourishing arts institutions is the 2,776-seat Arlene Schnitzer Concert Hall in the former Paramount. The ornate detail of the 1928 vaudeville–movie palace has been lovingly refurbished and first-rate acoustics built in. Home of the Oregon Symphony Orchestra, the hall also holds pop, country, and jazz concerts; shows films, and hosts conventions. Next door, two smaller theaters will open in June 1987. SW Broadway at Main (241-0788, for tours; 248-4496, for tickets).

Oregon Historical Society – Exhibitions on Oregon history, before and after the arrival of the white man. Also a fine series of dioramas on Indian life, plus a research library with open stacks for browsing; pioneer craft demonstrations for children. Closed Sundays. Free. 1230 SW Park (222-1741).

Ira Keller Fountain (and Civic Auditorium) – A series of pools and waterfalls a block wide, facing the Civic Auditorium. In hot weather, people splash around in its tons of swirling water. Designed by Lawrence Halprin, it is called Ira's Fountain. SW 3rd Ave at Clay.

Pioneer Courthouse – The first federal building in the Pacific Northwest, completed in 1875 and now restored to its original Victorian splendor. The interior includes a working post office, an elegant Victorian courtroom (where the US Court of Appeals meets), and adjoining rooms for the judges. The courtroom can be seen by asking the security guard to unlock the door. Enter at 555 SW Yamhill (no phone). Across the street is Pioneer Courthouse Square, an open city block that has become the hub of downtown. This is a place for music, flowers, food, and fanfare.

Portlandia – The cookie-tin Portland Building (designed by the Postmodern architect Michael Graves) is now crowned in glory. Over the main portico kneels a copper lady of heroic proportions. The new symbol of the city, the sculpture is by Raymond Kaskey. 1120 SW 5th Ave.

Old Town – When the Pioneer Courthouse was brand new, some folks thought it much too far from the downtown business section — a whole six blocks. Now "downtown" is called Old Town, a restored shopping and browsing area filled with craft, art, and antique shops. The area runs from First to Fifth avenues, on both sides of Burnside. Artists from all over the state sell their work at the Sunday and Saturday markets, under Burnside Bridge, from 10 AM to 5 PM, May to December.

Worth noting on Ankeny, south of Burnside: *Dan and Louis Oyster Bar* (see below, *Eating Out*), and *Le Panier,* on SW Second, whose Parisian chefs serve fresh French bread and croissants every day. North of Burnside, Couch Street, and beyond are numerous specialty shops. Best buys are Indian artifacts, toys, spinning and weaving supplies, original jewelry.

Washington Park – One of the city's oldest parks, it has 145 acres, all part of the 40-mile park system that thrives within the city limits. There are five points of special interest on the grounds: the Rose Test Gardens, the Japanese Garden, the Oregon Museum of Science and Industry, the Western Forestry Center, and Tera One, a totally solar home, as well as some magnificent views of the city and countryside. Plan to spend some extended periods of time here, but note: The only food available is hot dogs and hamburgers at the zoo, so think about taking along a picnic lunch (*Elephant's Delicatessen* will prepare one for you; 13 NW 23rd Pl., 224-3955).

The Rose Test Gardens offer hundreds of varieties of roses, all generously identified. June and September are the best months for seeing them. In summer, a zoo train runs from the Gardens to the zoo (admission charge), which (among other displays) has a children's petting zoo. At the Penguinarium you can see Humboldt penguins at close range. Open daily.

The zoo is part of a complex that includes the Oregon Museum of Science and

Industry (OMSI), the Planetarium, and Western Forestry Center. OMSI, closed only on Christmas, offers a giant walk-through reconstruction of a human heart, an authentic ship's bridge, hands-on computers, various traveling exhibitions. Admission charge. Western Forestry Center has displays, exhibitions on Oregon's largest industry. Admission charge. The entire complex is on SW Canyon (228-OMSI; zoo, 226-1561; Forestry Center, 228-1367).

Pittock Mansion – The imposing French Renaissance home built by Henry Pittock, a poor boy who made good as publisher of *The Oregonian* at the turn of the century. The grounds are open daily and are free; the house is open every afternoon for a fee. *The Gate Lodge* serves lunch and tea Tuesdays through Fridays. 3229 NW Pittock Dr. (mansion, 248-4469; lodge, 221-1730).

Tryon Creek State Park – The state's first metropolitan park, 2 miles south of central Portland, with 600 acres of wilderness for biking, hiking, and naturalists (horses are welcome, but there are none for rent). Adjoining Lake Oswego (636-4550).

EAST SIDE

The Grotto – An outdoor chapel, built in a grotto with a ten-story cliff, monastery, and gardens at the top. The 58 acres of grounds are open for contemplation, quiet walks, solitude. Sunday mass is celebrated in the chapel at 10 AM. 8840 NE Skidmore (254-7371).

Crystal Springs Gardens – More than 2,000 rhododendron plants, maintained by the Portland chapter of the American Rhododendron Society. No Portlander would miss the gardens during April and May when first the azaleas, then the rhododendrons, reach their peak. Adjacent is the campus of Reed College. SE 28th Avenue near SE Woodstock.

Mt. Tabor Park – Believed to be the only extinct volcano within a US city's limits. Some of the best views of the city. Between Yamhill and Division, east of SE 60th Ave.

■**EXTRA SPECIAL:** *Sauvie Island,* the largest island in the Columbia River, is just north of Portland on US 30. Devoted primarily to farmland, the island is ideal for biking, hiking, picnicking, fishing, or just lolling about for a day. Here, the Oregon Historical Society maintains the *Bybee–Howell House,* a restored pre–Civil War farmhouse, open to the public from June to October (free; donations appreciated). The last Saturday of September is the "Wintering-In" picnic and celebration at the house, when local farmers sell harvest goods.

The *Columbia River Highway* runs east and west of Portland. Drive east for a view of the Columbia River Gorge, with its 2,000-foot cliff and 11 waterfalls.

SOURCES AND RESOURCES

TOURIST INFORMATION: The Visitors Information Center at the Convention and Visitors Association is best for brochures, maps, general tourist information and personal help; if you arrive after hours, outdoor map dispensers and kiosks can provide a basic orientation. 26 SW Salmon (222-2223).

Oregon State Highway Division offers travel information at 12345 N Union Ave. (open May through October only, 285-1631).

The Portland Guidebook by Linda Lampman and Julie Sterling (The Writing Works; $5.95) is the best and most comprehensive guide to Portland and its environs.

Local Coverage – *The Oregonian,* morning and afternoon daily; *Willamette Week* offers a liberally opinionated study of the city.

Food – Check *The Portland Guidebook* and the weekly newspaper restaurant reviews.

Area Code – All telephone numbers are in the 503 area code unless otherwise indicated.

CLIMATE AND CLOTHES: The good news: It doesn't get too cold in Portland (snow is pretty rare); it doesn't get too hot here, either (summer temperatures above 90° only last two or three days). However, it certainly does rain. The months from October through May are the worst. June, July, August, and September are fairly clear, and the average temperature is in the 70s. That's the time when tourists visit the Portland area, so book ahead.

GETTING AROUND: Airport – Portland International Airport is a 20- to 30-minute drive from downtown, and cab fare should run $14 to $18. The Downtowner airport bus (236-0341) provides transportation to downtown's major hotels for $4. The trip takes about 45 minutes, 60 minutes during rush hour. Buses depart from in front of the airport every 20 minutes from 5:30 AM to midnight. Tri-Met city bus #72 also stops in front of the airport and connects to buses going downtown; the fare is 75¢ to $1.

Bus – Portland's Tri-Met system covers three counties; exact-change-only fare is zoned except within the 340-block downtown shopping area (including Old Town, major shopping malls, Art Museum and Historical Society, riverfront) which is free and called Fareless Square. Complete route and tourist information (and map of Fareless Square) is available from downtown Customer Assistance Office, 701 SW 6th Ave. (enter under the waterfall in Pioneer Courthouse Square).

Light Rail – The bus system is complemented by the Light Rail network of streetcars serving downtown and the eastern suburbs. Schedules are available at Light Rail stops along the streets as well as at the Pioneer Courthouse Square transit office.

Taxi – Cabs must be called by phone or picked up at taxi stations in front of the major hotels. They cannot be hailed in the street. Most hotels have direct phone connections to the two largest companies, Broadway Cab (227-1234), Radio Cab (227-1212).

Car Rental – National and local firms are represented in abundance. Everything from rental Lincolns to Rent A Wreck; check the yellow pages. Tropical Rent A Car, 7101 NE 82nd (257-3451), has one of the lowest weekly rates.

MUSEUMS: The Oregon Historical Society and the Pittock Mansion are both noted in *Special Places.* Other interesting museums are:

American Advertising Museum – The nation's best collection of persuasive media, from sandwich boards to videos. Through the evolution of advertising much of our country's history and progress is revealed. NW 2nd Ave. at Couch (771-4033).

Portland Art Museum – With an outstanding permanent collection of Northwest Indian art, the museum also features a representative group of Oregon's prolific contemporary artists and a wide variety of traveling shows. There's also an outdoor Sculpture Mall. Closed Mondays. Admission charge. SW Park and Madison (226-2811).

Portland Children's Museum – *The* place to be on a rainy day. Kids amuse themselves for hours with dozens of hands-on displays, exploring a cave and a tunnel, and more. Closed Mondays. Free. 3037 SW 2nd Ave. (248-4587).

MAJOR COLLEGES AND UNIVERSITIES: The jewel in Portland's academic crown is Reed College, 3203 SE Woodstock Blvd. (771-1112), a private, liberal arts college of the highest caliber. Other institutions of learning are the University of Portland, 5000 N Willamette Blvd. (283-7911);

Lewis and Clark College, 0615 SW Palatine Hill Rd. (244-6161); and Portland State University, 724 SW Harrison (229-3000).

 PARKS AND GARDENS: Even the freeways into Portland are divided by banks of wild roses and iris; the city is surrounded by green mountains and garlanded with 7,608 acres of parkland. Washington Park, Pittock Acres Park, Mt. Tabor Park, Crystal Springs Gardens, and Tryon Creek State Park are all described in *Special Places.* Other notable Portland parks are:

Council Crest Park – above Portland Heights, SW Fairmount Blvd.

Hoyt Arboretum – 400 SW Fairview Blvd.

Rocky Butte – I-84 east to NE 102nd.

Westmoreland Park – SE 22nd Ave. at Bybee.

 SPECIAL EVENTS: *The Portland Rose Festival,* featuring everything from beauty queens to bicycle races, runs during the first half of June. *Wintering-In Celebration,* on Sauvie Island, is a harvest festival on the last Saturday of September.

 SPORTS AND FITNESS: Baseball – The Portland *Phillies,* a farm team for the Philadelphia *Phillies,* play at Portland Civic Stadium, April-August. Tickets are sold at the stadium, 1844 SW Morrison (248-4345).

Basketball – The *Trail Blazers* play their home games at Memorial Coliseum from October through April; tickets at the Coliseum, 1401 N Wheeler (239-4422).

Bicycling – Rent from the Bike Route, NW Cornell Rd. at Murray (641-4195). Numerous city and country rides are described in *The Portland Guidebook.*

Fishing – For chinook salmon, try the lower Willamette or Willamette Slough from March through early May. Steelhead are found in the Clackamas River, and its tributary, Eagle Creek, from December through February. But best of all (for fly fishermen) are the Toutle, Washougal and Wind rivers in southwest Washington state, where you can do battle with the warrior steelhead.

Fitness Centers – The *Marriott* Health Club has a pool, Jacuzzi, weight room, and sauna; provides towels, and is open to all. 1401 SW Front Ave.; take elevator to 1st floor (226-7600).

Golf – The metropolitan area has 20 public courses. The best is Forest Hills Country Club, 20 minutes from downtown in Cornelius (a plus: it has showers; 648-8559).

Jogging – Run up Broadway or 5th Ave. to Duniway Park, then follow the bike path to Terwilliger Park; this route can range from 5 to 30 miles, as time or stamina permits. Upcoming running events are listed with the Oregon Road Runners Information Hotline (223-7867).

Racing – For racing and pari-mutuel betting, Portland Meadows Horse Race Track, 1001 N Schmeer Road (285-9144), with a season from October to April; and Multnomah Kennel Club Dog Race Track, 220 3rd Ave., Fairview (12 miles from city) (667-7700), from May to September.

Skiing – The closest is Mt. Hood Meadows; better is Mt. Bachelor, 180 miles from Portland at Bend.

Tennis – The Park Bureau runs 7 indoor and dozens of outdoor courts. The indoor courts may be reserved by calling 233-5959 or 248-4200. Otherwise, first come, first served. The major tennis center is in Buckman Park, Portland Tennis Center, 324 NE 12th Ave.

 THEATER: For up-to-date offerings and performance times, check the publications listed above. Portland has 15 theaters that offer performances, some locally produced, others traveling shows. Colleges and universities in the area also produce plays and musicals. Best bets for shows: *Portland Civic*

Auditorium (248-4496); *Portland Civic Theatre* (226-3048); *New Rose Theater* (222-2487); *Storefront Actors' Theatre* (224-4001); *Willamette Repertory Theater* (224-4491).

MUSIC: Concerts and opera are held by *Oregon Symphony Orchestra* (228-1353); *Portland Opera Association* (241-1401); free summer concerts in Washington Park between mid-July and mid-August, and at Waterfront Park from late August to mid-September (796-5100).

NIGHTCLUBS AND NIGHTLIFE: Pop music, jazz, Dixieland, folk, and rock are all offered at Portland's many pubs, taverns, and nightclubs. Current favorites: *Father's,* 309 SW 3rd (227-5492), for 1930s swing jazz; the *Jazz Quarry,* 1111 SW Jefferson (222-7422), for top jazz artists; *Starry Night,* 8 NW 6th Ave. (227-0071), for danceable new wave; *Last Hurrah,* 555 SW Alder (224-1336), for rock. *Maxi's* at the *Red Lion Motor Inn,* 909 N Hayden Island Dr. (240-8595), for disco top-40 music; and *Key Largo,* 31 NW 1st Ave. (223-9919), for blues and bluegrass; *Shanghai Lounge,* 0309 SW Montgomery (220-1865), for rock music and for meeting everyone in town.

SINS: Though residents claim resolutely that "there is no sin in Portland, we outlawed it years ago," there is; it just isn't very spirited. The mountains, the nearby sea, and the Oregon wildlands are too mesmerizing for most residents. Portland is a clean-living city, and so, while the lovelies stripped to bikinis for a swim in Ira's Fountain across from the Civic Auditorium, 222 SW Clay St., have been known to arouse *lust* in the hearts of men prone to that sort of thing, any one of those males — given a choice between the girl and a season ticket to the *Trail Blazers'* games — would take the tickets and run. *Pride* flourishes among those who know how to pronounce Glisan (the name of a street; rhymes with listen); and *envy* toward the first Portland gardener to produce a red tomato before September. *Gluttony?* It stirs over the Dungeness crab legs sold at $17 a pound at Green's Seafood, 6767 SW Macadam Ave. (246-8245).

LOCAL SERVICES: Babysitting – Wee-Ba-Bee Attendants (661-5966)
   Business Services – Contact the Business Service Bureau, 1208 SW 13th Ave (228-4107); Business Communication Center, 200 SW Market. (226-1007)
   Mechanic – Tune Up Specialties, 8060 NE Glisan (252-8096), ask for Tony; Alliance Goodyear, 333 SW 10th Ave. (227-2443)

■ **TAKE SOME PORTLAND HOME WITH YOU:** Fresh chinook and silver salmon are two of Portland's best known exports, and airlines are accustomed to seeing passengers board an outbound flight with a cold fin under one arm. Tony's Fish Market, 14th and Washington, Oregon City (656-7512), will supply fresh salmon and crab, specially packed to travel.

BEST IN TOWN

CHECKING IN: The choice of Portland hotels has become more interesting of late. With the addition of the *Heathman* and the *Alexis,* it is now possible to slumber in splendor as well as in the comfort and convenience always offered by the city's better hotels. Expect to pay $90 or more for a double room in one of the hotels we've noted as expensive; $50 to $90 in the moderate range; and under $50 in the inexpensive category. For B&B accommodations, contact: Northwest Bed & Breakfast, 610 SW Broadway, Suite 609, Portland, OR 97205 (503 243-7676).

Portland Marriott – More than a million dollars' worth of millwork went into this Northwest incarnation. It has 500 rooms, 2 restaurants (one with a view of the Willamette River), banquet facilities, indoor pool, whirlpool, sauna, and exercise rooms. 1401 SW Front Ave. (503 226-7600). Expensive.

Westin Benson – Built in 1913 by wealthy logger Simon Benson to be Portland's premier hotel. Although the lobby maintains a feeling of Old World luxury, the 330 rooms and suites don't really offer the kind of traditional atmosphere you might expect.Now managed by Westin Corporation, it is comfortable and convenient, with a quite good *London Grill* restaurant (open daily) and a respectable *Trader Vic's* as well (closed Sundays). Concierge; access to health club; 24-hour room service. Pay garage. 309 SW Broadway (503 228-9611). Expensive.

Heathman – Adjoining the Performing Arts Center are 160 of the most luxurious guest rooms and suites in town. After a two-year restoration and renovation, done by the same designer as San Francisco's *Stanford Court,* the *Heathman* has emerged as an authentic first-class property. Amenities include complementary video movie library for in-room use, concierge, valet parking, and access to a nearby health club. Its main restaurant is noted for its selections of fresh Pacific Northwest seafood and game. SW Broadway at Salmon (503 241-4100 or 800 551-0011). Expensive.

Alexis – The city's newest inn is one of its smallest: a mere 74 rooms and suites clustered on the waterfront. In the morning, guests awaken to views of the marina and to Continental breakfast. Marble, brass, fresh flowers, and classic furnishings produce an easy elegance. Six suites have wood-burning fireplaces and wet bars. Concierge, 24-hour room service, access to adjacent health club. The *Esplanade* restaurant prepares Northwest regional cuisine. 1510 SW Harbor Way (503 228-3233). Expensive.

Portland Hilton – Sitting snugly between the major streets of the downtown shopping district, the 455-room *Hilton* sports a skylit atrium lobby and a health club. *Alexander's* restaurant on the top floor offers good food with a glittery view. Amenities include room service, pool, and banquet facilities. 921 SW 6th (503 226-1611). Expensive to moderate.

Thunderbird–Red Lion Motor Inns – This giant complex on the Columbia River, just between Portland and Vancouver (Washington), is 10 minutes from the airport. These two inns, together with a third, also called the *Thunderbird Inn* (at the Quay on the Washington side), provide 830 rooms. Fine restaurants, free parking, live entertainment, a large convention center, two grand ballrooms, and room service. Pool, tennis, and mini-golf at *Red Lion.* For either *Thunderbird:* 1401 N Hayden Island Dr. (503 283-2111). *Red Lion:* 909 N Hayden Island Dr. (503 283-4466). Expensive to moderate.

Mallory Motor Hotel – A step down from the Jacuzzi tubs and poolside cabanas, but a comfortable, quiet 144-room hotel that offers a good room and adequate restaurant facilities at a reasonable price. Just across the street from the Civic Theater. Free parking. 729 SW 15th Ave. (223-6311). Inexpensive.

EATING OUT: Portland shines pretty brightly as an eating place. The impact of a certain style of restaurant — small, personal, with creative cuisine (often a mixture of several styles of food, like American and Oriental, macrobiotic and vegetarian) and inviting decor — has had dramatic effects on local eating habits. Residents are out of their own kitchens and around town as never before. Often, the new restaurants are owned by young people who are intensely interested in healthy food in a homey, comfortable atmosphere. Our restaurant selections range in price from $50 or more for a dinner for two in the expensive range, $20 to $40 in the moderate, and $20 or less in the inexpensive range. Prices do not include drinks, wine or tips.

Belinda's – No longer surrounded by dilapidated neighbors, *Belinda's* now finds itself among spiffy Old Town renovations. It continues to be one of the finest French restaurants in Portland. The wine list is extensive and the entrées — veal, pork, beef, and seafood — are gently coddled in rare French sauces. Look for fresh herbs in the salad (bought from local growers) and sample from the scrumptious dessert tray. The house pâté is another must. Open daily. Reservations recommended. Major credit cards. 112 SW 2nd Ave. (222-6606). Expensive.

Le Cuisinier – The late James Beard salivated in print over this very small French restaurant that puts the emphasis on eating (diners sit in straight-backed chairs). Appetizers include homemade pasta, steamed mussels, and paper-thin slices of chilled leg of lamb with mustard sauce. Main courses include sautéed salmon, braised sweetbreads in madeira sauce and roast beef tenderloin with green peppercorns as well as duckling confit. Dinners only, Tuesdays through Saturdays. Reservations requested. It's not easy to find, so take a cab. 1308 W Burnside (224-4260). Expensive.

Atwater's – Occupying the entire 30th floor of the US Bancorp Tower, one of the main lures is the only 360° view in all downtown. The restaurant does justice to the striking panorama, with an American menu that relies on only the freshest local products. The menu undergoes revision seasonally. Dinner daily, plus brunch on Sunday. Reservations required. Major credit cards. 111 SW 5th Ave. (220-3600). Expensive.

Harborside – The eclectic, 114-item menu ranges from Cajun pizza to peanut butter truffle cake, with a stop at fresh salmon along the way. The proprietors miraculously manage very high quality throughout. Tables on three tiers give all diners a view of the waterfront. Open daily. Reservations for six or more only. Major credit cards. 0309 SW Montgomery (220-1865). Moderate.

Rian's Eating Establishment – A favorite downtown lunch and cocktail meeting place. Sandwiches as well as quiche, chicken Kiev, crab. Closed Sundays. Reservations suggested. Major credit cards. In Morgan's Alley (downtown shopping mall), through the wrought-iron gate between SW Park and Broadway (222-9996). Moderate.

Sweet Tibbie Dunbar – A former golf course clubhouse that has achieved genuine charm as a redecorated English pub serving lunch (daily except Saturdays), dinner, and Sunday brunch. Reservations advised. Major credit cards. 718 NE 12th Ave. (232-1801). Moderate.

Rheinlander – A good spot to feed the kids on grand portions of good German food. Not the place to go for an intimate rendezvous, since it's filled with families who enjoy being serenaded by a strolling accordian player. Open daily. Reservations accepted. Major credit cards. 5035 NE Sandy Blvd. (288-5503). Moderate.

Jake's Famous Crawfish – Serving crawfish and other seagoing delectables since 1892, *Jake's* has occupied its current premises since 1908. Worth a visit for both quality food and interesting surroundings. Open daily. Reservations advised. Major credit cards. 401 SW 12th St. (226-1419). Moderate.

Chen's Dynasty – For Chinese specialties like stir-fried pork with pickled mustard greens and peanuts or cracked crab with Hunan black beans, this is the place. The menu of Chinese delights seems endless. Open daily. Reservations suggested. Major credit cards. 622 Washington (248-9491). Moderate.

Delphina's – Choose anything from pizza to tender milk-fed veal in this cozy Northwest neighborhood restaurant. The bread and pasta are *Delphina's* own, and justly famous throughout the city. Open daily. Reservations advised. Major credit cards. 2112 NW Kearney (221-1195). Inexpensive.

Dan and Louis Oyster Bar – A Portland institution. Clams, crab, oysters — quickly, simply, and deliciously prepared. Opened in the days when restaurants didn't worry about decor, and it's still the same today (which means it has a distinct, turn-of-the-century style). Open daily. Reservations for five or more. Major credit cards. 208 SW Ankeny (227-5906). Inexpensive.

Organ Grinder – Not so much a restaurant as a performance at which you can buy pizza and beer. The place has at least seven pipe organs connected to one keyboard, at which pop tunes are played to accompany silent films. Open daily. No reservations. Some credit cards. 5015 SE 82nd Ave. (771-1178). Inexpensive.

Original Pancake House – No kin to the national chain of nearly the same name. From lingonberry to German pancakes, these are Portland's best, and well loved in the city. Closed Mondays and Tuesdays. No reservations. No credit cards. SW Barbur Blvd at 26th (246-9007). Inexpensive.

Victoria's Nephew – Director's chairs, potted ferns, a huge old "fireside chat" radio on the counter, and tables on the sidewalk; a great place for lunch or English-style high tea. Closed Sundays. Reservations accepted. Major credit cards. 212 SW Stark (223-7299). Inexpensive.

Rose's Delicatessen – Delicate blintzes, delicious cakes, gigantic sandwiches. The food isn't kosher, but the atmosphere — and the quality of the sandwiches — is vintage New York. Open daily. Make reservations or expect a wait during prime meal times. Major credit cards. 315 NW 23rd Ave. (227-5181). Inexpensive.

The Skyline – Stuck on an island in the middle of Skyline Boulevard (a major road), this is a drive-in that serves hamburgers and the usual roadside fare. So why do we include it? Because the hamburgers are terrific, and because it's only a five-minute drive from the Portland Zoo complex. Open daily. No reservations. No credit cards. 1313 NW Skyline Blvd. (292-6727). Inexpensive.

Taco Houses No. 1 & 2 – Tacos and beer; the best in the city. Open daily. No reservations. Some credit cards. *No. 1:* 3255 NE 82nd Ave. (252-1695); *No. 2:* 3550 SE Powell Blvd. (234-6401). Inexpensive.

Carnival – Decorate your own hamburger and sample creamy milkshakes in an enticing variety of flavors. Indoor booths in a circus-tent atmosphere or picnic tables in the back garden are all family-pleasers. No credit cards. 2805 SW Sam Jackson Park Rd. (227-4244). Inexpensive.

ST. LOUIS

Long known as a great city in which to raise a family, the Gateway to the West is finally growing up and expanding in new directions. It now offers more than baseball and a scenic view of the Arch to both visitors and residents who want culture, entertainment, history, and fun.

The change has taken place during the early 1980s, as St. Louisans have started to realize they don't have to leave town for respect. Residents can hail the achievement of the St. Louis Symphony, recently acclaimed as number 2 in the nation by *Time* magazine. The Fabulous Fox, a movie palace resuscitated in all its glitzy greatness, has led to big-name entertainment and the best of Broadway touring companies coming to St. Louis' own Grand Boulevard.

Always a showplace for sports talent, the city is the home of major league teams: the baseball Cardinals, football Cardinals, soccer Steamers, and hockey Blues. The Bowling Hall of Fame, next to Busch Stadium, stands as a testimonial to yet another sport. Although the Mississippi is not itself a center of water sports, new marinas just east of Laclede's Landing provide some peaceful waves in which to play.

The city's cultural and entertainment rejuvenation has been spurred by an infusion of capital into the real estate market, especially downtown, where the entire skyline has changed significantly. Due to a strict city ordinance, no building near the famous Arch is allowed to tower above the gleaming steel structure's 630 feet, but the new 40-story-plus Southwestern Bell corporate headquarters is the city's first real skyscraper. Well, almost. Actually, the Wainwright Building, designed by Louis Sullivan, was known as the first skyscraper in the nation and was renovated by the State of Missouri as a state office building several years ago.

Renovation and rehabilitation have been the keys to St. Louis' renaissance. Neighborhoods such as Soulard, Lafayette Square, Shaw Park, Compton Heights, Washington Heights, and Benton Park have been given a facelift and revived by urban pioneers who turned their new blood and ideas to these old, dilapidated areas. Today they have become national landmarks and offer an architectural history lesson of the Midwest. Walking tours and home tours are offered regularly by the Landmarks Association.

St. Louis grew up along the river, and the mighty Mississippi has left its indelible mark on the city's music — jazz, gospel, and bluegrass are part of regularly held festivals. Another reminder of the city's river heritage is the warehouse district, where once goods were shipped en route to the rugged West. Restored right down to its original cobblestone streets, Laclede's Landing draws office traffic during the day, restaurant and bar patrons at night. The development is particularly appealing to conventioneers and college students.

ST. LOUIS
WEST END

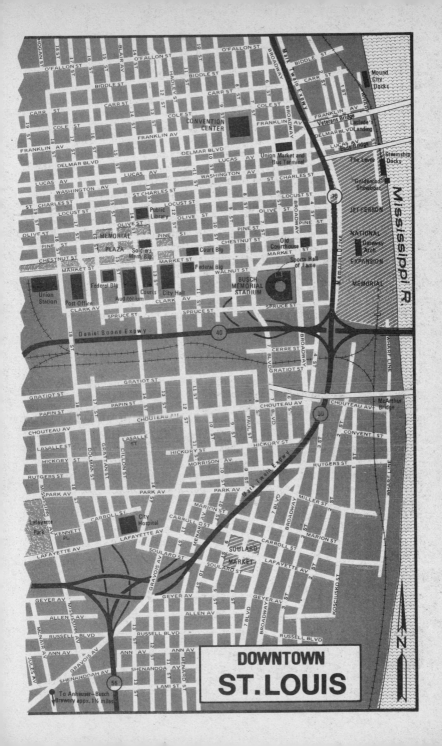

DOWNTOWN ST. LOUIS

More sophisticated palates travel to St. Louis' Central West End, very near Forest Park, for a little more diversity and, frankly, better food. Dedicated diners also know that a good meal may be found in the city's various ethnic neighborhoods, prime steakhouses downtown, and many new French restaurants scattered throughout the metropolitan area.

Along with good food, St. Louisans like good beer. They know that only a tourist orders anything that isn't an Anheuser-Busch product. The world's biggest brewery calls St. Louis home and the city takes as much pride in its beer heritage as in its architecture and sports teams. Not surprisingly, the brewery (which offers free tours) owns both the baseball team and the stadium. Grant's Farm, August Busch's home, is also a tourist attraction, complete with buffaloes and, at the end of the ride, what else — pretzels and beer.

This city, which in the 1940s was said to be "First in shoes, first in booze, and last in the American League" (referring to the hapless, now defunct St. Louis Browns), is moving back into the limelight. Union Station, an enormous train depot, was a busy hub in the 1940s, when hundreds of thousands of soldiers stopped on their way off to war. Dormant for years, the station has recently opened as a hotel/retail/restaurant complex, with its own lake as an extra attraction.

While St. Louis looks to its future, there remain the living monuments to its past. The 1904 World's Fair gave birth to the ice cream cone and hot dog and inspired a great Judy Garland flick, but, more important to St. Louisans, the fair brought to prominence Forest Park, one of the nation's largest urban parks, and the St. Louis Zoo. On the south side of town, the Missouri Botanical (Shaw's) Garden literally grew out of British immigrant Henry Shaw's generosity and dedication to beauty. In addition to being a botanical research center, it is also the home of the Climatron (a geodesic-domed greenhouse), a peaceful Japanese garden, rose gardens, the Desert House, Henry Shaw's town house, his herb garden, and the scented garden — especially popular with the visually handicapped.

And along the river, where St. Louis began, sits the stately Old Cathedral. The first cathedral built west of the Mississippi, it attracts members of all faiths. The immense and awe-inspiring building stands next to the Arch, a gleaming symbol of St. Louis' future, and near the Mississippi itself, a reminder of the strength of its past.

Recently, St. Louis was ranked the seventh best city in the country in which to live. At one time its citizenry would have been skeptical of the rating. Today they have faith in their city and its future.

ST. LOUIS AT-A-GLANCE

SEEING THE CITY: A tour of St. Louis must begin along the Mississippi River, where the city began, and the riverfront offers an irresistible focal point: the Gateway Arch, soaring 630 feet above the levee. From its top, you can see all of St. Louis and miles of countryside beyond, on both sides of the river. Ride to the top of the Arch in one of two capsule trams that form a trainlike vehicle running on special tracks to the 70-foot observation room, which affords a truly spectacular 30-mile view. While waiting for the tram, visit the Museum of Westward Expansion (11 N 4th St.; 425-4465), see a film on the construction of the Arch in the Tucker Theater, or browse in the Museum Shop, on the plaza between the two legs of the Arch.

Built in 1966 by architect Eero Saarinen, the Arch is so delicately engineered that its last segment — that bit of the arch that's farthest off the ground and connects the two columns — had to wait to be installed until the weather was perfect, so the steel would neither contract nor expand a fraction until it was in place.

 SPECIAL PLACES: Though it's most convenient to get around St. Louis by car, most areas lend themselves to a walking tour. You can park your car for free along the waterfront, for example, and explore on foot the levee, Laclede's Landing, and downtown. For the less energetic, Tram Tour (516 Cerre St.; 241-1400) offers a 2-hour narrated tram tour of the downtown area, which runs about every 30 minutes.

RIVERFRONT AND DOWNTOWN

The Levee – Moored on the river side of the cobblestoned levee are St. Louis' most famous riverboats: the *Goldenrod Showboat,* for dinners and old-fashioned "meller-dramers," and the *Huck Finn* and *Tom Sawyer,* for day and night trips up and down the Mississippi. You'll also find the *Delta Queen* (543-1949) and the *Robert E. Lee* (241-1282), luxurious sternwheelers from the golden era of steamboats, as well as the only floating *McDonald's.* Two new arrivals are the *President,* the world's largest excursion boat, which offers 2½-hour cruises twice daily, and the *Admiral,* a floating entertainment complex, with a 200-seat restaurant overlooking the riverfront, the Birdland Theater, the Admiral Bandathon, Admiral Ballroom, and five decks of promenades, eateries, and games.

On the city side of the levee is Jefferson Expansion Memorial Parkway, with the Arch at its center, and in one corner, the Old Cathedral, which is, naturally, the oldest cathedral west (just west) of the Mississippi, 2nd and Walnut sts. (231-3250). It started as a log cabin in 1764 when the city was founded and took its present form in 1834.

Laclede's Landing – In the 50 years after the Civil War, St. Louis became rich as well as famous, and the entire downtown section boomed and bloomed. What's left of the bloom is Laclede's Landing, a ten-block area just north of the levee on the far side of massive Eads Bridge with some fine examples of cast-iron-fronted buildings (Raeder Place, formerly the Old Missouri Hotel at 806 N 1st, is best of all). It's now the home of a new generation of restaurants and galleries, and one of the few areas in the city where liquor can be served until 2 AM. Some suggestions while wandering the area: *Kennedy's 2nd Street Company,* 612 N 2nd St. (421-3655), for a lunch of chili, burgers, and sandwiches; *The Old Spaghetti Factory,* 727 N 1st St. (621-0276), for inexpensive Italian dishes and an old European decor; or, for a good catfish dinner or oyster appetizer, *2nd Street Diner and Fish Market,* 721 N 2nd St. (436-2222). For food as well as entertainment, try *Hannegan's Restaurant and Pub,* 719 N 2nd St. (241-8877), or *Bogart's on the Landing,* 809 N 2nd St. (241-9380).

Old Courthouse – At one time a site of slave auctions, this courthouse was just two years old in 1847 when an American slave named Dred Scott tested the legality of slavery by suing his owner. The case was heard here; when he lost, the course of slavery was set. Inside are displays of Old St. Louis and courtrooms where great lawyers such as Thomas Hart Benton tried their cases. Most interesting today is the building's cast-iron dome, completed in 1859, and the mural that adorns its interior. Open daily. Free. 4th St. at Market (425-4465).

St. Louis Sports Hall of Fame – A must for sports fans, with short film clips of various World Series, and memorabilia of different sports and sports figures. Special emphasis, of course, on the Cardinals' own Stan Musial. Open daily. Admission charge. In Busch Memorial Stadium, between Gates 5 and 6, at Walnut St. (421-6790).

Eugene Field House – Primarily an antique toy collection, with some artifacts of the famous St. Louis author Eugene Field, who wrote *Little Boy Blue*. At Christmastime, the house prepares a complete Victorian Christmas display. Closed Mondays. Admission charge. 634 S Broadway (421-4689).

Campbell House Museum – A stately mid-Victorian town house containing original furnishings. 1508 Locust (421-0325).

Mercantile Money Museum – Here is everything you've ever wanted to know about money, including counterfeiting. A talking mannequin introduces you to the witticisms of Benjamin Franklin. Free. Mercantile Tower, 7th and Washington sts. (425-2050).

St. Louis Centre – One of the country's largest urban shopping complex, a four-level glass-enclosed mall consisting of 150 shops and 20 restaurants that connects two of the city's largest department stores, Dillard's and Famous-Barr. Between 6th, 7th, Washington, and Olive blvds.

SOUTH ST. LOUIS

South St. Louis is primarily German, Italian, and Eastern European. The most determinedly ethnic neighborhood in the area is the Hill (between South Kingshighway and Shaw). From its bocce courts and front yard shrines to its green, white, and red hydrants, the Hill is 20 blocks of solid Italian consciousness — great for walking and snacking. Two suggestions: *John Volpi & Co.,* 5256 Daggett (772-8550), closed Mondays, for salami, prosciutto, and Italian sausage; *Amighetti Bakery,* 5141 Wilson (776-2855), closed Sundays and Mondays, for fresh bread and carry-out "po' boys."

Anheuser-Busch Brewery – The makers of Michelob and Budweiser offer free one-hour tours of the brewery and grounds, featuring, naturally, a healthy sampling of the King of Beers. Best on the tour: the stables, a registered landmark building, where the mighty Clydesdale horses reside when they're not on parade. Closed weekends and holidays. Free. 610 Pestalozzi St. (577-2626).

Missouri Botanical Garden (Shaw's Garden) – After Henry Shaw got very rich with a hardware store in downtown St. Louis, he decided to repay the city by opening his Southside garden estate to the public. Since 1860 its reputation and its collection have grown apace. Highlights of the 79-acre park: the Climatron, a geodesic-domed tropical greenhouse; Seiwa-En, a beautiful Japanese garden; and the Scented Garden, a special collection of scented plants for the blind which may be touched and handled, with descriptions and explanations in Braille. Open daily. Admission charge. 2101 Tower Grove (577-5100).

Soulard Market – Soulard is the name of both the market and the neighborhood which surrounds it. Since 1847, when the ground was given to the city to be used as a public farmers' market, Soulard Market has been open for business — busiest on Saturday mornings, when everything from live rabbits to homemade apple butter is for sale, but offering something most days. The outside stalls around the main building open whenever fresh goods — meat or poultry, vegetables, fruit, farmers' canned goods or home specialties — come into the city. Closed Sundays and Mondays; most active Fridays and Saturdays. 7th St. and Lafayette (622-4180).

CENTRAL WEST END

Named for its location near famous Forest Park at the western edge of the city limits, Central West End is the St. Louis' most sophisticated and elegant section — a warren of small shops, pleasant restaurants, and ornate mansions in the fashionable "places" (private boulevards maintained by the residents; grandest of the grand are Portland and Westmoreland places). All is grist for the walkers' mill, even the private "places," so spend some time just exploring.

Maryland Plaza – A stroller's delight, between Kingshighway and Euclid Avenue, just around the corner from the *Chase Hotel* (see *Best in Town*). With the best people-watching in town, this area is a magnet for politicians, media types, and other glitzy characters. A potpourri of shops and restaurants makes for good food and great buys, too. Some suggestions: 26 Maryland Plaza, an arcade of boutiques featuring everything from seashells and antique clothing to herbs; *Tricia Woo,* 308 N Euclid (367-1869), selling beautiful handmade quilts, unusual toys, and children's and women's clothes. For a bite to eat, if you have money enough left over, try *Duff's,* 392 N Euclid (361-0522), for lunch of sandwiches and imported beer; *Llywelyn's Welsh Pub,* 4747 McPherson (361-3003), for a ploughman's lunch or soup (and of course British beers). The Central West End also sports several establishments that can satisfy more hearty appetites: *Balaban's,* 405 N Euclid (381-8085), for a dinner of seafood, French cuisine, or their unusual dinner crêpes; *Palm Beach Café,* 4755 McPherson (361-6190), an attractive Pasta House outlet decorated in a Florida beach motif; the *Magic Wok,* 1 Maryland Plaza (367-2626), a Hunan restaurant with the best Chinese food in town; or *Marilyn's Pie Parlor,* 27 Maryland Plaza (367-4752), with full lunch and dinner menus as well as a selection of their famous homemade pies. If you're at the *Chase Hotel* and elegant dining is what you want, you need go no farther; the hotel's *Tenderloin Room,* 212 N Kingshighway (361-2500), is the place for prime ribs, chops, and seafood in a Victorian setting. All stores in the area carry the *Maryland Plaza Guide,* which lists shops in the neighborhood. For monthly shows of photography and paintings, try *Norton's Fine Arts,* 325 N Euclid (367-9917).

St. Louis Cathedral – It is not just the size of the cathedral — immense — that is awesome; it is the mosaics that adorn almost the whole interior space — beautiful, ethereal, light bearing; millions of pieces of stone and glass in thousands of shades depicting saints, apostles, and religious scenes. Considered one of the finest examples of mosaicwork in this hemisphere, and not to be missed. Tours conducted on Sundays at 12:45 PM. Free. Lindell at Newstead (533-2824).

The Fabulous Fox Theatre – This recently restored 1929 movie palace now has all the gilt and glitz of its yesteryears. At night the house lights come on, and the Fox presents some of the biggest entertainment names in the country — Las Vegas–style shows at midwestern prices. Tours of the theater are given Wednesdays through Saturdays at 10:30 AM for $2. 527 N Grand Blvd. (534-1678, for entertainment information).

■**EXTRA SPECIAL:** An hour south from St. Louis just off Rte. 55 is *Ste. Genevieve,* one of the oldest permanent settlements west of the Mississippi (established in 1735) and a town that has maintained its bounty of old homes with admirable care. A number of the oldest homes are open daily, as is an excellent old inn, *St. Gemme Beauvais,* 78 N Main St. (314 883-5744). It's a beautifully furnished, 8-room village inn with the best food in town. And not to be missed, if you are in the area during the second weekend of August: Ste. Genevieve's Jour de Fête, when all the old homes are open for a festive two days.

For the young, or just the young at heart, take a day trip to *Six Flags Over Mid-America,* a 200-acre theme park with Looney Tunes Town (where you can shake hands with Bugs Bunny), the shooting rapids of Thunder River, the Screaming Eagle, and all sorts of unique shows and shops. Open daily, late May through late August, it's about a 20-minute drive from downtown, at I-44 and Allenton Rd. in Eureka (938-4800). Or visit the locale of Huck Finn and Tom Sawyer — *Hannibal, Missouri* (314 221-0114). Described as the "World's Most Famous Small Town," it was the home of Samuel Clemens, better known as Mark Twain. Another unusual attraction is *Silver Dollar City.* Tucked away in the heart of 2,000 acres overlooking Table Rock Lake, it is a unique community of good-time shows, old-time crafts, fun-time rides, and plenty of farm-fresh food in a variety of good restaurants.

SOURCES AND RESOURCES

 TOURIST INFORMATION: The Convention and Visitors Bureau publishes a free guide that lists special events (festivals, street fairs, house tours) and other tourist information; it also has maps, brochures and will help with individual problems. 1300 Convention Plaza (421-1023).

The *St. Louis Annual Guide* (published by *St. Louis* magazine; $3.50) is comprehensive. *St. Louis for Families,* by Paula Knoderer, Carol Hollander, and Bob Broeg (Bethany Press; $3.50), covers every possibility for "doing" the city with kids. The *St. Louis Symphony Society* arranges special tours of any part of the city, with proceeds going to the society's treasury; 712 N Grand Blvd. (533-2500). The American Institute of Architects has architectural maps of the city, pinpointing interesting buildings (621-3484). The Landmarks Association has information on neighborhoods and restoration projects (421-6474).

Local Coverage – *St. Louis Post-Dispatch,* daily (Thursday's edition carries a calendar of coming events); *The Argus* is the city's famous black community newspaper, published every Thursday; *St. Louis* magazine appears monthly. The *St. Louis Business Journal* is a weekly update on the business scene.

Area Code – All telephone numbers are in the 314 area code unless otherwise indicated.

 CLIMATE AND CLOTHES: From mid-June well into September the heat and humidity are wilting. Dress coolly and be prepared for the worst. Autumn is crisp, cool, and beautiful; winter, cold but with little snow. Spring is likely to be especially stormy, with sudden winds and hard rains blowing up quickly against ink-black skies during tornado season — May and early June.

 GETTING AROUND: Airport – Lambert–St. Louis International Airport is usually a 30-minute drive from downtown (up to an hour during rush periods), and cab fares should run $18. The airport limo service to downtown costs $5.90 and leaves the airport every 15 minutes. The city's Natural Bridge Airport bus leaves for downtown from the air terminal's main entrance every 45 minutes to an hour and costs 75¢.

Bus – The Bi-State bus system serves most of the metropolitan area. Route information, maps, 707 N 1st St. (231-2345).

Taxi – Cabs can be picked up at the major department stores and hotels, hailed in the streets, or ordered by phone. Major companies are Laclede Cab (652-3456); Yellow Cabs (361-2345); County Cab (991-5300); Allen Cab (531-4545).

Car Rental – St. Louis is served by all the major national companies; several have booths at the airport as well as around the city. A reliable local service is Enterprise Leasing, with nine locations around the city (231-4440).

 MUSEUMS: The story of the movement west is told in murals, graphic displays, and film sequences at the Museum of Westward Expansion under the Arch (*Special Places*). Other museums of interest in St. Louis are:
The Magic House – 516 Kirkwood (822-8900), dares children to have a good time and learn something too. Closed Mondays. Admission charge.

Medical Museum and National Museum of Quackery – 3839 Lindell Blvd. (371-5225). Closed Sundays, Labor Day through Easter. Admission charge.

St. Louis Art Museum – In Forest Park (721-0067). Closed Mondays.

St. Louis Science Center (McDonnell Planetarium) – 5100 Clayton Ave., Forest Park (289-4400). The McDonnell Planetarium and the Museum of Science and Natural History are both part of one entertainment and educational complex that will eventually include the Medical Museum. The Planetarium now features a Star Theater, hands-on science and natural history exhibitions, and a Discovery Room. Open daily. Exhibitions are free; small charge for Star Theater.

St. Louis Wax Museum – 2nd and Morgan sts. (241-1155). Over 130 lifelike wax figures, including those of movie stars, presidents, sports celebrities, religious leaders, and public figures. Open daily (call for hours). Admission charge.

 MAJOR COLLEGES AND UNIVERSITIES: There are three major universities in the St. Louis area: St. Louis University, founded by the Jesuits in 1818 and the oldest college in the United States west of the Mississippi, Grand at Lindell (658-2222); Washington University, founded by a predecessor of T. S. Eliot, too shy to name the school for himself (at the western end of Forest Park on a beautiful campus; 889-5000), and the University of Missouri, St. Louis, 8001 Natural Bridge Rd. (553-0111).

 PARKS AND GARDENS: Forest Park is America's third largest city park (Central Park and the Portland, Oregon, park system are larger) and it offers far too much to see in even a long day. Highlights are: the zoo, used for years by the much-loved Marlin Perkins. You can visit the exhibitions — "Big Cat Country," the famous Monkey House, the walk-through Bird Cage — on foot or by zoo train. The Children's Zoo charges a modest admission price, and you must buy a ticket for the train; all else free (781-0900). Art Museum, on Art Hill (closed Mondays), maintains a wide-ranging collection and hosts traveling exhibitions (721-0067). Laumeier International Sculpture Park, 12580 Rott Rd. (821-1209), features huge outdoor sculptures in a woodsy setting.

 SPECIAL EVENTS: *The International Festival* (432-4013) is held at Steinberg Rink in Forest Park during the three-day Memorial Day weekend. Authentic music, dance, food, and crafts of 35 nationalities are featured. The *Huck Finn* and the *Tom Sawyer* riverboats are the contestants in the *Memorial Day Riverboat Race.* On the *Goldenrod Showboat,* St. Louis ragtimers host the *National Ragtime and Jazz Festival* (621-3311) in June. The *Japanese Festival* (577-5100) at Missouri Botanical Gardens is an annual summer celebration of Japanese culture through music, dance, food, and crafts. The *Veiled Prophet Fair* (367-FAIR) on the Arch grounds is a four-day entertainment extravaganza, featuring a parade of 20 or more lavishly outfitted floats, fireworks, marathons, music, and air and water events, that takes place during the July 4 holiday. German food and culture is celebrated during the *Strassenfest,* a weekend celebration usually held the end of July in the area bordered by 11th, 13th, Pine, and Clark sts. *The Great Forest Park Balloon Race* (726-6896), an annual St. Louis tradition since 1904, begins in Forest Park and ends wherever the wind carries. Contact the Visitors Bureau (421-1023) for exact dates.

 SPORTS AND FITNESS: St. Louisans love their professional teams, and sports events are well attended.

Baseball – Busch Memorial Stadium (Broadway at Walnut St., downtown) is home for the National League *Cardinals* (421-3060). Tickets are available at the Stadium and from Famous-Barr department stores.

Bicycling – The largest biking event in St. Louis is the Moonlight Ramble, a 17-mile bike ride that starts at 2 AM on the last Sunday of every August and lasts until dawn. American Youth Hostel will have information (644-3560). Biking is always good in Forest Park and bikes can be rented from the Forest Park Boathouse from April to mid-October (367-3423).

Fitness Centers – The YMCA has a pool, racquetball courts, track, and exercise equipment, 1528 Locust St. (436-4100).

Football – The NFL's *Cardinals* (421-1600) play at Busch Memorial Stadium.

Golf – Forest Park has two public courses, 9 and 18 holes respectively. The 18-hole course has a reputation for being tough, but greens and tees are not in the best condition on either. Best public course in the city is the 9-hole course at Ruth Park, 8211 Groby Rd. (727-4800). It's open all year, modest greens fee.

Hockey – The *Blues* play NHL hockey at the Arena, 5700 Oakland (644-0900).

Horse Racing – Thoroughbred racing at Cahokia Downs, Rte. 460, about 20 minutes from St. Louis; harness racing at Fairmount Park, Rte. 40 East, Collinsville, IL (436-1517).

Jogging – Start at Wharf Street below the Gateway Arch and run the 2-mile stretch along the river; jog the 6-mile perimeter of Forest Park; or follow Wydown Road by the Washington University campus for about a 2-mile residential run.

Soccer – The St. Louis *Steamers,* 212 N Kirkwood Rd. (821-1111), one of the teams in the Major Indoor Soccer League, compete from November through April at the St. Louis Arena, 5700 Oakland.

Tennis – Best for the visitor are the courts at Dwight F. Davis Tennis Center in Forest Park, open during daylight hours; permits for daily play obtained at the center (367-0220).

 THEATER: For up-to-date offerings and performance times, check the publications listed above. For dinner and a show, especially if you are with children, visit the *Goldenrod Showboat,* prototype for Edna Ferber's *Showboat,* where nightly melodramas demand boos and hisses for the villain. Moored at the levee (information, 621-3311). Other choices are: the fine *Repertory Theatre of St. Louis,* 136 Edgar Rd. (968-4925); the *Fabulous Fox,* 527 N Grand Blvd. (534-1111), winter home of traveling Broadway shows and name entertainers; and the *Westport Playhouse,* 600 W Port Plaza (878-2424), one of St. Louis' newest and most attractive theaters, for productions ranging from plays to well-known entertainers. The *Municipal Opera House* in Forest Park offers its summer stock program of musicals. About 1,400 seats every performance are free; line up outside the Muny about 6:30 PM (361-1900).

 MUSIC: Concerts and opera from: *St. Louis Symphony* at Powell Hall (information, 533-2500); *Opera Theater of St. Louis,* Loretto-Hilton Theater (961-0171).

 NIGHTCLUBS AND NIGHTLIFE: The tempo of the St. Louis revival is ragtime, and you can hear it at the *National Ragtime Festival,* a five-day ragtime splurge, held in June every year. Call the Goldenrod Showboat (621-3311) for a schedule. *Muddy Water Saloon,* 724 N 1st St. (421-5335), has consistently good progressive jazz. *Fourth and Pine Blarney Stone,* 716 N 1st St. (231-8171), has Irish folk music and good Irish coffee and ale. *Goldenrod,* 400 N Wharf St. (621-3311), has live melodrama daily except Mondays. *Mississippi Nights,* 914 N

1st St. (421-3853), the only "nightclub" on Laclede's Landing, features a large dance floor and music from local as well as nationally known concert bands. The city's newest addition to this genre is *Jimmy's Cabaret,* 4905 Delmar (367-4471).

 SINS: The town whose *pride* is a baseball team, the St. Louis Cardinals, also likes to brag that its *sloth* is confined to the zoo (in Forest Park; 781-0900). *Gluttony* prevails at *Ted Drewes Frozen Custard,* an outdoor stand-up place that's a St. Louis institution. Locals have been known to drive 20 or 30 miles for a Concrete, the thickest milkshake imaginable. Two locations: 6726 Chippewa (481-2652), 4224 S Grand (352-7376).

 LOCAL SERVICES: Babysitting – A number of agencies are listed in the yellow pages, but most will be more expensive than two nonprofessional organizations that provide conscientious babysitters: Missouri Baptist Hospital (569-5193) provides nursing students with good references and their own transportation; and Maryville College sends trustworthy students only. During the day, contact the Dean of Student Affairs (576-9480). Both are tightly run, relatively strict, and careful.

Business Services – Clayton Business Service, 34 N Brentwood (721-3842)

Mechanic – Domian Standard Service, 814 S Lindbergh (993-4025), has 24-hour road service, and can work on most foreign cars as well as all American automobiles.

BEST IN TOWN

 CHECKING IN: Whether you want to be within walking distance of the levee, smack-dab downtown, on either end of Forest Park, or conveniently near Lambert Field Airport, quality hotels are available. Prices range from $80 and up for a double in our expensive category, $55 to $75 in the moderate, and $50 and under for an inexpensive hotel.

Marriott Pavilion – In the midst of rebuilt downtown. The "Pavilion" of its title is the Spanish Pavilion, jewel of the 1964 New York World's Fair, dismantled and moved to St. Louis by Mayor Alfonso Cervantes amid great controversy. The pavilion now makes up the 2-story lobby of the 671-room *Marriott,* where it is a great success. The hotel offers a coffee shop, 2 restaurants, and a bar. Free garage, pool, sauna. 1 Broadway (314 421-1776). Expensive.

Sheraton St. Louis – On the banks of the Mississippi, the hotel has many rooms with river views. All of them have color TV, telephones, and other standard amenities. There are also bars, a dining room and café, and a swimming pool. 910 N 7th St. (314 231-5100). Expensive.

Chase – The grand old hotel of St. Louis, where limousines routinely line the entrance drive and celebrities are regular guests. Made an official landmark in 1977, the *Chase* is beautiful to behold. It isn't an intimate little hotel, with 821 rooms carved from an original 1192, but it does have all the amenities one would expect of a grand hotel. Barber shop, 3 restaurants, 4 bars, shops, garage for guests next door. 212 N Kingshighway (314 361-2500 or 800 325-8989). Expensive.

Omni International – More than just a hotel, it's an event — part of the complex that includes the beautifully restored Union Station, originally built in 1894. Of its 546 rooms, 68 are in Head House, which was actually part of the station, and the remainder under the original roof of the train shed. All have phones and TV in the bath. There are 2 restaurants, the elegant *American Rotisserie* and the less formal *Café Potpourri,* and the *Grand Hall* bar. Surrounded by more than 11 climate-controlled acres of fine shops and marketplaces, it is truly an experience. 1820 Market St. (314 241-6664). Expensive.

Marriott Motor Hotel – At Lambert Field Airport, half an hour from downtown, this 433-room spot features extensive recreational facilities — 2 pools, tennis courts, putting greens, sauna and exercise rooms — and is good both for business people on short visits and families on the road who'd like to stretch after a day of travel. Free parking. I-70 at the airport (314 423-9700). Expensive.

Embassy Suites Downtown – One of St. Louis' newest and most stylish hostelries, it has 298 two-room suites, all with wet bar, refrigerator, color TV, and two phones. Guests receive complimentary cooked-to-order breakfasts and cocktails daily. Other features include an indoor pool, whirlpool, sauna, Jacuzzi, exercise room, steam room. 901 N 1st St. (314 241-4200). Expensive.

Cheshire Inn and Lodge – Aspires to an image of an English country inn, one block west of Forest Park. Close neighbors are no longer surprised by the English double-decker bus that fetches hotel guests from the airport; the theme is embellished with reproductions of English antiques in its 110 rooms. Beds set high off the floor. Pool, good restaurant, free parking. Clayton Rd. at Skinker (314 647-7300). Moderate.

Clayton Inn – This modern 220-room hotel in one of St. Louis's wealthy suburbs provides good service, spacious rooms decorated in contemporary style, and fine facilities. There are 2 restaurants, including the *Top of the Sevens* (closed Sundays), with a panoramic view of the city, a piano bar, health club with indoor and outdoor pools, sauna, exercise room, and whirlpool. 7750 Carondelet Ave. (314 726-5400). Moderate.

Forest Park – An older hotel undergoing successful renovation, just two blocks from the *Chase* in the Central West End. Half the hotel is given over to permanent residents, leaving about 100 rooms available for visitors. Hotel has a dining room, coffee shop, barber and beauty shops, cleaner's, outdoor pool, and free parking. 4910 W Pine Blvd. (314 361-3500). Inexpensive.

 EATING OUT: Considering St. Louis' large Italian community, it is hardly surprising that the city's premier restaurant serves Italian haute cuisine or that its name is *Tony's.* What is more surprising is the host of good restaurants that complement it and the wide variety of cuisines and reasonable prices charged. Our choices below are grouped into broad price categories — expensive, about $60 for a meal for two; moderate, $30 to $40; inexpensive, $15 to $25 — and are guaranteed to get you into the most interesting corners of the city for lunch or dinner. Prices do not include drinks, wine, or tips.

Tony's – According to the *Wall Street Journal,* owner Vince Bommarito is the Vince Lombardi of the restaurant world — a stickler for detail and a perfectionist. What started out as a spaghetti house and has grown into a first-rate eatery, with waiters who study food and drink the way medical students crib for finals. One warning: *Tony's* takes no reservations, and the wait on Saturday night can take more than three hours. Dinner only; closed Sundays and Mondays. Most major credit cards. 862 N Broadway (231-7007). Expensive.

Anthony's – Without knowing, you might be justified in assuming that *Anthony's* owner was trying to steal Vince Bommarito's thunder; you might even suspect bad blood between the two. Blood there is, but not bad, one hopes; *Anthony's* is owned and run by Tony Bommarito, Vince's brother and partner in that original spaghetti-house-that-became-king. It's dedicated to light, French cuisine, fresh seafood (a rarity in St. Louis), and service that matches brother Vince's place. Open for lunch weekdays as well as dinner daily except Sundays.

Reservations accepted. Most major credit cards. 10 S Broadway (231-2434). Expensive.

Al's Restaurant – Just north of Laclede's Landing, an unlikely but successful combination of riverboat decor and Italian (and American) dishes. Arguably, it has the best steak in town as well as a very respectable rack of lamb and an excellent shrimp de jonghe. Dinner only; closed Sundays. No reservations on Saturdays. Most major credit cards. 1st St. at Biddle (421-6399). Expensive.

Cunetto's House of Pasta – On The Hill, where everything Italian prospers, and where the heart and soul of good food is pasta, hot, fresh, in a variety of styles, augmented by veal, steak, and Italian specialties. Weekdays, lunch and dinner; Saturdays, dinner only. No reservations (long waits at dinnertime). Major credit cards. 5453 Magnolia (781-1135). Moderate.

The Lettuce Leaf – A former business school professor decided to put his marketing theories into practice and opened up a few restaurants that serve tasty salads, sandwiches, and soups, and a very good cheesecake. Open daily. Major credit cards. Three locations: 7823 Forsyth (727-5439); 107 N 6th (241-7773); and 600 West Port Plaza (576-7677). Moderate.

Empanadas – It's cafeteria-style for lunch and sit-down in the evening and features (what else?) empanadas, a pastry stuffed with meat and vegetables. After dark, other meat, seafood, and chicken dishes are served. Closed Sundays. Some credit cards. 32 N Euclid Ave. (367-1300). Moderate.

Edibles – Not much to look at, but the food more than makes up for appearances. Also a cafeteria by day and café by night. Try the beef bourguignon or a lighter spinach pita, and don't miss the chocolate cheesecake for dessert. Closed Sundays. No credit cards. 7816 Forsyth (721-0822.) Inexpensive.

Bobby's Creole – Here the specialty is New Orleans–style seafood. Soups, salads, and *beignets* (fritters) are served until 1 AM on weekends. Closed Sundays. Most major credit cards. 6307 Delmar (725-6985). Inexpensive.

Two chains in the St. Louis area to keep in mind for feeding children cheaply but well:

Miss Hulling's Cafeterias – 11th St. at Locust (436-0840). Inexpensive.

Flaming Pit Restaurants – Steak and hamburger stops well above average that offer special children's menus, there are seven *Flaming Pits* throughout the city. Inexpensive.

SALT LAKE CITY

Salt Lake City was born when two great natural forces, history and geology, came together in an accident of fate. To its current residents, it was a fortuitous cosmic collision. This kind of epic overview has a particular appeal to the residents of this gleaming oasis in the desert, since Salt Lake City is the headquarters of the Church of Jesus Christ of Latter-Day Saints. Known to most of us as Mormons, disciples of this church believe in divine revelation. And they believe God guided them here. Although the church tries to keep a low profile, evidence of its past work is everywhere, and visitors are immediately aware of the influence of its teachings. All the streets, for example, run at right angles to each other, and are numbered in a grid scale from the center point of Temple Square. This is the plan ordered by Mormon leader Brigham Young in 1847, when he followed the plans envisioned by Mormon prophet Joseph Smith years before.

It was Brigham Young who led persecuted and desperately weary Mormons across 1,000 miles of wind-swept prairie and mountains in search of a refuge where no one would bother them. When they arrived, Salt Lake City was a place no one else would covet. The transformation of barren desert into a habitable urban environment was the Mormons' major task, and their history is the legacy of the city.

Geology played its part by placing the Wasatch Mountains to the west of the Great Salt Lake basin. Rising abruptly from the Great Salt Lake Desert, their peaks snatch eastward-bound clouds and wring water from them. This makes the mountains good for skiing, but creates problems for the valley-bound city. The mean precipitation for Salt Lake City itself is 16 inches a year, while the mountains annually reap about 450 inches of precipitation in the form of snow. Even so, Utah is the second driest state in the nation. (First is next-door Nevada.) But the scarcity of water has stimulated irrigation engineers to come up with a number of ingenious, creative solutions. Now there are dams in the mountains to trap the winter snowfall so that upon melting it can be delivered to the farmers in the valleys, who desperately need water to harvest their crops.

Although the lack of water is a problem, scarcity of population is not. In fact, it's quite an advantage, infinitely preferable to the overcrowding which is characteristic of most cities. The heart of the Intermountain area, Salt Lake City absorbs a sizable number of Utah's 1,461,000 residents. The largest city in the state, the city proper houses 167,000 people. More than 660,000 live in the larger Wasatch Front metropolitan district, sandwiched between the mountains to the east, the Great Salt Lake, and its desert to the west.

For a city of its size and relative isolation, the cultural scene is surprisingly active. The Utah Symphony, an important North American orchestra, tours Europe regularly. Ballet West is one of the outstanding ballet groups in the country, and the illustrious Mormon Tabernacle Choir is so well known it needs no description. Several dance companies, the Utah Opera company, and half a dozen theater groups perform throughout the year. The new Salt Lake County arts complex has three special buildings designed for concerts, ballet, and art exhibitions. Monday, a slow night in most cities, is a lively time in Salt Lake City, thanks to the Mormon Church. Mormon families are asked to set aside Monday as Family Home Evening, which makes it a good night for family movies and visits to local ice cream parlors. (Mormons have large families, so the emphasis on family togetherness is good for business.)

Brigham Young designed the city so its wide streets and tree-lined boulevards would be its most prominent features. His architectural foresight has stood the test of time, although the home of the Mormon pilgrims, like most other places, has yielded to the tyranny of progress. Ten years of intense building programs have changed the face of Salt Lake City. Main Street has been torn up and completely redesigned, with sparkling fountains, patterned sidewalks, hundreds of new trees, and flower planters. Other streets have received the same treatment, and rundown areas have given way to new buildings like the Salt Palace arena, convention center, and ZCMI and Crossroads malls, enclosed downtown shopping centers. Some delightful, old Victorian mansions remain; portions of others have found a new home at Trolley Square, a shopping center patterned after San Francisco's Ghirardelli Square. The ten beautifully landscaped acres of Temple Square surrounding the Salt Lake Temple and Tabernacle still attract more than 4 million visitors a year, making it Utah's greatest tourist site.

Although most Salt Lake City residents are Mormons, other ethnic communities exert strong cultural influences. The Guadalupe Center provides a base for the Mexican-Americans' civic activities. The Japanese community's Obon Festival and the annual Greek Festival contribute that eclectic, cosmopolitan flair generally associated with much larger cities. Even in other neighborhoods, many Salt Lake City residents are multilingual. Independent, pragmatic, and idealistic, Salt Lake City people prefer to do things themselves rather than ask for help. However, when other people need help, they will go out of their way. On a larger scale, their altruism is almost legendary. When neighboring Idaho's Teton Dam burst in 1976, thousands of people from Salt Lake City turned out in force to clean up the muck.

An attractive, well-organized city of good-natured people should be enticing enough for just these qualities alone, without the added incentive of the Great Salt Lake, without which, obviously, nothing would be the same. Floating in its briny, warm water is as much a part of the Salt Lake City experience as immersing oneself in its streets and buildings. Salt Lake City is unquestionably a splendid collaboration of nature, civilization, and people who refuse to accept the notion that kindness and what we commonly refer to as progress are mutually exclusive concepts.

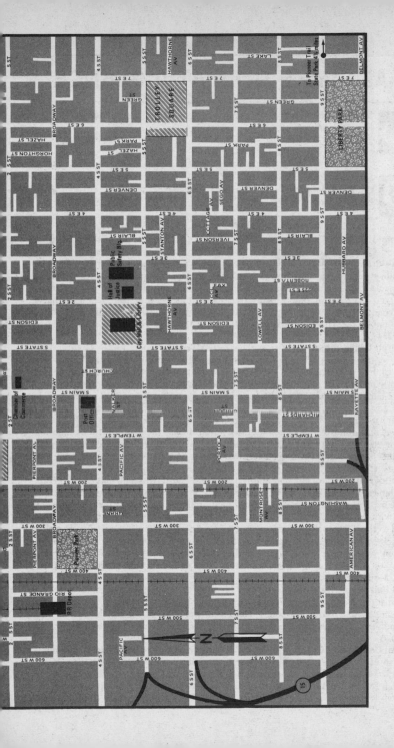

SALT LAKE CITY AT-A-GLANCE

 SEEING THE CITY: From the top of Capitol Hill, you can look out over the whole city.

 SPECIAL PLACES: Salt Lake City's grid pattern is simplicity itself. Everything radiates from Temple Square. Eighteen blocks south is 18th South, five blocks west is 5th West, etc.

CENTRAL CITY

Temple Square – The logical place to start, as it's the heart of the worldwide Mormon Church. Enclosed within a 15-foot wall, the 10 acres of Temple Square's grounds draw about four million visitors a year. Within the grounds are the Temple, a granite structure that took 40 years to build; the dome-shaped, acoustically perfect Tabernacle, home of the Mormon Tabernacle Choir; and the Information Center, where you can join any one of many free, daily guided tours. The great Tabernacle organ conducts public recitals every day at noon. Tabernacle Choir rehearsals are open to the public on Thursday evenings. Organ recitals and choir rehearsals are free (531-2534).

Church Office Building – Across the street at Temple Square East is Utah's tallest structure, the Church Office Building, housing the general offices of the Latter-Day Saints Church. Its Genealogical Library is used by thousands of people daily. It houses the world's largest genealogical collection, and chances are you or your ancestors are listed. Members of the staff will be happy to help you find out. Temple Square (531-2531).

Beehive House – Built by Brigham Young as his official residence in 1854, Beehive House is now a museum operated by the Church. It was the first governor's mansion and is open daily except Thanksgiving, Christmas, and New Year's Day. The patriarch himself is buried half a block northeast in a quiet park. Free. 67 E South Temple and State sts. (531-2671).

Capitol Hill – Capitol Hill contains the capitol, Pioneer Museum, and Council Hall, all within easy reach. There are free guided tours on weekdays through the granite and marble capitol, a splendid piece of Corinthian architecture, and its many exhibitions of Utah products and art (533-5900). Council Hall, across the street to the south, was moved to the hill stone by stone and now houses the Utah Travel Council, where you can pick up brochures and maps (see *Sources and Resources;* 533-5681). Pioneer Museum, west of the capitol, has one of the most complete collections of pioneer relics in the West. Closed Sundays from October to April. Voluntary contributions accepted. 300 N Main St. (533-5759).

Salt Palace and Bicentennial Center for the Performing Arts – Almost anything goes on at the 28,000-seat Salt Palace — conventions, sports events, rock concerts (100 SW Temple; 363-7681 or 521-6060). The Bicentennial Arts Center includes a concert hall and art center on the same grounds as the Salt Palace and Capitol Theater (1st South).

ZCMI Center and Crossroads Plaza – Returning to tree-lined Main Street, you'll find two of the largest downtown covered shopping malls in the West. The ZCMI Center, on the east side of the street (15 S Main St.), has over 60 stores inside, some of which serve old-fashioned refreshments like phosphates and iron port. Across the street to the west is the new Crossroads Plaza, with 70 stores and numerous theaters and fast-food eateries. 18 S Main St.

MID-CITY

SE Temple – Start at the Cathedral of the Madeleine, a Roman Gothic church completed in 1909, which has a beautiful series of German stained-glass windows. Farther along the street are dozens of exquisite old mansions built by mining magnates at the turn of the century. One of them, the marble and wood former Utah State Historical Society building at 603 E South Temple, is the governor's mansion.

Trolley Square – Trolley Square has won national acclaim as a restoration project. Ingeniously rebuilt in abandoned trolley barns, this collection of shops, theaters, restaurants, and boutiques attracts a fascinating stream of people. Wandering artists and troubadors entertain in the turn-of-the-century entries and courtyards. Open daily. 5th South and 7th East sts. (521-9877).

Liberty Park – Three blocks south on 7th East is 80-acre Liberty Park, with bowers, picnic areas, tennis and horseshoe courts, swimming pool, playground, the Tracy Aviary home for birds, an amusement park, and a boating center. 1302 South, 900 East (972-6714).

EMIGRATION CANYON

Pioneer Trail State Park – "This is the place," Brigham Young said when he and his entourage caught their first glimpse of the Valley of the Great Salt Lake. And this is where you'll now find the new Pioneer Trail State Park, with 11 renovated buildings from pioneer times, including the Brigham Young Farm Home and the Social Hall (533-5881). This is also the site of This Is The Place Monument and visitors center, with audio-visual exhibits showing the Mormon trek from Illinois to Utah. Tours of the buildings are available. The park is open daily, May through early October, but hours are quite variable; call in advance (533-5920). Emigration Canyon, 2601 Sunnyside Ave.

GREAT SALT LAKE

Great Salt Lake – The most important natural feature of the region, the 73-mile long lake is marshy, salty, sticky, and warm. As you approach it, it may look like nothing more than marshes and weird salt flats. Due to rising lake waters, all the old beaches have flooded, so swimming is difficult. But the boat harbor at Saltair Beach State Park, GSL (at the southern end of the lake) was saved, and there is some water access and minimal facilities. The rising waters have diluted the salt concentration, so while floating is still a unique experience, it's not the fantasy it once was. The water tastes awful and stings terribly if it gets in your eyes, so don't splash. We warn you, the brine flies are sometimes ferocious. 17 miles west on US 40, I-80.

■ **EXTRA SPECIAL:** The 848,000-acre *Wasatch National Forest* is one of the busiest forests in the country. In the High Uintas Primitive Area, the Wasatch National Forest is full of mountain lakes, rugged spruce, dramatic canyons, and mountain peaks as high as 13,400 feet. The Utah State Fish and Game Dept. operates a winter feeding ground at Hardware Ranch in Logan (245-3131). There are campgrounds at Little Cottonwood, Big Cottonwood, and Mill Creek canyons; call the Salt Lake Ranger Station for information (524-5042). Those closest to the city are the most crowded. Hunting conditions are excellent here. Deer, elk, and moose can be hunted in the fall. A variety of trout swim the streams. In winter, skiers flock to Alta, 25 miles southeast of the city on Rte. 210; Brighton, 27 miles southeast on Rte. 152; and Snowbird, in Gad Valley, 2 miles from Alta. To get to the eastern section of Wasatch, take US 40, and Rtes. 152, 210; to reach the northern part, follow US 89 and 91. For further information, contact the Supervisor's Office, 125 S State St., Salt Lake City 84138 (524-5030, or 942-4059 for campground information; 364-1581 for avalanche information).

SOURCES AND RESOURCES

TOURIST INFORMATION: For brochures and maps, contact the Utah Travel Council, Council Hall, Capitol Hill (533-5681). For information on winter skiing, summer recreations, and fuel availability, call 521-8102. For other events call 533-TIPS.

The best guide to Salt Lake City is *Great Salt Lake Country,* a free brochure available from the Utah Travel Council.

Local Coverage – *Salt Lake Tribune,* morning daily; *Deseret News,* evening daily; *Utah Holiday,* monthly.

Food – *Utah Holiday* has a full listing of restaurants in the Salt Lake area, and each issue has a number of articles describing restaurants.

Area Code – All telephone numbers are in the 801 area code unless otherwise indicated.

CLIMATE AND CLOTHES: Wintertime is for skiing. Spring is beautiful, but fickle, with apricot blossoms sometimes covered in snow. Summer is hot and dry, with temperatures climbing into the 90s. Fall is gorgeous, especially in the nearby canyons.

GETTING AROUND: Airport – Salt Lake City International Airport is a 15- to 20-minute ride from downtown; taxi fare should run about $8 or $9. Utah Transit Authority buses run hourly from the airport terminals into the city center for 40¢ (50¢ during peak hours). Special Downtowner buses run from the airport to downtown hotels on a regular basis.

Bus – For information on bus schedules in and around Salt Lake, call Utah Transit Authority (263-3737).

Taxi – The best way to get a cab is to call Yellow Cab (521-2100).

Car Rental – All major firms are represented; a cheap local alternative is Payless Car Rental System, 2080 W North Temple (596-2596).

MUSEUMS: Beehive House is described under *Special Places. Hansen Planetarium* features exhibitions on astronomy and natural science. On the University of Utah campus are the *Utah Museum of Natural History* (581-6927) and the *Utah Museum of Fine Arts* (581-7332). Another notable museum:

Salt Lake Arts Center – 100 SW Temple (328-4201)

MAJOR COLLEGES AND UNIVERSITIES: The University of Utah campus has a theater, a special events center, and two museums (see *Museums,* above). Between 14th East and 20th East, 1st South and 5th South (581-7200).

SPECIAL EVENTS: On July 24, Salt Lake City celebrates *Pioneer Day,* marking the arrival of the Mormon pioneers. In April and October, thousands of Mormons from all over the world converge on Temple Square for the conferences of the Church of Latter-Day Saints. In July, the *Japanese Obon Festival* is held at the Buddhist Temple, 211 W 1st South. In September, the *Greek Festival* takes place at the Hellenic Memorial Building. For information on special events, call 521-8102 in nonskiing season, or 533-5681.

SPORTS AND FITNESS: Baseball – The minor league *Salt Lake Trappers* play from mid-April to Labor Day at Derks Field, 65 W 1300 South (584-9900).

Basketball – The NBA *Utah Jazz* plays in the Salt Palace (363-7681).

Fishing, Hunting, Camping, Backpacking, River Running – At Wasatch National Forest (524-5030), you can fish, hunt, camp, and backpack (see *Extra Special*). For hunting and fishing regulations, contact Utah Division of Wildlife Resources, 1596 W North Temple (533-9333). For information on backpacking, river running, and primitive wilderness areas in general, call the Bureau of Land Management Office of Public Affairs, 136 E South Temple (524-5330).

Fitness Centers – The Deseret Gym has a pool, sauna, steam room, track, and racquetball and squash courts, 161 N Main (359-3911). Sports Mall Metro (328-3116) features a track, sauna, exercise equipment and classes, and squash, racquetball, and handball courts in Crossroads Plaza, near the *Marriott.*

Golf – There are 8 public courses in the Salt Lake valley. The best is Mountain Dell (582-3812), in Parley's Canyon.

Hockey – The Salt Lake *Golden Eagles* play at the Salt Palace (363-7681).

Ice Skating and Sleigh Riding – Sugarhouse Park, 21 S 16th East, for sleigh riding; Bountiful Recreation Center, 150 W 6th North, Bountiful (298-6120) for ice skating year-round, or Triad Center outdoor ice rink, 50 S 300 West, open late November through April (575-5423).

Jogging – Run in Memory Grove Park, about a mile from the *Marriott,* or in Liberty Park (1-mile perimeter), about 2 miles from downtown.

Skiing – Utah claims to have the "Greatest Snow on Earth." And certainly, skiers from all over the world enthusiastically attest to its excellence. The season runs from mid-November to May or June. For a recorded ski report, call 521-8102. The major ski resorts within half an hour's drive of Salt Lake City are:

Alta: The granddaddy of them all, Alta, in Little Cottonwood Canyon, has the best and most consistent snow conditions. 25 miles SE of city on Rte. 210 (328-8589, 742-3333).

Brighton: At the top of Big Cottonwood Canyon. The average annual snowfall here is 430 inches. 27 miles SE on Rte. 152. (359-3283).

Deer Valley: Utah's newest and classiest ski resort, where the number of skiers is limited, making for short lift lines. Reservations recommended. 2 miles above Park City (649-4149).

Park City: The US Ski Team's National Training Center, with the longest night-skiing run in the nation. 20 miles east on I-80, up Parley's Canyon (649-9571).

Snowbird: Also in Little Cottonwood Canyon, Snowbird is a jet-set resort, with a spectacular tram lift to Hidden Peaks at 11,000 feet. The lift runs in summer, too. Gad Valley, 2 miles from Alta (521-6040).

Swimming – The Great Salt Lake accesses are essentially closed because of rising lake level. For freshwater swimming try the Raging Waters, a huge aquatic park at 1200 W 1700 South.

Tennis – There are 17 parks in the city with tennis courts. The most popular are the 16 courts (14 lighted) at Liberty Park. Lessons are available (535-7994). The University of Utah has quite a few outdoor public courts.

THEATER: *Promised Valley Playhouse,* 132 S State (364-5677), features free performances during the summer of productions with mass appeal as well as more esoteric fare. Tickets are available at Temple Square Information Center. The *Pioneer Memorial Theater* and adjacent *Babcock Theater* at the University of Utah stage all kinds of plays, University of Utah campus (581-6961). *Theater 138* is at 138 S 2nd East (332-0093). *Salt Lake Acting Company,* 168 W 500 North (363-0525), features all types of plays. *Triad* theater at the Triad Center (575-5123) has a number of plays year-round.

MUSIC: Salt Lake City has many concerts and dance events. For information, call 533-8477. The *Mormon Tabernacle Choir* rehearsals are open to the public on Thursday evenings. Free. Temple Square. *Utah Symphony Orchestra, Ballet West, Rine-Woodbury Dance Co.,* and *Repertory Dance Theater* perform at Symphony Hall and the Capitol Theater. Big-name rock and country artists perform at the Salt Palace, 100 S West Temple (363-7681).

NIGHTCLUBS AND NIGHTLIFE: *Room at the Top* in the *Salt Lake Hilton,* 150 W 5th South, has a piano bar and fine food (532-3344). The *Zephyr,* 301 S West Temple (355-9913), features live jazz and blues. More comfortable but less trendy is Salt Lake City's oldest private club, *D. B. Cooper's,* 19 E 200 South (532-2948). Utah liquor laws require that tourists buy a 2-week membership ($5) for clubs, which entitles you to bring four friends.

SINS: Outside the city, in the ski resort towns of the surrounding Wasatch Mountain wilderness, women and money abound; Salt Lake City's beggars can be choosers there. But around the great Mormon Tabernacle, the influence of the church is so strong that neither the "thou" or the "jug of wine" are readily bought. And since the Mormon work ethic has banished *sloth* to the ski slopes, *pride* (mainly over the Tabernacle) holds the fort with *gluttony* (with *Snelgrove's* ice cream, and the long, jam-packed menu of frozen concoctions, supplying most of the fuel). "It seems," says one Salt Lake City resident, "that ice cream is the Mormons' biggest vice."

LOCAL SERVICES: Business Services – Aztec Typing Service, 211 E 3rd South (364-6806).
    Mechanic – Andy Stevens Automotive, 458 Montague Ave. (328-9222).

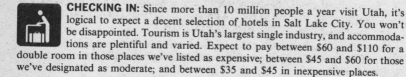

BEST IN TOWN

CHECKING IN: Since more than 10 million people a year visit Utah, it's logical to expect a decent selection of hotels in Salt Lake City. You won't be disappointed. Tourism is Utah's largest single industry, and accommodations are plentiful and varied. Expect to pay between $60 and $110 for a double room in those places we've listed as expensive; between $45 and $60 for those we've designated as moderate; and between $35 and $45 in inexpensive places.

Westin Utah – Still the grande dame of the state, the *Utah* is elegant in the traditional sense of the word. Its multimillion-dollar facelift hasn't disturbed the old crystal chandelier that still hangs from the mezzanine. *The Roof,* one of the city's more elegant restaurants, and *The Grill* are open daily. The *Bowl and Basket,* open until 5 PM, serves great soups. Corner of Main and South Temple sts. (801 531-1000). Expensive.

Salt Lake Hilton – The 352-room *Salt Lake Hilton* exudes an aura of contemporary sophistication. Suites have sunken baths; there is an outdoor swimming pool, therapy pool, sauna, and 5 dining rooms. A package store on the premises sells liquor. Pets are welcome. 150 W 5th South (801 532-3344). Expensive.

Salt Lake Marriott – The 518-room hotel has 2 restaurants, a lounge, an indoor pool, saunas, a liquor store, and direct access to the Crossroads Mall. Guests have privileges at an adjoining health spa for racquetball, squash, and tennis. The 16-story structure is opposite the Salt Palace on the corner of West Temple and 1st South (801 531-0800). Expensive.

Radisson – This 380-room, 13-story high-rise is built in an unusual arc to give every room a view of the valley. The panoramic view from the top is spectacular. Amenities include 24-hour movies, sports, and news in addition to usual TV fare. With its own heliport and an outdoor pool. The *13th Floor Supper Club* and the *Golden Spike* restaurants are popular with residents (open daily). Children under 14 free. 161 W 6th South (801 521-7373). Moderate.

Best Western Little America – On the city's main thoroughfare, within walking distance of the downtown shopping area and convention center. This 850-room hotel has year-round swimming in an indoor-outdoor pool, plus another outdoor pool, wading pool, saunas, and weight-lifting room. Children under 12 free. Free bus service to the airport. 500 S Main St. (801 363-6781). Expensive to moderate.

Temple Square – Another centrally located hotel, this is the city's best modest hostelry. It offers free parking, and has a coffee shop on the premises. The keynote here is functional rather than fancy. Across the street from Temple Square at 75 W South Temple (801 355-2961). Inexpensive.

 EATING OUT: Salt Lake Valley restaurants offer a number of different cuisines, from Continental to seafood, steaks, and chops. Expect to pay between $40 and $50 for two at those places we've listed as expensive; between $20 and $30 at those places designated moderate; under $20, inexpensive. These prices do not include drinks, wine, or tips. *Special note:* The larger restaurants have liquor licenses; otherwise you'll have to bring your own from the nearest state liquor store (closed on Sundays). You can expect a small setup fee at many restaurants.

La Caille at Quail Run – One of Utah's finest restaurants, in a château (styled as an 18th-century French *maison*) a few miles from the city, serves food commensurate with its well-appointed surroundings. The dining room, overlooking the formal gardens of the estate, features French cuisine and a popular Sunday brunch. Reservations are a must. Major credit cards. 9565 Wasatch Blvd. (942-1751). Expensive.

Five Alls – If you're willing to make the transition from 20th-century Salt Lake to medieval England, drop into the *Five Alls* for a meal. Waitresses in old-fashioned costumes will rush to serve you anything from prime ribs to sweet English trifle. Closed Sundays. Reservations recommended. Major credit cards. 1458 Foothill Dr. (582-1400). Expensive.

Bratten's Grotto – This restaurant serves only seafood and steaks and is extremely popular with Salt Lake City residents, who willingly stand in line at least 20 minutes to be seated. The complete dinner includes a relish bowl, appetizer, soup, choice of breads, entrée, and dessert. Closed Sundays. Reservations accepted. Major credit cards. 644 E 4th South (364-6547). Moderate.

Lamb's – In business since the early 1900s, this old-fashioned downtown restaurant has become an institution. This is where the city's power brokers power lunch. A surprisingly extensive menu, good seafood. 169 S Main St. (364-7166). Moderate.

Mullboon's Restaurant – A recent hit with Salt Lakers, most of whom think it's worth the half-hour to two-hour wait for a table. Prime rib, steaks, and fresh seafood are served, and a one-pound bowl of shrimp accompanies each dinner. Terrific homemade desserts and bread as well. Open daily. No reservations. Major credit cards. 515 S 7th East (363-9653). Moderate.

Market Street Grill – A popular gathering spot, especially at lunchtime, it's in a handsomely renovated old building. The menu features fresh seafood (flown in four or five times a week) as well as steaks, prime rib, and lamb. There's also an oyster bar. Open daily. Reservations at lunch only. Major credit cards. 60 Post Office Pl. (322-4668). Moderate.

Ristorante della Fontana – A remodeled church with stained-glass windows provides a lovely setting for six-course dinners combining Italian and American dishes; the halibut casserole and broccoli and chicken casserole are the most popular. Closed Sundays. Reservations necessary on weekends. Major credit cards. 336 S 400 East (328-4243). Inexpensive.

The Old Spaghetti Factory Restaurant – One of the more popular inexpensive eating places in town, it has lots of friendly ambience. You may find yourself dining on an old brass bed or in a trolley car, with turn-of-the-century furnishings and memorabilia around. Spaghetti comes in all styles, but try the clam sauce. Open daily. No reservations. 189 Trolley Square (521-0424). Inexpensive.

Two Guys from Italy – Italian food from salads to pizza, with a pasta bar, close to the Salt Palace downtown. 165 S West Temple St. (532-4897). Inexpensive.

SAN ANTONIO

Fed up with politics after failing to win reelection to Congress in 1835, Davy Crockett told his Tennessee constituents, "You kin all go to hell, I'm a-goin' to Texas." And so he did. He ended up in San Antonio just in time to join the Texians at the Alamo in their struggle to gain independence from Mexico. (The citizens became "Texans" after severing their ties with Mexico.) He fought alongside Colonels William Travis and James Bowie, who showed Crockett the original bowie knife and said, "You might tickle a fellow's ribs a long time with this instrument before you'd make him laugh." And certainly Santa Anna and his 5,000 soldiers did not go away laughing when the 187 Texas heroes withstood their might, and greatly weakened their ranks, before finally succumbing to the greater force. Though all the fighters for Texas went down in the battle, Crockett (among the last surviving) made his final stand with a lunge at the Mexican general and was promptly dispatched by the swords of the Mexican soldiers.

Today the Alamo still stands, at the center of a cosmopolitan area that blends the old Texas, with its classic Spanish influence, and the largely Texan-Mexican (Tex-Mex) style of today. Alongside numerous well-preserved reminders of days gone by, the missions and lovely adobe buildings, stand modern steel skyscrapers. Established in 1718 by Spanish missionaries who came to convert the Indians, San Antonio drew thousands of pioneers from around the world. Many ethnic groups remain today, but the largest is the Mexican Americans, who make up over half of the city's population of just over 1 million. The city is largely bilingual, but beyond this mix of cultures is a great disparity in economics; San Antonio is a city of poverty and wealth, with pockets of posh suburbs sharing the same pair of pants with pockets of poverty. Here, where the great post–Civil War cattle boom originated, rich Texas ranchers and bankers live in fabulous homes, which are as far as you can get from the public housing units occupied by the poor. But over the past few years the Mexican-Americans have gained political power, and, in fact, over half of San Antonio's state legislative delegation and City Council is of Mexican descent, including Mayor Henry Cisneros, who received a remarkable 91% of the votes in the last election.

Military tradition runs deep in the city's blood. Teddy Roosevelt recruited his famous Rough Riders in the bar of the Hotel Menger. Several aviation "firsts" were established at Fort Sam Houston in 1910 by Lt. Benjamin D. Foulouis when he reported, "My first takeoff, my first solo, my first landing, and my first crash on the same day." San Antonio's current military record is somewhat more stable if less flamboyant. Five military installations with more than 60,000 active duty personnel and civilian employees make the federal government the city's major employer. More than 70,000 enlisted men

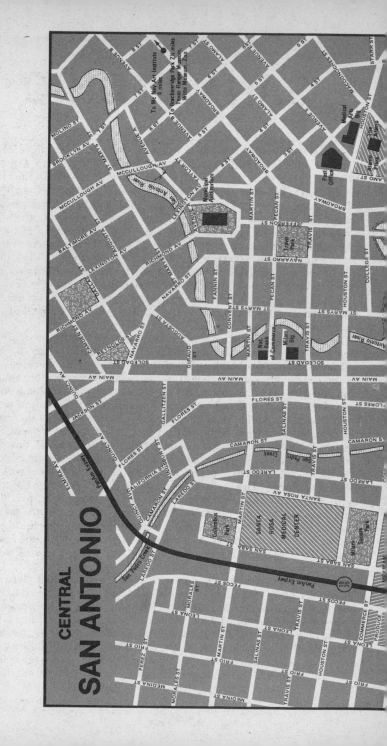

CENTRAL
SAN ANTONIO

and women a year undergo basic training at Lackland Training Center, the cradle of the Air Force.

Since 1968, San Antonio has been an authentic tourist magnet. That was the year of HemisFair, a World's Fair celebrating San Antonio's 200th birthday, which left the city with a valuable convention center, the Lila M. Cockrell Theater for the Performing Arts, and the Institute of Texan Cultures. Even more important, the year-long celebration focused attention on the city's forgotten architectural treasures. La Villita, San Antonio's oldest residential neighborhood, was restored with lovely adobe buildings housing authentic Mexican artisan shops. Homes in the King William section, where the German community lived in grandeur in the 19th century, were restored and feature German stone masonry as well as almost every notable style of American architecture of the past century. And to walk on the Paseo del Rio, the river walk that traces the horseshoe course of the San Antonio River in town, is to step into a people-scale tropical paradise of banana palms and bougainvillea only steps away from apartments, shops, cafés, and San Antonio's business center.

SAN ANTONIO AT-A-GLANCE

SEEING THE CITY: The Tower of the Americas, San Antonio's most visible landmark, at 622 feet, offers the best vantage point from which to view the city and the surrounding countryside. From the observation deck you see flatland stretching to the south and gently rolling hills to the northwest, leading to the Texas Hill Country. Directly below are the buildings of HemisFair Plaza, the site of the '68 World's Fair, and a branch of the San Antonio River that cuts a horseshoe path through town and branches into HemisFair Plaza.

SPECIAL PLACES: The heart of San Antonio is great for walking, with the lovely Paseo del Rio (River Walk) tracing the course of the river, and short distances between many of the attractions. Other sights, including the missions along Mission Trail and the zoo, are best reached by car or bus.

CENTRAL CITY

The Alamo – Where Davy Crockett, Col. James Bowie, Col. Travis, and the 184 other Texas heroes fought against Mexican dictator Santa Anna and his force of 5,000 in Texas' 1836 struggle for independence. Established in 1718 by Spanish priests as Mission San Antonio de Valero, the original mission has been restored and the site turned into a block-square state park that includes a museum with displays on the Alamo and Texas history, with an excellent weapon collection featuring derringers, swords, and an original bowie knife. Open daily. Free. Alamo Plaza (222-1693). After visiting the Alamo, it's easy stroll along the Paseo del Rio, which now reaches the west side of S Alamo St., directly across from the park; the steps from street level are bounded by a series of waterfalls that lead to the *Hyatt* hotel.

La Villita – This little Spanish town in the center of the city looks very much as it did 250 years ago, when it was San Antonio's first residential area. Girded by a stone wall and surrounded by banana palms and bougainvillea, the stone patios and adobe dwellings have been authentically restored and now house artisans' shops where many of the old crafts — glass blowing, weaving, dollmaking, and pottery — are still practiced. Among the other buildings are the restored Cos House (1835), where General Cos, commander of the Mexican forces, surrendered to the Texians; and the Old San Antonio Museum, featuring displays on Texas history and pleasant outdoor cafés. Open daily. Free. One square city block bounded by the river on the north, Nueva St. on the south, S Alamo St. on the east, and Villita St. on the west. Main office, 416 Villita St. (299-8610).

Paseo del Rio – A branch of the San Antonio River winds like a horseshoe through the central business district. Stone stairways lead down to the River Walk which, only 20 feet below street level, is as far from the world of the business district as you can get. Tall trees, tropical foliage, and banana palms line the walks dotted with curio and craft shops, night spots and cafés, and an increasing number of fashionable apartments. You can experience the river in a paddleboat or a barge (paddleboat booth at the river under the Market St. Bridge), and dine by candlelight aboard some. Make arrangements through barge office, 430 E Commerce St. (222-1701).

HemisFair Plaza – A legacy of the 1968 World's Fair, HemisFair Plaza features the Tower of the Americas with its panoramic view of Texas countryside, a convention center, the Lila M. Cockrell Theater for the Performing Arts, shops, and several modern buildings that have exhibitions. The Institute of Texan Cultures examines the influence of 26 different ethnic groups — including the Mexicans, Germans, Poles, Hungarians, and Irish — who developed the state. There are films, slide shows, and exhibitions of artifacts including Mexican stone cooking equipment and examples of the dress of each of the groups. Closed Mondays. Free (226-7651).

The Museum of Transportation – Shows how people got around in the days of the open country with classic and antique carriages, stagecoaches, hearses, horse-drawn pumpers, until the range gave way to highways and autos. Closed Mondays and holidays. Admission charge (ticket stubs serve as admission to the Witte Museum and the San Antonio Museum of Art). Bounded by Commerce, Market, Durango, and Alamo sts. (226-5544).

El Mercado – Though the original marketplace has been renovated, it is still lined with Spanish buildings and retains its old market flavor, with Mexican merchants who do their best to lure you into shops offering handcrafted objects like baskets, piñatas, pottery, silver jewelry. Open daily. 515 W Commerce St. (299-8600).

Spanish Governor's Palace – The only Spanish colonial mansion remaining in Texas. Built in 1749 for the Spanish governors when Texas was a province of Spain, the palace has 3-foot-thick walls, a keystone above the door bearing the Hapsburg coat of arms, original Spanish furnishings, and a floor of native flagstone. Open daily. Small admission charge. 105 Military Plaza (224-0601).

Hertzberg Circus Collection – If you're a circus fanatic, you'll go ring crazy here with displays of artifacts tracing the development of the circus from its English origins to P. T. Barnum and the American three-ring extravaganza. Particularly strong in miniatures featuring the original carriage of Tom Thumb and an entire circus in one room. Closed Sundays. Free. 210 W Market St. in Library Annex (299-7810).

SOUTH SIDE

Missions – The Alamo was the first of five missions established under Spanish rule. All except the Alamo are still active parish churches and are located along the well-marked Mission Trail, starting at the southern tip of the city. Most notable are:

    Mission Concepción – The oldest unrestored church in the country is remarkably well preserved with original frescoes made by the padres and Indians from a mixture of vegetable and mineral dyes. Open daily. 807 Mission Rd. (532-3158).

    Mission San José – Called the Queen of the Missions, it's the finest and largest example of early mission life. The original parish church, built of limestone and tufa, features Rosa's Window, an impressive stone carving, and is surrounded by a 6-acre compound including a restored mill, Indian quarters, and granary. Open daily. 6539 San José Dr., 6 miles south on US 281 (922-2731).

Buckhorn Hall of Horns – Once an old shoot'em-up saloon, this hall was transported lock, stock, and barrel by the Lone Star Brewing Company to tamer grounds. The collection is as wild as ever — some of the fastest guns in the West, and hunting trophies of everything imaginable from horns and antlers of elk, buffalo, and antelope to whole polar bears and grizzly bears. Open daily. Admission charge. 600 Lone Star Blvd. on the company's grounds (226-8303).

NORTH SIDE

Brackenridge Park – This 343-acre park includes the Southwest's largest zoo. Rock cliffs provide a backdrop for fine displays of animals in their natural settings. Over 3,500 specimens of 800 species are represented and best are the Monkey Island, an outdoor hippo pool, open bear pits, and a children's zoo nursery. Open daily. Admission charge. 3903 N St. Mary's (734-7183).

McNay Art Institute – Small but fine collections include works by Picasso and Chagall among displays of international scope and exhibitions of regional artists. Open daily. Free. 6000 N New Braunfels (824-5368).

■**EXTRA SPECIAL:** *The Grey Moss Inn,* in Grey Forest, a wildlife sanctuary only a few minutes from downtown, offers outdoor dining on a shaded patio where you can have charcoal-broiled steak, seafood, or chicken prepared on an open grill. You may see a white-tailed deer grazing nearby as you dine. Indoor dining centers around a fireplace. Dinner only; closed Mondays. Reservations advised. Major credit cards. Scenic Loop Rd., 12 miles from the Bandera Rd./Loop 410 Interchange (695-8301).

SOURCES AND RESOURCES

TOURIST INFORMATION: General tourist information, brochures, maps, and events calendars are available at the Convention and Visitors Bureau, 210 S Alamo St. (299-8123). More convenient is the San Antonio Visitor Information Center, directly across from the Alamo at 317 S Alamo St. The *San Antonio Convention & Visitor's Guide* (free) is a good area guide.

Local Coverage – *The San Antonio Express-News,* morning and afternoon daily and *The San Antonio Light,* morning and afternoon daily. Both papers available at newsstands. Paseo del Rio Association's *Showboat* lists upcoming events. Available at Visitors Bureau and in hotel lobbies.

Area Code – All telephone numbers are in the 512 area code unless otherwise indicated.

CLIMATE AND CLOTHES: Known as the place where "sunshine spends the winter," San Antonio winters are, naturally, sunny and mild with temperatures averaging above 50°. If you like hot weather, summers are pleasant too, with temperatures over 90° and lots of sunshine except for an occasional tropical storm from the Gulf of Mexico.

GETTING AROUND: Airport – San Antonio International Airport is about a 15-minute drive from downtown; a taxi ride will run about $12. VIA Metropolitan Transit (227-2020) provides limo service to the city's major hotels every half-hour and costs $5. VIA buses also run between the airport and downtown during certain hours in the morning and afternoon for 75¢; call for schedules.

Bus – San Antonio Metropolitan Transit System serves all sections of the city, with the system's streetcars covering a 25-square-block downtown area for 10¢. Complete route and tourist information is available from the Transit Office, 800 W Myrtle St. (227-2020).

Streetcar – Attractive reproductions of antique trolleys (on rubber wheels) follow five distinct tourist and traffic loops to and through major points of interest around the city. The fare is 10¢. Free maps are available from any visitor center.

Taxi – Cabs may be ordered by phone or picked up at taxi stations in front of major hotels. Some will answer a hail in the street, most will not. Two of the largest companies are Checker (222-2151) and Yellow (226-4242).

Car Rental – All national firms are represented, but one of the best for the budget-minded is Budget Rent-A-Car, at San Antonio International Airport (9245 John Saunders; 349-4441), and 338 NE Loop (349-4441).

 MUSEUMS: The Alamo Museum, the Museum of Transportation, the Hertzberg Collection, the McNay Institute, the Buckhorn Hall of Horns, and the Institute of Texan Cultures are described in *Special Places.* Other interesting museums are:

San Antonio Museum of Art – Closed Mondays; 200 W Jones Ave. (226-5444)
Texas Ranger Museum – Closed Mondays, Tuesdays; 3805 Broadway (822-9011)
Witte Memorial Museum – Closed Mondays; 3801 Broadway (226-5544)

 ART GALLERIES: Artists and craftsmen from all over the world are finding that San Antonio is an accommodating place to live and work. The art colony is growing rapidly, and galleries are numerous. Try the *Raul Gutierrez Gallery of Fine Arts* for Western oils, acrylics, and bronzes (8940 Wurzbach; 696-5356), and the *Southwest Craft Gallery* for handcrafted pieces by well-known Southwest craftsmen (420 Paseo de la Villita; 222-0926). At the Southwest Craft Center, 300 Augusta (224 1848), you can watch artists at work.

 MAJOR COLLEGES AND UNIVERSITIES: With ten colleges and universities, San Antonio has a large student population. The major educational institutions are the University of Texas at San Antonio, Loop 1604, 17 miles north of downtown (691-4011); St. Mary's University, One Camino Santa Maria (436-3011); Trinity University, 715 Stadium Dr. (736-7011); the University of Texas Health Science Center, 7703 Floyd Curl (691-6011); Incarnate Word College, 4301 Broadway (828-1261); and Our Lady of the Lake University, 411 SW 24th (434-6711).

 SPECIAL EVENTS: A city of fiestas, the most elaborate blowout is the 10-day *Fiesta San Antonio* in mid-April, celebrating Sam Houston's victory over Santa Anna with parades, the Battle of the Flowers, the Fiesta Flambeau in the streets, and the Fiesta River Parade with lighted floats on the river, a king and queen, and lots of food and drink for the subjects. The *Starving Artists Show* in early April has works of art by hungry local artists for nothing much more than $20; everyone is trying to make ends meet so they can eat at the fiesta.

 SPORTS AND FITNESS: Baseball – The San Antonio *Dodgers* minor league team plays at V. J. Keefe Field, St. Mary's University (434-9311).
Basketball – The NBA *Spurs* play at the Convention Center Arena from October through March; tickets at the Arena in HemisFair Plaza (224-9578).

Fitness Centers – The YMCA has a pool, track, weights, and handball and racquetball courts, 903 N St. Mary's and Lexington (227-5221).

Football – The San Antonio *Gunslingers* joined the USFL in 1984 and now play at Alamo Stadium from September through November; tickets at the stadium, 110 Tuleta Dr. (734-USFL).

Golf – There are 17 courses in the city in constant use all year round. Best for visitors is Olmos Basin Municipal Course, 7022 McCullough (826-4041).

Jogging – Run along the River Walk early or late in the day; up Broadway to Brackenridge Park; or follow the Mission Trail, along Mission Road (the marathon route), to the missions.

Swimming – There are 17 municipal pools open May through Labor Day (299-3000). Best is Alamo Heights Pool, 229 Greeley St.

Tennis – McFarlin Tennis Center is a municipal facility. Courts are $1.50 per person per hour, but call for reservations, 1503 San Pedro Ave. (732-1223).

 THEATER: More than a dozen theaters offer a continuing and varied fare of traveling and locally produced shows, the most impressive of which is the *Majestic Theater,* 214 E Houston St. (226-2626). This incredibly ornate structure has been restored to its 1920s grandeur and now hosts everything from traveling national theater companies to rock concerts. The area's colleges and universities also produce plays. For shows: *San Antonio Little Theater,* off the 1500 block of San Pedro (733-7258); *Harlequin Dinner Theater,* Fort Sam Houston (221-5953); *Actors Theater,* 1150 S Alamo St. (224-4085); *Arneson River Theater* on Villita St. and the river (299-8610), where the stage and terraced hillside of the audience are separated by the river, and an occasional passing barge upstages the actors.

 MUSIC: The *San Antonio Symphony* performs with guest stars from September through May at 109 Lexington Ave. (225-6161).

 NIGHTCLUBS AND NIGHTLIFE: Pop music, jazz, Dixieland, folk, rock, and country-western are all offered at San Antonio's many pubs, taverns, and nightclubs. For a little country, try the *Farmer's Daughter,* 542 N W. W. White Rd. (333-7391). For jazz, try *Jim Cullum's Landing,* 522 River Walk (223-7266). You may want to try the nostalgia of *Larry Herman's Roaring 20's,* 13445 Blanco Rd. (492-1353).

 SINS: The aristocrats who make up old San Antonio society have fortunes based on land and cattle in a city where oil money is still considered nouveau. Every year cattle baron *pride* reaches the sublime with the Order of the Alamo's election of a Queen of the Fiesta, a celebration held in honor of Texas' victory at the Battle of San Jacinto.

This event attains a level of *gluttony* not in food consumed but in costumes displayed. The cost of gowns for the Queen and her court run into five or six figures; the outfits are so elaborate that their hapless wearers have to be shuttled from function to function standing up in moving vans, like, uh, cattle.

With San Antonio's military population regularly roaming downtown, there often seems to be an equal population of hookers available to satisfy *lustful* urges.

If you want to see some good Texan *anger,* attend a weekly meeting of the current City Council. These take place on Thursdays, and usually run quite long. The various ethnic groups represented have interests divergent enough to keep tempers short, voices high, and manners nonexistent.

LOCAL SERVICES: Babysitting – Northside Sitters Club, 7918 Jones-Maltsberger (341-9313)

   Business Services – Manpower, Interfirst Plaza Bldg., 300 Convent (224-9251)

Mechanic – The Bexar Engine and Transmission Service, 707 S Flores St. (226-9114)

(BEST IN TOWN)

 CHECKING IN: You can find all of the things you're probably looking for in San Antonio's hotels, like comfortable and convenient accommodations. Expect to pay $95 or more for a double room for a night in the expensive category, $60 to $85 in the moderate range, and $40 in the inexpensive.

Four Seasons – This spacious garden hotel is on nearly 5 acres accented by tropical gardens, tall native Texas trees, and sparkling fountains. Its 250 rooms have balconies overlooking La Villita Historic District. There are 4 distinctive restaurants with international menus. Incorporated into the complex are three restored 19th-century bungalows, which are a functional part of the hotel's dining and entertainment facilities. Pool, exercise rooms, sauna, and tennis courts. 555 S Alamo (512 229-1000). Expensive.

La Mansion del Rio – This hotel combines a Spanish-style building with a restored 1852 building that was originally part of St. Mary's University. Nicely designed, with 373 rooms overlooking either the river or an inner courtyard. Features the *Capistrano Room* and *Las Canarias* restaurants and the *El Colegio Bar.* Also a pool and free parking. 112 College St. (512 225-2581). Expensive.

Hilton Palacio del Rio – Right on the riverside, at the liveliest corner of Paseo del Rio, the *Hilton* makes the best use of its prime location. The *El Comedor Dining Room* serves al fresco on the River Walk, some of the rooms in this attractive Spanish-style building have river views, and there is an elevator stop that lets you off at river's edge. Also features a rooftop pool, free coffee in rooms, 24-hour room service, meeting rooms, shops, and *Durty Nellie's* pub, where you can let loose with an Irish lullaby. 200 S Alamo St. (512 222-1400). Expensive.

Hyatt Regency of San Antonio – Most of the 633 rooms in this 16-story hotel built around an atrium have views of the San Antonio River and Old San Antonio. For dining and drinking, there's the *Crescendo Restaurant, La Puerta* on the River Walk, and *Caps* and the multilevel *River Terrace Lounge* in the atrium. Pool. 123 Losoya (512 222-1234). Expensive.

San Antonio Marriott on the River Walk – Directly across the street from the convention center, the *Marriott* is the city's largest and one of its newest hotels, nestled in a bend of the San Antonio River. The most striking feature is its 7-story atrium with an indoor-outdoor heated swimming pool. *Gambits on the River Walk,* a 2-story nightclub, opens up onto the river; *The Cabrillo* features live entertainment; and the *Cactus Flower Café* has riverside dining on its patio. 711 E River Walk (512 224-4555). Expensive.

Inter-Continental San Antonio – Richness envelops guests who enter the lobby, a by-product of the Empire chandeliers, Oriental rugs, marble and hand-painted Mexican tiles, and a rosewood and gold-leaf grand piano. This is the old, landmark *St. Anthony,* handsomely restored. The *Jefferson Manor* restaurant (one of the city's best) serves traditional American specialties in the setting of a Monticello estate; the hotel also has another restaurant, several bars, a rooftop garden, 24-hour room service, and a pool. 300 E Travis St. (512 227-4392). Expensive.

Wyndham – This 328-room property, with an exterior of polished pink granite, opened in February 1985. With its 20,000 square feet of meeting space, the hotel is a boon to business travelers, though anyone can appreciate its two large swimming pools, exercise room and sauna, and attractive two-story lobby with brass sculptures and a marble bar. 9803 Colonnade (512 691-8888). Expensive.

The Gunter – Opened in 1909, this hotel was twice declared a Texas landmark. A turn-of-the-century atmosphere still pervades the lobby, with its crystal chandeliers, marble floor, and dark mahogany paneling. More modern are the 326 high-ceilinged rooms with tile baths. International and Texas specialties are served in the *Café Suisse* restaurant; *Pâtisserie Suisse* is a European-style bakery; and there's dancing at *Padre Muldoon's,* a Victorian saloon. 205 E Houston St. (512 227-3241). Moderate.

The Crockett – Behind the Alamo since 1909, the *Crockett* recently emerged from a $15 million renovation as one of the nicest of San Antonio's "old" hotels. Some of the 200 rooms are small, but all are beautifully decorated. The most impressive accommodations are the luxurious 7th-floor suites overlooking the Alamo grounds. *Lela B's* restaurant serves meat salads (turkey, duck, steak) and the like at lunch, weekdays, and Continental fare for dinner, daily. 320 Bonham (512 225-6500). Moderate.

El Tropicano – Six blocks from the heart of downtown, at the north end of the River Walk, and thus a good place from which to tour the river on foot or by water taxi. 110 Lexington Ave. (512 223-9461). Moderate.

La Quinta – Two blocks from the river, this two-story Spanish building offers comfortable, convenient accommodations at good prices. Pool, TV, café. 130 rooms. 1001 E Commerce St. (512 222-9181). Inexpensive.

 EATING OUT: Some 26 ethnic groups pioneered Texas, and its current large military population has brought back a taste for exotic dishes from remote areas of the globe, resulting in a wide variety of restaurants. However, most folks would agree that San Antonio's best restaurants are Mexican. Non-Texans (outlanders, as they're called down here) are generally surprised (happily) by the prices. Our selections range in price from $65 or more for dinner for two in the expensive range, $20 to $30 in the moderate range, and under $15, inexpensive. Prices do not include drinks, wine or tips.

La Louisiane – When it opened in 1935, this fine French and Créole restaurant offered full dinners for 75¢ to $1.25. Imminent failure was forecast by residents, who said it was too expensive for San Antonio. Today, a couple can go all out with an elegant $65 to $75 production that includes pompano en papillote (poached with oyster and shrimp in white wine sauce), frogs legs sauté meunière, and three vintage wines; or some excellent dishes on a less grand scale. *La Louisiane* has won many national awards for its food and service. Closed Sundays and Mondays. Reservations advised. Major credit cards. 2632 Broadway (225-7984). Expensive.

The Fig Tree – Long, leisurely dinners with excellent service are the rule at this 19th-century adobe house. In the rare event that you have to wait for a table, have a drink on the balcony overlooking the San Antonio River. Specialties are seafood and beef. La Villita section, a few blocks from the Alamo site. Open daily for dinner only. Reservations advised. Major credit cards. 515 Paseo De La Villita (224-1976). Expensive.

Arthur's – Expert service amid stylish surroundings, with a menu of seafood, meat, and poultry dishes. Shipments of white asparagus from France, fish from Boston, and strawberries from Peru arrive daily, adding further gustatory interest. The *Cabaret Bar* is a good spot for jazz, with Nobuku at the piano. Open daily.

Reservations advised. Major credit cards. 4001 Broadway on the Boardwalk (826-3200). Expensive.

PJ's – New to the River Walk scene, *PJ's* prepares a buffet luncheon of roast beef, soup, and innovative salads. But the fish, desserts, and homemade pasta are what's making this place one of the city's latest hot spots. *PJ's* can be reached by river taxi from the Casa Rio boat dock, but complimentary parking is also available. Closed Sundays. Reservations advised. Major credit cards. 1 River Walk Pl. at St. Mary's (225-8400). Expensive to moderate.

Cadillac Bar & Restaurant – An import from Nuevo Laredo, featuring dishes most often found in Mexican border towns. Beware of the salsa sitting innocently on the table; it has vaporized more than one palate. Ramos gin fizzes are the drink of choice; fish dishes are the best menu items. Strolling mariachis add to the atmosphere of this very friendly, informal eatery. Lunch and dinner; closed Sundays. Major credit cards. 212 S Flores (223-5533). Moderate.

Texas Tumbleweed – You say you've worked up a hunger flying in? Then try a little belt-bustin' right here, just 5 minutes from the airport. Steaks are Texas big, juicy, and tender. Try the Wagonwheel (bacon-wrapped filet) or the Grub Steak (sirloin); both are house specialties. Open daily. Major credit cards. 13311 San Pedro Ave. (496-1122). Moderate.

Mario's – A popular West Side eatery often described as a piece of Mexico that mistakenly strayed across the border. It's a 24-hour operation where patrons warm up on a breakfast of chilaquiles (scrambled eggs with tortilla strips) and tackle grilled sweetbreads and a dessert of capirotada (bread pudding) for lunch. Mariachis keep the place lively. Two blocks from El Mercado. Open daily. Visa and MasterCard accepted. 325 S Pecos (223-9602). Moderate to inexpensive.

Mi Tierra Café and Bakery – When you tire of souvenir hunting at El Mercado, you can go to the heart of the market square for the real thing — great Mexican food at low prices. The cheese enchiladas are terrific, and the cabrito (kid) is good here too. Open daily. No reservations. Major credit cards. 218 Produce Row (225-1262). Moderate to inexpensive.

La Fogata – Authentic recipes and foods from Mexico. Cooking is exclusively by charcoal, and though the menu sounds exotic, the prices are down to earth. (No liquor is served.) Closed Mondays. No reservations. Major credit cards. 2427 Vance Jackson (341-9930). Moderate to inexpensive.

El Mirador – Citizens say the best (and most authentic) Mexican food in the city is served here. It's a special favorite at lunchtime on Saturdays, when the entire citizenry seems to visit. Caldo Xochit (a chicken-cum-vegetable soup) is a special treat. Breakfast 6:30 to 10:45 AM. Closes at 6 PM on weekdays and 3 PM Saturdays. No credit cards. 722 S St. Mary's (225-9444). Inexpensive.

El Bosque – Excellent Mexican food in a country setting 15 minutes from downtown. Try the menu's Extra Special No. 1, which includes the works: enchiladas, refried beans, Spanish rice, tamales, tortillas, chile con queso, guacamole salad. The chiles rellenos are a house specialty. Cocktails and Mexican beer. Open daily. Major credit cards. 12656 West Ave. (494-2577). Inexpensive.

Earl Abel's – After feeding hungry families for almost half a century, Earl has gotten pretty good at it. The place is a godsend for those who have been watching the ravenous animals at the nearby zoo. Offers big servings of standard American fare — broiled filet of trout from the Coast, a chicken liver dinner, a full line of hamburgers, big T-bones, and terrific homemade pecan pie. No reservations. No credit cards. 4200 Broadway (822-3358). Inexpensive.

Church's Fried Chicken – Fast food with a hot twist — chicken and jalapeños. Both spicy and cheap. The headquarters of the national chain, San Antonio has more than 30 Church's so you can't miss them. Open daily. Inexpensive.

Mama's – Good food in a family atmosphere with everything from burgers to steaks. Specialty of the house is chicken-fried mushrooms. A volleyball court and basketball hoop are set up in the fenced backyard so kids can work off their energies while mom and pop have a leisurely after-dinner drink. Open daily. Major credit cards. 9907 San Pedro (349-2314). Inexpensive.

SAN DIEGO

Sparkling and white against a classic aquamarine sea, San Diego looks like what a first-timer to California imagines Los Angeles to be. It's clean, sunny, and radiates glowing self-satisfaction. It is archetypal Southern California. San Diego residents call it paradise. (Really.)

Strangers in paradise are usually flabbergasted by the terrific climate. This is one place that really lives up to its outrageously positive reputation. Residents in this land of eternal spring (71° is the average annual temperature) tend to gripe when even the merest wisp of cumulus mars the turquoise heaven. Never mind that days without sunshine are few and far between; nothing short of perfect weather will do. You can get spoiled living in Eden.

A lot of people do. About 950,000 live in the city, while the San Diego metro area has 2 million people. Although the unemployment rate is higher here than the national average, people would rather be out of work and live in San Diego than work and have to live somewhere else. When the aerospace industry declined toward the end of the Vietnam War, thousands of highly trained engineers, research scientists, and technicians suddenly found themselves out of work. The fact that they did not pick up and leave is generally attributed to the "laid back" San Diego lifestyle. Many of these highly qualified professionals chose to take jobs like washing carpets or fixing washing machines and cars rather than forsake those splendid afternoons lounging on the beach. And why not? More than 150,000 visitors come to San Diego every day to do just that.

Tourism is the city's third largest industry. The US government is number one. In fact, 25% of the San Diego labor force works for Uncle Sam. The San Diego Navy complex includes the largest naval air station on the West Coast. Second most important is the aerospace equipment and missile industry. About 1,000 firms manufacture aviation equipment. (The military-industrial complex thrives in Southern California as much as anything else.) San Diego's present size is a direct consequence of the incredible mobilization during World War II. After the Japanese attack on Pearl Harbor, the US moved its Pacific naval headquarters from Honolulu to San Diego. Here were manufactured thousands of B-24 Liberators, which, in turn, pounded thousands of tons of high explosives into the very heart of occupied Europe. Millions of people passed through town during the war years, and many returned to settle when there was peace. This influx swelled the city to the bursting point, necessitating a series of building projects. Then, as America entered the space age, thousands more engineers, rocket specialists, and physicists poured into the area. San Diego gave birth to the Atlas missile, one of the earliest of the sophisticated rockets used to launch man into space.

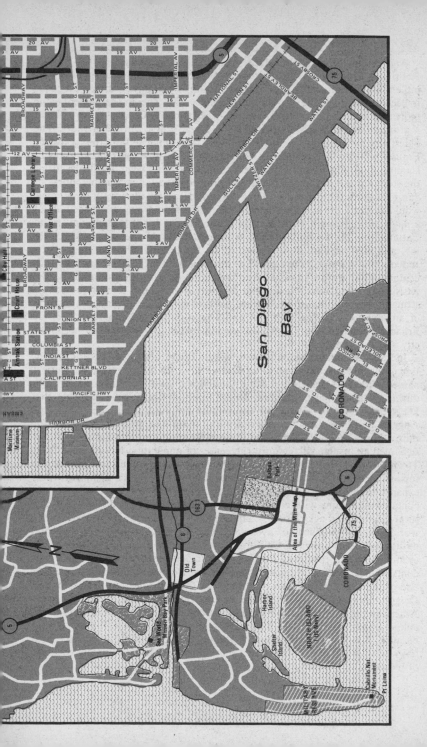

And originally, it is the place where California began. In 1542, Juan Rodriguez Cabrillo, the Portuguese explorer sailing under a Spanish flag, pulled into the natural shelter formed by San Diego Bay. Cabrillo was later to become known as the "Columbus of California." The first settlement came more than two centuries later, however, when explorer Gaspar de Portolá and a group of Spanish settlers planted San Diego's first European roots. The oldest city in California includes on its list of original settlers the legendary Franciscan, Fray Junipero Serra, founder of the 21-mission trail known as El Camino Real. The first of Fray Serra's missions, San Diego de Alcala, forms the southern end of the chain that lines the coast as far as Sonoma, north of San Francisco. (One wonders what the gentle, pacifist disciple of St. Francis would think of the missiles that are manufactured here now.) Spaced about a day's journey apart, each mission housed about 1,000 Indian converts to Catholicism. The Indians worked as farmers and craftspeople. Food, clothing, and medical care were dispensed by the priests, who also taught the Indians how to irrigate the fields. The missions were the kibbutzim of the 18th century. They were also established with military priorities in mind. As the Russians pushed into Alaska, the Spanish government looked toward its string of religious settlements and outposts as strategic bulwarks in the event of an invasion. To the north of San Diego de Alcala, San Luis Rey de Francisco and San Juan Capistrano stood between California's southernmost city and Los Angeles.

In 1810, Mexicans gained control of San Diego, after a successful revolution in the northern Mexican town of Querétaro, led by a revolutionary priest named Hidalgo. The United States seized the land from Mexico in 1846 during its expansionist "manifest destiny" period. Under American rule, San Diego grew slowly, taking a back seat to the mercantile centers of Los Angeles, San Francisco, and Sacramento, the state capital, located on major railroad lines and at the juncture of two of the state's major rivers. San Diego remained an insular village until the center of population moved from "Old Town" to the "New Town" (designed by sugar heir John Spreckels) at the turn of the century. Modern San Diego follows Spreckels's plan, but it has expanded more than 20 miles to the north, south, and east. San Diego County contains mountains with enough snow for winter skiing and fertile agricultural land. In fact, agriculture is San Diego's fourth largest industry. It is the world's largest producer of avocados. The majority of the more than 500 million avocados grown in California last year came from San Diego. Many eventually found their way into guacamole consumed by visitors and residents. Guacamole is a Mexican hors d'oeuvre, a culinary influence that is just one of the many Mexicanisms permeating the San Diego atmosphere. San Diego's Mexican-Spanish heritage is also reflected in its large Mexican-American population and in its modern architecture as well as in its remarkable old buildings. The Mexican border is only 17 miles to the south, and because of it, San Diego retains a unique character: a blend of American hospitality, traditional border-town sensuality, and the best climate this side of paradise.

SAN DIEGO AT-A-GLANCE

SEEING THE CITY: Cabrillo National Monument, where Juan Rodriguez Cabrillo first saw the West Coast in 1542, still offers the most spectacular view of San Diego. It's the most visited national monument in the US — more popular than the Statue of Liberty. Museum and Visitor Center open daily. Free. Catalina Blvd. on the tip of Point Loma (293-5450).

SPECIAL PLACES: San Diego stretches from the fashionable northern suburb of Del Mar to the Mexican border: all in all, a span of more than 30 miles along the Pacific Coast. It's advisable to concentrate your sightseeing efforts in one particular area at a time. There's no way you can see everything in just a day.

SAN DIEGO

Shelter Island – A manmade resort island in the middle of San Diego Bay lined with boatyards, marinas, and picturesque, neo-Polynesian restaurants. Between July and November, marlin sportfishers haul their giant catches into port here to be weighed and photographed. Stop off at Marlin Club Landing, 2445 Shelter Island Drive. If the sight of these monsters makes you yearn for the tug of a giant fish on the line, sign on for a marlin expedition at any of the sportfishing marinas two blocks away on Fenelon Street. You can also fish for albacore and yellowtail. To get to Shelter Island, follow Rosecrans Street until you see signs pointing to Shelter Island.

Harbor Island – This is a super deluxe, $50 million resort island. Actually, it started as a landfill project in 1961 when the US Navy offered surplus harbor muck to the Port of San Diego. The Navy was deepening a channel through the Bay. Port officials took them up on their offer and used the 3½ million tons of waste to create Harbor Island. You'd never know, to look at the place. Humble beginnings have yielded fancy beachside promenades, traffic-free malls, restaurants, and hotels. Take Rosecrans to Harbor Drive, then follow signs to Harbor Island.

Mission Bay Park – A 4,600-acre waterfront recreation area. Here you'll find manmade tropical islands, channels, and specific areas where you can water ski, swim, and sail. There are golf courses, hotels, and restaurants here, too. The 2-mile stretch of Mission Beach, along the western edge of the park, is one of San Diego's oldest beach communities. A Visitor Information Center is open daily. Take Rte. 5 to Mission Bay Drive exit. The Information Center is right off the exit ramp (276-8200).

Sea World – This 80-acre oceanarium is the highlight of the Mission Bay recreation complex. Performing dolphins and Shamu, the three-ton killer whale, entertain regularly. The water show includes the Ding-a-Ling Brothers' Seal and Otter Circus, too. Backstage you can feed the dolphins and meet the walruses. Yes, there are sharks, too. Open daily. Admission charge. Mission Bay Park (224-3562).

Old Town Plaza – The best way to see Old San Diego is by walking through it. Old Town Plaza (also known as Washington Square) used to be the scene of violent cockfights and bullfights. Duelists chose this as their site for shooting it out. One-hour guided walking tours leave Old Town Plaza daily. Free. San Diego Ave., Mason, Calhoun, and Wallace sts. (For general park information, call 237-6770.)

Casa de Estudillo – The former commandante of San Diego, José Maria Estudillo, lived here while the city was under Mexican control. It was also the site of Helen Hunt Jackson's book *Ramona*, which describes how the Indians were mistreated. It was built in 1829. Open daily. Free. San Diego Ave. and Mason St. (no phone).

San Diego Union Newspaper Museum – Still going strong, the *San Diego Union* started out in this small, 1860s building. In fact, the newspaper is responsible for restoring it, and for setting up the editorial offices and printing press. Copies of the first *Union* ever printed are still on sale for 25¢. Open daily. Free. 2626 San Diego Ave. (297-2119).

Old California Museum – Right in back of the Newspaper Museum, this is a good place to get an idea of what Old Town looked like a hundred years ago. A scale-model diorama is on display. Across the alley, you can see Seeley Stable, barns, and a fine collection of horse-drawn wagons and carriages. There's also a slide show of San Diego history. Open daily. Free. 2626 San Diego Ave. (297-2119).

Whaley House – The first brick house in San Diego, built by New Yorker Thomas Whaley. The house is supposed to be haunted by a man who was hung on the grounds in 1852. Haunted or not, the house was the scene of many lively high society parties in its day. Ornate 19th-century furnishings still fill the halls. Closed Mondays and Tuesdays. Admission charge. 2482 San Diego Ave. (298-2482).

Derby-Pendleton House – Behind the Whaley House, this home was built in Portland, Maine, then taken apart, shipped around Cape Horn, and reassembled on this site. Lt. George H. Derby lived here during the Civil War era. On the grounds of this house and Whaley House are a restored trolley car, a pharmacy collection of apothecary paraphernalia, and an herb shop. Closed Mondays and Tuesdays. Free. 4017 Harney St. (298-2482).

El Campo Santo – At the southern end of San Diego Avenue is a cemetery containing the graves of many pioneers, soldiers, and bandits. One of the latter, Antonio Garra, was actually executed next to his grave. Unfortunately many of the headstones are missing, but there's enough history here to make a visit compelling. San Diego Ave. and Noell St. (no phone).

Mormon Battalion Memorial Visitors Center – This military museum marks the longest infantry march in US history: 1846 to 1847, when 500 Mormons left their home in Illinois and trekked more than 2,000 miles to San Diego. Only 350 made it. It also has a number of exhibitions of the Church of Latter-Day Saints and historical displays. Open daily. Free. In Heritage Park at 2510 Juan St. (298-3317).

Heritage Park – A pocket of preserved Victoriana. The County Parks and Recreation Dept. has its offices in the Sherman-Gilbert House. There are several other mansions to explore. Open daily. Free. Heritage Park Row (565-3600).

Serra Museum – Named after Fray Junipero Serra, this lovely mansion houses documents, books, and artifacts on the history of the region during its Spanish colonial, Mexican, and early US periods. The tower gallery is especially fascinating. The museum is on the site of the original European settlement. Open daily. Free. Presidio Park (297-3258).

Horton Plaza – The first major project in San Diego's downtown redevelopment program, this multilevel shopping plaza comprises major department stores, movie theaters, restaurants, entertainments, and over 150 specialty shops. The newly reopened, almost legendary *U. S. Grant Hotel* is adjacent on Broadway. Stretching from Broadway to G St. between 1st and 4th aves.

Balboa Park – A definite must — the cultural heart of the city. Within its 1,200 acres of lawns, groves, lakes, and paths are a complex of fine museums, set in an area of the park known as the Prado, a Shakespearean Theater, and the world-famous San Diego Zoo (each listed below). Open daily. Free. Park Blvd. (239-0512).

San Diego Zoo – Incomparable. One of the finest zoos in the world. For more than 60 years, San Diego has been home to more than 4,000 animals. The zoo covers more than 125 acres, with animals ranging from Australian koala bears to the only New Zealand kiwis in captivity in the country to Indonesian Komodo dragons. Very few of the animals are caged in. The Skyfari Aerial Tramway gives you a great bird's-eye view of everything. Guided bus tours leave frequently from the gate. Open daily. Admission charge. Balboa Park (234-3153, 231-1515).

Timken Art Gallery – Controversial when it was built in 1965 because some people felt it clashed with the prevalent Spanish adobe architecture, the modern Timken houses French, Spanish, Flemish, Russian, and Italian Renaissance art. You'll find Rembrandt, Bruegel the Elder, and Cézanne on the walls. Open daily. Free. Plaza de Panama, Balboa Park (239-5548).

Fine Arts Gallery – Donated by the Appleton Bridges family in 1926, the original section of the gallery was built to resemble the university at Salamanca, Spain. Two newer wings have since been added. Diego Rivera, the Mexican muralist, Rubens, the painter of big nudes, Rembrandt, and Dali are represented. Closed Mondays. Admission charge. Plaza de Panama, Balboa Park (232-7931).

Museum of Man – Concerning itself primarily with anthropology and archaeology, this museum bears the distinction of being the only remaining permanent structure from San Diego's 1915 Exposition. Its Spanish colonial tower is remarkable in itself. Exhibitions focus on the Southwest Indians. Open daily. Admission charge except Wednesdays. El Prado, Balboa Park (239-2001).

Aerospace Hall of Fame – San Diego's noted collection of antique planes and gliders. Ford Bldg., Balboa Park (232-8322).

Reuben H. Fleet Space Theater – The first of its kind. Simulated space travel is the attraction here. Images projected on the 360° screen give you the impression you're moving in zero-gravity conditions. The Science Center also has exhibitions on astronomy and technology. On weekends there's a free demonstration of lasers. Open daily. Admission charge. Off Park Blvd., Balboa Park (238-1168).

Museum of Natural History – More than a century old, this museum has a collection of birds that nest in the San Diego area, and sharks, whales, and fish who make their home in the surrounding seas. A Sefton seismograph measures tremors and earth movement. Open daily. Admission charge except Tuesdays. Across from the Fleet Space Theater, Balboa Park (232-3821).

Seaport Village – The city's new waterfront complex of restaurants and specialty shops built around three main plazas edging San Diego Bay is designed to look much like a New England fishing village. A main attraction is the wonderfully restored Flying Horses Carousel, with its hand-carved wooden animals, originally constructed around 1900 for the amusement park at Coney Island, New York. It's nice to stroll through the village in the evening and have dinner in one of the restaurants here. *Papagayo's* (232-7581) has very good Mexican seafood dishes and reasonable prices. Seaport Village, Harbor Dr. at Pacific Hwy. (235-4013).

Embarcadero – Another interesting place to walk. From the pier you can see the activities on North Island Naval Air Station across the bay and watch the hundreds of sailboats cruising. Navy ships are open to visitors on weekends, off the Broadway Pier.

Maritime Museum – The oldest square-rigged merchantman afloat, the 100-plus-year-old *Star of India* is berthed here, along with the turn-of-the-century ferryboat *Berkeley* and steam yacht *Medea*. Open daily. Admission charge. Broadway Pier at Harbor Dr. (234-9153).

LA JOLLA

Tidepool – La Jolla, an uncommercial beach 12½ miles north of San Diego, offers opportunities to observe marine life in a natural setting. Visit the tidepools just beyond Alligator Head at La Jolla Cove at low tide to see a veritable profusion of hermit crabs, anemones, and starfish clambering over one another. Make sure you wear tennis shoes — the jagged rocks can cut your feet. From San Diego, take Rte. 5 to Ardath Rd. exit. Take Ardath west until it becomes Torrey Pines Rd. Take

Torrey Pines west, turn right on Prospect and follow it to Coast Boulevard. Follow signs to La Jolla Cove.

Whale Point – If you visit La Jolla during December, January, or February, visit Whale Point. Every year the giant whales migrate south along this route. Since they've been doing this for the past 8 million years or so, we have no reason to believe they'll stop before you read this chapter. To get to Whale Point, follow the shore south from Alligator Head. Opposite the only large building on the beach, there's a small cove known as Seal Rock. From Seal Rock, you'll be able to see another cove, marked by a lifeguard stand and a wall. That's Whale Point.

La Jolla Museum of Contemporary Art – Dramatically situated near the beach, between Seal Rock and Whale Point, the gardens and building are well worth a look. You'll find paintings and sculpture from all over the world. A good place to contemplate art and nature. Closed Mondays. Free. Prospect and Silverado (454-3541).

Sea Caves – A natural formation of seven caves hollowed out by the waves. You get there by walking along the cliffs facing the ocean. To get to the caves, take Coast Boulevard to the tunnel leading to Coast Walk.

Scripps Institute of Oceanography – One of the most highly esteemed marine study institutes in the world. You can stroll through the grounds, or relax on the Scripps beach. You can't walk on the pier, but the Thomas Wayland Vaughn Aquarium Museum is open to the public. You can watch the fish being fed at 1:30 PM Wednesdays and Saturdays. Open daily. Free. La Jolla Shores Dr. (452-6933).

Torrey Pines State Reserve – In order to avoid crowding, admission is limited. Get there early. The strange-looking, bent pine trees, which are the outstanding feature, date back to the period when Southern California was a vast pine forest. On the northern side of the park, Los Penasquitos Lagoon offers a spectacular vantage point for watching blue herons and rare egrets. Mule deer come to the southern part of the lagoon to feed. Open daily. Admission charge. Torrey Pines Rd. (755-2063).

■ **EXTRA SPECIAL:** No tour of San Diego would be complete without a visit to *Mexico.* The bustling border city of *Tijuana* is just 17 miles south of downtown. Many visitors and residents drive there, park their cars on the US side of the border, and walk into Tijuana. (The Tijuana taxis are infamous for overcharging. If you refuse to pay, you can end up in jail.) San Diego's new trolley system is a good alternative to driving. The trip to Tijuana takes about 40 minutes and costs $1.50 each way. It's possible to hop on the trolley at various points along the route, but the trip originates at the Amtrak Terminal, C St. and Kettner Blvd., and terminates at San Ysidro (200 feet from the border). Trolleys leave the main stations (in either direction) every 15 minutes from 5 to 1 AM daily; tickets are purchased at vending machines at all pickup points. Tijuana has many crafts shops selling finely wrought ironwork, pottery, and jewelry. Prices are a fraction of what the same items cost in the US. You can bring back $400 worth of goods duty-free, once every 30 days. Goods must be declared at retail value at the checkpoint for reentering the US. (At press time, currency exchange regulations limited purchases and items allowed.) If you're driving into Mexico, it's wise to purchase insurance at one of the many insurance offices near the border. It will prevent you from unpleasant detention should you happen to have an accident. Conventional US auto insurance is *not* valid in Mexico. Tijuana also offers year-round thoroughbred racing, dog racing, jai alai, and bullfighting.

A short drive down a scenic toll road from Tijuana is *Ensenada,* a resort and fishing village. From Ensenada, the road stretches south to the most famous Mexican Pacific coast resort cities or to Baja California. No visas or tourist cards are needed for US citizens in the border areas. You do need a tourist card to travel south of Ensenada.

SOURCES AND RESOURCES

 TOURIST INFORMATION: The San Diego Convention and Visitors Bureau distributes brochures and maps. 1200 3rd Ave., Suite 824 (232-3101). There's a Visitor Information Center on E Mission Bay Drive off Rte. 5, Mission Bay (276-8200). If you want advance information, write: Mission Bay Lessees Assn., 1702 E Mission Bay Dr. For maps and brochures on walking tours of the historic district, stop at the visitors center at Old Town Plaza (237-6770).

Barry Berndes' The San Diegan (San Diego Guide; $1.95) is the most complete guide to the area; write to *The San Diegan,* PO Box 99127, San Diego 92109, or call 275-2213.

Local Coverage – *Evening Tribune,* evening daily; *Union,* morning daily; *Del Mar News-Press,* weekly.

Food – *Barry Berndes' The San Diegan.*

Area Code – All telephone numbers are in the 619 area code unless otherwise indicated.

 CLIMATE AND CLOTHES: Rainstorms are few and far between, and almost invariably occur in December, January, and February. During these months, the temperature might drop down into the high 40s at night, so bring a sweater. Daytimes are generally in the 60s. The rest of the year, you can expect bright days and cool evenings with daytime highs in the 70s, lows at night in the 50s. Bathing suits are de rigueur all year round.

 GETTING AROUND: Airport – San Diego International Airport is within sight of downtown. The cost of a cab ride between the airport and downtown varies but should run $6 or $7, $11 or $12 to Mission Valley. San Diego Tranxit (233-3004) bus #2 leaves from the airport every 20 minutes and runs along Broadway, downtown; fare, 80¢.

Bus – The San Diego Transit System operates frequent buses connecting downtown with the suburbs (233-3004).

Taxi – You can get a cab by calling Yellow Cab (234-6161); Radio Cab (232-6566); Checker Cab (234-4477); Co-Op Cab (280-2667).

Car Rental – The best way to see everything at your convenience is by car. All major national car rental firms are represented. For lower rates, try American International Rent A Car (234-8343).

Trolley – The San Diego Trolley is a new, inexpensive way to get around. There are pickup points throughout the city, but the line originates at the Amtrak Terminal, C St. and Kettner Blvd., and leaves every 15 minutes from 5 to 1 AM daily. Tickets are dispensed from machines at all trolley stops and cost from 50¢ to $1.50, depending on your destination, with discounts for senior citizens and the handicapped (231-8549).

 MUSEUMS: Balboa Park contains most of the city museums: the Timken and Fine Arts Galleries, Museum of Man, Aerospace Museum, Reuben H. Fleet Space Center, and Museum of Natural History. The Maritime Museum, Serra Museum, San Diego Union Newspaper Museum, Heritage Park, historic Old Town houses, and La Jolla Museum of Contemporary Art are given fuller descriptions in *Special Places. Palomar Observatory*'s giant telescope was, for many years, the most powerful in the world. It's still in use. Photographs of the cosmos are on display. Open daily. County Rd. S6, east of Escondido (742-3476).

MAJOR COLLEGES AND UNIVERSITIES: Scripps Institute of Oceanography (see *Special Places*) is only a part of the University of California at San Diego. The rest of the campus is at University City, La Jolla (452-2230). Other colleges and universities include: US International University, Pomerado Rd. (271-4300); San Diego State University, Alvarado Freeway (265-5200); University of San Diego, Alcala Park (260-4600); Point Loma College, 3900 Lomaland Dr. (222-6474); San Diego Community College District (junior colleges), 3375 Camino del Rio S (230-2000).

SPECIAL EVENTS: San Diego is a summer festival almost all year.

January: Andy Williams San Diego Open Golf Tournament, Torrey Pines Golf Course (272-0851; 276-6145); *Rugby Tournament,* Robb Field, 2525 Bacon St. (224-7581).

February: Indoor Games, Sports Arena, 3500 Sports Arena Blvd. (224-4176).

March: Kite Festival, Ocean Beach (223-1175); *La Costa Tennis Tournament,* La Costa Country Club, Costa del Mar Rd., Carlsbad (438-9111, ext. 431); *Pacific Coast Soaring Championships,* Torrey Pines Glider Port, La Jolla (457-9093).

April: San Diego Crew Classic, Bahia Point, Mission Bay Park (488-3642); *Jumping Frog Jamboree* (preliminaries for Calaveras County annual contest), Del Mar Fairgrounds (755-1161); *PGA Tournament of Champions,* La Costa Country Club, Costa del Mar Rd., Carlsbad (438-9111, ext. 431).

May: Fiesta de la Primavera, citywide.

June: Model Yacht Regatta, Model Yacht Basin, West Vacation Isle, Mission Bay Park (238-2140); *Annual Camp Pendleton Rodeo,* Camp Pendleton, Area 16 (725-4lll); *Shakespeare Festival,* Balboa Park (239-2255).

July: God Bless America Week; La Jolla Tennis Championship, 7632 Draper St. (459-9950); *Southern California Exposition,* Del Mar Fairgrounds (755-1161; 297-0338); *Jazz Festival,* San Diego Stadium (281-1330); *Festival of the Bells* to celebrate founding of the California missions (574-6300).

August: Annual celebration of *America's Finest City Week.*

September: Mexican Independence Day (15 and 16 September); *Cabrillo Festival* (293-5450); *Fiddle and Banjo Contests,* Frank Lane Memorial Park (765-0323).

October: Oktoberfest, La Mesa (469-4129); *Borrego Springs Desert Festival,* Borrego Springs (767-3114).

November: Starlight Yule Parade, Chula Vista (420-6602); *National Senior Hardcourt Tennis Championships,* La Jolla Beach and Tennis Club (454-7126).

December: Mission Bay Parade of Lights, from Quivira Basin to Sea World (276-2800).

SPORTS AND FITNESS: There's just about everything for everybody.

Baseball – The National League *Padres* (283-4494) play at San Diego's Jack Murphy Stadium, 9449 Friars Rd. (281-1330).

Bicycling – Hamel's Cyclery and Surf Shop, 704 Ventura Pl., Mission Beach (488-5050); California Bicycle, 633 Pearl St., La Jolla (454-0316); Wheels 'n Things, 2910 Navajo Rd., El Cajon (465-3976).

Fishing – The longest fishing pier on the West Coast is at Point Loma. There are also piers at Mission Bay, San Diego Harbor, and Shelter Island. You don't need a license, and there is no fee for pier fishing. For deep sea fishing, however, you do need a permit. Write to the California Department of Fish and Game Resources Building, 1416 9th St., Sacramento 95814. Marlin, yellowtail, and sailfish run in the spring. Seaforth Sportfishing offers day and overnight excursions, 1717 Quivira Rd. (224-3383).

Fitness Centers – San Diego Sports Medicine Center offers aerobics classes and workout equipment, 6699 Alvarado Rd. (287-4446); the YMCA has a pool and weight room, 1115 8th Ave. and C St. (232-5181).

Flying – You can rent a Cessna or take flying lessons at Gibbs Flite Center, Montgomery Field (277-0310).

Football – The NFL *Chargers* (280-2121) and San Diego State University *Aztecs* (283-7378) play home games at the Stadium, too.

Golf – For tournaments, see *Special Events,* above. Torrey Pines municipal golf course alongside the ocean is the site of the annual Andy Williams Open. It's also the most famous of the more than 60 public courses in San Diego County. Mission Bay Golf Course is lit up for night games, Mission Bay Park (273-1221).

Ice Skating – The House of Ice, 11001 Black Mountain Rd. off Mira Mesa Blvd. W (271-4001), has day and night skating.

Jogging – Run along Laurel Street to Balboa Park, where there are six different courses, ranging from less than ½ mile to 9 miles. It's possible to jog along Harbor Drive in the direction of the airport, but avoid rush hours because of the fumes. Mileage (8 miles' worth) is marked around Mission Bay. In La Jolla, run along the shore and boardwalk or the La Jolla cove.

Racing – Thoroughbreds race at Del Mar Race Track, July to September, I-5 to Fairgrounds exit (755-1141 or 299-1340), also at Caliente Race Track, Tijuana (260-0060; see *Extra Special*). Jai alai is played at Fronton Palacio, Tijuana, Fridays through Wednesdays (282-3636)

Sailing and Boating – The City Recreation Dept. rents motorboats and rowboats for use on lakes (236-5740). They also give sailing courses (488-1004). Seaforth Boat Rentals has sailboats, rowboats, and power boats as well as boats rigged for water skiing. They also rent fishing gear, 641 Quivira Rd., Mission Bay (223-1681). You can rent sailboats and take sailing lessons at Harbor Island Sailboats, 2040 Harbor Island Dr., Harbor Island (291-9568) and Vacation Village Boat Rentals, West Vacation Isle (274-4630).

Skiing – The Torrey Pines Ski Club organizes trips to nearby mountains. Write PO Box 82087, San Diego 92138

Surfing and Scuba Diving – La Jolla Cove is the most popular scuba diving spot because the water is particularly clear. Boomer Beach, so named because of the rumbling sound of surf crashing to shore, is the body surfers' first choice. Surfboarders ride the waves at La Jolla Shores.

Swimming – There are 70 miles of public beaches, not to mention Mission Bay Park's manmade lagoons. La Jolla and Torrey Pines State Park beaches are especially beautiful (see *Special Places*). There are ten municipal swimming pools: Kearney Mesa, Kearns Memorial Park, Vista Terrace, Swanson, King, Colina del Sol, Mission Beach Plunge, Memorial, Clairemont, and Allied Gardens. For information call the Aquatics Department of the City Recreation Office (270-3932).

Tennis – For special tennis tournaments, see *Special Events,* above. The best public courts are at La Jolla Recreation Center, 615 Prospect St. (454-2071). Others can be found at Morley Field, 2221 Morley Field Dr., Balboa Park (298-0920). Standley Park, 3585 Governor Dr. (452-8556); and Robb Field, 2525 Bacon St. (224-7581).

Whale Watching – You can watch the migrating sea mammals from Cabrillo National Monument, Whale Point in La Jolla, or you can take a whale-watching excursion from H & M Landing (222-1144) or Islandia Sport Fishing (222-1164). December, January, and February.

 THEATER: *The Old Globe Theater* stages Shakespearean festivals every summer. The Elizabethan theater reproduction housing the festival was destroyed in 1978 by an arson fire but has been rebuilt with public donations (239-2255). The rest of the year, the company performs at the next-door Cassius Carter Center Stage in modern musicals and dramas, Balboa Park (239-2255). *Mandeville Center* offers plays, dance concerts, and musical events by members of the University of California San Diego Campus and professional touring groups at Torrey

Pines Rd., La Jolla (452-2380). *Marquis Public Theater,* 3717 India St. (295-5694), does classics, modern, and experimental plays. For intimate cabaret-style musicals, *Coronado Playhouse,* 1775 Strand Way, Coronado (435-4856).

MUSIC: San Diego Convention and Performing Arts Center consists of three separate theaters. Symphony Hall (Fox Theater) is the new home of the *San Diego Symphony* (694-4200). The *San Diego Opera Company* performs at the Civic Theater. Golden Hall is the stage for big-name rock artists. Plaza Hall hosts trade expos and exhibitions like the annual antiques show. All at 202 C St. (236-6510). *California Ballet* does the *Nutcracker Suite* at Christmas, other classics the rest of the year, 8276 Ronson Rd. (560-5676). The *Ballet Society of San Diego* performs classics, too, at their home, 337 W Washington St. (299-9001). *San Diego Youth Symphony* also performs at Civic Theater (233-3232). Free organ concerts are played every Sunday afternoon at the Organ Pavillion, Balboa Park. For jazz, visit the *Catamaran,* 3999 Mission Blvd., Mission Beach (488-1081).

NIGHTCLUBS AND NIGHTLIFE: *The Halcyon* is a very popular disco in town at 4258 West Pt. Loma Blvd., Ocean Beach (225-9559). *Bali Hai South Pacific Room* has a Hawaiian nightclub act, 2230 Shelter Island Dr. (222-1181). *Bacchanal* has live music nightly throughout the week and is a popular spot with young singles, 8022 Clairemont Mesa Blvd. (560-8022).

SINS: You really can't blame San Diego residents for puffing up with *pride* over their city's sunshine, its space, its utter cleanliness, and its fantastic zoo (the best in the country); the city even has good restaurants, and *gluttony* thrives in Old Town State Park, a historic restoration of old San Diego where there are seven Mexican restaurants nearly side by side.

There are thorns in every paradise, however; and lest you overlook *lust,* you should be reminded of Lower Broadway, where virile young men fresh from the frustrations of the nearby naval base let themselves get worked up over a not particularly outstanding assortment of porn palaces.

LOCAL SERVICES: Babysitters – Baby Sitter Service, 4138 30th St. (281-7755); Reliable Babysitter Agency, 3435 Camino del Rio (298-0856)
Business Services – Economic Development Corp. of San Diego, 701 B St. (234-8484)
Mechanics – Tenth Avenue Garage, 843 10th Ave. (232-1428); Jimmy on the Spot Mobile service — he comes to you (560-1140)

■ **WHEN THE SWALLOWS COME BACK:** Yes, the swallows come back to Capistrano. Every year. Stop in at the Mission of San Juan Capistrano in March for a serenade. It's also open daily the rest of the year. Free. Follow Rte. 5 north for 47 miles to Capistrano exit (493-1111).

BEST IN TOWN

CHECKING IN: San Diego has some fine hotels and resorts, with outdoor athletic facilities and super views. Expect to pay $100 and up for a double at those places noted as expensive; between $60 to $80, moderate; about $50 at places listed as inexpensive. For B&B accommodations, contact Bed & Breakfast Directory for San Diego, PO Box 3292, San Diego, CA 92112 (619 297-3130).

The Westgate – A modern, deluxe, 225-room property considered among the finest in the US. Its location near the San Diego Convention Center makes it convenient as well. Consistent with the $1 million worth of antiques decorating the premises, the hotel also offers superb service. The *Fontainebleau Room* is one of the best restaurants in town (see *Eating Out*). 1055 2nd Ave. (619 238-1818). Expensive.

Inter-Continental – The new elliptical tower of the *Inter-Continental* rises 25 floors above San Diego Bay and the hotel's own 19-acre marina. Inside are 681 rooms and suites, a shopping arcade, and half a dozen restaurants and bars. Also on the premises are 4 lighted tennis courts and a large outdoor pool. 333 W Harbor Dr. (619 234-1500). Expensive.

Sheraton-Harbor Island – This 500-room resort and convention hotel has tennis courts, saunas, a swimming pool, and complete convention facilities. Harbor Island has more of the same. 1380 Harbor Island Dr. (619 291-2900). Expensive.

Half Moon Inn – On Shelter Island, overlooking the bay and the marina with all its sleek and shining boats. There are 137 luxury rooms, a pool, and it's within walking distance of boatyards and sport-fishing operations. 2303 Shelter Island Dr. (619 224-3411; 800 532-3737 in California; 800 854-2900 elsewhere). Expensive.

Hotel del Coronado – One of the world's most picturesque hotels. When it opened in 1888, it was the largest wooden building in the country and the first hotel in the world to have electrical lighting and elevators. Thomas Edison himself supervised the electrical installation. Today, this turreted, rambling, 339-room resort is such a landmark that the management offers tours on Saturday afternoons. Rooms in the historic building are regrettably less impressive than the exterior architecture, and there is a modern annex that's downright pedestrian. Then there are those early morning flights buzzing out of the naval air station. . . The nearby *Chart House Restaurant* is very good (see *Eating Out*). Two health clubs, two pools, tennis courts. On the Coronado Penninsula, 1500 Orange Ave. (619 435-6611). Expensive.

Town and Country – One of the best in Mission Valley. Its 1,000 rooms make this the largest hotel in the city. A popular convention hotel; facilities include pools, saunas, barber shop, beauty parlor, and 24-hour coffee shop. 500 Hotel Circle (619 291-7131). Expensive to moderate.

Torrey Pines Inn – A spectacular location overlooking the Pacific and right next door to the famous Torrey Pines Golf Course. Surfers and hang gliders are visible from the hotel windows, and La Jolla's beaches are just out the door. Swimming pool and lounge with entertainment on the premises. 67 rooms. 11480 Torrey Pines Rd., La Jolla (619 453-4420). Moderate to inexpensive.

EATING OUT: San Diego has a wide range of restaurants, the most prevalent menu items being Mexican and seafood. Two local chains are excellent — *Anthony's Fish Grottos* and *Chart House.* Expect to pay $55 or more at those places listed as expensive; $30 to $50, moderate; under $20, inexpensive. Prices are for a meal for two, not counting drinks, wine, or tips.

Anthony's Star of the Sea Room – One of the best on the West Coast. Overlooking San Diego Harbor, Anthony's serves fresh-from-the-ocean abalone, and other fish and shellfish. Their clams Genovese is often ordered as an entrée. Open daily except major holidays. Reservations required a day or two in advance. Major credit cards. Harbor Dr. at foot of Ash St. (232-7408). Expensive.

Top o' the Cove – Looking out onto La Jolla Cove, a favorite of show-biz types from LA. If you're in the mood for experimenting, order langosta con guacamole (lobster with avocado and mushrooms in white wine sauce). The restaurant is famous for its hot bread puffs. Closed Mondays and holidays. Reservations necessary. Major credit cards. 1216 Prospect St., La Jolla (454-7779). Expensive.

Prince of Wales Grille – Interestingly enough, this is where the Prince of Wales met the woman for whom he abdicated his throne. Grilled dishes are the specialty here. We suggest the crown roast rack of lamb — it's appropriately regal. Closed Sundays and holidays. Reservations required. Major credit cards. *Hotel del Coronado,* 1500 Orange Ave. (435-6611). Expensive.

Coronado Chart House – One of the chain. This one, in the *Hotel del Coronado*'s boathouse, has Tiffany lamps, antique tables, and a very friendly atmosphere. The view looks out at Glorietta Bay. Steak and lobster are served, and everything is charcoal broiled. Open daily. No reservations. Major credit cards. Near *Hotel del Coronado,* 1701 Strand Way (435-0155). Expensive.

Fontainebleau Dining Room – Waiters wearing white gloves quietly serve superlative Continental dishes such as veal with bay shrimp. The dessert cart is fabulous. One of San Diego's very best. Open daily. Reservations necessary. Major credit cards. *Westgate Hotel,* 1055 2nd Ave. (238-1818). Expensive.

Lubach's – For many years this was considered San Diego's best restaurant. Now, there are other contenders for the title, but *Lubach's* is still in the ring. Shrimp brochette and calf's sweetbreads financière highlight a menu which includes some fabulous beef and duck dishes. Closed Sundays and holidays. Reservations advisable. Major credit cards. 2101 N Harbor Dr. (232-5129). Expensive.

Butcher Shop – If, after the theater or other late activity, you crave a good steak, this is the place. The menu is actually a tray filled with the cuts of meat you can order. Meals are served until 1 AM. Open daily. Reservations advised. Major credit cards. 1515 Hotel Circle (291-8405). Moderate.

Nino's – Unpretentious surroundings and superior food. The deep-fried zucchini and eggplant are served as an appetizer with every meal. Follow that with spaghetti in butter and garlic and veal Fiorentina and you've got a meal to remember. Closed Mondays and Tuesdays. Reservations advisable. Major credit cards. 4501 Mission Bay Dr. (274-3141). Moderate.

China Camp – The cooking is not Chinese, but it's not quite American either. Specialties such as drunk steak, begger's hen, and immigrant beef are based on the recipes of the Chinese immigrants who came to California in 1849 to pan for gold. Open daily. Reservations advised. Major credit cards. Pacific Hwy. at Hawthorne (232-1367). Moderate.

El Chalan – If you've never sampled Peruvian food, this is a good place to start. Start with spicy ceviche, a marinated cold fish salad. You can follow it with papas rellenas — potatoes stuffed with meat, or pescado à la chorrillana, fish sautéed with garlic, onions, peppers and tomatoes. Closed Tuesdays. Reservations suggested. Major credit cards. 5621 La Jolla Blvd. (459-7707). Moderate.

Alfonso's – The Mexican dishes here are probably the most popular in town. Try carne asado Alfonso or one of the burrito or taco combination plates. Every dish comes with a marvelous house salad and bread baked in Mexico earlier that day. Ask for Alfonso's Secret — it changes every day, but it's not on the menu. Open daily. Reservations advisable. Major credit cards. 1251 Prospect St., La Jolla (454-2232). Inexpensive.

Aztec Dining Room – Another hit with aficionados. There are combination plates and five dinner plates, as well as standard à la carte tacos, chiles relleños, and enchiladas. The guacataco contains shredded beef, guacamole, and hamburger. Mexican beer is available. The atmosphere is informal and some outdoor dining is available. Open daily. No reservations necessary. No credit cards. 2811 San Diego Ave., Old Town (295-2965). Inexpensive.

Bit of Sweden – All you can eat — and then some — in a help-yourself smorgasbord. There are more salads than you can decently consume, and hot dishes that include roast beef, turkey, baked ham, Swedish meatballs, Swedish pancakes, and stuffed cabbage. Then there's dessert. Closed Mondays. Reservations advisable. No credit cards. 2850 El Cajon Blvd., East San Diego (284-7893). Inexpensive.

SAN FRANCISCO

"San Franciscans are the luckiest people on earth; they not only get a vacation with pay, they have San Francisco to come home to." A Chamber of Commerce press release? No, just the sentiments of one of the lucky ones, *San Francisco Chronicle* columnist Herb Caen, who, like most of its residents, is in love with this city. It is a characteristic of genuine San Franciscans, whether native or transplanted, that they simply can't hear enough praise of the place. And such is the nature of San Francisco that they are very rarely disappointed. A visitor commented on her last day in the city, "I feel sorry for children born here. How sad to grow up and find out the whole world isn't like this." And even Billy Graham has stated publicly that "the Bay Area is so beautiful I hesitate to preach about heaven while I'm here."

Any place that can give pause to Billy Graham must be a remarkably well-endowed piece of geography. And so San Francisco is. The city occupies a hilly peninsula of 47 square miles, shaped something like a slightly crooked thumb pointing northward. On its western border is the Pacific Ocean; to the east is huge, beautiful San Francisco Bay. The waters of the Bay join the Pacific through the narrow northern strait that Golden Gate Bridge spans so spectacularly. When the Bay fills with fog, as it often does, the bridge becomes a single strand of lights riding over clouds. By choosing an inland suburb or an area on the coast, residents can have either the Sun Belt warmth of California's eternal spring or the sharper, foggier weather bred along the shoreline.

Either way, the city's climate is universally desirable for walking, if you can handle the incredibly steep hills. Hidden lanes, small houses circled by picket fences and surrounded by large commercial buildings, stately Victorian façades, stunning murals and other public art, and historical plaques reward even a casual stroll. Grant Avenue provides a tour of Chinatown; Columbus, a glimpse of Italian North Beach and the birthplace of the Beat Generation; and Sutter, a taste of San Francisco's high fashion shops and art galleries.

More demanding is a climb up the city's hills. To live "uphill" in any part of town is more prestigious than downhill, and to live on a famous hill tops all. Nob Hill, original home of the railroad nabobs and now site of several of the city's luxury hotels, is a most elegant address, and Russian Hill has renowned views of the city and the Bay. Along Telegraph Hill's eastern side, Filbert and Greenwich streets create a series of steps that become wooden sidewalks fronting New England–style cottages, surrounded by gardens and filled with an impressive quiet.

For a city so generously festooned with views, vistas, and vantage points, San Francisco was a long time being discovered. Explorers seeking a northern strait and new lands, among them Sir Francis Drake and Juan Rodriguez Cabrillo, sailed up and down the California coast without spying the great, but hidden, inner bay. In 1769, a Spanish land expedition led by Gaspar de Portolá blundered onto San Francisco Bay on a trek north from Mexico. Their goal had been Monterey, and their excitement at discovering one of the world's finest natural harbors was exceeded only by their confusion. The discovery, once made, did not go unexplored. In 1775, another Spaniard, Juan Manuel de Ayala, sailed through the rugged portals that had hidden the bay for so long, and for the first time the full potential of the inlet was realized.

Soon after, the area was fully incorporated into Spain's American empire when Father Junipero Serra built Mission Dolores. San Francisco was an early center for the Pacific fur trade, and the 19th century brought New England whalers, Russian trappers, and, when gold was discovered at Sutter's Mill in 1849, nearly everyone else and his brother. By 1850, the population of San Francisco had grown from 900 to 56,000 — prompting Will Rogers to observe a century later that it was "the city that never was a town." (The population is 690,000 today.) Ten years after the gold strike, silver was found in the Comstock Lode, and San Francisco was caught in a second wave of prosperity that carried it to the end of the century. While Levi Strauss made a minor fortune providing Nevada miners with blue jeans, Leland Stanford, Charles Crocker, Collis P. Huntington, and Mark Hopkins financed the transcontinental railroad.

In many ways this uncompromising history influences the city's character today. The Gold Rush brought adventurers from around the world; they were violent, hard men, but they lived together with a certain graceless tolerance. The railroad brought Chinese into the city, and later came Japanese. Russians, Greeks, Mexicans, Filipinos, Scandinavians — all settled in larger and smaller communities around the city over the years. The result is an admirable harmony, and a kind of hodgepodge culture both pleasing and natural: In what other city is the longtime chef of the town's best pizza parlor Chinese? The basis for this culture is respect and tolerance among individual citizens. The city gives birth to new lifestyles, in part, because the civic body politic doesn't get choleric over diversity. It is a natural center of gay life, for example, and gays have been incorporated into the city's mainstream.

What is life like here? Consider this anecdote: In this city of hills, full buses occasionally have trouble negotiating the steepest inclines. A bus driver with a full load may be forced to stop before beginning ascent, to ask a few passengers to get off. Remarkably enough, some always do. This is an absolutely true story, but it is also a parable of sorts, a conundrum to contemplate when standing on Golden Gate Promenade. From there you will see the fine spires of the bridge, with the gold dome of the Palace of Fine Arts shining below, and in the distance, framing the picture, the blue Pacific. If that's not a sight worth getting off the bus for, you're just not resident material.

SAN FRANCISCO AT-A-GLANCE

 SEEING THE CITY: Coit Tower, on the summit of Telegraph Hill, offers a spectacular panorama of San Francisco and the surrounding area: to the north are the waterfront and San Francisco Bay, the Golden Gate Bridge, Alcatraz Island, and on the far shore, Sausalito; downtown San Francisco lies to the south; to the east are Berkeley and the East Bay hills; and Nob Hill and Russian Hill rise to the west. The tower itself, a 210-foot cylindrical column built in 1934 under the Work Projects Administration, is a striking landmark against the city's skyline. Open daily. Small admission charge. Follow Telegraph Hill Blvd. to the top from Lombard and Kearny sts. Twin Peaks is another excellent vantage point from which to view the city. Follow Twin Peaks Blvd. to the top. Several cocktail lounges offer fine views, too; the highest, at 779 feet, is the *Carnelian Room,* the restaurant and bar atop the Bank of America building. 555 California St. (433-7500).

 SPECIAL PLACES: San Francisco is a compact city and easy to get around. Most of the attractions are concentrated within a few areas, and the mild weather year-round makes walking pleasant. San Francisco Discovery Walks offers visitors a close look at the city's fine architecture, gardens, views, and Victorian interiors for $25, including lunch. Contact Fred Baumeister, 1200 Taylor St., #32 (673-2894).

DOWNTOWN

Civic Center – This seven-square-block area encompasses several attractive buildings and a nicely designed fountain and plaza. Among the buildings are City Hall, a notable example of Renaissance-style grandeur with a 300-foot-high dome; the War Memorial Opera House, site of the signing of the UN Charter in 1945 and current home of the San Francisco Opera and Ballet; the Civic Auditorium, scene of cultural and political events since 1915; and the Louise M. Davies Symphony Hall. The War Memorial Veterans Building houses the San Francisco Museum of Modern Art. Its fine permanent collections include works by Matisse, Klee, Calder, and Pollock, while changing exhibitions include works by internationally known modern and contemporary artists. Closed Mondays. Admission charge except Thursday nights. McAllister St. and Van Ness Ave. (863-8800). Bounded by Van Ness Ave. and Hyde, McAllister, and Grove sts., the Civic Center is also a good place to start the 49-Mile Drive, a well-marked trail that takes in many of the city's highlights. Just follow the blue, white, and orange seagull signs.

Union Square – Right in the shopping area, Union Square offers respite from the crowds of people in its throngs of pigeons. You can feed the pigeons, relax on the benches, watch the fashion shows, concerts, and flower displays that are held there in good weather. The elegant *St. Francis Hotel* is on the west side of the square, while the surrounding area contains sidewalk flower stands and the city's finest shops. (Gump's has a beautiful collection of jade pieces among its many rare imports; 250 Post St.) Bordered by Geary, Post, Powell and Stockton sts. (982-1616).

Bank of California Museum – Perhaps you've been wondering what makes those ticker-tape machines tick and what's really behind all the action. You'll find the answer while looking at the Gold Rush artifacts, the silver ingots, and the privately minted gold coins in this fine exhibition of western currency. Open weekdays from 10 AM to 2 PM. Free. 400 California St. (765-0400).

Wells Fargo History Room – The history room features more of Old California, with photographs and relics from Gold Rush days, and the Wells Fargo Overland Stage, the wagon that brought pioneers west, as well as coins from Mother Lode mines. Open weekdays from 10 AM to 3 PM. Free. 420 Montgomery St. (396-2619).

Embarcadero Center – This 8½-acre area, housing shopping malls and offices, between the financial district and the waterfront features several notable sculptures, including the Vaillancourt Fountain (100 abstractly arranged concrete boxes with water pouring out of the ends) and a 60-foot sculpture by Louise Nevelson. At noon, street merchants set up stalls and you can pick up a variety of handcrafted goods — leather items, jewelry, macramé, paintings, and sculptures. At the foot of Market St.

Chinatown – The largest Chinese community outside of the Orient, Chinatown is an intriguing 24-block enclave of pagoda-roofed buildings, excellent restaurants, fine import shops featuring ivory carvings and jade jewelry from the Orient, temples, and museums. Grant Avenue is the main thoroughfare — enter through an archway crowned with a dragon (Grant at Bush St.). Best to go on foot or take the California Street cable car, because the area is quite congested and difficult to park in. The Old St. Mary's Church, built in 1854 of granite from China, is the city's oldest cathedral. It survived the earthquake, perhaps because of its warning on the façade above the clock dial: "Son Observe the Time and Fly from Evil" (Grant Ave. and California St.). More words of wisdom, as well as regional artifacts, including tiny slippers used for the bound feet of Oriental ladies, pipes from Old Chinatown opium dens, and photographs of some famed telephone operators who memorized the names and numbers of 2,400 Chinatown residents in the old days, can be found at the Chinese Historical Society of America Museum. Closed Sundays and Mondays. Free. 17 Adler Pl. off Columbus Ave. (391-1188). For information on walking tours of Chinatown, contact the Chinese Cultural Foundation, 730 Kearny St. (986-1822), Tuesdays through Saturdays.

You haven't really experienced Chinatown fully until you've had dim sum, a brunch or luncheon feast of a variety of delicate morsels — chopped mushrooms in half-moons of rice dough, deep-fried sweet potato, meat dumplings; try either the original *Yank Sing,* 671 Broadway (781-1111), or the *Hong Kong Tea House,* 835 Pacific Ave. (391-6365). Bordered by Kearny, Mason, Bush sts. and Broadway.

North Beach – There is no longer a beach here, but this traditionally colorful neighborhood remains intact — mostly Italians, Basques, and Chinese. The area's great for strolling and eating — there are bakeries and bread shops selling cannolis, rum babas, marzipan, and panettone (a round, sweet bread filled with raisins and candied fruit). There are numerous restaurants and cafés where you can have dinner, espresso, or cappuccino. For lunch or dinner, the *Washington Square Bar and Grill,* 1707 Powell St. (982-8123), has great pastas, fresh fish, and veal as well as a popular bar. Or if you want to make it yourself, you can pick up noodle machines and espresso makers at *Biordi's,* 412 Columbus Ave. (392-8096). At night, the Broadway district offers everything from Italian opera and jazz to *Finocchio's,* 506 Broadway (982-9388), for its famous female impersonators. Day or night, *Enrico's Sidewalk Café,* 504 Broadway (392-6220), is perfect for sipping, snacking, and people-watching. One of the best times of year to visit North Beach is in early June, during the street bazaar, when local artists display their wares. Other times, numerous galleries and studios exhibit crafts, paintings, jewelry, and unusual clothing. Washington Square is a nice place to sit in the sun or have lunch with the paisanos under the statue of Benjamin Franklin (Columbus and Union sts). Extends north and northwest from Chinatown to San Francisco Bay.

Japan Center – This attractive modern complex is the focal point in culture and trade of San Francisco's substantial Japanese community. The 5-acre area contains the Kabuki Theater, teahouses, restaurants, sushi and tempura bars, art galleries, a school where you can learn Japanese dollmaking and flower arranging, and the Japanese consulate. The elegantly landscaped Peace Plaza with its five-tiered Peace Pagoda in the center of a reflecting pool is the scene of the April Cherry Blossom Festival and traditional Japanese celebrations, like the Mochi-Pounding Ceremony (in which much preparation and even more pounding result in delicious rice cakes). Speaking of pounding, the Kabuki Hot Springs' shiatsu massage, traditional Japanese baths, whirlpool, saunas, steam bath, and the works will make you feel good as a newly made rice cake (1750 Geary Blvd.; 922-6000). Bounded by Laguna, Fillmore, Geary, and Post sts.

FISHERMAN'S WHARF AND VICINITY

Fisherman's Wharf – This rambling waterfront section is at once the center of the commercial fishing industry and California's major tourist attraction, second only to Disneyland. On the wharf at Jefferson Street you walk through an open-air fish market where you can partake in an old San Francisco tradition. Buy a loaf of freshly baked sourdough bread at *Boudin's Bread Company* and create the ultimate urban picnic by adding Dungeness crab purchased at one of the numerous sidewalk stalls. The fishing boats return in the afternoon and hoist their crates of fish to the pier at the foot of Jones and Leavenworth sts. If you're up late (about 3 AM), there are few sights at that hour more impressive than the San Francisco fleet leaving the harbor for a day's catch. The wharf restaurants are often crowded and expensive, and you would do better to have a seafood dinner elsewhere (see *Eating Out*). But the wharf vicinity does have many sidewalk stalls selling handcrafted items, and interesting sights have sprung up around this fishing base. Among things to see:

Pier 39 – Reconstructed with wood salvaged from other (demolished) piers, Pier 39 is a new entertainment complex on the northern waterfront. A pleasant hour or two can be spent ambling through the plethora of shops — crafts, bakery, import, clothing, specialty, toy, jewelry, camera, fine food, crystal and silver, and many others. For lunch or dinner, there's an international roster of cuisines from which to choose — Mexican, Italian, Japanese, Chinese, Swiss, French, Polynesian; grab a bite at one of the numerous, stand-up, take-out fresh seafood booths; or simply indulge your sweet tooth at *Swensen's,* the famous ice cream parlor. Children can run off excess energy at the Pier's playground and park; weekend sailors and fishermen can charter boats at the marina. Pier 39, on the Embarcadero, just east of Fisherman's Wharf. (Parking garage across the way on Beach St.)

Balclutha – This British three-masted squarerigger, first launched from Scotland in 1886, had a long and full life as a trading ship, rounding Cape Horn 17 times to San Francisco carrying rice and wine, working as an Alaskan salmon trader, and even doing a stint in Hollywood as a rather oversized prop in sea films. Today *Balclutha,* restored by the San Francisco Maritime Museum Association, is open for public inspection. You can see the wheelhouse, the red-plush upholstered chart house, the captain's cabin, and the hull with its collection of sailing and Barbary Coast memorabilia. Open daily. Admission charge. Pier 43, Fisherman's Wharf (982-1886).

National Maritime Museum and Historic Park – This huge ship-shaped building is sure to catch your eye. The museum, now run by the National Park Service, is a treasure trove of photographs tracing shipping development from Gold Rush days to the present: figureheads, massive anchors, shipwreck relics, and beautiful model ships. Open daily. Free. At the foot of Polk St. (673-0797). Just north, along the Hyde Street Pier, is the Historic Park — five old ships, including the *Eureka,* the *Eppleton Hall,* and the *C. A. Thayer.* Open daily. Free. At the foot of Hyde St. at Jefferson (556-6435).

Bay Cruises – The Blue and Gold Fleet (Pier 39; 781-7877) and the Red and White

Fleet (Pier 43½, near Fisherman's Wharf, and Pier 41, near the *Balclutha;* 546-2810), cruise year-round past Alcatraz Island and the Golden Gate Bridge and then to the shoreline of Marin County rimming the Bay. Departures every day, all day, year-round. Admission charge.

Alcatraz Island – This famed escape-proof federal penitentiary stands out grimly in the Bay 1½ miles from Fisherman's Wharf. Such notorious criminals as Al Capone, "Machine Gun" Kelly, and Doc Barker never returned from their stays here. The prison was closed in 1963 because of exorbitant operating costs and has been open to the public since 1973. The National Park Service runs tours of the prison block, where you see the "dark holes" in which rebellious prisoners were confined in solitude, and the tiny steel-barred cells. Two-hour tours depart daily on a first-come, first-served basis; tickets may be purchased in advance through Ticketron. Departs from Pier 41 (546-2805).

Ghirardelli Square – Originally a chocolate factory, these stately red brick buildings now house import shops where you can find anything from Persian rugs to Chinese kites, outdoor cafés, art galleries, and fine restaurants. *The Mandarin* serves excellent Chinese food; *Maxwell's Plum* has a flashy setting and a stunning bay view; but perhaps sweetest of all is the *Ghirardelli Chocolate Manufactory* (771-4903), where you can watch chocolate being made and then eat the spoils afterward, and, if you're truly inspired, the Golden Gate banana split, which tops all — three scoops of ice cream, three flavors of syrup, and a banana bridge rising above mountains of whipped cream. Open daily. Bounded by Beach, Larkin, North Point, and Polk sts.

The Cannery – Similar to Ghirardelli Square, but canned fruits and vegetables were the products made here. Today this three-level arcade features chic boutiques and restaurants and an olive tree–shaded central courtyard where street musicians and mimes strut their stuff. Open daily. Bounded by Beach, Leavenworth, and Jefferson sts.

Lombard Street – Often referred to as the most twisting urban street in the world, Lombard St. has ten hairpin turns in a single block. Drive down slowly or, better yet, stroll, taking time to appreciate the lovely residential façades, colorful flowers, and lush plantings. Between Hyde and Leavenworth sts.

GOLDEN GATE — THE PROMENADE AND THE PARK

Golden Gate Promenade – This 3½-mile shoreline trail is among the most spectacular walks (or jogging paths) in America. You meander from Aquatic Park past lush green trees, eroding rocky points, a classy yacht harbor, a grassy park beside an old cobbled seawall, all the while approaching that ultimate of bridges, the Golden Gate. A number of interesting museums line the way. Fort Point, built in 1863 as the West Coast's only Civil War outpost, is now a National Historic Site. Free (under the bridge, 556-1693). The Presidio Army Museum, established in 1776 as a Spanish garrison, has artifacts from the Civil War and Spanish-American War. Closed Mondays. Free. Lincoln and Funston Ave. (561-4115). Most unusual is the Palace of Fine Arts, a grand Beaux-Arts building constructed for the Panama-Pacific Exhibition of 1915. It houses the Exploratorium, a collection of 400 displays on perception, which demonstrate just how deceiving the senses can be. Closed Mondays and Tuesdays. Admission charge for adults. 3601 Lyon St. (563-7337).

The Golden Gate Bridge – The loftiest and one of the longest single-span suspension bridges ever constructed. At the bridge, climb to the toll plaza for the view. From here you have several options: You can catch a bus back downtown; turn around, and walk back with the view of the city skyline accompanying you all the way; or follow in the footsteps of great coast trekkers across the Golden Gate Bridge and beyond — north along trails on the ridges and shoreline for 60 miles to Tomales Point. You can walk across the bridge (or under it); if you are driving, take the very first exit north of the bridge, park, and enjoy the terrific view of San Francisco.

California Palace of the Legion of Honor – A memorial for America's World War I dead, modeled after its namesake in Paris, this beautiful classic Greek building houses a fine collection of French art, particularly strong on Impressionist paintings by Monet, Manet, and Degas and Rodin sculptures. Closed Mondays and Tuesdays. Admission charge includes entry to the de Young Museum (see below). Lincoln Park (221-4811).

Golden Gate Park – Developed from 1,000 acres of rolling sand dunes, Golden Gate Park has all the amenities of a large recreation area. There are bike paths, hiking and equestrian trails, three lakes (where you can sail model boats, or rent real ones, or practice casting), sports fields, and a 25-acre meadow. The park also features a Rose Garden, a lovely Rhododendron Dell, the Strybing Arboretum — over 70 acres rich with 5,000 species of plants and trees from all over the world — and the Conservatory, a greenhouse with lush tropical growth. (Arboretum and Conservatory open daily. Free. Along South Drive and Conservatory Drive respectively.) The *Japanese Tea Garden* is a masterpiece of Oriental landscaping with a half-moon wishing-well bridge, a bronze Buddha, a temple, a teahouse serving jasmine and green tea, and, in the spring, magnificent blooms of cherry blossoms. Open daily. (Off South Drive just west of the de Young Museum.) No such lyrical setting could be complete without music, and the Music Concourse offers this with free open-air Municipal Band concerts on Sunday afternoons when weather is good (between the de Young Museum and the California Academy of Sciences). The park also has two fine museums:

M. H. de Young Memorial Museum – The West Coast's major art museum contains the Western world's finest Oriental collection. Donated by Avery Brundage, the wing contains Chinese jades, bronzes, ceramics, Japanese paintings, delicate lacquered woodwork, and art from India, Korea, and Southeast Asia spanning 6,000 years of Eastern civilization. Also, exhibitions of European and Classical works. American Galleries contain the extensive Rockefeller Collection of paintings and furniture. Closed Mondays and Tuesdays. Small admission charge. On the Music Concourse (221-4811).

California Academy of Sciences – The state's oldest scientific institution offers a wide variety of exhibitions ranging from the Steinhart Aquarium, with dolphins, piranhas, talking fish, penguins, and 14,000 other species, to the farthest reaches of space in the Morrison Planetarium's changing shows on black holes and UFOs. Open daily. Small admission charge. On the Music Concourse (221-5100).

Cable Car Museum – This lovely brick building is the powerhouse for the current system and the storehouse for cable car history. The first cable car, invented in 1873 by Andrew Hallidie, and exact scale models of cars servicing all the various lines are on display here at their middle stop. Open daily. Free. Washington and Mason sts., near Chinatown (474-1887).

San Francisco Zoo – The new Primate Discovery Center and Koala Crossing make a visit here more worthwhile than ever. More than 1,000 birds and animals can be viewed on foot or from aboard the motorized tour train. Adjacent to the main zoo is the Children's Zoo, a 7-acre nursery where children can stroke barnyard aniamls or watch baby lions being bottle fed. The spectacular primate center has dozens of exotic and/or endangered species as well as a sophisticated discovery center full of hands-on experiments and informative, fun-to-do computer/slide programs. Open daily. Admission charge. Sloat Blvd. and 45th Ave. (661-4844).

■**EXTRA SPECIAL:** Within an hour's drive of San Francisco (north along US 101, Rte. 37, then Rte. 21) is California wine country — the gently rolling hills of *Napa Valley* and *Sonoma County.* This major wine-producing region has numerous wineries, most of which are open daily for tours and tastings. The beautiful weather is accommodating not only for the vineyards but also for outdoor activity. Among the wineries, the most interesting to visit are Beringer Wines (St. Helena), where you enter the old hillside's aging tunnels and then attend a tasting in the Gothic Rhine House; the Christian Brothers (Mont LaSalle); and the Sterling Vineyard (south of Calistoga), with its striking Aegean-style architecture. You can pick up bread and cheese at one of the shops facing the Sonoma town square or along Highway 29 and head to Bothe–Napa Valley State Park (via Rte. 29), 1,000 wooded acres of broad-leafed trees, conifers, and redwoods, lovely for picnicking, hiking, and swimming. A few miles farther north is the town of Calistoga, home of the famous health spas and mineral baths, resorts, the interesting Napa County Historical Society Museum, and, best of all, an "Old Faithful" geyser, a 60-foot shower of steam erupting every 50 minutes.

SOURCES AND RESOURCES

TOURIST INFORMATION: The San Francisco Convention and Visitors Bureau, at 1390 Market St., is best for brochures, maps, general tourist information, and personal help. If you write ahead, it will send you a valuable package of information, including a three-month calendar of events. Call 391-2000 anytime for the lowdown on what's going on in town. Its downtown Visitor Information Center provides multilingual service. Powell and Market sts. (974-6900).

San Francisco at Your Feet by Margot Patterson Doss (Sunset Books; $5.95) is a good walking guide.

Local Coverage – *San Francisco Chronicle,* morning daily; *San Francisco Examiner,* evening daily. Sundays, the two publish a joint edition, including a comprehensive entertainment section, the Datebook.

Food – Check the *San Francisco Menu Guide* by Dan Whelan and Bella Levin (Danella Publications; $2.95) or *Restaurants of San Francisco* by Patricia Untermann and Stan Sesser (Chronicle Books; $7.95).

Area Code – All telephone numbers are in the 415 area code unless otherwise indicated.

CLIMATE AND CLOTHES: Daytime temperatures average 60° to 65° in summer and 45° to 57° in winter, so residents vary their springlike wardrobes of knits and lightweight woolens only slightly from season to season. In summer, morning and evening fogs make parts of the day very cool, so a jacket or sweater is a good idea. Traditional summery cottons are still useful outside the city, however, because while it is 65° in San Francisco, it can be in the 80s in the suburbs. In winter, a topcoat — preferably a lined raincoat (downpours are common between November and March) — should be adequate.

GETTING AROUND: Airports – San Francisco International Airport is about 16 miles south of the city, a 30-minute drive when it's not rush hour. Taxi fare from downtown to the airport should run about $20. Airporter (673-2432 or 877-0345) coaches leave from the airport and from San Francisco's Downtown Terminal (at Taylor and Ellis sts.) every 15 minutes and cost $6. Lorrie's (826-5950 or 800 762-2600) provides transportation to and from the airport for $8; a reservation is required 6 hours before pickup. SAMTRANS buses (761-7000) serve both the peninsula and downtown San Francisco (the Transbay Terminal at Mission and First sts.). Buses depart from the airport every half-hour during the day, hourly at night; the fare is $1.15. For more information on the airport's facilities, consult one of its teleguide terminals.

Oakland International Airport is a 20-minute drive from San Francisco's Financial District; cab fare should run about $30. Bus transportation into downtown San Francisco is provided by AC Transit (839-2882) for $1.50, and rail service via the BART system (464-6000) for $1.55. For airport information, call 444-4444.

Bus – Efficient and inexpensive buses serve the entire metropolitan area. Bus maps appear at the front of the yellow pages in the telephone book. For detailed route information contact MUNI (Municipal Transit) of San Francisco, 949 Presidio Ave. (673-MUNI).

Streetcar – Five lines of the MUNI Metro streetcar system run under Market Street, one level above BART, and branch off toward various parts of the city. For route information, call 673-MUNI.

Cable Car – The best way to travel up and over the hills of the city is aboard these famous trademarks; they are pulled along at 9½ miles an hour. There are three lines, and the most scenic is the Hyde Park line, which you can pick up at the turntable at Powell and Market sts. It will take you over both Nob and Russian Hills to gaslit Victorian Square. For route information call 673-MUNI.

BART – If you really want to move, this ultra-modern, high-speed rapid transit rail network will whisk you from San Francisco to Oakland, Richmond, Concord, Daly City, and Fremont at up to 80 miles an hour. The system is easy to use, with large maps and boards in each station clarifying routes and fares. For information, contact Bay Area Rapid Transit, 800 Madison St., Oakland (788-2278).

Taxi – Cabs can be hailed in the street or called on the phone. Major cab companies are Yellow Cab (626-2345); Veteran's Cab (552-1300); Luxor Cab (552-4040).

Car Rental – There are a few things to remember if you plan to drive in San Francisco: Cable cars and pedestrians always have the right-of-way; curb your wheels when parking on a hill to prevent runaway cars. The national firms all serve San Francisco.

 MUSEUMS: The city's major museums are all described in *Special Places*. Others are:

Archives for the Performing Arts – Weekdays; War Memorial Opera House, near Fulton and Franklin sts. (431-0717)

California Historical Society – 2090 Jackson St. (567-1898)

Mexican Museum – Wednesday through Sunday afternoons; Fort Mason Center, Bldg. D (441-0404)

 MAJOR COLLEGES AND UNIVERSITIES: Two of the country's most prestigious universities are near San Francisco: University of California at Berkeley, Sproul Hall, Berkeley (642-6000), and Stanford University in Palo Alto (497-2300). San Francisco State College, 1600 Holloway Ave. (469-2141), and the University of San Francisco, Golden Gate Ave. and Parker Ave. (666-6886), are in the city.

 SPECIAL EVENTS: The *Chinese New Year,* a week-long celebration in January or February (depending on the fullness of the moon) begins with numerous private observances — settling of debts and honoring of ancestors — and then Chinatown goes public with festivals that draw thousands to the streets for the colorful Dragon Parade featuring a block-long dragon, Miss Chinatown USA pageant, marching bands, and elaborate fireworks. To buy reserved bleacher seats, contact the Chinese Chamber of Commerce, 730 Sacramento St. (982-3000).

The *Cherry Blossom Festival,* held on two weekends in April at Japan Center (Post and Buchanan sts.; 922-6776), features traditional tea ceremonies, flower arranging and doll-making demonstrations, bonsai displays, and performances by folk dancers from

Japan. The crosstown parade highlights the events with over 50 Japanese performing groups and intricate floats of shrines and temples.

The *Grand National Livestock Exposition, Horse Show, and Rodeo*, held in late October and early November at the Cow Palace (6 miles south of city on Rte. 101), is one of the biggest events in the country with all manner of rodeo events, equestrian competitions, and the best livestock in the West.

SPORTS AND FITNESS: The San Francisco Bay Area has everything in professional sports.

Baseball – The San Francisco *Giants* play from April to October in Candlestick Park (467-8000). Gilman Ave., on the southern edge of the city on Rte. 101. The *Oakland A's* play at the Oakland Coliseum Stadium (638-0500).

Basketball – The NBA's *Golden State Warriors* play from October to March at the Oakland Coliseum Arena (638-6000).

Bicycling – Rent from Avenue Cyclery, 756 Stanyan, across from Golden Gate Park (387-3155). The park has good bike trails.

Fishing – Fine salmon fishing in the sea beyond the Bay. Season is mid-February to mid-October. Charter boats leave daily early in the morning and return in the afternoon. For information contact Captain Ron's Pacific Charters, 300 Jefferson St. at Fisherman's Wharf (771-2800). You can also cast off San Francisco's municipal pier at Aquatic Park, anytime. No license required.

Fitness Centers – Fitness Break, 30 Hotaling Pl. near Washington and Montgomery sts. (788-1681), has weekday aerobic workouts, mornings, noons, and evenings; showers and lockers available. The YMCA, 166 Embarcadero (392-2193), has a pool, sauna, and weight room, along with racquetball and handball courts.

Football – The San Francisco *49ers* play at Candlestick Park from August to December (468-2249). The USFL *Oakland Invaders* play at the Oakland Coliseum (352-9700).

Golf – There are fine courses at Golden Gate Park (751-8987), Lincoln Park (221-9911), and Harding Park (664-4690).

Horseback Riding – Rent from Golden Gate Stables, Kennedy Dr. at 36th Ave. (668-7360). Seven miles of equestrian trails wind through the park.

Jogging – Run along the Embarcadero to the Marina Green; jog back and forth across the Golden Gate Bridge (1½ miles each way) and enjoy the fore and aft views as well as the one directly below. Take the #5 bus, which stops on Market, out to Golden Gate Park, where there are numerous dirt and concrete trails, not to mention plenty of other joggers. (It's not recommended to run alone in the park).

Racing – For horse racing, Bay Meadows is the place, in San Mateo (574-7223). Seasons are: harness racing — last week of December through mid-February; quarter-horse racing — third week of February through the third week of May; thoroughbred racing — first week of September through the first week of February. In the East Bay, Golden Gate Fields features thoroughbred racing from early February through late June (526-3020).

Skating – Roller skating is very popular in San Francisco, especially in Golden Gate Park on Sundays, when traffic is detoured off the park's main roads. You can rent skates at the park entrance on Fulton and 10th sts., or from Aji Skates, 1269 Ninth Ave. at Lincoln (566-6700).

Swimming – Though much of San Francisco's waters are too rough and cold for swimming, Phelan Beach is good when the weather permits and the current is safe, at Sea Cliff Ave. and El Camino Del Mar (221-5756).

Tennis – Good public tennis courts are in Golden Gate Park on John F. Kennedy Dr. (478-9500, for reservations).

Yacht Racing – The Yacht Racing Association holds several races each year in San

Francisco Bay. Good observation points are the Marina and the Vista Point area on the north side of the Golden Gate Bridge (for information, call 771-9500).

 THEATER: The *American Conservatory Theater* is an excellent resident repertory company and performs classical productions and modern plays from October to June at the *Geary Theater,* 415 Geary St. (673-6440). The *Curran Theater* is best for musicals and often stages traveling Broadway productions, 445 Geary St. (673-4400). The *Orpheum Theater,* 1192 Market St. (474-3800), and the *Golden Gate Theater,* Golden Gate and Taylor sts. (775-8800) also feature Broadway shows. *Club Fugazi,* an old North Beach landmark, has camp productions in a nightclub setting, 678 Green St. (421-4222).

 MUSIC: The *San Francisco Opera Company,* featuring celebrated guest artists, performs at the War Memorial Opera House (Civic Center) from September to early December and again in summer (usually June and July). Since tickets are difficult to get, it's best to write in advance: War Memorial Opera House, Box Office, San Francisco 94102 (864-3330). The *San Francisco Ballet,* the country's oldest company and among the finest, moves into the Opera House with its *Nutcracker* production in December, followed by a repertory season from January through May (621-3838). The *San Francisco Symphony* season runs from September through May at Davies Symphony Hall in the Civic Center (431-5400), but the orchestra can be heard at other times, too, such as during its June Beethoven Festival or its July Pops Concerts in the Civic Auditorium. The *Midsummer Music Festival* is a series of free Sunday ballet, symphony, opera, jazz, and ethnic programs from mid-June to mid-August at Stern Grove, 19th Ave. and Sloat Blvd.

Tickets for most music, dance, and theater events can be obtained through BASS ticket centers (893-2277). In addition, half-price tickets to many events can be bought (cash or traveler's checks only) on the day of performance at the STBS booth on the Stockton Street side of Union Square, Tuesdays through Saturdays from noon to 7:30 or 8 PM (433-STBS for recorded information).

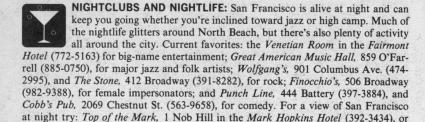 **NIGHTCLUBS AND NIGHTLIFE:** San Francisco is alive at night and can keep you going whether you're inclined toward jazz or high camp. Much of the nightlife glitters around North Beach, but there's also plenty of activity all around the city. Current favorites: the *Venetian Room* in the *Fairmont Hotel* (772-5163) for big-name entertainment; *Great American Music Hall,* 859 O'Farrell (885-0750), for major jazz and folk artists; *Wolfgang's,* 901 Columbus Ave. (474-2995), and *The Stone,* 412 Broadway (391-8282), for rock; *Finocchio's,* 506 Broadway (982-9388), for female impersonators; and *Punch Line,* 444 Battery (397-3884), and *Cobb's Pub,* 2069 Chestnut St. (563-9658), for comedy. For a view of San Francisco at night try: *Top of the Mark,* 1 Nob Hill in the *Mark Hopkins Hotel* (392-3434), or *Starlite Roof* in the *Sir Francis Drake Hotel* (392-7755).

 SINS: San Francisco is a beautiful city, but it also rates as one of the prime porno capitals of the world, where *lust* is easily satisfied. Here an enormous number of films are made as well as shown, and San Francisco's Broadway was one of the first places in the country to really develop an empire of topless bars and sleaze joints. But now, the nude female mud wrestlers, naked love dancers, and female impersonators share Broadway with little theaters and an interesting mix of restaurants, making the street a bit tamer than it once was.

LOCAL SERVICES: Babysitting – Bay Area Baby Sitters Agency, 758 San Diego Ave., Daly City (991-7474)

Mechanics – California Garage, for American cars, 1776 Green St. between Gough and Octavia sts. (474-0279). Foreign Car Repair, for imports, 6027 Geary between 24th and 25th sts. (752-8305)

BEST IN TOWN

CHECKING IN: President Taft called San Francisco the town that knows how, and though he probably wasn't talking about hotel accommodations, his statement applies. Accommodations range from ritzy Nob Hill to more modest downtown digs. Expect to pay from $120 to $150 and up for a double room in the expensive bracket; $60 to $80, moderate; and under $60, incxpensive. For B&B lodgings, contact American Family Inn/Bed & Breakfast San Francisco, PO Box 349, San Francisco, CA 94101-0349 (415 931-3083).

Stanford Court – Built on the site of 19th-century Governor Leland Stanford's mansion, in the tradition of Nob Hill elegance and with a touch of original flair, this may be the best hotel in the entire US. The drive-in courtyard is covered by a Tiffany-esque glass dome; the 402 rooms and suites have rattan furniture, canopied beds, etchings of old San Francisco, and private baths complete with miniature TVs and heated towel racks. The hotel's restaurant, *Fournou's Oven,* specializes in racks of lamb roasted over an oakwood fire and fluffy baked potatoes topped with golden caviar. Its well-stocked wine cellar features a tasting room and private wine bins where residents can store their personal favorites. You can have coffee or tea in the lobby bar or the fine café. 905 California St. (415 989-3500). Expensive.

Campton Place – A small luxury hotel in the European tradition, it opened in 1983 half a block north of Union Square. Its sumptuously decorated (if smallish) 125 rooms and suites offer extras such as armoires, writing desks, remote control TV, and a second telephone in the marble and brass bath. There's a roof garden for sunning and small receptions, and two conference rooms. On the lobby level, wonderfully innovative and impeccably prepared American cuisine is served at breakfast, lunch, and dinner in the *Campton Place Restaurant;* cocktails and coffee are available in the adjacent bar. Other amenities include concierge, telex, cable, and valet services. 340 Stockton St. (415 781-5555). Expensive.

Mark Hopkins – In the heights of extravagance at Number 1 Nob Hill, with some of the original gables and turrets of railroad magnate Mark Hopkins's 19th-century mansion, and a guest list that has included everyone from Haile Selassie to Frank Sinatra. Now operated by Inter-Continental hotels, the 400 suites and rooms feature either classical or contemporary decor, commodious baths and closets, possibly a grand piano (the Presidential Suite has one). The tower rooms have especially fine views, but the glass-walled *Top of the Mark* lounge is best for a 360° panorama of the city. The *Nob Hill Restaurant* serves noteworthy French cuisine, with outstanding lamb and duck dishes. For an elegant breakfast, including freshly baked Danish pastries, or for lunch, try *Café Vienna,* a brasserie on the arcade level. Open daily. 1 Nob Hill (415 392-3434). Expensive.

Fairmont – Just on the other side of the cable car tracks, but on Nob Hill neither side is the wrong one. Adjoining the distinctive old-fashioned main building is a modern tower topped by the *Fairmont Crown,* which serves lunch, dinner, and Sunday brunch. The facade is best known for its appearance on TV's *Hotel* series, and Mrs. Swig's old apartment is now America's largest and most expensive hotel suite. Among the other features are the *Squire Room* for Continental cuisine, the *Tonga Room* for Polynesian fare and dancing, *Mason's* restaurant, the ornate *Venetian Room* (closed Mondays) for supper and top name entertainment, the *New Orleans Room* for nightly jazz, the *Brasserie* for 24-hour coffee shop service, and the *Sweet Corner* for ice cream. 700 rooms and suites. California and Mason sts. (415 772-5000). Expensive.

Four Seasons Clift – A multimillion-dollar renovation has polished this traditional favorite to near perfection. An air of subdued elegance prevails, from the lobby sitting areas, reminiscent of an Edwardian salon, to the traditionally furnished guestrooms. No hotel in San Francisco provides friendlier service. The *Redwood Room* bar and lounge is a 1933 Art Deco original, paneled in redwood burl and set off with smart chandeliers, wall sconces, and Gustav Klimt prints. Its restaurant, the *French Room,* serves French cuisine in an innovative California translation, plus a menu of low-calorie, low-cholesterol, low-sodium alternatives, and it has an award-winning list of predominantly California wines. Many of the 332 rooms are unusually spacious, with color TV, extension phones in baths; gift shop, garage. Geary and Taylor sts. (415 775-4700). Expensive.

Huntington – One of the best values on Nob Hill, with an atmosphere of understated elegance. The 151 rooms are each distinctively decorated and comfortable, and many have good views. The *Big Four* restaurant (the name refers to the four Gold Rush millionaires) looks like a turn-of-the-century men's club and serves fish, chops, and steaks, plus a fillet of buffalo. *L'Étoile* is a fine French restaurant (closed Sundays). 1075 California St. (415 474-5400). Expensive.

St. Francis – A San Francisco landmark. Since 1904 this grand old hotel has entertained royalty, presidents, and international celebrities with its Old World charm. As a 75th birthday present, the *St. Francis,* now owned by the Westin chain, underwent a massive renovation and added the 32-story *Tower,* which keeps to the hotel's theme of red velvet, glimmering crystal, and polished rosewood. At the top of the *Tower* are *Victor's* restaurant, featuring nouvelle cuisine, and the chic *OZ* disco; both have lovely panoramic views of the city. The older sections of the hotel house the restaurants, cocktail lounges, and convention facilities. Union Square (415 397-7000). Expensive.

The Inn at Union Square – Four floors of tranquillity in the middle of downtown San Francisco, this stylish hotel has 30 rooms graced with Georgian antiques and brass fixtures, warm printed fabrics and pastel colors, down pillows and thick bathrobes. The penthouse suite has a sauna, whirlpool, and fireplace. Each day of one's stay here is punctuated with breakfast (in bed, if you wish), tea and cucumber sandwiches, and wine and hors d'oeuvres. 440 Post St. (415 397-3510). Expensive.

Donatello – One block west of Union Square, this elegant hotel offers 140 spacious rooms (including 9 suites), an atmosphere of serenity, and special touches such as live plants, terrycloth robes, complimentary local telephone calls, parking facilities, conference rooms, and a concierge. On the mezzanine level is a restaurant — also called *Donatello* — highly regarded for its North Italian cuisine. 501 Post St. (415 441-7100). Expensive.

San Francisco Suites on Nob Hill – A block down from the Big Four hotels atop Nob Hill, this former apartment building has been revamped into a combination time-share/hotel. Each of its 7 parlor suites and 9 one-bedroom suites is tastefully and thoughtfully decorated and outfitted with a stereo, bar, and kitchen. 710 Powell St. (415 433-9700). Expensive.

Hyatt on Union Square – Quite luxurious, quite elegant. The view from the lavish suites on the 34th floor is simply breathtaking. *Hugo's One-Up* is a top-floor restaurant and cocktail lounge, and *Nappers Too*, off the plaza deck, is popular for weekday lunches. 700 rooms. 345 Stockton St. (415 398-1234). Expensive.

Meridien – The epitome of commercial luxury, with a distinctly French atmosphere, this 36-floor, 700-room hotel is in the spruced-up South-of-Market area, just a block from the Moscone Convention Center. It features a fine restaurant, *Pierre*, whose consulting chef, Alain Chapel, owns a fabled three-star restaurant near Lyon. There is also a hotel brasserie, open from 6:45 AM to 11 PM. 50 Third St. (415 974-6400). Expensive.

Hyatt Regency – Inside this futuristically designed structure is an 18-story atrium lobby with all the activity of a three-ring circus, plus glass elevators that whisk you to the top, where a revolving bar looks out on San Francisco. The 803 rooms are attractive and modern, and the *Hyatt* offers all the amenities: convention facilities, shops, color TV, and, for a small extra fee, in-room movies. The lobby is particularly lively, with jazz concerts on weekend afternoons, big-band dancing on Friday evenings, and the Regency Strings nightly. Embarcadero Center (415 788-1234). Expensive.

Spreckels Mansion – Actually two adjoining 19th-century houses, offering 10 distinctive guest rooms furnished with French and English antiques, oversize brass beds, and eye-lingering views through leaded-glass windows. Fantasize about the days when Jack London frequented the place as you savor a sumptuous breakfast in bed or the late-afternoon wine hour. On a hill overlooking Buena Vista Park, at 737 Buena Vista (415 861-3008). Expensive.

Petite Auberge – Near Union Square but closer to the heart of France, this inn, complete with an antique carousel horse in the foyer, manages to be both rustic and elegant. A sweeping staircase (and a small elevator for the less athletic) leads to 26 rooms on five floors, furnished with French country antiques. Full concierge service is provided. Reserve a month or more in advance. 863 Bush St. (415 928-6000). Expensive.

Union Street Inn – This Edwardian inn in a chic neighborhood has 5 distinctly different guest rooms — all feature either a brass or a canopied bed and two have a private bath — plus a separate, quite lovely, and potentially very romantic carriage house. On pretty days, breakfast can be taken in the pleasant back garden. 2229 Union St. (415 346-0424). Expensive.

The Sherman House – This ornate, white 19th-century mansion, overlooking San Francisco Bay from Pacific Heights, has been transformed into one of the city's most luxurious small inns. Exquisite antiques, marble woodburning fireplaces, four-poster beds swathed in tapestries, deep window seats, wet bars, wall safes, TV and cassette systems, whirlpool baths, and down comforters are standard amenities in most of the 15 rooms and suites. One even has a large deck with a 300° bay view, and one of the three carriage house rooms has its own gazebo. Dining rooms look out on the bay and a formal garden designed by Thomas Church. Concierge, 24-hour room service. 2160 Green St. (415 563-3600). Expensive.

The Mansion Hotel – Better called the Fantasy Hotel, this Queen Anne–style historical landmark will provide a stay unlike any other, with larger-than-life murals of local personages on some walls, a pervasive pig motif (ask for the story behind this one) on others (*not* in the 16 bedrooms, fortunately), a nightly musical hour or magic show that features Claudia the Ghost on piano, and a huge dining room dwarfed by a backlit stained-glass window. Beyond (or despite) this, the food and service are excellent. 2220 Sacramento St. (415 929-9444). Expensive.

Victorian Inn on the Park – Known as the Clunie House, it was built in 1897 in honor of Queen Victoria's Diamond Jubilee and now has guests reserving two or three weeks in advance for one of its 10 bedrooms. Inlaid oak floors, mahogany woodwork, charming period pieces, a handsome oak-paneled dining room (which serves an excellent Continental breakfast), and a lavish parlor are only some of the drawing cards of this registered historic landmark. Across from Golden Gate Park, at 301 Lyon St. (415 931-1830). Expensive to moderate.

York – This hotel got its start during Prohibition, and in the 1950s it was the setting of Alfred Hitchcock's *Vertigo*. Now it's been renovated to sport a contemporary look, and all that remains of its colorful past is the *Plush Room* — once a speakeasy, now a nightclub with live entertainment. The 99 rooms all have a wet bar, and there is a gym and complimentary limousine service. No restaurant, but Continental breakfast and snacks are available. 940 Sutter St. (415 885-6800; in California, 800 327-3608; elsewhere in the US, 800 227-3608). Expensive to moderate.

Marina Inn – This bed-and-breakfast inn, as the place bills itself, has Italian marble floors, a crystal chandelier, and textured pastel wall coverings in the lobby; the rooms have antique beds in brass or wood and handwoven Peking rugs that set the color scheme for each room. Complimentary Continental breakfast is served in the sitting room, beer and wine in the parlor. 3110 Octavia at Lombard (415 928-1000). Expensive to moderate.

Galleria Park – An affordable European-style hotel in the heart of the shopping and financial district is just what the city needed. For starters, there's a 3rd-floor park, a jogging track, an Art Nouveau lobby, and an 8-story atrium. Other features, like a sundries shop, concierge, bar, and two restaurants (including *Bentley's* for fresh seafood), make this hotel quite impressive for the price. 177 rooms (with refrigerators) and 20 suites. 191 Sutter St. (415 781-3060 or 800 227-4248). Moderate.

Lombard – Built in 1925, this 99-room hotel has recently undergone an extensive facelift that, ironically, evokes the past — in this case, the elegant turn-of-the-century hotels in London. The main public room has a fireplace, piano, and marble floors, and hand-etched glass doors open into the high-ceilinged lobby. Complimentary limousine service, a redwood sun deck, and a restaurant, the *Gray Derby*, are among the amenities. 1015 Geary St. (415 673-5232; in California, 800 327-3608; elsewhere in the US, 800 227-3608). Moderate.

Canterbury – Plenty of charm if you don't mind the downtown street noise. In the lobby there is a grandfather clock, a terrarium, two aquariums, and lots of human life as well — most on its way to or from *Lehr's Greenhouse,* a tropical garden restaurant with good shrimp Créole, a salad bar, and very popular Sunday brunch. 250 rooms. 750 Sutter St. (415 474-6464). Moderate.

Washington Square Inn – Within walking distance of Ghirardelli Square and Chinatown. Only 15 rooms, each individually decorated, in a turn-of-the-century house in the North Beach area. Three rooms overlook Washington Square Park and are more expensive. 1660 Stockton St. (415 981-4220). Moderate.

Cartwright – An efficiently run 114-room hotel with sparkling clean and cheerfully furnished rooms and very reasonable prices. The new *Town and Country Room* serves breakfast and lunch. Continental breakfast is also available through room service. 524 Sutter St. (415 421-2865). Moderate.

Andrews – This recently renovated Victorian building retains some original brass fixtures and beveled glass windows plus a sense of old-fashioned hospitality in its 48 rooms. Wicker trays are available on each floor for carrying Continental breakfasts back to the room. The *Post Street Bar and Café* off the lobby serves California favorites at lunch and dinner. 642 Post St. (415 563-6877). Moderate.

Beresford – For European charm at a reasonable price. Old-fashioned service, a writing parlor off the Victorian lobby, flower boxes in the street windows, and pleasant rooms. The *White Horse* tavern uses fresh vegetables from the hotel's garden, and fish caught by its own boat (open for breakfast and lunch only). 112 rooms. 635 Sutter St. (415 673-9900). Inexpensive.

EATING OUT: The city has over 2,600 restaurants serving every kind of ethnic fare, seafood, and over 50 kinds of hamburgers. Many of the restaurants are well-known institutions; some, like *Trader Vic's,* have branched out across the country while leaving their very best cooks in San Francisco. Our restaurant selections range in price from $75 or more for a dinner for two in the expensive range; $50 to $75, moderate; $25 or less, inexpensive. Prices do not include drinks, wine, or tips.

Campton Place Restaurant – In the *Campton Place Hotel* but a legitimate magnet for diners in its own right. A relatively small room, decorated in soft shades of rose and gray, with a menu that is an outstanding example of American dishes done to perfection — without excessive fuss or fanfare. Breakfast, lunch, and dinner are served daily, and each is marvelous. Reservations at least a week in advance are a must. Major credit cards. 340 Stockton St. (781-5555). Expensive.

Trader Vic's – The late Victor Bergeron traveled far and wide to procure recipes and concoctions for his flagship San Francisco restaurant. The atmosphere is as homey as a South Seas paradise: lush jungle foliage, Polynesian batiks, spears, and big-game trophies and skins won by the Trader himself. After one drink (sip one of the tropical rum concoctions), try bongo bongo soup (cream of puréed oyster), Malay peanut chicken, breast of peach blossom duck, or barbecued double pork loin luau-style. The service is good, and if you're having trouble deciding, the waiters offer informed suggestions. If you really want to penetrate the heart of things, try to make reservations for the Captain's Cabin, a favored meeting place of the city's social set. Open daily. Reservations. Major credit cards. 20 Cosmo Pl. (776-2232). Expensive.

Le Club – This intimate French restaurant tucked away in a ritzy Nob Hill apartment house treats all guests elegantly whether they're regulars or first-timers. The atmosphere is that of a fancy private club, with two small dining rooms and a handsome mahogany bar. The French chef renders any classic French dish in addition to house specialties. Closed Sundays and major holidays. Reservations required. Major credit cards. 1250 Jones St. (771-5400). Expensive.

Ernie's – Perhaps the best known name on the local scene. Dining here is a leisurely affair, so you have plenty of time to enjoy the atmosphere — Victorian yet tasteful. Traditional French dishes have been replaced by nouvelle cuisine. Open daily. Reservations required. Major credit cards. 847 Montgomery St. (397-5969). Expensive.

Maurice et Charles Bistro – A half-hour north of San Francisco in San Rafael is this very popular bistro-style restaurant with scrumptious food. Try the wild boar with chestnut purée or duck breast in green peppercorn sauce. Closed Sundays and Mondays. Reservations. Major credit cards. 901 Lincoln Ave., San Rafael (456-2010). Expensive.

Masa's – Although the famous chef Masa Kobayshi died in 1985, his namesake restaurant, now headed by his protégé Bill Galloway, still ranks as one of the city's finest. Masa was a master of perfect presentation, extravagant sauces, and creative combinations, and Galloway has carried on that tradition. Open for dinner only Tuesdays through Saturdays, 6 to 9 PM. Reservations are essential; call at least 3 weeks in advance. Visa and MasterCard only. 648 Bush St. (989-7154). Expensive.

The Mandarin – A Chinese palace with thick beamed ceilings, a delicate cherrywood lotus blossom carving, Mandarin antiques and embroideries — and excellent Chinese food which you watch being barbecued in the Mongolian fire pit. To be set up in style, call owner and hostess Madame Cecilia Chiang a day in advance and order the Mandarin duck (a whole duck prepared with scallions and plum sauce), beggar's chicken, sharkfin soup, or anything she may recommend. Open daily. Reservations advised. Major credit cards. 900 North Point, in Ghirardelli Square (673-8812). Expensive.

Chez Michel – Here you'll find French cuisine in a chic but casual setting. The brass bar is stunning, the wooden tables are topped with fresh flowers daily, and the ceiling is brightly canopied. *Chez Michel* has nightly specialties that are all wonderfully prepared by their Swiss chef. Closed Mondays. Reservations recommended. Visa and MasterCard. 804 North Point (771-6077). Expensive.

Maxwell's Plum – The San Francisco branch of the New York landmark; perhaps the most elaborately decorated restaurant in the country. Stained glass, ornate crystal chandeliers, a rocking disco complete with a fabulous in-wall fountain, all on a site overlooking San Francisco Bay and the Golden Gate. The menu ranges from hamburgers to haute cuisine, and the desserts are a special treat. Open daily. 900 North Point, Ghirardelli Sq. (441-4140). Expensive to moderate.

California Culinary Academy – Primarily involved in teaching classic French cuisine to prospective chefs, the public is invited to sample the students' creations. Sumptuous four-course dinners are served Mondays, Tuesdays, Wednesdays, and Saturdays. We gluttons prefer the Thursday and Friday night buffets — especially the table littered with more than 40 desserts. Open weekdays for lunch and dinner; dinner only on Saturdays. Reservations required. Major credit cards. 625 Polk St. near Turk (771-3500). Moderate.

Hayes Street Grill – In a city famous for its seafood, this is one of the best seafood restaurants it has to offer. Everything is fresh, nothing is overcooked, and there is always a long list of daily specials. Along with great sourdough bread and an unusually good crème brulée for dessert, it is a quintessential San Francisco dining experience. Open for lunch and dinner weekdays; dinner only on Saturdays. Reserve at least a week in advance. Visa and MasterCard only. 320 Hayes St. (863-5545). Expensive to moderate.

Modesto Lanzone's – Two things are magnificent here — the view of the Bay and the pasta. Modesto, who's around all the time, makes sure that everything's up to par. And so it is — the agnolotti (rounds of dough stuffed with chicken and covered with cream), cannelloni, fettuccine, and gnocchi (pasta made with potato and flour). Closed Mondays. Reservations. Major credit cards. Two locations: 900 North Point in Ghirardelli Square (771-2880); Opera Plaza, 601 Van Ness (928-0400). Expensive to moderate.

Rosalie's – One of the most exciting new restaurants in the city, it is almost as popular for its southwestern-influenced food as for its decor. Aluminum palm trees soar toward the 40-foot ceilings; each wall is a different bold color. The lunch and dinner menus, which feature wildly imaginative salads and appetizers as well as more traditional veal, fish, and chicken dishes, change monthly. Open daily. Reservations advised. Major credit cards. 1415 Van Ness Ave. (928-7188). Expensive to moderate.

Yoshida-Ya – This stunning Japanese restaurant is known for its excellent yakitori — a selection of meats, fish, and vegetables, all marinated, skewered, and grilled over charcoal. Upstairs and weekends are less crowded. Open daily. Reservations suggested. Major credit cards. 2909 Webster at Union (346-3431). Moderate.

Jack's – A landmark for nearly as long as San Francisco has been on the map. Because of its location in the financial district, many visitors don't know about it and its excellent American and French food. All the grilled entrées are recommended, but the banana fritters with brandy sauce are unbeatable. The decor is unpretentious, as are the prices (particularly the dinner special), and the service is good. Open daily. Reservations necessary. No credit cards. 615 Sacramento St. (986-9854). Moderate.

Tadich's Grill – San Francisco's oldest restaurant (since 1849), and still going strong with what clientele maintain is the freshest seafood in town. Best bets: baked avocado with shrimp diablo, rex sole, salmon, sea bass. Don't pass up the homemade cheesecake for dessert. Closed Sundays. No reservations. No credit cards. 240 California St. (391-2373). Moderate.

Maye's Original Oyster House – The other traditional seafood favorite in San Francisco. After 100 years, owned by the same family using the same secret recipes for broiled calamari, baked creamed crabmeat, and poached salmon in egg sauce. The decor's also original, though there's not much to it (large leather booths). Open daily. Reservations suggested. Major credit cards. 1233 Polk St. (474-7674). Moderate.

MacArthur Park – Fresh seafood, barbecued steaks and spare ribs, and a good California wine list. Open daily. Reservations advised. Major credit cards. 607 Front St. (398-5700). Moderate.

Schroeder's – Fast, friendly service and large portions of good German food: sauerbraten, potato pancakes, sausages, German beer, and, for dessert, its famous apple strudel. Closed weekends. Reservations advised. American Express. 240 Front St. (421-4778). Moderate.

Fog City Diner – A sleek chrome and neon restaurant with a creative approach toward food called American dim sum — an array of American-style (from Cajun to Tex-Mex) appetizers that are meant to be passed around the table — which include deep-fried catfish fingers and Buffalo chicken wings. Entrées for diners who prefer a plate to themselves range from spicy chicken adobo to homemade sausage with polenta. Like any self-respecting establishment that calls itself a diner, *Fog City* has milkshakes, hamburgers, and similar fare, but even these are done differently. Open daily for lunch and dinner. No reservations. Major credit cards. Third and Folsom sts. (546-6297). Moderate.

Le Central – For a variation on the Continental theme, a brasserie-style restaurant with bright lights, brick walls hung with French art and the menu written on mirrors and blackboards. Food is in the best brasserie fashion: cassoulet (navy beans simmered with sausages, duck, pork, and lamb), choucroute Alsacienne (sauerkraut cooked in wine with bacon, pork, and sausage), and saucisson chaud (thinly sliced sausage with hot potato salad). Closed Sundays. Reservations advised for lunch and dinner. Major credit cards. 469 Bush St. (391-2233). Moderate.

Empress of China – The Szechwan, Hunan, and Cantonese dishes served here are tasty (Peking duck is the house specialty), and the rooftop garden adds spectacular views to the dining experience. Open daily. Reservations advised. Major credit cards. 838 Grant St. (434-1345). Moderate.

Rings – A tiny, straightforward café of the kind locals try to keep to themselves. House standards include dishes such as chicken breast marinated in orange juice and achiote; the ever-changing list of specials might have corn, pepper, and goat cheese frittata or grilled king salmon with honey-pepper glaze. Open for lunch weekdays; for dinner Tuesdays through Saturdays. Reservations accepted for parties of five or more only. Visa and MasterCard. 1131 Folsom St. (621-2111). Moderate to inexpensive.

Garibaldi Café – An intimate dining room tastefully decorated in high-tech neon and an equally tasteful, clever kitchen make this restaurant a standout. Specialties such as roast pork loin stuffed with apricots and veal-stuffed tortellini in a creamy Champagne pesto, change daily, but they're always excellent. Open for lunch weekdays; for dinner Tuesdays through Saturdays. Visa and MasterCard. 17th and Wisconsin sts. (552-3325). Moderate to inexpensive.

Far East Café – Don't let the neon-lit exterior fool you — inside there are ornate Chinese lanterns and private, curtained booths. The extensive Cantonese menu features all the old classics and, if you call in advance, an excellent family banquet. Open daily. Reservations suggested. Major credit cards. 631 Grant Ave. (982-3245). Inexpensive.

Pier 23 – With all the charm of an authentic waterfront dive but with food that makes up for the absence of fancy surroundings. A perfect lunch stop for weary Fisherman's Wharf sightseers. The menu generally features a few fresh seafood specials, such as crab salad with lemon basil dressing, as well as regular items like Mexican-style quesadillas stuffed with cheese and walnuts. Open for daily for lunch and Sunday brunch only. Near Fisherman's Wharf (362-5125). Inexpensive.

David's – Cheese blintzes with sour cream and jam, stuffed cabbage, gefilte fish with challah, chicken liver with schmaltz, or hot pastrami on Siberian soldiers' bread. And if you really can't get enough, you can move in — adjoining the restaurant is David's hotel, where guests receive a 10% discount on all meals. Open late daily. No reservations. Major credit cards. 474 Geary St. (771-1600). Inexpensive.

La Rondalla – Christmas decorations are left in place all year at this usually festive corner "Mexicatessen." A mariachi band makes Saturday nights particularly lively. Beyond all the tinsel is good, hearty food, and specials like the beef dishes and chile relleños are deserving of the name. Closed Mondays. Reservations only for ten or more. No credit cards. 901 Valencia St. (647-7474). Inexpensive.

Magic Pan Restaurant – For late supper or brunch, featuring hearty soups, avocado or melon salad, and crêpes filled with ratatouille, creamed chicken, beef bourguignon. Best of all is the Southern praline crêpe, with vanilla ice cream, spiced whipped cream, toasted pecans, and hot praline sauce. There's also a spacious bar up front. Open daily. Reservations advised. Major credit cards. 341 Sutter St. (788-7397). Inexpensive.

The Hippo – More variations on the good old American hamburger than there are states in the Union. Open daily. No reservations. Major credit cards. Van Ness Ave. at Pacific (771-3939). Inexpensive.

Buena Vista – This saloon has built its reputation on Irish coffee — which some say is the best in the world — and an extensive imported beer selection. The diverse clientele comes to drink, be merry, and then eat. Food, although a secondary consideration, is very good here and ranges from steak and veal to hot dogs and enchiladas; breakfasts are a treat and are served all day. Community tables are half the fun. Overlooks the bay with views of Alcatraz and Marin County. Open daily. No reservations. No credit cards. 2765 Hyde St. (474-5044). Inexpensive.

Caffè Trieste – A relaxed and homey place that is a popular early morning hangout. Customers start the day with strong Italian coffee and fresh sticky pastries. Around noon, the clientele comes to eat simple meals — quiche, sandwiches — or simply linger over cappuccino. Impromptu operatic arias are sung by the Giotto family on Saturday afternoons, and you can buy fresh coffee beans at the next-door annex. Open daily. No reservations. No credit cards. 601 Vallejo (392-6739). Inexpensive.

Isobune – At this sushi and sashimi restaurant there's counter service only — but what counter service! Japanese-style wooden boats glide by bearing all sorts of Japanese wonders, and customers take what they want. Each dish contains two or three pieces of sushi and costs from $1 to $2. The tab is figured by counting plates. Count on a worthwhile wait. Open daily. No reservations. Visa and Master-Card. 1737 Post St. (563-1030). Inexpensive.

SANTA FE

The Pueblo Indians had a village on the site of Santa Fe several centuries before Europeans settled in the New World. According to legend, they called the town "the dancing ground of the sun," an apt description of a splendid setting. The city sprawls across a 7,000-foot-high plateau in the middle of the vast sagebrush-swept southwestern desert. To the east rise the massive, forested peaks of the Sangre de Cristo mountains, and to the west, those of the Jemez Mountains. The sky is a shimmering turquoise blue and the air, clear and dry. Sunlight, which is dazzling in intensity, dominates the perspective, casting ever-shifting patterns of light and shadow across the monumental landscape.

The ancestors of the Pueblos, the Anasazi people, settled in this area thousands of years ago. Anthropologists are uncertain of their origins, but the Pueblos believe they came from an underworld beneath the earth's surface. This place was dark, ugly, and damp, and they struggled to get out. After many vicissitudes, they finally emerged through the earth's navel onto the land and into the light. The point of emergence is represented by a small opening, or *sipapu,* constructed in the sacred underground ceremonial chambers called *kivas,* which are still found in pueblos today.

The Spanish established modern Santa Fe a decade before the Pilgrims landed at Plymouth Rock. In contrast to the English settlers, who came to America to escape poverty and religious persecution at home, the Spanish came to the New World to reshape it in the image of the Old. Their interests were, quite simply, God, gold, and glory; however, their settlement here was a serious miscalculation. La Villa Real de la Santa Fe de San Francisco, the Royal City of the Holy Faith of St. Francis, yielded little gold or glory, and the Pueblos took to the Spanish ways of worshiping God in only limited and frustrating ways. When Spanish demands and oppression became too great, the Indians rose up in the Pueblo Revolt of 1680, when they burned most of Santa Fe and drove the Spanish away. They did not return until twelve years later, and even then the Reconquest, led by Don Diego de Vargas, was bloody and many Indians were killed. Although the Palace of the Governors was intact and the walls of the San Miguel Mission were standing, everything else had been razed. The Spanish colonists had to rebuild Santa Fe totally, using construction concepts borrowed from the Pueblos. Many of these early-18th-century structures have survived to the present.

The frontier period of Santa Fe life, which began in 1821, with the opening of the Santa Fe Trail, had less influence on the city than the Spanish, but looms large in America's mythology of the West. At its peak of activity, trade on the Santa Fe Trail employed 10,000 men a year and grossed millions of dollars. When American traders reached Santa Fe at the end of the 70-day journey from Missouri, they poured into the gambling halls that lined the

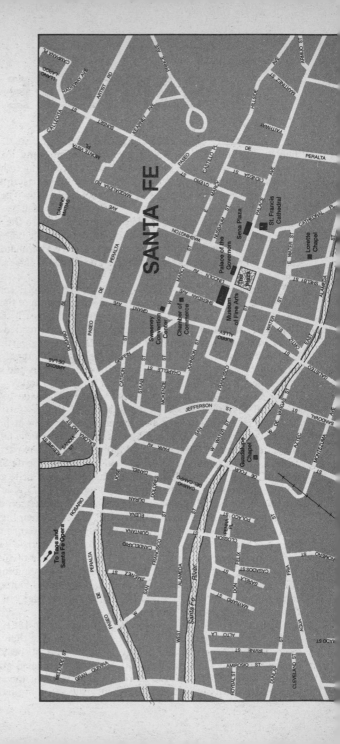

plaza to drink, play monte, and dance fandangos with lavender-scented senoritas in black veils. The trail made Santa Fe a natural target for the US Army in its march westward to fulfill the country's Manifest Destiny. In 1846 General S. W. Kearny seized the city from Mexico, and two years later the Treaty of Guadalupe Hidalgo was signed, giving the territory of New Mexico to the US. Santa Fe at first resisted then gradually adapted to the change.

Shortly thereafter, a new breed of settler began to arrive from the East. Anthropologists came here to continue the work of Adolph Bandelier, a Swiss scholar of international reputation who lived in Santa Fe in the 1880s. Bandelier's studies of the Pueblos stimulated considerable interest in North American prehistory. By the first decade of the 20th century, the anthropologists had established Santa Fe as a research center for Indian culture and had initiated a successful campaign to preserve the city's historic adobe architecture as well.

They were energetically assisted in their preservation efforts by the painters and writers who settled in the area beginning around 1910. These artists, attracted by the serenity and primitive charm of New Mexico and by the quality of its light, were the single most important outside influence on the city in this century. Through them, Santa Fe became nationally known as an art colony, where young artists were developing new techniques as well as working in traditional styles. The Museum of Fine Arts was founded with the philosophy that any local artist might exhibit his work there.

The leading figures of the first decade were Robert Henri and John Sloan, both of whom continued to live mainly in New York, though Sloan maintained a summer home in Santa Fe for more than 30 years. In the 1920s, Mabel Dodge Luhan moved her radical salon from New York City to Taos, bringing such visitors as the English novelist D. H. Lawrence and the early American modern painters Max Weber, John Marin, Georgia O'Keeffe, Marsden Hartley, and Andrew Dasburg. Two of Luhan's guests, O'Keeffe and Dasburg, stayed in the area and became legendary presences. Georgia O'Keeffe, who lived in Abiquiu, was known for her elemental New Mexico landscape paintings. Andrew Dasburg, who settled in Taos, once compared the pureness of the light to that in the Garden of Eden. Seldom given to understatement, D. H. Lawrence wrote that "the moment I saw the brilliant, proud morning shine high up over the deserts of Santa Fe, something stood still in my soul and . . . the old world gave way to a new." And Marsden Hartley claimed the area was the only place in America where true color exists. For these artists, and for anyone who cares to linger, Santa Fe remains, as the original settlers knew it, "the dancing ground of the sun."

SANTA FE AT-A-GLANCE

SEEING THE CITY: Visitors with lots of time and stamina should hike the trail up Tesuque Peak (12,040 feet) from the Aspen Vista Picnic Area. The trailhead is on the paved road to the Santa Fe Ski Basin, a drive that also provides fine views for those who prefer to stay in the car.

SPECIAL PLACES: The downtown area of Santa Fe is very compact and can easily be explored on foot. A car would be helpful for visiting the museums on Camino Lejo or for taking day trips to Taos, Acoma, and other nearby places of interest.

The Plaza – The plaza has been the center of Santa Fe life for almost four centuries, ever since the day in 1610 when mounted Spanish soldiers in medieval armor first used it as a parade ground. Throughout the centuries the plaza has been the scene of the most important public events in the city: markets, fiestas, proclamations, parades, and even, at one time, bullfights. An obelisk now marks the center of the lovely, tree-shaded square. Along the footpaths emanating from the obelisk are benches where weary shoppers rest, sightseers fiddle with their cameras, and office workers enjoy picnic lunches. The Palace of the Governors dominates the north side of the square; the three other sides are lined with shops, restaurants, and galleries.

Palace of the Governors – Erected in the first year of Spanish settlement, it's the oldest government building in the US and has been occupied by more than 100 Spanish, Mexican, and American rulers. Originally, all of the palace was made of mud except the roof beams, or vigas. The walls, then as now, were adobe. The dirt floor was mixed with animal blood to pack it and produce a sheen. Even the roof above the vigas was simply several feet of mud until relatively recent times. As late as the 1880s, one US territorial governor complained that the "rafters, as rain-stained as those in the dining hall of Cedric the Saxon, and overweighted by tons and tons of mud composing the roof, had the threatening downward curvature of a shipmate's cutlass." Today the palace houses historical exhibitions for the Museum of New Mexico, which makes it a natural starting point for a tour of the city. The museum shop has a small but interesting collection of Indian crafts as well as many books on the subject. Closed Mondays during the winter. The Plaza (827-6483).

Museum of Fine Arts – Next door, moving west from the palace, is this museum, which features changing exhibitions of work by various southwestern artists. The contrast between the two buildings is a striking comment on the architectural continuity and integrity of the city. Completed in 1917, some 300 years after the palace, the museum was a successful effort to combine traditional adobe design and materials with modern comfort and efficiency, and it became a model for the architectural style that still dominates Santa Fe construction. Closed Mondays during the winter. W Palace Ave. (827-4455).

Sena Plaza – To the east of the palace is Sena Plaza, a charming, tree-shaded and flower-brightened courtyard surrounded by the four wings of the 19th-century Sena hacienda. The 33-room adobe structure is now divided into shops and offices. E Palace Ave.

St. Francis Cathedral – Directly across Palace Avenue, this structure built between 1869 and 1886 is the legacy of the French bishop Jean Baptiste Lamy, the most influential person in local history and the subject of Willa Cather's *Death Comes for the Archbishop.* The Romanesque style of the building is, like many of Lamy's ideas, imported and a little out of place. Its most interesting feature is the adobe chapel that existed here before the cathedral, most of which was incorporated into the larger structure built of local quarry stone. In continuous use since 1718, the chapel is dedicated to La Conquistadora (Our Lady of the Conquest), protector of the early Spanish settlers. The carved wooden statue of La Conquistadora, said to be the oldest madonna in North America, was brought here from Mexico by the Spanish in 1625. Cathedral Pl.

Barrio de Analco – The Santa Fe River is as slow, irregular, and inexpedient as the town it crosses, yet because it was the main source of water in the early days, almost all the homes were built along it. Noting how the town followed the path of the river, one 19th-century visitor described Santa Fe as "three streets wide and a mile long."

Many of the old homes on the narrow streets in the Barrio de Analco (as the quarter on the other side of the river was called) have been preserved, particularly on East De Vargas. Although these homes are still private residences, visitors can stroll by for a look.

"Oldest House" – The foundations of this structure are thought to have been laid by the Pueblo Indians in the 13th century, although the tree rings in the ceiling beams only date to about 1750. However accurate the claim to be the "oldest house in the US," the western portion of this structure is in fact a good example of primitive adobe construction. Most early Santa Fe residents had similar dwellings, with low log ceilings, dirt floors, thick mud walls, and a corner fireplace for heating and cooking. 215 E De Vargas.

Chapel of San Miguel – This chapel is as old as the Palace of the Governors. Originally built in 1610-12, it was practically razed by the Pueblo Indians in the 1680 Revolt. When the Spanish rebuilt it in 1710, they covered over what remained of the earlier walls, placed the windows up high, and added adobe battlements to the roof. The most prominent feature of the interior is a fine old reredo, or colonial Spanish altar screen, made in 1798. Most of the paintings on the altar screen were done in Mexico in the 18th century. Old Santa Fe Trail and De Vargas St.

State Capitol – A bit south of San Miguel's Chapel is this unusual structure, intended by architects to evoke a Pueblo kiva (the ceremonial chamber in which religious rites are performed). Old Santa Fe Trail.

Canyon Road – One of the most romantic and picturesque streets in the US, it's also the oldest still in use; it was well established as a Pueblo trail long before the Spanish arrived. By the 18th century, residents were building adobe homes and cultivating farms along Canyon Road, which follows the river east from downtown. Sections of some of the current buildings date from that period, and the style of the street's architecture was established in a way that has not changed substantially since. In the early 20th century, Canyon Road became the center of the Santa Fe art colony. Though few artists can afford to live here today, the street is still zoned for "residential arts and crafts," limiting its use to galleries, studios, restaurants, and homes. It's an ideal place to see both the residential character of the old city and the latest work of Santa Fe artists.

Cristo Rey Church – Built in 1940, this church was designed by architect John Gaw Meem in classical Spanish mission style. Nearly 200,000 adobe bricks were used in its construction, all made from soil on the site — the traditional practice. One of the largest adobe structures in existence, it was scaled to house the most famous piece of Spanish colonial art in New Mexico, an ornately carved stone reredo, commissioned in 1760. Upper Canyon Rd.

■**EXTRA SPECIAL:** Santa Fe is the best place in New Mexico (and perhaps in the entire Southwest) to shop for *Indian art:* jewelry, pottery, weavings, paintings, kachina dolls, beadwork, and baskets. As you travel, even a cursory browse will quickly reveal that Indian art can be very expensive: Pueblo pottery may cost several hundred dollars, while Navajo rugs can run into the thousands. We recommend that you begin by visiting the area's museums — the Indian Pueblo Cultural Center in Albuquerque as well as the Wheelwright Museum of the American Indian and the Laboratory of Anthropology in Santa Fe. They all display the very distinctive work produced by the various tribes and you'll soon learn to recognize the traditional patterns and techniques each one employed. You'll also become familiar with the names of certain families or individuals who have become well known for a particular style. The museum shops at the Indian Pueblo Cultural Center, the Palace of the Governors, and the Wheelwright Museum (called the Case Trading Post) all carry fine Indian art as well as numerous books on the subject. They are also usually attended by salespeople who are willing to part with a few pointers about how to tell the real from the fake (some cheaper, imitation crafts are imported from Mexico), what's special about the pieces they carry, and how to care for what you buy. In addition to the museum shops, there are a number of stores and galleries along the plaza and elsewhere in the city that sell Indian art. Among those to look for are: *Cristof's* (106 W San Francisco), *Dewey-Kofron Gallery* (74 E San Francisco), *Kiva Trading Post* (57 Old Santa Fe Trail), *Mudd-Carr Gallery* (924 Paseo de Peralta), *Packard's Indian Trading Co.* (61 Old Santa Fe Trail), *Santa Fe East* (200 Old Santa Fe Trail). It's also possible to visit the several pueblos in the area — Jemez, Zia, Santa Clara, San Ildefonso, Acoma, Zuni, Taos — to buy pottery and jewelry directly from the Indians. Two final bits of advice: Buy what you like when you see it; each piece is handmade and unique and if you hesitate, you will not find it elsewhere. Also, be prepared with lots of cash because many stores — not to mention Indians, who sell from their living rooms — seldom take credit cards.

SOURCES AND RESOURCES

TOURIST INFORMATION: The Santa Fe Chamber of Commerce can provide a map and a limited range of free tourist information, 200 W Marcy St. (983-7317). For a free copy of the Santa Fe Visitor's and Convention Bureau's *Visitors Guide,* call 800 528-5369. A better but more expensive alternative is the newsstand at *La Fonda Hotel* (100 E San Francisco), just off the plaza, which carries all available guides and major works of fiction and nonfiction about the area. For a lively literary introduction to the city and vicinity, pick up Willa Cather's *Death Comes for the Archbishop* and John Nichols's *The Milagro Beanfield War.*

Local Coverage – *The New Mexican* is published daily; look at Friday's Pasatiempo section for information on events of the coming week. Do not, however, rely on the paper for restaurant recommendations.

Area Code – All telephone numbers are in the 505 area code unless otherwise indicated.

CLIMATE AND CLOTHES: Santa Fe's climate is shaped by both the Rocky Mountains and the southwestern desert. The sun is usually shining, the air is very dry, and the sky is very clear and turquoise blue. During the day, the air temperature always feels warm, even when there's snow on the ground, although as soon as the sun sets the air cools quickly. The average daily temperature in the summer is about 80° and about 40° in the winter. Dress is generally informal.

GETTING AROUND: Although it's the state capital, Santa Fe does not have a major airport. Visitors usually fly into Albuquerque International Airport, about 70 miles south, and then either rent a car or rely on the bus service provided by a firm called Shuttlejack (243-3244, or 982-4311 from Santa Fe). Departures are from the east end of the airport approximately every 2 hours; the trip costs $15 and takes about 80 minutes.

There is no public transportation in Santa Fe, and although the downtown area is small enough to see enjoyably by foot, you'll need a car to visit the farther-flung points of interest.

Car Rental – All the major car rental agencies are represented at Albuquerque airport. Cars may be rented in Santa Fe after arrival, but the rental offices can be scattered and rather inconvenient. *Avis* has an office at *Inn of the Governors,* 234 Don Gaspar (982-4361), and *Hertz* at 855 Cerrillos Rd. (982-1844).

Taxi – The cab companies in Santa Fe are fairly new and small and operate in sync with the city's slow pace. There is no central taxi stand, but you might call 24 Hour Taxi, 215 S El Rancho (982-9990).

 MUSEUMS: The Palace of the Governors and Museum of Fine Arts are described in *Special Places.* Also of interest are the following, all of which are on Camino Lejo, just off the Old Santa Fe Trail:

Laboratory of Anthropology – An extensive collection of Pueblo and Navajo artifacts dating back many centuries (827-8941).

Museum of International Folk Art – One of the finest collections of folk crafts from around the world (827-8350).

Wheelwright Museum of the American Indian – Indian arts and artifacts (982-4636). *Note:* The Case Trading Post downstairs sells high-quality and award-winning Indian pottery, jewelry, and weavings.

 MAJOR COLLEGES AND UNIVERSITIES: College of Santa Fe, St. Michael's Dr. (473-6011); St. John's College, Camino de Cruz Blanca (982-3691).

 SPECIAL EVENTS: Summer is the performing arts season, with cultural events staged by the Santa Fe Opera, the Santa Fe Chamber Music Festival, and the British American Theatre Institute nightly in July and August. The annual *Indian Market* is held the third week in August in the plaza; at this very popular juried event, Indians from the surrounding pueblos sell a wide variety of crafts — jewelry, pottery, sand paintings, weavings, kachina dolls, and so on. The *Fiesta de Santa Fe,* celebrated the weekend after Labor Day, originated in 1712. It opens with the ritual burning of a 40-foot puppet, called *Zozobra,* representing Old Man Gloom. After two days of parades, dancing, eating, and partying, the fiesta ends with mass at St. Francis Cathedral. The pueblos near Santa Fe have very different but equally interesting fiestas and other celebrations; the Santa Fe Chamber of Commerce (983-7313) usually has information about the ones visitors are allowed to attend.

 SPORTS AND FITNESS: Camping and Hiking – For maps and advice about the Santa Fe area, write to the US Forest Service, PO Box 1689, Santa Fe, NM 87501, or call 988-6940. For information about the Bandelier National Monument, write to the Superintendent, Bandelier National Monument, Los Alamos, NM 87544 (672-3861). Also refer to the book *Day Hikes in the Santa Fe Area,* published by the local chapter of the Sierra Club.

Fitness Centers – Courthouse and Spa of Santa Fe, 1931 Warner Ave. (471-5011); Tom Young's Racquet Clubs and Nautilus Fitness Centers, 1601 St. Michael's Dr. (988-4446) and at two other locations.

Horse Racing – The season at the *Downs,* just south of the city on I-25, extends from early May to Labor Day, with races on Wednesdays and weekends (471-3311).

Jogging – The most pleasant run is along the Santa Fe River, on Palace Avenue or Canyon Road. A more strenuous route is up Bishop's Lodge Road, into the Tesuque valley.

Skiing – Northern New Mexico usually has good powder from mid-December until early March and sunny spring skiing for several weeks after that. The *Santa Fe Ski Basin* is close, moderate in size and challenge, and relatively uncrowded (982-4429). Advanced skiers often prefer the long, steep runs at the *Taos Ski Valley,* 1½ hours away (776-2291).

Tennis – There are 32 courts in nine locations around town (984-6500, for information). Nonguests are sometimes allowed to use (for a fee) the courts at the *Bishop's Lodge* and *Rancho Encantado* hotels.

THEATER: The *British American Theatre Institute,* a project of the National Theatre of Britain, stages small-scale, experimental summer productions at the Greer Garson Theatre on St. Michael's Dr. (473-6511).

MUSIC: The *Orchestra of Santa Fe* performs at the Lensic Theatre downtown (988-4640) from October to May; in February the orchestra performs a *Bach* or *Mozart Festival,* alternating composers every year. In July and August the *Santa Fe Chamber Music Festival,* widely recognized for its posters reproducing the work of Georgia O'Keeffe, takes place at the St. Francis Auditorium in the Museum of Fine Arts on W Palace Ave. The 7-week festival begins in early July and features eminent artists from around the world (983-2075). The internationally acclaimed *Santa Fe Opera* offers lavish, adventuresome performances in a dramatic outdoor theater from early July to late August (982-3851). For details on lectures and backstage tours, call 988-7089. The theater is on Hwy. 84/285, about 8 miles north of town.

NIGHTCLUBS AND NIGHTLIFE: Santa Fe is not known for its throbbing nightlife; the summertime arts festivals can be exciting, but for the most part, it's a pretty quiet town. There are, however, some diversions. Maria Benitez, one of the world's great flamenco artists, dances most summer nights at the *Sheraton de Santa Fe,* (982-5591). Live music (usually rock) and dancing can be found at *Club West,* 213 W Alameda (982-0099). If you're not up for dancing, consider soaking at *Ten Thousand Waves,* a Japanese bathhouse in the mountains with communal and private hot tubs, Ski Basin Rd. (982-9304).

SINS: Exuberant public sin died out about a century ago, as the railroad displaced the Santa Fe Trail. Opportunities for today's visitors are pretty much limited to *gluttony* at the dinner table, *avarice* at the racetrack, and *envy* of those who live here.

BEST IN TOWN

CHECKING IN: Santa Fe sees a tremendous influx of visitors every summer, so it's best to book well in advance. Expect to pay up to $200 a day in the hotels listed in the expensive category, $60 to $90 in moderate, and under $50 in inexpensive. The resorts characterized as expensive are closed in the winter; during this time the rates for the others drop between 10% and 25%.

The Bishop's Lodge – Originally the retirement home of Bishop Lamy in the late 19th century, this comfortable hotel has its own stables and breakfast horseback rides, tennis courts, pool, and sauna, trap and skeet shooting range, and an all-day program for children. The tariff includes three meals a day, with ample buffets of American and Continental food and a steak fry on Friday nights. Open April to November. Bishop's Lodge Rd. (505 983-6377). Expensive.

Rancho Encantado – The "Enchanted Ranch" is a gracious small resort in the Tesuque hills. Within the original adobe buildings are Santa Fe–style rooms, the most attractive in the area, with fireplaces, *vigas,* Indian rugs, and hand-painted tiles. Recently built condominiums can also be rented: one or two bedrooms, with living and dining rooms as well as a kitchen. The ranch offers facilities for a range of outdoor activities, such as horseback riding, tennis, archery, and swimming. Open April through December. Rte. 22 in Tesuque, 8 miles north of Santa Fe (505 982-3537). Expensive.

La Posada – A few blocks from the plaza, this southwestern inn is spread out over 6 landscaped acres. The center of the complex is the Staab House, a Victorian home dating from 1882 that's been tastefully converted into a good restaurant and a popular lounge. Rates depend on the size and charm of the room, some of which are fairly conventional and some romantically southwestern, with adobe fireplaces, vigas, and Indian rugs. 330 E Palace (505 983-6351). Moderate.

La Fonda – A Santa Fe landmark just off the plaza, it's less notable for service than for a striking appearance and historic character: Though the present hotel was built in 1920, an inn called *La Fonda* has existed on this site since the opening of the Santa Fe Trail, almost 200 years ago. The rooms are best described as Spanish colonial rustic, while the restaurant *La Plazuela*, in a pretty enclosed courtyard, is worth a look. 100 E San Francisco St. (505 982-5511). Moderate.

The Inn at Loretto – The exterior of this modern hotel near the plaza is distinctively Spanish Pueblo in style, although the rooms are quite standard, with no surprises. It's named for the historic spot it occupies, that of the old Loretto Academy, established in the 1850s by Bishop Lamy and the Sisters of Loretto. 211 Old Santa Fe Trail (505 988-5531). Moderate.

Grant Corner Inn – One of several small bed-and-breakfast inns recently opened in old homes in the downtown area. This one may be the nicest, with 9 comfortable rooms and a terrific breakfast. 122 Grant Ave. (505 983-6678). Moderate.

Preston House – Another good bed-and-breakfast option downtown. Two of the 5 rooms have fireplaces. 106 Faithway (505 982-3465). Moderate to inexpensive.

El Rey Inn – This is the best bargain in town for Santa Fe charm; if it were downtown (instead of on motel row), prices would at least double. Many of the individually decorated rooms have adobe fireplaces, vigas, and tile murals; some are solar heated and overlook a garden. 1862 Cerrillos (505 982-1931). Inexpensive.

EATING OUT: Expect to pay $30 or more for a meal for two (without drinks, wine, or tip) in a restaurant listed below as expensive; between $15 and $25 at moderate; and around $10 or $15 in inexpensive.

The Compound – Santa Fe's best known restaurant may no longer be depended upon to deliver consistently excellent meals on every occasion, but the (Continental) food served usually is very good and there's a fine wine list. Housed in a converted 19th-century hacienda, the eatery also provides a delightful dining environment. Jackets required for men. Closed Mondays. Reservations necessary. American Express. 653 Canyon Rd. (982-4353). Expensive.

The Periscope – Although lunch is available Tuesdays through Saturdays, dinner is only served here on Saturday nights, and these seven-course extravaganzas — featuring dishes from around the world — are always carefully prepared and usually delicious. Reservations necessary. No credit cards. 221 Shelby (988-2355). Dinner expensive; lunch moderate.

The Pink Adobe – One of the city's best restaurants for many years, "the Pink" (as it's known) features an unusual menu that includes steak, Créole dishes, and New Mexican specialties. Try the steak Dunnigan, with green chile, or the chicken enchiladas with green chile and sour cream. Reservations necessary. Major credit cards. 406 Old Santa Fe Trail (983-7712). Expensive to moderate.

Victor's Ristorante Italiano – This is the place to go for good Italian food served in an attractive southwestern setting. The antipasto is filling, the pastas are made with skill and dedication, and one house specialty, braciole falso magro (beef stuffed with prosciutto, egg, and pine nuts, braised in a wine sauce), is unusual for Santa Fe. Open daily. No reservations. Major credit cards. 423 W San Francisco St. (982-1552). Expensive to moderate.

La Tertulia – The classiest of the city's restaurants serving New Mexican cuisine, housed in a converted convent. The native dishes tend to be mild but tasty, and the homemade sangria is excellent. Closed Mondays. Reservations necessary. Major credit cards. 416 Agua Fria, near Guadalupe (988-2769). Moderate.

Shohko Cafe – One of several Japanese restaurants that have become very popular in Santa Fe, it offers what must be the only green chile tempura in the world. The rest of the menu includes more traditional dishes — sukiyaki, teriyaki, and so on – - and there's a large, crowded sushi bar. Closed Sundays. Reservations advised. Major credit cards. 321 Johnson St. (983-7288). Moderate.

Rancho de Chimayo – Generally agreed to be the best New Mexican-style restaurant anywhere, it's in an old adobe hacienda about 25 miles north of Santa Fe. The drive, the setting, and the food are all delightful. Those who especially like hot dishes should try carne adovada, pork cooked in red chile. The flan (custard with caramel syrup) may be the area's best. Closed Mondays in winter and most of January. Major credit cards. Reservations necessary. Rte. 4 in Chimayo (351-4444). Moderate to inexpensive.

Josie's Casa de Comida – A rare example of a dying breed — the small, plain, downtown luncheon café. The chile rellenos, enchiladas, and other regional dishes are terrific, and the more standard American lunches are pretty good, too. *Josie's* is so popular that people will line up and wait patiently on the street for a table. Lunch only. Closed weekends. 225 E Marcy St. (983-5311). Inexpensive.

The Shed – It's the most popular place in town for lunch. There is usually a line after 11:30 AM, but the wait is pleasant in the front courtyard, originally the central patio of a large hacienda. The red chile served on blue corn enchiladas, tacos, and burritos is unmatched, the posole and beans very good, and the desserts fine. Lunch only. Closed Sundays. No reservations or credit cards. 113½ Palace Ave. (982-9030). Inexpensive.

Tecolote Cafe – Despite the inauspicious location, it serves the best breakfast in town, complete with a basket of homemade biscuits and blueberry muffins. The Santa Fe omelette — filled with green chile and cheese — will get anyone moving. Closed Mondays and Tuesdays. Dinner served weekends only. No reservations. Major credit cards. 1203 Cerrillos Rd. (988-1362). Inexpensive.

Tomasita's – At this local favorite, the selection of dishes is limited but the flavors authentic, the portions large, and the service friendly. Unless you arrive early, the wait for a table can easily be as long as your dinner. Closed Sundays. No reservations. Major credit cards. 500 Guadalupe (983-5721). Inexpensive.

SAVANNAH

Savannah is where Georgia began. Here is the quintessential southern city, possessed of just the right amount of atmosphere and ambience. Nowhere is there total urban dominance by the modern architectural behemoths — skyscrapers etching a skyline while virtually ignoring history and heritage closer to earth. Savannah's roots are too deeply sown in the Georgian soil to permit any such thing. Savannah *is* the South.

The city's beginnings were hardly as auspicious as the present state of restoration would suggest. The site chosen for Savannah had originally been part of a royal grant made in 1663 to the Lord Proprietors of Carolina, but frequent Indian raids (and constant threat of invasion from the Spanish colonists close by) discouraged the Carolina colonists from extending their boundaries to the fullest possible extent. Thus the last of the British colonies in the New World (and likewise last of the 13 original settlements) was ordained by royal proclamation in 1732, when George II turned the rights to these lands over to the "Trustees for Establishing the Colony of Georgia in America."

The leader of these trustees was General James Oglethorpe, who literally began the colony as an experiment in regimentation. His intention was to turn English debtors into American citizens by regulating even the most minute segments of their daily lives. The equipment carried to the New World by each would-be settler was meticulously detailed: "To every Man, A Watch-Coat, A Musket, and Bayonet, An Hatchet, An Hammer, An Handsaw, A shod Shovel or Spade . . . And a publick Grindstone to each Ward or Village."

Savannah scarcely survived its colonial period, and the judicious choice of its site was no doubt the reason it ultimately did. Set on Yamacraw Bluff, 15 miles above the mouth of Savannah River, its protected topographical position precluded a substantial number of conventional calamities. But it is the physical layout of the city itself which is Savannah's most enduring heritage. Eschewing the more conventional grid pattern most often used in fledgling colonial urban developments, Oglethorpe chose instead a visionary plan that included separate wards and public squares in regular conformation.

And today, one of the city's many sobriquets is "city of squares." (Others are "the walking city," because everything can be seen on foot; and "forest city," because of the city's treasured Spanish moss–hung trees.) These squares are more than public parks. Landscaped and kept immaculate by a park and tree department nearly as old as the city itself, the squares provide places for shoppers to rest and for bands to play noontime concerts while downtown office people munch brown-bag lunches. Visitors ask, "Why so many squares?" Residents are hard-put to supply an answer. Some say the squares were intended as rallying points in case of Indian attack. Others insist the squares are small versions of English commons. And researchers have substantiated that the pattern of Savannah's squares holds a more than coincidental likeness to those of Old Peking!

Somehow, finding a plausible answer to "Why squares?" is simply not as important as enjoying them. The city has worked hard to beautify them, planting trees and azaleas, and installing benches. In some stand monuments to Georgian heroes: General Oglethorpe (whose name also graces the snobby Oglethorpe Club, which some residents crave to join and others thank the heavens they don't have to), preacher John Wesley, and William Washington Gordon, whose Central of Georgia Railroad first linked seaport Savannah to the midlands and uplands when cotton was king and the pine tree — source of turpentine and resin products — was crown prince.

Cotton is king no longer. The pine tree is, but because of paper pulp, not resin. Savannah's main industry is papermaking, but the city of 178,000 has a number of strings to its economic bow. With a marvelous deepwater port 18 miles from the Atlantic, the world comes right to Savannah's ocean door.

Most people — as opposed to most industries — come to Savannah not for business but to see the city itself. They come mainly to view the historic preservation and restoration that has been going on for a long time. In the late 1940s, when the postwar trend toward "modernization" threatened to deprive the city of physical evidences of its heritage, a few citizens took countermeasures. Convinced of the economic, historic, and aesthetic value of keeping the city's beautiful architecture intact, they formed the Historic Savannah Foundation as a private undertaking.

With seed money provided by individual members, the agency began to purchase homes and offices (Regency, Georgian, and Victorian buildings) otherwise slated for the wrecking ball. The properties were then sold to private buyers who were required to restore and repair them. Proceeds from each sale went toward further purchases by the Foundation.

Instead of parking lots or high-rises, Savannah now enjoys refurbished mansions, town houses, and distinctive offices that not only retain, but *are,* the character of a outhern city that otherwise might have gone with the wind. Most fascinating is that this restoration is a viable, working, and living museum. Functional as well as beautiful, Savannah's buildings are enjoyed by everyone in the community. They are not museum pieces. Restorers literally live in the houses they have nurtured back to life, and many property owners have been lured from the suburbs back to the city to live and work within the restoration area. Although various homes are periodically placed on public view — the owners are understandably proud of what they have done and are quite willing to share their delight with others — the houses in historic Savannah are all mostly just *homes.* As you ramble through the area (we hope on foot), you may find a home owner blithely washing the car in the front yard of a house more than a century and a half old. Show any real interest, and you will likely be invited in to see what hard work and patience have lovingly wrought.

As a result of this restoration effort, a 2½-mile section of the "old" city has been designated a national landmark district, the largest of its kind in the country. In 1968, Savannah embarked on a multiphased downtown revitalization program to round out the restoration within this district. The city built

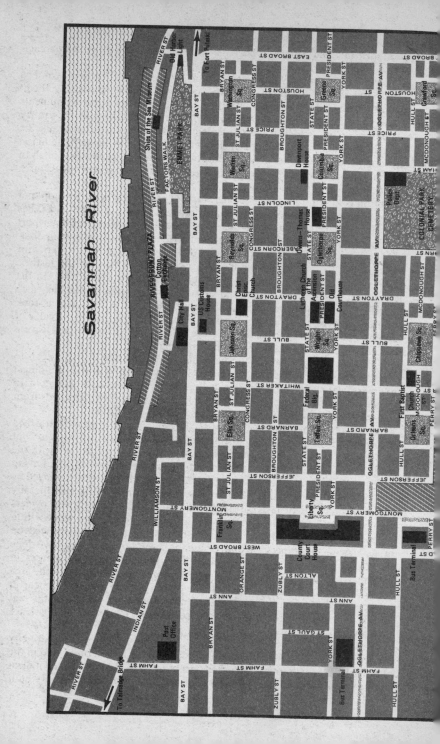

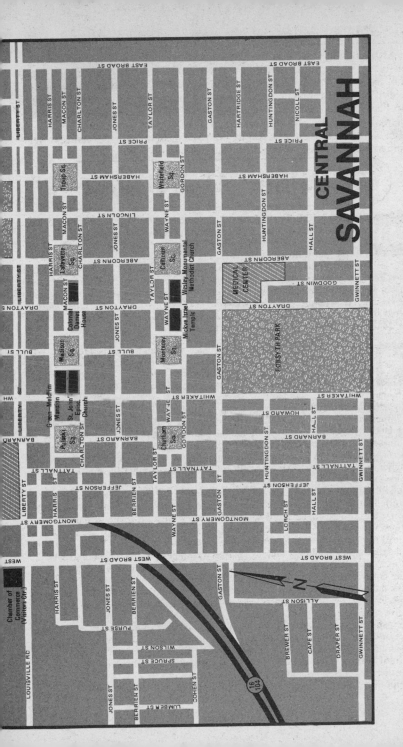

CENTRAL
SAVANNAH

the $10.4 million Civic and Convention Center, and completely rebuilt the nine-block River Street waterfront. Riverfront Plaza, the cobblestone and brick esplanade that replaced the rotting docks and its eroded shoreline, is an ideal place for romantic strolls, ship watching, or shopping and roaming. The Plaza is lined with more than 65 shops, restaurants, cafés, boutiques, galleries, nightclubs, and the new *Hyatt Regency Savannah* hotel.

In all, Savannah is an opportunity not to be missed. Which explains, in yet another sobriquet, why it is called "the magnetic city."

SAVANNAH AT-A-GLANCE

SEEING THE CITY: Driving into Savannah across Talmadge Bridge offers a fine introductory view of the city. For the best view from on high, visit the *De Soto Hilton*'s *Harborview Room,* a banquet room on the top floor at Liberty and Bull sts. (232-0171).

For a pleasant introduction to Savannah, take a cruise on one of the Cap'n Sam Cruise Line sightseeing boats. Cap'n Sam runs regular daily tours of the harbor (a 20-mile, 2-hour trip); twilight cocktail cruises in the evenings; and on summer nights, special dinner/dance cruises. The boats — *Harbor Queen I, Waving Girl, Harbor Queen II,* and the *Cap'n Sam* — depart from the foot of Bull Street behind city hall. Call 234-7248 for the cruise schedule and reservations.

SPECIAL PLACES: Historic Savannah is appealingly negotiable on foot. We recommend at least four walking tours; and count on a minimum of two days to see everything. You can squeeze it all into a morning and afternoon, but by nightfall, exhaustion will be the undisputed victor. Herewith, four walking tours:

Riverfront Plaza – A logical place to start, Riverfront Plaza leads eastward along the Savannah River shoreline. Bordering the thriving seaport's 40-foot-deep channel, the 9-block, brick Plaza is alive with commercial establishments in the 19th-century buildings which were formerly cotton warehouses. Waterfront browsers may be treated to a rock concert or a chamber music recital by an ensemble from the Savannah Symphony. A Riverfront Plaza day tour will undoubtedly whet the appetite for an evening excursion.

Bull Street – If you spend a morning at the Plaza, the afternoon can be spent walking down Bull Street, from City Hall to Forsyth Park, 12 blocks south. Bull is Savannah's principle north-south street, and it contains the city's five most beautiful squares. The six-story City Hall, on River and Bay streets, stands alongside two brass cannons captured from Cornwallis at Yorktown. The cannons were presented to the Chatham Artillery, a Savannah military unit, by George Washington, in 1791. East of City Hall, Factors Walk, with its iron bridges and narrow street, runs along the city side of the former cotton buildings. After passing City Hall, you will come to the US Customs House, built in 1852 on the same site where Georgia's founder, James Edward Oglethorpe, lived in 1733. It's also where evangelist John Wesley first preached in America. The five squares, not to be missed, are:

Johnson Square – Here, two fountains flow and decks of azaleas are in dazzling flower in spring. Christ Episcopal Church, the first church established in the Colony of Georgia (1773), stands here, too. The present building dates from 1838.

Wright Square – The exquisite Ascension window of the Lutheran Church of the Ascension (1878) is internationally known as a work of art.

Chippewa Square – Here you'll find the First Baptist Church, the oldest of its denomination in Georgia; the Barrow Mansion, which now houses an insurance firm; and the Savannah Theater, one of the oldest theaters in continuous use in the country (233-7764).

Madison Square – The carillons and stained-glass windows of St. John's Episcopal Church (1840) are well known to church lovers. Here, too, is the former Green-Meldrim mansion, which served as Sherman's headquarters after Savannah was captured in the Civil War.

Monterey Square – Temple Mickve Israel, consecrated in 1878 for Georgia's oldest Jewish congregation (1773), contains a Torah scroll more than 800 years old. The Gordon and Taylor Street houses facing Monterey Square are outstanding examples of historic preservations.

From Abercorn to St. Julian Street – Starting at Calhoun Square, at Abercorn and Gordon streets, walk north toward Massie School (1885), a Greek Revival structure that is the public school system's education museum. Alongside stands Wesley Monumental Methodist Church. Four blocks north, at Lafayette Square, is the Colonial Dames House (1849). Two blocks east, beside Troup Square and on parallel Charlton and Macon streets, are Savannah's two best examples of slum conversion properties, now first-rate town houses. A block and a half north of Troup Square, Colonial Park Cemetery contains the graves of Georgia colonists, with priceless tombstone inscriptions. From the cemetery, it's a two-block walk up Abercorn Street to the Owens-Thomas House (1816) at the corner of State Street, hailed as "America's finest example of English Regency architecture." Now a museum, the house was visited in 1825 by Revolutionary hero Marquis de Lafayette. One block east of Owens-Thomas House, facing Columbia Square, Davenport House, now a museum, is the first architecturally important structure to have been reclaimed by the Historic Savannah Foundation. From here, it's a three-block walk north to St. Julian Street, which splits three squares: Reynolds Square at Abercorn Street, Warren Square at Habersham Street, and Washington Square at Houston Street. This section has one of Savannah's largest clusters of restored 18th- and 19th-century homes. Facing Reynolds Square is the *Pink House* (c. 1790), now a fashionable restaurant.

Fort Pulaski – A national monument named for the Revolutionary hero killed in the 1779 Battle of Savannah. Built between 1829 and 1847, the fort was captured by Union forces in 1862. Open daily. Free. US 80 near Savannah Beach. (785-5787).

■**EXTRA SPECIAL:** The *Great Savannah Exposition,* a new multimillion-dollar attraction in the former train yards behind the Savannah Visitors Center, is a pleasant way to absorb a little history. Two theaters feature films, animated historical characters, and sound-and-light effects; Exposition Hall contains a 19th-century steam locomotive, a replica of the cotton gin (invented in Savannah), and many other interesting artifacts. *The Crossing,* an informal café next to the exposition, serves dishes from the city's fine restuarants. Open daily. Admission charge (238-1779).

Hilton Head Island, a luxury resort area in South Carolina about 40 miles northeast of Savannah, has 16 golf courses, pretty beaches, deep-sea fishing, tennis courts, a private airstrip, and plenty of nightlife. Reservations are advised if you plan to stay overnight. Sea Pines Plantation, a resort community of private villas and a 204-room, oceanfront inn, has beaches, 3 championship golf courses (including famed Harbour Town), tennis courts, bicycle paths with rental facilities, swimming pools, marinas, and a 625-acre forest preserve. For information, contact Sea Pines Plantation, Hilton Head Island, SC 29928 (800 845-6131 or 803 785-3333). Reservations islandwide may be made through the Hilton Head Reservation Service (800 845-7018). For information on Hilton Head activities, call the Chamber of Commerce (803 785-3673).

SOURCES AND RESOURCES

 TOURIST INFORMATION: Before starting off on a walk, be sure to pick up a map of the city at the Savannah Visitors Center. Its offices are in a former 1860 railroad station. Take an extra 15 minutes to watch its film, which will help give you a feel for the city. Before visiting, you can write to 301 W Broad St., Savannah, GA 31499, for information. W Broad and Liberty sts. (233-6651).

Sojourn in Savannah by Betty Rauers and Franklin Traub (Historic Savannah Foundation; $3) offers detailed information on places of interest around town.

Local Coverage – *Savannah Morning News* and *Savannah Evening Press,* dailies.

Area Code – All telephone numbers are in the 912 area code unless otherwise indicated.

 CLIMATE AND CLOTHES: Warm and sunny is the forecast for Savannah most of the year, with temperatures mostly in the 70s. From December through March, you can expect the mercury to drop into the 50s and 40s, and in the height of summer, to climb to the high 80s or low 90s. You can also be pretty sure of afternoon thunderstorms between June and September. Apart from the rains, however, the humidity is hardly ever greater than 60%.

 GETTING AROUND: Airport – Savannah International Airport is about 8 miles from the downtown area, and the 20-minute drive by taxi should cost about $12. For $8 per person, Host Savannah Transportation (964-0332) takes passengers to downtown hotels. Two other companies provide service to Hilton Head Island, an hour's drive away, for $16: Low Country Adventures (803 681-8212) and Regal Limousine (803 785-5466).

Bus – Savannah Transit Authority operates the municipal bus system, 900 E Gwinnett St. (233-5767).

Taxi – Cabs can be hailed in the streets, downtown. There are taxi stands at the main hotels, but you may prefer to call Yellow Cab (234-2330).

Car Rental – Avis and Hertz have offices in town. Thrifty Rent-a-Car is a reliable local service (236-6316).

 MUSEUMS: Savannah is a treasury of historic and cultural elegance. On your way through the streets of the historic district, the *Telfair Academy of Arts and Sciences* on Barnard St. (232-1177) recommends itself as one of Savannah's outstanding museums. Other notable museums are:

Museum of Antique Dolls – 505 President St. E (233-5296)
Savannah Art Association – 107 E Hall (232-7731)
Savannah Science Museum – 4405 Paulsen (355-6705)
Ships of the Sea Maritime Museum – 503 E River St. (232-1511)

 MAJOR COLLEGES AND UNIVERSITIES: Armstrong State College, 11935 Abercorn St. Extension (927-5211); Savannah State College, Thunderbolt (356-2186). Both are four-year colleges within the Georgia state university system.

 SPECIAL EVENTS: Savannah has three major annual festivals. *Georgia Day,* February 12, celebrates the founding of the colony. Festivities last for a week. *St. Patrick's Day* (March 17) features the biggest street parade south of New York. The fourth weekend in April, *"A Night in Old Savannah,"* is a three-day ethnic fun and food festival in Johnson Square.

SPORTS AND FITNESS: Savannah is at the head of one of the country's most popular vacationland areas. Names like Hilton Head, Sea Island, St. Simons, and Jekyll Island are all familiar to lovers of the outdoor life, and all are less than a day's drive from Savannah.

Bicycling – Cycling through the historic district can be an unforgettable experience. The *De Soto Hilton* hotel rents bikes.

Fitness Centers – There is an outdoor pool, operated by the YMCA, at 6400 Habersham (354-6223).

Golf – The *Savannah Inn* course, one of the best known in the South, is also open to the public on Wilmington Island (897-1612). The best municipal course is at Bacon Park, Skidaway Rd. and Shorty Cooper Dr. (354-2625). (Shorty Cooper was one of the original golf caddies at Bacon Park.)

Jogging – Run around the perimeter of Forsyth Park, 1 mile, or along the waterfront in the early morning or evening when it isn't heavily trafficked; Lake Mayer, reachable by car, has an asphalt track. A jogging map is available at the *De Soto Hilton.*

Swimming and Fishing – Tybee Island (formerly Savannah Beach), nostalgically remembered as one end of a rollicking railroad that connected the mainland to the beach, has been a favorite haunt for many years. Here, you can indulge your penchants for swimming, fishing, surfing, crabbing, boating, picnicking, or beachcombing among the dunes. It's 18 miles from downtown Savannah.

Tennis – Best public tennis courts are at Bacon Park, Lake Mayer, Forsyth Park, and Daffin Park.

THEATER: For complete performance schedules, check the publications listed above. *Savannah Civic Center* is the largest auditorium in the city, Orleans Sq. (234-6666). *Little Theater,* Chippewa Sq. downtown (233-7764), is another place for good drama. It occupies the historic Savannah Theater, the oldest theater in continuous use in the US.

MUSIC: The Savannah Civic Center is the home of the *Savannah Symphony Orchestra,* and offers the best concerts, ballets, touring Broadway productions, and dance theater performances, in Orleans Sq. (234-6666).

NIGHTCLUBS AND NIGHTLIFE: Riverfront Plaza is alive with discos and clubs. Three of the most popular are *Night Flight,* a restaurant with live music (233-1959), *Port Royal* (233-2462), and *Spanky's* (236-3009).

SINS: *Gluttony* has made far deeper inroads than *lust* in Savannah life. For while red lights flicker here and there all over town, with only the most eager lechers seeking out the fancy women and pornographic books stashed away in the odd corners of this fairly conservative city, *gluttony* flourishes in the open. Residents and tourists alike crowd the restaurants to overdose on exotic seafood dishes at the *Pirate's House,* E Broad and Bay sts. (233-5757). The city's *pride?* A St. Patrick's Day celebration that ranks with those of New York, Boston, and Cleveland.

LOCAL SERVICES: Babysitting – Angels and Imps, 614 Jackson Blvd. (355-1068)

    Business Services – Tempo Secretarial Services, 6606 Abercorn St. (355-5511)

Mechanic – Complete Auto Repair, 1141 W Gwinnett St. (236-0631)

BEST IN TOWN

CHECKING IN: Savannah has over 3,600 rooms for guests, most of them scattered among the motels within and around the fringe of the city. The city also has four hotels that offer a special elegance. Expect to pay between $80 and $100 or more for a double at those places we've listed as expensive; between $60 and $80 in the moderate range; under $50 for an inexpensive hostelry.

De Soto Hilton – On the site of the former *De Soto Hotel,* this retains much of the decor that made its predecessor the queen of the gaslight era's carriage trade. The 264-room present property was built from the ground up after the old hotel was razed in the mid-1960s. Its *Red Lion* cocktail lounge (closed Sundays) is almost an exact replica of the old Sapphire Room; its *Pavilion Restaurant* is one of Savannah's finest. The *Harborview Room,* a banquet room on the top floor, offers unquestionably the best panoramic north-south view of Savannah. The *De Soto* has a bicycle rental desk, arranges golf and tennis games, and offers free garage parking. At the intersection of Liberty and Bull sts. (912 232-0171). Expensive.

Hyatt Regency Savannah – This 350-room hotel rises above the Riverfront Plaza, giving guests a view of the oceangoing ships cruising in and out of the harbor. *The Windows* restaurant, overlooking the river, has quickly become a favorite dining spot, along with the more casual *MD's Lounge* and *Patrick's Porch.* Guests can arrange tours and other activities at the concierge's desk in the lobby. Indoor parking. 2 W Bay St. (912 238-1234). Expensive.

Sheraton Savannah Resort and Club – Ten miles from Savannah on the Wilmington River, this was one of the Roaring Twenties' great resort hotels, and succeeding owners have kept it in first-class condition. Its 210 rooms are distributed between the 8-story hotel, a number of small cottages, and some villas. It has a swimming pool, sauna, restaurant, nightclub, and fishing and boating. Its pride is its 18-hole golf course, one of the South's finest. A modified American plan is available for those who want meals included in the price. Wilmington Island (912 897-1612). Expensive.

Eliza Thompson House – This quaint 3-story 1847 town house in the Historic District has been restored and converted to an inn by Laurie and Jim Widman. Some of the 25 rooms are filled with antiques as well as with Savannah history books so you can brush up on Georgia's oldest city during your stay. Others also have fireplaces, kitchenettes, or private entrances. Complimentary sherry makes things even cozier. 7 W Jones St. (912 236-3620). Expensive.

Foley House Inn – Just 20 rooms, with fine antique furnishings and fireplaces, on historic Chippewa Square. Amenities include private baths with Jacuzzis and an outdoor hot tub. 14 W Hull (912 232-6622). Expensive.

Magnolia Place – Savannah's latest bed-and-breakfast gem. Facing Forsyth Park, the 13-room inn is in the heart of Old Savannah and has antique furnishings along with Jacuzzis, limousine service, and video disc players. 503 Whitaker St. (912 233-1094). Expensive.

Royal Colony Inn – Originally built in the 1920s, the inn has recently been taken over by a company that respects historic landmarks. After undergoing a thorough renovation, it's rather like a comfortable home with Georgian furnishings and tasteful decor throughout. The penthouse rooms even have working fireplaces. 29 Abercorn St. (912 232-5678 or 800 554-1187). Expensive to moderate.

Downtowner – Five blocks west of the *De Soto Hilton,* built of Savannah gray bricks salvaged from older buildings. Ornamented with wrought-iron balconies, the 204-room, 6-story hotel blends in with the architecture of the surrounding historic landmark district. Next to the Civic Center, with a swimming pool. Its *Regency Restaurant and Tavern* is a favorite of residents. 201 W Oglethorpe (912 233-3531). Moderate.

Best Western/Savannah Riverfront – This recently renovated motel has 142 rooms and overlooks River Street. Its *Bottle Works Restaurant* is open for all meals. 412 W Bay St. (912 233-1011). Moderate.

Days Inn Savannah – A new hotel with 253 rooms, it's across the street from the city's famous waterfront. A good choice for families since there's a swimming pool, game room, and a 24-hour restaurant where kids under 12 eat for free. 201 W Bay St. (912 236-4440). Inexpensive.

Quality Inn/Heart of Savannah – Its romantic name and size (53 rooms) create a certain intimacy, in contrast to larger hotels. The two great things about it, though, are the free Continental breakfast and the price, about $40 for two. 300 W Bay St. (912 236-6321). Inexpensive.

 EATING OUT: Savannah's restaurants range from elegant to home-style. The seafood here is excellent, and the prices are good, too. Two people can eat very well for about $40 or less. Anything between $25 and $35 is moderate; under $20, inexpensive. Prices do not include drinks, wine, or tips.

Pirates' House – In Savannah's oldest standing building, this made literary history in Robert Louis Stevenson's *Treasure Island.* In any of its 23 dining rooms, a meal is an authentic experience. Choices include oysters Savannah, several flaming dishes, local seafood, steak, red rice, and exotic desserts. Open daily. Reservations advised. Major credit cards. 20 E Broad St. (233-5757). Expensive.

The Windows – This exquisite restaurant in the *Hyatt Regency Savannah* overlooks the Savannah River. Diners can watch merchant ships come and go while choosing from a Continental menu featuring seafood, duck, and stir-fried Oriental dishes. Open daily; brunch only on Sundays; no lunch on Saturdays. Reservations advised. Major credit cards. 2 W Bay St. (238-1234). Expensive

45 South Restaurant and Bar – In an environment as traditional as old Savannah, this new suburban eatery is surprisingly contemporary. The New American menu features grilled seafood and chicken as well as creative soups, salads, and pastas. Open daily for lunch and dinner. Reservations. Major credit cards. 45 S Eisenhower Dr. (354-0444). Expensive.

La Toque – This popular dining spot features Continental cuisine and fresh local seafood. All entrées are cooked to order and there's a good wine list. A specialty food shop, *Swiss Affair Ltd.,* is also on the premises and serves light dinners (omelettes, soups, and salads). Closed Sundays. Reservations advised. Major credit cards. 420 E Broughton St. (238-0138). Moderate.

Johnny Harris – Specialties here are steaks, prime ribs, barbecues, and chicken. They do their own baking on the premises. In its third generation of continuous ownership, this is where the nationally marketed Johnny Harris Barbecue Sauce originated. Jacket and tie are required on Friday and Saturday nights, but, surprisingly, reservations are not necessary. Closed Sundays. Major credit cards. 1651 E Victory Dr. (354-7810). Moderate.

Elizabeth on Thirty-Seventh – In a lovely old Savannah mansion, the dining room has been widely acclaimed. Freshly prepared seasonal foods are offered along with sumptuous desserts. Closed Sundays and Mondays. Reservations not necessary. Some credit cards. 37th at Drayton (236-5547). Moderate.

The Pavilion – Another well-known Savannah restaurant, featuring traditional "Old South" recipes from land and sea, with a great buffet. When you're finished eating, go up to the *Harborview Room* on the top floor for the best view of the city. Open daily. Reservations advised. Major credit cards. *De Soto Hilton Hotel,* Bull and Liberty sts. (232-0171). Moderate.

17 Hundred 90 – The setting is normal in this 19th-century house, which can accommodate around 100 diners. Savannah residents consider this to be one of their best restaurants: dress appropriately. The seafood casserole is especially good. Closed Sundays. Reservations advised. Major credit cards. 307 E President St. (236-7122). Moderate.

Anna's Little Napoli – This is the only Italian restaurant in town that offers a complete Italian menu of pasta, veal, and seafood. We recommend the lasagna and veal parmagiana. Open daily. No reservations. Major credit cards. 2308 Skidaway Rd. (234-5083). Inexpensive.

Crystal Beer Parlor – For the last half-century this place has been famous for its sandwiches, burgers, and casual, friendly atmosphere. Closed Sundays. 301 W Jones St. (232-1153). Inexpensive.

Palmers Seafood House – On Wilmington Island, just 15 minutes from downtown; residents consider this the best place in the area for fresh seafood. The atmosphere is casual, and no reservations are taken. Open daily. 80 Wilmington Island Rd. (897-2611). Inexpensive.

Mrs. Wilkes' Boarding House – This is one of Savannah's culinary landmarks. Mrs. Wilkes advertises by word of mouth, and while some people are critical, they admit that it is only because when they want home cooking they eat at home. When you walk into Mrs. Wilkes, you'll find set out on dining room tables food enough to stagger Sherman's army: grits, biscuits, sausage, and eggs for breakfast, or fried chicken, swordfish steak, potatoes, rice, peas, cornbread, and other down-home treats for lunch. To serve yourself, just spread your arm in that proverbial boarding-house reach. Open weekdays for breakfast and lunch. No reservations or credit cards. In the basement of 107 W Jones St. (232-5997). Inexpensive by any standards — about $5 for all you can eat.

SEATTLE

Visitors often feel they have "discovered" Seattle: Because the Emerald City is less well known than many of its West Coast counterparts, travelers are surprised and delighted to find a booming city with a striking skyline, a surfeit of green spaces, lovely residential neighborhoods, lots of cultural events, and a host of outdoor and adventure activities, all very accessible. It is not unusual hereabouts to go skiing in the nearby mountains in the morning and go sailing or salmon fishing in Puget Sound in the afternoon.

Seattle occupies a rich corner of the western frontier, seven hills tucked away by imposing mountain ranges to the east and west. The Olympic Mountains lie on the western horizon line, and the Cascades, with their jagged cliffs crowned by the snow-capped summit of the 14,410-foot Mt. Rainier, on the eastern. Immediately to the west is Elliott Bay of the Puget Sound, which leads outward to the vast expanse of the Pacific, and on the east is a 24-mile length of fresh water, Lake Washington.

The earliest inhabitants of the region were the Northwest Indians, who were generally more content to trade than to make war with neighbors. Their territory was covered with thick forests, watered by the Puget Sound and Lake Washington, and they lived in comfortable harmony with their surroundings. They had fish and clams for the taking, a moderate climate year-round, and plenty of bark available for the construction of their superb, long canoes.

The European settlers who came in the 1850s couldn't leave well enough alone. They harvested the readily available timber and sent it south to San Francisco. Then they leveled a couple of the more prominent hills to make north-south travel easier. One of those hills, now a concrete canyon in Seattle's downtown, was the lumberjacks' principal source of timber. When teams of oxen skidded the new-cut logs down the street to the sawmill, a new American expression was born — Skid Road (now Row). On either side of the Road, you can now hear the strains of rock and jazz from nightclubs where once only the music of box-house bands played. Lumbering, of course, is still one of Seattle's major industries, but the oxen are gone.

Seattle seems to owe its rise to having been in the right place at the right time. There was nothing inevitable about its growth. Olympia, to the south, was an established town when Seattle was little more than a collection of rude huts; Port Townsend was better situated on the Sound; and Tacoma, though it didn't develop as early, was named as the terminus of the Northern Pacific Railroad. Seattle had a fine deepwater harbor on the Sound, but so did several other 19th-century Washington towns. But in 1897 a "ton of gold" was brought back from Alaska aboard a ship that docked at a Seattle pier, and the town was, well . . . golden. Gold fever spread, and the city naturally became a boom town because of its easy access to riches — a protected inland

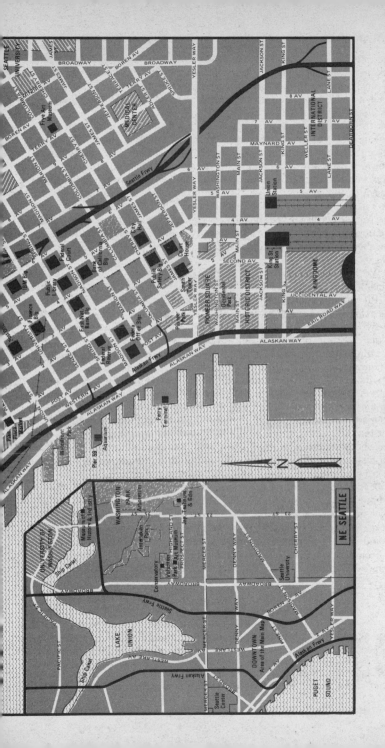

passage to Alaska. Vice flourished in this raw frontier town, if you consider brothels a way of flourishing. The confluence of Seattle lumberjacks and miners on their way to find their fortune in gold in the Klondike brought about a demand for prostitution, which was best satisfied in all the West along Seattle's Skid Road.

After the Gold Rush days, Seattle seemed almost ashamed of itself for its extravagances. It was quick to embrace Prohibition in 1916, three years before the rest of the nation capitulated. Even before World War II, it was a conservative, one-industry town, depending far too heavily on plane production.

Things began to change in 1962, when a group of businessmen put together an audacious undertaking, a World's Fair in Seattle. There had been the Alaska-Yukon Pacific Exposition in 1907, which had created quite a stir, but this was something else. Even the backers were dubious of its success. But the venture turned out profitably and left the city with a different attitude toward itself — a feeling that the city could be first class in more ways than it thought possible.

The World's Fair gave the city a real boost culturally, too, leaving it with the valuable legacy of the Seattle Center, a complex that includes an Opera House, Playhouse, Arena Coliseum, the Pacific Science Center with its wide-ranging exhibitions, and the futuristically designed Space Needle. The Seattle Repertory Theater is a strong professional group; the Seattle Symphony under the direction of Gerard Schwarz is of world class; and the Seattle Opera, culminating its season with a Wagner Ring Festival in the summer, is outstanding.

In sports, too, Seattle hit the big league. The basketball SuperSonics play their games at the Coliseum, while the football Seahawks and baseball Mariners play at the Kingdome. The Dome sits on land reclaimed from Elliott Bay.

With all of its progress toward the future, Seattle still is concerned with its past heritage and has maintained the "old town" alongside the new. Pioneer Square, where the city was founded in 1852, has been renovated and designated a historic preservation area. The old brick buildings surrounding the square are protected from the ruthless movements of progress and the bulldozer. Beyond the stately facades lie galleries, boutiques, and restaurants.

The inner city is unusually healthy; people are moving back into the city to enjoy a new sense of belonging. Off in the distance, the snow-capped peaks of the Cascades and Olympic Mountains, and the expansive stretch of Puget Sound and Lake Washington, create a magnificent backdrop. But it is the scene of current Seattle — the dynamic activity of a rising city — that is attracting residents.

SEATTLE AT-A-GLANCE

 SEEING THE CITY: The best view of Seattle and the magnificent Washington landscape is from the top of the *Space Needle* (447-3100). The observation deck and revolving restaurant offer 360° views of the city, Puget Sound, Lake Washington, and beyond to the snow-covered peaks of the Cascade and Olympic Mountains. Admission charge unless dining. Seattle Center.

SPECIAL PLACES: Don't be confused by the geographical designations in street addresses, like north or south. The directions that follow avenue names and precede street names (5th Ave. North or North 5th St.) give location in relation to downtown (where only street names and numbers are used).

Seattle Center – The legacy of the 1962 World's Fair, this 74-acre area contains some of the city's finest facilities. Dominating the 50 buildings and the grassy plazas is the Space Needle, a futuristic steel structure that spires 607 feet upward from its tripod base. Among the other highlights are the *Food Circus* (Center House, 305 Harrison St.) where you can sample inexpensive international delicacies, two playhouses, the Opera House, Arena (adjoining buildings on Mercer St.), and Fun Forest Amusement Park (370 Thomas St.) for a variety of entertainment. Information for Seattle Center theater tickets and activities at booth in Center House Bldg., 5th Ave. N between Denny Way and Mercer St. (625-4234). There are two notable museums in the Center:

Pacific Science Center – Designed by Minoru Yamasaki, the center features astro-space displays, with a large fiberglass moon and a full-scale model of a lunar module, an operating oceanographic model of the Puget Sound that simulates waves, a laserium that uses laser beams to form images, a reconstruction of a Northwest Indian longhouse, and a popular science playground with hands-on exhibitions for children. Open daily. Admission charge. 200 2nd Ave. N (443-2001).

Seattle Art Museum Pavilion – Changing exhibitions of photography and regional and contemporary artists, including Harry Callahan and Andy Warhol. Closed Mondays. Admission charge. 2nd Ave. N and Thomas St. (447-4670).

Seattle Aquarium – Next to the public fishing pier at Waterfront Park, the aquarium offers a close view of what's swimming in Puget Sound. In the domed viewing room — actually a 400,000-gallon tank — you are surrounded by octopus, starfish, dogfish sharks, rock cod, red snapper, scallops, shrimps, anemones, and sea pens. There are also tropical fish, a touch-me exhibition, and a wonderfully captivating family of sea otters. Open daily. Admission charge. Pier 59 (625-4357). All along the waterfront there are fish bars where you can pick up a good regional lunch.

Puget Sound Ferry Ride – If looking out at the Sound and up at its marine life isn't enough, you can have the full Sound experience by taking the 45-minute ride to Winslow or to Victorian Port Townsend or as far as Victoria, BC, Ferry Terminal (464-6400).

Pike Place Market – Founded in 1907, this public market is now a historic site full of lively vendors and a colorful array of produce, flowers, and fresh fish. There are also musicians, craftspeople, and specialty restaurants. Closed Sundays. 1st Ave. between Pike St. and Virginia St.

Seattle Art Museum – The exceptional Oriental collection of Richard E. Fuller features beautiful Chinese jade and bronzes, delicately crafted pottery and snuff bottles, and Indian stone sculptures. Also changing displays of modern and Northwest Indian art. Closed Mondays. Admission charge except Thursdays. Volunteer Park (447-4670).

Museum of History and Industry – Extensive collection of Pacific Northwest artifacts traces the history of Seattle's first 100 years. A mural depicts the fire that leveled the city in 1889, and the displays include almost everything that came afterward — mementos of the Gold Rush, old firefighting equipment, a maritime display, and a Boeing exhibit that follows its development over the past 60 years. Open daily. Admission charge except Mondays. 2161 E Hamlin St. (324-1125).

Pioneer Square – The site where the city was founded in 1852 has become a historic preservation area, and remains in all its Victorian grandeur today. The classic old brick buildings house some of the city's best boutiques, galleries, and restaurants (for fresh seafood at a moderate price, try lunch at *La Galleria;* see *Best in Town,* below). When fire ravaged the district in 1889, the city rebuilt atop the rubble, leaving an underground town, 10 feet below. Bill Speidel's Underground Tours guide visitors through the subterranean five-block area, which has some storefronts, interiors, and old waterlines intact. Tours daily. Admission charge. Reservations advised. (610 1st Ave.; 682-4646). For gold rush nostalgia, visit the Klondike Gold Rush National Historic Park (117 S Main; 442-7220), which traces the history of Klondike gold fever with murals, exhibitions, and a slide show.

International District – Often called the Gateway to the Orient, Seattle has a large Chinese and Japanese community concentrated in this interesting old section of the city. There is a Buddhist temple, many craft shops, and Asian restaurants. Shop at *Uwajimaya* (6th Ave. S and S King; 624-6248), the West Coast's largest Asian retail store, for gifts and specialty food items. The Wing Luke Memorial Museum has a collection tracing the emigration of the Chinese to the Northwest from the 1860s on. Closed Sundays and Mondays. Free. 414 8th Ave. S (623-5124).

University of Washington Arboretum – Some 200 lakeside acres contain over 5,000 species of plant life from all over the world. Features the largest Japanese Tea Garden outside Japan. Open all year. Admission charge. Lake Washington Blvd. between E Madison and Montlake (543-8800).

■**EXTRA SPECIAL:** Just an hour and a half south of Seattle is the spectacular *Mt. Rainier National Park,* with its 14,410-foot summit of the Cascade range. There are over 300 miles of trails ranging from the super-rough 90-mile Wonderland trail, which circles up to the peak, to short nature walks for mere earthlings. On the way home, stop at *The Wild Berry Restaurant* in Ashford for a colossal club sandwich made with three slices of fresh sourdough bread, and a jar of delicious Mountain Blackberry jam. Also on Route 161, you can stop at Northwest Trek Wildlife Park (325-5566), where moose, elk, buffalo, mountain goat, and caribou roam free. The zoo belongs to the animals; visitors tour from a tram and are not allowed off.

SOURCES AND RESOURCES

TOURIST INFORMATION: The Seattle Visitors Bureau offers daily events schedules, maps, and information. 1815 7th Ave. (447-7273).

The Seattle Guidebook by Archie Satterfield, available at the Elliott Bay Book Co. (624-6600) for $4.95, is a good guide to Seattle and the surrounding area.

Local Coverage – *Seattle Post-Intelligencer,* morning daily, publishes *What's Happening* on Fridays with coming week's events; *Seattle Times,* afternoon daily, publishes *Tempo* magazine on Fridays. Both are available at newsstands. *Seattle Guide* is available at hotels and some restaurants.

Food – *Seattle's Best Places* by David Brewster (The Weekly Press; $11.95).

Area Code – All telephone numbers are in the 206 area code unless otherwise indicated.

CLIMATE AND CLOTHES: Seattle's proximity to Puget Sound keeps the climate mild and moderately moist. Winters are relatively warm, with average temperatures around 40° and little or no snow. The wet season is from October to April, so carry an umbrella. Seattle is best in summer and early fall when city and countryside are most accessible.

GETTING AROUND: Airport – Seattle-Tacoma International Airport (known as Sea-Tac) is about a 25-minute drive from downtown; taxi fare from the center of the city will run about $18 to $20. Evergreen Trails Airport Express (626-6088) offers service every half-hour and costs $4.75. Stops are made at the *Madison, Holiday Inn Crowne Plaza, Four Seasons, Olympic, Westin, Sheraton,* and *Warwick* hotels. Metro buses #174 and #191 leave for Sea-Tac from 9th Ave. and Stewart St.; fare, 85¢ ($1 during rush hours).

Bus – Metropolitan Transit provides extensive service in the metropolitan area with an added attraction: Metro's Magic Carpet Service offers free transportation in the downtown-waterfront area. Route information is available at its office, 821 2nd Ave. (447-4800).

Monorail – The quickest and most exciting way to get from downtown to Seattle Center is via the World's Fair monorail. Leaves every 15 minutes from Westlake Mall, 4th and 5th aves. at Pine St.

Taxi – Cabs can be hailed in the street or ordered on the phone. Major companies are Farwest (622-1717) and Yellow Cab (622-6500).

Car Rental – Seattle is served by the major national firms.

 MUSEUMS: Exhibitions on the history, art, industry, and even marine life of the Pacific Northwest and the world are well represented in Seattle's cultural institutions. The Seattle Art Museum, the Pacific Science Center, the Museum of Science and Industry, and the Aquarium are described above under *Special Places.* Other interesting museums are:

Bellevue Art Museum – American and regional art, Bellevue Sq. (454-3322).

Frye Art Museum – Contemporary regional works, Terry Ave. and Cherry St. (622-9250).

 MAJOR COLLEGES AND UNIVERSITIES: The University of Washington, founded in 1861, is the area's oldest and largest educational institution, at 17th Ave. NE and NE 45th St. (543-2100). Also in the city are Seattle University, 12th Ave. and E Columbia St. (626-6200), and Seattle Pacific University, 3rd Ave. W and W Nickerson St. (281-2000).

 SPECIAL EVENTS: The *Seattle Seafair* is a citywide celebration in early August featuring everything from a hydroplane race, a torchlight parade, a beauty contest, and a marathon run to a special appearance by the Pacific Fleet. Check the papers for exact dates.

 SPORTS AND FITNESS: Seattle is in the big leagues, with three professional teams. The best bet is to order tickets by phone and later pick them up at the team's ticket office.

Baseball – The *Mariners'* baseball season is April through September at the Kingdome (628-3300).

Basketball – The NBA *SuperSonics* play from October through April at the Seattle Center Coliseum (ticket office, at the west entrance, 281-5850).

Bicycling – Rent from Gregg's Green Lake Cycle, 7007 Woodlawn Ave. NE (523-1822). Green Lake Park and Burke-Gilman Trail are good areas for biking.

Fishing – You can wet a line from the public pier of Waterfront Park or go after the big salmon by renting a boat or taking a charter into the deep sea from Ray's Boathouse, 6049 Seaview Ave. NW (783-8873).

Fitness Centers – The Clark Hatch Fitness Center (624-9020) has a pool, Jacuzzi, sauna, steam room, exercise equipment, and weights; athletic clothing is provided; 2001 6th Ave., across from the *Westin Hotel.* The YMCA has a pool, weight room, and track, 909 4th Ave. and Madison (382-5000). The private Seattle Club (2020 Western Ave.; 443-1111) is available to guests of several downtown hotels. Among the many facilities are racquetball courts, track, pool, Nautilus, massage, tanning, exercise classes, and a restaurant.

Football – The NFL *Seahawks'* season is from August through December at the Kingdome, 201 S King St. (827-9766).

Golf – The city has three good 18-hole municipal courses: Jackson Park, 1000 NE 135th St. (363-4747); Jefferson Park, 4101 Beacon Ave. S (762-4513); West Seattle Course, 4470 35th Ave. SW (932-9792).

Horse Racing – Longacres Racetrack is 11 miles SE via I-5 and I-405 in Renton (226-3131). The season is from mid-May to late September.

Jogging – Run the 3-mile course at Myrtle Edwards Park on the waterfront, at Alaska Way between W Bay and W Thomas. Or follow many Seattle residents and run around Green Lake (2.8 miles); to get there, take the #6 or #16 northbound bus from 3rd and Pine.

Skiing – Close by is Alpental on the Snoqualmie Pass via I-90 (434-6112). Also popular is Crystal Mountain 120 miles away near Mt. Rainier (663-2265).

Tennis – City parks have outdoor courts.

THEATER: For current offerings check the publications listed above. The *Seattle Repertory Theater* performs classical and modern productions from September through April at the new *Bagley Wright Theater* at the Seattle Center, 225 Mercer St. (443-2222). *Intiman Theatre Co.* performs at the *Broadway Performance Hall,* 1625 Broadway Ave. (624-2992). *A Contemporary Theater* plays at 100 W Roy (285-5110). The *5th Avenue Theater,* 1308 5th Ave. (625-1900), features pop concerts and touring Broadway plays; and the restored *Paramount Theater,* 907 Pine St. (622-6089), brings in top concert artists. The *Empty Space Theatre,* 95 S Jackson (467-6000), showcases new plays. The *Bathhouse Theatre,* 7312 W Green Lake Dr. N (524-9109), stages experimental productions, the *New City Theatre,* 1634 11th Ave. (323-6800), features works by up and coming playwrights, and the *Group Theatre,* 3940 Brooklyn Ave. NE (543-4327), focuses on ethnic plays.

MUSIC: *The Seattle Symphony* and the *Seattle Opera Association* perform at the Opera House from September through April. The Opera's Wagner Ring Festival is in August. The ticket offices for both are in Center House, Seattle Center (Symphony, 447-4736; Opera, 447-4711).

NIGHTCLUBS AND NIGHTLIFE: Some of the area's hottest nightspots are *Astor Park,* 415 Lenora (625-1578), for new wave; *Jazz Alley Bistro,* 4135 University Way NE (441-9729), for jazz; and *Swannie's,* 222 S Main St. (622-9353), for headline comedy acts. Favorite discos are *Sunday's,* 620 1st Ave. N (284-0456), and *Brass Connection,* for gays, 718 E Pike (322-6572).

SINS: To *gluttons,* Seattle offers the Pike Street Market, chockablock with fresh fish, fruits, vegetables, and other ingestible goodies. *Dilettante Chocolates,* 416 Broadway E (329-6463), is a remarkable spot for chocohol- ics who would like to linger over an espresso and a plate of hand-dipped chocolates. The city's *pride?* An occasional sunny day. If you're so lucky as to encoun- ter one, scurry along to the Bank of California building and take the elevator to the top for a view of Mt. Rainier through the glass wall. Or go up the water tower at Volunteer Park off 15th Avenue for a view of Lake Washington, Puget Sound, the Cascades, and the Olympic Mountains.

LOCAL SERVICES: Business Services – Secretarial Assistants, Bank of California Bldg. (682-6072)
Mechanics – Rhodes Automotive Service, 164 S Michigan St. (762-5007)

BEST IN TOWN

 CHECKING IN: Seattle has an abundance and wide variety of accommodations. Those we rate as expensive begin at $90 for a double room; moderate, from $45 to $60. For information about B&B accommodations, contact: Pacific Bed & Breakfast, 701 NW 60th St., Seattle, WA 98107 (206 784-0539).

Westin Seattle – Two imposing 40- and 47-story towers in the heart of the shopping district that are difficult to overlook. The 875 rooms offer spectacular views of Puget Sound, Mt. Rainier, and the Cascade and Olympic Mountains. Restaurants include a *Trader Vic's,* the *Market Café,* and the *Palm Court.* Shops, airport bus. 5th Ave. at Westlake (206 624-7400). Expensive.

Sorrento – This small first-class hotel with just 76 rooms offers many extras: terry bathrobes, plants and potpourri in every room, a hot water bottle in your bed in winter, and complimentary limousine service into downtown. Dine at the highly acclaimed *Hunt Club* or enjoy English tea in the afternoon. Terry Ave. and Madison St. (206 622-6400). Expensive.

Four Seasons Olympic – A splendid restoration of a historic city landmark (the *Olympic Hotel*) that blends the old and new seamlessly. Highlights include the guest rooms, elegantly decorated with Henredon furnishings; the Solarium, a sparkling new health spa; and the *Georgian Restaurant,* a favorite for special occasions. Many of the city's most popular attractions are within walking distance. 411 University (206 621-1700). Expensive.

Alexis – For the sophisticated traveler who needs to be pampered, this 51-room hotel is the place. The management claims service to be its top priority and it shows, from the optional butler who will do your unpacking to the free shoeshines. 1st and Madison (206 624-4844). Expensive.

Pacific Plaza – An older hotel, smartly updated to appeal to businesspeople and others who want to be in the center of downtown at a reasonable price. It features 168 quiet rooms and complimentary Continental breakfast. 400 Spring St. (206 623-3900). Moderate.

Mayflower Park – In the downtown shopping district, providing convenient accommodations in a recently refurnished and renovated setting. Children under 17 stay free with their parents. Free parking, a coffee shop, and a cocktail lounge. 4th Ave. and Olive Way (206 623-8700). Moderate.

 EATING OUT: Seattle's food industry did not really get moving until the 1962 World's Fair. Being in the international spotlight spawned a wide variety of ethnic restaurants and boosted the quality of existing establishments. Our selections run from $50 for a dinner for two in the expensive range to from $30 to $45 in the moderate and from $25 in the inexpensive category. Prices do not include drinks, wine, or tips.

Mirabeau – Its lofty perch — atop the 50-story Seattle–First National Bank Building — is entirely fitting, as it is simply one of the city's best restaurants. The French cuisine is complemented by a good wine list. Closed Sundays. Reservations necessary. Major credit cards. 1001 4th Ave. (624-4550). Expensive.

Rosellini's Four-10 – Victor Rosellini aims at a big target, not wild game, but the Old World, which he covers admirably with classic Continental and Italian dinners, elegant service and surroundings. The pasta specialties are from old Rosellini family recipes, executed by European-trained chefs. Luncheon specialties include roast duckling and poached salmon stuffed with shrimp sauce. Closed Sundays. Reservations advised. Major credit cards. 4th and Wall sts. (728-0410). Expensive.

Canlis' – Features excellent dishes, including several cuts of charcoal-broiled steaks, poached fresh salmon in hollandaise sauce, pan-fried Quilcene oysters from nearby Quilcene Bay, and a sweeping view of Lake Union. Closed Sundays. Reservations advised. Major credit cards. 2576 Aurora Ave. N (283-3313). Expensive.

Daniel's Broiler – A small, intimate, and usually crowded restaurant on the shores of Lake Washington, *Daniel's* has a pretty view and some of the finest stir-fried vegetables and prawns you'll find in the Northwest. Steaks are also favorites. Open daily for dinner only. Reservations advised. Major credit cards. 200 Lake Washington Blvd. (329-4191). Expensive.

Baffert's – Actually, three places in one: A New York-type bar where wealthy, young Seattleites gather; the *Palm Court* for casual dining; and the *Club Room,* with a more intimate and formal atmosphere. The menu features creative Northwest cuisine and the wine list is extensive. Open daily. Reservations advised. Major credit cards. 314 Broadway E (323-1990). Expensive to moderate.

La Galleria – The decor of this Pioneer Square restaurant will make you feel as if you were dining on a street in Italy. Fresh seafood, pasta, and veal specialties are served in the indoor garden; and set aside some time for wine tasting in the underground wine cellar. Closed Sundays. Reservations suggested. Major credit cards. 83 King St. (467-1660). Moderate.

The Mikado – From its sushi bar, with delectable raw fish, through a dinner menu featuring shioyaki seafood, the *Mikado* is an experience. Tatami rooms, where you feel a part of the Japanese culture, are available for parties of six or more. Dinner only; closed Sundays. Major credit cards. 514 S Jackson St. (622-5206). Moderate.

Settebello – Northern Italian cuisine is featured here, with daily pasta, veal, and seafood specialties. Red floor tiles brighten the room, and, though not noisy, the restaurant has an appealing liveliness. Closed Sundays. Reservations advised. Major credit cards. 1525 E Olive Way (323-7772). Moderate.

Metropolitan Grill – Aged beef, served a variety of ways, is the chef's specialty, as is the ever-popular salmon. Open daily. Reservations advised. Major credit cards. 820 2nd Ave. (624-3287). Moderate.

Ray's Boathouse – On the waterfront at Shilshole Bay, a great place to have a leisurely dinner while watching the sun go down behind the Olympic Mountains. Seafood offerings are fine and varied. Open daily. Reservations advised. Major credit cards. 6049 Seaview Ave. NW (789-3770); also *Ray's Downtown,* 999 3rd Ave. (623-7999). Moderate.

Jake O'Shaughnessey's – A taste of the old Seattle, with booze bottles lining the mirrored bar walls, the decor of the turn-of-the-century saloon, and six beef and seafood entrées. Specialties are fresh salmon roasted over alder wood, saloon beef, roasted for eight hours in a cast of pure grain roasting salt, and Puget Sound sea stew with ten Sound ingredients. Open daily. Reservations suggested. Major credit cards. 100 Mercer St. in Hansen Baking Co. (285-1897). Moderate.

Boondock's, Sundecker's, & Greenthumbs – Have a cocktail before starting to peruse the menu — it's a small book. This is one of the Broadway district's first fine restaurants, and it manages to make the meals big — and tasty. You can't go wrong with *Boondock's* Joe's Special, spinach salad, quiches, or wine salami sandwich. There's also a good selection of wines. Open daily. Reservations advised. Major credit cards. 611 Broadway (323-7272). Moderate.

WASHINGTON, DC

In the 1950s, during one of the thaws in the Cold War, President Eisenhower was showing the visiting Nikita Khrushchev around Washington. Every time Eisenhower pointed out a government building, the Soviet leader would claim that the Russians had one bigger and better that took only half as long to build. Eisenhower, so the story goes, got pretty weary of this civic one-upmanship, and when they passed the Washington Monument, he said nothing, forcing Khrushchev to ask what the structure was. Eisenhower replied, "It's news to me. It wasn't here yesterday."

Well, the story may be somewhat apocryphal, but it does indicate something important about Washington: It is a city filled with imperial architecture — grand, expansive, deliberate — of a kind that simply doesn't happen overnight or by chance. And yet it is a city that did, indeed, happen almost by chance; a city that until World War II seemed to resist almost in its bones being what it has today become: the international showplace of the United States.

A walk along the Mall will remove any doubts you have about the quality of Washington's cityscape. The Mall is the grand promenade of the capital, connecting the Capitol to the Lincoln Memorial by two miles of open green and reflecting pools, lined by the excellent Smithsonian museums. Gleaming marble and massively columned buildings on and surrounding this expanse signify that this *is* the seat of the imperial power of the United States of America. These structures, familiar to everyone from picture postcards, take on real dimensions and fulfill the promise of grandeur (particularly at night when they are bathed in floodlights). But this city of wide tree-lined avenues offers enough open space for varied architectural styles to appear truly consistent. Newer government buildings of modern design and neat rows of town houses fit in with Federal and Greek Revival structures. And Washington will retain its impressive mien. A city ordinance limits the height of buildings to 13 stories, so the Capitol remains the city's tallest building. Though others approach it, none surpasses the splendor of this domed edifice.

The fact that Washington is so impressive is especially remarkable if you consider its stormy birth at the turn of the 18th century. Its future then couldn't have looked more bleak. Were it not for a band of disgruntled Continental soldiers who marched into Philadelphia on June 20, 1783, to demand back pay, Congress might well have remained in that most civilized of American cities, and Washington would probably still be a marshy swamp.

For the next seven years, Congress wrangled over the location of the new federal city. In 1790, as a result of a compromise between the North and the South, a site on the Potomac shore was selected, far enough inland to protect against surprise attack, yet accessible to ocean vessels, and at the head of a tidewater. Maryland agreed to give 69.25 square miles of land and Virginia

30.75 square miles to form the square to be known as the District of Columbia. The city was named for George Washington, who as first president was authorized to oversee its development.

Washington appointed Major Pierre L'Enfant, a French engineer, to lay out the city. L'Enfant arrived on the scene in 1791 and on viewing Jenkins's Hill, the present Capitol Hill, he pronounced it "a pedestal waiting for a monument." He also set about designing avenues 160 feet wide which were to radiate out from circles crowned with sculpture. The city's two focal points were to be the Capitol and the president's house, with Pennsylvania Avenue the principal ceremonial street between.

L'Enfant soon became involved in a controversy over the sale of lots which were to have raised money to finance construction of government buildings, and was fired before the year was out. He spent the rest of his life in relative obscurity, living off the charity of friends. George Washington died in 1799 before the development of the federal city was assured. But President Adams's resolve was firm and Congress was pried from its comfortable surroundings in Philadelphia to the howling wilderness of Washington in November of 1800. Abigail Adams was none too happy with the choice, and wrote to her sister from the new White House: "Not one room or chamber of the whole is finished. . . . We have not the least fence, yard or other convenience without, and the great unfinished audience room I make a drying room of, to hang the clothes in." Abigail was displeased by the White House, and nobody was pleased with the city. The streets were unpaved and mud-rutted, the sewers, nonexistent, and the swampy surroundings infested with mosquitoes (better to stay in the drying room).

During the War of 1812 the city underwent a devastating setback when British troops marched in and succeeded in burning the White House and gutting the Capitol. A torrential thunderstorm saved the city from total destruction, but much was burned beyond repair.

Ironically, for the showplace of democracy, just about the most constructive period of the capital's history took place 50 years later, when Alexander "Boss" Shepherd, governor of the District of Columbia, decided to make Washington worthy of being the capital city in fact as well as in name. Between 1871 and 1874 he succeeded in having the streets paved, gas, sewer mains, and street lights installed, and parks laid out. He thought big, lived high, and used cronyism as his modus operandi. The results were spectacular, as was the debt — $20 million — which left the city bankrupt. The "Boss" was fired; he fled to Mexico, but returned later to a hero's welcome.

Events did not turn out so badly after all for Pierre L'Enfant — or at least for his plans (he, unfortunately, died a pauper in 1825). In 1901 the McMillian Commission was instituted to resurrect L'Enfant's original plans and treat the capital as a work of civic art. Railroad tracks were removed from the Mall, plans were made for the construction of the Lincoln Memorial and Arlington Bridge, and 640 acres of swampland were converted into Potomac parklands. The remains of Pierre L'Enfant were transferred to a grave in Arlington National Cemetery overlooking the city that still bears the stamp of his magnificent design.

First-time visitors to Washington may well wonder if there's a life in Washington beyond the monuments, buildings, fountains, and statues. Behind the handsome facades lie many Washingtons, but it would take the combined skills of a historian, political analyst, city planner, expert on international, race, and social relations, and a master satirist to explain each one. The writer Ben Bagdikian observes: "In many respects, Washington, DC, is a perfectly normal American city. Its rivers are polluted. The air is periodically toxic from exhaust fumes. It has traffic jams, PTA meetings, and other common hazards of urban life. . . . Beyond its official buildings the natives rise each morning, crowd into buses and car pools, go to work, return at night, to the naked eye no different from the inhabitants of Oklahoma City or Pawtucket, Rhode Island."

All true, but Washington has something no other city has — the federal government. The District is something of a one-industry town, but the industry is government and that has made all the difference. Nearly half of the 640,000 people living in Washington and its immediate surroundings work for some branch of government (the population of the entire metropolitan area is close to 3.5 million). As civil servants, they earn relatively high incomes, a factor which provides a solid economic base for the city. Contrary to popular opinion, the population is relatively stable. Even during a change of administration, only about 3,000 officeholders lose their positions. In addition to the permanent government employees, diplomats from more than 137 countries serve in Washington — considered to be the world's top post. The embassies lend a cultural sophistication to the capital, and further diversify the population.

In response to these influences, Washington has developed as a major cosmopolitan center. Restaurants offer nearly as wide a representation of nationalities as do the embassies, and in some cases, even wider — you can eat in a Cuban restaurant, but try to find the Cuban embassy (if you do, it's news to us; it wasn't there yesterday). In the Smithsonian Institution museums you can see anything and everything, from the US's only Leonardo da Vinci painting to something even da Vinci, in his wildest dreams, never imagined: the film *To Fly* (at the National Air and Space Museum), projected on a huge screen with dazzling camerawork that scans the countryside and the globe from dizzying heights as if the viewer were in the cockpit of a plane or a spacecraft. (Perhaps this *was* da Vinci's wildest dream.) The cultural picture has never been brighter (remember that it used to be an "event" to have a visiting ballet troupe squeeze onto the stage of a downtown movie theater, or a post-Broadway road show visit Washington's only theater, the National). But today the Kennedy Center draws star artists and provides a home for music, theater, and dance companies. And what better proof of being an established cultural center than having branches of Bloomingdale's, I. Magnin's, and Neiman-Marcus?

Still, there are some shadows across this bright horizon. Washington has a fairly high crime rate, though due to greatly increased police patrols it's no longer the town of after-dark terror it once was said to be. Cold FBI statistics place it 18th on the list of high crime metropolitan areas. Of the District's resident population, which is largely black, there is a distressingly high rate of unemployment among unskilled workers and teenagers. Following the assassination of Martin Luther King, Jr., in 1968, extensive parts of downtown Washington were burned, precipitating a white flight to the suburbs. But recently many families have returned to the city and are renovating homes in formerly seedy neighborhoods that are becoming stable integrated communities. Many of the city's worst slums, particularly in the southwest section, have been torn down and replaced by apartment houses, theaters, restaurants, town houses, and a redeveloped waterfront area.

The forecast ranges from overcast to sunny. With home rule a reality (since 1973), Washington has abandoned its status as "the last colony." Residents may now vote for president, a mayor, a city council, and a nonvoting representative to Congress. Congressional committees that used to have sole discretion on District spending must share the purse strings with elected officials who have the best interests of their Washington constituency in mind, so the future promises further progress.

And so it goes with Pierre L'Enfant's city. It is the Washington he envisioned which you see today. Every visitor to the Capitol should stand on its west terrace and appreciate one of the finest cityscapes in the world. And as you gaze, you might contemplate the words of Henry Adams. Over a century ago, he wrote, "One of these days this will be a very great city if nothing happens to it." Something has, but nevertheless it is.

WASHINGTON AT-A-GLANCE

 SEEING THE CITY: The 555-foot Washington Monument commands a panorama of the capital in all its glory. To the north stands the White House, below stretches the green Mall with the Lincoln Memorial in the west and the Capitol perfectly aligned with it to the east. Beyond to the south and west flows the Potomac, and across the river lies Virginia. Open daily. 15th St. between Independence and Constitution aves. (426-6839).

 SPECIAL PLACES: In Washington, all roads lead to the Capitol. The building marks the center of the District. North/south streets are numbered in relation to it, east/west streets are lettered, and the four quadrants into which Washington is divided (NW, NE, SW, SE designated after addresses) meet here.

An easy way to get around the principal sightseeing area is by Tourmobile. These 88-passenger shuttle trams allow you to buy your ticket (good for all day) as you board, get on or off at any of the 15 stops, listen to highlights of the sights along the way, and set your own pace. Tourmobiles pass each stop every 30 minutes. For complete information contact the office at 1000 Ohio Dr., SW (554-7950).

Gray Line offers narrated bus tours of the District and outlying areas (479-5900). Museum tours as well as special group tours emphasizing historic Washington are run by National Fine Arts Associates, 4801 Massachusetts Ave., NW (966-3800). From April until mid-October, Washington Boat Lines has sightseeing tours, including trips to Mount Vernon. 6th and Water sts., SW (554-8000). Washington à la Carte, 1706 Surrey Lane, NW (337-7300), offers tailor-made tours for any size group.

CAPITOL HILL AREA

The Capitol – The Senate and House of Representatives are housed in the Capitol, which is visible from almost every part of the city. When the French architect L'Enfant first began to plan the city he noted that Jenkins's Hill (now called Capitol Hill) was "a pedestal waiting for a monument." And though Washington laid the cornerstone in 1793, the pedestal had to wait through some 150 years of additions, remodelings, and fire (it was burned by the British in 1814) to get the monument we know today. The 258-foot cast-iron dome, topped by Thomas Crawford's statue of Freedom, was erected during the Civil War; beneath it, the massive Rotunda is a veritable art gallery of American history featuring Constantino Brumidi's fresco, *The Apotheosis of Washington* in the eye of the dome, John Trumbull's Revolutionary War paintings on the walls, and statues of Washington, Lincoln, Jefferson, and others. The rest of the building also contains many artworks, and though you are free to wander about, the 40-minute guided tours that leave from the Rotunda every quarter hour are excellent and provide access to the visitors galleries of Congress (congressional sessions start at noon). Open daily from 9 AM to 4:30 PM (last tour at 3:45). Free. You can also ride the monorail subway that joins the House and Senate wings with the congressional office buildings and try the famous bean soup in the *Senate Dining Room.* 1st St. between Constitution and Independence aves. (225-6827).

The Supreme Court Building – This neoclassical white marble structure, surrounded by Corinthian columns, and with the inscription on its pediment "Equal Justice Under Law," was designed by Cass Gilbert and completed in 1935. Until then however, the highest judicial body in the nation and one of three equal branches of government met in makeshift quarters in the basement of the Capitol. Now the Court receives equal treatment under the law and meets in an impressive courtroom flanked by Ionic columns when it is in session intermittently from October through June. Sessions are open to the public on a first come, first served basis. Open weekdays; courtroom presentations are on the half-hour from 9:30 AM to 3:30 PM, except when court is in session. Free. 1st St. between Maryland Ave. and E Capitol St., NE (479-3030).

The Library of Congress – These magnificent Italian Renaissance buildings house the world's largest and richest library. Originally designed as a research aid to Congress, the Library serves the public as well with 80 million items in 470 languages, including manuscripts, maps, photographs, motion pictures, and music. The exhibition hall displays include Jefferson's first draft of the Declaration of Independence and Lincoln's first two drafts of the Gettysburg Address. Among the Library's other holdings are one of three extant copies of the Gutenberg Bible, Pierre L'Enfant's original design for Washington, and the oldest known existing film — the three-second *Sneeze* by Thomas Edison. The Coolidge Auditorium has regular concerts and literary events. Forty-five-minute guided tours are offered on weekdays. Open daily. Free. 1st St. between E Capitol and Independence sts., SE (287-6400).

Folger Shakespeare Library – The nine bas-reliefs on the facade depict scenes from Shakespeare's plays, and inside you can find out anything you want to know about Shakespeare and the English Renaissance. The world's finest collection of rare books, manuscripts, and research materials relating to the foremost English-language playwright is here. The library, an oak-paneled, barrel-vaulted Elizabethan palace, also has a model of the Globe Theater and a full-scale replica of an Elizabethan theater complete with a trap door (called the "heavens" and used for special effects). Visitors can see how productions were mounted in Shakespeare's day and how they are done today. Poetry, concerts, and plays by Renaissance and modern authors are presented here. The bookstore features the fine Folger series on the Elizabethan period as well as editions of Shakespeare's plays. Open daily; closed Sundays from Labor Day to April 15. Free (544-4600). For information on attending a play see Theater, *Sources and Resources*. 201 E Capitol St., SE (546-4000).

The National Museum of African Art – The most extensive collection of African art in this country is on display in the restored town house that was the first home of Frederick Douglass, who worked his way up from slavery to become a noted orator and government official. Exhibitions include figures, masks, and sculptures in ivory, wood, bronze, and clay from 20 African nations; also color panels and audio-visual presentations on the people and environment of Africa. One gallery has an intriguing display concerning the influence of Africa's cultural heritage on modern European and American art, and another focuses on the career of Douglass. Delightful gift shop. Open all day weekdays and weekend afternoons. Donations suggested. 316-318 A St., NE (357-1300).

Botanic Gardens – If you feel like you are overdosing on history, the Botanic Gardens provides a pleasant antidote with its azaleas, orchids, and tropical plants, and we're not even going to tell you how big they are or where they're from. Open daily. Free. 1st St. and Maryland Ave., SW, at the foot of Capitol Hill (225-8333).

THE WHITE HOUSE AREA

The White House – Probably the most historic house in America because George Washington never slept here, though every president since has. It has been the official residence of the head of state since 1800. Designed originally by James Hoban, the White House still looks like an Irish country mansion from the outside; inside there are elegant parlors decorated with portraits of the presidents and first ladies, antique furnishings of many periods, and many innovations added by various presidents, like the revolving tray in the Green Room — an invention of Thomas Jefferson's that revolved between pantry and dining room, allowing him to serve such novelties as macaroni and ice cream and waffles without fear of eavesdropping servants. The five state rooms on the first floor are open to the public, and though you won't actually see the business of government going on, you'll be very close to it.

Visitors line up at the East Gate on E Executive Ave. Open Tuesdays through Saturdays from 10 AM to noon. (Tickets, required during summer months, are available from the tent on the Ellipse.) VIP tours of seven rooms, instead of the usual five, are available by writing to your congressman in advance. Be sure to specify alternate dates. From 8 to 10 AM, Tuesdays through Saturdays. Free. 1600 Pennsylvania Ave., NW (456-7041).

Lafayette Square – If you do not enter the White House, you can get a fine view of it from this square, which was originally proposed by city planner L'Enfant as the mansion's front yard. Statues commemorate Andrew Jackson and the foreign heroes of the American Revolution — Lafayette, de Rochambeau, von Steuben, and Kosciusko. Flanking the square are two early-19th-century buildings designed by Benjamin Latrobe, Washington's first public architect. St. John's Church, constructed along classically simple lines, is better known as the Church of Presidents because every president since Madison has attended services here. Open daily. Free. 16th and H sts. NW (347-8766). The Decatur House, built for Commodore Stephen Decatur and occupied after his death by a succession of diplomats, is a Federal town house featuring handsome woodwork, a spiral staircase, and furniture of the 1820s. Open Tuesdays through Fridays, 10 AM to 2 PM; weekends, noon to 4 PM. Closed January and February except weekends in February. Small admission charge. 748 Jackson Pl., NW (673-4030). Near the southwest corner of the square at 1651-1653 Pennsylvania Ave., NW, is Blair House, the president's official guest house since 1942 and home of the Trumans from 1948 to 1952 when the White House was being renovated (Blair House is not open to the public).

The Ellipse – This grassy 36-acre expanse is the location of the zero milestone from which all distances in Washington are measured, the site of everything from demonstrations and ball games to the national Christmas tree. 1600 Constitution Ave., NW.

Corcoran Gallery of Art – If you think you've seen the Athenaeum portraits of George Washington before, you're probably not experiencing déjà vu. Check your wallet and with luck you'll see several more reproductions and maybe a few of Jackson, too. This outstanding collection of American art contains some less familiar works as well, including a beardless portrait of Lincoln (a $5 bill won't help you here). The Corcoran also offers the opulent Grand Salon from the Hôtel d'Orsay in Paris, built by Boucher d'Orsay during the reign of Louis XVI and moved and reconstructed here in its entirety. Closed Mondays. Free. 17th St. and New York Ave., NW (638-3211).

Renwick Gallery – This beautiful French Second Empire building — designed by Smithsonian "Castle" architect James Renwick in 1859 to house W. W. Corcoran's art collection — is the nation's first art museum. Now run by the Smithsonian Institution, it is worth a visit for its changing exhibitions of contemporary American crafts and design. The gallery's other noteworthy sights are the entrance foyer, with its impressive staircase, and the 1870 Grand Salon, with overstuffed Louis XV sofas and potted palms. Open daily. Free. Pennsylvania Ave. at 17th St., NW (357-2700).

Daughters of the American Revolution Museum – Though any member of the DAR must prove that she is descended from those who served the cause of American independence with "unfailing loyalty," the museum is open to everyone regardless of the color of their blood. Exhibitions feature 28 period rooms, including the parlor of a 19th-century Mississippi River steamboat. There's also an extensive genealogical library. Open on weekdays and Sunday afternoons; closed Saturdays and most of April. Free. 1776 D St., NW (628-1776).

Octagon House – This stately red brick town house is a notable example of Federal architecture. The house in which President James and Dolley Madison lived for 6 months after the British burned down the White House in 1814 is maintained as a museum to give a picture of the high style of the early 19th century and features American antique furnishings from the Federal period. Closed Mondays. Donations suggested. 1799 New York Ave., NW (638-3105).

The Organization of American States – In the Pan American Union Building. Its architects, Paul Cret and Albert Kelsey, have blended the styles of North and South America in this building of imposing formality and inviting elegance. The Museum of Modern Latin American Art is just behind the Aztec Garden. Closed Sundays and Mondays. Small fee. 17th St. and Constitution Ave., NW (789-3000).

THE MALL

This two-mile stretch of green from the Lincoln Memorial to the Capitol forms something of the grand avenue envisioned by Pierre L'Enfant in his original plans for the city.

Lincoln Memorial – From the outside, this columned white marble building looks like a Greek temple; inside the spacious chamber with its colossal seated statue of Lincoln, sculpted by Daniel French, it is as inspiring. Carved on the walls are the words of the Gettysburg Address and the Second Inaugural Address. National Park Service guides present brief talks at regular intervals. Open daily. Memorial Circle between Constitution and Independence aves. (426-6841).

Washington Monument – Dominating the Mall is the 555-foot marble and granite obelisk designed by Robert Mills (completed in 1884) to commemorate George Washington. The top (reached by elevator) commands an excellent panoramic view of the city. You can ride down or descend the steps, where you see many stones donated by such groups as the "Citizens of the US residing in Foo Chow Foo, China." Open daily. Free. 15th St. between Independence and Constitution aves. (426-6839).

Vietnam Veterans Memorial – Maya Ying Lin, a Yale architecture student, designed this simple but immensely moving memorial to the American soldiers who died or are missing as a result of the Vietnam War. The two arms of the long, V-shaped polished black granite walls point toward the Washington Monument and the Lincoln Memorial. A sculpture depicting three soldiers stands a short distance from the memorial. Constitution Ave., NW and Henry Bacon Dr. (426-6700).

Bureau of Engraving and Printing – If you're interested in money and how it is really made, the 25-minute self-guided tour that follows the entire process of paper currency production will prove enlightening if not enriching. Everything of a financial character from the one-cent postage stamp to the $500 million Treasury Note is designed, engraved, and printed here. Though it costs only a penny to produce a single note, there are no free samples. Open weekdays, 9 AM to 2 PM. Free. 14th and C sts., SW (447-9709).

National Archives – The repository for all major American records. The 76 Corinthian columns supporting this handsome building designed by John Russell Pope are nothing compared to the contents. Inside, in special helium-filled glass and bronze cases, reside the very pillars of our democracy — the Declaration of Independence, the Constitution, and the Bill of Rights. Open daily. Free. Constitution Ave. between 7th and 9th sts., NW (523-3000).

Jefferson Memorial – Dominating the south bank of the Tidal Basin, this domed temple-like structure (also designed by John Russell Pope) is a tribute to our third president and the drafter of the Declaration of Independence. The bronze statue of Jefferson was executed by Rudulph Evans and inscribed on the walls are quotations from Jefferson's writings. Open daily. Free. South Basin Dr., SW (426-6822).

J. Edgar Hoover Building – If you want to find out a little more about an organization that already knows everything about you, take a tour of the FBI. In addition to a film on some past investigative activities, you'll get to see the laboratory and a firearms demonstration. Open weekdays. Free. Pennsylvania Ave. between 9th and 10th sts. NW (324-3447).

The National Gallery of Art – One of the larger jewels in Washington's rich cultural crown, this gift to the nation by Andrew Mellon, financier and former Secretary of the Treasury, houses one of the world's finest collections of Western art from the 13th century to the present. Among the masterpieces in this huge and opulent white marble gallery are a grand survey of Italian painting including da Vinci's *Ginevra de' Benci,* Fra Filippo Lippi's *The Adoration of the Magi,* Raphael's *Saint George and the Dragon,* works of French Impressionists, a self-portrait by Rembrandt, Renoir's *Girl With a Watering Can,* Picasso's *The Lovers,* and an extensive American collection. The 7-story East Building, designed by I. M. Pei, is something of an architectural masterpiece itself. An intriguing structure of interlocking triangular forms, it houses the Center for Advanced Study in the Visual Arts as well as exhibition halls. Several visits are necessary to see the whole gallery; there are also tours, films, lectures, and weekly concerts. Open daily. Free. 4th St. and Constitution Ave., NW (737-4215).

Smithsonian Institution – Before James Smithson died in 1829 he willed his entire fortune of half a million dollars "to found in Washington, an establishment for the increase and diffusion of knowledge among men." The wealthy English scientist had never even been to America and probably had no idea how much knowledge would be increased and diffused here in his name. Today the Smithsonian administers numerous museums, galleries, and research organizations; has an operating budget of over $90 million, a staff of over 4,000, and 75 million items in its total collection. The Romanesque red sandstone building, known as the Castle, is the best place to get visitor information on any of the Institution's activities. All buildings are open daily. Free. 1000 Jefferson Dr., SW (357-2000, for information on all 13 Smithsonian museums). Among the Smithsonian Museums on the Mall are:

National Museum of Natural History – Only 1% of the museum's collection is on display but, with a total of some 60 million specimens, there's still plenty to see. Features eyefuls of the biggest and the best of most everything from the largest elephant on record — 12 tons from the African bush — to the precious Hope Diamond, at a hefty 44.5 karats, the largest blue diamond known (its only flaw is that it has brought tragedy to all its possessors). The Hall of Dinosaurs has mammoth skeletons. And there's even Martha, who died in the Cincinnati Zoo in 1914 and is now stuffed, the last of the extinct Passenger Pigeons. Open daily. Free. Constitution Ave. at 10th St., NW.

National Museum of American History – Everything that has to do with American ingenuity in craftsmanship, design, and industry can be found here along with some things that bear only the most tenuous link. (That's where the real fun begins.) Hall after hall features such items as Eli Whitney's cotton gin, a gargantuan pendulum which was used by French physicist Jean Foucault to demonstrate the rotation of the earth, and a full gallery of First Lady mannequins dressed in Inaugural Ball gowns. Open daily. Free. Constitution Ave. at 14th St., NW.

National Air and Space Museum – The largest of the Smithsonian's museums, with displays of aircraft in its vast, lofty interior. Exhibitions include the Wright Brothers' plane, Charles Lindbergh's *Spirit of St. Louis,* the Apollo 11 command module, and a walk-through model of a Skylab orbital station. The films *To Fly* and *The Dream Is Alive,* shown on a huge screen, are as spectacular as they are dizzying. Planetarium shows are presented in the Albert Einstein Spacearium. Open daily. Free. Independence Ave. between 4th and 7th sts., SW.

Hirshhorn Museum and Sculpture Garden – Smaller but also superb is this collection donated in 1974 by a Latvian immigrant and self-made millionaire. The Hirshhorn is worth a visit not only for its fine collection but also for the building itself, a circular concrete structure with an open core in which a bronze fountain shoots water 82 feet into the air. Displays include 19th- and 20th-century European and American works, and an attractive sculpture garden that features Rodin's *The Burghers of Calais* and Picasso's *Baby Carriage.* Open daily. Free. Independence Ave. at 8th St., SW.

Freer Gallery of Art – This prime collection of Far and Near Eastern art was amassed by the Detroit industrialist Charles L. Freer. Includes Chinese bronze, jade, and porcelain pieces, Greek biblical manuscripts, Japanese ceramics, and Egyptian glassworks. Freer also gathered over 1,000 works of James Whistler. The Peacock Room, Whistler's only known attempt at interior decorating, should not be missed. Open daily. Free. 12th St. and Jefferson Dr., SW.

The Arts and Industries Building – Just east of the Castle, this is the second oldest Smithsonian building on the Mall. Open daily. Free. Jefferson Drive and Independence Ave. at 9th St., SW.

DOWNTOWN

National Portrait Gallery and The National Museum of American Art – Inside the National Portrait Gallery, an excellent example of Greek Revival architecture, many Americans who have gone down in the history of this country have gone up on the walls ,(in portrait form, that is). Among those hanging are all the American presidents, Pocahontas, Horace Greeley, and Harriet Beecher Stowe. The National Museum of American Art features American painting, sculpture, and graphic arts, including Catlin's paintings of the Indians and a choice group of works of the American Impressionists. Both museums (also administered by the Smithsonian) are open daily. Free. 8th St. at F and G sts.

Ford's Theatre – The site of Lincoln's assassination in 1865 by John Wilkes Booth is a national monument, and in the 1960s it was restored and decorated as it appeared on that fatal night. In the basement is a museum of Lincoln memorabilia, including displays showing his life as a lawyer, statesman, husband and father, and president, and the clothes he was wearing when he was shot, the derringer used by Booth to shoot him, and the assassin's personal diary. For theater tickets, call 347-4833. Open daily. Free. 511 10th St., NW (426-6927).

Peterson House – Directly across the street from the theater and museum is the house in which Lincoln died the morning after the shooting. The small, sparsely furnished house appears much the way it did in 1865. Open daily. Free. 516 10th St., NW (426-6830).

GEORGETOWN

There's not much tobacco left in this area, once the Union's major tobacco port. It's particularly nice in the spring when it's pleasant to walk along the Chesapeake and Ohio Canal. The whole area's great for strolling. Besides the Canal (between Jefferson and 31st sts.) the streets off Wisconsin Avenue house the city's social and political elite in beautiful restored town houses with prim gardens and lovely magnolia trees. The main drags are Wisconsin Avenue and M Street, with boutiques, restaurants, and ice cream parlors (try an old-fashioned sundae at *Swensen's,* 1254 Wisconsin Ave.). Most of the action, including the city's hottest nightlife, takes place here. In the area at the top of the hill (along R St. east of Wisconsin Ave.), large 18th-century country estates survive and mingle with smaller row houses. The Dumbarton Oaks Garden has beautiful formal gardens, and in the Dumbarton Oaks Museum is a fine collection of early Christian and Byzantine art. The entrance to the museum is at 1703 32nd St., NW; the entrance to the gardens is at 31st and R sts., NW. The museum is open Tuesday through Saturday afternoons; free. The gardens are open every afternoon; small admission charge from April to October (338-8278).

■**EXTRA SPECIAL:** Just 16 miles south of Washington on George Washington Memorial Parkway is *Mount Vernon,* George Washington's estate from 1754 to 1799 and his final resting place. This lovely 18th-century plantation is interesting because it shows a less familiar aspect of the military-political man — George Washington as the rich southern planter. The mansion, overlooking the Potomac, and the outbuildings that housed the shops that made Mount Vernon a self-sufficient economic unit have been authentically restored and refurnished. Some 500 of the original 8,000 acres remain; all are well maintained, and the parterre gardens and formal lawns provide a magnificent setting. There's also a museum with Washington memorabilia; the tomb of George and Martha lies at the foot of the hill. In the spring or the summer, start out early to avoid big crowds. Open daily. Admission charge (703 780-2000).

Also beautifully landscaped and overlooking the Potomac, but with many more tombs and monuments is *Arlington National Cemetery,* a solemn reminder of this country's turbulent history. Here lie the bodies of many who served in the military forces, among them Admiral Richard Byrd, General George C. Marshall, Robert F. Kennedy, Justice Oliver Wendell Holmes, and John F. Kennedy, whose grave is marked by the Eternal Flame. The Tomb of the Unknown Soldier, a 50-ton block of white marble, commemorates the dead of World Wars I and II and the Korean and the Vietnam wars and is always guarded by a solitary soldier. Changing of the guard takes place every hour on the hour. The grounds of the cemetery were once the land of Robert E. Lee's plantation but were confiscated by the Union after Lee joined the Confederacy. Lee's home, *Arlington House,* has been restored and is open for public inspection. Cars are not allowed in the cemetery, but you can park at the Visitor Center and go on foot or pay and ride the Tourmobile. Open daily. Directly west of Memorial Bridge in Arlington, Virginia (703 692-0931).

SOURCES AND RESOURCES

 TOURIST INFORMATION: The Washington Convention and Visitors Assn., 1575 Eye St., NW, Washington, DC 20005 (789-7000), has pamphlets and other information on where to stay, eat, and shop. The International Visitors Information Service, 733 15th St., NW, Suite 300, Washington, DC 20005 (783-6540), has free information for foreign visitors. The new Visitors Center in the Great Hall of the Dept. of Commerce, 14th and Pennsylvania Ave., NW (789-7000), provides maps, brochures, and other help for tourists. The Travelers Aid phone number is 347-0101.

Local Coverage – The *Washington Post,* morning daily; *The Washington Times,* morning daily; and *Washingtonian* magazine, monthly.

Food – *The Shoestring Gourmet* by Erik Kanin, Nancy Turner, and Andrea Lubershane (Andrik Associates; $5.95) describes where two can dine for $20 or less.

Area Code – All telephone numbers are in the 202 area code unless otherwise indicated.

 CLIMATE AND CLOTHES: Washington has four distinct seasons. Summers are Amazonian, falls New Englandish and lovely, winters cold with some snow and lots of slush (wear boots or suffer), and spring — when the cherry blossoms bloom, and all is sublime.

 GETTING AROUND: Airports – Washington is served by three major airports. National is the city's primary facility, and the 20-minute drive to downtown by taxi will cost about $7. The Washington Flyer (685-1400) provides limo service every half-hour from National to most downtown and Capitol Hill hotels for $5. The Metro's Blue Line connects downtown with the airport; Metro Center, at 11th and G sts., NW, is the system's main terminal (637-2437).

Dulles International Airport is about 25 miles west of the city, in Virginia. The ride from downtown DC to Dulles usually takes about an hour, and cab fare should run between $30 and $35. The Washington Flyer (685-1400) leaves Dulles about every half-hour for the *Mayflower,* the *Capitol Hilton,* and the *Washington Hilton* hotels; fare, $10.

Baltimore/Washington International Airport (BWI) also serves the DC area and is a 45-minute trip from downtown by car. Cab fare from BWI to DC should run about $35 to $40. The Washington Flyer (441-2345) airport limo runs between BWI and the *Capitol Hilton* and *Washington Hilton* hotels for $10.

Bus – The Metro Bus system serves the entire District and the surrounding area. Transfers within the District are free and the rates increase when you go into Maryland and Virginia. For complete route information call the Metropolitan Area Transit Authority office (637-2437).

Taxi – Cabs in the District charge by the zone and are relatively inexpensive. Sharing cabs is common, but ask the driver whether there is a route conflict if you join another passenger. Cabs may be hailed in the street, picked up outside stations and hotels, or ordered on the phone. By law, basic rates must be posted in all taxis. Major cab companies are Yellow (544-1212) and Barwood, serving the Maryland suburbs (984-1900).

Car Rental – All the national firms serve Washington.

Subway – The newest way to get around Washington is by Metrorail, the subway system. The lines that are in operation provide a quick and quiet ride. New lines to the suburbs and other areas of the city open as they are completed, and buses deposit or pick up passengers at these stations. For complete route and travel information and a map of the system, contact the Washington Metropolitan Area Transit Authority office, 600 5th St., NW (637-2437).

 MUSEUMS: When it comes to museums, Washington is one of the nation's major showplaces, with the Smithsonian Institution's outstanding museums leading the way. Described in some detail in *Special Places* are the National Gallery of Art, the Smithsonian, Hirshhorn Museum, Freer Gallery of Art, National Air and Space Museum, Arts and Industries Building, National Museum of Natural History, National Museum of American History, National Portrait Gallery, National Museum of American Art, and the Renwick Gallery. Also described are the Corcoran Gallery and the Museum of African Art. Other notable museums are:

Hillwood – Russian icons, portraits, and Fabergé creations are housed in the elegant former home of Marjorie Merriweather Post. Tours by appointment only; call well in advance for reservations. 4155 Linnean Ave., NW (686-5807).

National Building Museum – A new museum in the old but wonderful Pension Building. 4th St. and Judiciary Sq., NW (272-2448).

National Geographic Society Explorers Hall – 17th and M sts., NW (recorded information: 857-7588; general information: 857-7589).

The Phillips Collection – 19th- and 20th-century art, 1600 21st St., NW (387-2151).

Washington Doll's House and Toy Museum – 5236 44th St., NW (244-0024).

Woodrow Wilson House – A memorial to our 28th president and his wife. 2340 S St., NW (673-4034).

 MAJOR COLLEGES AND UNIVERSITIES: Washington has several universities of high national standing — George Washington University, 19th to 24th sts., NW, F St. to Pennsylvania Ave. (676-6000), American University, Massachusetts and Nebraska aves., NW (686-2000), Georgetown University, 37th and O sts., NW (625-0100), Howard University, 2000 6th St., NW (636-6100), and Gallaudet College (for the deaf), 7th St. and Florida Ave., NE (651-5000).

 SPECIAL EVENTS: Any town that inaugurates a new president every four years is in good standing when it comes to special events. The president takes the oath of office every fourth year on January 20. Usually the swearing-in is followed by a parade down Pennsylvania Ave.

In between inaugurations there's plenty to keep the District going for four more years. The publications above list exact dates. When you start noticing white single blossoms and a flood of pink double blossoms, it's *Cherry Blossom* time in Washington. In early April, a big festival celebrates the coming of the blossoms and the spring with concerts, parades, balls, and the lighting of the Japanese Lantern at the Tidal Basin.

Around the same time (give or take a few blossoms), is the *Easter Monday Egg Rolling*, when scads of children descend on the White House lawn; adults are only admitted if accompanied by a child.

House, garden, and embassy tours are given in April and May, allowing entrance to some of Washington's most elegant interiors. For information on the tours, see the Weekend section in Friday's *Washington Post.*

During the summer, the *American Folklife Festival* sponsored by the Smithsonian Institution sets up its tents on the Mall near the reflecting pool, and groups from all regions of the country do their stuff with jug bands, blues, Indian dance and handicraft demonstrations.

The city is especially festive at Christmas. Special music programs are presented at the Kennedy Center and at many other spots around town.

SPORTS AND FITNESS: Basketball – The NBA's Washington *Bullets* hold court from October to April at the Capital Centre, Capital Beltway and Central Ave. in Landover, Md. (301 350-3400). Tickets are available at Ticketron outlets.

Bicycling – Rent from Thompson Boat Center, Rock Creek Pky. and Virginia Ave., NW (333-4861). The towpath of the Chesapeake and Ohio Canal, starting at the barge landing in Georgetown, is a good place to ride.

Boating – The Ambassador's Cup Regatta draws the world's fastest speedboats to the Potomac River off Hains Point the first weekend in June.

Fitness Centers – Office Health Center has separate exercise classes and whirlpool for men and women; its assistants all have master's degrees in health education or related fields; 1990 M St. and 20th, off Connecticut (872-0222).

Football – The NFL's *Redskins* play at Robert F. Kennedy Stadium from September to December. Tickets during the season are hard to come by and there is usually a waiting list for season tickets, but if you're in town during late July or August for pre-season games, chances are much better. Try the Ticketron outlet, 1101 17th St., NW (659-2601), or the stadium box office, E Capitol and 22nd sts., SE (546-2222).

Golf – The best public golf course is the East Potomac–Hains Point Course. In East Potomac Park off Ohio Dr. (863-9007).

Hockey – The *Capitals,* Washington's pro hockey team, play at Capital Centre from October to April. Tickets are available at Ticketron outlets or by calling 301 350-3400.

Jogging – Join plenty of others in making a round trip from the Lincoln Memorial to the Capitol (4 miles); also run in Rock Creek Park and in Georgetown, along the C & O Canal.

Skating – From November to April you can skate on the rink on the mall between 7th and 9th sts., NW (347-9041).

Swimming – Year-round facilities are available at the East Capitol Natatorium, 635 North Carolina Ave., SE (724-4495).

Tennis – Washington has some fine public courts and the best bets are the District tennis facilities at 16th and Kennedy sts., NW (723-2669).

 THEATER: The opening of the *Kennedy Center* in 1971 gave the District a real cultural boost; it's off Virginia Ave., NW (254-3600). The center's *Eisenhower Theater* offers musical and dramatic productions, including Broadway previews and road shows (254-3670). The *Terrace Theater,* on the top floor of the center, offers many different productions — modern dance, ballet, dramas, poetry recitals, and so on (254-9895). The *National Theater* presents major productions throughout the year, 1321 Pennsylvania Ave. NW (628-6161). During the fall, winter, and spring the *Arena Stage* and the *Kreeger Theater* host classical and original plays, 6th and M sts., SW (488-3300), and the *Ford's Theatre* offers American productions at 511 10th St., NW (347-4833 or 638-2367). The *Folger Theatre Group* offers innovative interpretations of Shakespeare's plays as well as more contemporary works at the Folger Library's classical theater, 201 E Capitol St., SE (546-4000). During the summer the *Olney Theater,* about a half-hour drive from the District, offers summer stock and well-known casts (Rte. 108, Olney, Md.; 301 924-3400) and the *Wolf Trap Farm Park for the Performing Arts* presents musicals, ballet, pop concerts, and symphonic music in a lovely outdoor setting (Rte. 7 near Vienna, Virginia, accessible via Dulles Airport toll road Rte. 267; 703 255-1860). Unsold theater and concert tickets are available on the day of the performance at half price from the *TICKETplace* stand in F Street Plaza, 12th and F sts., NW (842-5387).

MUSIC: The *National Symphony Orchestra*, conducted by Mstislav Rostropovich, performs at the Kennedy Center Concert Hall from October through April (254-3776). The *Opera Society of Washington* (857-0900) presents four operas a year at the Kennedy Center Opera House. The *Juilliard String Quartet* and other notable ensembles perform chamber music concerts on Stradivarius instruments at the Library of Congress Auditorium, 1st St. between E Capitol St. and Independence Ave., SE, Thursday and Friday evenings in the spring and fall (for tickets, call 287-5502). During the summer there's music under the stars at *Wolf Trap Farm Park* (703 255-1860) and free concerts by the service bands on the plaza at the West Front of the Capitol, or in front of the Jefferson Memorial. Consult newspapers for where and when. Army and Navy Band concerts are presented at different locations in the winter. Information for Army Band Concerts, 692-7219; for Navy Band concerts, 433-2394.

 NIGHTCLUBS AND NIGHTLIFE: For some, Washington is an early-to-bed town, but there's plenty of pub crawling, jazz, bluegrass, soul, rock, and folk music going on after dark. You just have to know where to look for it, and best bets are Georgetown, lower Connecticut Ave., and the Capitol Hill areas. Current favorites: *F. Scott's*, one of the classiest bars in town, 1232 36th St., NW (965-1789); *Blues Alley*, for mainstream jazz and Dixieland, 1073 Wisconsin Ave., NW (337-4141); *Charlie's Georgetown*, for dining and listening to Charlie Byrd, a popular jazz guitarist, 3223 K St., NW (298-5985); *Numbers*, a huge modern club with three bars, three dance floors, and a restaurant, 1330 19th St., NW (463-8888); *Jenkins Hill*, for the District's longest bar, where everyone from public servants to students slake their thirst, 223 Pennsylvania Ave., SE (544-6600); and *The Dubliner Restaurant and Pub*, with old Irish and Celtic tunes and jigs, 520 N Capitol St., NW (737-3773).

 SINS: No matter how you look at it, Washington is a great place for *anger*. Tempers often flare, with lobbyists fighting for their various causes, and senators and members of Congress trying to convince one another that their side is the "right" side of an issue.

Most of Washington's "red light" *lust* takes place on K St. near Lafayette Park and 14th St., NW, a pretty rough area by day and especially so by night. The newest hooker haven seems centered around M Street and 14th, with ladies of the evening varying from the conventional hot-pants-clad types to elegantly dressed damsels who serve as escorts to embassy parties.

LOCAL SERVICES: Babysitting – Child Care Agency, 733 15th St., NW (783-8573)

Business Services – WSS Secretarial Service, 2020 K St., NW (457-1848)

Mechanic – Call Carl (24-hour service), 1112 Half St., SW (479-7200)

BEST IN TOWN

CHECKING IN: Hotel building is currently going on at a dizzying pace, relieving the room shortages that have prevailed for years, except during weekends. Still, accommodations at the best stopping places can dwindle fast, so reservations should be made in advance. Visitors in town for only a few days should stay downtown to make best use of their limited time; weekends offer the best package deals. Inexpensive taxis, the Metro system, and buses facilitate getting around without a car, which is difficult and expensive to park. However, if you have a car, major motel chains have facilities at all principal entry points to the district — Silver Spring and Bethesda in Maryland, Arlington, Rosslyn, and Alexandria in Virginia. Expect to pay $125 and up (sometimes way up) for a double room in the expensive range, $75 to $100 in the moderate range, and $40 to $70 in the inexpensive range. For information about B&B accommodations, contact: The Bed and Breakfast League, 2855 29th St., NW, Washington, DC 20008 (202 232-8718), or Sweet Dreams & Toast, PO Box 4835-0035, Washington, DC 20008 (202 483-9191).

Madison – With 374 luxurious rooms, excellent service by a well-trained staff, amid gracious Federal decor; extras including interpreters, refrigerators, saunas, and bathroom phones. The *Montpelier Room* is quite a good restaurant. Open for buffet on weekdays and Sunday brunch. There are also two more informal restaurants and a cocktail lounge. 15th and M sts., NW (202 862-1600). Expensive.

Hay Adams – An incomparable location just off Lafayette Square, within a silver dollar's throw of the White House. This older 166-room hotel with Old World dignity maintains the standards of the neighborhood with antique furnishings, a paneled lobby, a fine dining room, cocktail lounge, and good service. The entire hotel was renovated in 1984. 16th and H sts., NW (202 638-2260). Expensive.

Ritz Carlton – Restored to an elegance beyond even its original standard. The same management that operates Chicago's distinguished *Tremont* and *Whitehall* hotels has been at work here, and the same taste is evident everywhere. This is as close to an evocation of a classic European hotel as exists in Washington. Facilities include the *Jockey Club* restaurant, the *Fairfax Bar,* as well as a ballroom and 7 meeting rooms. A new addition brings the room total to 230. 2100 Massachusetts Ave., NW (202 293-2100 or 800 424-8008). Expensive.

Four Seasons – Georgetown's answer to the *Madison.* Its exterior looks a lot like a penitentiary, but the interior is bright and beautiful, and the appeal of its rooms has got visitors returning whenever possible. The *Aux Beaux Champs Restaurant* also deserves high praise. A traditional concierge offers many personal services including mail delivery. 2800 Pennsylvania Ave., NW (202 342-0444). Expensive.

Grand – A distinctive copper dome wedged between walls of brick and granite marks this West End hostelry (formerly the *Regent*). In architecture and ambience, it is reminiscent of a small European hotel: a white marble staircase cascades through the lobby, the inner courtyard is meticulously landscaped, and all 262 rooms feature Italian marble baths, 3 phones, remote control TV, and working fireplaces in some suites. The elegant *Mayfair* serves cuisine courante, a step beyond nouvelle with a menu that changes daily; the *Promenade Lounge* features lunch, brunch, and a High Tea in a more informal atmosphere; and burgers and grilled items are the fare in the club-like *M Street Grille.* Besides a multilingual concierge and currency conversion service, the *Grand* offers 24-hour room service, in-house valet and dry cleaning, valet parking, and Godiva chocolates with nightly turndown service. 2350 M St., NW (202 429-0100 or 800 848-0016). Expensive.

Mayflower – Four blocks from the White House, this 720-room hotel, which hosted Calvin Coolidge's inaugural ball, has undergone a very satisfying facelift. The lobby and public areas are light, airy, and filled with flowers. Two excellent new restaurants: the elegant *Nicholas* specializes in nouvelle cuisine with a wide variety of seafood, and the less formal *Café Promenade* has a buffet lunch and scrumptious desserts. The cocktail lounge also serves a light lunch and dinner. 1127 Connecticut Ave., NW (202 347-3000). Expensive.

Sheraton-Carlton – Host to many presidents and dignitaries, most making somewhat more of an impression than ribbon-cutter Calvin Coolidge. Truman used to hold his affairs of state here while the White House was being redone, and Jimmy

Carter announced his intention to run here. The hotel's Italian Renaissance lobby is elegant, the 235 rooms comfortable, the Sunday brunch terrific, and the bar good enough to win approval from Jimmy Breslin. And if you find anything unsatisfactory, the White House is only three blocks away. There are two excellent dining rooms and a cocktail lounge. 923 16th St., NW (202 638-2626). Expensive.

Sheraton Grande – Relatively new on the scene, this 272-room hotel has a 4-story atrium with marble columns and a waterfall as well as the *Signature Room,* a restaurant offering New American cuisine at serious prices (dinner for two costs $90 to $100). The hotel also offers limousine service, exercise equipment, and guest privileges at a nearby squash club. Near the Capitol. 525 New Jersey Ave. (202 628-2100). Expensive.

Vista International – François Mitterrand and Elizabeth Taylor are among those who have stayed at this 413-room hotel, only six blocks from the White House. Its 6 one-bedroom suites, designed by Givenchy, sport full-length mirrors and bathrooms in opalescent tile (cost: $375 a night). Favorite recipes of past presidents are on the menu at the *American Harvest* restaurant; cardiovascular fitness gear is available at the health club. 1400 M St. (202 429-1700). Expensive.

Bristol – It's all suites — 240 of them. There's also a restaurant, the *Bristol Grill,* and a specialty food shop with seating for snacks and sandwiches. Cordials and chocolates that appear in the suites at night are among the hotel's appealing touches. 2430 Pennsylvania Ave., NW (202 955-6400). Expensive.

JW Marriott – Connected with a mall complex of 160 stores and the National Theater, this is the flagship of the Marriott chain. There are 744 rooms, a pool and health spa. 1331 Pennsylvania Ave., NW (202 393-2000). Expensive.

Watergate – Though this modern hotel-apartment-office complex doesn't look too historic, appearances can be deceiving (as can small pieces of tape). With 238 large contemporarily furnished rooms, indoor swimming pool and health club, the excellent *Watergate Restaurant* (open daily), cocktail lounge, Les Champs shopping mall with even more dining possibilities, and a location adjacent to Kennedy Center. 2650 Virginia Ave. (202 965-2300). Expensive.

Loews L'Enfant Plaza – This imposing modernistic structure is one of Washington's best hotels, occupying the top floors of an office complex. A huge fountain cascades on the plaza; below there is a large shopping mall with chic boutiques and a Metro station, and on the 12th story there's an outdoor swimming pool. The service is high quality, the location conveniently near the Mall, and there are 372 rooms, 2 restaurants and a cocktail lounge. 480 L'Enfant Plaza, SW (202 484-1000). Expensive.

Willard Inter-Continental – Nine president-elects stayed at this Beaux-Arts landmark while awaiting completion of the White House, and Charles Dickens and Julia Ward Howe were regulars. But the "crown jewel" of Pennsylvania Avenue fell into disrepair (and was almost razed in the late 1960s). New manager Inter-Continental has just completed a thorough $70 million renovation and modernization of all public spaces and 394 rooms, restoring it to its turn-of-the-century grandeur. Amenities include a mini-bar, direct-dial telephone, and hairdryer in all rooms. Those on the upper three floors have french doors opening onto private terraces. The property adjoins the new Willard Complex of 20 boutiques and restaurants. Corner Pennsylvania Ave. and 14th St., NW (202 628-9100) Expensive.

Georgetown Inn – In the middle of one of Washington's most historic areas, this handsome brick building is unusually classy for a motor inn. All 95 rooms are well appointed with large beds and bathroom phones. Free parking. 1310 Wisconsin Ave., NW (202 333-8900). Expensive.

Canterbury – Near the downtown business district and not far from the White

House, this small hotel has 99 suites with a stocked bar in each. Amenities include a complimentary Continental breakfast, underground parking, nightly turn-down service with a Godiva chocolate placed on your pillow, and *Chaucer's* restaurant. Lower weekend package rates are available. 1733 N St., NW (202 393-3000). Expensive.

Washington – One of the city's older hotels, recently refurbished and offering an incomparable view of the White House and various monuments from its rooftop restaurant. Always comfortable, but great during an inaugural parade. Nearby downtown shopping, TV, bathroom phones. 370 rooms. 15th St. and Pennsylvania Ave., NW (202 638-5900). Moderate.

Tabard Inn – On a charming semi-residential street near the heart of the business district. Guests enjoy an ambience rare in an American city; there is a library and small dining room on the first floor. The rooms are furnished with antiques and some of them share baths. 1739 N St., NW (202 785-1277). Moderate.

Georgetown Dutch Inn – Near the C&O Canal and within a block of the best restaurants and shopping that Georgetown has to offer, this small inn has 47 housekeeping units. 1075 Thomas Jefferson St., NW (202 337-0900). Moderate.

Wellington – This pleasant hotel between Georgetown and the Washington Cathedral has 150 rooms, 120 of them efficiencies. 2505 Wisconsin Ave., NW (202 337-7400). Inexpensive.

Allen Lee Hotel – At this hotel in the heart of the George Washington University campus near the downtown area, some of the rooms don't have private baths, but it's a popular spot with young people. 2224 F St., NW (202 331-1224). Inexpensive.

Harrington – This 310-room, older hotel in the center of Washington's commercial area has seen better days but provides clean accommodations and is within walking distance of the Mall. High school students flock here on their Big Outing to the nation's capital, and family groups are also drawn because the *Kitcheteria* makes feeding the troops easy and inexpensive. 11th and E sts., NW (202 628-8140). Inexpensive.

Rock Creek Hotel – This small, 54-room hotel is a well-kept secret. not too far from downtown, adjacent to Rock Creek Park, it offers quiet lodging with few amenities. 1925 Belmont Rd., NW (202 462-6007). Inexpensive.

Windsor Park Hotel – A modest, 43-room property within walking distance of the subway and near the French Embassy. Convenient and basic. 2116 Kalorama Rd., NW (202 483-7700). Inexpensive.

 EATING OUT: Considering the international aspects of Washington — 2,000 diplomats and a large number of residents who have lived abroad and brought back a taste for foreign cuisines — it's not too surprising that the District can provide an international gastronomic tour de force. What is surprising is that this wasn't the case until just a few years ago. The greatest local meals even two decades ago were served in private homes or in embassies (Jefferson was known to treat his guests to such delicacies as ice cream and imported French wines). The change began when the Kennedys brought a French chef to the White House, and this awakened a broad interest in food and spawned a restaurant boom that hasn't stopped yet. Though it's always helpful to have an ermine-lined wallet or, better yet, an expansive expense account, those who have only the yen for good food needn't go hungry. Our restaurant selections range in price from $100 or more for a dinner for two in the very expensive restaurants to about $80 in expensive places, $40 to $60 in the moderate ones, and $30 and under in the inexpensive bracket. Prices do not include drinks, wine, or tips. Reservations are a must at the top-flight restaurants.

Jean-Louis – Named for its chef, this is a small (only 14 tables) and elegant restaurant with gracious service and fine nouvelle cuisine. Fixed price dinners. Closed

Sundays. Reservations necessary. Major credit cards. In the Watergate Hotel, 2650 Virginia Ave., NW (298-4488). Very expensive.

Maison Blanche – The "in" spot for the Reagan White House, where Washington's famous and powerful meet amid an elegant Parisian dining room decor. Classical French dishes are served, but there are touches of nouvelle cuisine as well. An extensive list of lunch and dinner specials is offered daily. Closed Sundays. Reservations necessary. Major credit cards. 1725 F St., NW (842-0070). Very expensive.

Le Pavillon – Though this restaurant may have the highest prices in town, French chef Yannick Cam offers nouvelle cuisine to those who know and appreciate the best. Closed Sundays. Reservations necessary. Major credit cards. 1050 Connecticut Ave., NW (833-3846). Very expensive.

Le Lion d'Or – Reputed to have the finest French food in town, although some say that the service isn't up to par. Don't leave without tasting one of the spectacular desserts. Open Saturdays for dinner only; closed Sundays. Reservations necessary. Major credit cards. 1150 Connecticut Ave., NW (296-7972). Very expensive.

Jockey Club – Originally (but no longer) operated under the direction of the management of New York's *"21" Club,* this *Ritz Carlton* restaurant is a favorite meeting and eating spot for local movers and shakers. The decor looks more like *"21"* than the original, though the food preparation is of even higher quality. Open daily. Reservations necessary. Major credit cards. 2100 Massachusetts Ave., NW (659-8000). Very expensive.

Cantina d'Italia – Still the longest running hit among Italian restaurants (North Italian cuisine), the changing menu offers new culinary delights but retains the old showstoppers like fettuccine con salsa di noci (homemade noodles with puréed walnuts, pine nuts, ricotta cheese, and parmesan). The only drawback is the small and somewhat confining basement location. Closed weekends. Reservations required. Major credit cards. 1214A 18th St., NW (659-1830). Expensive.

Dominique's – This restaurant has elegant French food, a lively and friendly atmosphere, and if you insist, such exotic items as wild boar, rattlesnake, and buffalo. For a great bargain, try the pre- and post-theater prix fixe menu. Closed Sundays. Reservations necessary. Major credit cards. 1900 Pennsylvania Ave., NW (452-1126). Expensive.

Aux Beaux Champs – The restaurant in the *Four Seasons* hotel is the best in Georgetown. The service is stylish and the food first rate. 2800 Pennsylvania Ave., NW (342-0810). Expensive.

Le Gaulois – Though small and sometimes overcrowded, it has a top-notch French menu including a full page of daily specials. Closed Sundays. Reservations suggested. Major credit cards. 2133 Pennsylvania Ave., NW (466-3232). Expensive to moderate.

Harvey's Restaurant – A fixture in Washington since 1858, it's reputation for fine seafood is well deserved. Try the crab imperial, lobster and shrimp Norfolk, or the shad roe in season. Closed Sundays in July and August. Reservations suggested. Major credit cards. 1001 18th St., NW (833-1858). Expensive to moderate.

La Colline – Charming and moderately priced, this restaurant serves adventurous French food and daily specials as well as wonderful desserts. Open daily. Reservations suggested. Major credit cards. 400 N Capitol St. (737-0400). Moderate.

Lafitte – Classic French and authentic Créole specialties are served in an atmosphere reminiscent of 18th-century New Orleans. The chocolate raspberry torte is a must. Brunch only on Sundays. Reservations advised. Major credit cards. 1310 New Hampshire Ave., NW (466-7978). Moderate.

Morton's of Chicago – This is one of the best places in Washington to get a steak with all the trimmings. Closed Sundays. Reservations advised. Major credit cards. 3251 Prospect St., NW (342-6258). Moderate.

Gusti's – A downtown standby with consistently good service and traditional Italian specialties. Open daily. Reservations not necessary. Major credit cards. 19th and M sts., NW (331-9444). Moderate.

The Broker – A bit off the beaten track in Southeast Washington, this stunning restaurant deserves a visit for its unusual and beautifully prepared Swiss dishes. Sunday brunch is a specialty. Open daily. Reservations advised. Major credit cards. 713 8th St., SE (546-8300). Moderate.

House of Hunan – Relatively new in town, this restaurant already ranks among the finest in the city. Unusual appetizers include shrimp balls and vegetable curls, and special main dishes are crisp whole fish Hunan style, and honeyed ham. Open daily. Reservations necessary for dinner. Major credit cards. 1900 K St., NW (293-9111). Moderate.

Old Europe – Features the best German wine list in the District with some French and American labels; standard German dishes as well. Open daily. Reservations advised. Major credit cards. 2434 Wisconsin Ave., NW (333-7600). Moderate.

The Bread Oven – There's nothing like it in downtown Washington — a combination bakery, pastry shop, and restaurant. Stop by for a croissant and coffee in the morning, or the lunch and dinner specials (a standard is rib steak). Closed Sundays. Reservations advised for dinner. Major credit cards. 1220 19th St., NW (466-4264). Moderate.

Germaine's – *Germaine's* features a varied Oriental menu — including Japanese, Korean, Vietnamese, and Indonesian foods. Specialties are lemon chicken and squirrel fish. Open daily. Reservations suggested. Major credit cards. 2400 Wisconsin Ave., NW (965-1185). Moderate.

Au Pied de Cochon – An informal place for a good meal at a decent price 24 hours a day. If pied de cochon (pig's feet) aren't your style, try asparagus vinaigrette, coq au vin, and other bistro specialties. No reservations. Major credit cards. 1335 Wisconsin Ave., NW (333-5440). Moderate to inexpensive.

Old Ebbitt Grill – An old-timer in a new and elegant Victorian setting. Tasty appetizers lead off a menu ranging from hamburgers to filet mignon. Try the hot fudge sundae for dessert. Open daily. Reservations advised. Major credit cards. 675 15th St., NW (347-4800). Moderate.

Roma – Solid Italian family-style place, best in warm weather when the large outdoor garden is open and musicians and singers add to the relaxed ambience. All the old favorites are there from pasta to pizza. Open daily. Reservations. Major credit cards. 3419 Connecticut Ave., NW (363-6611). Inexpensive.

Astor – Consistently good Greek food at consistently rock-bottom prices. Known more for its food (try the poililia hors d'oeuvre platter, moussaka, pastitso, or styfado — beef stew) than its atmosphere, the restaurant provides bellydancers upstairs amid electric blue vinyl and marbled Formica. An inexpensive wine list has Greek and Mediterranean offerings. Open daily. Reservations advised. Major credit cards. 1813 M St., NW (331-7994). Inexpensive.

Iron Gate Inn – A former stable now dedicated to Middle Eastern food: shish kebab, couscous, and stuffed grape leaves. Speaking of which, there's a charming little grape arbor over the outdoor dining area where you can be served in warm weather. Open daily. Reservations suggested. Major credit cards. 1734 N St., NW (737-1370). Inexpensive.

Vietnam Georgetown – Small and intimate, this simple restaurant serves the best Vietnamese food in town with subtle French overtones. Specialties include deep-fried crispy rolls, shrimp with sugar cane, and beef in grape leaves. Open daily. No credit cards. 2934 M St., NW (337-4536). Inexpensive.

The American Café – A Georgetown favorite, popular for informal meals of light fare (salads, sandwiches, and soups served in imaginative ways). There are also some luscious desserts. Open daily. Major credit cards. Two locations: 1211 Wisconsin Ave., NW, Georgetown (337-3600); on Capitol Hill at 227 Massachusetts Ave., NE (547-8500). Inexpensive.

Patent Pending – The best cafeteria near the Mall. Run by a graduate of the École de Cuisine Française in Dijon, with such dishes as Tomatoes Alice B. Toklas (half a scooped-out tomato stuffed with chick peas vinaigrette, the other half with dill egg salad), Courtyard Salad (fresh mushroom slices, tiny cauliflowers, and tomatoes on a bed of salad greens, under a subtle but spicy yogurt-based dressing), and great soups (lentil, zucchini, or corn chowder). You can dine in a courtyard or in one of two vaulted rooms; there's Dijon mustard on each table. Open daily for lunch. No reservations. No credit cards. At 8th and G sts., NW, in the National Museum of American Art (638-7895). Inexpensive.

Clyde's – This lively place is frequented by Georgetown students and trendy types. *Clyde's* serves omelettes, pasta, and steaks but is known mostly for its terrific bacon cheeseburgers and its weekend brunch. There's also Guinness stout on tap that's served at just the right temperature. Open daily. Reservations advised. Major credit cards. 3236 M St., NW (333-0294). Inexpensive.

You can satisfy your sweet tooth by saving dessert for a visit to either *Häagen-Dazs* or *Swensen's* ice cream parlors. Both have two locations: *Häagen-Dazs*, 1524 Connecticut Ave., NW (667-0350), and 1438 Wisconsin Ave., NW (333-7505); *Swensen's*, 1254 Wisconsin Ave., NW (333-3433), and 5310 Wisconsin Ave., NW (966-8606). Inexpensive.

DIVERSIONS

For the Body

Downhill Skiing

 You don't have to be particularly athletically inclined to ski or even particularly rich. People all over the US are taking to the hills, with some 1,200 ski areas around the country to practice their art. For no other reason than the sheer number of runs, knowing where to go can be a problem.

If you're only going for a day or a weekend, the primary consideration will be to find a nearby resort that meets your budget and doesn't have long lift lines. For a list of those near you, write to the state travel directors or see magazines like *Ski* and *Skiing; Ski*'s monthly "Where to Ski in Your Region" is full of information on lift rates, kids' programs, tips on avoiding lift lines, and more. If you have a week to spend, the problem of choosing an area becomes more difficult. California, Colorado, Idaho, Montana, New Hampshire, New Mexico, Utah, Vermont, and Wyoming all have resorts with terrain that is diverse enough and nightlife, restaurants, and other amenities that are abundant enough to prove alluring. The *White Book of Ski Areas, U.S. & Canada* (Inter-Ski Services, PO Box 3635, Georgetown Station, Washington, DC 20007; 202 342-0886) lists all the ski areas in the US and Canada, with brief descriptions. It's revised annually and can be found in bookstores ($12.95) or by mail from the publisher ($15).

The first decision involves choosing the particular part of the country where you most want to ski — East, Midwest, Rockies, or the Far West. California and the Pacific Northwest get the most snow, with hundreds of inches' accumulation every winter, but because of the high moisture content of the clouds that bring it from the sea, it is often heavy and slushy. The East often endures long lift lines, and the relatively low altitudes at which most skiing there (and in the Midwest) is done, combined with weather patterns, result in a lot of between-snowfall freezing and thawing that often make for icy trails.

For the kind of powder snow that makes for the best skiing, there's no place like the Rockies. That these mountains are the only great land barrier for storms moving inland from the West Coast means that they get huge quantities of snow, and the area's basic overall dryness makes the moisture content low, so that the snow is light and skis skim across it with almost no resistance. Because the water density per cubic centimeter is high (particularly in Utah), the snow has enough body to support a skier through deep powder. The northern Rockies get more snow than the southern Rockies; but snow in the south is drier.

Mountains are smallest in the Midwest, where vertical drops (the perpendicular height from the highest lift-served point to the base of the ski area) may amount to only a few hundred feet, but midwestern resorts are just the place if you are learning.

The mountains are highest in the West; the vertical drops are larger and the runs somewhat longer. In the West, too, you will find wide-open bowls. Though their slopes are steep at the top, most intermediates can get down them in good shape by taking long traverses. In the East, trails have been cut narrow to keep snow from blowing off and to provide shelter from the wind. As a result, skiing that is already difficult because of the snow conditions can be even more demanding because the skier must always ski the fall line. Not all the fall lines are horrendously steep, of course, but going straight down takes fortitude even on a gentle slope.

Eastern mountains range in size between the hills of the Midwest and the Western giants. As a rule, if you're just learning to ski, you won't need access to difficult terrain that only a big mountain can provide; what matters will be whether the beginners' area has terrain varied enough to keep you interested. You don't want to spend a week on the slope with a view of the world's biggest parking lot.

Where you go will also depend on what sort of lodgings you like: not all resorts have condominiums or housekeeping units. Not all have inexpensive ski dorms or, for that matter, those friendly rustic old inns where everybody eats in the lodge every night. Most resort towns have modern motels and ski lodges with private baths, saunas, swimming pools, and the like. In New England, in addition, you'll find old country inns — long on charm but not much for plumbing and not always as convenient as some people like.

Some resorts are better for families. Most families are made up of skiers of varying abilities, and if all the hard runs are in one place, and all the easy runs are a five-minute drive away, families are going to have a hard time getting together for lunch or at the end of the day, even if there's some sort of shuttle-bus transportation. If you're taking your family, pick a resort that has a centralized lift layout on one mountain. (Check the trail map in the area's brochures.) Check, too, to see whether nurseries and children's ski schools in which you want to park your kids for the afternoon require that you pick them up for lunch; some resorts provide all-day supervision, and some don't.

Nearly every ski resort worth the name has a ski school — and some are quite good. In addition, a number of other resorts sponsor Woman's Way Ski Seminars, which deal with ski problems that seem particularly troublesome to women — stiffness, fear, and motivation; for further information, write Box 1182, Tahoe City, CA 95730 (916 583-2904).

The resorts listed below include a few of the major destinations in the country. At all of them, you'll find an abundance of lifts, with rates from $10 to $30 a day (considerably less when you purchase a full week pass), lodging places in all price ranges, a variety of packages, and seasons that run generally from mid-November into April. Note that most resorts are extremely crowded at Christmastime, over the Washington's Birthday holiday, and during the Easter holidays. Always reserve well in advance.

EAST

SUGARLOAF USA, Kingfield, Maine: With a 2,637-foot vertical drop, plus 56 trails and slopes and above-timberline skiing in the spring, this is the third biggest ski mountain in the East, but with plenty of terrain (125 acres of it covered by snowmaking) to suit beginners and intermediates as well as experts. Recent additions include a triple chair lift, 4 new trails, increased snowmaking coverage, and a new hotel — *The Lodge at Sugarloaf.* Best skiing is in February, March, and April. There's a definite Down East feel to the place, and you can stay right on the mountain in condos or comfortable lodges. Information: Sugarloaf USA, Kingfield, ME 04947 (207 237-2000).

THE MT. WASHINGTON VALLEY, North Conway and Jackson, New Hampshire: With four ski mountains (and interchangeable lift tickets), better than half a dozen ski villages (including *Jackson,* which one ski writer called the most beautiful in all New England), a bounty of country inns, one of the region's best XC trail networks, and striking scenery at the base of the Northeast's tallest mountain, this is quite a ski area. *Black Mountain,* with a 1,200-foot vertical, offers easy, family-type skiing. At *Attitash,* the narrow, looping trails draw a fashion-oriented family crowd, and limited lift-ticket sales keep down the weekend crowds. *Mt. Cranmore,* friendly, easy, and wide open, is great for intermediates; its oddball Skimobile is one of the oldest lifts in New England. *Wildcat* has narrow, hair-raising trails (built to keep Mt. Washington's winds from denuding the slopes) and a 2,100-foot vertical. All have snowmaking; and since the area is not well known outside Boston, it's not as crowded as some others, and many good packages are available. Information: Mt. Washington Valley Chamber of Commerce, PO Box 385, North Conway, NH 03860 (603 356-3171).

WATERVILLE VALLEY, Waterville Valley, New Hampshire: Known for its snowmaking and careful slopes grooming, this resort also boasts varied terrain on a maximum 2,020-foot vertical; a self-contained "village" full of spiffy condos; daytime shuttle bus service; reciprocal lift privileges with three nearby ski areas midweek; and a friendly ski week program for adults as well as children. In the indoor sports center, swimming, ice skating, and other activities are available. Information: Waterville Valley Ski Areas, Waterville Valley, NH 03223 (603 236-8311, 603 236-4144 for snow information; 800 552-4767 from New Hampshire, 800 258-8988 from the rest of the East, 603 236-8371 elsewhere for reservations).

KILLINGTON, Killington, Vermont: The home of the longest ski lift and the longest trail in North America, this trail-veined basin has been called a "department store of skiing" for the huge variety of terrain it offers. There are wide long runs, steep and narrow ones (100 trails in all), six interconnected peaks, seven lodge facilities, one of the best novice slopes in the East, Vermont's longest vertical drop (3,160 feet), and acres and acres of gladed skiing, which you don't usually find outside the West and Europe. The Bear Mountain area, where the US Alpine Ski Team trained for the 1980 Olympics, offers New England's steepest skiing terrain. It also has fantastic snow conditions (which mean skiing from October to June), and the standout snowmaking operation, now the world's most extensive, has been expanded every year so that 60% of the skiable terrain is now covered, 38 miles in all. Killington also has some of the East's best learn-to-ski weeks. Information: Killington Ski Resort, Killington, VT 05751 (802 422-3333, information; 802 422-3711, reservations).

MAGIC MOUNTAIN, near Londonderry, Vermont: The miniature Switzerland that Hans Thorner established as a ski resort in 1960 never grew as quickly as nearby Stratton and Bromley. But it is a comprehensible, friendly place, and notably smooth-running. The lower half of the mountain is for novices or intermediates; the top will challenge the very best skiers; and there's snowmaking from top to bottom on both the east and west sides, with coverage of some 70% (soon to be 100%) of the terrain. Five hostelries are available, each with its own personality and all within walking distance of the slopes; also available for rental are 17 condos, most of them with three or four bedrooms. Information: Magic Mountain, Londonderry, VT 05148 (802 824-5566).

STRATTON, Stratton, Vermont: With its 2,000-foot vertical drop, Stratton's mountain, in the Green Mountains of southern Vermont, is the tallest in the region. It is a smooth classic cone divided into two separate areas, each with steep sections that are wide, interestingly contoured, and unfailingly well groomed. Its 57 trails and 10 lifts offer something for skiers at every level. There are four lodges within walking distance of the base and a number of condominiums at the area. It also offers a special carousel that tows beginners around in circles until they get the feel of their skis, and, in the glittering Sports Center, indoor tennis, racquetball, swimming, and Nautilus equipment. And construction is now under way on *Stratton Mountain Village,* a $60 million base expansion that features a new hotel, luxury villas and town houses, a proposed conference center for 500, covered parking, and a shopping center — the whole thing scheduled to be completed by 1987. Information: Stratton Corporation, Stratton Mountain, VT 05155 (802 297-2200).

BROMLEY, Manchester Center, Vermont: Marketed by the Stratton Corporation until recently, this fine ski resort now stands completely on its own. It offers a 1,334-foot vertical drop; wide trails; long, well-groomed runs; snowmaking that covers over 83% of the terrain; and one of the best ski schools in the East. The lift setup is such that it's easy to ski off nearly all the chair lifts (there are seven altogether) covering different sections of the mountain from the base. Information: Bromley Mountain, PO Box 1130, Manchester Center, VT 05255 (802 824-5522).

MT. SNOW, near West Dover, Vermont: Walter Schoenecht, the eccentric who founded *Mt. Snow,* left as his legacy a batch of interesting trails and a reputation as a skier's Disneyland that the present owner, the Sherburne Corp., has been hard put to live down, even as the funds that once went into frills were diverted to essentials such as snowmaking and lifts. More than 80% of the 1,700-vertical-foot mountain's skiable terrain is now covered by snowmaking, and the lifts layout is operating more smoothly than ever thanks to a double handful of carefully thought out improvements to serve the 57 trails. Proximity to the East's major metropolitan areas and an abundance of restaurants and nightspots all up and down the valley make *Mt. Snow* one of Vermont's most popular — and busiest — resorts. Information: Mt. Snow Ski Resort, Mt. Snow, VT 05356 (802 464-3333).

THE MAD RIVER VALLEY (SUGARBUSH, SUGARBUSH NORTH, MAD RIVER GLEN), near Warren and Waitsfield, Vermont: *Sugarbush,* the most famous in this trio of topnotch resorts in north-central Vermont, has a certain classy style that makes it less frenetic than, say, *Stowe.* The runs are as long, steep, narrow, and twisting, and the 2,400-foot vertical as impressive as anything you'll find further north. Some 80% of the skiing is rated intermediate or advanced. There is snowmaking coverage to the top of the mountain, as well as two new triple chair lifts. And the Sports Center offers an abundance of other diversions, including indoor tennis, racquetball, and swimming. With a 1,985-foot vertical, *Mad River* is, according to some, the toughest mountain in the state. Moguls and expert skiing abound, and — increasingly rare — most of the skiing is on trails rather than slopes. But the centralized layout and uncommercial family orientation make this a good place to take novice youngsters as well. *Sugarbush North* (known as *Glen Ellen* before its 1978 takeover by Sugarbush Management) has the longest vertical of the three (2,600 feet) but is also the easiest. Accommodations in the valley — guest houses and inns, condominiums, motels, hotels, and the posh *Sugarbush Inn* (802 583-2301) — overlap; each resort has a housing office that can place you. Information: Sugarbush Valley, Warren, VT 05674-9993 (802 583-2381; 800 451-5030 for reservations) and Mad River Glen, Waitsfield, VT 05673 (802 496-3551).

STOWE, Stowe, Vermont: When one journalist poked fun at *Stowe*'s lift lines and its variable snow conditions, letters of indignation poured in. This is the East's premier ski resort, and its regulars don't take that position lightly. Nowadays, they have even more to puff up about. A massive snowmaking installation covering more than half the resort's terrain, two new trails, and a new high-speed, high-capacity triple chair lift on Mt. Mansfield have resolved situations that most skiers were willing to tolerate only because the skiing on the 2,350-foot vertical was so good. Meanwhile, a well-coordinated children's ski school–day care setup has added terrific appeal for young families; and the famous tough runs share the limelight with the 70% of the slopes and trails rated for novices and intermediates. The restaurants, nightlife, and accommodations are as varied and lively as ever. Lodging information: Stowe Area Association, PO Box 1230, Stowe, VT 05672 (802 253-7321; 800 24-STOWE for reservations). Area information: Mt. Mansfield Co., Stowe, VT 05672 (802 253-7311).

WEST

SKI LAKE TAHOE, near Lake Tahoe, California: On the shores of this incredibly deep-blue body of water, *Heavenly Valley, Northstar, Alpine Meadows, Squaw Valley* (for more about which, see below), and *Kirkwood* have banded together to offer the greatest concentration of skiing available in America. Alone, each resort offers magnificent terrain; the assemblage is simply mind-boggling. *Heavenly Valley* (800 822-5922), straddling the California-Nevada state line, calls itself America's largest ski resort. The intermediates' haven is on the Nevada side, the beginner/intermediate terrain mainly in California. This is also the resort closest to major league gambling and low-cost, high-quality lodging in South Lake Tahoe. *Alpine Meadows* (8 0 824-8557; 800 822-5959 in California) is somewhat smaller, with a smooth lift layout, a respectable 1,800-foot vertical, and 30 acres covered by snowmaking. The upper mountain is full of steep bowls and narrow chutes, but there's usually enough space for traversing; the lower slopes are wide, gentle, beautifully groomed. *Kirkwood* (209 258-7247), whose 2,000-foot vertical has been developed relatively recently, focuses on skiing and other outdoor pleasures rather than après-skiing. Olympic and Sentinel bowls and the snow-filled saddles of the ridges have established *Kirkwood*'s reputation as a place for experts. *Northstar* (800 824-8516; 800 822-5987 in California), with a 2,300-foot vertical, is more like a private club attached to condominiums. Information: Ski Lake Tahoe, PO Box 17346, South Lake Tahoe, CA 95706 (916 541-5950).

SQUAW VALLEY, Olympic Valley, California: Some 6,000 acres of bumps, chutes, gulleys, headwalls, saddles, bowls, and meadows graded for experts, intermediates, and novices make this resort a good bet for a long ski week. The 1960 Olympic site and its bustling Olympic Village are still lively — and lots of fun once you find your way around. Information: Squaw Valley, PO Box 2007, Olympic Valley, CA 95730 (916 583-6985; 800 824-7954; 800 545-4350 in California).

MAMMOTH MOUNTAIN, Mammoth Lakes, California: Mammoth it is. This 11,053-foot blown-out volcano is skiable from late October until early July; the bottom sections are excellent for beginners. Elsewhere, there are rugged runs designed to chill experts on 3,100 feet of vertical served by 32 lifts. Information: Mammoth Mountain, PO Box 24, Mammoth Lakes, CA 93546 (619 934-2571).

ASPEN, Aspen, Colorado: The biggest action town in ski-dom, an old mining center, and the granddaddy of American ski resorts, *Aspen* has a little something for everyone. Aspen Mountain, with its 3,370-foot vertical, is known for its powder, its steep runs, and celebrated toughies like Silver Queen. Aspen Highlands, with its 3,800-foot vertical, has runs of up to 3½ miles. Its terrain is well balanced, with half intermediate and the other half divided equally between beginner and expert. Buttermilk Mountain, with its 2,030-foot vertical, is a beginners' and intermediates' paradise not only for the quality of the snow but also for the width and gentleness of its trails. And there's nightlife and good eating in a quantity and variety that you'll find at few other ski resorts in the world. Information: Aspen Mountain and Buttermilk Mountain, PO Box 1248, Aspen, CO 81612 (303 925-1220); Aspen Highlands, PO Box T, Aspen, CO 81612 (303 925-5300).

BRECKENRIDGE, Breckenridge, Colorado: Some 85 miles (90 minutes) west of Denver and associated with *Copper Mountain* and *Keystone* through a "Ski the Summit (county)" lift ticket exchange program, *Breckenridge,* one of Colorado's first great skiing finds, does a brisk business among skiing families — and everybody else lucky enough to have discovered it. There are three mountains (with a fourth being planned), three base areas, a 2,583-foot vertical rise, 1,441 skiable acres comprising 50 miles of trails (which even on the busiest days can seem empty), 300 acres of snowmaking, and a Nordic center and snowmobiling close by. Besides all of this, *Breckenridge Resort* has the distinction of being part of a town that is over 120 years old, with its own history, character, and appearance. The town boasts 350 historic Victorian structures as well as many newer homes designed to harmonize with their older neighbors — perfect for a walking tour to loosen up sore muscles. There is a variety of available lodgings, including three bed-and-breakfast establishments, and an active nightlife. In town, public transportation is plentiful, but a car is better for real mobility. Information: Breckenridge Ski Area, PO Box 1058, Breckenridge, CO 80424 (303 453-2368).

COPPER MOUNTAIN, Copper Mountain, Colorado: About 75 miles from Denver, the mountain soars above a compact conduminium village, including the only cold-weather *Club Med* in North America. Three base lift stations, within walking distance of accommodations, lead, respectively, to beginner, intermediate, and advanced terrain. The vertical is 2,760 feet; the 1985-86 expansion into Spaulding Bowl added 290 acres, bringing the total to 1,160. Together with *Breckenridge* and *Keystone,* this resort is part of the "Ski the Summit (county)" exchange program. Information: Copper Mountain Resort, PO Box 3001, Copper Mountain, CO 80443 (303 968-2882 or 800 525-3878).

KEYSTONE and ARAPAHOE BASIN, Keystone, Colorado: Only 75 miles from Denver (the closest major ski area to Stapleton Airport), *Keystone* has been immaculately designed to take advantage of the natural contours of its mountain. Even the easy slopes, like the 2,000-foot vertical Schoolmarm, are interesting, and the difficult slopes, while hard, are not impossible. The snowmaking system, which covers more than three fourths of the mountain, is the Rockies' most extensive. *Arapahoe Basin,* the longtime favorite of Denver day-trippers that is now owned by Keystone's parent corporation, Ralston Purina, has added late (into June) skiing to Summit County's offerings. Its vertical is 1,640 feet; *Keystone's* is 2,400. *Keystone's* third, newest mountain, *North Peak,* with 200 acres of advanced intermediate and expert terrain, brings the resort's skiable acreage to 1,335. *Keystone* and *North Peak* can be reached by six-passenger gondola, another part of *Keystone's* expansion program. All three areas participate in the "Ski the Summit" lift exchange program with *Copper Mountain* and *Breckenridge.* Shuttle buses available, but a car is helpful. Information: Keystone Resort Association, PO Box 38, Keystone, CO 80443 (303 968-2882).

SNOWMASS RESORT, Snowmass Village, Colorado: Whereas *Aspen* is best known for its appeal to singles, nearby *Snowmass* is a family-oriented place that has won a reputation for itself as a Cadillac among family ski areas. One of the largest intermediate mountains in the country, with more than 1,560 acres of skiing, it has over 90 runs ranging down its 3,600-foot vertical. Most accommodations are right on the slope. Information: Snowmass Resort Association, Box 5566, Snowmass Village, CO 81615 (303 923-2000).

STEAMBOAT, Steamboat Village, Colorado: A relaxed family area on the outskirts of an archetypal Old West town named for its whistling hot springs. The runs (91 of them) are roomy and varied; there are trails, bowls, and powder fields for skiers of all skills; good children's programs; and a 3,600-foot vertical. The recently opened Sunshine Bowl adds 400 acres of skiable terrain, a triple chair lift, and the *Rendezvous Saddle* restaurant. *Steamboat's* celebrated, ultra-light "champagne powder" is best experienced in January and February; March and April are good for sunny, warm spring skiing. Information: Steamboat, PO Box 774408, Steamboat Springs, CO 80477 (303 879-0740).

VAIL, Vail, Colorado: One of the most magnificent ski complexes in the US, this pioneer of modern American skiing takes up 10 square miles of a mountain up and down a 3,000-foot vertical. There's so much skiing that even experts can spend a week at *Vail* and never repeat a run, and a major expansion plan has already added new terrain and high-speed lifts and will, when complete, include a new gondola in Lions-Head, more lifts, and the opening of over 800 *more* new acres of skiing. *Beaver Creek* — the carefully developed new Vail Associates resort 10 miles away — adds still more. Lodging in the area ranges from small, simple inns and lodges to full-service hotels at Vail Village and LionsHead — both within skiing distance of the lift bases. Information: Vail Resort Association, 241 E Meadow Dr., Vail, CO 81657 (303 476-5677).

SUN VALLEY, Sun Valley, Idaho: The ne plus ultra of destination ski resorts, this grande dame offers something for everyone on its 3,400 vertical feet — steilhangs for the brave and ballroom slopes for the tyro. Baldy, famous for steep-bowl skiing, now boasts an equal variety of intermediate terrain, more like that of Dollar (*Sun Valley*'s other mountain — accessible by shuttle bus). Lodging is in Sun Valley proper, at the base of Dollar where there's a self-contained village full of shops and restaurants, and at Baldy's base in the old mining town of Ketchum. Information: Sun Valley, Sun Valley, ID 83353-0010 (208 622-4111 or 800 635-8261).

THE BIG MOUNTAIN, Whitefish, Montana: It's often been said that the farther you have to go to get to a resort, the friendlier it's bound to be. And though remarkably *accessible* thanks to decent transportation, The Big Mountain is a good example. Singles can have a great time because of the coziness of the lodges (within walking distance of lifts) and a schedule of parties, and families enjoy it because of the centralized, manageable layout of its 35 miles of runs. A new slope and triple chair lift were added in 1985. Because the mountain is in the northern Rockies, it gets enough snow that you can ski from Thanksgiving until mid-April. Whitefish, 28 miles from the west entrance to Glacier National Park, is an old logging town turned resort; après-ski can be lively. Information: The Big Mountain, Box 1215, Whitefish, MT 59937 (406 862-3511).

TAOS SKI VALLEY, Taos, New Mexico: The deep powder for which *Taos* has always been famous is still here, and the lift lines are still notably absent; but the relentlessly steep runs down parts of this 2,613-vertical-footed mountain are no longer the sadistically narrow demons of yore. This, thanks to an extensive and painstaking trail-revamping project that also included smoothing the slopes to take snow cover earlier and keep it longer. Après-ski centers on several cozy American-plan lodges at the mountain's base. The ski school — also famous — is as good as ever; virtually everyone participates. Information: Taos Ski Valley, Taos, NM 87571; 505 776-2291; for reservations, 800 992-SNOW).

ALTA, Alta, Utah: Two things are generally known about this rustic resort hidden away in Little Cottonwood Canyon since 1938, not far from *Snowbird* and Salt Lake City. First, this is the mother nest for powder skiers; second, the famous Alf's High Rustler run, a ¾-mile chute with a 40° slope, no trees, and frequent avalanches, is possibly the scariest trail in the West. However, not all the runs are steep, and the novice and intermediate bowls offer wonderful views of jagged peaks and forests. *Alta* is also one of the cozier of American ski resorts, since all après-ski life revolves around the several lodges at base. Lift rates are among the lowest you'll find at any major ski resort. Information: Alta Ski Area, Alta, UT 84092 (801 742-3333; 801 742-2040 for lodging information).

DEER VALLEY, Park City, Utah: This highly unusual ski resort believes that skiers care as much about the flakiness of their croissants as they do about the grooming quality and steepness of their slopes; it's like a superb big resort at which a major ski mountain is just one of the amenities. Accordingly, the base lodge and the midmountain lodge are tastefully done up with pine, cedar, fir, and real antiques; the restrooms are fitted out with pink Carrara marble and brass fixtures. Accommodations are in the luxurious fieldstone and stucco *Stein Erikson Lodge* and in superb condos with hillside views, big Jacuzzis, sunporches, and the like. As for the skiing, it's ideal — thanks to an annual 300 inches of the type of powdery snow only Utah can deliver, trails that unfold like a good novel, and a limited lift ticket sales policy that keeps lift lines down to five minutes. Add the great cuisine (the preparation and serving of which require the effort of a third of all *Deer Valley* employees), and you've got a ski vacation option like no other in the US. Information: Deer Valley Resort, Box 1525, Park City, UT 84060 (801 649-1000).

PARK CITY SKI AREA, Park City, Utah: With its many varied trails, night skiing, and snowmaking, *Park City* has always been terrific for skiers of all levels, with some of the steep snowfields a particular challenge to experts. On the eastern slopes of the

Wasatch Mountains, it is Utah's largest ski area, with some 2,200 acres of skiable terrain. The maximum vertical is now 3,100 feet. The town is an erstwhile mining settlement full of shops, health food emporiums, saloons, fancy steak joints — and lots of atmosphere to spare. Information: Park City Ski Area, PO Box 39, Park City, UT 84060 (801 649-8111).

SNOWBIRD, Snowbird, Utah: Like *Alta,* well known for powder skiing. Where *Alta* is old-fashioned and home-grown, *Snowbird,* just a mile to the west, is high-tech and elegant; the fact that it's a multimillion-dollar project shows in the slick condominium towers of unadorned concrete and in the aura of luxury that surrounds the whole scene. As for the 1,900 acres of skiing, there are superb runs for experts on *Snowbird*'s 3,100 vertical feet, and a respectable quota of runs for novices and intermediates as well. Among the resort's special ski programs are the Mountain Experience (five hours of steep going in the backcountry for experts), free guided skiing tours, and helicopter skiing in the backcountry with the *Wasatch Powderbird Guides.* Information: Snowbird Ski and Summer Resort, Snowbird, UT 84092 (for reservations: 801 742-2222 from Utah; 800 453-3000 elsewhere).

JACKSON HOLE SKI AREA, Teton Village, Wyoming: That the resort has America's biggest vertical drop (4,139 feet) and its longest runs does not explain why it also ranks among the country's least crowded. That is because the first lifts here went up on redoubtable Rendezvous Mountain, and its first reputation was as not only the biggest but also the toughest. Energetic development of the 2,200 vertical feet of Après Vous, the resort's other, far more forgiving giant, is only beginning to dispel the scare stories. High time: half of *Jackson Hole*'s skiable acreage is rated for experts, its nonexpert terrain is bigger than the entirety of 90% of other US ski resorts. That, plus a compact lift-base arrangement of resorts (so that cars are optional) makes *Jackson Hole* a good vacation bet for *any* skier. Information: Jackson Hole Central Reservations, PO Box 510, Teton Village, WY 83025 (307 733-4005 or 800 443-6931).

Cross-Country Skiing

You can go striding and gliding across almost anywhere when there's even a little snow on the ground. Or you can spend an afternoon tooling down a frozen river or canal, around the edge of a cemetery, or through a city park. You can cross-country in most forests, national and state parks, and even in wildlife management areas. All you need is a pair of cross-country skis. As long as there is enough snow to cover the grass, the pavement, or the underbrush, those long, skinny skis will glide right along.

The special cross-country skiing centers springing up around the country not only offer lessons and cross-country ski rentals but also suggest marked trails that are tracked by machines to make the going easier and distribute trail maps. In very wild areas, some will also provide guides.

EAST

ACADIA NATIONAL PARK, Bar Harbor, Maine: The 50 miles of carriage roads on Mt. Desert Island, which are not plowed in winter, take you up and down the rugged mountains of the interior and along the coast, and when conditions are right, this is a winter wonderland par excellence. However, because the ocean moderates the temperatures, you can't count on snow; call before traveling. Information: Acadia National Park, Box 177, Bar Harbor, ME 04609 (207 288-3338).

SUGARLOAF AREA, Kingfield, Maine: Two miles from *Sugarloaf USA,* Maine's largest downhill skiing area, the *Carrabassett Valley Touring Center* has some 65 miles of trails along old logging roads, through forests, down an old narrow-gauge railroad track, to a pond surrounded by hills and mountains, and around some condominiums at *Sugarloaf.* Lodgings are in cabins, condominiums, and motels nearby. Information: Carrabassett Valley Touring Center, Carrabassett Valley, ME 04947 (207 237-2205).

THE BERKSHIRES, around Lenox, Massachusetts: Miles and miles of trails through the forests here, some in state parks, some at resorts, and some maintained by special touring centers. Country inns are like hotels with personality or else intimate resorts or house parties at somebody's exceptionally wonderful country home. You'll find a number of major touring centers with ski rental shops and special activities — some of them adjoining state forest lands that also have trails. For general information on the area, contact Berkshire Hills Conference, Berkshire Common, Pittsfield, MA 01201 (413 443-9186 or 800 237-5747).

MT. WASHINGTON VALLEY, around North Conway, New Hampshire: Inns, a couple of ski centers, the Appalachian Mountain Club (AMC), and the Jackson Ski Touring Foundation maintain over 150 miles of trails at the base of some of the highest peaks in the East. Some curl through the valley, weaving between country inns and art galleries, shops, and quaint restaurants; some plunge into the forests. The most distinctive lodging is at the AMC's *Pinkham Notch Camp,* off by itself at the northern end of the valley, beloved of rugged outdoor types (although with thick wool blankets and freshly ironed sheets on the narrow bunk beds and shiny tile in the bathroom down the hall, it's not all that spartan). The AMC also maintains two backcountry huts (supply your own food and sleeping bag); reservations are required. Information: Appalachian Mountain Club, PO Box 298, Gorham, NH 03581 (603 466-2727); Mt. Washington Valley Chamber of Commerce, PO Box 385, North Conway, NH 03860 (603 356-3171).

THE ADIRONDACKS, around Lake Placid, New York: This 6-million-acre region offers some of the most varied touring in the eastern US; the area around the site of the 1980 Olympics at Lake Placid is one of its centers. The *Bark Eater Lodge* (Box 139, Keene, NY 12942; 518 576-2221) offers a variety of guided tours into the wilds and on its own trail system, which is linked to that of the 12-mile-distant *Adirondak Loj,* a rustic log structure named by the inventor of phonetic spelling and favored by gung-ho cross-country types (PO Box 867, Lake Placid, NY 12946, 518 523-3441). Both systems connect with the 30 miles of trails at the Mt. Van Hoevenberg Recreation Area, where each trail has been very carefully designed to help skiers of varying ability levels perfect their skills. Various sections of the Northville–Lake Placid Trail, a famous wilderness hiking trail through the valleys between the two towns, are also suitable for cross-country skiing. For a free booklet describing them as well as others in the Adirondacks, write the New York Dept. of Environmental Conservation, 50 Wolf Rd., Albany, NY 12233-0001 (518 457-7433). Also contact the Lake Placid Chamber of Commerce, Olympic Arena, Lake Placid, NY 12946 (518 523-2445), or Olympic Regional Development Authority, Lake Placid, NY 12946, 518 523-1655).

NORTHEAST KINGDOM, Vermont: This still-quiet, unspoiled section of the Green Mountain State is one of the US's up-and-coming ski-touring areas. You can ski-tour through woods and fields, across lakes, on old logging roads or unplowed secondary roads, or along hiking trails or hunting trails — as well as on a number of trails that are prepared and maintained as part of the ski-touring at *Burke Mountain Recreation,* a downhill ski resort with a 20-mile cross-country trail network (East Burke, VT 05832; 802 626-3305). The *Inn on the Common,* a fancy, antiquey establishment on the green in one of those picture-postcard towns presided over by a white-steepled clapboard church (Craftsbury Common, VT 05827; 802 586-9619), uses the extensive facilities — including over 30 miles of trails — at the 2½-mile-distant *Craftsbury Ski Center* and at the wonderfully homey *Highland Lodge* (Caspian Lake, Greensboro, VT 05841; 802 533-2647).

BLUEBERRY HILL INN, Goshen, Vermont: In the central part of the state, this small inn — a countrified sort of place except for the English paintings on the walls and the French faience pottery from Quimper in the antique corner cabinet — has always catered to cross-country skiers (and, in warmer months, to hikers). There are nearly 50 miles of trails — some in loops, some running through the woods to nearby inns — and many special programs. Information: Blueberry Hill, Goshen, VT 05733 (802 247-6535).

STOWE, Vermont: The more-Austrian-than-in-Austria chalet that was always such an attraction of the *Trapp Family Lodge* (owned by the *Sound of Music* Trapp family) burned in 1980. But the Trapps never took setbacks lying down, and the cross-country ski center reopened within a week of the fire — much to the satisfaction of Stowe XC-ers: The center was the oldest in the US and one of the finest. A brand-new lodge opened in December 1983 (Stowe 05672; 802 253-8511). Linking up with its 37 miles of especially well groomed trails are the paths at prim and proper *Edson Hill Manor* (Stowe 05672; 802 253-7371); those at the *Mt. Mansfield Touring Center* at the base of the alpine facilities; and 20 miles of trails at *Topnotch-at-Stowe,* a very fancy, well-done contemporary resort (Stowe 05672; 802 253-8585 or 800 451-8686). Various other trails connect the *Stowe* networks to those at *Bolton Valley* and *Smugglers' Notch* ski areas. Information: Stowe Area Association, PO Box 1230, Stowe, VT 05672 (802 253-7321; 800 24-STOWE for reservations).

INN-TO-INN XC, Vermont: Through the woods, fields, and high country, the inn-keepers take care of your luggage. *Country Inns Along the Trail* and *Vermont Voyageur Expeditions* offer self-guided trip packages that include accommodations, meals, car shuttles, and directions. Guided tours are also available. Information: Country Inns Along the Trail, c/o Churchill House Inn, RD 3, Brandon, VT 05733 (802 247-3300); Highland Lodge, Caspian Lake, Greensboro, VT 05841 (802 533-2647); Vermont Voyageur Expeditions, Montgomery Center, VT 05471 (802 326-4789).

MIDWEST

SUPERIOR NATIONAL FOREST, north of Duluth, Minnesota: Some of Minnesota's most concentrated touring opportunities are on the eastern edge of this vast forestland on the Canadian border. There are hundreds of miles of groomed and ungroomed trails in the forest, some under the care of the Forest Service, others maintained by the rustic lodges and inns of the region, and many are connected; the "Ski Thru" program lets you travel from inn to inn while the owners take care of your luggage. For a list of lodges and details, contact the Superior National Forest, 515 W First St., Duluth, MN 55801 (218 720-5324), and the Minnesota Arrowhead Association, 734 E Superior St., Duluth, MN 55802 (218 722-0874).

CHEQUAMEGON NATIONAL FOREST, Park Falls, Wisconsin: This north-central Wisconsin woodland has about 64 miles of mapped and marked loop trails, ranging in length from about 1 mile to about 10, designed primarily for cross-country skiers. But it's also possible to set out along hundreds of miles of unplowed roads or along the 60-mile section of the North Country National Scenic Trail that runs through the forest. This is a straight-line affair, but you can camp en route at Adirondack-style shelters; the scenery certainly warrants the efforts. Information: Chequamegon National Forest, 157 N Fifth Ave., Park Falls, WI 54552 (715 762-2461).

WEST

LASSEN VOLCANIC NATIONAL PARK, Mineral, California: There are about 30 miles of trail marked for cross-country skiing around the park. It's also possible to ski on just about any of the 150 miles of hiking trails (with topography map and compass or guide) or to glide along the park roads (which aren't plowed or groomed). These features, along with a comfortable warming hut, make this an especially great place for a cross-country ski vacation. The trip through the deep pine woods to the Bumpass Hill thermal area — where mud pots and hot springs roar, bubble, and throw great clouds of warm steam into the cold air — is especially memorable. It's important to check with the park rangers upon entering. Information: Lassen Park Ski Area, 2150 N Main St. #7, Red Bluff, CA 96080 (916 595-3376).

SEQUOIA AND KINGS CANYON NATIONAL PARKS, near Visalia, California: *Sequoia Ski Touring*'s extensive trail network takes you through groves of the magnificent giant sequoia trees, across white-carpeted meadows, and to overlooks that give you wonderful vistas of the Sierra high country. Day-long guided tours are available out of two centers. Information: Sequoia Ski Touring, Sequoia & Kings Canyon Hospitality Service, Sequoia National Park, CA 93262 (209 565-3461).

YOSEMITE NATIONAL PARK, Yosemite, California: The sequoias drown in the snow, the waterfalls freeze into fantastic sculptures, and everything sparkles. *Yosemite Mountaineering School* (209 372-1244; October to May) takes groups on easy overnight trips through just such wonderlands. Special clinics teach you touring, winter camping, touring survival, cross-country racing techniques, ice climbing — and how to handle that XC anathema, a real downhill run. The first weekend in March, the whole place is jammed for two days of anyone-can-do-it "citizens' races" and the Nordic Holiday Race. Lodgings: anything from the primitive cabins at *Curry Village* to the posh high-ceilinged *Ahwahnee*. Information: Reservations Office, 5410 E Home Ave., Fresno, CA 93727 (209 252-4848).

STEAMBOAT SPRINGS, Colorado: Some of the best tours in the state can be found around the *Scandinavian Lodge,* one of the country's first to emphasize cross-country skiing, and the *Steamboat Ski Touring Center;* Sven Wiik, the former US Olympic Nordic Team coach who set up both of them, knew what he was doing when he planned them. Especially on Rabbit Ears Pass, you've got the advantages of being up at 10,000 feet — the great views and November-to-May powder — and none of the steep pitches or, for that matter, avalanche danger. The lodge — where you'll eat Scandinavian favorites and après-ski in big public rooms decorated with the weavings and the pottery of Mrs. Sven Wiik — manages to stay low key despite the fact that there's a downhill resort practically within schussing distance. Information: Scandinavian Lodge, PO Box 774484, Steamboat Springs, CO 80477 (303 879-0517).

VAIL, Colorado: The *Vail Cross Country Center,* directed by Jean Naumann, has been the focus of ski touring in the area; it now shares the spotlight with its companion resort 10 miles west, *Beaver Creek Cross Country Center;* both have complete ski schools. At *Vail,* there are easy marked and packed trails on the gentle terrain of a golf course east of town. Guides are available to take beginners through the aspen forests in the valley not far away, and to lead better skiers into the steep country up the valley to the high country of the White River National Forest for half- and full-day tours. At *Beaver Creek* there's a 12-mile set track at McCoy Park and a complete touring program. Information: Vail/Beaver Creek Cross Country Ski Centers, 458 Vail Valley Dr., Vail, CO 81657 (303 476-5601, ext. 4380), and the Vail Resort Association, 241 E Meadow Dr., Vail, CO 81657 (303 476-5677).

SUN VALLEY, Idaho: This is one place you don't have to climb to get to the high country: Helicopters take you up to the Douglas fir–covered mountains for trips to Boulder Basin or Corral Creek, or you can go on your own to the Pioneer Cabin near Hyndman Peak, where you can picnic in the sun. In addition there are some hundred miles of marked trails which you can do on your own or with guides. Information: Nordic Ski Touring Center, Box 272, Sun Valley, ID 83353 (208 622-4111).

GRAND TETON NATIONAL PARK, near Jackson, Wyoming: There are miles and miles of touring in this park — along roads as well as on countless trails around and in the Jackson Hole Valley, with splendid views of the jagged-tooth mountains; up gentle hills and across frozen flatlands. More experienced skiers may register at park headquarters for trips into the canyons, up the steeper slopes, and through high-country tundra. *Flagg Ranch Village,* between Grand Teton and Yellowstone national parks, is open for lodging, meals, and cross-country skiing equipment December 15–March 15. The *Jackson Hole* valley outside the park contains a handful of special cross-country touring centers, with lodges, restaurants, rentals, tours, and instruction. You can also find helicopter skiing through *High Mountains Helicopter Skiing* (PO Box 2217, Jackson, WY 83001; 307 733-3274), and backcountry tours during which you help build your own shelter out of snow with *Timberline Tours* (Box 855, Wilson, WY 83014; 307 733-2565). *Spring Creek Ranch* has good beginner terrain. Especially nifty and away-from-it-all is the *Togwotee Mountain Lodge,* on a pass about 45 miles from Jackson in the middle of some of the snowiest forests and meadows anywhere (PO Box 91, Moran, WY 83013; 307 543-2847). The average yearly snowfall is 600 inches, and there is unlimited backcountry and telemark skiing in the surrounding Bridger-Teton National Forest (PO Box 1888, Jackson, WY 83001; 307 733-2752) and the neighboring Teton Wilderness Area. Or you can stay in a sleek condominium in *Teton Village* at the base of the big downhill mountain about 7 miles from town. Information: Jackson Hole Chamber of Commerce, PO Box E, Jackson, WY 83001 (307 733-3316); Grand Teton National Park, PO Drawer 170, Moose, WY 83012 (307 733-2880); Jackson Hole Nordic Association, PO Box 3483, Jackson, WY 83001 (307 733-7013).

YELLOWSTONE NATIONAL PARK, Yellowstone, Wyoming: There's an otherworldly look to the place in winter — partly because of the clouds of steam rising from the flats almost everywhere, partly because of the overwhelming emptiness of it all: Geysers roar, fumaroles rumble, and blue pools mild as morning glories explode into showers of scalding water, without a soul to witness the spectacle. There are bison, Canada geese, and elk in such profusion that you stop noticing them after a while. You can make cross-country tours out of the *Old Faithful Snow Lodge* or *Mammoth Hot Springs Hotel* in the northern section of the park. Rental snowmobiles are available to get you to more distant trailheads. Information: TW Services, Yellowstone National Park, WY 82190-0165 (307 344-7311; 800 421-3401).

The Best Tennis Vacations

Got some vacation time coming and want to work on your game? You can visit a camp or clinic, or just hole up at a resort with good tennis facilities and play away.

The 5-to-8-hour-a-day programs known as camps are particularly intensive. Usually held at colleges, private schools, or camps that cater to children in other seasons, they don't offer much in the way of accommodations, but there's always plenty of tennis. Cost for room, board, and instruction is about $90 per day. Clinics, usually held at hotels or resorts, are special weekend or week-long programs with instruction provided by the establishment's own pros or by visiting experts. Clinics may cost $30 to $100 per day more than camps.

But in either case you're guaranteed a certain number of hours of court time every day. At the beginning of the program you're graded, grouped with others of similar ability, and then worked — hard — by instructors who drive you like boot camp drill sergeants. Usually you tackle one stroke at a time. First there will be a demonstration, then simple hitting drills, then more complicated hitting drills in which the stroke is made part of a more complex sequence of moves. You'll end each day with varying degrees of sunburn, blisters, and sore muscles. (One New York jogger arrived at his camp feeling smug and fit; he ended his first day so bushed he could hardly focus on his *Times.*) How successful the course is will depend on where you start. Intermediates who want to add some muscle and bite to their game probably will. But beginners won't leave as Pancho Segura.

Resorts are probably the most relaxing places to spend a tennis vacation. Sign up for a couple of lessons, play tennis when you want, and use the resort's saunas, whirlpool baths, swimming pools, golf courses, and activity programs the rest of the time. In other than clinic situations it's often true that larger resorts catering to groups attract so many beginners that advanced players may be bored; that older, more established resorts attract more advanced players and may not be much fun for beginners; and that a high courts-to-rooms ratio and the presence of a tennis host who arranges games usually means that the tennis program is well enough organized that you won't spend all your time waiting around for a court.

Find out where the resort you're considering fits into this scheme. Also look into the court situation. How many are there, and what kind? How many are lighted? (In some areas, it's just too hot to play during the day.) Can you reserve courts? How far in advance? Can you do it on the phone or must you present yourself in person? Is there any limit to how long you can play? And if you're not taking your own partner, is it easy to scare up a game?

For a complete and up-to-date list of clinics and camps, check the annual January issue of *Tennis* ($1.75 from *Tennis* magazine, 5520 Park Ave., PO Box 0395, Trumbull, CT 06611-0395; 203 373-7000). For tennis resorts, see *Tennis*'s November 1984 listing of the US's 50 greatest or its annual February treatment of places to play.

Here are some good bets for a first-rate tennis vacation:

TENNIS CLINICS

These organizations sponsor clinics and camps at a number of resorts, schools, and college campuses. Each outfit has its own teaching style and methods.

RAMEY TENNIS SCHOOLS: Headquartered in Owensboro, Kentucky, this organization puts on spring and summer clinics for youth and adults in stroke development and, for better players, tournament camps and competitive play and drill programs at college campuses in Galesburg, Illinois; South Bend and Franklin, Indiana; Springfield, Ohio; and Sewanee, Tennessee. Adult weekend programs and ladies-only programs are held at an indoor club, with deluxe hotel housing, in Owensboro. Computer stroke charting and videotape analyses are special features. Information: Ramey Tennis Schools, Rte. 6, Owensboro, KY 42301 (502 771-5590 or -4723).

VAN DER MEER TENNIS UNIVERSITY: Billie Jean King's onetime coach Dennis Van der Meer, one of the most knowledgeable and influential of the nation's teaching pros, personally supervises all clinics held by his organization at Hilton Head, South Carolina, and Sweet Briar, Virginia. Information: Van Der Meer Tennis University, PO Box 5902, Hilton Head Island, SC 29938 (803 785-9602 in South Carolina; 800 845-6138 elsewhere).

ALL AMERICAN SPORTS: Adult programs emphasizing strategy and stroke development, and featuring intensive drill sessions and liberal use of video replay equipment and ball machines, are offered at resorts in Amelia Island, Florida; Windham, New York; Warren and Stowe, Vermont; plus one in Loreto, Mexico, and three in the Caribbean. Participants may opt for anywhere from two to four hours of court work per day. On the other hand, at the camp in Amherst, Massachusetts, the tennis program is very intensive, with five hours of instruction daily. Information: All American Sports, 45 Kensico Dr., Mt. Kisco, NY 10549 (914 666-0096 in New York; 800 223-2442 elsewhere).

JOHN GARDINER'S TENNIS: The celebrated ranches in Scottsdale, Arizona, and Carmel Valley, California, have spawned a whole new group of tennis clinics at resorts in Keystone, Colorado; West Palm Beach, Florida; a junior summer camp in Sun

Valley, Idaho; and Jackson, Wyoming. The method has you hitting lots of balls under the supervision of well-trained and well-disciplined instructors who hammer the basics into you as you hammer balls. Information: John Gardiner's Tennis, 5700 E McDonald Dr., Scottsdale, AZ 85253 (602 948-2100).

TENNIS RESORTS

EAST

MT. WASHINGTON HOTEL, Bretton Woods, New Hampshire: This immense classic resort, housed in an old white Edwardian structure, gives you spectacular views into the Presidential Range of the White Mountains. Private and group lessons (some using video) are available, and facilities include 12 clay courts; court reservations are possible. Information: Mt. Washington Hotel, Bretton Woods, NH 03575 (603 278-1000).

WATERVILLE VALLEY RESORT, Waterville Valley, New Hampshire: A condominium and lodge development snuggled in the White Mountain National Forest, popular with families. Facilities: clinics and private instruction; 18 clay courts; 2 indoor courts; court reservations possible. Information: Waterville Valley Resort, Waterville Valley, NH 03223 (603 236-8311).

THE CONCORD, Kiamesha Lake, New York: With 1,200 rooms scattered through several high-rise hotel structures on 4,000 acres in the Catskills, this place is like a city — but you *can* play all winter long. Facilities: 40 Latexite courts, 16 of them indoor and open 24 hours a day; ball machines and other teaching aids; courts available by reservation only; private and group lessons. Information: The Concord, Kiamesha Lake, NY 12751 (914 794-4000 ext. 1655).

TOPNOTCH AT STOWE, Stowe, Vermont: An elegant, modern resort. Facilities: All-American Sports clinics; 4 courts indoors, and 10 out; reservations possible. Information: Topnotch At Stowe, PO Box 1260, Stowe, VT 05672 (802 253-8585 or 800 451-8686).

STRATTON MOUNTAIN RESORT, Stratton Mountain, Vermont: Tennis is booming at Stratton, with 23 courts presently available in the area; 4 Plexi-Cushion indoors and 19 outdoors (9 Har-Tru, 2 red clay, and 8 Deco-Turf II). From mid-May to late September there are 2- and 5-day instructional programs and court reservations are available year-round. The inn itself is a modern, newly renovated 125-room ski and summer resort. Information: Stratton Mountain Resort, Stratton Mountain, VT 05155 (802 297-2200).

SUGARBUSH INN, Warren, Vermont: A chic resort in the Green Mountains that manages to be gracious, elegant, and informal all at once. Wonderful food. Facilities: 11 courts — 5 clay, 6 Har-Tru; video replay and ball machines; reservations possible; private instruction and clinics. Information: Sugarbush Inn, Warren, VT 05674 (802 583-2301; for reservations, 800 451-4320).

THE GREENBRIER, White Sulphur Springs, West Virginia: One of the few turn-of-the-century resorts that hasn't lost even a little of its class. Facilities: 20 courts — 15 Har-Tru outdoors, 5 air-conditioned Dynaturf courts indoors; private lessons and clinics. See also *Resort Hotels.* Information: The Greenbrier, White Sulphur Springs, WV 24986 (304 536-1110).

SOUTH

AMELIA ISLAND PLANTATION, Amelia Island, Florida: This 900-acre development offers terrific beaches, wonderful subtropical forest scenery, plenty of peace and quiet, and facilities outstanding enough to have put the place on *Tennis* magazine's list of America's top 50 tennis resorts. You'll find 19 clay composition courts (3 lighted), 2 Deco-Turf hard courts, 4 Omni courts, video replay and ball machines, clinics by

All-American Sports, and private and group lessons. Court reservations are available. See also *Beaches.* Information: Amelia Island Plantation, Amelia Island, FL 32034 (904 261-6161, or 800 874-6878; 800 342-6841 from Florida).

GRENELEFE GOLF AND TENNIS RESORT, Cypress Gardens, Florida: A handsome, fast-growing resort development in the pines and citrus country a half-hour southwest of Walt Disney World. The tennis facilities and services include: 13 courts — 8 Har-Tru (all lighted), 5 Laykold (3 lighted); videotape and ball machines; and clinics and private lessons. In addition, it offers a range of activities guaranteed to divert even a tennis fanatic: three 18-hole golf courses, four swimming pools, 6,400-acre Lake Marion with its full-service marina, saunas, Jacuzzis, bike rentals, and jogging trails. Information: Grenelefe Golf and Tennis Resort, 3200 State Rd. 546, Grenelefe, FL 33844-9732 (800 237-9549; in Florida, 800 282-7875).

THE SHERATON ROYAL BISCAYNE BEACH HOTEL AND RACQUET CLUB, Key Biscayne, Florida: The courts at this good-sized resort off the Miami shore around the corner from Nixon's old haunt draw locals as well as vacationers; you can almost always find a tennis partner. Facilities: 10 Laykold courts (4 lighted); video replay and ball machines; court reservations necessary; private and group lessons. Information: The Royal Biscayne, 555 Ocean Dr., Key Biscayne, FL 33149 (305 361-5775 or 800 325-3535).

THE DORAL HOTEL & COUNTRY CLUB, Miami, Florida: A veritable city of a resort, this ultra-posh establishment on a 2,400-acre estate offers just about any diversion (including five 18-hole golf courses) that you could ask for, except a beach of its own. But there's one just 15 minutes away at a sister property, the *Doral Hotel On-the-Ocean,* not to mention a swimming pool, 80 acres of fishable lakes, a health club, three restaurants, and a cocktail lounge with dancing. Tennis facilities: 15 well-kept courts (5 hard surface, 10 clay — 4 lighted); backboard and ball machines; court reservations available; tennis hostess; private and group lessons. Arthur Ashe is director of tennis. Information: The Doral Hotel & Country Club, 4400 NW 87th Ave., Miami, FL 33178 (305 532-3600 in Florida; 800 327-6334 elsewhere).

HARDER HALL GOLF AND TENNIS RESORT, Sebring, Florida: An old-line central Florida resort turned tennis hot spot whose total renovation and restoration was completed in 1986. Facilities: 10 Plexipave and 2 Har-Tru courts — 5 lighted; ball machines and video replay; guaranteed unlimited play; clinics and group and private lessons. Information: Harder Hall, Sebring, FL 33870 (813 385-0151 or 800 282-1650 in Florida; 800 237-2491 elsewhere).

INNISBROOK, Tarpon Springs, Florida: Near the famous sponge market, a thousand acres of pine woods, citrus groves, moss-hung cypress trees, and 950-odd rooms make this quite a big place — but it's well managed and friendly all the same. Facilities: 18 courts — 11 Har-Tru, 7 Laykold — 7 lighted; video replay and ball machines; backboards; court reservations possible; clinics, and private and group lessons. Home of the Australian Tennis Institute. Information: Innisbrook, PO Box 1088, Tarpon Springs, FL 33589 (813 937-3124 or 800 282-9813 in Florida; 800 237-0157 elsewhere).

HILTON HEAD ISLAND, South Carolina: Along with its stunning white beaches, quietly elegant villas, homes, and marinas, and subtropical forests, this island also has lots of tennis. You'll find most of it at two resorts: the *Palmetto Dunes* and the *Sea Pines Plantation. Palmetto Dunes* has 25 courts, 23 of them clay, and 6 of them lighted, and offers Rod Laver Tennis clinics in addition to private and group instruction; the emphasis is on the Australian method, which brought up so many great players of Laver's generation. At *Sea Pines* — the largest tennis-oriented resort in the world — there are 43 courts (most Har-Tru) clustered in primarily three locations, each a short distance from the beach, shopping, restaurants, and swimming pools. Private lessons are available if you don't want to join one of the resort's own impressive roster of tennis clinics, which include a "Tiny Tots" program for children aged four to seven (life-size cartoon characters are incorporated into the drills), and clinics that focus on singles and doubles strategy, the contact point, preparation, and the like. In addition, there are full-time tennis hostesses and almost daily round-robin tourneys for players of all ages and skill levels. Otherwise, the difference is mainly a matter of style and layout: *Sea Pines* is big, spread out enough that you need at least a bike to get around, while at the smaller *Palmetto Dunes* nearly everything is within walking distance. Information: Palmetto Dunes, PO Box 5606, Hilton Head Island, SC 29938 (803 785-1194 in South Carolina; 800 845-6130 elsewhere); and the Rod Laver Tennis Center, PO Box 4798, Hilton Head Island, SC 29938 (803 785-1152 in South Carolina; 800 845-6130 elsewhere); or Sea Pines Plantation, Hilton Head Island, SC 29928 (800 922-7042 in South Carolina; 800 845-6131 elsewhere).

THE RESORTS OF LAKEWAY, Austin, Texas: Town houses cluster around the groups of courts in the Texas hill country. You feel as if you've got your own courts (almost). Facilities include 26 Laykold courts — 24 lighted, 2 indoors; reservations possible; private lessons and clinics are available. Information: Resorts of Lakeway, One World of Tennis Sq., Austin, TX 78734 (512 261-6000 or 800 LAKEWAY).

JOHN NEWCOMBE'S TENNIS RANCH, New Braunfels, Texas: Quiet and unpretentious — but the video replays are in color. At John Newcombe's home base, where he appears five or six times yearly, you lodge in comfortable condos or motel rooms. Facilities: 28 Laykold courts — 8 lighted and 4 covered; ball machines and video replay; practice alleys; many clinics. Information: John Newcombe's Tennis Ranch, PO Box 469, New Braunfels, TX 78130 (512 625-9105).

MIDWEST

THE FRENCH LICK SPRINGS HOTEL, French Lick, Indiana: The venerable resort in the hills of the southern part of the state, once *the* spot to sip mineral waters and take a cure, and the first place in America where a chef served tomato juice, is now doing a booming business in conventions — and tennis. Facilities include 21 courts — 8 indoor, 10 outdoors, all lighted; ball machines; court reservations possible, some limits may apply; private lessons. Information: French Lick Springs, French Lick, IN 47432 (812 935-9381).

BOYNE MOUNTAIN LODGE, Boyne Falls, Michigan: A complex of villas, chalets, and lodges in the northern Michigan hills that caters to skiers in winter and to golfers and tennis players in summer. The tennis program was originally designed by the Laver organization, and *Tennis Digest* magazine rated it among the top 50 private tennis facilities in the country. Facilities: 12 Laykold courts; ball machines; reservations possible; clinics and private lessons. Information: Boyne Mountain Lodge, Boyne Falls, MI 49713 (616 549-2441).

WEST

THE ARIZONA BILTMORE, Phoenix, Arizona: This ultra-posh, large-scale, superstar resort is well known for the fact that the gold leaf dining room ceiling, the glass mural in the lobby, and the texture of the walls in the lobby were all inspired by or based on designs of Frank Lloyd Wright; the tile-bottomed Olympic-sized swimming pool compares favorably to the no-holds-barred paradise at San Simeon. Facilities include 17 Supreme surface courts, 16 lighted; plus video replay and ball machines; reservations possible; private lessons and clinics. Information: Arizona Biltmore, 24th and Missouri, Phoenix, AZ 85016 (602 955-6600; 800 528-3696 from outside Arizona).

JOHN GARDINER'S TENNIS RANCH, Scottsdale, Arizona: Some people call this Papa Bear of the tennis world the most complete and professional training establishment in the world — and there's good reason for that. Facilities and services include: 22 Plexipave outdoor courts and 2 Omni courts; video replay and ball machines (plus other instructional aids); tennis clinics; private lessons; complimentary court time for guests. You can lodge in small casitas or in three- or four-bedroom casas, some with their own pool and court; the court at the Casa Rosewall is on the roof. Champagne on the house when it rains. Information: John Gardiner's Tennis Ranch, 5700 E McDonald Dr., Scottsdale, AZ 85253 (602 948-2100; 800 245-2051 for reservations).

JOHN GARDINER'S TENNIS RANCH, Carmel Valley, California: Luxurious. The first Gardiner ranch is still the ultimate tennis resort; and Gardiner himself is on hand with his team of top instructors to take care of the 28 guests who can be accommodated at any given time in the week-long clinic programs (offered April through November). There are 14 Plexipave courts. Information: John Gardiner's Tennis Ranch, PO Box 228, Carmel Valley, CA 93924 (408 659-2207).

LA COSTA HOTEL AND SPA, Carlsbad, California: This super-spa, a favorite among stars of all stripes, has equally well developed tennis facilities: 23 hard-surface courts — 4 lighted; 4 brand-new courts — 2 grass, 2 clay; ball machines; reservations possible but usually not necessary; private lessons by members of a pro staff headed by Pancho Segura. Information: La Costa, Costa Del Mar Rd., Carlsbad, CA 92008 (619 438-9111 or 800 542-6200 in California; 800 854-6564 elsewhere).

VIC BRADEN TENNIS COLLEGE, Trabuco Canyon, California: The licensed psychologist and tennis ace whom no less than Jack Kramer called the greatest tennis teacher in the world holds forth here, delivering pre-drill lectures that some standup comics would envy. ("Get to know your navel." "Air your armpits.") The facilities are equally impressive: 16 concrete courts — 12 lighted; ball machines; specially designed hitting lanes; a tall teaching tower and video screening rooms; and a huge array of newfangled teaching devices. Classroom lectures are also part of the program. Information: Vic Braden Tennis College, PO Box 438, Trabuco Canyon Rd., Trabuco Canyon, CA 92678 (714 581-2990).

SUN VALLEY, Idaho: Guests at the *Sun Valley Inn*, the *Sun Valley Lodge*, and condominiums in Sun Valley and in *Elkhorn* (the smaller resort community a mile away) have access to more than 50 Laykold courts. Reservations are available, as are clinics; videotaping and closed-circuit TV facilities are used. Information: Elkhorn Resort at Sun Valley, PO Box 6009, Sun Valley, ID 83354-6009 (208 622-4511 or 800 635-6356), and Sun Valley Company, Sun Valley, ID 83353-0010 (208 622-4111 or 800 632-4104 in Idaho; 800 635-8261 elsewhere).

Golf: The Greening of America

 Golf can be a most frustrating sport for travelers in America, especially those who've spent any appreciable time in front of a television set watching the pros cavort in all their glory on some of the world's finest courses. Not only are the courses attractive to the point of distraction, but seeing them so temptingly displayed only heightens their allure.

One would think that the willingness to travel to each course's locale would permit a golfer to satisfy his or her fondest longings. Not so. The fact is that only about half a dozen of the golf courses listed by *Golf Digest* magazine among the country's top 50 are open for public play on any regular basis, and tourists don't do that much better with the rest.

Nonetheless, there are still a host of top courses that are open to traveling players. What follows is a list of a few of those that are truly worth traveling a significant distance to experience.

EAST

TACONIC GOLF CLUB, Williamstown, Massachusetts: One of the least-known championship courses in the US, in the northwest corner of Massachusetts. Though it is the home of the Williams College golf team and the preferred turf of an active membership, it is open to transient players on weekdays (except from noon to 1:30) and on weekend and holiday afternoons after 1:00 PM. Especially on a fall afternoon, with the leaves just turning on the trees covering the beautiful Berkshire hills, this landscape is right out of America's past, although the very real teeth of this course are apparent in any season. Information: Taconic Golf Club, Water St., Williamstown, MA 01267 (413 458-3997).

THE CONCORD, Kiamesha Lake, New York: One of the very best courses in the country is part of the three-course *Concord Resort Hotel* complex on Kiamesha Lake in the Catskill Mountains. It is a track well worth its nickname, "the Monster." It is nearly unconscionably long and almost intolerably difficult, and that's probably why great numbers of masochistic golfers from New York City and points north trudge up to its first tee every weekend. These crowds usually include a number of Japanese players (the most avid, most polite, and sometimes, it seems, most painstakingly slow golfers in the world), so you should plan your own assault for a weekday. Information: The Concord, Kiamesha Lake, NY 12751 (914 794-4000).

HERSHEY COUNTRY CLUB, Hershey, Pennsylvania: It's difficult to take seriously a course so close to Cocoa and East Chocolate avenues, but that doesn't change the fact that the two courses at the *Hershey Country Club* are among the best in the Northeast. The West course is especially challenging. Chocolate freaks may find the scent in the air a bit distracting, but no one can quarrel with the quality of the golfing challenge. Information: Hershey Country Club, 1000 E Derry Rd., Hershey, PA 17033 (717 533-2360).

THE HOMESTEAD, Hot Springs, Virginia: Three superior courses are the focus of attention at this magnificently kept dowager of a hotel, and the fact that the redoubtable Sam Snead makes his home nearby gives you an idea of just how good they are. The Cascades course, a couple of miles from the Homestead's front door, is the best of the trio of tracks; it was the site of the USGA's 1980 Senior Men's Championship. The newer Lower Cascades course is longer. Information: The Homestead, Hot Springs, VA 24445 (703 839-5500).

THE GREENBRIER, White Sulphur Springs, West Virginia: Anyone who regularly attends any sort of meeting or seminar will inevitably trip over the immense, elegant Greenbrier; but golfers tend to look forward to these conferences with particular relish. The resort's trio of Charles Blair MacDonald courses provide a more than adequate variety of play, and now that Jack Nicklaus has finished his renovation of the Greenbrier track (the site of the Ryder Cup matches in 1979), its appeal has become even greater. A special attention-getter is the lavish buffet lunch served every day in season in the clubhouse — oh, those peach halves with the freshly whipped cream! See also *Resort Hotels.* Information: The Greenbrier, White Sulphur Springs, WV 24986 (304 536-1110).

SOUTH

WALT DISNEY WORLD, Lake Buena Vista, Florida: Veteran golfers seldom consider this resort complex for their vacations, but this ambitious attempt to be all things to all people has three courses. The 7,222-yard Magnolia was named for the 1,000 magnolia trees scattered around its lakes and elevated trees; the 6,951-yard Palm is rated among the nation's most challenging golf tests. There's also the 6,540-yard Lake Buena Vista. The trio hosts the Walt Disney World Golf Classic, a $400,000 PGA event, each October. Added attractions include the Golf Studio instructional program and the courses' relative removal from the frenzy of the park proper: it's not unusual for the adults in a *Walt Disney World* vacation group to hide out on the course while the youngsters try to bring the Magic Kingdom to its knees. Having succeeded, they may then try their luck with the six-hole Wee Links, designed to introduce the game to the junior set. Information: Walt Disney World Central Reservations, PO Box 78, Lake Buena Vista, FL 32830 (305 824-8000).

GRAND CYPRESS GOLF CLUB, Orlando, Florida: Completed in 1984, this new Jack Nicklaus course at the *Grand Cypress Resort* somehow transcends its relatively flat terrain by creating dunelike rough on which high grass grows; the sensation of playing in a Scottish environment is inescapable. Perhaps the most notable design element of the landscape is the number of two-tiered fairways. These unusual hazards make position play all important and add a new dimension to a round here. Double greens are another unusual aspect. An additional 9 holes, completed in 1985, brings the total to 27. It's a pity that access to the course is currently restricted to hotel guests only. Information: Grand Cypress Golf Club, One North Jacaranda, Orlando, FL 32819 (305 239-4700).

THE DORAL HOTEL & COUNTRY CLUB, Miami, Florida: At the moment, this establishment stands like a last bastion against the general decay that has gripped most of the Miami–Miami Beach tourist axis. But *Doral*'s superb golf facilities (five championship 18-hole layouts, plus an executive course) thus far remain unassailed, and the fabled Blue Monster is still the most formidable challenge in the state. It is the site of the annual Doral-Eastern Open, and the Gold Course offers little diminution in challenge. Information: The Doral Hotel & Country Club, 4400 NW 87th Ave., Miami, FL 33178 (305 592-2000 in Florida; 800 327-6334 elsewhere).

SAWGRASS OCEANSIDE GOLF CLUB, Ponte Vedra Beach, Florida: For six years this was the site of the Tournament Players Championship, and anyone who watched Jack Nicklaus pump a couple of drives into the drink during the 1979 installment knows that this is one of the premier places to play. When the wind blows here, the task can be all but impossible. You also have the opportunity to make the experience as difficult as you choose, for two of the three 9s (the East and West courses, which made up the original 18 here) have four sets of tees from which one can play. It's one of the South's toughest golf tests. Information: Sawgrass, PO Box 600, Ponte Vedra Beach, FL 32082 (904 285-2261 or 800 432-1270 in Florida; 800 874-7547 elsewhere).

TOURNAMENT PLAYERS CLUB AT SAWGRASS, Ponte Vedra Beach, Florida: This may well be Pete Dye's consummate masterpiece. The 17th hole became a classic after only one televised tournament was played here, and this 132-yard island par 3 drove the pros crazy. It won't treat you any more kindly, so bring enough golf balls when you attempt to conquer the sculptured fairways and unkindly undulating greens. It's not likely that you'll score very well, but it's a comfort to know the pros did little better. A private club owned and operated by the PGA Tour and hosting the Tournament Players Championship every spring, the establishment allows any visiting golfer to play the course through reasonably priced associate memberships or residence at the Sawgrass resort. Information: Tournament Players Club at Sawgrass, 112 TPC Blvd., Ponte Vedra Beach, FL 32082 (904 285-3301).

SEA ISLAND GOLF CLUB, St. Simons Island, Georgia: This is only the most important part of the 10,000-acre resort complex known as the *Cloister*. The 36 holes of golf (divided into four distinct 9s) all have ocean views, and the landscape is dominated by magnolias and pampas grass. The Seaside nine is probably the most challenging of the available four, which may be played in any order or combination. Davis Love, Jr., is on the pro staff. The neighboring *St. Simons Island Club*, which has its own 18-hole course and a Low Country–style clubhouse, is also a part of the *Cloister* complex. Information: The Cloister, Sea Island, GA 31561 (912 638-3611).

PINEHURST HOTEL AND COUNTRY CLUB, Pinehurst, North Carolina: There is no golf community in the US more devoted to the game than *Pinehurst.* Nongolfers often can't grasp what all the hushed reverence is about, but believers happily play two rounds a day on the seven courses here, visit the World Golf Hall of Fame in between rounds, and attend golf clinics at the *Pinehurst Hotel* after dinner. Donald Ross's Pinehurst #2, named among the top ten courses of the world by leading golf publications, is the class of the circuits here; George and Tom Fazio built a tough but scenic #6. A #7 course designed by Rees Jones opened in April 1986. Instruction is also available. See also *Resort Hotels.* Information: Pinehurst Hotel, PO Box 4000, Pinehurst, NC 28374 (800 672-4644 in North Carolina, 800 334-9560 elsewhere).

HYATT DORADO BEACH, Dorado Beach, Puerto Rico: Though the Rockresort management team no longer minds the tees here, this superb golf center still retains its place as the island's most luxurious escape. There's lively debate about which of the two Robert Trent Jones courses offers the sterner test, but a middle-handicap golfer will be hard pressed to discern the differences as he battles his way through this former coconut and grapefruit plantation. Both courses were upgraded in 1986. Chi Chi Rodriguez is director of golf. Information: Hyatt Dorado Beach, Dorado Beach, PR 00646 (800 545-4000 or 809 796-1600).

HARBOUR TOWN GOLF LINKS, Hilton Head Island, South Carolina: Golfers have long known what the general public is just discovering: This island, the second largest (after New York's Long Island) among the East Coast's barrier chain, holds some of the country's best resort terrain. Golfers have their choice of 2 dozen courses; but the magnet is usually the *Harbour Town Golf Links,* part of the marvelous *Sea Pines Plantation* development (See *Beaches; Tennis*) and the site of the annual PGA Sea Pines Heritage Golf Classic. With a whopping course rating of 74 — one of the highest in the country — its difficulty needs no elaboration. Only the laid-back environment provides some small salve to soaring scores. Designed by Pete Dye with Jack Nicklaus consulting; Dye is our personal choice for the game's most creative craftsman, and his talent and handiwork are nowhere better displayed. Information: Harbour Town Golf Links, Sea Pines Plantation, Hilton Head Island, SC 29928 (800 922-7042 in South Carolina; 800 845-6131 elsewhere).

WEST

THE BOULDERS, Carefree, Arizona: Of the three 9-hole courses at this former Rockresort (now a part of the CSX resort group), which opened in January 1985, the "Boulders" nine is the most scenic and challenging. The green of #1 is set in an amphitheater of boulders, while the tee at #2 is at the very foot of a sheer, high, boulder-strewn hill. Each hole of the Saguaro nine offers four sets of tees, and the combination of the Saguaro and Boulders nines provides the opportunity to play a course of 6,851 yards from the professional tees — though only the longest-hitting, lowest-handicap players should attempt this feat. The Lake nine has had a substantial facelift, making it consistent with the dramatic desert look that makes the other two courses so fascinating. See also *Resort Hotels.* Information: The Boulders, PO Box 2090, Carefree, AZ 85377 (602 488-9009).

THE WIGWAM, Litchfield Park, Arizona: In a state that is rapidly becoming one of the golfing centers of the nation, none is better than the Gold Course, one of a trio of courses at this Phoenix-area resort, operated by the Goodyear tire organization. See also *Resort Hotels.* Information: The Wigwam, Litchfield Park, AZ 85340 (602 935-3811).

LA COSTA HOTEL AND SPA, Carlsbad, California: At this famous Southern California health spa, the late Dick Wilson created a course that bedevils even the pros, so you'll probably welcome the opportunity to repair to the steamroom after your first foray. That's especially true now that *La Costa* has added an additional nine, bringing the total number of available holes to 36. Information: La Costa, Costa Del Mar Rd., Carlsbad, CA 92008 (619 438-9111 or 800 542-6200 in California; 800 854-6564 elsewhere).

PEBBLE BEACH GOLF LINKS, Pebble Beach, California: If there is a leading contender for the title of Most Photographed Golf Course, it has to be the ocean-hugging *Pebble Beach Golf Links* on the windswept Monterey Peninsula. This is one of the rare instances where a truly first-class US tournament track is actually accessible to the public, and it's an opportunity not to be missed. Information: Pebble Beach Golf Links, Pebble Beach, CA 93953 (408 624-3811).

SPYGLASS HILL, Pebble Beach, California: Just 2 miles from Pebble Beach and considered so difficult that even the touring pros complain about its difficulty. But tromping through the local plants is a botanical education in itself. Information: Spyglass Hill, Pebble Beach, CA 93953 (408 624-3811).

TORREY PINES, La Jolla, California: San Diego is the golfing capital of Southern California, with nearly six dozen public courses to satisfy its golf-crazed citizenry. The best of these is the course at *Torrey Pines* (where the Andy Williams tournament is held every year), and both the North and South courses are worth attention. Information: Torrey Pines Inn, 11480 N Torrey Pines Rd., La Jolla, CA 92037 (619 453-4420 for lodging and golf packages; call the starters, 619 453-0380, for golf course information).

KEYSTONE RESORT, Keystone, Colorado: At first glance, *Keystone Ranch* looks like something out of a John Wayne movie — and it is. The first-class golf course, opened in June 1980, is laid out on a 9,300-foot plateau framed by snow-capped peaks; several holes run around old ranch buildings, while some are tree-lined like those at Hilton Head; water hazards resemble those at Pebble Beach, and the overall design bears a similarity to Pine Valley's. Former PGA champion Dave Stockton is the resident pro. The *Keystone Resort,* owned by Ralston Purina, has fine condominium and hotel facilities. Perhaps the greatest attraction of all is the thin air; you'll find your shots going considerably farther than at sea level. Information: Keystone Resort, Box 38, Keystone, CO 80435 (303 468-4242).

MAUNA KEA GOLF CLUB, Kamuela, Hawaii, Hawaii: Part of the premier resort of the same name is built on lava flows that have somehow solidified to give the course a linksland character. This is a warm, arid corner of these islands, and much care (and water) is needed to keep the terrain green and true. The spectacular volcanic peak that gives the resort its name is the backdrop for nearly every shot, and the Mauna Kea fairways are among the most scenic in the world. See also *Resort Hotels.* Information: Mauna Kea Beach Hotel, PO Box 218, Kamuela, HI 96743-0218 (808 882-7222).

MAUNA LANI RESORT GOLF COURSE, Kohala Coast, Hawaii, Hawaii: Built atop jagged black lava flows, using thousands of tons of imported topsoil, this is considered one of the most beautiful courses in the islands. Oceanfront hole #6 has perhaps the most dramatic setting, including a 199-yard clifftop carry over a small bay. Beauty aside, the course provides a true test of golfing skill. Hazards range from the conventional complement of sand traps to huge lava boulders that evoke images of Japanese gardens. Information: Mauna Lani Resort, PO Box 4959, Kohala Coast, HI 96743 (808 885-6655; 800 367-2323 for golf/hotel packages).

PRINCEVILLE AT HANALEI, Hanalei, Kauai, Hawaii: The garden spot of the Garden Island, with three spectacular 9s (Ocean, Woods, and Lake) in the same terrain you saw in the film *South Pacific.* An additional 18-holer planned by Robert Trent Jones, Jr., will eventually make this one of Hawaii's biggest golf resorts. Weather can be uneven here — the lush forests are the by-product of plentiful rainfall — but the quality of the courses merits the risk. Information: Princeville at Hanalei, PO Box 3040, Princeville, HI 96722 (808 826-6040 or 800 367-7090).

GOLF CLINICS

Regular practice under the supervision of a pro on your own home course can't be beat for reducing your handicap. But there's no substitute for an occasional look at your weaknesses from a new point of view. That's the purpose of the golf clinics that have sprouted up all over the country.

GOLF DIGEST INSTRUCTION SCHOOLS, headquartered in Trumbull, Connecticut: The Harvard of golf schools holds its courses — taught by some of the best teaching pros in the business — at resorts all over the country, year-round. Information: Golf Digest Instruction Schools, 5520 Park Ave., PO Box 0395, Trumbull, CT 06611-0395 (203 373-7000 or 800 243-6121).

WALT DISNEY WORLD GOLF SCHOOL, Lake Buena Vista, Florida: Directed by WDW golf professional Eric Fredericksen, this program aims to help golfers develop their own styles by building on current skills. Videotapes help you chart improvement, and the instructor's audiotape of his pointers, which participants can take home, can add punch to subsequent practice. Unlike many other programs, WDW "Golf Studios" last only 2 hours; sign up for more than one to get best results. Information: Walt Disney World, PO Box 40, Lake Buena Vista, FL 32830 (305 824-3625).

THE GOLF SCHOOL AT MT. SNOW, Mt. Snow, Vermont: These thorough and well-organized programs, offered from May until October, concentrate on making your clinic experience enjoyable as well as instructive — and attract a high repeat business as a result. Unique to this school is a four-to-one student-teacher ratio. Information: Golf School at Mt. Snow, Mt. Snow, VT 05356 (802 464-3333).

STRATTON GOLF SCHOOL, Stratton Mountain, Vermont: At this 22-acre facility, director Keith Lyford and his staff focus on the basics — grip, stance, alignment, and swing — during 2- and 5-day sessions from mid-May to September. Information: Stratton Golf School, Stratton Mountain, VT 05155 (802 297-2200).

Sailing America's Coastal Waters

WINDJAMMER CRUISES

 There's no better way to get a feeling for the great age of sailing than on one of the big windjammers that were built during the first quarter of this century, mostly for oystering, fishing, or cargo and later converted to handle passengers. You spend your days swimming off the side or dozing in the sun, and you eat big meals, family style, that may include muffins and pastries cooked on old-fashioned wood stoves. You cruise at least a few hours every day, sometimes all day, then stop for awhile — to go sightseeing, have a cookout, or to take hot showers at a marina. When you fall asleep at night, it's to the creaking of the ship's oak beams.

Otherwise, what a specific cruise is like depends a lot on the boat. On smaller vessels, the atmosphere is bound to be chummy (or confining, depending on your psyche) and somewhat more informal; each passenger has more say about where you go, what you do, and when you do it.

When considering the different windjammers, a selection of which follows, look into their size, ports of call, price (usually from $375 to $535 for a week aboard, including meals), means of power, and the policy on children (there may be minimum ages of, say, 14 or 16). Also investigate the plumbing facilities: many boats simply supply wash water on deck, while others have washbasins or showers right in their cabins.

MARY DAY, Camden, Maine: This 83-foot schooner carries 28 passengers in single to triple cabins on weekly cruises among Maine's coastal islands. A small power boat is supplied for excursions ashore, but the *Mary Day* herself has no engine. Each cabin provides a keg of fresh water; there's no running water. Four nonsmoking cruises are scheduled each season. Information: Coastal Cruises, PO Box 798, Camden, ME 04843 (207 236-2750).

ADVENTURE AND ROSEWAY, Camden, Maine: Largest windjammers of the US coast. Built during the Roaring 20s, the 120-foot *Adventure* is a Gloucester fishing vessel; the 112-foot *Roseway* was built as a yacht and was used for many years as a pilot boat in Boston Harbor. Today, both cruise the Maine coast and carry 37 passengers each (no children under 16). Hot and cold running water belowdecks. Information: Yankee Schooner Cruises, PO Box 696, Camden, ME 04843 (207 236-4449).

STEPHEN TABER, Camden, Maine: This family-operated, two-masted, 68-foot gaff schooner was built in 1871, and is the oldest continuously active US merchant vessel. It used to carry bricks and cord wood, but it has been cruising Maine's Penobscot Bay region with up to 22 passengers since 1946 (no children under 14). Running water in cabins. Listed on the National Register of Historic Places. Information: Schooner *Stephen Taber*, 70 Elm St., Camden, ME 04843 (207 236-3520).

HARVEY GAMAGE, Rockland, Maine: Launched in 1973 and supplied with running water, this 95-foot schooner is one of the most technologically advanced of all the windjammers. The two showers aboard are cold, but only a few windjammers have any at all. The ship is also unusual in welcoming children of any age among its 32 passengers. Cruises take in the New England coast in summer, the Virgin Islands during the winter. Sailing instruction is provided. The *Rachael & Ebenezer*, Dirigo Cruises' other vessel, also sails lower New England in the summer, but in wintertime it's based in the Florida Keys. Information: Dirigo Cruises, 39 Waterside Lane, Clinton, CT 06413 (203 669-7068).

ISAAC H. EVANS, Rockland, Maine: Built in 1886, this 64½-foot, two-masted schooner spent most of its life oystering and freighting in Delaware Bay. Now completely rebuilt, it has cold running water in the cabins, a potbellied stove for heat in the public room back aft, one hot- and cold-water shower, and a small push-boat for going ashore (or getting to safe harbor) if there's no wind: The ship itself has no engine. Up to 22 passengers at a time (minimum age 16). Information: Captain Edward Glaser, PO Box 482, Rockland, ME 04841 (207 594-8007).

LEWIS R. FRENCH, Rockland, Maine: This two-masted, 64-foot schooner, built in 1871 as a cargo vessel, is the oldest schooner still sailing in this country. It has been completely rebuilt so that it is essentially a new ship on an old design. The small cabins have reading lights and running water; up to 22 guests can be accommodated. Also on board is one hot shower — "to ensure lasting friendships," as the ship's brochure puts it. Information: Captain Dan Pease, PO Box 482, Rockland, ME 04841 (207 594-8007 or 207 594-7617).

SHENANDOAH, Vineyard Haven, Massachusetts: This topsail, engineless schooner, launched in 1964, is the only square-rigger in the US windjammer fleet. At 108 feet at the rail, it carries up to 29 passengers at a time in cabins for one to four. It puts in at ports throughout southern New England, between Nantucket on the east and Mystic on the west. Everybody has a washbasin; hot water comes from the galley. No children under 10. Information: Coastwise Packet Co., Vineyard Haven, MA 02568 (617 693-1699).

BILL OF RIGHTS, Newport, Rhode Island: One of the newest of America's windjammers, this 125-foot replica of a topsail schooner that ran contraband during the Civil War carries 32 passengers in 16 staterooms, with running water. It puts in at southern New England harbors like Mystic, Nantucket, and Block Island. It also runs sail training weeks in the summer. Information: Schooner *Bill of Rights*, PO Box 477, Newport, RI 02840 (401 849-4980).

SAILING SCHOOLS

ANNAPOLIS SAILING SCHOOL, Annapolis, Maryland: Based in Annapolis, America's first and largest sailing school has branches in all parts of the country and on St. Croix in the US Virgin Islands. The basic two-day beginners' course includes four hours in the classroom and eight hours on the water; the three- and five-day beginners' courses give you extra time to practice your skills. Several other programs are available, including many advanced courses (handling auxiliary cruising boats, coastal navigation and piloting, racing, and preparation for bareboat chartering), but are not offered at all of the school's locations. Fees range from about $150 for the two-day course to $300 for the five-day course; on week-long cruises, you pay $645 to $1,095 per boat, depending on its size. Information: Annapolis Sailing School, PO Box 3334-US86, Annapolis, MD 21403 (301 267-7205 in Maryland; 800 638-9192).

THE OFFSHORE SAILING SCHOOL, City Island, New York City, New York: Founded by ex-Olympian Steve Colgate, this school offers week-long Learn to Sail courses ($395 to $495) for beginners, with classroom sessions from Sunday (when all courses begin) through Wednesday, and half-day on-water instruction alternating mornings and afternoons Monday through Saturday. The courses cover all the basics, including navigation and some spinnaker work on 27-foot extra-stable Solings. Advanced courses ($375 to $525) are offered on the same week-long schedule and include Sailing and Cruising for small-boat sailors, Bareboat Preparation for sailors desiring to get into chartering and big-boat handling, Live Aboard Cruising for Bareboat Certification, and Racing and Intensive Racing for beginning and advanced racers. Locations include the Atlantic Oakes in Bar Harbor, Maine; South Seas Plantation on Captiva Island, Florida; Newport, Rhode Island; Tortola, in the British Virgin Islands; and City Island, New York. The last is not so much a vacation school as a place for residents to learn in their spare time — but occasionally, Midwesterners on a Big Apple vacation stop in for an intense dose of sailing skills. The boats range from 27 to 50 feet. Intensive Racing is taught by a different internationally known guest expert every week. Information: Offshore Sailing School, E Schofield St., City Island, NY 10464 (212 885-3200; 800 221-4326 outside New York).

GREAT SAILING AND CRUISING

Some parts of the US coastline are so sail-happy that you'd think everybody there owns a boat; if you don't, you can usually charter. Expect to be asked about your sailing experience; most are handled by brokers for private owners. Your experience will determine which boat you get; which you want will depend on how long you plan to cruise, since boats under 26 feet can be a little too cozy for a week on the water.

MARINA DEL REY, California: Ever since this marina, the largest manmade recreational-boat harbor in the world, was built in the 1960s, pleasure boaters have been passing through in droves; there are 6,000 slips and plenty of rentals and sailing schools. Information: Department of Beaches and Harbors, 13837 Fiji Way, Marina del Rey, CA 90292 (213 823-4571).

NEWPORT BEACH, California: Joey Bishop and some 10,000 others keep boats in this big, beautiful, busy Southern California harbor, the largest pleasure-boat harbor in the world. There are dozens of marinas; for a list, contact the Newport Harbor Area Chamber of Commerce, 1470 Jamboree Rd., Newport Beach, CA 92660 (714 644-8211).

SACRAMENTO–SAN JOAQUIN RIVER DELTA, near Stockton, California: Better than 1,000 miles of sloughs, cuts, canals and other streams tunnel through the tules (the tall rushes that give this flatland its distinctive appearance), and for some local folk, weekend cruising is a way of life. Most rentals are houseboats, which just about anyone can handle. Information: Stockton/San Joaquin Convention and Visitors Bureau, 46 W Fremont St., Stockton, CA 95202 (209 943-1987).

SAUSALITO, California: Sausalito is the yachting center for San Francisco Bay, with space for over 2,000 boats in its marinas. For a list of yacht brokers, contact the Redwood Empire Assn., One Market Plaza, Spear Street Tower, Suite 1001, San Francisco, CA 94105 (415 543-8334).

LONG ISLAND SOUND, Connecticut and New York: Between the notched shoreline of Connecticut and the rocks and sand edge of Long Island, there are literally hundreds of square miles of protected cruising water. The Sunday *New York Times* classified section always contains an extensive listing of boats available for charter. For crewed yachts, contact Sparkman & Stephens, 79 Madison Ave., New York, NY 10016 (212 689-9292).

THE MAINE COAST: Straight and bold in the southwest, deeply notched near Boothbay Harbor, and scattered all over with islands like Matinicus (ultra-wild) and Monhegan (crisscrossed with walking paths that take you to bluffs and boulders where you can sun yourself) — the Maine coast offers enough variety to make it among the country's best spots for cruising — provided, that is, you can handle the frequent fogs, the tides, the rocky shores, and the scarcity of marinas. Information: Sparkman & Stephens, 79 Madison Ave., New York, NY (212 689-9292), for crewed yachts; Cape Dory Charters, c/o Robinhood Marine Center, Robinhood, ME 04530 (207 371-2525); and Seal Cove Boatyard, PO Box 99, Harborside, ME 04642 (207 326-4422).

THE CHESAPEAKE BAY, Maryland and Virginia: The sine qua non of cruising in America, 185-mile-long Chesapeake Bay, America's largest estuary, is notched by river mouths, little coves, and harbors where you can tie up and go ashore for a walk through 300-year-old towns; and scattered with quaint islands like Smith and Tangier, where the people started losing their Elizabethan accents in the 1960s. The cruising season, which begins in April, continues well beyond October, when the Annapolis In-the-Water Boat Show, the largest in the world, is held. For information and charters (bareboats from 28 to 42 feet): Hartge Chesapeake Charters, Church Lane, Galesville, MD 20765 (301 867-7240).

America's Most Surprising Ocean Beaches

Along America's thousands of miles of lake and ocean shores, you'll find beaches for everyone. Most of the East Coast between the brief busy coast of New Hampshire and Miami Beach is beach-edged; a dotted line of slim barrier beaches, which protect the mainland from the brunt of the ocean's force, extends from Long Island to Florida. There, and along the Gulf Coast of Florida, Texas, and Mississippi (which has bluer, warmer waters, more gently sloping bottoms, and less surf than East Coast shores), beach grass backs the sand; behind that, further inland, grow scrubby trees and, in the South, tropical vegetation. Often, incredible as it may seem, the deep roots of these fragile plants are all that keep the islands from washing away in storms (as, indeed, they sometimes do anyway).

Beaches up and down the Pacific Coast are, as a rule, better for beachwalking and fishing than for swimming because of riptides and heavy undertow. However, there are exceptions. Water at beaches below Santa Barbara is generally warm enough for dips. Above Santa Barbara it's for the hardy only because of the proximity of the Alaska Current. Around Carmel, the shore is scalloped with coves; north of Fort Ross, it's gravelly and driftwood collecting is terrific. Still farther up the coast, the beaches are edged by forests. The coastlines of Oregon and southern Washington make up one solid strip of beach cut by occasional headlands; but the best concentrations are between Pacific City and Florence, Oregon. Stormwatching in winter is popular there, as is beachwalking afterward to pick up the leavings — driftwood, most commonly, but occasionally brightly colored Japanese fishing floats as well. As for Hawaii, it has some of the best beaches of all; the one on Waikiki is only the most famous.

In addition to the beaches described below, which are some of the country's best, there are still others described elsewhere in this book. Consider, for instance, Acadia National Park, in Maine; Assateague Island, Maryland; Cape Cod, Massachusetts; the New Jersey coast, including Victorian Cape May; the Outer Banks of North Carolina; Padre Island, off the Texas Gulf Coast; Carmel, California; and the entire western edge of Oregon.

Some American beaches allow nude sunbathing; if you're interested, consult the *World Guide to Nude Beaches and Recreation* ($16.95 postpaid from The Naturists, PO Box 132, Oshkosh, WI 54902) or the quarterly *Clothed with the Sun* (sample copy $5; $18 annually). Nancy Bruning's *The Beach Book* discusses American beaches at length (out of print; check your library).

EAST

OGUNQUIT BEACH, Ogunquit, Maine: This little harbor town is also the site of a 3-mile-long strand that is one of the best in New England — partly for its length, partly for the gentleness of the drop-off. The water is "refreshing," as you must expect in Maine. Information: Chamber of Commerce, Box 2289, Ogunquit, ME 03907 (207 646-2939).

OLD ORCHARD BEACH, Old Orchard Beach, Maine: This 7-mile strand — 700 feet wide — is the state's longest; the low surf makes it one of the safest on the Atlantic for swimming. Motels, cottages, condos, and amusements abound. Information: Chamber of Commerce, Box 600, Old Orchard Beach, ME 04064 (207 934-2091).

CRANE BEACH, Ipswich, Massachusetts: This resort town also boasts a wonderful 7-mile-long sweep of dune-backed sand. There's not much surf, so swimming is possible. The most interesting lodgings can be found 30 minutes away at Rockport. Information: Ipswich Chamber of Commerce, PO Box 456, Ipswich, MA 01938 (617 356-3231); lodging information: Chamber of Commerce, PO Box 67, Rockport, MA 01966 (617 546-6575).

FIRE ISLAND, New York: Walk-on ferries from Patchogue, Sayville, and Bay Shore, Long Island (May through October only), take passengers by the thousands to this slip of land, where there are communities for families and gay and heterosexual singles, and the 19,000-acre Fire Island National Seashore, where you can camp (by reservation), swim, hike, take a guided nature walk, surf-cast, or just sit in the sun. Information: Fire Island National Seashore, 120 Laurel St., Patchogue, NY 11772 (516 289-4810).

THE HAMPTONS, Long Island, New York: A great attraction to artists and writers since the 1920s, these towns offer superb beaches, plus restaurants, art galleries, markets, bookstores, gourmet food shops, and parties that keep the area swinging until the wee hours. Rooms are difficult to come by on short notice. However, after Labor Day, the beaches are almost completely deserted. Information: Chamber of Commerce, PO Box 64, Hampton Bays, NY 11946 (516 728-2211).

WATCH HILL BEACH, Watch Hill, Rhode Island: A fine surf beach open to the public in a town so exclusive that little else is. Presiding over the entrance to the beach is the century-old Flying Carousel, one of the oldest in New England. More beaches can be found nearby at Misquamicut and Weekapaug. Rentals and information: Chamber of Commerce, 159 Main St., Westerly, RI 02891 (401 596-7761).

SOUTH

GULF STATE PARK, Gulf Shores, Alabama: These 2½ miles of sugary sand, lapped by the aquamarine Gulf, make up only one short section of the 32-mile stretch between Alabama and Mobile Points — but it's the best section for vacations because of the quality of the facilities (which include an 18-hole golf course and a saltwater fishing pier) at the modern, well-run *Gulf State Park Resort.* Information: Gulf State Park Resort, PO Box 437, Gulf Shores, AL 36542 (205 968-7531).

AMELIA ISLAND PLANTATION, Amelia Island, Florida: One of the finest beach developments in existence, this one nestled in groves of live oak and surrounded by salt marshes and dunes has really caught on, and from March through May and again from June through August the 25 tennis courts, 27-hole golf course, 14 swimming pools, health spa, bike trails, charter fishing, horseback riding on the beach, youth program, restaurants, and comfortable condominiums beside the 4-mile-long Atlantic strand are all bustling. Near Jacksonville. Information: Amelia Island Plantation, Amelia Island, FL 32034 (904 261-6161; 800 342-6841 in Florida; 800 874-6878 elsewhere).

THE NORTHWEST COAST, Florida: This may be the whitest sand you'll ever see; it's white like snow, white like sugar. West of Panama City, in the panhandle, US 98 runs next to these beaches (but low dunes protect sunbathers from the sound of the traffic). One US government–owned 6-mile stretch, between greater Fort Walton Beach (pop. 68,000) and Destin (pop. 7,000), is completely undeveloped; there's no parking lot — you just stop your car anyplace along the road. Between Destin and Panama City, there are all kinds of handsome new hotels, motels, and condos, many available for rent in summer. Some of the towns east of Panama City are just being discovered as the great tourist destinations they are. St. George Island, near Apalachicola, has 20 miles of beaches, a state park, and a couple of hundred beach houses on stilts, some of which are available for rent through *Alice D. Collins Realty* (Box 16, St. George Island, Eastpoint, FL 32328, 904 670-2758) and *Suncoast Realty* (Box 7, St. George Island, Eastpoint, FL 32328, 904 670-2247). The loudest noise you'll hear on a busy summer's day is the occasional banging of a screen door. Not far away, the T. H. Stone State Memorial St. Joseph Peninsula State Park has another 20 miles of pure white sand, nice campsites in a grove of trees, and facilities for biking, boating, clamming, and fishing. As for temperatures, late March and early April begin the warm-weather season, and especially around Fort Walton Beach, the crowds, such as they are, stay until Labor Day. But even on July 4 you can get off to yourself on the empty strands. September and October are the best months for deep-sea fishing, and November through March is known as snowbird season, when northerners come to worship the sun and swim in waters that rarely get below 58°. Information: Destin Chamber of Commerce, PO Box 8, Destin, FL 32541 (904 837-6241), and Greater Fort Walton Beach Chamber of Commerce, PO Drawer 640, Fort Walton Beach, FL 32549 (904 244-8191).

SANIBEL-CAPTIVA ISLANDS, Florida: The 20-mile stretch of white sand on this two-island chain off the coast of Fort Myers offers some of the finest, perhaps even *the* finest, seashell collecting in the US, especially after storms with heavy northwest winds, usually following a cold snap, between January and March. Some good areas to search are around the lighthouse at the eastern tip of Sanibel; Bowman's Beach at the island's western end; the southerly tip of Captiva; and the northerly tip of Captiva. The water averages about 72° in winter, 80° in summer. Temperatures range between 65° and 86° in April, between 61° and 77° in November. Motels on the island are hidden away in groves of trees, so the atmosphere is low key, even during the busy Christmas and spring school holidays. Always reserve in advance, however. Information: Chamber of Commerce, PO Box 166, Sanibel, FL 33957 (813 472-1080).

CUMBERLAND ISLAND NATIONAL SEASHORE, Cumberland Island, Georgia: The interior of this 16-mile-long, 3-mile-wide barrier island, the most southerly of Georgia's Sea Islands, is covered with marshes alive with fiddler crabs, oysters, long-legged wading birds like ibis and wood stork, and with groves of weirdly contorted live oak, willow oak, magnolia, holly, and pine. The 18 miles of beaches that rim these wildlands are golden and (since the ferry that serves the island from St. Marys, Georgia, makes the 45-minute trip on a fairly limited basis) fairly empty as well. All you've got to do is walk a little farther from the ferry dock than anybody else and you'll be alone. Or, plan well in advance to reserve one of the handful of campsites on the island or a room at *Greyfield,* a small inn (904 261-6408; see *America's Special Havens*). Information: Cumberland Island National Seashore, PO Box 806, St. Marys, GA 31558 (912 882-4335).

GULF ISLANDS NATIONAL SEASHORE, near Ocean Springs, Mississippi: In this 70,800-acre portion of the Mississippi and Florida preserve there are some 52 miles of sugary sand beaches, all of them on four barrier islands off the Mississippi coast — Horn, Petit Bois, and East and West Ship islands. The first two, once national wildlife refuges because of the richness of the wildlife inhabiting the brackish and freshwater ponds and marshes and now classified as Wilderness Areas, are accessible only by private or chartered boat, as is the east section of Ship Island (split in two by Hurricane Camille in 1969); you can go out and camp in your boat or on the shore and have the island to yourself. (Charter boats are widely available through concessions in Gulfport and Biloxi.) Ship Island is accessible by private craft or, from April through September, by a twice-daily ferry from Gulfport or Biloxi; each boat accommodates 250. That may sound like a lot of people, but once on the island the crowds scatter to the right and left of the boardwalk that leads to the Gulf Coast beach, and you can end up practically alone. For those who prefer more company — and comfort — the mainland headquarters in Ocean Springs has a 51-site campground with water and electrical hookups and a boat dock and ramps. Take plenty of sunscreen, a lightweight long-sleeved shirt, and trousers: You'll need the protection since there's scarcely a bit of shade on the islands. Information: Gulf Islands National Seashore, 3500 Park Rd., Ocean Springs, MS 39564 (601 875-9057).

HILTON HEAD ISLAND, South Carolina: Not as porcelain white as the beaches of southern Florida, the 12 miles you find here are clean, gently sloping, and almost completely free of crushing waves and strong undertow (except at South Beach, where you've got to be careful). They're also wide — 600 feet at low tide — and hard-packed. You can bicycle along them as well as hike, bird-watch, beachcomb (best after fall and winter storms), and swim (April into October). When the weather is too cold for splashing in the surf, you can always take a dip in one of the pools at the several resort developments that made this island famous in the 1950s; among them are *Sea Pines Plantation* (woodsy, spread out; 803 785-3333 in South Carolina; 800 845-6131 elsewhere), and *Palmetto Dunes* (everything in walking distance; 803 785-1161 in South Carolina; 800 845-6130 elsewhere). Some of the best golf and tennis facilities in the country are also on the island, along with sailing schools and fishing schools, bike paths, stables, shops, restaurants, and much more. Information: Chamber of Commerce, Box 5647, Hilton Head Island, SC 29938 (803 785-3673).

KIAWAH ISLAND, South Carolina: This 10,000-acre barrier island is like a wilderness, as you'll see when you sign up for one of the resort's 2-hour jeep safaris. But when you've had your fill of the tangled jungles, you can stroll down the 10 miles of wide, hard ocean beach (among the best spots on the East Coast for shelling) and pick up elegant disks and stiff pen shells, lettered olives, whelks, and such. Or play tennis or golf; bike along the more than 12 miles of bicycle paths; or swim in the ocean or any of three large resort pools. From May through August, loggerhead turtles lay their eggs on the beach in the dark of the night. The climate is subtropical and balmy, with average highs in the 80s in August and September and in the 60s in

February and March. Lodgings are available in the posh *Kiawah Island Inn* and in condominiums, cottages, and private homes; restaurants and shops are nearby. Information: Kiawah Island Co., PO Box 12910, Charleston, SC 29412-0910 (800 845-2471).

THE GRAND STRAND, Myrtle Beach, South Carolina: Stretching for 60 miles from the North Carolina border to Georgetown, South Carolina, this white strand is one of the most popular seaside resorts on the entire Atlantic coast. Accommodations range from modest motels to plush oceanfront villas and condominiums, and literally dozens of hotels and motels crowd the boardwalk — great for people-watching. And the recreational possibilities are virtually endless, what with three dozen 18-hole golf courses, 150 tennis courts, 10 fishing piers, more than 700 restaurants, and all sorts of amusements and attractions. If that doesn't appeal, Grand Strand also has nine campgrounds and two state parks with more than 10,000 sites. Naturally, the Strand's peak activity is during summer, but a mild year-round climate makes it pleasantly visitable in fall and early spring as well. Information: Chamber of Commerce, Box 2115, Myrtle Beach, SC 29578 (803 626-7444).

WEST

HUNTINGTON BEACH, California: The "Surfing Capital of the U.S.A.," with its 1,800-foot-long pier (built in 1902 as the Pacific's answer to Atlantic City), is one of the top spots on the coast to watch surfers catching some of the Pacific's best waves, sometimes right under the barnacle-spiked pilings; a good surfer can stay on top for the distance of two city blocks. Information: Greater Los Angeles Visitors and Convention Bureau, 505 S Flower St., Los Angeles, CA 90071 (213 239-0200).

PISMO BEACH, California: The giant Pismo clams once found in such numbers that farmers plowed them up for hog and cattle feed are still plentiful enough on this wide, 21-mile-long strand that it's not so difficult to get your limit — 10 per day of at least 4½ inches in width. Best shelling is at extreme low tides, year-round. Otherwise, you can swim (best from August through November) and go surfing or fishing or just drive down the beach. ATCs (all-terrain cycles) are available to rent nearby, and there are dozens of special events. Motels are mainly at the north end of the strand, atop rocky cliffs; some have their own short narrow beaches, accessible by twisty wooden staircases. Information: Pismo Beach Chamber of Commerce, 581 Dolliver St., Pismo Beach, CA 93449 (805 773-4382).

POINT REYES NATIONAL SEASHORE, Point Reyes, California: A 40-minute drive north of San Francisco, the westernmost point of this triangle of land holds the US Weather Bureau's record for the foggiest, windiest station between Mexico and Canada. So, though it's safe to swim at 4-mile Drake's Beach and at 3-mile Limantour, Point Reyes is not where you come for fun in the sun. Rather, you come for the solitude and great walks — especially along Pacific-pounded Point Reyes and McClure's beaches. People stop for picnics on the former, the more sheltered of the pair, then move on; McClure's is nearly deserted most of the time because of its more difficult access (a steep, though navigable, trail). Inland, where weather is less changeable, 140 miles of hiking trails show off wildflowers, marshes, and wildlife. Also visit the self-guided Earthquake Trail, Kule Loklo (Miwok Indian Exhibition), the Morgan horse ranch, and the historic Point Reyes Lighthouse, a good spot for whale-watching. Motels are in Inverness. Information: Point Reyes National Seashore, Point Reyes, CA 94956 (415 663-1092).

KAANAPALI, Maui, Hawaii: The longest of all Hawaii's great beaches, this one takes in about 3 miles of golden sand near Lahaina, the old whaling port; flat water makes it good for swimming. Edging the beach: an area full of hotels and golf courses on land owned by the Amfac Corporation, whose careful master plan has kept the architecture handsome and harmonious. Information: Maui Visitors Bureau, PO Box 1738, Kahului, Maui, HI 96732 (808 871-8691).

Scuba: The Wild Blue Under

 Just about anyone can use a snorkel, mask, and flippers (invented, incidentally, by Benjamin Franklin) wherever the water is clear enough — in Hawaii, along the coast of Block Island, Rhode Island, or at Florida's John Pennekamp Reef State Park (see DIRECTIONS). The Virgin Islands offer some fine snorkeling as well.

Scuba diving is something else. Handling everyday procedures and emergencies with equal aplomb takes training and practice. And so, to buy scuba gear, refill tanks, and rent equipment at any dive shop, you have to be able to show proof of having passed special certification courses that require one or two nights a week for four to six weeks, partly in a swimming pool and partly in open water. For details, contact the certifying organizations: the *National Association of Underwater Instructors* (NAUI), PO Box 14650, Montclair, CA 91763 (714 621-5801); *PADI International,* 1243 E Warner Ave., Santa Ana, CA 92705 (714 540-7234); or your YMCA.

Longtime divers should note the recent publication of a series of wreck charts that pinpoint the locations of explorable shipwrecks in the Atlantic, the Gulf of Mexico, and the Pacific between San Diego and Vancouver. Just $15 each, the charts are accompanied by booklets that explain why the ship sank and when. Information: Wreck Charts, 11 Creek Bend Dr., Fairport, NY 14450 (716 377-1061).

SHORT COURSES

You can get your certification (or C card) on your vacation if you work at it every day. Several establishments in Hawaii offer short courses, with a good deal of work in the clear warm waters around the coral reefs. They include the *Sea Sage Diving Center,* 4-1378 Kuhio Hwy., Kapaa, Kauai, HI 96746 (808 822-3841); and *Gold Coast Divers,* Hotel King Kamehameha, Suite P-1, 75-5660 Palani Rd., Kailua-Kona, HI 96740 (808 329-1328).

SOME GREAT DIVING SPOTS

Check local diving shops for up-to-the-minute particulars.

LA JOLLA COVE, La Jolla, California: Starting in this 50-yard-deep, 100-yard-wide notch in the Southern California coastline, the San Diego–La Jolla Underwater Park takes in about 7 miles of underwater scenery up the coast as far as Torrey Pines; within that area there's a look-but-don't-touch area where you can see vast quantities of kelp, abalone, and lobster. One of the best sites is at the edge of a 20-mile-long submarine canyon that borders the underwater park; the drop-off is 11,000 feet. Information: Parks and Recreation Dept., Coastal Division (619 236-6652), and, for details about La Jolla hostelries, the San Diego Convention and Visitors Bureau, 1200 Third Ave., Suite 824, San Diego, CA 92101 (619 232-3101).

JULIA PFEIFFER BURNS STATE PARK, Big Sur, California: Some 42 miles south of Monterey, where the mountains shoulder down to the sea, divers in wet suits watch sea lions, some 50 varieties of fish, and occasional whales coming by to scrape barnacles from their backs on rocky chimneys in the sea floor. All this and kelp beds, too. Partington Cove, where the diving takes place, is extremely rugged, so only experienced divers should venture in. *Nepenthe,* a redwood pavilion designed by a Frank Lloyd Wright disciple on a cliff 800 feet above the sea, is the place to eat and see what's going on in the area (408 667-2345). Information: Pfeiffer Big Sur State Park, Big Sur, CA 93920 (408 667-2315).

HAWAII'S KONA COAST, Hawaii, Hawaii: On the leeward side of Hawaii Island there's good diving in the Pine Trees area (lava-tube caves big enough to drive a Volkswagen through, lionfish, lobsters, and a spectacular canyon) and the Red Hills area (good caves, including one in which you'll almost always see a shark, shrimp, and banded coral). Everywhere there are arches, coral, clear warm water, and fish. This island is good for diving because it's new in geologic terms and there's not a lot of sand to cover up food for the fish. *Gold Coast Divers* sponsors several night dives, plus a unique manta ray dive that gives participants the opportunity to ride these big graceful creatures. Information: Gold Coast Divers, Hotel King Kamehameha, Suite P-1, 75-5660 Palani Rd., Kailua-Kona, HI 96740 (808 329-1328).

BUCK ISLAND REEF NATIONAL MONUMENT, St. Croix, Virgin Islands: A mile and a half off the coast, this island has one of the finest marine gardens in the Caribbean. Half- and whole-day trips, on sailboats and motorized vessels, are widely available in Christiansted. The monument also offers a hiking trail, picnic areas, and an underwater snorkel trail that's off-limits to scuba divers. A scuba area has been designated on the north side of the island, away from snorkelers. Information: PO Box 160, Christiansted, St. Croix, VI 00820 (809 773-1460).

VIRGIN ISLANDS NATIONAL PARK, St. John, Virgin Islands: Snorkelers as well as scuba divers can marvel at the coral reefs (flowerlike, vivid, full of tiny organisms); National Park Service Rangers lead underwater snorkel tours for beginners. Information: Superintendent, Virgin Islands National Park, PO Box 7789, St. Thomas, VI 00801 (809 776-6201).

TRIPS

The establishments that sponsor scuba courses for beginners usually also run extensive dive trip schedules to sites accessible only by boat, for experienced divers; for lists of these operators in the area you want to visit, write the national scuba-instruction certification organizations, PADI and NAUI (above), or the YMCA. The following outfits also sponsor trips:

CALIFORNIA: *The Diving Locker,* 1020 Grand Ave., San Diego, CA 92109 (619 272-1120), sponsors dive trips to San Clemente Island and Coronado Island as well as offering local beach dives.

FLORIDA: Diving trips to the Keys are sponsored by the *Reef Shop Dive Center,* Rte. 2, Box 7, Islamorada, FL 33036 (305 664-REEF); *The Diving Site,* 12399 Overseas Hwy., Marathon, FL 33050 (305 289-1021); *Hall's Diving Center,* 1688 Overseas Hwy., Marathon, FL 33050 (305 743-5929); and *Key West Pro Dive Shop,* 1605 N Roosevelt Blvd., Key West, FL 33040 (305 296-3823). In the Palm Beach area, contact *Norine Rouse Scuba Club of the Palm Beaches,* 4708 N Dixie, W Palm Beach, FL 33407 (305 844-2466), for trips to colorful reefs and to sunken ships full of porkfish, grunts, coneys, and other exotic fish. Around Pompano Beach, where the waters have reefs and drop-offs, contact *Pro Dive,* 2507 N Ocean Blvd., Pompano Beach, FL 33062 (305 942-3000).

TEXAS: Along the coast of Padre Island not far from Corpus Christi, you can dive off oil platforms or three sunken Liberty ships; the water is warm and very clear. Information from *Padre Island Dive Shop,* 7336 S Padre Island Dr., Corpus Christi, TX 78412 (512 993-6000).

Touring America's Waterways

In the days before cities were strung together by highways, people traveled from one settlement to another along rivers and chains of lakes. Quite a few have been dammed up, polluted, or defaced by highways and factories. But there are still enough open and visible water courses to suit the needs of most recreationists, and you don't have to be an expert paddler to enjoy them. Some are easy enough for beginning canoeists in open-deck canoes. Others — whitewater torrents as wild now as they were 200 years ago — are serviced by experienced boatmen who will take you down in big rubber rafts.

FLATWATER CANOEING

The following waterways offer extensive opportunities for paddling trips easy enough for almost anyone — though you should check on conditions before you put in, since recent rainfalls or strong winds can turn normally navigable lakes and streams into trouble spots. Canoes are usually available at about $10 to $30 a day, with packages and reductions available for multiday tours. Liveries are usually your best source of information about campsites en route. Most provide shuttle services from point of entry to final landing.

EAST

THE ALLAGASH, Maine: As much a region as a 92-mile-long river and chain of lakes, the Allagash sweeps and swirls through one of the mightiest woodlands in the East as it heads north from Telos Lake near Baxter State Park to its confluence with the St. John River along the Canadian border. Countless other lakes and streams, in equally wild country, are accessible by portages, so you can canoe and fish to your heart's content. May and June are high-water months; fall foliage, which flames bright in early October, changes the scene once again. Information: Maine Bureau of Parks and Recreation, Station 22, Augusta, ME 04333 (207 289-3821).

THE ADIRONDACK CANOE ROUTES, New York: You feel like a 19th-century woodsman when you paddle through this hundred-mile-long chain of river-and-portage-connected lakes in New York's North Country. The waters are on the cold side, but lovely for swimming and fishing. You can camp in three-sided log lean-tos on the shores of the lakes and on islands in the middle. The terrain along the route is mountainous, rocky, forested, and, except for the shelters, virtually undeveloped. Information: New York State Dept. of Environmental Conservation, 50 Wolf Rd., Albany, NY 12233-0001 (518 457-7433).

THE DELAWARE RIVER, Pennsylvania, New York, New Jersey: From the foothills of the Catskill Mountains in southern New York state to the Delaware Water Gap on the border of Pennsylvania and New Jersey, the Delaware ripples through some 120 miles of dense woodlands — the sort you wouldn't expect to find so close to the East's big cities. Liveries include *Bob & Rick Lander's Delaware River Canoe and Raft Trips* (RD 2, Box 376, Narrowsburg, NY 12764, 914 252-3925); *Jerry's Three River Canoe Rentals and Campgrounds* (PO Box 7, Pond Eddy, NY 12770, 914 557-6078); *Kittatinny Canoes* (Silver Lake Rd., Dingmans Ferry, PA 18328, 717 828-2338 or -2700).

THE SHENANDOAH RIVER, Virginia: Snaking between the Massanutten Mountains and the Blue Ridge on this majestic stream, you will almost always have a panorama of forested hills in view — though occasionally the banks are given over to farmlands or summer homes. This goes on for nearly 100 miles, but the most popular trip is the 45-mile stretch between Luray and Front Royal, which can be paddled in a long weekend. Foliage peaks in mid-October, while the fish (and, alas, the blackflies) are most active in early June. Information: Shenandoah River Outfitters (RFD 3, Luray, VA 22835, 703 743-4159).

SOUTH

BUFFALO NATIONAL RIVER, Arkansas: This 148-mile-long stream in northern Arkansas is speckled by gravel bars and edged by forests and cliffs full of waterfalls, caves, and fern falls. The seasons — from the pink and white springs to the lush summers and through the stunning orange and red autumns — make each trip down the Buffalo a delight. Current is no problem; long pools alternate with rapids and riffles. Camping is permitted on the gravel bars and at most river accesses; hiking is available in wilderness areas and on developed day-use trails. Information: Buffalo National River, PO Box 1173, Harrison, AR 72602-1173 (501 741-5443).

THE WHITE RIVER, Arkansas: With its ghostlike morning fogs, cave-pocked shoreline bluffs, mountains, wildlife, and good trout fishing, this 100-mile stream provides a beautiful trip. Information: Batesville Area Chamber of Commerce, 409 Vine St., Batesville, AR 72501 (501 793-2378).

EVERGLADES NATIONAL PARK, Florida: In still water, the paddling is more strenuous, but the scenery — mangroves, big buttonwood trees, bays, and tunnels — is worth the effort. There are several short trails and one 100-miler that will keep you paddling for days. Winter months are best; there are fewer bugs, you see more birds, and the weather is more invigorating. You need a back-country use permit for overnight stays. Information: Everglades National Park, PO Box 279, Homestead, FL 33030 (305 247-6211).

OKEFENOKEE NATIONAL WILDLIFE REFUGE, Georgia: Leachings of decaying vegetation stain these still south Georgian waters black as a moonless night; and, smooth as glass, they reflect every twig of the moss-veiled cypress forests through which many of the canoe trails will take you. (Others cut through "prairies" — water-rooted versions of those in Kansas.) A limited-permit system ensures that when you canoe through the swamp, you'll have the campsite all to yourself. Information: US Fish and Wildlife Service, Rte. 2, Box 338, Folkston, GA 31537 (912 496-3331).

BLACK CREEK, Mississippi: Canoeing this stream through forests of cypress, pines, and oaks, you can simply float along on the gentle current; at night, you can camp on snow-white sandbars. The longest trip is about 45 miles, about 3 days, starting at Big Creek. Half the trip runs through national forest. Information: De Soto National Forest, Black Creek Ranger District, PO Box 248, Wiggins, MS 39577 (601 928-4422).

MIDWEST

BLUE RIVER, Indiana: From Fredericksburg to this southern Indiana stream's confluence with the Ohio, there are 58-plus miles of clear deep green water edged by forests of redbud, oak, maple. Good rock bass fishing, especially in early summer. Information: Old Mill Canoe Rental, PO Box 60, Fredericksburg, IN 47120 (812 472-3140).

AU SABLE RIVER, Michigan: Along the 240 canoeable miles of this twisting Midwestern waterway you'll find quiet wooded shores, some in the Huron National Forest, and plenty of good fishing. Information: Oscoda–Au Sable Chamber of Commerce, 100 W Michigan Ave., Oscoda, MI 48750 (517 739-7322).

BOUNDARY WATERS CANOE AREA WILDERNESS, Minnesota: Wild and vast, this system of streams, narrows, and island-dotted lakes created by glaciers eons ago offers — with surrounding Superior National Forest (of which it is a part), nearby

Voyageurs National Park, and Ontario's Quetico Provincial Park — some of the most extensive canoeing on the continent. Guides, liveries, and complete outfitting services are widely available in Grand Marais, Ely, and Crane Lake, Minnesota. Information: Superior National Forest, PO Box 338, Duluth, MN 55801 (218 720-5324).

OZARK NATIONAL SCENIC RIVERWAYS, Missouri: The Current River and its tributary the Jacks Fork together offer some 140 miles of woods, caves, springs, sinkholes, and pleasant, easy-to-negotiate pools and riffles. Information: Ozark National Scenic Riverways, PO Box 490, Van Buren, MO 63965 (314 323-4236).

WEST

RUSSIAN RIVER, California: Fast enough to be fun, but not too fast, the 60 miles of this California stream from the Lake Mendocino Dam to the Pacific are safe almost year-round and understandably popular. The waters — deep pools, small riffles, and moderate rapids — swirl you between steep forested banks, past shores full of vineyards, orchards, and stands of redwood that hide summer cottages, to open spaces where you can smell the salt air. And it's all just an hour north of San Francisco. Rentals and information: Burke's Russian River Canoe Rentals, PO Box 602, Forestville, CA 95436 (707 887-1222).

MISSOURI RIVER, Montana: Central Montana's wonderfully stark sagebrush-and-sandstone-cliff wilderness encompasses the 149-mile length of this National Wild and Scenic River. It's a great place for sun, and it's also among the best in the West (where most streams are wildwater torrents) for easy canoeing. May, June, and September are best for wildlife watching; the cottonwoods turn to gold in late September and October. Information: Missouri River Outfitters, PO Box 1212, Fort Benton, MT 59442 (406 622-3295).

WHITEWATER RAFTING

When you're knifing through the 20-foot-high waves of a river racing downstream at the rate of 50,000 or 60,000 cubic feet per second, and your clothes are drenched with the spray, and you can hardly hear the screams of your fellows for the noise of the river (something like the roar of a dozen freight trains), and when the same scenario repeats itself day after day — even the wildest roller coaster seems tame.

But even when the same river is flowing at its normal 5,000 cubic feet per second, and even in the East, where the torrential stretches of wilderness rivers are so short that whitewater trips usually last only a day, it's not hard to understand why river-running can get into your blood. Few other means of wilderness travel put you so close to the forces of nature. And if you're not the rugged, hardy type, another way to get deep into the wilderness without some kind of noisy motor simply doesn't exist. Many of the following have been designated National Wild and Scenic Rivers, which means that their route passes through true wilderness and also that it is advisable to apply for a permit (or sign up with an outfitter) well in advance — at many, early in the preceding winter — as access is strictly limited, ensuring that the word "crowd" will never pass anyone's lips. Most of the country's mightiest rivers are accessible on trips run by commercial operators — both small outfits who take their craft down one or two streams in a given region and larger organizations that have developed programs nationwide. Among the latter are the *Sierra Club,* 730 Polk St., San Francisco, CA 94109 (415 776-2211); the *American River Touring Association,* 445 High St., Oakland, CA 94601 (415 465-9355); and *OARS,* PO Box 67, Angels Camp, CA 95222 (209 736-4677). *Adventure Bound* (649 25 Rd., Grand Junction, CO 81505; 303 241-5633) runs several trips on the Green, Lower Colorado, and Yampa rivers in Colorado and Utah.

Depending on where you go and when and who takes you, you may wield a paddle (with the guide in the rear shouting out instructions) or you may go along as just a passenger. In the very wildest waters, you'll probably go in big catamaran rafts. On other trips down other rivers, the outfitter will pack along inflatable canoes or kayaks, and you can get out and do some paddling on your own, even closer to the water level, when you tire of watching the cliffs, rocky banks, and forests go by — that is, if you're not worn out from the swimming, picnicking, hiking, fishing, and other diversions that the outfitters normally program into excursions. Between the river, the sourdough pancake breakfasts, the steaks and spuds dinners, the companionable evenings around the campfires, and the lullaby the river sings to you through the quiet canyon nights — a trip down a great waterway is one of those memorable vacation adventures that brings out the poet in you.

THE COLORADO RIVER (GRAND CANYON SECTION), Arizona: The most challenging of all river trips, and one of the most popular, is also, some people will tell you, one of the great moments of human experience. You shoot some 100 rapids — Badger Creek, Soap Creek, 25 Mile, House Rock, Unkar, Nevills, Crystal, Lava, Sockdolager, Grapevine, and dozens of others — as you run the 277 miles between the put-in area at Lee's Ferry and the headwaters of Lake Mead. The soaring sculptured walls and the glowing colors of their rock layers are as grand when seen from below as they are when you stand on the Canyon rim. And, though the flow is controlled by the Glen Canyon Dam upstream, the river itself changes all the time. Summers are busy and hot; in spring you'll find temperatures in the comfortable 70s and 80s, blooming desert plants, and smaller crowds. For a complete list of outfitters (who go downstream in everything from dories to motor-powered rafts), write the River Subdistrict, Grand Canyon National Park, PO Box 129, Grand Canyon, AZ 86023 (602 638-7843).

THE MAIN SALMON, Idaho: A good trip for beginning your river-running career, Lewis and Clark's "River of No Return" offers enough deep-rolling rapids to keep you interested, but not so many that you'll spend your river hours in terror. On the 100-mile stretch between Corn Creek and Spring Bar, not far from Riggins — the stretch most commonly floated by commercial outfitters — there are warm springs and quiet pools where you can get out and splash, sandy beaches, spectacular canyons, big horn sheep and other wildlife, and, on the north-facing slopes, stands of Douglas fir. In one 10-mile stretch, the banks rise so steeply from the water's edge that there's not even a trail along the shore. Runs during high water in May or June are wildest; the following months through Labor Day are quieter on the water. Actually, the river is floatable for 237 miles between North Fork and the confluence of the Salmon and the Snake. Private parties require permits to float the Wild section, from Corn Creek to Long Tom Bar, but only from June 20 to September 7. For a list of outfitters, including some who will take you the whole route, write the Idaho Outfitters and Guides Assn., PO Box 95, Boise, ID 83701 (208 342-1438), or the Salmon National Forest, Box 780, North Fork, ID 83466 (208 865-2383).

THE MIDDLE FORK OF THE SALMON, Idaho: The 100-mile stretch floated by most outfitters — a Wild and Scenic River, which runs between Boundary Creek and the Main Salmon — this waterway takes you through the Frank Church River of No Return Wilderness, over 80 or more wild rapids, and into the second deepest gorge on the continent (Hell's Canyon on the Snake is the deepest). During rest stops and overnights, you can explore creeks and waterfalls, side canyons, and hot springs. Information: Middle Fork District, Challis National Forest, PO Box 404, Challis, ID 83226 (208 879-4321); and the American River Touring Assn., 445 High St., Oakland, CA 94601 (415 465-9355).

THE SELWAY RIVER, Idaho: From Paradise Guard Station at the mouth of White Cap Creek to Selway Falls, this river drops an average of 28 feet per mile. Too rocky for floating most of the time, it is among the most challenging whitewater courses in the country during peak spring runoff in the last two weeks in June and the first two in July. (Trips book up well in advance; applications for permits to float from May 15 to July 31 should be submitted between December 1 and January 31 to the West Fork Ranger Station, for a random drawing.) You wouldn't want to pit yourself against the Selway on a first river trip, but it's a good bet for veterans. The river's course takes you through the 1,337,681-acre Selway-Bitterroot Wilderness, among the country's largest, most of which is passable only on foot or by boat. Information: Bitterroot National Forest, West Fork Ranger Station, Darby, MT 59829 (406 821-3269); and the Nezperce National Forest, Moose Creek Ranger Station, Grangeville, ID 83530 (208 983-2712).

THE ROGUE RIVER, Oregon: A National Wild and Scenic River, the 33 miles between Grave Creek and Watson Creek, about 25 miles from the Pacific, offer Class III rapids, high canyons, rock gorges, wildlife, good fishing (for steelhead, chinook, and silver salmon), and historic sites — Zane Grey had a cabin at Winkle Bar. There's whitewater on rapids like Mule Creek Canyon and Blossom Bar, but since there are long stretches of smooth water between them, commercial trips on the Rogue are good for families. Most operators run between Grave Creek and Foster Bar. Information: River Permits/Information, 14335 Galice Rd., Merlin, OR 97532 (503 479-3735); for private, commercially guided trips: BLM, 3040 Biddle Rd., Medford, OR 97504 (503 776-4190).

YOUGHIOGHENY RIVER, Pennsylvania: The trip down the 7½-mile wild section of this famous eastern whitewater stream lasts only a little over half a day, but you get quite a run for your money. The scenery is beautiful: laurel and rhododendron in the spring, wraithlike mists and lush forests in summer, and bright leaves in autumn. Information: Ohiopyle State Park, PO Box 105, Ohiopyle, PA 15470-0105 (412 329-8591).

THE CHATTOOGA, South Carolina: This National Wild and Scenic River, considered to be among the most beautiful in the world, can be rafted from March through October. After seeing *Deliverance,* which was filmed here, a lot of people who didn't know any better tackled the whitewater in metal canoes, and the canoes usually ended up on the river's bottom, torn to pieces or wrapped around rocks. In other words, this is no canoe trip for beginners. But in a raft, and with a guide, almost anyone can shoot the rapids. *Wildwater* (Long Creek, SC 29658, 803 647-5336) will show you how to scout them — great for helping you understand swift water. There are also stretches suitable for beginners and intermediates in these 47 miles (spanning two national forests). Other outfitters include *Nantahala Outdoor Center,* US 19 West, Box 41, Bryson City, NC 28713 (704 488-2175), and *Southeastern Expeditions,* 1955 Cliff Valley Way, No. 220, Atlanta, GA 30329 (404 329-0433).

THE RIO GRANDE, Texas: A stretch of the Rio Grande within Big Bend National Park takes you through some of the most isolated country in America. You won't find much whitewater, but the floating is spectacular. Most trips run through either Santa Elena Canyon, Boquillas Canyon, or Mariscal Canyon. Santa Elena is deepest, and, because of Rockslide Rapids, wildest; Mariscal, most remote; Boquillas, 16 miles from end to end, the longest and great for sunsets. Raft trips of at least 30 miles include non-canyon stretches. Go in April to see a spectacular wildflower display, in May to see the bird migrations, or in October, which is the residents' favorite time because of the great weather and the ordinarily reliable water flows. One portion of the river was recently designated a Wild and Scenic River. Information: Big Bend National Park, TX 79834 (915 477-2251).

THE GREEN RIVER (GRAY AND DESOLATION CANYONS), Utah: Were you to put in on the Green below Flaming Gorge and float all the way to Lake Powell, several hundred miles later, you wouldn't find more interesting river country than this stretch between Sand Wash (about 35 miles southwest of Myton) and Green River City (some 96 miles later). Gray Canyon has the biggest rapids by far, but there are some in Desolation which, in the words of one river rat, will "eat you up if you don't know what you're doing." Views from the boat take in stands of Douglas fir, cottonwood groves, and petroglyphs from the Fremont culture of 1,200 years ago. Floating season is May through late September; spring is wildest, July and August hottest. Information and permits: Bureau of Land Management, PO Box AB, Price, UT 84501 (801 637-4584).

THE COLORADO RIVER (CATARACT CANYON SECTION), Utah: In all of the immense Colorado River system, this stretch of water in Canyonlands National Park offers some of the most technically demanding whitewater and some of the most exciting rafting in the country — even if you don't go in the spring, when the flow is many times normal. Cataract Canyon lies just downstream of the Green's confluence with the Colorado; trips through the canyon begin either on the Green or the Colorado, and continue downstream to Lake Powell. Permits required — for the Cataract Canyon section only — for private parties. Information: Canyonlands National Park, 125 W Second South, Moab, UT 84532-2995 (801 259-7164).

WHITEWATER STREAMS, West Virginia: The Mountain State's geographical position and topography conspire to dump abundant rain and snow on the Allegheny Highlands, a region of misty mountains, ridges, and deep gorges cut by eons of runoff. Major streams born here include the Cheat, Tygart, Greenbrier, Elk, Gauley, Meadow, and the three sisters of the Monongahela National Forest — the Cherry, Williams, and Cranberry rivers. All feature whitewater stretches suitable for various skill levels. In the south, New River and its rowdy tributary, the Bluestone, drain a huge, sparsely populated, and ruggedly beautiful watershed. In eastern West Virginia, the Potomac and its tributaries, the South Branch and the Cacapon, and the gentle Shenendoah combine whitewater and stunning landscapes rich in American history. Professional outfitters run trips on many of these streams in spring, summer, and fall, and also teach paddling and kayak skills to individuals. Information: Travel West Virginia, State Capitol Complex, Charleston, WV 25305 (304 348-2286 in West Virginia; 800 624-9110 elsewhere).

Goin' Fishing: The Best Spots in America

America's number one participation sport has hooked 25% of the US population, so it's no wonder that huge amounts of money, not to mention bureaucratic time and effort, go into massive stocking programs. Just where you'll find all these fish at any given time can vary from year to year, depending on water conditions, weather, chemicals, and season.

A long familiarity with the habits of fish in a single lake is almost a guarantee of hefty stringers, but, as the professional bass fishermen who fish many different lakes can tell you, it's enough to have reliable knowledge of the species' habits, and of the water temperatures, bottom conformations, shoreline, and so on, of the area you're fishing — information that is easily obtained from local fish and game authorities and from area marinas and bait and tackle shops.

EAST

Ocean fishing is big in all the coastal states — mainly for bluefish and stripers that migrate up and down the coast as they seek out congenial water temperatures. Inland, fishermen work the lakes and stalk the wily trout in streams and rivers.

MOOSEHEAD LAKE, Greenville, Maine: The largest body of water in Maine, a sportfishing resort for over a century, provides landlocked salmon and brook and lake trout; deep waters (246 feet) and good oxygenation make the fishing good throughout the season — despite some fishing pressure from a variety of fishing camps around the shores. The steamer *Katahdin* cruises the lake daily in season. Call the Moosehead Marine Museum for reservations (207 695-2716). Area information: Moosehead Lake Region Chamber of Commerce, Box 581, Greenville, ME 04441 (207 695-2702).

OCEAN CITY, Maryland: The white marlin capital of the world sends fishermen out to the Baltimore and Washington Canyons, about 50 miles off shore, for dolphin, bonita, tuna, and wahoo. Surf casting and jetty fishing can also yield good results. Information: Chamber of Commerce, Rte. 1, PO Box 310A, Ocean City, MD 21842 (301 289-8559).

LAKE WINNIPESAUKEE, near Laconia, New Hampshire: The largest body of water in New Hampshire (72 square miles) offers some of the best stringers of lake trout and landlocked salmon in New England. Some 240 miles of shoreline on the mainland, and still more on 278 scattered islands, provide good habitat for bass and pickerel. Salmon are most active in April, May, and June (at the surface); later you've got to fish deeper. Lake trout are liveliest in April and May. And there's ice fishing from January through March. Information: Lakes Region Association, PO Box 300, Wolfeboro, NH 03894 (603 569-1117), and the New Hampshire Fish and Game Dept., 34 Bridge St., Concord, NH 03301 (603 271-3211).

BATTENKILL RIVER, near Manchester, Vermont: This famous Vermont fishing stream, a forest-edged, sun-dappled angler's idyll, is heavily fished, but its long, slow, waist-deep pools give the brookies and browns who inhabit it "a two-day look at every visitor" (according to one veteran), and since the fish are not hatchery-bred, they don't regard man as a friend. The upshot is that the average fisherman doesn't get much: The stream is what you'd call a challenge. A nationally known tackle company based nearby can answer your questions about when and where. Information: Orvis, 10 River Rd., Manchester, VT 05254 (802 362-3166).

NEW RIVER, near Hinton, West Virginia: This fascinating fishing stream produces good creels of trophy white bass, hybrid striped bass, smallmouth bass, muskellunge, walleye, rock bass, and channel catfish. Best spots are downstream of the Bluestone Dam and at the New/Gauley confluence. Information: Dept. of Natural Resources/Wildlife, 1800 Washington St., East Charleston, WV 25305 (304 348-2771).

SOUTH

The southern fisherman heads for the Gulf or the Atlantic, where offshore oil rigs and artificial reefs draw huge populations of big fish, or for the huge Arkansas, Kentucky, and Tennessee impoundments, which are managed with fishing in mind. Crappie and largemouth bass are usually available, but depending on the area, you'll also get smallmouth, trout, stripers. Try western North Carolina and northern Georgia for trout.

LAKE EUFAULA, near Eufaula, Alabama: One of the finest largemouth fisheries in the country, not just for the quantity of fish available for the taking but also for their size. This impoundment of the Chattahoochee River along the Georgia-Alabama line is the site of many annual tournaments. Spring and fall are best. Information: Chamber of Commerce, PO Box 347, Eufaula, AL 36027 (205 687-3879).

THE WHITE RIVER, Lakeview, Arkansas: Local fishermen call this wilderness Ozarks stream the trout capital of the world; the lake water released below the Bull Shoals Dam is ideal for trout propagation, and record catches of rainbows and browns are not uncommon. For a list of outfitters, request the *Ozark Mountain Region Guide* from the Arkansas Dept. of Parks and Tourism, One Capitol Mall, Little Rock, AR 72201 (501 371-1511 or 800 482-8999 in Arkansas; 800 643-8383 elsewhere).

BOCA GRANDE PASS, Boca Grande, Florida: One of the world's most famous fishing grounds, for the silvery legions of fighting tarpon that invade the Gulf every summer, will give you the liveliest action in June; the season extends from March through October. Information: Charlotte County Chamber of Commerce, 2702 Tamiami Trail, Port Charlotte, FL 33952 (813 627-2222).

TEN THOUSAND ISLANDS, near Naples, Florida: This trackless mangrove wilderness of creeks, oyster-bottomed coves, and rivers, stretching 60-odd miles along the Gulf Coast, is one of the best US spots for snook, a battling tropical fish found only in southern Florida; May through July is the season. Information: Naples Area Chamber of Commerce, 1700 N Tamiami Tr., Naples, FL 33940 (813 262-6141).

DESTIN, Florida: Residents call Destin "the world's luckiest fishing village," and with more than 75 party boats and charters (the state's largest fishing fleet) charging into the Gulf every day, they just may be right. The quarry: pompano, grouper, king mackerel, sailfish. Information: Chamber of Commerce, PO Box 8, Destin, FL 32541 (904 837-6241).

THE KEYS, Florida: Islamorada, Marathon, and Key West are the three main centers in the area for bonefish, permit, and tarpon; Islamorada's sport fishing fleet is one of the US's largest. And that doesn't include the deep-sea fishing — for marlin, sailfish, grouper, and the other big ones. Information: Chamber of Commerce, 3330 Overseas Hwy., Marathon, FL 33050 (305 743-5417); Greater Key West Chamber of Commerce, 402 Wall St., Key West, FL 33040 (305 294-2587); Chamber of Commerce, PO Box 915, Islamorada, FL 33036 (305 664-4503).

ALLIGATOR ALLEY, between Naples and Fort Lauderdale, Florida: Along the canal that parallels Rte. 84, bass and bluegills feed and reproduce in nearly ideal conditions (it's said that more tolls have been paid by fisherman than by cross-state drivers). Fishing is best at low water. Information: Naples Area Chamber of Commerce, 1700 N Tamiami Tr., Naples, FL 33940 (813 262-6141).

LAKE OKEECHOBEE, Okeechobee, Florida: Some of the world's finest black crappie fishing can be found at this inland sea, the second largest body of fresh water entirely within the US; you can also take bluegill and bass, plus catfish that sometimes take two hands to display. The season runs from November to April. Information: Okeechobee County Chamber of Commerce, 55 S Parrott Ave., Okeechobee, FL 33472 (813 763-6464).

BILLFISH ALLEY (DE SOTO CANYON), south of Fort Walton Beach, Florida: Paralleling the coast for a hundred miles, this offshore depression offers an abundance of white and blue marlin, sailfish, tuna, dolphin, wahoo, and swordfish. (Best fishing is May through October.) Information: Chamber of Commerce, PO Drawer 640, Fort Walton Beach, FL 32549 (904 244-8191); Panama City Beach Resort Council, PO Box 9473, Panama City Beach, FL 32407 (904 234-6575).

LAKE JACKSON, near Tallahassee, Florida: There is an interesting reason for the legendary catches of big largemouth bass at this angling hot spot. Every 25 years or so, three or four sinkholes, part of an underground river system, open up and drain the lake, thereby exposing the bottom to sunlight, rejuvenating plants, and thus improving the habitat for fish — so that they grow bigger. The most recent sinkhole, though no more than 4 or 5 feet wide, drained three quarters of the lake like a bathtub in less than a week. Information: Office of Informational Services, 620 S Meridian St., Tallahassee, FL 32301 (904 488-4676).

LAKE BARKLEY and KENTUCKY LAKE, near Cadiz, Kentucky: The 220,000 acres of water (with 3,500 miles of shoreline) shared by these two impoundments offer some of the state's most consistently fine bass fishing — with an abundance of smallmouth, largemouth, and spotted bass (the last two are especially plentiful in Kentucky Lake). The area has also been called the "crappie capital of the world." March through November is the season. Information: Land Between the Lakes, TVA, Golden Pond, KY 42231 (502 924-5602).

GRAND ISLE, Louisiana: Internationally known for its deep-sea fishing, especially around offshore oil rigs, this angling center offers quantities of party and charter boats.

The surf fishing — for trout, flounder, sheephead, tarpon, reds, and mackerel — is also great. Information: Nez Coupe Souvenir & Tackle Shop, PO Box 171, Grand Isle, LA 70358 (504 787-3352).

OUTER BANKS, North Carolina: The proximity of the Gulf Stream to this slender finger of sand has brought good fishing close to shore. There are blue and white marlin, flounder, weakfish, bonito, tuna, dolphin, barracuda, wahoo, sailfish, Spanish and king mackerel, and bluefish aplenty. Best fishing is from April through November. Information: Outer Banks Chamber of Commerce, PO Box 90, Kitty Hawk, NC 27949 (919 261-2626).

CURRITUCK SOUND, Knotts Island, North Carolina: This huge shallow expanse of water between Kitty Hawk and the Virginia line offers some of the best freshwater fishing in the country — largemouth plus rock bass, speckled trout, and white perch. The sound's size and its hundreds of islands make a guide essential. Good catches are the rule April through November, especially during southerly winds. Information: Elizabeth City Area Chamber of Commerce, PO Box 426, Elizabeth City, NC 27909 (919 335-4365).

LAKES MARION and MOULTRIE, near Santee, South Carolina: This 171,000-acre impoundment of the Santee River, the first in the country with a landlocked striped bass program, offers some of the best fishing for these fighters, and has produced world-record channel catfish, black crappie, and bowfin. Crappie and largemouth are especially plentiful. Information: Santee-Cooper Country, Drawer 40, Santee, SC 29142 (803 854-2131).

MIDWEST

Michigan, Minnesota, and Wisconsin together boast nearly 5 million fishing license holders, so it's not surprising that the angling is lively. The best fishing is for trout on Michigan's Au Sable, Manistee, Pine, Rifle, and upper Muskegon Rivers; for steelhead in April; and for smallmouth bass in lakes in the northwest part of the lower peninsula.

In Minnesota, on the other hand, walleye is the fish — but you can also get smallmouth on the waters along the Canadian border; pike in the north, muskie in the Boy River chain, the Mantrap chain, and Big Lake and Leech Lake; and kamloops and native steelhead in the streams that empty into Lake Superior.

Missouri's fishing is mainly in the big southwestern reservoirs, but there's also float fishing for bass and panfish on the Jack's Fork, the Meramec, the Eleven Point, Niangua, James, Big Piney, and Current Rivers. Ohio's western basin produces some of the US's best walleye fishing in spring and summer — off reefs, island shorelines, and submerged shoals.

Wisconsin produces salmon beginning in August around Kenosha, Milwaukee, and Racine. Fishermen troll for lake trout in summer and go for cohos and brown trout between Bayfield and Washburn. There are smallmouth in all the northern lakes, especially on the Door County peninsula in July and August.

LAKE MILLE LACS, near Brainerd, Minnesota: The fact that between opening day and late July the harvest of walleyes allegedly ran to 2½ tons of fish a day (or about 400,000 over the whole period one year) gives you an idea of the scope of the fishing here. Information: Chamber of Commerce, Brainerd, MN 56401 (218 829-2838; 800 432-3775 in Minnesota).

WEST

Salmon fishing in Alaska is the standard by which all other salmon fishing is matched; you can get kings in May and June and silver salmon in autumn. But California is the bigger fishing state, with over 2 million holders of fishing licenses and 500 charter boats leaving from ports up and down the coast — for salmon in the north, and for yellowtail, albacore, and bonito in the south.

Trout reigns as king in Colorado. Ditto for Idaho, the Black Hills of South Dakota, western Montana, and the mountain lakes of California and Washington. Idaho's Snake, Clearwater, and Salmon Rivers are visited every year by huge quantities of steelhead and chinook in October, November, March, and April.

Hawaiian catches hold more than half of the International Game Fish Association records for blue marlin — but there's also adventure to be had in going for bonefish (not in the flats as in Florida but in deep water) and surf-casting.

In Oregon and Washington, charters go for salmon and tuna from June through September. Chinook and silver run in summer and early fall, and steelhead in winter.

Meanwhile, there are walleye in Missouri River impoundments in South Dakota, and in North Dakota, smallmouths around islands and flooded butte tops of the various impoundments. In Utah, 200-mile-long Lake Powell has crappie, striped bass, and walleye; bass are active March through May and late September and early November.

THE SACRAMENTO RIVER, Redding, California: Especially from Redding to Hamilton City (September through March), this river offers some fine king salmon fishing. Hefty 25- to 30-pounders are common, and 40-pounders are occasionally pulled out. The Balls Ferry area south of Redding and the mouths of the American and Feather Rivers are also good, as is the steelhead fishing in the Klamath River: This is outdoor country par excellence. Information: Chamber of Commerce, PO Box 850, Red Bluff, CA 96080 (916 527-6220), and the Shasta-Cascade Wonderland Assn., 1250 Parkview Ave., Redding, CA 96001 (916 243-2643).

THE KONA COAST, Hawaii, Hawaii: All but one of those record fish caught in Hawaii were pulled in off the Kona coast. Charters are plentiful around the port of Kailua. Information: Hawaii Visitors Bureau, 75-5719 W Alii Dr., Kailua-Kona, HI 96740 (808 329-7787).

COLUMBIA RIVER, below the Bonneville Dam, Oregon: May and June shad runs are so huge that nearly everyone catches one of these strong-running, high-leaping fish; stringers of 25 (the limit) are not uncommon. Walleye fishing is a recent major attraction. Information: Chamber of Commerce, Port Marina Park, Hood River, OR 97031 (503 386-2000); Colombia River Wholesale, PO Box 371, Cascade Locks, OR 97014 (503 374-8214); or Smith's War Surplus, 1737 Cascade St., Hood River, OR 97031 (503 386-3040).

PORT ARANSAS, Texas: Some 70 charter boats operate out of this small town on Mustang Island, one of a handful of long, skinny islands that skim Texas' Gulf Coast. Sportsmen come by the dozen to cruise out to sea in search of finned fighters like tarpon, sailfish, tuna, marlin, and the like. But you don't have to be a diehard fisherman to have a great time here. Party boats accommodating anywhere from 18 to 100 passengers sail out to the snapper banks, about 1½ hours offshore, allowing anglers to haul in fish by the basketful. The so-called electric reels provided on the boats going out after snapper may take away some of the sport — just press a button and the reel whirs into action, bringing in a hooked fish in a thrice. But until the novelty wears off, it's great fun. If you don't want to have to give away all your catch, be sure to stay in a motel with housekeeping facilities. Information: Chamber of Commerce, Box 356, Port Aransas, TX 78373 (512 749-5919).

ILWACO, Washington: From mid-April to October, a fleet of charter boats goes out into the Pacific for kings and silvers at the Salmon Capital of the World; 300,000 salmon are caught offshore every year. Some fishermen, in fact, complain that they get their limit almost as soon as they leave shore, and don't know what to do with the rest of the day. The area is also famous for its razor-clam digging. Information: Peninsula Visitors Bureau, PO Box 562, Long Beach, WA 98631 (206 642-2400).

FIREHOLE RIVER, Yellowstone National Park, Wyoming: With headwaters near Old Faithful, this river is small by Western standards; the rainbows and browns that inhabit it are most commonly just 10 to 16 inches long; and the fish big enough to keep (those over 16 inches) are hard to catch, even in late May and June and again from late August until season's close in late October, when the Mayfly and caddis-fly hatches bring the trout into action. But the Firehole is one of the nation's great "total experience" rivers: Rarely will you fish here without seeing wildlife, and the scenery — forests, mountains, and clouds of steam rising from the great meadows that flank the stream — is superb. Information: Bud Lilly's Trout Shop, Box 698, West Yellowstone, MT 59758 (406 646-7801).

FISHING SCHOOLS

In the last few years, a number of fishing pros and tackle manufacturers have taken it upon themselves to teach the bumbling angler the fine art of filling up a stringer — so even if you didn't grow up in a fishing family, you can quickly begin acquiring the skills necessary to keep you hauling them in with the best. Some provide instruction in fly-fishing and concentrate on trout; others teach you bait- and spin-casting techniques.

FENWICK FLY FISHING SCHOOLS, based in Westminster, California: The company that took the lead in mass-producing first-rate fly rods some 20 years ago now turns out top-notch fishermen at the two- to five-day courses it offers at locations all over the US and Mexico. The emphasis differs with the school locale; you can learn fly-fishing, bass and muskie tactics, steelhead techniques, and more. Information: Peggy Noe, Fenwick/Woodstream Company, 14799 Chestnut St., Westminster, CA 92683 (714 897-1066).

BUD LILLY'S FLY-FISHING SCHOOL, West Yellowstone, Montana: Complete two- and three-day programs are offered. More informal programs are run daily in this scenic area; special courses are offered for ladies. Information: Bud Lilly's Trout Shop, Box 698, West Yellowstone, MT 59758 (406 646-7801).

JOAN AND LEE WULFF FISHING SCHOOLS, Lew Beach, New York: Two of the nation's most famous fishermen share their expertise with anglers of all skill levels at their school in the Catskills, just 120 miles from New York City. The Beaverkill is one of several productive waters where you can practice. Weekend courses are offered in not only trout fishing but also Atlantic salmon fishing and fly casting. Late April through the end of June. Information: Joan and Lee Wulff Fishing School, Lew Beach, NY 12753 (914 439-4060).

ORVIS FLY-FISHING SCHOOL, Manchester, Vermont: This manufacturer of fine fishing gear, in business since 1856, has taught the intricacies of the sport to such luminaries as Supreme Court Justice Potter Stewart, and in the opinion of some who know the field, its program — which includes practice in the company's stocked ponds, dry runs on the famous Battenkill (see above), and classroom sessions — is one of the best of its kind. Students stay at the now reopened colonial *Equinox Inn.* In fall, Orvis sponsors a shooting school. Information: Orvis, 10 River Rd., Manchester, VT 05254 (802 362-3900).

Mountain Climbing and Mountains

Like all great sports, mountaineering allows the participant to choose the severity of the test — to match skills to challenge. Climbs can range from simple but rugged hikes requiring some technical work (that is, the use of chocks, nuts, ropes, ice axes, and crampons to get over vertical rock faces and icy surfaces) to high-altitude expeditions lasting weeks and requiring specialized skills, great reserves of strength and endurance, and sophisticated equipment. But one rule applies to all climbing: You are only as safe as your judgment and training are good. And it is always exhilarating.

Climbing is not a forbidding sport for a beginner, but the only way to start is with training. Best is a beginner's one-day course; in the West, with either the *Exum Mountain Guides* in Grand Teton National Park, Box 56, Moose, WY 83012 (307 733-2297, seasonal), or at the *Yosemite Mountaineering School* in Yosemite National Park, Yosemite, CA 95389 (209 372-1335, June to mid-September; 209 372-1244, rest of the year). In the East there's a school sponsored by *Eastern Mountain Sports,* Main St., North Conway, NH 03860 (603 356-5433). A one-day course will give a not too strenuous introduction to belaying, anchoring, rappelling, and moderate-angle climbing; and even with these modest skills you will be able to take rocks which in your pre-course life you'd have judged unclimbable.

Better than a one-day course (which is really more orientation and encouragement than adequate training for more rigorous climbs) is a week or multiweek course, which provides an active, exciting vacation. The one you pick will depend on where you want to be and what you want to learn — rock work, snow and ice techniques, or expedition planning. Some courses concentrate on one subject; others combine the three.

CLIMBING SCHOOLS

PALISADE SCHOOL OF MOUNTAINEERING, Bishop, California: Week-long courses and guided climbs are offered during summer, operating out of a base camp in the Palisades, a 10-mile-long crest of jagged peaks and glaciers. You can learn ice and snow climbing, rock climbing, and expedition planning. Also offered are expeditions to the Mexican volcanoes, the Ecuadorian and Peruvian Andes, and Nepal. Information: Palisade School of Mountaineering, PO Box 694, Bishop, CA 93514 (619 873-5037).

COLORADO MOUNTAIN SCHOOL, Estes Park, Colorado: Basic to advanced ice-, snow-, rock-climbing, and mountaineering seminars, lasting from 1 to 7 days, are offered year-round by this establishment, as well as several expeditions and special programs. Information: Colorado Mountain School, PO Box 2106, Estes Park, CO 80517 (303 586-5758).

NANTAHALA OUTDOOR CENTER, Bryson City, North Carolina: This wilderness adventures center, the largest whitewater canoe and kayak instruction facility in the US, also offers a program of weekend and five-day rock climbing clinics for beginners and intermediates. Information: Nantahala Outdoor Center, US 19W, Box 41, Bryson City, NC 28713 (704 488-2175).

RAINIER MOUNTAINEERING, Tacoma, Washington: Seminars in snow and ice climbing and guided summit climbs of Mt. Rainier are offered at this northwestern institution. Information: Rainier Mountaineering, 201 St. Helens St., Tacoma, WA 98402 (206 627-6242).

AMERICA'S MOUNTAINS — FOR THE CLIMBING

LONGS PEAK, near Estes Park, Colorado: One way to reach this 14,255-foot summit in Rocky Mountain National Park involves a long, challenging trek from the Longs Peak Ranger Station through aspen stands and conifer forests, tundra, alpine meadows, and boulder fields through the Keyhole (about 8 miles). The north face route is less crowded, but climbing skills are required. Information: Backcountry Office, Rocky Mountain National Park, Estes Park, CO 80517-8397 (303 586-2371).

MT. KATAHDIN, near Millinocket, Maine: The 5,267-foot peak in Baxter State Park, the northern terminus of the Appalachian Trail, rises sharply as you get close to the 4,000-foot timberline. Most routes don't require ropes, and the climb takes a day — but slopes full of loose rock can make the going tough. Information: Baxter State Park, 64 Balsam Dr., Millinocket, ME 04462 (207 723-5140).

MT. WASHINGTON, near North Conway, New Hampshire: The view from the 6,288-foot summit — the "second greatest show on earth," according to no less than P. T. Barnum — attracts hikers by the thousands. The trails up are steep, but not *that* steep. The danger, instead, lies in the weather, reputedly the worst in the world. It is treacherous, and ferocious snowstorms *do* blow up on a regular basis with practically no warning — even in summer. Information: Appalachian Mountain Club, Pinkham Notch Camp, PO Box 298, Gorham, NH 03581 (603 466-2725).

MT. MARCY, near Lake Placid, New York: This 5,344-foot Adirondack peak can be reached in a day over a variety of routes — most of them steep trails that make many climbers wish they were in better shape. The forests at the bottom — full of ferns and trees whose foliage seems almost electric green — may remind you of the Pacific Northwest rain forests. Information: New York State Dept. of Environmental Conservation, License Sales/Information Office, 50 Wolf Rd., Albany, NY 12233-0001 (518 457-3521).

MT. HOOD, near Government Camp, Oregon: The 11,235-foot summit of this inactive volcano has been conquered by a blind man, a man with no legs, several adventurers with artificial limbs, a 5-year-old, a 79-year-old woman, and travelers on skis, bikes, and in tennis shoes; only Mt. Fuji is more popular as a summit destination. Nonetheless, this climb takes technical know-how and preparation; it is the inexperienced, poorly equipped climber who is most apt to be injured (and well over. a hundred people have lost their lives on the mountain). Most people follow the southside route, which departs from the new Wy'East Day Lodge, where you can register and get current conditions at a 24-hour climbing station. Then you're off for the beautiful trip — beginning at midnight, past scenic glaciers and fumaroles. The climbing season is from mid-December to mid-June. Information: Mt. Hood National Forest, 2955 NW Division St., Gresham, OR 97030 (503 666-0700).

MT. RAINIER, near Ashford, Washington: Visible on a clear day for over a hundred miles in all directions, this 14,410-foot mountain, the fifth highest in the lower 48 states, is lush with wildflowers and giant forests below the 6,800-foot timberline, heavily glaciated above it. The two-day trip to the top, which takes you over glaciers and crumbling lava, is long, strenuous, demanding, and not without hazards — but anyone in good condition can do it with a guide. Information: Mt. Rainier National Park, Tahoma Woods, Star Route, Ashford, WA 98304 (206 569-2211).

THE GRAND TETON, near Jackson, Wyoming: Looking at it from below, you'd never think that relatively inexperienced climbers could safely scale the awe-inspiring 13,770-foot summit. However, the granite rock (solid enough that you can trust it) offers plenty of handholds and footholds — everything you need to climb a mountain, one step at a time, with some training, the proper equipment, and a guide (which more experienced climbers will be able to do without). *Exum Mountain Guides,* which operates the School of American Mountaineering (Box 56, Moose, WY 83012, 307 733-2297 from June to mid-September) and *Jackson Hole Mountain Guides* (PO Box 547, Teton Village, WY 83025; 307 733-4979), will take you up on the two-day climb to the top after you've spent a few days in the climbing school. Information: Grand Teton National Park, PO Drawer 170, Moose, WY 83012 (307 733-2880).

Wilderness Trips on Foot

Building your backpacking skills to the point that you can go deep into a trackless wilderness for a few weeks and come out none the worse for wear takes some time. But it's not impossible. Day hikes, for example, are a good introduction. All the national parks and forests, state parks and forests, and various other public lands have trails of various lengths that are perfect for simple walks. You'll be breaking in your boots so that over extended treks blisters will be less likely to develop, and you'll be building up your stamina.

From there, short trips close to home are your best bet. Or you can sign up for one of the various outdoor programs that school tenderfeet in wilderness and hiking skills. Guided trips build confidence and provide companionship. A few areas of the US have the counterparts of the hikers' huts scattered all over the Alps; you don't have to carry a tent or even food.

Then there are thousands of square miles of hikable terrain all over the country, with easy trails for novices, more rugged ones (steeper, less well maintained) for better hikers, and huge wildernesses where you can hike cross-country with just a topographic map and compass.

OUTDOOR TRAINING SCHOOLS

Some adults are lucky enough to have learned how to handle themselves in the wilderness when they were young — in the company of backpacking-loving relatives. Others must acquire camping skills on their own, and learn about everything from tree identification to back country first aid from books. For the very timid, however, there's no better introduction to woodcraft than one of the handful of outdoor training schools offered by a number of organizations around the country. The *National Outdoor Leadership School* (NOLS) and *Outward Bound,* listed below, are among the most important. You can find out about others in magazines like *Backpacker* (1515 Broadway, New York, NY 10036) and *Outside* (1165 N Clark, Chicago, IL 60610), where most advertise their services.

OUTWARD BOUND, based in Greenwich, Connecticut: With schools on Hurricane Island in Maine, and in Colorado, Minnesota, North Carolina, and Oregon; at each, the aim is to help you grow by challenging you. Information: Outward Bound, 384 Field Point Rd., Greenwich, CT 06830 (203 661-0797 or 800 243-8520).

NATIONAL AUDUBON SOCIETY ECOLOGY CAMPS, based in Boulder, Colorado: These June, July, and August programs held in Connecticut, Maine, Wisconsin, and Wyoming focus on area ecosystems; you lodge in cabins and bungalows in each area and do your learning on field trips. Great for both adults and children. Information: National Audubon Society, 4150 Darley, Suite 5, Boulder, CO 80303 (303 499-0219).

BOULDER OUTDOOR SURVIVAL SCHOOL, Provo, Utah: The mountains, deserts, and canyonlands of Utah are the setting for this small but venerable institution's 12-, 15-, and 26-day programs. You learn primitive fire-building techniques, trap-and-snare construction, plant identification, primitive direction finding, shelter construction, and more. But increased self-confidence and personal awareness, and enhanced interpersonal relationships, are equally important benefits. Information: BOSS Booking Offices, PO Box 905, Rexburg, ID 83440 (208 356-7446).

AMERICAN HIKING SOCIETY, based in Washington, DC: This nonprofit hikers' association sponsors 2-week trail maintenance and construction trips from May until the end of August. Information: American Hiking Society, 1701 18th St., NW, Washington, DC 20009 (202 234-4609).

NATIONAL WILDLIFE FEDERATION CONSERVATION SUMMITS, based in Washington, DC: Week-long programs with self-designed schedules in North Carolina, Maine, and Colorado, held from June through August, focus on natural history and outdoor recreation; the programs and activities are wonderful for families. Information: National Wildlife Federation, 1412 16th St., NW, Washington, DC 20036 (703 790-4363).

NATIONAL OUTDOOR LEADERSHIP SCHOOL (NOLS), based in Lander, Wyoming: This organization, originally established to school wilderness-trip leaders in certain outdoor skills, offers courses in backpacking, minimum-impact camping, cross-country skiing, sea kayaking, and climbing, in Alaska, Washington, and Wyoming, as well as Mexico and Africa, all year. Information: NOLS, PO Box AA, Lander, WY 82520 (307 332-6973).

EASY LONG TRIPS

On these trips, you don't have to pack anything more than the clothes you'll need for the time you're away from home. Hikers' huts and inns provide your shelter.

YOSEMITE NATIONAL PARK, Yosemite, California: The High Sierra camps in this park are among the few places in the US where you can stay in the mountains overnight without having to camp out. The five tent-dormitory groups are roughly 9 miles apart; hot showers, linen, blankets, soap, and towels, and breakfast and dinner are provided for about $60 per person per night. Reservations (available in writing beginning December 1, and usually gone within two weeks) are required. Information: Yosemite Park & Curry Co., High Sierra Desk, 5410 E Home Ave., Fresno, CA 93727 (209 252-3013).

GLACIER NATIONAL PARK, West Glacier, Montana: You can't exactly backpack from Sperry to Granite Park — the two rugged stone chalets in this park — but you can do overnight backpacks first to one and then to the other, returning to your car between times. Only the restrooms, in separate buildings, and the kitchens at both chalets have been modernized, so they're much as they were when built around World War I. Both are lit after dark by candlelight, both are in the National Register of Historic Places, and both are open only in July and August; rates are around $45 a night including three meals. Reserve well in advance. Information: Belton Chalets, PO Box 188, West Glacier, MT 59936 (406 888-5511 from April to mid-September).

WHITE MOUNTAINS NATIONAL FOREST, around North Conway, New Hampshire: In the heart of the Presidential range, a system of hikers' huts maintained by the Appalachian Mountain Club gives you almost unlimited hiking variety — both above and below tree line. No two are quite alike: Lakes of the Clouds, situated at the edge of two icy blue lakes above tree line, seems relatively new; the Madison Hut, just above tree line, is built of stone and seems almost ancient. Blankets (but not linen), dinners, and breakfasts are provided for the nightly charge, about $30 a person. Reservations are essential. Information: AMC, Pinkham Notch Camp, PO Box 298, Gorham, NH 03581 (603 466-2727).

INN-TO-INN HIKING, around Vermont: A group of country inns along an 80-mile section of Vermont's Long Trail have teamed up to offer special trips during which you sleep in big brass beds under antique quilts, soak off your sore muscles in claw-footed bathtubs, and bring your gear and car to the selected finish each morning, where it will await your later arrival as the innkeeper drives you back to the day's starting point. Information: Country Inns Along the Trail, c/o Churchill House Inn, Brandon, VT 05733 (802 247-3300).

GUIDED HIKES

Not all organizations that sponsor trips for groups furnish the gear you'll need; some provide everything, while some will set you up with everything but a sleeping bag. Make sure to confirm this in advance, and find out whether the rates — usually from about $35 to $100 per day — include food, sleeping gear, lodging the night before the trip begins (if necessary), guides, equipment, and the like. For extensive lists of organizations offering group backpacking trips and hiking trips with pack stock carrying your gear, read *Outside* magazine, or consult Pat Dickerman's *Adventure Travel North America*, $13.95 postpaid from Adventure Guides, 36 E 57th St., New York, NY 10022 (212 355-6334). Dickerman has also begun an advisory service that can book spaces on established trips or plan trips on request.

AMERICAN FORESTRY ASSOCIATION, based in Washington, DC: Trips lasting five to ten days are offered in wilds of both the East and West — with pack stock carrying the gear. Information: AFA Trail Riders, 1319 18th St., NW, Washington, DC 20036-1802 (202 467-5810).

APPALACHIAN MOUNTAIN CLUB, Gorham, New Hampshire: This group's guided overnight hikes give you insight into the White Mountains' natural and social history. Information: AMC, Pinkham Notch Camp, PO Box 298, Gorham, NH 03581 (603 466-2727).

CAMP DENALI, Denali National Park, Alaska: Expeditions and seminar-type wilderness workshops give you a chance to explore subarctic tundra, rocky ridges, cross glacial streams with groups of up to 16. The first two weeks in June offer superb birding and wildflower viewing (under 24 hours of daylight); in late August and early September, sandhill cranes can be seen in migration, one of nature's great spectacles. May through September is the season to see moose, caribou, and grizzly bears. In all, over 35 species of mammals roam free here. Information: Camp Denali, Denali National Park, AK 99755 (907 683-2302 September through May, 907 683-2290 the rest of the year).

KENAI GUIDE SERVICE, Kasilof, Alaska: Backpacking above timberline, June through August, at the base of dark, rocky pinnacles, alpine meadows and gorges, glaciers and cliffs, snowfields. Information: Kenai Guide Service, PO Box 40, Kasilof, AK 99610 (907 262-5496).

SIERRA CLUB, headquartered in San Francisco, California: The conservation organization offers a variety of trips. Information: Sierra Club, Outing Dept., 730 Polk St., San Francisco, CA 94109 (415 776-2211).

UNIVERSITY OF THE WILDERNESS, based in Evergreen, Colorado: Five- to ten-day trips take you through the mountains, deserts, and river canyons of the southern and western US; workshops and classes on the Snowy Range Campus near Laramie, Wyoming, cover wilderness photography, art, music, Rocky Mountain flowers, wildlife, and related environmental subjects. Information: University of the Wilderness, PO Box 1687, Evergreen, CO 80439 (303 674-9724).

WILDERNESS SOUTHEAST, Savannah, Georgia: This active organization offers naturalist-led hiking, flatwater canoeing, camping, snorkeling, and backpacking programs in southeastern woodlands, islands, coral reefs, and swamps. Information: Wilderness Southeast, 711-G Sandtown Rd., Savannah, GA 31410 (912 897-5108).

BEST BACKPACKING SPOTS

There's good backpacking all over the country — even in the Midwest, where most of the forests have given way to farms and pastures. Best hiking and backpacking, however, lie in one of 11 general regions — Alaska, the Northwest Coast ranges, the Cascade range (slightly inland in Washington, Oregon, and northern California), the Columbia Plateau (just slightly inland from the Cascades), the Rockies (swooping through Idaho, western Montana, most of Wyoming and Colorado, and northern New Mexico), the Great Desert (covering most of Nevada), the Sierra (in California), the Colorado Plateau (northern Arizona, northwestern New Mexico, the southern two thirds of Utah), the Ozarks of northern Arkansas and southern Missouri, the Appalachians (extending from northern Maine through Tennessee and Virginia), and the north woods of northern Michigan and Wisconsin and Minnesota. Each area has its particular characteristics.

Alaska's mountains, valleys, forests, and oceans are all wilderness; the climate is wet and temperate in the southern part of the state, drier and much colder (with winters that fall to 50° below) north of the Alaskan range, and drier and colder yet north of the Brooks range, where large trees simply do not exist and the vegetation has to hug the ground to survive the winds. Trails and cross-country travel are both possible, but mosquitoes, bad in June, sometimes make the wilds unpleasant.

The Northwest Coast ranges, with peaks less than 8,000 feet, are primarily distinguished by their weather — wet, with about 200 inches of rain each year — and the resultant lush growth of cedars, firs, hemlocks, spruces, redwoods, ferns, mosses, shrubs. Summer is the driest season; trail use is usually moderate. The Cascade range, paralleling the Northwest Coast range, has peaks up to 10,000 feet, somewhat lighter precipitation, dense forests except in areas covered by relatively recent lava flows, good trails — and all-around fine wilderness. The Sierra, made famous by John Muir, are known for their good hiking — and with reason. Not only are there awesome glaciated granite peaks (which are characteristic), but the climate is somewhat drier than along the coast, with low-altitude forests of ponderosa, yellow, and lodgepole pine, and white and red fir giving way to alpine lakes and lichen-covered granite boulders as you follow uphill trails (which are plentiful); in addition, mosquitoes and other pests are usually absent. It's not hard to understand why the area is heavily trafficked.

The Columbia Plateau, on the other hand, gets relatively little use. Home of some of the largest populations of cougar in the country, of eagles, hawks, salmon, and sturgeon (and relatively insect-free because of the overall aridity), it has areas of recent volcanic activity, like moonscapes; ponderosa pineland; alpine terrain; and canyons like the celebrated Hell's Canyon and Snake River Canyon. A good many people float the streams, but scarcely anyone ventures uphill. The Great Desert area, cut by mountain ranges of sculptured rock, is the wildest and least used. People think of it as hot and boring. Actually, it boasts a wide variety of terrain: handsome stands of the weird Joshua tree (in the Mojave Desert), the cactus of the Sonora Desert (archetypical desert), and sagebrush and cottonwood country in its Great Basin section. There aren't many designated backpacking trails, but if you've got the experience to go cross-country, this is a place to do it.

The Colorado Plateau is characterized by its weirdly shaped buttes, canyons, mesas, and a range of environments from desert to alpine. It's hikable so long as you're prepared.

The Rockies, on the other hand, require less experience. More than 40 monuments, forests, and parks make this Valhalla for foot travelers; there are snow-capped peaks, fields of wildflowers, alpine lakes, icy streams, slopes full of conifers and deciduous trees. With the Sierra, this is the US's prime backpacking territory.

The Ozarks offer some backpacking through dense forests in low mountains and shallow valleys, scattered with caves and underground rivers; this is especially good if you want to travel cross-country, though long trails have recently become more abundant. The north woods, on the other hand, are full of trails. Flat and rolling countryside makes the going fairly easy as well, and huge numbers of lakes offer fine campsites.

In the East, the Appalachians make for the best backpacking. The peaks are lower and more rounded than those in the West, but many of the grades are just as steep as those in the rest of the country. The Appalachian Trail runs the length of the chain for 2,100 miles from Maine to Georgia; the Long Trail runs for 263 miles along the spine of the Green Mountains in Vermont. (For details about these long trails, contact the *Appalachian Trail Conference,* PO Box 807, Harpers Ferry, WV 25425, 304 535-6331; or the *Green Mountain Club,* PO Box 889, Montpelier, VT 05602, 802 223-3463.)

In addition to these long trails, there is yet a third — the recently designated North Country Trail, the country's longest, which runs for 3,246 miles from Crown Point, New York, across seven states to the Lewis and Clark National Historic Trail at Lake Sakakawea in North Dakota. Information: *North Country Trail Assn.,* PO Box 311, White Cloud, MI 49349 (402 221-3371).

OUACHITA NATIONAL FOREST, Hot Springs, Arkansas: Some of America's best hiking is to be found along the ridge-climbing, scenic, 175-mile-long Ouachita National Recreation Trail and its 40-odd miles of spurs. Information: Ouachita National Forest, PO Box 1270, Hot Springs, AR 71902 (501 321-5202).

OZARK NATIONAL FOREST, Russellville, Arkansas: The Ozark Highlands Trail stretches for 130 miles across the forest, which is most beautiful in spring, when dogwoods bloom by the thousand, and during fall foliage season. Information: Ozark National Forest, PO Box 1008, Russellville, AR 72801 (501 968-2354).

TONTO NATIONAL FOREST, Phoenix, Arizona: This is the largest national forest in the state, with more than 2.8 million acres, an 800-mile trail system, and eight wilderness areas that take in everything from desert at an altitude of 1,500 feet to fir and pine forest at 8,000 feet. You'll find desert, grassland, piñon, a maze of box canyons and arid mountains covered with chaparral, and, in the higher elevations, some ponderosa pine and mixed conifer. Experience in desert travel is important (and you must carry water). Trail conditions vary from excellent to very poor. Information: Tonto National Forest, PO Box 5348, Phoenix, AZ 85010 (602 225-5200).

KLAMATH NATIONAL FOREST, Yreka, California: Largely unused, because the many other national forests one must pass through on the way tend to absorb the majority of visitors, here are outstanding backpacking possibilities in a state that is full of them, because of the size (almost 1.7 million acres) and the fine forests of pine, cedar, fir, and hemlock that cover mountains ranging up to 8,000 feet. You can hike hundreds of miles of trails, most just moderately steep, and cross-country in the roadless areas of the Salmon-Trinity Alps Wilderness, Russian Wilderness, Siskiyou Wilderness, Red Buttes Wilderness, and the Marble Mountain Wilderness (pine and fir forests, meadows, icy streams, alpine lakes). In the spring and fall, you'll see a spectacular wildfowl show, as birds from Canada and Alaska, moving along the Pacific flyway, converge on the eastern part of the forest. The Pacific Crest Trail also runs through the Klamath. Information: Klamath National Forest, 1312 Fairlane Rd., Yreka, CA 96097 (916 842-6131).

NEZPERCE NATIONAL FOREST, Grangeville, Idaho: An incredible trail system — over 2,300 miles — makes this 2.2-million-acre forest one of the best for backpacking in the Rockies. An elevation range from 1,000 feet to 10,000 feet makes for plenty of variety — river canyons, lowland meadows, and cool mountain forests. A portion of the Frank Church River of No Return Wilderness Area, the largest classified wilderness in the US, lies within the Nezperce. Information: Nezperce National Forest, Rte. 2, Box 475, Grangeville, ID 83530 (208 983-1950).

SUPERIOR NATIONAL FOREST, Duluth, Minnesota: One of the finest forest areas in the country, these 3 million acres take in a million acres of wilderness scattered with lichen-covered granite outcrops and lakes — about two thousand of them, with rocky shorelines, islands, and occasional sand beaches. And there are over 250 miles of maintained hiking trails varying in length and difficulty. The fishing — for walleye, northern pike, trout, and bass — is superb; some people come for that alone. Information: Superior National Forest, PO Box 338, Duluth, MN 55801 (218 720-5324).

TOIYABE NATIONAL FOREST, Reno, Nevada: The largest national forest in the lower 48 states, the Toiyabe is scattered across central, southern, and western Nevada, and the east slopes of the Sierra Nevada Range in eastern California. The Toiyabe has High Sierra environments with alpine lakes, icy streams, and coniferous forests; and desert country with cactus, creosote bush, yucca, and above that juniper and piñon pine. Hundreds of miles of trails poke into every corner of its 3.4 million acres; those in California's Hoover Wilderness near Yosemite are heavily used, while those in the high desert ranges of central Nevada are quiet. Temperatures are not as forbidding as you might expect. For a few brief weeks, generally in October, you can gather the tasty piñon pine nuts, long an important food staple for the native Americans of Nevada and California, and a great delicacy nowadays. Information: Toiyabe National Forest, 1200 Franklin Way, Sparks, NV 89431 (702 784-5331).

WILLAMETTE NATIONAL FOREST, Eugene, Oregon: You can do outstanding backpacking on good trails through over 1,675,000 acres, 379,000 of which have been designated as wilderness: the Diamond Peak Wilderness, a cluster of volcanic peaks covered with fir, hemlock, pine, and meadows, scattered with lakes; the Bull of the Woods Wilderness, a terrain of rocky ridgetops and forested dells; the Mt. Jefferson Wilderness, which surrounds an extinct, glacier-covered volcano; the Three Sisters Wilderness, whose extensive trails take you through vast forests, sub-alpine terrain, meadows, and expanses of basalt and obsidian left from recent volcanic activity; the Mt. Washington Wilderness, much of which is lava flow; and more. Information: Willamette National Forest, PO Box 10607, Eugene, OR 97440 (503 687-6521).

SISKIYOU NATIONAL FOREST, Grants Pass, Oregon: The low mountains in the southwestern corner of the state are covered by wonderful flowering bushes — wild lilac, azaleas, and rhododendrons among them — and crossed by fine fishing streams, including the celebrated Rogue. You can hike along the Rogue River Trail, a part of the new 36,038-acre Wild Rogue Wilderness, through the rugged Coast Range; but the prime backpacking area is the Kalmiopsis Wilderness, 179,650 acres of rocky hills and low canyons where you'll see interesting hardwoods and shrubs, some quite rare. Hornets, yellow jackets, and rattlesnakes are common. Superb fishing in the Rogue during fall's massive salmon and steelhead migration. Information: Siskiyou National Forest, PO Box 440, Grants Pass, OR 97526 (503 479-5301).

ASHLEY NATIONAL FOREST, Vernal, Utah: The 460,000-acre High Uintas Wilderness — a wonderful expanse of lakes, forests, meadows, and rocky mountains, which the Ashley National Forest shares with the Wasatch National Forest — is what most people come to hike, but similar environments can be found throughout the forest, particularly on the east, and they're far less crowded. Lakes, streams full of trout, and many exposed geologic formations are also here. Information: Ashley National Forest, Ashton Energy Center, 1680 W Highway 40, Suite 1150, Vernal, UT 84078 (801 789-1181).

For the Mind

Regional American Theaters

A note in the program tells you to keep the aisles free of obstructions, and when the lights go down and the actors come whooping down the aisles around you, you know why.

Regional theater isn't always so exuberant, but it's not provincial either. The old situation, in which all you had in the hinterlands was dinner theater and summer stock of varying quality, no longer exists. Regional theater — theater out of New York City — has entered its prime, and some of the most exciting and innovative productions, the kind that "lower the drawbridge between actor and audience," in the words of one critic, go onto stages outside Manhattan. Regional theaters provide actors with a year-round opportunity to get back to the basics, and give talented local authors and first-timers a chance to get their works produced. Meanwhile, whether the play ends up on Broadway or never gets more than a reading, audiences get some lively dramatic experiences.

EAST

THE HARTFORD STAGE COMPANY, Hartford, Connecticut: Housed in a $2.5 million structure designed by Robert Venturi, this innovative organization presents an eclectic assortment of six plays during its season in productions that are generally noteworthy for their style, verve, and aesthetic vision; the focus is on presenting new works and rediscovering the classics. Information: Hartford Stage Co., 50 Church St., Hartford, CT 06103 (203 527-5151).

LONG WHARF THEATRE, New Haven, Connecticut: This prestigious regional theater welds fine ensemble performances by some of America's best actors to what the artistic directors like to call "plays of character," which are produced in two intimate theaters. Numerous Long Wharf productions go on to New York stages. Among past hits: *The Gin Game, Sizwe Banzi Is Dead, The Shadow Box,* and *Joe Egg.* Information: Long Wharf Theatre, 222 Sargent Dr., New Haven, CT 06511 (203 787-4282).

TRINITY SQUARE REPERTORY COMPANY, Providence, Rhode Island: Eleven major productions of modern, classic, and original dramas are staged annually in two theaters. Trinity Rep makes headlines for itself as much for its characteristic vigorous ensemble style — verging on the flamboyant — as for the plays themselves. The theater won a Tony award for outstanding repertory in 1981 and, in 1984, the first Ensemble Grant from the National Endowment for the Arts. Information: Trinity Square Repertory Company, 201 Washington, Providence, RI 02903 (401 351-4242).

ARENA STAGE, Washington, DC: One of the oldest and most consistently admired American theater companies and the first outside New York to receive a Tony for theatrical excellence, this institution founded in 1950 is noted for developing American drama and for introducing foreign (particularly Eastern European) plays to the US. The theater's three stages seat 827, 514, and 180; the last is used for small musical revues and experimental works. Robert Prosky and James Earl Jones have performed here; past productions include *After the Fall* by Arthur Miller, *Happy End* by Berthold Brecht and Kurt Weill; *Women and Water* by John Guare, *A Lesson from Aloes* by Athol Fugard, *Tomfoolery* by Tom Lehrer, George Bernard Shaw's *Major Barbara,* and *On the Razzle* by Tom Stoppard. Reservations essential. Information: Arena Stage, 6th and Maine Ave., SW, Washington, DC 20024 (202 554-9066; box office, 202 488-3300; TDD number for deaf patrons, 202 484-0247).

SOUTH

ACTORS THEATRE OF LOUISVILLE, Louisville, Kentucky: In recent years, the two stages here have become bright spots on the American theater scene. The annual Humana Festival of New American Plays, initiated in 1977, has gained international critical attention and has sent graduates on to successful runs on both coasts: *Agnes of God, Crimes of the Heart, Extremities,* and *Getting Out* all premiered here. The four dozen or so productions each season, both classics and innovative new works, are presented in a main auditorium and a smaller upstairs theater — both in a grand old columned building that has been designated a National Historic Landmark. Information: Actors Theatre of Louisville, 316-320 W Main St., Louisville, KY 40202 (502 584-1265; box office, 584-1205).

DALLAS THEATER CENTER, Dallas, Texas: Conventional dramas and plays by contemporary authors, many of them premieres, alternate between the Frank Lloyd Wright Theater and the Arts District Theater, the latter an immense, open performance space. Preston Jones's *A Texas Trilogy* got its start here. Besides the six works presented each season on both stages, an additional two plays, considered by the Center to be somewhat more controversial or just plain "different" (*Cloud 9* among them), are staged at a downstairs cabaret theater. Information: Dallas Theater Center, 3636 Turtle Creek Blvd., Dallas, TX 75219 (214 526-8210; box office, 526-8857).

ALLEY THEATRE, Houston, Texas: Classical drama, notable contemporary revivals, and new works chosen for ideas and language (usually 12 each season) are presented on both a large thrust-stage theater and a smaller arena theater. Both are in a stunning concrete and glass structure downtown. The Alley is one of the country's oldest resident professional theaters. Information: Alley Theatre, 615 Texas Ave., Houston, TX 77002 (713 228-9341; box office, 228-8421).

MIDWEST

CINCINNATI PLAYHOUSE IN THE PARK, Cincinnati, Ohio: World premieres of plays by new American playwrights, classics, rarely presented works, musicals, and comedies are the staples in the two theaters of this much-praised regional professional company. Information: Cincinnati Playhouse in the Park, PO Box 6537, Cincinnati, OH 45206 (513 421-5440; box office, 513 421-3888 and, in Ohio only, 800 582-3208).

GOODMAN THEATRE, Chicago, Illinois: The second oldest regional theater in the country, the Goodman mounts frequent productions of works by living writers, brings classics up to date in eye-opening ways, and stages that colorful favorite, *A Christmas Carol,* at the end of the year. The Goodman also hosts the Merrill Lynch Dance Series, featuring the world's finest dance companies, from classical to contemporary. There are two theaters, one small and one large. Information: Goodman Theatre, 200 S Columbus Dr., Chicago, IL 60603 (box office, 312 443-3800).

ORGANIC THEATER, Chicago, Illinois: Dedicated to producing world premiere theater, this creative ensemble of actors and designers has been described as "imaginative," "funny," and "original." The troupe has used the improvisational process to create such hits as *Bleacher Bums; E/R Emergency Room,* Chicago's longest running comedy; and *Warp!,* the country's first science fiction trilogy. David Mamet's *Sexual Perversity in Chicago* started out here, too. Information: Organic Theater, 3319 N Clark St., Chicago, IL 60657 (312 327-5588).

GUTHRIE THEATER, Minneapolis, Minnesota: With 1,441 seats, the Guthrie is the largest of the country's regional theaters. It also has the longest season, and its house, which shares a handsome contemporary building with the Walker Art Center, is one of the most unusually designed, with a unique thrust stage that gives audiences access to three sides of the production; no member is more than about 50 feet from the actors. Classical drama, European revivals, and American plays are presented Tuesdays through Sundays. Hume Cronyn, Jessica Tandy, Frank Langella, and Michael Moriarty are among scores of actors who got their start, or polished their skills, on the Guthrie stage. Information: Guthrie Theater, 725 Vineland Pl., Minneapolis, MN 55403 (612 377-2224 or 800 328-0542).

MILWAUKEE REPERTORY THEATER, Milwaukee, Wisconsin: In a six-play season, classics alternate with premieres of new works by talented contemporary playwrights, at the Todd Wehr Theater in the Performing Arts Center and the intimate Court Street Theater. The MRT's annual production of Charles Dickens's *A Christmas Carol* is a Milwaukee holiday favorite. Information: Milwaukee Repertory Theater, 929 N Water St., Milwaukee, WI 53202 (414 273-7121).

WEST

MARK TAPER FORUM, Los Angeles, California: One of the nation's best-respected resident theaters, the Mark Taper Forum won Tony awards for best play, best actor, and best actress for *Children of a Lesser God* in 1979 and for overall theatrical excellence in 1977, the same year Michael Cristofer's *The Shadow Box,* which was produced here, won a Pulitzer. On the main stage, you'll see many premières and an occasional revival; the subject matter tends towards the timely, the currently problematical. Also under the Taper wing are the Improvisational Theatre Project, the Taper Lab (where new works are developed), the intimate Taper, Too, house, the annual Taper Repertory Festival, and the James A. Doolittle Theatre in Hollywood. Information: Mark Taper Forum, 135 N Grand Ave., Los Angeles, CA 90012 (213 972-7211).

AMERICAN CONSERVATORY THEATRE (ACT), San Francisco, California: A bit of Shakespeare, some Ibsen, some Shaw, works by Lanford Wilson and Terence Rattigan, and world premieres by a slew of others have played to capacity audiences at this San Francisco theater, which started out in Pittsburgh and moved to the coast in the mid-sixties. There are also signed performances for the hearing impaired, and the annual year-end production of *A Christmas Carol* is now a Bay Area tradition. Information: ACT, 450 Geary St., San Francisco, CA 94102 (415 673-6440).

SEATTLE REPERTORY THEATRE, Seattle, Washington: Modern and contemporary comedies and dramas, both classics and premieres, are performed at the 860-seat Bagley Wright Theatre at Seattle Center and in the Poncho Forum, a large rehearsal room–cum–studio theater seating 170. Information: Seattle Repertory Theatre, Seattle Center, 155 Mercer St., Seattle, WA 98109 (206 443-2210; box office, 206 443-2222).

Outdoor Dramas

Paul Green, who in his long career as a dramatist wrote some of the best of these native American epic plays, called this dramatic form "a people's theater," and anticipated the day when it would ripen into something like outdoor drama of the Greeks. Whether we ever see that day, 1¾ million travelers every year are pilgrimaging to woodland amphitheaters across the country to watch these spectacles of war and peace, statesmen and villains, heroes and plain folk, prejudice, feuds, murder, night riders, love and suffering — the very stuff of American history acted out a lot larger than most of it was lived.

Outdoor drama is not a subtle art form, but pageants are not meant to be. These summer spectacles have two compelling virtues that would win audiences in any case: They are natively American, based on legends, stories, tall tales, and real history told in the very places where the legends occurred, the history was lived; and they are exciting — colorful, enthusiastically acted, compulsively produced with horses charging, guns and cannon exploding, flames leaping, and extravagant costuming and good music. And they are also generally inexpensive; reserved seats (which you should consider) usually cost less than $10 a head; unreserved even less. For a complete list of American outdoor dramas (there are more than 60), send a self-addressed and stamped envelope to Institute of Outdoor Drama, 202 Graham Memorial 052A, University of North Carolina, Chapel Hill, NC 27514 (919 962-1328).

EAST

TRAIL OF THE LONESOME PINE, Big Stone Gap, Virginia: The love story of a mountain girl and a mining engineer from the East, set in the days when coal and iron discoveries were changing the lives of the mountain people. It's a true story, presented not far from where the couple wooed, in this part of the state so deeply affected by mining. Mid-June through August. Information: June Tolliver Playhouse, PO Drawer 700, Big Stone Gap, VA 24219 (703 523-1235).

HATFIELDS AND McCOYS and HONEY IN THE ROCK, Beckley, West Virginia: The saga of the most famous feuding families in America (complete with a runaway daughter, a stillborn baby, killings, bounties, and betrayal) alternates in repertory with the story of the formation of West Virginia during the Civil War. Indians coined the phrase "honey in the rock" to refer to natural gas which escaped from cracks in rocks and which they worshiped (as you'll see in a scene in which gas jets under the stage are ignited). Late June through early September. Information: PO Box 1205, Beckley, WV 25801 (304 253-7313; 800 642-2766 in West Virginia in summer).

SOUTH

THE GREAT PASSION PLAY, Eureka Springs, Arkansas: The quaint hillside town where Carry Nation made her last temperance speech also puts on a pageant about Christ's last days, complete with camels, horses, sheep, donkeys, doves, and a cast of over 200. May through October. Information: Elna M. Smith Foundation, Box 471, Eureka Springs, AR 72632 (501 253-9000).

THE ARKANSAW TRAVELLER FOLK AND DINNER THEATRE, Hardy, Arkansas: An evening of Ozark food, good country music, and comedy based on the 1840 legend of the Arkansaw Traveller. (When visiting a fellow mountain man, the Traveller asks about a leaky roof; the man explains that when it's raining he can't fix it, and when it's not, he doesn't need to.) Late May through early September. Information: Arkansaw Traveller, PO Box 536, Hardy, AR 72542 (501 856-2256).

CROSS AND SWORD, St. Augustine, Florida: Paul Green's production of Pedro Menéndez de Avilés' founding of St. Augustine, the oldest permanent settlement in the US, was first seen in 1965, the year the city celebrated its 400th birthday; it now plays mid-June through mid-August. Information: Cross and Sword, PO Box 1965, St. Augustine, FL 32085 (904 471-1965).

THE STEPHEN FOSTER STORY, Bardstown, Kentucky: A musical about how the composer wooed and won his Jeannie with the light brown hair (whose real name, it turns out, was Jane). At the town's *Talbott Tavern*, you can visit the room Louis Philippe of France occupied during visits in the late 1790s, and stuff yourself on fried chicken, biscuits, and some of the richest pies in the South (107 W Stephen Foster Ave., Bardstown, KY 40004, 502 348-3494). Mid-June to Labor Day. Information: Stephen Foster Story, PO Box 546, Bardstown, KY 40004 (502 348-5971).

THE LEGEND OF DANIEL BOONE, Harrodsburg, Kentucky: This popular drama focuses on the history of the great pioneer, at the James Harrod Amphitheatre in Old Fort Harrod State Park — a 28-acre preserve set up to honor the first permanent white settlement in Kentucky. (*Lincoln,* the amphitheater's other outdoor drama, focuses, naturally, on the history of the great president.) Mid-June through late August. The *Trustees' House,* the Shaker restaurant and inn at nearby Shakertown at Pleasant Hill (606 734-5411; see *America's Special Havens*), and the lovely *Beaumont Inn,* which is also a restaurant serving traditional Kentucky fare (Harrodsburg, KY 40330, 606 734-3381), are area musts. Information: Legend of Daniel Boone, PO Box 365, Harrodsburg, KY 40330 (606 734-3346).

HORN IN THE WEST, Boone, North Carolina: This story of how the earliest American pioneers rebelled against the royal governor and went west was written by Kermit Hunter, a celebrated creator of outdoor dramas. Late June through mid-August. Information: Horn in the West, PO Box 295, Boone, NC 28607 (704 264-2120).

UNTO THESE HILLS, Cherokee, North Carolina: Kermit Hunter also wrote this piece about the Cherokee Indians from 1540 until 1838, when they were herded westward over the Trail of Tears; it's presented mid-June through late August at the Mountainside Amphitheater, on the edge of the Oconaluftee Indian Village, a replica of a Cherokee settlement of 200 years ago (see *Indian America*). Information: Unto These Hills, PO Box 398, Cherokee, NC 28719 (704 497-2111).

THE LOST COLONY, Manteo, North Carolina: A fixture of the summer season on the Outer Banks since 1937, America's first symphonic outdoor drama tells the story of the mysterious disappearance of Sir Walter Raleigh's first English colony in 1587 with Indian dances, fireworks, and grand court scenes. Mid-June through late August. Information: The Lost Colony, PO Box 40, Manteo, NC 27954 (919 473-2127 or 919 473-3414).

TEXAS, Canyon, Texas: The struggle between farmers and cattlemen in the not-always-so-gay 1880s, and how it affected a batch of young lovers, is presented at Palo Duro State Park, near Amarillo, mid-June through late August, in a 1,000-foot-deep, 100-mile-long canyon so impressive that in many ways it turns out to be the star of the show. Information: Texas, PO Box 268, Canyon, TX 79015 (806 655-2181).

THE LONE STAR, Galveston, Texas: The story of the Texas fight for independence features a cast of over 80 (including six horses), cannon and gunfire, and a couple of really spectacular battle scenes. The hero of the production is Sam Houston, general of the Texas army that defeated Mexican general Santa Anna and his forces; Alamo heroes Davy Crockett and Jim Bowie are also on hand. The drama plays in repertory with a Broadway musical (which is changed from time to time) from late June through early August. Information: The Lone Star, PO Box 5253, Galveston, TX 77551 (713 737-3440).

MIDWEST

TECUMSEH!, Chillicothe, Ohio: The Shawnee war chief's struggle with William Henry Harrison over the Northwest Territory involves a cast and crew of 120, a dozen horses, and thirteen stages, in performance mid-June through the end of August. Information: Tecumseh!, PO Box 73, Chillicothe, OH 45601 (614 775-4100).

TRUMPET IN THE LAND, New Philadelphia, Ohio: Moravian missionaries, Indian converts, and the Revolutionary War on America's first frontier, complete with horses, a massacre, dances, and humor. It's presented from late June to early September about a mile from Schoenbrunn Village, a restoration of the settlement where many of the events took place. Information: Trumpet in the Land, PO Box 567, Dover, OH 44622 (216 339-1132).

SHEPHERD OF THE HILLS, Branson, Missouri: Harold Bell Wright's novel of this name is reenacted on the farm where the 1902 Ozarks drought it depicts actually took place. Branson is near 43,100-acre Table Rock Lake and Silver Dollar City, an amusement park themed around crafts. The drama is staged late April through October. Information: Shepherd of the Hills Farm, Rte. 1, Box 770, Branson, MO 65616 (417 334-4191).

THE BLACK HILLS PASSION PLAY, Spearfish, South Dakota: The same man, one Josef Meier, has been playing Christ since 1939, backed by an ensemble of some 180 players. Meier also produces and directs the show, which runs June through August in Spearfish and mid-February through mid-April in Lake Wales, Florida. Information: PO Box 489, Spearfish, SD 57783 (605 642-2646), or PO Box 71, Lake Wales, FL 33853 (813 676-1495).

WEST

TRAIL OF TEARS, Tahlequah, Oklahoma: The story of the Cherokees from the end of the tragic march over the Trail of Tears until the beginning of this century. The story is presented at Tsa-La-Gi, the Cherokee Heritage Center, where, among other attractions, you can tour a re-creation of an early 18th-century Cherokee village, where Cherokees in costume work at crafting baskets, weapons, pots, and tools. Mid-June through late August. You can lodge nearby at the pleasant *Tsa-La-Gi Lodge* (918 456-0511). Information: Trail of Tears, PO Box 515, Tahlequah, OK 74464 (918 456-6007).

THE RAMONA STORY, Hemet, California: Townspeople turn out in droves for the barbecues and assorted goings-on held to honor this dramatization of the Helen Hunt Jackson novel, a sort of Indian *Romeo and Juliet.* Raquel Welch played Ramona a few years back. Six performances are presented in late April and early May; to get tickets, it's best to reserve by the preceding January, through the Ramona Pageant Assn., PO Box 755, Hemet, CA 92343 (714 658-3111).

America's Music Festivals: Summers of Sound

 All over the country, throughout the summer, musicians get together to regale audiences with the glorious sounds of music — not just symphonies, string trios, chorales and cantatas, but also breakdowns, rags, gospel choruses, and a lot of country fiddling and picking. They're playing in mansions and amphitheaters, rustic gardens and antique opera halls, huge band shells, and even the California vineyards. Some festivals are one-day happenings. Some mean round-the-clock music for a weekend or more.

State tourist organizations can tell you about the ones in the area you want to visit. Or, for a list of bluegrass events, you can contact *Bluegrass Unlimited* magazine for its annual festival edition ($1.50; PO Box 111, Broad Run, VA 22014; 703 361-8992).

Expect to pay from about $5 to $45 for tickets, depending upon where, what, when, and whom. Should you order in advance? By all means, most especially if the object of your trip is to hear a specific performance. Usually, you will be able to get seats at the last minute (and at the big festivals you can always sit on the lawn), but advance planning will ensure your sitting where you want. Remember, too, that tickets for seats under a sheltering roof eliminate the chance that rain will wash out your enjoyment.

EAST

TANGLEWOOD, Lenox, Massachusetts: The Boston Symphony Orchestra, summering at this old Massachusetts mountain estate, performs Friday and Saturday nights and Sunday afternoons, June through August, in an enormous covered amphitheater surrounded by lawns. Music students — the Barenboims and Horowitzes of the future — present professional chamber music concerts and chamber symphony programs at the Tanglewood Music Center. You'll find a bounty of great country inns in the area. Information: Tanglewood, Lenox, MA 01240 (617 266-1492).

CHAUTAUQUA INSTITUTION, Chautauqua, New York: Founded in 1874 as a training camp for Sunday school teachers, this lakeside community of quaint Victorian guesthouses and hotels is a learning festival where music keeps company with operas, plays, lectures, and courses in the fine and performing arts, psychology, politics, philosophy, crafts, and just about any other subject you can name. Late June to late August. Information: Chautauqua Institution, Colonnade Bldg., Chautauqua, NY 14722 (716 357-6200).

THE LAKE GEORGE OPERA FESTIVAL, Glens Falls, New York: Favorite operas are sung in English by internationally recognized performers during July and August in this most delightful of American vacation areas; Sunday evenings, there are Opera-on-the-Lake cruises. Information: Lake George Opera Festival, PO Box 425, Glens Falls, NY 12801 (518 793-3858).

CARAMOOR FESTIVAL, Katonah, New York: On weekends from late June through late August, chamber and orchestral concerts are presented on an Italian Renaissance style estate — the large works in an outdoor theater surrounded by 15th-century Venetian columns, the chamber concerts in a Spanish-style courtyard. Information: Caramoor, PO Box R, Katonah, NY 10536 (914 232-5035).

JVC JAZZ FESTIVAL, New York, New York: America's first and oldest jazz festival, born in 1953 as the Newport Jazz Festival and held in New York City since 1972, is now under the sponsorship of this large electronics company. It offers mostly big-name performers, with a few up-and-comers along the way, the last week in June and the first week in July at various spots in the city, including a boat cruise. Information: JVC Jazz Festival, PO Box 1169, New York, NY 10023 (212 787-2020).

THE SARATOGA PERFORMING ARTS CENTER, Saratoga Springs, New York: The watering hole of the horsey set, this genteel old town is also the home of the giant amphitheater where the New York City Ballet performs in July and the Philadelphia Orchestra in August. Popular special events are presented from June through September. And throughout the summer programs of theater and dance are presented in SPAC's Little Theatre. Information: SPAC Box Office, Saratoga Springs, NY 12866 (518 587-3330). The *Gideon Putnam Hotel*, on the grounds of the Saratoga Spa State Park (where you can still take the waters orally or in a variety of mineral baths), is posh and comfortable in that particular way that spells affluence (518 584-3000).

NEWPORT MUSIC FESTIVAL, Newport, Rhode Island: Three times daily, for two weeks every July, first-rate artists perform classical music in the gilt and marble ballrooms of the town's glorious mansions. For lodgings by the sea, don't miss the *Inn at Castle Hill* (401 849-3800; see *America's Special Havens*). Information: Newport Music Festival, 50 Washington Sq., Newport, RI 02840 (401 846-1133).

MARLBORO MUSIC FESTIVAL, Marlboro, Vermont: Fine musicians playing earnestly together under the direction of Rudolf Serkin make such music every weekend from mid-July through mid-August that most tickets sell out within a couple of weeks of an early April mailing. You may latch onto one of the hundred available for seating under a canopy outdoors by presenting yourself at the box office about an hour before curtain time (8:30 PM on Saturday, 2:30 PM on Sunday). To get on the mailing list, write the Marlboro Music Festival at 135 S 18th Street, Philadelphia, PA 19103 (215 569-4690) before mid-June and after mid-August, or at Marlboro, VT 05344 (802 254-8163) in the summer. The *Inn at Sawmill Farm* in West Dover, about 20 miles from Marlboro (802 464-8131), offers especially pleasant lodgings (see *America's Special Havens*).

OLD FIDDLERS' CONVENTION, Galax, Virginia: One of the largest and best-known festivals devoted to traditional music, this institution of half a century's duration is held annually during the second full weekend in August. Information: Old Fiddlers' Convention, Box 655, Galax, VA 24333 (703 236-6355).

THE ANNUAL HAMPTON KOOL JAZZ FESTIVAL, Hampton, Virginia: The Hampton Coliseum, where this event is held, sells out well in advance for performances by top names in soul and jazz, annually the last weekend in June; generally Friday through Sunday. Information: Hampton Kool Jazz Festival, PO Box 7309, Hampton, VA 23666 (804 838-4203).

FILENE CENTER AT WOLF TRAP FARM PARK, Vienna, Virginia: At this national park for the performing arts, you'll get a cross section of what's going on in the American and international music scene: Big-name performers in the world of classical and popular music, ballet, opera, and modern dance may fill up the lawns and the big open-air pavilion, while next the air reverberates with the music of folk singers or bluegrass musicians like Bill Monroe or Doc Watson, or even tap-dance groups or country-and-western performers like Tammy Wynette — all of whom have been on stage in the last few years. Early June into September. Information: Wolf Trap Foundation, 1624 Trap Rd., Vienna, VA 22180 (703 255-1916).

NATIONAL FOLK FESTIVAL, based in Washington, DC (changing locations): An annual event since 1934, this noncommercial festival is the oldest and largest multicultural folk festival in the US. Crafts demonstrations and storytelling are part of the goings-on, and a few other traditional arts are represented as well; but the real emphasis is on the music — bluegrass, blues, gospel and ballad singing, old-time fiddling, Tex-Mex, ethnic, and country music — and the nation's best performers in each genre appear. Joint sponsors are the National Council for the Traditional Arts and the National Park Service; the site changes yearly, as does the date — anytime between late July through late September. Information: NCTA, 806 15th St., NW, Suite 400, Washington, DC 20005 (202 639-8370).

SOUTH

MOUNTAIN DANCE AND FOLK FESTIVAL, Asheville, North Carolina: Square dancers and cloggers keep time to the music of mountain pickers, fiddlers, ballad singers, dulcimer players every August for this event, the oldest of its type in the country — it's been going strong since 1927. Information: Chamber of Commerce, PO Box 1011, Asheville, NC 28802 (704 258-3916 or 800 548-1300 in North Carolina; 800 257-1300 from other eastern states).

SPOLETO FESTIVAL USA, Charleston, South Carolina: Gian Carlo Menotti's important Italian arts festival made its stateside debut in 1977, and has been going strong ever since, every year for seventeen days beginning in late May. Performances of all types of dance, theater, jazz, opera, and symphonic, choral, and chamber music endow this event with extraordinary breadth. Information: Spoleto Festival USA, PO Box 157, Charleston, SC 29402 (803 722-2764).

MIDWEST

THE RAVINIA FESTIVAL, Highland Park, Illinois: The Chicago Symphony Orchestra holds forth in the open-air pavilion of a 36-acre woodland park beginning in late June, and stands as the star attraction of this international festival of all the arts. Visiting orchestras, recitals and chamber music programs, ballet and dance, and concerts of pop, jazz, and folk music are also a part of a long and varied summer season that lasts into September. Information: Ravinia Festival, PO Box 896, Highland Park, IL 60035 (312 RAVINIA). •

BEANBLOSSOM BLUEGRASS MUSIC FESTIVAL, Beanblossom, Indiana: This blink-and-you-miss-it settlement in the hilly southern part of the state really hops in June, when bluegrass music star and festival organizer Bill Monroe brings his musicians to town for a big bluegrass marathon. Of the thousands who come to watch the scheduled concerts in the wooded amphitheater, many set up tents and park their campers in a nearby field, and the air rings with the fiddling and picking of their jam sessions into the wee hours. Information: Monroe Festivals, 3819 Dickerson Rd., Nashville, TN 37207 (615 868-3333).

THE BLOSSOM MUSIC CENTER, Cuyahoga Falls, Ohio: When the Cleveland Orchestra isn't playing at this woods-rimmed, cedar-shingled shell halfway between Akron and Cleveland, you'll find pop concerts — everything from the Beach Boys and Barry Manilow to jazz and ballet. All in all, some 80 musical events are held every summer. Early June through mid-September. Information: Blossom Music Center, 1145 W Steels Corners Rd., Cuyahoga Falls, OH 44223 (216 920-8040 or 216 231-7300).

CINCINNATI MAY FESTIVAL, Cincinnati, Ohio: A 200-voice chorus and opera superstars perform cantatas and other ambitious choral works annually during the last two weekends in May in what claims to be the oldest continuing choral festival in the Western Hemisphere. Information: Cincinnati Music Festival Assn., Music Hall, 1241 Elm St., Cincinnati, OH 45210 (513 621-1919).

WEST

CARMEL BACH FESTIVAL, Carmel, California: Works by Bach and others are performed in recitals (sometimes two a day), daily evening concerts, and matinees at the halls and churches of this lovely sophisticated village on the northern California coast, for three weeks in mid-July to early August every year. Information: Carmel Bach Festival, PO Box 575, Carmel, CA 93921 (408 624-1521). Information about the many interesting hotels and restaurants in the area is available from the Carmel Business Assn., PO Box 4444, Carmel-by-the-Sea, CA 93921 (408 624-2522).

MONTEREY JAZZ FESTIVAL, Monterey, California: The sellout concerts that make up this event held annually the third weekend in September, the oldest continuously presented jazz festival in the nation, feature some of the biggest names in the business. Season tickets ($79) sell out by May 31; ground admission available through the festival weekend. Information: Monterey Jazz Festival, PO Box JAZZ, Monterey, CA 93942 (408 373-3366).

ASPEN MUSIC FESTIVAL, Aspen, Colorado: Constant musical activity of one sort or another — jazz, choral, orchestral, and operatic pieces, chamber works, and about anything else you can name — makes this festival, which is held annually from late June through late August, one of the nation's liveliest, and the town of Aspen an important American cultural center. Sometimes the performers are name soloists on the order of Pinchas Zukerman and Maureen Forrester; sometimes you'll be hearing students. No matter. The repertoire of medieval through contemporary works is always interesting, and the performances are thoughtful and well executed. There's plenty of backpacking, hiking, swimming, fishing, horseback riding, and other outdoor activity going on during the off-hours. Information: Aspen Music Festival, PO Box AA, Aspen, CO 81612 (303 925-3254).

CENTRAL CITY OPERA, Central City, Colorado: American talent shows its stuff in imaginative productions sung in English in a tiny, acoustically perfect 19th-century opera house. Some of America's finest operatic singers began here. Performances take place in July and August. Information: Central City Opera Festival, 1615 California St., Suite 614, Denver, CO 80202 (303 623-7167).

NATIONAL OLD-TIME FIDDLERS' CONTEST, Weiser, Idaho: Parades, BBQ dinners — and near-nonstop fiddling at daytime and nighttime competitions, and jam sessions in between — keep this town of 4,000 hopping every year the third full week in June. Weiser is the self-styled "fiddling capital of America" and the home of the Fiddlers' Hall of Fame, and the contest attracts some 300-plus contestants aged 5 to 92 and nearly 5,000 spectators from all over the US and Canada. Information: Chamber of Commerce, Weiser, ID 83672 (208 549-0452).

SANTA FE OPERA, Santa Fe, New Mexico: Familiar and unfamiliar works, plus

American and world premieres and an abundance of unusual compositions, alternate in repertory at this open-air theater during July and August. Tickets in advance are a must: Santa Fe is staging some of the nation's best opera. Information: Santa Fe Opera, PO Box 2408, Santa Fe, NM 87504-2408 (505 982-3851; box office, 505 982-3855).

PETER BRITT FESTIVALS, Jacksonville, Oregon: In the spectacular outdoor Britt Music Pavilion, the northwest's oldest music festival, founded to honor pioneer vintner, horticulturist, and daguerrotypist Peter Britt, now offers five festivals every summer; classical, bluegrass, jazz, dance, and musical theater. Reserve lodgings well in advance because of the concurrent Oregon Shakespearean Festival, some 15 miles away in Ashland. Information: Peter Britt Festivals, PO Box 1124, Medford, OR 97501 (503 779-0847).

GRAND TETON MUSIC FESTIVAL, Teton Village, Wyoming: From mid-July until late August, for seven weeks, you'll find great music in these oft-climbed mountains — small ensembles during the week, a full symphony orchestra on Saturdays; sometimes the artist or composer talks about the pieces beforehand. Information: Grand Teton Music Festival, PO Box 310, Teton Village, WY 83025 (307 733-3050).

Restored Towns and Reconstructed Villages

Williamsburg, Virginia, is only the most famous of America's restored towns: All over the country historical villages have been reconstructed — some simply repaired and restored, others pieced together from brand-new buildings or from original structures collected from numerous sites — to graphically re-create the day-by-day life of earlier periods in American history. At the best of these, curators hire craftspeople to demonstrate everyday tasks of the era, and provide lectures, walking tours, and special events. In general, the larger the restoration, the wider the variety of special activities.

And though not all museum villages are as authentic as Williamsburg, where the quest for historical accuracy extends to making male craftspeople's shoes from the same kind of leather that would have been used in the 18th century, curators at most museum villages take considerable pains to make sure that at least the most obvious things are correct. There's no better place to enjoy yourself learning history.

EAST

MYSTIC SEAPORT, Mystic, Connecticut: Gulls wheel and cry overhead while you're walking around the 17 acres of this re-created New England sea village, where, along with blacksmithing, woodcarving, fireplace cooking, and weaving, there's a ship's chandlery, sail loft, ship model shop, printers' shop, general store, tavern, and more. You may see shipwrights at work on 19th-century ships and boats; the recently restored *Charles W. Morgan,* America's last surviving wooden whaleship and a National Historic Landmark, towers proudly over it all. And there's more: more ships; the US's largest collection of small boats; formal exhibits of scrimshaw, marine art, and figure-heads; steamboat cruises; children's games; demonstrations of sail-setting and furling and other marine skills; and, at Christmas, a lively program of lantern-light tours and other period merriment. Information: Mystic Seaport, Mystic, CT 06355 (203 572-0711). (See also *Mystic Seaport,* DIRECTIONS.)

PLIMOTH PLANTATION, Plymouth, Massachusetts: This reconstruction of the Pilgrims' village now includes a dozen-plus houses, fort, farm buildings, and the famous replica of the *Mayflower* (2 miles north at State Pier). Its sails are made of flax and sewn by hand, its beams pegged together with "tree nails" made from 120-year-old cider vats. Both aboard ship and in the Village, men and women in period dress portray actual residents of the early colony through speech, manner, and attitude, while pursuing the daily routine of the farming community. The Pilgrims, it turns out, did not wear somber clothes, but instead, like other 17th-century farmers and working folk, colorful garments often decorated with lace and stitchery. In the Wampanoag Summer Campsite, museum staff recount the history and traditions of the native people who befriended them. Closed December through March. Information: Plimoth Plantation, PO Box 1620, Plymouth, MA 02360 (617 746-1622). As for actual colonial landmarks, nearby Duxbury and Kingston have street upon street of old homes. In Plymouth itself you can visit the houses of the Pilgrims, their burial sites, a grist mill, and the town's two wineries (one of which, aptly enough, produces only cranberry wine). Thanksgiving is a particularly good time to go; there's a public feast at the town's Memorial Hall, and a reenactment of the Pilgrims' Progress to church. Information: Plymouth Area Chamber of Commerce, 85 Samoset St., Plymouth, MA 02360 (617 746-3377).

OLD STURBRIDGE VILLAGE, Sturbridge, Massachusetts: Things are so authentic at this re-created village that sheep help to trim the grass on the village green, and the general store is stocked with just those items an early-19th-century shopper would have expected. Hard-working ladies cook up savory goodies on open hearths, using 19th-century "receipts," and blacksmiths, broom-makers, coopers, printers, shoemakers, and other artisans go about their work the traditional way. The purpose is to show rural America turning into industrial America, and so in addition to the farm and the grist mill, there are exhibits like the water-powered wool carding mill and the 1830s sawmill. Sturbridge is one of the most respected establishments of its type, the largest living history center in the Northeast, and even without its huge assortment of period theatricals, speechmakings, church services, and other special events, you could go back many times and never see it all. At Thanksgiving, Ballard Tavern puts on a traditional feast. Reservations are necessary. Information: Old Sturbridge Village, Sturbridge, MA 01566 (617 347-3362). At the *Publick House,* a quaint inn outside the restoration area, Christmas brings a wonderful Edwardian Yule feast-cum-pageant complete with scarlet-coated beefeaters and a boar's head (617 347-3313; see *America's Special Havens*).

STRAWBERY BANKE MUSEUM, Portsmouth, New Hampshire: Beginning in the 1630s, this neighborhood flourished for some 200 years, only to sink into what seemed a lasting decline in the mid-1800s. But a ten-acre area was rescued from demolition in the 1950s and has since been largely restored. Five houses are furnished and open for tours, and about 30 others are in various stages of completion. Some of the antique structures are being scraped and painted, others exhibit textile and tool collections, early photographs, architectural details, and archaeology. In all, there are 85 exhibition rooms in 4 different buildings as well as several period gardens, 7 working craft shops, and 5 houses furnished to illustrate different eras in local history. Information: Strawbery Banke, PO Box 300, Portsmouth, NH 03801 (603 436-8010).

THE FARMERS' MUSEUM AND VILLAGE CROSSROADS, Cooperstown, New York: The message here is how, in the 75 years between the end of the Revolution and the beginning of the Civil War, the plain people of America built a nation where only forests had stood. The museum's Main Barn section has displays on farm technology, village life, domestic economy, and outdoor activities, and crafts from broommaking to cabinetmaking to spinning are demonstrated nearby. Outside, there's a dirt-laned village where you'll see more of the same in period buildings while cows, chickens, and sheep have been known to wander around on the lawns. Special programs include a Harvest Festival in the fall; seminars dealing with American culture during the first two weeks of July; and scattered throughout the year, craft workshops for the interested amateur as well as the professional. Lodgings in the area include the fine Georgian-style *Otesaga* (607 547-9931; see *America's Best Resort Hotels*). Information: The Farmers' Museum, PO Box 800, Cooperstown, NY 13326 (607 547-2533).

GENESEE COUNTRY MUSEUM, Mumford, New York: Some 50 19th-century American buildings gathered from upstate New York and restored on this rolling 125-acre site reflect American life in the early 1800s. New additions include an elegant Italianate home, its two-story carriage house, and handsome sunken formal gardens (a gunsmith shop and two-story Shaker building were scheduled to open in 1986). You'll also see a pottery, bandstand, farm, parsonage, pioneer settlement, a variety of homes, an inn, a Methodist church, and a score of shops and offices, all peopled by costumed "villagers." The unusual Gallery of Sporting Art explores man and his animals. Open from mid-May through the third week of October. Information: Genesee Country Museum, Box 1819, Rochester, NY 14603 (716 538-6822).

HOPEWELL FURNACE NATIONAL HISTORIC SITE, near Elverson, Pennsylvania: This settlement, dating to 1770, is the most far-ranging restoration of the kind of iron-producing center that flourished in this corner of southeastern Pennsylvania in the 18th and 19th centuries. The ironmaster's home, charcoal house, waterwheel, blast machinery, casting house, cold-blast furnace, tenant houses, and barns are all open year-round. Blacksmithing, metal casting, carpentry, and other skills and crafts of the early 19th century are demonstrated from late June through Labor Day. Information: Hopewell Furnace, RD 1, PO Box 345, Elverson, PA 19520 (215 582-8773).

SHELBURNE MUSEUM, Shelburne, Vermont: In these collections of Americana housed in 36 historic buildings moved to the 45-acre site from all over the state, you'll see hundreds of carousel figures, cigar store Indians, cradles, dolls, dresses, horse-drawn vehicles, quilts, rugs, ship figureheads and shop figures, tin bathtubs, tools for farming and woodworking, and toys. The collection of decoys is the largest in the US. The massive steamship *Ticonderoga,* now landlocked, presides over it all. To see it all, go between mid-May and mid-October; only a few buildings are open in winter — and only on Sundays. The best lodgings are at the classy *Basin Harbor Club,* on Lake Champlain, open mid-June through mid-October (802 475-2311; see *America's Best Resort Hotels*); eat at the handsome, antique-filled *Dog Team* — and don't miss those great sticky buns (802 388-7651). Information: Shelburne Museum, Shelburne, VT 05482 (802 985-3344).

JAMESTOWN, Jamestown, Virginia: Foundations, property ditches, a church tower dating to 1639, and a few streets in the Jamestown National Historical Site are all that remain of the city that served as Virginia's capital and cultural center for 92 years; the liveliest area is the Glasshouse, reconstructed and fitted out so that craftsmen can make glass as they did here three centuries ago. The museum contains one of the largest collections of 17th-century artifacts in the country, part of which is on display at the visitors center. Three- and 5-mile drives provide access to the marshes and pine forests of Jamestown Island. Nearby, at the 25-acre Jamestown Festival Park, are museum buildings, a reconstructed fort and 17th-century Indian village, exhibitions and demonstrations of skills as performed in the 17th century (agriculture, medicine, seamanship, carpentry), and reproductions of the three famous ships which, though hardly bigger than yachts, transported 104 men and boys to Virginia in 1607. Information: Jamestown Festival Park, PO Drawer JF, Williamsburg, VA 23187 (804 229-1607); Colonial National Historical Park, PO Box 210, Yorktown, VA 23690 (804 229-1733). (See also *Tidewater Virginia,* DIRECTIONS.)

COLONIAL WILLIAMSBURG, Williamsburg, Virginia: All the superlatives apply to this restoration of Virginia's 18th-century cultural, social, and legislative center — not just for the sheer size of the collection (150,000 items, 173 acres, 88 colonial and early-19th-century buildings, several hundred reconstructions, and a formal museum), but also for the variety of crafts demonstrated (36 in all), the historical authenticity, and the craftworkers' knowledge. Summer days and spring and autumn weekends are the busiest time here, which may mean standing in line to get into the tavern. Information: Colonial Williamsburg Foundation, PO Drawer C, Williamsburg, VA 23187 (800 582-8976 in Virginia; 800 446-8956 elsewhere). (See also *Tidewater Virginia*, DIRECTIONS.)

SOUTH

HISTORIC ST. AUGUSTINE, St. Augustine, Florida: The Spanish in some parts of the New World were cruel, but here their settlement was quite civilized in other ways — or so it will seem when you tour this restored section of the US's oldest permanent settlement. The plain stucco houses line a narrow street across from the Castillo de San Marcos (the fort which protected the town) and fill a couple of side streets as well. At work in some buildings are a candlemaker, carpenter, Spanish cigarmaker with lightning-fast hands, and a weaver who crafts marvels out of the loveliest of wools. The settlement's story is told at an information center — a good place to begin any visit — and at the outdoor drama *Cross and Sword* (see *Outdoor Dramas*). Special events include an annual Blessing of the Fleet on Palm Sunday weekend and, on Easter Sunday, a "Parada de los Caballos y Coches," an Easter parade of horse-drawn carriages. Information: St. Augustine and St. Johns County Chamber of Commerce, PO Drawer O, St. Augustine, FL 32085 (904 829-5681).

WESTVILLE 1850, Lumpkin, Georgia: Life in the South wasn't all barbecues and 16-inch waistlines. Some people lived in modest homes, gathered eggs in the baskets they crafted, made pottery jugs and bowls, repaired buggies, dried fruits, stored vegetables, made syrup from sugarcane, and ginned cotton and baled it — all things you'll see demonstrated at this nifty re-created village. Extra craftsmen are on hand for the Fair of 1850, held the first week in November, and there are Maypole dances on May Day, a barbecue on July 4, and Christmas activities every Saturday in December. Information: Westville 1850, PO Box 1850, Lumpkin, GA 31815 (912 838-6310).

MIDWEST

LINCOLN'S NEW SALEM STATE PARK, Petersburg, Illinois: Edgar Lee Masters's home, the setting for his *Spoon River Anthology*, is a mere 2 miles from the town where Abraham Lincoln courted Ann Rutledge, tended store, worked as a postmaster, studied law, learned surveying, and, in 1837, got himself elected to the legislature. A variety of buildings have been reconstructed next to the Onstott Cooper Shop (an original structure which has been restored) on a site presented to the state by William Randolph Hearst. There are craft workers on hand during the summer and for special events throughout the year. Nearby, Ann Rutledge and Edgar Lee Masters are buried in Petersburg's Oakland Cemetery. Information: Lincoln's New Salem State Park, RR 1, Box 244A, Petersburg, IL 62675 (217 632-7953).

HENRY FORD MUSEUM & GREENFIELD VILLAGE, Dearborn, Michigan: The Henry Ford Museum's phenomenal collections of American decorative arts, musical instruments, tools, household furnishings and appliances (whole collections of washing machines, vacuum cleaners, and sewing machines, for instance), and implements of agriculture, communications, lighting, transportation, and power cover 12 acres — but that's only what you'll see in the museum. Set in Greenfield Village, on an adjacent 240 acres are, for starters, a courthouse where Abe Lincoln practiced law as a circuit rider; Edison's laboratories; homes or birthplaces of the Wright Brothers, Luther Burbank, Noah Webster, Harvey Firestone, Henry Ford, William Holmes McGuffey (of *McGuffey's Reader*); and nearly 100 other structures that tell the story of American life from the colonial period to the turn of the century. Most were moved from their original sites. The emphasis is on the changes that occurred in America with the new processes and inventions of the Industrial Revolution. Depending on the season, you can ride in a horse-drawn carriage or sleigh, an antique car, a steam train, a steam-powered paddlewheel boat — or even take a spin on a 1913 carousel. Best lodgings in the area are at the Georgian-style *Dearborn Inn* (313 271-2700; see *America's Special Havens*). Information: Henry Ford Museum and Greenfield Village, PO Box 1970, Dearborn, MI 48121 (313 271-1620).

LUMBERTOWN USA, Brainerd, Minnesota: The town that calls itself Paul Bunyan's home is also the site of a re-created 1870 logging center with bunkhouse, mess hall, saloon, and nearly 30 other buildings. Closed mid-September through late May. Information: Chamber of Commerce, Brainerd, MN 56401 (218 829-2838).

STUHR MUSEUM OF THE PRAIRIE PIONEER, Grand Island, Nebraska: The cottage in which native son Henry Fonda was born is on display here along with some 60 other structures — and an operating steam train — that give a vivid impression of what life was like for the ordinary pioneers here on the south-central Nebraska prairie. The village is open from May through September only; you can visit two museums also on the property year-round. Nearby are Harold Warp's Pioneer Village and the 1864 Fort Kearny State Historical Park, once an important stop on the Oregon Trail. Information: Stuhr Museum, 3133 W Hwy. 34, Grand Island, NE 68801 (308 384-1380).

HAROLD WARP'S PIONEER VILLAGE, Minden, Nebraska: This antique collection installed in a collection of 26 buildings compactly arranged on a 20-acre site shows you "man's progress since 1830." That means, in part, that you'll see not one old kitchen setup, but several (from 1830, 1860, 1890, 1910, 1930, 1950, and 1980). Stoves, refrigerators, autos and trucks, farm machinery, farm tractors, bikes, boats, planes, fire engines, streetcars, steam engines, locomotives, and many other familiar objects get the same thorough treatment. Information: Harold Warp Pioneer Village Foundation, PO Box 68, Minden, NE 68959 (308 832-1181; 800 445-4447 outside Nebraska).

WEST

BODIE STATE HISTORIC PARK, near Bridgeport, California: Within 20 years of the discovery of gold in 1859, Bodie was, in the words of its pastor Reverend F. M. Warrington, "a sea of sin lashed by the tempests of passion." It had 30 mines, breweries, 65 saloons, ale stoops, pothouses, restaurants, gin mills, and opium dens; and, on Maiden Lane and Virgin Alley, plenty of ladies — Eleanor Dumont (alias Madame Mustache), Nellie Monroe, French Joe, and Rosa May. Very little of Bodie has withstood the years of fire and heavy snowstorms since its heyday; the buildings that have survived are maintained by the California State Park system in a state of "arrested decay" — that is, minor repairs are made and walls are shored up, but no attempt is made to make Bodie look any different than it did when it was at last abandoned. Peering through windows as you take the mapped-out walking tour, you'll spot old-fashioned condiments and canned goods on a general store shelf; caskets inside the morgue; a pipe organ in the Methodist church. It can all be enormously eerie. Open all year but inaccessible except in summer. Information: Bodie State Historic Park, PO Box 515, Bridgeport, CA 93517 (no phone).

COLUMBIA STATE HISTORIC PARK, Columbia, California: The "gem of the southern mines" never quite died out like Bodie but only decayed, so restoration was relatively simple. Walking tours mapped out by the state take you past all the important structures. After your tour, you can pan for color in Matelot Gulch, ride a stagecoach, sip sarsaparilla, or get a haircut at California's oldest barbershop. Plenty of camping and hiking is available in the surrounding Stanislaus National Forest, and there are lively special events during Easter, the first weekend in May, the July Fourth weekend, and the second and third weekends of December. Open year-round. Best lodgings are at the restored 1851 *Gunn House* in Sonora (209 532-3421) and at the very Victorian *City Hotel* (209 532-1479; see *America's Special Havens*). Information: Columbia State

Historic Park, PO Box 151, Columbia, CA 95310 (209 532-4301); Tuolumne County Chamber of Commerce, PO Box 277, Sonora, CA 95370 (209 532-4212); Stanislaus National Forest, 19777 Greenley Rd., Sonora, CA 95370 (209 532-3671).

POLYNESIAN CULTURAL CENTER, Laie, Oahu, Hawaii: Studying at the Mormon-operated Brigham Young University Hawaii Campus, students from all over the South Pacific put themselves through school by working at this 42-acre reconstruction of traditional villages of Fiji, Hawaii, New Zealand's Maori culture, Samoa, Tahiti, the Marquesas, and Tonga. The crafts, singing, dancing, and food preparation are all things the students have grown up with, so it couldn't be more authentic. Some 150 young Islanders make up the cast of *This Is Polynesia,* a special twice-daily performance. Information: Polynesian Cultural Center, 2301 Kalakaua Ave., Ste. C304, Honolulu, HI 96815 (808 293-3333 or 800 367-7060).

Utopias and Religious Settlements

 Ever since the Pilgrims fled England for the New World, Americans have been leaving settled areas for wildernesses where they could set up their own civilizations, far from corrupting influences. Sometimes the new settlements survived. For instance, the Amana Colonies — founded over a century ago — still thrive, even though the communal ownership of property was dissolved in the 1930s. In parts of Ohio, Pennsylvania, and Maryland, the Amish still live by the old ways, though buggies are not quite so common as they once were.

A good many others were not so successful. All through American history, religious settlements and attempted Utopias have come and gone like Christmas shoppers through a revolving door. Often, however, the communities that they built have withstood the ravages of time, and the last few years have seen a number of these settlements restored as museum villages. Some are open year-round, some only in summer; it's wise to call before you go. Admission fees are low — $6 or less for passes that will allow you to tour all the buildings, or 50¢ to $1 or so for each restored structure. Some are free.

BISHOP HILL, near Galesburg, Illinois: The first major Swedish settlement in the US, this community near the Mississippi River was not a big success. Eric Jansson, the dissident Swedish Lutheran who came here in the early 1840s and persuaded some 800 of his fellows to follow him in 1846, was assassinated in 1850 — and it was all downhill after that. In 1861, communal ownership of property was dissolved. Dissidents among the dissidents withdrew. Mismanagement of remaining property ensued. The community went into debt and Bishop Hill crumbled. However, a good many of the descendants of the original settlers stayed on, so the buildings did not all decay. By the 1960s, when people got interested in the colony, 13 of the 16 original structures were still standing, among them the Bjorklund Hotel, the blacksmith shop, the Greek Revival Steeple Building (topped by a one-handed clock), and the Colony Church, which could seat 1,000 worshipers. An 11-mile path leads visitors past that structure — where, early every Christmas morning, a traditional Julotta service is held by candlelight — and other structures. The nearest motels are in Galesburg, where you can visit Carl Sandburg's birthplace, see the granite boulder under which his ashes were placed, and, on the campus of Knox College, tour the site of the Lincoln-Douglas debates. Information: Bishop Hill State Historic Site, Box D, Bishop Hill, IL 61419 (309 927-3345).

NAUVOO, Nauvoo, Illinois: Chicago was little more than a one-horse town when the followers of Mormon leader Joseph Smith arrived here and started building simple frame houses with wood from Wisconsin forests and brick they were soon manufacturing themselves. By 1846, the town was 20,000 strong, full of gardens, and topped by an immense white marble temple. Schisms developed, partly because of disagreements within the Mormon band itself over the polygamy issue. Joseph Smith ended up lynched at the jail in Carthage, and Brigham Young, another Mormon, led the group westward just as in the famous old grade B movie on the subject. Over the years, while Salt Lake City was abuilding, the houses in Nauvoo were burning, one by one. But the neat grid of streets is still as clear as ever, and scattered here and there are enough surviving buildings to provide a pretty good idea of how it all was. Many have been reconstructed, and most of them are open for tours and manned by Mormon missionaries, who, it seems, are attempting conversion just by presenting facts (almost always interesting). Jonathan Browning, maker of the famous rifles, was a Mormon, as you'll learn; you'll tour his studio and home and see an interesting device he worked out that would churn butter and rock a baby in a cradle at the same time. The Mormons were replaced in Nauvoo by a group of French Utopian thinkers called Icarians. They did not flourish, and most left in about 10 years. Following them came a very traditional group of Germans, who found that the land would grow grapes and built 35 wine cellars, which in 1937 were discovered to be perfect for ripening blue cheese. These businesses flourish in Nauvoo today, and when you eat a meal at the *Hotel Nauvoo* you can sample them both in one of their seven dining rooms. The hotel also has comfortable rooms with private bath (open mid-March through October; phone 217 453-2211). A good time to visit, if you can plan for lodgings well in advance, is the weekend before Labor Day, when the annual Grape Festival takes place. Among the parades for grownups and kids and other small-town doings, there's a ceremony called the Wedding of the Wine and Cheese. Information: Nauvoo Chamber of Commerce, PO Box 341, Nauvoo, IL 62354 (217 453-6648).

NEW HARMONY, Indiana: This quiet little town in southwestern Indiana near the confluence of the Wabash and Ohio rivers has been the home of two Utopian settlements. The first was led by Harmonist George Rapp, who, with his 700-plus followers, turned the forests and swamplands they found here in 1814 into 30,000 acres of farms, factories, and homes in a bare ten years. The later venture was led by Robert Owen, a Scottish intellectual who drew distinguished scholars, writers, and educators to New Harmony, established free kindergartens, education for women, a library, and many other firsts. That settlement declined, but many sturdy Harmonist buildings survived and are open year-round. Particularly fascinating are the Workingmen's Institute, founded in 1838 as a trade school and now filled up with Indian artifacts, lacy antique underwear, a stuffed eight-legged calf, and the oddest lot of other knickknacks you'll see in a long time; and the re-created Labyrinth, a maze made out of hedges that you can actually try to walk through. The original, built by George Rapp's Harmonists, was supposed to represent the choices taken during a lifetime. A variety of special programs take place in the striking Atheneum, designed by architect Richard Meier and opened to the public in 1979. The carefully designed *New Harmony Inn,* modern but Shaker-simple, a real symphony of polished woods, itself is worth the trip (812 682-4491; see *America's Special Havens),* and there's good food at the *Red Geranium* (812 682-4431). Information: Historic New Harmony, New Harmony, IN 47631 (812 682-4474 or 812 682-4488).

AMANA COLONIES, Iowa: The Community of True Inspiration, a Lutheran splinter group, founded this group of seven villages — now a National Historic Landmark — in 1855 as a communal society in which everybody shared all goods, all gains, and even ate together. Reorganized some three quarters of a century later in 1932, the Amana Colonies today have a good deal more community feeling than you find in other parts of the US. The story of life in the good old days is told at the Barn Museum in South Amana (a scale-model village), and at the Museum of Amana History in Amana (exhibitions of potting, ice-cutting, bookbinding, woodworking, wine making, soap making, along with an Amana doctor's washhouse and woodshed, and a schoolhouse).

Amana, West Amana, South Amana, Middle, High, and Homestead all have interesting little shops where you can buy local produce — fruit wines, woolens, furniture, baked goods, sausages, and other foods and crafts. And several have atmospheric restaurants that are great for German-American food served family style; *Bill Zuber's Restaurant* is one (319 622-3911). Information: Amana Colonies Travel Council, Box 303, Amana, IA 52203 (319 622-3828).

SHAKER VILLAGE OF PLEASANT HILL, near Harrodsburg, Kentucky: A belief in celibacy effectively guaranteed the demise of this outgrowth of the Quaker religion founded by Mother Ann Lee, but the legacy has been enormous. The Shaker conviction that religion should not be separated from the secular concerns of human life meant that much effort and ingenuity were expended on the tiniest details of life; every physical object was considered a prayer, and engineered for perfection. The tools and furniture that resulted fetch high prices at auctions today; they're bound to make an impression on you when you see them in this restoration's 27 original buildings. There are many special events including 1-hour riverboat excursions. Information: Shaker Village of Pleasant Hill, Harrodsburg, KY 40330 (606 734-5411).

HANCOCK SHAKER VILLAGE, near Pittsfield, Massachusetts: The best place in the East to see Shaker architecture. The standout is the three-story Round Stone Barn, designed for efficiency but beautiful enough to bring Le Corbusier and other great architects to mind. In all, 21 buildings on the property are filled with Shaker furniture and "spirit drawings." The four-story Brick Dwelling House held a hundred men and women; and there's a laundry and machine shop, wash house, and icehouse. Once a year, for a week in August, the museum stages Worlds' People's Dinners, which are open to the public (by reservation only), along with cooking and craft demonstrations daily, the end-of-July Kitchen Festival, and other special events. Country inns are plentiful nearby. Information: Hancock Shaker Village, PO Box 898, Pittsfield, MA 01202 (413 443-0188).

SHAKER VILLAGE, Canterbury, New Hampshire: One of two remaining active Shaker communities. The 22 white frame structures that stand here now were once the home of 400 Shakers. Meeting House Lane is lined with enormous sugar maples planted for the orphans for whom they cared. Tours of the village lead through the Ministry, Sisters' Shop, Laundry, Schoolhouse, and Meetinghouse (with separate entrances for men and women). Friday evenings offer candelight dinners and tours. Authentic Shaker food is served at the *Creamery Restaurant.* Information: Shaker Village, Canterbury, NH 03224 (603 783-9977).

OLD SALEM, Winston-Salem, North Carolina: Founded in 1766 by a group of Moravians from Pennsylvania, Salem's church directed not just spiritual life but also secular doings — and business prospered. At the restoration, you can see decorative arts and household items, plus craft shops, the oldest tobacco shop still standing in America, and the immense Single Brothers House, where 14-year-old boys came to live while they learned a craft. Special events are planned throughout the year. Information: Greater Winston-Salem Chamber of Commerce, PO Box 1408, Winston-Salem, NC 27102 (919 725-2361).

SCHOENBRUNN VILLAGE STATE MEMORIAL, near New Philadelphia, Ohio: Concerned about spreading the Gospel to the Indians, the Moravian church sent missionaries into the wilderness, and this was the first of six separate settlements that were established here. David Zeisberger and his force of Christian Indians, converts, and missionaries cleared the wilderness and within a couple of years had put up some 60 log structures. But by that time, England and the colonies were at war, and Schoenbrunn was caught between the firing lines. The missionaries and their congregations departed, leaving the settlement to crumble. What you see now — a church, school, and a baker's dozen other structures — is a re-created area built since the 1920s. On occasional special weekends, craftspeople are on hand to demonstrate spinning and weaving, candle-dipping, or tending the gardens, planted with red and calico corn, sweet corn, herbs, turnips, and pumpkins. *Trumpet in the Land,* an outdoor drama presented during July and August in an amphitheater nearby, tells the story (see *Outdoor Dramas*). Information: Schoenbrunn Village State Memorial, PO Box 129, New Philadelphia, OH 44663 (216 339-3636).

ZOAR STATE MEMORIAL, Zoar, Ohio: Another group of German Separatists who, like George Rapp, refusing to accept the Lutheran doctrine, found themselves alternately ignored and persecuted until it seemed easier to leave the Old World than to stay; and on Rapp's example, they crossed the ocean and bought a tract of land on the Tuscarawas River. The system of communal ownership under which the community eventually flourished in Zoar was not inspired by the Bible so much as by necessity imposed during the very lean times of the settlement's first years. When you visit today, you see it as it was during the lifetime of leader Joseph Baumeler: the red brick houses with their tile roofs and bright trim are spic and span; the bakery, tin shop, and garden house look for all the world as if they were still open for business; and the fantastic community garden, geometric in design, which is still so neat you'd say it had been laid out by some Prussian drill sergeant. A good time to see it all is during the Zoar Harvest Festival, held annually on the first weekend in August, when there are art and music festivals and tours of private homes in the area. Zoar State Memorial is closed from November through March. There are several bed-and-breakfasts in private historic houses. The nearby *Atwood Lake Lodge* in Atwood Lake Park is modern, comfortable, beautifully situated, and quite reasonable (216 735-2211). Information: Zoar State Memorial, PO Box 404, Zoar, OH 44697 (216 874-3211 or 216 874-3011).

OLD ECONOMY VILLAGE, Ambridge, Pennsylvania: When Father George Rapp left New Harmony, Indiana, he came here — and proceeded to create something even grander than the settlement he had left. There was, first of all, his own Great House, which was as imposing as the domicile of the society's leader should be. Then there was the Feast Hall, a single room which could seat 1,000 diners. Both structures, plus the wine cellar, shoe shop, cabinetmakers' shops, community kitchen, and a number of dwellings have been restored and are open to the public. Why did this enormously successful settlement finally die out? The policy of celibacy eventually rang the death knell, and the society was dissolved in 1905. Information: Old Economy Village, 14th and Church Sts., Ambridge, PA 15003 (412 266-4500).

EPHRATA CLOISTER, Ephrata, Pennsylvania: This religious experiment, begun in 1732 by a German Seventh-Day Baptist named Conrad Beissel, lasted until 1813 — despite celibacy and despite the rigorous lifestyle demanded of its practitioners: They slept on beds which were more like narrow benches, laid their heads on wooden pillows, walked down straight and narrow hallways and through doorways so low they had to stoop. There was, of course, plenty of symbolism behind all of it — and that, among other things, is what you learn about when you tour the handsome buildings. You'll also learn why singing was permitted, and, at the *Vorspiel* historical pageant, presented in summer, you'll hear some of the original music of Ephrata. For information about visiting Ephrata, in the heart of Pennsylvania Dutch country, contact: Ephrata Cloister, 632 W Main St., Ephrata, PA 17522 (717 733-6600).

America's Great Museums

Some of the best museums in the world can be found in the US — not just art museums, but natural history museums and science museums where the visitor is invited to touch, climb, experiment, try out, push buttons, and learn. Most have fascinating shops where you can buy reproductions of objects in the collections — postcards, statuary, textiles, jewelry, knickknacks.

For a complete listing of both major and minor museums of the urban areas you plan to visit, see the individual city reports in THE AMERICAN CITIES. Herein, a distillation of the best: art museums, museums of science and industry, natural history museums — the country's very best.

Those listed here are worth some time — a half-day is usually adequate — and return visits. They're popular, especially on weekends. To get the most from your time, try to visit midweek. Most have special exhibits for the holidays, changing exhibitions that supplement the permanent collections, and a schedule of concerts, lectures, and short courses that are well worth investigating, even on a short visit. Hours usually vary with the season; most are closed one day a week. Admission prices are low; in Washington, DC, many of the museums are free; in New York City, there's often a "pay what you wish but you must pay something" donation "requested."

EAST

BALTIMORE MUSEUM OF ART, Baltimore, Maryland: Strong on modern art, thanks to the Cone Collection — paintings, prints, and sculptures of Matisse, Picasso, and other French post-Impressionists donated by the two wealthy Cone sisters — the museum also has period rooms that highlight the architectural, artistic, and historic growth of Maryland, through furniture and decorative arts objects, some dating to the 1600s; the Wurtzburger collection of African, pre-Columbian, and Oceanic art; a vast print collection; fine 19th- and 20th-century American paintings and sculpture, a spectacular new outdoor sculpture garden; a stunning new wing with galleries for changing exhibitions and a café overlooking the garden; and the Jacobs wing of Old Masters painting and sculpture. Information: Baltimore Museum of Art, Art Museum Dr. (N Charles and 31st sts.), Baltimore, MD 21218 (301 396-7101).

MUSEUM OF FINE ARTS, Boston, Massachusetts: This great, vast old museum in the heart of Boston, not far from Fenway Park, sits alongside a lovely 12-acre park near the bank of the Charles River; on sunny days, you can spot artists with sketch pads in hand on the green. Inside, you'll find an extensive permanent collection of Impressionists (including many Monets), works by American portrait and landscape painters, and American decorative arts (Duncan Phyfe chairs, Paul Revere silver, and other such blue-blooded items). The collection of Egyptian architectural casts and artifacts is the largest outside Cairo; the Asiatic collection is the earth's largest under one roof. And the I. M. Pei addition is the talk of the architectural world. Information: Museum of Fine Arts, 465 Huntington Ave., Boston, MA 02115 (617 267-9300 or, for weekly events, A-N-S-W-E-R-S).

ISABELLA STEWART GARDNER MUSEUM, Boston, Massachusetts: One of the world's magnificent private galleries. The collections are housed in a 15th-century-style Italianate mansion built between about 1899 and 1903, with capitals, columns, fireplaces, fountains, staircases, and other architectural elements imported from Europe by the museum's founder, Mrs. Jack Gardner, a not-so-proper Bostonian who drank beer as well as tea, and further disgraced herself in the eyes of Boston society by being born in New York City. Mrs. Jack — as she was called — lived on the top floor of her four-story mansion during her lifetime, maintaining the rest of the house as a museum, which by the terms of her will is open to the public, with the proviso that the arrangement of paintings, furniture, and other objects remain as it was during her lifetime. As a result, objects that seem to have as much sentimental as aesthetic value are exhibited alongside Rembrandts, Titian's *The Rape of Europa,* and other pieces collected with the advice of Bernard Berenson, the art scholar who coined the term "squillionaire." (The museum *Guide* is a good thing to have.) The sounds of the lovely fountain in the marble and plaster courtyard in the center of the palace, and the smell of the flowers growing around it, are almost always with you as you inspect the results of Mrs. Gardner's acquisitiveness — Tintorettos, Manets, Botticellis, Whistlers, one Corot, and one of the 36 surviving works of Vermeer. When your feet are tired, you can take lunch or tea at a café on the premises. Information: Isabella Stewart Gardner Museum, 2 Palace Rd., Boston, MA 02115 (617 566-1401).

AMERICAN MUSEUM OF NATURAL HISTORY and THE HAYDEN PLANETARIUM, New York, New York: In the 40 halls and galleries of this behemoth, you'll find rooms and rooms of dinosaur bones; one of the largest collections of minerals and gems in the world (including the 563-carat Star of India sapphire); fabulous life-size dioramas of animals and vegetation; a fine exhibition about reptiles from the prehistoric days to the present, and much more. Especially interesting is the Margaret Mead Hall of Pacific Peoples, which preserves aspects of these peoples' traditional cultures. Don't miss the great whale — a huge replica of a blue whale hanging from the ceiling of the Hall of Ocean Life. The largest meteorite ever retrieved from the earth's surface is displayed in the Arthur Ross Hall of Meteorites. And recently the museum installed a stupendous screen for showing nature films; four stories high and 66 feet wide, it surrounds you with images. The adjoining Hayden Planetarium (212 873-8828) has lively shows daily and two floors of astronomical exhibitions. Information: American Museum of Natural History, Central Park West at 79th St., New York, NY 10024 (212 873-4225).

FRICK COLLECTION, New York, New York: Henry Clay Frick, a coke and steel magnate who died in 1919, commissioned the architect Thomas Hastings to design a house that could function equally well, later on, as a museum, and so it's not surprising that the surroundings, sumptuous with their elegant furnishings and thick carpets, are so perfectly suited to the elegant collection of sculpture, fine furniture, porcelains, enamels, and paintings — among them Renoir's *Mother and Children*, Fragonard's *The Progress of Love*, Rembrandt's *Self-Portrait* and *Polish Rider*, Giovanni Bellini's *St. Francis in the Desert*, three canvasses by Vermeer, Holbein's portraits of Sir Thomas More and Thomas Cromwell, and works by Gainsborough, Goya, Lawrence, Reynolds, Turner, and nearly everyone else (or so it sometimes seems) who ever inspired an art lover to rapture. All in all, the Frick is relaxing, hospitable, and among the most accessible museums anywhere. Information: Frick Collection, 1 E 70th, New York, NY 10021 (212 288-0700).

METROPOLITAN MUSEUM OF ART, New York, New York: Home of America's most extensive art collection. There are works of great masters from the Middle Ages to the present day, a vast assemblage of Greek and Roman sculptures, Oriental art, prints and photographs, musical instruments, decorative arts from all ages, and special exhibitions of stunning quality. The Lila Acheson Wallace Gallery has an extensive Egyptian collection; the Sackler Wing contains a whole temple. The American Wing comprises three centuries of American period rooms, paintings, sculpture, and decorative arts. The Michael C. Rockefeller Wing has works from Africa, the Pacific Islands, and pre-Columbian America. A variety of tape-recorded audio tours that hit the high spots of the collections will help you handle the mind-boggling presentation. At Christmas, a tree is hung with 18th-century Neapolitan ornaments — each one a sculpture in its own right. Closed Mondays. Information: Metropolitan Museum of Art, 5th Ave. at 82nd St., New York, NY 10028 (212 535-7710).

MUSEUM OF MODERN ART, New York, New York: The museum that is possibly the most complete museum of modern art in the world is more beautiful than ever since the completion of a major renovation in mid-1984. The permanent collections — concerned with 20th-century art — include works of abstractionists, expressionists, conceptualists, film-makers (there are daily film programs), industrial designers, photographers, and others. It is not a showplace of works of the very avant-garde; but then neither will you encounter Botticellis or Titians. Information: Museum of Modern Art, 11 W 53rd St., New York NY 10019-5486 (212 708-9480).

SOLOMON R. GUGGENHEIM MUSEUM, New York, New York: The first visual encounter you'll have when you come to this museum will be with the Frank Lloyd Wright structure that houses the collection. Perfectly round, with a domed roof, the building is constructed so that the exhibits are ranged along the walls of a quarter-mile-long ramp that spirals upward for six floors. Standing at the bottom, looking toward the skylight at the top, you can't help but wonder if Wright had read William Butler Yeats' "Turning and turning in the widening gyre . . ." It's also hard to understand the criticism that greeted the new building in October 1959; it was dubbed "a marshmallow" and even "a clothes washer." More charitable commentators said only that the building overpowered the art on display. Whether you agree will depend on how you feel about Wright vis-à-vis Kandinsky (one of the largest assemblages of his work in the world is here), Chagall, Delaunay, Picasso, and other Impressionist, modern, contemporary, and avant-garde artists represented in the permanent collections and in the ever-changing exhibitions that make the Guggenheim so lively. Information: The Guggenheim, 5th Ave. and 89th St., New York, NY 10128 (212 360-3500).

WHITNEY MUSEUM OF AMERICAN ART, New York, New York: Devoted to American art, primarily that of the 20th century, and the work of living artists, the Whitney presents about 15 exhibitions annually. The permanent collection includes works by Calder, de Kooning, Hopper, Johns, O'Keeffe, Nevelson, Prendergast, Segal, Sheeler, and Warhol. Information: Whitney Museum of American Art, Madison Ave. at 75th St., New York, NY 10021 (212 570-3676).

FRANKLIN INSTITUTE, Philadelphia, Pennsylvania: This huge, vital, hands-on science museum, in the final stages of a major renovation, has all kinds of new exhibits on subjects from aviation and astronomy to mechanics, light, math, patterns, and electricity. Watch light bend as it passes through concave and convex mirrors, walk through a 15,000-times-lifesize heart, board a Boeing 707, and take a ride on Philadelphia's beloved 350-ton Baldwin locomotive. Daily demonstrations show how lightning works and what energy is all about. Planetarium shows discuss black holes, satellite technology, and the constellations. And there's much, much more. Information: Franklin Institute, 20th St. and the Parkway, Philadelphia, PA 19103 (215 564-3375).

PHILADELPHIA MUSEUM OF ART, Philadelphia, Pennsylvania: In an imposing edifice of Minnesota dolomite, which Lord Dunsany called the most beautiful building in America, are Van Gogh's *Sunflowers*, Cézanne's *Bathers*, Marcel Duchamp's *Nude Descending a Staircase*, Picasso's *Three Musicians*, and the famous statue of Diana that topped New York City's first Madison Square Garden. Along with the excellent Impressionist collection, there's a Japanese Tea House, designed to convey the atmosphere as well as the art of Japan, a Chinese scholar's study, a large collection of arms and armor, and distinguished collections of china, porcelain, glass, jade, graphics, sculpture, and decorative arts. Information: Philadelphia Museum of Art, 26th St. and the Parkway, Philadelphia, PA 19130 (215 763-8100).

CORCORAN GALLERY OF ART, Washington, DC: In its gracious, skylit halls full of American art — among the finest collections of 18th- and 19th-century American art anywhere, in fact — are prestigious assortments of works by Sargent and Copley. You'll also find European paintings, however (some by Corot, some by the animal sculptor Antoine Barye, as well as Renaissance drawings), and a variety of changing exhibitions of contemporary art and photography. One block beyond the White House. Information: Corcoran Gallery of Art, 17th and New York Ave., NW, Washington, DC 20006 (202 638-3211).

SMITHSONIAN INSTITUTION, Washington, DC: Completed in 1855, the red Gothic castle on the Mall now functions mainly as office space for the staff that oversees the Smithsonian's scattered museums and galleries — seven on the Mall, six (including the National Zoo) in other parts of DC, one in New York City, and a half-dozen scientific research facilities around the country. The total collection contains almost 100 million items and gains almost a million more every year; only an infinitesimal percentage are displayed at any given time, so there's always something new to see. The museums of American History, Natural History, and Air & Space are among the most popular in Washington. Information: Smithsonian Institution, 1000 Jefferson Dr., SW, Washington, DC 20560 (202 357-2700).

HIRSHHORN MUSEUM AND SCULPTURE GARDEN, Washington, DC: One of the newer museums under the Smithsonian's wing and the most modern of the city's museums of modern art, the Hirshhorn houses, in part, the ever-astonishing collections amassed by Joseph H. Hirshhorn, who grew up in such poverty that he never even owned a toy. He spent much of the fortune he made in stocks and uranium buying art (the way some people buy clothes). The painting collection focuses on American art, and includes works by Eakins, Davis, Estes, Golub, Gorky, Henri, Hopper, de Kooning, Noland, and Stella; European masters like Bacon, Balthus, and Magritte are also represented. The extraordinary vitality of the sculpture collection reflects the greatness of Calder, Degas, Matisse, Moore, Rodin, and David Smith — many of whose works are displayed in the Hirshhorn sculpture garden — and the innovations of more recent sculptors. For this variety alone the Hirshhorn would be fascinating; the building itself — circular and fortresslike — is intriguing as well. Information: Hirshhorn Museum, Independence Ave. at 8th St., Washington, DC 20560 (202 357-2700).

NATIONAL GALLERY OF ART, Washington, DC: In a John Russell Pope building whose 500,000 square feet make it one of the world's largest marble structures, this museum built to introduce Americans to the cream of European art is what one local critic called "the sort of place paintings would aspire to if masterpieces went to heaven." Columns of Tuscan marble, floors of green marble from Vermont and gray marble from Tennessee, and walls of Indiana limestone and Italian travertine produce an effect that is unadulteratedly sumptuous, especially since a recent renovation; the museum's contents are, if possible, even more awe-inspiring. Leonardo da Vinci's *Ginevra de Benci* (America's only Leonardo), Jan Vermeer's *Woman Holding a Balance,* a Rembrandt *Self-Portrait,* Jean-Honoré Fragonard's *A Young Girl Reading,* Auguste Renoir's *A Girl with a Watering Can,* and Claude Monet's *Rouen Cathedral, West Façade* are among literally thousands of breathtaking canvases and sculptures — gifts of hundreds of donors — housed in the original building and the striking East Building, designed as a grouping of interlocking triangles by I. M. Pei & Partners. It can all be a bit bewildering, so, as an introduction, you might want to join one of the regular tours; rent a tape tour; or pick up the excellent *Brief Guide.* A monthly calendar of events includes free films, lectures, and concerts. Information: National Gallery of Art, 4th St. and Constitution Ave., NW, Washington, DC 20565 (202 737-4215).

MIDWEST

ART INSTITUTE OF CHICAGO, Chicago, Illinois: El Greco's *Assumption of the Virgin,* Seurat's *Sunday Afternoon on the Island of le Grand Jatte,* and Grant Wood's *American Gothic* are among the works in the Art Institute's outstanding collections, which also include excellent post-Impressionist and Impressionist works, Japanese prints, Chinese sculpture and bronzes, European and American prints and drawings, and more. The American Galleries are wonderfully conceived to show off the development of US culture; the Chagall stained glass windows and the Trading Room, from the old Chicago Stock Exchange Building, are not to be missed. The museum's renovated photography department is one of the most sophisticated facilities of its kind in the world. Information: Art Institute of Chicago, Michigan Ave. at Adams, Chicago, IL 60603 (312 443-3600).

FIELD MUSEUM OF NATURAL HISTORY, Chicago, Illinois: The more than 13 million artifacts and specimens displayed in 42 exhibition halls and 6 galleries are organized around anthropology, botany, ecology, geology, and zoology. The most famous are the pair of fighting elephants in the main hall, the butterflies, Bushman (the gorilla from the Lincoln Park Zoo, now stuffed but looking otherwise remarkably alive), and an exciting reproduction of a Pawnee earth lodge. At Place for Wonder, you can touch less precious specimens of the types of things you see in the museum. The new Maritime Peoples of the Arctic and the Northwest Coasts exhibit documents the life and culture of these peoples with some 2,500 objects. Information: Field Museum, Roosevelt Rd. at Lake Shore Dr., Chicago, IL 60605-2496 (312 922-9410).

MUSEUM OF SCIENCE AND INDUSTRY, Chicago, Illinois: Chicago's most popular attraction has computers to question, buttons to push, rides to ride, and so on, as part of some 2,000 exhibitions examining the principles of science (as well as other subjects). High points: Colleen Moore's fairy castle of a doll house; the computerized nutrition exhibition Food for Life; and the Sears circus exhibit, full of dioramas of circus scenes, piped-in circus music, and a dynamic short film (the kind you want to sit through twice in a row). The working coal mine, the walk-through human heart, and the German submarine are every bit as much fun as they always have been. And there are new exhibits on chemistry, physics, the post office, the life sciences, newspapers and Nobel Prize winners, not to mention the exciting and long-awaited offering from IBM on computers. The brand-new Crown Space Center features the Omnimax Theater and other space exhibitions. Information: Museum of Science and Industry, 57th St. and Lake Shore Dr., Chicago, IL 60637 (312 684-1414).

MILWAUKEE PUBLIC MUSEUM, Milwaukee, Wisconsin: The basic theme here is how man and other living creatures adapt to the environment, but there are a lot of variations, and exhibits relate not only to Indians, history, geology, and world cultures of the distant past, but also to aspects of American society. This sprawling institution really shines, however, when it comes to the making of dioramas. At a Northwest Coast Indian exhibition, for instance, smells and sounds come at you from all sides. In the Great Plains area, a rattlesnake rattles a warning, and when the buffalo charge, you can hear the thundering of their hooves on the earth — getting louder and louder. The geese honk overhead in a wildlife exhibit. In the Metasequoia Swamp, flashes of lightning illuminate hulking dinosaurs, and a loon calls out plaintively. At a portrayal of an East African bamboo forest, you hear the sounds of an elephant come crashing through the trees. Particularly interesting is the Streets of Old Milwaukee section, where the 19th-century city has been re-created, right down to flickering gaslights, telephone poles wrapped with wire to keep horses from chewing them, and a kite tangled up in the treetops. The same ingenuity is at work in the European village of shops and homes, which portrays 33 cultures of the Old World, and at the stunning new exhibit that documents the history, anatomy, and behavior of the Planet Earth (and stars two life-size dinosaurs). The new Wizard Wing Discovery Center offers a hands-on way to learn about air, collecting, pioneering skills, and a variety of natural history and cultural subjects. Information: Milwaukee Public Museum, 800 W Wells St., Milwaukee, WI 53233 (414 278-2700).

THE MINNEAPOLIS INSTITUTE OF ARTS, Minneapolis, Minnesota: The exterior of this highly esteemed institution is architecturally classic, and it houses an equally classic variety of Old Masters and other paintings, sculpture, decorative arts, photographs, and Asian, African, Oceanic, ancient, Oriental, and American objects. In addition, the museum presents films, concerts, and lectures. Information: The Minneapolis Institute of Arts, 2400 3rd Ave. S, Minneapolis, MN 55404 (612 870-3046).

WALKER ART CENTER, Minneapolis, Minnesota: Offering a vivid overview of major 20th-century art styles, this art center housed in a striking contemporary building complements the Institute's classic collections; originates many touring exhibitions; and conducts a lively program of music, dance, film, theater, and educational activities. Information: Walker Art Center, Vineland Pl., Minneapolis, MN 55403 (612 375-7600).

DETROIT INSTITUTE OF ARTS, Detroit, Michigan: One of the US's most comprehensive collections fills the 101 galleries of the institute, which is the fifth largest fine arts museum in the country. Italian art is only one of the areas in which the museum has large holdings; French painting and decorative arts and the Dutch and Flemish painters are also well represented. Diego Rivera's spectacular *Detroit Industry* frescoes cover the walls of a central court. There are several Egyptian mummies and suits of medieval armor on display, as well as a large collection of African and native American art. A permanent photography gallery opened not long ago, and Tony Smith's contemporary *Gracehoper* straddles the lawn. On Sundays, there is Brunch with Bach, and there are frequent special exhibitions, lectures, gallery talks, and films. Information: Detroit Institute of Arts, 5200 Woodward Ave., Detroit, MI 48202 (313 833-7900).

CLEVELAND MUSEUM OF ART, Cleveland, Ohio: One of the major American museums and one of the few of its kind that is still free to the public, this privately owned institution boasts an enviable collection that takes in all periods and cultures. Under the long directorship of the renowned Oriental art scholar Sherman E. Lee, who retired in 1983, galleries were organized chronologically, with the decorative arts pieces displayed alongside paintings and sculpture of the same era and area. A new wing, organized on the same basis, presents important collections of 19th- and 20th-century European and American art. The constantly growing collection currently numbers over 45,000 objects; the arts of the Near and Far East, India, pre-Columbian America, Europe, America, Africa, and ancient Egypt, Greece, and Rome are represented. The Oriental collection is one of the finest in the Western world, and the museum has particularly fine medieval, European painting, and decorative arts collections; of late, the collection of contemporary paintings has been growing rapidly. Throughout the year there are frequent concerts and films, with gallery talks every afternoon except Mondays. The original 1916 building overlooks a garden and lagoon; a wing designed by Marcel Breuer houses special exhibitions galleries, the musical arts department, and the education department (one of the largest professionally staffed education departments in the country); the most recent addition is a research library, open to the public on Wednesdays. A number of Cleveland's other cultural institutions face the museum across a grassy oval. Information: Cleveland Museum of Art, 11150 East Blvd. at University Circle, Cleveland, OH 44106 (216 421-7340).

WEST

LOS ANGELES COUNTY MUSEUM OF ART, Los Angeles, California: One of the best museums in the state and the largest built in the US in over 30 years, the Los Angeles County Museum has three separate pavilions — one devoted to changing exhibitions, one given over to the Leo S. Bing Theater (where there are weekly film presentations and frequent lectures and concerts), and the third — the Ahmanson Gallery — mainly to an eclectic permanent collection that encompasses exhibits of ancient times, the present, and years in between. The Robert O. Anderson Gallery, which should be open in 1987, will house a collection of classic modern and contemporary art. Though the collections are relatively recent, they're excellent, particularly the Indian and Islamic holdings and the European painting and sculpture. A sculpture garden contains works by Moore, Calder, and others. The Pavilion for Japanese Art is also scheduled for completion in 1987. Information: Los Angeles County Museum of Art, 5905 Wilshire Blvd., Los Angeles, CA 90036 (213 937-2590 or 213 857-6111).

ASIAN ART MUSEUM OF SAN FRANCISCO, San Francisco, California: The Avery Brundage Collection — one of the world's finest of Oriental objects — represents most of the museum's holdings, which include some 10,000 sculptures, architectural elements, paintings, bronzes, ceramics, and decorative objects illustrating stylistic developments of Asian art. There are also special temporary exhibitions and free docent tours. The museum shares an entrance with the M. H. de Young (below), but the two are distinct institutions. Information: Asian Art Museum of San Francisco, Golden Gate Park, San Francisco, CA 94118 (415 558-2993).

CALIFORNIA PALACE OF THE LEGION OF HONOR, San Francisco, California: The collections housed in this graceful building in the French neoclassical style (based on the Legion of Honor in Paris) are predominantly French, but you'll also find the largest graphics collection in the western US. With the M. H. de Young Memorial Museum (below), it is part of the Fine Arts Museums of San Francisco. Information: Lincoln Park, San Francisco, CA 94121 (415 750-3659).

M. H. DE YOUNG MEMORIAL MUSEUM, San Francisco, California: One of the western US's largest art museums, its collections include paintings, sculpture, and decorative arts from ancient Egypt through the 20th century. There are galleries devoted to American painting and decorative arts; to the traditional arts of Africa, Oceania, and the Americas; and to period rooms from Europe and America. Fra Angelico, Rembrandt, Rubens, Titian, El Greco, Goya, Hals, Van Dyck, Gainsborough, and Reynolds are represented. Information: M. H. de Young Memorial Museum, Golden Gate Park, San Francisco, CA 94118 (415 221-4811).

DENVER ART MUSEUM, Denver, Colorado: Besides having an excellent collection that takes in the period from AD 1100 to the present, the Denver Art Museum has top collections of pre-Columbian art and artifacts, native American art, Oriental art, and textiles, plus holdings in American, European, and contemporary art. The seven-story $6.5 million structure, which looks something like a medieval castle with its slitlike windows, was designed around the exhibits; some display halls completely re-create another time and place. Information: Denver Art Museum, 100 W 14th Ave. Pkwy., Denver, CO 80204 (303 575-2793).

AMON CARTER MUSEUM, Fort Worth, Texas: This museum started out chronicling America's westward expansion, with a huge collection of paintings and sculpture by Frederic Remington and Charles Russell. But gradually the museum has adopted American art as a whole as its theme, and, in addition to western pieces, you'll also see 19th-century landscapes and genre paintings by such artists as Winslow Homer, Albert Bierstadt, Mary Cassatt, and Thomas Moran; a selection of the 250,000-item American photography collection is also always on view. A new theater provides a home for films, lectures, and symposia. Information: Amon Carter Museum, 3501 Camp Bowie Blvd., Fort Worth, TX 76107 (817 738-1933).

FORT WORTH ART MUSEUM, Fort Worth, Texas: This museum concentrates on the 20th century, and outstanding examples of the work of Picasso, Louis, Warhol, Rothko, Stella, de Kooning, Rauschenberg, Motherwell, Pollock, and others hang in its galleries. It is also within a block of the Amon Carter and Kimbell museums. Information: Fort Worth Art Museum, 1309 Montgomery St., Fort Worth, TX 76107 (817 738-9215).

KIMBELL ART MUSEUM, Fort Worth, Texas: This result of a bequest by Kay Kimbell contains an incredible array of works by Cézanne, El Greco, Goya, Gainsborough, Picasso, Rembrandt, Van Gogh, and others, not to mention African sculputre and Asian ceramics, sculpture, screens, and scrolls. Recent acquisitions have expanded the collection. Information: Kimbell Art Museum, 3333 Camp Bowie Blvd., Fort Worth, TX 76107 (817 332-8451).

Space Centers: The Future Now

 The Saturn V Rocket on display at the Alabama Space and Rocket Center — one of three such space centers in the US — is as long as a football field and as wide as a two-lane highway; the sheer size of it is adequate testimony to the scope of the space program. There are plenty of reasons to visit. At each center you will be given facts and figures that may give you pause the next time you start to agree with someone who calls the space exploration program a waste of money. You'll be offered the opportunity to take over the controls of a rocket; experience weightlessness in a zero-gravity machine; and in a dozen other ways retrace the small steps that were such great leaps for mankind. Outside there are "rocket parks" — greenswards where mammoth spacecraft grow like so many monster asparagus stalks.

NASA SPACE AND ROCKET CENTER, Huntsville, Alabama: The feature attractions at Earth's Largest Space Museum tell you what's happening on the space scene — and looks into the future as well. The current emphasis is on the Space Shuttle and the Space Station, scheduled for orbit in 1993. Visitors can walk through a full-scale model of the Space Station being developed by NASA in Huntsville. On the grounds is the first full-scale mockup of the Space Shuttle orbiter: the 122-foot Pathfinder used for clearance tests at the nearby Marshall Space Flight Center, where NASA develops rockets for the space program. Visitors to the Spacedome Theater feel as if they are riding with shuttle astronauts during presentations of the Omnimax film *The Dream Is Alive*. The thunderous roar at launch from a 48-speaker sound system and inspiring views back at Earth on the planetarium-type ceiling provide a unique experience. Because the Saturn V rocket that launched Neil Armstrong to the Moon was made in Huntsville, Apollo spacecraft, space suits, and astronaut training gear are popular museum displays. The original moon rocket dominates the 20-acre park of NASA rockets ana army missiles. Bus tours that depart from the museum enter the Space Station development cneter and various astronaut training facilities. From March to Labor Day, the center holds the US Space Camp for children, with weekly astronaut training activities and simulated space shuttle missions; activities can be viewed from an elevated walkway. Information: NASA Space and Rocket Center, Tranquility Base, Huntsville, AL 35807 (205 837-3400 or 800 633-7280).

THE JOHN F. KENNEDY SPACE CENTER, Kennedy Space Center, Florida: The Kennedy Space Center is on Merritt Island and is the home of all Space Shuttle launchings; Cape Canaveral, across the Banana River, is the site for launchings of Department of Defense flights and NASA unmanned launchings. This 220-square-mile spaceport is a hotbed of space-related activity — everything from data-gathering and tracking to fuel storage and manned-flight launches. The best way to see it is on the 2-hour bus tour, which takes in the launching site of the Space Shuttle, Mission Control, and more. Spaceport USA, where you meet the tours, itself offers abundant attractions, including a lunar roving vehicle, a replica of an Apollo Lunar Module, and a baker's dozen theaters, minitheaters, and tape programs that tell you about flights past and future. Its newest attraction is the IMAX Theater, where viewers can watch a Space Shuttle launch on a screen 5 stories high and 70 feet wide; six-track stereo delivers the audio sensation of actual takeoff. If you opt for a tour around Christmas or in summer, be sure to arrive as close as possible to the center's 8 AM opening to avoid lines.

Afterward, you can swim off unspoiled beaches along the 25-mile Canaveral National Seashore, go deep-sea fishing, and, at the Merritt Island National Wildlife Refuge, see alligators, panthers, and some 200 species of birds. Cocoa Beach, where most motels are just a shell's throw from the Atlantic, is the place to lodge. Information: Spaceport USA, Visitor Center TWS 810, Kennedy Space Center, FL 32899 (305 452-2121).

THE LYNDON B. JOHNSON SPACE CENTER, Houston, Texas: An important research and development center for the US's Space Shuttle flight program. You can learn about the subject at the visitors center, where you see moon rocks, space suits, rocket engines, and spacecraft from the Mercury, Gemini, Apollo, Skylab, and Apollo-Soyuz test missions, and other impedimenta of the space age. NASA films shown all day long show you what each mission was like. Self-guided walking tours of the JSC take you to the Mission Simulation and Training Facility (Building 5), where astronauts practiced their complex Skylab tasks as well as Building 9A (devoted to Space Shuttle training) and Building 31A (where lunar samples are studied). Briefings at Mission

Control are also available daily. Information: NASA Johnson Space Center, AP4/Public Services Branch, Houston, TX 77058 (713 483-4321).

TO SEE A LIFT-OFF

"It's like being inside a flame — no heat, but your entire body shakes, your bones and organs shake, the earth shakes." That is one writer's description of watching a launch: They're definitely worth seeing. There are usually about ten a year from Cape Canaveral and Kennedy Space Center, and you can watch from either site along Rte. A1A, which passes between Cape Canaveral and Patrick Air Force Base. (For launch information, call 800 432-2153 in Florida.) It is hard to plan a vacation around a launching, because variable weather conditions make a strict schedule impossible. There is a special viewing area, 3 miles from the launching pads, for which you can make reservations through the Kennedy Space Center.

Factory Tours: Watching the Work

 Every year, literally hundreds of companies welcome thousands of visitors to their plants. Newspapers show off their printing presses, breweries their mash tubs, distilleries their warehouses and their quality-control systems, soft-drink companies their bottling plants, wineries their vineyards and aging rooms. Each region has a specialty. There are maple sugar houses and marble quarries in Vermont, tobacco warehouses and cigarette factories in Kentucky and North Carolina, glass factories in West Virginia, petrochemical works in Louisiana, oil fields and coal mines in Wyoming, lumber mills and wood products plants in the Pacific Northwest. Most big companies have plants in several parts of the country. If you're interested in seeing how a specific product is made, write the corporate headquarters and ask about tours.

Below, you'll find a very brief sampler of some industrial tours available to the general public. There are hundreds more, however. To find out about them, contact the state tourist offices and chambers of commerce in the areas you plan to visit. More than 2,500 factory and business tours are listed and described in the *Tours and Visits Directory*, a reference book published in 1981 by the Gale Research Company, available in many libraries.

And always phone ahead. Companies may need to line up someone to take you around, and that takes time. Even when the operation does have a regularly scheduled tour program, you've got to be sure that it will not be temporarily closed down because of vacations or model changeovers. If you have children, you need to make sure they are old enough to go on the tour. (There's usually an age limit of anywhere from 7 to 16.) This may seem a lot of trouble, but the excitement of the factories — the speed of the machines, the clanks and the screeches, the roars and the buzzes — will make all the planning worthwhile.

EAST

SCOTT PAPER COMPANY, Skowhegan, Maine: This mill takes tree-length logs, cuts them up into sections, chops them into chips, conveys them to a digester, treats them with chemicals, cooks them, bleaches them, and then bales up the soft, whitish fibers that result — wood pulp. The resemblance of the stuff to cotton is just one of the more interesting parts of the process, the first step in the manufacture of paper. Tours run from June 1 through August 1. Information: Bill Pasha, Scott Paper, Skowhegan, ME 04976 (207 453-9301).

SCOTT PAPER COMPANY, Winslow, Maine: Wood chips are turned into pulp, then slushed up in blenders, beaten with chemicals, and turned into rolls of Scottowels and other products and stocks. The complex has bark-burning and hydroelectric energy generation facilities as well as a new recycled fiber processing plant. Tours run late June through late August. Information: Scott Paper, Benton Ave., Winslow, ME 04902 (207 872-2751).

HARRISON OYSTER COMPANY, Tilghman Island, Maryland: In the heart of the fishing country of Maryland's Eastern Shore, watch oystermen unloading their briny catch and view an assembly line of oyster shuckers — as nimble-fingered a group as you can imagine. Though the tour lasts only half an hour, the process is fascinating and offers a pleasant diversion during a journey through one of the East's quaintest corners. Afterward, sample some of the local specialty in the adjacent restaurant, *Harrison's Chesapeake House.* Mid-September to mid-March, mornings only; restaurant open mid-March to end of November. Information: Harrison Oyster Company, PO Drawer J, Tilghman Island, MD 21671 (301 886-2530).

ANHEUSER-BUSCH, Merrimack, New Hampshire: One of the Anheuser-Busch breweries where the tour is guided (rather than self-guided), this brewery is also notable for being the East Coast home of the famous Clydesdales. Information: Anheuser-Busch, PO Box 610, Merrimack, NH 03054-4807 (603 889-6631).

CORNING GLASS CENTER, Corning, New York: Visitors get a ringside seat in the Steuben Glass factory to watch artisans transform gobs of red-hot molten glass into beautiful Steuben objects. Adjacent is a museum that houses one of the world's best glass collections and a science center where hands-on exhibitions, live demonstrations, and films show how glass is made and used. Corning itself is one of the country's more remarkable small towns, with its restored, master-planned main streets and handsome shops. Information: Corning Glass Center, Corning, NY 14831 (607 974-8271).

EASTMAN KODAK, Rochester, New York: With 300 buildings and grounds that are 1 mile across and 7 miles long, this town-sized plant, which houses the company's largest manufacturing operation, would probably take weeks to tour in its entirety, so the audio-visual presentation that begins a visit here and summarizes the whole operation makes a lot of sense; the bus tour that follows provides only an overview of a part of the roll and sheet film finishing operations. You actually see part of the inspection and packaging operations. Information: Eastman Kodak, Kodak Park Division, Visitor Services, 200 Ridge Rd. W, Rochester, NY 14650 (716 722-2465). For details about tours to the Kodak Apparatus Division plant, which manufactures cameras, projectors, and copier duplicators, phone 716 726-3426.

JULIUS STURGIS PRETZEL COMPANY, Lititz, Pennsylvania: At America's first pretzel bakery, built in 1784, visitors are given the history of the pretzel, along with a piece of dough, which they're taught to twist into a pretzel. In the half-hour tour that follows, a machine does more or less the same thing with lumps of dough (for hard pretzels only; soft ones are still made by hand), which, newly shaped, are baked for 7 minutes, then packaged. Visitors have first crack at buying the results. Closed Sundays and major holidays. Information: Julius Sturgis Pretzel Co., 219 E Main St. (State Rte. 772), Lititz, PA 17543 (717 626-4354).

FAIRDALE FARMS, Bennington, Vermont: This is really two tours in one. First, there's pigs, goats, ducks, and chickens; then there's the processing plant, where you watch cooled and pasteurized milk being bottled in gallons and half-gallons. Guided or self-guided tours run from May through October. Information: Fairdale Farms, PO Box 9, Bennington, VT 05201 (802 442-6391).

BUREAU OF ENGRAVING AND PRINTING, Washington, DC: At the world's largest securities manufacturing establishment, you can watch the making of currency on 25-minute self-guided tours. Information: Bureau of Engraving and Printing, Washington, DC 20228 (202 447-9709).

SOUTH

GERBER PRODUCTS, Fort Smith, Arkansas: Everything from baby cereal to strained spinach and applesauce, at every stage, through canning, packaging, and shipping. Winter is least active. Book at least one week ahead of time. Information: Personnel, Gerber Products, PO Box 1547, Fort Smith, AR 72902 (501 782-8671).

VILLAZON AND COMPANY, Tampa, Florida: Cigars, hand- and machine-made, from leaf to banding. Mornings are most active, and production peaks during September, October, and November. Closed mid-December to mid-January, during other holidays, and the first two weeks of July. Information: Villazon and Company, 3104 N Armenia, Tampa, FL 33607 (813 879-2291).

McILHENNY COMPANY, near New Iberia, Louisiana: An aged mash made of fermented red peppers is mixed with 100-grain vinegar in barrels, then put through three progressively finer strainers to make Tabasco sauce, and, finally, bottled, labeled, and packed into cartons. All in the middle of the mysterious Bayou Petit Anse. Information: McIlhenny Company, Avery Island, LA 70513 (318 365-8173).

CANNON MILLS COMPANY, Kannapolis, North Carolina: These tours take in the entire manufacturing process, from the opening of the cotton and polyester bales to carding, spinning, warping, weaving, labeling, dying, bleaching, finishing, and packing. Terrycloth gets its loops simply as a part of the process. Children under 12 are not admitted. Information: Cannon Mills, 200 West Ave., Kannapolis, NC 28081 (704 938-3200).

MIDWEST

CHICAGO TRIBUNE, Chicago, Illinois: Some years ago, the production operation moved from the Tribune Tower on North Michigan Avenue to Freedom Center at 777 West Chicago Avenue, where the tours take place. (The editorial, advertising, marketing, and public relations offices at the Tower are not open to the public.) Visitors are shown a 20-minute film on the history of printing, then guided through the Press Room, where papers are printed and bundled, and the Mail Room. The *Tribune* claims to have the world's largest offset facility under one roof. Reservations must be made at least a week in advance. Closed weekends. Information: *Chicago Tribune,* Public Service Office, 435 N Michigan Ave., Chicago, IL 60611 (312 222-3080).

CATERPILLAR TRACTOR CO., Peoria, Illinois: When the immense yellow tractors roar off the assembly line like so many mechanized elephants, everything shakes, even the concrete floor. By appointment only; closed weekends, holidays, and the last 2 weeks of July. Information: Tour Coordinator, Caterpillar, 100 NE Adams St., Peoria, IL 61629 (309 675-4578).

HALLMARK CARDS, Kansas City, Missouri: Although you don't go through the actual production area, you can watch employees at work: engravers creating metal dies, pressmen running cards through a press that applies shiny foil, and so on. Particularly enticing is a bow-making machine that visitors can activate. The visitors center features exhibitions of the company's products, including cards from the Depression and World War II. Closed Sundays and major holidays. Information: Hallmark Cards, PO Box 580, No. 132, Kansas City, MO 64141 (816 274-5672).

W*USA, Minneapolis, Minnesota: The TV studios and newsrooms — especially the weather department — are this tour's most popular attractions, which also includes control booths, master control, and the art department. Tours run from 9 AM to 2 PM, which avoids the most hectic part of the day but still provides a real sense of how a television station operates. Children under 10 not admitted. Closed weekends. Information: W*USA, 441 Boone Ave. N, Minneapolis, MN 55427 (612 546-1111).

SENECA FOODS, Rochester, Minnesota: Peas, corn, and lima beans can be inspected in their natural state before visitors view the canning process, which includes filling, cooking, casing, and labeling. The half-hour tours run from July to mid-September; Saturday tours most weekends. Information: Seneca Foods, 1217 Third Ave. SE, Rochester, MN 55904 (507 289-3926).

THE HOMESTAKE MINE, Lead, South Dakota: Here, you can see the aboveground operations of the largest underground gold mine in the Western Hemisphere. No tours on Saturdays or Sundays and from November through April. Information: Lead Civic Association, Lead, SD 57754 (605 584-1020).

KOHLER COMPANY, Kohler, Wisconsin: Ball clay is piped through miles of tubing into plaster molds of toilets, sinks, and drinking fountains. After two days of drying, this "greenware" is smoothed by hand, then sprayed with colored glazes. Thus are born the beautiful Kohler bath and kitchen fixtures on exhibit at the Kohler Design Center, a three-level showcase of the company's past, present, and future. What comes as a particular surprise to the 8,000 to 10,000 who visit annually is how much the plant resembles the studio of a ceramic artist and how much of the work is still done by hand — the punching of the holes for the fittings, the smoothing of the edges, and even some of the glazing. The town of Kohler — a planned community, one of the first in America, with strict guidelines about green space, parks, and construction — is interesting in its own right. Reservations required; children under 14 not admitted. No plant tours in late July and early August. Information: Kohler Company, Kohler, WI 53044 (414 457-4441).

WEST

HERSHEY CHOCOLATE COMPANY, Oakdale, California: This isn't the main Hershey factory, which is in Hershey, Pennsylvania, but since the main plant stopped giving public tours in 1973, this is the one to visit to see the sweet, rich stuff being mixed, molded, and packaged. Cravings can be satisfied at the store on the premises, where Hershey products are sold. Closed weekends and holidays. Information: Hershey Chocolate Co., 1400 S Yosemite Ave., Oakdale, CA 95361 (209 847-0381).

US MINT, Denver, Colorado: On a busy day, this money-making plant might turn out 32 million coins, enough to bring out the Scrooge McDuck in almost everyone. Huge, 6,000-to-8,000-pound coils are put on a punch press and uncoiled into a cutter that punches out disks that eventually end up as nickels, dimes, quarters, and half dollars. Pennies, which constitute up to 70% of the plant's production, are only stamped here. Closed holidays and weekends. Information: US Mint, 320 W Colfax Ave., Denver, CO 80204-2693 (303 844-3582).

PENDLETON WOOLEN MILLS, Pendleton, Oregon: Visitors to this plant watch wool production from fleece to fabric. And most are impressed with the huge kettles and percolators, each one holding some 500 pounds in which the stock is dyed; the special cylinders that comb the wool and turn it into yarn; and the subsequent winding of that same yarn onto bobbins or cones. The strands are then fed into sophisticated looms that transform it into the colorful plaid fabrics seen in the factory salesroom. Information: Pendleton Woolen Mills, 1307 SE Court St., Pendleton, OR 97801 (503 276-6911).

AUSTIN BAKING CO., Austin, Texas: Thousands of loaves of bread and rolls are turned out each day, and visitors can view their creation, from the mixing of dough to baking and packaging. Tours run Wednesdays and Fridays from October to May. Information: Austin Baking Co., 5800 Airport Blvd., Austin, TX 78752 (512 453-6606).

THE BOEING CO. (747/767 PLANT), Everett, Washington: By virtue of being big enough to hold 50 planes in various stages of completion, the final assembly building that plant visitors tour is the largest building in the world by volume — 62 acres under one roof! Children under 12 not admitted. Closed weekends. Information: The Boeing Co., PO Box 3707 (OE-44), Seattle, WA 98124-2207 (206 342-4801).

For the Spirit

National Parks: A Checklist

 Set aside by Congress for their exceptional array of one-of-a-kind scenic, geological, and historic features, the national parks are the Metropolitan Museums of America's natural history. You won't find *all* of the country's most marvelous natural features in the system — but almost.

Nevertheless, park boundaries are drawn arbitrarily, and usually take in only the areas where the marvels are found in greatest concentration. National forests, national wildlife refuges, state parks, and other government-protected preserves often surround the parks or take in similar countryside — and they're far less crowded.

Here is a list of the parks and adjacent recreation areas and attractions. Unless otherwise indicated, all of them offer camping and ranger programs; permits are usually required for overnight hiking trips into the backcountry.

Almost all parks will be crowded during a mid-July to mid-August summer "rush hour," and it may be necessary to reserve your campsite in advance. But you will also find naturalist programs scheduled with a frequency that you wouldn't encounter at other times of year — say, in other summer months, or during spring, fall, and winter. Then, on the other hand, you may have the country's most marvelous natural features almost all to yourself.

For folders on the individual areas, you can write the superintendents of the parks you're interested in, or address your query for information about more than one park to the National Park Service, Public Inquiries Office, PO Box 37127, Washington, DC 20013-7127 (202 343-4747). The Superintendent of Documents, US Government Printing Office, Washington, DC 20402, sells a good booklet on camping in the national park system as well as an interesting publication describing the dozens of less-used parks and a comprehensive listing of parks. Michael Frome's excellent *National Park Guide* (Rand McNally; $9.95) describes all 48 national parks plus the more than 300 National Park Service areas.

EAST

ACADIA NATIONAL PARK, Bar Harbor, Maine: With its fjord, towering shoreline cliffs, rocky coves, trail-crossed inland forests, and mountains, this 35,065-acre national park, the only one in New England, offers some of the most spectacular scenery in a beautiful state. Ocean Drive, the sea-hugging section of the 27-mile-long Park Loop Road, takes you to Thunder Hole, where waves crash on the shore with impressive fury when the surf is strong; to tidepools full of brightly colored marine life; to Otter Point, where you can watch the lobster boats and pleasure craft out at sea; to brief but golden Sand Beach; and to Cadillac Mountain, whose summit is the highest on the US's eastern seaboard. Somes Sound, the East Coast's only fjord, is also in the park. Acadia National Park, Box 177, Bar Harbor, ME 04609 (207 288-3338). See also *Acadia National Park,* DIRECTIONS.

SHENANDOAH NATIONAL PARK, Front Royal, Virginia: Crisscrossed by some

500 miles of trails — 94 of them along the Appalachian Trail — Shenandoah National Park's 195,353 acres are about as close to paradise as a hiker can get. The 105-mile-long Skyline Drive, which crosses and recrosses the top of the ridge along which the park sprawls, makes the place wonderful for Sunday drivers as well — particularly in May, when the pink azalea is in bloom; in June, when the mountain laurel is blossoming; and from mid- to late October during the fall color display. You can go riding, cycling, or fishing, or join the rangers for nature walks and campfire talks — and even today, when you look up into the night sky, you won't have any trouble figuring out why the Indians named the area "Daughter of the Stars." The ridge drive continues for nearly 500 miles more as the Blue Ridge Parkway. You can follow it or find other diversions closer at hand in the George Washington National Forest, which flanks the park. Information: Shenandoah National Park, Rte. 4, Box 292, Luray, VA 22835 (703 999-2243). See also *Shenandoah National Park,* DIRECTIONS.

SOUTH

HOT SPRINGS NATIONAL PARK, Hot Springs, Arkansas: Five thousand acres in the Ouachita Mountains, 47 mineral hot springs, and 3 spas at Bath House Row (where baths go for about $7 each) make this one of the nation's most unusual national parks. Nearby: DeGray and Ouachita lakes, immense impoundments where you can swim, fish, go boating; and the Ouachita National Forest, great for backpacking and hiking. From mid- to late May, the magnolias bloom; mid-October brings the equally spectacular fall foliage show. Information: Hot Springs National Park, PO Box 1860, Hot Springs, AR 71901 (501 624-3383). See also *Hot Springs National Park,* DIRECTIONS.

EVERGLADES NATIONAL PARK, Homestead, Florida: The park's 1½ million acres of mangrove swamps and watery plains provide a wonderful feeding ground for waterbirds, ducks, and all manner of tropical bird life: egrets, brown pelicans, yellow-crowned and black-crowned night herons, roseate spoonbills, great white herons, wood ibis, bald eagles. Go in summer to see giant loggerhead turtles laying their eggs on the beaches at Cape Sable (it may be difficult to find them but not impossible), or in winter and early spring for the best bird-watching. Nearby is the Audubon Society's 6,000-acre Corkscrew Swamp Sanctuary, home of the largest remaining stand of virgin bald cypress in the US. Information: Everglades National Park, PO Box 279, Homestead, FL 33030 (305 247-6211). See also *Everglades National Park,* DIRECTIONS.

MAMMOTH CAVE NATIONAL PARK, Mammoth Cave, Kentucky: The 52,000-plus acres of woodlands take in what used to be known as "the greatest cave that ever was." That was back in the days ladies had to don bloomers to visit, but a trip along the cave's 300-plus miles of mapped corridors will convince you that it isn't far from true, even today. Information: Mammoth Cave National Park, Mammoth Cave, KY 42259 (502 758-2251). See also *Mammoth Cave National Park,* DIRECTIONS.

GREAT SMOKY MOUNTAINS NATIONAL PARK, near Gatlinburg, Tennessee: The committee who picked the area for a park site called it "Exceptional, for the height of the mountains, depths of the valleys, ruggedness of the area, and unexampled variety of trees, shrubs, and plants." That this statement remains true is particularly amazing when you consider that the park lies within a day's drive of almost all the major cities in the East and the Midwest; the Smokies get the heaviest use of any national park in the system. Yet, with about 520,000 acres, 800 miles of hiking trails, and scenic parkways which never seem to end, you can usually get off by yourself, even in summer, the busiest season. Spring, fall, and winter are also lovely — spring for the wildflowers (late April) and rhododendrons and azaleas (June and early July); fall for the crisp air and flaming colors; winter for the solitude. Information: Great Smoky Mountains National Park, Gatlinburg, TN 37738 (615 436-5615). See also *Great Smoky Mountains National Park,* DIRECTIONS.

BIG BEND NATIONAL PARK, on the Mexican border near Terlingua, Texas:
The park's canyons were formed as the Rio Grande wore away at the hardened
sediments of an inland sea that covered the area millions of years ago. Big Bend is one
of the best places in the park system to study desert life. From the desert floor to the
rocky, pine- and juniper-covered Chisos Mountains — which change colors as the sun
moves through the sky — one finds coyotes, ringtails, mule,and white-tail deer, lizards,
snakes, and some 400 species of birds; because of the wide range in elevation, from
about 1,800 feet at river level to 7,835 feet atop Mt. Emery, habitats and wildlife are
exceptionally diverse. Hiking trails, primitive roads, and commercial rafting trips provide access. Information: Big Bend National Park, TX 79834 (915 477-2251). See also
Big Bend National Park, DIRECTIONS.

GUADALUPE MOUNTAINS NATIONAL PARK, near Salt Flat, Texas: Just south
of the New Mexico line, this 76,293-acre 1972 addition to the park system preserves
a spectacular exposure of what some geologists consider the world's most significant
and extensive fossil reef, a reminder that many years ago the entire area was covered
by a sea. Guadalupe Peak, Texas's highest (8,749 feet, accessible by trail), is here, as
are the whitish, thousand-foot cliffs known as El Capitan; the rugged countryside takes
in desert vegetation, ponderosa pine, southwestern white pine, and Douglas fir. The last
week in October and the first two weeks in November, when the canyon maples, oaks,
and walnuts take on their autumn colorations, are particularly beautiful. Information:
Guadalupe Mountains National Park, 3225 National Parks Hwy., Carlsbad, NM 88220
(915 828-3251).

VIRGIN ISLANDS NATIONAL PARK, St. John, Virgin Islands: Nearly two thirds
of tiny St. John Island is taken up by the tropical forests, sparkling beaches, and Danish
ruins of this 12,750-acre national park. Offshore, in 5,650 acres of park waters, are
wonderful coral reefs, vividly colored and full of neon-bright fish. Swimming, snorkeling, scuba diving, and hiking through the forests to former plantations and pre-Columbian Indian petroglyphs are the main pastimes; it's possible to camp just a stone's throw
from the beach. Information: Virgin Islands National Park, PO Box 7789, St. Thomas,
Virgin Islands 00801 (809 776-6201).

MIDWEST

ISLE ROYALE NATIONAL PARK, near Houghton, Michigan, in Lake Superior:
With some 166 miles of trails, this 539,280-acre park on the largest island in Lake
Superior is one of the best places for hiking in the US — and certainly in the Midwest.
You can also go boating, or fish in inland streams, bays, and in Lake Superior for trout,
northern pike, or perch. Information: Isle Royale National Park, 87 N Ripley St.,
Houghton, MI 49931 (906 482-0984). See also *Isle Royale National Park*, DIRECTIONS.

VOYAGEURS NATIONAL PARK, International Falls, Minnesota: While it is possible to drive to the edge of this 218,000-acre park, access to most of the forests, bogs,
and lakes (five big ones and some two dozen smaller ones) is almost entirely by
houseboat, runabout, cruiser, and canoe: Backpacking will never be as popular here as
it is, say, at Isle Royale, though exploring the Kabetogama peninsula on the Cruiser
Lake Trail on foot can be fun. For the moment, powerboating on the big lakes is the
main activity, along with fishing for walleye, northern pike, sauger, and smallmouth
bass, and, in winter, cross-country skiing, snowmobiling, and ice fishing. Pleasant
resorts and outfitters who rent everything from boats to camping gear are abundant on
the park's perimeter. Information: Voyageurs National Park, PO Box 50, International
Falls, MN 56649 (218 283-9821). See also *Voyageurs National Park*, DIRECTIONS.

WEST

GLACIER BAY NATIONAL PARK, Gustavus, Alaska: With over 3 million acres,
this meeting place of water, ice, and land is one of the widest expanses of terrain in

the national park system; inland peaks that rise to 15,300 feet are home to bear, coyote, wolf, and wolverine, while the shoreline is inhabited by whales and seals. Hiking is on 4 miles of trail near park headquarters or — for the venturesome — cross-country. The monument is accessible only by airplane or boat. Information: the Superintendent, Glacier Bay National Park, Gustavus, AK 99826 (907 697-3341).

DENALI NATIONAL PARK AND PRESERVE, Denali Park, Alaska: North America's tallest mountain, 20,320-foot Mt. McKinley, towers over the spectacular Alaska Range, which dominates the scenery in this 9,375-square-mile subarctic wilderness — but if you come specifically to see Denali, "the high one," you may be disappointed: the mountain is cloud-covered for more than half of every summer season. However, the park does offer an excellent opportunity to hike in both tundra and taiga and to look for grizzly, moose, caribou, Dall sheep, and wolf, as well as many other species of mammals, birds, and flora. The landscape will quite simply take your breath away. Information: Denali National Park, Box 9, Denali Park, AK 99755 (907 683-2294). See also *Denali National Park,* DIRECTIONS.

GRAND CANYON NATIONAL PARK, Grand Canyon, Arizona: "The world's most wonderful spectacle," according to naturalist John Burroughs. True or not, no other natural formation in the US comes close to equaling the Canyon's size, color, or geological significance. Information: Grand Canyon National Park, PO Box 129, Grand Canyon, AZ 86023 (602 638-7888). See also *Grand Canyon National Park,* DIRECTIONS.

PETRIFIED FOREST NATIONAL PARK, near Holbrook, Arizona: Part of the Painted Desert — a vast area of bright-colored sandstone, shale, and clay formations — 93,493-acre Petrified Forest National Park is made up of six areas where the fallen trees of 200-million-year-old forests have gradually filled with minerals stained brilliant red, purple, and blue by traces of iron, carbon, and manganese and have fossilized. The logs of jasper, agate, and other quartzes that resulted — some 100 feet long — lie helter-skelter on the ground. The 50,000 park acres designated as wilderness make for great hiking and primitive back-pack camping; best seasons are late spring and early fall, when desert wildflowers are in bloom and temperatures are moderate. Information: Petrified Forest National Park, AZ 86028 (602 524-6228). See also *Petrified Forest National Park,* DIRECTIONS.

LASSEN VOLCANIC NATIONAL PARK, near Mineral, California: This park has mud pots, fumaroles, hot springs, and such, just like Yellowstone; but Lassen is far less crowded. The park's center, 10,457-foot Lassen Peak, is one of the most recently active volcanoes in the lower 48 states. Information: Lassen National Park, Mineral, CA 96063-0100 (916 595-4444). See also *Lassen Volcanic National Park,* DIRECTIONS.

REDWOOD NATIONAL PARK, near Crescent City, California: Northern California's 106,000-acre park, 1 to 7 miles wide, stretches for 46 Pacific-pounded miles adjoining a section of Six Rivers National Forest, and takes in sand and pebble beaches, creeks, cliffs, and huge stands of virgin redwoods, including the earth's tallest tree, measured in 1963 at 367.8 feet. In 1980, UNESCO added the park to its prestigious World Heritage List of places worthy of preservation for the good of mankind. Most of the other mature redwoods reach 200 feet. Information: Redwood National Park, 1111 Second St., Crescent City, CA 95531 (707 464-6101). See also *Redwood National Park,* DIRECTIONS.

SEQUOIA AND KINGS CANYON NATIONAL PARKS, near Three Rivers, California: The two parks, administered as one, take in a 65-mile-long, 1,300-square-mile expanse of rugged canyons, peaks, and gorges. But the purpose of the park is to preserve groves of giant sequoia, which, with the coastal redwoods, are among the last surviving members of a large group which was widespread eons ago. Information: Sequoia and Kings Canyon National Parks, Three Rivers, CA 93271 (209 565-3341). See also *Sequoia and Kings Canyon National Parks,* DIRECTIONS.

YOSEMITE NATIONAL PARK, Yosemite, California: A 1,189-square-mile parkland, with groves of sequoias, mountain meadows, alpine vegetation, immense waterfalls (at their most thunderous in May and June), and huge monoliths. One of them, El Capitan, is among the world's largest masses of visible granite. You can take naturalist trips led by rangers or mule and horseback trips operated by the park's concessioner; go to mountain climbing school (see Climbing Schools, *Mountain Climbing and Mountains*); or take a summer photography workshop with the Ansel Adams Gallery. Ranger-led backpack trips are limited and are offered through the Yosemite Association. Information: Yosemite National Park, PO Box 577, Yosemite, CA 95389 (209 372-4461; recorded road, weather, lodging, camping, and skiing information, 209 372-4605). See also *Yosemite National Park*, DIRECTIONS.

MESA VERDE NATIONAL PARK, near Durango and Cortez, Colorado: Fourteen hundred years ago, Indians came to this land; built and lived in homes on the mesa tops and in elaborate dwellings set into the sides of the area cliffs; and then, possibly having overused their environment, they abandoned the area. Modern anthropologists and archaeologists believe that they probably moved south into northern New Mexico and Arizona, where they are represented now by various groups of Pueblo Indian people. Current visitors can explore some of the most dramatic of the cliff dwellings, including Long House and Step House on Wetherill Mesa; the 200-room Cliff Palace, the largest cliff dwelling in North America; Spruce Tree House, amazingly well preserved; and Balcony House. Whether you tour these on your own or in the company of a ranger will depend on which site you visit and when you travel. But either way, even history haters can't fail to get hooked on matters archaeological. Other area attractions: The old Durango and Silverton narrow-gauge railroad, which runs from Durango, through deep forested canyons, to the quaint old mining town of Silverton (call 303 247-2733 for train information); the San Juan National Forest, great for hiking and fishing; and a variety of other national monuments: the Aztec Ruins, Chaco Canyon, and other nearby towers, pueblos, and cliff dwellings scattered around the Four Corners area; Navajo, near Kayenta and Tuba City, Arizona; and Canyon de Chelly, near Chinle, Arizona, in the Navajo reservation. Lodgings are available in Mesa Verde at *Far View Lodge,* modern, beautifully situated, and aptly named (303 529-4421), which also offers 3-hour tours. In Durango, you'll find the refurbished Victorian *Strater Hotel* (303 247-4431) along with some 50 other hostelries. For park information, contact the superintendent in Mesa Verde National Park, CO 81330 (303 529-4465); for details about the surrounding area, write the Cortez Chamber of Commerce, Box 968, Cortez, CO 81321 (303 565-3414).

ROCKY MOUNTAIN NATIONAL PARK, Estes Park, Colorado: The 265,229 acres — 414 square miles — of high peaks and luxuriant forests that were set aside as a park in 1915 are today virtually unspoiled and make excellent hiking. Some visitors like to make the trek to the top of 14,255-foot Longs Peak, one of the park's 104 named peaks over 10,000 feet; others like to stroll to lovely Emerald Lake, its shores formed by towering peaks. Information: Estes Park Chamber of Commerce, PO Box 3050, Estes Park, CO 80517 (303 586-4431 or 800 654-0949 in Colorado; 800 621-5888 elsewhere), and Superintendent, Rocky Mountain National Park, Estes Park, CO 80517-8397 (303 586-2371). See also *Rocky Mountain National Park,* DIRECTIONS.

HALEAKALA NATIONAL PARK, on the island of Maui, Hawaii: Whether, after your trip to this 28,665-acre preserve, you'll remember the spectacular drive to the summit over the highest paved road in the mid-Pacific, or the stunning emptiness of the 19-square-mile crater of this now-dormant volcano, is a toss-up. The highway clings precariously to the mountainside, and offers views of mists, cloud banks, pastureland, ocean. The vast, silent area — ribboned with hiking trails where you can stay overnight in primitive cabins or at campgrounds — is dotted by cinder cones, lava flows, and spatter vents. In the Kipahulu District of the park, on the Pacific, you can splash in waterfall pools that tumble into each other on the way to the sea. Information: Haleakala National Park, PO Box 369, Makawao, Maui, HI 96768 (808 572-9306; for recorded weather information, 808 572-7749; for recorded cabin and hiking information, 808 572-9177). See also *Haleakala National Park,* DIRECTIONS.

HAWAII VOLCANOES NATIONAL PARK, near Hilo, Hawaii: Rising to 4,090 feet, Kilauea has been dubbed the drive-in volcano because of its accessibility. It's just one of two that are still active in this 229,177-acre park; and between it and 13,680-foot Mauna Loa, something is usually acting up. You may see Kilauea letting out fountains of lava (once, a fountain sprayed 1,900 feet into the air). You may see rivers of lava. You may feel Mauna Loa's tremors. You will probably see steam; along Steaming Bluff it will swirl around you like a fog. And at the Hawaiian Volcano Observatory, you can watch seismographs at work. The modern *Volcano House* is a good place to lodge; it's not fancy — but not every motel can boast a dining room with a view of a steaming crater (808 967-7321). On the opposite side of the island, on the Kona Coast, is Puuhonua-o-Honaunau National Historic Park, at Honaunau, the site of an ancient Hawaiian temple. Information: Hawaii Volcanoes National Park, HI 96718 (808 967-7311).

GLACIER NATIONAL PARK, West Glacier, Montana: Properly called Waterton-Glacier International Peace Park, because it adjoins Canada's Waterton National Park, this Montana area's million-plus acres — a phenomenal 1,600 square miles — take in precipitous peaks, knife-edged ridges, 40 glaciers, and approximately 700 miles of hiking trails. Grizzlies live here in abundance, along with bighorn sheep, mountain goats, mule and white-tail deer, and hawks. Fifty-mile-long Going-to-the-Sun Road provides magnificent vistas. There are marvelous places to stay in the park as well: *Sperry* and *Granite Park Chalets,* built around World War I and hardly modernized since, are accessible only by footpath — but if you can get there, you can see what it feels like to live in a house without electricity. Far fancier are the bigger local establishments — *Lake McDonald Lodge* and *Many Glacier Hotel* inside the park, and *Glacier Park Lodge,* just outside — which are like sets for a Nelson Eddy musical. Nearby: a chairlift ride at Big Mountain, near Whitefish; Flathead Lake, south of Kalispell, the largest natural freshwater lake west of the Mississippi; Flathead National Forest; and Bigfork, a tiny artsy town. Good lodgings are available at Big Mountain and at the *Flathead Lake Lodge* (406 837-4391; open May through September), a mile south of Bigfork. Time your visit for early summer and you'll catch the resort full of rodeo cowboys, who come to improve their skills at a special rodeo school. Information: Glacier National Park, West Glacier, MT 59936 (406 888-5441). See also *Glacier National Park,* DIRECTIONS.

CARLSBAD CAVERNS NATIONAL PARK, near Carlsbad, New Mexico: Lying underneath the rugged foothills of the Guadalupe Mountains, Carlsbad Cavern is only the best known of the dozens of caves in this 46,753-acre national park; the cave is as noteworthy for its immensity as for its variety of formations. From May through September, you can watch hundreds of thousands of bats leaving their underground lairs each evening. In another part of the park, lantern tours through an undeveloped cave are available. Information: Carlsbad Caverns National Park, 3225 National Parks Hwy., Carlsbad, NM 88220 (505 785-2232). See also *Carlsbad Caverns National Park,* DIRECTIONS.

THEODORE ROOSEVELT NATIONAL PARK, Medora, North Dakota: Some 70,374 acres of the badlands that so enchanted the future president when he first came to the area as a big game hunter in 1883 are preserved in this park, and when you visit, you'll easily comprehend the attraction that led Roosevelt to purchase two ranches in the area: The buttes and canyons, carved by wind and water into fantastic shapes, make the scenery extraordinarily beautiful, and the countryside is full of buffalo, prairie dogs, eagles, and more. Information: Superintendent, Theodore Roosevelt National Park, Medora, ND 58645 (701 623-4466).

CRATER LAKE NATIONAL PARK, near Crater Lake, Oregon: Formed by the collapse of a volcano some 6,840 years ago, 21-square-mile, 1,932-foot-deep Crater Lake is the deepest in the United States (and second deepest, next to Canada's Great Slave Lake, in the Western Hemisphere), and boasts some of the most brilliantly blue waters anywhere. Bordering the park are the Umpqua, Winema, and Rogue River National Forests; the Oregon Shakespearean Festival in Ashland; quaint Jacksonville, home of Peter Britt Festivals; and the whitewater raft trips down the Rogue. Information: Crater Lake National Park, PO Box 7, Crater Lake, OR 97604-0007 (503 594-2211). See also *Crater Lake National Park,* DIRECTIONS.

WIND CAVE NATIONAL PARK, near Hot Springs, South Dakota: Set in the Black Hills, this 28,260-acre park is home to bison, prairie dogs, pronghorn antelope, and an unusual cave full of exotic crystal formations — frostwork crystals made of calcite, aragonite, and boxwork, a honeycomb affair made of crystalline fins. You can see these on traditional walks through the cave, on special candlelight tours through unelectrified sections, and on spelunking tours where you do your locomoting on all fours. Nearby, there are hot springs; Mt. Rushmore National Memorial (where the heads of Washington, Teddy Roosevelt, Lincoln, and Jefferson are carved in granite cliffs); aptly named Jewel Cave National Monument; Custer State Park, home of one of the world's largest herds of bison; and Black Hills National Forest. You shouldn't miss the *State Game Lodge* in Custer State Park, where Coolidge and Eisenhower once summered and where you can now eat buffalo steaks and South Dakota pheasant (605 255-4541). According to one commercial buffalo rancher, buffalo tastes like beef wished it did — flavorful, but tender as a filet mignon. Information: Wind Cave National Park, Hot Springs, SD 57747 (605 745-4600); Black Hills National Forest, Box 792, Custer, SD 57730 (605 673-2251); Custer State Park, Star Rte. 3, Box 70, Custer, SD 57730 (605 255-4515).

BADLANDS NATIONAL PARK, Interior, South Dakota: Erosion has left the landscape of this 244,300-acre preserve sculpted into canyons and cliffs, spires and gullies, all banded with the bright colors of the many layers of clay and sandstone deposited here over millennia. On the Fossil Exhibit Trail you can see embedded in rock what remains of fleet-footed rhinos and other mammals that prowled the area 23 million to 37 million years ago. Also preserved here is the short grass prairie and its inhabitants — bison, pronghorn, bighorn sheep, deer. Information: Superintendent, Badlands National Park, PO Box 6, Interior, SD 57750 (605 433-5361).

ARCHES NATIONAL PARK, near Moab, Utah: Through some of the numerous arches already discovered in Arches National Park's 73,379 acres, you can see the park's vast expanse of canyons and, off in the distance, the snow-capped peaks of the LaSal. Trim, tapered Delicate Arch, the park's most celebrated landmark, is higher than most houses. Landscape Arch is among the world's longest known natural stone arches. Though only a few miles north of Canyonlands, the formations here have their own distinct character, and a visit to both will teach you a lot about how the earth came to be what it is. Information: Arches National Park, Moab, UT 84532 (801 259-8161) and the Grand County Travel Council, PO Box 550, Moab, UT 84532-2995 (801 259-8825).

BRYCE CANYON NATIONAL PARK, Bryce Canyon, Utah: The Paiutes called the stunning giant rock formations along the edge of the Paunsaugunt Plateau here "red rocks standing like men in bowl-shaped canyons." But when you drive along the 18-mile-long parkway on the plateau's edge, you may think the results of 60 million years of silt and clay deposits and water action resemble castles and cathedrals, Hindu temples and skyscrapers, chessmen and such. The colors — pink, orange, and scarlet, sometimes striped with lavender and blue, or cream, white, and yellow — are even more vivid at sunset. Information: Bryce Canyon National Park, Bryce Canyon, UT 84717 (801 834-5322). See also *Bryce Canyon National Park,* DIRECTIONS.

CANYONLANDS NATIONAL PARK, near Moab, Utah: The Green and Colorado rivers, which meet in this area, have carved deep and winding gorges in the reddish-orange sandstone. The buttes, cliffs, mesas, spires, columns, and pillars — like mad Ludwig's castles in Bavaria — are truly fantastic. The still relatively untrammeled 337,570 acres, full of juniper and pinyon, can be seen on jeep tours out of Moab, on float trips down the Green and Colorado rivers (see *Touring America's Waterways*), as well as on foot or horseback and by car from a number of overlooks. Nearby, you'll find Arches National Park; the cool woodlands of Manti-LaSal National Forest; the fine recreational waters of Glen Canyon National Recreation Area and Lake Powell; Natural Bridges National Monument; and Hovenweep National Monument, a chain of prehistoric Indian dwellings. Lodgings are available in Moab and Monticello. Information: Canyonlands National Park, 125 W 2nd South, Moab, UT 84532 (801 259-7164), and Grand County Travel Council, PO Box 550, Moab, UT 84532-2995 (801 259-8825).

CAPITOL REEF NATIONAL PARK, near Torrey, Utah: According to local legend, Butch Cassidy once used this isolated area as a hiding place, but it was only recently that the rest of America woke up to its beauties: sandstone monoliths, colored in deep rich reds that in some light seem almost luminous, and soaring up to 1,000 feet above the valley floor; petroglyphs and pictographs of prehistoric Indians that keep company with names that the early pioneers carved on the cliffs; and subtle, lovely desert vegetation. You can see it all either from your own car or on foot — along short hiking trails or by going cross-country. Backpacking is also possible. Information: Capitol Reef National Park, Torrey, UT 84775 (801 425-3871).

ZION NATIONAL PARK, near Springdale, Utah: It was the Mormons, settling here in the 19th century, who called the central feature of this 230-square-mile park "Zion," or "heavenly city of God," and who gave many of its features their unusual names — Kolob Canyons and Mt. Moroni. Backcountry trails can be rugged but full of marvels, like Kolob Arch, which claims to be the world's largest natural span at 310 feet, or "Hanging Gardens" — rock walls draped, in season (late April-September), with columbine, monkey flower, maiden-hair ferns, and scarlet lobelia — which you see along the Gateway to the Narrows Trail. Park roads provide terrific views of the canyon walls, colored crimson, purple, pink, orange, and yellow. Horseback trips are also available. Within a 125-mile radius, you can also visit the North Rim of the Grand Canyon; Bryce Canyon National Park; Cedar Breaks National Monument; the Dixie National Forest; and the Utah Shakespearean Festival on the campus of Southern Utah State College at Cedar City (801 586-7880). Information: Zion National Park, Springdale, UT 84767 (801 772-3256). See also *Zion National Park*, DIRECTIONS.

MT. RAINIER NATIONAL PARK, Longmire, Washington: The dormant ice-clad volcano that is the raison d'être of this park is only its most striking feature. The 235,404 acres also have cathedral-like forests of Douglas fir and Pacific silver fir, western red cedar, and western hemlock. The park is a wonderland of glaciers and boasts the lower 48's most extensive single-peak glacier system as well as its longest glacier (Carbon) and its largest (Emmons). Nearby are the Mt. Baker–Snoqualmie National Forest, the Gifford Pinchot National Forest, and the *Crystal Mountain Resort*, a ski and summer resort development that does a brisk business even when the weather is warm. Most accommodations — motels, inns, and lodges — are along Routes 7 and 706 from Tacoma. Information: Mt. Rainier National Park, Tahoma Woods Star Route, Ashford, WA 98304 (206 569-2211). See also Mt. Rainier National Park, DIRECTIONS.

NORTH CASCADES NATIONAL PARK, near Sedro Woolley, Washington: Ice falls and waterfalls, hanging valleys and ice caps, and some 300 glaciers, plus canyons, granite peaks, and mountain lakes and streams make this a rugged 789 square miles. It's not for that reason only, however, that you'll find some of the most extensive opportunities for outdoor recreation in the area. In addition to the park, you'll find the

184-square-mile Ross Lake National Recreation Area (which lies between the park's north and south units); the 97-square-mile Lake Chelan National Recreation Area (adjoining the south unit on its southern border); and surrounding the four units, the Mt. Baker–Snoqualmie, Wenatchee, and Okanogan national forests. You'll find especially interesting lodgings at the rustic *North Cascades Lodge* (509 682-4711) in Stehekin, at the north end of Lake Chelan and accessible only by boat or float plane from the town of Chelan. Lodgings can also be found at *Diablo Lake Resort* (Everett operator, area code 206; ask for Newhalem 5578) and *Ross Lake Resort* (Everett operator, area code 206; ask for Newhalem 7735); Ross Lake Resort is not accessible by car. Information: North Cascades National Park, 800 State St., Sedro Woolley, WA 98284 (206 855-1331).

OLYMPIC NATIONAL PARK, near Port Angeles, Washington: These 1,419 square miles lay claim to some of the wettest weather in America; sixty living glaciers; alpine meadows; deep lush valleys; exquisitely green rain forests full of fungi, lichens, and some 70 species of moss, draped over branches and growing on tree trunks. There are stands of Sitka spruce and Douglas fir, sometimes 300 feet tall and 1,000 years old. Huge Roosevelt elk, the largest remaining herd in the country, inhabit the park Seals, sea lions, and whales can be seen along the beaches in the Pacific coast section. Nearby are the Olympic Highway, which circles the peninsula; Olympic National Forest; and the San Juan Islands, a still fairly unspoiled resort area in Puget Sound, accessible by ferry from Anacortes, Washington, and Sidney, British Columbia. Information: Olympic National Park, 600 E Park Ave., Port Angeles, WA 98362-6798 (206 452-4501). See also Olympic National Park, DIRECTIONS.

GRAND TETON NATIONAL PARK, Moose, Wyoming, and environs: This 40-mile-long string of snow-capped and glaciated mountains dominates the skyline as do few other mountains in the nation. The 13,770-foot Grand Teton simply towers over Jackson Hole, the valley to the east of the Teton Range. Surrounding are Teton and Targhee national forests, both heavily forested and trail-crossed. Information: Grand Teton National Park, PO Drawer 170, Moose, WY 83012 (307 733-2880). See also Grand Teton National Park, DIRECTIONS.

YELLOWSTONE NATIONAL PARK, in the northwest corner of Wyoming: Old Faithful is the most famous thermal feature in this park full of thermal features. There are countless geyser basins, mud pots, bubbling springs, hot pools that are blue, red, orange, and yellow, depending on the temperature of the water and the plants (algae) that can survive there. What many people don't know is that Yellowstone also boasts beautiful mountains, abundant wildlife, and rich forests that make for some of the US's finest backpacking. Yellowstone has a reputation for being crowded — and it is, during July and August at its major points of interest. Go into the backcountry, however, and you can have trails almost to yourself. Information: PO Box 168, Yellowstone National Park, WY 82190 (307 344-7381). See also *Yellowstone National Park,* DIRECTIONS.

America's Most Exciting Amusement Parks and Theme Parks

Seventy or eighty years ago, the American Sunday changed forever. Until then, America's amusement parks were run as sedate adjuncts to picnic groves, usually owned by the companies that ran trolleys and interurban train lines. At some unrecorded moment, a trolley line executive realized that people loved the rides a lot more than the picnics, and before long picnicking as a Sunday afternoon pastime went the way of oil lamps. Huge entertainment complexes sprang up beside piers and boardwalks across the country. Roller coasters didn't go very fast (one attendant was chided for eating his lunch on board), but they stirred the masses. "It was something dreadful," scrawled a shaken Agatha Wales on the back of a postcard after her ride on the Venice, California, roller coaster. "I was never so frightened in my life. And if the Dear Lord will forgive me this time, I will never ride it again." Most folks were simply thrilled.

Today, more time, money, and talent is going into the business than ever before — and the results are spectacular. Not only are the parks clean, green, and flowering, but you can take in zippy, chills-down-the-spine shows and even top-name entertainers after you've whirled over some of the scariest roller coaster tracks in history.

Admission fees — usually around $15, with reductions for children — generally buy all the rides and shows you want, though occasionally you'll have to pay extra to play games at the penny arcade.

EAST

SIX FLAGS GREAT ADVENTURE, Jackson, New Jersey: The company that brought America Six Flags Over Texas (and with it, the concept of rides-and-live-shows entertainment complexes behind all those listed below) has completely changed the face of the park (the largest in the Northeast) since it took over; but the great rides — the coasters, the 15-story-high Ferris wheel, the giant log flume — are still there, along with a dual wooden coaster, the terrifying Free Fall, the Lightning Loops (a loop coaster that shuttles forward and backward), the Looping Starship, and the new Ultra Twister. And additional stomach churners are added every year. A 350-acre drive-through safari park adjoins the rides area, bringing the total acreage to 1,700. Information: Six Flags Great Adventure, PO Box 120, Jackson, NJ 08527 (201 928-3500).

HERSHEYPARK, Hershey, Pennsylvania: Though Hershey Bars and Reese's Cups stroll the grounds, the park's theme is Pennsylvania's German, Dutch, and English cultural heritage — carried out through an artfully reconstructed Tudor castle and food shops offering local specialties like Belgian waffles and funnel cakes; there are also personable craftspeople on hand — candlemaker, blacksmith, and leathercrafters. The fast, old wooden roller coaster known as The Comet is among the best in the US; the sooperdooperLooper, a steel-tube coaster that shoots you around steeply banked turns and upside down through one enormous vertical loop was the first of its kind on the East Coast. And there are over three dozen other rides. Also included in your admission is a trip through ZOOAMERICA, a small but high-quality zoo that showcases the plants and animals of five different North American environments; its prairie dogs, pumas, bison, timber wolves, and other home-grown mammals look as exotic to most visitors as the African creatures displayed at other parks. Information: Hersheypark, 100 W Hersheypark Dr., Hershey, PA 17033 (717 534-3900). See also *Pennsylvania Dutch Country,* DIRECTIONS.

THE OLD COUNTRY, Williamsburg, Virginia: Run by the people who operate Busch Gardens in Tampa, this is one of the most beautiful US parks. The site — 360 acres of ravine-cut woodlands — is one large reason. Not much of it has been manicured or tamed, and the rides (Rhine cruises, steam train trips, a log flume, and the like) have been chosen and installed to make the most of the scenery. The Loch Ness Monster — an absolutely terrifying double-looped, upside-down roller coaster that drops riders 114 feet in 5 seconds — is one of the best rides in the country, and the new Big Bad Wolf roller coaster travels seemingly out of control through the wooded ravines. The food stands out, too; you'll find not only hamburgers, but also European specialties — sausages, cheeses, pastas, tortes. And, as befits a park with a European theme, there are musical revues, oompah bands, strolling entertainers, concerts by top performers, import shops, and a giant Festhaus — a party hall like those in Munich, except that this one is twice the size of a football field. Visiting the Old

Country makes a fine complement to sightseeing around Colonial Williamsburg. (See *Tidewater Virginia*, DIRECTIONS.) Information: PO Drawer FC, Williamsburg, VA 23187 (804 253-3350).

KINGS DOMINION, Richmond, Virginia: Great roller coasters — not just the double, wooden racing roller coaster (one of three similar chillers in the US), but also a loop-the-loop that catapults you through a vertical loop, and then reverses the whole procedure and drops you into a 168-foot-long slide. The newest attractions are the fifth coaster, a whitewater raft ride, a stand-up looping coaster, and the 17-story-high Lost World, a manmade mountain that conceals three different adventures. Fred Flintstone and other Hanna-Barbera characters entertain. Information: Kings Dominion, Doswell, VA 23047 (804 876-5000).

CAROWINDS, Charlotte, North Carolina: The theme is Carolina's history, with a good assortment of rides and shows and five coasters, including one that turns riders upside down four times and a wild whitewater rapids ride. There's also Smurf Island. Information: Carowinds, PO Box 240516, Charlotte, NC 28224 (704 588-2600).

SOUTH

OPRYLAND, Nashville, Tennessee: The 120-acre wooded site on the banks of the Cumberland River on the edge of this southern city was pretty to begin with, and the architects made the most of the landscape by leaving all but a handful of the original trees while adding dozens of their own, and hundreds of flowers. The park is a treat to behold. But Opryland really shines when it comes to music — not just country and bluegrass, as you might expect, but also rock 'n' roll, gospel, Broadway show tunes, and more; up to a dozen stage shows each year, with over 350 performers. There are thrill rides, too: a twisting corkscrew roller coaster; the wild Grizzly River Rampage (a/k/a G-R-R), a huge and satisfyingly long whitewater rafting adventure; a bobsled adventure; and more. Every Memorial Day weekend, the big Opryland Gospel Jubilee brings some of the country's top-name gospel groups to the park; throughout the year, television specials are taped in the park (and tickets are free to park guests). The park is part of Opryland USA, a complex which also includes the Grand Ole Opry and the General Jackson showboat, an entertainment palace that cruises the Cumberland River. Information: Opryland Information Center, 2802 Opryland Dr., Nashville, TN 37214 (615 889-6611).

SIX FLAGS OVER GEORGIA, Atlanta, Georgia: Loosely themed around the six countries whose flags have flown over Georgia, Six Flags climbs a forested hillside on the western edge of the city. There are graded paths for strolling, gazebos for sitting and inhaling the sweet Southern air, and plenty of Coca-Cola and watermelon. The roller coaster, the Great American Scream Machine, ripples around a reflecting lake that makes it seem even higher than it really is; one of the scariest around. In addition to that, a *triple* loop coaster, a whitewater raft trip, and 39-odd other rides, there are Looney Toons characters, live shows, magicians, and, in summer, fireworks. By the way, the six flags belong to Britain, France, Spain, the US, the Confederacy, and of course, the state of Georgia. Information: Six Flags Over Georgia, PO Box 43187, Atlanta, GA 30378 (404 948-9290).

WALT DISNEY WORLD, Lake Buena Vista, Florida: Phenomenally successful in its first decade, this 43-square-mile resort complex holds even more promise for its second since the October 1, 1982, opening of the $1 billion EPCOT Center. More than twice the size of the Magic Kingdom — WDW's Disneyland-like rides and attractions area — this new "thinking man's theme park" examines technology and global cultures in a number of pavilions that feature some of Disney's most advanced special effects to date. Yet the 45 attractions of the Magic Kingdom, presided over by that fairytale castle, and River Country, the ultimate in old-fashioned swimming holes, look as terrific as ever. So do the three golf courses, the tennis courts, the one-of-a-kind campground, the dinner shows, the shopping village, and the spiffy resorts. Information: Walt Disney World, PO Box 40, Lake Buena Vista, FL 32830 (305 824-4321; for reservations, 305 824-8000). See also *Orlando,* THE AMERICAN CITIES.

BUSCH GARDENS, THE DARK CONTINENT, Tampa, Florida: Africa, the Dark Continent, is the theme of this 300-acre family entertainment center, where even the names of the seven distinctly different amusement areas evoke the exotic — Nairobi, Marrakech, the Congo, and so forth. A pair of rare white Bengal tigers (2 out of less than 100 existing in zoos worldwide) are among the more than 3,000 animals here, many of whom roam freely among the park's plains and waterways. Bird gardens, bazaars, belly dancers, and snake charmers are among the dazzling array of attractions. And of course there are rides, the newest being the Phoenix, a looping boat swing. Information: Busch Gardens, 3000 Busch Blvd., Tampa, FL 33612 (813 971-8282).

SIX FLAGS OVER TEXAS, Arlington, Texas: Also developed around the theme of six countries that have, over the years, called Texas their colony (Mexico, Spain, France, the Republic of Texas, the Confederacy, the US), Six Flags Over Texas, halfway between Dallas and Fort Worth, was the first of the successful theme parks. When it was founded in 1961, it would have been called "Texas Under Six Flags" but for the protest of a Texas director that "Texas ain't never been under nuthin'." Summers are hot — but nearly everything that can be air conditioned is. The assortment of rides and good clean fun entertainment is similar to that at its sister park in Atlanta. Information: Six Flags Over Texas, PO Box 191, Arlington, TX 76010 (817 640-8900).

ASTROWORLD, Houston, Texas: Another member of the Six Flags organization, this park is big, clean, as glossy as the Space City itself, and full of rides (over 100 of them) and attractions for the entire family, including a replica of the famous Coney Island Cyclone — one of the most exciting roller coasters ever built — a stomach-churning shuttle loop coaster, a wild river rapids ride, and Houston's only water recreation park, WaterWorld, as well as the Southern Star Amphitheatre, a 9-acre concert facility. Information: Astroworld, 9001 Kirby Dr., Houston, TX 77054 (713 799-8404).

MIDWEST

CEDAR POINT, Sandusky, Ohio: While many other old-fashioned amusement parks went into decline around 1960, this fixture of the Great Lakes summer scene was just getting renovated, with the finest of results. There's a midway that really looks like one instead of some make-believe European country and a host of nifty one-of-a-kind rides: Gemini (a traditional racing wooden coaster whose 125-foot-high first hill drops 118 feet at a 55° angle); one of the tallest Ferris wheels in the world (with views out over Lake Erie, which laps at the boundaries of the park); a movie theater with a 67-by-88-foot screen that makes you feel you're part of the action; five theaters of live shows; five carousels; an enormous arcade; and a marine complex where you can watch performing dolphins and sea lions. Cedar Point has 54 rides, the newest being Thunder Canyon, in which 12-passenger rafts splash through 1,600 feet of rapids, waterfalls, and canyons. Stay at the big, rambling *Hotel Breakers,* built in 1905 and fitted out with Tiffany stained glass windows and chandeliers. Knute Rockne, who perfected the forward pass on the Cedar Point beach, married an employee of the hotel. Information: Cedar Point, CN 5006, Sandusky, OH 44870 (419 626-0830).

KINGS ISLAND, near Cincinnati, Ohio: A family entertainment center with more than 100 rides and attractions, Kings Island features the world's longest, highest, and fastest wooden roller coaster, the Beast, and the country's first stand-up coaster, the incredible King Kobra. On the 1,600-acre grounds, there are also two golf courses, the College Football Hall of Fame, a 275-room resort hotel, and a campground. Information: Kings Island, Kings Island, OH 45034 (513 241-5600).

SIX FLAGS OVER MID-AMERICA, Eureka, Missouri: Like the other parks in the chain, this one near St. Louis will show you a something-for-everyone good time. The 200-acre park also features Thunder River, a whitewater raft ride, Colossus: The Giant Wheel, and the Screamin' Eagle roller coaster — no longer the highest and fastest of them all, but still plenty exciting. Information: Six Flags Over Mid-America, PO Box 60, Eureka, MO 63025 (314 938-5300).

SIX FLAGS GREAT AMERICA, Gurnee, Illinois: This addition to the ever-growing Six Flags chain has added some rides and attractions — in 1986, a giant water slide, and in 1985, Z Force, a state-of-the-art roller coaster with six vertical loops — but the Americana-drenched rest of it hasn't changed. It still has the same theme areas — Orleans Place, Yukon Territory, and so on; plus a Farmers' Market (food stands where you can get Mexican and Italian specialties, Belgian waffles, deli sandwiches, made-from-scratch french fries, and more, in a compact area); bands playing march music and Dixieland; giant loop roller coasters; a reproduction of an antique 100-foot-high double-decker carousel; and the Pictorium, a movie theater where the image projected measures 70 by 96 feet. Also a variety of Broadway-style original show productions. Other highlights include an exciting whitewater raft ride and one of the world's largest double-racing wooden roller coasters. Information: Six Flags Great America, PO Box 1776, Gurnee, IL 60031 (312 249-1776).

WEST

DISNEYLAND, Anaheim, California: This original dream of Walt Disney's is as fantastic as you've probably heard, as magical as Tinker Bell's fairy dust, and perfect to the last detail. Thrill rides aren't the big deal. Instead, you have "adventures" — you get bombarded by cannonballs fired by pirates in the Caribbean, visit a haunted mansion, explore the frontier, or fly through outer space. The special effects are truly astounding. During the summer Main Street Electrical Parade, floats and creatures are outlined in thousands of tiny white lights — supercalifragilisticexpialidocious. Ditto for the renovated Fantasyland, whose old-fashioned kiddie attractions were treated to some $55 million of Disney's most magical special effects. Speaking of special effects, *Captain EO,* a 3-D musical space video produced by George Lucas, directed by Francis Ford Coppola, and starring Michael Jackson, is the park's newest attraction, appearing in Tomorrowland. For a list of nearby lodgings and other vacation aids, write to the Anaheim Area Visitor and Convention Bureau, PO Box 4270, Anaheim, CA 92803 (714 999-8939). For Disneyland information: Guest Relations Office, 1313 Harbor Blvd., Anaheim, CA 92803 (714 999-4565).

KNOTT'S BERRY FARM, Buena Park, California: This park just down the road from Disneyland started out as, yes, a berry farm, then grew like Topsy when Mrs. Walter Knott began serving chicken dinners and Mr. Walter Knott took to concocting entertainments to amuse people who queued up for Mrs. Knott's chicken. It isn't another Disneyland. Nor is it an Opryland. Old things — antiques — are scattered throughout two of the five sections (a Mexican village, a Roaring 20s area and airfield, a ghost town, and Camp Snoopy, a children's park), so here and there you'll spot an old wagon wheel, some airplane parts, narrow-gauge locomotives, or an antique carousel powered by mules. In addition to the rides (about 30 in all, including some real white-knucklers), you can watch can-can dancers, marionettes, a summer ice show, a singing and dancing extravaganza; and play games in the largest arcade west of the Mississippi. And there's plenty of good eating right on the grounds: Sicilian pizza, extra-juicy hot dogs, barbecued ribs, among other things — if you don't want Mrs. Knott's fried chicken, that is. Information: Anaheim Area Visitor and Convention Bureau (address above) for area information; Knott's Berry Farm, 8039 Beach Blvd., Buena Park, CA 90620 (714 220-5200).

SIX FLAGS MAGIC MOUNTAIN, Valencia, California: The third in a trio of Southern California diversions, Magic Mountain is the place to go to get spun around, shaken like a rag doll, and flipped head over heels till you almost wished you'd stayed home. There are, in fact, so many coasters and spinning wheel rides that for years the place looked more like a test ground for scaffolding than a place to have a good time. No longer, though: It's green and clean as a whistle. And one area, Spillikin Handcrafter's Junction, is almost funky: You can watch craftsmen turning pots, blowing glass, working with leather and wood — and then buy the products. And since the Six Flags organization took over, the place has really blossomed, with a new dolphin and dive show, a water skiing pageant, the Animal Farm and Petting Zoo, and music and dance revues, so that the offerings are more balanced than ever before; you can have a good time even if you don't go on the rides. Looney Toons cartoon characters are the new park mascots. Lodging information: Greater Los Angeles Visitors and Convention Bureau, 505 S Flower St., Los Angeles, CA 90071 (213 239-0200). Information: Magic Mountain, 26101 Magic Mountain Pky., PO Box 5500, Valencia, CA 91355 (805 255-4100 or 818 992-0884).

GREAT AMERICA, Santa Clara, California: Though no longer owned by the Marriott Corporation, this 100-acre park — the largest family entertainment center in northern California — continues to offer a crowd-pleasing combination of live stage shows, games, shops, and thrill rides. Most breathtaking of the latter is The Edge, a free-fall ride that drops you 60 feet in 2½ seconds. Among the other attractions are a double-decker carousel, a 200-foot skytower, and the IMAX film 'An American Adventure,' projected onto a screen that's 7 stories high and 500 feet wide. The film's overall effect — in which you actually *feel* as if you're bobsledding in Lake Placid, New York, or swooping down over the Grand Canyon in a plane — can be dizzying. Information: Great America, PO Box 1776, Santa Clara, CA 95052 (408 988-1776).

America's Best Resort Hotels

American resorts are playgrounds for adults — full of golf courses, tennis courts, horseback riding trails and horse stables, bike paths, hiking paths, swimming pools, lake beaches, and other facilities too costly for the average homeowner's backyard.

Any decent resort should offer these kinds of activities. The list below is a selection of American resorts that give just a bit more — more activities, better service, greater style — or simply have just a bit more panache than their competitors. For any resort you will pay more than for a hotel or motel. At our choices, prices are likely to be even higher. But remember: Rates are usually reduced — sometimes cut in half — during off-season (the timing of which will vary depending upon where the resort is, and when it experiences its heaviest crowds). When you are budgeting, be sure to ask whether greens fees, tennis court fees, and the costs of other activities are included in the price of your room. If not, they can add as much as $25 or $30 a day or more to your budget.

EAST

THE BALSAMS GRAND RESORT HOTEL, Dixville Notch, New Hampshire: This fairy-tale castle — immense and white, with red tile roofs — sits at the base of 800-foot cliffs alongside a manmade lake, surrounded by 15,000 acres of the forests and stony peaks of northernmost New Hampshire. The 6,842-yard Donald Ross 18-hole golf course, built against the side of a mountain and full of sloping fairways, is a challenge; even the 9-hole executive course, a mere 2,020 yards long, will require every club in your bag. There's also tennis, swimming, hiking, trout fishing, and, in winter, downhill and cross-country skiing. Information: The Balsams, Dixville Notch, NH 03576 (603 255-3400 or 800 255-0800 in New Hampshire; 800 255-0600 elsewhere).

MOUNTAIN VIEW HOUSE, Whitefield, New Hampshire: In continuous operation since 1865, this hostelry set on a plateau overlooking the Presidential Range reflects every bit of the care that has been bestowed on it. Witness the magnificent flower arrangements on all the tables in the comfortable but well-put-together public rooms, and the immaculate grooming of the golf course, a 9-holer that can be played off two sets of tees as 18 holes. There's also tennis, hiking, an Olympic-sized swimming pool, movies, and nightly entertainment. Information: Mountain View House, Whitefield, NH 03598 (603 837-2511; 800 THE VIEW, from other New England states).

SPALDING INN & CLUB, Whitefield, New Hampshire: Not far from *Mountain View House,* this snug resort shares its certain feeling of gracious but unpretentious elegance that's encountered at few other hotels in the country. The maintenance is superb, from the lawns and gardens and white-trimmed clubhouse and cottages to the 4 clay tennis courts, the 9 holes of par 3 golf, and the heated swimming pool. But the *Spalding Inn & Club* is perhaps best known for its lawn bowling green, and several national competitions have been held here. The resort runs on the full American plan, and the food is good and interesting enough to quell any desire you may have to eat around. Information: Spalding Inn & Club, Whitefield, NH 03598 (603 837-2572).

THE OTESAGA, Cooperstown, New York: The building's fine turn-of-the-century Georgian exterior with its large columns and its stately colonnaded lobby is a good deal more formal than the resort itself, which is mannerly but not straight-laced. You can swim in Lake Otsego, at the foot of the resort's lawns, or go sailing, fishing, golfing, or tennis playing. There's a wonderful noontime buffet, a heated pool, nightly dancing. Cooperstown, of course, is a village of museums: the Farmers' Museum, the Baseball Hall of Fame, the Fenimore House. Information: The Otesaga, Box 311, Cooperstown, NY 13326 (607 547-9931).

GROSSINGER'S, Grossinger, New York: At this giant Catskills resort, you won't find just one Olympic-sized swimming pool but two; not one golf course but two; and health clubs for both men and women; 16 tennis courts; all kinds of activities, lectures and demonstrations, and after-dark entertainment; a lively day camp for youngsters through age 17; skating, skiing, snowmobiling, and tobogganing in winter; and so many other facilities that it's difficult to take advantage of everything. But it's a rare guest who, upon returning home, doesn't give top billing to the food. For as long as anyone can remember, a stay at *Grossinger's* has been nearly synonymous with great food and lots of it. There's more food at breakfast, lunch, and dinner than you can possibly eat — but it's so good that few have the inclination to leave it untouched. And when the waiters and waitresses (who won't take no for an answer) scurry to the kitchen and bring more, gourmands in the crowd polish their plates once again. The kitchen is kosher (meat and dairy products are prepared and served separately). Information: Grossinger's Hotel, Grossinger, NY 12734 (914 292-5000 or 800 874-7480 in New York State; 800 431-6300 elsewhere).

THE BASIN HARBOR CLUB, Vergennes, Vermont: In its tenth decade of summer resort operation, and in the fourth generation of the Beach Family proprietorship, the *Basin Harbor Club* sits right on the banks of Lake Champlain some 20 miles from the Shelburne Museum in Shelburne. It's clearly an operation designed for a well-heeled clientele but appears far more informal than most, more like an assemblage of summer homes at an exclusive lake resort. Which makes sense, since lodging is in 77 cottages (some beautifully appointed, some as modest as most people's lake resort places) and a modestly sized lodge. You'll find a 3,200-foot grass airstrip, tennis courts, swimming pool, boats for rent, a children's program, and a maritime museum. The golf course was treated to a massive, 5-year reconstruction program, and the rocks along the shore of Lake Champlain are great for sunning. On July 4, the resort celebrates with a buffet breakfast, brass band performances and a big fireworks display. Open from mid-June to mid-October. Information: Basin Harbor Club, Vergennes, VT 05491 (802 475-2311).

WOODSTOCK INN, Woodstock, Vermont: The town, a picture-postcard affair whose village green is rimmed by colonial homes and presided over by church steeples boasting four Paul Revere bells, deserved an inn like this; but when the old Woodstock Inn burned, nobody really expected a new hostelry quite so fine as this Rockresort. You can swim, play tennis on any of 10 courts or golf on a superb Robert Trent Jones course, go biking — or, in the area, shop for antiques, go horseback riding, or hike in the forests. In winter, you can ski downhill at Suicide Six, cross-country on any number of trails, go for sleigh rides, and more. There are special holiday celebrations for Thanksgiving, Christmas, and Washington's Birthday. Information: Woodstock Inn & Resort, Woodstock, VT 05091 (802 457-1100).

SOUTH

MARRIOTT'S GRAND HOTEL, Point Clear, Alabama: A rambling structure of weathered cypress occupies a corner of a 600-acre expanse of live oaks and spreading pines that grow right down to the soft white sand that edges Mobile Bay. The extensive facilities include 36 holes of golf, card rooms, a swimming beach and a freshwater pool, sailboats for sailing, speedboats for water skiing, courts for tennis, bikes for cycling, greens for lawn bowls, and a big air conditioned yacht for Gulf of Mexico fishing trips. But the atmosphere is low key and nobody feels obliged to scurry around to take advantage of it all. Information: Grand Hotel, Point Clear, AL 36564 (205 928-9201).

BOCA BEACH CLUB, at Boca Raton Hotel & Club, Boca Raton, Florida: You know you're entering a special place from the moment you arrive: Cozy armchairs and a goblet of champagne or a flagon of fresh orange juice are offered even before you check in; and registration is accomplished at lovely antique desks attended by a smiling, attentive staff. The guest rooms are large and tastefully furnished, and the club's site on a spit of land between the Intracoastal Waterway and the Atlantic guarantees a watery vista no matter where your room is. The best rooms in the house, however, are those on the ground floor: they offer lanais for lounging and direct access to the beach on the Atlantic side. There are also two large pools, and guests have access to the numerous tennis courts, the golf course, and the considerable other amenities of the sprawling 940-room resort complex of which it represents just one section. Information: Boca Raton Hotel and Club, 501 E Camino Real, Boca Raton, FL 33432-6127 (305 395-3000).

THE BREAKERS, Palm Beach, Florida: American millionaires built this great marble palace of a hotel — the third on the property — in 1925-26 to show Europeans that they had taste, and so it is filled with Flemish tapestries, watercolors and oils, crystal chandeliers, hand-painted and vaulted ceilings, and other works by some 1,200 craftsmen. On the 140-acre property are some large cottages, rental apartments, condominiums, two 18-hole golf courses including the Breakers Ocean (one of the best courses on Florida's east coast), 14 tennis courts, a croquet lawn, a private beach, and a heated, Olympic-size outdoor pool. Information: The Breakers, Palm Beach, FL 33480 (305 655-6611).

THE WORLD OF PALM-AIRE, Pompano Beach, Florida: This low-slung white stucco hotel and spa, whose sweeping lawns are brightened by an explosion of begonias, impatiens, and orange trees loaded with ripe fruit, has been around since 1971 — and attracting spa lovers like Elizabeth Taylor ever since. Just 15 minutes from the beach, it offers a complete range of spa facilities, from the Olympic-size pool and Nautilus equipment to the steam rooms, saunas, whirlpools, Swiss showers, and racquetball courts. Massages, salt-glow treatments, loofah scrubs, exercise classes, stress management seminars, and other special programs keep guests busy between rounds on the five golf courses and 37 tennis courts. Information: The World of Palm-Aire, 2501 Palm-Aire Dr. N, Pompano Beach, FL 33069 (305 972-3300; 800 327-4960 outside Florida).

DON CESAR BEACH RESORT, St. Petersburg Beach, Florida: Away from the noise and traffic downtown, this pink, Moorish-style establishment on the National Register of Historic Places was renovated not long ago — with such a lavish hand that it's now unsurpassed in the area. The rooms are plush, with thick carpeting, solid traditional furnishings, and Italian marble; the public rooms are done up in Mexican tiles and marble and include a couple of the fountains that were installed when the hotel was built in 1928. Activities include swimming in the heated pool (right on the Gulf of Mexico), health club treatments and workouts, bicycling, sailing, tennis, fishing, and even windsurfing. Information: Don Cesar Beach Resort Hotel, 3400 Gulf Blvd., St. Petersburg Beach, FL 33706 (813 360-1881).

THE KING AND PRINCE, St. Simons Island, Georgia: The centerpiece of this unpretentious 1930s Spanish-style palacio-by-the-sea is the splendid dining room, a former ballroom hung with a quartet of vast brass chandeliers and lined on both sides with arched windows that look out over the surf-pounded Atlantic (illuminated after dark). The resort has beautiful rooms with lazy ceiling fans, suites with sunken living rooms and entrances directly on the beach, contemporary villas, and lounges full of Chinese Chippendale and Queen Anne furniture with a panoramic view of the ocean. It's all very quietly elegant, but not so stuffy that you feel embarrassed to walk barefoot outside. Activities: golf, tennis, swimming, riding, biking, surf fishing. Information: King and Prince Hotel, PO Box 798, St. Simons Island, GA 31522 (912 638-3631).

THE CLOISTER, Sea Island, Georgia: This famous old Georgia shore resort — one of the East Coast's most noteworthy — is the kind of almost clubby place to which young people who came here originally on vacation with their parents return on their honeymoon, then come back time and time again, bringing their own youngsters; where, even when guests don't know each other at the start, conversations come easily, simply because everyone shares (if nothing else) a dedication to the resort's old-fashioned good manners. That means dressy evenings of dinner and dancing, and afternoons on the tennis courts or the links (absolutely superb; see *Golf*), or riding, shooting, fishing, boating, cycling, or swimming (either at the beach or in two lovely pools). The facilities are first-class all the way, the grounds are immaculately kept, and the 260-plus rooms all look so fresh that even regulars marvel. Information: The Cloister, Sea Island, GA 31561 (912 638-3611; 800 SEA ISLAND).

PINEHURST HOTEL AND COUNTRY CLUB, Pinehurst, North Carolina: Founded by a Yankee soda fountain manufacturer named James Tufts, Pinehurst quickly became known as a golf center; even before the turn of the century, there were complaints from dairy workers about golfers harassing the cows. But Pinehurst offers an abundance of delights in addition to golf (for more about which, see *Golf*): the 13,000 acres of grounds, laid out by the firm of Frederick Law Olmsted (the landscape architect who gave New York its Central Park), for instance. The tennis. The gun club, which is the site of more than a dozen trap and skeet tournaments annually. And the sailing on 200-acre Lake Pinehurst; the archery range; the hay rides, carriage tours, and trail rides; the jogging trails; the rental bicycles; and the complete health spa. It all adds up to one of the most invigorating — as well as one of the friendliest — big resorts around. Accommodations are in a gracious hotel furnished with antiques and in a couple of hundred spiffy, well-fitted-out villas. Information: Pinehurst Hotel and Country Club, PO Box 4000, Pinehurst, NC 28374 (800 672-4644 in North Carolina, 800 334-9560 elsewhere).

THE HOMESTEAD, Hot Springs, Virginia: One of the very finest American resorts, this complex of impressive red brick buildings has immense colonnaded salons where piano music accompanies high tea every day and health clubs where you can soak in mineral baths or take saunas or get massaged within an inch of your life. You can go swimming, play tennis or golf on any of three wooded courses, go riding through the 15,000 acres of Allegheny Mountain forests that belong to the resort, or pass an evening dining and dancing in dressed-up style. This is a big hotel (600 rooms), but it's so well ordered that you can hardly tell when the house is full. Information: The Homestead, Hot Springs, VA 24445 (703 839-5500).

THE TIDES INN, Irvington, Virginia: A gracious establishment founded in 1947 on a peninsula on the western shore of Chesapeake Bay about an hour's drive from Williamsburg or Richmond, this resort follows the best tradition of family-owned resorts, with fine service and elegant facilities — yachting, all-weather and fast-dry tennis courts, a swimming pool overlooking the Rappahannock River, a putting green, a 9-hole par 3 golf course, Sir Guy Campbell's 6,500-yard 18-hole course, George Cobb's 7,000-yard championship 18, and dining salons where the cutlery is real silver. The feeling at the *Tides Lodge,* across the inlet, is rustic-modern, casual — completely different. Information: Tides Inn, Irvington, VA 22480 (804 438-5000 or 800 552-3461 in Virginia; 800 446-9981 elsewhere).

THE GREENBRIER, White Sulphur Springs, West Virginia: Staying here will take you back to the Ginger Rogers–Fred Astaire era: You can't help but feel like dressing for dinner and going dancing in the Old White Club afterward — despite the fact that it's also difficult not to wear yourself out on the riding trails, hiking paths, tennis courts, and golf courses that fill up the hotel's 6,500 acres. Everything about this place is elegant, from the endless string of parlors ornamented with Chinese vases and priceless screens, centuries-old oil paintings, real English antique furniture and such, to the long menu full of every conceivable fish, fowl, meat, salad, appetizer, dessert, to the accommodations in comfortable bedrooms and "cottages," a short walk away from the hotel, like Fifth Avenue apartments. Information: The Greenbrier, White Sulphur Springs, WV 24986 (304 536-1110 or 800 624-6070).

MIDWEST

GRAND HOTEL, Mackinac Island, Michigan: The fact that there are no cars on this island gives it a turn-of-the-century feel you'll seldom find elsewhere in the US today; the hotel simply completes the picture. A rambling white structure with 275 rooms, set on 500 acres of lawns, gardens, and trees adjoining a 2,000-acre state park and overlooking the Straits of Mackinac, the recently renovated *Grand Hotel* is old-fashioned from the pillared veranda (so long you could barely recognize a friend standing at the opposite end) to the horse-drawn surreys that meet guests at the ferry, the afternoon teas, the ornate staircase, and the 19th-century furnishings. By some accounts, this is the world's largest summer resort. Cycling, riding, golf, and tennis are the activities. Closed November to mid-May. Information: Grand Hotel, Mackinac Island, MI 49757 (906 847-3331).

WEST

THE BOULDERS, Carefree, Arizona: This is a Rockresort in both senses. Opened in January 1985 by the organization whose name is synonymous with luxurious enclaves, it is set on 1,300 acres of desert foothills, at the base of towering piles of immense rocks that gave the *Boulders* its name. The resort's 120 adobe-colored casitas blend remarkably well with the surrounding stones, and while the landscape has been tamed slightly to allow for construction, the proliferation of desert vegetation has actually been enhanced. Walking from any guest room to the nearby lodge for a meal is to stroll through an entire spectrum of cactus varieties, to say nothing of sage and desert honeysuckle. The interior landscape is equally impressive: each casita contains a room with wet bar, large oval tub, and mesquite-log-burning fireplace. For recreation, there are six tennis courts, three first-class 9-hole golf courses, and access to horseback riding on desert trails. Information: The Boulders, PO Box 2090, Carefree, AZ 85377 (602 488-9009).

THE WIGWAM, Litchfield Park, Arizona: One of the top resorts in the country, founded around World War I as an R&R spot for Goodyear Tire and Rubber Company executives, this establishment offers 225 rooms in one- and two-story adobe casitas surrounded by palm- and eucalyptus-shaded gardens. Golf is the main activity because of the two excellent Robert Trent Jones courses — the 7,220-yard Gold Course, cleverly filled with sand traps, and the much easier 6,107-yard Blue Course, par 70, which offers well-bunkered fairways and many water holes. A third course designed by Robert Lawrence plays 6,861 yards (par 72). There are also 8 tennis courts (6 of them lighted), plus ball machines, practice alleys, and a good program of clinics and private instruction. Other activities: horseback riding, steak broils, shuffleboard and lawn sports, swimming in two big pools, and full health club facilities. Closed from June to mid-September. Information: The Wigwam, Litchfield Park, AZ 85340 (602 935-3811).

ARIZONA BILTMORE, Phoenix, Arizona: Frank Lloyd Wright's ideas were part of the inspiration for this grand duchess of desert resorts designed by his admirer Albert Chase McArthur. The place sports some very Gatsby-esque features, including the gold-leaf ceiling in the dining room and the glass mural in the lobby. The kitchen is good enough to bring diners from all over the valley, and there are afternoon teas in season and an endless assortment of facilities — 17 lighted tennis courts, two 18-hole golf courses, three swimming pools (one of them lined with Catalina tile, comparable to the one at William Randolph Hearst's San Simeon). Information: Arizona Biltmore, 24th St. and Missouri, Phoenix, AZ 85016 (602 955-6600; for reservations, 800 528-3696 outside Arizona).

MARRIOTT'S CAMELBACK INN, Scottsdale, Arizona: This resort at the foot of Mummy Mountain, facing its namesake across the valley, was built in 1935 of adobe mud dug up for the foundation; and in recent years, the total number of rooms on the 120 acres has expanded to about 420. To accommodate all the guests there are 2 swimming pools, 10 tennis courts, 2 of the fancier of the area's 18-holers, as well as a staff big enough to make room service and overall maintenance head and shoulders above that of most far smaller establishments. You can also go biking, hiking, riding on an Indian reservation a few miles away; play Ping-Pong, billiards, shuffleboard — or get massaged by the whirlpools. Information: Marriott's Camelback Inn, PO Box 70, Scottsdale, AZ 85252 (602 948-1700).

SONOMA MISSION INN & SPA, Sonoma, California: A $7.5 million renovation in 1980 rescued this three-story, 97-room wine country establishment built in 1926 from a sorry post-Depression decay. And the result — as proclaimed by magazines from *W* and *Vogue* to *Money* and *Interior Design* — is one of the most spectacular resorts on the West Coast. Another major refurbishing in 1986 added 70 rooms, many with fireplaces and balconies. The mission decor of the original building is still there, but the effect is at the same time very up-to-the-minute. The guest quarters, done up in shades of terra cotta, camel, or taupe, are both warm and contemporary; they have shutters, ceiling fans, and half canopies on the beds. The inn's spa has become northern California's answer to the Golden Door; its packaged weight loss and conditioning programs have attracted celebrities such as Albert Finney, Margaux Hemingway, Joel Grey, James Garner, and Linda Evans. Information: Sonoma Mission Inn & Spa, PO Box 1447, Sonoma, CA 95476 (707 938-9000).

THE LODGE AT PEBBLE BEACH, Pebble Beach, California: The California coast — "The finest meeting place of land and water in existence," according to one admirer — deserves no less than this magnificent hotel. The interior is only a part of the charm. The Pebble Beach Golf Links, a leading contender for the title of "most photographed golf course," and the Robert Trent Jones Spyglass Hill golf course are among the most famous in existence, for good reason; they're also among the few tournament-class courses open to the public. And there are still other courses in Pebble Beach. If you don't like golf, you can go shopping in nearby Carmel; sightseeing along the celebrated Seventeen Mile Drive, with magnificent views of the rocky shore; horseback riding through the private 5,328-acre Del Monte Forest, which surrounds the lodge; swimming; or play tennis at the nearby Beach and Tennis Club. Information: The Lodge at Pebble Beach, Seventeen Mile Dr., Pebble Beach, CA 93953 (408 624-3811).

MARRIOTT'S SANTA BARBARA BILTMORE, Santa Barbara, California: The sections of the hotel's 21 Montecito acres not taken up with the Spanish mission–style buildings that house the guest rooms are filled with gardens of eucalyptus, junipers, monkey trees, and oaks. The rooms are luxurious — with oversize beds, good mattresses, oversize showerheads, and Royal Velvet bath towels. There's an Olympic-sized swimming pool across from the hotel, plus an additional one on the property, 3 lighted tennis courts, and a ¼-mile-long beach. In the area, there's golf, fishing, and tennis. Summer, when daytime temperatures are in the eighties are moderated by a constant ocean breeze, is the prime season. Information: Marriott's Santa Barbara Biltmore, 1260 Channel Dr., Santa Barbara, CA 93108 (805 969-2261).

THE BROADMOOR, Colorado Springs, Colorado: When this magnificent hostelry was built by mining magnate Spencer Penrose and Charles Tutt in 1918, it was with the idea that this would be one of the world's most fashionable hotels, that it would be "permanent and perfect." It is. One of the interesting things about the *Broadmoor* is that in late winter and early spring you can sometimes enjoy winter and summer sports in the same day — skiing in the morning, for instance, golf or tennis in the afternoon. As for the venerable main building itself, it's everything you'd expect of a structure put up with the assistance of hundreds of European craftsmen: Not only are there art objects from around the world in all the public rooms, but incredible ornamentation embellishes walls, ceilings, and floors alike. Information: The Broadmoor, PO Box 1439, Colorado Springs, CO 80901 (303 634-7711).

THE WESTIN MAUNA KEA, Kamuela, Hawaii, Hawaii: Some say this is the most fantastic work yet of Laurance Rockefeller, the major domo of the Rockresorts group that originally developed this property along with a handful of other fantastic, one-of-a-kind, built-from-scratch luxury resort hotels. Now managed by Westin Hotels, the *Mauna Kea* seems to have grown up out of the landscape; it's an asset to the surroundings rather than an eyesore. There are many diversions: an infuriating Robert Trent Jones golf course with stupendous Pacific views from every green, 13 tennis courts, a splendid white sand beach, a swimming pool, a 65-foot catamaran, riding, snorkeling, scuba diving, and windsurfing. Hunting expeditions can be arranged, as can helicopter sightseeing trips, launched from the hotel's own helipad. All over the hotel there are artifacts from Asia and the Pacific — food implements and ancient ceremonial bowls, tapas, masks, tikis — and art conservators from the staff of the Bishop Museum to take care of them. Information: Mauna Kea Resort, Kohala Coast, HI 96743 (808 882-7222).

MAUNA LANI BAY HOTEL, Kawaihea, Hawaii, Hawaii: Even before its opening in 1983, it was widely predicted that this 350-room arrow-shaped hotel, built on 3,200 acres atop a prehistoric lava flow where the early Hawaiians settled around AD 750, would be Hawaii's most luxurious. And, as it has turned out, that is not far from true. Guests are greeted with fresh orange juice and leis. The lobby resembles a rain forest, complete with palm trees, waterfalls, and a credible lagoon. The guest rooms, done up in ivory and burgundy, are no less striking. The same goes for the four restaurants, including the elegant Bay Terrace, which serves mullet from the ancient spring-fed fish ponds that once provided fish to the *alii.* Some 40 acres of the property have been preserved as a historic park and can be explored on a number of walking trails. Those of a less studious bent may opt for swimming at the pool or beach, the outrigger canoe rides, the helicopter tours, tennis on one of the 10 courts, or the golf on 18 holes whose green fairways snake through black lava broken by coastal inlets; though the course is not as imposing as it may first appear, the occasional cavorting of migrating whales not half a mile from the sixth tee can be distracting. An interesting children's program, Camp Mauna Lani, is run at various times each year. Information: Mauna Lani Bay Hotel, Box 4000, Kawaikea, HI 96742 (808 367-2323 or 808 885-6622).

HALEKULANI, Honolulu, Oahu, Hawaii: Many generations of Waikiki visitors who have noted the truth in this venerable hostelry's name, which means "house befitting heaven," should be more than pleased with the recent $125 million renovation and expansion that have transformed a rather intimate 190-room establishment into a modern, but still remarkably personable, 456-room resort. The new design incorporates the restored two-story main building of the original hotel into a complex of multilevel structures surrounding tranquil courtyards and gardens. The *House Without a Key* restaurant, immortalized in one of Earl Derr Biggers's Charlie Chan novels, has been rebuilt on the same spot, and the old bungalow rooms have been replaced by large, luxurious, expansively balconied guest rooms, most facing the Pacific. All three restaurants overlook the ocean and Diamond Head, and the famous century-old kiawe tree continues to preside. The striking tiled orchid design accenting the large oceanside pool has come to be a symbol for the hotel itself. Information: The Halekulani, 2199 Kalia Rd., Honolulu, HI 96815 (808 923-2311; 800 367-2343 outside Hawaii).

KAPALUA BAY HOTEL AND VILLAS, Kapalua, Maui, Hawaii: With its fringe of pineapple fields bordered by neat rows of Cook pines, its view of Molokai (looming like a mirage on the horizon), and the landscapes distinguished by banyan trees and delicate yellow oleanders, this northwestern Maui resort hotel is the centerpiece of 750 acres as magnificent as any in Hawaii. And from the latticework of white pillars and bougainvillea-decked crosspieces out front to the grand, open-air, multilevel lobby full of hanging plants, it is as quietly luxurious as the landscape is beautiful. In addition to an array of water sports, there are 10 tennis courts, a pair of 18-hole golf courses that rank among the most distractingly scenic in existence, and a beach right on the doorstep. (The name means "arms embracing the sea.") Exercise classes, wine tastings, garden tours, ikebana (the art of Japanese flower arrangment), and a spectacular daily luncheon that positively invites excess round things out. Information: Kapalua Bay Hotel, One Bay Dr., Kapalua, Maui, HI 96761 (808 669-5656; 800 367-8000 outside Hawaii).

Inn Sites: America's Special Havens

 When standardization finally overtook the hotel industry, at least one great anxiety — where to stay — was removed from travel. Travelers could be assured of finding acceptable accommodations in even the most remote corner of the country. But a new worry arose: What happened to those *special* places, the inns and hostelries with special charm, with atmosphere, with a personal spirit and style and history all their own?

They still exist. The trend toward cookie-cutter construction simply increased the number of hotel and motel rooms; it didn't destroy those unique lodgings that still grace this country from Maine to Oregon. They tend to become the "finds" of lucky patrons who would publish their credit card numbers before they would broadcast the name and location of their favorite hideaway.

But being made of sterner stuff, we offer a listing of *our* favorite places all across this country. Some are traditional New England inns, perfect for a ski weekend or a trip through the forests when the foliage is at its most brilliant; some are luxurious hideaways; some are rugged western lodges where the horses are spirited and the campfire stories tall.

EAST

GRISWOLD INN, Essex, Connecticut: The "Gris" is a favorite port of call for Connecticut River sailors, who may tie up just a few steps from the inn's front door. Landlubbers arriving by car are just as welcome, and all are quickly infused with the friendly spirit radiating with the warmth from the potbellied stove. There's much to catch the eye — an outstanding collection of historic lithographs, steamboat relics, a large collection of historic firearms, many ships' name plaques, and a fine group of marine oils by Antonio Jacobsen. The beds, mostly brass, are in rooms that long ago developed port or starboard lists. But the hospitality and fine New England food more than make up for the absence of plumb joints. Sunday is a special eating day, featuring a buffet-style Hunt Breakfast. The all-you-can-eat groaning board seems about to buckle under everything from eggs and bacon to creamed beef and lamb kidneys. No less than Lucius Beebe acclaimed the Tap Room as "the most handsome barroom in America," and the description is not far from wrong. But it has a rival for the title in the adjacent Covered Bridge Room, which is hung from floor to ceiling with the prints and the paintings in the inn's standout collection. Nightly entertainment ranges from sea chanteys to Dixieland, and throughout December "A 1776 Country Inn Christmas" gives guests a taste of that era, with a special game menu, magicians and madrigal singers, and the staff outfitted in colonial costumes. Information: Griswold Inn, Essex, CT 06426 (203 767-0991). William G. Winterer, innkeeper. 22 rooms.

COPPER BEECH INN, Ivoryton, Connecticut: The decor of this elegant, charming, and immaculate inn installed in a turn-of-the-century Victorian home and now run by Paul and Louise Ebeltoft looks more like your rich old aunt's country estate than a commercial enterprise. There are five airy guest rooms in the house, and the bathrooms have huge, old-fashioned, claw-footed bathtubs; an additional nine rooms are in a restored carraige house on the property. The old greenhouse has been converted into a lounge (with a piano), and the three dining rooms are full of fresh flowers, crystal, gleaming silver, and the incredible smells of baby pheasant, rack of lamb, pâté, lobster bisque, bouillabaisse, and other delights that have put the inn on Connecticut's culinary map. Big breakfasts are not part of the picture, which is just as well because lunch and dinner are so good. Information: Copper Beech Inn, Main St., Ivoryton, CT 06442 (203 767-0330).

CURTIS HOUSE, Woodbury, Connecticut: The inn, reputedly Connecticut's oldest, is in a town with more than 30 antique shops, 20 on Main Street alone. Original beams and fireplaces set the atmosphere in the spacious dining rooms. The bedrooms have colonial furniture, a number of them with pretty canopied beds. Specialties on the regional American menu include roast duck, sweetbreads, and roast leg of lamb. Beef dishes are also available. Information: Curtis House, Woodbury, CT 06798 (203 263-2101). Chester C. Hardisty, innkeeper. 18 rooms.

BLUE HILL INN, Blue Hill, Maine: In operation on Blue Hill Bay since 1840, this inn is, according to the innkeepers, "the only inn in Maine which has never been operated as anything but an inn." Wingback armchairs, fireplaces, traditional wallpapers, ruffled curtains, and extra wool blankets make the bedrooms as cozy as they can be. But the real attraction here is the Maine coastline, best seen on foot, but accessible by bicycle, Moped, or car. The sea reaches into the meadowland all along this crabbed and twisting shoreline, so you keep seeing bits of the Atlantic wherever you go. Craft shops in Blue Hill carry famous Rowantrees pottery as well as other ceramic goods. Chamber music is performed several times a week in the summer by the students of Kneisel School of Music. The inn serves country-style breakfasts every morning, after which you are free to explore the coast or visit beautiful Deer Isle and Mt. Desert Island not far away. The inn's first-rate dinners are rich in chowders and fresh seafood; you'll also dine well on veal marsala, roast beef, mandarin chicken, and homemade breads and desserts. Information: Blue Hill Inn, Blue Hill, ME 04614 (207 374-2844). Ted and Rita Boytos, innkeepers. 10 rooms.

THISTLE INN, Boothbay Harbor, Maine: It's not the rooms (which are plain and old-fashioned) that make up this inn's attraction, so much as the warm and friendly atmosphere. In the tavern, a hangout for natives as well as a drawing card for weekenders, an upturned dory supports the bar and a piano player seldom has trouble getting together a chorus. The drinks are so hearty that most people are surprised by their size. In the restaurant, specialties include extra thick lamb chops, baked lobster pie, prime rib, and a fresh seafood platter. Information: Thistle Inn, Boothbay Harbor, ME 04538 (207 633-3541). Jim and Linda MacCormac, innkeepers. 8 rooms.

CENTER LOVELL INN, Center Lovell, Maine: This house was over 160 years old when William Mosca, a graduate student in sociology and children's literature in New Haven, came up and decided to turn the place into the kind of friendly bed-and-breakfast he had encountered in England. But Mosca's family is Italian, and so what he ended up with turned out to be, in his words, "a typical New England home — except Italian," a place of "bed-and-breakfast friendliness with Italian food." The food, all of it cooked as his grandmothers would have done it, is a point of pride with Mosca. He drives all the way to New York just to get the right cheeses and the right salami for his antipasto platters. Other specialties include Nicolo Firenze, a boneless half of chicken with an unusual stuffing, and gamberi al forno Roma, baked shrimp stuffed with crab. Three or four times a year — for New Year's Eve, Memorial Day, July 4, and one evening during the week of the big, locally famous Fryeburg Fair every autumn — Mosca lays out an eight-course banquet. Even if your timing is off for this feasting, however, there's plenty to keep you busy when you visit: hiking and antiquing in summer; craft-shopping at the Fryeburg Fair and leaf-peeping in the fall; and, in winter, alpine and cross-country skiing on an extensive network of old logging roads that begins right at the back door. (One Boston writer called the trails here New England's best.) Information: Center Lovell Inn, Rte. 5, Center Lovell, ME 04016 (207 925-1575). William and Susan Mosca, innkeepers. 10 rooms.

THE GREENVILLE INN, Greenville, Maine: Dominating this town on the edge of the wilderness surrounding giant Moosehead Lake, this rambling old mansion built by lumber barons in 1895 seems a lonely outpost of civilization, with its elegant paneling, leaded-glass windows, and fine detailing (ceramic tile fireplaces, for instance, and a shower arranged so that the spray comes at you from all sides). But the turn-of-the-century life that the structure was built to serve no longer exists. The furniture that replaced the lumber barons' is more comfortable than spiffy; and the style is informal and low key; the *Greenville Inn*, whose rooms are set up to handle families as well as couples, is a very friendly, very family-oriented sort of place. There are two dining rooms, one with a wonderful cherry mahogany ceiling, the other with views of Moosehead Lake and Squaw Mountain. Nowadays, the food is a bit fancier: the gourmet menu changes daily. Information: Greenville Inn, Box 1194, Greenville, ME 04441 (207 695-2206). Bob and Alice Stein, innkeepers. 9 rooms.

THE ISLAND INN, Monhegan Island, Maine: The century-old frame structure sitting on a picturesque bluff overlooking the tiny harbor between Monhegan and its satellite island of Manana is open summers only. Operated by a Monhegan native and his wife, the inn has a large, bright dining room where boiled lobster is the specialty, and fresh, simply prepared fish — striped bass, haddock, bluefish — fills the menu. An all-you-can-eat buffet on Sunday nights draws scores of Monhegan visitors who have spent the day exploring the awesome, 150-foot cliffs that face the pounding surf to the east. Although the inn has its own generator, most of the island goes without electricity. The yellow gleam of the kerosene lamps through the windows of the surrounding wood-shingled houses makes a pretty sight as you walk along the village's single dirt road. More than 600 varieties of flowering plants — including the trailing yew, unique to the island — and up to 200 species of birds may be seen along the many woodland trails. Information: The Island Inn, Monhegan Island, ME 04852 (207 596-0371). Bob and Mary Burton, innkeepers. 45 rooms.

ROBERT MORRIS INN, Oxford, Maryland: The most famous Robert Morris used his wide connections to raise money for the American Revolution, and when other backers failed to appear, he did not hesitate to pay the troops out of his own pocket. Alas, what the war couldn't do bad speculations accomplished a few years later, when he went bankrupt from a series of frontier land deals. His father's home, carefully preserved over the years, today is Tidewater Maryland's finest inn. Many of the rooms are decorated in vintage Americana, and you may climb into a high four-poster with the aid of a small stepladder or snuggle into a trundle bed. The slate on the tavern floor was quarried in Vermont, and public rooms and guest rooms alike are decorated with early braided or rag rugs. Best known to sailors, who tie up at the inn's anchorage on the Tred Avon River; to fishermen, who use the inn as a headquarters for excursions up and down the Chesapeake Bay shore; and to local gourmands, who swear its restaurant does the best things possible to bay crabs and the local oysters, the inn is a must for anyone touring the area. Information: Robert Morris Inn, Oxford, MD 21654 (301 226-5111). Ken and Wendy Gibson, innkeepers. 35 rooms.

WHEATLEIGH, Lenox, Massachusetts: This 33-room Italianate palazzo was built in 1893 by an American railroad man and banker, and ranks as the most elegant inn in all New England — if not in North America. Surrounded by formal gardens and lawns, the structure is all blond bricks and terra cotta and limestone detailing. There are loggias and arcades, stained-glass windows, a magnificent swooping staircase, lovely fireplaces, a proper library with glass-fronted bookcases and rich dark paneling, and, everywhere, ornately carved ceilings, moldings, mantelpieces, and walls. Travelers with a weakness for such things have reason to rejoice at the inn's restaurant, with cuisine appropriate to the setting. The four front bedrooms upstairs are extra special and commensurately costly. Information: Wheatleigh, PO Box 824, Lenox, MA 01240 (413 637-0610). Susan and Linfield Simon, innkeepers. 18 rooms.

· JARED COFFIN HOUSE, Nantucket, Massachusetts: The gas lamps ornamenting the façade of this inn have been converted to electricity, but they still cast a flattering glow on the 1845 brickwork — and give you an inkling of the marvels you will find inside: high ceilings; wonderfully ornate moldings; elegant chests and desks in Chippendale, Sheraton, and American Federal style; many canopied beds, several draped with crewel-embroidered fabric; oriental rugs; scrumptious seafood; and, most important of all, the extraordinary warmth and friendliness evinced by every staff member from the chambermaid to the desk clerk to the waitresses and the innkeepers themselves. Spring, summer, and fall are busy; winter — except during the year-end holidays, when the innkeeper stages a special celebration — is delightfully peaceful. This is the island's best-known and most popular inn, and you'll need reservations well in advance. But the planning always pays off when you return from a day of soaring along some cliff's-edge road on your bike, or tennis, golf, or soaking up the sun at the beach. Information: Jared Coffin House, Nantucket, MA 02554 (617 228-2405). Philip Whitney Read, innkeeper. 58 rooms in six buildings.

HANCOCK INN, Hancock, Massachusetts: Now that the venerable structure of this hostelry is like new again, owner-manager Chester Gorski, who once spent a good deal of his time toiling over burst pipes and ancient wiring and other maladies of a long-neglected building, has turned his full attention to culinary matters, earning quite a reputation for himself in the process. Dinner offerings are elaborate and tasty. There's billi bi (a cream of mussel soup) and medallions of fresh veal and jumbo shrimp in Dijon mustard sauce, duckling braised in port wine with grapes, and fresh lemon sole wrapped around a bay scallop and served in a shallot and Muscadet wine sauce. Ellen Gorski has a way with salads, and the white wine vinaigrette in which she tosses some unusual mixtures of vegetables (perhaps watercress and endive with a bit of romaine and shredded raw beets) is a standout; her cheesecake, whipped- ream-filled chocolate mousse torte, and frozen white chocolate mousse rank among guests' favorites. Exactly what you'll find on the menu depends on the season and the availability of ingredients — but it will always be Continental and so good that you'll pity the poor soul who comes here on a diet. The guest rooms are modest but comfortable. Information: Hancock Inn, Rte. 43, Hancock, MA 01237 (413 738-5873). Chester and Ellen Gorski, innkeepers. 8 rooms.

OLD FARM INN, Rockport, Massachusetts: When Antone Balzarini, a recent emigrant from northern Italy, rented the property that now surrounds this neat inn, he must have known about its long history and its several owners — the initials of one of them, one James Norwood, are chiseled on an old granite gate post together with a date, 1799. But he could not have foreseen its future as one of the most prosperous and popular establishments in a village where the visitors are more often discerning than not. He himself purchased the farm down the road, but one of the dozen children he raised later came back to the property, which by then was known as the Babson Farm, and began restoring the farmhouse, filling it with antiques, converting the erstwhile barn into guest accommodations, and adding new dining space to handle the increased numbers of guests. The inn's kitchen turns out food that is as tasty as ever — roast duckling, baked stuffed lobster, lobster pie, lobster Newburg, crabmeat-mushroom pie, and various New England–plain steaks and seafood platters. With their open hearths and old-fashioned lamps, the dining rooms are just as attractive as the meals. Information: Old Farm Inn, 291 Granite St., Rockport, MA 01966 (617 546-3237). The Balzarini family, innkeepers. 7 rooms.

RED LION INN, Stockbridge, Massachusetts: This fine rambling three-story old clapboard structure occupies a prominent place on Main Street, which, except for the traffic that clogs the intersection during the busy summer season, looks just as if Norman Rockwell ought to have painted it. He did. His home was just across the road, and the country's largest and finest collection of his paintings can be seen not far away, in the Old Corner House. Still, there's more to Stockbridge than Rockwelliana — Lenox's Berkshire Music Festival (a/k/a Tanglewood) and Berkshire Theater Festival, and the Jacob's Pillow Dance Festival at Lee, among other things — and the inn hums throughout the hot-weather months with overnight guests, diners, and a good many other folk who have simply stopped in to ogle the high-ceilinged Victorian parlors and their gleaming silver and mahogany embellishments; or to sit on the long front porch, where two rows of rocking chairs bob back and forth from early morning until well after dusk. The inn is well worth seeing, even if you can't get a bed for the night. Certainly, the inn's restaurants — the outdoor patio restaurant, all cool and green; the cozy, dark *Widow Bingham's Tavern*, with its candles and checkered tablecloths; and the main dining room, full of sparkling silver and white napery — are among the most charming spots for meals in an area that is full of appealing cateries. Hearty soups begin many dinners here; they conclude with one of New England's spiciest Indian puddings. Information: Red Lion Inn, Stockbridge, MA 01262 (413 298-5545). Betsy Holtzinger, innkeeper. 100 rooms.

COLONEL EBENEZER CRAFTS INN, Sturbridge, Massachusetts: In the eighteenth century, the finest homes were always built on the highest points of land — which gave their owners not only a commanding view of their property and herds but also the distinction of being set somewhat apart from their contemporaries. The circa 1786 farmhouse that the owners of the *Publick House,* described below, transformed into an inn a few years ago was one of those distinguished buildings. Its new role in life has not diminished its preeminence in the community, however, since this structure on the summit of Fiske Hill makes as lovely an inn as it was a farmhouse. Antiques and fine reproductions, afternoon tea or sherry in the library or the sunroom, fruit and cookies in the evening, and Continental breakfasts in the morning — by the pool in warm weather — make this an exceptionally pleasant place. The inn's namesake — a strong man who studied theology at Yale, established the *Publick House* as a tavern in 1770, and later equipped and drilled a cavalry company during the Revolution — later founded the town of Craftsbury, Vermont. Information: Colonel Ebenezer Crafts Inn, c/o Publick House, PO Box 187, Sturbridge, MA 01566 (617 347-3313). Patricia and Henri Bibeau, innkeepers. 8 rooms.

PUBLICK HOUSE, Sturbridge, Massachusetts: This is not one of those cozy country inns where it's you and the innkeeper against the rest of the world. Instead, this hostelry — which opened as one of our not-quite-yet-a-nation's finest restaurants in 1771 — is most popular for its food; and the hungry pour by the bus- and carload through its doors, then chow down on fresh fish and lobster pie and wonderful sticky buns. Some have had the foresight to reserve in advance, and, when they're sated on the innkeeper's savory offerings, they can simply waddle up the creaky, crooked stairs to one of the cozy rooms — or step outside to the Country Motor Lodge in back and collapse in one of the Colonial-style rooms. Recently purchased and totally renovated by the *Publick House,* the 100-room *Lodge* also sports an outdoor pool, tennis court, and jogging course, so visitors can work off at least some of the calories they've consumed. Some time ago the Publick House innkeeper initiated a splendid pageant-cum-feast, a revival of the Yuletide celebration known in merrie Olde England, with a Boar's Head Feast, a Yule Log Procession, and the telling of moving tales of the season; held thrice daily on the two Saturdays and Sundays preceding Christmas, it now sells out well in advance. A newer event, Yankee Winter Weekends, keeps the inn filled from January through March. You're welcomed with syllabub (chablis with cream) and Joe Froggers (giant ginger cookies), then fed goodies nearly around the clock: breakfasts of fried mush and deep-dish apple pie and hickory-smoked bacon; snacks of curried meatballs, aged cheddar, roasted chestnuts, codfish cakes and chowder and hot buttered rum; and dinners of roasted venison and other exotic concoctions. Then, as in summer (when a flock of sheep keep the grass short on the meadow behind the inn), you can visit Old Sturbridge Village, a reconstruction of a New England village that might have existed at about the time of the Industrial Revolution (see *Restored Towns and Reconstructed Villages*). Information: Publick House, PO Box 187, Sturbridge, MA 01566 (617 347-3313). Buddy Adler, innkeeper. 25 rooms; Country Motor Lodge, Publick House, PO Box 187, Sturbridge, MA 01566 (617 347-9555). Carol Young, manager. 100 rooms.

LONGFELLOW'S WAYSIDE INN, Sudbury, Massachusetts: Originally known as the Red Horse Tavern, the inn changed its name in 1863, the better to bask in the fame Longfellow created for it when he wrote *Tales of a Wayside Inn,* a series of poems whose most celebrated section begins, "Listen, my children, and you shall hear . . ." The building in which Longfellow set his work, which had been purchased by Henry Ford in the 1920s, was partially destroyed by fire, after some two and a half centuries of existence, in the mid-50s; but with Ford Foundation help it was soon restored. The former plans were somewhat modified: Many of the original guest rooms were turned into museumlike room settings showing how the inn probably looked in the early 18th century, and eight new rooms were added and fitted out with fine bathrooms and reproduction furnishings in early American color schemes. The surrounding 106 acres insulate you from the highway hubbub, and, because the inn's principal trade is in meals, when the diners are gone you it's as though you're on your own private estate. Meals consist of sturdy New England fare, including tasty breads, cakes, and pies out of the inn's own ovens, made from flour ground by the mill on the premises. Also on the grounds is the schoolhouse that inspired "Mary Had a Little Lamb" and a classic

New England chapel complete with white clapboards and soaring steeple, where countless New England sweethearts have tied the knot. Information: Wayside Inn, Sudbury, MA 01776 (617 443-8846). Francis J. Koppeis, innkeeper. 10 rooms.

FITZWILLIAM INN, Fitzwilliam, New Hampshire: The "Rules of the House" provide an accurate insight into what you're likely to find: "This is a New England country inn, in the heart of a New England country village, and we have some customs that may seem strange to you. Please try to understand our ways and abide by our requests." If you find this off-putting, you'll be encouraged by rule number one: "We have no room keys to give you — everyone trusts everyone else in the country. However, we do lock the outside doors early. If you're going to be out, please pick up a house key at the desk. The innkeeper is shy about answering the door in his PJs." Modern intrusions are unwelcome in this wooden hostelry dating from 1796. The innkeeper has been quoted as saying that when a prospective guest asks if the rooms have television sets, they're referred to "the nice motel just down the road." Information: Fitzwilliam Inn, Fitzwilliam, NH 03447 (603 585-9000). Charles and Barbara Wallace, innkeepers. 25 rooms.

JOHN HANCOCK INN, Hancock, New Hampshire: John Hancock never slept here or even stopped for a short mug of ale while inspecting the nearby landholdings left to him by a rich uncle. But the inn does boast that its 1789 opening makes it New Hampshire's oldest inn operating in the same building. In the Monadnock region, the "Currier and Ives corner of the Granite State," in one of those quintessentially New England towns with a white-steepled church, a bandstand on the green, and a half dozen bright clapboard houses stuck away in a fuzz of leaves, the inn is full of small neat rooms with twin canopy beds or white ruffled curtains and tiny-print wallpapers. But number 16 happens to be more beautiful than nearly any other room in any other inn in the region. The murals that are its most striking feature, creations of an itinerant artist named Rufus Porter, depict the scenes of the area in heavenly blues. The furniture is mahogany, the bedspread and curtains are white; but the work is so lively that you get an odd, you-are-there feeling. The only other remnant of Porter's work is found inside the closet of one of the rooms down the hall. The restaurant serves food that is basically New England plain; offerings include roast duckling, seafood casserole, and prime rib — served daily, not just once or twice a week as in many similar small restaurants. The bar, with buggy seats for benches and giant bellows for tables, is exceptionally homey. Information: John Hancock Inn, Hancock, NH 03449 (603 525-3318). Glynn and Pat Wells, innkeepers. 10 rooms.

LYME INN, Lyme, New Hampshire: Lyme is as delightful a New England village as you'd ever want to find, with its big green common, its fine clapboard church, its well-stocked country store — not to mention its handsome inn, a favorite lodging place for parents of students at nearby Dartmouth College and a tourist attraction in its own right. All the rooms are furnished with antiques. The structure itself, put up in 1809, is full of walls that slant, hallways that narrow then inexplicably widen, and stairways that twist and climb every which way, apparently without rhyme or reason. A fascinating collection of framed samplers, hanging on the walls of the dining rooms, is worth close scrutiny, not only for the workmanship but perhaps for the messages as well, from "God Bless Our Home" to more religious aphorisms. Information: Lyme Inn, Lyme, NH 03768 (603 795-2222). Fred and Judy Siemons, innkeepers. 15 rooms.

NEW LONDON INN, New London, New Hampshire: You may travel through New England for the length of a normal lifetime and assume you've seen most of what is good and fair when, suddenly, you discover a delight like New London. Here is a perfection of New England towns, not so much restored, one senses, as preserved. And in the middle of all this beauty, across from the town green, sits the three-story, clapboard-sided, antique-furnished *New London Inn*. Built in 1792, it is famous for a deal made in 1941 with a retired town tax collector named Calvin Sargent. Sargent, grandson of the original builder of the hostelry, had a hankering for security. Moreover, he liked the old place. So he offered the innkeepers $5,000 to room-and-board him for life (he was 73 at the time); the offer was accepted — and Sargent outlived the owners, enjoying the fruits of his contract well into his hundredth year. You may not stay so long, but there's plenty to keep you busy while you're there: in summer, water sports on three lakes; and, in winter, downhill and cross-country skiing. Information: New London Inn, New London, NH 03257 (603 526-2791). Maureen and John Follansbee, innkeepers. 26 rooms, all with private baths.

THE MAINSTAY INN, Cape May, New Jersey: Cape May, one of our nation's oldest seaside resorts, is a treasure of Victorian architecture, and the *Mainstay Inn* — just a few blocks from the Atlantic — is one of its gems. From the inn's buff-colored picket fence to the green wicker chairs that sit on its veranda, to the 12-foot mirror in the entrance hall, this late-19th-century former gambling house has been lovingly restored and exquisitely furnished in pure Victorian style by a dedicated young couple. Information: The Mainstay Inn, 635 Columbia Ave., Cape May, NJ 08204 (609 884-8690). Tom and Sue Carroll, innkeepers. 12 rooms.

THE INN AT THE SHAKER MILL FARM, Canaan, New York: When Ingram Paperny uncovered this abandoned early-19th-century mill, it had neither bedrooms nor public rooms and was sorely in need of an expert carpenter. But the structure, set beside a hillside waterfall, so tempted its discoverer that he set up his own wood shop and began its careful conversion to inn. The simple but comfortable rooms reflect the heritage of austerity left by the Shakers who lived in the area — in Old Chatham, New York, where there's now an extraordinary collection of material on display, and just across the state line in Hancock, Massachusetts, now home to the popular Shaker Village. The setting in the foothills of the Berkshires is one of great beauty, and so the inn attracts an interesting crowd, everyone from magazine editors to mycologists. Information: The Inn at the Shaker Mill Farm, Canaan, NY 12029 (518 794-9345). Ingram Paperny, innkeeper. 20 rooms.

THE 1770 HOUSE, East Hampton, Long Island, New York: Like so many other American inns, the *1770 House* has had several lives (in this case, first as a home, later as a store, then as a boarding house, and finally as the dining hall of a boys' school), and over the years hardly anybody bothered to give it the care it required. And so, when Sid and Miriam Perle bought the place, the building was a wreck. Thanks to their efforts, however, the structure has never looked better. The exterior, clapboards painted white with coal-black shutters at the windows, makes the inn a creditable addition to a venerable neighborhood. Inside, the old and the new work together to delightful effect. (Especially striking: the large colonial fireplace in the taproom, a popular spot for cozy dinners; the Perles' wonderful clock collection; and the stained glass that is used as a decorative accent throughout the inn.) The *1770 House* is open year-round but serves meals only on weekends in winter. Information: The 1770 House, 143 Main St., East Hampton, NY 11937 (516 324-1770). Sidney and Miriam Perle, innkeepers. 7 rooms.

GURNEY'S INN, Montauk, Long Island, New York: If you define an inn as a colonial hostelry on an elm-shaded New England street, this may not be the place for you: You won't find the antique lamp or the ancient patchwork quilt, the spinning wheel or the stenciled wall. You lodge in cottages or motel-type rooms with ocean-view balconies or terraces, set among trees and country gardens; dress up for dinner and dance to live music in the lounge after you've supped; or just hole up in your room and take in a television show when you've had your fill of the spa facilities (excellent enough to attract the likes of Cheryl Tiegs and Alvin Ailey). But *Gurney's Inn* is a personable place, and when you go out on the beach, one of those endless, surf-pounded Atlantic strands, you put civilization thousands of miles behind you. The shore is delightful for jogging or sunbathing in summer, and even better for walks in the fall — if you don't mind the whip of the wind, the tingle of the cold, and spray in the face as the price of a beach to call your own. Information: Gurney's Inn, Montauk, NY 11954 (516 668-2345). Nick and Joyce Monte, innkeepers. 128 rooms.

1740 HOUSE, Lumberville, Pennsylvania: Built around an early-18th-century stable by two other refugees from urban America, the *1740 House* is one of the best inns in Bucks County, which is full of inns — not so much because it's particularly quaint (because it isn't: the rooms are air conditioned, the floors are carpeted wall to wall, the baths are tiled, and the furnishings are W. & J. Sloane's finest). Rather, the *1740 House* prospers year after year because it is one of those unfailingly well-managed places where everything works, and because it is in the kind of countryside where everyone dreams, at least once, of making a second home: a woodsy region that shelters antique houses, run through by a mighty river and a placid canal where you can canoe or ice skate; where the towns have grown just enough so that there are interesting shops, movie theaters or playhouses, and restaurants and snack bars where you're as apt to find quiche on the menu as hamburger. In Bucks County, as at the *1740 House,* you can have your comforts and get away from it all, too. Hearty breakfasts (served in a sunny room overlooking the canal) and dinners are available at the inn; you'll have to go elsewhere for lunches and BYOB. Information: 1740 House, River Rd., Lumberville, PA 18933 (215 297-5661).

CLIFF PARK INN, Milford, Pennsylvania: This early-19th-century farmhouse-turned-inn, a venerable mountain resort hotel set not far from a 900-foot cliff that towers over the Delaware River, has been run since 1900 by five generations of the same family — so if you come here expecting someplace homey, you won't be disappointed. The beds in one room are covered with lace spreads. And there are cushy sofas in the parlors and antiques and polished floors throughout. But the *Cliff Park Inn* also has something of the elegance of a country club, in part because, ever since the golf course was added in 1913, back in the days that golf was just catching hold in America, golf has been one of the guests' favorite pastimes. (In fact, the resort is open only when the weather is temperate enough for a round, from Memorial Day to mid-October.) Most rooms are upstairs in the main building; three cottages are also available nearby. Information: Cliff Park Inn, Milford, PA 18337 (717 296-6491). Harry Buchanan, innkeeper. 20 rooms.

THE 1661 INN, Block Island, Rhode Island: The uniqueness of this pretty, simple structure perched above the village that clusters about the harbor, comes mostly from the beauty of its site on a meadow rising up 12 miles off Point Judith, an hour's ferry ride away. But the atmosphere — informal enough that before-dinner wine-and-nibbles hours seem to make perfect sense — figures strongly as well; the special house drinks — the Monhegan Moro, a wild combination of sweet and dry vermouth, and the Island of the Little Gods Mind Boggler, white wine with cranberry juice — are something else again. An abundant breakfast buffet offers eggs, ham, bacon, corned beef hash, home-grown potatoes, fresh fish, muffins and breads, and fruit. Lunches and dinners are served at the owners' other property, the mansard-roofed, Victorian *Manisses Hotel* inside the Garden Terrace room or on the breezy deck outside. That sister establishment now boasts 17 guest rooms, all with private bath and 4 with Jacuzzis. Block Island is one of the best places in the East for biking; there's also good snorkeling, picnicking, salt- and freshwater fishing, bird-watching, and beachcombing — below the steep Monhegan cliffs for shells, driftwood, and other flotsam. Information: The 1661 Inn and Hotel Manisses, Block Island, RI 02807 (401 466-2421). Joan and Justin Abrams, innkeepers. 25 rooms.

INN AT CASTLE HILL, Newport, Rhode Island: This three-story Victorian mansion, built on a 32-acre water's-edge site in 1874 by the son of the Swiss-American naturalist Louis Agassiz, is one of those mansions which Newporters call, inexplicably, "cottages." However, though it's a plain sort of place by the standards of William Wetmore's Stanford White–designed Château-sur-Mer and Cornelius Vanderbilt's

Richard Morris Hunt–designed The Breakers, you may have a tough time stretching your imagination to call it a cottage. In the first place, it's huge; and in the second place, it's more elegant than most Fifth Avenue apartments. The chestnut paneling gleams. Tiffany lamps shed their soft glow on fantastically carved Victorian furniture, much of it original to the house. Oriental rugs protect the polished floors. In the dining room, you'll sit on velvet-covered chairs, drink coffee poured from silver urns, and eat with silver cutlery. Innkeeper Paul McEnroe is a thoroughgoing professional and a gracious human being, and knows how to make every guest feel at home; the wonderful New Year's Eve dinner dance sells out well in advance as a result. The menu offers a Neptune's bounty of clams and lobsters and other seafood prepared with a Continental flair. Rooms are in the main house and in a newer area out back; for charm, the former are best. Information: Inn at Castle Hill, Ocean Dr., Newport, RI 02840 (401 849-3800). Paul McEnroe, innkeeper. 16 rooms.

THE OLD TAVERN, Grafton, Vermont: Restored, along with some 25 other Grafton buildings, by the Windham Foundation, as a part of one of the country's most extensive restoration projects, the *Old Tavern* is one of America's most beautiful inns. Everything gleams: the wooden floor boards throughout the main building and the annex across the street, the furniture, the tops of the tables in the dining room, the silver tableware, the glasses, and the china. All of the sleeping rooms are furnished with the loveliest sort of antiques — lace tester beds, wing chairs covered with chintz, Chippendale-style highboys, and such. When you consider all that, and the delightful setting in picture-postcard-perfect Grafton, you may call the *Old Tavern* one of your favorite inns, despite the fact that it's more elegant than cozy; so many people love the place so well, in fact, that you'll be hard put to get a room at the last minute. It's important to reserve well in advance and to ask the desk clerk carefully about the rooms: No two are alike, and some are more wonderful than others. The surrounding area is gorgeous, too: In Grafton alone there's the general store, the cheese company, and a lovely covered bridge. Information: The Old Tavern, Grafton, VT 05146 (802 843-2231). Richard Ernst, innkeeper. 36 rooms.

NORWICH INN, Norwich, Vermont: Just across the Connecticut River from Dartmouth College, the *Norwich Inn* has been in operation since 1797, and the people of the town take a proprietary interest in the establishment. When you visit the handsome *Terrace Dining Room,* glassed-in porch, carpeted and filled with plants so that it seems almost like a greenhouse, you can order roast duckling, fresh salmon, or lamb noisette. And you can order from one of the most extensive wine lists in the area — fine Champagne, first-growth French wines, and reasonably priced bottles both imported and domestic, some of which you usually can't get anymore. Norwich, one of those immaculately kept towns whose clapboard and brick homes and tall trees define most people's idea of how a New England town should look, is as charming as ever; and Dan & Whitt, a big old general store where you can buy hardware and grain for yourself and your animals, rifles and flannel and soaps and just about anything else you can name, is still doing its booming business. In summer, you can go hiking and biking, and in winter you'll want to go for a ski. Rooms, all with private bath, are both in the inn and in a motel unit directly behind it. Information: Norwich Inn, Norwich, VT 05055 (802 649-1143). Tom Spalding, innkeeper. 27 rooms.

KEDRON VALLEY INN, South Woodstock, Vermont: In operation since the early 1800s, this pleasant, relaxing inn — under the proprietorship of Max and Merrily Comins since the end of 1985 — has been updated to the point where, among other things, all rooms now have private baths and the new chef, a lifelong Vermonter, prepares local products in "nouvelle Vermont" style. Horseback riders are still able to ride the 250 miles of trails at the nearby stables — operated by the inn's former owners — which continue to make Kedron Valley one of their favorites. But even if you don't ride, there is much to do. In summer you can sit out by the spring-fed pond before taking a dip or hike on numerous trails; and golf, indoor and outdoor tennis, aerobics, a swimming pool, and other athletic facilities are just up the road. In winter, miles of cross-country trails are maintained in the area, and downhill skiing is available in almost every direction. Afterward, the innkeepers suggest you "settle back in your rocker, pull the antique quilt a little closer, and put your feet up by the potbelly stove in your room." Or you can take a horse-drawn sleigh ride through the countryside. Information: Kedron Valley Inn, Rte. 106, S Woodstock, VT 05071 (802 457-1473). Max and Merrily Comins, innkeepers. 30 rooms.

HARTNESS HOUSE, Springfield, Vermont: A cockamamie jumble of dormers, arched windows, fieldstones, bay windows, and other fancies of the typical Victorian architect, this mansion was originally the home of an inventor and "machine tool genius" who at one time held the post of governor of Vermont, one James Hartness. Some of the rooms, including a wonderfully handsome turret room, are in this house; other more modern quarters can be found in an addition in the back. The inn also has three stately dining rooms and the attractive *Crown Point Pub.* Outside, under a spreading maple, there's a swimming pool, with a lighted clay tennis court nearby and, just beyond, a weird object that looks like a tank turret tipped partly over — James Hartness's telescope, a nightly attraction. The area around Springfield, along the Black River, was for many years a center for the manufacture of precision machine tools, and Springfield came to be known as "the cradle of invention." The American Precision Museum, in nearby Windsor, is well worth visiting to learn the story. Also in the area is the St. Gaudens National Historic Site, across the river in Cornish, New Hampshire. Information: Hartness House, 30 Orchard St., Springfield, VT 05156 (802 885-2115). George and Cherrill Staudter, innkeepers. 46 rooms.

THE INN AT WEATHERSFIELD, Weathersfield, Vermont: Mary Louise Thorburn had spent years entertaining a house full of people (and loving it), and after the nest emptied out, running an inn seemed the natural thing to do. She and husband Ron looked all over for the perfect place, and in 1978 they came to Weathersfield, a perfect gem of a New England town some 19 miles from Woodstock. They saw this inn with its six white pillars and wavy-paned glass; fell in love with the design, the layout, and the setting on 12 acres of lawns and trees back from the road; bought the place practically on the spot; and in 1980 opened for business as one of those very special places where visitors feel like welcome guests in someone's home. And what a home: The floors are wide-planked throughout, the rooms are all furnished in antiques — some with four-posters, one with a magnificent old bedstead canopied with a single piece of hand-crocheted lace. Half the guest rooms have working fireplaces. There are enough antique quilts in the house to dazzle a museum textiles curator, and the bedsheets are flowered, ruffled, or edged with lace. (Atop every mattress, Mrs. Thorburn has laid an electric pad: just the thing to warm your toes on a cold Vermont night after the fire on your hearth has died down.) Afternoons are given over to bountiful English teas, served in sterling and accompanied by salmon mousse on bread rounds, fresh vegetables with a dip, and some wonderful sweet treat — perhaps an English trifle or a tipsy pudding. This is such a friendly occasion that guests who have met here often join up later for sightseeing, dinner company, and other activities. Breakfasts — sausage or ham and Grand Marnier–and–orange–water French toast, well-sauced fines herbes omelettes, eggs Benedict, Scotch eggs, or shredded cheddar cheese eggs — are so generous that you may be able to make tea do for lunch, especially if you know you have one of the Thorburns' delightful dinners, confected of imaginative appetizers, soups, entrées, and desserts, to look forward to. Carriage and sleigh rides are available with Dick, the inn's amiable horse. Information: Inn at Weathersfield, PO Box 165, Weathersfield, VT 05151 (802 263-9217). Mary Louise and Ron Thorburn, innkeepers. 12 rooms.

INN AT SAWMILL FARM, West Dover, Vermont: Abandoned barns, uniquely adaptable because of their huge open spaces, seem to make a special sort of inn — or so you would conclude upon seeing this fine establishment, the creation of Rodney Williams, an architect, and Ione, his wife, a professional decorator. The spaces are good, to begin with: the living room is high-ceilinged, just big enough for two sitting areas, but not so big that you can't sit and see the fire burning in the huge hearth; the dining rooms are small enough that you can almost feel you're at someone's very elegant dinner party; and there are all manner of comfortable nooks and crannies where you can go to read a book or just lie down and snooze. Ione has furnished the whole place with bright fabrics, and, because the Williamses' daughter is married to a Fieldcrest executive, everything from the towels and the sheets to the blanket covers, the carpets, and the bedspreads is color-coordinated. Meanwhile, the Williamses' son Brill has become quite a chef, and the ingredients he uses are always just a little fresher and a little more perfect than the garden variety. The food reflects that fact. The Marlboro Music Festival is nearby, and keeps the inn full in summer; and in fall, the flaming foliage draws crowds. In winter, people come to ski on Mt. Snow, just down the road, or to cross-country over the river and through the woods. So, no matter when you want to visit, reserve well in advance. Information: Inn at Sawmill Farm, PO Box 367, West Dover, VT 05356 (802 464-8131). Rodney, Ione, and Brill Williams, innkeepers. 22 rooms.

SOUTH

ROD AND GUN CLUB, Everglades City, Florida: Times have changed since the 1920s, when industrialist Barron Collier converted an old gulfside house, popular with hunters and fishermen for years, into a private club, and made it a hideaway for very important persons (including a scattering of US presidents). So the club is now open to the public. But much of the flavor of the early days remains, and there are mounted sport fish and hunting specimens on the walls; the emphasis here is still on the water and its creatures. A marina serves private boats. Charters and guides are available, as are skiffs and canoes for some fine fishing — for grouper, tarpon, or the battling snook; the chef will prepare your catch for a small fee. The inn is a mile from the entrance to Everglades National Park, and in February the place hops with a special seafood festival. There's a pool (screened because of the mosquitoes), and tennis courts are nearby. Information: Rod and Gun Club, Box G, Everglades City, FL 33929 (813 695-2101). Martin Bowen, innkeeper. 18 rooms in separate cottages.

CHALET SUZANNE, Lake Wales, Florida: The style of many places can be suggested in a word or phrase — Victorian, early American, motel modern. *Chalet Suzanne* is what you'd call eclectic. Left to her own devices in the depths of the Depression, with two children to care for, a tiny young widow named Bertha Hinshaw decided to start serving meals to the public. Talent and energy made this central Florida endeavor a huge success over the years, and by the time Bertha Hinshaw died not long ago, in her 90s, the inn had its own orange groves, a private airstrip, one of the finest and most original kitchens in the state, and a reputation for being one of the oddest-looking inns this side of paradise, for the *Chalet Suzanne,* as the establishment came to be called, after Mrs. Hinshaw's daughter, eventually came to reflect her passion for collecting anything and everything, but particularly tiles, and her penchant for putting together elements of architectural styles from all around the globe, everything from turrets to bare-wood decks. What could have been garish is here simply exquisite. Information: Chalet Suzanne, PO Box AC, Lake Wales, FL 33859-9003 (813 676-6011). Carl and Vita Hinshaw, innkeepers. 30 rooms.

GREYFIELD INN, Cumberland Island, Georgia: A one-of-a-kind inn on a one-of-a-kind island in the Atlantic, just northeast of the Georgia-Florida state line, this establishment was built by the Thomas Carnegies around the turn of the century for their daughter and her husband, and, substantially unaltered, was opened as an inn several years ago by a Carnegie granddaughter, Mrs. Lucy Ferguson. If something this far off the beaten track, accessible only by boat or chartered plane, appeals to you, then you may not mind that there are no tennis courts or swimming pool, and that the only recreation on the island, really, is reading, conversation, shelling, walking, and looking for birds, armadillo, and alligators. And when you've had enough of that, you can just sit around in the house and savor the lifestyle of one sort of turn-of-the-century rich. Information: Greyfield Inn, Drawer B, Fernandina Beach, FL 32034 (904 261-6408). Ferguson family, innkeepers. 9 rooms.

THE INN AT PLEASANT HILL, Harrodsburg, Kentucky: The Shakers — an ascetic, communal sect that originated in England in the mid-18th century — are usually associated with upstate New York and Massachusetts, where more than 200 years ago Mother Ann Lee established the country's first major Shaker settlements. However, the Shakers went west in the 19th century and eventually settled in Kentucky — at Auburn and near Harrodsburg at Pleasant Hill (see *Utopias*). As part of the nationwide revival of interest in the Shakers, particularly in their architecture and design, all 27 of the original buildings at Pleasant Hill have been restored, and 14 of them are fitted out with guest rooms and appropriate reproductions of Shaker furniture — chairs and trundle beds, sconces, mirrors, and, everywhere, pegs to hang things up as the Shakers did. The nonprofit organization that administers Pleasant Hill has provided every room with its own tiled bath, air conditioning, and a television set; but otherwise the feeling is one of authenticity. A dining room in the Trustees' House offers big Kentucky-style breakfasts with grits, eggs, sausage, biscuits, and the rest; lunches and dinners are also belt-looseners. Information: Inn at Pleasant Hill, 3500 Lexington Rd., Harrodsburg, KY 40330 (606 734-5411). Ann Voris, innkeeper. 72 rooms.

THE COLUMNS HOTEL, New Orleans, Louisiana: The unusual hotel where director Louis Malle filmed Brooke Shields's notorious film *Pretty Baby* has become no less than one of the city's most evocative stopping places thanks to a recent renovation. In the Garden District, with the St. Charles streetcar passing its front door, it started out as a wealthy tobacco merchant's home, became a boardinghouse in 1914, and was transformed into a hotel in the 1940s. Now it has a kind of luscious decadent splendor, from its Victorian lounge and ballroom-restaurant to its grand, free-standing stairwell and its abundant touches of Honduras mahogany. Information: The Columns Hotel, 3811 St. Charles Ave., New Orleans, LA 70115 (504 899-9308). Dale Michael, innkeeper. 16 rooms.

LaMOTHE HOUSE, New Orleans, Louisiana: Built in the early 1800s by a successful planter named Jean LaMothe, this exquisite early New Orleans town house is a delightful place to call home while visiting this exciting city. From the stately foyer to the lushly planted courtyard and throughout the elegantly antique-furnished establishment, you can't help but find yourself transported to the city's earlier, gentler days. But you won't find the discomforts: all of the rooms are air conditioned, and each has a private bath, a color TV, and a phone. Continental breakfast, the only meal served, is always an event: everyone sits at a long banquet table and lingers over chicory coffee drawn from a Sheffield urn at least two centuries old. At night you'll find a praline on your pillow — the candies are made fresh daily. New owners have refurbished the house to make a good thing even better, with American Victorian antiques and color schemes. The inn is just a few blocks from the heart of the French Quarter and its jazz, good food, and intriguing shops. Information: LaMothe House, 621 Esplanade Ave., New Orleans, LA 70116 (504 947-1161 or 800 367-5858). Ralph and Freda Lupin, innkeepers. 20 rooms.

MAISON DE VILLE, New Orleans, Louisiana: This gem of a hotel in the heart of the French Quarter offers you a choice of accommodations: There's the *maison*, with magnificent antique-furnished rooms with balconies and street or courtyard views. Or out back, there are the remodeled circa 1743 slave quarters. And then, a stroll away on Dauphine Street, there are the delightful *Audubon Cottages,* where John James Audubon lived and worked from 1821 to 1826 and where Tennessee Williams did his final draft of *Streetcar.* Built in the Creole brick-and-post style (something like the old European half-timbered buildings), they have perhaps the most elegant rooms of all, with luxuriously furnished bedrooms, kitchens with stocked refrigerators, and private gardens. The entire *Maison de Ville* complex stands out, however, for the service: Tables in restaurants and space on sightseeing tours are booked by an omniscient concierge; shoes left outside your door are shined; a classic French breakfast is served on a silver tray, along with a copy of the *Times-Picayune* and a rose. And when you return after a night on the town, you find a piece of chocolate on your pillow. Information: Maison de Ville, 727 Toulouse St., New Orleans, LA 70130 (504 561-5858 or 800 634-1600). Bonnie Leigh, general manager. 12 rooms, 2 suites, 7 cottages, 5 town house apartments.

SONIAT HOUSE, New Orleans, Louisiana: Installed in a pair of remarkable town houses built around 1830 and recently restored to the tune of nearly a million dollars, *Soniat House* blends the American and the Créole to the credit of both. While the bathrooms are marbled, modern, and equipped with telephones, the lofty-ceilinged bedrooms are filled with English and French antiques, including canopied or French empire beds and antique oriental rugs; many have their own balcony or terrace, and five have Jacuzzis. The three-story spiral staircase, the rocking chair–equipped balcony that spans the façade, the lush garden courtyard, and the location near the French Market are bonuses, as is the breakfast of biscuits with homemade strawberry preserves, fresh-squeezed orange juice, and rich Créole coffee. Information: Soniat House, 1133 Chartres St., New Orleans, LA 70116 (504 522-0570). Rodney Smith, innkeeper. 25 rooms.

HOUND EARS LODGE AND CLUB, Blowing Rock, North Carolina: Skiing down south? Yep, up here in the Blue Ridge Mountains. It can be pretty good, too, both here at the lodge and nearby. Open all year, this friendly resort has a fine 18-hole golf course as well as swimming, tennis, and other outdoor activities — for children as well as adults. The lodge operates on the modified American plan, and meals are served to overnight guests only. Information: Hound Ears Lodge and Club, Blowing Rock, NC 28605 (704 963-4321). David Blust, manager. 25 rooms.

NU-WRAY INN, Burnsville, North Carolina: If you like to get high on mountains and you're east of the Rockies, this is the place. Nearby are the Pisgah National Forest, one of the wildest woodlands in the East (don't miss Linville Gorge), and Mt. Mitchell, at 6,684 feet, the highest east of the Mississippi. The inn, at about half that altitude, will keep your feelings on the up side with its good food (meals are served family-style) and friendly atmosphere — despite the fact that you're awakened every morning without fail at 8 by the ringing of a bell and summoned to a country ham breakfast a half hour later by that same bell. The meal is worth it. The call to dinner (reservations suggested) is less jarring; a Reginaphone, an old-fashioned music box that is just one of the many Wray family antiques scattered around the inn, is your summons. Information: Nu-Wray Inn, PO Box 156, Burnsville, NC 28714 (704 682-2329). Betty Souders, innkeeper. 32 rooms.

SNOWBIRD MOUNTAIN LODGE, Robbinsville, North Carolina: As the name implies, this is a place for the birds — and those who love to watch them. From the inn's 3,000-foot setting bordering the Nantahala National Forest, the views above and below are breathtaking. Birders and hikers have their choice of trails, from the gentle to the rugged. The forest covers 450,000 acres, including a 50,000-acre Cherokee reservation with a restored village and many exhibits and demonstrations for visitors. Moreover, there are some spectacular driving tours in the area, most notably to 30-mile-distant Fontana Dam and its 30-mile-long lake. The inn serves all meals but has no bar.

Information: Snowbird Mountain Lodge, Joyce Kilmer Forest Rd., Robbinsville, NC 28771 (704 479-3433). Bob and Connie Rhudy, innkeepers. 22 rooms.

SWORD GATE INN, Charleston, South Carolina: Charleston is known for its glorious old homes, and the carefully restored Sword Gate Inn, housed in an 18th-century mansion in the heart of the city's historic section, is ideal for getting you into the spirit of the city. The furnishings were selected with sensitivity and great care for detail, and everything, from the gingham comforter to the freshly cut flowers, is directed toward a guest's comfort and delight. Breakfast — delicious and informal — is the only meal offered. Bikes and tours of the city are arranged upon request. Information: Sword Gate Inn, 111 Tradd St., Charleston, SC 29401 (803 723-8518). Walter E. Barton, innkeeper. 6 rooms.

THE RED FOX TAVERN, Middleburg, Virginia: Jefferson slept here; Washington surveyed the land; and Civil War rebels used the building, constructed in 1728, as headquarters. (The bar is made from the table used by J. E. B. Stuart's surgeon.) Later, because Middleburg lies in the heart of the Virginia hunt country, the inn prospered as a social center for the horsey set. But then for some reason it went into a decline and might well have gone the way of countless other old American buildings had it not been for the energetic ministrations of a local lady who wanted to do some good for the community and have a little fun at the same time. And so it was that the *Red Fox Tavern* was filled up with Williamsburg wallpapers and with antique furniture and paintings which, like so many of the people who come here once again for their hunt breakfasts, speak of horses as if there were no other subject in the world. In the dining room (pegged floors; stone wall; fireplaces; Windsor chairs), the innkeeper serves classic southern breakfasts and wonderful lunches and dinners that mix local specialties like crabcakes and peanut soup with steaks, chops, and Continental offerings such as veal with mushrooms and cream. Music and lighter fare are available in the pub out back. Horses are for rent, and there's plenty to watch — if not the National Beagle Trials, then plenty of races and shows. Information: Red Fox Tavern, Washington and Madison sts., PO Box 385, Middleburg, VA 22117 (703 687-6301). Turner Reuter, Jr., innkeeper. 17 rooms.

THE COUNTRY INN, Berkeley Springs, West Virginia: The six imposing white pillars on the front of this building suggest formality. But don't be deceived; this country inn is about as friendly as an inn can be and is a great place to stay when you come into the area — to visit 5,000-acre Cacapon State Park (where there's hiking, riding, cross-country skiing, swimming, and tennis); to tour hour-distant Harpers Ferry National Historical Park, where John Brown staged his notorious raid, or Charlestown, with its Shenendoah Downs; or simply to take the waters in Berkeley Springs, where, at one of the oldest spas in the country, the administering state parks department offers Turkish and Roman baths, massages, and mineral baths at rates that are almost unbelievably low. Moreover, the eating at the inn could hardly be better. Concoctions like chicken-cucumber-onion soup keep company on the menu with a great array of dishes. The plant- and flower-filled *Country Garden* dining room is a delight; the art gallery in the lobby displays some 140 works, from rural scenes painted by local artists to the Old Masters. The inn's adjoining Colonial-style three-story property called *Country Inn West* offers an additional 36 rooms. Information: The Country Inn, 207 S Washington St., Berkeley Springs, WV 25411 (304 258-2210). Jack and Adele Barker, innkeepers. 72 rooms.

THE GENERAL LEWIS INN, Lewisburg, West Virginia: What started out as a private home on a hilltop back in 1834 and grew over the years into a magnificent mansion, with columns in the front and a sweep of beautiful lawns all about, has been a classic inn in a lovely, old-fashioned town since 1929 — much to the delight of traveling Americans enamored of antique-furnished rooms and hearty country meals.

Information: General Lewis Inn, Lewisburg, WV 24901 (304 645-2600). John McIlhenny, innkeeper. 27 rooms.

MIDWEST

ABE MARTIN LODGE, Nashville, Indiana: Like many other Indiana state park lodging places, the rustic stone and log Abe Martin Lodge at Brown County State Park is not long on antique-filled sleeping accommodations and fancy cuisine. Guest quarters both in the lodge and in the surrounding cabins tend toward the plain but comfortable, and food toward the homestyle; fried chicken and biscuits are the order of almost every day. But few far more sumptuously furnished hostelries can boast such a setting — in the midst of 15,000 acres of wooded hills (a landscape that gives the lie to stories about Indiana being pancake-flat); the scenery is gorgeous during the pink and white springs, when the dogwoods and redbuds deluge the hills with a rosy blizzard, and in the blazing autumns, when the hardwoods turn scarlet, yellow, and all the colors in between. The scene brings the Great Smokies to mind, if on a smaller scale. Nearby Nashville, a small town gone touristy with galleries and antique shops, is quaint and distinctively Hoosier. Information: Abe Martin Lodge, PO Box 25, Nashville, IN 47448 (812 988-4418).

NEW HARMONY INN, New Harmony, Indiana: Associated with a restoration of two 19th-century communes that flourished here (see *Utopias*), the *New Harmony Inn* may be the most beautiful new hostelry in America: The lines are spare and clean, like those of a Shaker building, and the variety of woods used as furniture, floors, stairways, and moldings provides a visual treat. The spreads on the high beds are in natural colors as well; only the bathroom tiles are colored — and they are vivid indeed, as bright blue as the unusual glass-roofed swimming pool out back. Apart from Continental breakfasts available at the *Entry House,* no meals are served. But you can get a terrific lunch or dinner at the *Red Geranium,* a couple of minutes' walk from the inn. Information: New Harmony Inn, New Harmony, IN 4763d (812 682-4491). Gary Gerard, innkeeper. 45 rooms.

DEARBORN INN COLONIAL HOMES AND MOTOR HOUSES, Dearborn, Michigan: Built by Henry Ford in 1931 for very important visitors and Ford corporate officials, this cluster of motor houses and colonial homes (faithful reproductions of the finest examples of American Georgian architecture) is now an interesting inn open to the public. All the rooms are fine, but the homes, with their reproductions of early American decor and furniture, are particularly charming. The inn serves all meals, offers room service, has a heated pool and courts for tennis and shuffleboard, and livens up with a seafood buffet on Fridays and dinner and dancing on Saturdays. Nearby is Mr. Ford's grand display of Americana, Greenfield Village and the Henry Ford Museum. A public golf course is also nearby. Information: Dearborn Inn Colonial Homes and Motor Houses, 20301 Oakwood Blvd., Dearborn, MI 48123-4099 (313 271-2700 or 800 221-7237 in Michigan; 800 221-7236 elsewhere). Adrian A. de Vogel, innkeeper. 179 rooms.

NATIONAL HOUSE INN, Marshall, Michigan: The one-man preservation drive launched by a former Marshall mayor, one Harold Brooks, over a half century ago is finally bearing fruit, and hundreds of people are now actively involved in breathing new life into the town's beauty spots. Brooks bought several choice homes — the finest examples of 19th-century architecture in the area — and held them until he found buyers willing to restore and preserve the structures in their original style. Later, thanks to an enlightened zoning code and community cooperation, more and more homes were saved, so that by now 12 of them are in the National Register and 35 more are listed by the state as historic landmarks; all are examples of fine Victorian workmanship. The *National House* (1835) is the oldest operating inn in Michigan. It started as a hotel, served as a stop on the Underground Railroad (with abandoned tunnels and a hidden cellar room to show for it), went through several transformations — once into a windmill factory and another time into an apartment house — and has in recent years been restored in the Victorian style of its distinguished neighbors. From the doorknobs to the bed linens, everything has been done with a reverence for the original. The highlight of the year is the town's annual Historic Home Tour, the first weekend after Labor Day, when thousands come here to inspect the restored houses. Information: National House Inn, 102 S Parkview, Marshall, MI 49068 (616 781-7374). Jack and Sharlene Anderson, innkeepers. 16 rooms.

LOWELL INN, Stillwater, Minnesota: Built more than half a century ago, this gracious, Colonial-style inn, with its 13 columns and high portico, has been run by the Palmer family since 1930 with a greater-than-usual degree of sensitivity to the proper care and feeding of guests. The bedrooms have been recently redone (but no televisions were added to disturb the peace), and each of the three popular dining rooms has a different motif: The Garden Room, stone-floored, with wrought-iron tables and chairs, has a pretty trout pool from which you can pick your supper; the George Washington Room, full of bright napery and gleaming silver, reflects the colonial period; and the Matterhorn Room, whose specialty is fondue, is full of Swiss woodcarvings that seldom fail to evoke *oohs* and *ahs* from about everyone who sees them. Lowell, which is just about 18 miles from St. Paul, is chockablock with antique shops; and after the bustle of the Twin Cities seems about the most heavenly place on earth. Information: Lowell Inn, 102 N 2nd St., Stillwater, MN 55082 (612 439-1100). Arthur and Maureen Palmer, innkeepers. 21 rooms.

ST. GEMME BEAUVAIS, Ste. Genevieve, Missouri: A number of the late-18th- and early-19th-century buildings in this surprise of a town, whose founding in 1732 makes it Missouri's first permanent settlement, have been restored — among them the Amoureaux House, part of which dates from 1770; the 1790 Green Tree Tavern, the town's first inn; and *St. Gemme Beauvais,* its only operating inn. As befits the town's French heritage, the hostelry's breakfasts and lunches (the only meals served) feature Continental concoctions like quiche, crêpes, and omelettes; in keeping with the age of the structure, the parlors and guest accommodations are almost entirely done up in Victorian antiques — immense carved bedsteads that make you feel small no matter how much you ate for lunch, ornately framed mirrors, dressing tables with marble tops, a handsome old dining table and chairs. Lace curtains, flowered wallpapers, and draperies in the Victorian manner complete the effect, which is every bit as charming as the town itself. No wonder the citizens of St. Louis, less than two hours away, are so fond of the place. And for those who don't mind making the short walk to the inn for meals, a 5-room annex in an 1850 house provides equally luscious accommodations. Open all year. Information: St. Gemme Beauvais, 78 N Main, Box 231, Ste. Genevieve, MO 63670 (314 883-5744). Frankye and Boats Donze, innkeepers. 8 rooms, with an additional 5-room annex.

BUXTON INN, Granville, Ohio: Granville — in the middle of the state, near Denison University, the Heisey Glass Museum, and the Indian Mound Museum — is anybody's idea of how a Middle American town should look: spotlessly clean, with tree-lined streets, graceful buildings, inviting homes, and pleasant shops. It's a perfect setting for the growing *Buxton Inn* (not to be confused with its larger neighbor, the *Granville Inn*). The rooms have been furnished with a keen eye for the right antiques; several of the chandeliers are especially worth noting. And so, too, is the food. There's a fireplace in the front dining room, which has low ceilings to enhance its cozy atmosphere. Lunch and dinner, served every day in its atmospheric dining rooms, include French-American specialties like seafood coquille cardinale, Louisiana chicken (rolled in seasoned flour, sautéed, and served with a cream sauce, toasted almonds, and artichoke hearts), tournedos chasseur, and chocolate mousse cake. Also don't miss the bean soup. Information: Buxton Inn, 313 E Broadway, Granville, OH 43023 (614

587-0001). Orville and Audrey Orr, innkeepers. 3 rooms, with an additional 12-room annex.

GOLDEN LAMB INN, Lebanon, Ohio: Midway between Cincinnati and Dayton in a town of 10,000, Ohio's oldest inn has, since its founding in 1803, provided lodging to ten presidents, DeWitt Clinton, Henry Clay, Mark Twain, and a very cross Charles Dickens (who visited when the *Golden Lamb* was a temperance hotel and complained that he couldn't get a drink). The location, smack in the middle of town, is its single unappealing characteristic nowadays — but the antique-furnished rooms, some fitted out with four-posters, are among the most pleasant in the area, and the inn makes a fine base for a couple of days' canoeing or fishing on the Little Miami River, or visiting the nearby museums. The food at the inn is good, and overnight guests get preferred seating. Try some of the Shaker items on the menu. Information: Golden Lamb Inn, 27 S Broadway, Lebanon, OH 45036 (513 932-5065). Jackson B. Reynolds, innkeeper. 19 rooms.

WHITE GULL INN, Fish Creek, Wisconsin: Fish Creek is just what it sounds like, Door County's gift to those who just want a small, far-out-of-the-way place near water where things are fairly quiet and the eating's good, something like Montauk or Cape Cod. As for the food you can't beat the Fish Boil dinner, the best of the day's catch from Lake Michigan with boiled potatoes, a tasty coleslaw, and homemade cherry pie. Wash it down with a beer and amble down to the harbor and then back to bed for a good night's sleep to prepare for another day of the same. Information: White Gull Inn, PO Box 159, Fish Creek, WI 54212 (414 868-3517). Andrew and Jan Coulson, innkeepers. 14 rooms and 4 cottages with fireplaces.

WEST

ARIZONA INN, Tucson, Arizona: When Isabella Greenway (a bridesmaid of Eleanor Roosevelt and the state's only woman congressional delegate) opened this as an inn in 1930, it was primarily a desert oasis for the mighty, the mighty rich, and the well-heeled well-knowns — Rockefellers, Windsors, movie stars, and such. But the inn, no longer off in the desert by itself and no longer beyond the reach of lesser souls, has found itself surrounded by Tucson. No matter, it goes its own luxurious way in the manner and spirit in which it was conceived.

The gardens will astonish you first: flourishing amid the arid desert environment are 14 acres of lawns and flowers scattered with bushes and trees and crisscrossed by lovely footpaths; to take care of them, the inn employs more gardeners than some inns welcome as guests. Inside, the color scheme is a Mexican-American symphony of corals, beiges, grays, and reds that harmonize with the desert surroundings. A full-time staff decorator keeps things looking their best. A vivid blue heated pool is shaded on one side (to the delight of those for whom the glaring sun can be too much). You can play tennis (and the courts are floodlit) or, not far away, go riding or enjoy a round of golf. A good portion of the staff has worked here for a couple of decades or more, reflected in their unfailingly professional service. The Continental menu attracts diners from all over the state. Information: Arizona Inn, 2200 E Elm St., Tucson, AZ 85719 (602 325-1541; 800 421-1093). Robert Minerich, innkeeper. 85 rooms, 8 suites.

TANQUE VERDE RANCH, Tucson, Arizona: When is a dude ranch a country inn? When the dude ranch is, like this one 12 miles outside Tucson on the edge of the 1.4-million-acre Coronado National Forest and the lovely 63,000-acre Saguaro National Monument, the last word in luxury and personable charm. No run-of-the-mill dude ranch, the *Tanque Verde*, part of which used to be a stagecoach stop, has five tennis courts, indoor and outdoor swimming pools and a therapy pool, saunas, exercise rooms, and other luxuries. Most rooms have fireplaces and patios, and all have phones (but no TVs). Antiques are scattered throughout the inn. Some 200 species of birds, from the bridled titmouse to the bald eagle, have been identified in the area, and the inn is so popular with bird-watchers that bird-banding is a regular activity. Riding, however, is still the big deal, and you can do it to your heart's content (or your bottom's protest) on your choice of some 100 horses, on supervised trail rides that take place several times daily. And when all is said and done, there's the *Dog House Bar,* a bunkhouse converted to a bottle club. Information: Tanque Verde Ranch, Rte. 8, PO Box 66, Tucson, AZ 85748 (602 296-6275). Bob Cote, innkeeper. 47 rooms, 13 suites.

VENTANA INN, Big Sur, California: Boasting a setting as stupendous as any in the country — an expanse of staggeringly beautiful meadows in the rugged Santa Lucia Mountains that drop precipitously down to the rocky shoreline of the California coast 150 miles south of San Francisco — the *Ventana Inn* is quintessentially California modern. That means pale natural cedar, plenty of wicker, patchwork quilts, Franklin stoves and window seats, patios and private balconies, cathedral ceilings with giant beams, a swimming pool long enough for healthful laps, Japanese hot baths and a sauna. Sybarites can take the pleasure even further — by choosing one of the rooms with a hot tub or indulging in a massage or facial. Hiking in the woods is literally right outside the door; the beach, but a short walk away. Breakfast is served on a tray in your room or buffet style in the lobby in front of the fireplace — fresh juice and fruits, homemade breads and pastries, honey, coffee, and both herbal and caffeinated tea. But perhaps best of all are the sweeping vistas that take in all that splendid natural scenery. The silence — broken only, in the breakfast room, by classical music and the ticking of the clock and, in the guest quarters, by the rush of the wind through the pines — is not bad, either. Information: Ventana Inn, Hwy. 1, Big Sur, CA 93920 (408 667-2331). Randy Smith and Robert Bussinger, innkeepers. 40 rooms.

MOUNT VIEW HOTEL, Calistoga, California: Built in 1918, enlarged in 1938, and renovated in 1980, this two-story, beige stucco wine country establishment is a showplace of the art deco style. The lobby, warmed by a big fireplace and decked out with potted palms, is full of overstuffed sofas and chrome-trimmed chairs. The lounge is all black and silver, from the patterned wallpaper to the ebony cocktail tables and the chrome chairs. The dining room, where innovative California cuisine is the star, has deco light fixtures. And the bedrooms are full of original furniture that has been relacquered or otherwise refinished. Especially noteworthy is the Tom Mix Suite, whose brown velvet settees trimmed with curled Texas longhorns are said to have belonged to the famous cowboy movie star; and the Carol Lombard Suite, in which the bed has a fan-shaped headboard paved with beveled mirrors that match the mirrored façades of the bedside tables. Sunday brunches featuring Dixieland and swing music bring visitors from miles around. Also, don't miss the mudbaths for which the town is famous. Information: Mount View Hotel, 1457 Lincoln Blvd., Calistoga, CA 94515 (707 942-6877). Scott Ulrich, innkeeper. 34 rooms and suites.

VAGABOND'S HOUSE, Carmel-by-the-Sea, California: It's one thing to restore a neglected but fundamentally magnificent old building. It's a trick of quite another sort to take a group of efficiency units from the early 1940s and transform them into a charming inn worthy of unique natural surroundings. But that's what the innkeepers have done here on the loveliest part of the northern California coast. Antiques collected over the years crowd the inn's rooms. The ticking of old clocks is one of their characteristic sounds, along with the chattering of the squirrels who inhabit a wonderful main garden patio centered on an immense old live oak, dotted with rhododendron and camellia bushes, and hung here and there with baskets of ferns, begonias, and fuchsias. Most rooms face that patio, and each has a character all its own, depending on the particular mix of maple and wicker, bentwood and books, brass and quilts; most of the rooms have a fireplace. The combination of such details makes the inn one of the loveliest places to stay when you come to this area to see the much-photographed Point Lobos and the redwoods at Big Sur and to browse through the Carmel shops. The inn serves only Continental breakfast. Nearby, under the same management, the newly renovated *San Antonio House Inn* offers private two- and three-room suites with antiques and original art, a patio or garden, refrigerator, fireplaces, and fresh flowers. Information: Vagabond's House Inn, 4th and Dolores sts., PO Box 2747, Carmel-by-the-Sea, CA 93921 (408 624-7738 or 408 624-4334). Bruce Indorato, innkeeper. 12 rooms.

CITY HOTEL, Columbia, California: Thanks to a State Parks Department historic preservation project, this once fabulously prosperous Gold Rush town three hours from San Francisco is a living museum of the area's mid-19th-century boom days, and from spring through fall the town is jammed with sightseers. A highlight of nearly everyone's visit is a stop at this two-story brick hotel, restored in the 70s to the tune of over $500,000. The gold diggers of those long-gone days liked their comforts every bit as much as the tourists do, and when they struck it rich, they would usually go all out to treat themselves. And so a hotel in a town like this was apt to be just as grand as you find the *City Hotel,* the passion for the good life reflected in the furnishings — tufted settees, marble-topped washstands and bureaus, Victorian bedsteads in burled wood or brass, Oriental rugs, a rosewood piano, brass hat racks and chandeliers gleaming at every turn. What you don't expect is a wine list as excellent and extensive as the one you find in the gorgeously furnished restaurant, or a kitchen that is not only so competent but so talented; some people come to Columbia just for the food. Information: City Hotel, PO Box 1870, Main St., Columbia, CA 95310 (209 532-1479). Tom Bender, innkeeper. 9 rooms.

ST. ORRES, Gualala, California: The shoddiness of most contemporary building notwithstanding, a renaissance of interest in fine workmanship has quietly been taking place in America. As just one example, consider this inn on the northern California coast, a Russian palace of a structure built of redwood and salvaged materials around a tumbledown old guest house by a couple of carpenters-with-a-dream, and then named for the family that homesteaded the land. The interior is an exercise in woodworking virtuosity. Redwood paneling on the bedroom walls is meticulously tongue-in-grooved and laid in intriguing patterns that are as distinguished as those of an ancient fresco, or, for that matter, the ones you find in the velvet quilts that were hand-stitched by a talented local craftswoman for the beds. And the dining room — a three-story space walled partially in redwood-framed stained glass and topped by another copper onion dome — may be more arresting than any other restaurant in the country. In such a setting, you expect original meals, and you get them — wonderful variations on Continental classics for which some people drive all the way from San Francisco; a concoction known as chocolate decadence may make a chocoholic of you even if you don't have a sweet tooth. There is even a spa next to the creekside cottages. The totality is so marvelous that the peaceful setting amongst the beaches, coves, and redwoods is just icing on the cake. Information: St. Orres, PO Box 523, Gualala, CA 95445 (707 884-3303). Eric Black, Ted Black, Rosemary Campiformio, innkeepers. 8 rooms, 9 cottages.

TIMBER COVE INN, Jenner, California: Set on a rocky sea-view promontory 90 miles north of San Francisco, this establishment has a lobby with a full-length window at one end, a massive "walk-in" fireplace at the other, and a beamed, 40-foot ceiling overhead. Most of the rooms have hot tubs, fireplaces, and ocean views. Throughout, natural woods, walls of stone or whitewashed barn siding, and exposed beams lend a rustic feel. There's a meditation pool, a redwood grove, and a fern-fluffed canyon right on the grounds, and 26 acres of oceanside hiking trails. The whole place is utterly quiet and peaceful, in perfect harmony with the spectacular surroundings. Information: Timber Cove Inn, 21780 North Coast Hwy., Jenner, CA 95450 (707 847-3231; the inn itself is 14 miles north of Jenner). Richard Hojohn, innkeeper. 49 rooms.

HERITAGE HOUSE, Little River, California: Because so many early California settlers were homesick when they first arrived here from New England, they built their houses in styles that would remind them of the East Coast, and left this part of the West liberally sprinkled with New Hampshire cottages and Down East farmhouses like the one at the core of the main building of this inn on California's northern coast (which, incidentally, Baby Face Nelson once used as a hideout). But even though the original structure has been added to many times over the three decades since the present innkeeper came here in 1949, most of the rooms are not in the farmhouse but in small, medium, large, and extra-large guest cottages surrounding it. Each set of quarters is different. Some of the old ones, originally sited elsewhere in the coast region, were knocked down, transported to Little River, reassembled with varying degrees of fidelity to the original, and then luxuriously furnished; others were built from salvaged lumber. All the rooms have private baths; many have fireplaces or pot-bellied stoves and — most important of all — views of the ocean, which is what you come here for in the first place. As for the kitchen, it eschews the Continental in favor of the best of American cuisine — everything from the tiny pancakes to the cream soups and meat and fish entrées. Information: Heritage House, 5200 N Highway 1, Little River, CA 95456 (707 937-5885). L. D. Dennen, innkeeper. 65 rooms.

UNION HOTEL, Los Alamos, California: This old hotel, originally built in 1880 and rebuilt, after a fire, in 1915, had gone through more than 25 owners and nearly as many incarnations — as pool hall, dance hall, rooming house, and candidate for the wrecker's ball — when, in 1972, a meat wholesaler from not-far-distant Los Angeles, casting about for a new career, discovered the place and decided that running an inn was just what he had always wanted to do. He hired a carpenter and bought a couple of old barns, a trio of old sheds, and a garage to use as lumber to re-create the facade of the first Union Hotel as portrayed in an old print. And then he went out antique hunting. When he came home from his travels, he had enough furniture and knickknacks to give the empty building the cluttered look that a structure of its vintage deserved. Look around you, and marvel: Here are century-old gaslights from Mississippi and chairs hand-carved in Alabama, a mantelpiece from a Pasadena mansion and a vintage Singer sewing machine; there you see the chandeliers that once graced the home of Lee J. Cobb, a lamp used in the filming of *Gone With the Wind*, a grandfather clock, a 150-year-old bar made of African mahogany and an ivory-inlaid Brunswick pool table. Scattered around the guest rooms are a mahogany armoire that conceals a Murphy bed, a brass and iron bedstead inset with cloisonné work, and countless antique four-posters, quilts, crocheted bedspreads, and vintage Bibles. After all this Victorian clutter, the spacious dining room (where unpretentious home cooking is the order of the day) and the rough-paneled Western bar (which you enter through swinging doors that once admitted customers to a southern bordello) are a welcome change. The inn and restaurant are open only Friday through Sunday nights (year-round). Kids are charged for their food according to how much they weigh on a big butcher scale. A hundred feet west of the hotel, an 1864 three-story Victorian house should be open by 1987 after extensive restoration work. Information: Union Hotel, 362 Bell St., Los Alamos, CA 93440 (805 928-3838). Richard Langdon, proprietor. 15 rooms.

THE MacCALLUM HOUSE, Mendocino, California: East is East and West is West and they meet here, three hours north of San Francisco. Mendocino, Nantucket West to many, is another example of how the early California settlers brought New England to the coast. *The MacCallum House* happens to be one of the prettier expressions of the Easterners' homesickness. Built in 1882 by lumber magnate William H. Kelley as a wedding present for his daughter Daisy and her husband Alexander MacCallum, this three-story Victorian mansion, trimmed with jigsaw-cut woodwork and fronted by a wonderful expanse of windows, was bought by two San Franciscans in 1974, about 20 years after Daisy's death. With the house, they purchased almost all of the furnishings, and so, when you visit, you can browse through Daisy's library (which includes some handsome leatherbound books, some volumes in French and German, some books on travel and religion, and a good many romantic novels) and admire the Tiffany lamps, Persian carpets, and carved footstools that belonged to the MacCallums themselves until not long ago. Some of the guest rooms are in the main building, but the old carriage house, the barn, and the greenhouse have also been rebuilt, and most guests are accommodated there. The elegant Continental dinners devised by Tim Cannon have become a tradition. A short walk from town are the headlands at Russian Gulch State Park that can be described by only one word — spectacular. Information: The MacCallum House, PO Box 206, Mendocino, CA 95460 (707 937-0289). Melanie and Joe Reding, innkeepers. 20 rooms.

HOTEL LEGER, Mokelumne Hill, California: Restored and refurbished in 1960 and again in 1984, the pleasant Victorian interior of this century-old former beer hall and its two-storied veranda (pillars below and railing above) seem to re-create, for a moment, the Gold Rush days of the mid-19th century, and sometimes you can almost imagine how it was in Mok' Hill that famous weekend of legend when no less than 17 hangings took place in one night. The rooms are old-fashioned, with flowered wallpaper, high Victorian beds, and plenty of rocking chairs. The surrounding Mother Lode Country is less gussied up than some other sections of California's former mining regions, and it's a welcome change. But if you don't want to go out exploring, you can just laze around the swimming pool out back among the orange trees. French food is served in the dining room on weekends. Information: Hotel Leger, PO Box 50, Mokelumne Hill, CA 95245 (209 286-1401). Brandy Clark, innkeeper. 13 rooms.

SAN YSIDRO RANCH, Montecito, California: Originally owned by the Franciscan Missions, this 540-acre resort near Santa Barbara, which opened in 1893, enjoyed a long season as the choice vacation spot of the rich and the famous: Laurence Olivier and Vivien Leigh were married here; John F. Kennedy honeymooned with Jackie here; John Galsworthy, Aldous Huxley, Sinclair Lewis, Winston Churchill, Somerset Maugham, Bing Crosby, Jack Benny, and many others stayed here; and Ronald Colman owned the place from the mid-30s until his death in 1958. But in the 60s, the legend began to fade, and the inn started to fall apart and was well down the road to total ruin when Jim Lavenson, former president of New York's great Plaza Hotel, put up the money to clean up, fix up, and paint up. And so, when you visit today, the three tennis courts, stables, restaurant, and swimming pool are all as spiffy as they were when Galsworthy revised his *Forsyte Saga* there (if not more so: nine of the guest cottages have their own Jacuzzis). You can hole up in front of your fireplace, order room service, and never see the day, or mix with fellow guests in the bar and dining room. The kitchen, whose specialties include a smattering of both the French and the American, is good enough that among those who drop in to say "Hi!" to the chef are none other than Julia Child and Danny Kaye. Special meals grace the tables on holidays. The ranch is one of only six American inns listed in the prestigious Relais et Châteaux guide. Information: San Ysidro Ranch, 900 San Ysidro La., Montecito, CA 93108 (805 969-5046). Jim and Susie Lavenson, innkeepers. 39 cottages.

THE INN AT RANCHO SANTA FE, Rancho Santa Fe, California: It was one of those classic corporate bloopers: The Atcheson, Topeka and Santa Fe Railroad bought up some 9,000 acres of cheap land to plant 3 million eucalyptus trees to provide — company officials hoped — an endless supply of railroad ties. Nobody had bothered to think, however, that eucalyptus trees grow crooked, not straight — and though the trees took off, there wasn't a tie to be had in the bunch. The railroad then went into the citrus business, and, later, started up a residential development, one of the first planned communities in the country. The inn was first built to house prospective purchasers and it just kept on growing until it became what you find here today — a sedate and very restful complex of unpretentious cottages nestling in the luxuriant shrubbery on the grounds surrounding the original building. There are three tennis courts, a heated swimming pool, an English croquet court, and, nearby, two fine golf courses and a beach. The inn will pack you a box lunch. There's a wonderful library and a high-ceilinged lounge; and the whole thing is just 27 miles from San Diego. Information: The Inn at Rancho Santa Fe, PO Box 869, Rancho Santa Fe, CA 92067 (619 756-1131). Dan D. Royce, innkeeper. 75 rooms.

WINE COUNTRY INN, St. Helena, California: Here in Napa Valley, some 70 miles from San Francisco, is a rarity: a brand-new, built-from-scratch, old-fashioned country inn. Ned and Marge Smith spent years dreaming, talking, sketching, and planning inns; they traveled to classic inn country, lived there as guests, and picked the brains of innkeepers. And when they were ready a few years ago, they built their own, a marriage of the old and new made in inn Heaven. Each room is different; most have fireplaces and all have character. Thanks to the careful attention to detail, it all works as it should. Breakfast is the only meal, and it's served in a large, attractive common room. There are many fine restaurants in the area, and the menus for most of them are available for your perusal. Information: Wine Country Inn, 1152 Lodi La., St. Helena, CA 94574 (707 963-7077). Jim Smith, innkeeper. 25 rooms.

MANSION HOTEL, San Francisco, California: Unlike many other cities of its size, San Francisco is blessed with an inn — and a highly unusual one it is. The *Mansion Hotel,* created by a former ad man, boasts 18 rooms with private bath — some almost *House & Garden* charming. There's the lovely John Muir Room, for instance, and the elegant Empress Josephine Room, with its Louis XIV canopy bed and matching mirrored armoire, private sundeck, and bar; Barbra Streisand and Robin Williams have been among recent guests. Some rooms have a marble fireplace, some a private terrace, some a slanted, garret-like ceiling. All are named for some historic personage (a mural on the wall depicts his or her life) and all have speakers so you can tune into classical music. Downstairs, there's more of the same elegance — crystal chandeliers, original art, and beautiful paneling, for starters. Victorian memorabilia — beaded bags, lace shawls, antique clothing — is all around. Among the most interesting features, however, are the ghostly spirits whose presence was certified by the same demonologists that exorcised the celebrated house in Amityville, New York. Room rates include fresh flowers in the room; complimentary wine upon arrival, and coffee and tea nightly; Mansion Magic Concerts — and, of course, breakfast in bed. Other features include a music parlor, game room and library, billiard room, and an elegant restaurant open only to hotel guests and friends; chef David Coyle, who served the Duke and Duchess of Bedford in Woburn Abbey Palace for more than a decade, turns out ambitious entrées like prime New York cut steak accompanied by wine, mushroom, and truffle sauce; fettuccine tossed with shrimp and a basil, garlic, and Romano cheese sauce; boneless trout stuffed with smoked roe and doused with a Chablis sauce; and venison and juniper berry pâté marinated in port and fines herbes. In a toncy residential neighborhood, the *Mansion* is San Francisco's only designated Landmark Hotel. Information: Mansion Hotel, 2220 Sacramento St., San Francisco, CA 94115 (415 929-9444). Robert Pritikin, innkeeper. 18 rooms.

SONOMA HOTEL, Sonoma, California: This old wood and adobe structure, which started out in the 1870s as a dry goods store and meeting hall, was carefully restored in 1976 by the present owners, so that it now has a delightful Gay Nineties ambience. All of the rooms are furnished in turn-of-the-century European and American antiques; Room 3 is named after the Mexican General Vallejo (who founded the town) and furnished with his own exquisitely carved rosewood bedroom suite, which is currently on loan from the Sonoma League for Historic Preservation. In the morning, when you go downstairs for Continental breakfast in the inn's charming lobby, the management will help you plan a good tour of the surrounding wine country and nearby points of interest like the Jack London State Historic Park at Glen Ellen, where you can see the ruins of London's own Wolf House as well as the home of his widow, filled with London memorabilia. They can also help you arrange horseback or hot air balloon rides, picnics, and massages in your room. Information: Sonoma Hotel, 110 W Spain St., Sonoma, CA 95476 (707 996-2996). Dorene and John Musilli, innkeepers. 17 rooms.

SUTTER CREEK INN, Sutter Creek, California: One of the oldest country inns in the West, this green-shuttered bit of New England in California, built in 1859 by a wealthy merchant for his eastern bride, came into the possession of Jane Way, a somewhat psychic palm reader, graphologist, and former housewife, in 1966. Jane turned the place into an inn. She installed canopy beds, queen-size beds, and beds that swing, ever so gently, by chains from the ceiling. (If you can't get used to the motion, you can stabilize your bed.) Some of the bathtubs were sunk into the floors. Fireplaces and Franklin stoves were installed. Outbuildings were converted to guest rooms. Chintz by the yard was swathed around squashy sofas, draped over beds, and hung at the windows. There are plenty of antiques, but they're the kind that look as if they don't mind being used. The place feels comfortable, reflecting (with a greater degree of fidelity than is usual) the personality of the innkeeper herself. Jane doesn't serve lunch or dinner — she leaves that to other innkeepers in the area — but instead she offers her guests the chance to congregate first thing in the morning over a big eggs-and-sausage breakfast in the brick-walled kitchen, a room as warm as the flash of the copper utensils hung from beams and walls alike. When the conversation lags, Jane may add brandy to your coffee (if you haven't already done so), or swirl it with a cinnamon stick, just because it's more festive that way. Or she might be persuaded to tell you how she came to terms with the ghost she encountered when she first arrived at the inn, or about her father, who is known locally for having brought France's Colombard grape to California. Or, because she is well versed in local history, she might tell you the sad tale of John Sutter, who had built up one of the state's biggest ranches when a carpenter working in the area discovered gold in one of his streams in 1848 and set off a gold rush that had prospectors killing his cattle, destroying his land, and ruining his hopes for a comfortable old age. Only the memory remains: Sutter Creek today is beautifully kept, an antiquer's delight. Information: Sutter Creek Inn, 75 Main St., Box 385, Sutter Creek, CA 95685 (209 267-5606). Jane Way, innkeeper. 19 rooms.

AHWAHNEE HOTEL, Yosemite National Park, California: Built in 1927 in a deep wide valley guarded by granite mountains, ostensibly to accommodate the growing number of visitors arriving in the park by automobile, this marvelous establishment is rustic but luxurious, with slate floors, beamed ceilings, a cavernous lobby, and immense windows in even the smallest sitting rooms to give you views into the park. The *Ahwahnee* is the kind of place where dressing for dinner is the order of the day. Yet the old stone structure manages at the same time to so harmonize with the surroundings that even Frank Lloyd Wright admired it. Meals in the vast and imposing dining room, especially notable for its towering picture windows and heavily beamed ceiling, are highlighted by salmon (sometimes broiled, sometimes poached in white wine) and prime rib. Like the park, the hotel is open all year. But you'd be hard-pressed to say which season is best for a visit. In summer, there's hiking all through the Sierra, and you can sign up for rock climbing schools or special programs dealing with high-altitude ecology. In winter, the favored pastimes include downhill and cross-country skiing, snowshoeing to some of the frozen waterfalls, or races and winter games sponsored by the park concessionaire. At Christmastime, usually the high point of the *Ahwahnee*'s season, the hotel hosts the annual Bracebridge Dinner, wherein a section from Washington Irving's *Sketch Book* is reenacted in song and drama: The good Squire Bracebridge, an English country gentleman who is seated at the head of the dining room on a table set up on a dais, entertains his guests (you, a few hundred others, and assorted satin-, velvet-, and fur-clad actors and singers) over a fabulous six-course dinner that includes a flaming plum pudding and a peacock pie. The pageantry is gorgeous, so the limited number of tickets are hard to come by. Currently, they're sold by lottery during the January preceding each dinner, but the procedure changes occasionally, so write in advance for particulars. Information: Yosemite Reservations, 5410 E Home Ave., Fresno, CA 93727 (209 252-4848). 121 rooms.

BURGUNDY HOUSE, Yountville, California: The rolling hills, bucolic landscapes, and usually sunny skies of California's three great wine-producing areas — the Mendocino, Napa, and Sonoma valleys — seem a world apart from usually congested, often foggy or rainy San Francisco, even though they're just an hour or so north. And so, when you come to the Napa Valley town of Yountville, which recently celebrated its sesquicentennial, you have scenery, delightful weather, and the Burgundy House besides. This luxurious inn — installed in a circa 1872 former antique shop, brandy distillery, and speakeasy with two-foot-thick fieldstone walls — has been decorated in eclectic style by innkeeper Mary Keenan, with all manner of antique pieces, many of them French. One room has its own patio, a few have private baths, and all have fine views over treetops or vineyards. No matter which you get, you'll be welcomed with a decanter of wine. And there's more of the same in a big common room, where many guests gather in the late afternoons or evenings and for breakfast; this is the kind of place where strangers become fast friends fast. (Nearby *Bordeaux House,* under the same management, is every bit as companionable, despite its sleek, contemporary look; this establishment is your best bet if you want your own bath. And all its rooms have fireplaces.) Between meals at any number of fine restaurants, you can shop for antiques, go ballooning or soaring; visit one of the several nearby spas for massages or steam or mud baths; or taste some wine. Information: Burgundy House, 6711 Washington St., PO Box 2766, Yountville, CA 94599 (707 944-2855). Mary and Bob Keenan, innkeepers. 14 rooms.

MAGNOLIA HOTEL, Yountville, California: Built in 1873 and probably used as a bordello and a rumrunners' headquarters at various times during its checkered past, this small, stylish, stone-walled wine country establishment is fitted out with marble-topped tables, brass or walnut beds covered with crocheted lace bedspreads, and other French antiques; about a third of the rooms have fireplaces, and all have private baths. But what put the place on the map originally was the brick-and-stone-walled dining room, where a single entrée, a different one each night, was served as the centerpiece for five-course meals to accompany wines from a 20,000-bottle cellar. This meal service may or may not have recommenced after a recent hiatus, but the breakfasts of French toast (doused with a special port wine syrup) or various egg dishes are excellent. The Jacuzzi and large swimming pool complete the experience. Information: Magnolia Hotel, 6529 Yount St., PO Drawer M, Yountville, CA 94599-1913 (707-944-2056). Bruce and Bonnie Locken, innkeepers. 12 rooms.

C LAZY U RANCH, Granby, Colorado: This establishment, at about 8,200 feet just west of the Continental Divide, is the real thing, a working ranch as well as the western version of a country inn. The emphasis, of course, is on horseback riding, and you're given your own personal mount to ride for the duration of your stay. But other horsing around also figures: ranch riding competitions and rodeos, to be specific. The *C Lazy U* is also a guest ranch, though, and so you'll find a heated pool, a whirlpool and sauna, tennis and racquetball courts, a skeet-shooting range, Ping-Pong tables, and miles of trails for hiking (and cross-country skiing in winter). And if that won't keep you busy, you can always go fishing — or just take a drive through the mountains. The large lodge, which faces a lake where you can ice-skate in winter, is surrounded by guest cottages. All the rooms are cozy and comfortable; the food is solid and plentiful; and evenings are convivial. Information: C Lazy U Ranch, PO Box 378, Granby, CO 80446 (303 887-3344). Randy George, ranch manager. 16 rooms, 23 suites.

RANCHO ENCANTADO, Tesuque, New Mexico: Surrounded on three sides by the Tesuque Indian Reservation and on the fourth by the Santa Fe National Forest, this top-notch Old Southwest resort hotel came into being in the 1930s as a very ordinary sort of desert lodge. But in the late 60s, Betty Egan, a Cleveland widow with four children, came here to start life over again. She took the place in hand and turned it into the exciting complex it is today, a luxurious Western guest ranch — more than a hotel, more than an inn; the sort of establishment where you expect to find cowbells and dried peppers and Indian weavings hanging here and there, the occasional rawhide chair, and lots of red tile. The guest rooms, all furnished with antiques and Southwestern Indian art and artifacts, all have their own patios; most have fireplaces. The tri-level dining room, walled in white adobe, looks out across the desert, some 170 acres of which make up the *Rancho Encantado* spread. For fun, you can swim in a heated outdoor pool, play tennis, go riding (on horses you hire by the hour), or join in many other indoor or outdoor activities. Food is Mexican, American, and Continental. (Be sure to try the sour cream chicken enchiladas and the carne asado, steak marinated with chili strips.) There are big feasts for Thanksgiving and Christmas. European Plan rates, which include no meals, prevail except in November and December. Information: Rancho Encantado, Rte. 4, Box 57C, Santa Fe, NM 87501 (505 982-3537). Betty Egan, innkeeper. 22 rooms, 36 vacation condominiums.

SALISHAN LODGE, Gleneden Beach, Oregon: A dedicated environmentalist who was also a thoroughgoing sybarite couldn't find a better spot for a vacation than this unusual modern resort on the Oregon coast about 90 miles west of Portland. Here, everything harmonizes with the spectacular landscape of lagoons, woods, beach, and ocean. Every bedroom, lounge, and dining room is further testimony to the good taste of the resort's designers and the architectural integrity of the complex. The creation of Oregon manufacturer John D. Gray, Salishan stands as one proof that good design and reverence for the environment can also be good business.

Rooms — all with fireplaces, big bathrooms, and oversized windows that frame forest or bay and ocean views — are in 15 villas that are connected by bridges and covered walkways. The dining room is also exceptionally handsome, and the kitchen is noted for its way with seafood, particularly salmon, which comes barbecued, baked in puff pastry, and fixed just about any other way you can imagine. The wine list is so extensive that it has an index; it enumerates everything from an unpretentious Beaujolais to a Lafite-Rothschild that costs more than a whole weekend's stay at some very nice places. The new wine cellar stocks some 30,000 bottles, and is available for tours, tastings, and even catered dinner parties. The resort even has its own art gallery and publishes a botanical guide to the flora on the grounds and in the area. And every guest is assigned his own parking space (a feature much appreciated by the Cadillac-Mercedes-BMW crowd that gravitates here). To round things out, there is an indoor swimming pool, therapy pool, and a variety of health club facilities (exercise rooms, saunas, and such); tennis courts, both indoors and outdoors; and golf. Bird- and whale-watching, deep-sea fishing, collecting driftwood, and studying the trees and the wildflowers on the nature trails can keep you plenty busy, however. Information: Salishan Lodge, PO Box 118, Gleneden Beach, OR 97388 (503 764-2371). Hank Hickox, innkeeper. 150 rooms, 3 suites.

TIMBERLINE LODGE, Timberline, Oregon: Those who lived through the Great Depression remember that the WPA (Works Progress Administration) was the whipping boy of everyone who condemned the New Deal as a waste, and that the men who worked for the organization were widely considered no better than a bunch of lazy bums. *Timberline Lodge,* built by the WPA with youths from the CCC (Civilian Conservation Corps) more than halfway up snow-capped, 11,246-foot Mt. Hood, puts the lie to that notion. Hundreds of Oregonians — trained to chisel stones, blacksmith, carve, and carpenter by locals and by craftsmen imported from Europe — created a structure that is truly monumental, from its 400-ton chimney (a hundred feet high) and its 750-pound bronze and brass weather vane, to the cathedral of a lobby, the massive staircases, and the giant doorway. Even the details are dazzling: the chairs made of hardwood, wrought iron, and rawhide; the newel posts carved with animals and birds from sawed-off telephone poles; stained glass murals portraying local scenes and creatures; hand-wrought chandeliers and lamps; rugs hooked from the blankets and uniforms used by the workers; and on and on. The ensemble is a structure in harmony with the mountain it calls home, a work of unusual architectural design and impressive craftsmanship — and a monument to American determination. When you visit, you'll lodge in rooms filled up with sturdy blond furniture, hand-woven rugs, and appliquéd spreads and curtains. Every room has a private bath and a good view (either of valley or peak). There's a heated pool and a sauna; you can ski in both summer and winter, and when the weather permits, you can hike or climb as well. At Christmastime, Richard Kohnstamm, who has been here since the 1950s, celebrates the season with such verve that even stay-at-homes don't miss the hearth fires back home. Information: Timberline Lodge, Timberline Lodge, OR 97028 (503 272-3311). Richard Kohnstamm, area operator. 57 rooms.

EXCELSIOR HOUSE, Jefferson, Texas: In the 19th century, this community 170 miles east of Dallas on the Louisiana border was a booming cotton-shipping center. But then the world, in the person of the railroads, passed it by. Business suffered, "progress" ceased, and Jefferson came into the 1950s virtually unscarred by the wrecker's ball. The brick and timber, grillework-embellished *Excelsior House,* a New Orleans style construction that was one of the town's most prominent buildings, was bought in 1961 by the Jesse Allen Wise Garden Club, and its members set about sanding and painting, polishing and papering, to return the hotel to the grandeur it knew back in the days when it was welcoming the wealthy and the famous (even a few presidents). The rooms are now furnished with warm cherry, mahogany, and maple dressers and sleigh beds, canopy beds, and Jenny Lind–style spool beds. In the public rooms, there are oriental rugs underfoot and chandeliers of crystal and porcelain overhead. Some of the ceilings are pressed tin, some are plaster. The windows are draped in the Victorian style. Breakfast, for which you convene on the sun porch, is the only meal served — but what a meal it is: ham and eggs, grits, and heaps of the fluffy, bite-sized Orange Blossom Muffins for which the hotel is famous. Also memorable are a visit to Jay Gould's luxurious private railway car, which was restored by the garden club after it was found rotting away in a field, and a leisurely tour of the town's several other historical sights. Information: Excelsior House, 211 W Austin St., Jefferson, TX 75657 (214 665-2513) Mary Ann Rhodes, manager. 14 rooms.

CAPTAIN WHIDBEY INN, Coupeville, Washington: The chief claim to fame of the peaceful, wooded island 50 miles north of Seattle where venerable Coupeville is located is this resort built in 1907, high above the sea, of the reddish logs of the locally plentiful madrona tree. A fixture of the Pacific Northwest vacation scene almost since the beginning, it is popular, however, not so much because of any superabundance of activities (it's as quiet as the island itself) but because it is a personality kid, a one-of-a-kind through and through. Dominating the lobby is a huge stone fireplace surrounded by easy chairs. The shelves of the library are jammed with books. The window-walled dining room, where you can order from a wine list as distinguished as any in the area and a menu that features all kinds of fish and crustaceans fresh from the cold local waters, gives you views of the ocean and beyond it in the east, the snowy summit of Mt. Baker. And the ceiling of the bar, a favorite watering hole in this part of the world, is hung with hundreds of empty bottles whose labels bear inscriptions testifying to the good times had during the consumption of their contents. Rooms in the main building, all of them furnished simply but with some antiques and all with down comforters, are like miniature log cabins; they share the baths at the end of the hall. For privacy and space, you want the equally charming rooms facing the lagoon. Information: Captain

Whidbey Inn, 2072 W Capt. Whidbey Inn Rd., Coupeville, WA 98239 (206 678-4097). John Stone and Geoff Stone, innkeepers. 25 rooms.

JAMES HOUSE, Port Townsend, Washington: Dreaming of a future as the West's greatest port, this community boomed as rich men working on getting richer poured into town. Of the great houses they built along the city's streets to show off their substance, Francis Wilcox James's was the most impressive. Built in 1889, at a cost of around $10,000 — back in the days when $2,000 or $3,000 would pay for more than adequate living quarters, and $4,000 was all that was required to construct something really splendid — this porticoed, dormered, many-chimneyed, peak-roofed, shingle Queen Anne mansion fell on hard times in the years after the railroads passed Port Townsend by, and left the early dreams unrealizable. The ceilings were lowered, the large rooms were partitioned into cubicles. Then, in the 1960s, Bill and Frances Eaton saw the house, loved it, bought it, and over the course of a decade restored it. The present owners, Rod and Deborah LaMontagne, have also given it heavy doses of TLC, as you can see when you visit: From the banisters and the parquet floors to the carved settees and the high-standing bedsteads, the *James House* gleams. Information: James House, 1238 Washington St., Port Townsend, WA 98368 (206 385-1238). Rod and Deborah LaMontagne, innkeepers. 12 rooms.

BED-AND-BREAKFAST

The day that stateside travelers had to really hunt for the inexpensive pleasures of Europe's B&Bs is fast becoming a memory as the B&B movement continues to boom. One B&B reservation service has placed more than 10,000 guests in private homes in the last 5 years, and it is only one of over 150 organizations in 1,000 American cities. In 1983, the yellow pages of the telephone book began including a heading for B&B reservations services.

The *American Bed and Breakfast Assn.* (PO Box 23294, Washington, DC 20026) can send you more information if you include a large, self-addressed, stamped envelope. Or you can consult any of several guidebooks on the subject: the association's *A Treasury of Bed & Breakfast* ($14.95; $17.95 postpaid first class) includes over 3,000 homes in the US and Canada, lists of reservation services, and a chapter on starting your own establishment. *Bed & Breakfast USA,* updated annually, by Betty Rundback and Nancy Kramer (Dutton; $9.95) includes some 600 listings; *Bed & Breakfast North America* (Betsy Ross Publications, 3057 Betsy Ross Dr., Bloomfield Hills, MI 48013; $8.25 postpaid) indexes 2,000 cities; *The Bed & Breakfast Guide* (National Bed & Breakfast Association, PO Box 332, Norwalk, CT 06852; $9.95; $11.20 postpaid) lists between 800 and 1,000 B&Bs in the US and Canada; and *Bed & Breakfast America: The Great American Guest House Book,* by John Thaxton (Burt Franklin, 235 E 44th St., New York, NY 10017; $8.95) lists 350 homes and inns in 38 states, recommended through the author's personal experience.

A number of organizations can help you reserve accommodations around the country:

Bed & Breakfast Company, PO Box 262, S Miami, FL 33243 (305 661-3270). B&Bs around Florida

Bed & Breakfast International — San Francisco, 151 Ardmore, Kensington, CA 94707 (415 525-4569); B&Bs nationwide

The Bed & Breakfast League, 3639 Van Ness St., NW, Washington, DC 20008 (202 363-7767); bookings in East Coast cities and California

Northwest Bed & Breakfast, 610 SW Broadway, Suite 609, Portland, OR 97205 (503 243-7616); 300 homes from California to British Columbia

Sweet Dreams and Toast, PO Box 4835-0035, Washington, DC 20008 (202 483-9191); B&Bs in Washington, DC, Maryland, and Virginia

Vacations on Farms and Ranches

 In the country, city people rediscover the sound of songbirds and the smell of grass. Suburbanites get the chance to poke around an area where the nearest neighbors live miles away. Parents can say to their children, "No, milk does not start out in cartons" — and then prove it. Youngsters can see people who live differently, think differently, and have different values. But even if there were no lessons to be learned, however, a stay at a farm or ranch would be a decidedly pleasant way to pass a couple of weeks, so it's no wonder that all over the country there are hundreds of farms and ranches welcoming guests.

No two are quite alike. On the one hand, there are the guest farms and dude ranches with tennis courts, fancy swimming pools, square dances, hayrides, jam-packed recreation programs, and the like; guests are the main business. On the other hand, there are family farms and working ranches where raising animals or crops is the central activity, and the owners take guests only to bring in extra money.

In the sampling below, inexpensive means you'll pay about $135 to $195 per person per week, moderate about $200 to $345, and expensive about $350 and up. However, sometimes the rates include unlimited use of facilities and all the riding you want — and sometimes one or more of the activities cost extra. Be sure to find out what's included when you price the ranches.

For a comprehensive description of farms and ranches of all kinds, plus addresses, phone numbers, rates, size, activities, and previous guests' comments, see Pat Dickerman's *Farm, Ranch & Country Vacations* ($13.95 postpaid from Farm & Ranch Vacations, 36 E 57th St., New York, NY 10022; 212 355-6334); Dickerman can also dispense advice and make reservations. Herewith, a short list of some of the most typical:

FAMILY FARMS

THE RODGERS DAIRY FARM, West Glover, Vermont: About 35 miles from the Canadian border in Vermont's unspoiled Northeast Kingdom, three generations of the Rodgers family run a 350-acre dairy farm on the same property which their Scottish ancestors settled in the early 1800s — and provide lodgings to city folk in a century-old, 17-room, white clapboard farmhouse surrounded by maple-shaded lawns ringed with an old-fashioned split-rail fence. Daytimes, you can watch the cows being milked by machine and learn to ride the pony and to reach under the clucking hens to gather eggs — scary but fun. You can make friends with the dogs and the kittens, pull weeds in the gardens, and gather vegetables which will appear on the big dinner table within the hour. If it's haying time you can help pick up bales of hay, stack them on the haywagons, and unload them in the barn. Or, if you want, you can drive a few miles to Shadow Lake for a swim, or to Barton, 12 miles away, to see what it's like to be in a town with 1,051 inhabitants (many more than in the villages of Glover and West Glover, pop. 650, combined), take in an auction or two, or just sit in lawn chairs under the maple trees. Information: James and Nancy Rodgers, Rodgers Dairy Farm, RFD 3, Box 57, West Glover, VT 05875 (802 525-6677). Inexpensive.

WILSON'S PINTO BEAN FARM, Yellow Jacket, Colorado: Everything at this southwestern Colorado establishment is comfortable and homey — but don't expect luxury: The trailer guests occupy is not a late model, and the three guest rooms in the farmhouse are not large. Yet to visit Esther, Art, and the Wilson children (in their teens and twenties) is to experience real, honest-to-goodness farm life — 1,100 acres of pinto beans, wheat, and alfalfa; an assortment of farm animals; and a shed with the huge modern farm machinery used for planting and harvesting crops. The Wilsons grow much of their own food, and Esther's home-churned butter, home-baked bread, kosher dills, sweet pickle chips, apricot jam, and chokecherry jelly turn up on the big family table like clockwork, along with apple, cherry, and plum pies. Biking and horseshoe pitching are favorite activities, as is hiking to Canyon Pasture, where you can see the remains of a settlement, now overgrown with sagebrush, that once housed more people than similar, better-preserved structures at nearby Mesa Verde National Park (see *National Parks,* DIRECTIONS). Also nearby in the red earth country of the Four Corners region are the Hovenweep and Canyon de Chelly National Monument. Open March through November. Information: Arthur and Esther Wilson, PO Box 252, Yellow Jacket, CO 81335 (303 562-4476). Inexpensive.

DUDE RANCHES

WHITE STALLION RANCH, Tucson, Arizona: Yot get the feeling of wide-open spaces on this 3,000-acre spread northwest of Tucson, at the foot of the rugged Tucson Mountains, within a 100,000-acre game preserve. The White Stallion is the only guest ranch in the area that can also claim a Longhorn cattle operation — but riding is the point here — owners Allen and Cynthia True raise quarter horses, and once a week the cowboys stage a rodeo in the ranch arena. Wranglers will take you into the saguaro-dotted desert around the ranch house up to four times a day. And when you are not on horseback, the time is filled with hayrides, barbecues and cookouts, shuffleboard, and hikes. Or you can stake out a spot at poolside or in the cozy library, or visit the hot tub therapy room, or have a round of golf nearby, or a game of tennis on the ranch's Laykold courts. Everyone is on a first-name basis; the place is friendly and very informal, despite the size (about 45 guests in all). Open October through the first Sunday in May. Information: Allen and Cynthia True, White Stallion Ranch, 9251F W Twin Peaks Rd., Tucson, AZ 85743 (602 297-0252). Expensive.

COLORADO TRAILS RANCH, Durango, Colorado: See the Old West, hear its tales, and get the flavor of cowboy life — and at the same time lodge in a tidy little cabin with your own bath, carpeting, and electric heat, at this 525-acre mountain ranch just outside Durango, in the southwestern corner of Colorado. With up to 75 other vacationers, you can take riding lessons, go on trail rides and hayrides and overnight pack trips (the horse operation is one of the best of its kind), swim in a heated pool, lounge in the whirlpool, play tennis, fish for trout, water-ski on 10-mile-distant Vallecito Lake, or square dance. The staff puts on steak fries, variety shows, and powwows around the campfire. But there's never any pressure to do anything, and though sing-alongs may at first seem corny, somehow everyone ends up enjoying them. Counselors take kids (with groups of their peers) on special activities each day; the arrangement seems to give each generation just the right amount of time together and apart. Open June to early September; plan to reserve several months in advance. Information: Ginny and Dick Elder, Colorado Trails Ranch, PO Box 848E, Durango, CO 81302 (303 247-5055). Expensive.

WORKING RANCHES

DEER FORKS RANCH, Douglas, Wyoming: It takes about an hour to drive through the rangelands of eastern Wyoming from the town of Douglas to the 5,900-acre spread where the Middleton family grazes cows, grows hay, and welcomes guests. The two rustic housekeeping cabins with private baths and fully equipped kitchens where guests stay are quite comfortable. You can eat in the cabin or, if you prefer, share some meals with Ben and Pauli Middleton and their two children; the fare usually includes beef from the family's cattle, vegetables from their garden, and homemade breads and pies. Besides the milk cows, there are plenty of animals here to delight children — lambs, cats, even a cowdog (an Australian shepherd with an instinctive ability to herd cattle). If you can ride, you may be rounding up cows from the far corners of this mountainous ranch, and if you can't, you'll soon learn how. Hiking, arrowhead-hunting, and trout fishing will also keep you busy. Too, depending on the season, you may find yourself stacking bales of hay, separating steers from heifers, or helping the vet do pregnancy tests. One day you may drive in to see the rodeo, or state fair, or a cattle auction; another, you may join the Middletons and their friends and relatives for a branding. Open year-round. Information: Ben and Pauli Middleton, Deer Forks Ranch, Rte. 6, 1200 Poison Lake Rd., Douglas, WY 82633 (307 358-2033). Inexpensive.

THE G BAR M RANCH, Clyde Park, Montana: One of the few remaining cattle ranches in the West to cleave to the old lifestyle and welcome vacationers, this establishment in the Bridger Mountain foothills just east of Bozeman has 3,300 acres mainly given over to cattle, plus four rooms in the ranch house and two outlying log cabins fitted out for visitors. Riding, of course, is the main feature; you'll go out to check fence and water holes, help doctor calves that got too curious about porcupines, carry salt to the cattle on summer range in the high country, and so on; and George Leffingwell, one of the owners, puts even the most inexperienced rider at ease. Because part of the ranch is a private game sanctuary, you'll often see mule deer, golden eagles, and coyotes, along with moose, elk, and bear on occasion. You can also go fishing or hiking, hunt fossils, and photograph wildflowers. Once every week there's an all-day ride and on Saturday nights there's music and a steak fry. Otherwise, you won't find much of an activities program — and most people like it that way: "It's like coming home after being away for a long time," one visitor explains. Everyone — ranch family, vacationers, and ranch hands — has meals (including breakfasts of sourdough pancakes and chokecherry syrup) together, and in the course of mealtime talk, you'll learn about the area's history and ecology, the economics of operating a cattle ranch, and the independent spirit of the Western rancher. Open from mid-May to mid-September. Information: the Leffingwells, the G Bar M Ranch, PO Box AE, Clyde Park, MT 59018 (406 686-4687). Moderate.

THE HALTER RANCH, Big Sandy, Montana: In the center of the Missouri River Wilderness Waterway, 80 miles east of Great Falls, Montana, the Halter family raises cattle, horses, hay, and barley on 3,000 acres of meadows and rugged breaks along the White Cliffs of the Missouri River, described in Lewis and Clark's journal. Gay Halter Pearson and husband Ron will show you how to ride, or take you on overnight trail rides or trips in inner tubes down the Judith River. Gay's father, Jerry Halter, who is active in efforts to make the area a wild river waterway, can regale you with tales of the homesteads, forts, and Indian ruins in the area, some of which you'll see when (ranch work permitting) he takes you on float trips down the Missouri. All the guests — usually one family at a time, never more than two — seem to fit easily into the Halters' life, and they're exceptional people. Open from April into November. Information: Gay Halter Pearson, Box 408, Big Sandy, MT 59520 (406 378-2549). Moderate.

A Short Tour of Indian America

When people discuss early American history, their starting point is usually the 17th or 18th century, and the founding of Jamestown, the colonial settlements, or George Washington and the heroics of the American Revolution. But long before any of this took place, long before the white man ever arrived, the real history of this country was the story of the American Indian. During the period of the last glaciation, some 25,000 to 50,000 years ago, the area which is now the Bering Strait was a broad plain about 1,000 miles wide. Nomadic peoples wandered across this land bridge from Siberia into what is now Alaska. Before them stretched a vast uninhabited land, as diverse as it was silent, from the frozen ice caps of the north to the primordial swamp of the southeastern tropics. These people roamed freely over the land and truly discovered what we have come to call North America. They lived in direct and respectful relationship to the soil. In the far North, they became ice-hunters. In the rich forests of the North, hunting bands tracked the caribou, deer, beaver, and small fur-bearing animals. In the eastern woodlands and warm southeast-ern region, agriculture reached a high stage of development and was the center of ceremonial life. The Great Plains was inhabited by both farmers and hunters, people who would become great warriors after the introduction of the horse in 1750. Along the Pacific coast settled tribes who were primarily fishermen. The culture of native North America reached its most sophisticated point among the Pueblos, who lived in communal villages in the Southwest, and developed a hardy strain of maize capable of surviving in this arid region.

All of these people came to be known as Indians, for no better reason than that Christopher Columbus, landing one day in Santo Domingo, thought he was in the Indies, off the coast of Asia. As the Indians settled in different parts of North America, they adopted diverse lifestyles; but they remained fundamentally similar in many ways. They were a most remarkably resourceful people. Isolated from the rest of the world, they not only survived on their own, but they created rich cultures around the mysteries and miracles of nature. In addition to the wide variety of maize grown by different tribes, Indians developed pumpkins, beans, squash, tobacco, potatoes, sweet potatoes, chocolate, tomatoes, vanilla, and peanuts — all native and unique to this continent. The different tribes spoke their own languages, and though these may have derived from several parent tongues, at one time at least 200 mutually unintelligible languages were spoken by the American people. In these languages, the Indians told stories of the wonders of creation. The Navajo mythology involves a series of ascents through differ-ent worlds inhabited by spirits and beings of both good and evil. The story of emergence from the Black World that was "darker than the darkness of all the moonless nights of many winters" is as beautiful and rich as the story of Adam and Eve. Other tribes created their own legends, songs, dances, and ceremonies. Some lived in fear of nature, others praised its benevolence, but all reacted to it directly, channeling tremendous amounts of physical and emotional energy into their rituals. In New Mexico the Indians painted a series of murals with iron oxide to glorify nature. Elsewhere in the Southwest, they built subterranean chambers of worship, called kivas. In the Southeast, immense ceremonial mounds of earth were filled with sculpture, and many stand today, still protecting the secrets of the rituals for which they were created.

The European explorers who came to the Americas in the 16th, 17th, and 18th centuries came for conquest, and with their arrival, the story of the American Indian takes a tragic turn; it becomes, to a great extent, a tale of exploitation. In 1492, Columbus sailed to the New World and encountered the Indians; he remarked on the "artless and generous quality" they had "to such a degree as no one would believe but he who had seen it." In return for their good will, Columbus sent 600 Indians back to Spain to work as slaves. During the following centuries the Spanish, British, and, in their turn, Americans waged nearly constant war against the Indians. There was outright massacre, exemplified by the 1890 incident at Wounded Knee, when 300 unarmed Sioux men, women, and children, gathered to celebrate a Ghost Dance (itself a frenetic ritual which Indians believed would save them from decimation by the white invaders), were surrounded and gunned down by the Seventh Cavalry of the United States Army. Less horrific, but just as pernicious, was systematic subjugation by the government of the United States. In 1835, the Five Civilized Tribes of the East (Chero-kee, Seminole, Creek, Choctaw, and Chickasaw) were forcibly relocated to Indian

Territory in Oklahoma, only to have most of the land taken away from them by the government for white homesteading after the Civil War. From 1887 to 1934 the General Allotment Act divided communal Indian lands, and reduced the total number of Indian-owned acres in America from 138,000,000 to 48,000,000. Even in pathetic reservation enclaves, civil rights were denied the Indians. (Not until 1968, with the Civil Rights Act, were the provisions of the Bill of Rights extended to reservation Indians.)

Though many tribes have become extinct, the American Indian still survives (with a population of 830,000), a testament to human dignity and endurance. Except in the Southwest, the Indian tribes no longer occupy their original lands, and their members are beset with problems — discrimination, as well as extremely high unemployment and high alcoholism and suicide rates. But the story of the real discoverers of America is not finished. In recent years, many young Native Americans have become radicalized by the plight of their people: In 1969 Indians occupied Alcatraz Island; in 1972 many marched on Washington, presenting the federal government with a list of demands (called the Trail of Broken Treaties paper); and in 1973, Indians occupied the Pine Ridge Reservation on the site of the Wounded Knee Massacre, bringing broad international recognition to their plight.

But improvement in Indian affairs demands more than recognition; the gap is one of understanding that can only be bridged by direct contact. In recent years, this has become possible with the growth of tourism in Indian communities. Even some militant members of Indian society believe that this is a positive trend, one which will allow their tribes to practice their own unique lifestyles while sustaining themselves economically. And so, from the commercialized Seminole reservations in Florida to the settlements in the Southwest, where tribes still inhabit the lands of their ancestors — some of the most beautiful country in America — you can glimpse the complex dances and ceremonies and examine the magnificent handcrafted baskets, jewelry, patchwork, and painting of these ancient civilizations. The cultures that you'll encounter in this Indian America — though at the root of our nation's heritage — are as foreign as those of remotest Egypt and the Orient.

When you enter Indian America, it is best to meet the people on their own terms. Do not take photographs of ceremonies, rituals, or individuals without express permission. Similarly, do not use recording devices, sketch pads, and notebooks. It is advisable to behave as unobtrusively as possible, refraining from applause, loud talking, or even questions about the significance of rituals. In some cases, explanations may be offered. Otherwise it is best to watch what is going on around you and do research before or afterward. Keeping these few things in mind, you will undoubtedly find an adventure in Indian America truly rewarding.

Described below are several highlights of Indian America — reservations and other Indian lands, ceremonies, beautiful natural settings, and excellent museums.

For information about arts and crafts businesses owned and operated by Native Americans, get a copy of the free *Source Directory* published by the Indian Arts & Crafts Board (Room 4004, US Dept. of the Interior, Washington, DC 20240, 202 343-2773).

And for an overview of American Indian heritage, consult the following:

Indians of North America, by Harold E. Driver (University of Chicago Press; $15.95 in paperback), a reconstruction of the native American culture with an emphasis on the 20th century and the post-60s era.

I Have Spoken: American History Through the Voice of the Indians, edited by Virginia L. Armstrong (Athens, Ohio: Ohio University/Swallow Press; $7.95).

EAST

MICCOSUKEE TRIBAL ENTERPRISE, near Miami, Florida: Some 550 members of the Miccosukee tribe (which was not officially recognized until 1962) live on this reservation on the northern border of the Everglades National Park. A museum has exhibits tracing the history of the tribe, which shares a language and hunting and fishing techniques with the Seminoles, who also live in Florida, and craftspeople are on hand to demonstrate doll making, wood carving, and basketweaving; daily alligator-wrestling shows are presented as well. The lifestyle on the reservation is still fairly traditional. In the school system, English takes second place to Mikasuki, the tribal language. Many Miccosukees live in chickees, which are palmetto thatched-roof dwellings, and some work as artists, making baskets, cypress wood carvings, and clothing of patchwork cloth (available at the Cultural Center). A quarter-mile east of the museum is the Miccosukee restaurant, which serves traditional Indian fare — frybread, pumpkin bread, catfish, and Everglades' frogs' legs — as well as hot dogs, burgers, and such. One of the best times to visit is at the end of December during the annual Indian Arts Festival, when musicians and artists and craftsmen from many tribes around the world converge on the reservation to play everything from traditional music to Indian rock. On US 41, 26 miles west of Miami. Information: PO Box 440021, Miami, FL 33144 (305 223-8380 or 305 223-8388).

CHEROKEE, North Carolina: Adjacent to the Great Smoky Mountains National Park, this beautiful area is the country where the Cherokees lived before they were forcibly relocated to Oklahoma in 1835 along a route now called the Trail of Tears. But some Cherokees remained, hiding in the mountains, and others returned later. Today, this is the center of the Cherokee people, and many work here in the tribal government, in factories that produce moccasins and quilts, and in tourist businesses. One of the best times to visit is in the fall during the Fall Festival when Cherokees from all over return home and participate in traditional dances, games, and arts and crafts demonstrations. The event customarily begins the Tuesday of the first full week in October. For exact dates, check with the Cherokee Visitor Center, PO Box 465, Cherokee, NC 28719 (704 497-9195; 800 438-1601 in the eastern US). Of interest at Cherokee are:

Oconaluftee Indian Village – This replica of a Cherokee village depicts the life of the 18th century, with guided tours. Included are a seven-sided council house, ceremonial chambers, and lectures at various sites where members of the tribe, dressed in authentic costumes, demonstrate crafts, cooking, and weapon-making. Open mid-May through October. Off Rte. 441 on Drama Rd. For a little more history come to life, see the drama *Unto These Hills,* which recounts the story of the Cherokee people in an amphitheater during the summer (see *Outdoor Dramas*). Mountainside Theater on Drama Rd. Information: Oconaluftee Indian Village, Cherokee, NC 28719 (704 497-2315 or 704 497-2111).

Museum of the Cherokee Indian – Owned by the Eastern Band of Cherokee Indians, this museum has multimedia theaters and innovative exhibitions, including a new hands-on exhibit for small children, that focus on the history of the tribe with examples of clothing and implements used for farming, hunting, and fishing. Open daily year-round. Admission charge. On Drama Rd. Information: Museum of the Cherokee Indian, PO Box 770A, Cherokee, NC 28719 (704 497-3481).

Qualla Arts and Crafts Mutual – Best of the area's many craft shops, this is the official cooperative marketing center of the Cherokees. The work is authentic, and many items here are rarely available elsewhere, such as white oak, river cane, and honeysuckle vine baskets, animal sculptures made of buckeye, walnut, and wild cherry, pottery, and beadwork. On Rte. 441 near the Museum. Information: Qualla Arts and Crafts Mutual, PO Box 277, Cherokee, NC 28719 (704 497-3103).

WEST

Some 16.5 million acres in northeastern Arizona and neighboring New Mexico and Utah form the Navajo nation, the largest Indian reservation in America. The Navajos are the most populous of the Indian tribes, with over 160,000 members, many of whom live in traditional dwellings called hogans, hexagonal houses built of logs, cemented with clay, and covered with earth. The Navajos were primarily a pastoral rather than agricultural people, but they did pick up farming, weaving, and sand-painting from the Pueblos. They are also more open about their ceremonies than the Pueblos, providing visitors with an opportunity to observe a few sacred rituals.

WINDOW ROCK, Arizona: The town is the seat of Navajo tribal government and is a good place to begin a trip into Navajo land. You can view displays about the tribe's history and culture at the newly renovated Tribal Museum; learn a bit about how the Navajos see their environment and live in harmony with it at the Navajo Zoological and Botanical Park; shop for crafts at the Navajo Arts and Crafts Enterprise; and take any number of excursions into the surrounding countryside. The Navajo Tourism Development Office of the Navajo Division of Resources can suggest destinations and give you dates for various events and activities. Among the biggest festivities are the Navajo Nation Fair, staged in Window Rock the first Wednesday through Sunday after Labor Day, and the Fourth of July celebration and rodeo, held annually during the July Fourth weekend from Thursday through Sunday. The *Window Rock Motor Inn*'s restaurant offers southwestern dishes like Navajo tacos and frybread (602 871-4108). Information: Navajo Tourism Development Office, Navajo Division of Resources, PO Box 308, Window Rock, AZ 86515 (602 871-6436 or 602 871-6437).

MONUMENT VALLEY NAVAJO TRIBAL PARK, Arizona and Utah: The valley is a classic western scenic wonder with high mesas, sculptured buttes, natural bridges, earth arches, chiseled canyons and gorges, huge sandstone monoliths, and has been used in filming innumerable Westerns, including a few early John Wayne films. A 16-mile road (a 1½-hour drive) winds its way through the valley and can be negotiated by most cars, except during the winter, when four-wheel-drive vehicles are advisable. Visitors should not photograph Navajos or their possessions without permission. Camping is available at the park headquarters, where there is also a Navajo arts and crafts shop. 25 miles north of Kayenta off Rte. 163. Information: Box 93, Monument Valley Tribal Park, UT 84536 (801 727-3287).

NAVAJO NATIONAL MONUMENT, Tonalea, Arizona: The largest and most intricate of Arizona's cliff dwellings are preserved in this rugged country. There are two areas, each of which contains a remarkable 13th-century pueblo ruin. Betatakin Area is the site of the monument headquarters, and the visitor center offers exhibitions on the Anasazi culture, a slide show and film, a Navajo arts and crafts shop, and a campground. Betatakin is the more accessible of the areas, and the ruin across the canyon may be viewed from a foot trail, or visited on a four-hour guided tour (daily in summer; no tours in winter). The other area, Keet Seel, may be reached via horseback (reserve from headquarters in advance) or by a strenuous 8-mile hike, also in summer only. 28 miles southwest of Kayenta off Rte. 160. Information: Navajo National Monument, HC-71, PO Box 3, Tonalea, AZ 86044-9704 (602 672-2366).

HUBBELL TRADING POST NATIONAL HISTORIC SITE, Ganado, Arizona: Dating back to the 1870s, this is the oldest continuously active trading post on the Navajo reservation. The post and Hubbell home depict the life of an unusual trader and his family, and have displays on the history of the area, and beautiful Navajo sand paintings, handwoven rugs, silver work, and other jewelry. The National Park Service runs guided tours of the site, and there are usually Navajo weaving and silversmithing demonstrations at the Visitor Center. 1 mile west of Ganado on Rte. 264. Information: Hubbell Trading Post National Historic Site, PO Box 150, Ganado, AZ 86505 (602 755-3475).

FIRST, SECOND, AND THIRD MESA, Arizona: The Hopis are exceptional jewelry makers and farmers and live in a close communal relationship in apartment villages on three isolated ridges of land high above the northeastern Arizona desert. The best place to stay is on the Second Mesa, at the *Hopi Cultural Center,* which has a motel, museum, and restaurant where traditional Hopi foods such as hominy stew, frybread, and piki are served along with hamburgers and such. At the Hopi Arts and Crafts Guild, you can purchase the finest of Hopi crafts — silver jewelry, pottery, kachina dolls, and baskets. The studio of Charles Loloma, the most prominent contemporary Indian jeweler, and Old Oraibi, the oldest continuously occupied village in the US, are on the Third Mesa. A variety of ceremonies are open to visitors, but the exact dates are usually not announced till very close to the event, so check at the Cultural Center. Motel reservations should be made at least 3 weeks in advance. On Rte. 264 at Pinon Rd., 4 miles northwest of Rte. 87. Information: Hopi Cultural Center, PO Box 67, Second Mesa, AZ 86043 (602 734-2401).

Nowhere in the United States do you get a better sense of the Indian past than among the Pueblos, the desert peoples of New Mexico. The aridity of the climate has left many ancient ruins intact, and the tribes live among them on the land of their ancestors in pueblos, communal villages of adobe or sandstone dwellings that blend unobtrusively into their surroundings. The pueblos described below are within driving distance of Santa Fe or Albuquerque.

ACOMA, New Mexico: Perhaps the most spectacular of the pueblos, this village sits on a 367-foot-high mesa, commanding a panoramic view of the New Mexico plain. The pueblo has been inhabited for some 1,000 years, and though many of the families have homes in nearby farming villages, Acoma is open to visitors year-round except during religious ceremonies. Among the buildings are the mission of San Esteban, established in 1629 and constructed of adobe walls 10 to 14 feet thick; a subterranean ceremonial chamber known as a kiva on the main plaza (off-limits to visitors); and several small craft shops where delicate Acoma pottery with geometric and bird pattern motifs can be purchased for prices lower than at trading posts elsewhere. Tribal members lead tours daily. Small admission charge and photographic fee. On I-40, Exit 102, 60 miles west of Albuquerque. Information: PO Box 309, Pueblo of Acoma, NM 87034 (505 552-6606).

TAOS, New Mexico: Sitting at the base of the Sangre de Cristo range, which culminates in New Mexico's highest point, the Taos pueblo is a stronghold of tribal tradition. The people are devout in their religious observances, and subsist as farmers. Near the multistoried adobe dwelling, craftsmen display moccasins and drums as well as mica clay pottery. The San Geronimo Fiesta in late September is open to the public and features extraordinary dancing, a greased-pole climbing contest, and other festivities. The town of Taos, 2½ miles south, is primarily an artists' colony, and the work of residents and of other artists is displayed at some 55 galleries all over town. Area information: Taos County Chamber of Commerce, Drawer I, Taos, NM 87571 (505 758-3873 or 800 732-8267).

Once dominant on the northern plains, the Sioux — nomadic buffalo hunters who lived in conical tents of animal hide called teepees — were the prototype for the American Indian image. Today, the buffalo no longer roam, and the tribe is beset with economic problems, but the Sioux still maintain their dignity. The area is not highly developed commercially, but if you do visit, the rewards will be great.

OGLALA SIOUX PINE RIDGE RESERVATION, South Dakota: This 2.3-million acre reservation — where, at Wounded Knee, some 300 unarmed Sioux were slaughtered in 1890 in a massacre commemorated by a simple gravesite — is now the home of nearly 15,000 Sioux. You can visit the Holy Rosary Mission, where there are exhibits on Sioux culture and displays of fine Sioux crafts: bead work, quill work (an intricate type of weaving employing porcupine quills), and magnificent paintings on buffalo hide that display a visionary quality — despite the fact that life in the past was beset by tragedy, they depict a happy life that might have been. The Tribal Office can give you information about ceremonies to which the public is welcome — among them the Sun Dance. Held the first week of August, it is a religious observance of both atonement and thanksgiving that involves much elaborate drumming and dancing. There are also powwows and rodeos throughout the summer. The reservation is 120 miles south of Rapid City on Rte. 18. Information: Oglala Sioux Pine Ridge Reservation, PO Box 468, Pine Ridge, SD 57770 (605 867-5821).

MUSEUMS

HEARD MUSEUM OF ANTHROPOLOGY AND PRIMITIVE ARTS, Phoenix, Arizona: One of the world's best, this museum founded in the late 1920s focuses on the Indian cultures of the Southwest. Its centerpiece is the recently built wing devoted to a permanent exhibit on native Americans of the Southwest — the largest exhibit of its kind in North America. Tracing the history of the region from 15,000 BC to the present, its many displays include everything from prehistoric pottery vessels to contemporary Navajo textiles. A special gallery features most of the museum's collection of Hopi kachina dolls — perhaps its best-known collection — many of which were donated by Barry Goldwater. These painted and feathered dolls, according to Hopi lore, are handed to children by the kachina spirits, who represent ancestors and things of nature. The museum also has exhibitions of jewelry, baskets, textiles, ceramics, and artifacts of the area's ancient inhabitants. Of a pair of additional galleries devoted to changing shows, one focuses on contemporary Native American fine art — the museum is one of the leading institutions of its kind concerned with the work of today's artists and craftsmen — while the other compares this native culture to others around the world. Information: Heard Museum, 22 E Monte Vista Rd., Phoenix, AZ 85004 (602 252-8840).

MUSEUM OF THE AMERICAN INDIAN, New York, New York: One of the world's largest anthropological museums, this institution houses an immense, uniquely representative collection of the artifacts of the aboriginal peoples of North, Central, and South America; it ranks among the world's biggest such collections and represents everything from precious ornaments to commonplace tools, from paleo-Indian projectile points to abstract paintings by contemporary Indian artists, covering the hemisphere from Atlantic to Pacific, from the Arctic to the Antarctic. In the gift shop, you can buy original Indian hand-crafted objects as well as books on native American culture. Information: Museum of the American Indian, Broadway at 155th, New York, NY 10032 (212 283-2420).

WHEELWRIGHT MUSEUM OF THE AMERICAN INDIAN, Santa Fe, New Mexico: Changing exhibits focus on the history, culture, and art of Native Americans. The museum is modeled after a traditional Navajo residence, the eight-sided hogan. At the heart of the permanent collection are the stunning Klah and Manuelito sandpainting tapestries. Downstairs is a re-created 19th-century trading post, where Indian arts and crafts of exceptional quality are for sale. Information: Wheelwright Museum, 704 Camino Lejo, Santa Fe, NM 87502 (505 982-4636).

SIOUX INDIAN MUSEUM, Rapid City, South Dakota: This fine facility, operated by the Indian Arts and Crafts Board of the Department of the Interior, transmits a feeling for the Sioux past with its collection of 19th-century Sioux artifacts — clothing, games, moccasins, pipe bags, and baby carriers. Another gallery broadens the scope with changing exhibits, usually shows of contemporary artists from many different tribes. Information: Sioux Indian Museum, PO Box 1504, West Blvd. between Main and St. Joseph St., Rapid City, SD 57709 (605 348-0557).

Dam Nation

The politics of water and the ecology of America's "big dams" are just beginning to be understood, but the bane of environmentalists can, for all that, make quite a pleasant vacation experience. First of all, dams are clean-lined and beautiful to look at; they're impressively huge. All the bigger ones — including those listed here — offer tours of the powerhouses of pumping stations, or at least have visitors' centers with exhibits that explain what the dams do. Often, you can also watch boats being locked through navigation systems or see fish fighting their way up fish ladders to their upstream spawning grounds. And when you've seen the dam, you can enjoy yourself on the huge reservoirs they impound.

GLEN CANYON DAM, near Page, Arizona: Five million cubic yards of concrete, 1,560 feet across, rise 710 feet above the bedrock across the Colorado River between sheer walls of red Navajo sandstone. Behind: Lake Powell, 186 miles long and with more than 1,900 miles of shoreline. You can fish for crappie or striped and largemouth bass; the largest stripers are nearing 36 pounds. Around the lake is the million-acre Glen Canyon National Recreation Area. Information: Glen Canyon National Recreation Area, PO Box 1507, Page, AZ 86040 (602 645-2471).

OROVILLE DAM, Oroville, California: Rising 770 feet above Oroville's business district, this is the highest dam in the US and the highest earth-fill dam in the US. Lake Oroville, with 162 miles of shoreline, backs up behind the dam, and there's good boating and fishing — for king salmon, rainbow and brown trout, largemouth and smallmouth bass, crappie, bluegill, and catfish. Information: Lake Oroville State Recreation Area, 400 Glen Dr., Oroville, CA 95966 (916 534-2409).

KENTUCKY DAM, near Gilbertsville, Kentucky: The 206-foot height and 8,422-foot length make this structure across the Tennessee River the largest in the TVA system; together with the Barkley Dam on the Cumberland River nearby, it impounds some 220,000 acres of water with 3,500 miles of forested, cove-notched shoreline. Both Kentucky Lake and Lake Barkley are great for crappie and largemouth bass fishing as well as white bass, catfish, sauger, and bluegill; and a multitude of activities are available at Kenlake, Kentucky Dam Village, and Lake Barkley State Resort Parks, and at the TVA's own 170,000-acre Land Between the Lakes, all on the shores of the two impoundments. Information: Department of Travel Development, Capitol Plaza Tower, Frankfort, KY 40601 (502 564-4930 or 800 225-TRIP).

FORT PECK DAM, near Glasgow, Montana: The largest earth-fill dam in the US, the second largest in the world, this $75 million, 21,026-foot-long structure rises 250½ feet above the Missouri River. Fort Peck Lake, with 1,520 miles of shoreline, is the world's fourth largest reservoir. And the Glasgow mayor said it could be built for $1 million! Information: Chamber of Commerce, Box 832, Glasgow, MT 59230 (406 228-2222).

HOOVER DAM, Boulder City, Nevada: This 726-foot-high structure, the Western Hemisphere's highest concrete dam, was selected by the American Society of Civil Engineers as one of the country's Seven Modern Wonders of Civil Engineering — and when you take the 528-foot, 52-story elevator ride to the power plant, you'll probably agree. Some 110 miles long, with 822 miles of shoreline when full, Lake Mead (behind the dam) is by volume one of the world's largest manmade reservoirs. Information: Lake Mead National Recreation Area, 601 Nevada Hwy., Boulder City, NV 89005 (702 293-4041).

JOHN DAY DAM, near Biggs, Oregon: For this $487 million project, the US Army

Corps of Engineers rerouted highways and moved a pair of towns and parts of two others (Boardman, Roosevelt, Arlington, and Umatilla, respectively). The most impressive part of a visit is a viewing window in the fish ladder by which adult salmon and steelhead make their way upstream to spawn. But all kind of sv￼perlatives apply. Lake Umatilla stretches for about 75 miles behind the dam. Information: The Dalles–John Day Project, Resources Section, PO Box 564, The Dalles, OR 97058 (503 296-1181).

FLAMING GORGE DAM, near Vernal, Utah: In the Green River's Red Canyon, this $66 million, 502-foot-high dam impounds a 91-mile-long reservoir in the Flaming Gorge National Recreation Area — 154,475 acres of bright red and orange rock chimneys and spires, rust-colored canyons, pine-clad mountains. Information: Ashley National Forest, Dutch John, UT 84023 (801 885-3315).

GRAND COULEE DAM, Coulee Dam, Washington: The world's largest concrete dam, this one completed in 1942 is higher than a 46-story building and nearly a mile long, used up 11,975,521 cubic yards of concrete, and has a spillway twice as high as Niagara Falls. Yet it's dwarfed by the immense granite cliffs on either side. The spillway is floodlit on summer nights. Recreational opportunities are available in the 100,059-acre Coulee Dam National Recreation Area, Box 37, Coulee Dam, WA 99116 (509 633-1360).

Historic Canals

 When Charles Dickens traveled through Ohio in the 1840s, he did it on a canal boat — and returned to scribble the tale of the cramped quarters and the odoriferous companionship of the mules brought aboard between stints of pulling.

But until the advent of the railroads, the canals that linked inland cities to lakes and rivers from Maine to Chicago provided the fastest transportation. Then canal boomtowns died out, and many canals (like much of the original Erie Canal, which linked Lake Erie and the Atlantic Ocean) were filled in and paved over or left to crumble.

Still, canals have not been forgotten. Cruising on these wave-free waterways is relaxing, and several short trips are available for only a few dollars a person. Also, *Midlakes Navigation Co.,* PO Box 61, Skaneateles, NY 13152 (315 685-5722), has 2- and 3-day cruises on the canals of New York State — Champlain, Erie, Oswego, and Seneca-Cayuga. And *American-Canadian Line,* Box 368, Warren, RI 02885 (401 245-1350), runs 12-day trips between Warren, Rhode Island, and Montréal, Québec, via the Erie and Oswego canals, the Saquenay River, and the St. Lawrence Seaway. The *American Canal Society,* 809 Rathton Rd., York, PA 17403, keeps its members posted on what they can see where with a newsletter (annual membership, $10). Here are a few canal sites you can visit:

EAST

THE C & D CANAL MUSEUM, Chesapeake City, Maryland: An old stone pumphouse on the Chesapeake and Delaware Canal has working models of a lock, a brief slide show that relates the story of the still-busy 150-year-old canal for which it is named, and a wooden waterwheel, a mechanical marvel fitted out with buckets that transferred water from Back Creek into the canal at the rate of 1.2 million gallons an hour. Information: US Army Corps of Engineers, Chesapeake City, MD 21915 (301 885-5622).

OLD ERIE CANAL STATE PARK, DeWitt to Rome, New York: Some 35 miles of the celebrated Erie Canal are maintained by the State for recreational use, and in summer you can go hiking and biking, and in winter, snowmobiling. Picnic areas and connecting paths to nearby recreation areas are strategically placed. Information: Central Region–New York State Office of Parks Recreation and Historic Preservation, Jamesville, NY 13078 (315 492-1756).

CANAL TOWN MUSEUM, Canastota, New York: In a yellow clapboard building directly across the street from the canal, this small, decade-old museum is filled with artifacts related to canal days, models of canal boats, and displays on Canastota history. Information: Canal Town Museum, Canastota, NY 13032 (315 697-3451).

ERIE CANAL VILLAGE, Rome, New York: At an 1840s canal village on a restored section of waterway, you can take steam train rides and cruises on the horse-drawn packet boat *Chief Engineer of Rome*. A dozen restored buildings — among them one set up as a farm vehicle museum with over 25 contraptions on view — plus a canal museum can be visited. Open May through October. Information: Erie Canal Village, 5789 New London Rd., Rome, NY 13440 (315 336-6000).

THE ERIE CANAL MUSEUM, Syracuse, New York: Changing exhibitions of life on the canals are set up in the last surviving building where canal boats were weighed to determine the tolls they'd pay. A full-size canal boat has been reconstructed, participational exhibitions organized, and a weighmaster's office re-created. Information: Erie Canal Museum, 318 Erie Blvd. E, Syracuse, NY 13202 (315 471-0593).

ALLEGHENY PORTAGE RAILROAD NATIONAL HISTORIC SITE, Cresson, Pennsylvania: The eastern and western divisions of the state-run Pennsylvania Canal were linked by this railroad. Visitors see some of the stone railroad ties, a quarry where they were made, a full-scale model of a locomotive, and a couple of the engine houses; demonstrations of stone cutting, spinning, weaving, and other period crafts are presented in summer. Slide programs at the visitors center set up in the old Lemon House Tavern tell the story. Information: Allegheny Portage Railroad National Historic Site, PO Box 247, Cresson, PA 16630 (814 886-8176).

CHESAPEAKE AND OHIO CANAL NATIONAL HISTORICAL PARK, near Washington, DC: A 1924 flood put an end to the uneven career of this 184-mile-long waterway between Georgetown and Cumberland, Maryland. The woodsy towpath is ideal for hiking and biking; the sections of the canal that aren't dry (22 miles) are great for canoeing. Exhibitions in the visitors center near Great Falls, Maryland, in an old tavern, tell the story. Information: C&O Canal National Historical Park, PO Box 4, Sharpsburg, MD 21782 (301 739-4200).

MIDWEST

ILLINOIS AND MICHIGAN CANAL HEADQUARTERS BUILDING, Lockport, Illinois: What some people call the best-preserved canal town in America has a number of old canal locks (as well as a modern one), a fine 19th-century block of storefronts, some stone sidewalks — and the only canal museum in the US that illustrates the construction, operation, and demise of a single waterway. Exhibits relating to the history of the settlement and the lifestyle of the area's pioneers round out the extensive display. Information: Will County Historical Society, 803 S State St., Lockport, IL 60441 (815 838-5080).

CANAL FULTON, Canal Fulton, Ohio: A full-sized replica of the mule-drawn canal barges that once plied the Ohio-Erie Canal rides you up and down that same waterway today. A festival held every July re-creates the era. Information: Canal Fulton Heritage Society, Canal Fulton, OH 44614 (216 854-3808).

ROSCOE VILLAGE, Coshocton, Ohio: This once-busy 1800s community on the Ohio-Erie Canal, now restored, is a fine place to get an idea of what rough-and-ready canal life was like. In season, you can ride a horse-drawn trolley and canal boat replica, and year-round you can visit a blacksmith shop, general store, old-fashioned hardware store, tavern, period home, and several antique shops and craft studios — plus a wonderful peppermint-pink ice cream parlor with one of those tinkling Vox Regina music boxes. Many lively special events. Information: Roscoe Village, 81 Hill St., Coshocton, OH 43812 (614 622-9310).

America's Military Academies

 From the establishment of West Point in 1802 to the opening of the Air Force Academy in April 1954, the academies have always provided a variety of spectacles from pomp-and-circumstance full-dress parades to museums of military equipment, cannon, and guns. The grounds are manicured, delightful for walking; the settings usually breathtaking. Be sure to time your visit to catch a parade; and ask about athletic events and guided tours which are often available.

US AIR FORCE ACADEMY, Colorado Springs, Colorado: After you've seen the visitors center and its displays about cadet life, a self-guided tour (which takes about 2 hours) of the 18,000-acre grounds will include the Academy's chapel — a "chapel of the future" when it was built in 1963 in the shape of a 17-spired tetrahedron pyramid 150 feet high, with separate chapels inside for various faiths. Every weekday (except during summer vacations and some other breaks), the cadets — in uniform — assemble, then march in formation to the dining hall to the accompaniment of martial music. A real goose-bump raiser. You can lodge in Colorado Springs — the state's second biggest city — at any number of motels; most prestigious is the *Broadmoor,* a very posh, very old, and very famous resort (303 634-7711; see *Resort Hotels*). Information: US Air Force Academy, Colorado Springs, CO 80840-5151 (303 472-4040).

US COAST GUARD ACADEMY, New London, Connecticut: Your visit to this pretty campus begins at the modern visitors center, where you can browse through exhibits and watch a multimedia show depicting cadet life, then pick up a map for a self-guided tour that takes in the chapel; the academy's museum, notable for its intriguing collection of vessel models; and when it's in port, the sailing bark *Eagle,* now used for cadet training cruises. Once weekly in spring and fall, usually on Friday afternoons, cadets parade in review. An added attraction of this nautically minded corner of Connecticut is the interesting selection of inns, the best of which includes the venerable *Griswold Inn,* a bustling place on Main Street in Essex that has been putting up travelers for centuries (203 767-0991), and the *Copper Beech,* in Ivoryton, the former home of a Connecticut ivory trader, full of high-ceilinged, four-postered sleeping chambers (203 767-0330). See *America's Special Havens.* For academy information, contact the US Coast Guard Academy, New London, CT 06320 (203 442-1092).

US MERCHANT MARINE ACADEMY, Kings Point, New York: On Long Island's picturesque North Shore, and overlooking Connecticut, Long Island Sound, and New York City and its bridges, this academy occupies what used to be the Chrysler estate (as well as parts of others on Long Island's Gold Coast). At the Main Gate, you can get maps and information about what to see — displays about the history of the Merchant Marine and their ships at the American Merchant Marine Museum, and regimental reviews, held on some Saturdays in fall and spring at 10 AM. Information: US Merchant Marine Academy, Kings Point, NY 11024 (516 482-8200).

US MILITARY ACADEMY, West Point, New York: Founded on March 16, 1802, with an initial enrollment of ten, this academy is probably the most famous and most visited of the service schools, and for good reason. It fairly oozes military tradition. The campus is beautiful, as manicured as any parkland, full of Gothic buildings, and magnificent views like the one from Trophy Point, above the Hudson River. ("The fairest of the fair and lovely Highlands of the North River, shut in by deep green heights and ruined forts, and looking down upon the distant town of Newburgh," according to Charles Dickens, who visited in 1842.) The Cadet Chapel, a lofty granite Gothic structure which seems even more majestic because of the several flights of stairs you've got to trek up to get into it, houses the largest church pipe organ in the country. The museum — filled with military artifacts from the Stone Age to the present — is the largest of all military museums in the world. At Trophy Point, you can see a few links of the heavy iron chains the American revolutionaries stretched across the river to block British ships during that war. Cadet parades are held during spring and fall; for times and dates, call ahead. Country inns come and go in the area. Among the nicest are the *Bird and Bottle Inn* in Garrison (914 424-3000) and the *Beekman Arms* in Rhinebeck (914 876-7077). You can eat or lodge in any of these. Also interesting, for food: the Culinary Institute of America's *Escoffier Room* and *American Bounty* restaurants, in Hyde Park, where top chefs of the future are in rigorous training (914 471-6608; closed July). Information: Visitors Information Center, US Military Academy, West Point, NY 10996 (914 938-2638).

US NAVAL ACADEMY, Annapolis, Maryland: On certain Wednesday afternoons during fall and spring, and during commissioning week, the 4,500 spit-and-polished midshipmen have a 3:45 PM dress parade on Worden Field. During the academic year when the temperature is above 55°, the Brigade of Midshipmen assembles in Tecumseh Court for reports, a drum and bugle performance, and a march to lunch. There's more to see: the crypt of John Paul Jones, somewhat like Napoleon's in Paris; the chapel, really a large cathedral, complete with stained glass windows; trophies in the fieldhouse (and an explanation of how the goat came to be the navy's mascot); a museum full of naval history exhibits. Pamphlets outlining a self-guided walking tour are available, as are guided tours. Information: US Naval Academy, Annapolis, MD 21401 (301 263-6933).

Great Horse Races

Ever since President Washington closed Congress on October 24, 1780, so that he and the senators could attend the races at this country's first racetrack, Baltimore's Pimlico, Americans have been competing against each other on horseback.

Every breed has its set of competitive events. Standardbreds, bred to trot (with diagonal legs moving in synchronization) or, more commonly, to pace (with lateral legs moving together), pull sulkies around dirt ovals. Thoroughbreds ridden by tiny jockeys in bright-colored silks charge down flat tracks or leap their way over steeplechase courses. Quarter horses run for million-dollar purses, while Western horses work out at rodeos.

ALL ABOUT HORSES

KENTUCKY HORSE PARK, Lexington, Kentucky: Possibly the best place in the country to get a feeling for American horse life, this $35 million facility which opened in September 1978 on 1,032 acres in the heart of the Kentucky bluegrass country represents not just the thoroughbreds which are born and bred in the area, but also Morgans, Arabians, Appaloosas, and just about any other breed you can name. With a stirring 25-minute film on the history of man and horse, and a 40,000-square-foot museum full of dioramas, computers, and various displays about horses the size of dogs, horses and Roman chariots, horses in the wild West, and more. A motorized tram ride gives you an overview and takes you through the back paddock areas. At the Walking Farm Tour, you can see a farrier, a harnessmaker, and over 25 different breeds of horses, and learn about the day-by-day care of the horses in residence. You can go horseback riding, take pony rides, cruise the grounds in horse-drawn omnibuses, watch appropriately costumed drivers hitch up landaus — and take in dozens of special events: polo games, steeplechase meetings, dressage exhibitions, horse pulling contests, quarter horse sprints, cross-country races (the kind in which Britain's Princess Anne competed in the Olympics). Also available are 265 sites for camping, tennis courts, recreation areas, a fine lively activities program, and a good-size swimming pool. Information: Kentucky Horse Park, 4089 Iron Works Pike, Lexington, KY 40511 (606 233-4303).

GREAT RACES

Of the hundreds of races that give horse racing the largest paid attendance of any US sport, these are among the biggest.

THE BLUE GRASS STAKES, Lexington, Kentucky: With a $150,000-added purse, this is the biggest event of the 15-day spring meeting at Keeneland Race Course — old, famous, and very beautiful at this time of year with the dogwoods and flowering crabs in full bloom. Because the race is run nine days before the Kentucky Derby, over a course just an eighth of a mile shorter than the Derby's mile and a quarter, it is a steppingstone to the Triple Crown. The $150,000-added Spinster, for fillies and mares three years old and up, highlights a 16-day October season and determines, at least in part, which horse will be named champion in her respective division. Four times a year there are thoroughbred sales — yearlings in July and September, breeding stock in November, all ages in January. The highest price ever paid for a horse at public auction — $13.1 million — was paid here at Keeneland in 1985 for a colt by Nijinsky II. Tickets and information: Keeneland Assn., PO Box 1690, Lexington, KY 40592 (606 254-3412).

THE KENTUCKY FUTURITY, Lexington, Kentucky: The Red Mile, named for the color of the clay on the track, has two seasons every year — the first from late April through June at night, the second from mid-September through early October; the first weekend are races, the rest afternoons. The Kentucky Futurity — a mile-long, $200,000 race for three-year-old trotters, the third leg of the Triple Crown for trotters — comes at the end of September or early October. The fact that the fillies and colts who enter have raced against each other for months by the time they get here makes for exciting races. The Red Miles is known as the fastest standardbred track in the world. Right in the middle of the October meeting is the Tattersalls Sale (the equivalent of Keeneland's big yearling sale). On Show Day, the Sunday halfway through the October meeting, all the horse farms in the area hold open houses, complete with burgoo (a kind of oatmeal gruel) and music — and anyone can come. Information: Tom White, The Red Mile, PO Box 420, Lexington, KY 40585 (606 255-0752; 800 354-9092).

THE KENTUCKY DERBY, Louisville, Kentucky: Always the highlight of the spring meet, always on the first Saturday in May, this race, modeled after England's English Derby, was established in 1875 and has been run over the same course ever since (though the original mile-and-a-half distance was trimmed to 1¼ miles in 1896). It's a big deal for the horse owners because of the big purse (some $700,000); for the horses because of the competition and the distance (which is considerable for a three-year-old so early in the season); and for all of Louisville, for which this is a social as well as a sporting event. Reserved seat tickets are sold on an invitational basis — which means that tickets rarely change hands from year to year. However, general admission tickets are sold on the day of the race. Information: Churchill Downs, Louisville, KY 40208 (502 636-3541).

THE PREAKNESS, Baltimore, Maryland: The middle jewel of the Triple Crown is raced the third Saturday in May for more than $350,000 on the 1³⁄₁₆-mile dirt track at the Pimlico Race Course. The Preakness, one of the oldest races in America, started in 1873 and attracts the best three-year-old thoroughbreds from all over the country — not to mention crowds of more than 80,000. The regular racing season at Pimlico runs mid-February through May and mid-July through October on both the flat track and the ⅞-mile turf course. Information: Maryland Jockey Club, Pimlico Race Course, Baltimore, MD 21215 (301 542-9400).

THE HAMBLETONIAN, East Rutherford, New Jersey: Named for the greatest sire of them all (every trotter and pacer is said to be related to this famous horse), this jewel in the Triple Crown for trotters was moved to the Meadowlands in 1981 from its home of 25 years at the Illinois Du Quoin State Fair. Held the first Saturday in August, it is one of the most prestigious races of them all, with a purse of $1 million. Information: The Meadowlands Racetrack, E Rutherford, NJ 07073 (201 935-8500).

WOODROW WILSON PACE, East Rutherford, New Jersey: The richest event in harness racing, this contest for two-year-old pacers — a midsummer annual at the Meadowlands — carries a purse of approximately $2 million. Information: The Meadowlands Racetrack, E Rutherford, NJ 07073 (201 935-8500).

ALL-AMERICAN FUTURITY, Ruidoso Downs, New Mexico: The richest race of its kind since the dawn of civilization, with a $2.5 million gross purse ($1 million of which goes to the winner), is not a race of thoroughbreds but of quarter horses — originally bred primarily for ranch work with powerful hind quarters that make them superb sprinters, and now infused with thoroughbred blood. Between 10,000 and 15,000 people make their way every summer to southern New Mexico to watch over 300 horses go through eliminations that leave the 10 fastest to compete on a quarter-mile dash down a straight track. Held on Labor Day. Information: Ruidoso Downs Race Track, Ruidoso Downs, NM 88346 (505 378-4431).

THE BELMONT STAKES, Elmont, New York: The third and final leg of the races for the Triple Crown by the best of the country's three-year-old thoroughbreds. Held every year in the first half of June, with the highest purse and the longest distance (1½ miles) in the Crown. Secretariat holds the record at 2:24. The regular racing season at Belmont Park, where the race is held, is mid-May through July, and late August to mid-October. Information: New York Racing Assn., PO Box 90, Jamaica, NY 11417 (718 641-4700).

THE TRAVERS, Saratoga Springs, New York: The oldest active stakes race in the country — a 1¼-mile run for three-year-old thoroughbred colts — is held at the oldest active racetrack in the country, the Saratoga Race Course, where they've been racing almost every year since 1864. Many US tracks have been designed after Saratoga. In the Travers, which is worth $250,000, the colts are so closely matched that it's usually a pretty exciting race. The Saratoga season runs for four weeks, from about the end of July until about the end of August, and there are stakes races of one sort or another almost every day, with big races on Saturdays: the Alabama, $125,000 for three-year-old fillies; the Whitney, $200,000 for three-year-olds and up; and the Hopeful, a $100,000 race for two-year-olds whose winner, historically, has often gone on to win the Triple Crown races the following year. Information: New York Racing Assn., PO Box 90, Jamaica, NY 11417 (718 641-4700).

THE INTERNATIONAL TROT, Westbury, New York: In Europe, trotting trainers are more concerned with gait and style, and a European trotting race is a pretty race. You can see the difference between European trotters and American at the $250,000 International Trot, the world championship of trotting, held at Roosevelt Raceway every July or August during the summer meet (other meets are held late February through April and mid-October to early December). Information: Roosevelt Raceway, Westbury, NY 11590 (516 222-2000).

THE MESSENGER STAKES, Westbury, New York: The second most important race of the Roosevelt Raceway year, this one held at the end of October or beginning of November is the third leg of the Triple Crown for three-year-old pacers and helps decide who gets divisional honors and who gets named the horse of the year. The purse is $275,000. Information: Roosevelt Raceway, Westbury, NY 11590-0978 (516 222-2000).

THE CANE PACE, Yonkers, New York: This $560,000 race, usually held in mid-summer, with the Little Brown Jug (Delaware County Fair, Delaware, Ohio) and the Messenger Stakes (see above), make up the Triple Crown of pacing; the race is similar to the Messenger in many ways, right down to the half-mile track (somewhat slower, because of the turns required, than the mile-long track at the Meadowlands, in East Rutherford, New Jersey). As for all other staked races, competitors have been entered (and payments made to keep their entrance status current) almost from birth. Information: Yonkers Raceway, Yonkers, NY 10704 (914 968-4200).

THE YONKERS TROT, Yonkers, New York: Worth an estimated $400,000, this is one of the three glamour events of trotting (with the Kentucky Futurity and the Hambletonian described above) held in summer. Information: Yonkers Raceway, Yonkers, NY 10704 (914 968-4200).

THE MARION du PONT SCOTT COLONIAL CUP INTERNATIONAL STEEPLE-CHASE, Camden, South Carolina: The $50,000 cup makes this late fall event, first held in 1970, the very biggest in steeplechase racing; with the American Grand National at Charlottesville, Virginia, and the Temple Gwathmey at Belmont Park, New York, it is one of the jewels of the Triple Crown of steeplechase racing. But unlike its fellows, the Colonial Cup is an international race, and participants come from around the world. There are no timber races, but instead special "national fences" made of plastic brush — 17 obstacles in all. The Carolina Cup, held in the spring, is older and draws bigger crowds (though the purse is not so large). Information: Colonial Cup, PO Box 280, Camden, SC 29020 (803 432-6513).

RODEOS

Beyond the fact that the rodeo cowboy's skills are rooted in the life of the Wild West, the rodeo system today has very little to do with that romantic era. In the first place, there's big money involved — hundreds of thousands of dollars in prizes for all the different events. Then, too, the cowboys are more like Olympic athletes: They train hard and work hard to get where they are. All rodeos sanctioned by the Professional Rodeo Cowboys' Association (PRCA) — the larger of the two cowboy "leagues" — include bareback, saddle bronc, and bull riding; calf roping and team roping; and steer wrestling. Often there's also barrel racing (for women), sanctioned by the Girls' Rodeo Association; plus chuckwagon races and the like. All of these rodeos — the US's biggest and most important — are associated with livestock shows or big state or county fairs.

NATIONAL WESTERN STOCK SHOW AND RODEO, Denver, Colorado: At this venerable annual, the largest indoor rodeo in the country, some 1,000 entrants vie for over $300,000 in prize money every January. But as the biggest of the US's livestock exhibitions, it also has plenty of exhibits that tell you everything you never knew about livestock matters from saddles to beef production. All over the place there are kids grooming animals in preparation for judging and onlookers numbering in the thousands. Information: National Western Stock Show and Rodeo, 1325 E 46th Ave., Denver, CO 80216 (303 297-1166).

NATIONAL FINALS RODEO, Las Vegas, Nevada: At the end of the year, the top 15 money-winners who have competed in the more than 640 Professional Rodeo Cowboy Association–sanctioned rodeos qualify for the National Finals — and from there they all have equal chances for the championships in the various divisions. At stake are nearly $2 million in prizes and the NFR and world titles, and the competition is fierce. The 10 performances are held beginning the first Friday in December; most tickets sell out a year in advance. Information: Las Vegas Events, PO Box 72556, Las Vegas, NV 89170 (702 731-2115).

SOUTHWESTERN EXPOSITION AND FAT STOCK SHOW RODEO, Fort Worth, Texas: The world's oldest indoor rodeo, held in the heart of cowboy country at the end of January every year, pays over $400,000. Information: Southwestern Exposition, PO Box 150, Fort Worth, TX 76101 (817 335-9346).

HOUSTON LIVESTOCK SHOW AND RODEO, Houston, Texas: This event, which runs for two weeks beginning in late February, features a Texas-size rodeo, held in the Astrodome; and the world's largest livestock show, which fills up the Astrohall and Astroarena with horses, chickens, pigs, and cattle, for display and for sale at auction. In 1983, five chickens went for $61,000 and, in 1984, the grand champion steer for $150,000. Tickets and information: Houston Livestock Show, PO Box 20070, Houston, TX 77225 (713 791-9000).

CHEYENNE FRONTIER DAYS RODEO, Cheyenne, Wyoming: The biggest US rodeo and the granddaddy of them all is a long-standing tradition in Wyoming. In addition to the usual competitive events, there are night shows (generally featuring country and western performers like Charley Pride or Dolly Parton), chuckwagon races; and parades, Indian dancers, and various exhibitions and entertainments at the associated ten-day celebration. Last full week in July. Information: Frontier Days, PO Box 2666, Cheyenne, WY 82003 (307 778-7200).

FOR MORE INFORMATION

There are complicated systems for the way the thoroughbreds and standardbreds race; an understanding will help you enjoy the races more and make wiser bets. The *Thoroughbred Racing Associations,* 3000 Marcus Ave., Suite 2W4, Lake Success, NY 11042 (516 328-2660), publish lists of major races. The *US Trotting Assn.,* 750 Michigan Ave., Columbus, OH 43215 (614 224-2291), publishes a history of the sport and free booklets that tell you how to pick a winner, purchase a horse, or pursue a career in racing. Steeplechasing information: *National Steeplechase and Hunt Assn.,* PO Box 308, Elmont, NY 11003 (516 437-6666). Rodeo information: *PRCA* (Professional Rodeo Cowboys Association), 101 Prorodeo Dr., Colorado Springs, CO 80919 (303 593-8840).

Oddities and Insanities

America is full of offbeat attractions — museums given over to one subject (cartoons, buttons, soup tureens), whole festivals entirely devoted to matters that you'd consider entirely inconsequential, big blowouts or festivals that completely take over a town, and "world's best," "world's only," "world's first," etc. Around every corner there's something unexpected. Here are some of particular note.

EAST

BARNUM FESTIVAL, Bridgeport, Connecticut: A ten-day flurry each June/July of contests, concerts, fireworks, circus parades, flea markets, an antique auto show, and an air show in the great showman's home town. Information: Barnum Festival, 804 Main St., Bridgeport, CT 06604 (203 367-8495).

THE NEWSPAPER HOUSE, Rockport, Massachusetts: A cabin made entirely of pasted, folded, and pressed newspapers — with furniture made of rolled newspapers

— is at 52 Pigeon Hill in this shop-crammed resort town north of Boston. Information: Chamber of Commerce, Rockport, MA 01966 (617 546-6575).

LAKE CHARGOGGAGOGGMANCHAUGGAGOGGCHAUBUNAGUNGAMAUGG, Webster, Massachusetts: The name, in the language of the Nipmuc Indians, means "I fish on my side, you fish on your side, and no one fishes in the middle." Local fishermen call it Lake Webster. Largemouth and smallmouth bass, pickerel, and rainbow and brown trout have an almost ideal environment. Information: Webster-Dudley-Oxford Chamber of Commerce, Box 100, Webster, MA 01570 (617 943-0558).

LUCY THE MARGATE ELEPHANT, Margate, New Jersey: Constructed around 1881 along with similar curiosities by one James Lafferty, Lucy is a 75-foot-long and 65-foot-tall elephant building, a former hotel. Now she stands as a National Historic Landmark. There's a small museum inside, and you can climb onto her howdah, an observatory. Seasonal, so be sure to check first. Information: Save Lucy Committee, PO Box 3000, Margate, NJ 08402 (609 822-6519).

NATIONAL POLKA FESTIVAL, Hunter, New York: Top bands, a band competition, a dance floor that holds 1,000 in the largest tent in the US, ethnic foods, and daily dance contests. August. Information: National Polka Festival, Bridge Street, PO Box 297, Hunter, NY 12442 (518 263-3800).

MUSEUM OF CARTOON ART, Rye Brook, New York: Exhibitions of historical and contemporary cartoons, with examples of over a thousand different cartoonists — not to mention cartoon animations on film and video. The collection, the largest of its kind in the world, is housed in Ward's Castle, the first house in the world to be constructed entirely of reinforced concrete. Information: Museum of Cartoon Art, Comly Ave., Rye Brook, NY 10573 (914 939-0234).

WORLD CHAMPIONSHIP SNOW SHOVEL RIDING CONTEST, Ambridge, Pennsylvania: You sit on shovels or spades, then slide down a 153-foot snow-covered slope; the idea is to get down before your opponents — still sitting on the shovel. Held every winter in January. Information: Beaver County Tourist Promotion Agency, 14th & Church sts., Ambridge, PA 15003 (412 266-2226).

BEAN SOUP FESTIVAL, McClure, Pennsylvania: Thousands of gallons of bean soup are stirred up in 35-gallon iron kettles to accompany 25 roast hogs and the usual small-town festival doings every year in September. It's a great feast. Information: Bean Soup Festival, Box 8, McClure, PA 17841 (717 658 8425).

UNITED CHURCH OF CHRIST GAME SUPPER, Bradford, Vermont: A church supper where the goodies on the table are beaver, boar, bear, coon, pheasant, rabbit, venison, Moufflon ram, and whatever else is available that year, the sittings sell out within days of tickets going on sale. November. Information: United Church of Christ, Bradford, VT 05033 (802 222-4418).

CONVENTION OF THE AMERICAN SOCIETY OF DOWSERS, Danville, Vermont: A gathering of novice and experienced dowsers with reports, workshops, meetings, and speakers. One four-day weekend in September preceded by a two-day dowsing school. Information: American Society of Dowsers, Danville, VT 05828-0024 (802 684-3417).

WORLD'S FAIR, Tunbridge, Vermont: A country fair with pony pulling contests, oxen judging, and fiddlers' and band concerts (among other things) — it gets pretty lively. Mid-September. Information: Vermont Dept. of Agriculture, 116 State St., Montpelier, VT 05602 (802 828-2428).

FEAST OF THE RAMSON, Richwood, West Virginia: The publisher of this town's newspaper once threatened to put the juice of the ramp — a wild onionlike vegetable peculiar to the shady coves of Appalachia — in the printing ink, and the townspeople panicked. Once you've eaten ramps, the smell hangs around you for days, but the annual feast devoted to the green is much loved nonetheless. There is also a mountain-related arts and crafts display. April. Information: Chamber of Commerce, 50 Oakford Ave., Richwood, WV 26261 (304 846-6790).

SOUTH

NATIONAL PEANUT FESTIVAL, Dothan, Alabama: Peanut recipe contests, parades, arts and crafts shows, soapbox derbies, hog herding contests, sheep dog trials, and greased pig scrambles are the staples at this two-week small-town bash grown to state fair size. And the nuts themselves are for sale everywhere. Mid-October. Information: National Peanut Festival Assn., 1691 Ross Clark Circle, SE, Dothan, AL 36301 (205 793-4323).

WORLD'S CHAMPIONSHIP DUCK-CALLING CONTEST, Stuttgart, Arkansas: The competition for the title of Queen Mallard is followed by various duck-calling competitions, some for kids, some for women, some for men in hale, mating, feed, and comeback calls. All of this is the kick-off for a week-long festival and carnival. Annually, starting the weekend of Thanksgiving. Information: Chamber of Commerce, PO Box 932, Stuttgart, AR 72160 (501 673-1602).

NATIONAL WILD TURKEY CALLING CONTEST AND TURKEY TROT FESTIVAL, Yellville, Arkansas: Miss Turkey Trot presides over this big (and cacophonous) October contest, further enlivened by dancing, a parade, live entertainment, and lots more. Information: Chamber of Commerce, Box 369, Yellville, AR 72687 (501 449-4676).

WORLD CHAMPIONSHIP SWAMP BUGGY RACES, Naples, Florida: With their high wheels, these homemade conveyances that can get through mud and water under nearly any conditions are a way of life in this part of the country; a flooded 40-acre marshland on the edge of the Everglades provides the racecourse twice a year, usually the last Sundays in October and February. Information: Swamp Buggy Days, PO Box 3105, Naples, FL 33939 (813 774-2701).

WORLD'S CHICKEN PLUCKIN' CHAMPIONSHIP, Spring Hill, Florida: Teams compete at this small community northwest of Tampa to establish new world records (to be listed in *Guinness*) the first Saturday in October. Also part of the goings-on is a Miss Drumstick Contest, in which competitors' torsos are enveloped in flour sacks; and there's plenty of music, singing, dancing, and food. Information: Spring Hill VFW–Post 10209, 15166 Spring Hill Dr., Spring Hill, FL 33526 (904 796-0398).

MULE DAY, Calvary, Georgia: Mule-judging contests here have spectators casting their ballots for the ugliest, most stubborn, and prettiest mules — but only after a big and very lively mule parade has gotten everyone in the mood. And tobacco-spitting contests, cakewalks, sugarcane grinding, greased-pig-chasing competitions, and plenty of live country entertainment round out the program. November. Information: Chamber of Commerce, Box 387, Cairo, GA 31728 (912 377-MULE).

GREAT EASTER EGG HUNT, Stone Mountain, Georgia: One of the world's largest Easter egg hunts, with 62,000 brightly colored hard-boiled eggs hidden in a meadow. The park where it is held, on the outskirts of Atlanta, also has two Easter sunrise services, one at the mountain's base, the other at its peak. Information: Stone Mountain Park, PO Box 778, Stone Mountain, GA 30086 (404 498-5600).

INTERNATIONAL BANANA FESTIVAL, Fulton, Kentucky: The twin cities of Fulton, Kentucky, and South Fulton, Tennessee, celebrate the area's role as "Banana Crossroads of the United States" and "Banana Capital of the World" with banana-eating contests, a banana bake-off, and a one-ton banana pudding that serves 10,000 — half to a third of the people who put in an appearance in these communities about 50 miles from Paducah and 127 miles from Memphis. And it's free — and so are the bananas handed out to all comers. September. Information: International Banana Festival, PO Box 428, Fulton, KY 42041 (502 472-2975).

THE CRAWFISH FESTIVAL, Breaux Bridge, Louisiana: Such a major event is involved in serving up these little crustaceans in all imaginable forms that the townspeople can put on the festival only every other year. In May in even-numbered years.

Information: Breaux Bridge City Hall, 101 Berard St., Breaux Bridge, LA 70517 (318 332-2171).

LOUISIANA FUR AND WILDLIFE FESTIVAL, Cameron, Louisiana: Trapshooting, retriever dog trials, duck- and goose-calling and oyster-shucking contests, nutria- and muskrat-skinning contests, fur judging, and more. Second weekend in January. Information: Secretary, Louisiana Fur and Wildlife Festival, PO Box 19, Cameron, LA 70631 (318 775-5718).

NATIONAL HOLLERIN' CONTEST, Spivey's Corner, North Carolina: Left over from the days before telephones, when each man had his own holler. In 1976, a three-legged dog barked along with the hollerers. Third Saturday in June. Information: Ermon Godwin, PO Box 332, Dunn, NC 28334 (919 892-4133).

EASTER EGG FIGHTS, Sugar Hill, North Carolina: Descendants of this Piedmont town's early German settlers, following a 160-year-old custom, test the durability of their hard-boiled brightly colored eggs by banging the small ends together. The contestant that ends up with the least damage wins. Early on Easter Sunday. Area information: Chamber of Commerce, PO Box 305, Cherryville, NC 28021 (704 435-3451).

CHITLIN' STRUT, Salley, South Carolina: The chitlin' capital of the world serves up over ten tons of these boiled, deep-fried hog intestines every year on the Saturday after Thanksgiving. Information: E. W. Clamp, PO Box 482, Salley, SC 29137 (803 258-3331).

WORLD'S BIGGEST FISH FRY, Paris, Tennessee: Some four tons of catfish hauled out of the Tennessee River are cooked up at this big affair to serve with an equally staggering quantity of coleslaw, hushpuppies, and baked beans. Late April. Information: Chamber of Commerce, Box 82, Paris, TN 38242 (901 642-3431).

ZILKER PARK KITE FESTIVAL, Austin, Texas: The oldest of America's dozen or so celebrations of this favorite childhood toy is held annually in mid-March; some 10,000 spectators usually show up to watch the 200 fliers send up craft as small as a square on a Rubik's cube and as large as a master bedroom. Information: Parks and Recreation Dept., 1500 W Riverside Dr., Austin, TX 78704 (512 499-2000, ext. 2737).

EASTER FIRES PAGEANT, Fredericksburg, Texas: Costumed Easter bunnies, fireworks, and bonfires in a pageant which got its start back in the days when parents told their youngsters that what were actually the bonfires of watchful Indians were the cookfires of Easter bunnies boiling eggs. Easter Eve. Information: Chamber of Commerce, PO Box 506, Fredericksburg, TX 78624 (512 997-3444).

THE WURSTFEST, New Braunfels, Texas: Crowds of over 140,000 come around to gobble mettwurst, blutwurst, bratwurst, leberwurst, wurstkabobs, pork hocks, sauerkraut, dumplings and all the rest at a 10-day extravaganza that nods to the heritage of the people who settled here. Late October through November. Information: Wurstfest Assn., PO Box 180, New Braunfels, TX 78130 (512 625-2385).

EASTERN SHORE SEAFOOD FESTIVAL, Chincoteague, Virginia: The 3,000 or so tickets to this big affair sell out nearly a year in advance, and you'll see why: The savory Chincoteague oysters are served here by the ton, along with clams (steamed, raw, in fritters), and plenty of coleslaw, french-fried sweet potatoes, hush puppies, and other goodies. Early May. Information: Eastern Shore Chamber of Commerce, Box 147, Accomac, VA 23301 (804 787-2460).

MIDWEST

NATIONAL HOBO CONVENTION, Britt, Iowa: Thousands of vacationers and even some hobos converge on this little town every year in August — and have been doing so since 1900. A king and queen are selected, and 500 gallons of Mulligan stew are dished out for free. Information: Chamber of Commerce, Britt, IA 50423 (515 843-3867).

INTERNATIONAL PANCAKE DAY, Liberal, Kansas: The main event is a foot race in which women in house dresses, aprons, and head scarves run a 415-yard S-shaped course through town while flipping flapjacks in skillets — a strange activity that got its start some 500 years ago in England. Shrove Tuesday. Information: International Pancake Day, PO Box 665, Liberal, KS 67901 (316 624-1106).

WORLD'S LONGEST BREAKFAST TABLE, Battle Creek, Michigan: Where else but in the Breakfast Capital of the World would you find four blocks of end-to-end picnic tables laden with products of the Big Three (Kellogg's, General Foods, and Ralston-Purina)? And it's all free. June. Information: Greater Battle Creek/Calhoun County Visitor and Convention Bureau, 172 W Van Buren St., Battle Creek, MI 49017 (616 962-2240).

THE MAGIC GET-TOGETHER, Colon, Michigan: After the great illusionist Harry Blackstone moved here in the '20s, the town became a magicians' colony of sorts; Abbott's Magic Company puts on this extravaganza of "illusions," as magic tricks are known in the business. August. Information: Abbott's Magic, Colon, MI 49040 (616 432-3235).

NATIONAL CHERRY FESTIVAL, Traverse City, Michigan: Nearly a quarter-million visitors journey here annually for one of the nation's biggest festivals — where they can enjoy cherry sundaes at an ice cream social, cherry desserts made by area cherry growers' wives and a cherry smorgasbord luncheon, cherry pie eating contests, cherry orchard tours, two band competitions, and three big parades. One week in July. Information: National Cherry Festival, PO Box 141, Traverse City, MI 49685 (616 947-4230).

NATIONAL FENCE PAINTING CONTEST, Hannibal, Missouri: Kids dressed up like Tom Sawyer compete as part of the Tom Sawyer Days, held every year the first week in July. Supremacy among fence-painters is determined by the judges' opinion of the authenticity of a contestant's costume — and the speed and thoroughness with which he applies the whitewash. There's also frog jumping, a baby beauty contest, a mud volleyball game (played in a pit full of pure Mississippi mud), and raft race. Information: National Fence Painting Chairman, c/o Hannibal Jaycees, PO Box 484, Hannibal, MO 63401.

THE PUMPKIN SHOW, Circleville, Ohio: Crowds up to half a million come for what Ohioans call "the greatest free show on earth" — and down piles of pumpkin ice cream, pumpkin pie, pumpkin fudge, pumpkin candy, pumpkin milk shakes, pumpkin cookies, and even pumpkin burgers. October. Information: Chamber of Commerce, PO Box 462, Circleville, OH 43113 (614 474-4923).

BUZZARD DAY, Hinckley, Ohio: Buzzard Town USA got its name because of a flock of 75 or so of the big birds that spend most of the warmer months here; the day they return from their wintering grounds (or a day close to it) every March there are bazaars where you can buy chocolate buzzards, buzzard cookies, T-shirts, and bumper stickers, and a big pancake breakfast. Information: Chamber of Commerce, Box 354, Hinckley, OH 44233 (216 278-4242 or 216 661-1020).

INTERNATIONAL CHICKEN FLYING MEET, Rio Grande, Ohio: An organized version of what farm boys have been doing from hay lofts, trees, cliffs, and other high places for years, on Bob Evans' farm. May. Information: ICFM Secretary, 3776 S High St., Columbus, OH 43207 (614 491-2225).

LUMBERJACK WORLD CHAMPIONSHIPS, Hayward, Wisconsin: Events in sawing (single-man bucking, two-man bucking, power sawing), log rolling, speed climbing, ax throwing, canoe jousting, lumberjack relays, and chopping contests at a museum village, Historyland, that traces the history of the area. July. Information: Historyland, Hayward, WI 54843 (715 634-4811).

WEST

THE FUR RENDEZVOUS, Anchorage, Alaska: This action-packed festival features the World Championship Sled Dog Race, an Eskimo blanket toss exhibition, fur auction, fur style show, and over 130 other events, including a downhill canoe race, Grand Prix car racing, a cross-country snowmobile race, and more. One of the nation's ten largest festivals. Ten days in February. Information: Fur Rendezvous, PO Box 100773, Anchorage, AK 99510 (907 277-8615).

CALAVERAS COUNTY FAIR & JUMPING FROG JUBILEE, Angels Camp, California: This ordinary county fair features the International Frog Jump Finals, which climax a season of frog-jumping events across the country. The 2,800 contestants jump bullfrogs in an attempt to beat Weird Harold's 1984 21-foot-1½-inch record. Frogs are available for rent. Third full weekend in May. Information: Frogtown, PO Box 96, Angels Camp, CA 95222 (209 736-2561).

MULE DAYS, Bishop, California: The Mule Capital of the World puts on a Mule Days Parade with an assemblage of over 200 entries — mule teams, riding teams, pack strings and comedy entries (in which mules carry outhouses or beds); plus mule shoeing contests, mule and chariot races, a Mule Sale, a braying contest (for people), and a variety of other events. Memorial Day weekend. Information: Chamber of Commerce, 690 N Main St., Bishop, CA 93514 (619 873-8405).

INDIO DATE FESTIVAL, Indio, California: A ten-day county fair with some unusual entertainment: races of camels and ostrich (who behave so unpredictably that everybody else is upstaged), not to mention the Arabian pageant. February. Information: National Date Festival, PO Drawer NNNN, Indio, CA 92202 (619 342-8247).

INTERNATIONAL SURF FESTIVAL, Manhattan Beach, California: Also at Hermosa, Torrance, and Redondo beaches, this event is the big deal of a surfer's year. Late July or August. Information: Chamber of Commerce, 425 15th St., Manhattan Beach, PO Box 3007, CA 90266 (213 545-5313).

NATIONAL BASQUE FESTIVAL, Elko, Nevada: The population of this little town skyrockets as merrymakers from all over come to chorus the Basque national anthem, watch Basque games and contests (walking weight carries, tugs of war, handball, woodchopping and sheephooking contests, and 250-pound granite-ball lifts), and enjoy Basque meals and dancing and singing. It all culminates on Sunday afternoon with the Basque "Irrintzi" (war cry) contest. July. Information: Chamber of Commerce, PO Box 470, Elko, NV 89801 (702 738-7135).

WORLD CHAMPIONSHIP COW CHIP THROWING CONTEST, Beaver, Oklahoma: Pasture discus fans from around the world compete in this highly specialized athletic event, also known as the Organic Olympics. There's a special division for men and women champions and a very special division for politicians. Also on the schedule: an amateur talent show, an antique show, parade, carnival, street festivals, and a Wild West shootout. April. Information: Chamber of Commerce, PO Box 878, Beaver, OK 73932 (405 625-4726).

WORLD POSTHOLE DIGGING CHAMPIONSHIP, Boise City, Oklahoma: Men, women, and children compete. The event is part of the annual Santa Fe Trail Daze festival the first weekend in June. Information: Chamber of Commerce, PO Box 1027, Boise City, OK 73933 (405 544-3344).

INTERNATIONAL BRICK AND ROLLING PIN THROWING CONTEST, Stroud, Oklahoma: Hurlers from this small town compete against teams from Stroud, England, Stroud, Canada, and Stroud, Australia, for the best throws with bricks (for men) and rolling pins (for women). July. Information: Chamber of Commerce, PO Box 633, Stroud, OK 74079 (918 968-3321).

NATIONAL ROOSTER CROWING CONTEST, Rogue River, Oregon: Roosters from across the nation attempt to best the 1979 record set by White Lightning — 112 crows in 30 minutes. Last Saturday in June. Information: Chamber of Commerce, PO Box 457, Rogue River, OR 97537 (503 582-0242).

LEBANON STRAWBERRY FESTIVAL, Lebanon, Oregon: Bigger than the National Strawberry Festival (Manistee, Michigan, in early July), this festival stars the World's Largest Strawberry Shortcake (a 5,700-pounder that is 36 feet long, 10 feet wide, 5 feet high and served with 25 cases of whipped cream and 3,000 pounds of strawberries, and feeds 18,000 people). First full weekend in June. Information: Chamber of Commerce, 1040 Park St., Lebanon, OR 97355 (503 258-7164).

WORLD'S CHAMPIONSHIP SNOWSHOE SOFTBALL TOURNAMENT, Winthrop, Washington: Teams from all over the Pacific Northwest battle it out on snowshoes one day every February in this tiny, old-fashioned western town. Besides the softball, there's a sled-bed race, jousting, a relay tourney, and a chariot race — all on snowshoes. Information: Chamber of Commerce, Box 402, Winthrop, WA 98862 (509 996-2411).

DIRECTIONS

East

Mystic Seaport, Connecticut, to Providence, Rhode Island

Mystic Seaport, a restored whaling village and nautical museum, is off I-95 in Mystic, Connecticut, about 150 miles northeast of New York City. A driving tour will take you through several grimy, industrial New England towns, but you can escape the interstate at exit 71, South Lyme. Bear left at the end of the ramp, then left again at the junction of Rte. 156, going toward East Lyme (the sign is very confusing). This is a charming back road that winds through forgotten little towns of country stores, antiques shops, and boatyards fronting Long Island Sound.

NIANTIC, Connecticut: A village of New England Gothic wood-frame homes. Cross a drawbridge flanked by marinas and restaurants. As you reach the opposite side of the bridge, you'll pass the entrance to the Millstone Nuclear Power Plant. One wooded interlude beyond, you'll find yourself in a long strip of curio shops, gas stations, and shopping centers. This is antiques country, too, and there are innumerable places to stop and browse. In the distance, that inviting cluster of soft spruce hills punctuated by a church spire is New London.

NEW LONDON, Connecticut: An 18th- and 19th-century whaling port, now home of the US Coast Guard Academy, so there are lot of military jeeps and rugged seamen. In all, New London has a rather faded air, similar to some of the waterfront industrial districts in London, England, for which the town was named. Follow the signs to the business district and park on Bank Street near the Fishers Point Ferry Landing, with its polished wood waiting room. In winter, a fierce, wet wind blows in from Long Island Sound, but in warmer months the cool breeze is ideal. You can stroll along the Captain's Walk, a cobblestone promenade offering a view of the water. Caruso's Music Shop sells drums decorated with garishly colored windmills. Some of the main sites in New London are the Lyman Allyn Museum, a hodgepodge collection of Egyptian, Greek, Roman, medieval, Renaissance, and antique furniture (625 William St., 443-2545); Tale of the Whale, a museum with whaling implements (3 Whale Oil Row, 442-8191); Ye Olde Towne Mill, in use in 1650, with a museum room containing the grindstones and the gears operated by the waterwheel (Mill and State Pier Rd.; 203 444-2206).

MYSTIC, Connecticut: Take I-95 12 miles north to exit 90. Leaving the interstate, you'll pass the Mystic Marine Life Aquarium, with sea lions, seals, and more than 2,000 species of marine life (536-3323). About ½ mile south of I-95 on Rte. 27 is Mystic Seaport Museum (572-0711). Even in the winter the parking lot is crowded, but then it is possible to wander through the seaport without encountering hordes of people. In summer, the place is jammed. It takes at least three hours to see everything. Mystic Seaport consists of neat rows of sparkling white buildings along the banks of the Mystic

River, which feeds into Long Island Sound. There are four major historic ships, a working shipyard, a re-created 19th-century community area with craftspeople, and a formal exhibition area. You may board the 1882 training ship *Joseph Conrad;* the fishing schooner *L. A. Dunton;* and the fully restored 1841 whaling ship *Charles W. Morgan.* In summer, there are daily demonstrations of sail setting and furling, chantey singing, and other maritime skills. You'll probably gasp in astonishment as you enter the exhibition building with an assortment of giant ships' figureheads. Exhibitions of scrimshaw (engraved whale teeth) depicting old clipper and whaling ships bear testimony to years of patient craftsmanship. Also open to visitors are the chandlery, the ropemaking factory, rigging and sailmaking lofts, and model ships. Be sure to stop at the Mystic Scale Model, to see the town as it was in the 19th century. Stepping outside again, you'll realize how much love and care has gone into preserving the peaceful beauty and dignity of the village.

WESTERLY, Rhode Island: About 12 miles east of Mystic on Rte.1, this town of dignified, white Colonial mansions stretches to the coast of Block Island Sound. Westerly includes Watch Hill, an exclusive residential community, and Misquamicut State Beach. Florence Nightingale's cap is on display at Westerly Hospital, Wells St. (596-6000). Be careful driving around town. Westerly has only five principal streets, but you can easily get lost and end up back in Pawcatuck, Connecticut. Keep bearing right around the circle to avoid this.

PROVIDENCE, Rhode Island: The capital of Rhode Island, about 50 miles from Westerly on I-95 or Rte. 1, another delightfully empty road that hugs the coast, is a city with a low skyline. Take the Broadway exit off I-95 and bear right. Drive straight along that street and then bear left until you get to Kennedy Plaza and the US Courthouse on Exchange St., a building with several interesting classical sculptures depicting Justice. Circle the plaza, take a left on Dorrance, and when you pass the Westminster Mall, a pedestrian shopping plaza, turn left on Weybosset St. to the Crawford St. Bridge. Bear right at the intersection; at the end of the bridge, turn left and left again on S Main St. to Waterman St. Head up the hill, past the Rhode Island School of Design's Museum of Art (110 Benevolent St.; 331-3511). This area, known as College Hill, includes Brown University, whose main gate is on George St. (863-1000), and the Rhode Island School of Design, known as RISD, at 2 College St. (331-3511). Both campuses have concerts, films, plays, lectures, and cultural exhibitions throughout the year. Brown plays in the varsity Ivy League. Interspersed with the college buildings are a number of historical houses. These splendid Colonial estates, columned mansions, and gardens are like entering another world. Some of the houses are open daily. By the way, George Washington really did sleep in the Stephen Hopkins House (15 Hopkins St.; call the Providence Preservation Society at 831-7440). The easiest way to return to I-95 is by following Thayer St. to I-195, which feeds into I-95. I-95 will take you back to New York or on to Boston, about 45 miles northeast.

BEST EN ROUTE

Larchwood Inn, Wakefield, Rhode Island – Built in 1831, this country inn is known for its delicious, fresh seafood, elegant yet comfortable furnishings, and cozy atmosphere. Close to swimming, boating, fishing, and surfing as well as bicycling and cross-country ski routes. 176 Main St., Wakefield, RI 02879 (401 783-5454).

The Biltmore Plaza, Providence, Rhode Island – A major renovation has revived this lovely old hotel. Its rooftop restaurant, *L'Apogée,* has notable Continental food. Kennedy Plaza, Providence (401 421-0700; 800 228-2121).

The Ancient Mariner, Mystic, Connecticut – After wandering around the seaport, a seafood meal is a must. Chowder here is hearty, homemade, authentic New England clam. Seafood Thermidor is well stocked with scallops, shrimp, and other shellfish. 34 W Main St., Mystic (203 536-2581).

The Maine Coast and Acadia National Park, Maine

To drive along Maine's coastline is to spend some honest time with nature. Not the kind of ski lodge nature that seems to be little more than an entertainment, letting you come and go as you will and ending conveniently at the doors of a warm lodge. Nature in Maine comes mostly on its own terms, and those are terms of force — the fundamental power of the open Atlantic, the obdurate resistance of the rocky coastline against which it washes.

What makes this an honest trip, if you are observant, is a single revelation: that the forces at work here are totally oblivious to human beings. Watch eddies of the sea suck and slap against some stark slab of stone, perhaps at Acadia National Park, where the process is particularly well defined; the edge of the continent is being constantly, imperceptibly worn away, altered, but it is not an action within the scope of our time scale. It is not something that happens for any motive. It is natural force; it is nature. We don't even have language to describe such a process and its relation to us. Words like indifferent or oblivious imply knowledge, intention, will. They don't begin to represent the implacable force of water and stone, its inhuman beauty. Only by seeing it does this become comprehensible.

Perhaps the best road in the country to see this sea and stone contest — east of the California/Oregon coastal road — is Maine's Rte. 1. It stretches from Kittery to the Canadian border, but the most interesting section for a short two- or three-day drive is from Portland to Acadia National Park.

This route allows you to stop along the way at any number of villages and towns of unique Maine flavor. All along this craggy coast, America's history is evident. Not so much the history of great battles or the sites of events that altered destiny, but in a sense of one's own past. We are all, in some part, Yankees. There's more than a little twinge of recognition while viewing something studied but never before seen, like the widow's walks on the roofs of so many of the houses. It's this kind of familiar history that nudges your consciousness all along this coastal route.

Anyone in search of a few days' respite from the current century will hardly be disappointed by the state of Maine.

PORTLAND: A good place to begin your drive along the coast. It's a city, like countless others, with the requisite number of hotels and places to eat. The true flavor of Maine, however, lies beyond the city limits. Head out on I-95 due north, which in Maine is known as "Down East."

BATH: Now — and always — a shipbuilding center. A Marine Museum (963 Washington St.) portrays local history in a unique way — you are ferried down the Kennebec River and stop at four separate museum sites en route, each dealing with a different phase of Maine's maritime past. You can also explore the antique fishing boat *Sherman Zwicker*.

WISCASSET: An ideal place to sample life as it was in the late 1800s. Many of the homes of that era are still occupied today. Originally built by wealthy merchants and shippers, they are lovingly maintained by their present owners. The Nickels-Sortwell House (Main and Federal sts.), one of several homes open to the public, offers a good example of 19th-century Federal elegance — at least as it existed in Maine.

BOOTHBAY HARBOR: This town has been discovered by tourists, but that should not detract from its interest as a place to visit. It is, rather, a tribute to the Yankee ingenuity that early recognized the salability of picture-postcard scenes, incomparable lobster suppers, and singular charm. Enjoy the appealing (albeit commercial) displays that have been concocted for your amusement, among them the Railway Village (just north of town) with its narrow-gauge train that carries passengers. There's also the public aquarium (admission free) at McKown Point. And be sure to eat your fill of the local delicacy — lobster. You'll find it served in a variety of styles, delicious and relatively inexpensive.

While there are several fine places to stay right in Boothbay Harbor, there's something quite special just across the bay on Monhegan Island, the *Island Inn*. It's family-owned and over a century old, and there's a sort of time-stood-still feeling about the entire island. Most of the island has no electricity; peace and seclusion are the main elements of island entertainment, and you can explore in solitude, discovering the wildflowers and birds on your own. It's only a short ferry ride from the mainland to this gentler time.

ROCKLAND: This modern port city is the world's largest lobster distribution point and the takeoff place for the ferry to two very special Maine islands — North Haven and Vinalhaven. North Haven has a number of summer estates. Vinalhaven is a fishing village of about 1,100 Down East residents. There are no tennis courts, swimming pools, or movies; but there are church suppers (with baked beans, brown bread, and homemade pies), walks along the often foggy shores, and the constant coming and going of fishermen. Both islands are accessible via the Maine State Ferry Service from Rockland (207 594-5543). North Haven has no commercial accommodations; Vinalhaven has two: *Bridgeside Inn* (207 863-4854) and *Tidewater Motel* (207 863-4618); but local families also take in travelers.

CAMDEN: Stop here between Rockland and Mt. Desert Island (described below) simply because it is such a beautiful harbor town. Surrounded by high hills (there is good skiing here in the winter, and winter sports at Camden Snow Bowl) and a number of beautiful old homes, it is a town for walking around in, for a long lunch, or for shopping — especially if you are shopping for one of Maine's 3,344 islands. The town is something of a center for real estate agents dealing in islands, and the place to start is with the ads in *Down East* magazine, published in neighboring Rockport and available throughout the state.

MT. DESERT ISLAND: An exceptional place, one of the most wildly beautiful spots in the country, with 35,000 acres devoted to spectacular Acadia National Park; the peak for which it was named (by the French explorer Champlain in 1605) is Mt. Cadillac, the highest spot on the Atlantic coast (which, at 1,530 feet, is hardly gargantuan, but offers a marvelous view of Frenchman's Bay from its height); its major town, Bar Harbor, has been synonymous with wealth and society since the 1920s.

In its heyday — from the 1890s through the 1940s — Bar Harbor was simply too posh for the likes of most folks; the old wealth, certainly, is still on the island (as you will see when you peek at the mammoth estates in the hills as you drive the park's loop road). But today Bar Harbor is far too open, too raucous, too egalitarian to appeal to its original crowd. It opens and closes with the summer season, and for people on the way to the splendors of Acadia, it offers trendy shops (wander along Main Street and note especially the Rock Shop), many hotels, and a host of good seafood restaurants. But the real attraction of Mt. Desert is Acadia. It is the only national park that was purchased with private funds, an effort organized by Dr. Charles Eliot of Harvard and George Bucknam Dorr when lumber interests threatened the island. The nation accepted the gift in 1916. Parts of the park are off the island, on Isle au Haut and Schoodic Point on the mainland, but the main attractions are accessible from the 19-mile loop road that circles Mt. Desert's portion of Acadia.

Start a tour at the visitors center (at the entrance near Bar Harbor), with exhibitions on the ecology and history of the island. You can also pick up information on camping and sports (golf, cycling, horseback riding, hiking, swimming, and an array of winter activities) and maps of the driving routes as well as the hundreds of trails that score the island's "mountains." The Ocean Drive loop culminates in the crown of Mt. Cadillac; along the way there are ample opportunities to stop for a descent straight to rocky shore, where sea and stone meet.

Special treats, available at the harbors of the island's towns (Bar Harbor, Northeast Harbor, Bass Harbor), are sea cruises of nearby islands directed by naturalists. You search for eagle's nests or signs of porpoises and seals, go whale-watching, learn about the lobster trade, or make forays to historical museums on out islands. Get information at the visitors center or from the companies that offer the cruises, on the harbors mentioned above. Acadia is New England's only national park and it is a major treasury of authentic wilderness. Information: Superintendent, Acadia National Park, Box 177, Bar Harbor, ME 04609 (207 288-3338).

BEST EN ROUTE

There is a delicate art to planning a trip to New England, and Maine is no exception. Summer and winter are high seasons; book well in advance. The three weeks from late September to mid-October are leaf-peeping season, a magic time to be here but crowded, especially in the delightful New England inns — themselves incentive enough for a trip. An optimal time to visit is after the leaves turn and before winter, when life has returned to nontourist normal, and with luck the weather is fine. But that is just the period (mid-October to mid-November) when the Maine inns begin closing for the season, and you must plan in advance to get the ones you want. (An incentive: Rates during this period can be cut in half.) Our favorite Maine inns:

Homewood Inn, Yarmouth Beyond Portland on beautiful, foggy Casco Bay, this traditional inn has hearty food, a popular Monday night clambake, tennis, pool, boating, and gameroom. Closed from mid-October to early June. PO Box 196, Yarmouth, ME 04096 (207 846-3351).

The Island Inn, Monhegan Island – This frame structure on a bluff over the tiny harbor is open summers only. Fresh fish — striped bass, haddock, bluefish — are regulars on the menu; the cooking is not fancy, but the service is cheerful and quick. An all-you-can-eat buffet on Sunday nights brings in hikers. See also *America's Special Havens,* DIVERSIONS. Monhegan Island, ME 04852 (207 596-0371).

Whitehall Inn, Camden – A classic Maine house, wrapped around by a deep, cool porch decorated with lots of potted plants. It was here that Edna St. Vincent Millay (a resident of the town from the time she was 18) gave the first public recitation of *Renascence.* Closed in winter. PO Box 558, Camden, ME 04843 (207 236-3391).

Asticou Inn, Northeast Harbor, Mt. Desert Island – An elegant but comfortable resort that maintains its style in simple ways. It encourages repeat visits and likes to get to know its visitors. Open from mid-June to mid-September. In the very backyard of Acadia National Park. Asticou Way, Northeast Harbor, Mt. Desert Island, ME 04662 (207 276-3344).

Maryland's Eastern Shore

On the eastern coast of Maryland, set between the Chesapeake Bay and the Atlantic Ocean, is the peninsula called the Eastern Shore, one of the most charming and unspoiled historic sections of the country. Dating from pre-Revolutionary times, the Eastern Shore has retained the simple elegance that characterized the region when Lord Baltimore and his followers established their settlements. Although part of the eastern seaboard, the environment is surprisingly remote from urban and suburban 20th-century America.

The Eastern Shore is more than just a few scattered plantations separated by open green. It retains a neat harmony of spreading rivers and streams, large and small farms, fine homes, with grounds that stretch to the water's edge. Mention the bay in this part of the country and you'll find it means only one thing: the Chesapeake, 200 miles long, from 4 to 30 miles wide, fed by 150 rivers, and containing more than 7,000 miles of tidewater shoreline. Here, you can taste some of the best oysters, crabs, and clams in the country, within sight of fishermen on the bay to remind you of the region's most important occupation. Take US 40 or I-95 northeast from Baltimore about 35 miles, then head 5 miles south on Rte. 213 to Chesapeake City.

CHESAPEAKE CITY: The Maryland port of the Chesapeake and Delaware Canal. Built in 1829 for $2 million, the canal shortens the water route between Baltimore and Philadelphia by more than 275 miles and has been a constant source of jobs for people in the surrounding community. The canal was purchased by the US government in 1919 and lowered to sea level in 1927 for $10 million. Since then, it has served as an important commercial line in the inland waterway connecting Maine to Florida and has been used for leisure vessels as well. The largest waterwheel in the world can be found in the stone pumphouse, along with a scale model of the original canal, on the government property. The wheel was used to control water levels until the early 1900s. Information: Old Lock Pump House (301 885-5621).

EARLEVILLE: About 5 miles west of Rte. 213 overlooking the Sassafras River is Mount Harmon Plantation, an 18th-century tobacco plantation with a brick mansion, formal boxwood and wisteria gardens, and a tobacco house. The restored 1730 manor house is furnished with American and English antiques. The 386-acre property is almost entirely surrounded by water and recalls life and work in the 17th and 18th centuries on Maryland's Eastern Shore. More than 200 acres continue to be farmed, although tobacco no longer is raised. Owned by the Natural Lands Trust, Mount Harmon is open to the public from April through October. Information: Mount Harmon Plantation, PO Box 65, Earleville, MD 21929 (301 275-2721).

CHESTERTOWN: About 22 miles south of Warwick on Rte. 213, this tranquil, pretty, pre-Revolutionary town facing the Chester River contains several historic two-story brick houses. Across town, away from the river, Washington College spreads over 20 acres. Founded in 1780 by the Reverend William Smith, this small liberal arts college, named after George Washington (who served on the Board of Visitors and Governors), now has an enrollment of about 800 students (Washington Ave.). Pre-Revolutionary buildings include: the Wickes House (100 E High St.), Palmer House (532 W High St.), Geddes-Piper House (Church Alley), and Widehall and the Customs House (both at High and Front sts.). On the third Saturday in

September, there's a candlelight walking tour that takes you past the wide, sweeping lawns of the town's homes into the public and Colonial homes decorated with ornate, carved mantelpieces and unusual Americana. For information, call Mrs. Robert Bryan at 301 778-1141. For general information on historic homes and tours, call the Chestertown Town Hall (301 778-0500) or the Kent County Chamber of Commerce (301 778-0416).

WYE MILLS: About 25 miles south of Chestertown on Rte. 662 (via Rte. 213), this tiny colonial town grew up around an early-18th-century gristmill that has now been restored and is operated by college students. The Wye Church, built in 1721, is also in use. Nearby stands the Wye Oak, the official state tree. It has provided shade for 450 years and is one of the tallest white oaks in the country.

EASTON: About 12 miles south of Wye Mills on US 50 is the self-proclaimed "Colonial Capital of the Eastern Shore." Easton is often swamped with envious Northerners, some of whom become so enchanted that they return to purchase old estates upon retirement. Easton has some fine local antiques, artwork, and artifacts. During the second week in November, the town celebrates the Waterfowl Festival, which attracts wildfowl artists and carvers from all over the East Coast. Historic attractions in town include the Third Haven Meeting House, built in 1682, and the Talbot County Historical Society and Museum. Information: Easton Chamber of Commerce (301 822-4606).

OXFORD: Take Rte. 333 southwest from Easton until you reach the end of land. Here, you can ride on the oldest "free running" ferry in the nation. The Oxford-Bellevue ferry shuttles across the Tred Avon River, offering a fine view of the enclosed port and this small boating community.

ST. MICHAELS: When you leave the ferry, take Rte. 329 to Rte. 33 northwest about 8 miles. St. Michaels has an authentic 19th-century lighthouse at the Chesapeake Bay Maritime Museum, which contains maritime exhibitsion, a boatbuilding workshop, and Chesapeake Bay sailing craft. Narrated cruises of the Miles River can be taken from the museum aboard *The Patriot.* Information: Chesapeake Bay Maritime Museum (301 745-2916).

TILGHMAN ISLAND: Continue southwest on Rte. 33 to its southern tip. Tilghman Island is the home port for a portion of the Chesapeake Bay skipjack fleet, the last commercial sailing fleet in North America. The island is a haven for fishermen, and fishing boats and a skipjack are available for charter.

BLACKWATER NATIONAL WILDLIFE REFUGE: Returning to Easton, pick up Rte. 50 south through Cambridge to Rte. 16, and past Church Creek to Rte. 335, about 20 miles. Blackwater is a winter refuge for Canada and snow geese, ducks, and birds of prey. There are driving tours, walking tours, and a visitors information center. For information, call the refuge at 301 228-2677.

CRISFIELD: About 55 miles south of Cambridge, this is where you can catch boats to two excellent retreats, Smith and Tangier islands. Several boats take passengers, mail, and freight to the islands, where colonies of Chesapeake Bay watermen live and work. Both islands are flat, sandy, and surrounded by marshland. Smith Island, Maryland, a miniature version of the mainland, has tiny frame houses with small gardens, wharves, crab shanties, and very little commercialism. There's no town hall here because there's no local government. Nearly everything is part of the United Methodist Church. Tangier Island, Virginia, is more developed, with a new anchorage for visiting sailors, a high school, and a local government headed by a mayor. For more information, contact the Somerset County Tourism Commission (301 651-2968).

BEST EN ROUTE

Tidewater Inn, Easton – Almost a legend, certainly a landmark. Activities in town center around this 120-room Colonial inn, especially during Waterfowl Festival.

The restaurant is famous for fish and other local produce; Dover and Harrison sts., PO Box 359, Easton, MD 21601 (301 822-1300).

The Robert Morris Inn, Oxford – In the former home of a financier, the inn is next to the Tred Avon River ferry. Close to tennis, golf, sailing, swimming, and bicycling. Dining room open to the public. Oxford, MD 21654 (301 226-5111).

Chesapeake House, Tangier Island – Another secluded guest house close to nautical activities. Tangier Island is in Virginia waters. Tangier Island, VA 23440 (804 891-2331).

Francis Kitching's, Smith Island – A 5-room guest house and small motel that serves dinner and breakfast. Near all water sports. Ewell, Smith Island, MD 21824 (301 425-3321).

The Berkshires, Massachusetts

Up and down the East Coast, the Berkshires are famous for art and music in the summer, foliage in the fall, and downhill and cross-country skiing in the winter. Nobody seems to be quite sure how it all began — whether vacationers began going to the Berkshires because of the excellence of the music and art or whether artists and musicians began going because that's where the summer people went — or whether it's simply that everybody loves a vacation in the Berkshire Mountains.

More correctly referred to as the Berkshire Hills (although you'll swear they look just like mountains), Berkshire County fills the western quarter of the state, stretching from Connecticut to Vermont along the 50-mile border Massachusetts shares with New York. However, the Berkshires begin in earnest west of I-91, from Great Barrington in the south to the Mohawk Trail and Vermont in the north. Running straight through this area is Rte. 7, connecting the major towns (major in influence, not in size; only Pittsfield is a city of any size): Great Barrington, Stockbridge, Lenox, Pittsfield, Williamstown, and, slightly to the east, North Adams. Rte. 7 is a good road on which to start a trip, but remember the special advantage of Berkshire geography: The outside boundaries of the Berkshires form an almost perfect square, which in turn makes an almost perfect driving route. Follow the square and you can take in all the significant cultural, educational, and historical activities that give the Berkshires its special cachet.

Summer is, of course, prime time for artistic offerings. From the world-famous Tanglewood concerts and the Jacob's Pillow dance performances to the less well known theatrical offerings and the galleries presenting works of art and crafts, the Berkshire area is synonymous with both excellence and innovation in the arts.

A formidable rival to summer is the fall season, when the Berkshire Hills explode into color. The season starts in late September, but finding foliage at its colorful peak is about as chancy as finding perfect snow on a ski trip: You never know if nature will cooperate. Still, there are some general rules about when foliage will peak in a particular area. In late August, the harbingers stand out as solitary spots of gold or scarlet against the green hillsides. By mid-September, swamp maples are ablaze at the higher elevations and the northern part of the region. Most of the area, however, doesn't peak until October.

Snow always changes the face and appeal of a northern area, and the Berkshires are no exception. Mt. Greylock, the state's highest peak, provides a glorious setting for cross-country skiing and snowmobiling.

During the summer months there's so much going on that even old-timers have to consult the newspaper to plan their cultural days. You'll find an exhaustive list of events in local papers, divided into areas, each providing a complete rundown on what's happening in any location. For advance information on the whole area, any season, write to the Berkshire Hills Conference, Berkshire Common Plaza Level, Pittsfield, MA 01201 (413 443-9186). Request the *Berkshire Vacation Guide* and the *Circle Tours* booklet, which describes nine trips through the Berkshires. Information on the Mohawk Trail area: Northern Berkshire Chamber of Commerce, 69 Main St., N Adams, MA 01247 (413 663-3735); and Mohawk Trail Association, PO Box 7, N Adams, MA 01347 (413 664-6256).

STOCKBRIDGE: This beautiful town is the archetypal Berkshire village, in part because of the many famous paintings by its late resident Norman Rockwell. Its buildings and its people have graced the covers of the *Saturday Evening Post* and *McCall's* dozens of times. You can see the originals of many famous covers (*The Four Freedoms,* for example) at the Norman Rockwell Museum (Main and Elm sts.; 413 298-3822), a lovingly preserved collection of Rockwell work. Just down the street is the marvelous *Red Lion Inn,* justly one of New England's most famous hostelries.

Two interesting stops are Chesterwood, the home of sculptor Daniel Chester French, and the Mission House. Chesterwood (2 miles northwest of town off Rte. 183, Glendale; 413 298-3579) is maintained by the National Trust for Historic Preservation. You can visit the home, its gallery, and the gardens. Mission House (in town, Main and Sergeant sts.; 413 298-3239) was built in 1739 by the Reverend John Sergeant, who preached to the Berkshire Indians. (Relations were warm between the Indians and white settlers. Today, about a mile out of town, stands a marker reading: "The Ancient Burial Place of the Stockbridge Indians, Friends of Our Fathers.") Today the house is a museum of early Colonial life.

BECKET: Here is the home of Jacob's Pillow, the oldest dance festival in America. For nine weeks in summer, it draws dance groups from all over the world; its own resident company performs as well. PO Box 287, Lee, MA 01238 (413 243-0745), for schedule and reservations.

LENOX: Generally acknowledged as the star town of the Berkshires, Lenox is the summer home of the Boston Symphony Orchestra. Every summer, the Tanglewood concerts draw crowds of thousands each weekend. And there's more than one way to take your music at Tanglewood: at the Music Shed you can join the throngs picnicking, dreaming, and enjoying the symphony concerts; Chamber Music Hall offers more intimate programs to smaller audiences; Theater also presents chamber music programs. All these — and more — take place on the 210-acre estate of Tanglewood, near where Nathaniel Hawthorne lived and wrote. You can tour the manicured grounds and the Hemlock Gardens as well. For Tanglewood's schedule: Symphony Hall, 251 Huntington Ave., Boston, MA 02115 (617 266-1492) or, from June, Festival Ticket Office, Lenox, MA 01240 (413 637-1940).

Nearby is the Pleasant Valley Wildlife Sanctuary (W Mountain Rd.), maintained by the Massachusetts Audubon Society. Guided trails show you much of western Massachusetts nature and a beaver colony as well. There are small jewel-like lakes at almost every turn in this part of the Berkshires. One of the nicest is Stockbridge Bowl (south off Rte. 183).

PITTSFIELD: Its main summer event is the South Mountain Concerts, which feature opera, chamber music, and young people's concerts (call 413 442-2106 for schedules and information). Other attractions are open all year. Hancock Shaker Village, 5 miles west of town, is an original Shaker community built around 1790. There's a restored round barn, homes and buildings, and many exhibitions of Shaker life. The Berkshire Museum (39 South St.) has an impressive collection of Old Masters, early American works, and some very modern works as well as natural history exhibitions. If you loved *Moby Dick,* you'll want to visit Arrowhead (780 Holmes Rd.), Herman Melville's home from 1850 to 1863. The Berkshire Historical Society maintains this home with its Melville memorabilia, furniture, and period costumes.

WILLIAMSTOWN: The home of Williams College also offers the Williamstown Theater Festival (Main St.) and the Clark Art Institute (South St.), a jewel box of a museum with outstanding examples of French Impressionists, old silver, porcelains, and sculpture.

It is at Williamstown that you turn the "corner" of the Berkshire route and join the Mohawk Trail toward North Adams and Greenfield. Before reaching North Adams, to the south nature provides some spectacular attractions with the proximity of Mt. Greylock and its lookout tower; the Natural Bridge formation (scientists estimate that it's been around for about 55 million years!); and the Savoy Mountain State Forest and Mohawk Trail intersection, with a host of camping, picnicking, swimming, hunting, and fishing.

NORTH ADAMS: The Fall Foliage Festival is held here in the last weeks of September to celebrate the coming of color with a no-holds-barred Oktoberfest blowout. It's a perfect time to visit. Contact the Northern Berkshire Chamber of Commerce (address above) for details.

BEST EN ROUTE

Below are our choices from a wide variety of eating and lodging places. The Berkshires have some of the best inns in the country — truly an embarrassment of riches (see *Inn Sites,* DIVERSIONS). We suggest you also examine a couple of the inn books listed in *For More Information,* GETTING READY TO GO. In the meantime, you should note:

The Red Lion Inn, Stockbridge – The atmosphere here is homey, friendly, and full of small-town charm. The inn dates from 1773; some rooms have original antiques. Rates are higher during summer weekends; in winter, fewer rooms are open. The restaurant serves all meals and is noted for good, dependable, Yankee cuisine. See also *America's Special Havens,* DIVERSIONS. Rte. 7, Stockbridge, MA 01262 (413 298-5545).

The Williamsville Inn, West Stockbridge – Dating from 1797, this former farmhouse is the center of a 10-acre property that includes a pool, tennis court, pond for fishing, and skiing and antiquing nearby. The 15 guest rooms (only 9 in winter) include one with a fireplace. The inn is particularly known for its fine Continental cuisine. Children over 10 welcome. Rte. 41, West Stockbridge, MA 01266 (413 274-6580).

The Springs, New Ashford – Your hosts, the Grossos, have been feeding visitors for almost 60 years in informal, hearty style. Rte. 7, New Ashford, MA 01237 (413 458-5945).

Mill on the Floss, New Ashford – An 18th-century house is the setting for this restaurant. The food is Continental and good. Dinner only; closed Sundays. Rte. 7, New Ashford, MA 01237 (413 458-9123).

Le Jardin, Williamstown – Country inn combines gracious surroundings with fine

French cuisine. Closed in November. 777 Cold Springs Rd., Williamstown, MA 01267 (413 458-8032).

Cape Cod, Martha's Vineyard, and Nantucket, Massachusetts

When you look imaginatively at a map of Massachusetts, Cape Cod takes on the shape of a squat foot — wrapped in an elfin slipper that rises and curls at the toes — taking a step into the Atlantic. The cape is 70 miles long, from Buzzards Bay, where it leaves the mainland of southern Massachusetts, to the tip of its toe at Provincetown. It juts at least 30 miles into the Atlantic, far enough to be washed by the warmer waters of the Gulf Stream; consequently, the cape has cooler summers and milder winters than the mainland.

Below it, accessible by ferry and plane, are the two famous islands of Martha's Vineyard and Nantucket, where the homes and villages of America's 19th-century seafaring community are still intact and inhabited.

What is special about the cape and the islands has everything to do with the sea. It is the sea that provides the sailing, swimming, and beaches so attractive in summer. (Cape Cod has 300 miles of beaches — almost all clean and beautiful — and two kinds of water: on its northern, protected shore, waters are calm and warmer; southern and eastern beaches, facing the open Atlantic, are cold, with high, exciting waves.) It is the sea that is responsible for its history. The Pilgrims landed at Provincetown about a month before they reached the mainland at Plymouth, and its beautiful, perfectly preserved 19th-century homes and villages are products of the area's successful ventures into worldwide shipping 150 years ago. (There was a time when Nantucket captains were as likely to meet one another in the Banda Islands as on the streets they shared at home.) And it is the sea — and the sand it torments — that makes Cape Cod one of the most interesting ecological studies a layman is likely to stumble across.

That's the good news. The bad news is, of course, that nasty commercialism has corrupted much of this tranquillity — filling up the open spaces with fast-food chains, assaulting the eyes and ears of the beholder with a concrete barrage. But only in some places! Two specific areas of the cape are protected by law from 20th-century excesses: the 28,000-acre Cape Cod National Seashore, with its 35-mile stretch of untamed shoreline; and old Rte. 6A along the north coast of the cape. Here you'll be able to discover villages with their heritage intact. Village elders must give their okay for so much as a shingle to be changed. Consequently, very few changes take place.

For a look at what might have happened without these protective laws, take a drive along Rte. 28 (along the south shore), which is up to its neon in the 20th century. Nothing has escaped modernization here. Rte. 28 is lined on both sides with drive-ins, stores, and restaurants with names like Leaning Tower of Pizza.

And so the formula for sightseeing on Cape Cod can be shaped according to your preference: If you're looking for up-to-the-minute action, follow Rte. 28; if you seek peace and a sense of history, take Rte. 6A; and if you're in a rush to get to Provincetown, take Rte. 6, which bisects the cape.

In order to see both Cape Cod *and* the neighboring islands, it makes sense to sweep the northern shore up to Provincetown (Rte. 6A), and return via the outer shore along the southern coast as far as Hyannis Port (Rte. 28). Here, pick up the ferry for the two offshore islands and later return to the cape at Woods Hole.

One further caveat: Everybody loves Cape Cod. In peak season, the whole area fairly groans under the weight of all its adoring visitors (Provincetown leaps from a population of 5,000 to 55,000 in summer). If you can time your trip for either spring or late fall, you'll be able to see much more nature. And you'll be able to find some local folks with time to sit and chat. However, if you want crowds, excitement, and big names, July and August are your time.

SANDWICH: The first town along Rte. 6A, it is rewardingly historic. The Sandwich Glass Museum (Rte. 130) has remarkable examples of the town's famous glass. The First Church of Christ (1848) features a spire that was copied from a design by England's Christopher Wren. Everything American from antique cars to a Civil War gristmill can be seen at the Heritage Barn Plantation (Rte. 6A, Grove and Pine sts.). And children will be delighted with the Yesteryears Doll Museum (River and Main sts.).

YARMOUTH PORT: Here are three restored original houses: Capt. Bangs Hallet House (18th century) on Strawberry La.; Col. John Thatcher House (1680) on Rte. 6A; and Winslow Crocker House (1780), also on 6A.

"THE DENNISES": Four towns — Port, South, East, and West Dennis — together offer a combination of old and new: historical houses to tour, and, June through Labor Day, current theater offerings at the Cape Playhouse (Rte. 6A; 385-3911 for schedule and reservations). The Dennis Pines Golf Course, in East Dennis, has an 18-hole course (617 385-8347).

BREWSTER: This town offers two interesting museums: Drummer Boy (2 miles west), a 35-acre site with Revolutionary scenes; and the Cape Cod Museum of Natural History (Main St.) with live animals and marine exhibitions. Sealand of Cape Cod (3 miles on 6A in West Brewster) has marineland shows and a penguin rookery.

EASTHAM: The gateway town to the Cape Cod National Seashore. In addition, the Historical Society maintains several restored homes for touring. It is just off Rte. 6 in an 1869 schoolhouse, with exhibits.

CAPE COD NATIONAL SEASHORE: Cape Cod is a peninsula without bedrock — it is all sand. Before white men came here in any numbers, the cape had stands of hardwood and topsoil, which protected the Atlantic shoreline from the sea's fury. When the hardwood went, the sea and the wind played havoc with the sand — shores around Truro and Wellfleet were eaten away, and the same sand was deposited along the moors surrounding Provincetown. The Cape Cod National Seashore came into being in 1961 after years of appalling disregard almost put an end to this 28,000-acre chunk of the cape. It now runs from Eastham to Provincetown and includes six towns, much private property, and four public areas. No camping is allowed except in privately owned campgrounds. There are four picnic areas. From June through Labor Day the National Park Service conducts guided tours and evening lectures. There are many self-guided trails. For more information: Superintendent, Cape Cod National Seashore, South Wellfleet, MA 02663 (617 349-3785); Province Land visitors center at Race Point Rd., Provincetown (617 487-1256); Salt Pond visitors center on Rte. 6, Eastham (617 255-3421).

WELLFLEET: Numerous beaches for swimming and a wealth of inland freshwater ponds dot the area. Fishing and sailing are also well provided for here — the town marina can accommodate 150 boats. Wellfleet Bay Wildlife Sanctuary runs a summer day camp for kids with the emphasis on natural history appreciation. The Massachusetts Audubon Society sponsors the sanctuary and maintains its many self-guided nature trails.

PROVINCETOWN: The town most familiar to first-timers on the cape, it attracts artists and celebrities and is exceedingly liberal and easy-going — in rather startling contrast to the town's early history as the first landing site of the Pilgrims.

In 1899 Charles Hawthorne established the Cape Cod School of Art in Provincetown, and its reputation as an art center was established. Several leading artists summer here (including Robert Motherwell), and the town's long Commercial Street has at least a dozen good galleries side by side with museums (Provincetown Museum adjoining the Pilgrim Monument overlooking the city, the Heritage Museum, and the city's oldest house at 27 Commercial St.). The Provincetown Playhouse on the Wharf gained national recognition for its excellence and innovation in theater. Unfortunately, a tragic fire in 1976 destroyed the theater as well as the Eugene O'Neill Theater Museum.

To return via the south shore (Rte. 28) you must backtrack for a period of time. An interesting stop, which you would have passed on your way to Provincetown, is Truro.

TRURO: A real change from Provincetown's hustle and commotion. Sparsely settled, Truro is known for the excellence of its fishing and swimming and for the Highland Light, which dates to 1795 and can be seen 20 miles out to sea. Less well known is the fact that a large part of Truro's summer population comprises New York City and Boston psychiatrists.

CHATHAM: Is one of the many towns on the cape with a working gristmill that offers for sale the corn you can see being ground into meal. This one dates to 1797 (Shattuck Pl. off Cross St.).

HYANNIS: Now synonymous with the Kennedy family, but long before the clan and its compound, Hyannis drew its share of visitors because of its marvelous swimming beaches. There's an annual Antiques Fair in July (National Guard armory) and musical theater-in-the-round is held in the Melody Tent (W Main St.; 617 775-9100 for schedule and prices). Hyannis is also a terminus for the ferry services to the islands. There are day trips for sightseeing as well as auto ferry service. You must reserve well in advance for space on the ferries by calling the Steamship Authority (617 771-4000). Hy-Line (617 771-2220) also serves the islands, and the *Island Queen* leaves from Falmouth (617 548-4800), but goes only to Martha's Vineyard.

NANTUCKET: It is not by chance that both Captain Ahab and First Mate Starbuck of the ill-fated *Pequod* were Nantucket men. Nothing could have seemed more likely to Melville's readers, and besides, one Captain George Pollard of Nantucket did lose a ship to an enraged sperm whale. Nantucket was once the whaling capital of the world, and you know it the instant the ferry gets within sight of Nantucket town. Main Street is lined with elegant 19th-century homes (many open for viewing); the Whaling Museum offers a whaling boat among other exhibits.

Some 30 miles south of Cape Cod, the island is only 49 square miles and can boast 50 miles of sand-dune-protected beaches. The Gulf Stream hovers offshore, warming the waters to an amazing 70° or more much of the summer. There are eight beaches, most with lifeguards, bathhouses, and food facilities. Sailing enthusiasts can rent all sizes of boats. Bicycle lanes coexist peacefully with roads for cars.

MARTHA'S VINEYARD: If you've ever heard that New Englanders are feisty and independent, consider some former goings-on on Martha's Vineyard. In 1977, the state legislature decided to take away the island's individual representation, incorporating it into a single district with Cape Cod. Natives of the island didn't take too kindly to this, and they formed a group to push for secession. They received offers from other US states for annexation — including Hawaii. A compromise was finally worked out so you won't have to say you've been to Martha's Vineyard, Hawaii!

Five miles by sea from Cape Cod, a sprawling 10 miles wide and 20 miles long, this island requires you to have some wheels to see it all. You can rent cars, bikes, or mopeds. Shuttle buses scurry between the main resort towns, and taxis and tour buses are available.

The main towns are Vineyard Haven, shopping center for the island; Gay Head, famous for its multicolored clay cliffs looming above the ocean; Oak Bluffs; Menemsha; and Edgartown.

Edgartown is the oldest settlement on the island, a fact well documented by the Dukes Historical Society Museum (School and Cooke sts.). Built in 1765, it has some marvelous examples of Colonial architecture, a Jacobean fireplace, and seven open fireplaces. You return to the mainland via the ferry (remember to reserve!), this time arriving at Woods Hole on Cape Cod.

MASHPEE: Route 28A leads northward and back to mainland Massachusetts. But before leaving Cape Cod, detour inland to Mashpee, which is in the heart of the cape and in the heart of cranberry country. Descendants of the Mashpee Indians still gather cranberries from the many bogs. There's also the Wampanoag Indian Museum (Rte. 130), with a diorama and exhibitions of Indian lore; the Old Indian Meeting House (1648); and the Mashpee burial grounds (Rte. 28, south of town).

BEST EN ROUTE

Old Yarmouth Inn, Yarmouth Port – The oldest place (1676) on the cape, you won't find the inn advertised anywhere. It doesn't need to — its delighted clientele does it for them. It's good for rooms and meals — 14 rooms in all, each with private bath. Food is, happily, mainly seafood caught locally, vegetables are similarly fresh. Open all year. Old King's Highway, Yarmouth Port, MA 02675 (617 362-3191).

Jared Coffin House, Nantucket Island – Numerous celebrities have stayed here, beginning in 1821 when it was built. Now historically restored, the 58-room hotel offers old-time elegance to its guests — a formal dining room complete with piano during evening meals. During December (21st through New Year's Day) a gala "Twelve Days of Christmas" celebration — that folks have been reserving for a year ahead — keeps things running in high gear on this now year-round island. See also *America's Special Havens,* DIVERSIONS. 29 Broad St., Nantucket, MA 02554 (617 228-2405).

White Mountains, New Hampshire

There's a pleasant, comfortable feeling about the White Mountains, similar to the pleasing quality of a George Gershwin tune. As you drive along roads that wind through deep, tree-lined gorges and sparkling clear mountain brooks, breathing the clean, fresh smell of pine everywhere, you get an inescapable sense that "all's right with the world."

Smack in the center of the state, some 140 miles north of Boston on I-93 (the only interstate through the area), the White Mountains offer New Hampshire countryside at its best. Our route starts at Plymouth and wanders through some of the best sightseeing and skiing land in the state.

PLYMOUTH: As you approach the White Mountain National Forest, 1,600 square miles of one of the oldest mountain ranges in the Appalachian chain, you can take a brief detour onto Rte. 25 at Plymouth, about 60 miles north of Manchester, for a quick look at the Polar Caves. As the name implies, these caves are reminders of the great glaciers that passed this way around 50,000 years ago, then retreated to the north. The Hanging Boulder, an 80-ton rock that seems to hang in midair, has been suspended that way for countless thousands of years; it isn't likely to fall on your head. You can also glimpse some of the glacial ice left behind during the great retreat. It's still sticking to the cavern floor.

WHITE MOUNTAIN NATIONAL FOREST: As you return the 8 miles to I-93, you'll pass the southern boundary of the national forest. There are 20 campgrounds here; Pinkham Notch is the headquarters of the Appalachian Mountain Club Huts System (for information and reservations, call 603 466-2727). If you're here in the fall, you'll be overwhelmed by the foliage, reds and oranges fanning out in all directions like spectacular flames, and you might wonder why they're called the White Mountains. In summer, the subtle green leaves of the white birch ripple with those of the brown sugar maple, giving the mountains an unforgettable depth and richness. Since the White Mountains are older than the Rockies, geological forces have had more time to smooth them into rounded formations. Information: White Mountain National Forest, PO Box 638, Laconia, NH 03247 (603 524-6450).

THE FLUME: The Flume is a narrow natural gorge flanked on both sides by 70-to-90-foot granite walls and set in the fir, spruce, and birch forest of Franconia Notch State Park. Intertwined along the cliffs is an intricate set of catwalks that allows you to get several unusual perspectives of the Flume Brook and its waterfall.

THE OLD MAN OF THE MOUNTAINS: As you leave the Flume, driving slowly, take in the view of Mt. Liberty. Just 3 miles north you'll see the Old Man of the Mountains, a magnificent, craggy, Lincolnesque profile carved naturally into the side of a mountain. New Hampshire's most famous landmark, it is often used as a symbol of the state. Skiers are no doubt more familiar with this part of the world as the site of the Cannon Mountain Aerial Tramway.

FRANCONIA NOTCH: Known as "the Switzerland of America," Franconia Notch is between the Kinsman and Franconia mountain ranges and is traversed by I-93. The Old Man of the Mountains is on the west side of the notch. The southern flank of the Franconia Range stretches across the horizon, sedate as those grand men of history for whom the Presidentials are named. Mt. Lincoln and Mt. Lafayette are the closest to Franconia, but as you proceed northeast on Rte. 3, you'll pass Mt. Cleveland, then the approach to Mt. Washington, the tallest peak. Jefferson, Adams, and Madison stand to the north; Monroe, Franklin, Eisenhower, Clinton, Jackson, and Webster to the south.

MT. WASHINGTON: Ascending this mountain is an adventure whether you climb, take the cog railway or chauffeured car, or drive yourself. All of these dramatic, rugged paths lead to the rocky summit at 6,288 feet. That might not sound high to you, and certainly it's not by Rocky Mountain standards, but Mt. Washington is the tallest peak in the Northeast. Unless you're an expert climber, we recommend going up in a vehicle. Mt. Washington is known as "Misery Mountain" because of its foul weather. There's the chance of snow no matter when you go, and the average temperature for the year is about 26°F. Even if you're there in mid-August, when the neighboring valleys are in the humid 80s, you'll need a heavy sweater before you get to the top. Washington. If you're climbing, be sure to check weather conditions before setting out. The mountain has taken many lives over the years; there are some very slippery, dangerous spots along the way. If you are driving, make sure to stop frequently while descending to let your brakes cool off. The road is so steep that it is possible to burn the lining from brake drums before reaching the bottom. If you don't want to risk it, take the Cog Railway. Working since 1869, it's a safe way to reach the stark, windswept mountain peak.

CRAWFORD NOTCH: Another good vantage point for gazing at the Presidentials, Crawford Notch State Park has camping, fishing, hiking, and picnicking facilities (in Bartlett on Rte. 302; 603 374-2272). Traveling southeast on Rte. 302, you'll pass Attitash Ski Area and Alpine Slide (a 4,000-foot-long ride down a mountain).

NORTH CONWAY: About 20 miles south of Crawford Notch you can ride up a mountain on a skimobile at the Mt. Cranmore Ski Area (603 356-5543). There's also a restored Victorian railway in town.

KANCAMAGUS HIGHWAY: North Conway and Conway have grown into resort towns of pinewood shopping centers and motels. If it seems overdeveloped for your taste, head west on Rte. 112, known as the Kancamagus Highway. This is one of the most glorious drives anywhere in the US, going into the deep recess between the mountains to take you closer to what you've already seen from a distance, returning you to I-93 45 miles later.

BEST EN ROUTE

Dana Place Inn, Jackson – A 16-room hotel, with swimming pool and river swimming, tennis courts, fishing, close to cross-country and downhill skiing and golf. Pinkham Notch Rd., Jackson, NH 03846 (603 383-6822).

Lovett's Inn by Lafayette Brook, Franconia – Guest house and cabins, some with fireplaces in living rooms, a swimming pool, pond, and cross-country skiing. Close to golf, tennis, and fishing. Personal service and excellent cooking. 32 rooms. Profile Rd., Franconia, NH 03580 (603 823-7761).

The Jersey Shore: Atlantic City to Cape May, New Jersey

There are good beaches all along the 127-mile intercoastal waterway of New Jersey's Atlantic Ocean shoreline, but the most famous section is the 50-mile stretch of wide, beautiful seashore and gentle surf that begins just south of Atlantic City and ends at Cape May Point. It has some of the best beaches on the eastern seaboard and an unusual geographic conformation that makes for fabulous fishing: The oceanfront land is actually a series of narrow islands that run parallel to the mainland, with a tidal bay in between. Fishermen can choose deep-sea fishing or the calmer waters of the protected bays.

This section of the Jersey shore was *the* place to summer in the late 1800s for anyone who was anyone. This popularity — exemplified most by Atlantic City, made famous by the Depression game of Monopoly — ultimately led to overexposure and a recession; since World War II, as successive waves of "beautiful people" flocked first to Florida and then to European and Caribbean beaches rather than prosaic New Jersey, the major resorts suffered severe setbacks.

In desperate attempts to lure tourists back, many of these towns began casting about for other means of excitement — amusement parks, convention facilities, special activities. This is good news and bad news for the visitor today. Good news because it makes the shore — with its quiet surf and wide beaches — a great place to take small children; bad news because amid the hurly-burly you might just overlook the very best aspect of some shore towns — the lovely Victorian and Edwardian houses hidden in the streets behind the gaudy boardwalks.

These islands and mainland communities form what is called the Jersey Cape. The islands themselves are connected by Ocean Drive — actually a series of bridges designed as a scenic, efficient beltway for traffic up and down the cape. The towns along Ocean Drive stir the memory of anyone raised on the East Coast — Atlantic City, Ventnor City, Margate City, Strathmore, Sea Island City, Avalon, Stone Harbor, Wildwood, Cape May. A stop at any one of them will prove entertaining, but the high points are certainly Atlantic City, America's newest gambling center; Wildwood; and beautiful Victorian Cape May. Information: Atlantic City Convention and Visitors Bureau, 16 Central Pier, Atlantic City, NJ 08401 (609 348-7100); Wildwood Bureau of Publicity, PO Box 609, Wildwood, NJ 08260 (609 522-1407); Cape May County Chamber of Commerce, PO Box 74, Cape May Courthouse, NJ 08280 (609 465-7181).

ATLANTIC CITY: On November 2, 1976, New Jersey legalized casino gambling, and Atlantic City slammed into high gear to become Las Vegas's East Coast competition. So far, the project has received mixed reviews. While the casinos are generating high revenues and are successfully competing with their Vegas counterparts, benefits to the community such as a bolstering of the local economy and a facelift for areas outside the Boardwalk (where the new building is concentrated) are slow in materializing. Nonetheless, Atlantic City is the only spot in the eastern two thirds of the country in which Americans can legally gamble in a casino. The first casino to open was the lavish *Resorts International* at North Carolina and Boardwalk, followed in 1979 by the *Caesar's Boardwalk Regency* at Arkansas and Boardwalk and *Bally's Park Palace Hotel and Casino*. There are now ten in all, with a couple more under way. The city's latest noncasino attraction is Ocean One, a sparkling new shopping complex built to resemble an ocean liner with open decks and a nautical motif, which juts out over the water on one of the Boardwalk's former piers. Of course, you can also enjoy the rest of the Boardwalk (all 6 miles of it) — its piers, teeming with amusement centers; the Miss America pageant; and of course the saltwater taffy.

WILDWOOD: This town strikes something of a balance between the quieter pleasures of a visit to Cape May and the ritz, swank, and swizzle of Atlantic City. Wildwood has a fine, wide beach, an appropriately lively boardwalk with six amusement piers, and a reputation for good evening entertainment, offered by a varied array of nightclubs with comedians and singers, jazz bands and Dixieland groups.

CAPE MAY: The clocks here all stopped somewhere toward the end of the 19th century — and that suits the townsfolk just fine. That particular time warp has proved to be a gold mine for tourism. The determined and dogged theme of this town is Victoriana. There are so many original and preserved Victorian wood-frame buildings still in mint condition that Cape May has been declared a national landmark. Attempts at modernization are squashed as quickly as possible.

Indeed, authenticity is lovingly protected in this town. Its 600 Victorian buildings stand busily side by side, each resplendent in its gingerbread excess, scalloped widow's walks traced along scalloped rooftops, columned verandas with latticework trims; even the gardens seem just right for a nosegay framed with a lace doily.

Visitors can enjoy this old-fashioned community in a number of ways. There's a 1¼-hour historic walking tour four days a week that leaves from the information booth at Washington and Ocean streets. A horse-drawn tourist trolley covers a similar route. There's a delightful Victorian pedestrian mall and even a Victorian bandstand where weekly concerts are presented, a free offering by the community. At Convention Hall, visitors are treated to entertainment ranging from free ballroom dancing, teen discos, and concerts to antiques shows, cartoon shows, and so on. Consult the calendar of events posted at the information office just outside the hall on Beach Drive at the boardwalk.

But for pure self-indulgence and excess you just can't beat the experience of living in one of these authentic Victorian mansions during your stay. A Victorian guest house might well feature afternoon tea served on the veranda, an antique fourposter bed in your room, or a tour of the house.

Probably the most famous of these guest houses is the *Mainstay Inn,* known locally as the Victorian Mansion. Authenticity is fiercely maintained by the present owners, a young couple who delight in sharing their wealth of Victoriana with interested visitors. This house was built in 1872 as an Italian villa and has gone through some fascinating changes. Your room might be one of the "front rooms," which means you'll luxuriate in 12-foot ceilings and a splendid view. Or you might choose one in the "new wing," which was built in 1896 to accommodate the six housemaids.

At the very tip of the cape is the Cape May Point State Park. Although no swimming is allowed here due to the insidious currents, called "Cape May rips," visitors love to search the beach for "diamonds" — bits of wave-polished quartz that shine brilliantly in the sand. There's also a nearby bird sanctuary and lighthouse.

Also at the tip of the cape is the Cape May–Lewes, Delaware, ferry. Passengers may embark here for the 70-mile ride to Delaware. Make reservations by writing to PO Box 827, N Cape May, NJ 08204 (609 886-9699).

BEST EN ROUTE

The Mainstay Inn, Cape May – Built in 1872, with original furnishings, a grand dining room, and veranda. A few blocks from the ocean. Rates include a Continental breakfast on the porch (in summer) and afternoon tea at 4 PM. Closed November through March. See also *America's Special Havens,* DIVERSIONS. 635 Columbia Ave., Cape May, NJ 08204 (609 884-8690).

Seventh Sister Guest House, Cape May – A 6-room inn built in the late 1800s. Most rooms have an ocean view, and the house has a comfortable porch facing the sea. Baths are shared. 10 Jackson St., Cape May, NJ 08204 (609 884-2280).

Windward House, Cape May – A shingled cottage in the heart of the historic district with 7 rooms and 1 small efficiency apartment. 24 Jackson St., Cape May, NJ 08204 (609 884-9609).

Hotel-Casinos, Atlantic City – *Resorts International,* N Carolina at Boardwalk (609 344-6000 or 800 GET-RICH, from most East Coast states); *Caesar's Atlantic City,* Arkansas Ave. at Pacific (800 582-7600 in New Jersey, 800 257-8555 elsewhere); *Bally's Park Place,* Park Pl. at Boardwalk (800 225-5977); *Golden Nugget,* Boston and Pacific aves. on the Boardwalk (800 257-8677); *Harrah's Marina,* 1725 Brigantine Blvd. (800 242-7724); *Sands,* S Indiana Ave. between Pacific Ave. and Boardwalk (800 257-8580); *Claridge Hotel and Hi Ho Casino,* Indiana and Boardwalk (800 582-7676 in New Jersey; 800 257-8585 elsewhere); *Trump Casino,* Mississippi Ave. and Boardwalk (800 441-0909). *Trump Castle,* Huron Ave. and Brigantine Blvd. (800 441-5551); *Tropicana,* Iowa Ave. and Boardwalk (800 257-6227 or 800 THE TROP).

Adirondack Park and Mountains, New York

For some people the ideal vacation is a complete return to nature. They seek out rugged wilderness locations and gently ease their "civilized" bodies into the comforting natural rhythms. The Adirondack Park offers almost unlimited challenges and opportunities for this sort of communion with the elements. Of the six million acres in this area, nearly half are protected by law from the "modern improvements" of man. There are mountains; more lakes than you can count, several of them very famous (Saranac Lake, Lake George, Lake Champlain, Lake Placid); many campsites tucked away in the miles of forests; and the old Indian Canoe Route.

The Adirondack Park and Mountains encompass just under 9,000 square miles, just about filling the entire northeastern section of New York State, from Lake Champlain and the Vermont border to as far south as Glens Falls. The area is popular year-round; in winter for skiing and other snow sports (Lake Placid was the site of the 1932 and the 1980 Winter Olympics); in summer for its lakes, forests, and fishing; in autumn for the spectacular foliage of its wooded mountains. It's an especially attractive vacation area because among the isolated fields, lakes, and mountains of the interlaced parklands are cities of reasonable size, which can be visited — or avoided — as you choose.

The deliberate underdevelopment of the Adirondack Park is the very foundation of its charm and appeal. However, roads are few and they don't always lend themselves to a straight route, especially if you really want to get a sense of the scope of the area. However, with some backtracking and patience you can circle the entire parkland in a few days, allowing plenty of flexibility for stopping, looking, enjoying, and relaxing.

The Adirondack Mountains are about 4 hours from New York City. Our route starts at Lake George and makes a counterclockwise loop through the area; along the way you will have ample opportunity for exploring on your own. Information: Division of Tourism, Dept. of Commerce, 1 Commerce Plaza, Albany, NY 12245 (518 474-4116 or 800-CALL-NYS in all states north of Virginia and east of Michigan); or New York State Office of Parks Recreation, Historic Preservation, Empire State Plaza, Albany, NY 12238 (518 474-0456); for camping information: call the Summer Recreation Office (518 457-2500) or write for brochures to the New York State Dept. of Conservation, 50 Wolf Rd., Albany, NY 12233.

LAKE GEORGE VILLAGE: The most populous (30,000 accommodations for tourists) and most commercial town in the area. The lake itself is a 32-mile jewel set comfortably at the base of some very impressive mountains. There are dozens of state-owned islands in the lake. Lake George Village is an active, exciting place, with some of the drawbacks of a tourist center. The natural pleasures of swimming, boating, and fishing have almost been superseded by more profitable ventures like the Great Escape (5 miles south on Rte. 9), a theme park with six fairy-tale areas.

The entire Adirondack area is a mine of early American history, especially from the French and Indian War period. Lake George is no exception. Fort William Henry (Canada St.) is a reconstructed 200-year-old fort, with interesting displays. You will be shown a 45-minute edited version of *The Last of the Mohicans* as part of the tour. An impressive number of war relics are on display.

Explore the scenic beauty of Lake George on one of the cruise vessels operated by the *Lake George Steamboat Co.* (Steel Pier and Beach Rd.). There are twilight cruises, long and short versions as well, aboard powerboats or the paddlewheel *Minne-Ha-Ha* (518 668-5777 for times). An eagle's-eye view of the area is yours for the driving. Take Rte. 9 a half mile south to Prospect Mountain State Parkway. At the end of the spectacular 5-mile climb, you transfer to the free viewmobile for the final ascent to Prospect's peak.

BLUE MOUNTAIN LAKE: Take Rte. 28 west from Lake George. In addition to the glorious scenery you'll also find the Adirondack Lake Center for the Arts (in the village), with an art gallery, concerts, films, and exhibitions. The Adirondack Museum (1 mile north on Rte. 30) has 20 buildings of treasures (mostly on the history of the area). Nearby Blue Mountain has nature trails and some overlooks at its peak.

Rte. 30 north will take you past Long Lake. Tupper Lake lies just north. The chief attraction is Big Tupper Mountain with its excellent skiing facilities, including a chair lift (which operates in summer for sightseeing), T-bar, beginners' lift, and various snack bars. There is golfing, boating, swimming, and camping all around the lake.

SARANAC LAKE: World famous as a health resort, Saranac's spas have been visited by a host of celebrities (including Robert Louis Stevenson, whose cottage is open to the public) and a lot more just plain folks. This area, too, is a winter and summer sports resort. There are boat races, art exhibitions, and concerts. The Dickert Memorial Wildlife Collection (in the Saranac Lake Free Library, 100 Main St.) has some marvelous mounted specimens of local wildlife. In winter, Mt. Pisgah Ski Center — at the end of the village — has a ski lift.

LAKE PLACID: This largest town in the Adirondacks is synonymous with the 1932 and 1980 Winter Olympics, and the sports facilities are superior here. At the Olympic Arena and Convention Hall (Main St.) there are winter and summer skating as well as ice shows, concerts, and other performances. On the famous Mt. Van Hoevenberg Bobsled Run (7 miles southeast on Rte. 73) you can skim down in an Olympic-type bobsled. During the winter there are afternoon races (December to March). It's also a good cross-country ski area.

The Center for Music, Drama, and Art (Saranac Ave. at Fawn Ridge) offers concerts, performances by the repertory company, and art exhibitions (518 523-2512 for specific information).

John Brown's Farm Historical Site (John Brown Rd. off Rte. 73) gives you a glimpse into the famous abolitionist's life — his furnishings, his home, and his gravesite.

Lake Placid, too, has a variety of lake cruises. Trips leave from Holiday Harbor (north on Rte. 86 to Mirror Lake Drive). General tourist information is available from the Lake Placid Chamber of Commerce, Main St., Lake Placid, NY 12946 (518 523-2445).

AUSABLE CHASM: A scenic wonder on Rte. 9 north not to be missed. There are any number of ways to view this incredible gorge, which slashes from 100 to 200 feet deep along its route. Footbridges cross its 20-to-50-foot width. You can take a self-guided walking tour and see the quaintly named rock formations: "pulpit rock," "elephant's head," "cathedral rock." From May to September, you can also take a guided boat ride down a natural flume through the rapids. (Just to settle any arguments, it's pronounced Oh-*say*-bl.)

FORT TICONDEROGA: This fort played a strategic part in our nation's history. Originally built in 1675 by the French, it changed hands in its active life about a dozen times, was burned, and almost destroyed. Now restored according to the original French plans, it houses a museum with many original weapons, uniforms, and other war trappings. Live fife-and-drum performances and cannon firings add realistic touches.

Although there is much to do in Adirondack towns, there is much more to do in the Adirondack countryside, and chances are you're here to camp, fish, swim, and hike. Below are a list of some of the campgrounds in the area with telephone numbers for more information and reservations. For complete information: Division of Tourism, Dept. of Commerce, 1 Commerce Plaza, Albany, NY 12245 (518 474-4116 or 800-CALL-NYS in all states north of Virginia and east of Michigan).

Lewey Lake at Indian Lake (209 sites). Climb Snowy and Blue Ridge mts., fish, swim, canoe, hike (518 648-5266).

Moffit Beach at Lake Pleasant (257 sites). Camp on Sacandaga Lake. Swim, fish, hike, canoe (518 548-7102).

Luzerne at Lake Luzerne (165 sites). Swim and hike (518 696-2031).

The Glen Island Group at Bottom Landing (398 sites). Register at Glen, boat to any of 55 islands. Sites all have fireplace, tent platform, semiprivate dock. Four different boat launching sites. Swim, hike, fish, canoe (518 644-9696).

Rogers Rock at Hague (304 sites). Supervised hikes up the 1,000-foot Rogers Rock. View over Lake George. Swim, fish, hike, canoe (518 585-6746 or 585-9728).

Putnam Pond at Chilson (56 sites). Miles of trails branch out from here to forest ponds and lakes (518 585-7280).

Cranberry Lake at Cranberry Lake (173 sites). Over 50 miles of wilderness trails, some with rustic lean-tos. 20 miles of Oswegatchie Inlet for boaters. Swim, fish, hike, canoe (315 848-2315).

Ausable Point at Peru (121 sites). Remote area, near rapids. Swim, fish, canoe (518 561-7080).

Higley Flow at Colton (143 sites). Fishing and swimming in the Raquette River (315 262-2880).

BEST EN ROUTE

The Lodge, Lake Clear – German food in rustic and woodsy surroundings. The lodge itself is pure old-Adirondack, with mounted moose heads hung on the walls. The menu is fixed and served family style — and everyone gets to know everyone else over a hearty meal. Reservations are a must for dinner and for the few available rooms. The Lodge on Lake Clear, Lake Clear, NY 12945 (518 891-1489).

Hotel Saranac, Saranac – A learning laboratory for students of hotel administration at nearby Paul Smith College. If you have a complaint, an army of folks will hear you out. 101 Main St., Saranac Lake, NY 12983 (518 891-2200).

Hudson River Valley, New York

Rip Van Winkle slept here. So did George Washington. And you can, too, in any number of charming inns and hotels as you explore the magnificent Hudson River and the valley that surrounds it. There is so much scenic beauty, so many historical reference points, and so many downright fascinating bits of folklore that you will find yourself totally caught up in the charm and mystery of this area.

Our route follows the east bank of the Hudson from New York City to Rip Van Winkle Bridge, about 20 miles south of Albany. This is the entry point to the Catskill Mountain area to the west and the Adirondacks to the north. At the bridge, our itinerary crosses from the east to the west bank, and returns toward New York City. For a comprehensive, mile-by-mile guide to this route, see *The Hudson River Tourway* by Gilbert Tauber (it's out of print; try your public library).

This is a compelling route for the sheer beauty of the Hudson, if for no other reason. In its 315-mile course from the Adirondacks to the sea, the Hudson changes style from a shimmering, 3-mile-wide expanse (called Tappan Zee by the early Dutch; *zee* is Dutch for sea) to a sinuous serpent squeezed by the towering Palisades downriver nearer New York City. To see the river reflect the setting sun is one of the enchantments of New York life.

Throughout local history men have compared the Hudson to Germany's Rhine. And men of great wealth, seeking to exploit the similarities, built palatial estates along its banks. Lacking any definable style, these pseudo-villas and châteaux have been lumped together into the tongue-in-cheek category of Hudson Valley Gothic. Many of these mansions are open to the public and are well worth a look.

British and American forces fought for this area inch by inch during the Revolutionary War. The Hudson was the key to holding the great northern territories beyond, and the towns up and down the valley held in turn patriots and king's men.

Finally, less tangible but very real, is the air of folklore and mystery — the delicious shiver of the supernatural — that cloaks the high mountains and heavily forested valleys. There's the goblin who sits atop Dunderberg whose churlish moods control the winds whipping up the river below. And, of course, there's the Headless Horseman; this is his turf.

TARRYTOWN: Just 25 miles north of New York City is Washington Irving's "Sleepy Hollow" country. Sunnyside, Irving's home for 24 years, is open to the public. You can see his books, manuscripts, household furnishings, and some statues of his characters (W Sunnyside La., off Broadway). Nearby is one of those incredible Hudson Gothic mansions, Lyndhurst (635 S Broadway), built in 1838 by Alexander Jackson Davis and the home of railroad tycoon Jay Gould from 1880 to 1893. The 67-acre estate, now run by the National Trust for Historic Preservation, offers stunning interiors and vistas as well as outdoor concerts and festivals in the warm months (914 631-0046).

GARRISON: Two mansions here must not be missed. Boscobel, built by S. M. Dyckman for his wife in 1806, remains a glorious villa housing a collection of rare and beautiful antiques. The grounds are manicured in English formal style, and the view of the Hudson is spectacular. Nearby is Dick's Hilltop Castle, intended as a near-replica of the Alhambra by its owner, dreamer Evans Dick. The poor soul lost all his money in the stock market disaster of 1911 and his dream house — after four years of work and $3 million — was never finished. What's there, however, is quite enough to behold.

POUGHKEEPSIE: Two families have immortalized their names as well as their town: the Vassars, for their prestigious college, and the brothers Smith, for their cough drops.

Be sure to visit the Glebe House (635 Main St.), built about 1767 as a rectory for the Episcopal church, and the Clinton House (Main St. at White St.), home of the governor during the brief period in 1777 when Poughkeepsie was the state capital. There are also some beautiful old houses in town.

HYDE PARK: This town is familiar to most Americans as the home of Franklin Delano Roosevelt. He spent most of his life here and, with his wife, Eleanor, is buried here in the rose gardens on the Roosevelt estate. Visitors may browse through FDR's books, collections, and other personal treasures in the estate's museum and library. The admission price here also entitles you to visit the Vanderbilt Mansion down the road. Designed by Stanford White and built in 1895, this Gothic is a study in lavish excess. New for visitors is the Eleanor Roosevelt retreat and homestead, just a short shuttle bus ride from the FDR home and library.

RHINEBECK: For a bit of history-come-alive don't miss the Old Rhinebeck Aerodrome (off Rte. 9 on Stone Church Rd.). In addition to a spiffy collection of World War I aircraft still in working order, there's a Waldo Pepper–type simulated dogfight overhead staged Sunday afternoons, May through September, and Saturday afternoons as well from early July to the end of the season. It's very real. And what with the aviators in goggles and flowing white scarves, you'll find yourself searching the cast for a glimpse of Robert Redford — or at least the Red Baron. Rhinebeck is a lovely old town, with the oldest inn in the country, the *Beekman Arms.*

KINDERHOOK: Just east of Kinderhook (Rte. 66) is the Old Chatham Shaker Village, a restoration of the 18th-century community. Visitors can go into the homes and see the marvelously simple items created by these people. There are also an herb garden, bookstore, and gift shop. From this point one either continues north into the Adirondacks or crosses the river (via the Rip Van Winkle Bridge, 20 miles back, near Hudson) and returns south along the west bank of the Hudson.

CATSKILL: The gateway to the famous mountain resort area is also the site of Mr. Van Winkle's famous nap. The Catskill Game Farm (12 miles west, off Rte. 32) delights kids with its touch-and-feed areas for tame deer and other animals. Catskill Park is a forest preserve that contains six campgrounds, hundreds of miles of marked nature trails, a ski run with chair lift, and all the glories of nature. Hunter Mountain is a popular ski area here and well known for its summertime international festivals.

WOODSTOCK: Now associated with the flower children of the 60s, the town was established in 1895 by a wealthy Englishman as a colony for intellectuals and artists. The Art Students League of New York set up a summer program here a few years later. Still healthy and active today, Woodstock continues to be synonymous with the arts. Each summer cultural events are presented to the public: Woodstock Artists Association Gallery (28 Tinker St. at Village Green) features traveling shows by local and nationally known artists; and the Woodstock Playhouse (Rte. 212 at Rte. 375, 914 679-2436).

KINGSTON: One of New York's oldest towns, it has survived every curve ball thrown by history — and there have been a number. First a Dutch trading post, then an English colony, and finally American (the state constitution was signed here in 1777), the city suffered attacks by various parties at every juncture — Indians, Dutch, British, Americans. A century ago its major industry was cement; that played out, but today it still prospers with a diverse economy, including a large IBM complex. This town has more than 15 original early American homes in the old stockade area (the stockade was built in 1658) that can be toured. Some of the houses on the tour made up a segment of the Underground Railroad for escaped slaves headed for Canada. After the tour, you can peek into the New York State Senate House and Museum (312 Fair St.).

NEW PALTZ: Today restored homes and a church from the original settlement, founded by French Huguenots in 1768, are open to the public. An equal attraction is the marvelous *Mohonk Mountain House,* a delightful inn nearby.

NEWBURGH: For more than a year (between April 1782 and August 1783), George Washington and the Continental Army made their headquarters here, and it was from here that the successful conclusion of the war was announced. The headquarters are a fascinating place to visit — the Jonathan Hasbrouck House (Liberty St.), where Washington stayed, and the New Windsor Cantonment (off Rte. 32), a reconstruction of the army's winter camp. Ironically, it's not open in the winter.

MOUNTAINVILLE: Not far away is the Storm King Mountain Art Center, a cut-stone French château housing some important pieces of sculpture, including some by David Smith, and 200 acres outdoors. The view is quite Alpine in feeling — the river narrows between towering mountains, and one is impressed with the distant vistas.

For a change in perspective, visit the Brotherhood Winery (North St. in Washington-ville, off Rte. 94). Established by monks many years ago, it remains America's oldest functioning winery. Tour the caverns where the aging casks lie in state, learn a bit about winemaking, and then sample some of the products (914 496-9101 for hours).

WEST POINT: The United States Military Academy, founded in 1802, was the training ground for some of our nation's top military leaders. There are some places you'll want to see, spots remembered from all those movies: the chapel with its stained glass windows, the kissing rock, and Trophy Point, with its crow's-eye view of the Hudson.

BEST EN ROUTE

Beekman Arms, Rhinebeck – This just might be the oldest continuously operating inn in the US. It is built over an original stone tavern (c. 1700); the main portion of the existing hotel was built in 1760. During the Revolution it was known as Bogardus Tavern to its regulars — among them Washington and Lafayette. Rhinebeck, NY 12572 (914 876-7077).

Bear Mountain Inn, Bear Mountain – Renovated a few years back at a cost of millions, this charming old inn was built to resemble a Swiss chalet. Besides the main inn, accommodations are available in the Overlook Lodge and in small rustic cabins. Open all year. Bear Mountain Inn and Conference Center, Bear Mountain, NY 10911 (914 786-2731).

Mohonk Mountain House, New Paltz – Open year-round, this world-famous resort offers a wide variety of sports, a relaxing, rustic atmosphere in the 1869 Victorian mansion, and overwhelming panoramic scenery. Rooms include three meals a day; the dining room is open to the public as well. Miles of nature trails lead guests on self-guided tours. Cross-country skiing and horseback riding are two favorite sports. New Paltz, NY 12561 (914 255-1000; 212 233-2244 in New York City).

La Crémaillère, Banksville – Owned and operated by one of New York City's finest French restaurateurs, this inn captures the best of a French country inn. The rustic walls are hung with original oils depicting various French provinces, open fire-places warm body and soul, lovely china pieces decorate the small wood bar. The food is outstanding, worthy of the multi-star ratings the restaurant has received. Closed Mondays and the month of February. Call for directions and reservations. Banksville, NY (914 234-9647).

Escoffier Restaurant of the Culinary Institute of America – Combining the best of creative cooking with a new experience in dining out, the institute offers a two-year cooking course to serious chefs. The final phase includes cooking for the public in one of two dining rooms on the premises: the *Escoffier Room,* formal and extremely serious in its approach to haute cuisine, and the *American Bounty,* for à la carte American regional cuisine. Lunches and dinners are served Tuesdays through Saturdays. (Dinners, it should be noted, are lengthy, 3-hour affairs.) Rte. 9, Hyde Park, NY 12538 (914 471-6608).

Niagara Falls and Buffalo, New York

If you're searching for an unspoiled vacation paradise far from crowds and confusion, Niagara Falls is definitely not your destination. It is, in fact, a major tourist attraction, second only to New York City in the entire eastern US. Big and bawdy, Niagara Falls generally makes things seem larger than life — its commercialism is tackier and somehow more annoying than in other areas, its industrial pollution more offensive. Despite all these excesses, Niagara Falls manages, quite literally, to rise above it all.

It is ironic that the single most devastating threat to the future of the falls comes not from the abuses of man but rather from a weakness in nature. The shale and limestone foundations of the riverbed are slowly being washed away by the sheer force of the water plunging over the falls. As this erosion continues, the falls will be forced backward until they flatten out altogether and become little more than a series of rapids in the river.

But there's still time to pack the car and leave a note for the newspaper boy to say you're leaving. (Scientists estimate that all this will take another few tens of thousands of years.) So visit the falls. And while you marvel at their massive beauty, you might even have a kind thought or two for the commercial-minded folks whose various enterprises make it so ridiculously easy for you to see the attractions.

You can also shuttle over the several bridges across the Niagara River and see the whole thing from the Canadian vantage points.

Once you've had enough of the wonders of nature and crave some intellectual stimulation, you can drive to nearby Buffalo, an upstate cultural oasis complete with major art galleries, museums, and a symphony orchestra — not to mention three professional sports teams.

NIAGARA FALLS: The falls are formed as the waters of Lake Erie race downhill to join Lake Ontario, becoming en route the Niagara River. The river gathers strength and power in the narrows, then plunges almost 200 feet to form the world-famous falls. A small island in the river splits this whitewater juggernaut at the point of its mighty dive, dividing it into two falls instead of one: the American Falls — 182 feet high and 1,076 feet wide; and the Horseshoe (Canadian) Falls — 176 feet high and 2,100 feet wide. There is a minor falls, much smaller, called Bridal Veil.

The indomitable little island responsible for this twofold masterpiece is Goat Island, named for its former residents. Its 70 acres are prime viewing locations, making it a popular attraction. In addition to scenic walks almost at the brink of the falls, the island features a heliport for sightseeing choppers and an elevator that takes visitors to the falls' base. From here the fearless may don the heavy-weather gear provided by the tour leader and walk along the path just behind the incredible wall of water — as drenching as it is deafening.

If you can dream up an offbeat angle from which you'd like to view the falls, chances are someone has already thought of it and has turned it into a prosperous business. An aerial view? The selection includes: Spanish Aerocars, cable cars that cross over the whirlpool and rapids; helicopter rides; or any of several observation towers. The two best viewing towers are on the Canadian side, on a 250-foot escarpment across from the falls. They are the 524-foot Skylon Tower (viewing height about 770 feet above the falls) and the 416-foot Panasonic Tower (viewing height about 665 feet).

At ground level there are any number of ways to view. The View-mobile offers miniature trams that run a 30-minute course between Prospect Point and Goat Island, allowing passengers to get on and off at any of several stops along the route. Of the various boat trips, the *Maid of the Mist* is the most famous. (Actually, there are three sightseeing boats named *Maid of the Mist,* so you won't have too long to wait.) For the very daring, giant rafts depart from below the falls and make a whitewater tour of the downriver rapids.

And don't forget night viewing. The Horseshoe Falls is lighted by four billion candlepower in rainbow colors every night. The energy for this Technicolor extravaganza is provided by the falls itself.

Residents of the American side will grudgingly but honestly admit that the Canadian side is more pleasant (meaning less commercial). Several bridges span the river, and crossovers are made as hassle-free as both countries' Customs can manage. The Canadian side offers a wide range of falls-oriented attractions in addition to the towers already mentioned. The Niagara Power Project (4 miles north of town, Rte. 104) uses displays and demonstrations to help the layperson understand how all this raw natural power is harnessed and put to work for us. Another learning experience is at the Geological Museum (Prospect Park), where audiovisual presentations illustrate the various rock formations in the area, specifically how they affect the future of the falls. The museum also has a lovely rock garden and a nature trail.

Many festivals and special events are scheduled during the peak summer months. At the huge Artpark (7 miles north of town; Robert Moses Parkway at Lewiston) there are 200 acres where dance performances, concerts, and other artistic presentations are held (716 745-3377 for schedules; in summer, 716 754-9061).

The Tuscarora Indian Reservation is nearby (5 miles northeast of town) and invites the public to two annual events each summer: Maid of the Mist Festival, with authentic dances, parades, and folklore; and the Picnic, which is a sharing of Indian foods and a celebration of the lifestyles of this offshoot tribe of the mighty Iroquois nation. Information: the Niagara Falls Convention and Visitors Bureau, 300 4th St., PO Box 786, Niagara Falls, NY 14303 (716 278-8112 for recorded information, or 716 278-8010).

BUFFALO: The second largest city in New York (pop. 463,000) has all the cultural, industrial, and other urban trappings you would expect in a large city. What's surprising is the breadth of its fine arts centers and its physical beauty. Virtually surrounded by parks, Buffalo is most proud of Delaware Park, designed by the famed landscape architect Frederick Law Olmsted (best known for New York City's Central Park). Delaware boasts not only spectacular grounds and landscaping but also a golf course, a zoo (with some buffalo, of course), and two museums: the Albright-Knox Art Gallery (1285 Elmwood Ave.), with an impressive collection of contemporary American and European works as well as 18th-century English and 19th-century French and American artists; and the Buffalo and Erie County Historical Society (25 Nottingham Court at Elmwood Ave.), which plunges you into the rich history of the area.

There's boating and fishing on nearby waters, including Lake Erie, and skiing within an hour of the city. For sports fans, Buffalo has three professional teams: the *Bills* (football), who play in Rich Stadium (Abbott Rd. and US 20); the *Bisons* (baseball) and the *Sabres* (hockey), who play in Memorial Auditorium (Main and S Park sts.).

Famous in its own right, the Buffalo Philharmonic Orchestra now boasts guest appearances by its former conductor, the illustrious Michael Tilson Thomas. Home base is the Kleinhans Music Hall, known for its superior acoustics (26 Richmond Ave.; 716 885-4632 for schedules).

BEST EN ROUTE

Red Jacket Inn, Niagara Falls, NY – Some rooms have private patios overlooking the Niagara River (which at this point is actually an island strait). A pool and weekend entertainment. 7001 Buffalo Ave., Niagara Falls, NY 14304 (716 283-7612).

Ameri-Cana, Niagara Falls, Ontario, Canada – About 4 miles outside the hustle and bustle of downtown, amid spacious grounds with a play area, this motor inn has rooms as well as several efficiencies and kitchen units. It makes a great base if you've got a small mob with you. 8444 Lundy's La., Niagara Falls, Ont. L2H 1H4 (416 356-8444). Moderate.

Old Red Mill, Clarence, NY – Some 11 miles northeast of Buffalo, this restaurant has several interesting dining areas: a lovely old house with fireplaces and a few converted railroad cars. Mailing address: 8326 Main St., Williamsville, NY 14221 (716 633-7878).

Old Orchard Inn, East Aurora, NY – Converted into a fine restaurant, this old home serves family style in a warm, rural atmosphere. Blakely Rd., East Aurora, NY 14052 (716 652-4664).

Pennsylvania Dutch Country, Pennsylvania

The Pennsylvania Dutch aren't Dutch at all. They came here in the 18th century from Germany seeking the freedom to worship as they wished, and in William Penn's country they found it. They also found natives who couldn't pronounce the word *Deutsch* ("German" in the German language) — so Dutch it has been ever since. The center of this large area — which encompasses the counties of Lancaster, York, Dauphin, Lebanon, Berks, and Lehigh — is Lancaster, the middling-size city in southern Pennsylvania almost halfway between Philadelphia and Harrisburg.

The freedom these devout people sought was the right to observe and practice Jesus's teachings as they interpreted them — their interpretation being highly literal. With typical brevity, they summed up their beliefs: "God said it/ Jesus did it/ I believe it/ And that settles it!"

In reality, what we mean by "Pennsylvania Dutch" actually incorporates three bodies of faith: the Amish, most rigid in their interpretation of the Bible, shunning all things modern and living physically austere lives based on the style of their forefathers; the Mennonites, more accepting of the outside world but still what is called in the area "plain"; and the Moravians, also called the "fancy Dutch," mainly German Lutherans and Reformed Church members whose farms are set apart by the "hex signs" that adorn their barns.

Some Amish will not speak to strangers; their homes may not be toured;

they may not be photographed. Despite their refusal to use any modern technology (they travel by horse and buggy), they are superior farmers. Each year droves of tourists sample their distinctive and now famous foods — shoofly pie, scrapple, and chicken-corn soup.

Luckily, all is not buttoned up in Pennsylvania Dutch country. There are many Mennonites whose source of income is the tourist trade, and it is possible to rent rooms in a Mennonite farmhouse rather than stay in a hotel. You can hire a Mennonite guide for a personal tour of the countryside, thereby gaining an edge on commercial tour groups. These unusual and interesting additions to your visit can be arranged at the Mennonite Information Center (2209 Millstream Rd., Lancaster, PA 17602; 717 299-0954). Because the area is so large, to get a true feeling for the plain and fancy peoples you should have a plan — an organized idea of what you want to see, buy, or eat. Information: Pennsylvania Dutch Visitors Bureau, 1799 Hempstead Rd., Lancaster, PA 17601 (717 299-8901).

LANCASTER: The largest concentration of authentic Pennsylvania Dutch sights are clustered here and just outside town along Rtes. 30 and 340. Farmers markets are one of the biggest draws — with good reason. Here the prize of the crops are offered for sale — along with flowers, plants, homemade baked goods, canned relishes, and old-country-style sausage and bologna. There are six such markets, but the most popular is the Central Market (Penn Sq.), open from 6 AM to 2 PM on Tuesdays and Fridays. Almost as lavish in its abundance is the Southern Market (106 S Queen St.), open Saturdays from 6 AM to 2 PM.

For a better understanding of Amish life, you can visit several simulated Amish communities. The Amish Homestead (1½ miles east on Rte. 462) shows the farming techniques practiced by the first Amish settlers and has a tour of an 18th-century house; the Amish Farm and House (3 miles east on Rte. 30) offers a tour and a lecture, "The Plain People"; and the Amish Village (7 miles east, just off Rte. 30 on Rte. 896 south) has a tour through a farmhouse, blacksmith shop, one-room school, and smokehouse. There are several ways to get an overall view of Lancaster. Many commercial sightseeing tours offer planned itineraries. Or you can take a self-guiding auto tape tour. The tape and player can be rented for about $9 from many commercial establishments. (Ask at the Information Center for one nearby.)

BIRD-IN-HAND: Here you can learn about the traditional folk-art hex signs. At the Hex Barn (off Rte. 340) you can watch them being made and then buy some of the finished products. At the Folk Craft Center (west on Rte. 340, north on Mt. Sidney Rd.) there's a charming display of antique toys, dower chests, and other folk furnishings. And on many roads in this area, you'll cross ancient covered bridges, many in their original state. Outside Bird-in-Hand is the excellent *Plain 'n' Fancy Farm* restaurant (on Rte. 340) with a representative menu of Pennsylvania Dutch favorites. Almost anywhere you stop to eat in Pennsylvania Dutch country is an experience in overabundance as well as plain good cooking, in a culture that traditionally equates well stuffed with good health. Be prepared to be as dazzled by the sheer size of the spread as by the flavor of the food.

HERSHEY: Milton Hershey was a Mennonite whose lifestyle appears to have been pretty worldly — and if not his lifestyle, at least his sweet tooth, which has also affected just about every American since the Hershey Chocolate Factory was built in 1903. The townsfolk and descendants of Milton Hershey don't appear to be overly modest either. Much of this town bears his name, from the Hershey Gardens to Hersheypark (a theme park with rides and amusements), to Hershey Stadium (sporting events), to just about everything else. One thing you'll want to see is the tour of Chocolate World, where you'll watch a simulated step-by-step version of how chocolate is made, from cacao bean to Hershey Kiss.

KUTZTOWN: Famous for its Pennsylvania Dutch Folk Festival held every year in early July, the town welcomes the serious shoppers who throng here to buy the many handicrafts, sample the culture and food, and enjoy historic exhibitions of the plain and the fancy Dutch. Be sure to visit the Crystal Cave, a natural phenomenon discovered in 1871 and now improved with indirect lighting and safe walkways. You'll see crystal formations, natural bridges, and caverns.

While the annual events and farmers markets are warm-weather major attractions, remember that the crowds they draw create a distraction and a disadvantage. So you might want to time your visit during the off-season (spring, fall, or winter), when the tourist traffic is lighter and you stand a better chance of fading into the background and gaining truer insights.

Regardless of season, your stay will be much more enjoyable if you do your homework in advance. Brochures and detailed maps are easily obtained from the tourist bureaus, and they are absolutely essential. There are 220 noteworthy sights to see and visit in Lancaster County alone!

BEST EN ROUTE

Visiting a Mennonite Farm – If you wish to do this, you must call or write ahead to the Mennonite Information Center or the Pennsylvania Visitors Bureau (address above). They will send you an up-to-date listing of the participating farms. Some serve breakfast; others do not. A double room (no private bath) costs about $16 and up. The Mennonites are afraid of publicity and are fearful to say in print that they will serve meals because of the avalanche of tourists in the area. Individual tourists are often lucky enough to form their own personal relationships with their Mennonite hosts. Information: Mennonite Information Center, 2209 Millstream Rd., Lancaster, PA 17602 (717 299-0954).

Americana Host Farm Resort, Lancaster – A large resort for a total family vacation. Guests choose from a barrage of activities — sports, amusements, even cabaret shows — something for everyone. 2300 Lincoln Hwy. E, Lancaster, PA 17602 (717 299-5500).

General Sutter Inn, Lititz – The inn has been around since 1764 and accommodations are comfortable, clean, unfancy; the food is marvelous. 14 E Main St., Lititz, PA 17543 (717 626-2115).

Groff's Farm, Mt. Joy – In a 1750s home, the food is all made from the freshest ingredients. The wine is made here and housed in the cellar. There are two seatings, 5 PM and 7:30 PM, and if it happens to be your birthday, Betty Groff will grab her huge trumpet and march through the house's many dining rooms serenading your good health. If her music doesn't turn you on but her cooking does, you can take home a copy of one of her cookbooks. Reservations are a must. Pinkerton Rd., RD 3 Box 912, Mt. Joy, PA 17552 (717 653-2048)

Newport and Block Island, Rhode Island

Newport, America's first resort town, is so crammed with history that you can take a leisurely stroll past a row of 19th-century millionaire's mansions, stop by a tavern that has been in business since 1673, and visit the Old Colony

House, where George Washington conferred with French strategists during the Revolutionary War. Like old sedimentary rock, the town is composed of different time layers. There is Colonial Newport — a refuge from religious intolerance; 18th-century Newport — a bustling and prosperous seaport; and late-19th-century Newport — the summer playground of the super-rich. And thanks to the work of the Preservation Society of Newport County and the Newport Restoration Foundation, they all coexist in 20th-century Newport, an architectural museum of glittering mansions, impressive 17th- and 18th-century homes, and some of the oldest houses of worship in America. Add a pleasant shoreline and snug harbor in Narragansett Bay and you have a place where history and recreation are in fine balance.

Founded in 1639 by victims of the Massachusetts elders' religious intolerance, Newport attracted settlers of all religious convictions, including Quakers and Jews. In the 17th and 18th centuries, the town prospered as a seaport and merchants built fine homes with the profits they made from transporting rum to the West Indies and slaves from Africa. It was during this period, in the 1720s, that wealthy planters and merchants from the Carolinas and West Indies began to spend their summers here, making Newport America's first resort. The British occupation during the Revolution put an end to Newport's first golden age; the second did not begin until after the Civil War, when people like the Astors, the Belmonts, and the Vanderbilts began to build their summer "cottages" — modeled after the grand palaces and châteaux of Europe.

A center for yachting and all kinds of sea sports, Newport is on the tip of the large island for which the state is named, in Rhode Island Sound. It has several excellent beaches, but even better ones are on Block Island, about 12 miles south of the mainland and accessible by ferry from Newport (as are Providence, New London, Connecticut, and Montauk Point, New York). Newport and Block Island are a morning's drive from Boston and New York.

NEWPORT: To get oriented at once, stop at the Chamber of Commerce (10 America's Cup Ave.) for a free visitors guide, maps, and information on current happenings. There are frequent musical programs, especially in summer. Newport's bookstores carry many guidebooks to the town; an excellent one is *Newport: A Tour Guide* by Anne Randall, which offers well-planned walking routes. Newport is so compact that you can walk or bicycle just about everywhere, but if you like your sightseeing sitting down, *Viking Tours* (401 847-6921) offers a two-hour city bus tour and a one-hour harbor/bay boat ride as well as walking tours.

If you have come to Newport, you have come at least in part to see its mansions. The Preservation Society of Newport (118 Mill St.) offers a very good tour of some of Newport's most stunning "summer cottages." Hunter House (54 Washington St.), built in 1748, is the only Colonial mansion on the tour. This stately home once served as the headquarters of the commander of French forces in the American Revolution. The Breakers (Ochre Point Ave.), a 70-room mansion overlooking the Atlantic, is the most splendid of Newport's great houses. Built in 1895 for Cornelius Vanderbilt, the building resembles a northern Italian Renaissance palace. In the course of a stroll down Bellevue Avenue, you will pass the finest examples of Newport's "cottages" from the Gilded Age. The Elms, built in 1901 for a Philadelphia coal magnate, was modeled after the

Château d'Asnières near Paris. After touring the house, which is completely furnished with museum pieces, you can walk around the grounds and see the formal French gardens and collection of rare trees and shrubs from all over the world. Marble of all kinds and colors was used to build Marble House, completed in 1892 for William K. Vanderbilt. This palatial home contains all of its original furnishings. Château-sur-Mer, built in 1852, is one of the finest examples of ornate Victorian architecture in America. Rosecliff, where scenes from Paramount's *Great Gatsby* were filmed, was designed by Stanford White after the Grand Trianon at Versailles and built in 1902. Also on Bellevue Avenue are the International Tennis Hall of Fame and Tennis Museum, an 1881 casino where the first tennis matches were played, and Belcourt Castle, with the largest stained glass collection in the world.

Another way to see Newport's mansions is to take the Cliff Walk, a 3-mile trail between the mansions and the sea.

Away from mansion row, you step back in time to the Federal and Colonial eras. At the Old Colony House (Washington Sq.), Washington conferred with Rochambeau. The Wanton-Lyman-Hazard House (17 Broadway), built in 1675, is the oldest residence in Newport. The Newport Historical Society (82 Touro St.) houses a fine collection of old Newport silver, porcelain, furniture, toys, and dolls as well as a marine museum. Nearby is the Touro Synagogue (85 Touro St.), considered an architectural gem as well as a symbol of religious liberty. Built in 1763, the synagogue is the oldest in the US. (Open daily except on Saturdays and religious holidays.)

At the corner of Church and Spring streets, Trinity Church, built in 1726, is the most perfectly preserved Colonial wooden structure in the country. The church, modeled after the London churches of Christopher Wren, contains many artifacts of early American life. A few blocks away is the Redwood Library, built in 1748 and a National Historic Site. Legend has it that the Old Stone Mill next to the library was built by Norsemen, but excavation dates this building at about 1673.

At the Samuel Whitehorne House (416 Thames St.), you can see some of the exquisitely crafted furniture, silver, and pewter that once graced the homes of wealthy Newport merchants.

If you crave a few of Newport's treasures for yourself, you can shop for fine reproductions of Colonial furniture, silver, and brassware at the Brick Market (Thames St.). Antiques shops line Franklin and Spring streets, and the boutiques on cobblestoned Bowen's Wharf at the waterfront (off Thames St.) carry everything from sweaters to scrimshaw. (Be sure to try some of the seafood restaurants, too.)

BLOCK ISLAND: An antidote to too much shopping and sightseeing, this pear-shaped bit of rolling meadowland is 12 miles at sea in Block Island Sound and just an hour's ferry ride from Newport. There are a few historical things to see on Block Island: Settler's Rock, where the first settlers landed in 1661; the Palatine Graves, where an ill-fated ship met a watery grave (commemorated in a poem by Whittier); the Block Island Historical Society, with exhibitions on the island's history. (The island has a bad reputation with sailors. The site of over 200 shipwrecks, it was for a good part of the 18th century a haven for pirates, smugglers, and sea thieves.) But mostly this is a place to loll on the beach, take long walks by the sea, or do some serious fishing. The waters off Block Island support tuna, bluefish, cod, and flounder, and there are over 300 inland ponds. Block Island is an excellent vantage point for bird-watching: It is filled in fall and spring with migrations of birds on the Atlantic flyway. At the southeastern end of the island, Mohegan Bluffs, 200 feet above sea level, offer long ocean vistas. You can leave your car on the mainland and rent a bike to get around; the whole island covers only 11 square miles. It has a fine harbor, and sailors up and down the coast put up here for a day, biking around the beaches for a day, picnicking, and shopping.

BEST EN ROUTE

Inn at Castle Hill, Newport – Formerly the home of Alexander Agassiz, the son of the famous 19th-century naturalist. Rooms have excellent views of Narragansett Bay. The inn itself has been declared a historical monument. The restaurant here is quite good; there's a varied menu, but the specialty is, of course, seafood. See also *America's Special Havens,* DIVERSIONS. Ocean Dr., Newport, RI 02840 (401 849-3800).

The 1661 Inn and Hotel Manisses, Block Island – The 1661 is a Block Island tradition. While only breakfast is served at the inn, the owners have restored their *Manisses* restaurant to its 1870s appearance and serve breakfast, lunch, and dinner here through October; breakfast and dinner only through December. The inn is open year-round. See also *America's Special Havens,* DIVERSIONS. PO Box I, Block Island, RI 02807 (401 466-2421).

Vermont: A Short Tour

"Winter or summer," one Vermonter says, "being here is the name of the game." It's true. You can't go wrong in Vermont, no matter when you go. From the beautiful southern villages that inspired Norman Rockwell to the elaborate ski resorts flanking the Green Mountains, it's all stunning. There are several routes to the Green Mountain State. From Boston, take I-93 to I-89 directly to Burlington, Vermont's largest city, on Lake Champlain. With Burlington as your base, you can explore the northern part of the state, wander along the Canadian border, then journey through the southern section on your way back to Boston.

BURLINGTON: This town dates back to the Revolution, and Revolutionary War hero Ethan Allen is buried here in Greenmount Cemetery. Burlington's location on Lake Champlain makes it a major navigational center for ship traffic between the US and Canada. It was the site of a major naval battle during the War of 1812. From Battery Park, you can get a marvelous view of the tranquil lake and spruce-lined shores. It's hard to believe that any place this peaceful could have been a battlefield. Lake Champlain and Vermont's inland lakes provide a variety of catch, plentiful and safe for consumption. Ferries cross Lake Champlain every hour from the end of May through mid-October to reach Port Kent, New York. The crossing takes 2½ hours round-trip (contact *Lake Champlain Transportation Co.,* King St. Dock; 802 864-9804). There is a swimming area at North Beach. Apart from the lake itself, the highlight of Battery Park is Beansie the hot dog man. Beansie sells hot dogs, chili, and french fries from his van during the warmer months. In winter, he takes his van and his hot dogs to Florida. In town, the University of Vermont (802 656-3480), Trinity College (802 658-0337), and St. Michael's College (802 655-2000) offer films, concerts, plays, and sports activities throughout the academic year.

SOUTH HERO: Just north of Burlington on one of Lake Champlain's islands. Allenholm Farms sell fresh apple cider and hot apple and pumpkin pies in late September–early October, when Vermont's foliage is at its height. The apples come from the Allenholm orchards. Pick up some milk at a country store and feast while gazing at the lake. To get to South Hero, take Rte. 7 to Rte. 2 northeast. You'll pass through Sand Bar Wildlife Area and State Park, another good spot for picnicking.

STOWE: If you ski, you've undoubtedly heard of Stowe. Even if you don't, it's worth a trip. Take Rte. 7 north to Rte. 104A east. (When you pass Cambridge, keep your eye out for a genuine Vermont covered bridge. No longer in use, it's now standing off to the side of the highway.) Head south on Rte. 108 at Cambridge Junction–Jeffersonville, the prettiest part of the state, according to many residents. A few miles south of the turnoff, you'll pass through Smugglers Notch, an important hideout for contraband goods passing between the US and Canada during the War of 1812. The rugged, hairpin road through the notch is impassable during winter, but you can cross-country ski (a detour to Stowe when Smugglers Notch is closed would be I-89 east to Rte. 100). There are downhill ski areas at Smugglers Notch, Mt. Mansfield — the tallest peak in the state — and nearby Underhill and Bolton Valley. Mt. Mansfield explodes into view as you round a hill. When the sun is shining behind its snow-covered peak in winter, the mountain is, in the words of one resident, "most amazing." (High praise from a Vermonter.) Marking the end of the Green Mountains, Mt. Mansfield's 4,393 feet are laced with trails and caves. In August, you can pick blueberries as you hike. Stowe, one of the most famous ski areas in New England, is just down the road on Rte. 108.

HUNTINGTON GORGE: From Stowe, continue south to Rte. 89 west, toward Burlington, taking the Richmond exit. Follow Rte. 2 toward Jonesville, take a right on the steel bridge crossing the Winooski River (Winooski is an Indian word for onion), and follow the road to Huntington Gorge, a secluded picnic and swimming spot. Here, the Huntington River narrows to a waterfall. But be careful — there are no lifeguards.

JAY PEAK: Alternately, from Stowe, you can head north on Rte. 100 all the way to Canada. Just before you reach the border, take the turnoff for Rte. 101 north to the Jay Peak ski area. To return to Burlington, head west on Rte. 105 to St. Albans, formerly an important railroad stop along the route to Canada. Here you can pick up I-89 south to Burlington.

SHELBURNE: Just south of Burlington, this is the home of the Shelburne Museum, with restored Americana from the 1880s (802 985-3344). You can see what an old Vermont village used to look like. There are farm buildings, a grocery store, a pharmacy, feed shops, a dentist's office, and even the steamboat *Ticonderoga,* which used to ply its way across Lake Champlain. If you're fortunate enough to be here at sunset, go to Shelburne Point, the tip of a little finger of land pointing northwest on the shores of Lake Champlain. The sunsets are no less than magnificent from this vantage point, and there's a beach and a restaurant at the marina.

LINCOLN GAP: Wandering south along Rte. 7, through Vergennes, you'll encounter a number of good restaurants and inns. South of Vergennes, you can detour east on Rte. 17, through Bristol, to Lincoln Gap, a winding passageway.

MIDDLEBURY: On the western boundary of the Green Mountain National Forest, here is the site of Middlebury College and the Bread Loaf Writers' School, where Robert Frost taught. There's a Robert Frost Mountain, a Robert Frost Wayside Recreation Area, and Middlebury College Snow Bowl, a family ski area popular with residents but not yet familiar to out-of-staters. There's a good climbing trail at neighboring Ripton. Continue southeast on Rte. 125, which runs into Rte. 100 south, to get to the Killington and Pico Peak ski areas.

PLYMOUTH: The birthplace of President Calvin Coolidge, his former home is now a museum. His son, John Coolidge, runs Plymouth Cheese, a small factory where everything is made by hand. Coolidge and his team of hardy Vermonters keep the place open even when the world is covered with snow. The cheddar is delicious. (Speaking of Vermont specialties, if you're in the state in late winter, take a special trip to St. Johnsbury, home of the Maple Grove Maple Factory, the world's largest maple candy factory. For Vermonters, maple sugaring time is a celebration of spring. To get to St. Johnsbury, take Rte. 2 east from Burlington.)

ROUTE 100A: This scenic road takes you past Calvin Coolidge State Forest to Plymouth Union and Round Top ski area, which is usually not overrun with tourists.

At Ludlow, the Okemo Mountain ski area has good conditions. From Ludlow, take Rte. 100 south to its end at South Londonderry, site of Ball Mountain Dam Recreation Area, and pick up Rte. 30 southeast to Brattleboro.

You've probably noticed by now that Vermont has no billboards on its highways and very few bottles littering the roadsides. Vermonters are very proud of their state and have passed a number of strict conservation laws designed to protect the countryside from abuse. Visitors are welcome, but must share this respect for the land.

BRATTLEBORO and STRATTON: In the winter, Stratton is a very popular ski resort and Brattleboro the biggest town near another major ski area, Mt. Snow. If you're here during the summer months, you can check on the area's special summer events, such as Brattleboro's Annual Arts and Crafts Show or Stratton's lovely Annual Art Festival. In the fall, the foliage displays are quite spectacular; pack a picnic lunch and set off through the trees. For information on scenic autumn foliage tours, skiing, and more: Vermont Travel Division, 134 State St., Montpelier, VT 05602 (802 828-3236).

BEST EN ROUTE

Cortina Inn, Killington – This 61-room resort is best known for its intensive tennis school held on 8 clay and Plexipave courts, but there are also hunting, fishing, golf, horseback riding, and skiing nearby. Owners Bob and Breda Harnish have also opened a spa on the premises, with an indoor pool, sauna, and whirlpool and classes in weight training, martial arts, calisthenics, and sportsmedicine. Rte. 4, Killington, VT 05751 (802 773-3331).

North Hero House, Champlain Islands – A 23-room inn with tennis and water sports facilities, with an ideal lakefront location. Bicycles provided. Champlain Islands, North Hero, VT 05474 (802 372-8237).

Middlebury Inn, Middlebury – Close to the college and the Shelburne Museum, this 75-room inn is near golf, tennis, bicycling, skiing, and swimming. The dining room is open to the public. Court Sq., Rte. 7, Middlebury, VT 05753 (802 388-4961).

Waybury Inn, East Middlebury – Built in 1810 as a stagecoach stop, it has 12 rooms. This is a popular spot for hearty meals, even if you don't plan to spend the night. Rte. 125, East Middlebury, VT 05740 (802 388-4015).

Okemo Inn, Ludlow – Built in 1810, this has a homey feel, with a grand New England fireplace and 12 rooms, 10 with private bath. Rte. 103, RFD 1, Box 133, Ludlow, VT 05149 (802 228-8834).

Walloomsac Inn, Bennington – A fine old-timer dating from 1764. Large rooms, some with four-poster beds, old-fashioned bathtubs on legs, and a sprawling porch. Open mid-May through October. 67 Monument Ave., Old Bennington, VT 05201 (802 442-4865).

The Creamery, Danville – It's a good choice for well-prepared steaks and fresh fish and seafood as well as homemade breads and pies (the maple cream in particular has received raves). Closed Mondays during winter. Hill St., Danville (802 684-3616).

Shenandoah National Park, Virginia

For 80 miles along the spine of the Blue Ridge Mountains in northwestern Virginia, overlooking the beautiful valley of the Shenandoah River, lies Shenandoah National Park. More than 95% of the park's 190,000 acres are

wooded — stands of deciduous hardwood (oak, hickory, maple) that explode
into color during the first short, cold days of autumn. Through the park runs
the 105-mile Skyline Drive as well as a 95-mile section of the Appalachian
Trail, the entire length of which winds from Georgia to Maine.

Bounded by the Blue Ridge Mountains on the east and the Alleghenies to
the west, the Shenandoah Valley is the heart of the mighty Appalachian
Mountain chain, an area loved and revered by Indians and white men for
centuries (Shenandoah is Indian for "daughter of the stars"). George Washington surveyed land here and was so awed by its special splendor that he
became a large landowner. Eventually he required all of his tenants to plant
at least four acres of apple trees — a legacy Americans can still enjoy while
gazing from the park's overlooks and trails to the glorious apple orchards that
blanket the valleys below. The park was established in 1935 to make inviolate
a goodly portion of the Shenandoah area. It extends from the town of Front
Royal in the north to just east of Waynesboro in the south, and is only a
couple of hours' drive from the Washington, DC, area. Waynesboro is connected by I-64 to Richmond and the "historic triangle" towns of Williams-
burg-Yorktown-Jamestown.

FRONT ROYAL: Take in some of the attractions at the northern edge of the park
before entering. Most interesting is the Thunderbird Museum and Archaeological Park
(6 miles south of town on Rte. 340). The Blue Ridge Mountains here form the most
southeasterly wave of the Appalachians, formed of lava a billion years old. The area
has nature walks, picnic facilities, and craft shops. Warren Rifles Confederate Museum
(Chester St., Front Royal) has many relics of the Civil War, including furniture, rare
photographs, weapons, and other typical war memorabilia.

If you're visiting in the fall, plan to attend the annual Festival of Leaves held in Front
Royal the second weekend in October (when the foliage is at its peak). The festival,
one of the largest in all Virginia, offers a wide variety of attractions, including craftsmen
and an art show with over 50 artists exhibiting. Information: Chamber of Commerce,
PO Box 568, Front Royal, VA 22630 (703 635-3185).

And if you find yourself seduced by the beauty of the Shenandoah River and want
to get to know it better before entering the park, a short drive north into West Virginia's
eastern panhandle will bring you to Harpers Ferry, where you can join a Shenandoah
River whitewater rapids expedition. Each trip takes about 5 hours, including a Southern hospitality-style picnic, and is organized by *Blue Ridge Outfitters* (304 725-3444
in Harpers Ferry) between late March and November.

SHENANDOAH NATIONAL PARK: Every autumn the park produces just about the
most spectacular show of fall foliage to appear anywhere in the country. The Skyline
Drive charges straight along the crest of the Blue Ridge for the entire length of the park,
surrounded by successive waves of Appalachian hills — the Blue Ridge nearest, Alleghenies to the west — rising and falling into the distance. It is an unparalleled
leaf-peeping experience, marred only by the inconvenience of having to share it with
so many other people. Park vistas are as beautiful in the spring and summer as they
are in autumn. Flowers and blossoming trees carpet the valleys in infinite varieties of
color and depth. If you want to see the foliage, by all means brave the park in October;
if you want to see the park, however, avoid the autumn crowds.

The park has two visitors centers: Dickey Ridge, just within the northern entrance
at Front Royal, and Byrd Visitor Center at Big Meadows, where rangers have deliber-
ately checked the growth of the forest to allow a huge, green meadow to flourish in

the sunshine. There, myriad varieties of park plants — orchids, violets, wildflowers — grow in profusion. A visit to the park should include a stop at one of the centers — preferably first — to pick up literature and check out daily activities. Rangers lead nature walks through different parts of the park, advise on trails, and provide information on camping. Shenandoah has two lodges, five campgrounds, and a policy allowing off-trail camping. However, campers must have permits, available from rangers.

There are two distinct ways of seeing the park. Skyline Drive has numerous stops and overlooks, many with short trails leading from them, which allow visitors to drive the park's length, stopping where they wish. Certainly you can enjoy the many beautiful vistas along the route doing this, and with some luck even see some of the park's wildlife — deer or perhaps a bear. However, the only way to get more than a passing acquaintanceship with Shenandoah is simply to plunge into it, and with more than 500 miles of hiking trails and paths — some quite arduous, others little more than strolls — as well as the Appalachian Trail, Shenandoah is a park made for hiking.

Available at the visitors centers is a free newspaper called *Shenandoah Overlook*, with daily activities and a list of services and facilities and points of interest. The trail up Hawksbill Mountain is rigorous (3 miles long) but very rewarding: Along its route are numerous stopping points that offer spectacular views of the valley.

A walk around Stony Man Mountain reveals something about the underpinnings of the entire mountain chain in this area. Formed of ancient lava galvanized by eons of slow heat, along Stony Man (and elsewhere in the park) high cliffs of lava break into great columns of stone, called columnar jointings, which developed as the lava that made them cooled and separated. Here and wherever stone is exposed, you will see strange, circular bubbles of color in the rock. These were caused by gas that percolated through the lava as it cooled, nearly a billion years ago.

Though 95% forest, the park has very little virgin woodland left. When it was established in 1935 and the last of the residents were moved nearby, almost nothing was left of the original Blue Ridge forests; generations of farmers had practiced the time-honored method of quick-burning to clear forests and prepare fields for planting. Today's woodlands represent a masterwork of reforestation. A real tragedy was the loss of the area's native chestnut trees. Once the most common tree in the mountains, they were certainly the most useful. Their wood was excellent for furniture, their foliage provided tannic acid required for tanning, and their nuts were a cash crop. But 70 or 80 years ago a fungus deadly to the trees entered the US from the Far East and devastated the native forests. Today scientists are trying to develop resistant breeds, but nothing has appeared to replace the thousands of acres of chestnuts.

At Limberlost, in Whiteoak Canyon, you can see some of the very few virgin trees left in the park. There is a stand of original hemlock trees and some 500-year-old white oaks. Information: Superintendent, Shenandoah National Park, Box 292, Rte. 4, Luray, VA 22835 (703 999-2266).

BEST EN ROUTE

Shenandoah has five major campgrounds. It also has a unique off-trail "camp where you like" system, but, as noted above, all campers must have permits; they specify how many people are allowed in the party and for how long it may be out. The park also has two excellent lodges, *Skyland* and *Big Meadows*. For reservations at either, write ARA Virginia Sky-Line Co., PO Box 727, Luray, VA 22835 (703 743-5108). *Skyland* is a Shenandoah tradition, begun in 1894 by George Pollock. It has 158 rooms, a full dining room, a stable, and craft shops. *Big Meadows* offers the same features, with only 96 rooms. Lodging is available from March through December, with reservations required about 2 months in advance for any time except foliage season (then 8 months, minimum).

Tidewater Virginia

One of the richest historical areas in the country is Virginia's coast — traditionally called Tidewater Virginia — on the Chesapeake Bay. Here, almost within call of one another, are Williamsburg, Jamestown, and Yorktown; the beautiful 18th-century plantation homes along the James, York, Rappahannock, and Potomac rivers; and to the west and north, Richmond and Fredericksburg, with a wealth of surrounding Civil War sites. There is hardly a period of early American history, from initial exploration to the War Between the States, not represented by some vital detail here.

Begin a tour of Tidewater Virginia at the beginning. The "historic triangle" between the James and the York rivers is the most highly concentrated area of historical sites in the whole country. The three points of the triangle are: Jamestown, where America began; Williamsburg, where patriots plotted the future of the nation-to-be; and Yorktown, where the Revolutionary War ended and the nation was born. And all three are conveniently linked by the Colonial Parkway.

WILLIAMSBURG: The first restoration of a historical area ever undertaken in the US, it is still the best. Work was begun in 1926; no detail was too insignificant, no project too large, in this staggering task. Visitors to Williamsburg can actually experience life as it was lived in Colonial days. Craftsmen ply their trades exactly as they did then, sheep graze on the green, a horse-drawn cart takes you down Duke of Gloucester Street, with its array of taverns and shops all busy at their 18th-century businesses. Take a stroll over to Market Square and watch the militia train and drill. A good introduction to Colonial Williamsburg can be found at the visitors center (Colonial Pkwy. and Rte. 132 Y). Of the 400 buildings that have been restored there are some you won't want to miss: the Governor's "Palace," as it was called by the disgruntled colonists whose taxes paid the bills for this luxurious mansion; the College of William and Mary, built in 1693 and the second oldest college in America; and two jovial and famous meeting places, Raleigh and Wetherburn's taverns.

Make reservations well in advance, for Williamsburg is a very popular destination for families. There are a great many motels and hotels near town. Within the town itself is the *Williamsburg Inn* (Frances St.), a joy to see or visit for its painstaking authenticity. (See *Restored Towns and Reconstructed Villages*, DIVERSIONS, for more information about Williamsburg.)

JAMESTOWN: Williamsburg became the seat of the royal government in 1699. Before that, Jamestown had been the center of the royal colony and the site of the first successful English settlement in America. John Smith and his group of 103 settlers arrived in Jamestown in May 1607. Today it is an island; at the time, it was connected to the mainland by a narrow isthmus that the James River eventually ate away. The first years of the colony were extremely hard, with little help from the London Company, which sponsored the journey; and, in general, fate dealt the town a rather hard hand. By 1699, when the government was moved, it had been burnt down once, set afire another time, and finally abandoned.

Today the area is part of the Colonial National Historical Park. For the most part, one sees diggings indicating where buildings were and how extensive the settlement was. The one remaining building of the period is the church tower of 1639, around which the church has been reconstructed. Also reconstructed on its original site is the Glasshouse, fitted out as it was originally, with craftspeople blowing glass. But history comes most vividly alive at Jamestown Festival Park, in the harbor of the James River (not part of Jamestown itself). Here are full-scale replicas of the three tiny ships on which the first settlers made their journey: the *Susan Constant,* the *Godspeed,* and the *Discovery.* You can actually board one of them and see the cramped quarters that housed those courageous families. There is also a re-creation of James Fort, which you can tour, as well as several special exhibition houses. For more information, see *Restored Towns and Reconstructed Villages,* DIVERSIONS.

YORKTOWN: The third city of colonial significance, Yorktown was an important tobacco shipping port until the Revolutionary War began. In the autumn of 1781, British Commander Cornwallis got boxed in here by a combination of the French fleet along the coast and French and American ground troops, led by George Washington. On October 9 a siege began, and ten days later Cornwallis surrendered. The Revolutionary War was over. Unlike Jamestown, however, Yorktown is a functioning city today, surrounded on all sides by the Yorktown Battlefield. The Yorktown Victory Center (on Rte. 238) has information and brochures as well as Revolutionary War exhibitions and a display of archaeological material raised from one of Cornwallis's ships that sank in the York River during the war. After a visit here, you can walk through the battlefield, which is carefully designed to explain the battle and its significance. Of special interest is the Moore House (on Rte. 238), where the capitulation papers were drawn up (they were signed in the adjacent trenches), and the Swan Tavern (Main St. and Ballard), a reconstruction of an early-18th-century tavern, now a shop. Before leaving the area, consider a visit to Busch Gardens, The Old Country, a theme park outside Williamsburg (5 miles on Rte. 60); see *Amusement Parks,* DIVERSIONS.

TIDEWATER PLANTATIONS: Along any and all of the rivers, inlets, bays, and peninsulas of Tidewater Virginia and the Chesapeake Bay you will find lovely Georgian homes, fully restored and inhabited, which date from the tobacco trade days of the mid-1800s. However, from Williamsburg west along the north shore of the James River are a number of the most famous plantation homes in America. Most are open to visitors, and even if one house is closed on the particular day you visit, the grounds are always open. About 8 miles outside Williamsburg is Carter's Grove, built in the 1750s and restored as part of the Colonial Williamsburg project. Across the river from Jamestown is Smith's Fort Plantation, built almost 100 years earlier, on land given by the Indian Chief Powhatan to his daughter Pocahontas and her groom John Rolfe. Just east of Smith's Fort lies Chippokes Plantation State Park, a plantation dating to 1619. Along the James River north shore route are Sherwood Forest, the home of President John Tyler; Westover, the home of William Byrd II, built in the 1730s as the focal point of his 179,000-acre fiefdom; Berkeley, the birthplace of President William Henry Harrison; and Shirley, the seat of the immensely powerful Carter family.

PORT OF HAMPTON ROADS: This port incorporates three cities — Newport News, Portsmouth, and Norfolk — and is a center for shipping and shipbuilding. It is also the entry point to Virginia's beaches, either around Cape Henry to Virginia Beach or through the Chesapeake Bay Bridge-Tunnel to the peninsula of Virginia that hangs below Maryland.

From Yorktown, Rte. 17 and I-64 lead into the center of these seafaring towns. A fitting stop is the Mariner's Museum (Clyde Morris Blvd., Newport News). It offers a wealth of ships' fittings, models, cannon, maps, and instruments. In Newport News you can take a the harbor cruise (from the Boat Harbor at the end of Jefferson St.) which takes you around Hampton Roads and historic Fort Monroe, in the very waters where the *Monitor* met the *Merrimac.*

BEST EN ROUTE

Williamsburg Inn, Williamsburg – Genteel luxury in a perfectly restored and maintained 18th-century atmosphere. In the center of Williamsburg, the inn offers history outside the front door and a golf course outside the back. Reservations Office, Colonial Williamsburg Foundation, PO Box B, Williamsburg, VA 23187 (804 229-1000).

Tides Lodge, Irvington – Primarily a golf establishment that offers numerous outdoor activities (yachting, tennis, canoeing, jogging, swimming, fishing) for the family. Associated with the elegant *Tides Inn* nearby. See also *Resort Hotels,* DIVERSIONS. Irvington, VA 22480 (804 438-6000).

Harpers Ferry and Monongahela National Forest, West Virginia

West Virginia really is the stuff that country music is made of — country roads, rocky cliffs, Blue Ridge Mountains, almost heaven. But it's much more than mountaintops and John Denver lyrics. The small towns built into these old hills are strongholds of America's history. This is where John Brown's ill-fated raid on Harpers Ferry took place, where one of the bloodiest and most crucial battles of the Civil War was fought, and where hundreds of mule-drawn barges navigated the Chesapeake and Ohio Canal, carrying coal to fuel the young nation. The towns are within a few hours' drive of each other through beautiful backcountry, including the Monongahela National Forest, a thickly wooded area with both tranquillity and wild and woolly whitewater canoeing.

HARPERS FERRY, West Virginia: Though this lovely hillside town overlooking the confluence of the Potomac and Shenandoah rivers appears tranquil today, it was the site of John Brown's raid on the federal arsenal in 1859 as part of his plan to arm a slave rebellion and to establish a free state in the Blue Ridge Mountains. The abolitionist force succeeded in capturing the arsenal, but it was surrounded by the local militia, and Brown was captured by Colonel Robert E. Lee and hung for treason and murder a month and a half later. A ½-mile walking tour through the Harpers Ferry National Historical Park (Shenandoah St.) links several restored homes, a gunmaking museum, the engine house where Brown was caught, a blacksmith shop, confectionary, tavern, and Jefferson Rock, which commands a fine view of the area's rivers and hills.

SHARPSBURG, Maryland: The headquarters of the Chesapeake and Ohio Canal National Historical Park (the park itself is 10 miles south of US 70 along Rte. 65). This 185-mile canal was begun in 1828 to link Washington, DC, and Pittsburgh. It never reached its final destination; construction was halted at Cumberland, Maryland, in 1850 because the railroad had become a more efficient means of transportation. The canal is still among the longest and best preserved canals built during the early 1800s. It was used until 1924 to carry coal, crops, and lumber from the West Virginia mountains to Georgetown. At its peak, some 500 mule-drawn barges navigated the waterway and were raised and lowered through its 75 locks. Many of the locks and aqueducts have been restored, and interesting old buildings line the banks of the canal, now run by the National Park Service. Trails and campsites along the entire length of the canal are available for hikers and bicyclists.

The Antietam National Battlefield and Cemetery Site lies 1 mile north of Sharpsburg on Rte. 65. Here the Union forces stopped the first Confederate invasion of the North in one of the bloodiest battles of the war. Iron tablets and battlefield maps describe the events. The visitors center houses a museum; musket and cannon demonstrations, historical talks, and bicycle tours are scheduled throughout the year.

CHARLES TOWN, West Virginia: Charles Washington, brother of George, founded and designed this town in 1786. Of interest here are numerous historic homes as well as the Jefferson County Courthouse (N George and E Washington sts.), the site of the 1859 trial of John Brown and his gallows (S Samuel and Hunter sts.). The Jefferson County Museum (N Samuel and E Washington sts.) has everything of John Brown's that's not a-moldering in the grave. Just outside town is Harewood, an estate built by another Washington brother, Samuel, and the site of the wedding of James and Dolley Madison. Nearby are Claymount Court (Summit Point Rd.), built by George's grand-nephew, Bushrod; and Happy Retreat (Blakely Pl.), an earlier home of Charles.

BERKELEY SPRINGS, West Virginia: For many years, this resort city was called Bath, after the English spa. George Washington noted the mineral springs while surveying the region for Lord Fairfax, who donated the springs to Virginia in 1756; they have been public property ever since. Not one to mingle with the commoners, Fairfax bathed in a private hollow that's known as the Fairfax Bathtub. Today, however, the hoi polloi bathe right at the center of town in the Berkeley Springs Park, a state-run facility with health baths, warm springs, a swimming pool, and even a Roman bathhouse.

Cacapon Park, 10 miles south of town (off Rte. 522), is a 6,155-acre park at the base of Cacapon Mountain with excellent facilities for golf, tennis, horseback riding, fishing, swimming, and boating.

LOST RIVER STATE PARK, near Moorefield, West Virginia: These parklands were once a vacation spot of the Lee family of Virginia and now have facilities for swimming, tennis, picnicking, and riding. One of the original cabins has been restored and turned into a museum. Nearby stands unusual Ice Mountain (it has ice at its base even on the hottest summer days). The mountain is honeycombed with cold underground passages that keep the ice frozen.

MONONGAHELA NATIONAL FOREST, West Virginia: The forest covers over 850,000 acres in the heart of the Alleghenies, stretching southwest from the Maryland border for 100 miles through the West Virginia backcountry, a region of rounded mountains and twisting valleys. Much of the Monongahela is a "reconstructed" forest. In the early part of this century, large forest fires and indiscriminate logging practices stripped it of its huge stands of timber. The regeneration and planting program began in 1920 and the region is blanketed once again with deep forests inhabited by whitetail deer, black bear, wild turkey, and many other wildlife species.

A popular route through Monongahela starts at Petersburg, at the northeast corner of the forest, and heads southwest via Rte. 28 to Bartow. The road runs along the north fork of the Potomac. Seneca Rocks, towering 1,000 feet above the river, is a major landmark (there's also a visitors center here). Mountain climbers from all over come here to claw their way up the rugged face of this immense rock cliff. Nearby is Spruce Knob, at 4,862 feet the highest peak in West Virginia. (West Virginia's average altitude is the highest of any state east of the Mississippi.) This area of the forest is being managed as a national recreation area. The 100,000 acres have facilities for hiking and camping. Starting at the Seneca Rocks, there's whitewater canoeing for 15 miles along the headwaters of the Potomac.

Near Greenbank is the National Radio Astronomy Observatory, a huge radio telescope with which astronomers are recharting the heavens. Tours of the complex are given during the summer and a film explains the work done at the observatory. The facility is open daily from mid-June through Labor Day; weekends only from Memorial Day to mid-June and in September and October.

At Cass (just south of Greenbank, off Rte. 7) is the depot of a state-owned railroad with a steam locomotive that runs through the rugged mountains along an old logging track up to the summit of Bald Knob, the second highest mountain in the state. The trip to the top of the mountain takes 4½ hours.

In the southwestern portion of the forest, west of Mill Point and north of Rte. 39, lies Cranberry Glades, a large outdoor botanical laboratory centered around a big cranberry bog. The area is particularly beautiful during the fall but worth a visit at any time. Nearby, the Cranberry Mountain visitors center has instructive displays. While you're there, take a short hike down Hills Creek, where within half a mile there are three lovely waterfalls.

The Monongahela National Forest now has 24 campgrounds. There are about 700 miles of streams with excellent trout and bass fishing. In season, there is hunting for bear, deer, grouse, cottontail rabbit, snowshoe hare, squirrel, and wild turkey. There are also about 600 miles of hiking trails and four wilderness areas totaling approximately 78,000 acres. Information: Monongahela National Forest Headquarters, USDA Bldg., Sycamore St., PO Box 1548, Elkins, WV 26241 (304 636-1800).

BEST EN ROUTE

The Greenbrier, White Sulphur Springs, West Virginia – Just south of Monongahela, this magnificent resort has been favored by celebrities ranging from Robert E. Lee to the Duke of Windsor and 20 American presidents since the springs were first used in 1778. Originally a mineral spa, the Greenbrier has been a resort for more than 200 years and is famous for having as many employees as guests — a standard few modern resorts can match. There are three 18-hole golf courses, one of which was recently redesigned by Jack Nicklaus, 20 tennis courts, 2 Olympic-sized pools, miles of riding trails, skeet and trap shooting, an art colony, theaters, nightclubs, restaurants, and a spa. There's also a notable diagnostic clinic on the premises. After roughing it in the Monongahela National Forest, nothing could be better than being pampered here for a day or two. See also *Resort Hotels*, DIVERSIONS. Station A, White Sulphur Springs, WV 24986, just west of town on Rte. 60 (304 536-1110; 800 624-6070).

Cacapon Lodge, near Berkeley Springs, West Virginia – This state-run facility in the park provides good standard accommodations and easy access to all the park activities. Berkeley Springs, WV 25411 (304 258-1022).

Watoga State Park, south of Marlinton, West Virginia – This state facility offers 88 campsites, cabins, restaurant, swimming pool, horses for hire, picnicking, fishing, and hiking. Information and reservations: 304 799-4087.

South

Hot Springs National Park, Arkansas

If you've only thought of Hot Springs, Arkansas, as a place to bring your aching joints when they seem to creak, you're in for a huge surprise. Hot Springs is the hottest tourist attraction in Arkansas. And it's only 50 miles from Little Rock, the state capital.

A city of some 35,000, Hot Springs is the center of Hot Springs National Park. This, in itself, is unusual, since most national parks are miles from large, populated centers. The place has certainly come a long way from the day in 1541 when the explorer Hernando de Soto christened it "the valley of vapors." At that time, it was a secluded section of Indian territory, and it was supposedly the Indians themselves who led de Soto and his exhausted team to the bubbling pools of water, where they were rejuvenated after a bath. The legendary curative properties of these 47 thermal springs became known all the world over. In 1832, 4 square miles of Hot Springs were declared a federal reservation. In 1921 they became a national park, which now covers almost 5,000 acres.

The fabled Bathhouse Row has been offering regimens of baths and massages long enough to be listed on the National Register of Historic Places. There are six bathhouses, two of them on Bathhouse Row (the others are in nearby hotels). Before you step into the mineral baths, it's recommended (not required) that you be examined by a physician. You do need a referral from a licensed physician for physiotherapy sessions at any of the hydrotherapy facilities. The springs themselves are on the western slope of Hot Springs Mountain. A reservoir collects the 800,000 gallons flowing through 45 of the thermal springs daily and channels them to the bathhouses. (You can see two of the bubbling springs behind the Maurice Bathhouse on Central Avenue; another flows down the hillside above Arlington Lawn at the north end of Bathhouse Row. The rest are not visible to the public.)

You might be surprised at the blue-green algae floating on the surface of the springs, since algae traditionally make their home in colder waters. The springs puzzle geologists, too, but for other reasons. They theorize that rain seeps through an aquifer and then rises along layers of rock to bubble out through a fault at the base of Hot Springs Mountain. But how is it heated? Perhaps by molten rock deep inside the earth or by radioactive minerals. It could be the result of inner seismic friction or unexplained chemical reactions.

The spa is merely one aspect of this vacation area. From February to April, thoroughbred horses race at Oaklawn Park, a handsome track. The season reaches its climax during the week-long Racing Festival of the South in the third week of April. It culminates in the running of the Arkansas Derby on the final day. The races kick off a lively, diversified summer and fall season. In June, Hot Springs is the scene of the Arkansas Fun Festival; in July, the Miss Arkansas Pageant; in October, the Arkansas Oktoberfest; in November, the Healthfest/Spa 10K Run. Special performances of an outdoor drama are staged at the 1,600-seat Mid-America amphitheater.

Other places of interest include: Arkansas Alligator Farm (847 Whittington Ave.); IQ Zoo (600 Central); Wildwood 1884 (Victorian Mansion, 808 Park Ave.); Josephine Tussaud Wax Museum (250 Central Ave.); the Magic Springs Family Fun Park (Rte. 70 east); Educated Animals (380 Whittington Ave.); the Fine Arts Center (815 Whittington Ave.); and the Mid-America Center Museum.

For a touch of tranquillity, follow Rte. 270 west to the gently rolling Ouachita Mountains, one of the oldest mountain ranges on the continent. Here, you'll find three manmade lakes on the Ouachita River: Lakes Ouachita, Hamilton, and the smallest, Catherine. These lakes are the pride of Hot Springs, each offering fishing, swimming, water skiing, sailing, and scuba diving. You can camp at Lake Catherine, 12 miles west of Malvern. There are also campsites along the southern shores of Lake Ouachita and an unbeatable 18 miles of hiking trails through the forests. You can join guided nature walks during the summer. Lake Ouachita offers a unique camping opportunity. If you rent a Camp-a-Float motorized barge, you can take your car or camper onto the water and travel around the 48,000-acre lake without having to land.

For complete information on accommodations and facilities, call the Hot Springs Chamber of Commerce (800 272-2081 in Arkansas; 800 643-1570 elsewhere). For a free travel kit, write to the Oot Springs Advertising Commission, PO Box 1500, Hot Springs National Park, Hot Springs, AR 71902, or contact the Arkansas Dept. of Parks and Tourism, 1 Capitol Mall, Little Rock, AR 72201 (501 371-1511 or 371-7777; 800 482-8999 in Arkansas; 800 643-8383 elsewhere). Since it attracts people from all over the world, Hot Springs isn't one of those national parks where you can look forward to hot dogs on stale rolls and rubbery hamburgers. There's an abundance of restaurants: American, German, Italian, Czechoslovakian, French, Mexican, and kosher. Information: Superintendent, Hot Springs National Park, PO Box 1860, Hot Springs, AR 71902 (501 624-3383).

BEST EN ROUTE

Arlington Hotel, Hot Springs – In the middle of the city, with its own hot mineral water bathhouse, the hotel has 2 swimming pools, 3 restaurants, and 500 rooms. Central and Fountain sts., Hot Springs, AR 71901 (501 623-7771; 800 643-1502 outside Arkansas).

The Ozarks, Arkansas

They call it "the Natural State" — down home, pickin' and strummin', come-as-you-are Arkansas. It's an unpretentious part of the world, when you get right down to it. The home of the Ozarks is one of the great capitals of American folk myth and heritage. This is the land of country roads leading through gentle, blue-green mountains, twisting along the edges of gorges that catapult into white, frothy rivers. If you can imagine a banjo or fiddle in the background, you've got the whole picture. To get to the Ozarks from Little Rock, the capital, take I-30 and Rte. 67 north about 110 miles.

NEWPORT-JACKSONPORT: On the banks of the White River, famous for its fine trout. You can stop at Jacksonport State Park, just north of Newport, to picnic. If you have enough confidence in your casting ability, you can fish in the river for your meal. Jacksonport was once a rough-and-ready frontier river town, and its old courthouse is now a museum. The *Mary Woods II*, a White River paddlewheel tugboat, is also on display. According to local history, Jacksonport citizens liked the river city so much, they refused to let the railroad come in; so the station was built 3 miles south, in Newport. As a result, Jacksonport declined.

BATESVILLE: Follow the river northwest along Rte. 14, about 35 miles up the road, and you'll be able to step back into the 19th century, since this town is very much as it was during the days when the paddlewheelers steamed into dock, full of passengers and cargo. For two weeks during the summer, Arkansas College holds Folklore Workshops in conjunction with the Ozark Folk Center, 40 miles away in Mountain View.

MOUNTAIN VIEW: The home of the Ozark Folk Center, this is a good place for first-timers to get acquainted with the crafts, customs, and music of the Ozarks. Since it opened in 1973, the center has been a country music and folk history lover's dream. In addition to mountain craft displays and workshops, the 80-acre center is alive with music. If you're visiting in April, you'll probably be swept up in a crowd of about 100,000 people, all flocking to town for the Arkansas Folk Festival, two weekends of jug band, fiddle, jew's harp, mountain dulcimer, and banjo strummin' sessions. If you don't like crowds but hanker after that foot-stompin' music, stop by between late spring and October. The Ozark Folk Center's 1,043-seat auditorium has concerts almost every night. There are also free concerts at the county courthouse every Saturday night, and, in October, a two-week Family Harvest Festival at the center. Traditional pottery, quilting, shucking, spinning and weaving — you can see it all at the folk center. And you can take some home — from the center's shop. For information call the Ozark Folk Center, 501 269-3851.

BLANCHARD SPRINGS CAVERN: Blanchard is in the Sylamore District of the Ozark National Forest, about 15 miles north of Mountain View on Rte. 14. Considered one of the most spectacular underground natural environments in the state, it has only been open to the public since 1973. You can walk along Dripstone Trail, an intricate labyrinth that crisscrosses the palatial subterranean caverns and takes you past stalactites. More difficult is the Discovery Trail, with a Christmas-tree-shaped stalagmite, a frozen waterfall, and a cavern called the Ghost Room (open all year long). There are nature trails and camping areas here, too. Be sure to make reservations (501 757-2213) at least three days in advance during the summer months, even if you only want to tour.

MOUNTAIN HOME: Some fabulous river and lake country lies just to the north of Blanchard Springs. If you stay on Rte. 5, you'll pass the junction of the rushing waters of the White and Buffalo rivers. About 50 miles north of Mountain View is Mountain Home, sitting between Norfork Lake and Bull Shoals, two of the Ozarks' most famous lakes. Both are great for canoeing, swimming, and water skiing. Bass, bream, crappie, catfish, stripers, and rainbow trout swim around in the clear water just waiting to be caught, and there are Ozark guides who'll take you to where the fish are biting. You can even join a night fishing expedition on a pontoon boat. On the shores of Bull Shoals Lake, Bull Shoals State Park has campsites and a dock (on Rte. 178). Near Buffalo Point National Recreation Area, on the shores of the Buffalo River, you can rent a canoe for an unforgettable trip along one of America's wild rivers. The 132-mile Buffalo River flows through spectacular blue mountains, and there are no artificial dams to obstruct the water's flow. The National Park Service maintains cabins and campsites along the riverbanks.

HARRISON: "The hub of the Ozarks," Li'l Abner country. Here you'll find Dogpatch, USA, a theme park filled with cartoonist Al Capp's notable characters (on Rte. 65).

EUREKA SPRINGS: This delightful Victorian town is just east of 28,000-acre Beaver Lake. A fashionable health spa in the 1880s, Eureka Springs has 63 natural springs within the city limits, more than Hot Springs, the state's most popular thermal spa resort. The kids will love the shuttle bus, designed to look like a trolley car. Here, too, you can hear country music concerts during the summer in Basin Spring Park bandshell on weekday nights. From May through October, the Great Passion Play is performed near the seven-story-tall Christ of the Ozarks statue in a 4,200-seat amphitheater (daily except Mondays and Thursdays). Information: Eureka Springs Chamber of Commerce, PO Box 551, Eureka Springs, AR 72632 (501 253-8737).

BEAVER LAKE: Rte. 62 loops around the north shore of Beaver Lake. Here you can visit Pea Ridge National Battlefield Park, site of a decisive 1862 Civil War battle, after which Missouri stuck firmly to the Union.

OZARK NATIONAL FOREST: On your way back to Little Rock, take Rte. 62 south to Fayetteville, home of the University of Arkansas's main campus (501 575-2000). Then follow Rte. 71 south, past Devil's Den and Lake Fort Smith state parks, to I-40 east. (There's a Travel Information Center to the west of the intersection of Rte. 71 and I-40.) On your way back to Little Rock, you can stop at Clarksville, the heart of the 1.1-million-acre Ozark National Forest. You can get off the interstate and wander north along Rte. 21 through dense, uninhabited forest. As you breathe in the scent of pine, you might find yourself humming to the tune of some banjo song you heard a few nights earlier. This is the time to enjoy the cool, rushing sounds of the forest. Information: the Forest Supervisor, Ozark National Forest, PO Box 1008, Russellville, AR 72801 (501 968-2354).

BEST EN ROUTE

Ozark Folk Center Lodge, Mountain View – A 60-room lodge in woodsy surroundings right next to the folk center. A good place to choose if you want a rustic environment and a chance to be where it's all happening. Mountain View, AR 72560 (501 269-3871).

Crescent Hotel, Eureka Springs – A landmark, built in 1886. Most of the 76 rooms have different Victorian furniture. The limestone hotel has a restaurant, swimming pool, tennis court, ice cream parlor, and rooftop garden lounge. Close to 12 springs. From January through March it's open weekends only. 75 Prospect St., Eureka Springs, AR 72632 (501 253-9766).

Everglades National Park, Florida

In most of America's national parks you have little more to do than arrive and open your eyes to be impressed. The Everglades is far more demanding. Here you must know something about ecology, and something about what you're looking at, to appreciate the full splendor of this magnificent swamp wilderness.

The Everglades is America's only subtropical wetlands. Fed by the waters of southern Florida's huge Lake Okeechobee, the entire southern tip of the state was once more or less like the Everglades today — a huge tract of mangrove swamps, seas of saw grass, hammocks of hardwood trees, and millions of birds, fish, snakes and alligators, and insects (especially mosquitoes). As southern Florida developed, the slow-draining waters of Okeechobee were channeled for irrigation and swamps drained. Bit by bit, southern Florida dried out.

In 1947, alarmed by the destruction of these unique wetlands, the federal government set aside 1,400,533 acres 30 miles west of Miami as Everglades National Park. Despite various (and continuing) threats, the park remains today: the third largest of America's national parks, 2,188 square miles of the world's most delicate ecological system, stretching to Florida's southern and western Gulf coasts.

You must understand the delicacy of the Everglades to enjoy its understated pleasures. It is actually a freshwater river (its Indian name is Pa-Hay-Okee, "River of Grass") 100 miles long, 50 miles wide, and just inches deep. This strange stream travels along an incline of only three inches a mile, mvoing so slowly that a single drop of water takes years to reach the Gulf from Lake Okeechobee. This slow river provides nourishment for a vast and complex system of life and is a perfect laboratory in which to see the interdependence and sensitivity of an ecosystem. Where the earth rises so much as three inches, the plant life in the 'glades changes from saw grass to hardwood forest. Where ripples appear in a pond, a small fish is eating mosquito larvae; a large fish, a bream perhaps, will dine on the larvae-eater; bass hunt the bream; gar will feed on the bass; and the gar is menu fodder for the alligator who originally made (or deepened) this pond with his tail in the winter.

About 200 miles north of the Tropic of Cancer, the Everglades is the meeting point of subtropical and temperate life forms. In this it is unique in the US: Here you see mangrove, West Indian mahogany, and the poisonous manchineel tree, and in a nearby hammock rising from the saw grass, pine and hardwood trees. Alligators and whitetail deer share the same stomping ground.

The entrance to the Everglades is on Route 9336 about 12 miles southwest of Homestead. Route 9336 ends at the park entrance; from here follow the main park road for a 38-mile journey through the park to Flamingo, on the

Florida Bay. There are several ways to see the 'glades: by car, you can drive to various stops along the road; on foot, where trails follow into the heart of things (with or without ranger guides); by small outboard or canoe, following the water routes. In any case, the first stop is at the visitors center at the park entrance, where you can see exhibitions on park wildlife and ecology and pick up information on guided tours, "swamp tromps" (more about these later), and park activities and rules.

If you are driving, the next stop is Royal Palm Station (about 2 miles beyond the center), where you can follow boardwalks over the saw grass and watch for animal life. (That saw grass has mean, serrated edges on three sides. It chews clothes or flesh with equal ease, so be careful.)

Beyond Royal Palm the road runs through pine forests to Long Pine Key Area, a good picnicking spot. Note the pines. They manage to survive only because they are sturdily fire resistant. You may see a number of them with fire-blackened trunks. In both summer and winter fires sweep through parts of the 'glades. Many trees are killed, but pines burn only on the outside; their corky bark protects them. In summer, the saltwort marshes that flank many of the forests dry out and are torched by summer lightning, but since it is the rainy season, when water levels are high, these fires do little damage. It is the fires during the winter dry season — usually caused by man — that do the most harm.

Pa-Hay-Okee is the next stop on the car route. From here you have access to a high platform and boardwalks that overlook Shark River Basin, where alligators and fowl gather. The alligators form an important link in the chain of life in the Everglades. During the dry season — autumn through spring — they settle into sloughs and dig deep holes with their tails. In late winter, as the marshes dry out, fish get caught in these " 'gator-holes," which become teeming pools of fish life. This is crucial for the wading birds, which nest near these ample sources of food and are assured a food supply.

Seven miles beyond Pa-Hay-Okee is Mahogany Hammock, the largest stand of mahoganies in the US. Boardwalks allow you to wander into it. A bit farther is Paurotis Pond, where you encounter the first mangrove trees. Here salt and fresh water begin to mix, and the mangrove is the only tree that thrives in salt water. It is a great colonizers and lives in a constant drama of creation and destruction all along the Gulf shore. It settles into the swampy salt water of the coast, and as it drops seeds and throws out breathing roots it captures material and actually begins "building" earth bulwarks against the sea. As seagulls and other sea birds collect around it, dropping guano, this earth becomes rich and fertile. Then hurricanes sweep the coast, and everything is ripped out of the swampy ground and thrown inland.

The main park road ends at Flamingo, where you'll find a hotel, campgrounds, and boats for hire (including houseboats) for excursions into portions of the 'glades only accessible by waterway.

Serious visitors should plan to spend most of their time out of their cars, on marked foot trails or on a "swamp tromp" into the very heart of the marshes. (There is also a tram ride available at Shark Valley off Rte. 41, which skims the northern border of the park.) For the less hardy, foot trails are a comfortable way to have an intimate experience of the 'glades.

Gumbo Limbo Trail begins at Royal Palm and explores the interior of Paradise Key, where exotic air plants and hardwood trees grow; also at Royal Palm, Anhinga Trail is a likely route to spot a number of alligators and a variety of birds from an elevated walkway. You might just be lucky enough to spot some of the delicate Virginia whitetail deer along the Pineland Trail (beginning about 2 miles from Long Pine Key area). (These little deer are the prey of the Florida panther, which, sadly, lives in dwindling numbers here in the Everglades.) At the Pa-Hay-Okee Overlook you'll get a perspective of the expanse of saw grass that makes up the Shark River basin.

For the more intrepid who would like to meet nature's challenge, from December through March there are the frequent "slough slogs" or "swamp tromps" — walking expeditions led by park naturalists which get you into things. Quite literally. You'll need old clothes and shoes that you don't mind getting muddy and wet. And be sure to have plenty of mosquito repellent handy. There are several possible destinations: out to a 'gator hole, a tree island, or a major mangrove stand. Ask for schedules at the visitors center.

The Wilderness Waterway is just about the most challenging test the Everglades can cook up for the outdoors person. It is a 99-mile water trail that corkscrews through the Ten Thousand Islands area. Although the water lanes are well marked, there is sufficient room for error that travelers are asked to take all precautions when undertaking this journey. By powerboat it is quite possible to complete the course in about 6 hours. However, any serious nature observer will opt for the canoe and the serenity it offers en route. There are minimally outfitted campsites, each wryly nicknamed, along the water lanes: "Hell's Bay" ("hell to get into and hell to get out of"); "Onion Key," the bare-bones remains of a 20s land developer's dream; and a crude pit outhouse and fireplace campsite known as "the Coming Miami of the Gulf." The waterways begin at Everglades City and extend to Flamingo.

The somewhat less athletic and daring boater might prefer to take a guided boat cruise. One such cruise departs every evening from Flamingo to tour Florida Bay; this is a good opportunity to view Florida's blazing sunsets and watch the indigenous birds returning to roost for the evening. From November through May, there are daily cruises from Everglades City to explore Upper Chokoloskee Bay.

The not-so-visible members of the Everglades family run the gamut from the lowly and much-hated mosquito all the way to the signature 'gator, who is most often spotted when his eyes break water while the rest of him hides beneath the surface. Fish are tropical and abundant, each with a role in the food cycle that maintains the Everglades. Schools of dolphin can usually be spotted from the coastal shorelines. Recreational fishing is permitted, but all plants and animals are protected by law from any molestation or harm by man. Information: Superintendent, PO Box 279, Homestead, FL 33030 (305 247-6211).

BEST EN ROUTE

Fontainebleau Hilton – Still the glittering standard by which most Miami Beach hotels are measured. Some say the hotel's lagoon-like pool with grotto bar is the best swimming hole in South Florida. 1,250 rooms. 4441 Collins Ave., Miami Beach, FL 33140 (305 538-2000).

Key Biscayne – The Key's first and still most delightful hotel, with a quiet and peaceful atmosphere amid soft tropical decor. It features a long private beach, tennis courts, pitch-and-putt golf course, and a good dining room. 103 rooms and villas. 701 Ocean Dr., Key Biscayne, FL 33149 (305 361-5431).

Holiday Inn – Across from the University of Miami, this motel is a good choice for visitors to the southwest area. The rooms are comfortable and there's a popular restaurant. 1350 S Dixie Hwy,, Miami, FL 33146 (305 667-5611).

Omni International, Miami – This 553-room hotel is in a large shopping mall. The Treasure Island Amusement Park is also in the mall, promising to lure and amuse the kiddies with a variety of rides, bumper cars, and the like. 16th St. and Biscayne Blvd., Miami, FL 33132 (305 374-0000).

Florida Keys and John Pennekamp Coral Reef State Park, Florida

Curving 150 miles out into the Gulf of Mexico from the southern tip of mainland Florida, the Florida Keys dot the waters like an ellipsis following a phrase. And in many ways this archipelago is an afterthought to that great landmass above, centered around Miami, with its glittering nightlife and crowded swimming beaches. The 45 islands that make up the Keys are generally tucked soundly away by 11 at night, have very few swimming beaches despite the availability of water (the shallow waters coupled with fierce coral discourage swimming), and few glamorous resorts. The local hotel with five stories — a midget by Miami standards — is a skyscraper hereabouts.

What the Keys do have, however, are some of the finest seascapes around — the blue waters of the Atlantic to the east and south and the green seas of the Gulf of Mexico on the northern side. As you drive along the Overseas Highway (US 1), a toll-free highway that spans the islands with 43 bridges (some only 100 feet long, one stretching as far as 7 miles), you'll be surrounded on all sides by sea and sky. Even on the Keys themselves, many of which are only a few hundred yards wide, you can see through the mangroves, Caribbean pine, and silver palmetto to the sea, which is the overwhelming presence here. And though you can't see it from the car, below the surface the view is even more dramatic. The Keys are surrounded by an offshore coral reef, a section of which can be seen close up at the John Pennekamp Coral Reef State Park in Key Largo. It is a slightly hallucinogenic underwater scene as bright blue and green tropical fish move in and out of the sculptured reefs of white, pink, and orange coral.

The story of the Overseas Highway is interesting. In the late 1880s, Henry

Flagler, an associate of John D. Rockefeller, aimed to establish a "land" route to Cuba by extending the Florida East Coast Railroad line to Key West. From there he planned a ferry shuttle for the final 90 miles to Havana. He invested some $20 million in the construction of tracks, but the 1929 crash destroyed his project. Six years later, the Labor Day Hurricane of 1935 wiped out most of what remained of the tracks. At that point, the government stepped in and began building the Overseas Highway along the same route. In 1982, 37 bridges were replaced with wider, heavier spans, including the well-known Seven-Mile Bridge at Marathon.

Of the 45 keys linked by the highway, several are major islands with accommodations, restaurants, shops, and their own unique characteristics. Much of this local flavor has to do with the natives of the area. They're Floridians, but they call themselves Conchs. Descended from the London Cockneys who settled in the Bahamas, the Conchs also incorporate Cuban, Yankee sailor, and Virginia merchant blood. Conchs have always been people of the sea — fishermen, boatsmen, underwater salvagers. (They could hardly be otherwise, living as they do, surrounded by water.) And when you are in their territory, you can easily share their pleasures. Fishing is king in these parts, with over 300 varieties of fish in the surrounding waters. Besides the challenges to anglers, the availability of fresh fish has stimulated Key chefs to dream up such creations as Conch chowder and, in their landbound flights of fancy, Key lime pie — which must be yellow, not green, to be genuine.

JOHN PENNEKAMP CORAL REEF STATE PARK and KEY LARGO NATIONAL MARINE SANCTUARY, Key Largo: Key Largo is the first of the keys and the longest, but what is most interesting here is under water. Running parallel to the Key for 21 miles is the country's only underwater state park and the sole living coral reef in the continental US. The park is a snorkeler's and scuba diver's heaven, encompassing 170 square miles of the Atlantic Ocean, hundreds of species of tropical fish, and 40 different varieties of coral. Laws forbid taking anything from the water so that the area will be preserved for others to see.

To get an overview of the reef and surrounding sea, take the discovery tour boat and look through the eye-level windows lining the hull. Though somewhat commercial, it provides valuable information on the ecological balance of the reef and journeys several miles out onto the high seas to the reef's most spectacular section, where you'll see beautifully colored coral formations and other marine life, including barracuda, giant sea turtles, and sharks, from a dry vantage point. But as the water gets bluer and bluer, the ride gets rougher and rougher, so take the antiseasickness tablets they offer at the beginning of the trip.

You can also venture into the water under better circumstances for scuba diving tours of the reef. You can rent gear at one of Key Largo's many dive shops or at park headquarters.

Closer to shore, water trails for canoeing in the mangrove swamp offer alternatives for those who want to stay above water. And for those who want to go in, the swimming beach has a roped-off area that is good for a dip or some casual skin diving.

There are 47 campsites, all with tables, charcoal grills, electrical hookups, and water. Reservations for the sites should be made one month in advance — the park is a very popular destination. Reservations and information: John Pennekamp State Park, PO Box 487, Key Largo, FL 33037 (305 451-1202).

ISLAMORADA, Upper Matecumbe Key: A sportfishing center in an area that's famous for fishing, the many coral reefs in the surrounding shallow waters attract scuba and skin divers as well. The Underwater Coral Gardens, two colorful coral deposits and the wreck of a Spanish galleon, offer underwater exploration and photography and can be reached by charter boat.

LONG KEY: Stop here for some underwater hunting (in season) of crawfish — lobsterlike crustaceans without the pincers. There are dive shops all along the route, indicated by the red-and-white-striped divers' flags, which arrange private or group snorkeling expeditions to nearby reefs where you stalk (swim after) your prey.

MARATHON: This large key, midway down the archipelago, has been developed as a tourist center and has an airport and an 18-hole golf course. Nevertheless, Marathon retains much of the original character of a fishing town. There are over 80 species in the Gulf and ocean waters which can be taken with rod and reel or nets from charter boats or the key's bridges. For information on the many fishing contests held throughout the year, write to the Chamber of Commerce, 3330 Overseas Hwy., Marathon, FL 33050 (305 743-5417). The competition is rough and the fish smart. *Hall's Diving Center* (1688 Overseas Hwy., 305 743-5929) is a good place to rent gear.

BIG PINE KEY: The largest of the Lower Keys contains 7,700 acres thick with silver palmetto, Caribbean pine, and cacti. Tiny Key deer were thought to be extinct until they reappeared here, and it is possible to spot rare white heron. The Bahia Honda State Recreational Area (5 miles east on US 1) has camping, boating, picnicking, and coral-free swimming.

KEY WEST: The southernmost community in the US and the point closest to Cuba (a 90-mile swim), this famous key combines Southern, Bahamian, Cuban, and Yankee influences in a unique culture that can be seen in its architecture, tasted in its cuisine, and felt in its relaxed, individualistic atmosphere. Traditionally, fishermen, artists, and writers are drawn to this tranquil slip of sand and sea. Ernest Hemingway, among its early devotees, lived here during his most productive period, when he wrote *To Have and Have Not, For Whom the Bell Tolls, Green Hills of Africa,* and one of his greatest short stories, "The Snows of Kilimanjaro." His Spanish colonial–style house of native stone, surrounded by a lush garden of plantings from the Caribbean, is now a museum with many original furnishings and Hemingway memorabilia (907 Whitehead St.). Among others who have been attracted to Key West are Harry Truman (who established a "Little White House" here), John James Audubon, Tennessee Williams, John Dos Passos, and Robert Frost.

To get your bearings, take the Conch Tour Train, a 90-minute narrated tram ride that covers 14 miles, passing all the highlights of town. The train leaves several times a day from one of two depots: Duval and Front streets and Old Mallory Square. Since Key West is best for strolling, afterward you can visit the places that sounded most interesting or walk to the galleries, craft, and shell shops.

The Lighthouse Museum (Truman Ave. and Whitehead St.) has many military displays, including a Japanese submarine captured at Pearl Harbor. The Audubon House (205 Whitehead St.), where the artist worked on paintings of Florida Keys wildlife in 1831 and 1832, has a complete set of *Birds of America* engravings.

Fishing dominates sports here as elsewhere in the Keys. In addition to fishing, there is a collection of local marine life at the Municipal Auditorium (Whitehead St. on Mallory Sq.). For scuba diving around the coral reefs, the *Key West Pro Dive Shop* sponsors trips and rents gear (1605 N Roosevelt Blvd., PO Box 580, Key West, FL 33040, 305 296-3823). Information: Key West Chamber of Commerce, 402 Wall St., Key West, FL 33040 (305 2949-2587). Area information: Florida Keys Visitors Bureau, PO Box 1147-PR, Key West, FL 33041 (800 FLA-KEYS).

BEST EN ROUTE

Hawk's Cay Resort – This 178-room hotel has 4 dining rooms, a new cocktail lounge, tennis courts, marina, and fresh- and saltwater pools. Marker 61, Marathon, FL 33050 (800 482-2242 in Florida; 800 327-7775 elsewhere).

Pier House, Key West – In the heart of the restored Old Town Key West area, this 120-room hotel has 3 dining areas and a pool. 1 Duval St., Key West, FL 33040 (305 294-9541; 800 327-8340 in Florida; 800 432-3414 elsewhere).

Eden House, Key West – An old guest house, built back in the early 1920s, now stands as the best of traditional designs and the price is right. 1015 S Fleming St., Key West, FL 33040 (305 296-6868).

Okefenokee Swamp, Georgia

If you've ever hummed "Way Down Upon the Suwannee River," you already have a connection to the Okefenokee Swamp. In fact, you're even ahead of Stephen Foster, who'd never seen the Suwannee River when he wrote the song. He originally called it "Way Down Upon the Pedee River," but luckily for Okefenokee lovers, he switched names, thereby immortalizing a curious wandering waterway that begins in this southeast Georgia marshland and flows 230 miles through northeast Florida into the Gulf of Mexico. If you've ever hummed "Way Down Upon St. Marys River," you are already no doubt familiar with the aquatic interrelationships within the 660 square miles of the Okefenokee Swamp. St. Marys is the other Okefenokee river.

The powerful, mysterious marshland of watery caverns lined with elegant, luxurious cypress trees dripping with moss is known as the "land of the trembling earth," a name bestowed upon it by its early inhabitants, the Seminole Indians. Many thousands of years earlier, the swamp had been a vast expanse of salt water. Trail Ridge, now Okefenokee's eastern border, was then an ocean reef. But shifting land formations locked the water in, and it became a breeding ground for swamp vegetation. The first white settlers arrived in 1853 and made their living by fishing, hunting 'gators, and picking wild herbs to sell. The swampers led a fairly rugged life, plying their boats up and down the Suwannee in search of cooters, the giant turtles they sold in local markets. Youngsters earned pocket money by catching snakes for people to keep as pets and crayfish for fishermen's bait. The worn, wooden porches of swampdwellers' cabins were very often covered with the drying leaves of a plant called deer's tongue, used as a medicine and to flavor pipe tobacco.

There are several ways to get to the Okefenokee Swamp from Savannah, Georgia. If you take I-95 south along the coast, you'll find any number of interesting places to stop. At Brunswick, 60 miles south of Savannah, pick up Rte. 84 east for about 50 miles, to Okefenokee Swamp Park, the northern entrance to the Okefenokee National Wildlife Refuge.

SAPELO ISLAND: About 50 miles south of Savannah is the Sapelo Island National Estuarine Sanctuary — the island's official name. The number of visitors allowed here is restricted because it has been set aside by the Georgia Department of Natural Resources to study and protect the salt marshes — and their marine life — surrounding the island. This island is so unspoiled that ecologists use it as a base for measuring the pollution levels of other areas. Along with lots of deer and wild turkey and the University of Georgia Marine Institute laboratories, the lovely South End mansion is here. Originally built as a plantation house in the 1800s and once owned by the tobacco tycoon R. J. Reynolds, South End is sometimes used by former President Carter and his family for vacations. Tours of the island are given on Wednesdays, Fridays, and Saturdays only from June through Labor Day; no Friday tours the rest of the year (reservations required; phone the Darien Chamber of Commerce, 912 437-6684); you get to the island by ferry from Darien (it's a 45-minute boat ride).

MARSHES OF GLYNN: About 30 miles farther south, the Marshes of Glynn stretch west from the highway. Georgia-born poet Sidney Lanier composed an epic poem to the marsh in 1878; "The Marshes of Glynn" is not exactly something you would hum at a bus stop, but "Glooms of the live oaks, beautiful-braided and woven/With intricate shades of the vines that myriad-cloven/Clamber the forks of the multi-form boughs" gives you a pretty good idea of life in the sea-marsh.

SEA ISLANDS: Barely 10 miles farther south, these legendary islands hug the Georgia coast. Fabled for their exquisite resorts and superior outdoor sports facilities, St. Simons, Jekyll, and Sea islands have a unique charm. Jekyll, the most southerly island, was a private club for millionaires until 1946, when it became a state park, with 9 miles of beach, a wildlife refuge, and restored millionaire's cottages.

OKEFENOKEE NATIONAL WILDLIFE REFUGE: Follow I-95 south from St. Simons about 30 miles to the Okefenokee turnoff (Rte. 40), then go approximately 22 miles west to Folkston. Follow Rte. 121/23 south for 8 miles to the Suwannee Canal Recreation Area. Here, at the eastern entrance to the National Wildlife Refuge, you can take guided boat trips or rent a boat yourself. There are also hiking trails, a visitors center, and a wildlife observation drive. Interpreters out at the Chesser Island Homestead will explain how families settled the area and describe what life was like in the swamp. In 1937, the government declared Okefenokee a National Wildlife Refuge. Since then, rare species of woodpecker, reptiles, amphibians, and wading birds nest here, protected by law. Mud turtle, snapping turtle, and Florida cooter swim among the water lilies, along with an inordinate variety of frogs, toads, and snakes. Although some, like the king and black racer snake, are not dangerous, others, such as the diamondback rattler and cottonmouth, are venomous and can be hazardous. If you're taking a guided excursion in a flat-bottomed boat, the swamp guide will explain how to watch out for these and other reptiles. Most snakes are scared of people and won't go out of their way to attack. Within the boundaries of the refuge is Stephen C. Foster State Park, which offers camping, picnicking, fishing, and boat tours and rentals. Outside the northeastern refuge boundary is Laura Walker State Park, near Waycross, Georgia, which also offers recreational facilities as well as swimming. Okefenokee Swamp Park, in Waycross, is the site of the Swamp Ecological Center and takeoff point for boat journeys through the swamp. Information: Okefenokee National Wildlife Refuge, Rte. 2, Box 338, Folkston, GA 31537 (912 496-3331).

BEST EN ROUTE

The King and Prince Beach Hotel, St. Simons Island – A 96-room resort inn alongside the sea with a good beach, swimming pool, tennis courts, and bike rental. Close to golf, horseback riding, fishing, sailing, and skeet shooting. Dining room open to visitors. See also *Resort Hotels,* DIVERSIONS. PO Box 798, St. Simons Island, GA 31522 (912 638-3631).

Hilton Inn, Jekyll Island – As you'd expect from a former millionaires' paradise, Jekyll Island resorts are still deluxe. This beachfront resort complex has a restaurant, disco, and many other facilities. There are also 9 tennis courts and 63 holes of championship golf on the island. 975 N Beachview Dr., Jekyll Island, GA 31520 (912 635-2531).

Mammoth Cave National Park, Kentucky

An ancient Chinese sage, believing that it is better to be soft and yielding than hard and inflexible, was fond of pointing out that stone, the most rigid of substances, always gives way to water. If Lao-tse were around today, he would find the perfect example of his teachings in Mammoth Cave, a huge system of underground chambers and passageways in central Kentucky that has been hollowed out of stone entirely by the seepage of rainwater and the flowing and dissolving action of underground streams.

Mammoth Cave National Park is off I-65, about 100 miles from Louisville and the same distance from Nashville. The entrance to the main cave is about 9 miles west of Cave City, Kentucky. The longest known cave in the world, Mammoth contains chambers that are two-thirds the length of a football field. Its tallest dome is 192 feet high; its deepest pit is 106 feet deep. Although the entire cave complex lies beneath an area only 10 miles in diameter, its known passageways and chambers wind and twist through five separate levels for more than 300 miles.

If its size alone isn't enough to impress you, consider the cave's fantastic formations: Disney-like shapes in stone that twist and turn, ripple and flow, in infinite variation. Most of these natural sculptures, like strange yet familiar objects in a dream, remind you of a hundred different things at once, but some — usually the larger ones — so strongly suggest particular objects that they have been named: King Solomon's Temple, the Pillars of Hercules, Frozen Niagara, the Giant's Coffin, the Bridal Altar (which has actually been used for weddings). Adding to the dreamlike effect, clusters of gypsum crystals, like rare flowers, hug many of the cave's walls, turning them into exotic hanging gardens.

National Park Service rangers conduct daily tours (except on Christmas) of the most interesting parts of the cave. (No solo exploring is allowed.) And if you weary of the park's subterranean wonders, aboveground are 52,000 acres of beautiful Kentucky woodlands to roam.

The origins of Mammoth Cave go back more than 240 million years to a time when a succession of seas covered this part of the country. The seas left layers of mud, shells, and sand that hardened into limestone and sandstone. After the last sea drained away, rainwater, containing small amounts of carbonic acid, seeped into fissures in the limestone layers, dissolving some of the stone as it percolated down. Over time, the cracks widened and a system of underground streams developed which hollowed out the cave. As the streams cut deeper and deeper into their beds, they continuously lowered the floor of the cave, allowing more and more of the upper regions to dry.

Water not only carved out this mammoth house of stone, it furnished and decorated it as well. As it seeped through the limestone in the dry parts of the cave, it evaporated, leaving a mineral deposit called travertine (also known as cave onyx). Water dripping from the ceiling of the cave over centuries formed chemical icicles of travertine, or stalactites. Water flowing over rock formed waterfalls of travertine, or flowstone. In a similar way, water shaped the cave's pillars, temples, and altars. Even as you marvel at these formations and gasp at the vastness of this underground palace, water, seeping through the limestone and flowing in underground streams, continues the process begun eons ago.

Human beings knew about Mammoth Cave 3,000 years ago. The remains of a mummified man who was apparently killed by a falling boulder while he was chipping minerals from the cave walls indicate that the woodland Indians used to mine gypsum here.

Kentucky pioneers discovered the cave in 1798; since then it has had a varied history. During the War of 1812, saltpeter, an ingredient in gunpowder, was extracted from dirt found on the floor of Mammoth Cave. As almost the only source of saltpeter in the entire country, the cave played an important role in winning the war.

In the 1840s, when the cave was privately owned, a doctor attempted to cure tubercular patients by having them live in the constant temperature (54°F) and humidity (87%) of the cave for several weeks. A few patients died and the rest emerged sicker than before.

Throughout the 19th century, the curious came from far and near to see the cave's wonders by the flickering light of whale-oil lamps. Occasionally, the famous were drawn as well. Edwin Booth, the celebrated Shakespearean actor, recited Hamlet's soliloquy in a chamber of the cave now called Booth's Amphitheater.

There are five main entrances to the cave: the natural or Historic Entrance and four manmade entrances known as Frozen Niagara, Carmichael, Violet City, and New Entrance. You can purchase tickets for a variety of different tours at the visitors center near the Historic Entrance or at Ticketron outlets throughout the US. (Beware of official-looking solicitors who offer to sell you tickets on the way to the visitors center; these people are usually employed by owners of small private caves nearby.)

There are six main tours to choose from — one to suit just about every age and level of endurance. (All tours require sturdy shoes and a warm sweater.) The easiest trip is the Presidential (½ mile, 1½ hours), which takes you to a variety of formations, the largest of which is Frozen Niagara. On the Historic Trip (2 miles, 2 hours) you will see the Rotunda Room, where mineral-laden dirt was processed into saltpeter during the War of 1812, and Mammoth Dome, the highest dome in the cave.

To see some of the most beautiful gypsum formations in the cave, take the Half-Day Trip (4 miles, 4½ hours), on which you will stop for lunch in the Snowball Room, 267 feet underground. It ends at Frozen Niagara.

You will see the cave in an entirely different light when you take the Lantern Trip (3 miles, 3 hours). While electricity makes it easy to see everything, only lantern light creates the proper shadowy atmosphere for cave viewing.

For a shorter tour by lantern light, take the Great Onyx tour (1 mile, 2½ hours), with views of dripstone and gypsum formations and a bus ride through a hardwood forest.

The Echo River tour (3 miles, 3 hours) includes a boat ride on the river but is somewhat strenuous, since it also means enduring steep hills and deep sand.

Persons in wheelchairs need not miss out on Mammoth Cave. A special tour (½ mile, 1½ hours) is available for the physically handicapped.

When you finally emerge from your tour, blinking in the sunlight and dazzled by all the wonders underground, you can restore your senses with a short (1 mile) walk on the Cave Island Nature Trail, which begins and ends near the Historic Entrance. Giant sycamores and beech trees line this trail, which leads to the bottomlands of the Green River. There, underground streams emerge from the caverns belowground. Several other trails wind through the woods on this side of the park.

The least developed and, in many ways, the most beautiful part of the park is its north side. Here, you can walk along the stream beds past waterfalls and natural bridges or meander along the steep bluffs that afford lovely views of the Kentucky hills. To get to this little-known side of the park, take the free car ferry run by paddlewheel and guided by cables across the Green River.

If you have just returned from a cave and have had enough hiking for the day, you can board the *Miss Green River* for a leisurely cruise. The twilight cruise is the best for seeing wildlife: As you sit in comfort, you glide past beaver, turtles, deer, and snakes on the riverbank. Not as exciting as the *African Queen* maybe, but a very pleasant way to pass an hour. You can buy tickets for the cruise at the visitors center.

If your fishing gear is just languishing in the trunk of the car, you can put it to good use in the Green River or in the scenic Nolin River, which runs along the park's western boundary. Fishing permits are not required in the park.

Before you head north to Louisville for the Kentucky Derby (held on the first Saturday of May at Churchill Downs), northeast to the beautiful Bluegrass Country around Lexington, or west to the lake country that borders Tennessee, don't forget to stop at the craft shop at Mammoth Cave National Park. Here you can buy woven items, pottery, metal crafts, baskets, brooms, wood carvings, and dulcimers handmade in the Kentucky hills. Information: Superintendent, Mammoth Cave National Park, Mammoth Cave, KY 42259 (502 758-2328).

BEST EN ROUTE

There are numerous hotels and motels in the area, at Cave City and Bowling Green. Farther afield in central Kentucky, in the general direction of Louisville and Lexington, are a couple of inns of interest that could be comfortably incorporated into a Mammoth Cave visit.

Doe Run Inn, Brandenburg – Close to the Indiana-Kentucky border near the Ohio

River, 40 miles southwest of Louisville, the inn incorporates the remains of an early Kentucky mill, and it is simple, unadorned, and comfortable. One reason for visiting is to eat — chicken, ham, biscuits — traditional Kentucky fare done with great attention. Hwy. 448, Brandenburg, KY 40108 (502 422-2982).

Boone Tavern Hotel, Berea – Run by Berea College and staffed by students; guests are welcome at all college activities. About 40 miles south of Lexington. Main St., Berea, KY 40403 (606 986-9358).

Bayou Country, Louisiana

Technically, a bayou is a bit of waterway that has wandered away from — or been left by — a main river. A huge, slow river will create bayous as it flows across any flat plain, cutting new waterways as rising sediment changes its course, then abandoning them when it changes direction yet again.

That's the dictionary definition of a bayou, but it doesn't begin to describe the bayou country of southern Louisiana, where the Mississippi River flows so slowly, and over such a wide and meandering course, that it has bred bayous like bastard children, a whole world of them, filled with swampgrass patrolled by alligators and cypress forests festooned with Spanish moss. Bayou country — called Acadiana — starts west of New Orleans and covers 22 parishes (counties) from Avoyelles Parish down to the Gulf Coast.

Bayou is actually the French mispronunciation of the Choctaw word *bayuk,* meaning creek or stream. The Choctaw Indians were the first inhabitants of this region. In the mid-1700s they were joined by the Acadians, French inhabitants of Nova Scotia whom the British exiled from Canada. (You may remember *Evangeline,* Longfellow's tragic poem about their trek.) These Acadians — "Cajuns," as they came to be known down here — adapted to the temperate climate, settled in, and gradually turned the bayou country into a French-American enclave unlike anything in the world.

The marriage of bayou and French was felicitous; today the culture remains, though not untouched, still unique. Whimsical Cajun French crops up everywhere: horse races at Evangeline Downs begin with the cry *"Ils sont partis"* instead of "They're off." The unofficial motto of this part of the country is *Laissez les bons temps rouler,* which, if not authentic French, nonetheless translates into an accurate summary of Cajun attitudes — "Let the good times roll."

On a map, Acadiana is in south-central Louisiana, west of Baton Rouge. Its eight parishes include a few largish cities, some spectacular gardens, some local oddities like salt islands that you're not likely to see anywhere else, and a lot of history kept alive by the Cajuns.

Due to its sprawling size, Acadiana does not lend itself to an organized driving route. Part of the charm of a visit here is in meandering like the bayous themselves, traveling wherever highways lead you. A detailed map of Acadiana is absolutely essential, as some of the roads here will not even show up on large state maps. Request a driving map from the Lafayette Convention and Visitors Commission, PO Box 52066, Lafayette, LA 70505 (318 232-3737).

There are dozens of little towns, each with its own festival or its special claim to fame. Remember that you are in the South, where the pace is much less hectic than in other regions of the US. The people are very outgoing — friendlier and more willing to sit for a spell and chat. Add to this Southern hospitality and French charm — and you have the basic ingredients for a memorable vacation. Allow enough time to let yourself get into the slow swing. Certainly try some of the regional cuisine, like crawfish. Join in the local festivals. In short . . . *Laissez les bons temps rouler!*

ATCHAFALAYA BASIN: Running down the eastern third of Acadiana, the Basin is a good place to begin getting familiar with the country — and incredible country it is. The Basin is a swamp of 1,300 square miles, stretching from near Lafayette south to the Gulf. Three times larger than Okefenokee Swamp in Georgia, it receives little notice outside the state because it is totally undeveloped for tourists, with one exception. For an adventure through Atchafalaya Basin, you can board the boat tour that leaves from McGee's Landing near the town of Henderson (take exit 115 off Rte. I-10).

LAFAYETTE: At the intersection of US 167 and I-10, this is the undisputed center of Acadiana. A city with a population of some 100,000, it boasts the usual variety of municipal auditoriums, centers, and museums. But these are not the things that have drawn you to bayou country. There are special Cajun places and events here you'll not want to miss. The Acadian Village (1½ miles off Hwy. 167, north on Ridge Rd.) is a bayou town that has been relocated and restored to reflect life in the 19th century. Visitors can walk through town, stopping at the general store, several open houses, the trading post, and a blacksmith shop. The heart of the village is the Chapel of New Hope; the chapel remains a symbolic heart today because this village exists not only as a historic restoration but also as a fund-raising center for the Alleman Center for Louisiana's handicapped citizens.

In March and April, Lafayette holds the Azalea Trail festivities, when antebellum homes throughout the area open to the public and millions of azaleas grown in the area burst into bloom; it is the perfect time to visit the town.

BREAUX BRIDGE: Here the Crawfish Festival is held in May in even-numbered years. This "crawfish capital of the world," 9 miles northeast of Lafayette (Rte. 94 and I-10), is actually a picturesque Acadian town on the banks of the Bayou Teche. Up to 50,000 hungry visitors come to enjoy this delicacy that restaurants serve in dozens of different ways, all Cajun and all delicious.

ST. MARTINVILLE: This is the area where a great many Acadians first settled, and the town is filled with references to that epic story and Longfellow's poem. (If you read the poem before you visit, it will heighten your appreciation of the town.) In town you can visit Evangeline's grave. The city has a life-size bronze statue of Evangeline, a gift from actress Dolores del Rio after filming the movie here. The town courthouse has a small, intriguing display of early French aristocratic coats of arms, but even more interesting is the Acadian Museum, on the grounds of the Longfellow-Evangeline Commemorative Area just outside town, with live demonstrations of early crafts. The museum is said to be in the house of the man who was Gabriel in the poem. The grounds of the area cover 157 acres.

NEW IBERIA: At the junction of Highways 90 and 14 is the center of the sugar cane industry as well as the home of the romantic Bayou Teche. Here, too, is Shadows-on-the-Teche, a stately old mansion very much like those always associated with the Old South. It's vintage 1830 and is now one of 12 properties owned and maintained by the National Trust for Historic Preservation.

Just outside town are two of those geographical oddities mentioned earlier — islands formed by salt domes that pushed up from the sea-level marshlands millions of years ago. These dome-islands are, as you might imagine, rich in salt. In fact it is mined right there. (Salt from here served the entire Confederate army for the duration of the war.) But there is also an astonishing amount of other natural resources, including oil reserves, and some of America's most fertile earth.

AVERY ISLAND: Though small, it is packed with things to see and marvel over. Jungle Gardens and Bird Sanctuary were both developed by the late Edward Avery McIlhenny. The Gardens are a 200-acre landscaped paradise, featuring exotic growing things from all over the world. The Bird Sanctuary is famous for its huge rookery for egrets. Enormous flocks of herons and egrets and other birds protected here can be seen in warm months. Ducks and other migrating fowl can be seen in winter. Here on Avery Island grow all those tiny but fiery little peppers that go into the supersecret recipe for Tabasco sauce. You can tour the Tabasco plant if you like, but they guard their secret formula jealously.

A final note about Avery Island: It is one of the primary US producers of fur-bearing nutria. Nutria, lest you ask, are fur-bearing mammals also known as coypus, originally from South America. A number of years ago a hurricane allowed some domestic nutria to escape from their cage. They discovered that the bayou agreed with them and proceeded to overpopulate. They are caught today for their fur.

BEST EN ROUTE

Lafayette is basically an ordinary city when it comes to lodgings; an exception is the *Sheraton Acadiana.* Many hotels and motels are comfortable, reasonable, and handy but offer little more than convenience. Outside the city, you can stay in an old plantation house, which will provide a more interesting atmosphere.

Mintmere Plantation House, New Iberia – Built in 1857 and restored in 1976, the guest rooms in this lovely home are decorated with antiques and look out over Bayou Teche. 1400 E Main, New Iberia, LA 70560 (318 364-6210).

Sheraton Acadiana, Lafayette – A modern 6-story, 300-room hotel with 2 restaurants, an outdoor swimming pool, and other amenities, including hot tubs. 1801 Pinhook Rd., Lafayette, LA 70505 (318 233-8120).

Asphodel, near Jackson – A plantation village in the heart of plantation country, close to bayou country. Asphodel is the plantation, open for tours only; the village has smaller buildings: an inn/restaurant, antique train depot used for dinner theater, gift shop, and breakfast room. The cuisine is interesting, mixing Créole cooking with the best of others. Rooms come with "Southern breakfast" (grits, eggs, bacon, and much more). Asphodel Plantation, Rte. 2, Box 89, Jackson, LA 70748 (504 654-6868).

Natchez Trace Parkway, Natchez, Mississippi, to Nashville, Tennessee

For several hundred years before white men settled in the Mississippi and Ohio valleys, the Natchez, Choctaw, and Chickasaw Indians used one major trail to pass north and south. Worn down to a permanent roadbed, the trail — or Trace — wandered for 500 miles from the lower Mississippi River into what was to become central Tennessee. When Kentucky and Tennessee filled up with hunters and trappers, then settlers, the Trace entered the history of commerce. "Kaintuck" boatmen floated their goods downriver on flatboats carried by the Mississippi's currents, but they were obliged to return home on foot (sometimes on horseback). Between the late 1700s and about 1820, the Natchez Trace was a constant thoroughfare. The coming of steamboats changed the history of the Trace. By 1819 there were 20 steam-driven ships plying the Mississippi, eliminating the need for overland portage.

Parts of the Natchez Trace still exist, and today the entire route is commemorated by the Natchez Trace Parkway, a modern highway being built under the auspices of the National Park Service and still under construction, that will run from Natchez, Mississippi, northward through a slip of Alabama, to Nashville, Tennessee. The parkway does not replace the Trace, but it does follow the original route as closely as possible, and there are numerous spots along the way where travelers can park and actually walk (or ride horseback) on the Trace. The parkway's longest continuous section stretches from Jackson, Mississippi, to Shady Grove, Tennessee, 303 miles of quiet two-lane highway with numerous points of interest — Indian mounds, sites of Civil War battles, areas of natural interest, and above all, portions of the Trace that cross the parkway's route — marked by signs. You can follow the Natchez Trace Parkway from Nashville south to Natchez (realizing that the entire route is not yet completed) or from Natchez to Nashville. We start our itinerary, as did the boatmen who used the Trace, at Natchez, traveling north to Tennessee. Information: Superintendent, Natchez Trace Parkway, RR 1, NT 143, Tupelo, MS 38801 (601 842-1572).

NATCHEZ: Before beginning the journey north, spend some time in Natchez itself. When the boatmen ended their downriver journeys here in the first decades of the 19th century, they found a city on its way to getting rich, obsessed with elegance and style, supported by the profitable cotton trade. The rivermen saw little of this elegance or opulence, however. With their wages stuffed in their pockets, they spent most of their time in Natchez-Under-the-Hill, everything a shantytown river city should be. Gamblers, killers, adventurers, and traders gathered there to pursue their respective businesses.

There is little of Natchez-Under-the-Hill today, but there is a great deal to see and do in Natchez itself. It is known as the city "where the Old South still lives," and in town are two antebellum homes of note: Stanton Hall (401 High St.) and Rosalie (100 Orleans St.). Rosalie is the earlier of the two, built about 1820. There are a number of antebellum homes in the area open to the public; a list is available from the Pilgrimage Headquarters (PO Box 347). There's an annual Christmas Pilgrimage for a week in December and for a month every spring — early March to April (and/or two weeks in early October) — when the Pilgrimage and Natchez garden clubs sponsor a daily tour that includes some 30 of the finest antebellum homes in the country. Everything possible is done to create the aura of the Old South: ladies in hoop skirts greet visitors in their spacious parlors, formal gardens are pruned, preened, and open to the public, and the evenings are given over to an annual Confederate Pageant.

Within city limits is the Grand Village of the Natchez Indians (US 61, on Jefferson Davis Blvd.), a National Historic Landmark that has yielded archaeological proof that Natchez is the site of the Natchez Indians' largest village (the "Grand Village"). The Natchez culture peaked in the mid-1500s and came to a disastrous end in 1730, when the French wiped out most of the tribe.

NATCHEZ TRACE PARKWAY: When completed, the parkway will run the full 450 miles between Natchez and Nashville, crossing and recrossing the Trace many times in its course. Today only three segments are open (a total of almost 380 miles): between Lorman and Jackson, Mississippi (about 57 miles); between Jackson and Shady Grove, Tennessee (about 303 miles); and a shorter segment north of Natchez. However, roads leading to these sections are clearly marked, so it is possible to leave from either terminus and follow the route of the Trace.

The parkway is completely free of commercialism. There are no hotels or restaurants along the road. Park rangers patrol the road to provide visitor assistance. There are picnicking facilities at frequent scenic spots and campsites at three campgrounds. Campsites can't be reserved, and there is a 15-day limit on camping. The parkway headquarters is 4 miles north of Tupelo. There you can get maps and information and see a film on the Trace and its history. The parkway features self-guiding tours along the Trace; ask about them at the headquarters.

Today the significance of the Natchez Trace is the history that is buried on or near it. The parkway offers a way of following the Trace while having the most significant aspects of it pointed out as you go. Indian mounds, remains of inns or "stands," as they were called, and talks presented by rangers give a sense of what the Trace was like when it was a footpath that cut through steaming swamps and flatlands, plagued by insects, disease, roving bands of cutthroats (the boatmen who used the Trace were returning home from profitable trading ventures on the Mississippi; as they walked along the dark lane of the Trace, sometimes through sections up to 15 feet below ground level, they would be set upon by thieves), and unfriendly Indians.

Just 12 miles outside Natchez on the parkway is Emerald Mound, one of the largest Indian ceremonial mounds ever found in the US. Built sometime in the 300 years before 1600, Emerald Mound covers nearly eight acres and is representative of the Mississippian Indians who predated the Natchez and Choctaws, who still lived in the area when white explorers discovered it.

Outside Tupelo is Chickasaw Village, the site of a fortified Chickasaw camp. Much of the country around the Trace saw action during the Civil War, and numerous markers note points of historical interest. Though it is off the parkway, anyone interested in the war will certainly want to visit the Tupelo National Battlefield, where some 10,000 Confederate horsemen met 14,000 Union troops. The cavalry engaged the Union forces three times on July 14, 1864, and was defeated each time at a ghastly price in men and horses. Finally the Union troops retreated north, after buying enough time for General Sherman to move his force by rail to begin the attack on Atlanta.

A segment of the parkway 109 miles beyond Tupelo has one special feature, a short section of the actual Trace that can be driven, called the Old Trace Loop Drive. About 2½ miles of the Trace have been paved (though very narrow) and turned into a one-way loop drive for automobiles, featuring several scenic overlooks. Trailers are not recommended to try the loop.

BEST EN ROUTE

Texada, Natchez – Pronounced "te-hada." This fully restored 1792 mansion, part of the yearly Pilgrimage Tour, offers accommodations for overnight guests. Rooms are in the main house, and one has twin sleigh beds. There is also a 3-bedroom guest cottage. 222 S Wall St., Natchez, MS 39120 (601 445-4283).

The Burn, Natchez – Antebellum elegance; 6 rooms for guests. 712 N Union St., Natchez, MS 39120 (601 445-8566).

Carriage House Restaurant, Natchez – In the courtyard of Stanton Hall, the restoration project of the Pilgrimage Garden Club. The menu emphasizes early Southern food and is excellent. 401 High St., Natchez, MS 39120 (601 445-5151).

Cock of the Walk, Natchez-Under-the-Hill – The atmosphere comes from the flatboat days, when boatmen fought one another to earn the right to wear the red feather, signifying they were "cock of the walk." The tavern features red-shirted waiters who serve only one dish — the Mississippi specialty of catfish, with all the trimmings. Natchez-Under-the-Hill, Natchez, MS 39120 (601 446-8920).

Outer Banks and Cape Hatteras National Seashore, North Carolina

The elements reign supreme on the Outer Banks, a 175-mile ribbon of sandy islands — linked by ferries and bridges — running faintly parallel to the North Carolina coast. The ocean and the wind lash at the shoreline, changing its shape, washing away and replacing sand. Storm waves falling across the sand at a particularly narrow point can make two islands where once there was one, and there are spots where only a few hundred feet separate a crashing Atlantic from the calm Pamlico Sound. The visitor will gaze in awe at what the ocean and the wind can do, because a trip to these islands (north to south: Bodie, Pea/Hatteras, Ocracoke, and Cape Lookout) is a trip not of doing but of simply being there and witnessing the ever-writing hand of nature.

Except for one stretch of superhighway — the "motel row" from Kitty Hawk to Nags Head, an area tolerated for the tourists it brings — the Outer Banks are America's seaside wilderness, where man has been defeated by nature and has admitted it. And a good thing, too. With almost all the motels in one area, the rest of the land is under the auspices of the National Park Service and is protected from development (except for some small villages on the islands).

Ghosts haunt the Outer Banks. More than 500 ships sank within just a few miles of its shores, earning it the title "Graveyard of the Atlantic." It began with Sir Richard Grenville's *Tiger* in 1585 and continues today; its most recent victim was the *Lois Joyce* in January 1982. Most famous was the Federal gunboat *Monitor;* it survived a match with the Confederacy's *Merrimac* in March of 1862, but on December 31 of that same year it went under in a Hatteras storm.

The irregular coastline and manic weather made these shores the perfect lair for pirates. In the early 1700s, Edward Teach (Blackbeard) and his band holed up in Ocracoke. It was here, in 1718, that Blackbeard was killed.

This section of ocean offers excellent sport, with scores of fish to be pulled in by surf casters: drum, bluefish, trout, and mackerel.

There's no telling what nature will do next: Birds stop here by the thousands on their way north and south in warm and cold seasons, making the Outer Banks one of the country's prime bird-watching spots. The trees that held the sands in place centuries ago are gone, having been felled for New England shipbuilding by the fishermen who lived here. Today, several picturesque fishing villages remain, accented by wildflowers — thousands of them — whipping in the breezes.

Three approaches link the banks with the mainland: from the north, two bridges, one at Point Harbor at the end of Rte. 158; the other, the extension of Rte. 64, running across Roanoke Island and through Manteo before coming out near Nags Head. From the south, a toll ferry connects Cedar Island and Ocracoke Village. Free ferry service runs from Ocracoke Island to the village of Hatteras. For more information and to make reservations on the ferry from Swanquarter call 919 926-1111; from Ocracoke, call 919 928-3841 or from Cedar Island, call 919 225-3551; reservations are accepted by phone or in person within 30 days prior to the crossing. For details on free ferry service to Hatteras, call 919 986-2353.

KITTY HAWK: A visit can start from either end of the Outer Banks islands, but we'll begin in the north, at Kitty Hawk, because there isn't a schoolchild alive who doesn't associate this little town with Wilbur and Orville Wright and that day in 1903 when a new era began. Commemorating the two bicycle makers from Dayton is a majestic monument, the Wright Brothers National Memorial, 2 miles south of town on the Rte. 158 bypass. Farther south on Rte. 158 is a visitors center (open year-round, except Christmas; free) that displays full-scale reproductions of the 1902 glider and the 1903 "flying machine"; nearby are the reconstructed hangar and living quarters.

The drive south through Nags Head is disappointing; simply ignore the motels that line the road and contemplate the scenery to come. Nags Head is the last town before the Cape Hatteras National Seashore officially begins, and the beach just south of town boasts spectacular sand dunes.

CAPE HATTERAS NATIONAL SEASHORE: A visitors center near the southern end of Bodie Island (signs point the way) is open daily in summer and intermittently in fall and spring; closed in winter. Also stop at the Bodie Island Lighthouse visitors center. Nearby is a nature trail with an observation platform for viewing the bird life.

Before continuing south, cross the bridge to Manteo on Roanoke Island. Just north of town is the Fort Raleigh National Historical Site, commemorating the English colonies settled in 1585 and 1587 by Walter Raleigh and found empty and mysteriously abandoned in 1590. Historians are still puzzled by the disappearance of the colony and the single word *croatoan,* found carved on a palisade post. Today, visitors can tour a reconstruction of the earthwork fort and a nature trail by Roanoke Sound. The site is open daily (except Christmas). Next to the site is the Elizabethan Gardens, a memorial to the colonists, featuring an herb garden, flower gardens, and sculpted lawns. A nightly presentation (in summer, except Sundays) of the historical drama *The Lost Colony* takes place at the Waterside Amphitheater at Fort Raleigh. (See *Outdoor Dramas,* DIVERSIONS.) The gardens are closed from mid-December to early January.

Pea Island is the next bit of land south of Bodie, home of the Pea Island National Wildlife Refuge, 5,880 acres maintained by the US Fish and Wildlife Service. All year long this is one of the East Coast's most populated avian roosting places, but it's especially exciting in late fall, winter, and early spring when birds head south or north. Expect to see great snow geese, gadwalls, Canada geese, loons, grebes, herons, brant, whistling swans, and countless other species of aquatic and migratory birds.

The drive south on Rte. 12 on Hatteras Island deserves unhurried attention because each spot is worth a stop. Markings along the road indicate places for swimming, fishing, viewing hulls of wrecked vessels, and spying on wildlife. At the "elbow" of the island is the village of Buxton, and just south is the Cape Hatteras Lighthouse, America's tallest at 208 feet. It is now closed for safety reasons. If you spend enough time watching the waves and the shifting sands, you'll feel that you're watching the shape of the island change, sand washing away and returning in different configurations. Nearby is the Hatteras Island visitors center, with programs and displays on the island's centuries of maritime activity and industry (open daily except Christmas).

The town of Hatteras, south of Buxton on Rte. 12, is known only as a place to stop for a bite to eat or a quick look around. Stop and talk to some natives and listen for their cockneylike accent. The story goes that Hatteras Village was settled by the survivors of a ship that left Devon, England, and capsized off the coast. To this day, villagers have a "Devon" twang to their speech. A more prosaic explanation made by some is that the sheer isolation of the colonial settlers from Virginia cemented their Elizibethan accents.

The final island in the national seashore chain is Ocracoke, physically the most beautiful. The only town is Ocracoke Village, at the island's southern tip, where ferries from Cedar Island and Swanquarter dock and pick up passengers for the return trip. Stop in the visitors center there (open daily in summer) to pick up brochures on the island's many walks and sights. You should also be sure to visit Cape Lookout National Seashore, the next set of islands to the south. Ferries leave from Harker's Island (passengers only) and the towns of Davis and Atlantic (passengers and four-wheel-drive vehicles) for Cape Lookout. There are no roads on this newly cited national monument to nature, but you can walk around and see unfettered vegetation and the remains of abandoned fishing villages. Of all the areas in the Outer Banks, this is one of the most fascinating and well saved for last. There is little to do, but so very much to see and experience. Information: Cape Lookout National Seashore, PO Box 690, Beaufort, NC 28516.

For more information on campgrounds and anything else in the Outer Banks: Superintendent, Cape Hatteras National Seashore, Manteo, NC 27954 (919 473-2111). National Park rangers are more than willing to help with all your questions by mail, on the phone, or in person. They'll even teach the novice how to surf cast (in summer only); just bring your own bait. For lodging information outside the park: Dare County Tourist Bureau, PO Box 399, Manteo, NC 27954 (919 473-2138).

BEST EN ROUTE

Make reservations to stay in either Kill Devil Hills or Nags Head at the northern end of the island chain outside the seashore park; there is a wide choice of motels and restaurants. (Most establishments close from mid-October to early April; be sure to call or write for exact dates.)

Sea Ranch, Kill Devil Hills – Has an indoor-outdoor pool, indoor tennis, golf privileges, and a nightclub with entertainment. It is north of town, on Rte. 158 at milepost 7, PO Box 325, Kill Devil Hills, NC 27948 (919 441-7126).

Chart House, Kill Devil Hills – In the same area, with comfortable accommodations and a selection of recreational activities — private beach, pool, golf, picnic facilities. Also on Rte. 158 at milepost 7.5. PO Box 432, Kill Devil Hills, NC 27948 (919 441-7418).

Quality Inn Sea Oatel, Nags Head – On its own beach, with most of its rooms overlooking the sea, on Rte. 158 at milepost 16.5. PO Box 489, Nags Head, NC 27959 (919 441-7191).

Blue Heron, Nags Head – Has its own beach as well and bargain rates, very near the *Sea Oatel* on Rte. 158. RR.1, PO Box 741, Nags Head, NC 27959 (919 441-7447).

Hatteras Island Motel, Rodanthe – On the north end of Hatteras Island on Rte. 12. It offers one- and two-bedroom apartments and has a pool and a playground. Write to the motel at PO Box 8, Rodanthe, NC 27968 (919 987-2345).

Island Inn, Ocracoke – A surprise in the town of Ocracoke on Ocracoke Island, with very comfortable rooms overlooking the harbor and, best of all, perhaps the best food in the area. PO Box 9, Ocracoke, NC 27960 (919 928-4351).

While in the area be sure to try *Port O' Call* restaurant, an especially good seafood place with daily specials. On Rte. 158 at milepost 9 (919 441-7484). Another good seafood restaurant is *Evans' Crab House* at the Rte. 158 bypass at milepost 10 (919 441-5994).

There is a choice of clean and well-managed campsites on the Outer Banks: Oregon Inlet (on Bodie Island), Cape Point (Buxton, on Hatteras Island), in Ocracoke, in Salvo (south of Rodanthe), and in Frisco (northeast of Hatteras). The first three are open in late spring, summer, and early fall; the other two, summers only. Information from the Cape Hatteras National Seashore (address above). There are also many private camping facilities available on Hatteras Island.

Great Smoky Mountains National Park, Tennessee and North Carolina

When most people consider US national parks, their thoughts turn to nature's spectacles — shooting geysers, roaring rivers carving out vast canyons, forests turned to stone. The most popular of the national parks has no such superstars but still attracts nearly 9 million visitors annually with its almost perfect serenity. Spread across the southwestern corner of North Carolina and the southeastern tip of Tennessee, the Great Smoky Mountains National Park offers 800 square miles of quiet beauty — virgin forest blanketing a third of the land; 16 rounded ancient mountains reaching 6,000 feet or higher; drives with inspiring views; more than 800 miles of marked trails for hiking and horseback riding; over 600 miles of streams for fishing; lush and varied vegetation; and a romantic, bluish mist from which the Great Smokies derive their name. They are the oldest mountains in America and among the oldest on earth, formed during the Appalachian Revolution, a period that began about 230 million years ago and which lasted many millions of years. The Great Smokies rose as the earth's crust gradually buckled and thrust upward. Whipped, worn, and shaped by eons of storms, winds, and rains, the Smokies survived the weather's onslaught, and today their altitude is better than 5,000 feet for 36 miles along the main crest. Clingmans Dome, the highest peak, arches 6,643 feet upward, and, like its neighbors, almost always wears a veil of blue "smoke." Therein lies one of the Smokies' mysteries. What the Indians once called "smoke" we now know is a mist formed by a mixture of water vapor and oils secreted by plants.

The Smokies support an incredible variety of plants. Nurtured by 60 inches of rain a year, more than 130 species of trees flourish in the park. Some trees here were seedlings when the Europeans came to America, including giants with trunks measuring 25 feet in circumference. Hemlocks, pines, oaks, yellow poplars, mountain laurel, and rhododendrons can be seen as you drive along US 441, which bisects the park. As you drive or climb upward, you encounter diverse flora — southern, New England, and Canadian plant life all on one mountain.

Mt. Le Conte (6,593 feet) is one of the Smokies to explore thoroughly. You can enjoy the view from a distance, but a mountain is more than a big thing to be seen from a car window. To fully appreciate its beauty, ascend Mt. Le Conte by foot or on horseback. There is no road. At its base, southern plants (like dogwood) abound. Higher up, New England sugar maples and yellow birches appear. And thriving near the top are spruce and fir trees, native to southern Canada. During the Ice Age, the glacier advance stopped north of the Smokies. As a result, northern plants migrated south in order to survive and mingled with local species.

On the way up Mt. Le Conte, you can follow the Alum Cave Trail. Crossing Alum Cave Creek, you confront another of the park's mysteries: the laurel hells. Laurel and rhododendron tangle together so inextricably as to be almost impenetrable. Actually, "hellish" is hyperbolic — this vegetation is interesting and beautiful. No one knows why no trees grow on this ground. Perhaps fires swept the area and the rhododendron–mountain laurel brush established itself before trees could. But getting out of a hell can be tricky off the paths. Even bears have difficulty breaking through any other way.

Did someone say bears? Yes, there are many black bears in the Smokies. The black bear is the smallest species of bear in North America, weighing 200 to 300 pounds. However, there is no need to practice 100-yard dashes. Chances are you won't come across any bears, since they tend to shy away from humans, and hikers on trails rarely encounter them. Occasionally, backcountry bears will raid hikers' packs and food supplies, so when camping at night, hang your packs on tree limbs over ten feet high and four feet between the tree trunks. Bolder bears will sometimes beg for food from tourists. Avoid feeding or approaching them. Bears that rely on handouts forget how to forage for food when the tourist season ends. Certainly do not imitate the man who tried to push a bear into his car so that he could take the bear's picture next to his wife. As gentle as bears may seem, they can suddenly turn mean.

Back on the main track, the Alum Cave Trail leads not to Alum Cave (there is none) but to a bluff with a good view. Legend has it that Confederate soldiers came up here to mine alum for gunpowder. What is here is an overhang of black slate 150 feet high and about 300 feet long. On the summit there is a glorious view and a resting spot — *Le Conte Lodge* — well worth the trek up.

Clingmans Dome, the highest peak in the Smokies, is another worthwhile climb. The winding road up leads to a parking lot. From there a paved half-mile trail leads to the summit, continues spiraling up the ramp of an observation tower, and ends in a serene and beautiful view from the Smokies' highest point. The smooth asphalt trail provides access to the view for those in wheelchairs.

Another tranquil spot is Cades Cove, a green Tennessee valley in the park's western reaches. A one-way road circles past cabins, barns, and a gristmill from the days of the pioneers. Many of the 19th-century pioneers who settled this area now rest in the Cades Cove church graveyard.

Gregory Bald is a good example of the kind of wide, green, open meadowland typical of the Smokies' mountaintops and something of a mystery. There is no obvious reason for mountaintop meadowlands, and none of the explanations put forward by park naturalists — wind, fire, or prolonged dry spells killing tree life, making way for meadows — is entirely satisfactory.

Gregory Bald and Clingmans Dome are among the park sites on the famous Appalachian Trail. Stretching from Maine to Georgia, the Appalachian Trail zigzags for 70 miles along the park's crest. Altogether, there are about 870 miles of trails in the Great Smoky Mountains National Park, and many of them can be hiked easily in a day or less. Horseback riding is permitted on about half of them.

For motorists, there are 215 miles of paved roads in the park. The main one, US 441, called Newfound Gap Road, affords splendid views of the mountains as it winds across the park between Gatlinburg, Tennessee, and Cherokee, North Carolina.

Gatlinburg, the northern entrance to the park, sees a large share of the park's visitors. Having just 3,500 permanent residents, Gatlinburg is wall-to-wall motels and tourist shops.

On the park's southern side is Cherokee, the capital of the Cherokee Indian reservation, with the Oconaluftee Indian Village, a replica of an 18th-century Cherokee village, and the Qualla Arts and Crafts Mutual, which has high-quality crafts. (For more information, see *A Short Tour of Indian America,* DIVERSIONS.)

The Great Smoky Mountains National Park is open year-round. The blue mist is thickest in the heat of summer, but the mountains are smoky and majestic in any season. Even on the busiest summer day you can find peace and seclusion here. There is no mystery about why the Great Smoky Mountains National Park is so popular. Information: Superintendent, Great Smoky Mountains National Park, Rte. 2, Gatlinburg, TN 37738 (615 436-5615).

BEST EN ROUTE

Visitors have several lodging options. The park runs seven developed campgrounds, three of which can be reserved in summer (contact park headquarters for information). Those at Cades Cove, Elkmont, and Smokemont are open year-round. Some 98 primitive backcountry campsites can be reserved (at least 30 days ahead), most of which are simply clearings with water; there are also 17 shelters (with chain link fencing fortified against bears) along the Appalachian Trail and other trails for which you must obtain a permit before setting out. Listed below are other lodgings inside the park and nearby. For more information on park facilities and reservations, contact Park Headquarters, Great Smoky Mountains National Park, Rte. 2, Gatlinburg, TN 37738 (615 436-5615).

Le Conte Lodge, Great Smoky Mountains National Park – This secluded retreat atop Mt. Le Conte is accessible only by foot or horse trail. The lodge is on park grounds but privately run, and it can accommodate 40 people with plenty of fresh mountain air and hearty mountain fare. Open from late March through October, space must be reserved. PO Box 350, Gatlinburg, TN 37738 (615 436-4473).

Wonderland Club Hotel, Great Smoky Mountains National Park – Old-fashioned atmosphere with good service and food in a quiet setting. Similar to *Le Conte,* but this hotel can be reached by car. Open late May through October; reservations recommended. Rte. 2, Gatlinburg, TN 37738 (615 436-5490).

Big Bend National Park, Texas

If the call of the wild has got your number, strike out for Big Bend National Park. It's as remote as you can get in the Southwest without actually setting foot into one of the more obscure sections of northern Mexico. About 300,000 visitors come to Big Bend National Park every year — not a huge crowd as parks go, but still more than the intrepid handfuls who braved it in 1944, when this area came under federal jurisdiction. But the national park is only part of a mammoth, exquisite stretch of land, known as the last surviving huge wilderness of Texas. It's still as raw here today as it was when the frontiersmen and women arrived to conquer the Wild West.

Big Bend is literally just that — a big bend in the Rio Grande in southern Texas. If you look at the map, you can see that it's set in that little pocket of Texas that sags slightly to the left of the main body of the state. Although it's not as far south or as far west as you can go by any means, it hugs an interesting corner of the state. It's also nowhere near anyplace you're likely to call civilized. The closest town is Marathon, Texas, about 41 miles north. And the only thing really noteworthy about Marathon is that you have to go through it to get to Big Bend. If you're coming from Dallas/Fort Worth, 545 miles northeast, take I-20 to Rte. 18 south at Monahans. Rte. 18 runs into Rte. 385 south at Fort Stockton, which takes you through Marathon, all the way to Persimmon Gap Ranger Station. Continue on to the administration building and visitors center at Panther Junction in Big Bend National Park.

Because it's so out of the way, lots of people don't get out here. Not that the folks and wildlife in Big Bend really mind — they adore having these isolated, 740,118 acres of canyons and desert all to themselves. You might not understand why anyone would want to live here at all if you go down to the park's lower elevations in summer, when the scorching heat makes it almost too hot to breathe. Dust fills the air, whirling in conical clouds with only an occasional thunderstorm to break the dry agony. Legends about the intolerable July temperatures include the one about a Big Bend coyote chasing a Big Bend jackrabbit. Even though both are swift animals, the story goes, it was so hot, "they was both walkin'." But since the park's altitude ranges from 1,850 to 7,835 feet, there are places to cool off.

If you visit in the spring, there's a good likelihood you'll experience a jubilant awe in the presence of rocky cliffs overflowing with white and crimson blossoms. Although the scenery is a knockout, we can't promise you a sunny garden; Big Bend is notoriously unpredictable when it comes to climate. In February, it can hit the 90s on a Monday and snow six inches or more later in the week. And very often, the temperature climbs 40° during the day, only to drop faster than a stone falls off a cliff after dark.

Millions of years ago the entire area was covered with water. Layers and layers of sand filtered down to the bottom, forming sedimentary rock — in some places, more than 1,000 feet thick. When the ocean dried, the Rio

Grande poked its wet nose into the neighborhood and began winding its way through the rocky plains, wearing a groove in the earth along its path. This same process of water eroding rock was a part of the making of the Grand Canyon.

Any trip to Big Bend should begin at the visitors center at Panther Junction. From there, continue along the road to Chisos Basin, where you can rent horses, pack animals, and guides for day or overnight expeditions. You can also camp here, at the Chisos Basin campground. (Since the Chisos Basin is more than 5,000 feet high, be sure to bring a sleeping bag even in the summer.) You can see spectacular sunsets from here, as the sky cascades into a medley of pink, orange, and purple. Because the desert atmosphere is especially clear, the shimmering changes of color are intense and powerfully moving. White-tail deer occasionally wander past; skunk and javelina also make this their home. You can hear the coyote wail as it gets dark, an eerie, echoing prelude to a harmonious serenade of night birds. Lizards come out in the morning, which is really the best time for human exploration, too. The park takes in an entire mountain range — the Chisos Mountains. The shallow Rio Grande cuts its way through the gorges of Boquillas Canyon and the 1,500-foot-high Santa Elena Canyon. It's a great place to land catfish.

You don't have to rough it to see these canyons, although many people prefer the greater intimacy of traveling on foot. A good driving road leads to Santa Elena and Boquillas canyons. In fact, you can drive for 187 miles through Big Bend. If you want to hike, the rangers will tell you about the trails. There's one to Lost Mine Ridge that takes about 3 hours, round-trip, and another good one to the South Rim. Inquire at Panther Junction visitors center. Information: Superintendent, Big Bend National Park, Big Bend, TX 79834 (915 477-2251).

BEST EN ROUTE

Chisos Mountains Lodge, Big Bend National Park – A small lodge with motel-type units, restaurant, and a supply store, dramatically situated within the park at 5,400 feet. Reservations required year-round. Big Bend National Park, TX 79834 (915 477-2291).

Indian Lodge – This rustic inn in nearby Davis Mountain State Park has 39 air conditioned rooms, pool, restaurant, parking. State-run; access to all park facilities. PO Box 786, Fort Davis, TX 79734 (915 426-3254).

Padre Island National Seashore, Texas

Like the coasts of New Jersey and the Carolinas, Texas's Gulf of Mexico shoreline is blessed with a series of long, lean islands that lie just offshore and follow the great arc of the Gulf Coast with almost perfect fidelity. The last and longest of these islands is Padre Island, 115 miles of sand and grass that stretch along the south Texas coast, roughly from Port Aransas just above

Corpus Christi to Port Isabel, where Mexico and Texas meet like two lips puckering to kiss the Gulf.

Padre Island is really two islands separated by a tiny channel of sea: South Padre Island, the southernmost 35 miles of the island; and North Padre Island, covering 80 miles, 65 miles of which is designated as the Padre Island National Seashore. The national seashore is a stretch of sand, grass, dunes, and sea where you stand a good chance of witnessing nothing but the work of nature — waves beating against the shore, acres of grasslands, and, if you're lucky, not another human being, just the thousands of birds and shore animals that live here or visit during migrations.

Development is contained in settlements predominantly confined to the northern and southern extremities of Padre Island, where you will find the motels, hotels, restaurants, resort communities, condominiums, and highways that have made the south Texas coast famous. As if it weren't enough to have these civilizations coexisting, Padre Island is an anomaly because the two ways of life get on together very well.

The "port" cities — Port Aransas in the north and Port Isabel in the south — are the main points of development as well as being two of the three gateways to Padre; the third gateway is park road 22, which runs east out of Corpus Christi. If you've come to visit the seashore, you'll almost have to stay in or near one of the port cities; that's not so bad. If you've come to visit the cities and enjoy their very relaxed, sun-filled, pleasure-dome existence, that's not so bad, either, so long as you make some time to visit what nature has wrought.

PORT ARANSAS: Actually on Mustang Island, an "adopted" part of the Padres. The University of Texas Marine Science Institute is here, a reminder of the area's primary — if not only — industry, the sea. Charter trawlers crowd the town's small harbor, waiting to plow the bountiful Gulf waters in search of tarpon, sailfish, snapper, tuna, and countless other breeds of fighters. A hefty catch is almost guaranteed every time you set out with rod and reel. (Many of the deep-sea party boats are equipped with motorized reels: Get a nibble, flick the switch, and land your catch. If, like many people, you feel this method eliminates the sport in fishing, be sure to check out the equipment when you rent.) May through July, the town is filled with anglers in for the Deep-Sea Roundup, a contest to see who can land the biggest and who can land the most. Other attractions center on the 18 miles of sparkling white beach, focal point for surfers, surf casters, swimmers, and surfside drives.

There is direct access to the national seashore from Port Aransas, but before going over, visit the Aransas National Wildlife Refuge on the mainland. To get there take Rte. 35 through Aransas Pass and go just beyond the tiny hamlet of Lamar. The 54,000 acres of the Aransas National Wildlife Refuge have been set aside for the nearly extinct whooping crane, visible in the colder months, when the cranes come down from Canada. (The refuge is open daily; admission is free.) There is an observation tower and an information station as well as trails for spying on the natives by foot or car. An alternative to a park visit is a cruise up Aransas Bay past the water side of the refuge for less obstructed views of the cranes. Cruises leave from Rockport and must be arranged at its harbor.

PADRE ISLAND NATIONAL SEASHORE: Return to Port Aransas and take Rte. 53 south, the single highway that links Mustang Island with North Padre. After making the crossing, one of the first sights is Malaquite Beach, with a visitors center that's open year-round and an excellent campground for trailers and the hearty few who tent on the beach. (Up and down Padre the beaches are open for overnight guests, but camping is not allowed in the dunes or grasslands. For more information, contact the Superintendent, address below.)

There are no towns or any other signs of man's existence in the national seashore park. Once upon a time, the grasslands that cover the inland portions of the island — from the beaches of Laguna Madre in the west to the beaches of the Gulf of Mexico in the east — were grazing land for cattle. Padre Nicholas Balli, the Spanish monk after whom the island chain is named, started raising livestock here in 1800, but the cattle, cowboys, and monks are gone, and the grasses are returning to the sandy soil.

Other men have been here in the last 500 years, mostly Spaniards in the 16th, 17th, and 18th centuries, chasing or being chased by pirates. And the shallow waters of the Gulf side took their toll of vessels, including many a royal treasure ship. It's acknowledged by the residents and seashore personnel that millions of dollars in silver and gold are probably buried in the Padre sand or lost just off the coast. For this reason, the seashore is off limits to metal detectors and today's treasure hunters. The natural splendor will not be violated by fortune seekers.

To travel around the greater part of the national seashore other than on foot assumes that you own or have rented a four-wheel-drive vehicle. But note that driving on the dunes and in the grasslands is prohibited.

However you go, watch for the diverse and utterly fascinating collection of animal life. On the ground, the island is crawling with creatures like coyote, ground squirrels, gophers, and kangaroo rats. At least 12 different types of snakes are known to reside in the tall grasses, including two species of rattlers. Watch out for these unfriendly fellows. (Campgrounds and other areas designated for two-legged guests can be assumed safe from potentially dangerous visitors.) In the air and alighting everywhere are hundreds of birds of different species: herons, willets, black skimmers, marsh hawks, pelicans, avocets, horned owls, peregrine falcons, and swarms of sanderlings. They come from Mexico and Central America in the spring or pass through on their way south in fall and early winter. Year-round, Padre is an avian amusement park.

Of course, wherever you go, there is fishing. The beaches of Padre are regarded as among America's best for variety and sheer volume. Standing on the beach throwing your tackle to the surf, you may be the only person visible for miles. There may not be another soul to hear your victory shout after a half hour fight with a shark — a fairly common catch in this part of the Gulf.

Near Malaquite Beach is the Grasslands Trail, a well-marked trek through the tall grasses (visitors are forbidden to walk on the dunes). The walk offers a look at many types of the island's native growth, including sea oats, railroad vines, croton, wild indigo, and a last vestige of Virginia live oak. The walk is also impressive for its museumlike representation of how dunes are formed. You may think that the dunes — in every stage of formation from small sand drifts to hills — have been prepared as some kind of exhibit. But no, these are real drifts, in the normal and natural process of being shaped by wind, weather, and sand shifts. For Grasslands Trail information, call the Malaquite Beach visitors center, 512 949-8068. General information: Superintendent, Padre Island National Seashore, 9405 S Padre Island Dr., Corpus Christi, TX 78418 (512 937-2621).

SOUTH PADRE ISLAND: Because no road runs the full length of either North or South Padre, you'll have to get back on mainland roads to reach South Padre. The southern tip of the island is being carefully developed as a vacation paradise, so hotels and motels and miles of sporting pleasures line the white-yellow beach and turquoise water. The causeway through Port Isabel comes out near Isla Blanca Park. There you'll find a bathhouse and cabanas, plus overnight accommodations for sleeping under the stars. There are also food concessions, water-skiing facilities, a trailer park, and a children's recreation area.

PORT ISABEL: Just across the Laguna Madre and connected to South Padre by the Queen Isabella Causeway is Port Isabel, a growing but still peaceful resort town — one of the South's first vacation centers, the favorite of Texas society dating back to the mid-1800s. Port Isabel is primarily a fishing town, with the world's largest shrimping fleet tying up here and a little farther into the bay at the port of Brownsville, and the harbor is home port for many deep-sea charter fishing boats.

Just west of town on Rte. 100 is the smallest state park in this state famous for big things, the Port Isabel Lighthouse Historic Site. The lighthouse dates from the 1850s when gold rush fever made Port Isabel a popular stop for folks on the way west. The lighthouse also overlooks the site of Fort Polk, a Mexican War camp and depot that was commanded by General Zachary Taylor. The last land battle of the Civil War was also fought in the neighborhood, at Palmito Hill. The lighthouse is open daily, 9 AM to 5 PM, with an admission charge.

If you're in Port Isabel, take a quick drive across the Mexican border to Matamoros, a town featuring markets for jewelry, leather, and clothing as well as some authentic Spanish restaurants and nightclubs. They accept American currency, and only proof of citizenship is necessary to cross the border.

At the end of any visit through the untamed, natural, sandy expanses of North Padre Island, you'll find South Padre, and especially Port Isabel, quiet, relaxed enclaves perfect for enjoying a warm sun, sparkling water, and deluxe accommodations. For more information on accommodations and activities on South Padre: The South Padre Island Tourist Bureau, PO Box 2095, South Padre Island, TX 78597 (512 943-6434).

BEST EN ROUTE

There is no shortage of top-flight accommodations in either Port Aransas or Port Isabel.

The Beachhead, Port Aransas – Just a boardwalk away from the beach. One- and two-bedroom apartments available with kitchens; parking, a coin laundry, and a heated pool. Balcony views look over the Gulf. PO Box 1577, Port Aransas, TX 78373 (512 749-6261).

Executive Keys, Port Aransas – On the Gulf, with balcony views from almost every room. Recreation facilities include lawn games, golf privileges, volleyball. All of the two- and three-bedroom kitchen-equipped suites have dishwashers and such amenities. PO Box 1087, Port Aransas, TX 78373 (512 749-6272).

Island Retreat, Port Aransas – A fisherman's delight, offering fish cleaning and freezing facilities for guests. Most apartments have balconies on the Gulf and convenience appliances. Also has two pools, access to the ocean, and a raft of recreational activities. PO Box 637, Port Aransas, TX 78373 (512 749-6222).

South Padre Hilton Resort Hotel, South Padre Island – The cream of South Padre Island's hotel-apartment offerings, with a large new condominium tower, a private beach, a club for dining and dancing, an Olympic-sized pool, and tennis. PO Box 2081, South Padre Island, TX 78597 (512 943-6511).

Bahia Mar, South Padre Island – The *Hilton*'s competition, with two pools and saunas, tennis courts, a putting green, and entertainment nightly. Choice of accommodations from rooms to apartments and town houses. PO Box 2280, South Padre Island, TX 78597 (512 943-1343).

Most people on the island cook for themselves, and there is a shortage of good restaurants besides the cafés and roadhouses that line the highways. For first-class meals, locals and long-time summer residents drive into Corpus Christi or Brownsville.

When on South Padre Island, you might try the *Jetties* (Rte. 100; 943-6461) for a wide choice in seafood; its known especially for fresh jumbo Gulf shrimp.

For more information, contact these local service organizations: Corpus Christi Area Convention and Tourist Bureau, PO Box 2664, Corpus Christi, TX 78403; Cameron County Park Board, PO Box 666, Port Isabel, TX 78578.

Midwest

The Lincoln Heritage Trail, Illinois, Indiana, and Kentucky

The Lincoln Heritage Trail blazes 2,200 miles along the folkloric roads of Illinois, Indiana, and Kentucky, Abraham Lincoln's home states. Here, his voice still echoes around every bend: eloquently in government chambers, softly in great Victorian mansions, and jokingly in the backwood cabins of his close friends. Along the trail, memories of Mr. Lincoln are vividly recollected through reenactments of scenes from America's past and reconstructions of stately buildings, quaint homesteads, and entire 19th-century towns. The route that follows is a living history book, tracing Lincoln's footsteps through frontier America.

SPRINGFIELD, Illinois: Here you will see and hear more about Abraham Lincoln than anywhere else in the US. Start with Lincoln's own residence (the only house he ever owned) on 8th and Jackson sts. One of a row of handsome period homes, it has been repainted in its original colors of Quaker brown and apple green and furnished with some Lincoln family possessions. Informative tour guides minutely detail Lincoln's home life. Open daily.

The Old State Capitol on Public Square, where Lincoln gave his famous "House Divided" speech, has been completely rebuilt, and the stunning second-floor legislative chamber looks as if a session had just adjourned. The Illinois State Historical Library is on the bottom floor. Open daily except Sundays. On summer evenings a sound and light show colorfully depicts Lincoln's accomplishments in Springfield. Presented on the mall facing the building at 9 PM except Mondays.

A 117-foot granite obelisk marks the Lincoln Tomb site in Oak Ridge Cemetery. The tomb's rotunda contains a single statue of Lincoln and a few bronze plaques, creating a solemn and dignified tribute; at the rear of the memorial, a monument to Lincoln is enclosed in a semicircular chamber, flanked by flags and remnants of the longest funeral procession in history. On the opposite wall are the crypts of Mary Todd Lincoln and three of the couple's four sons.

A few miles from Springfield I-55, in the city of Lincoln, are the Lincoln College Museum, which houses an impressive array of memorabilia, and the Postville Courthouse, where almost-7-feet-tall Charlie Ott impersonates Lincoln and relates anecdotes of his travels as a circuit court lawyer. Maps outlining the route Lincoln rode and documents stating the bylaws of this early court system cover the walls.

NEW SALEM, Illinois: The next site on the trail is the village of New Salem, reconstructed to look exactly as it did when Lincoln lived here in the 19th century. You'll see mammoth oxen pulling covered wagons along dirt roads lined with tiny log cabins, and a visit to the cabins finds period-costumed women kneading dough, cooking over flaming hearths, and spinning wool. During the summer months, beginning at sunset, you can watch one of the three outdoor dramas held nightly, except Mondays: *Your Obedient Servant, A. Lincoln; Even We Here;* and *Abraham Lincoln Walks at Midnight.* (If it rains, performances are held at the Senior Citizens Center at Petersburg, a 5-minute drive away.)

VINCENNES, Indiana: The trail through Lincoln country cuts into Indiana at the border town of Vincennes, the original capital. Called "the Birthplace of the West," it's a tribute to early American growth. Visit the George Rogers Clark Memorial and Visitors Center, an awesome structure that contains several massive murals by Ezra Winter. Headsets, distributed at the entrance, explain each mural and its relevance to the American past.

The Log Cabin visitors center provides tickets for the Trailblazer tour on a trolley-like bus that winds its way through the Mile of History in the old state capital.

HISTORIC NEW HARMONY, Indiana: Take a break from Lincoln and visit New Harmony, another landmark in American history. Originally a tract of wilderness on the banks of the Wabash, the village grew from settlements of religious and utopian communal sects. First came the Rappites (or Harmonists), led by Father George Rapp, who preached that the second coming of Christ would occur in their lifetime. Later came the Owenites, a group of experimenting intellectuals looking to improve the quality of life.

The placid walkways of New Harmony are lined with restored, sparsely furnished houses and Harmonist dormitories. Ticket books purchased at the visitors center provide access to many buildings, including the Atheneum, an architectural award winner, the Roofless Church, and the Opera House. Be sure to wander through the labyrinth — a reconstruction of the sect's maze symbolizing the twisting road of life to perfect harmony.

LINCOLN CITY, Indiana: Now pick up the Heritage Trail in Lincoln City (on Rte. 162, off US 231) at the Lincoln State Park and the Lincoln Boyhood National Memorial. The memorial features a museum, a working pioneer farm on the site of the farm Lincoln's father owned from 1816 to 1830, and the burial place of his mother. The state park has many recreational facilities, and both areas have self-guided history-nature trails. Entrance fee for the state park. The grounds are open daily except on Christmas and New Year's.

JEFFERSONVILLE, Indiana: Shortly before reaching Jeffersonville you can take a side trip to Wyandotte Cave in Harrison Crawford Wyandotte Woods and Cave, on Rte. 62 in Leavenworth. It is one of the largest cave complexes in North America. Then, off I-65, is the town of Jeffersonville. Perched on the banks of the Ohio River, the Howard Steamboat Museum (in James Howard's former home) displays intricately carved models of his 19th-century masterpieces. Outside the window, the *Belle of Louisville* steamboat still chuffs by.

Cross the Ohio River into Louisville. For a complete report on the city and its attractions, see *Louisville,* THE AMERICAN CITIES.

HODGENVILLE, Kentucky: Abe Lincoln's life in Kentucky began in a tiny cabin nestled among the bluish-green, "Knob" hills of north-central Kentucky. Take I-65 to Hwy. 61 and the Abraham Lincoln Birthplace and National Historic Site in Hodgenville. A section of this national park is actually Sinking Springs Farm, where Lincoln was born in 1809. An elaborate memorial building has been erected around the original family cabin. A faulty land deed uprooted the family when Lincoln was only two and provoked their move to Knob Creek, where the family lived for seven years. The primitive Lincoln log cabin stands reconstructed among the lushest of bluegrass hills.

BARDSTOWN, Kentucky: Continue northeast on Hwy. 31E for a pleasant stop at Bardstown, where you'll find the Federal Hill estate better known as "My Old Kentucky Home." Tour the grand estate and its mansion, where Stephen Foster supposedly wrote the famous song. Have lunch in Bardstown under the cozy brick arches of *La Taberna Restaurant*, at 5th St. and Xavier Dr.

LEXINGTON, Kentucky: Next, it's northeast to Lexington via US 150 and US 68, the scenic palisades road. In Lexington, off Rte. 68 (which becomes Broadway) on West Main Street, is Mary Todd Lincoln's childhood home. This grand house personifies her life in the aristocracy and contradicts Lincoln's background completely: Meticulously crafted antiques and exquisitely detailed carpets crown the polished wooden floors. 578 W Main St. Open from April to mid-December; closed Sundays and Mondays. Admission charge.

BEST EN ROUTE

New Harmony Inn, Historic New Harmony, Indiana – This inn's 45 rooms all have simple wood furnishings and some have working fireplaces, kitchenettes, and small balconies. The atmosphere reflects the quiet, easy pace of the community. No television or radio. Complimentary Continental breakfast served in the adjoining building. New Harmony Inn, Box 581, New Harmony, IN 47631 (812-682-4491).

Overlook Restaurant, Leavenworth, Indiana – This restaurant has a wonderful view of the Ohio River and the best in home-style cooking: Heaping portions of mashed potatoes, vegetables, and biscuits accompany Southern fried chicken and other entrées. Hwy. 62, Leavenworth, IN (812-739-4264).

Isle Royale National Park, Michigan

Imagine yourself on a remote island where there are no cars, no roads, and where the only sound you are likely to hear at night is the call of a loon, the cry of a wolf, or the wind in the trees. If the thought appeals, your destination should be Isle Royale, largest of the 200 islands and islets that make up Isle Royale National Park in Lake Superior. Isle Royale — the dominant island for which the park was named — lies parallel to the northwest shore of Lake Superior, like a long candle flame pointing north, 44 miles long and between 5 and 9 miles wide. Open in summer only, this isolated bit of wilderness in Lake Superior has changed little since French trappers took possession of it and named it in honor of Louis XIV.

Though closer to the Minnesota-Canada border, the park officially is part of Michigan. You can reach Isle Royale from both the Michigan and the Minnesota shores of Lake Superior. Access from Michigan is through the town of Houghton, by seaplane or ferry. (It is about a 6-hour ferry ride to Isle Royale; a splendid grace period in which to leave civilization behind and contemplate the real isolation of the island.) The route to Houghton from St. Ignace (the town at the northern end of the Mackinac Straits Bridge, which links Michigan's Upper and Lower peninsulas) takes you through the land of Hiawatha, the Ojibwa Indian immortalized in Longfellow's poem.

The shorter route to Isle Royale is from Minnesota. The ferry leaves Grand Portage, just below the Canadian border, 150 miles north of Duluth. The Duluth–Grand Portage section of US 61 offers one of the most scenic shore drives in the US. And in Grand Portage you can visit the national monument that marks the site of the "great depot" of early fur trading days.

Another ferry runs from Copper Harbor, about 50 miles north of Houghton; the trip takes about 4½ hours. The ferry accommodates passengers only; cars are not allowed on the island. There are ample parking facilities. For information on ferry schedules and reservations, write the Superintendent of the park.

Hundreds of millions of years ago, lava flows formed the earliest rock of Isle Royale. During the glacial period, a layer of ice a mile high covered the island, but when the ice melted and the resulting lake receded a bit, Isle Royale emerged — "an island of rock rising abruptly from the lowest depths of the lake in irregular hills to a height varying from 100 to 450 feet above the level of the lake," as Michigan's first state geologist put it in 1841. A thin layer of soil, in some places no more than a few inches deep, covers the rock like icing on a cake, but it is enough for spruce, balsam, pine, aspen, and birch to thrive.

As you make your way across the water to Isle Royale, leaving the mainland shore farther and farther behind, you will begin to get a sense of the isolation that has deeply affected the island's ecology. Only birds and animals that have been able to fly, swim, or drift across from the mainland are found on Isle Royale. Moose suddenly appeared for the first time on the island around 1912 and, without a predator, multiplied so fast that the plant browse became scarce on the island and overpopulation threatened to reduce the herds. A fire in 1936 stimulated the growth of new browse and, in the winter of 1948-49, wolves crossed the ice from Canada, restoring the ecological balance.

Over 160 miles of hiking trails, springy with moss and spruce needles, take the place of roads on Isle Royale. The trails lead to lookout towers with sweeping views, sheltered inlets along the pebbled shore, abandoned copper mines now buried deep in blueberry thickets, and silent inland lakes (over 20 of them), where at sunrise or sunset you are likely to glimpse a moose. More than 30 campgrounds are scattered across the island.

Hiking offers an opportunity to observe some of the island's abundant wildlife, which includes beaver, muskrat, mink, weasel, squirrels, the snowshoe hare, and red fox as well as moose. There are also wolves, but they are extremely shy of human beings. Herring gulls and warblers are plentiful, but you will also see pileated woodpeckers, osprey, and loons among the 200 species of birds on the island. There are hundreds of common wildflowers as well as such rarities as yellow lady's slipper, bog kalmia, swamp candle loosestrife, and some 30 different species of orchids.

Such unspoiled wilderness has its price. You won't, for example, find flush toilets at the campgrounds. Noncampers can stay in the comparative luxury of the *Rock Harbor Lodge,* but in general, if you turn pale at the thought of roughing it, Isle Royale is probably not for you.

One of the best ways to explore the island's interior is to walk its length. To do this, take the Greenstone Ridge Trail, which connects *Rock Harbor Lodge* at the eastern end of the island with Washington Harbor at the western end, 40 miles away. This hike will take you several days. A much shorter but very rewarding walk is the trail to Mt. Franklin, where you can continue on to Ojibway Lookout, offering a fine view of the Canadian mainland from the tower. If you take the trail that leads to Monument Rock, a 70-foot-high natural tower that has been sculpted by waves and ice, you can continue past the rock to Lookout Louise, which offers the best views in the entire park.

A fine trail leads to the old Rock Harbor Lighthouse, built in 1855 to guide the boats sent by mining companies to take out the island's copper. The lighthouse guards what one member of the team on the US Linear Survey of 1847 called "the most beautiful harbor in Lake Superior." This same gentleman reported seeing mirages of islands and mountains off Isle Royale's coast.

On the west end of the island, a trail leads from Washington Creek to an abandoned copper mine that was worked until the turn of the century, when it was no longer considered profitable. A boat makes a full circuit around the island several times each week. (For information, write Isle Royale Transportation Lines, PO Box 754, Duluth, MN 55801, 218 728-1237.) There are also shorter excursions to nearby islands, boat rentals at *Rock Harbor Lodge,* and a marina for small private craft at Rock Harbor. If you want to canoe, bring your own or rent one at Rock Harbor or Windigo. The park's canoeing brochure indicates the best routes.

Anglers will find pike, walleye, perch, and even some whitefish in the island's inland lakes, brook trout in its streams, and lake trout in Lake Superior. You don't need a license for the inland waters of the park, only for Lake Superior. If you plan to camp overnight, you must obtain a permit from the headquarters in Rock Harbor.

To learn more about the flora and fauna you have seen during the day, you can attend one of the evening programs that are given at Windigo, *Rock Harbor Lodge,* and Daisy Farm Campground. Information: Superintendent, Isle Royale National Park, Houghton, MI 49931 (906 482-0984).

BEST EN ROUTE

Rock Harbor Lodge, Isle Royale – At the eastern end of the island, this offers 20 housekeeping lodges, 60 rooms, a dining room and snack bar. You can buy camping supplies and food here as well. Reservations between mid-June and Labor Day: National Park Concessions, PO Box 405, Houghton, MI 49931 (906 337-4993); the rest of the year: National Park Concessions, Mammoth Cave, KY 42259 (502 773-2191).

Isle Royale Campsites – There are 36 campgrounds along the shores and inland lakes. Some offer screened shelters and minimal facilities. There are usually enough shelters for all, but it's best to bring your own tent just in case. A park ranger or camping brochure will tell you how long you will be able to stay at each site.

St. Croix River, Minnesota and Wisconsin

Many people say the territory around the St. Croix River is haunted. They say that spirits of the Indians who lived here for many generations are still a strong presence in the birch and pine forests lining the riverbanks. There are even some who say the Indians' shadowy birchbark canoes still make their way through the tributaries and creeks feeding into the St. Croix, and that you can hear the rustle of paddles breaking water if you listen in the silence.

More prosaic travelers, less inclined to give credence to tales of ghostly wanderers, are nonetheless enchanted by the magic of the St. Croix — a 164-mile stretch of water separating Minnesota and Wisconsin that was one of the first to be granted federal protection under the Wild and Scenic River Act of 1968. It's surprising to find such a relatively unspoiled section of country close to a big city, but you don't have to travel very far from the cosmopolitan Twin Cities, Minneapolis–St. Paul, to get to the lower St. Croix. It's just 25 miles northeast of St. Paul on Rte. 36.

Although the lower St. Croix valley is dotted with attractive villages, the untamed upper St. Croix hasn't changed much from Indian times. In fact, the Ojibwa (or Chippewa), descendants of the Algonquin, still harvest wild rice from the fertile crannies hidden among the small inlets lacing the surrounding marshes. But the placid waters bear a history of conflict.

The Dakota Indians lived here first, treasuring the river for its fish, the land for its wild rice, and the forest for its many kinds of game. (Otter, beaver, raccoon, fox, and deer still make their home in these woods. After more than 350 years of wars, the Dakota were driven out by the Ojibwa, who had moved in from the East after unsuccessfully trying to defend their land from Iroquois attack. While the Ojibwa and Dakota battled, the French explorers and traders arrived, calling the Dakota a derogatory Ojibwa name, Sioux. After the Ojibwa victory, the Sioux fled south and west, eventually to be vanquished by the whites.

The French used the St. Croix as a fur connection, establishing many trading posts along its banks and developing the waterway into a flourishing commercial route. Beaver pelts were sold and shipped to Canada, and from there to Europe, where they found their way to the haberdashers of the fashionable. The intense struggle to control this resource-rich territory was not confined to the Indians and the French. The British were avid for supremacy, too, and in 1763, when the French and Indian wars were finally over, the Union Jack flew from the masts and flagpoles along the St. Croix. The Hudson Bay Company and other trading enterprises of the period conducted a brisk business until the War of 1812, when the US imposed a ban on foreign trading activity in the area. Then the loggers arrived. Thousands of men felled hundreds of thousands, perhaps even millions, of trees, mostly white pine, and the river was used to float logs. Innumerable lumberjacks perished while dynamiting logjams that clogged the river's flow. The lumbering era is a strong part of the historic legacy of the valley, and St. Croix residents still compete in logrolling contests. The logging came to an end when there were no longer enough trees for the industry to operate profitably. Since then, the region has been marked for conservation, and many people are working through a number of organizations to prevent further exploitation and destruction of the forest.

STILLWATER: The birthplace of Minnesota is a riverfront town 25 miles from St. Paul. Stillwater's the kind of place where they consider you a newcomer unless at least

one generation of your family is in the cemetery. But don't let that throw you —
it's a great place to visit, full of charming old buildings, fine antiques shops, emporiums,
and cafés. If you'd like to charter an old twinstack steamwheel boat, go to the Stillwater
Levee in Lowell Park, where you can rent the 200-passenger *Andiamo Showboat* or the
60-passenger yacht *Andiamo Too*. If you're visiting in May, be sure to take in the
Rivertown Arts Festival, at which artists from all across the US display their works;
it's held for two days in Lowell Park on the banks of the St. Croix. For information
on logrolling contests, fireworks, and the pageantry of Stillwater's annual Lumberjack
Days (midsummer), contact Stillwater Area Chamber of Commerce, 101 W Pine,
Stillwater, MN 55082 (612 439-7700). For sightseeing tours of the upper and lower St.
Croix, call Valley Tours (612 439-6110).

MARINE-ON-ST. CROIX: At one time a dynamic lumberjack town, Marine-on-St.
Croix has lost much of that rip-roaring, freewheeling atmosphere that characterized its
formative years during the tree-tumbling era, but you can muse about what the old days
must have been like in William O'Brien State Park overlooking the river.

TAYLORS FALLS and ST. CROIX FALLS: Canoe enthusiasts will probably head
straight for these two towns sitting across the river from each other about 28 miles
north of Stillwater. This is the dividing line between the upper and lower St. Croix.
Here, the picturesque, tranquil southern stretch becomes rugged whitewater. (Actually,
it's the other way around, since the St. Croix flows from north to south, but as you're
most probably driving from the south, it will seem as if the peaceful part of the river
ends and the wild section begins.) The land is relatively unsettled from this point north,
which makes it ideal for back-to-the-woods people. The dramatic disparity between
upper and lower St. Croix has its roots in the glacial and postglacial era, which formed
two great lakes out of melting ice about 10,000 years ago. The water melting from
glacial Lake Grantsburg, which covered much of Minnesota, flowed south, forming the
St. Croix. When the entire mass of ice covering the hemisphere began to recede, glacial
Lake Duluth, the predecessor of Lake Superior, was unable to drain east because of
a huge section of ice that refused to melt. The excess water began cutting its way
through sand, gravel, and boulders of what is now the St. Croix Valley, in the process
forming the great gorge known as the Dalles. The path of the new glacial river also
bored giant kettle holes, which are responsible for the tricky currents that challenge
today's canoeists. (For a list of outfitters and other information, contact State of
Wisconsin Dept. of Development, Madison, WI 53707; 608 266-2161; 800 ESCAPES
in the Midwest.) If you are unwilling to tackle the frothy, churning waters of the Upper
St. Croix in a canoe, you might consider a day trip on the St. Croix Dalles as a safer
alternative. Excursions take you past geological formations in the river while guides
explain what each is and how it was formed. Taylors Falls Scenic Boat Tours (PO Box
225, Taylors Falls, MN 55084; 612 465-6315 or 612 291-7980) run these trips daily
from June through October. They also operate the *Kathy M* (an imitation paddlewheeler), the *Taylors Falls Queen* (the genuine article), and the 250-passenger *Taylors
Falls Princess* (also authentic). For information about a houseboat vacation on the St.
Croix, write to Great River Harbor, Route 1, Box 189A, Alma, WI 54610 (608
248-2000; 800 328-8303). For maps showing canoe routes throughout Minnesota,
contact the Minnesota Office of Tourism (240 Bremer Bldg., 419 N Robert, St. Paul,
MN 55101; 800 652-9747 in Minnesota, 800 328-1461, elsewhere). If you enjoy looking
at the great outdoors but don't care to spend the night, you can head back to Minneapolis–St. Paul on Rte. 8 west to I-35 south.

BEST EN ROUTE

Lowell Inn, Stillwater – More than 50 years old, this hotel and restaurant built in
red brick Colonial style is known as the "Mount Vernon of the West." It's run

by the 11 members of the Palmer family. 102 N 2nd St., Stillwater, MN 55082 (612 439-1100).

Voyageurs National Park and Boundary Waters Canoe Area, Minnesota

Centuries before there were roads in North America, the Indians in their birchbark canoes traveled a network of lakes, streams, and connecting portage trails that stretched from the Rocky Mountains to the St. Lawrence River. In the heyday of the great fur trade, French-Canadian voyageurs plied this natural highway, paddling and portaging huge quantities of furs east to Montréal and great numbers of soldiers, explorers, and missionaries west to the frontier. The last of the voyageurs disappeared in the 1830s, but in Voyageurs National Park and the Boundary Waters Canoe Area in northern Minnesota, you can still get a taste of what it was like on the old voyageur highway in the days when the splash of a paddle was the only manmade sound on these waters and the wilderness stretched as far as the eye could see.

Voyageurs National Park and the Boundary Waters Canoe Area are part of the oldest landmass in the world. Glaciers shaped this land, scooping out its lake basins, scoring its surface with an intricate maze of waterways, polishing its ancient boulders smooth. Except for an occasional sandy beach or rocky cliff, a canopy of trees — spruce, pine, fir, balsam, aspen, and birch — covers the land to the water's edge.

Voyageurs National Park, one of the country's newest national parks (it was established in 1975), extends almost 50 miles along Minnesota's northeast border. Numerous streams and 30 lakes — ranging in size from Rainy Lake, 35 miles long, to Quarterline Lake, about 350 yards across — make up a third of the park's 217,000 acres. At the heart of the park lies the wild and scenic 75,000-acre Kabetogama Peninsula. You can hike, fish, and of course boat here, and stay in accommodations that range from tentsites accessible only by water to fine lakeside resorts. As in the days of the voyageurs, wild rice grows in the shallow waters of the park, and deer, moose, wolves, beaver, and bear inhabit its deep woods. No fees are charged for using the park and no permits are required. Motorboats are the park's most popular means of transportation; there are no restrictions on their use.

Just east of Voyageurs National Park lies the vast Boundary Waters Canoe Area (BWCA), one million acres of Minnesota's Superior National Forest, most of which have been reserved exclusively for the use of canoeists. The BWCA stretches nearly 100 miles along the border between Minnesota and Ontario's million-acre Quetico Provincial Park, another protected canoeing area. With its myriad lakes interconnected by innumerable streams and portage trails and its access to Quetico's waters, the BWCA offers the canoeist an almost infinite number of route possibilities. Motorboats and cars are allowed only in certain parts of this canoeist's paradise, and even the air space is restricted. Travel permits are required.

VOYAGEURS NATIONAL PARK: Access to the park's perimeter is from Crane Lake, Ash River, and Kabetogama Lake resort areas east of Rte. 53 and from International Falls, Minnesota, via Rte. 11 east. To enter the park, a boat or floatplane is needed. They can be hired at the many resorts surrounding the park. In the winter, ice roads, snowmobiles, and skis provide access. Voyageurs is unique to the national park system in that it provides an opportuy for visitors to motorboat and camp at one of the more than 100 primitive campsites scattered on islands and bays throughout the park.

At the east end of Rainy Lake, the well-preserved *Kettle Falls Hotel,* built in 1913, recalls the days when only trappers, traders, fishermen, and lumberjacks passed through these parts. Because of a quirk in the boundary line here, you can stand at Kettle Falls on the Minnesota side and look south to Canada.

Canoeing is possible in the park as long as you pay attention to the weather. Fast-rising storms can generate dangerous waves on the larger lakes. Experienced canoeists use islands for shelter from the winds and avoid crossing the biggest open stretches of water. You can obtain maps and the services of a guide at local resorts, canoes and supplies from outfitters at a number of places.

Another major Voyageurs recreation is fishing. The waters of Lakes Rainy, Namakan, Sand Point, and Kabetogama are known for their walleye, northern pike, and smallmouth bass. In the smaller lakes and streams are lake trout, and Shoepack Lake on Kabetogama Peninsula has the famed muskellunge.

Park visitors usually stay at one of the sixty resorts rimming the park, where there is a full range of accommodations, including campsites. You'll also be able to arrange for anything from water skiing to backcountry fishing via floatplane.

For information on naturalist-guided activities, camping, and recreational facilities in and adjacent to the park: Superintendent, Voyageurs National Park, Box 50, International Falls, MN 56649 (218 283-9821).

BOUNDARY WATERS CANOE AREA: The main gateway to BWCA is through Ely, Minnesota (other routes are through Grand Marais or, by canoe, through the Voyageurs lake system). If you go by paddle and portage, it is possible to follow the Canada-US border all the way from Rainy Lake at the western end of Voyageurs to the eastern end of BWCA and beyond to Grand Portage, on the shores of Lake Superior.

This 275-mile route retraces the final leg of the 2,000-mile journey made annually by the northwestern voyageurs, who transported furs from the northwest trading posts in the Rockies to the central depot of the fur trade in Grand Portage. Here, the "Montrealers," who had paddled across the Great Lakes to meet them, collected the furs to take east. The voyageurs used to paddle 18 hours a day, but assuming you will be traveling at a more leisurely pace, this trip should take about three weeks.

Within the BWCA, any number of routes are possible, from a day-long excursion to a summer-long voyage. Almost all of them are listed in *Suggested Canoe Routes,* available from Boundary Waters Canoe Area, Forest Service, US Dept. of Agriculture, PO Box 338, Duluth, MN 55801. Maps of all major canoeing trails in Minnesota and Quetico Provincial Park in Ontario are sold at W. A. Fisher Co., 123-125 Chestnut St., or PO Box 1107, Virginia, MN 55792 (218 741-9544).

If you are entering the BWCA from Ely, stop in at the Voyageurs visitors center, just east of town on Rte. 169, to see the full-sized replica of a voyageur's birchbark canoe. There are other displaysas well. Maps, travel permits (required for all canoeing), camping permits, and advice are dispensed here free of charge. (Travel permits are also available from district rangers and some canoe outfitters anywhere in the Superior National Forest.)

Like Voyageurs National Park, the BWCA doesn't offer many whitewater thrills. (Where there are rapids, they are generally too rough to navigate and you have to take a portage trail around them.) What it does offer, however, is the chance to canoe in solitude. If you choose one of the less traveled routes that require longer portages, you may be lucky enough to have almost the whole route to yourself.

The time of year can also make a difference: Peak months at BWCA are July and August, but the prime season for canoeing runs from May through October. Unfortunately, May and June are also the prime months for mosquitoes and black flies.

Canoe outfitters in Ely and Grand Marais can supply you with everything you might need for your trip, including guides, food, and the canoe itself.

If you plan to cross over into Canadian waters, you must check in at a US customs post at Ely, Crane Lake, or Grand Marais, as well as at a Canadian customs post. The Canadians charge a small daily fee for camping and canoeing permits.

After your canoeing adventure, you can rest your newly developed paddling muscles by taking a scenic drive on Honeymoon Trail or the Gunflint or Sawbill trails in the magnificent Superior National Forest. Wherever you travel in this huge wilderness preserve, you won't be far from one of its 2,000 lakes.

Not far from the eastern edge of the Boundary Waters Canoe Area in the Superior National Forest is Grand Portage and the Grand Portage National Monument, which marks the site of the central trading depot of the voyageurs. From Grand Portage, in the summer, you can take a ferry to Michigan's remote Isle Royale National Park, an island wilderness in Lake Superior. Information: Boundary Waters Canoe Area, Forest Supervisor, PO Box 338, Duluth, MN 55801 (218 365-3201).

BEST EN ROUTE

The Voyageurs National Park area abounds with fishing camps, lodges, and resorts. The Park Service will provide lists of them. Voyageurs is a new national park, and facilities are by no means complete, with many resorts and hotels still under construction or in the planning stages.

Kettle Falls Hotel, Rainy Lake – Long a favorite of fishermen, it's accessible only by boat and plane, on the east end of the 40-mile lake that stretches along the US-Canada border. Open from mid-May to October. Kettle Falls Hotel, PO Box 1272, International Falls, MN 56649 (218 374-3511).

West

Denali National Park and Preserve, Alaska

With the passage of the Alaska Lands Bill on December 2, 1980, the park's name was changed from Mt. McKinley National Park to Denali National Park and Preserve. Denali, an Athabascan Indian word meaning "the High One," refers, of course, to the commanding peak, Mt. McKinley.

Mt. McKinley is our giant. Nothing in our part of the world is higher, and at more than 20,000 feet, Mt. McKinley approaches — admittedly just barely — Himalayan altitudes. (The Greater Himalayas tower above it at 25,000 to 29,000 feet [Mt. Everest]; but McKinley competes handily with the Lesser Himalayas, whose peaks rise 7,000 to 15,000 feet above the Vale of Kashmir.) Just a couple of hundred miles from the Arctic Circle, Mt. McKinley is the heart and soul of surrounding Denali National Park and Preserve, about 6 million acres of the austere, wild tundra country that is one of the greatest natural wonders in the US.

McKinley is actually two peaks, its double summits separated by 2 miles of glacial ridge. It is an imposing sight: North Peak rises 19,470 feet, South Peak, 20,320. No matter how many pictures you see, how many articles you have read, nothing quite prepares you for it: the startled recognition, an audible gasp or sigh, unrestrained exclamations of wonder.

Climbers have been on the South Peak since the early 1900s when "sourdoughs," gold prospectors with some free time, decided to get to the top to see what the country looked like from up there. In a show of bicentennial enthusiasm, nearly 80 climbers made it to the summit of South Peak in July 1976. The fatality rate for McKinley climbers is low, but the last 7,000 feet are covered by sheer ice and snow, which make for very difficult climbing. (Parties interested in scaling McKinley or Mt. Foraker *must* apply to the National Park Service first. Because of the difficulty of the slope, only experienced, healthy climbers with tested skill and proper equipment should consider the challenge.)

Mt. McKinley is just one of the attractions of this huge, isolated tundra world — a world, alas, few get the opportunity to visit. The park is designed to protect its year-round, native inhabitants; man is an afterthought. There is one navigable road through the park; most of it is closed to private traffic, and the rest is restricted except for park shuttle buses. The park is open year-round, but its access road is closed from October until late May. Spring arrives late in the year, not until June or early July, when the wildflowers, nesting birds, and mosquitoes come out in full force. An added treat, as if calculated to give extra pleasure to the three or four months allowed to visitors, is that sunlight lasts 18 to 20 hours each day in the warm season; consequently, many activities are scheduled for 6 AM to take advantage of the early morning light, when the mountain shimmers cold-blue and ice-white, before clouds can obscure its uppermost 5,000 feet.

Perhaps the greatest attraction of the park is its vital animal life: caribou, grizzly bear, surefooted Dall sheep, wolf, and a huge variety of smaller, furred, warm-blooded beasts. One of the surprises of the park is its array of flora, including a variety of miniature trees — one-foot willows, knee-high birch — which have adapted to the incredible cold of winter and limited water by developing root systems reaching yards into the earth, where the temperature may be 50° warmer than on the surface. They literally grow down instead of up. Mosses and lichen grow like tufts of beard on the tundra's rough face, providing vital food supplies to caribou and other nonhibernating winter creatures. Visitors habitually learn to identify hundreds of plant species by their shapes and color when sighted across a broad meadow or hanging from a sheer canyon wall.

Denali National Park and Preserve is not a place to visit casually. The only road into the interior begins in the town of Denali Park, 123 miles south of Fairbanks, 240 miles north of Anchorage. For years after the park was established in 1917 it remained without direct road access to these main cities; a railroad and private aircraft linked it to the outside world (and still do, along with commercial air service from the two towns). Today, Rte. 3 passes the entrance to the park on its run from Anchorage to Fairbanks. The road into the park is almost 90 miles long, running due west past many scenic canyons, passes, and riverbanks. Only the first 15 miles are paved. The first sight of Mt. McKinley occurs a few miles in, but it isn't until mile 60, at Highway Pass, that you can get a full view of its magnificent peaks. Private vehicles are not allowed on the park road after Savage River Bridge, at mile 14.5 (except for visitors with confirmed reservations for more distant campsites).

Campsites are spread intermittently along the road, and a shuttle bus stops at them as well as at the many trails and sights. The bus is also something of a mobile social center, a place for picking up the latest on where caribou herds have been sighted. The shuttle bus runs from Riley Creek Information Center to Wonder Lake (at the northern edge of the park), making stops along the way wherever passengers request. Shuttle service runs regularly from 6 AM to 5 PM (check for exact times at the Information Center). There is also a bus stop near the railroad depot.

The Eielson visitors center sits just off the park road some 65 miles in from the entrance. At an elevation of 3,730 feet, it offers good views of the mountain's twin peaks and the awesome spectacle of the Muldrow Glacier, stretching from McKinley to within a mile of the park road. Exhibitions at the center explain glacial geology and describe past mountain-climbing expeditions. Make a point of stopping at the center, especially if you plan to hike or stay overnight. Information on weather conditions, animal activity, and other potentially lifesaving data are available from the rangers stationed there.

Along the park road you're sure to pass a number of places worthy of a stop. The Teklanika River is a classic example of the glacial rivers that flow on their curled courses north from the Alaska Range. Dall sheep, those surefooted mountain climbers, can be spotted as mere dots on the sides of Igloo Canyon. Grizzly bear activity centers around Sable Pass. (No matter where you spot grizzlies and other animals throughout the park, don't frighten them or attempt to pet or feed them. They only *look* friendly.) Wildflowers spreading across the vast fields of Stony Hill Overlook are a summer contribution to the scene. And at Wonder Lake, the last stop on the park road at the northern end of the park, magnificent reflections of the mountains are cast on the mirrorlike surface.

Hikers and backpackers should obtain a backcountry-use permit before setting out on their treks. Fishing licenses are not required, but a limit is imposed. (Fishing in the park is far from Alaska's best due to silty lakebeds and streams and shallow ponds.) Tours can be arranged at the *Denali National Park Hotel* for a full day's excursion into the park. For information on all aspects of park life and visiting, write: Superintendent, Denali National Park and Preserve, Box 9, Denali National Park, AK 99755 (907 683-2294).

BEST EN ROUTE

Denali National Park Hotel, Denali National Park – Filling meals are offered day and night — especially appealing to the early riser who wants to make that 6 AM appointment with nature. Information: From May to September, ARA Outdoor World, Denali Park, AK 99755 (907 683-2215); or, year round, ARA Outdoor World, 825 W 8th Ave., Suite 240, Anchorage, AK 99501 (907 276-7234).

In Denali National Park and Preserve – A choice of several campgrounds along the park road offers the best opportunity to see, and *feel*, tundra life. The camps are: Sanctuary River, Teklanika, Igloo Creek, Wonder Lake, Savage, and Riley Creek. Motorists can drive to Savage and Riley Creek without road permits, but other sites are on the controlled-access portion of the road. Bring warm clothing, a waterproof shelter, mosquito netting and/or repellent, camp stoves (no wood is available in the park). Information: Superintendent, Denali National Park and Preserve, Denali National Park, AK 99755 (907 683-2294).

Camp Denali – A wilderness camp north of Wonder Lake, in the park, *Camp Denali* features log cabins and a communal dining room. Guided tours are conducted daily from the site, as are 4-, 5-, and 9-day "Sourdough Vacations" into the wilderness. In summer, write Camp Denali, PO Box 67, Denali National Park, AK 99755 (907 683-2290). In winter, HCR 75, Box 106, Cornish, NH 03745 (603 675-2248).

Tongass National Forest, Alaska

John Muir, the Scottish naturalist who wrote eloquently about Yosemite and this country's western wilderness, was rendered almost speechless by the beauty of the southeastern panhandle of Alaska. "Never before this had I been embosomed in scenery so hopelessly beyond description," he said in *Travels in Alaska*. His words capture the nature of this area, much of which is still preserved as a wilderness in Tongass National Forest. The Tongass is the largest of the national forests, encompassing 16.9 million acres, reaching nearly the entire length of the rugged 400-mile coastline of southern Alaska from north of Juneau to south of Ketchikan, east from the outermost islands of the Alexander Archipelago to the border of British Columbia in the west. The panhandle is also bordered by two parallel mountain ranges. To the west, the peaks of the submerged Fairweather Range form the islands of the archipelago; to the east looms the Coast Range, with many peaks between 5,000 and 10,000 feet and numerous glaciers. In between is enough land to leave even the most blasé visitor breathless: America's only remaining frontier — more than 11,000 evergreen-covered islands, fjords whose flanks rise precipitously from the water's edge, huge walls of moving ice, glaciers carving and molding the coastline, and lush, moss-blanketed rain forests rising toward the Coast Range.

The Inside Passage runs the entire length of the Tongass. This waterway, which once provided gold seekers with access to the Klondike, is well protected from the bitter northwesterly winds by the outlying islands, and it's a pleasant passage by ferry along the foot of the Coast Range. Fjords and rivers flow into the passage, and the surrounding lowlands are blanketed by thick stands of hemlock, cedar, and spruce. In the summer, wildflowers abound: Fireweed, shooting stars, iris, and anemone color the marshes and meadows of the Tongass.

This region does not conform to stereotyped notions of Arctic harshness. If you expect huskies pulling sleds and boundless snow, the weather will disappoint you. Sitka, a city with a climate typical of the region, has an average temperature of 56° in August and 32° in January. This moderation is caused by the Japanese Current, which brings warm temperatures and plenty of rain. Sitka collects an average of 97 inches of rain annually, with June the driest month and October the wettest. During the summer it gets dark around midnight, so there is plenty of light for exploration of the Tongass.

The national forest is a rich wildlife area. Brown and black bear, trumpeter swans, deer, wolf, moose, and mountain goats roam many of the islands and coastal regions. The bald eagle, a bird that is close to extinction in the lower 48 states, thrives in Alaska and can be readily seen. Fishing is outstanding, with salmon up to 50 pounds not uncommon. In addition, many varieties of trout inhabit the freshwater lakes and streams of the Tongass.

Even bigger and better than a 50-pound salmon is another natural phenomenon of the Tongass — the glacier. Alaska possesses the largest expanse of glacial ice in the world outside Greenland and Antarctica. The panhandle's active glacier system offers a view of a broad succession of glacial stages. The glaciers that carved, shaped, and plowed much of this region are of fairly recent origin. Geologists estimate that about a million years ago, during the Pleistocene period, the sea level was hundreds of feet lower than it is today; glaciers moved from the heights of the Coast Range toward the sea, gouging the deep fjords and river valleys visible in the Tongass today.

Glaciers originate in snowfields in the higher regions of mountains. The only prerequisite for glacier formation is a snow cover that deepens over the years as more snow accumulates than melts. As successive layers build up, the accumulated weight exerts increased pressure on the underlying layers. When pressure is sufficient, snow crystallizes into ice. Movement of the glacier begins when the weight of the accumulation exceeds the strength of the ice. The immense pressure exerted by the sheer mass of the ice makes the ice "flow," something like cold molasses; glacial ice is not brittle.

The glaciers that exist in Alaska today are remnants of a "Little Ice Age," which began in the 14th century and lasted for some 300 years. Due to a warming trend in the climate during the latter half of the 19th and first half of the 20th century, the Alaskan glaciers are receding.

The only glacier in southeast Alaska accessible by highway, Mendenhall Glacier, is reached by Rte. 7 and Mendenhall Loop Rd., just 13 miles from Juneau. Mendenhall is over 12 miles long and 1½ miles wide at its face. The National Forest Service has a visitors center (open daily) at the glacier and also maintains trails alongside so that you can view the river of ice from excellent vantage points. If you're lucky, you'll see an example of calving: when a large slab of cobalt blue ice plummets from the glacier's face into Mendenhall Lake.

In Glacier Bay National Park and Preserve, the retreat of Muir Glacier, which bares the rocky deposits (glacial moraines) left in its wake, illustrates how virgin forest grows on seemingly barren soil. Only lichens and moss can survive in the most recently exposed regions. However, in the areas exposed during earlier years, small willows take hold and are followed by spruce and hemlock that mature into a forest. When the glacier moves inexorably forward during the next ice age, the forest will be swept aside.

The few major cities in the panhandle serve as excellent departure points for fishing, camping, and hiking forays into the Tongass, and also provide comfortable modern accommodations. Inaccessible by highway, the cities are reached by air, cruise ship, or the Alaska Marine Highway System, a state-run ferry service linking Seattle, Washington, and Prince Rupert, British Columbia, with the panhandle. Information: Division of Marine Transportation, Pouch R-DOT, Juneau, AK 99811 (907 465-3941).

Southernmost Ketchikan is renowned for its salmon fishing, and the many sportfishing lodges in the area offer anglers a chance to go after king salmon. The Tongass Historical Society Museum (629 Dock St.) has a collection of Indian artifacts and items used by southeastern Alaska pioneers. Petersburg and Wrangell are the next stops on the Marine Highway. The Clausen Memorial Museum (2nd and F sts.) in Petersburg has a good collection of historical fishing gear. The Bear Tribal House (on Chief Shakes Island) of the Tlingit Indians has a fine totem pole collection.

To the northwest lies Sitka, which was known as the Paris of the Pacific during the 19th century, when it was the major trading outpost of the Russian Empire. St. Michael's Russian Orthodox Cathedral (Lincoln St.) is one of the best surviving examples of Russian peasant cathedral architecture in the free world and contains ecclesiastical art and gifts from the czar. The Sheldon Jackson Museum (on the Jackson College campus) has an outstanding collection of Aleut, Eskimo, and Indian artifacts. In mid to late June, the city hosts the All-Alaska Logging Championships.

Juneau, the state capital, at the northern end of the Inside Passage, has the widest range of accommodations. A walking tour links fifteen points of historic interest. The Alaska State Museum (in the Subport area) has extensive collections of pioneer memorabilia from the Russian American period and Gold Rush era as well as Aleut, Eskimo, and Indian crafts and artifacts. Bus tours of the Mendenhall Glacier region are available from the city.

Only a boat or short plane ride away from these cities lies the wilderness of the Tongass. The Forest Service maintains campgrounds in these areas and close to the cities too. In addition, 143 cabins in the outlying areas, on the seacoast, or near rivers or lakes offer excellent opportunities to get back to nature. They have no bedding, plumbing, or electricity, but most of the lakeside cabins include a skiff. When you go this way, you see the Tongass for what it is — a gift from the earth. For further information and reservations write to the Tongass Forest Regional Forester, PO Box 1628, Juneau, AK 99802 (907 586-8806), or the US Forest Service and National Park Service Information Center, 101 Egan Dr., Juneau, AK 99811 (907 586-8751). For further information on the cities and the rest of the panhandle: Alaska Division of Tourism, Pouch E, Juneau, AK 99811 (907 465-2010).

BEST EN ROUTE

Hilltop Motel, Ketchikan – Some 46 rooms with restaurant and lounge, directly across from the airport and ferry terminal. 3434 Tongass Ave., Ketchikan, AK 99901 (907 225-5166).

Sheffield-Shee Atika Lodge, Sitka – On the waterfront, the facilities of this hotel include a restaurant and marina. 330 Seward St., Sitka, AK 99835 (907 747-6241 or 800 544-0970).

Baranof Hotel, Juneau – In the center of the city, this 226-room hotel has a restaurant, coffee shop, airport limousine service, meeting rooms, and nightly entertainment. 127 N Franklin St., Juneau, AK 99801 (907 586-2660).

Sheffield Juneau, Juneau – This 104-room hotel has a restaurant, lounge, and live entertainment. 51 W Egan Dr., Juneau, AK 99801 (907 586-6900).

Grand Canyon National Park, Arizona

On first looking at the Grand Canyon, even the firmest atheist may feel intimations of some higher power. An awesome force created this vast expanse of beautiful sculptures of the earth. Level upon level of rock of intricate and seemingly infinite formations rises out of this huge chasm in the earth and seems to be patterns of some master design. As your eye traces the layers and reaches the far rim of the canyon, your gaze keeps rising as if expecting to see a sign, perhaps the artist's signature emblazoned across the sky. And you may find confirmation of your beliefs. On the other hand, you may, at this point, begin searching for some scientific explanation. Whether the force was natural or supernatural, the instrument of the sculpting is right in front of you, at the bottom of the canyon. You've only to look at the Colorado River.

You may have overlooked the river, because the Colorado follows a winding course through the canyon and is not even visible at certain points along the rim, and where it is, it appears to be a narrow gentle stream. Looks have never been more deceiving. At the floor of the canyon, you see this gentle stream for what it really is — the wide and mighty Colorado. And only then do you begin to understand the tremendous force that has cut an awesome course through vast stretches of rock and time. The canyon is 277 miles long, from less than 1 mile to 18 miles wide, and more than a mile deep. While the area around it has been "under construction" for 2 billion years, the canyon itself is a relative newcomer, geologically speaking. The Colorado River began eroding layers of sediment about 10 to 20 million years ago, and its present course is no more than 6 million years old.

The story told by the multiple layers of the Grand Canyon is extraordinary. Initially, the area surrounding the canyon (long before it existed) was flat. Over millions of years heat and pressure buckled the land into mountains, which were then flattened over more millions of years by erosion. Mountains formed again, eroded, and were covered by shallow seas. All of this is recorded in the canyon, a great book written by the hands of time and force. The rock layers exposed to view are like steps in a staircase of natural history. At the bottom of the gorge is the first step, the Vishnu Group, the hard shiny black rocks of the Precambrian age, which are among the oldest exposed rocks on earth. As we move up the staircase, the changes in hue, texture, and fossil remains between layers are truly incredible; there is the Redwall limestone, a 500-foot-thick deposit of gray-blue limestone stained by higher layers, outstanding because of its sheer cliffs and traces fossils from a warm, shallow sea; above that is the Coconino sandstone, the solid remains of sand dunes in which fossilized footprints indicate lizard life. And at the top is the pale gray Kaibab limestone (at 250 million years, the toddler of the Grand Canyon family), a rich exhibition case for fossils from the shallow sea that once covered the area — sponges, sharks' teeth, corals, and bivalves.

Though geologists could spend lifetimes exploring the area, the canyon has attractions beyond. Hikers, bikers, river adventurers, naturalists, and just plain tourists have equal claim on the wonder. Between the South Rim and North Rim (about 9 miles as the crow flies, almost 23 miles by the rugged Kaibab hiking trail, and more than 200 miles by automobile) there is a vast expanse with something to see at every point, from the magnificent views to four distinct climatic zones to many species of plants and animals.

The South Rim is the more heavily visited of the two and the best place for an introduction to the Grand Canyon. Crowded in the summer but open year-round, it has extensive facilities for visitors amid a lovely background of juniper and piñon forest and open fields of Arizona blue lupine, yellow wild buckwheat, and purple asters. The South Rim visitors center, Yavapai Museum, and Tusayan Ruin and Museum offer orientation exhibits on the geological history of the area and the peoples who lived in the canyon. At the center you can pick up information on all the daily and weekly activities, from nature hikes along the rim led by rangers to more strenuous excursions into the canyon. South Rim drives cover 35 miles and have excellent overlooks. The 8-mile West Rim drive is closed to automobile traffic from Memorial Day Weekend to Labor Day but has a free shuttle bus service linking key points. Ranger-naturalists rove between Hopi Point, Maricopa Point, and Trailview for interpretive talks on the geology, botany, animal life, and peoples of the

Grand Canyon. The West Rim drive provides the best overview of the canyon, and the frequent buses that run from early morning till evening allow visitors to enjoy the sights at their own pace. Scenic airplane and helicopter flights are available year-round.

Trails for hiking down into the canyon start at the South Rim and, if you know your limits, can provide more intimate acquaintance with the wonders therein. The Bright Angel Trail, with rest stations at 1½ and 3 miles, and the steep South Kaibab Trail, a 6.4-mile hike with no water facilities, are best for hiking. You can take supervised nature walks or do it on your own, but remember that the canyon gets hotter as you descend and is hottest at midday. Take your hike in the early morning or late afternoon, be sure to have plenty of water and food and a hat for protection from the sun, and don't forget that going down is the easy part. Leave twice as much time for hiking back up. Note that hiking to the Colorado River and back in one day is not recommended.

One of the most interesting and certainly less strenuous ways to see the canyon is by muleback. There are one-day rides and overnight trips into the inner gorge; riders stay overnight at the small guest ranch alongside Bright Angel Creek, where comfortable cabins can soothe even the most saddlesore.

There are a wide range of lodgings at the South Rim from the private concessions in the park — the rustic *Bright Angel Lodge,* the modern *Yavapai* and *Thunderbird* lodges — to several park-run or privately operated campgrounds. Since the canyon is such a popular attraction, reservations should be made well in advance, particularly in the summer.

Less accessible from major highways and cities, the North Rim is also less crowded and offers different views of the canyon from a magnificent setting. Tall blue-green firs, scarlet gilias, and roaming deer can be seen on the North Rim, which is closed in the winter because of heavy snows (open from mid-May to mid-October). The 26-mile Cape Royal Drive has magnificent overlooks including Point Imperial, which at 8,801 feet is the highest point on the canyon rim and features spectacular views of the subtle hues of the Painted Desert, Marble Canyon, and the Colorado River. The North Rim has some organized activities (trail walks, talks, evening programs led by rangers, muleback trips) but is more a place for solitary communion with nature. The most outstanding vista is Toroweap Point, which, far off the beaten track (reached only by 60 miles of dirt road), offers an amazing view, 3,000 feet down a sheer vertical wall to the snake-shaped Colorado.

The *Grand Canyon Lodge* provides modest accommodations on the North Rim. A campground near the inn allows stays of up to one week.

Of all the ways to see the canyon, none is more exciting than rafting the roaring Colorado. Various commercial enterprises offer trips on relatively stable rubber rafts powered by outboard motors. On these, you get to see the canyon from the bottom up — cat's claw, yucca, blackbrush, the pink Grand Canyon rattlesnake — and above rise the sheer cliffs of rock almost older than time itself. Shooting along the rapids, you get a sense of the power that has revealed it all. Information: Superintendent, Grand Canyon National Park, Grand Canyon, AZ 86023 (602 638-7888).

BEST EN ROUTE

There is a variety of accommodations in the Grand Canyon National Park. The National Park Service runs several campgrounds on a first come, first served basis. For overnight hikes you need a permit and should make reservations by contacting the Backcountry Office at the address given above. Several concessions operate motels and hotels in the park. Rooms should be reserved 3 to 4 months in advance by contacting Grand Canyon National Park Lodges at South Rim, Grand Canyon, AZ 86023 (602 638-2401). Among the park's hotels, we think the best is:

El Tovar – This hotel is the oldest and most luxurious of the Grand Canyon accommodations. Some suites have balconies overlooking the canyon, and there is a good dining room serving prime ribs and filet mignon. South Rim.

Petrified Forest National Park, Arizona

In one of those great moments of cinematography, Humphrey Bogart, playing a desperate criminal in *The Petrified Forest,* allows his sensitive side to rule and frees his captive, Bette Davis, at the ultimate cost of his own life. But in this case it was more than the dame that compelled him. Certainly the desert landscape of the Petrified Forest, at once desolate and inhospitable, yet strangely beautiful in its harshness, can turn a person's head and heart. And such a change in conscience is not a special effect of the movie but part of the real life here as well. The Painted Desert visitors center has a display of apologetic letters, in some cases long confessionals written as many as 20 years later, from visitors who have broken the park rules and taken samples of petrified wood, only to find that the wood weighs more heavily on their minds than on their bookshelves. The Petrified Forest has a powerful impact on the minds and imaginations of those who see it.

You have simply to go there to feel its power; you will undoubtedly be surprised by what you find. The 147-square-mile Petrified Forest is nothing like a forest at all but rather a high arid desert region in northeastern Arizona. No living trees stand, and the predominant forms of vegetation are cactus and yucca growing sparsely around mesas and buttes that bake in the unrelenting sun. But there are trees, or at least the remains of trees, and thousands of them, lying supine and glowing in the desert heat. In fact, the park contains the richest collection of petrified wood in the world, ranging from huge prone logs to small brilliantly colored chips — burning oranges, deep reds, rusts, and yellows mixed with the dark shades of black, blue, and purple and lighter shades of white, gray, and tan. The only color you won't see much of is green, for forest has turned to stone. And the colors of the logs are part of the landscape as well. The northern portion of the park contains a portion of the Painted Desert, which really is just that, except that the colors are natural in this series of plateaus, buttes, and low mesas, remarkable for the bright reds, oranges, and browns in layers of sandstones, shales, and clays. The area is something of an outdoor gallery; the Painted Desert might more aptly be called the sculpted desert, for it exhibits nature's work in various media as the colors and forms change from minute to minute with the intensity of sun and the formidable shadows of late afternoon or early morning.

In the dawn of its history, the Petrified Forest was actually a forest. About 225 million years ago, what is now a high desert plateau was a low-lying swamp basin with dense beds of ferns, mosses, and trees growing in marshlands and along streams. Groves of conifers flourished on hills and ridges above this basin. Over long periods of time, natural forces felled the trees, and flooding streams transported them to the floor of the floodplain, where they were gradually buried under thousands of feet of mud, sand, and silica-rich volcanic ash. Water carrying the silica and other minerals seeped through the sediment and filled in each wood cell, retaining the details of the wooden mold. The silica left glasslike deposits of white, gray, and tan, while traces of iron in the water colored the logs yellow, orange, red, and rust, and manganese created the blacks, blues, and purples. During a period of mountain-building activity 70 million years ago, an upheaval lifted the layer high above sea level, and gradual erosion left the rainbow logs exposed. Geologists believe that more logs are buried below the surface to a depth of 300 feet. In 1985, the oldest dinosaur skeleton in the world was excavated from the Painted Desert.

Though more logs will be exposed in the continuing evolutionary process, what is on the surface is truly remarkable and can be seen in several hours. The park's major features, five separate forests with concentrations of chips and huge chunks of onyx, agate, and jasper, are linked by a 28-mile road. The two visitors centers, open year-round, are good places to stop first to see specimens of polished petrified wood, displays explaining the petrification process, and of course the letters from petty and grand petrified-wood thieves whose consciences got the better of them. Giant Logs, behind the Rainbow Forest Museum, is a magnificent highlight for its beautiful colors and the evidence of the petrification process; many trunks exceed 100 feet in length, and brilliant chips of onyx, agate, carnelian, and jasper tint the desert sand. At Long Logs, logs are piled on top of one another, and a partially restored Indian pueblo built of petrified wood chunks overlooks the area. One of the park's most unusual sights is Agate Bridge, a huge single log with over 100 feet exposed and both ends encased in sandstone. A parking lookout on a ridgetop above Jasper Forest provides a view of masses of logs, opaque in color, strewn on the valley floor. Be sure to stop at Blue Mesa, where a 1-mile loop of paved trail leads along a blue-gray ridge carved by the wind into intricate sculptures. Newspaper Rock is a mammoth chunk of sandstone with intriguing uninterpreted picture writings of prehistoric Indians (currently closed due to rock slides). Exploration of the vast unmarked surroundings should be arranged with park rangers; without natural water sources or trails, the Petrified Forest is not for casual hiking.

The Painted Desert is at the northern end of the park. After stopping at the visitors center to see displays showing how traces of iron have stained the layers of clay and sandstone many shades from bright red to pale blue, take a drive to one of the several overlooks and see it for yourself. The colors seem ever-changing and appear most vivid in early morning or late afternoon, or after rain, a most uncommon event.

There are no lodging facilities inside the park and camping is not permitted. Removing petrified wood from the park is also strictly forbidden. However, if you want a sample of petrified wood, you can purchase some taken from private lands outside the park at the Painted Desert Oasis and Rainbow Forest Curio near the park entrances. But leave the park intact as federal law, nature's law, and, as many have found, the law of the conscience dictates. The beauty of the Petrified Forest is there for all to behold. You really can't take it with you — except in your mind's eye. Information: Petrified Forest National Park Headquarters, AZ 86028 (602 524-6228).

BEST EN ROUTE

The park has no overnight facilities but there are many motels in Holbrook, 25 miles to the west, and one in Chambers, 21 miles east.

Budget Inn, Holbrook – This 38-room motel has an outdoor pool, TV and telephone in every room, and will accommodate pets. Within walking distance of two restaurants. 602 Navajo Blvd., Holbrook, AZ 86025 (602 524-6263).

Royal Motel, Holbrook – This 32-room motel has color TV in every room, a full-service restaurant, and accepts pets. 310 W Hopi Dr., Holbrook, AZ 86025 (602 524-2885).

Best Western Chieftain, Chambers – This 51-room motel is near the Navajo Reservation. Facilities include a pool, a service station, and a restaurant serving Spanish, American, and Indian food such as Navajo tacos — frybread sandwiches with beans and other vegetables. Reservations are advisable. PO Box 697, Chambers, AZ 86502, on I-40 (602 688-2754).

Big Sur and the Monterey Peninsula, California

Big Sur is a 50-mile stretch of Pacific coast south of the Monterey Peninsula and Carmel-by-the-Sea; its name is a corruption of a Spanish phrase meaning "big south." California Rte. 1 hugs the rugged coastline from Monterey, through Big Sur, to Morro Bay, 125 miles south. Convict chain gangs spent almost two decades carving the twisting highway out of solid cliffs, a highway that is unquestionably the most dramatic on the entire Pacific Coast.

The Monterey Peninsula and Carmel lie 125 miles south of San Francisco, 350 miles north of Los Angeles. Carmel is 4 miles south of the town of Monterey.

MONTEREY: California's first capital has more than 40 buildings built before 1850. The Old Custom House is the oldest government building in California, dating to 1827. It has historic material on display (Custom House Sq.). The Monterey Presidio, now a Defense Department language training center, dates from 1770, when it was built by Franciscan Father Junipero Serra, founder of California's Mission Trail (Pacific St.). California's first constitution was drafted in Colton Hall in 1849; the building dates from 1848 (Pacific St. and Colton Hall Park). Enamored with what he sensed as "the haunting presence of the ocean," Robert Louis Stevenson in 1879 lived and worked at the French Hotel, now called the Robert Louis Stevenson House (530 Houston St.). Cannery Row, the site of John Steinbeck's famous novel, has long since given way to chic shops and elegant eateries.

SEVENTEEN-MILE DRIVE: Despite its name it's only 12 miles long, but it takes you from the beaches and cypress trees of Pacific Grove to Carmel. Stop off at Seal Rock, Cypress Point, Pebble Beach Golf Links (site of the ATT-Pebble Beach National Pro-Am, formerly "the Crosby"), and Pebble Beach, enclave of the super-rich.

CARMEL-BY-THE-SEA: In this picturesque seaside artists' colony, about 25% of the permanent population are working artists. Carmel's quaint, untouched quality is attributable to some of the most stringent zoning laws in the country, passed in 1929. Since then, neon signs, traffic signals, and dozens of other garish accouterments have been prohibited. Carmel's narrow streets are lined with intriguing boutiques, shops, art galleries, and some excellent restaurants. The Carmel Mission, the most perfectly restored of all the California missions, was founded in 1770 by Father Junipero Serra, who loved it so much, he arranged to be buried here. In 1960, Pope John raised the mission to the status of a minor basilica, the second religious landmark so designated in the American West (Lasuen Dr. and Rio Rd.). South of Carmel, Point Lobos Recreation Area, a 1,255-acre park, has some of the most beautiful scenery along the California coast. Be sure to visit China Cove, Bird Island, and the wonderful stands of cypress. Colonies of seals and sea lions live on the rocks. Though there are no wolves in the area, the Spanish called it *lobos* (meaning "wolf") because the seals' barking reminded them of the sound of wolves. The park has a visitors center, hiking trails, campsites, and fishing spots (4 miles south of Carmel on Rte. 1). The Bach Music Festival takes place every July. For information on events in Carmel-by-the-Sea, contact the Carmel Business Association, Carmel, CA 93921 (408 624-2522).

CARMEL VALLEY: Follow the Carmel Valley Road east into the land of strawberry fields, orchards, grazing pasture, and artichoke farms. Because of its sunny, warm climate, the valley is an ideal choice for vacationers. You can play golf, ride horses, swim, play tennis, hunt wild boar and deer in season, or fish for trout in the Carmel River. Carmel Valley Begonia Gardens are ablaze with the colors of 15,000 flowers. The Korean Buddhist Temple is a good place to experience a contemplative foreign religion (Robinson Canyon Rd.). Most hostelries in the Carmel Valley are resorts. For information on accommodations and events, contact the Carmel Valley Chamber of Commerce, PO Box 288, Carmel Valley, CA 93924 (408 659-4000).

THIRTY-MILE DRIVE: The 30 miles between the Monterey-Carmel area and Big Sur are some of the most dramatic in the country. It takes about an hour to drive along the coast-hugging, twisting road where the Santa Lucia Mountains encounter the sea. Bixby Creek Bridge, just south of Carmel, is a 260-foot-high observation point where you can park, watch the ocean pound the beach, and gaze hypnotically at the Point Sur Lighthouse, which flashes every 15 seconds.

BIG SUR: This most famous piece of shoreline on the continent is so familiar to TV and movie audiences, it's almost unnecessary to talk about it. The rolling grassy hills of Big Sur end abruptly at cliffs towering high above the sea. There are many places to stop and watch sea otters, seals, and sea lions near the shore. You might even see whales spouting farther out to sea. Below the cliffs, waves crash over the boulders. You won't need to be told which spots on the road are especially scenic; when you round a hairpin curve and find yourself grabbing for your camera, you'll know you've found one.

In the town of Big Sur, you can stroll along the beach, have a picnic overlooking the water, browse in the art galleries, or visit the redwood trees, inland. Be sure to stop at *Nepenthe,* a restaurant on an 800-foot cliff that was built by a student of Frank Lloyd Wright. It has evolved over the years into Big Sur's main hangout and social center (408 667-2345). Pfeiffer–Big Sur State Park, a deep forest of redwood and other trees, provides a change of scenery from the bare, grassy hills of Big Sur. It has horseback riding, hiking trails, fishing spots, picnic areas, campgrounds, food service, and a lodge. At Jade Cove, you can hunt for jade at low tide. For information, contact Big Sur Information Center, Big Sur, CA 93920 (408 667-2100).

SAN SIMEON: About 40 miles south of Big Sur, William Randolph Hearst's fabled castle, San Simeon, contains sections of castles from other parts of the world which the newspaper tycoon shipped to his Pacific estate. Amazingly reconstructed, the majestic rooms, halls, courtyards, and swimming pools are no less than stunningly elegant. Tours will take you through this regal $50 million treasure house, now a state historical monument of 123 acres overlooking the ocean. Tickets may be purchased in advance through Mistix reservation service, by mail or phone: PO Box 85705, San Diego, CA 92138-5705 (800 446-PARK in California; 619 452-1950 elsewhere). For information only, call the Dept. of Parks and Recreation, Hearst Castle (800 452-5580 in California; 916 323-2988 elsewhere).

MORRO BAY: Named for the massive volcanic spire jutting out almost 600 feet above the sea. Morro Bay State Park, a 1,483-acre tract with horseback riding, hiking trails, picnic areas, and campsites, also has a natural history museum on local marine biology and ecology.

BEST EN ROUTE

Ventana Inn, Big Sur – Dramatic, contemporary elegance with exposed beams, high ceilings, balconies, patios, and windows looking over the mountains and ocean. All rooms have patchwork quilts and hand-painted furniture. Swimming pool, sauna, Jacuzzi, and hiking trails. Hwy. 1, Big Sur, CA 93920 (408 667-2331).

Pine Inn, Carmel – This Victorian establishment has stained glass, electrified gas lamps, marble-topped tables, wooden chests, and brass beds. A penthouse that sleeps eight has a fireplace. Each of the 49 bedrooms is furnished differently. PO Box 250, Carmel, CA 93921 (408 624-3851).

Sea View Inn, Carmel – Although the sea view is partially blocked by tall pines, this inn was built around 1906 and has retained much of its original atmosphere — if not its original $3 rate. There are 8 bedrooms, 6 with private bath; several have window seats and rocking chairs. A delicious breakfast is included. PO Box 4138, Carmel, CA 93921 (408 624-8778).

Death Valley National Monument, California

One of the largest of our national monuments, Death Valley National Monument covers 3,000 square miles, 550 of which are below sea level. It is 140 miles west of Las Vegas via Rtes. 95 and 373, 300 miles northeast of Los Angeles via I-14 to Rte. 395 to 190 or I-15 and Rte. 127, on the California side of the California-Nevada border, in the Mojave Desert. Originally, the 140-mile valley was called Tomesha ("ground afire") by the Indians, but was given its present name by a party of prospectors who got lost in the valley during the Gold Rush.

To the 49ers and the early settlers, Death Valley was a deadly obstacle to be overcome in order to reach the riches of California. Modern travelers find it an exciting, dramatic place that can be explored in relative safety. Death

Valley can be a special side trip on journeys from southern California to Las Vegas, Yosemite, or Sequoia–Kings Canyon national parks.

Death Valley is part of a region of extremes. At 282 feet below sea level, it is the lowest point in the entire Western Hemisphere. Only 70 air miles away stands the highest point in the continental US — Mt. Whitney, 14,494 feet above sea level. Death Valley is also one of the hottest places on earth, with temperatures recorded as high as 134° in the shade (the all-time world record is 136°, recorded in Libya, in 1922). Summertime is a good time to stay away unless you are well prepared.

Each of the canyons and mountains surrounding Death Valley seems to have its own special colors. Golden Canyon has bright golds and rich purples; Mustard Canyon is various shades of ocher. The Black Mountains have reds, greens, and tans. One particularly interesting canyon is Mosaic Canyon, whose gray rock surfaces are embedded with colorful pebbles that have been worn down by erosion, making the canyon look as if someone decorated it with brilliant mosaics.

If a scientist were to tell you he or she was going to Death Valley to study fish, you might raise an eyebrow. However, several species of fish in the streams of Death Valley do not exist anywhere else in the world. There are, in fact, more than 40 species of life indigenous only to Death Valley. Despite its great heat and minuscule rainfall (less than two inches a year), Death Valley has springs and several streams that flow all year. There's even a small swamp. During migration periods, Death Valley is visited by such unlikely guests as Canada and snow geese, herons, and ducks.

In addition to its valid claims on things that are the highest, the lowest, the oldest, and the biggest, Death Valley might also be the richest. There are many legends about the fabulous lost mines of Death Valley. They may or may not be true, but at one time it certainly had some of the nation's most lucrative mines. There were boom towns with colorful names like Bullfrog and Skidoo, towns that died when the mines played out, although today you'll pass what remains of these once-vibrant mining centers en route to monument headquarters, north of Furnace Creek. At the Furnace Creek visitors center, you can pick up brochures and maps explaining how to take a self-guiding auto tour. There are also slide shows, nature exhibitions, and lectures.

Death Valley is actually the floor of what was once a large inland lake fed by runoff from glacial retreats in the Sierra Nevada range. With the disappearance of the glaciers, the supply of new water couldn't keep up with the evaporation rate of 150 inches per year. Little in the way of rain makes it past the formidable barrier of the Sierra. The Devil's Golf Course is the name for a bed of salt pinnacles, some of which are as high as four feet and still growing.

If there's one mineral that Death Valley is famous for, it's borax. The borax mines were established in the 1880s, when roads in Death Valley were built for the legendary 20-mule team wagons that hauled the borax out of the valley. Three of the modern roads in Death Valley follow the route of the old mule teams. At the Harmony Borax Works, 1½ miles north of the visitors center, are the remains of one of the first processing plants.

However, the most famous landmark in Death Valley is Scotty's Castle.

Walter Scott (or "Death Valley Scotty," as he was known) had once been a performer in Buffalo Bill's Wild West Show. He built an elaborate, lavishly furnished castle in Grapevine Canyon at the north end of Death Valley, claiming he had paid for it with gold from a secret mine. The castle, standing like a mirage on the edge of the desert, has been famous ever since it was built. The romantic tale of a secret gold mine is, unfortunately, false. The castle was actually built by Albert M. Johnson, a wealthy Chicago businessman who came to Death Valley and quickly became friends with the flamboyant ex-cowboy. Other well-known Death Valley landmarks are Zabriskie Point, Titus Canyon, Telescope Peak — 11,049 feet high — and directly below it, Badwater, the lowest point in the valley. Nine campgrounds are scattered throughout the valley, among them: Furnace Creek, Mahogany Flat, Mesquite Spring, Sunset Campground, and Texas Springs. Reservations are not accepted, but there's almost always plenty of room for everyone. The tourist season runs from mid-fall to mid-spring, and the weather is pleasant during the winter. If you're planning to do any hiking, keep in mind at all times that Death Valley got its name for a reason. You should *always* carry plenty of extra water.

Death Valley's stark visual appeal evokes a strong emotional response. While other western national parks and monuments allow visitors to view the beauty of the West, Death Valley invites you to experience something of the spirit of the Old West — the determination, drive, and sense of hope that made this part of America what it is today. The original pioneers knew that they faced the very real possibility of death as they started out across this valley. Most of them made it and went on to new lives in California; one lies buried beneath its sands. You can't visit Death Valley without instinctively finding yourself thinking about these settlers. It's a monument to the American spirit and to the spirit of the pioneers who traveled the American West. Information: Superintendent, Death Valley National Monument, Death Valley, CA 92328 (619 786-2331).

Within a few hours' drive of Death Valley are a number of ski resorts, among them: *June Mountain, Mammoth Mountain,* and *Wolverton.* Just 120 miles from Death Valley lies the southernmost glacier field in the Northern Hemisphere, near the town of Big Pine on Rtes. 190 and 395.

BEST EN ROUTE

Reservations at both the inn and the ranch listed below can be made through Furnace Creek Inn, PO Box 1, Death Valley, CA 92328.

   Furnace Creek Inn, Death Valley – This luxurious, 69-room hotel has a swimming pool, tennis, lounge with entertainment, and palm-lined gardens. Open from mid-October through April. A mile south of the visitors center on Rte. 190 (619 786-2345).

   Furnace Creek Ranch, Death Valley – More casual accommodations in cottages and motel units, with a swimming pool, golf, tennis, horseback riding, restaurant, cocktail lounge, and service station. Adjacent to trailer park and landing strip for light planes. 225 rooms. Open all year. Next to the visitors center on Rte. 190 (619 786-2345).

Lake Tahoe, California

Lake Tahoe is so much more than a lake resort that its name is almost misleading. It is equally famous for its incomparable outdoor sports facilities, especially skiing, and for sophisticated gambling casinos offering the best nationally known entertainers. The largest mountain lake in North America, Tahoe is 22 miles long, 12 miles wide, and has 72 miles of shoreline. At an altitude of 6,229 feet, it is 1,664 feet deep and contains enough water to cover the entire state of California to a depth of more than one foot. Despite its size and the heavily populated sections of its shoreline, the water is pure enough to drink. In fact, it could supply every person in the US with five gallons of water every day for five years.

Lake Tahoe is nestled at the notch in the California-Nevada state line where California's eastern boundary starts to slant southeast. Actually, two thirds of the lake belongs to California, one third to Nevada. South Lake Tahoe is 198 miles from San Francisco, on I-80 to Sacramento, then Rte. 50. At South Lake Tahoe you have a choice: Rte. 50 to Rte. 28, north, along the undeveloped eastern shore in Nevada, or Rte. 89, which runs into Rte. 28, around the northern edge of the lake in California.

There are two theories about Lake Tahoe's origins. One argues that the lake was a huge crater gouged out of the crown of the Sierra Nevada range during the Ice Age. Another puts the lake's beginnings at 3 million years ago, when volcanic lava hardened, trapping the Tahoe waters in a deep, geological cup. Modern Tahoe offers something for nearly everyone. Luxury-seekers will find ultramodern hotels and casinos at the southern end of the lake. Sports enthusiasts will find skiing, boating, swimming, fishing, hiking, golf, and tennis in abundance. Campers seeking solitude and untrammeled nature have access to any of the three national forests around the lake — Tahoe, 696,000 acres to the north of the lake; Toiyabe, 3.1 million acres on the eastern edge in Nevada; and Eldorado, 886,000 acres to the southwest.

Starting at the US Forest Service visitors center (open from Memorial Day to June 28, weekends 10 AM to 6 PM; from June 28 to Labor Day, 8 AM to 6 PM daily; 916 541-0209), at the southern tip of the lake on Rte. 89, 1 mile north of Camp Richardson, you can trace the shoreline by car north and west through California or through Nevada. The corkscrew road winding through the ponderosa pine and spruce along the western edge of the lake is considerably more rugged than the strip facing the eastern shoreline. California offers much better sightseeing, since Rte. 89's intricate twists and turns reveal dramatic, panoramic views. You'll have to take it easy — the road is peppered with 10 mph zones, and, on a weekend, it's clogged with people. And take it *very* slow if the weather is foggy, rainy, or snowy — Rte. 89 can be treacherous.

EMERALD BAY: You might well experience déjà vu — the feeling you've been here before. This is one of the most photographed sites in the state. Eagle Falls, a canyon above the bay, has crystal-clear pools for swimming. Cruises of Emerald Bay are available aboard the *Tahoe Queen,* a glass-bottom paddlewheeler (916 541-3364) and MS *Dixie* (see Zephyr Cove, below).

DESOLATION VALLEY WILDERNESS: In startling contrast to Emerald Bay's fairyland splendor, these 41,000 forbidding acres of lake-dotted granite form a barren landscape laced with dozens of hiking trails. Experienced hikers have been known to gripe that the trails are as mannerly as a city park's.

TAHOE CITY: This is ski country. You can pick up interchangeable lift tickets for slopes at *Northstar, Alpine Meadows, Heavenly Valley, Squaw Valley,* and *Kirkwood.* For information, contact Ski Lake Tahoe, PO Box 17346, S Lake Tahoe, CA 95706 (916 541-5950). Tahoe North Visitors and Convention Bureau is at 850 N Lake Blvd., Tahoe City, CA 95730 (800 822-5959 in California, 800 824-8557 elsewhere).

SQUAW VALLEY: Five miles north of Tahoe City, the site of the 1960 Olympics, Squaw Valley is one of the most famous ski areas in the world, with 26 chairlifts, cable cars, and complete accouterments. The aerial tram operates during the ski season and for two months in the summer (916 583-6985).

INCLINE VILLAGE: At the northern end of the lake, this town is in Nevada. Lakeshore Boulevard is lined with expensive houses, showy hotels, casinos, and other attractions that make this "the Entertainment Capital of Lake Tahoe." Robert Trent Jones designed the two championship 18-hole golf courses, notorious for their water hazards. Golf Incline, as it's called (702 831-1821), becomes Ski Incline from December through April (702 831-3211). The Lake Tahoe Racquet Club has 26 courts (702 831-0360).

PONDEROSA RANCH: This ranch is probably as familiar to you now as your own living room, and you can catch a glimpse of the set of the TV series *Bonanza* from the Incline golf courses. More than 350,000 people visit every year. A pre-breakfast horseback ride leaves the Ponderosa Stables at 8 AM (702 831-0691).

MT. ROSE: Detour north on Rte. 27 for a bird's-eye perspective of the lake and environs. In winter, Mt. Rose has three ski slopes; in summer, there are 40 campsites in the Mt. Rose Campground (702 882-2766).

TOIYABE NATIONAL FOREST: Slightly to the east of the shoreline, the forest is known for its challenging hiking trails — so "uncontrolled" that inexperienced hikers are cautioned to stay away. Reservations must be made in advance for the 54 campsites, operated by the US Forest Service. Contact Ticketron in San Francisco (415 788-2828).

CAVE ROCK: Once used as a natural barrier against enemy attack by the Paiute Indians, today the cave is a tunnel for cars, with a lookout point.

ZEPHYR COVE: Cruise to Emerald Bay on the MS *Dixie,* a triple-deck ship offering dinner, cocktail, and midnight disco cruises as well as daylight passenger excursions. The ship can be hired for special charter cruises off-season, October through April. During the spring and summer, reserve well in advance (702 588-3508).

STATELINE: This is gambling country, what Tahoe is most famous for. Take your pick — you'll find slot machines, craps and keno tables, roulette wheels, and giant names in nightclub entertainment all over town. *Harrah's, High Sierra, Harvey's,* and *Caesar's Tahoe* are the most famous casinos. *Barney's,* next to *Harrah's,* has a smaller casino and gives discount coupons to guests at other hotels. *South Tahoe Nugget* also distributes coupons. It's about three quarters of a mile east of *Barney's* on Rte. 50. For information and reservations, contact the South Lake Tahoe Visitors Bureau, PO Box 17727, South Lake Tahoe, CA 95706 (800 822-5922).

BEST EN ROUTE

River Ranch Lodge, Tahoe City, California – A 21-room inn with a cocktail lounge and restaurant. PO Box 197, Tahoe City, CA 95730 (916 583-4264).

Hyatt Lake Tahoe, Incline Village, Nevada – Big casino and nightclub activity, plus water sports, tennis, and golf nearby. 460 rooms. PO Box 3239, Incline Village, NV 89450 (702 831-1111).

Coeur du Lac Condominiums, Incline Village, Nevada – For information on rentals, write PO Box 7107, Incline Village, NV 89450 (702 831-3318).

Harrah's, Stateline, Nevada – The world-famous 546-room super-resort has a 150-yard-long casino, famous entertainers, 4 lounges, and a full range of activities 24 hours a day. The *Summit Restaurant* has lake views and serves Continental specialties like pheasant with choucroute and champagne sauce. PO Box 8, Stateline, NV 89449 (800 648-3773, from Arizona, California, Idaho, Oregon, and Utah; everywhere else, 702 588-6611).

Del Webb's High Sierra, Stateline, Nevada – A casino with 1,200 slot machines, superstar nightclub/lounge, luxury facilities (540 rooms), and here, too, nonstop action. *Stetson's* serves filet mignon béarnaise and flambé desserts. PO Box C, Stateline, NV 89449 (800 648-3322 from Arizona, California, Idaho, Oregon, and Utah; everywhere else, 702 588-6211).

Harvey's, Stateline, Nevada – More than 1,600 slot machines, all gambling facilities, and several restaurants. *Top of the Wheel* serves Polynesian and American specialties. The *Sage Room* serves steak and seafood, and the *El Dorado Room* serves a buffet. Over 700 rooms. PO Box 128, Stateline, NV 89449 (800 648-3361; 702 558-2411 in Nevada, Hawaii, and Alaska).

Caesar's Tahoe Resort, Stateline, Nevada – This resort has 450 rooms, one Chinese and one Continental restaurant, a showroom, cabaret, and complete gambling facilities. PO Box 5800, Stateline, NV 89449 (702 588-3515 in Nevada; 800 648-3353 elsewhere).

Christiana Inn, South Lake Tahoe, California – If you're looking for quieter accommodations close to the scene, try this small(2 rooms, 3 suites), European-style chalet a mere 100 yards from the ski lifts at Heavenly Valley. The dining room offers an extensive Continental menu and wine list. PO Box 6870, S Lake Tahoe, CA 95729 (916 544-7337). In Heavenly Valley, try the *Top of the Tram* restaurant (steak, chicken, trout entrées). The price of Sunday brunch includes the tram. Keller Rd. (916 544-6263).

Palm Springs and Joshua Tree National Monument, California

Palm Springs is in Coachella Valley, 100 miles southeast of Los Angeles. It was at one time an important stop on the stagecoach route from Prescott, Arizona, to Los Angeles. Today, the drive from LA to Palm Springs takes about two hours on I-10, which in LA is the San Bernardino Freeway.

The sun shines an average of 350 days a year in Palm Springs and the air is pure. The average daytime temperature is 88°; nighttime average, a comfortable 55°. Since the humidity is always low, you can enjoy the heat without suffering from that muggy, clammy feeling that can accompany high humidity.

Palm Springs was discovered hundreds of years ago by the Agua Caliente Indians. Agua Caliente means "hot water" in Spanish, and it was, in fact, the discovery of hot springs in the earth which led to the area's development into a spa and, later, a resort, for the Indians considered the springs to have miraculous healing powers. They were opened to the public around the turn of the century, and, whether or not they healed anyone, they have provided a miracle for the Agua Caliente tribe, the largest single landowner in Palm Springs. The 180 members of this tiny tribe own over 10 square miles of tremendously valuable land within the city limits.

Today, people are more attracted to Palm Springs' warm, dry climate, its desert scenery, and superb resort facilities than to the springs themselves. For the rich, Palm Springs offers all the luxurious goods and services money can buy. For anyone, rich or poor, it offers what money cannot buy — a sparkling environment and delightful climate. Although Palm Springs has over 200 hotels and welcomes about 2 million visitors annually, it is still a very small town, with a permanent population of 38,000. It probably has the world's highest number of swimming pools per capita — over 7,400, one for every five people. Not everyone in Palm Springs is rich, although sometimes it seems that way. In winter, the wealthy, the famous, and the powerful come to play, and prices for everything soar as high as Mt. San Jacinto, the peak overlooking the city. During the summer, temperatures rise and prices drop.

No matter when you come, you'll find active nightclubs, dozens of fascinating (and expensive) boutiques, and sports activities that range from horseback riding through the nearby canyons to balloon trips through the desert. Known as "the Golf Capital of the World," Palm Springs has 60 golf courses and is the site of more than 100 major golf tournaments each year, including the Bob Hope Chrysler Classic and the Nabisco–Dinah Shore Invitational. There are hundreds of tennis courts and an increasing number of important annual tennis championships. The round of constant events and festivals includes rodeos, horse shows, the Desert Circus, art festivals, major league exhibition baseball games, charity balls, and designer fashion shows. Clothing designers often launch new styles in Palm Springs, so you can find next year's fashions this year. Check out the elegant specialty shops on Palm Canyon Drive, the main thoroughfare.

The main places of interest include the Palm Springs Desert Museum, a lavish cultural center with an excellent art museum, a history museum with unusual Indian artifacts, and outstanding facilities for the performing arts (101 Museum Dr.). The Living Desert has plants in natural settings with landscaped paths; Moorten Botanical Gardens offers more than 2,000 kinds of desert plants from all over the world (1701 S Palm Canyon Dr.). San Jacinto Wilderness State Park, atop the 10,780-foot mountain, has more than 50 miles of hiking trails, picnic areas, and six campgrounds. Its 13,000 acres can be reached only by an aerial tram ride. Part of the larger San Bernardino National Forest, the park is the site of numerous activities — some serious and some purely fanciful — throughout the year. Information: Palm Springs Convention and Visitors Bureau, 255 N El Cielo Rd., Suite 315, Palm Springs, CA 92262 (619 327-8411).

THE INDIAN CANYONS: Filled with plants, bubbling hot springs, magnificent waterfalls, ancient Indian cliff dwellings, and pictographs on the walls, the canyons may remind you of Shangri-la — they were used as the location of the original movie version of *Lost Horizon*, James Hilton's novel about the fabled hidden paradise. The canyons, part of the Agua Caliente Indian Reservation, are closed to visitors during the summer.

INDIO: "The Date Capital of the World" (the kind that grows on trees), Indio is also the site of the National Date Festival in February. Decor is neo–Arabian Nights, with camel and ostrich races. A movie called *The Sex Life of a Date* plays at Shield's Date Gardens.

JOSHUA TREE NATIONAL MONUMENT: Created in 1936 over howls of protest from mining companies that wanted to exploit the region, the monument is a haven for the strange Joshua tree and other desert wildlife and plants. The Joshua tree was given its name by early pioneers who felt that it resembled the prophet Joshua raising his arms in supplication to God or perhaps pointing the way for them to go.

Start your tour at the Twentynine Palms Oasis, site of the monument's headquarters, visitors center, and museum. A hike along the short nature trail will acquaint you with the plants and animals that live here. The park spreads over 870 square miles south of the oasis, with good major roads. Split Rock, one of the monument's best-known landmarks, is a giant split boulder more than three stories high with a natural cave underneath.

Ten miles south of Pinto Wye, Cholla Cactus Gardens and nature trail cover several acres. The gardens are filled with a species of cactus known as jumping cholla, so called because it seems to jump out at you to give you a painful sting. (It's probably a good place to skip if you have young children with you.) Wonderland of the Rocks in Hidden Valley is the most popular site on monument grounds. Thousands of years of desert winds have carved the rocks into bizarre shapes resembling sailing ships, monsters, cabbages, kings, and assorted other oddities. The best examples of Joshua trees stand at Keys View, which offers impressive views of the San Bernardino Mountains, San Jacinto, and the distant waters of the Salton Sea. Information: Superintendent, Joshua Tree National Monument, 74485 National Monument Dr., Twentynine Palms, CA 92277 (619 367-7511).

BEST EN ROUTE

Canyon Hotel Racquet and Golf Resort, Palm Springs – This 468-room luxury resort has 3 heated pools, golf, tennis, restaurants, coffee shop, and nightclub with entertainment. Children under 15 not admitted from mid-December through Easter except for Christmas and Easter days. 2850 S Palm Canyon Dr., Palm Springs, CA 92262 (619 323-5656).

Gene Autry Hotel, Palm Springs – Not as expensive as *Canyon*, with 3 heated pools, tennis, restaurant, nightclub with entertainment. 186 rooms, 12 cottages. Closed mid-June to mid-September. 4200 E Palm Canyon, Palm Springs, CA 92264 (619 328-1171).

La Siesta Villas Condominium Resort, Palm Springs – Eighteen rooms in self-contained villas, all with fireplaces and kitchen units, plus condominiums. Heated pool. No children under 14. 247 W Stevens Rd., Palm Springs, CA 92262 (619 325-2269).

Sun Spot Hotel, Palm Springs – Heated pool, laundromat, putting green, and airport transportation. Tennis and golf privileges; 19 rooms, some with kitchens. Southeast of downtown Palm Springs. 1035 E Ramon Rd., Palm Springs, CA 92262 (619 327-1288).

Sheraton Plaza Palm Springs, Palm Springs – Opened in 1981, this luxury resort is set on 13 acres with 258 rooms (about a third are suites), a lavish garden courtyard, swimming pool, tennis courts, and exercise room. Other amenities include a fine restaurant, poolside dining, and live entertainment nightly at *Harvey's Bar. The Wine Bar* features award-winning California wines by the glass or by the bottle. Within walking distance of the town's shops, restaurants, and attractions. 400 E Tahquitz Way, Palm Springs, CA 92262 (619 320-6868; 800 325-3535).

Redwood National Park and Lassen Volcanic National Park, California

Millions of years ago, redwoods grew throughout vast areas of North America. Now they're found only in a narrow band of land along the coast of northern California and southern Oregon, and they rarely grow more than 50 miles inland since the conifer needs the coastal fog's moisture, which it absorbs through its needles.

REDWOOD NATIONAL PARK: Established in 1968, Redwood National Park consists of several fragments of land in California near the Oregon border. About a quarter of the park's 106,000 acres is divided into three state parks — Jedediah Smith State Park, 9 miles northeast of Crescent City (where Redwood National Park maintains its headquarters and visitors center); Del Norte Coast Redwoods State Park, 7 miles southwest of Crescent City; and Prairie Creek Redwoods State Park, near the southern boundary of Redwood National Park at Orick. When the national park was created, the existing parklands were augmented with other redwood groves purchased from lumber companies and private owners. It now has about 40 miles of rugged shoreline with spectacular bluffs. Altogether, Redwood National Park is 55 miles long but only 10 miles wide at its widest point. If you're coming from San Francisco (326 miles to the south), you'll enter the park at Orick.

Just north of Orick is the site where the park was dedicated. Nearby stands Lady Bird Johnson Grove, a group of immense trees named in honor of the former First Lady. Along Redwood Creek are the tallest trees on earth. A redwood grove gives the feeling of a cathedral. The huge trees grow close together, shutting out the sunlight from above. The branchless trunks soar 80 to 100 feet straight up before the bows spread out to form the roof of the grove. Few smaller trees can grow in their shadow. Although redwoods are related to the giant sequoias of the High Sierra, it's quite simple to distinguish the two — the tall, slender trunk and dark brown bark of a redwood differs from the sequoia's bright reddish brown and comparatively massive trunk. The scientific name for the coast redwood is *Sequoia sempervirens*.

For over a century commercial logging has been active in this region, and since it began, more than 85% of the original redwood forest has been cut down. In 1978, vast new tracts of land were acquired by the park, almost doubling its size. Unfortunately, however, all but a few thousand acres had already been cut over by the lumber companies. A National Park Service study done in the 1960s estimates that virtually all of the original forest outside the parks will be gone by the 1990s. Presently, there are over 250,000 acres of redwood parks in the state.

Nature designed the redwood for durability. It can grow either from seeds or sprout from the roots and stumps of old trees. Its bark is often more than a foot thick, and there are natural chemicals in the fiber of the tree that make it incredibly resistant to decay, disease, and fire. The durable, everlasting quality of the redwood is the main reason for the demise of the original groves; it is superb for items like picnic benches and the siding of houses, and it has incredible insulation properties.

The Tall Tree is the tallest known tree on earth — 367.8 feet high and 44 feet in circumference. To the north of Redwood Creek, Prairie Creek State Park gets as much rain as an Amazon rain forest (about 100 inches a year, most of which falls in winter). The park is filled with redwood, big-leaf maple, Douglas fir, and luxuriant foliage and flowers. Fern Canyon's 50-foot-high walls are swathed with mosses and lichens, and 40 miles of trails stretch through the area's 12,000-acre forest. In the broad meadows of the state park, a herd of about 200 Roosevelt elk roams free. Gold Bluffs, at the western edge of Prairie Creek State Park, faces the sea. Rugged promontories jut into the Pacific and huge waves break over the jagged rocks. There are more than 100 campsites at Gold Bluffs and Prairie Creek. South of Eureka, there are 33 miles of majestic redwood groves on the Avenue of the Giants in Humboldt Redwoods State Park.

Del Norte Coast Redwoods State Park, 7 miles southwest of Crescent City, is unusual because its virgin redwood forest extends right to the steep bluffs overlooking the rocky shore. The best views are from the coast-winding Damnation Trail. In late spring, this section is ablaze with azaleas. There are campgrounds at Mill Creek. The northernmost section of the national park, Jedediah Smith Redwoods State Park, stands at the northeastern edge of the coastal redwood belt. It contains redwoods as well as inland species like Jeffrey pine. The largest trees are in the Frank Stout Memorial Grove, where the star attraction is the 340-foot Stout Tree. There are campsites and good swimming at a sandy beach along the Smith River (9 miles northeast of Crescent City). Information: Redwood National Park, 1111 Second St., Crescent City, CA 95531 (707 464-6101).

LASSEN VOLCANIC NATIONAL PARK: Lassen is about 160 miles southeast of Redwood National Park. Lassen Peak last erupted in 1914, making it one of the most recent active volcanoes in the continental US. After centuries of peace, Lassen's 20th-century eruptions lasted for seven years, highlighted by a massive explosion in May 1915 that catapulted five-ton rocks into the air, mowing down all life on the northeast side of the mountain for several miles. Volcanic dust fell as far away as Nevada. In 1916, the volcano and the surrounding area were set aside as a national park. (You could say it opened with a bang.) The smallest of the national parks in California, 106,000-acre Lassen is a tiny Yellowstone, with bubbling mud pots, boiling hot springs, and hissing steam vents known as fumaroles. Like Yellowstone, most of Lassen's major sites are easily accessible by car. The park headquarters are in Mineral, on Rte. 36, 9 miles from the entrance, where you can stop for information. Or you can take Rte. 44 east from Redding about 40 miles to the visitors center at Manzanita Lake. The 30-mile Lassen Park Road winds through the western section of the park, which contains the major attractions, including 10,457-foot Lassen Peak. More than 150 miles of hiking trails lead to thermal areas and lakes. Lassen Peak Trail will take you on a 2½-mile climb to the summit of Lassen Peak; a shorter, easier trail leads to Bumpass Hell, a section of hot springs, mud pots, and fumaroles in the southwestern corner of the park. (Bumpass is named for an early guide who plunged a leg into a steaming mud pot.) Nearby is the Sulphur Works, accessible by car. In winter you can downhill ski in the southwestern corner of the park or cross-country ski anywhere in the park.

Summit Lake, in the park's center, is the embarkation point for backpacking trips to the eastern areas. Cinder Cone, in the northeast corner, was set aside as a national monument several years before Lassen became a park. The stark, black cylindrical cone is surrounded by colorful formations of volcanic ash called the Painted Dunes. To the east of Cinder Cone lie the aptly named Fantastic Lava Beds, a mass of black volcanic stone deposited when Cinder Cone erupted in 1851. If you are intimidated by the thought of visiting volcanoes, keep in mind that Cinder Cone is considered dormant. That doesn't mean, however, that new eruptions are impossible. Information: Superintendent, Lassen Volcanic National Park, PO Box 100, Mineral, CA 96063-0100 (916 595-4444).

BEST EN ROUTE

The Benbow Inn, Garberville – Built in the 1920s to resemble an English Tudor mansion, the inn has dark wood paneling, a stone fireplace, and a shaded terrace. Facilities include a 9-hole golf course, hiking trails, fishing, hunting, swimming, canoeing. Closed January through mid-April. 445 Lake Benbow Dr., Garberville, . CA 95440 (707 923-2124).

Mineral Lodge, Mineral – Set in a valley with a mountain view, the lodge consists of several buildings, a swimming pool, restaurant, tennis, and gift shop. PO Box 160, Mineral, CA 96063 (916 595-4422).

Sequoia and Kings Canyon National Parks, California

Sequoia and Kings Canyon national parks are the backpackers' highway into the majestic Sierra Nevada of Southern California. By car you can see a bit — the giant sequoias, for which Sequoia is named, the forests that surround them, the lower-elevation sights. But only two major roads enter the 1,300 square miles of the parks: One is frequently closed during the winter by mammoth snowfalls; the other meanders into and out of the western corner of Sequoia so quickly that one feels it is intimidated by the mountains to the east. What you don't see by car is almost everything but the trees: the largest mountain peaks, especially Mt. Whitney, tallest peak in the continental US (at 14,495 feet), the animals, the streams, and the thousands of miles of backcountry, mountain trails for hiking, camping, horse and mule packing, fishing. These *are* the High Sierra experience.

Geographically and administratively, Sequoia and Kings Canyon are one park, covering about 860,000 acres. But the two boast radically different physical features. Sequoia, the southwestern corner of which is accessible by car, is the site of the world-renowned giant sequoia trees, the largest living things known on earth (and not to be confused with coastal redwoods — *Sequoia sempervirens* — which are taller than *Sequoriadendron* but not nearly so broad). Forests of the giant sequoia used to cover the hemisphere; now they are found only on the western faces of the Sierra Nevada, at middle elevations (still thousands of feet above sea level, however). East of the stands of sequoia, the park begins to rise with the Sierra Nevada, culminating at the park's eastern edge in Mt. Whitney, Mt. Muir (14,045 feet), and Mt. Langley (14,042 feet). Then, as quickly as they sprouted, the great peaks fall away to lower elevations, and outside the parks the country breaks into deep, long valleys.

Kings Canyon stretches north of Sequoia, sharing with it one entire border. Made a national park in 1940 (50 years after Sequoia), Kings Canyon has the same wild, rugged mountain beauty of eastern Sequoia, with the additional attraction of sheer canyon ledges for which it gained fame. Mountains of

13,000 feet are not at all uncommon in the eastern region of Kings Canyon, and running through them, from the northern reaches of Kings Canyon to Mt. Whitney in Sequoia, is the John Muir Trail, the 220-mile walking path that threads through the most spectacular, isolated, and peaceful vistas of both parks. Immediately to the east and north of the parks is the John Muir Wilderness Area, with Inyo National Forest just beyond.

There is no more fitting tribute to the naturalist than these trails and protected areas. It seems that most of America's beautiful parks and natural wonderlands have at some time in their histories required the guardianship of a farseeing and usually heroic protector; for many that person was John Muir. Sequoia and the High Sierra are perhaps his most remarkable testaments. Muir fought the government and the lumber companies to protect the sanctity of these natural treasures in the late 1880s, long before most people recognized their beauty and spiritual importance. In 1890, thanks to Muir's devotion, Sequoia National Park was officially created, the country's second such refuge. (Yellowstone Park had been established 18 years earlier. Yosemite Park followed Sequoia by a mere five days.)

Automobiles are given limited access in Sequoia and Kings Canyon; there is, however, a beautiful drive along the 46 miles of Generals Highway, which begins at the park entrance, 7 miles north of Three Rivers, winds through the mighty stands of sequoia in the park's southwestern corner, and ends at Grant Grove in Kings Canyon. (Sometimes the Generals Highway is closed in winter due to snow — as much as 20 feet at a time in some places; call 209 565-3351 for park weather and road conditions.)

If you start the driving tour at the western corner of Sequoia, you will drive past some of the most magnificent examples of sequoia in the world — several of the mightiest named for American generals. Based on its total volume, the General Sherman Tree is known as the largest living thing on this planet. It rises 274.9 feet on a 102.6-foot circumference, and it is the subject of thousands of photographs; not one expresses the sheer awe you'll feel standing next to its thick, reddish-brown trunk, wondering if it ever stops. Estimates of the age of General Sherman put it somewhere between 2,500 and 3,000 years. Estimates of the tree's weight place it at 2,000 tons, with enough wood to build 40 five-room houses. It is as high as the Capitol in Washington and no less a national treasure. The General Sherman Tree is part of Giant Forest, of special interest because it offers a view of sequoia in every stage of development, from sapling (they grow from seeds about the size of a pinhead) to high in the sky.

As you drive the full length of the Generals Highway you will pass several other magnificent trees, especially in Grant Grove (actually part of Kings Canyon), where the road joins Rte. 180 and turns north on the way to the heart of Kings Canyon. There stands the General Grant Tree, a full 7 feet shorter than Sherman, but 5 feet larger in circumference, and considered by many to be the more awe-inspiring spectacle. Robert E. Lee Tree is nearby, and a short drive (about 5 miles) from the grove is Big Stump Basin, where you can see what remains of these colossi after loggers get to them, as they did in the late 19th century despite Muir's efforts. Another well-known tree in the range is Hart Tree, standing in the Redwood Mountain Grove, west of Generals Highway in Kings Canyon National Park.

Halfway along Generals Highway you will come to Lodgepole visitors center, with displays on the trees and other aspects of park life. By all means plan to stop for a while. The visitors center (there is also one in Grant Grove and a visitor contact station at Cedar Grove in Kings Canyon) has information on a huge array of available activities and is a starting point for guided hiking tours. There is no question that the best way to see the parks is with backpack, tent, and time to hike around. Ranger-guided trips to the mountains and through the sequoia forests give a feeling for the land that is impossible to have from the road, even with frequent stops.

Making plans and seeing exhibitions is not the only incentive for stopping at Lodgepole visitors center. Rising some 6,725 feet above sea level (4,000 feet above the Kaweah River), Moro Rock offers a magnificent view of the parks and all their treasures. The eastward view is most impressive, looking toward the spiny backbone of the Sierra. A short walk from the rock is Crescent Meadow and Tharp's Log, the log cabin headquarters of the 19th-century explorer Hale Tharp. A climb up Beetle Rock is best saved for late afternoon and the experience of a sunset closing out the day over the park. And the strong-winded should hike down to Crystal Cave, a marble cavern highlighted by guided tours.

For an exciting overnight trip, get in a tour to Bearpaw Meadow. The walk on the High Sierra Trail is 11 miles of scenery that rivals the best of the Muir Trail. Make reservations with the park concession for facilities there. If you are roughing it, you must get a backcountry permit from the visitors center. Past Bearpaw, the High Sierra Trail continues eastward until it meets the Muir Trail at Wallace Creek. From there, you can make side trips to Mt. Whitney, Big Arroyo, or Kern Canyon. Be sure to tell park personnel where you plan to be and when you plan to return.

The center of activity in Kings Canyon is Cedar Grove, reached by Rte. 180. This area has four campgrounds with 351 sites, and the ranger station at Cedar Grove has the most current information on hikes. From Cedar Grove, hikes can go in almost any direction on miles of trails. The least explored areas are to the north, into the heart of Kings Canyon Park. You will find lakes of all sizes and mountain after mountain. It must be done on foot or horse or muleback. There is little stopping you from tackling the miles of trails and countless opportunities for individual exploration. After all, that's why John Muir fought for it. Information: Superintendent, Sequoia and Kings Canyon National Parks, Three Rivers, CA 93271 (209 565-3456).

BEST EN ROUTE

Although nothing in the Sequoia and Kings Canyon area really earns a place in *Best en Route*, there are ample alternatives for accommodations — in nearby hotels and motels, in park lodges, and in campsites throughout the national parks and forests.

There are more than a dozen in the two parks. The *Lodgepole Campground* is run on a reservation-only basis and they can be made through Ticketron outlets. Guest Services, Sequoia National Park, CA 93262 (209 561-3314), has information about the park's three lodges, *Giant Forest Lodge* in Sequoia Park and *Cedar Grove Lodge* and *Grant Grove Lodge* in Kings Canyon.

In the parks, a number of stores and supply stations can help outfit you for a hike or overnight. They are near the campsites and also sell the fishing licenses that are required if you plan to tackle the lakes and streams for the many varieties of native catch, especially the magnificent golden trout. Mules, burros, and horses can be rented at Giant Forest, Grant Grove, Cedar Grove, and Mineral King for pack trips throughout the parks.

Other campsites are available in the Sequoia National Forest, on *Hume Lake* (where boating, swimming, fishing, and other accommodations are the featured attractions), in *Inyo National Forest,* and at *Stony Creek Campground* (on Generals Hwy., south of Grant Grove in Kings Canyon).

Hotel and motel accommodations outside the park are limited to four nearby towns: Three Rivers, just south of Sequoia; Visalia to the west; and Porterville and Fresno.

Yosemite National Park, California

A good many of California's finest physical resources are the product of the Sierra Nevada, the mountain range that runs for 500 miles parallel to the Nevada border. The gem in this mountainous necklace is Yosemite National Park, 1,189 square miles of mountains, valleys, granite spires and monoliths, waterfalls and forests, in central eastern California.

Yosemite was established as a national park in 1890, but its natural history spans millions of years, starting during an ancient age when a shallow arm of the Pacific covered a section of western Nevada, the Sierra Nevada, and the great Central Valley of California. The sea dried up and subsequent volcanic activity caused molten rock to infiltrate the underlying sedimentary layers. In time, these layers were eroded and the igneous rock, granite, was exposed. Later upheavals of the earth tilted these layers to the west, creating the steep eastern flank and long western slope of the mountains we know today. As a consequence of the angle of the mountains, the flow of streams became more rapid, cutting deep V-shaped valleys into the granite. Then, during Ice Ages two or three million years ago, glaciers gouged the valley into a U-shaped trough with a round bottom and sheer sides. Finally, the melting glaciers formed a lake whose bed is the present valley floor.

Today the valley is Yosemite's main attraction, though by no means all the park has to offer. Carpeted with meadows and forests and watered by the Merced River, the valley is 7 miles long and up to 1 mile wide. Its walls rise 2,000 to 4,000 feet from the valley floor, featuring some of the geological wonders of the world. First and foremost is El Capitan, at 7,569 feet the largest known single block of granite in the world, a sheer outcropping that does not have a single fracture on its entire perpendicular wall, a challenge to even veteran rock climbers. Towering above the lower end of the valley, directly across from El Capitan, are the 6,114-foot Cathedral Spires. On the north side of the valley stand the Three Brothers, a trio of leaning peaks piled on top of one another to a height of 7,779 feet. Beyond, the upper valley broadens with a semicircle of granite domes — Sentinel, Basket, North

Dome, and the massive Half Dome. These huge granite deposits were formed by glaciation and exfoliation; in the latter process, the surface layers of rock released from subterranean pressures peel, chip, and crumble into rounded contours on their way toward ultimate dissolution. Though this shaping force is completely imperceptible, the valley's magnificent waterfalls demonstrate the process of gradual dissolution still at work. The most spectacular of the valley's falls is Yosemite, noted for its height; the Upper Fall plunges 1,430 feet over the north wall (a height equal to nine Niagara Falls), and the Lower Fall immediately below is a drop of more than 300 feet. Combined with the cascades in between, the fall's double leap measures 2,425 feet, making Yosemite the highest waterfall on this continent. With the valley's other water-falls — Ribbon, the misty Bridalveil, Nevada, Vernal, and Illilouette — Yosemite offers one of the most amazing water spectacles anywhere.

In September 1980, the Yosemite General Management Plan began to serve as the approved, long-term guideline for the park. It is likely that this plan will limit the number of visitors entering the park to avoid overuse. There is also a provision for the employee housing and maintenance and storage facilities to be relocated outside the park.

Yosemite Village, the center of activities in the park, with campgrounds, lodging, shops, and restaurants, is a good place to begin a visit. The Yosemite Valley visitors center, open year-round, offers exhibits on the geological devel-opment of the area and information on the wide range of activities — ranger-guided walks, lectures, and demonstrations (the Yosemite *Guide* pro-vides a schedule of the week's activities). After a stop at the visitors center and a tour of the valley via tram has oriented you, over 700 miles of trails outside the valley can be covered by horse, mule, or foot.

No matter how you see them, there are several highlights of the park that you should not miss. Glacier Point offers a sweeping 180° panorama of the High Sierra. Half Dome rises in front of you, Nevada and Vernal Falls are prominent, and in the background are the snowy peaks of Yosemite's back-country. The road to Glacier Point (closed in winter) winds through red fir and pine forest and meadow. You can hike to the valley floor along one of several trails. Four-Mile Trail (really 4.6 miles) zigzags down steeply, while Pohono Trail skirts the south rim and descends to the valley floor near Bridalveil Fall, a total of 13 miles.

Tuolumne Meadows is a major trailhead to the high country and, at 8,600 feet, the largest subalpine meadow complex in the High Sierra. Though it is closed in the winter, during the summer the park operates a campground here and a full-scale naturalist program exploring high-altitude ecological systems.

The Mariposa Grove is the largest of the park's three groves of mammoth sequoias. Over 200 of the beautiful old redwoods here measure more than 10 feet in diameter. Among them is the tunnel tree (now supine), which was so large that people used to drive through the hollow area at the base. The Grizzly Giant is not hollow; but if it were, a Mack truck carrying the tunnel tree could drive straight through it.

In addition to its scenic attractions, Yosemite offers a wide variety of summer and winter recreational activities. The miles of trails offer hiking for everyone from tenderfoot to trailblazer. Wilderness permits are required for overnight backcountry travel and are issued at the ranger station on a first come, first served basis or by mail reservation February through April. Stables at Camp Curry and Wawona rent horses and mules and offer a variety of guided trips from 1-day excursions to 6-day saddle trips through the High Sierra. If you're afraid of mules and horses, bike rentals at Yosemite Lodge and Camp Curry provide wheels. For those who like to live dangerously, the vertical granite walls of the valley beckon with some of the finest climbing areas in the world. Actually, the Yosemite Mountaineering School (209 372-1244) gives lessons on scaling a sheer cliff.

In wintertime, Yosemite becomes a snow-covered paradise, with Badger Pass for downhill skiing, over 90 miles of trails for cross-country skiing, an outdoor ice-skating rink at Camp Curry, and magnificent mountainous vistas.

At every time of year Yosemite has something to offer, and while you are there, you imagine how those cliffs would appear during another — perhaps covered with snow — or how the falls thunder as the snow melts. But no matter what you imagine about Yosemite, a visit will more than fulfill its promise. Information: Superintendent, PO Box 577, Yosemite National Park, CA 95389 (209 372-0264).

BEST EN ROUTE

The National Park Service runs 16 developed campgrounds in the park. Group campsites must be reserved in advance. Individual campsites are assigned on a first come, first served basis, except between April and October 31, when the Yosemite Valley campgrounds are on an advance campsite reservation system. Reservations can be made by mail through Ticketron Reservation Office, PO Box 2715, San Francisco, CA 94126. *Campsites cannot be reserved by phone.*

Ahwahnee Hotel – This classy structure of stone and native timber dates to 1927. It has a good dining room, 2 bars, entertainment, and lots of well-designed public areas. Yosemite Valley (209 252-4848).

Yosemite Lodge – A combination of cabins and modern hotel rooms built around a central area with 2 restaurants, a cafeteria, swimming pool, bike rental, shops, and, in the summer, an ice cream cone stand. Yosemite Valley (209 252-4848).

Camp Curry – Rustic tents, cabins, and hotel rooms have access to a cafeteria, public lounge, fast-food service, pool, and bike rental facility. The Mountaineering School has its headquarters here, and in the winter, there's an ice skating rink. Yosemite Valley (209 252-4848).

Wawona Hotel – A century-old Victorian structure 27 miles south of Yosemite Valley on Rte. 41. Roughly half of its 77 rooms have private baths and all are furnished with antiques. The dining room serves all meals; 9-hole golf course; tennis; swimming pool. Open April through Thanksgiving (209 252-4848).

Rocky Mountain National Park, Colorado

The North American Rocky Mountains stretch from northern New Mexico and southern Colorado to the Columbia Range and the Rocky Mountain Trench in Canada, 300 miles north of the US-Canada border. And this massive range is part of an even larger series of mountains, the North American Cordillera, which includes the Brooks Range in Alaska and Mexico's

Sierra Madre, the mountains that follow Mexico's eastern and western coasts.

In the US, the highest peaks in the Rockies are those of the Front range, so named because it is the first range of the chain to rise from the Great Plains in north-central Colorado. Some 410 miles of the Front range have been set aside as the Rocky Mountain National Park, and within its 265,229 acres are more than 104 named peaks over 10,000 feet, 49 above 12,000 feet, innumerable mountain valleys (averaging 8,000 feet above sea level), and Longs Peak at 14,255 feet. It is a spectacular area of glacial moraines (great piles of rocks where the advance of glaciers finally stopped), mountain lakes, alpine valleys, and tundras. The area has five small glaciers and myriad hiking and horse trails, peaks, canyons, and roads.

The Colorado Rockies began formation between 40 and 60 million years ago; they rose and were worn down by wind and water erosion over the next 30 million years. A 15-million-year period of volcanic activity and faulting threw them up once again. The mountains that appeared were at the mercy of wind and water for eons, but its present form was stamped on the chain during the past 2 million years, when the first of four glacial periods began. Portions of mountains were leveled by the incredible force of the glaciers; chasms appeared as mountain walls were cut through; cirques dug where the glaciers' heads buttressed against unyielding mountain faces. Many of the beautiful mountain lakes that dot the park today are the remnants of deep gouges dug by the inexorable force of glaciers grinding against bedrock.

The first human beings in the area were Indian tribes who traveled in nomadic bands more than 11 thousand years ago. In recent centuries the land was controlled by the Utes and the Arapahoes. Arrowheads, pottery, tools, and hand hammers are just some of the Indian artifacts that have been found in the park region. Some trails still in use today bear the marks of the earlier Indians who crossed this mountainous terrain.

However, the Louisiana Purchase brought ownership of this land to the US government in 1803. The first American pioneers, Colonel Stephen Long (1820), William Ashley (1825), and John C. Frémont (1843), paved the way for other adventurers. The mountains became the goal of many Easterners seeking gold in the late 1850s and early 1860s. In 1859, Joel Estes saw the Front Range and within a year had settled his family there, in Estes Park, the area now named for him (just 3 miles from the main entrance to the park). Estes loved the beauty and abundance of the area, but several years after he arrived, he became weary of the isolation and moved farther west. Within a year he was back again, unable to live without the rugged spectacle of the mountains surrounding him. He was not alone in his appreciation. An Irish earl built a huge estate in the Front Range and publicized the beauty of the area. In 1915, the region became a national park, thanks largely to the hard work and constant writing of Enos Mills, a great naturalist and author. He believed that this wonderful wilderness should be maintained, as a park, in order to preserve the clean air and lofty peaks. He once wrote: "He who feels the spell of the wild, the rhythmic melody of falling water, the echoes among the crags, the bird songs, the wind in the pines . . . is in tune with the universe."

Rocky Mountain National Park is open all year, though many facilities — and roads — within the park close during the snows, between October and May. The park is approached through the beautiful alpine valley, Estes Park. In the town of Estes Park you can take an aerial tramway, to the top of Prospect Mountain (8,900 feet) for your first, overwhelming view of the Rockies to the west. From the town, there are two possible entrances — through the Fall River entrance directly onto the Trail Ridge Road, the main driving route through the park, or through the more southerly entrance at Beaver Meadows. If it is your first visit, by all means take the slightly more roundabout route through the Beaver Meadows entrance, where you will be able to stop at the visitors center for orientation. Rangers will provide maps of the entire park. There are more than 355 miles of trails in the park, designed for amateurs as well as experienced hikers. There is a ½-mile trail at Bear Lake (at the end of the short drive south from Beaver Meadows) that circles the lake. If you are a serious hiker you may want to try the 15-mile (round-trip) route to and from the top of Longs Peak, the highest in the range. Though long, it is by no means an impossible feat; about 200 hikers a day reach the pinnacle during the summer. The view from the top is unsurpassed. Rangers at the Beavers Meadows visitors center have information on hikes, camping and campgrounds, activities, and facilities in the park.

There are two roads across the park: Trail Ridge Road, which starts at the Fall River entrance and meanders west and then south to Grand Lake (the park's western entrance point); and the shorter Fall River Road, an offshoot of the Trail Ridge that runs slightly north of the longer road. Fall River is a narrow, one-way dirt road with a 15 mph speed limit that is strictly enforced, but it offers marvelous opportunities for photographs, both of the peaks in the park, and of park wildlife. The entire park is a wildlife refuge, natural habitat of elk, deer, black bear, coyote, and the increasingly scarce mountain lion and bobcat. You may see bighorn sheep — called Rocky Mountain sheep — which are the park's emblem, and if you do any hiking, especially in spring (which comes late here), you will see the alpine wildflowers that flourish in the meadows above and below treeline. Summer is brief in the mountains — a few weeks in late July and August — and the winters are long and harsh, and above treeline flora is that of the tundra — lichen, tiny flowers, scrub trees with deep roots that can survive the freezing winters, deep snows, and rocky, barren terrain above 11,000 feet.

Trail Ridge Road, the park's main road, offers an exquisite view of Longs Peak and leads you by the Mummy Range, where you rise above the treeline and lose sight of the stands of spruce, pine, and fir. At Fall River Pass, where the road turns gradually southward, you can stop at the Alpine visitors center, where exhibitions explain the alpine tundra through which you are driving. The Trail Ridge Store has a snack bar for light meals. If you follow Trail Ridge Road to its end at Grand Lake you will cross the Continental Divide at Milner Pass (10,760 feet). The Divide is the weaving line that defines a basic North American watershed: all precipitation falling to the west of this ridge eventually winds up in the Pacific; to the east, it ends up in the Atlantic or the Gulf of Mexico. Farther north the Divide often appears as no more than a gentle rise in the road, but at Milner Pass, where the north fork of the Colorado River begins, you get a real sense of its significance. From here, Trail Ridge Road follows the Colorado to the western entrance and egress point of the park at Grand Lake and Lake Granby, which border the park on its southwest edge. Grand Lake has a good boat harbor. Information: Superintendent, Rocky Mountain National Park, Estes Park, CO 80517 (303 586-2371); Estes Area Chamber of Commerce, Estes Park, CO 80517 (800 621-5888 in Colorado; 800 654-0949 elsewhere); or Grand Lake Chamber of Commerce, Grand Lake, CO 80447 (303 627-3402).

BEST EN ROUTE

Hobby Horse Motor Lodge, Estes Park – Adjacent to a stable and golf course, with riding trails in the surrounding area. It has its own trout pool for children as well as a heated swimming pool. PO Box 40, Estes Park, CO 80517 (303 586-3336).

McGregor Mountain Lodge, Estes Park – At the entrance of Rocky Mountain National Park, overlooking Fall River Canyon. 2815 Fall River Rd., Estes Park, CO 80515 (303 586-3457).

Machin's Cottages in the Pines, Rocky Mountain National Park – Comfortable, well-appointed cottages that accommodate groups of up to 12 people. Cottages have completely equipped kitchens, fireplaces, and cozy living rooms. PO Box 88, Estes Park, CO 80517 (303 586-4276).

Hawaiian Islands: A Survey

Hawaii attracts almost 5 million visitors a year, and it is a tragedy that many of these people never get beyond the traditional tourist centers of Honolulu and Waikiki, Maui, or the Kona Coast on the Big Island. None of the major Hawaiian Islands are untouched by tourism, but several — Molokai, Kauai, and the less developed sections of Maui and the Big Island — genuinely reflect the original Polynesian and plantation cultures that are unique to the islands. This doesn't mean developed areas should be avoided. There is an allure and excitement in Honolulu and Waikiki which grab you the minute you step off the plane, and Maui's beautiful western coast has some of the finest resort hotels in the world, with unmatched facilities and activities. But it does mean there is another Hawaii, far closer than the historic islands, just beyond the resorts. By careful planning you can have both, and that makes Hawaii one of the most exciting vacation spots in the United States.

The State of Hawaii consists of 132 islands, some no more than bare rocks hardly above waterline, that stretch across 1,600 miles of the north Pacific Ocean from Hawaii island in the southeast to Kure and the Midway Islands in the northwest. The largest islands are clustered together in the southeastern end of the chain, about 2,500 miles southwest of Los Angeles, and these make up what most of us think of as Hawaii: Hawaii, Kahoolawe, Maui, Lanai, Molokai, Oahu, Kauai, and Niihau. There are direct flights from the US mainland to Maui (Kahului), the Big Island (Kona and Hilo), and Kauai

(Lihue). Inter-island travel is extremely easy, by jet or by "commuter" plane.

Of the eight major islands, only six are open to tourism. Kahoolawe, a 45-square-mile dot in the ocean between Hawaii and Maui, has been a US Navy bombing range since World War II and is uninhabited. Niihau, off Kauai's western coast, is privately owned (73 square miles) and devoted to a colony of pure Hawaiians living as did their ancestors. No tourists or journalists are allowed to visit without explicit permission from the owners. Herewith a brief survey of the six inhabited and accessible major islands:

HAWAII: Called the Big Island, with just about twice as much land area as the rest of the chain combined (just over 4,000 square miles) and a population of 108,000. The island has two active volcanoes, Kilauea and Mauna Loa.

MAUI: A fascinating combination of sophisticated resorts (along the western coast) and rural, mountainous inlands. The 729-square-mile island is dominated by Haleakala, a 10,023-foot dormant volcano surrounded by a large national park.

LANAI: The smallest island open to tourists (140 square miles) and in the early stages of developing tourist facilities. Much of the land is devoted to growing pineapples.

MOLOKAI: Most famous for the leper colony on the isolated peninsula of Makanalua. This early colony was taken over by Father Damien, a Belgian priest, in 1873, and he strove to make it a home for the people who were persecuted elsewhere. Molokai has some of the most spectacular cliffs in the islands, and today it is very much the plantation island that it was in the late 1800s, although Sheraton and other organizations have built luxurious resorts along one coast.

OAHU: The capital island, with Honolulu and Waikiki Beach and an infinite variety of activities, sights, and nightlife. The 608-square-mile island supports four fifths of the population of the entire state (see *Honolulu,* THE AMERICAN CITIES).

KAUAI: A splendid combination of plantation Hawaii and resorts, restaurants, and activities. The 533-square-mile island has some of the most beautiful country in the world, including the spectacular mountain coast of Na Pali, which is inaccessible by car.

Hawaii, Hawaii

Slightly smaller than Connecticut, Hawaii is the largest island in the Hawaiian chain, hence its nickname, the Big Island. It is also the youngest, and that makes it a living text of how, and of what, the entire chain was formed. It is the island of active volcanoes, where periodic eruptions of Kilauea and Mauna Loa (the two living volcanoes that form Hawaii Volcanoes National Park) pour tons of lava across the countryside and into the sea. The forces at work on this island have wrought a variety of landscape that typifies the natural processes gradually shaping and reshaping the entire chain; but here, because the island is large enough to feel like a small subcontinent, you can travel from the rich earth of the sugarcane fields (and on the famous southwestern Kona Coast, America's only coffee fields) to the strange, sparse moonlike rockbeds of lava in the park and along the eastern coast. Green tropical jungle and gray, twisted rock — those are the muscle and bone that form the face of the Big Island.

Kilauea has been erupting with some measure of frequency in recent years, and Mauna Loa last erupted in 1984. Eruptions are always anticipated by the scientists living in the park, who constantly monitor the moods of the volcanoes. Hundreds of people — sightseers, photographers, journalists, and the idly curious — fly over to the island to try to catch a glimpse of eruptions when they occur. During one of the more serious eruptions villages were evacuated, and the villagers waited calmly for the noise and fury to pass, secure in the knowledge that their prayers to Pele, the goddess of fire who lives in Kilauea, would not be unanswered. The eruption came as scheduled, the lava flowed as expected, and, as anticipated by the villagers, the damage was minimal.

The attractions of the Big Island are manifold. It has glittering resort areas on the western side — the Kona and Kohala coasts — which offer accommodations and activities of every sort; it has many, many small communities that are untouched by commercialism and that represent agricultural Hawaii as well as any in the islands; and it has the volcanoes, and thus the lava-torn landscape, which is unique in all the world. With an airport at Hilo, on the northeastern coast, and one outside Kona (Keahole Airport) on the western coast, either place can be the Hawaiian entrance or exit point for travelers.

Allow at least four days to see the Big Island. There are really three major areas to explore: Hilo and the northern Hamakua Coast; the Kona Coast; and the national park. The route described below starts at Hilo and circles counterclockwise past the Hamakua area, to the Kona Coast, and ends at the park.

HILO: Offers an opportunity to see Hawaii's thriving orchid industry nose-to-blossom. Some nurseries are designed to give the impression of being ornate formal gardens; a few are open to the public. These include *Nani Mau Gardens,* 421 Makalika St.; *Hilo Tropical Gardens,* 1477 Kalanianaole Ave.; and *Orchids of Hawaii,* 575 Hinano St.

The Lyman Mission House and Museum (276 Haili St.), built in 1839 as the home of an early missionary, has exhibits on the ethnic makeup of the islands, as well as artifacts of early Hawaiian culture. Nearby is a very genuine, and very large, artifact: the Naha Stone, which adorns the front yard of the Hilo Library (300 Waianuenue Ave.). The stone weighs more than two tons; according to an ancient legend, the man who could lift the stone would become king of all the islands. The man who did so was King Kamehameha I — known to history as Kamehameha the Great because he did indeed conquer all the islands (more with the help of cannon than brute strength). For shopping, try *Hawaiian Handcrafts,* 760 Kilauea Ave., with Hawaiian-made wood products at reasonable prices.

HAMAKUA COAST: North along Rte. 19 the views are staggering. Atop high pali (cliffs), the road looks over the windward coast and the not-very-peaceful Pacific Ocean. This road was constructed to accommodate nature, not man, and you will soon develop a rhythm in your driving as you curve, plunge, curve, and climb around waterfalls and valleys. All along the route you will see the state Hawaiian Warrior signs that indicate scenic overviews. Don't fail to stop. When Hawaiians think a view is good enough to warrant special note, mainlanders had better take them at their word. Off the highway at the small village of Honomu is Akaka State Park, with two of the most beautiful waterfalls on the island. The highest is Akaka Falls itself — a 442-foot ribbon of water that plunges daintily down a jungle cliff; the other is Kahuna Falls, which drops 400 feet. Nearby are jungle walks among lush, if eerie, plants. Laupahoehoe Point — a small "leaf of lava" that pushes into the brutal, angry Pacific — is an excellent spot for picnicking. The point is marked by a Warrior sign, and you must drive from the road down a small, winding road to the point itself. There the picnic area is bathed in a fine sea spray, and you can watch the sometimes terrifying fury of the sea smashing against the rocks. In 1946, a school with 20 children and 3 teachers inside was lost to the sea when a giant tidal wave washed over the point. A monument commemorates the spot.

The end point of the northward Rte. 19 road is Waipio Valley, where Rte. 19 joins Rte. 25, the only navigable point through the Kohala Mountains. Here there is a lookout tower with fine views of the northeastern end of the island, and drivers with four-wheel vehicles who offer tours through the rough roads of the valley.

PUUKOHOLA HEIAU NATIONAL HISTORIC SITE: Where Rte. 19 crosses the base of the Kohala Mountains and turns south to follow Hawaii's eastern coast stands this historic site, an ancient temple (approximately 15th century) and altar that young King Kamehameha I rebuilt in 1791, dedicated to a god of war. Behind this act of piety was cold and cunning ambition. He invited his chief island rival to the dedication cermony and there killed him. With that act Kamehameha initiated his drive to conquer not just the island of Hawaii but all the major islands in the chain. Just down the road from the heiau is one of the island's most elegant resorts, the *Westin Mauna Kea,* and beyond it Puako, a small village with some of the best examples of Hawaiian petroglyphs. At Puako, Rte. 19 becomes the Queen Kaahumanu Highway, cutting across a lava desert and skirting a number of beautiful, and as yet relatively undeveloped, beaches.

KAILUA-KONA: The major town on the Kona Coast and the starting point of a series of resorts that stretches to Keauhou. Most of the town's contemporary attractions — hotels, shops, restaurants, and bars — are on Alii Drive. There, also, is Hulihee Palace, a summer resort built in 1837 for the Hawaiian royal family that today houses a museum of furnishings and memorabilia of the period. Kailua-Kona is a major center for deep-sea fishing along the Kona Coast (one of the best fishing grounds for big game fish in the world), and there are numerous charter operations. This is also a fine place for a late afternoon stroll, to watch the charters return to port, and the weighing of the catches.

KEALAKEKUA BAY: British Captain James Cook was killed here in 1779. Cook was the first Western explorer to discover the Hawaiian Islands (which he called the Sandwich Islands) when he sailed into Kauai's Waimea Bay in 1778 in search of fresh water. He was greeted joyfully by the Hawaiians, who regarded him as something of a god and who recognized his courage and mastery of the sea. Cook's expedition stayed for only a few weeks, but returned in January 1779 to Kealakekua Bay on the Big Island. Here too he was accorded great respect. On February 4, 1779, Cook and his crew set sail but ran into a storm that damaged one ship and forced them to go back. This lapse in godliness, as well as the new demands for food and supplies, strained relations between the islanders and Cook and eventually a battle erupted, ending with Cook's death. It has become legend that the islanders dismembered and ate Cook, but this is not true. They gave him a hero's burial, which involved dismemberment and special burial in the earth. The spot where Cook fell is marked by a monument, and today the bay is a marine preserve.

CITY OF REFUGE NATIONAL HISTORICAL PARK: This ancient and sacred area was once a sanctuary for Hawaiian criminals. Fugitives had to swim the perilous Honaunau Bay to reach the City of Refuge. Once there, they were entitled to pardons from the resident priest and could then return home, free from stigma and the threat of death. Today visitors can explore this bit of antiquity, watch craftsmen carve canoes with the same tools and methods used by early Hawaiians, and marvel at the perfect remains of parts of the 6-foot-thick walls built of lava rock and locked in place without mortar, and at the formidable tikis, handcrafted copies of the 16th-century originals. Brochures are available at the visitors center.

HAWAII VOLCANOES NATIONAL PARK: When either of the Big Island's two active volcanoes — Kilauea, 4,077 feet, and Mauna Loa, 13,680 feet — rumbles, bubbles, or actually erupts, people flock from around the world to watch. Both volcanoes are in the park, which is dedicated to collecting and disseminating information on volcanic phenomena. The visitors center (about 2 miles inside the park's boundaries) has volumes of material on the effects of these two volcanoes as well as information on park activities — camping and hiking within Kilauea's crater, ranger-led hikes, special events. While you visit, anything could happen. You might see Kilauea releasing fountains of steam or rivers of lava; you might feel tremors from Mauna Loa; you certainly can watch the seismograph at the observatory. At *Volcano House* (the park's inn and restaurant, just across from the visitors center) you can spend the night on the edge of Kilauea crater and have a box lunch packed for a day's hike the next morning. Information: Superintendent, Hawaii Volcanoes National Park, Hawaii, HI 96785 (808 967-7311).

BEST EN ROUTE

Westin Mauna Kea, Kohala – This is as close to paradise as most of us will ever get. A valuable art collection is displayed throughout the main rooms and halls for all to touch and appreciate; gardens delight the eye at every turn. It has 3 fine dining rooms, very handsomely decorated rooms, and a Robert Trent Jones, Sr., golf course with a world-famous water hole over the crashing Pacific. Tennis, beach, horseback riding, and pool. PO Box 218, Kohala Coast, Hawaii, HI 96743 (808 882-7222 or 800 228-3000).

Kona Village Resort, Kona Coast – Some 100 bungalows dot the 65-acre expanse of this village, each designed and decorated in the style of one of the islands of the South Pacific. Facilities include tennis courts, water sports, sailing. The daily rate includes breakfast, lunch, and dinner. PO Box 1299, Kaupulehu-Kona, Hawaii, HI 96745 (808 325-5555 or 800 367-5290).

Volcano House, Hawaii Volcanoes National Park – This is the first place to fill up when scientists at the observatory predict a major eruption. This gracious, comfortable inn and restaurant requires reservations even during periods of quiet. Surely it must be one of the few hotels in Hawaii that routinely lights a cozy fire in the evenings. Hawaii Volcanoes National Park, HI 96718 (808 967-7321 or 800 325-3535).

Kauai, Hawaii

Kauai is a spectacular island by any standards: oldest in the archipelago — first formed, and, therefore, first to cool — most lush, verdant, and rich with soil, a land where anything will grow. Papaya, mango, coconut, hundreds of varieties of exotic plants and orchids, bougainvillea and cactus, litchi, banana trees, mimosa — an endless list. And every growing edible — as well as almost every other species — was brought by someone: the first Hawaiians, the missionaries, Western explorers, the Japanese, mainland visitors. Without human help, the islands get only one new species of plant every 10,000 years.

On the windward side, everything is green. The razor-sharp pinnacles of the volcanic fissures along Na Pali coast, the spectacular rock chasms that spill down the windward side of the island into dense jungle valleys, pouring forth myriad waterfalls, are covered with a light down of lichen. And that which is not green is red — the ferrous red of iron-permeated soil, further evidence (if any were needed) of the now utterly extinct volcanoes that heaved this island thousands of feet from the sea bed.

Even the misconceptions that visitors carry to the island are dominated by geography. Kauai is known as one of the wettest spots on earth. But, in fact, it rains only 60 to 80 inches a year on the northern, wetter, and windward side of the island; only 15 to 20 inches a year leeward. Way up on Mt. Waialeale (Why-ali-ali), it rains some 500 inches a year, easily one of the wettest places in the world and the source of Kauai's rotten weather reputation. But Waialeale is in the middle of the island, 5,000 feet up, and it actually acts as a rain barrier for the southern half of Kauai. Windward it is wet, especially in winter, but spring and summer bring good holidaying weather to the entire island.

LIHUE: By necessity most vacationers begin their visit to Kauai here, the island's commercial center and the site of its main airport (a 20-minute flight from Oahu). Whether coming for a week (advised) or a day (popular but a pity), Lihue is the point of arrival and offers the first glimpse of the marriage of sugarcane and tourism that characterizes Kauai right now. Best about Lihue is its location on Kauai's eastern coast, midway on the road that circles the island (Kauai is a slightly dented and bashed circle, 32 miles across; the road would make a complete circle around the island except for the interruption of the impassable Na Pali cliffs).

Once beyond Lihue — which is low on charm but does have some interesting sights and a few good restaurants — you plunge almost instantly into old Hawaii. The towns and villages still live in the grip of the two monoliths of island life, the missionary church and the plantation. Little towns like Hanapepe (which means "working babies") are part of a genuine frontier plantation culture. Scattered along the coast are numerous fine resorts and most of the historic and geological sights that make a driving tour enchanting.

South and west from Lihue the road leads to Waimea Canyon, a "must see," and eventually ends at Kokee State Park — quite literally perched over a 1,000-foot drop into the westernmost valley of Na Pali. That is the final destination of the drive south (perhaps a whole 19 miles from Lihue), but along the way there is much to see.

POIPU BEACH: Its waters (like those along most of the island's beaches) are shallow a long way out and subject to fits of rock along the sea floor where sand ought to be, but it's still a lovely beach for swimming and sunning. (All island beaches, even those of the posh resorts, are public, open, and free.) Poipu Beach has two of the best posh resorts on the island, the *Waiohai* and the *Kiahuna.*

SPOUTING HORN: An outjutting of volcanic rock, so eaten by the sea that when a strong roller comes in, the sea water spurts through a hole 10 to 15 feet into the air; a sad sigh whispers through this natural pneumatic tube with each spout. It provides a good illustration of the power the sugarcane companies have traditionally held on Kauai. Years ago, the spout shot as high as 80 feet into the air, high enough that salt spray was flung across the cane fields — perhaps 200 yards away — killing patches of cane. The plantation managers dynamited the horn, widening the hole so that the spout stayed within a reasonable height. Now the horn is protected by the state.

WAIMEA CANYON: Nowhere on the island are you so close to the staggering power of the earth itself as when peering into the depths of this 3,600-foot canyon, 10 miles long. The original Hawaiians believed this was the work of Pele, goddess of fire. It hardly makes more sense to try to imagine the force necessary to have left these huge wedges of mountain hanging just so; to have honed these cliffs to such sharp precision;

to have etched such regular and undeviating patterns across miles and miles of rock. When a helicopter swings across the canyon, hanging 1,000 feet or so above the Waimea River at the bottom of the ravine and whizzing along the length of the valley, you can suffer vertigo just watching.

KOKEE STATE PARK: The park has a lovely, tiny museum, a large picnic area, a restaurant (hamburgers and other sandwiches), and some comfortable cabins for about $10 a day (make reservations at least three months in advance, Kokee Lodge, PO Box 518, Kekaha, Kauai, HI 96752; 808 335-6061). It's a good place to stop after Waimea Canyon and before going the few miles more to the road's end at Na Pali lookout. It is also the starting point of miles of hiking trails that will be irresistible to botanists and backpackers.

NA PALI COAST: The highlight of any trip to Kauai. Here the windward side of the island breaks into a series of splendid, jagged, jungle valleys thousands of feet deep, like patterns cut into fine crystal. They stretch from the mountains to the sea and are accessible only by foot (and some not even by foot), air, or sea. Numerous legends and superstitions surround Na Pali. It was here that an entire tribe of Hawaiians disappeared forever several centuries ago. And here that the legendary Menehune — a race of dwarfs, credited with building much of the stonework on the island — are said to have hidden when they mysteriously disappeared. Some islanders believe they still live in Na Pali. (Lest you don't quite believe in the existence of the Menehune, Captain James Cook, who landed here in 1778, mentions in his report to the British Admiralty seeing a group of very light-skinned, diminutive women.) Late last century, a leper named Koolau fought off the entire state militia by guerrilla warfare waged from the jungles of Na Pali. He refused to go to the leper colony on Molokai and took his family into the depths of the jungle, where presumably they lived and died.

From the lookout 4,000 feet above the ocean, is a magnificent view down Kalalau Valley to the water. There are some hiking trails into Na Pali from the eastern side of the island, but most frequent access is from the other side, where Kauai's main, circular road ends at Hanalei and Haena. From there you can hike to beaches 2, 6, or 10 miles along the coast, following wave upon wave of valley. Or take the easy way out and hire a helicopter from Lihue or Princeville (companies charge about $95 and up for an hour's ride) to spin you through the valleys.

HANALEI: *South Pacific* was filmed here, and a marvelous old plantation town it is. The town has a thrown-together, informal museum, Hanalei Museum, but of more interest is Waioli Mission House, built in 1841 and filled with period furnishings. It's a piece of genuine New England Hawaii. There's also good scuba and snorkeling in the area.

BEST EN ROUTE

Waiohai, Poipu Beach – This super-deluxe resort is sleek and handsome and thoroughly devoted to pampering its guests. Bedrooms are spacious, done in fresh, cool colors and outfitted with well-stocked wet bars and luxurious dressing rooms. An early morning dip in one of its 3 swimming pools or a stroll along its lovely curve of sandy beach should be followed by breakfast on your lanai overlooking the sea; ask for the house specialty — macadamia nut muffins. Poipu Beach (808 742-9511 or 800 227-4700).

Kiahuna Plantation, Poipu Beach – A first-rate beach and tennis resort, this low-rise, plantation-style condominium covers 35 garden acres. Inside, the one- and two-bedroom apartments follow a tropical scheme, with cool pastel fabrics and lots of rattan furnishings. There's also an 18-hole golf course. Poipu Beach (808 742-6411 or 800 367-7052).

Makai Club Cottages and Condominiums, Princeville – The one- and two-bedroom apartments are large and well furnished with such amenities as two-level living rooms, fireplaces, Japanese furo baths, and spacious dressing rooms. Restaurants and shops, too. PO Box 3040, Princeville, Kauai, HI 96722 (808 826-3820 or 800 367-7090).

Maui, Hawaii

The second largest island in the Hawaiian chain has a very strange shape, an even more interesting history, and topography that accounts for some of the most beautiful country in the islands. Given only a day or two, you will undoubtedly end up on the beaches of West Maui, where beautiful hotels and condominiums stretch from Kaanapali to Kapalua, or on the resort strip farther south, from Kihei to Wailea. You could do worse. But with just a couple more days, and a car to help negotiate the long — for the islands — distances between stops, you can add to that the lush valleys around Wailuku and Kahului and the heights of Haleakala National Park. The result would be almost a small survey of Hawaii's geologic and cultural history — a dormant volcano; verdant, fertile valleys devoted to cane and pineapples; and a west coast village that was a standard stop on the whaling route more than 150 years ago, when missionaries and New England whalers literally fought for the hearts and minds of the Hawaiian people.

Maui has three distinct geographic areas. Picture the island in the form of a steer's head facing east. West Maui, with the gold coast strip of hotels and beach, and the well-preserved whaling town of Lahaina form the ear of this steer. Inland, West Maui is mountainous, wild, and, in part at least, unexplored. Where the ear joins the head, at Wailuku and Kahului, the mountains break and there is much flat and fertile farmland. To the east the island rises steadily along the slopes of dormant Mt. Haleakala, its summit 10,023 feet above the sea. At the snout of the hypothetical steer is the village of Hana.

Most tourists begin their visit to Maui at Kahului airport (a 20-minute jet flight from Oahu) and from there head west for Lahaina and the resorts beyond, south for Kihei and Wailea, or east on Rte. 37 to Haleakala.

LAHAINA: The capital of the Hawaiian islands from 1795 until 1843, when King Kamehameha III moved the court to Honolulu. Of far greater impact on the town and its people were the whaling ships, which made Lahaina a regular stop from the early 1800s until petroleum replaced whale oil as a source of light at the end of the century. For the 80 or 90 years of the whaling period, life was constant turmoil. Missionaries saved souls and sailors seduced and drank, and in general the Hawaiians were harassed and harangued on all sides. A great deal of the original whaling town still exists, in part due to the hard work of Lahaina's contemporary citizens, who have spent a good part of recent years in restoration work. An interesting place to visit is Baldwin House Museum, the home of the medical missionary Dr. Dwight Baldwin in the mid-19th century. In the vicinity is a huge, spreading banyan tree (in the town square near Front St.). It was planted in 1873 to commemorate 50 years of missionary work on the island, and it stands still strong and hale today. Across the street from the tree is the town's most famous manmade landmark, the *Pioneer Inn,* an old rake of a hotel that opened at the turn of the century; in the harbor in front is the *Carthaginian II,* a ship of recent vintage true-rigged like a brig of the whaling era. Visit anytime during the winter months, when the annual migration of humpback whales is under way and enjoy a wide choice of whale-watching cruises. The whales breed in Hawaiian waters in the winter (in summer they live much farther north, in Arctic seas), and standing on the dock you can see them cavorting between Maui and Lanai from December through April.

KAANAPALI TO NAPILI: This 4-mile stretch of beach has been called "a sort of rarefied Waikiki." Even "rarefied" does it a disservice. If the beach is not quite so spectacular as Waikiki, the resorts that line it have been far more sensitively and sensibly developed than those that pile up like a freeway crash along Honolulu's pride. The beach is neatly divided by a huge outcropping of black volcanic rock, called Black Rock in English and Kekaa in Hawaiian. At the base of this beauty is the *Sheraton Maui Hotel.* Five other hotels and an equal number of condominium complexes make up the *Kaanapali Beach Resort,* which also includes the famous Royal Kaanapali Golf Courses (two of eight 18-hole courses on the island) and Whalers Village. The full impact of the whaling industry on Maui is described in detail in the many exhibitions of this combination shopping bazaar and museum that allows adults to shop while kids entertain themselves with a huge whale skeleton and other such delectables.

KAPALUA: Beyond Kaanapali, the coast of West Maui is almost one uninterrupted stretch of holiday condominiums to the northwest tip of the island. Two particularly beautiful beaches can be found here, the beach at Napili Bay and Kapalua Bay, perhaps the most perfect crescent beach on the island. Kapalua Bay is surrounded by the exquisite scenery of another of Maui's planned resort developments, Kapalua, set on panoramic acreage formerly used to grow pineapples. *Kapalua Bay Hotel,* condominium communities, 2 Arnold Palmer golf courses, 10 tennis courts, and a small shopping center are the central features of the resort.

WAILUKU: Another early Maui city that has survived — and thrived — in the 20th century. On Maui's northern coast, close to Kahului and its airport, Wailuku has its own remnants of early Hawaii. A staunch emblem of Maui's missionary past is Kaahumanu Church (Rte. 30), the first version of which was built in 1832 (the present structure dates from 1876). It is a simple building that reflects much of the spirit and the form of early church work here and throughout the islands. Wailuku is also a good place to make forays to Iao Valley, in the mountains of inland West Maui. Along the way on Rte. 32 you pass the Maui Historical Society Museum, Hale Hoikeike, with exhibitions on all aspects of Maui history. It is a good place to stop before continuing to road's end a few miles farther west, at Iao Valley's Kepaniwai Park. The park is the approximate point where King Kamehameha the Great (grandfather of the King Kamehameha who moved the royal court from Maui to Oahu) finally trapped his Mauian enemies in the basin of Iao Valley and decimated them, assuring the loyalty of all the major islands in the chain. This happened in the 1790s, and the carnage was so great that the stream that runs through the valley was named Wailuku, "Bloody River."

KIHEI AND WAILEA: The southwestern coast of Maui is on the dry leeward side of Haleakala. Six miles of the coast are known as Kihei — and better known as "sunny" Kihei because of the sparse average annual rainfall. Kihei is almost one long strip of golden beach from beginning to end, and not too many years ago the land fronting the beach — the same land that is now chockablock with low- and high-rise condominiums — was virtually virgin territory. So while Kihei has its beach to recommend it, it is often pointed to as a worst-case example of unchecked development, while the planned resort of Wailea, just south, is considered a model of the way to go. Wailea, too, has glorious beaches, but they are backed by resort property irrigated to the ultimate in verdure, and the two 18-hole golf courses, a 14-court tennis center, shopping center, three condominium villages, and two first-class hotels complement rather than violate the landscape.

HALEAKALA NATIONAL PARK: "The House of the Sun" — Mt. Haleakala — dominates the entire eastern half of Maui. The approaches from the west are a peaceful contrast to the tourist frenzy of the coastal resort areas. Here is countryside virtually untouched by commercialism, a series of pastoral scenes that could represent almost any mountainous region in the world. Because of the mountain, Maui enjoys a unique climate system, hot on the coasts, fertile and moist on the flat plains between West Maui and the mountain, and progressively cooler weather as the altitudes increase. Some 10,000 feet high, Haleakala is the largest dormant volcano in the world. Its crater is an immense 19-square-mile hole 3,000 feet deep, honeycombed with trails and devoted to a national park. On the way to the park's entrance you will pass (on Rte. 377) the Kula Botanical Gardens, where experts will explain how Maui's unique climate is used to grow simple garden vegetables (the best in the islands) beside exotic tropical orchids.

Park headquarters, at about 7,000 feet, is a necessary stop to collect information on campgrounds, the mountain, and activities like horseback riding, hiking, and renting simple cabins maintained by the National Park Service in the crater. These must be reserved at least three months in advance (address below), and camping is strictly controlled; only 25 overnight campers are allowed in the park at one time. No matter how warm it may be at the base of Haleakala, you will need some light wrap at the summit or heavier clothing if you go at sunrise (a popular excursion).

The view from the top is spectacular. From there you see West Maui, and the neighboring islands of Hawaii, Lanai, Molokai, and Oahu. It was from the summit of Haleakala that Maui the god lassoed the sun to force him to make his daily trip across the sky more slowly. And dawn atop the mountain is one of the finest experiences a traveler can behold.

The park extends to Maui's eastern coast in a single 8-mile strip. The area encompasses a stretch of ecologically delicate jungle, where the rangers are struggling to maintain an environment that protects and encourages the tropical growths. The area also includes the Seven Pools, a series of pools and streams that spill into one another like a pyramid of champagne glasses filled to overflowing. This eastern area of the park, which encompasses the Kipahulu Valley, can be reached by circling East Maui on the Hana Highway, a scenic route that is in itself one of the island's sightseeing attractions. The road is rough, winding, and very narrow, which makes it difficult to stop to enjoy the views, but there are three lookout points along the way before it ends in Hana, a tiny village populated mainly by part-Hawaiians who work on the Hana Ranch and by out-of-town celebrities seeking seclusion. Beyond Hana, another 10 miles of rutted road leads to the park again, to where the lowest of the Seven Pools spills into the sea. Information: Superintendent, Haleakala National Park, PO Box 369, Makawao, Maui, HI 96768.

BEST EN ROUTE

Sheraton Maui Hotel, Kaanapali – Certainly one of the most dramatic locations on the island, with lobbies at the base and top of stark Black Rock. Facilities include the beach, swimming pools, tennis courts. Kaanapali Beach, Lahaina, Maui, HI 96761 (808 661-0031 or 800 325-3535).

Hyatt Regency Maui – Not just a hotel but a sightseeing attraction. Besides the 815 elegant rooms in three 7- to 9-story towers, the hotel's 20 landscaped acres contain tropical gardens, waterfalls, and Maui's largest swimming pool, fed by a 130-foot water slide. The hotel also boasts $2 million worth of Asian and Pacific art and a staff ornithologist to care for the many exotic birds on the property. Kaanapali Beach Resort (808 667-7474 or 800 228-9000).

Hotel Hana-Maui, Hana – This intimate hotel spreads across 20 acres on the island's far east coast; the only distractions from the perfectly blue Pacific are tennis courts, riding stables, a pool, and a pitch and putt golf course. It is currently completing a remodeling and expansion project; all 82 rooms have been renovated. Hana, Maui, HI 96713 (808 248-8211).

Molokai, Hawaii

There is a distinct hierarchy of development among the Hawaiian islands, and once you understand the forces at work it is a pretty accurate measure of the state of the local agricultural economy. Most of the major islands — Maui, Hawaii, Kauai, Molokai — have been dependent on agriculture at one time or another during this century. And time and again that industry has failed, forcing the islands, one after another, to develop adequate tourist facilities to replace the lost farming income. It has happened most recently on Kauai, which for years had a thriving sugarcane industry, with plantations of thousands and thousands of acres. In the last decade, however, the island has repeatedly lost business to the Far East, where cane is produced at perhaps one-tenth the cost (primarily because of low labor costs). And so Kauai began developing tourist facilities — very cautiously and with great consideration — to replace the vacuum left by sugarcane.

All this is happening right now on Molokai. Throughout the 19th century Molokai was known as "the Forgotten Island." Then, early in the 20th century, pineapples were introduced and the island began a gradual renaissance; Dole and Del Monte bought large chunks of the island, and people returned to Molokai for pineapple jobs. But as in the case of sugarcane on Kauai, impossibly cheap labor in the Far East has meant that island pineapples are simply too expensive, and Dole and Del Monte ceased operations in 1975 and 1983, respectively.

Right now Molokai has only one full-fledged resort, the *Sheraton Molokai.* More are on the drawing boards, but for the time being the island seems almost in a state of suspension, awaiting the future. The sense of quiet and solitude that has always characterized it has never been more marked than it is right now. In some places — the closed Dole Pineapple plantation town — there is an eerie sense of history just passed, of an era having closed so recently that it still vibrates in the air; yet elsewhere on the island this solitude is splendid and serene — for example, along the jagged, wild, inaccessible cliffs east of Makanalua Peninsula, or at the many coves and beaches that swimmers have entirely to themselves for hours on end. It is certainly an island that can be visited on a day trip from Oahu; the visitor flies either to Molokai airport (well outside the town of Kaunakakai) to see the whole island, or to Kalaupapa to visit the historical site and colony on Makanalua peninsula. But Molokai has wild roads and beautiful vistas as yet unmapped on any standard tourist itinerary, and a two- or three-day visit will offer a feeling of Hawaii unavailable on any of the more developed islands.

KAUNAKAKAI: Eight miles east of Hoolehua Airport, through which most tourists enter Molokai, is the island's main town of Kaunakakai. It may surprise you. With its main street and the wooden façade of its stores, it looks remarkably like a western frontier town. There is a distinct "cowboy" atmosphere about it typical of many towns throughout the islands. In the case of Kaunakakai, this atmosphere is more a reflection of the general character of Molokai towns than its proximity to the island's huge Puu O Huko Ranch. With a population of less than 1,000, the town has few tourist facilities, but much about it speaks of the island's recent history. You will note, for example, the fine, long wharf — extending a half mile into the sea — which is almost empty today. It was built to accommodate the huge barges on which pineapples were shipped for processing. Today little work is done on it.

PAPOHAKU BEACH: This is the west coast site of Molokai's *Sheraton Hotel* as well as some condominum resort development. The coast tends to be rocky, with occasional underwater coral reefs that can be an unpleasant surprise as you swim. Even the *Sheraton*'s beach is better for sunning than swimming. On the way to Papohaku, along Rte. 46, you will pass the former Dole plantation town of Maunaloa, where artists and craftspeople have settled. It is well worth a look as a living museum of contemporary company towns in Hawaii.

PALAAU STATE PARK: Along Molokai's northern coast, the park overlooks Makanalua Peninsula and the Kalaupapa settlement. The peninsula is 2,000 feet below the park, at the base of a series of jagged, wild cliffs that become inaccessible farther along the eastern coastline. The present view is not the original overlook. This can be found at the beginning of the Jack London Trail (also in the park), the tortuous switchback trail, navigable by foot or mule only, that leads from the overlook to the peninsula below, a trip of several hours.

HALAWA VALLEY: Filling Molokai's northeastern end. The valley is accessible only by Rte. 45, which begins in Kaunakakai and follows the island's coast east and north. At least a half-day's excursion from the airport, it offers a real sense of Molokai today — and the best views of the magnificent cliffs at road's end. (The road, by the way, becomes increasingly narrower as it heads north, twisting and turning along the mountains that rise like a ship's prow along the island's northern coast.) Immediately outside Kaunakakai on Rte. 45 are a number of ancient fish ponds. Dating as far back as the 15th century, they were built as fattening-up farms for the fish trapped inside, assuring the availability of a fresh fish meal whenever the royal whim desired one. All the major islands have ruins of these royal fish ponds, but the ones on Molokai are in the best state of preservation and are therefore worth a stop.

At the end of Rte. 45 is deserted Halawa Valley. Once a thriving community valley patchworked with taro farms, in 1946 the warnings of the giant tidal wave (tsunami) forced an evacuation from the valley. No one returned. The valley remains a tranquil, very tropical place popular with hikers and nature lovers. It's 4½ miles long, and a 2-hour hike that isn't too difficult leads to Moaula and Hipuapua Falls, which cascade 250 feet down into the head of the valley. The freshwater pool at Moaula Falls is cool but safe for swimming.

KALAUPAPA: In 1866 the entire Makanalua Peninsula was declared a leper colony by royal decree, and sufferers throughout the islands were forced to come here. Kalaupapa's isolation acted as a perfect buffer, protecting the healthy islanders from the disease they feared and shunned. The suffering inflicted on victims of the disease was intense: No provisions were made for food, shelter, clothing, or the basic necessities of life. Lepers were peremptorily dumped on the island and left to die (often with whatever family members consented to care for them in exile). In 1873 a Belgian priest, Father Damien Joseph de Veuster, chose to join the lepers, and for the next 16 years he labored to provide shelter and food for them and to build a living community where only disease and despair had ruled human relations. In 1889 he died of leprosy, but he left behind a real community. Today the peninsula is under the auspices of the Hawaii State Department of Health, and about 100 persons live here. It is their peninsula, but adult visitors are welcome (children under 16 are not allowed). Hansen's disease is completely under control today thanks to various sulfa drugs, and adults are completely safe. Several organizations offer tours of the peninsula, which can be approached by air, sea, or foot (a very tough hike) or mule from the overlook at Palaau State Park. One company is *Damien Tours,* PO Box 1, Kalaupapa, Molokai, HI 96742 (808 567-6171).

BEST EN ROUTE

Sheraton Molokai, Kepuhi Beach – *Sheraton* is the first in the sweepstakes to develop Molokai into a recognized tourist stop, and its entry is topnotch. With 292 rooms spread over 32 buildings, it has tennis courts, an 18-hole golf course, a beach (though not usually suitable for swimming), a pool, and shops. Its main dining room is beautifully designed, using some traditional Hawaiian building materials. PO Box 1977, Kepuhi Beach, Molokai, HI 96770 (808 552-2555 or 800 325-3535).

Hotel Molokai, Kaunakakai – In a palm grove about 2 miles from town, this resort has been converted into a condominium hotel. Rooms are distributed among buildings throughout the grounds, and though it hasn't the recreational facilities of the *Sheraton,* it is much more conveniently placed, in the center of the island rather than on the isolated western coast. PO Box 546, Kaunakakai, Molokai, HI 96748 (808 553-5347 or 800 367-5124).

Oahu, Hawaii

Oahu, home of four fifths of Hawaii's population, is quite appropriately nicknamed "the Gathering Place." Since Kamehameha III moved the royal court to Honolulu from Maui in 1843, Oahu has been the social, political, and industrial center of the entire archipelago. Since World War II it has also been the center of tourism, and several Oahu sites and cities have become synonymous with Hawaii itself: Honolulu, Diamond Head, Waikiki, and Pearl Harbor. (For a detailed report on these sites, see *Honolulu,* THE AMERICAN CITIES.) Just as you must get off Oahu to the Neighbor Islands to see all of Hawaii, you must get out of Honolulu to see all of Oahu. On the other hand, simply because of Honolulu, Oahu offers an immense variety of activities.

WAIKIKI BEACH: Not unlike Miami Beach, Waikiki is a miracle of shoulder-to-shoulder tall hotels with the expected complement of souvenir shops, restaurants, discos, bars, and other tourist attractions. The beach itself is the most extravagant stretch of sand in all the islands. It was the exclusive spot of the ancient Alii (royalty), who came here to sun and surf. The beach today remains as physically beautiful as any you will see in the world — when you can see it, that is. It is usually well hidden beneath a layer of supine bodies. Even sunrise joggers must jockey for a bare stretch of sand. Waikiki is not a deserted island paradise. There are some splendid hotels and restaurants along this strip. There are also honky-tonk traps and tacky stores.

From Honolulu and Waikiki the route we describe below roughly follows the southern, eastern, and northern coasts of the island in a large 110-mile loop. The first part of this loop, Rte. 72, covers the entire eastern tip of Oahu, from Diamond Head to Kailua. Ask at your hotel or at the desk of any car rental agency for a booklet of Oahu itineraries called the *Drive Guide.* It contains helpful maps and interesting descriptions of the routes.

OAHU'S SOUTHERN TIP: The road really starts at Diamond Head, the spectacular volcanic crater that has become the symbol of Hawaii. The volcano that formed this perfect crater has been extinct for at least 150,000 years, and early Hawaiians, for whom it was just as much a landmark as it is for Hawaiians today, thought it resembled nothing so much as a fish head. There are a number of relatively tough hiking paths in the crater that can be entered from a road between Makapuu Rd. and 18th Ave., off Diamond Head Road.

Rte. 72 passes through two affluent neighborhoods beyond Diamond Head, the Kahala district and Hawaii Kai, a development begun by Henry Kaiser, the man who during World War II turned the making of Liberty ships into a five-week project. Hanauma Bay Beach Park is where the Elvis Presley film *Blue Hawaii* was filmed; it has one of the most beautiful underwater parks in the country. It's an excellent place for snorkeling or scuba diving because the waters are so perfectly clear. Nearby is Halona Blow Hole, a submerged lava tube that turns sea water into a saltwater geyser as waves roll in.

Here, too, is Sea Life Park (259-7933), with a number of standard aquatic displays (dolphins, seals, whales) as well as a fascinating see-through tank filled with coral and various forms of sea life that would normally live in a coral reef. At feeding times you can watch scuba divers plunge into the water to lead a happy parade of turtles, multicolored fish, manta rays, eels, and small and larger sharks happily intent on the food being distributed. For confirmed landlubbers it is a fascinating performance. The easternmost point on the island is Makapuu Point, marked by a lighthouse. This is the point at which the trade winds divide, some continuing north, some south, across the island. At Kailua, to the north, it is possible to cut inland and return to Honolulu via the Pali Highway (Rte. 61). En route are the Nuuanu Pali Tunnels and the scenic masterpiece, Pali Lookout. This is where Kamehameha I drove the defenders of Oahu over the steep cliffs to their deaths. Today the view from these heights is as grand as it is fear-inspiring. The Pali Highway is mountainous, leading through lush tropical rain forests, numerous curves, and arriving abruptly in the teeming urban Honolulu.

EASTERN OAHU: The coastal loop continues beyond Kailua as Rte. 83, the Kamehameha Highway. This road takes you along the eastern and northern coasts of the island. Each of the islands has at least one — and usually several — mountains or ridges that form some familiar shape. On Maui there is the John F. Kennedy profile in Iao Valley; on Kauai, Queen Victoria's profile. All the islands are of volcanic origin, and in the fury of an eruption lava turns, twists, and tears into a fantastic variety of shapes. Oahu's major profile is the Crouching Lion, visible from Rte. 83. Like all of these figures, the resemblance is not exact and depends as much on the viewer's perspective and good will as on the actual shape of the formation. But what is interesting is that myths always collect around these profiles. A bit beyond the Crouching Lion is the lovely Sacred Falls, an 87-foot waterfall that plunges into a pool. You are welcome to swim in the pool and cavort in the falling water, but it is a hard mile's hike beyond the parking spot, and you should be prepared for about an hour's tramp.

The culmination of the drive along the eastern shore is the Polynesian Cultural Center in Laie (293-3333; in Waikiki, 923-1861). Though it is a commercial enterprise, the center has excellent reconstructions of villages of all the major cultures of the Pacific — Marquesas, Samoan, Tongan, Hawaiian, Tahitian, Fijian, Maori — with cultural performances and arts and crafts demonstrations in each village. There are lunchtime and evening Polynesian shows. A mixture of museum and Disneyland, the center is informative and a great deal of fun as well.

NORTHERN OAHU: Where Rte. 83 rounds the top of the island and turns southwest, it runs smack dab into a spot that is guaranteed to raise goose pimples on any surfer's surface — Sunset Beach, home of the Big Waves, including the notorious Banzai Pipeline. Here, every winter, international competitions are held. More cerebral, but thrilling in its own right, is nearby COMSAT — earth station for international commercial satellite communications. Ahead on the north shore is Waimea Falls Park (638-8511), another natural wonder gone professional. The famous and incredibly beautiful waterfall is now made easy to see on a round-trip tram ride. The 1,800-acre park offers a variety of botanical gardens, forests, and restaurants.

From here the highway turns south and heads toward Honolulu.

BEST EN ROUTE

Kahala Hilton, Honolulu – This deluxe hotel has a magnificent setting on a tropical lagoon inhabited by dolphins and turtles. Many of the 308 rooms have separate dressing rooms and lanais overlooking the lagoon, mountains, or beach. All have large baths and are decorated with interesting handmade wall hangings. The *Maile Restaurant* is one of the best in the Honolulu area. 5000 Kahala Ave., Honolulu, Oahu, HI 96816 (808 734-2211 or 800 367-2525).

Royal Hawaiian, Honolulu – Fondly known as "the Pink Palace" or "Pink Lady," this 525-room hotel was *the* place to stay in the 1930s, when luxury liners steamed into Honolulu with elegant passengers who stayed for months. The pink stucco Mediterranean-style building retains its glittering chandeliers and long corridors, although it has changed hands since then and is now managed by Sheraton. Avoid the new tower; it's the gracious, older rooms that really give this place its charm. 2255 Kalakaua Ave. (808 922-4422 or 800 325-3535).

Hyatt Regency, Honolulu – The two octagonal towers of this hotel atop the ritzy Hemmeter Center are a visual landmark in Waikiki, and its Great Hall with a tropical garden, three-story waterfall, and massive hanging sculpture is a sightseeing spot in itself. Each of the 1,234 rooms is handsomely furnished and decorated with some fine Hawaiian prints. 2424 Kalakaua Ave. (808 922-9292 or 800 228-9000).

Craters of the Moon National Monument, Idaho

Everyone wants to know what the moon really looks like. For centuries we lived with intense speculation, some of it informed by science, much indebted to imagination. Since 1969 we have lived with reality: those incredible pictures of a flat, gray, pockmarked surface scarred by all the flying debris of space for eons, flanked by strange, craggy rocks rising from Swiss cheese holes in the ground; and in front, standing with a flag unfurled in a vacuum, the astronaut, looking as awkward and out of place as a snowman learning to walk. These pictures have become part of our consciousness, our definition of what space travel is about. And while all the rigmarole of space is familiar — the liftoff, the orbit, the lunar module — the moon remains a mystery. What did the first astronauts feel? What would it be like to visit the moon?

It's not impossible. And no farther away than Idaho. When scientists wanted to familiarize prospective astronauts with the lunar surface, they brought them to Craters of the Moon National Monument, in the valley of the Snake River. The next best thing to actually being there, Craters of the Moon will give you an understanding of that extraterrestrial splendor we spend billions of dollars trying to reach.

It's not unfamiliar territory to many people, especially skiers. Some 70 miles to the west is Idaho's *Sun Valley,* one of the state's finest skiing centers. Coming south from Sun Valley, or north from I-84, you must drive at least a section of Rtes. 93 and 75 before getting to the turnoff for Craters of the Moon. Along the road are two diversions worth considering.

SHOSHONE INDIAN ICE CAVES: Idaho has a number of caves — some discovered, some not — related to its volcanic origins. The Shoshone Indian Caves are a constantly cool (about 32°) series of caves (or one long cavern really) that simply won't change temperature no matter how hot it is outside. There are tours every half hour between May and October. (Be sure to bring a sweater.) On the grounds are an Indian museum and the statue of Chief Washakie of the Shoshone tribe. Admission charge. About 43 miles south of Sun Valley, 15 miles north of Shoshone on Rte. 75.

SHOSHONE FALLS: Although quite a detour — 30 miles south of the town of Shoshone — the falls are well worth the drive. Larger than Niagara, these waterfalls drop 212 dramatic, turbulent feet into the Snake River. (Evel Knievel fans will remember Snake River because of his world-famous, daredevil jump across Snake River Canyon, which is farther along the meandering Snake.) Like all parts of the Snake, the drama of the falls is affected by the flow of water, which is, in its turn, affected by rainfall and, more important, the amount of irrigation along its course through Idaho. During the heat of the summer irrigation is at its height, the falls are at their nadir.

CRATERS OF THE MOON NATIONAL MONUMENT: Craters of the Moon is 60 miles northeast of Shoshone, along Rte. 93. You'll know you're in the right part of the country a few miles before you reach Carey, Idaho, when you pass a series of lava beds. If you miss them, don't worry; there'll be plenty more coming up.

Craters of the Moon is a land of lava on lava — stark, black, and cinder-blown. Its visual impact is stunning: miles of black lava rising and falling over the otherwise broad, flat valley, with abrupt, jagged peaks and huge cinder and lava cones — some 800 feet high — dotting the landscape. The entire area was the product of a series of volcanic explosions that over eons added successive layers of lava to rock and lava already laid down. So startling is the effect of seeing the monument that its equally startling geographic history takes some time to appreciate.

The monument sits atop a 60-mile fissure in the earth known as the Great Rift. In eight great epochs of upheaval, the Great Rift exploded in waves upon waves of white-hot magma — spewing molten rock at 2,000° out of the fissure itself — throwing tons of debris and rock into the air to form the volcanic cones that appear across the area. The cones belong to one of the earlier series of eruptions; lava flows within the monument date anywhere from 2,000 to nearly 15,000 years ago.

The human history of the monument is nowhere near as intriguing as its natural history. Indians certainly knew — and passed through — the area. You will see trail markers and cairns piled in various spots; they are Indian artifacts, though we do not know exactly how they were used. But it does not seem to have been an important part of the world for them. The area was discovered by white men in 1833 and proclaimed a national monument in 1924.

The place to start any tour is at the visitors center, where there are displays on the area's amazing formations and natural history which describe the process in detail. From there, a 7-mile loop drive will take you past most of the monument's best-known landmarks. Don't miss the Indian Tunnel, an 830-foot lava tube used as a cave by the Indians on treks through the lava fields, and Devils Orchard, one of the younger lava formations. Be sure to take along water, even when you are driving. In summer, the sun bakes the lava, burns the foot, and parches the throat. (In winter, the entire area is covered in deep snow and turns into marvelous cross-country ski terrain.)

For the more adventurous, numerous trails and walks let you explore the monument on foot and bring you face to face with the lava. There is much to recommend this approach. Since much of the monument can't be reached by car, it is the only way to really see the vast area of lava fields that are virtually unexplored. And by venturing into the (relative) unknown on foot, you will discover the monument's great secret: Far from being a sterile, hostile, bleak landscape, it is alive with plants, birds, and animals. Hundreds of species of flora have adapted to the area; there are mountain bluebirds, nighthawks, and sparrows galore; and in the backcountry you will see mule deer, hear coyote, and, if you're very lucky, spot a distant bobcat. Permits are required for overnight travel into wilderness areas. Information: Superintendent, Craters of the Moon National Monument, PO Box 29, Arco, ID 83213 (208 527-3257).

BEST EN ROUTE

You will certainly have no trouble finding hotels and motels within striking distance of Craters of the Moon. However, most recommendable are several lodges in the Sun Valley/Ketchum area.

Sun Valley Lodge and Inn – The lodge and inn are separate physical entities, but part of the *Sun Valley Resort*. The lodge is a classic, rustic redwood ski lodge (of recent vintage) with 141 rooms, some with fireplaces; also, 2 good restaurants. The inn is more family-oriented, with 115 rooms in a rambling, neo-Tyrolean building. Some shops and restaurants are in a mall separating the two buildings. Sun Valley Rd., Sun Valley, ID 83353 (208 622-4111; 800 632-4104 in Idaho, 800 635-8261 elsewhere).

Heidelberg Inn – More in the Alps tradition of Idaho resorts, the *Heidelberg* is a kind of Austrian Alps motel, pleasanter to visit than to try to describe. Some of its 30 rooms have fireplaces and kitchenettes. PO Box 304, Sun Valley, ID 83353 (208 726-5361 or 800 367-6820).

Tamarack Lodge – A very comfortable resort lodge with 27 rooms. PO Box 2000, Sun Valley, ID 83353 (208 726-3344).

Flint Hills, Kansas

The Flint Hills run from the Kansas-Oklahoma border into the northern third of the Sunflower State. The north-south axis of the hills lies about 45 miles east of Wichita, or about a quarter of the distance between the Missouri state line in the east and the Colorado foothills of the Rockies that form Kansas's western edge.

The Flint Hills, so named because of the chunks of flint in the soil, are among the last surviving plains of prairie grassland. Although at one time the plains formed a belt that ran from Chicago to the edge of the Rockies and from Canada to Texas, now scarcely 1% of the original 400,000 square miles of tallgrass remain. Most of the land has been razed to provide homes on the range or has been reduced to stubble by machines and grazing herds.

Once the plains were subject to long droughts and brush fires — the stereotypical picture of this area of Kansas. But modern technology has changed that image of the plains, with the planting of fire lines, the building of large reservoirs, and the construction of superhighways. Also, the Flint Hills are probably not as dry and devoid of plant life as you might have thought. Trees line the area's streams, which in turn nourish wild plums; wildflowers seem to thrive on the streams' grassy slopes with blooms for every warm season; Fremont's clematis, towering sunflower, evening primrose, larkspur, cornflower, indigo, and clover mingle on the hillsides.

For the most part, this section of Kansas looks much as it did when pioneers passed through on their way west, and settlers stayed to farm the rich soil in other parts of the state. The farms are vastly larger now, the fields tended by giant clanking machines, but the prairie that served as a home for herds of buffalo and pronghorn antelope is still prime grazing territory. The area is also known for its sprawling cattle ranches and rich oil deposits.

Cattle fed on the grasses of Kansas grow exceptionally large and healthy, although it was not until the turn of the century that agricultural scientists understood why. Under the prairie lies limestone chock full of protein and minerals. The prairie roots, going down into the earth as deep as six yards, tap this remnant of an ancient seabed and bring its nourishment to the stems and leaves, making extraordinarily rich fodder. Cowboys still ride the hills on horseback and in four-wheel drives, searching for the stragglers of their grazing herds. You can join these lone sailors in a sea of golden grass by driving through Flint Hills. If you have a jeep, you can get away from the paved highways that cross the plains here, but even if you stick to the civilized paths, you cannot help being transported, for a moment, to the simpler life of the past.

Although Kansas is known for its sudden, severe thundershowers and storms that often bring tornadoes, there are only a few twisters during the spring.

The route we suggest will lead you through Flint Hills en route from Kansas City to Oklahoma City.

TOPEKA: The state capital since 1861, Topeka was the site of bitter conflict between abolitionists and proslavery factions during the Civil War. After years of being known as Bleeding Kansas, the state joined the Union. Sites in town include: State House, housing artwork depicting pioneer and Civil War years (Capitol Square; 913 296-0111). The zoo has exhibitions that include a tropical rain forest and a new gorilla encounter (Gage Park; 913 272-5821). Nearby, the Reinisch Memorial Rose and Rock Gardens provide an oasis of fragrant tranquillity in spring, summer, and autumn (Gage Park). The Kansas State Historical Society has a new multimillion-dollar museum complex with displays on the state's history (take the Wanamaker North exit off I-70, west of Topeka).

EMPORIA, FLINT HILLS: Take I-35 about 50 miles southwest from Topeka. This is the heart of the Flint Hills region and its major cattle market. Tens of thousands of cattle are sent to the slaughterhouse from this town every year. Emporia was the home of William Allen White, publisher of the *Emporia Gazette* and one of America's most respected editors. His bust stands in Peter Pan Park. For information on activities, call the Emporia Chamber of Commerce (316 342-1600). Emporia State University presents concerts, plays, and films throughout the year (1200 Commercial). The Way College emphasizes biblical studies (1300 W 12th). Lyons County Lake and Park, a 528-acre recreation area, has swimming, boat launching, fishing, and camping. Campsites do not have hookups (11 miles north of town on Rte. 170). For information, call the State Forestry, Fish and Game Commission office in Emporia, 316 342-0658.

FLINT HILLS NATIONAL WILDLIFE REFUGE: About 5,000 acres form this refuge, primarily devoted to waterfowl. In winter, as many as 20 bald eagles nest on the grounds, as well as many other species. Among them: snow geese, blue geese, greater and lesser Canadian geese, mallard ducks, great horned and snowy owls. Whitetail deer, coyote, red fox, and rabbit live here too. The best time to visit is fall, either before or after the hunting season, when the refuge is closed to human visitors. Open the rest of the year. Free. From Emporia, take Rte. 99 south about 3 miles. After you cross the river bridge, you'll see an unnumbered county road running east to Hartford. Follow it for about 20 miles to the refuge (316 392-5553).

FALL RIVER AND TORONTO DAM AND LAKE STATE PARKS: Known as the twin reservoirs of the "Kansas Ozarks," the combined recreation area consists of 2,000 acres, with 40 miles of shoreline. Fishing, boating, swimming, hiking, and camping are available. The parks are 55 miles south of Emporia on Rte. 99, then east for 20 miles on Rte. 96 (316 637-2291).

WICHITA: Kansas's largest city and leading manufacturing center, Wichita is the headquarters of four aircraft companies. Places of interest include the Wichita Art Museum, containing American and European canvases and sculpture (619 Stackman Dr., Sim Park); Wichita Art Association, containing two modern galleries and a children's theater (9112 E Central); Wichita/Sedgwick County Museum, containing displays on home life in the 1800s (204 S Main); Wichita State University, with Frank Lloyd Wright buildings and a contemporary art museum (N Hillside and 17th sts.). Kids will enjoy the Old Cow Town Museum, a restored frontier village with Wyatt Earp's jail. Open daily, March through December; closed weekends in January and February (1871 Sim Park Dr.).

Glacier National Park, Montana

Montana's Glacier National Park is measured in millions: 1 million acres carved by the movement of massive glaciers millions of years ago, visited by about 2 million people every year. These 1,600 square miles shared by the US and Canada are known as Waterton/Glacier International Peace Park or simply Glacier, although the giant ice sheets to which the park owes its name and its geography have long since disappeared. There are still some 50 small glaciers throughout the park — snow masses deep enough to compact the lower levels into ice and heavy enough to creep downhill. The largest of these, Grinnell, covers 300 acres and contains ice 400 feet thick. In the summer, streams of water from Grinnell and the other glaciers cascade down the mountainside, gathering volume as they merge and tumble into the deep cold lakes. This spectacular descent and many other features of this Alpine wilderness in the northwest region of Montana (just west of St. Mary) merit at least a one-week visit.

Glacier's six large lakes (all at least 5 miles long) stretch from the park's edges into its interior; it has some 200 smaller lakes and glacial ponds, 1,000 waterfalls, over 50 streams, and 700 miles of trails and paths for hiking and horseback riding as well. The Blackfeet Indians considered the area sacred because of its awesome beauty.

The park is open all year long, although some roads are closed in winter due to heavy snow. Late fall brings visitors who come to observe the migrating bald eagles and other wildlife; winter brings cross-country skiers and snow-shoers. Others come merely to enjoy a snowball fight in summer, fish in a mountain stream, or watch a mountain goat appear to defy gravity in search of vegetation along a mountain slope.

Enter the park from West Glacier, along US 2 or from St. Mary on the park's east end along US 89. Within park boundaries, you will be urged to follow regulations, not only because of the geography of the park, which can be treacherous, but to protect its rich and abundant animal life. The 57 species of animals include the mountain goat, deer, moose, elk, beaver, muskrat, mink, bighorn sheep, coyote, wolf, and grizzly bear. Glacier is one of the few US parks that is home to grizzlies. Hikers are encouraged to make noises along the trail, indicating their presence in order to avoid surprising and frightening the bears.

In addition to the variety of animal life, there are at least 200 types of birds, from hawks and eagles that swoop overhead to grouse and dippers that inhabit the woods and streams. As in any wildlife preserve, these creatures are not easy to spot, and it is likely that you will leave having seen only an occasional mountain goat or sleepy marmot.

The best way to see the park is on foot, on short walks from the visitors centers at Logan Pass, St. Mary, or Apgar, or on longer treks, some of which are guided. In some areas you can rent horses for horseback journeys through the park. But if you have a few days to spare, the best assurance of getting a taste of the park's resources is to hike and camp in any of the 15 camp-grounds. What you discover on your own can be augmented by participating in one of the daily walks or campfire programs conducted by rangers at the visitors centers or campgrounds. They will point out the myriad plants and explain how the knife-edged ridges and glacial peaks were formed eons ago, an invaluable part of your visit.

If you cannot manage more than a drive through Glacier, you will still have the experience of one of the best routes in America. The park's Going-to-the-Sun Road, starting in St. Mary on Rte. 89, is an unforgettable 50 miles of twisting, cliff-hanging mountain roadway linking the east and west sides of the park. (Vehicles over 30 feet long or over 8 feet wide are banned from the road, and even a slight snow necessitates strict regulations.)

Along the way, you skirt the edge of St. Mary Lake, with its backdrop of snow-capped peaks and Douglas firs, reaching the first of 17 parking turnouts about 5 miles beyond the lake. Here you can see Triple Divide Peak, where — as the name implies — mountain waters divide and enter three larger water systems: the Arctic via Hudson Bay, the Gulf of Mexico via the Missis-sippi system, and the Pacific Ocean via the Columbia River.

After many other magnificent vistas and views of the park's towering peaks (including 10,080-foot Mt. Jackson), you reach the highlight of the drive, the crossing of the Continental Divide at Logan Pass. From this 6,680-foot elevation there's a 100-mile view of the countryside — a spectacular pano-rama that justifies Glacier's reputation as the Alps of America.

At the visitors center here, you can get directions to Hidden Lake overlook. The 1½-mile hike, part boardwalk and part trail, offers a fine view of the calm, deep blue lake 800 feet below — a perfect finale to a lovely walk.

Your drive on the Going-to-the-Sun Road eventually leads into McDonald Valley. For more hiking, head over to Avalanche Campground and pick up an easy 2-mile trail that leads to Avalanche Basin. Technically called a "glacial cirque," this is a natural amphitheater with 2,000-foot walls and six waterfalls — a spectacular sight that gives you a sense of the park's interior without making a longer trek.

The park's largest lake, McDonald is a center of activity. You can swim, take a boat tour from the dock at Lake McDonald Lodge, or hike to Sperry Glacier, where Sperry Chalets offer overnight stays complete with prepared meals and box lunches. Reservations are required. The chalets are also a good spot from which to plan a fishing expedition, an activity that requires a permit (free) at Glacier, and spans a season from mid-May through November (with some exceptions).

There is also fishing at Two Medicine Lake in Two Medicine Valley, southeast of Lake McDonald. Rainbow, brook trout, and mackinaw are caught commonly, while cutthroat and bull trout are available during seasonal migrations. Two Medicine Lake is a good place for camping, hiking, and boating as well.

For horseback riding, you should stay in Many Glacier Valley long enough to join the popular all-day trip through Alpine meadows filled with wildflowers to a lake.

There are many other sights in the park — Red Eagle Lake, with some spectacular falls and an impressive gorge; Flattop Mountain, near Lewis Range, where the juxtaposition of forest and meadow makes it a favorite for hiking; and Grinnell Lake, where a trail leads to the largest glacier in the park.

If you have driven through the park and would like even more wildlife adventure and/or isolation in the mountain pines, take Chief Mountain International Highway (Rte. 17) to Waterton Lakes National Park in Canada. An extension of Glacier, it offers more of the same, with fewer crowds. Information: Superintendent, Glacier National Park, West Glacier, MT 59936 (406 888-5441).

BEST EN ROUTE

If you prefer sheets and blankets to the stars above and mud below, there are several good hotels, motels, and lodges at the park. If you wish to stay at one of the chalets at Sperry or Granite Park, write to Belton Chalets, PO Box 188, West Glacier, MT 59936; otherwise information on accommodations in and around the park is available through Glacier Park, Inc., headquartered during the park season in the Glacier Park Lodge at the southeast corner of the park on Rte. 49, East Glacier, MT 59434 (406 226-5551), from October through May at Greyhound Tower, Reservations Dept., Station 5510, Phoenix, AZ 85077 (602 248-6000). In the park are:

   Lake McDonald Lodge – This lodge was originally built in 1914. In a setting of giant cedars, its cozy atmosphere and lakeside locale make this a good choice if you want to go fishing, boating, or riding. Make early reservations. The lodge is

often booked months in advance. Open mid-June to mid-September. 10.6 miles
northeast of West Glacier on Going-to-the-Sun Rd. (406 888-5431).
Glacier Park Lodge – Offers a pool, playground, attractive setting, and good restaurant serving prime ribs, mountain trout. Open mid-June through mid-September.
In the southeast corner of the park on Rte. 49 (406 226-9311).

Carlsbad Caverns National Park, New Mexico

If you're driving across the eastern part of New Mexico and those vast
horizontal stretches of land are beginning to appear endless rather than
beautiful, there's something nearby that can satisfy the direction of your fancy
— Bat Flight at Carlsbad Caverns. Here, every night at sunset from May
through September, 5,000 bats per minute spiral out of the open-mouthed
darkness of the cave, as many as 500,000 in one viewing. For an hour or more,
the bats, on their way out to feed for the night, create a blackening vortex
against the sky which widens into a gray streak as they set off into the stillness
of nightfall.

Carlsbad Caverns National Park is in New Mexico's southeastern corner,
just 15 miles from the Texas border to the south and 27 miles from Carlsbad,
New Mexico, to the northeast. As you approach Carlsbad Caverns, you begin
to sense something unique about the place; the monotony of the terrain is
broken by the rise of the foothills of the Guadalupe Mountains. But it is
underground in this hilly, desert region that everything spectacular is happening. Below the surrounding terrain (the national park encompasses 73 square
miles) is an intricate network of caves, with the main cavern one of the largest
known underground cavities in the world. In the late 1800s, New Mexico
residents noticed the nightly bat flights from a nearby cave and named it Bat
Cave. But they left the bats and the cave alone until 1901, when the deposits
of bat guano near the cave's entrance attracted commercial interest. A mining
operation was set up and, from then to 1923, 200 million pounds of guano were
extracted from the cave for fertilizer. During that time, James Larkin White,
a local boy, explored the inside of the cave and discovered its marvelous
limestone formations. White was only on the tip of an iceberg; inside the cave
lie acres of caverns and formations. Even now, some areas in the surrounding
network have still not been completely explored. But the main cavern, with
its stalagmite and stalactite formations of magnificent design and infinite
variety — some joining and creating monumental pillars, others densely clustered in fragile and delicate patterns — is a testament to nature's artistry.

The beginnings of this subterranean gallery go back more than 200 million
years when a vast inland sea covered the entire area. At the edge of this sea,
limestone-secreting organisms and mineral precipitates built the massive
Capitan Reef. In the course of millennia, the sea dried up and the reef was
buried under several thousand feet of sediment. Then, approximately 20
million years ago, cracks appeared in the rock. Rainwater, made slightly

acidic from carbon dioxide in the air and soil, seeped into the cracks and worked its way down to the water table. The acid eroded the rock and created the caverns. Mountain building activity raised the caverns above the water table, and the erosion was accelerated as massive blocks of porous rock, no longer supported by water, collapsed, increasing the size of chambers. The seepage of surface rain and melted snow from above continued, carrying dissolved limestone to the walls of the cavern, where it was deposited. Drop by drop, eon by eon, the water deposited more limestone, creating many formations — stalactites that hang like icicles from the ceiling and stalagmites that reach up from the ground. Where the two have fused stand massive pillars.

To get a good feeling for nature's work at Carlsbad Caverns, you will need about half a day. (The park is open all year.) After stopping at the visitors center to consult background displays on the history of the cavern, follow a short trail to the entrance of the cavern, where a self-guided tour begins (visitors are given portable radio receivers). Remember to wear a sweater — the cave stays a pleasantly cool 56° year-round. The natural entrance to the cave is imposing — an arch 90 feet wide and 40 feet high. The walk goes a total of 3 miles, beginning with a relatively steep descent down switchback trails to a depth of 829 feet. As you progress, the main points of interest are described on your radio receiver, but look all about and take your time to appreciate the immensity and beauty of what lies around you. You walk along the main corridor through a succession of amazing chambers — the circular King's Palace, with its ornate limestone decorations and curtains of glittering cave onyx, the Queen's Chamber, noted for its delicate "elephant ear" formations, and the Papoose Room, a low-ceilinged chamber with numerous stalactites. Larger than both the King's and Queen's chambers is the Big Room, which fulfills its title with a 255-foot ceiling in an area the size of 14 football fields. The room's magnificent and huge totem poles, pillars, and domes are most striking.

If you are pressed for time or cannot make the descent by foot, there is an elevator and a shorter tour of 1¼ miles, of the Big Room.

Incongruous as it may seem after walking through the cavern's natural chambers, there is a lunchroom at the bottom where you can have a meal. Except for the lunchroom and the elevator that brings you to the surface after you complete the tour, little has been done to alter the natural state of the caverns. The lighting is well hidden in underground cables and brings out the subtle hues in the limestone formations.

Lantern-lit tours are also available at New Cave — the ultimate in underground adventure — 25 miles from the visitors center and 36 miles from the city of Carlsbad. The trip also involves a trek up a steep ½-mile trail. The tour through the cave lasts from 1½ to 2 hours. You discover the spectacular formations only with the help of the lights you are carrying. Tours are given daily during the summer and weekends the rest of the year. Reservations are required (505 785-2232). You needn't be an experienced spelunker, but you should wear sturdy walking shoes.

At the visitors center, you can stroll along a self-guided nature trail or, in the summer, take the daily guided tour and view the arid desert vegetation and large variety of cacti, and with luck some of the area's wildlife — mule deer and lizards. For the more adventurous, there is backcountry camping with plenty of contact with the wilderness — the trails are poorly defined, and the desert, rugged and dry.

But neither trailblazer nor tenderfoot should miss the bat flight any evening from May through September (the bats migrate to Mexico in winter). Everyone sits in the amphitheater at the cave's mouth, waiting for the bats to come whirling out; a park ranger explains the flight but is usually upstaged in midsentence when thousands of bats pour out of the cave into the darkening horizon. Information: Superintendent, Carlsbad Caverns National Park, 3225 National Park Hwy., Carlsbad, NM 88220 (505 785-2232).

BEST EN ROUTE

Although you can get a permit at the visitors center for rugged backcountry camping, there are no developed overnight facilities in the park. The town of Carlsbad, 27 miles northeast of the park along US 62, offers a wide range of motels, hotels, and camping facilities. Whites City, a privately owned town 7 miles northeast of the visitors center, has a motel and a few shops as well.

Rodeway Inn, Carlsbad – This 107-room motel has a café, color TV, heated indoor pool, exercise room, playground, dancing, and entertainment on Saturday nights. PO Box 640, 3804 National Parks Hwy., Carlsbad, NM 88220 (505 887-5535 or 800 228-2000).

Motel Stevens, Carlsbad – Pool, attractive restaurant, free coffee in rooms, dancing and entertainment; 181 rooms. PO Box 580, 1829 S Canal St., Carlsbad, NM 88220 (505 887-2851).

Motel 6, Carlsbad – Pool, 80 rooms and low rates. 3824 National Parks Hwy., Carlsbad, NM 88220 (505 885-8807).

Cavern Inn, Whites City – This motel has 132 rooms, a restaurant, pool, and accepts pets. PO Box 128, Whites City, NM 88268 (505 785-2291).

Crater Lake National Park, Oregon

The Klamath Indians have their own explanation for the creation of this spectacular, brilliant blue, deep lake in the Cascade Mountains of southern Oregon. Llao, the god of the underworld who lived here, and Skell, the god who dwelt on Mt. Shasta, had a battle over an Indian maiden. Skell won and collapsed Llao's mountain. It was later filled with water to prevent Llao from escaping, thus creating the caldera that now is the focal point for more than 500,000 visitors each year.

Geologists offer an equally splendid version of the story. At least a half-million years ago, in the age of the Cascade Mountains — which include Rainier, Shasta, and Adams — Mt. Mazama began to build. Over the next 500,000 years a series of eruptions, interrupted by dormant periods, built Mt. Mazama to an estimated 12,000 feet. The eruptions came from a chamber of magma (hot molten rock) several miles beneath the mountain. A massive eruption of Mt. Mazama about 6,800 years ago virtually emptied the magma chamber and weakened the structure of the volcanic cone. The cone collapsed into the chamber, forming a caldera about 6 miles wide and nearly 4,000 feet deep. Continuing lesser eruptions within the caldera created smaller cones and helped seal off the basin with lava flows. Rain and snow began filling the basin and eventually formed a lake. Although the lake's surface temperature gets as warm as 60° to 67°F in summer, its depths remain very cold; and although the water is relatively pure, rangers advise visitors not to drink it.

Whichever version makes a believer of you, Crater Lake is a sight not to be missed. Oregon's only national park (established in 1902 after long years of lobbying), it is famous for animal and plant life, miles of hiking trails, a scenic road running 33 miles around the rim of the crater, and the lake, 1,932 feet deep, the deepest in the US. The park's vistas are unparalleled both for their natural beauty and for the many natural viewing places created as if expressedly for the visitors who flock here.

Although far from southern Oregon's few big cities (Medford is about 80 miles south, Roseburg a bit farther west), Crater Lake's Rim Road is as ideal a method for viewing this wonder as any man could have devised. Almost 100 miles of trails, many starting from the Rim Road, snake through the park, up adjacent mountains for panoramic views of the lake or down to the lake's shores. There you can find boat trips around the lake and to its two islands, Phantom Ship and Wizard.

Until 1853, Crater Lake was unknown to white men. Then a gold prospector, John Wesley Hillman, stumbled upon it while searching with a party of gold diggers for the famous Lost Cabin Mine. It was called Deep Blue Lake by the few who knew of it, and the discovery wasn't made public for 31 years. Official expeditions were made during that time, and in 1886 a government geologist sounded its depths at 1,996 feet, a respectable finding for the limited equipment of the day.

The man most crucial to the lake's fate first saw it in 1885. William Gladstone Steel was a Kansan transplanted to the great new West. Once he laid eyes on this spectacle, he committed his life to its preservation. He personally led a crusade to save it from homesteaders, lumber interests, and prospectors. Teddy Roosevelt, perhaps the greatest conservationist to inhabit the White House, made Crater Lake a national park on May 22, 1902. In 1913, Steel was rewarded for his long crusade with an appointment as the park's second superintendent.

Crater Lake National Park is a 286-square-mile tract surrounded on almost every side by national forests. There are three entrances. From the south (driving north from Klamath Falls, on Rte. 97), take Rte. 62 to the southern entrance and soon enter the Rim Road. From the north, you enter from Rte. 138, passing through the park's Pumice Desert before reaching the Rim Road.

Begin at the visitors center at Rim Village (open daily from mid-June until the first snow) and the nearby Sinnott Memorial, an excellent orientation point. Talks on the origin of the lake are given at the Sinnott Memorial daily, and exhibitions are open. Cross-country skiing is popular here during winter months; ask at the visitors center. During winter months, only the park's south and west entrances are open.

There are two reasons to go to Crater Lake: one is to take a boat tour *on* it (no private craft allowed), and the other is to get *above* it, to look down on it, as did the men — Indian and white — who discovered it. Two walking tours worth investigating start at the visitors center. A 1½-mile trail runs to the top of Garfield Peak, 1,900 feet above the lake's surface. The other trail is Discovery Point Trail, taking the modern explorer to the spot where John Hillman first laid eyes on this unexpected vision.

Fishing is allowed without a license, but there is a daily limit of ten fish per person; the lake has trout and a species of small salmon. Nightly campfire programs are held at Mazama Campground and the Rim Center at Rim Village.

From the visitors center you enter the Rim Road — you'll have to struggle to keep your eyes on the road and off the scenery. Fortunately, nature anticipated your needs, and numerous natural stopping places mark the circular route. There are also many trails and tracks that lead from stopping places up nearby summits (for even larger views).

The first stop on the mountain is called the Watchman, with a 4/5-mile trail to its summit, overlooking the lake from 1,800 feet. Farther along, on the northeast side, you'll run across Cleetwood Trail and its 1-mile path down to the lake's shores. It is a steep path down, steeper coming back up, and don't take more than you can comfortably carry. But do go down, for at the end of the trail the boat trips on Crater Lake begin, 2-hour circles around the lake and to the islands. Boat trips have guides on board explaining what you pass and what to look for. Inquire at the visitors center before heading down Cleetwood Trail as to times and availability of boat trips.

Other stops along the route include the 2½-mile trail up Mt. Scott, the highest point in the park. A little farther on is the turnoff for the drive to the top of Cloudcap, 1,600 feet above the lake. All these paths and roads give different perspectives on the vastness of the lake below, views of the Cascade Range to the north, and the full scope of Oregon scenery all around.

The major drawback to Crater is winter, for when it comes, the park closes almost totally. There are 50-foot accumulations of snow by the time winter has had its say, and the north entrance is closed almost the entire season. Though park accommodations close, a choice of ski facilities is open inside the park. The Rim Road opens sometime in July — when the snow is cleared. Certain roads and trails may be closed during peak season due to conservation considerations.

A last note: Although you'll undoubtedly have the experience of sneaking up on "tame" wild animals like deer, squirrels, chipmunks, marmots, and foxes, don't feed or try to pet them. For more information on facilities, park accommodations, travel suggestions: Superintendent, Crater Lake National Park, Crater Lake, OR 97604 (503 594-2211).

BEST EN ROUTE

Crater Lake Lodge, Rim Village – Just what you'd expect of a well-managed, comfortable, but rustic national park lodge. There are 76 rooms and a number of cabins available, plus some stores in Rim Village. There is nightly entertainment

— campfire programs — and easy access to information on ranger tours, boat rides, lectures, and other park activities. Open June 15 to mid-September. Reservations required. Crater Lake National Park, Crater Lake, OR 97604 (503 594-2511).

Also in Crater Lake National Park – Two campgrounds within the park offer a variety of camping facilities: *Mazama*, in the south-central area, and the primitive *Lost Creek*. All are run on a first come, first served basis; there is a nominal charge for Mazama, Lost Creek is free. Information: Superintendent, Crater Lake National Park, Crater Lake, OR 97604 (503 594-2211).

Diamond Lake Resort, Diamond Lake, Oregon – Just 7 miles north of the park's northern entrance, this lodge has 92 rooms, on the lakefront. Diamond Lake, OR 97731 (503 793-3333).

The Oregon Coast

One of the most awesome drives in the country is along Oregon's northwest Pacific Coast, from Astoria at the mouth of the Columbia River all the way to the California border at Pelican Beach. Here you can see how land has been — and is still being — sculpted by the enormous, slow force of the sea. Very little of the land along the coast is privately owned, so you can stop at hundreds of points along the road that are part of state and federal forests. Most of the coast is lined with steep cliffs; 20 million years ago, when the coastline was formed, the land was level with the Pacific. The route can be driven north to south or south to north; we start at the northernmost point, Astoria, and work south. To get from Portland to Astoria take Rte. 30, a 75-mile drive. The coast road is Rte. 101.

ASTORIA: At the mouth of the Columbia River, known for its salmon, Astoria is both a river fishing and a commercial deep-sea fishing center. On the waterfront, the Colombia River Maritime Museum has ship models, artifacts, and — moored outside — a restored lightship. From the top of the Astoria Column on Coxcomb Hill, you can see the harbor, ocean, and, inland, the wooded mountains. Astoria Column is a monument to the area's history. Four miles south on Rte. 101, Fort Clatsop National Memorial replicates the fort where Lewis and Clark spent the winter of 1805-6. Just west is the major charter fishing port of Warrenton. Ten miles south of Fort Clatsop, the small town of Gearheart has an excellent 18-hole golf course.

SEASIDE: Two miles south of Gearheart, this is one of Oregon's busiest shore resorts. A sea wall along the coast forms a 2-mile boardwalk above the beach. Tillamook Head, 5 miles from Seaside on an old logging road that juts west to the ocean, stands more than 1,200 feet above sea level and provides a sweeping view of the northern territories and the offshore Tillamook Lighthouse. South of Seaside, Rte. 101 turns east along the Necanicum River, through green lowlands where commercial farms grow lettuce and peas. At Cannon Beach Junction, a road lined with towering hemlocks leads to Cannon Beach, a community becoming known for its music, art, and theater programs.

ARCH CAPE: Arch Cape is carved into a bluff at Neah-kah-nie Mountain. Barely 5 miles down the road, Manzanita is both a beach and mountain resort, tucked in a cove protected by rugged headlands to the north. From here the road cuts inland with Nehalem Bay, crosses the Nehalem River, and passes through Wheeler. Seven miles south, Rockaway has broad beaches, the arched Twin Rocks, an offshore formation, and attractive resort facilities.

TILLAMOOK BAY: The bay's main town is Tillamook, a center of Oregon's inland dairy region. The Tillamook Cheese Factory here offers tours. Cape Meares, just west of town, offers a broad view of the ocean from a 700-foot-high overlook. Cape Meares is the first stop on the Three Capes Scenic Drive, which also leads to Cape Lookout and Cape Kiwanda, near Pacific City.

NESKOWIN: About 30 miles south, the beaches attract beachcombers who hunt for Japanese floats, colored glass balls used as net supports by Oriental fishermen. The floats cross the Pacific on the Japan Current. Cascade Head, southwest of Neskowin, stands 1,400 feet high and juts out to sea.

DEVIL'S LAKE: Some 14 miles south of Neskowin, the lake offers good fishing and claims to be the source of the shortest river in the world, "D" River, which flows only 400 yards from Devil's Lake to the Pacific. Just west, Lincoln City has the largest concentration of resort facilities on the coast.

DEPOE BAY: Go south for 15 miles. Before reaching Depoe Bay, just south of Boiler Bay State Park, huge (up to an acre) heaps of shells mark the remains of Indian feasts. The town's harbor is nearly always filled with trawlers, and charter boat fishing is available. Offshore, water spouts from an aperture in the rocks known as Spouting Horn. Look for the geyser of spray shooting skyward from the ocean. The Depoe Bay Aquarium has displays of local marine life (Rte. 101 in the middle of town). About 4 miles south, Cape Foulweather viewpoint overlooks an impressive stretch of ocean, and just south, Devil's Punch Bowl State Park looks out to Otter Rock, a seabird rookery that was once the home of thousands of sea otters. At the base of a sandstone bluff, waves rush through two openings and boil up inside the rocky caldron, receding in a wash of foam. This is the Devil's Punch Bowl. For information on Depoe Bay parks, contact City Hall Recreation Dept. (Depoe Bay, OR 97341; 765-2361). About 10 miles south of the Devil's Punch Bowl, Newport spreads across a steep, ridged peninsula between the ocean and Yaquina Bay. The resultant sheltered harbor offers year-round surfing, scuba diving, fishing, clamming, and crabbing. In Newport, be sure to sample the delicious Dungeness crab and Yaquina Bay oyster. Across the bay, the Mark O. Hatfield Marine Science Center has a variety of exhibitions and is popular with kids for its "handling pools."

FLORENCE: Here, the coastline alters in character. The steep, craggy headlands give way to a 50-mile stretch of sand dunes extending to the Coos Bay area. Behind the low foredunes along the shore stretches a chain of freshwater lakes. Beyond the lakes are huge dunes, some reaching as high as 250 feet and extending as far as 3 miles inland. Half-buried pine and spruce mark the dunes' eastward march. Jessie M. Honeyman State Park contains Cleawox Lake, locked in by the dunes, and a dense, evergreen forest laced with trails. South of Honeyman is Oregon Sand Dunes Recreational Area, part of Siuslaw National Forest. You can take a dune buggy ride or hike over the dunes, but be careful: It's easy to get lost. Winds can whip up and become blinding in a short time, covering your footprints. Dune hiking is also more taxing than hiking on hard-packed ground.

COOS BAY: South of the dunes area, mile-long McCullough Bridge crosses Coos Bay, site of the lumber town of North Bend. The Coos Bay region is the West's main lumber port. Shore Acres, Sunset Bay, and Cape Arago state parks, west of Coos Bay, overlook protected coves and Simpson's Reef offshore. Shore Acres has large formal gardens on view at a former estate. From the headland, sea otters and sea lions can be seen playing on offshore reefs.

BANDON: Some 17 miles south of Coos Bay, this diversified town features a restored Old Town and, a few miles south, a petting zoo/walk-through safari at the West Coast Game Park (347-3106).

CAPE BLANCO: Forty miles south of Coos Bay, a road leads to Cape Blanco, the most westerly point in Oregon. The flat, grassy cape juts 2 miles into the Pacific, overlooking Blanco and Orford reefs to the south. The Cape Blanco Lighthouse on the headland was built in the 1870s. Port Oxford, 6 miles south of the Cape Blanco turnoff, is a small harbor town protected by a cape to the north called the Heads. Many trails lead through underbrush to secluded beaches and tidal pools. Humbug Mountain, 6 miles farther south, rises 1,750 feet; Humbug Mountain State Park (part of Siskiyou National Forest) has fishing, swimming, and camping facilities.

GOLD BEACH: At the mouth of the Rogue River (which can be toured by jet boat), 22 miles south of Humbug Mountain, is Gold Beach. During the 1850s a good deal of gold was dredged from the Rogue, but in 1861 floods swept the deposits into the ocean. (Small amounts of gold can still be found along the beaches.) The stretch of coastline from here to the California line is probably the most rugged in Oregon. Innumerable coves and tidal pools remain, virtually untouched. Cape Sebastian, 7 miles south of Gold Beach and 35 miles from the California border, is a 700-foot promontory reaching out to the sea, with many trails branching inland from the coast. Harris State Park, 6 miles from California, has miles of beach and a view of offshore bird rookeries.

BEST EN ROUTE

Crest Motel, Astoria – On a hilltop overlooking the Columbia River, with mountains on the far shore. Accommodations are in three buildings, one of which houses two large suites — 26 rooms in all. 5366 Lief Ericson Dr., Astoria, OR 97103 (503 325-3141).

Tu Tu Tun Lodge, Gold Beach – In the woods on the banks of the Rogue River, all rooms overlook the water. A jet boat stops to pick up passengers at the lodge dock daily. Swimming pool, fishing, and hiking trips. 96550 N Bank Rogue, Gold Beach, OR 97444 (503 247-6664).

Jacksonville Inn, Jacksonville – Some 100 miles inland from Gold Beach, in the heart of what was once gold rush country. Built in 1863, the inn has been through several incarnations — a bank, hardware store, professional offices, and a repair shop. Each of the 8 bedrooms is lovingly furnished with antiques. The dining room serves substantial meals of steak, seafood, and Continental dishes. An interesting 19th-century town, Jacksonville has a number of frontier-era buildings to explore. PO Box 359, Jacksonville, OR 97530 (503 899-1900).

Badlands National Park, South Dakota

About 60 miles southeast of Rapid City, South Dakota, on I-90, Badlands National Park covers more than 170 square miles, haunting southwestern South Dakota with a presence of irregular, awesome hills carved in pastel colors brilliant enough to make even Dorothy's magical rainbow seem commonplace. It was raised in status from a national monument to a national park in 1978.

The Indians called this region Maco Sica, or "land bad," because of its barren terrain and weird shapes. Later, the French-Canadian explorers and trappers who passed through on their way south labeled the stark prairie *les mauvaises terres* — badlands. General Alfred Sully took one look at the place and called it "a part of hell with the fires burned out."

The journey starts in Rapid City.

RAPID CITY: Settled in the late 1870s after gold was discovered in the Black Hills, Rapid City now has a population of over 50,000 and spreads across a section of Black Hills plateau. Main sites in town include the South Dakota School of Mines and Technology, with displays of fossils and geological artifacts, including specimens of local minerals (St. Joseph St.); Dahl Fine Arts Center, with giant murals showing scenes of US history and assorted Americana (713 7th St.); Bear Country animal park, home of roaming buffalo, wolves, bison, deer, mountain lion, antelope, and various smaller furry native creatures (8 miles south on Rte. 16). At Black Hills Reptile Gardens you can see rattlesnakes being milked, alligators being wrestled, and snakes from all over the world (6 miles south on Rte. 16). Chapel in the Hills is a replica of an 800-year-old Norwegian church set among rolling hills in a tranquil valley (Chapel Rd.). The Horseless Carriage Museum offers old-fashioned cars, clothes, musical instruments, machinery, and other nostalgia; 10 miles south on Rte. 16. Before heading for the national park, look at the surrounding countryside from Skyline Drive, a scenic route in the southwest part of town. Then pick up I-90 southeast to the park. You can enter at Wall, 55 miles from Rapid City.

BADLANDS NATIONAL PARK: Over 80 million years ago this entire area was submerged, the underwater surface of a shallow sea. Sediment of rock, clay, and sand slowly swept across the plains from the west. Some 40 to 50 million years later the water disappeared, leaving marshy plains surrounding the powerful White River to the north. Slow-moving streams brought water through the more arid southern regions. This period was known as the Oligocene Epoch, an important segment of the period known as the Age of Mammals. A great variety and number of animals roamed the prairies and plains. Many, like their dinosaur predecessors, became extinct. Others, such as giant sea turtles, three-toed horses, and large, rhinoceros-like animals, evolved into species we know today. After these animals died, their remains sank into the soft marshes or settled on the bottom of a nearby riverbed. Gradually, winds and rivers from the west brought even greater quantities of sediment, most of which came from volcanic disturbances. Winds and infrequent rains continued, drying out the badlands even further. Grasslands replaced marshes. Strange, statuesque shapes produced by sediment took form. Today, the land is a sweeping sculpture garden with buttes rising above weaving gullies of dry sand. Different colored layers created by volcanic ash, clay, and stone stand in the open, clearly visible. Fossils lie imbedded in and underneath these geological structures. Nor has the process stopped. These strange formations are constantly changing shape, molded by easterly winds and sudden downpours.

No matter how desolate the landscape appears, there is plenty of wildlife. Occasionally, you can spot a juniper or red cedar among the stark surroundings. Likewise, yucca, green skunk, and rabbit brush thrive on the recently fallen slopes and valleys which hold greater moisture. Most animals in the area seek refuge in those moist prairies on the park's circumference, but in the badlands you can see buffalo, along with herds of deer and antelope. The jackrabbit, cottontail, and chipmunk keep close to the shrubs in an attempt to avoid their predatory neighbor, the coyote. Occasionally, you can catch sight of the golden eagle, cliff swallow, rock wren, and snowy owl.

In the late 1800s, the badlands were overrun with geologists seeking souvenirs and fossils. In an attempt to preserve the area, Congress passed legislation creating Badlands National Monument in 1929. In 1939, a presidential proclamation, in cooperation with the State of South Dakota, set aside 110,000 acres to be administered by the

National Park Service and the Department of the Interior. (Collecting fossils is not permitted.)

Though there are entrances at both sides of the Badlands National Park (40 miles apart), the entrance at the northeast corner, just south of Cactus Flat, takes you to headquarters and the visitors center, which is farther down the road on the left, near Cedar Pass. Inside are displays and recorded slide programs. In the summer, nature hikes are conducted and evening nature programs take place in the amphitheater.

You can drive for 22 miles along a paved road lined with parking areas and lookouts with markers describing geological and botanical phenomena. There are two main hiking trails: the ¾-mile Door Trail and the shorter Cliff Shell nature trail. Both take you into the middle of the multicolored plateaus and soft clay surroundings so you can see them at close range. If you are a photographer, be sure to set out in the early morning or late afternoon, when the rainbows and stripes carved into the jagged hills are clearest. There are campsites at Sage Creek and Cedar Pass.

If you enter at Cedar Pass, you can drive through the park and exit at the western Pinnacles entrance, picking up I-90 at Wall for the return trip to Rapid City. Or you can stop in Kadoka, about 20 miles east of Cedar Pass, on the far eastern boundary of the park. Information: Superintendent, Badlands National Park, PO Box 6, Interior, SD 57750 (605 433-5361).

KADOKA: Only 815 people live in this town, but if you're interested in looking at some of the biggest petrified logs in the neighborhood as well as fossilized fish from the period when South Dakota was partially underwater, stop in at Badlands Petrified Gardens, off the E Kadoka exit of I-90.

BEST EN ROUTE

Cedar Pass Lodge, Badlands National Park – In the heart of the rugged badlands, not far from the park's visitors center. Accommodations consist of 19 cabins and a main building with a restaurant and a gift shop. Cedar Pass Lodge, PO Box 5, Interior, SD 57750 (605 433-5460).

Black Hills, South Dakota

The fabled Black Hills cover about 6,075 square miles of southwestern South Dakota along the Wyoming border. Famous for mineral deposits and pure grazing land, the Black Hills are actually green: a blend of oak, elm, ash, pine, and aspen. They are, in reality, a far cry from the ominous-sounding name bestowed upon the hills by the Indians.

According to folklore, Paul Bunyan and his blue ox, Babe, created the Black Hills. Hungry, the huge Babe swallowed a stove in the hope of finding nourishment. Unfortunately, his stomach couldn't adapt to this hefty substance and he died. Unable to find a suitable burial ground, Paul Bunyan poured soil over his faithful companion. With time, the rain carved brooks and streams into the mound and brisk winds and birds brought seeds to the undeveloped hills. Thus the Black Hills. To tour the Black Hills from Rapid City, take Rte. 16 southwest for 13 miles to Rockerville.

ROCKERVILLE: This veritable ghost town was in its glory during the late 1870s, when $1 million worth of gold was mined out of the surrounding hills, but its supply of the valuable mineral ran dry as suddenly as it was found. By 1882, most residents moved farther west, leaving empty saloons and cabins to the animals that roamed the hills. But nowadays the town comes alive in summer, when tourists come to see the old-time saloon, general store, and soda parlor. Mock gunfights are held during the day. In the evenings, there's vaudeville at the Rockerville Meller Drammer Theater, a gaslight theater. All attractions are part of Rockerville Gold Town, Rte. 16.

KEYSTONE: One of the first pioneer towns in the area, it is the official address of Mt. Rushmore, 3 miles from the center of town (see *Mt. Rushmore,* in this section). You can see it from the Rushmore Aerial Tramway, ½ mile south of Keystone, on Rte. 16A. Also on Rte. 16A, you can mine for gold ore and keep anything you find at Big Thunder Gold Mine.

HILL CITY: About 10 miles west of Keystone on Rte. 16 is Hill City, where an 1880s steam train takes you through the Black Hills, past the settings used in the TV series *Gunsmoke.* You can go by train and connecting car to Keystone and back. To make reservations, write 1880s Train, PO Box 1880, Hill City, SD 57445 (605 574-2222). About 5 miles south stands 7,242-foot Harney Peak, the highest point in South Dakota. Look for the detour leading from Rte. 385; it will take you to the base of the mountain. From here you must hike to the summit. Harney Peak provides an elegant view of "the Needles," a section of granite pinnacles.

CUSTER: About 25 miles southwest of Keystone on Rte. 16 west and Rte. 385 south and nestled along French Creek, Custer is one of the oldest towns in the Black Hills. Though quartz, mica, beryl, and gypsum are mined in the immediate area, it was gold that brought the town its prosperity. In fact, the first gold strike in the state occurred in 1874 in Custer State Park (5 miles east on Rte. 16A, 7 miles north on Rte. 89), where you can swim, fish, and hike. Within the park's 72,000 acres roams one of the largest publicly owned buffalo herds in the world. The park has 4 state lodges that offer accommodations and meals and 11 campgrounds (also run by the state), four lakes, mountain streams, and many outdoor recreational facilities. Daily interpretive programs are held from Memorial Day through Labor Day. Entrance fee charged from May through September; open year-round. Information: Custer State Park, Star Rte. 3, Box 70, Custer, SD 57730 (605 255-4515).

JEWEL CAVE NATIONAL MONUMENT: About 14 miles west of Custer on Rte. 16. A myriad of crystal formations create beautiful images and designs. Walking tours and more rigorous spelunking tours are conducted during the summer, but you should be in good physical condition before considering one. The visitors center and exhibition room provide background on local geology (about 14 miles west of Custer on Rte. 16). The last weekend in July, the Gold Discovery Days Pageant at Custer attempts to re-create the time of the great gold discovery of 1874. Celebrations include a carnival, a rodeo, and a reenactment of Gold Rush events.

WIND CAVE NATIONAL PARK: Designated a national park by President Theodore Roosevelt in 1903, the cave got its name from the strong wind currents that blow through its entrance. The winds are believed to be caused by external atmospheric pressures. Most of the 28,000-acre park is above ground and consists of woodlands and open prairies. Elk, bison, and prairie dogs wander freely among the wildflowers and trees, making this area a favorite of photographers. It's about 15 miles south of Custer on Rte. 385.

BLACK HILLS NATIONAL FOREST: The forest covers more than a million acres of dense stands of pines and open meadows seemingly wedged into the crevices of the rugged, jagged hills. Established in 1897, Black Hills National Forest is home to elk, deer, antelope, and mountain goats. Camping, hiking, fishing, and picnicking facilities are available. A visitors center at Pactola Lake is open from Memorial Day to Labor Day. Information: Forest Supervisor, Black Hills National Forest, PO Box 792, Custer, SD 57730 (605 673-2251).

LEAD: Unlike neighboring towns, Lead (pronounced "leed") never ran dry of gold. The largest working gold mine in the Western Hemisphere, Homestake Mine, in operation since 1877, offers tours from May through October (on Rte. 14A and Rte. 85). In winter, Lead is an active ski resort as people challenge the slopes of Terry Peak, at 7,076 feet the highest ski mountain east of the Rockies. The chair lift to the summit gives you an unparalleled view of Montana, North Dakota, Nebraska, and Wyoming (1½ miles southwest on Rte. 14A).

DEADWOOD: Less than 5 miles east of Lead on Rte. 85, Deadwood is primarily a tourist town. Once, however, it was the "get rich quick" spot after Custer ran dry. Wild Bill Hickok, Calamity Jane, and Preacher Smith roamed the streets and caroused at the very well attended saloons. It was here that Wild Bill Hickok lost not only a game of poker but his life. He and other Wild West characters are buried at Mt. Moriah Cemetery. Every summer, Wild Bill Hickok's death is reenacted at the Old Town Hall (Lee St.) in a play called *The Trial of Jack McCall.* The first weekend of August, Deadwood holds a rodeo and a parade on Main St. to celebrate the "Days of '76." For information call the Chamber of Commerce (605 578-1876).

BEST EN ROUTE

Sylvan Lake Resort, Custer State Park – Near Sylvan Lake, a popular resort area, this hotel offers fishing and riding. You can stay in cabins or in a standard hotel room. There is a restaurant on the premises. Open May until October. For reservations, write to Sylvan Lake Resort, PO Box 695, Piedmont Rte., Piedmont, SD 57769 (605 574-2561).

State Game Lodge, Custer State Park – Motel units and cabins, stocked fishing streams, and fine horseback riding trails. Restaurant and cocktail lounge. Pets are welcome. State Game Lodge, Custer State Park, Custer, SD 57730 (605 255-4541).

Rushmore View Motor Lodge, Keystone – Provides a terrific view of Mt. Rushmore without crowds and traffic. Open May until October. PO Box 197, Keystone, SD 57751 (605 666-4466).

Mt. Rushmore National Memorial, South Dakota

Southwest of Keystone, off Rte. 16A, Mt. Rushmore National Memorial rests in the eastern portion of South Dakota's Black Hills, surrounded by trees and streams. The portraits of Presidents Washington, Jefferson, Lincoln, and Theodore Roosevelt, which are carved into the granite cliffs, rise above all else in the area. Mt. Rushmore, fittingly known as "the Shrine of Democracy," has become a symbol of America.

Looking at the site from nearby Harney Peak, a 7,242-foot mountain, Mt. Rushmore's designer, Gutzon Borglum, spotted the rectangular block that was later to serve as the base for his presidential masterpiece and became excited with the possibility. "There's the place to carve a great national memorial," Borglum exclaimed. "American history shall march along the skyline."

Upon closer inspection, Borglum found Mt. Rushmore was, indeed, ideal for his intended project. Despite a few minor flaws, the surface was smooth, rising 6,000 feet above sea level. The rock face that rested on the southeast corner of the slab was 1,000 feet long and 400 feet wide and provided maximum daylight and optimal illumination.

Curiously enough, Mt. Rushmore got its name by accident. In fact, there is no connection between the name and the shrine to the four presidents. In the late 19th century, the Black Hills became a haven for gold seekers. Inevitable land disputes followed. One miner, involved in a interminable conflict, hired the services of an eastern lawyer, Rushmore, to settle his claim. One day, riding past the rocky plateau with his client, the lawyer asked about its name. Kidding, the miner said it was Mt. Rushmore. And 45 years later, in 1930, Mt. Rushmore became the official name.

But the idea to construct a shrine was not as easily accepted. In 1923, Doane Robinson, South Dakota state historian and poet, proposed building a monument dedicated to famous western heroes such as Lewis and Clark, Kit Carson, and the famous Sioux Indian Red Cloud. But the citizens were reticent to support the idea, failing to grasp the potential significance of such a romantic memorial. Refusing to give up, Robinson finally managed to win the support of two influential and wealthy South Dakotans, Representative William Williamson and Senator Peter Norbeck. Both agreed that the giant sculpture would bring fame and fortune to the quiet midwestern state, known primarily for its mineral-rich Black Hills and never-ending prairies. Robinson and his colleagues found the needed support, and in 1924 Gutzon Borglum was called to survey the terrain and discuss the project. Foreseeing the possibilities and intrigued by the challenge, Borglum left Confederate Memorial, which he was carving at Stone Mountain outside Atlanta, Georgia, and headed for the Black Hills.

It was Borglum's idea to create a national memorial that would embrace the merits and symbolize the ideals of our most celebrated presidents. But many people were critical. Wanting no manmade sculpture to destroy the beauty of the rich Black Hills, they made fund raising difficult. Traveling extensively, Borglum finally found enough money to begin his greatest work. Aware that people might only react to its size, he declared, "I did not and don't intend that this shall be just a damn big thing, a three-day tourist wonder."

On August 10, 1927, President Calvin Coolidge rode a horse 3 miles from nearby Keystone to dedicate the beginning of Mt. Rushmore's construction. Sporadic funding and inclement weather forced the project to take 14 years, the actual construction requiring 6½ years. Borglum, with the help of his son, Lincoln, supervised throughout, overseeing an average crew of 30, some of whom came from the Stone Mountain sculpture in Georgia. Between 1927 and 1941, when the project was completed, nearly $1 million was spent, all but $153,992 from the federal government. Borglum died in March 1941, just before Mt. Rushmore's completion. Nevertheless, his lifelong dream became reality only a few months later, under his son's supervision. Since that time, no addition or refinement has been made, despite numerous proposals.

When looking at Mt. Rushmore, you can see the painstaking detail that Borglum inscribed into the tough granite surface; George Washington's jacket collar and Teddy Roosevelt's spectacles are two examples. The faces weren't sculpted by traditional methods. More than 450,000 tons of rock were removed; the outer surface was removed with dynamite. Drillers, lowered in "swing seats" from above, blasted away stone to rough out the faces. The remaining rock was chipped away by hand and smoothed by a technique called "bumping," using an air hammer.

However, even with all the fine detail, it is still the dimensions of the monument that create its impressive aura. The faces measure 60 feet from top of head to chin; the mouths stretch more than 18 feet across, and the average nose is 20 feet long. The finished project is a perfect example of that love of size that swept 20th-century America. Mt. Rushmore ranks as one of the largest sculptures in the world, comparable to the ancient Egyptian pyramids and sphinxes.

The symbolism in this "Shrine of Democracy" is as grand and potent as its physical dimensions. Addressing congressional peers in 1928, William Williamson stressed the symbolic, allegorical significance of the memorial. "Washington symbolizes the founding of our country and the stability of our institutions," he said. "Jefferson, our idealism, expansion, and love of liberty; Lincoln, our altruism and sense of inseparable unity. Roosevelt typifies the soul of America — its restless energy, rugged morality, and progressive spirit."

The memorial's visitors center is open daily, from 8 AM to 5 PM. In summer it remains open through early evening. No camping or picnicking permitted. Information: Mt. Rushmore National Memorial, PO Box 268, 57751 (605 574-2523).

BEST EN ROUTE

Palmer Gulch Lodge, Hill City – Down-home ranch accommodations with horseback riding, fishing, hiking, and swimming. Cabins can accommodate between 3 and 8 guests. PO Box 295, Hill City, SD 57745 (605 574-2525).

Powder House Lodge, Keystone – Only 4 miles from Mt. Rushmore, in a mountain setting. Accommodations consist of cabins and motel units. Restaurant has a salad bar and specializes in roast beef. Open May through September. Keystone, SD 57751; write to 320 Quincy, Rapid City, SD 57701 (605 666-4646).

Great Salt Lake, Utah

There's a stretch out west, familiar to anyone who has crossed the country on I-80 — that ultimate of American superhighways — where all life seems to stop. On both sides of the shimmering blacktop spread vast reaches of sand, blinding white in the unrelenting sun. The air is hot, dry, and stagnant, and the monotonous flatness inspires mirages. But sometimes the harsher a place seems, the more interesting it turns out to be, and this is the case with the Great Salt Lake Desert region in Utah.

As you continue driving you will encounter what looks like a gray-blue inland sea that is either the Great Salt Lake or the largest mirage you're ever likely to see. If you're still on I-80, west of Salt Lake City, the lake is no illusion. And as you get closer, you will find that it is no anomaly in relation to the surrounding landscape but only to our general concept of lakes and seas. This 30-by-80-mile body of water does not teem with life as one would expect. It is North America's dead sea by virtue of its high salt concentration — as much as 22% in the lake's northern reaches (almost seven times saltier than sea water). The only life that the lake supports is some primitive algae, bacteria, a kind of brine shrimp (¼ inch long and feathery, a semitransparent crustacean used for tropical fish food), and swarms of stingless brine flies that blacken the shores from June to September. Naturally, the water is unfit for drinking, hardly ideal for swimming, and not exactly a fisherman's dream. But it does offer 4.8 billion tons of salt, deposits of magnesium, lithium, gypsum, potash, boron, sulfur, and chloride compounds that have lured chemical firms to this liquid mine; and for everyone else, some of the most fantasy-fulfilling floating, wading, and bobbing imaginable.

With a little knowledge of natural history, everything begins to fall into place. The arid and desolate area that surrounds the lake appears as inhospitable as it does because it was once covered by the lake's salty waters. Today's Great Salt Lake is merely a drop in the bucket compared to this earlier sea. Only 23,000 years ago, freshwater Lake Bonneville (formed from the melting snows of successive ice ages) stretched from Salt Lake City west into Nevada, north into Idaho, and south into Cedar City, Utah, covering an area comparable to Lake Michigan. The lake reached depths exceeding 1,000 feet and encompassed 20,000 square miles. (The terraced striations marking its former shorelines are still visible today on the flanks of the Wasatch Mountains of the Rockies.) When the last of the glaciers waned and the ice retreated northward, weather in this region became hotter and drier. Lake Bonneville shrank below the level of its outlet, Red Rock Pass in southeast Idaho, and its feeder streams continued to bring in minerals that could not escape. Though some water flowed in, the amount was not sufficient to offset evaporation, and the lake grew saltier and saltier. Today, the remnant of this once vast inland sea is so salty that no swimmer can sink in it. The Southern Pacific's rail causeway, built in 1903, divides the lake into two sections of differing salinities. To the south of the dike-supported track, the lake appears bluer because the freshwater inflow dilutes the salinity; the north side approaches saturation. But either side of the tracks provides ample testing grounds for experiments in human buoyancy.

Great Salt Lake State Park Saltair Beach, at the southern end of the lake (16 miles west of Salt Lake City on I-80), is one of the two places the public has had access to the lake. Unfortunately, high water has covered all of the "beaches" and flooded the permanent facilities. The boat harbor has been saved and there is some water access and minimal facilities. (For a full report on the city, see *Salt Lake City*, THE AMERICAN CITIES.) In the summer the water will be quite warm, around 80°. Once you are in chest- or neck-deep water you can experiment as you wish (floating is still easy). But there are positions you shouldn't try — any that involve putting your face in or under the water. You won't sink, but that burning sensation in your eyes and nasal and oral passages will make you wish you never set eyes on the Great Salt Lake. The park is open year-round and you can still sunbathe on an adjacent beach (but keep your suit on because Utah law does not look kindly on nudity). There is a boat ramp and small sailboat rentals. Motorboats are not used because the high salt concentration has a corrosive effect on the motor and metal. Those with boats can get information from the rangers on how to reach some of the lake's islands.

Antelope Island, the other point for public access, is less crowded and can be reached via a 16-mile boat ride (leaving from Layton and Syracuse, 63 miles north along I-15 on the east shore). It also provides camping and picnic facilities all year. The island is a good jumping-off point for boat trips because it provides access to several other lake islands — Egg and Fremont, where you can see birds and other animals including horses and sheep that are brought here for summer grazing. Gunnison Island in the northwest quadrant of the lake can only be reached via boat and is a nesting site for the great white pelican. Amid these scrubby bushes and rock heaps, you can spot this magnificent bird as well as terns and gulls.

Though you'd hardly suspect it as you lie in the warm waters of the Great Salt Lake or watch the seagulls soar, there are a dozen well-developed ski resorts within an hour's drive in the Wasatch Mountain Range east of Salt Lake City. The base elevation is 8,000 feet and the season stretches from November to May, so when it gets too cold to float (although folks of polar bear habits do immerse themselves year-round), there are plenty of places to ski in what Utahns claim is the greatest snow on earth. There's a good cover of snow, and unlike on the lake, on the slopes the law of gravity prevails — if you fall, you're down. For more information on the Great Salt Lake: Superintendent, Saltair Beach State Park, GSL, PO Box 323, Magna, UT 84044 (801 533-4081).

BEST EN ROUTE

For information on camping in the Salt Lake area, contact Utah State Parks and Recreation, 1636 W North Temple, Salt Lake City, UT 84116 (801 533-6011). A wide range of accommodations are available in Salt Lake City.

Hotel Utah, Salt Lake City – Still the grande dame of the state; elegant from the crystal chandelier hanging above the mezzanine to the beautiful new Grand Ballroom. Main and S Temple sts., Salt Lake City, UT 84111 (801 531-1000).

Salt Lake Hilton, Salt Lake City – This hotel exudes an aura of contemporary sophistication. Suites have sunken baths; there is an outdoor swimming pool, therapy pool, sauna, and 5 dining rooms. 150 W 5th South, Salt Lake City, UT 84101 (801 532-3344).

Zion and Bryce Canyon National Parks, Utah

According to official Utah sources, one seventh of all the national parks in the US lie within a 200-mile circle in southern Utah. Two of the most spectacular, Zion and Bryce Canyon, are only 90 miles apart. From Salt Lake City, I-15 south proceeds 320 miles to Zion National Park. From there, Rte.

9 east to Rte. 89 north and Rte. 12 takes you to Bryce Canyon National Park. Another route is from Las Vegas, only 160 miles south of Zion National Park, by way of I-15 and Rte. 9.

ZION NATIONAL PARK: A series of dramatic gorges and canyons, Zion is geologically part of the area that includes the Grand Canyon, 125 miles to the south, and Bryce Canyon, 89 miles northeast. From the air, the three canyons look like a series of steps, with Grand Canyon the first, Zion in the middle, and Bryce Canyon, the top. The middle sibling of this vast natural canyon-scape is younger than the Grand Canyon and older than Bryce. It dates to the Mesozoic era, a period familiar to us as the time when dinosaurs stalked the earth. (It is possible to see dinosaur footprints in the rocks at Zion if you look diligently enough.) At first a sea, then a desert, Zion's layered buttes and canyons are actually the scars of incredibly harsh climatic changes. These shifts created psychedelic purple, lilac, yellow, and pink rock walls and gorges that shimmer in the clear light. When you see it, you'll know why they call this "the land of rainbow canyons." Geologists believe Zion Canyon was formed by the Virgin River, which carved a gorge out of deep layers of sediment left from the shallow seas that covered the area. We're not sure whether the river was named after explorer Thomas Virgin or the Virgin Mary. There seems to be a running debate among historians, just as there is among geologists. The 229 square miles of Zion National Park (established in 1919) were named by a 19th-century Mormon, Isaac Behunin. To the Mormons, Zion means "heavenly resting place."

Zion is most impressive for the intense and rugged beauty of its canyons, some of which are impassable even today just as they were when explorers began visiting the area last century, and for the splendid incandescence of the color of its rock formations. There is a breathtaking drive on the Zion–Mt. Carmel Highway, which runs along the canyon valley, zigzagging up Pine Creek Canyon and through the 5,607-foot-long tunnel. This road connecting I-15 and Rte. 89 is all the more remarkable when you consider that it was completed in 1930, the year Zion and Bryce canyons were first photographed from the air.

Any visit should begin at the Zion Canyon visitors center near the southern entrance, where there's a museum of geological exhibitions and an information desk. From the lobby, you'll have an excellent view of multicolored Zion Canyon. Another visitors center is to the north, at the Kolob Canyons exit off I-15. Overnight hikes on any of the 65 miles of trails require permits, which you can pick up at the visitors center before setting out. And be sure to check weather conditions — the trails around the canyon rim are sometimes closed due to snow. From the *Zion Lodge*, you can also embark on horseback trips on Sandbench Trail. For a combined driving-hiking expedition, drive to the Temple of Sinawava, 8 miles from the south entrance of the park. Inside the amphitheater-shaped temple are the two giant pillars for which the temple got its name: the Altar and the Pulpit. Once you reach the temple, the road stops, so you'll have to get out and walk. From here, it's a mile to the beginning of the Narrows, where the Virgin River, sometimes no more than 20 feet wide, races through the giant walls of rock where columbine and shooting star flowers grow in spring. You can join a guided nature hike during the summer or camp along the ash-, cottonwood-, and moonflower-lined banks of the river. It's 2½ strenuous miles to Angels Landing at the top of the canyon, but the view is worth it. There is a two-day backpacking trip along the 12-mile West Rim Trail. The southwestern section of Zion National Park is desert. Coalpits Wash is the home of lizards, cacti, and a small waterfall. Information: Superintendent, Zion National Park, Springdale, UT 84767 (801 772-3256).

KANAB: Southeast of Zion, this town of about 13 motels and a handful of restaurants has the distinction of being 20 miles east of a set of coral pink sand dunes used as a location for many a Hollywood movie.

BRYCE CANYON NATIONAL PARK: The Paiute Indians called the stone formations at Bryce Canyon "red rocks standing like men in a bowl-shaped canyon" and thought the twisted shapes had been cast into stone by a vengeful god. The configurations do look disturbingly human and many have been named after the things they resemble. Technically, Bryce's canyons are not canyons at all but breaks in the earth, tremendous pink and white limestone amphitheaters as deep as 1,000 feet. Standing at the eastern edge of the Paunsaugunt Plateau (Paunsaugunt means home of the beaver), Bryce Canyon National Park is laced by a network of tributaries (usually dry) of the Paria River. You can get a great view of the splintered rock plateau stretching to the north from the 9,105-foot-high Rainbow Point. (We recommend taking it easy at Bryce Canyon. The 8,000- to 9,000-foot altitude will tire you quickly.)

As at Zion, the best place to start your explorations of Bryce Canyon's 36,000 acres is the visitors center. Here you'll find some interesting geological and archaeological exhibitions as well as information on guided naturalist activities and horseback rides. In summer, there is also a minibus tour, which leaves from *Bryce Canyon Lodge*. There are 20 miles of driving roads around the rims of the canyon and 61 miles of hiking trails for exploring either the top or the bottom of the canyon. The most popular hiking trail is the Navajo Trail, a one- to two-hour excursion that takes you more than 500 feet into the canyon, past Thor's Hammer and other rock formations. Once at the bottom of the Navajo Trail, you can hike it back up or try the Peekaboo Loop Trail (a 3.5-mile loop), or take the Queen's Garden Trail back up to the top. Although the Paunsaugunt Plateau was given its name because of a preponderance of beaver, hunting for pelts has pretty much wiped them out. You should, however, be able to spot skunk, gray fox, marmot, chipmunk, and squirrel without too much difficulty. Hawk, swallow, and raven are among the more prevalent species of winged creatures that can be seen above Bryce Canyon. This is also one of the best places in the country for photography. Light sparkles here, illuminating the canyons so that they seem to glow from an inner fire. Dawn and dusk are the best times to take pictures. There are two campgrounds, each with a 14-day restriction. Information: Superintendent, Bryce Canyon National Park, Bryce Canyon, UT 84717 (801 834-5322).

BEST EN ROUTE

Zion Lodge, Zion National Park – A group of cabins with a total of 120 rooms. There are horseback riding facilities and a snack bar/restaurant. Managed by TW Services, PO Box 400, Cedar City, UT 84720 (801-586-7686).

Bryce Canyon Lodge, Bryce Canyon National Park – A collection of cabins and motel units with a total of 120 rooms, some with ornamental fireplaces. Managed by TW Services, PO Box 400, Cedar City, UT 84720 (801 586-7686).

Bryce Canyon Pines Motel and Restaurant, Bryce Canyon – About 8 miles from the park. Facilities include a restaurant and coffee shop, heated swimming pool, and horseback riding. Some of the 34 rooms have fireplaces. Bryce Canyon Pines, Star Route 1, Panguitch, UT 84759 (801 834-5336).

Mt. Rainier National Park, Washington

Swathed in glaciers, Mt. Rainier reaches 14,410 splendid, icy feet into the sky. A formidable, awesome presence, it is the tallest peak in Washington state (fifth tallest in the lower 48), 60 miles southeast of Seattle. Exploring Mt.

Rainier's perilous slopes might not be your idea of a holiday — not everyone likes to hang upside down from a precipice, fastened to firmament by the mere grace of rope and pick — but regardless, your first encounter with Mt. Rainier is sure to be unforgettable.

Even those who are not enamored of mountains, insisting that "when you've seen one, you've seen 'em all," almost invariably return from a visit to Mt. Rainier converted. A solitary giant laced with frosty crevasses, this mountain dominates the surrounding area. In fact, the 235,404 acres of Mt. Rainier National Park seem to have been selected specifically to provide natural settings of pine, wildflowers, and lakes against which the craggy Rainier can be seen to best advantage.

A curious combination of glacial and volcanic activity, Mt. Rainier is the product of relatively recent geological phenomena. One would be hard put to establish its precise age, since the mountain itself is the product of those momentous eruptions occurring within the last million years, which are also responsible for Mt. Baker, near the Canadian border, Lassen Peak in northern California, and the other peaks in the Cascade Range, to which Rainier belongs.

Climbers approaching Columbia Crest, Mt. Rainier's summit, have reported tiny geysers of steam spurting through the ice, a sign of volcanic activity below. The steam has carved intricate mazes in the mountain's ice, forming a labyrinthine network of ice tunnels and caves. In 1870, the first team to climb Mt. Rainier spent the night before their ascent to the pinnacle safely nestled in one of these burrows. Without these natural caves and tunnels to provide shelter, they probably would have died from exposure. Mt. Rainier's glacial system, the most extensive "single peak" network in the country (apart from Alaska), consists of 25 named glaciers and about 50 smaller, unnamed ones. Their age is estimated to be a mere 10,000 years, a legacy of the last, massive Ice Age Retreat. Carbon Glacier is Mt. Rainier's longest — 6 miles; Emmons Glacier, almost 4½ miles long by 1 mile wide, the largest. If you're curious about geological activity, this is the best place for observing icy and subterranean thermal forces in action. The Nisqually Glacier moves between 50 feet and 400 feet a year.

Declared a national park in 1899, Mt. Rainier is surrounded by national forests. Snoqualmie National Forest forms the eastern, northern, and western boundaries. Gifford Pinchot National Forest is to the south.

To get to Mt. Rainier National Park from Seattle, take I-5 south about 13 miles to exit 42B, then follow Rte. 161 south and pick up Rte. 7 to Rte. 706, which will take you directly to Mt. Rainier. This approach is open year-round.

MT. BAKER–SNOQUALMIE NATIONAL FOREST: This forest stretches 160 miles from the Canadian border to White Pass. Spruce and fir trees cover the 1.7 million acres that include Mt. Baker, a 10,778-foot dormant volcano, 390 glaciers, and 1,200 miles of trails, including sections of the Pacific Crest Trail. There are ski centers at Snoqualmie Pass, White Pass, Stevens Pass, Mt. Baker, and Mt. Pilchuck. Campsites open in summer. On Rte. 410, just north of Mt. Rainier National Park. Forest headquarters at 1022 First Ave., Seattle, WA 98104 (206 442-0170).

CRYSTAL MOUNTAIN: A year-round resort with excellent ski facilities in winter.

A year-round chair lift offers a breathtaking view, sweeping from Mt. Rainier to Mt. Hood in Oregon. The Washington Cascade Crest Trail leads to nearby mountains. Snoqualmie National Forest on Rte. 410 (206 663-2265).

MT. ST. HELENS: In August 1982, President Ronald Reagan signed a bill naming Mt. St. Helens a National Volcanic Monument and designating 110,000 acres of its surrounding area for recreation and research. Part of Gifford Pinchot National Forest, Mt. St. Helens had been dormant since 1842 until it stirred to life in March 1980. A series of earthquakes and minor eruptions culminated in a massive explosion that blasted over 1,300 feet off the top of the 9,677-foot mountain in May 1980. The story of the eruptions is presented in the Forest Service interpretive center at Lewis and Clark State Park on Jackson Highway, about 12 miles south of Chehalis. Also in Gifford Pinchot is Mt. Adams, a 12,326-foot monster with glaciers, forests, and lava flows, the Pacific Northwest's second largest peak. At its base, the Pacific Crest Trail leads from the western side of the mountain through Goat Rocks Wilderness. There are several campgrounds in different parts of the forest. Open most of the year. Borders Mt. Rainier National Park to the south. Headquarters at 500 W 12th St., Vancouver, WA 98660 (206 696-7500).

MT. RAINIER NATIONAL PARK: Enter the park via Mather Memorial Parkway, a 50-mile paved road that takes you to the White River entrance where the road forks. You can continue south, to Stevens Canyon and the Ohanapecosh visitors center and campground, or west, to the Sunrise visitors center and White River Campground, about a mile from the road. Stevens Canyon Road, a section of the 117-mile network of paved roads, takes you along the southern boundary, past the Tatoosh Range and 5,995-foot Eagle Peak. The road passes Longmire, Paradise, and the Nisqually entrance and ranger station, in the southwest corner of the park. The visitors center distributes free information on hiking and climbing. Be sure to pick up the booklet entitled *Fragile, Handle with Care* before setting out. Guides conduct expeditions from Paradise in summer. In winter, Paradise is headquarters for snowshoe walks and cross-country skiing. At Paradise, Longmire, or Sunrise visitors centers, you can pick up the Wonderland Hiking Trail, a 90-mile route that circles the base of Mt. Rainier. Wonderland takes you past Box Canyon, waterfalls, fields with wildflowers in season, Golden Lakes, Carbon River, Carbon Glacier, and the Mowich Glaciers. Campsites are spaced every 12 miles along the trail. Northern Loop Trail extends 17½ miles from Wonderland Trail through backcountry meadows to Chenuis Mountain, at an elevation of 6,400 feet. Pick up a permit at a visitors center if you intend to camp overnight.

The 1963 US Mt. Everest Expedition trained on Mt. Rainier, but you don't have to be preparing to tackle the world's largest mountain to get to Rainier's peak. You can take a 1- or a 5-day course in mountain climbing techniques at the national park's Paradise Guide House, Rainier Mountaineering (201 St. Helens, Tacoma, WA 98402; 206 627-6242). All climbers must register at one of the visitors centers before setting out, and there are restrictions on the number of people allowed in each party. Park officials have also set requirements for health, equipment, and leadership qualifications. All expeditions are monitored. Even in good weather, sudden storms can envelop the mountain in gales of Himalayan ferocity, and, on quiet days, the glacial movements sometimes form new crevasses. At any moment, sudden rockfalls can tear out hunks of trail. The best time to climb is mid-July, after the summer storms have passed but before the constant summer heat wears down the ice, causing unstable mountain conditions. Generally, the climb takes two days, with an overnight stop at Camp Muir, a shelter at 10,000 feet. You can rent or buy camping gear at Paradise Guide House. Information: Superintendent, Mt. Rainier National Park, Ashford, WA 98304 (206 569-2211).

BEST EN ROUTE

Crystal Mountain, Crystal Mountain – A self-contained Alpine village with Silver Skis Chalet and Crystal Chalets condominiums, with heated pool, night skiing, and grocery stores. Crystal House, Crystal Inn, and Alpine Inn, the three hotels on the premises, have 120 rooms. 100 condo units available all year. Off Rte. 410. Crystal Mountain, WA 98022 (206 663-2265).

Alta Silva, Crystal Mountain, Washington – A small, rustic, chalet-style apartment complex. Horses are available for summertime excursions. Fishing and hunting trips organized. At press time, Alta Silva was closed and in the process of being sold. Check if it's open before you visit. Rte. 410. PO Box 198, Star Route, Enumclaw, WA 98022 (206 663-2238).

Mt. Rainier National Park, Washington – Near Paradise, elevation 5,400 feet, *Paradise Inn* has a lodge-type lobby with two open fireplaces, cocktail lounge, snack bar. Dining room. 128 rooms. Open from late June to early October. Near Longmire visitors center, elevation 2,700 feet, *National Park Inn* offers meal service and a gas station. Open daily year-round. 16 rooms. For reservations, write Manager, Paradise Inn or National Park Inn, Mt. Rainier Guest Services, Star Route, Ashford, WA 98304 (206 569-2275).

Olympic National Park, Washington

The heart of the Olympic peninsula in western Washington State, Olympic National Park covers 1,400 square miles of diverse terrain. On the western edge of the peninsula lies a 57-mile stretch of wild Pacific beachfront. Hundreds of offshore islands nestle among the inlets and coves that shelter many communities of seals and other marine and amphibious creatures. Inland, numerous small lakes dot the landscape, filling glacial pits that scarred the earth when giant masses of ice withdrew to the north at the end of the Ice Age about 10,000 years ago. The lakes are part of a thriving water system, and the western slope of the Olympic peninsula is the wettest spot in the continental US, with an average annual precipitation of 133+ inches. It is cloudy more than 220 days each year and wet 160 days. Temperatures are in the 70s in summer, in the 30s in winter. Here, too, are junglelike, complex, and primeval rain forests, and not far from them glacier-capped mountains tower into the sky. The biggest is Mt. Olympus, a 7,965-foot peak in the center of the park. All told, about 60 glaciers cover some 25 square miles of mountainous terrain, in frosty juxtaposition to the lush vegetation nearby.

Discovered in 1592 by the Spanish explorer Juan de Fuca, for whom the strait connecting the Pacific with Puget Sound was later named, the Olympic Peninsula was the home of the Coast Salish Indians, an artistic civilization with an intense economic and spiritual kinship to the sea. A stream of trappers and traders found their way to the peninsula in the early 1800s, and they brought with them germs to which the Indians were not immune. A series of appalling epidemics and conflicts with the white settlers wiped out many of the original inhabitants. Today, the descendants of the Salish survivors live in reservations. The Quillayute and Hoh Indian reservations are adjacent to

Olympic National Park's coastal area. The Ozette and Makah Indian reservations are in the northwestern corner of the peninsula; the Skokomish and Nisqually Indian reservations, in the southeast. Olympic National Park itself was established in 1938, and the coastal area came under federal protection in 1953, with additional coastal land added in 1976.

Some 75 miles west of Seattle, Olympic National Park is accessible from Rte. 101, which loops around the peninsula. From Seattle, you can take a Washington State Ferry across Puget Sound to the Kitsap Peninsula, then take the Hood Canal floating bridge. Or take I-5 south from Seattle to Olympia and pick up Rte. 101 north. This road loops around the eastern, northern, and western coasts of the peninsula. You have to pick up Rte. 12 at Aberdeen to complete the circular route to Olympia, a distance of 50 miles.

The major entrance to Olympic National Park is Port Angeles, site of the largest of three visitors centers (Pioneer Memorial Museum) with exhibitions on local fauna and flora. Heart o' the Hills Road, an 18-mile paved road that ascends to an elevation of nearly a mile, begins here. Halfway up, at Lookout Point, you can see across the Strait of Juan de Fuca to British Columbia and to Mt. Baker when visibility is good. Perched at the top of the road, Hurricane Ridge Lodge is a good place to catch your breath and pick up more information. If you plan to explore the wilderness or camp, you must get a permit, available at all ranger stations and visitors centers. You can embark on Big Meadow Nature Trail on foot, or you can continue by car along an unpaved mountain road to Obstruction Point, at 6,450 feet. Unless it's shrouded in fog, Mt. Olympus should be staring you smack in the face. A number of hiking trails begin at Obstruction Point. One leads to Deer Park Campground. You can't reserve space at any of the campsites, so it's advisable to carry rain gear if you plan to sleep outdoors. The maximum stay permitted at any site is 14 days.

Lake Crescent is about 15 miles west of Port Angeles on Rte. 101, still in mountain country. West of the lake, you can pick up the road to Soleduck Hot Springs Resort, Soleduck Campground, and the Seven Lakes Basin.

Named after the mythological home of the Greek gods and covered by six glaciers, some as thick as 900 feet, 7,965-foot Mt. Olympus gets about 200 inches of snow and rain a year, making it the wettest spot of the lower 48 states.

On the western edge of the park stands the Hoh rain forest; the visitors center can give you information on the numerous species of shrubs, fungi, mosses, and trees. This is the home of the giant Sitka spruce, which often grows as high as 300 feet. Roosevelt elk, deer, bear, raccoon, and dozens of different species of birds live in this area.

One of the park's finest attributes is its Pacific Coast area, 57 miles of rugged beachfront studded with giant rocks and the home of seagulls, eagles, seals, and sea lions. Campsites are open year-round. Fishing boats can be chartered at La Push. Unlike the Makah Indians (below), the Quinault Indians at the reservation 5 miles to the south do not welcome tourists. Information: Superintendent, Olympic National Park, 600 E Park Ave., Port Angeles, WA 98362 (206 452-4501).

MAKAH INDIAN RESERVATION: About 10 miles west of Lake Crescent, pick up a small road running north from Sappho, bearing left onto Rte. 112 northwest to Clallam Bay. Continue to the northwesternmost tip of the peninsula at Neah Bay, a fishing village where the Makah Indians operate several charter fishing companies, motels, and crafts shops. There's a museum at Neah Bay containing the archaeological material excavated by teams from Washington State University. And there are campsites at Makah Bay, 1 mile south. For information contact the travel secretary at the Makah Tribal Office, PO Box 115, Neah Bay, WA 98357 (206 645-2201).

OLYMPIC NATIONAL FOREST: The forest forms the eastern, northern, and southern borders of the national park with 651,000 acres of rain forest vegetation. Campsites in the Quinault Lake and Hood Canal area are open in summer. For information, contact Olympic National Forest Headquarters, 801 Capital Way, Olympia, WA 98507 (206 753-9534).

BEST EN ROUTE

Olympic National Park – Lake Crescent Lodge has 33 one- and two-room cabins and 20 motel units and is near hiking trails, boating, and fishing areas. There are 16 campgrounds in the park; sites are available on a first come, first served basis only. For lodge information or reservations, write National Park Concessions, Star Route 1, Box 11, Port Angeles, WA 98362 (206 928-3211).

Makah Motel, Makah Reservation – Leased from the Makah Indian tribe, it has 11 rooms, some with kitchens. Open all year. PO Box 797, Neah Bay, WA 98357. Main St. (206 645-2366).

Makah Restaurant, Makah Reservation – Across the street from the motel, serving seafood, hamburgers, steaks, and french fries. Open daily. Main St., Neah Bay (206 645-2476).

Devils Tower National Monument, Wyoming

In the film *Close Encounters of the Third Kind*, François Truffaut holds up a picture of Devils Tower, asking, "Have you ever seen anything like this?" "Sure," says Richard Dreyfuss. "I've got one just like it in my living room."

If you've seen the movie, you undoubtedly know that Devils Tower is the site selected for encounters of the third kind (physical contact) with beings from another planet. And you're also aware that one aspect of the initial contact is the implantation of a psychic image of Devils Tower in the minds of American men and women, who then become obsessed with visions of the tower, which they are driven to reproduce by sketching, painting, or even sculpting a giant replica.

Whether or not you've seen the film, your first encounter with Devils Tower National Monument will most probably be overwhelming. A gargantuan landmark rising suddenly in the middle of a vast Wyoming plain, Devils Tower is the only outstanding physical feature in the northeastern sector of the state. On a clear day you can see it from as far as 100 miles away.

Devils Tower is close to the western edge of the Black Hills National Forest in South Dakota. If you're coming from Rapid City or the Black Hills, take

I-90 or Rte. 34 west (Rte. 34 becomes Rte. 24 when you cross the Wyoming state line). It's about 100 miles. You can also get there on Rte. 14. Devils Tower National Monument covers 1,346 acres of land between the towns of Sundance and Hulett.

Pioneers traversing the Great Plains by horse and wagon used it as a guidepost, as had the first white explorers and, before them, the Indians. Some of those Indians called it Mateo Tepee, meaning Grizzly Bear Lodge. The army misinterpreted Mateo Tepee to mean Bad God's Tower, and it was by this name the first US Geological Survey party became acquainted with it in 1875, later changing its name to Devils Tower. According to one legend, the Bad God (Satan) beats on the top of the tower as on a drum to frighten the land during thunderstorms. Kiowa Indians, however, mythologically ascribe the tower's origin to an incident in which several bears tried to attack seven young Indian maidens. The Great Spirit saved them by lifting the rock on which they were standing to a great height — thus, the tower. In this version, those deep, vertical ridges on the sides of the tower were formed by the bears' frustrated scratching in an attempt to reach their prey. When the animals died from exhaustion, the Great Spirit lifted the little girls to the sky and transformed them into the constellation Pleiades. We don't know if President Theodore Roosevelt was aware of these myths, but in 1906 he decided Devils Tower was important enough to become the country's first national monument.

Since then, it has intrigued visitors from all over the world. Geologists have come to its base at the foot of the Belle Fourche River, fascinated by the layers of sedimentary rock and vegetation. According to scientific estimates, the tower dates back about 50 million years, the product of a geological process involving molten rock bubbling up from the center of the earth and cooling. The fluted, strangely symmetrical sides of the monolith also provide a visible lesson in how plants are formed. Although the formidable, barren-looking tower hardly seems hospitable to botanical life, the rock attracts lichens that slowly erode the solid mineral surface into tiny fragments. As dust blows in from the prairie, little pockets of soil nestle in the cracks, attracting moss and liverwort. As the soil deepens, grass and wildflowers grow. Sagebrush and other shrubs cluster closer to the base while, lining the very bottom, aspen and pine trees take root. About a half mile from the base, a prairie dog community burrows intricate underground mazes. (Because they are on the grounds of a national monument, the colony at Devils Tower is one of the few protected communities of prairie dogs in the US.)

If you want to climb to the top of the tower, make sure you get permission from the supervisor at the visitors center. Scaling the sides has become a lot more feasible since 1893, when William Rogers reached the summit. Instead of climbing, he actually wedged a wooden ladder device between the vertical ridges of the rock. In 1937, the first team of three climbers reached the top by traditional methods. If you're contemplating the climb, remember there are now more than 98 ways to reach the 1½-acre top of the giant, tree-stump-shaped tower. And when you get there, you'll probably encounter falcons' and hawks' nests. If you're not up for an assault on the tower itself, you can wander along the Tower Trail and watch the prairie dogs burrow. You'll also catch glimpses of rabbit, chipmunk, and, if you're lucky, whitetail and mule deer. (Deer come out to feed at sunset.) The visitors center will give you a guide to the nature trail.

Although inclement weather tends to keep people away in winter, Devils Tower National Monument is open year-round. Because of its isolated location, you'll find yourself alone with the four staff members if you head out there between October and March. There are cross-country ski trails lacing the grounds and plenty of room to stretch, but the 51 campsites might well be closed due to snow since the rangers don't maintain the road in rough weather. Summer activities include campfire programs and nature walks.

Whether you come to climb, to explore the geology and nature, or to photograph the mysterious, dramatic rock, you'll be fascinated by Devils Tower's mystique, as have thousands of others. And who knows? After seeing the real thing, you might decide that you, too, want one in your living room. Information: Superintendent, Devils Tower National Monument, Devils Tower, WY 82714 (307 467-5370) or the Wyoming Travel Commission, I-25 at Etchepare Circle, Cheyenne, WY 82002 (307 777-7777 or 800 225-5996).

BEST EN ROUTE

Dampier's Hunting Valley, Four Corners – About 45 miles southeast of Devils Tower, with ranch house, trailer hookup, and cabins. Near hiking, rodeos, and trout fishing. Accommodations for 50 guests. James and Marilyn Dampier, General Delivery, Four Corners, WY 82715 (307 746-4797).

Grand Teton National Park and Jackson Hole, Wyoming

Grand Teton National Park is just south of Yellowstone National Park in northwestern Wyoming, near the Idaho border. The park encompasses over 310,000 acres, which include the most spectacular part of the Teton Range, the "youngest" stretch of peaks in the Rockies — less than 10 million years old.

Early French-Canadian fur trappers gave the Tetons their name, French slang for "big breasts." Perhaps their naming represented wishful thinking, for there is nothing smooth, soft, or voluptuous about the jagged, irregular spires of the Teton Range. The name is doubly ironic since there are three mountains named Teton: Grand, Middle, and South Teton. In 1806, when John Colter left the Lewis and Clark expedition to explore Yellowstone, directly north of Jackson Hole, he brought back fantastic tales of boiling springs, powerful geysers, and sulfurous fumes spouting from the earth. People back East didn't believe him and nicknamed the place "Colter's Hell." If Yellowstone is Colter's Hell, then by rights the Tetons, with their tranquil, majestic beauty, should be called Colter's Heaven. Although there are higher mountains in North America, the Tetons have a special visual impact because their sheer mass rises abruptly without foothills from the peaceful flat valley of Jackson Hole, Wyoming.

Jackson Hole ("hole" is an old fur trappers' term for an enclosed mountain valley) is about 50 miles long and 6 to 12 miles wide, with highways leading to different parts of the valley. The town of Jackson is south of Grand Teton National Park. Coming from Yellowstone National Park, take the Rockefeller Parkway, which runs alongside the Snake River from Yellowstone. Most of the valley is accessible by automobile year-round.

GRAND TETON NATIONAL PARK: As you head for park headquarters at Moose visitors center, be sure to stop at the spectacular Signal Mountain overlook. (The Moose and Colter Bay visitors centers and Jenny Lake Ranger Station distribute information on hiking, fishing, camping, and the history of the Tetons.) There are more than 200 miles of hiking trails in the park. One three-hour excursion includes a boat ride across Jenny Lake and a moderate hike of 2 miles to Hidden Falls and Inspiration Point. The boat leaves the East Shore Dock at Jenny Lake about every half-hour from 8 AM to 6 PM. More difficult is the Teton Crest Trail, which climbs to an elevation of 2 miles above sea level. Another strenuous hike, along the Indian Paintbrush Trail, is known for its resplendent wildflowers and wonderful views of the lakes and mountains. Both Teton Crest and Indian Paintbrush trails are suitable for people in reasonably good physical condition. (Be warned, however, that the park rangers' idea of "reasonably good physical condition" might well be considerably more rigorous than your own.) You can rent canoes and boats on Jackson and Jenny lakes or launch your own (you must buy a permit, available at the Moose and Colter Bay visitors centers). There are scheduled boat rides on Jackson Lake, the biggest lake in the valley. Guided rubber raft trips down the Snake River leave from *Jackson Lake Lodge* as well as other valley locations. There are over a dozen routes to the summit of Grand Teton Mountain, 13,770 feet high. Some are relatively easy technical climbs, but one is considered to be among the most difficult in the nation. *Exum Mountain Guides* of Jenny Lake offers a two-day mountain climbing course, with guides to take you up many peaks in the summer (Box 56, Moose, WY 83012; 733-2297). *Jackson Hole Mountain Guides* at Teton Village also provides climbing courses and guides (Teton Village, WY 83025; 733-4979). You can rent horses at Colter Bay, Jenny Lake, or *Jackson Lake Lodge.* There are six campgrounds, and permits are required for backcountry camping. Information: Superintendent, Grand Teton National Park, PO Drawer 170, Moose, WY 83012 (307 733-2880).

BRIDGER-TETON NATIONAL FOREST: Adjoins the national park to the east, and extends north to flank Yellowstone National Park. Bridger-Teton takes in more than 3 million acres of forest, river, mountain, and wilderness. Trout fishing in streams and mountain lakes, hunting, skiing, rafting, 3,000 miles of hiking trails, and the Teton and Bridger wildernesses are the major attractions. There are 37 campgrounds and an aerial tramway that rises to 10,500 feet — great for sightseeing in summer, skiing in winter. Information: Forest Supervisor, Bridger-Teton National Forest, FS Building, PO Box 1888, Jackson, WY 83001 (307 733-2752).

TARGHEE NATIONAL FOREST: Often called the back door to Grand Teton and Yellowstone national parks because it borders them, Targhee covers 1.8 million acres, most of it in southeast Idaho. Fishing, rafting, swimming, horseback riding, backpacking, and camping (at 35 campgrounds) are the activities in summer. In winter, there's snowmobiling on 750 miles of groomed trails and cross-country as well as downhill skiing at Grand Targhee Winter Sports Area in Alta, Wyoming. Information on Targhee: Forest Supervisor, Targhee National Forest, PO Box 208, St. Anthony, ID 83445 (208 624-3151).

JACKSON HOLE: With the biggest vertical drop and the longest runs anywhere in the US, two world-famous ski resorts attract people to the Jackson Hole area: *Teton Village,* on Rendezvous Mountain overlooking Jackson Hole, and *Grand Targhee,* on the west side of the range, both of which are in the national forest. *Teton Village,* 12 miles west of Jackson, has more extensive beginning and intermediate slopes than those found at 90% of the major ski resorts in the country as well as some of the toughest slopes around. It's an excellent place for a family whose members ski at different levels. *Grand Targhee* is an hour's drive from Jackson over Teton Pass, on Rtes. 22 and 33, but it offers excellent skiing from the very early fall to very late spring. Jackson Hole has more than just impressive ski facilities, excellent food, and après-ski entertainment. In fact, its most important feature is something other ski areas often lack — snow. One year, the US Forest Service had already recorded 161 inches of new snow by the opening day of the ski season — more than most ski resorts get in an entire year. In summer, more than 130,000 people come to Jackson Hole for quiet, leisurely Snake River floating excursions or more exciting whitewater trips. There are more than a dozen float trip operators in the area. Three of the best are *Barker-Ewing* (Box 100, Moose, WY 83012; 307 733-1800); *Triangle X* — also a first-rate working dude ranch (Box 120T, Moose, WY 83012; 307 133-2183); and *Jack Dennis Float Trips* — especially for fishing trips (PO Box 286, Jackson, WY 83001; 307 733-3270). The Jackson Hole area has the best fishing in the Rockies; local cutthroat trout are legendary. Information: Jackson Hole Area Chamber of Commerce, Jackson, WY 83001 (307 733-3316).

BEST EN ROUTE

Jackson Lake Lodge, Grand Teton National Park – Boating and fishing expeditions, swimming, horseback riding, and restaurant. 385 rooms. Grand Teton Lodge Co., PO Box 240, Moran, WY 83013 (307 543-2855).

Jenny Lake Lodge, Grand Teton National Park – Log cabins in a rustic setting. Boating and fishing expeditions, hiking trips, horseback riding, and restaurant. 30 rooms. Grand Teton Lodge Co., PO Box 240, Moran, WY 83013 (307 733-4647).

Colter Bay Cabins, Grand Teton National Park – Log cabins with full water sports and horseback riding; restaurant. 209 rooms. Grand Teton Lodge Co., PO Box 240, Moran, WY 83013 (307 543-2855).

Alpenhof, Teton Village – Chalet-style mountain lodge with pool, sauna, close to skiing. Fireplaces in lounge, good American and Continental restaurant. 40 rooms. PO Box 288, Teton Village, WY 83025 (307 733-3242).

Hitching Post Lodge, Jackson – Specializes in cookouts and chuck wagon breakfasts. Heated pool. 17 rooms. Open May through September. PO Box 521, Jackson, WY 83001 (307 733-2606).

Yellowstone National Park, Wyoming

Nowhere on earth is the raw power of nature more apparent than at Yellowstone National Park. We learn as schoolchildren that the face of the earth is constantly changing — mountain ranges are formed and then eroded; lakes are born and then slowly degenerate into swamps; ice ages come and go, forever changing the contour of the land. But all these things take thousands, even millions of years, and the inner forces that shape the earth we live on are rarely perceptible to us.

At Yellowstone, however, the awesome grandeur of the earth's primal forces can be seen, felt, smelled, and heard. The ground rumbles as a geyser shoots thousands of gallons of scalding water into the air, steam hisses and roars from crevasses in the earth, hellish sulfurous odors fill the air, mud flats boil and bubble. Yellowstone combines the grandeur of creation with the mightiness of destruction.

Yellowstone was the first national park to be established anywhere in the world (1872). It is the largest national park in the contiguous states, covering 3,472 square miles — larger than Rhode Island and Delaware combined. Although most of the park lies in northwestern Wyoming, it also stretches into Montana and Idaho. There are entrances at Gardiner, Montana (north), West Yellowstone, Montana (west), Jackson, Wyoming/Grand Teton National Park (south), Cody, Wyoming (east), and Cooke City, Montana (northeast). The entrance at Gardiner is open all year. The other entrances are closed to cars from early November through April. The John D. Rockefeller Memorial Parkway leads from Grand Teton National Park to the south entrance of Yellowstone. Western, Northwest Orient, Frontier, and Continental airlines serve nearby cities and provide bus transportation to the park. All entrances except the northeast are open in winter to snowmobiles and heated snow coaches and are also accessible on foot — skis or snowshoes. Yellowstone's winter season runs from mid-December through mid-March.

The superstar of Yellowstone is Old Faithful. The geyser has been erupting on an average of once every 70 minutes ever since it was discovered over 100 years ago. The average period between eruptions is deceptive; the period between performances has varied from a record low of 33 minutes to a record high of 2 hours. Though not the largest geyser in Yellowstone, Old Faithful is among the most dependable, shooting thousands of gallons of steaming water from 106 to 184 feet into the air for periods of two to five minutes.

More than 200 other geysers in the park make Yellowstone the greatest geyser region in the world. (Only three other areas in the world have concentrations of geysers — Iceland, New Zealand, and Siberia.) Yellowstone also has an estimated 10,000 hot springs, mud pots, and fumaroles (natural vents in the earth that shoot out superheated steam). The fuel for this thermal activity is thought to lie as close as 2 to 3 miles below the surface of the earth where a chamber of magma (molten rock) heats the overlying layers of stone. A geyser occurs where groundwater seeps into underground crevasses in the red-hot rocks. The water is superheated to over twice its boiling point. At first, the pressure of the thousands of gallons of overlying water prevents the superheated liquid from turning to steam. Finally the pressure becomes so great that some of the water is pushed out through the cone of the geyser. As the pressure drops, the superheated water instantly distills into steam and blasts out of the geyser's cone.

Geyser basins cover less than 2% of Yellowstone. Even without the geysers, Yellowstone would still be an important national park. The Grand Canyon of the Yellowstone, with a waterfall twice as high as Niagara and canyon walls splashed with multicolored rock, deserves that status by itself. There's also a unique petrified forest, with trees that remained upright just as they were when they were covered with volcanic dust and turned to stone millions of years ago. Yellowstone Lake is the largest mountain lake above 7,000 feet in North America and one of the highest lakes of its size in the world; only Lake Titicaca in Peru has a higher elevation.

Many of Yellowstone's major attractions are accessible by car. The famous Grand Loop is a 142-mile-long road that traces a circular route around the park. Counting the trip into and out of the park, your visit to Yellowstone will be about 200 miles long. You should plan on a minimum of two or three days to see the major attractions.

The park's headquarters and museum and the Mammoth Hot Springs Terraces are near the Gardiner entrance. At the springs you will see bizarre-looking terraced pools formed on the side of Terrace Mountain by mineral-rich water from the hot springs. Some of the terraces are growing at the rate of a foot a year as the hot springs dissolve the subterranean limestone beds under the mountain and redeposit the minerals on the surface. Terrace Mountain is quite literally turning itself inside out. Over the course of a few years, you could watch a mountain growing before your eyes.

The Norris Geyser Basin is 21 miles south of Mammoth Hot Springs. A museum has exhibitions and guided walks through the main basin. There's also a 2-mile trail through the lower basin.

The west entrance (via Rtes. 20 and 191) joins the Grand Loop at Madison Junction. Heading south, the Grand Loop goes along the banks of the Fire-hole River, a stream that's fed by dozens of hot springs in its bed.

Old Faithful is just 16 miles south of Madison Junction, where there is a visitors center with fine exhibitions. The surrounding geyser basins — Upper, Midway, and Lower — have some of the best geysers, hot springs, and mud pots in the park.

The south entrance road joins the Grand Loop 17 miles east of Old Faithful. The road hugs the shore of Yellowstone Lake all the way up to its northern end. Yellowstone Lake has great fishing for cutthroat trout (although there are strict catch limitations). Boats and tackle are available at Bridge Bay Marina on the northwest shore.

North of Fishing Bridge, the Grand Loop leads to the 24-mile-long Grand Canyon of the Yellowstone. The river has carved a twisting canyon 800 to 1,200 feet deep. The dominant color of the stone face of the canyon walls is, of course, yellow, but the canyon is also tinted with colors ranging from pale saffron to bright orange.

The Upper Falls of the Yellowstone mark the beginning of the canyon. The water moves with such force that it appears to arch through the air rather than fall. Farther along is the magnificent Lower Falls, which are twice as high as Niagara. The Upper Falls are easy to see; the best view of the Lower Falls is from a trail leading to them. Inspiration Point, which juts far out into the canyon, offers incredible views of the river raging below.

At Tower Junction, the northeast entrance road joins the Grand Loop. Nearby, the spectacular Tower Falls drop 132 feet.

There are several hotels/motels along the Grand Loop (see *Best en Route*) and some of the major campgrounds are at Bridge Bay, Grant Village, Lewis Lake, Madison Junction, Canyon, and Tower Fall. Keep in mind, however, that Yellowstone is packed to the treetops with tourists in the summer, especially in July and August. If you would like to visit at that time, make reservations well in advance of your trip. The park service has recorded messages about lodging, campsites, and other information (307 344-7381). Campgrounds are run on a first come, first served basis.

One message that is constantly repeated is a warning that *it is illegal and dangerous* to feed the animals, especially the bears. Bears can turn from seemingly tame creatures to the unpredictable wild animals they are in a split second.

Yellowstone presents the park service with a dilemma. It is one of the most popular national parks, and millions of people visit each year, causing traffic jams and leaving behind tons of litter. Visitors are constantly demanding that the park service expand the facilities. In doing that, however, some of the unique character of Yellowstone would be destroyed. The last major expansion program took place in the late 1950s. In 1959, Yellowstone was shaken by a series of huge earthquakes that knocked down half a mountain — almost as if the earth were reasserting its sovereignty over Yellowstone and cautioning those who wanted to exploit and commercialize this region that they should regard Yellowstone with awe and treat it with proper respect.

For more information on facilities in Yellowstone contact: National Park Service, PO Box 168, Yellowstone National Park, WY 82190, 5 miles south of the north entrance at Mammoth Hot Springs (307 344-7381).

BEST EN ROUTE

TW Services is a concessionaire that offers lodging, meals, and tours around the park. For further information, contact TW Services, Yellowstone Division, Yellowstone National Park, WY 82190 (307 344-7311).

Old Faithful Snow Lodge – For accommodations during the winter season (mid-December to mid-March) as well as the summer. 89 rooms. Loop Rd. next to Old Faithful.

Lake Yellowstone Hotel and Cabins – Overlooks the lake and provides easy access to boating and fishing. 185 rooms; 110 cabins. Open all year. 2 miles south of Fishing Bridge Jct.

Canyon Village – Centrally located near the Grand Canyon of the Yellowstone. 588 cabins, open in the summer. Loop Rd. at Canyon Jct.

Mammoth Hot Springs Hotel and Cabins – 95 rooms, 125 cabins, some with view of the springs. Open in summer and winter. 5 miles south of the north entrance on Loop Rd.

Index